Bioethics

Principles, Issues, and Cases

Lewis Vaughn

New York   Oxford

OXFORD UNIVERSITY PRESS

2010

Oxford University Press, Inc., publishes works that further Oxford University's
objective of excellence in research, scholarship, and education.

Oxford New York
Auckland   Cape Town   Dar es Salaam   Hong Kong   Karachi
Kuala Lumpur   Madrid   Melbourne   Mexico City   Nairobi
New Delhi   Shanghai   Taipei   Toronto

With offices in
Argentina   Austria   Brazil   Chile   Czech Republic   France   Greece
Guatemala   Hungary   Italy   Japan   Poland   Portugal   Singapore
South Korea   Switzerland   Thailand   Turkey   Ukraine   Vietnam

Copyright © 2010 by Oxford University Press, Inc.

Published by Oxford University Press, Inc.
198 Madison Avenue, New York, New York 10016
http://www.oup.com

Oxford is a registered trademark of Oxford University Press

Library of Congress Cataloging-in-Publication Data

Vaughn, Lewis.
    Bioethics: principles, issues, and cases/Lewis Vaughn.
       p. ; cm.
    Includes bibliographical references and index.
    ISBN 978-0-19-518282-8 (paper: alk. paper) 1. Medical ethics. 2. Bioethics. I.
Title.
    [DNLM: 1. Bioethical Issues. WB 60 V371b 2010]
    R724.V38 2010
    174′.957—dc22

                                                         2008053791

Printed in the United States of America
on acid-free paper

BRIEF CONTENTS

Preface ix

Part 1. Principles and Theories
Chapter 1 MORAL REASONING IN BIOETHICS 3
Chapter 2 BIOETHICS AND MORAL THEORIES 30

Part 2. Physician and Patient
Chapter 3 PATERNALISM AND PATIENT AUTONOMY 51
Chapter 4 TRUTH-TELLING AND CONFIDENTIALITY 105
Chapter 5 INFORMED CONSENT 144
Chapter 6 HUMAN RESEARCH 193

Part 3. Life and Death
Chapter 7 ABORTION 253
Chapter 8 REPRODUCTIVE TECHNOLOGY 354
Chapter 9 GENETIC CHOICES 460
Chapter 10 EUTHANASIA AND PHYSICIAN-ASSISTED SUICIDE 526

Part 4. Justice and Health Care
Chapter 11 DIVIDING UP HEALTH CARE RESOURCES 613

Glossary 683
Index 685

CONTENTS

Preface ix

Part 1. Principles and Theories

Chapter 1

MORAL REASONING IN BIOETHICS 3

Ethics and Bioethics 3

Ethics and the Moral Life 5

In Depth: Morality and the Law 7

Moral Principles in Bioethics 8

Autonomy 9

Beneficence 10

Utility 11

Justice 12

Ethical Relativism 13

In Depth: Anthropology and Moral Diversity 14

Ethics and Religion 17

Moral Arguments 18

Argument Fundamentals 19

Patterns of Moral Arguments 22

Review: Valid and Invalid Argument Forms 23

In Depth: Fallacies in Moral Reasoning 24

Evaluating Premises 26

Key Terms 28

Summary 28

Further Reading 29

Notes 29

Chapter 2

BIOETHICS AND MORAL THEORIES 30

The Nature of Moral Theories 30

Influential Moral Theories 31

Utilitarianism 32

In Depth: Utilitarianism and the Golden Rule 34

Kantian Ethics 34

Natural Law Theory 36

Rawls' Contract Theory 38

Virtue Ethics 39

The Ethics of Care 40

In Depth: Can Virtue Be Taught? 41

Feminist Ethics 42

Criteria for Judging Moral Theories 42

Review: Evaluating Moral Theories: Criteria of Adequacy 44

Applying the Criteria 44

Utilitarianism 45

Kant's Theory 46

Key Terms 46

Summary 47

Further Reading 47

Notes 48

Part 2. Physician and Patient

Chapter 3

PATERNALISM AND PATIENT AUTONOMY 51

Shades of Autonomy and Paternalism 51

Refusing Treatment 52

In Depth: The Hippocratic Oath 53

Futile Treatment 54

Legal Brief: Refusing Treatment for Children on Religious Grounds 55

In Depth: CPR and DNR 56

Applying Major Theories 56

Key Terms 57

Summary 57

Classic Case File: Elizabeth Bouvia 58
Cases for Evaluation 60
Further Reading 62
Notes 63

READINGS 63
"Paternalism," *Gerald Dworkin* 63
"The Refutation of Medical Paternalism,"
    Alan Goldman 73
"Why Doctors Should Intervene,"
    Terrence F. Ackerman 79
"Autonomy, Futility, and the Limits of Medicine,"
    Robert L. Schwartz 84
"Whose Body Is It Anyway?" *Atul Gawande* 88
Bouvia v. Superior Court, California Court
    of Appeal 98
"Fundamental Elements of the Patient-Physician
    Relationship," *AMA Council on Ethical and
    Judicial Affairs* 102
"Code of Ethics for Nurses," *American Nurses
    Association* 103

Chapter 4

**TRUTH-TELLING AND
CONFIDENTIALITY** 105

Paternalism and Deception 105
    *In Depth: Do Patients Want the Truth? Do
        Physicians Tell It?* 106
Confidential Truths 108
    *Legal Brief: Confidentiality and a Duty
        to Warn* 109
Applying Major Theories 110
Classic Case File: Carlos R. 111
Key Terms 112
Summary 112
Cases for Evaluation 112
Further Reading 114
Notes 114

READINGS 115
"Telling the Truth to Patients: A Clinical Ethics
    Exploration," *David C. Thomasma* 115

"On Telling Patients the Truth," *Mack Lipkin* 119
"On a Supposed Right to Lie from Altruistic
    Motives," *Immanuel Kant* 121
"Respect for Patients, Physicians, and the Truth,"
    Susan Cullen and Margaret Klein 122
"Why Privacy Is Important," *James Rachels* 130
"Confidentiality in Medicine—A Decrepit
    Concept," *Mark Siegler* 135
Tarasoff v. Regents of the University of California,
    Supreme Court of California 138

Chapter 5

INFORMED CONSENT 144

Autonomy and Consent 144
Conditions of Informed Consent 145
    *In Depth: Two Views of Informed
        Consent* 147
    *Legal Brief: Important Informed Consent
        Cases* 148
Applying Major Theories 149
Key Terms 149
Summary 149
Classic Case File: Jerry Canterbury 150
Cases for Evaluation 151
Further Reading 153
Notes 154

READINGS 154
"The Concept of Informed Consent,"
    Ruth R. Faden and Tom L. Beauchamp 154
"Informed Consent—Must It Remain a Fairy
    Tale?" *Jay Katz* 159
"Transparency: Informed Consent in Primary
    Care," *Howard Brody* 169
"Should Informed Consent Be Based on Rational
    Beliefs?" *Julian Savulescu and Richard W.
    Momeyer* 175
"Informed Consent: Some Challenges to the
    Universal Validity of the Western Model,"
    Robert J. Levine 183
Canterbury v. Spence, United States Court of
    Appeals 189

Chapter 6

HUMAN RESEARCH 193

The Science of Clinical Trials 194
  In Depth: The Tuskegee Tragedy 195
Beneficence, Science, and Placebos 196
Science and Informed Consent 199
  In Depth: Women in Clinical Trials 200
Research on the Vulnerable 201
  In Depth: Why Enter a Clinical Trial? 202
Applying Major Theories 205
Key Terms 206
Summary 206
Classic Case File: The UCLA Schizophrenia
  Study 207
Cases for Evaluation 208
Further Reading 212
Notes 212

READINGS 213
The Nuremberg Code 213
*Declaration of Helsinki: Ethical Principles for
  Medical Research Involving Human Subjects,*
  World Medical Association 214
"The Belmont Report," *National Commission for
  the Protection of Human Subjects of Biomedical
  and Behavioral Research* 217
"Final Report: Human Radiation Experiments,"
  *Advisory Committee on Human Radiation
  Experiments* 220
"Of Mice but Not Men: Problems of the
  Randomized Clinical Trial," *Samuel Hellman
  and Deborah S. Hellman* 226
"A Response to a Purported Ethical Difficulty with
  Randomized Clinical Trials Involving Cancer
  Patients," *Benjamin Freedman* 231
"How to Resolve an Ethical Dilemma Concerning
  Randomized Clinical Trials,"
  Don Marquis 235
"Clinical Trials: Are They Ethical?" *Eugene
  Passamani* 238
"The Ethics of Clinical Research in the Third
  World," *Marcia Angell* 242

"Ethical Issues in Clinical Trials in Developing
  Countries," *Baruch Brody* 246

Part 3. Life and Death

Chapter 7

ABORTION 253

Starting Point: The Basics 253
  Fact File: U.S. Abortions 254
  In Depth: Abortion and Public Opinion 256
The Legal Struggle 257
Persons and Rights 257
  In Depth: Late-Term Abortion 258
Applying Major Theories 262
Key Terms 263
Summary 263
Classic Case File: Nancy Klein 264
Cases for Evaluation 265
Further Reading 268
Notes 268

READINGS 269
"A Defense of Abortion,"
  Judith Jarvis Thomson 269
"Why Abortion Is Immoral,"
  Don Marquis 279
"On the Moral and Legal Status of Abortion,"
  Mary Anne Warren 291
"An Almost Absolute Value in History,"
  John T. Noonan, Jr. 301
"Abortion Decisions: Personal Morality,"
  Daniel Callahan 305
"Abortion and the Concept of a Person,"
  Jane English 310
"In Defense of Abortion and Infanticide,"
  Michael Tooley 316
"Abortion Through a Feminist Ethic Lens,"
  Susan Sherwin 333
Roe v. Wade, United States Supreme Court 342
*Planned Parenthood of Southeastern Pennsylvania
  v. Casey,* United States Supreme Court 347

Chapter 8

REPRODUCTIVE TECHNOLOGY 354

In Vitro Fertilization 354
  Fact File: Assisted Reproduction 355
Surrogacy 360
  *In Depth: IVF and Children's Future
    Children* 361
Cloning 362
  *Legal Brief: Surrogacy Contracts
    and the Law* 363
  In Depth: Cloning Time Line 365
Applying Major Theories 366
Key Terms 367
Summary 367
Classic Case File: Baby M 368
Cases for Evaluation 369
Further Reading 371
Notes 372

READINGS 373

"IVF: The Simple Case," *Peter Singer* 373
"IVF and Women's Interests: An Analysis
  of Feminist Concerns," *Mary Anne
  Warren* 377
"'Give Me Children or I Shall Die!' New
  Reproductive Technologies and Harm to
  Children," *Cynthia Cohen* 389
"Instruction on Respect for Human Life in Its
  Origin and on the Dignity of Procreation,"
  *Congregation for the Doctrine of the
  Faith* 400
"Surrogate Mothering: Exploitation or
  Empowerment?" *Laura M. Purdy* 409
"On 'Surrogacy,'" *Barbara Katz Rothman* 418
"The Wisdom of Repugnance,"
  Leon R. Kass 426
"Cloning Human Beings: An Assessment
  of the Ethical Issues Pro and Con,"
  Dan W. Brock 441
Opinion in the Matter of Baby M, New Jersey
  Supreme Court 452

Chapter 9

GENETIC CHOICES 460

Genes and Genomes 460
Genetic Testing 461
  *In Depth: Direct-to-Consumer Genetic
    Tests* 464
Gene Therapy 468
  Fact File: Genetic Tests 469
Stem Cells 471
  In Depth: Recent Research in Gene Therapy 472
Applying Major Theories 474
Classic Case File: The Kingsburys 475
Key Terms 476
Summary 476
Cases for Evaluation 477
Further Reading 479
Notes 479

READINGS 480

"Implications of Prenatal Diagnosis for the
  Human Right to Life," *Leon R. Kass* 480
"Genetics and Reproductive Risk: Can Having
  Children Be Immoral?" *Laura M. Purdy* 484
"The Morality of Screening for Disability," *Jeff
  McMahan* 491
"Disowning Knowledge: Issues in Genetic
  Testing," *Robert Wachbroit* 495
"The Non-Identity Problem and Genetic Harms—
  the Case of Wrongful Handicaps,"
  Dan W. Brock 499
"Is Gene Therapy a Form of Eugenics?,"
  John Harris 503
"Genetic Enhancement," *Walter Glannon* 509
"Germ-Line Gene Therapy," *LeRoy Walters and
  Julie Gage Palmer* 514
"What Does 'Respect for Embryos' Mean in the
  Context of Stem Cell Research?"
  Bonnie Steinbock 521
"Declaration on the Production and the Scientific
  and Therapeutic Use of Human Embryonic
  Stem Cells," *Pontifical Academy for Life* 524

Chapter 10

EUTHANASIA AND PHYSICIAN-ASSISTED SUICIDE 526

Deciding Life and Death 527
   Legal Brief: Euthanasia and Assisted Suicide: Major Developments 529
   In Depth: Euthanasia and Assisted Suicide: What Doctors Think and Do 530
Autonomy, Mercy, and Harm 530
   In Depth: Oregon's Death With Dignity Act 533
Applying Major Theories 534
   In Depth: Physician-Assisted Suicide and Public Opinion 535
Key Terms 536
Summary 536
Classic Case File: Nancy Cruzan 537
Cases for Evaluation 538
Further Reading 541
Notes 541

READINGS 542
"The Wrongfulness of Euthanasia,"
   J. Gay-Williams 542
"Voluntary Active Euthanasia,"
   Dan W. Brock 545
"When Self-Determination Runs Amok,"
   Daniel Callahan 556
"When Abstract Moralizing Runs Amok,"
   John Lachs 561
"Physician-Assisted Suicide: A Tragic View,"
   John D. Arras 565
"Active and Passive Euthanasia,"
   James Rachels 580
"The Distinction Between Refusing Medical Treatment and Suicide," *New York State Task Force on Life and the Law* 584
"The Philosophers' Brief," *Ronald Dworkin, Thomas Nagel, Robert Nozick, John Rawls, Thomas Scanlon, and Judith Jarvis Thomson* 592

Vacco v. Quill, United States Supreme Court 601
Washington v. Glucksberg, United States Supreme Court 604

Part 4. Justice and Health Care

Chapter 11

DIVIDING UP HEALTH CARE RESOURCES 613

Health Care in Trouble 613
   In Depth: Unequal Health Care for Minorities 615
   Fact File: U.S. Health Care 616
Theories of Justice 616
A Right to Health Care 617
   In Depth: Public Opinion: Obtaining Adequate Health Care 618
The Ethics of Rationing 620
Key Terms 622
Summary 622
Classic Case File: Christine deMeurers 623
Cases for Evaluation 624
Further Reading 626
Notes 627

READINGS 627
"Is There a Right to Health Care and, if So, What Does It Encompass?" *Norman Daniels* 627
"The Right to a Decent Minimum of Health Care," *Allen E. Buchanan* 634
"Multiculturalism and Just Health Care: Taking Pluralism Seriously," *Jeffrey Blustein* 640
"Rights to Health Care, Social Justice, and Fairness in Health Care Allocations: Frustrations in the Face of Finitude," *H. Tristram Engelhardt, Jr.* 652
"Rationing Fairly: Programmatic Considerations," *Norman Daniels* 661
"The Allocation of Exotic Medical Lifesaving Therapy," *Nicholas Rescher* 666
"QALYfying the Value of Life," *John Harris* 675

Glossary 683
Index 685

Only the teacher of bioethics can judge whether this book fulfills its outsized ambition. Its aim is to do what any good bioethics text is supposed to do—but to do it in a way that is more useful and rewarding to students and teachers than the norm for texts in this field. Like other books, it provides in-depth discussions of the medical, scientific, social, and legal aspects of controversial bioethical issues and combines this material with a varied collection of thought-provoking readings. But on this foundation are laid elements that other texts often forgo:

1. An extensive introduction to ethics, bioethics, moral principles, critical thinking, and moral reasoning
2. Full coverage of influential moral theories, including criteria and guidelines for evaluating them (the focus is on utilitarianism, Kantian ethics, natural law theory, Rawls' contract theory, virtue ethics, the ethics of care, and feminist ethics)
3. Detailed examinations of the classic cases that have helped shape debate in major issues
4. Collections of current, news-making cases for evaluation
5. Many pedagogical features to engage students and reinforce lessons in the main text
6. Writing that strives hard for clarity and concision to convey both the excitement and complexity of issues without sacrificing accuracy

TOPICS AND READINGS

Nine chapters cover many of the most controversial issues in bioethics, detailing the main arguments and filling out the discussions with background on the latest medical, legal, and social developments. The main issues include paternalism and patient autonomy, truth-telling, confidentiality, informed consent, research ethics, clinical trials, abortion, assisted reproduction, surrogacy, cloning, genetic testing, gene therapy, stem cells, euthanasia, physician-assisted suicide, and the just allocation of health care.

Every issues chapter contains 7 to 10 readings, with each selection prefaced by a brief summary. The articles—old standards as well as new ones—reflect the major arguments and latest thinking in each debate. They present a diversity of perspectives on each topic, with pro and con positions well represented. In most cases, the relevant court rulings are also included.

SPECIAL FEATURES

A two-chapter introduction to bioethics, moral reasoning, moral theories, and critical thinking. These chapters are designed not only to introduce the subject matter of bioethics but also to add coherence to subsequent chapter material and to provide the student with a framework for thinking critically about issues and cases. Chapter 1 is an introduction to basic ethical concepts, the field of bioethics, moral principles and judgments, moral reasoning and arguments, the challenges of relativism, and the relationship between ethics and both religion and the law. Chapter 2 explores moral theory, shows how theories relate to moral principles and judgments, examines influential theories (including virtue ethics, the ethics of care, and feminist ethics), and demonstrates how they can be applied to moral problems. It also explains how to evaluate moral theories using plausible criteria of adequacy.

Helpful chapter elements. Each issues chapter contains:

1. Analyses of the most important arguments offered by the various parties to the debate. They reinforce and illustrate the lessons on moral reasoning in Chapter 1.

2. A section called "Applying Major Theories" showing how the moral theories can be applied to the issues. It ties the discussions of moral theories in Chapter 2 to the moral problems and illustrates the theories' relevance.

3. A section titled "Classic Case File" that examines in detail a famous bioethics case. The stories covered in these sections include those of Elizabeth Bouvia, Jerry Canterbury, Nancy Klein, Baby M, Nancy Cruzan, the Kingsburys, Christine deMeurers, and the UCLA Schizophrenia Study. These are in addition to many other controversial cases covered elsewhere in the book—for example, the Teri Schiavo controversy, the Tuskegee tragedy, the Willowbrook experiments, the U.S. government's human radiation studies, and the AZT trials on HIV-infected women in Africa.

4. A bank of "Cases for Evaluation" at the end of each chapter. These are recent news stories followed by discussion questions. They give students the chance to test their moral reasoning on challenging new scenarios that range across a broad spectrum of current topics.

A diverse package of pedagogical aids. Each issues chapter contains a chapter summary, suggestions for further reading, a list of key terms, and a variety of text boxes. The boxes are mainly of three types:

(1) "In Depth"—additional information, illustrations, or analyses of matters touched on in the main text; (2) "Fact File"—statistics on the social, medical, and scientific aspects of the chapter's topic; (3) "Legal Brief"—summaries of important court rulings or updates on the status of legislation

ANCILLARIES

An Instructor's Manual and test bank on CD
An on-line Student Study Guide that includes study questions, flashcards with key words, essay questions for each reading, answers to the text's self-assessment quizzes, and helpful web links

ACKNOWLEDGMENTS

The faults of this text lie not in the stars nor in the editors but in the author. For the text's virtues I owe much to the good people at Oxford University Press—especially my hard-working editors Robert Miller and John Haber, as well as Sarah Calabi and Yelena Bromberg. A long roster of sharp reviewers critiqued this book and offered a host of helpful suggestions and great ideas. Many thanks to all of them:

Kim Amer, DePaul University
Jami L. Anderson, University of Michigan
Don Berkich, Texas A&M University
William Bondeson, University of Missouri, Columbia
David W. Concepción, Ball State University
Russell DiSilvestro, Assistant Professor, California State University, Sacramento
Denise Dudzinski, University of Washington School of Medicine
Craig Duncan, Ithaca College
John Elia, University of Georgia
Jacqueline Fox, University of South Carolina School of Law
Leslie P. Francis, University of Utah
Kathryn M. Ganske, Shenandoah University
Helen Habermann, University of Arizona
Margaret Levvis, Central Connecticut State University
Burden S. Lundgren, Old Dominion University
James Lindemann Nelson, Michigan State University
Thomas Nenon, University of Memphis
Laura Newhart, Eastern Kentucky University
Anthony Preus, Binghamton University
Susan M. Purviance, University of Toledo
Gladys B. White, Georgetown University

Principles & Theories

CHAPTER 1

Moral Reasoning in Bioethics

Any serious and rewarding exploration of bio-ethics is bound to be a challenging journey. What makes the trip worthwhile? As you might expect, this entire text is a long answer to that question. You therefore may not fully appreciate the trek until you have already hiked far along the trail. The short answer comes in three parts.

First, bioethics—like ethics, its parent disci-pline—is about morality, and morality is about life. Morality is part of the unavoidable, bitter-sweet drama of being persons who think and feel and choose. **Morality** concerns beliefs regarding morally right and wrong actions and morally good and bad persons or character. Whether we like it or not, we seem confronted continually with the necessity to deliberate about right and wrong, to judge someone morally good or bad, to agree or disagree with the moral pronounce-ments of others, to accept or reject the moral out-look of our culture or community, and even to doubt or affirm the existence or nature of moral concepts themselves. Moral issues are thus ines-capable—including (or especially) those that are the focus of bioethics. In the twenty-first century, few can remain entirely untouched by the press-ing moral questions of fair distribution of health care resources, abortion and infanticide, eutha-nasia and assisted suicide, exploitative research on children and populations in developing coun-tries, human cloning and genetic engineering, assisted reproduction and surrogate parenting, prevention and treatment of HIV/AIDS, the con-fidentiality and consent of patients, the refusal of medical treatment on religious grounds, experi-mentation on human embryos and fetuses, and the just allocation of scarce life-saving organs.

Second, it would be difficult to imagine moral issues more important—more closely gathered around the line between life and death, health and illness, pain and relief, hope and despair—than those addressed by bioethics. Whatever our view of these questions, there is little doubt that they matter immensely. Whatever answers we give will surely have weight, however they fall.

Third, as a systematic study of such questions, bioethics holds out the possibility of answers. The answers may or may not be to our liking; they may confirm or confute our preconceived notions; they may take us far or not far enough. But, as the following pages will show, the trail has more light than shadow—and thinking criti-cally and carefully about the problems can help us see our way forward.

ETHICS AND BIOETHICS

Morality is about people's moral judgments, principles, rules, standards, and theories—all of which help direct conduct, mark out moral prac-tices, and provide the yardsticks for measuring moral worth. We use *morality* to refer gener-ally to these aspects of our lives (as in "Morality is essential") or more specifically to the beliefs or practices of particular groups or persons (as in "American morality" or "Kant's morality"). *Moral*, of course, pertains to morality as just de-fined, though it is also sometimes employed as a synonym for right or good, just as *immoral* is of-ten meant to be equivalent to wrong or bad. *Eth-ics*, as used in this text, is not synonymous with *morality*. **Ethics** is the study of morality using the tools and methods of philosophy. Philosophy is a discipline that systematically examines life's big questions through critical reasoning, logical argument, and careful reflection. Thus ethics—also known as *moral philosophy*—is a reasoned way of delving into the meaning and import of moral concepts and issues and of evaluating the merits of moral judgments and standards. (As with *morality* and *moral*, we may use *ethics* to say such things as "Kant's ethics" or may use *ethical* or *unethical* to mean right or wrong, good or bad.) Ethics seeks to know whether an action is right or wrong, what moral standards should guide our conduct, whether moral principles can be justified, what moral virtues are worth cultivating and why, what ultimate ends people should pursue in life, whether there are good reasons for accepting a particular moral theory, and what the meaning is of such notions as *right, wrong, good*, and *bad*. Whenever we try to reason carefully about such things, we enter the realm of ethics: We *do* ethics.

Science offers another way to study morality, and we must carefully distinguish this approach from that of moral philosophy. **Descriptive ethics** is the study of morality using the methodology of science. Its purpose is to investigate the *empirical* facts of morality—the actual beliefs, behaviors, and practices that constitute people's moral experience. Those who carry out these inquiries (usually anthropologists, sociologists, historians, and psychologists) want to know, among other things, what moral beliefs a person or group has, what caused the subjects to have them, and how the beliefs influence behavior or social interaction. Very generally, the difference between ethics and descriptive ethics is this: In ethics we ask, as Socrates did, *How ought we to live?* In descriptive ethics we ask, *How do we in fact live?*

Ethics is a big subject, so we should not be surprised that it has three main branches, each dealing with more or less separate but related sets of ethical questions. **Normative ethics** is the search for, and justification of, moral standards, or norms. Most often the standards are moral principles, rules, virtues, and theories, and the lofty aim of this branch is to establish rationally some or all of these as proper guides for our actions and judgments. In normative ethics, we ask questions like these: What moral principles, if any, should inform our moral judgments? What role should virtues play in our lives? Is the principle of autonomy justified? Are there any exceptions to the moral principle of "do not kill"? How should we resolve conflicts between moral norms? Is contractarianism a good moral theory? Is utilitarianism a *better* theory?

A branch that deals with much deeper ethical issues is metaethics. **Metaethics** is the study of the meaning and justification of basic moral beliefs. In normative ethics we might ask whether an action is right or whether a person is good, but in metaethics we would more likely ask *what it means* for an action to be right or for a person to be good. For example, does *right* mean *has the best consequences*, or *produces the most happiness*, or *commanded by God*? It is the business of metaethics to explore these and other equally fundamental questions: What, if anything, is the difference between moral and nonmoral beliefs? Are there such things as moral facts? If so, what sort of things are they, and how can they be known? Can moral statements be true or false—or are they just expressions of emotions or attitudes without any truth value? Can moral norms be justified or proven?

The third main branch is **applied ethics**, the use of moral norms and concepts to resolve practical moral issues. Here the usual challenge is to employ moral principles, theories, arguments, or analyses to try to answer moral questions that confront people everyday. Many such questions relate to a particular professional field such as law, business, or journalism, so we have specialized subfields of applied ethics like legal ethics, business ethics, and journalistic ethics. Probably the largest and most energetic subfield is bioethics.

Bioethics is applied ethics focused on health care, medical science, and medical technology. (*Biomedical ethics* is often used as a synonym, and *medical ethics* is a related but narrower term used most often to refer to ethical problems in medical practice.) Ranging far and wide, bioethics seeks answers to a vast array of tough ethical questions: Is abortion ever morally permissible? Is a woman justified in having an abortion if prenatal genetic testing reveals that her fetus has a developmental defect? Should people be allowed to select embryos by the embryos' sex or other genetic characteristics? Should human embryos be used in medical research? Should human cloning be prohibited? Should physicians and nurses always be truthful with patients whatever the consequences? Should severely impaired newborns be given life-prolonging treatment or be allowed to die? Should people in persistent vegetative states be removed from life support? Should physicians help terminally ill patients commit suicide? Is it morally right to conduct medical research on patients without their consent if the research would save lives? Should human stem-cell research be banned? How should we decide who gets life-saving organ transplants when usable organs are scarce and many patients who do not get transplants will die? Should animals be used in biomedical research?

The ethical and technical scope of bioethics is wide. Bioethical questions and deliberations now fall to nonexpert and expert alike—to patients, families, and others as well as to philosophers, health care professionals, lawyers, judges, scientists, clergy, and public policy specialists. Though the heart of bioethics is moral philosophy, fully informed bioethics cannot be done without a good understanding of the relevant nonmoral facts and issues, especially the medical, scientific, technological, and legal ones.

ETHICS AND THE MORAL LIFE

Morality then is a normative, or evaluative, enterprise. It concerns moral norms or standards that help us decide the rightness of actions, judge the goodness of persons or character, and prescribe the form of moral conduct. There are, of course, other sorts of norms we apply in life—*nonmoral* norms. Aesthetic norms help us make value judg-

ments about art; norms of etiquette about polite social behavior; grammatical norms about correct use of language; prudential norms about what is in one's interests; and legal norms about lawful and unlawful acts. But moral norms differ from these nonmoral kinds. Some of the features they are thought to possess include the following.

Normative Dominance. In our moral practice, moral norms are presumed to dominate other kinds of norms, to take precedence over them. Philosophers call this characteristic of moral norms *overridingness* because moral considerations so often seem to override other factors. A maxim of prudence, for example, may suggest that you should steal if you can avoid getting caught, but a moral prohibition against stealing would overrule such a principle. An aesthetic (or pragmatic) norm implying that homeless people should be thrown in jail for blocking the view of a beautiful public mural would have to yield to moral principles demanding more humane treatment of the homeless. A law mandating brutal actions against a minority group would conflict with moral principles of justice and would therefore be deemed illegitimate. We usually think that immoral laws are defective, that they need to be changed, or that, in rare cases, they should be defied through acts of civil disobedience.

Universality. Moral norms (but not *exclusively* moral norms) have universality: Moral principles or judgments apply in all relevantly similar situations. If it is wrong for you to tell a lie in a particular circumstance, then it is wrong for everyone in relevantly similar circumstances to tell a lie. Logic demands this sort of consistency. It makes no sense to say that Maria's doing action A in circumstances C is morally wrong but John's doing A in circumstances relevantly similar to C is morally right. Universality, however, is not unique to moral norms; it's a characteristic of all normative spheres.

Impartiality. Implicit in moral norms is the notion of impartiality—the idea that everyone should be considered equal, that everyone's interests should count the same. From the perspective of morality, no person is any better than any other. Everyone should be treated the same unless there is a morally relevant difference between persons. We probably would be completely baffled if someone seriously said something like "murder is wrong . . . except when committed by myself," when there was no morally relevant difference between that person and the rest of the world. If we took such a statement seriously at all, we would likely not only reject it but also would not even consider it a bona fide moral statement.

The requirement of moral impartiality prohibits discrimination against people merely because they are different—different in ways that are not morally relevant. Two people can be different in many ways: skin color, weight, gender, income, age, occupation, and so forth. But these are not differences relevant to the way they should be treated as persons. On the other hand, if there are morally relevant differences between people, then we may have good reasons to treat them differently, and this treatment would not be a violation of impartiality. This is how philosopher James Rachels explains the point:

> The requirement of impartiality, then, is at bottom nothing more than a proscription against arbitrariness in dealing with people. It is a rule that forbids us from treating one person differently from another *when there is no good reason to do so.* But if this explains what is wrong with racism, it also explains why, in some special kinds of cases, it is not racist to treat people differently. Suppose a film director was making a movie about the life of Martin Luther King, Jr. He would have a perfectly good reason for ruling out Tom Cruise for the starring role. Obviously, such casting would make no sense. Because there would be a good reason for it, the director's "discrimination" would not be arbitrary and so would not be open to criticism.[1]

Reasonableness. To participate in morality—to engage in the essential, unavoidable practices of

the moral life—is to do moral reasoning. If our moral judgments are to have any weight at all, if they are to be anything more than mere personal taste or knee-jerk emotional response, they must be backed by the best of reasons. They must be the result of careful reflection in which we arrive at good reasons for accepting them, reasons that could be acknowledged as such by any other reasoning persons.

Both logic and our commonsense moral experience demand that the thorough sifting of reasons constitute the main work of our moral deliberations—regardless of our particular moral outlook or theory. We would think it odd, perhaps even perverse, if someone asserted that physician-assisted suicide is always morally wrong—and then said she has no reasons at all for believing such a judgment but *just does.* Whatever our views on physician-assisted suicide, we would be justified in ignoring her judgment, for we would have no way to distinguish it from personal whim or wishful thinking. Likewise she herself (if she genuinely had no good reasons for her assertion) would be in the same boat, adrift with a firm opinion moored to nothing solid.

Our feelings, of course, are also part of our moral experience. When we ponder a moral issue we care about (abortion, for example), we may feel anger, sadness, disgust, fear, irritation, or sympathy. Such strong emotions are normal and often useful, helping us empathize with others, deepening our understanding of human suffering, and sharpening our insight into the consequences of our moral decisions. But our feelings can mislead us by reflecting not moral truth but our own psychological needs, our own personal or cultural biases, or our concern for personal advantage. Throughout history, some people's feelings led them to conclude that women should be burned for witchcraft, that whole races should be exterminated, that black men should be lynched, and that adherents of a different religion were evil. Critical reasoning can help restrain such terrible impulses. It can help us put our feelings in proper perspective and achieve a measure of

IN DEPTH
MORALITY AND THE LAW

Some people confuse morality with the law, or identify the one with the other, but the two are distinct though they may often coincide. Laws are norms enacted or enforced by the state to protect or promote the public good. They specify which actions are *legally* right or wrong. But these same actions can also be judged *morally* right or wrong, and these two kinds of judgments will not necessarily agree. Lying to a friend about a personal matter, deliberately trying to destroy yourself through reckless living, or failing to save a drowning child (when you easily could have) may be immoral—but not illegal. Racial bias, discrimination based on gender or sexual orientation, slavery, spousal rape, and unequal treatment of minority groups are immoral—but, depending on the society, they may not be illegal.

Much of the time, however, morality and the law overlap. Often what is immoral also turns out to be illegal. This is usually the case when immoral actions cause substantial harm to others, whether physical or economic. Thus murder and embezzlement are both immoral and illegal, backed by social disapproval and severe sanctions imposed by law. Controversy often arises when an action is not obviously or seriously harmful but is considered immoral by some who want the practice prohibited by law. The contentious notion at work is that something may be made illegal solely on the grounds that it is immoral, regardless of any physical or economic harm involved. This view of the law is known as *legal moralism*, and it sometimes underlies debates about the legalization of abortion, euthanasia, reproductive technology, contraception, and other practices.

Many issues in bioethics have both a moral and legal dimension, and it is important not to confuse the two. Sometimes the question at hand is a moral one (whether, for example, euthanasia is ever morally permissible); whether a practice should be legal or illegal then is beside the point. Sometimes the question is about legality. And sometimes the discussion concerns both. A person may consider physician-assisted suicide morally acceptable but argue that it should nevertheless be illegal because allowing the practice to become widespread would harm both patients and the medical profession.

---

impartiality. Most of all, it can guide us to moral judgments that are trustworthy because they are supported by the best of reasons.

The moral life, then, is about grappling with a distinctive class of norms marked by normative dominance, universality, impartiality, and reasonableness. As we saw earlier, these norms can include moral principles, rules, theories, and judgments. We should notice that we commonly apply these norms to two distinct spheres of our moral experience—to both moral *obligations* and moral *values*.

Moral obligations concern our duty, what we are obligated to do. That is, obligations are about conduct, how we ought or ought not to behave. In this sphere, we talk primarily about *actions*. We may look to moral principles or rules to guide our actions, or study a moral theory that purports to explain right actions, or make judgments about right or wrong actions.

Moral values, on the other hand, generally concern those things that we judge to be morally good, bad, praiseworthy, or blameworthy. Normally we use such words to describe persons (as in "He is a good person" or "She is to blame for hurting them"), their character ("He is virtuous"; "She is honest"), or their motives ("She did wrong but did not mean to"). Note that we also attribute *nonmoral* value to things. If we say that a book or bicycle or vacation is good, we mean good in a nonmoral sense. Such things in themselves cannot have *moral* value.

Strictly speaking, only actions are morally *right* or *wrong*, but persons are morally *good* or *bad* (or some degree of goodness or badness). With this distinction we can acknowledge a simple fact of the moral life: A good person can do something wrong, and a bad person can do something right. A Gandhi can tell a lie, and a Hitler can save a drowning man.

In addition, we may judge an action right or wrong depending on the motive behind it. If John knocks a stranger down in the street to prevent her from being hit by a car, we would deem his action right (and might judge him a good person). But if he knocks her down because he dislikes the color of her skin, we would believe his action wrong (and likely think him evil).

The general meaning of *right* and *wrong* seems clear to just about everyone. But we should be careful to differentiate degrees of meaning in these moral terms. *Right* can mean either "obligatory" or "permissible." An obligatory action is one that would be wrong *not* to perform. We are obligated or required to do it. A permissible action is one that is permitted. It is not wrong to perform it. *Wrong* means "prohibited." A prohibited action is one that would be wrong to perform. We are obligated or required *not* to do it. A *supererogatory* action is one that is "above and beyond" our duty. It is praiseworthy—a good thing to do—but not required. Giving all your possessions to the poor is generally considered a supererogatory act.

MORAL PRINCIPLES IN BIOETHICS

As noted earlier, the main work of bioethics is trying to solve bioethical problems using the potent resources and methods of moral philosophy, which include, at a minimum, critical reasoning, logical argument, and conceptual analysis. Many, perhaps most, moral philosophers would be quick to point out that beyond these tools of reason we also have the considerable help of moral principles. (The same could be said about moral theories, which we explore in the next chapter.) Certainly to be useful, moral principles must be interpreted, often filled out with specifics, and balanced with other moral concerns. But both in everyday life and in bioethics, moral principles are widely thought to be indispensable to moral decision-making.

We can see appeals to moral principles in countless cases. Confronted by a pain-racked, terminally ill patient who demands to have his life ended, his physician refuses to comply, relying on the principle that "it is wrong to intentionally take a life." Another physician makes a different choice in similar circumstances, insisting that the relevant principle is "ending the suffering of a hopelessly ill patient is morally permissible." An infant is born anencephalic (without a brain); it will never have a conscious life and will die in a few days. The parents decide to donate the infant's organs to other children so they might live, which involves taking the organs right away before they deteriorate. A critic of the parents' decision argues that "it is unethical to kill in order to save." But someone else appeals to the principle "save as many children as possible."[2] In such ways moral principles help guide our actions and inform our judgments about right and wrong, good and evil.

As discussed in Chapter 2, moral principles are often drawn from a moral theory, which is a moral standard on the most general level. The principles are derived from or supported by the theory. Many times we simply appeal directly to a plausible moral principle without thinking much about its theoretical underpinnings.

Philosophers make a distinction between absolute and prima facie principles (or duties). An *absolute* principle applies without exceptions. An absolute principle that we should not lie demands that we never lie regardless of the circumstances or the consequences. In contrast, a *prima facie* principle applies in all cases unless an exception is warranted. Exceptions are justified when the principle conflicts with other principles and is thereby overridden. W. D. Ross is given credit for drawing this distinction in his 1930 book *The Right and the Good*.[3] It is essential to his account of ethics, which has a core of several moral principles or duties, any of which might come into conflict.

Physicians have a prima facie duty to be truthful to their patients as well as a prima facie duty to promote their welfare. But if these duties come in conflict—if, for example, telling a patient the truth about his condition would somehow result in his death—a physician might decide that the duty of truthfulness should yield to the weightier duty to do good for the patient.

Moral principles are many and varied, but in bioethics the following have traditionally been extremely influential and particularly relevant to the kinds of moral issues that arise in health care, medical research, and biotechnology. In fact, many—perhaps most—of the thorniest issues in bioethics arise from conflicts among these basic principles. In one formulation or another, each one has been integral to major moral theories, providing evidence that the principles capture something essential in our moral experience. The principles are (1) autonomy, (2) beneficence, (3) utility, and (4) justice.[4]

Autonomy

Autonomy refers to a person's rational capacity for self-governance or self-determination—the ability to direct one's own life and choose for oneself. The principle of autonomy insists on full respect for autonomy. One way to express the principle is: *Autonomous persons should be allowed to exercise their capacity for self-determination.* According to one major ethical tradition, autonomous persons have intrinsic worth precisely because they have the power to make rational decisions and moral choices. They therefore must be treated with respect, which means not violating their autonomy by ignoring or thwarting their ability to choose their own paths and make their own judgments.

The principle of respect for autonomy places severe restraints on what can be done to an autonomous person. There are exceptions, but in general we are not permitted to violate people's autonomy just because we disagree with their decisions, or because society might benefit, or because the violation is for their own good. We cannot legitimately impair someone's autonomy without strong justification for doing so. Conducting medical experiments on patients without their consent, treating competent patients against their will, physically restraining or con-

fining patients for no medical reason—such practices constitute obvious violations of personal autonomy.

Not all restrictions on autonomy, however, are of the physical kind. Autonomy involves the capacity to make personal choices, but choices cannot be considered entirely autonomous unless they are fully informed. When we make decisions in ignorance—without relevant information or blinded by misinformation—our autonomy is diminished just as surely as if someone physically manipulated us. If this is correct, then we have a plausible explanation of why lying is generally prohibited: Lying is wrong because it undermines personal autonomy. Enshrined in bioethics and in the law, then, is the precept of *informed consent*, which demands that patients be allowed to freely consent to or decline treatments and that they receive the information they need to make informed judgments about them.

In many ways, autonomy is a delicate thing, easily compromised and readily thwarted. Often a person's autonomy is severely undermined not by other people but by nature, nurture, or his or her own actions. Some drug addicts and alcoholics, people with serious psychiatric illness, and those with severe mental impairment are thought to have drastically diminished autonomy (or to be essentially nonautonomous). Bioethical questions then arise about what is permissible to do to them and who will represent their interests or make decisions regarding their care. Infants and children are also not fully autonomous, and the same sorts of questions are forced on parents, guardians, and health care workers.

Like all the other major principles discussed here, respect for autonomy is thought to be prima facie. It can sometimes be overridden by considerations that seem more important or compelling—considerations that philosophers and other thinkers have formulated as principles of autonomy restriction. The principles are articulated in various ways, are applied widely to all sorts of social and moral issues, and are themselves the subject of debate. Chief among these is the harm principle: a person's autonomy may be curtailed to prevent harm to others. To prevent people from being victimized by thieves and murderers, we have a justice system that prosecutes and imprisons the perpetrators. To discourage hospitals and health care workers from hurting patients through carelessness or fraud, laws and regulations limit what they can do to people in their care. To stop someone from spreading a deadly, contagious disease, health officials may quarantine him against his will.

Another principle of autonomy restriction is paternalism. **Paternalism** is the overriding of a person's actions or decision-making for her own good. Some cases of paternalism (sometimes called *weak paternalism*) seem permissible to many people—when, for example, seriously depressed or psychotic patients are temporarily restrained to prevent them from injuring or killing themselves. Other cases are more controversial. Researchers hoping to develop a life-saving treatment give an experimental drug to someone without his knowledge or consent. Or a physician tries to spare the feelings of a competent, terminally ill patient by telling her that she will eventually get better, even though she insists on being told the truth. The paternalism in such scenarios (known as *strong paternalism*) is usually thought to be morally objectionable. Many controversies in bioethics center on the morality of strong paternalism.

Beneficence

The principle of *beneficence* has seemed to many to constitute the very soul of morality—or very close to it. In its most general form, it says that *we should do good to others and avoid doing them harm.* (*Benevolence* is different, referring more to an attitude of goodwill toward others than to a principle of right action.) Its dual injunctions—to both do good and avoid harm—are distinct. The former (called *active beneficence* here) enjoins us to advance the welfare of others and prevent or remove harm to them; the latter (known as *nonmaleficence*) asks us not to intentionally or unintentionally inflict harm on them.[5]

In bioethics, nonmaleficence is the most widely recognized moral principle. Its aphoristic expression has been embraced by practitioners of medicine for centuries: "Above all, do no harm." A more precise formulation of the principle is: *We should not cause unnecessary injury or harm to those in our care.* In whatever form, nonmaleficence is the bedrock precept of countless codes of professional conduct, institutional regulations, and governmental rules and laws designed to protect the welfare of patients.

A health care professional violates this principle if he or she deliberately performs an action that harms or injures a patient. If a physician intentionally administers a drug that she knows will induce a heart attack in a patient, she obviously violates the principle—she clearly does something that is morally (and legally) wrong. But she also violates it if she injures a patient through recklessness, negligence, or inexcusable ignorance. She may not intend to hurt anyone, but she is guilty of the violation just the same.

Implicit in the principle of nonmaleficence is the notion that health professionals must exercise "due care." The possibility of causing some pain, suffering, or injury is inherent in the care and treatment of patients, so we cannot realistically expect health professionals never to harm anyone. But we do expect them to use due care—to act reasonably and responsibly to minimize the harm or the chances of causing harm. If a physician must cause patients some harm to effect a cure, we expect her to try to produce the least amount of harm possible to achieve the results. And even if her treatments cause no actual pain or injury in a particular instance, we expect her not to use treatments that have a higher chance of causing harm than necessary. By the lights of the nonmaleficence principle, subjecting patients to unnecessary risks is wrong even if no damage is done.

Active beneficence demands that we do more than just avoid inflicting pain and suffering. It says that we *should actively promote the well-being of others and prevent or remove harm to them.* In bioethics, there is little doubt that physicians, nurses, researchers, and other professionals have such a duty. After all, helping others, promoting their good, is a large part of what these professionals are obliged to do.

But not everyone thinks that *we all* have a duty of active beneficence. Some argue that though there is a general (applicable to all) duty not to harm others, there is no general duty to help others. They say we are not obligated to aid the poor, feed the hungry, or tend to the sick. Such acts are not required, but are supererogatory, beyond the call of duty. Others contend that though we do not have a general duty of active beneficence, we are at least sometimes obligated to look to the welfare of people we care about most—such as our parents, children, spouses, and friends. In any case, it is clear that in certain professions—particularly medicine, law, and nursing—benefiting others is often not just supererogatory but obligatory and basic.

Utility

The principle of *utility* says that *we should produce the most favorable balance of good over bad (or benefit over harm) for all concerned.* The principle acknowledges that in the real world, we cannot always *just* benefit others or *just* avoid harming them. Often we cannot do good for people without also bringing them some harm, or we cannot help everyone who needs to be helped, or we cannot help some without also hurting or neglecting others. In such situations, the principle says, we should do what yields the best overall outcome—the maximum good and minimum evil, everyone considered. The utility principle, then, is a supplement to, not a substitute for, the principles of autonomy, beneficence, and justice.

In ethics this maxim comes into play in several ways. Most famously it is the defining precept of the moral theory known as utilitarianism (discussed in Chapter 2). But it is also a stand-alone moral principle applied everywhere in bioethics to help resolve the kind of dilemmas just mentioned. A physician, for example, must decide whether a treatment is right for a patient, and that decision often hinges on whether the possible benefits of the treatment outweigh its risks by an acceptable margin. Suppose a man's clogged artery can be successfully treated with open-heart surgery, a procedure that carries a considerable risk of injury and death. But imagine that the artery can also be successfully opened with a regimen of cholesterol-lowering drugs and a low-fat diet, both of which have a much lower chance of serious complications. The principle of utility seems to suggest that the latter course is best and that the former is morally impermissible.

The principle also plays a major role in the creation and evaluation of the health policies of institutions and society. In these large arenas, most people aspire to fulfill the requirements of beneficence, but they recognize that perfect beneficence is impossible: Trade-offs and compromises must be made, scarce resources must be allotted, help and harm must be balanced, life and death must be weighed—tasks almost always informed by the principle of utility.

Suppose, for example, we want to mandate the immunization of all school children to prevent the spread of deadly communicable diseases. The cost in time and money will be great, but such a program could save many lives. There is a down side, however: A small number of children—perhaps as many as 2 for every 400,000 immunizations—will die because of a rare allergic reaction to the vaccine. It is impossible to predict who will have such a reaction (and impossible to prevent it), but it is almost certain to occur in a few cases. If our goal is social beneficence, what should we do? Children are likely to die whether we institute the program or not. Guided by the principle of utility (as well as other principles), we may decide to proceed with the program since many more lives would likely be saved by it than lost because of its implementation.

Again, suppose governmental health agencies have enough knowledge and resources to develop fully a cure for only one disease—either a rare heart disorder or a common form of skin cancer. Trying to split resources between these two is sure to prevent development of any cure at all. The heart disorder kills 200 adults each year; the cancer occurs in thousands of people, causing them great pain and distress, but is rarely fatal. How best to maximize the good? On which disease should the government spend its time and treasure? Answering this question (and others like it) requires trying to apply the utility principle—a job often involving complex calculations of costs and benefits and frequently generating controversy.

Justice

In its broadest sense, *justice* refers to people getting what is fair or what is their due. In practice, most of us seem to have a rough idea of what justice entails in many situations, even if we cannot articulate exactly what it is. We know, for example, that it is unjust for a bus driver to make a woman sit in the back of the bus because of her religious beliefs, or for a judicial system to arbitrarily treat one group of citizens more harshly than others, or for a doctor to care for some patients but refuse to treat others just because he dislikes them.

Questions of justice arise in different spheres of human endeavor. *Retributive justice*, for example, concerns the fair meting out of punishment for wrongdoing. On this matter, some argue that justice is served only when people are punished for past wrongs, when they get their just deserts. Others insist that justice demands that people be punished not because they deserve punishment, but because the punishment will deter further unacceptable behavior. *Distributive justice* concerns the fair distribution of society's advantages and disadvantages—for example, jobs, income, welfare aid, health care, rights, taxes, and public service. Distributive justice is a major issue in bioethics, where many of the most intensely debated questions are about who gets health care, what or how much they should get, and who should pay for it.

Distributive justice is a vast topic, and many theories have been proposed to identify and justify the properties, or traits, of just distributions. A basic precept of most of these theories is what may plausibly be regarded as the core of the principle of justice: *Equals should be treated equally.*

(Recall that this is one of the defining elements of ethics itself, impartiality.) The idea is that people should be treated the same unless there is a morally relevant reason for treating them differently. We would think it unjust for a physician or nurse to treat his white diabetic patients more carefully than he does his black diabetic patients—and to do so without a sound medical reason. We would think it unfair to award the only available kidney to the transplant candidate who belongs to the "right" political party or has the best personal relationship with hospital administrators.

The principle of justice has been at the heart of debates about just distribution of benefits and burdens (including health care) for society as a whole. The disagreements have generally not been about the legitimacy of the principle, but about how it should be interpreted. Different theories of justice try to explain *in what respects* equals should be treated equally.

Libertarian theories emphasize personal freedoms and the right to pursue one's own social and economic well-being in a free market without interference from others. Ideally the role of government is limited to night-watchman functions—the protection of society and free economic systems from coercion and fraud. All other social or economic benefits are the responsibility of individuals. Government should not be in the business of helping the socially or economically disadvantaged, for that would require violating people's liberty by taking resources from the haves to give to the have-nots. So universal health care is out of the question. For the libertarian, then, people have equal intrinsic worth, but this does not entitle them to an equal distribution of economic advantages. Individuals are entitled only to what they can acquire through their own hard work and ingenuity.

Egalitarian theories maintain that a just distribution is an *equal* distribution. Ideally, social benefits—whether jobs, food, health care, or something else—should be allotted so that everyone has an equal share. Treating people equally means making sure everyone has equal access to certain minimal goods and services. To achieve this level of equality, individual liberties will have to be restricted, measures that libertarians would never countenance. In a pure egalitarian society, universal health care would be guaranteed.

Between strict libertarian and egalitarian views of justice lie some theories that try to achieve a plausible fusion of both perspectives. With a nod toward libertarianism, these theories may exhibit a healthy respect for individual liberty and limit governmental interference in economic enterprises. But leaning toward egalitarianism, they may also mandate that the basic needs of the least well-off citizens be met.

In bioethics, the principle of justice and the theories used to explain it are constantly being marshaled to support or reject health care policies of all kinds. They are frequently used—along with other moral principles—to evaluate, design, and challenge a wide range of health care programs and strategies. They are, in other words, far from being merely academic.

ETHICAL RELATIVISM

The commonsense view of morality and moral standards is this: There are moral norms or principles that are valid or true for everyone. This claim is known as **moral objectivism,** the idea that at least some moral standards are objective. Moral objectivism, however, is distinct from **moral absolutism,** the belief that objective moral principles allow no exceptions or must be applied the same way in all cases and cultures. A moral objectivist can be absolutist about moral principles, or she can avoid absolutism by accepting that moral principles are prima facie. In any case, most people probably assume some form of moral objectivism and would not take seriously any claim implying that valid moral norms can be whatever we want them to be.

But moral objectivism is directly challenged by a doctrine that some find extremely appealing and that, if true, would undermine ethics itself: **ethical relativism.** According to this view, moral standards are not objective but are relative to what individuals or cultures believe. There simply are

no *objective* moral truths, only *relative* ones. An action is morally right if endorsed by a person or culture and morally wrong if condemned by a person or culture. So euthanasia is right for person A if he approves of it but wrong for person B if she disapproves of it, and the same would go for cultures with similarly diverging views on the subject. In this way, moral norms are not discovered but made; the individual or culture makes right and wrong. Ethical relativism pertaining to individuals is known as **subjective relativism,** more precisely stated as the view that right actions are those sanctioned by a person. Ethical relativism regarding cultures is called **cultural relativism,** the view that right actions are those sanctioned by one's culture.

In some ways, subjective relativism is a comforting position. It relieves individuals of the burden of serious critical reasoning about morality. After all, determining right and wrong is a matter of inventorying one's beliefs, and any sincerely held beliefs will do. Morality is essentially a matter of personal taste, which is an extremely easy thing to establish. Determining what one's moral views are may indeed involve deliberation and analysis—but neither of these is a necessary requirement for the job. Subjective relativism also helps people short-circuit the unpleasantness of moral debate. The subjective relativist's familiar refrain—"That may be *your* truth, but it's not *my* truth"—has a way of stopping conversations and putting an end to reasoned arguments.

The doctrine, however, is difficult to maintain consistently. On issues that the relativist cares little about (the moral rightness of gambling, say), she may be content to point out that moral norms are relative to each individual and that "to each his own." But on more momentous topics (such as genocide in Africa or the Middle East), she may slip back into objectivism and declare that genocide is morally wrong—not just wrong for her but wrong *period.*

Such inconsistencies hint that there may be something amiss with subjective relativism, and indeed there is: It seems to conflict violently with commonsense realities of the moral life. For one

IN DEPTH
ANTHROPOLOGY
AND MORAL DIVERSITY

Many moral philosophers have been quick to point out that differences in moral judgments from culture to culture do not in themselves prove a difference in moral standards. Some anthropologists have made the same argument. Solomon Asch, for example, says,

> We consider it wrong to take food away from a hungry child, but not if he is overeating. We consider it right to fulfill a promise, but not if it is a promise to commit a crime.... It has been customary to hold that diverse evaluations of the same act are automatic evidence for the presence of different principles of evaluation. The preceding examples point to an error in this interpretation. Indeed, an examination of the relational factors points to the operation of constant principles in situations that differ in concrete details....Anthropological evidence does not furnish proof of relativism. We do not know of societies in which bravery is despised and cowardice held up to honor, in which generosity is considered a vice and ingratitude a virtue. It seems rather that the relations between valuation and meaning are invariant.[6]

thing, the doctrine implies that each person is morally infallible. An action is morally right for someone if he approves of it—if he sincerely believes it to be right. His approval makes the action right, and—if his approval is genuine—he cannot be mistaken. His believing it to be right makes it right, and that's the end of it. If he endorses infanticide as a method of population control, then infanticide is morally permissible. His sincere approval settles the issue, and he cannot be in error. But our commonsense moral experience suggests that this relativist account is absurd. Our judgments about moral matters—actions, principles, and people—are often wide of the mark. We are morally fallible, and we are rightly suspicious of anyone who claims to be otherwise.

There is a more disturbing way to frame this point. Suppose former Iraqi leader Saddam Hussein approved of slaughtering thousands of Iraqis during his reign. Suppose Hitler approved of killing millions of Jews during World War II. Suppose American serial killer and cannibal Jeffrey Dahmer approved of his murdering 17 men and boys. Then by the lights of subjective relativism, all these mass killings were morally right because their perpetrators deemed them so. But we would find this conclusion almost impossible to swallow. We would think these actions morally wrong whether the killers approved of their own actions or not.

Subjective relativism also implies that another commonplace of the moral life is an illusion: moral disagreement. Consider: Hernando tells Sophia that allowing seriously impaired infants to die is morally right. Sophia replies that allowing seriously impaired infants to die is morally wrong. We may think that Hernando and Sophia are having a straightforward disagreement over an important moral issue. But according to subjective relativism, no such disagreement is happening or could ever happen. In stating his approval of the actions in question, Hernando is essentially expressing his personal taste on the issue, and Sophia is expressing her personal taste. He is saying he likes something; she says she does not like it—and they could both be correct. Subjective relativism implies that they are not uttering conflicting claims at all—they are discussing different subjects, their own personal feelings or preferences. But this strange dance is not at all what we think we are doing when we have a moral disagreement. Because subjective relativism conflicts with what we take to be a basic fact of the moral life, we have good reason to doubt it.

Cultural relativism seems to many to be a much more plausible doctrine. In fact, many people think it obviously true, supported as it is by a convincing argument and the common conviction that it is admirably consistent with social tolerance and understanding in a pluralistic world. The argument in its favor goes like this:

1. If people's moral judgments differ from culture to culture, moral norms are relative to culture (there are no objective moral standards).
2. People's moral judgments do differ from culture to culture.
3. Therefore, moral norms are relative to culture (there are no objective moral standards).

Is this a good argument? That is, does it provide us with good reason to accept the conclusion (statement 3)? For an argument to be good, its conclusion must follow logically from the premises, and the premises must be true. In this case, the conclusion does indeed follow logically from the premises (statements 1 and 2). The truth of the premises is another matter.

Let us look first at premise 2. All sorts of empirical evidence—including a trove of anthropological and sociological data—show that the premise is in fact true. Clearly, the moral beliefs of people from diverse cultures often do differ drastically on the same moral issue. Some societies condone infanticide; others condemn it. Some approve of the killing of wives and daughters to protect a family's honor; others think this tradition evil. Some bury their dead; others cremate them. Some judge the killing of one's elders to be a kindly act; others say it is cold-hearted murder. Some think polygamy morally permissible; others believe it deplorable. Some consider it a solemn duty to surgically remove the clitorises of young girls; others say this is immoral and cruel. Some commend the killing of people who practice a different religion; others believe such intolerance is morally reprehensible. We are forced to conclude that diversity of moral judgments among cultures is a reality.

But what of premise 1—is it also true? It says that because cultures have different moral beliefs, they must also have different moral standards, which means morality is relative to cultures. If diverse moral standards arise from each culture, then morality cannot be objective, applying to all people everywhere. There is no objective morality, just *moralities*.

Premise 1, however, is false. First, from the fact that cultures have divergent moral beliefs on an issue, it does not logically follow that there is no objective moral truth to be sought, that there is no opinion that is objectively correct. People may disagree about the existence of biological life on Mars, but the disagreement does not demonstrate that there is no fact of the matter or that no statement on the subject could be objectively true. Disagreements on a moral question may simply indicate that there is an objective fact of the matter but that someone (or everyone) is wrong about it.

Second, a conflict between moral beliefs does not necessarily indicate a fundamental conflict between basic moral norms. Moral disagreements between cultures can arise not just because their basic moral principles clash, but because they have differing nonmoral beliefs that put those principles in very different light. From the annals of anthropology, for example, we have the classic story of a culture that sanctions the killing of parents when they become elderly but not yet enfeebled. Our society would condemn such a practice, no doubt appealing to moral precepts urging respect for parents and for human life. But consider: This strange (to us) culture believes that people enter heaven when they die and spend eternity in the same physical condition they were in when they passed away. Those who kill their parents are doing so because they do not want their elders to spend eternity in a state of senility but rather in good health. This culture's way is not our way; we are unlikely to share these people's nonmoral beliefs. But it is probable that they embrace the same moral principles of respect for parents and life that we do. According to some anthropologists, diverse cultures often share basic moral standards while seeming to have little or nothing in common.

The argument we are considering, then, fails to support cultural relativism. Moreover, many considerations count strongly against the view. Specifically, the logical implications of the doctrine give us substantial reasons to doubt it.

Like subjective relativism, cultural relativism implies moral infallibility, a very hard implication to take seriously. As the doctrine would have it, if a culture genuinely approves of an action, then there can be no question about the action's moral rightness: It is right, and that's that. Cultures make moral rightness, so they cannot be mistaken about it. But is it at all plausible that cultures cannot be wrong about morality? Throughout history, cultures have approved of ethnic cleansing, slavery, racism, holocausts, massacres, mass rape, torture of innocents, burning of heretics, and much more. Is it reasonable to conclude that the cultures that approved of such deeds could not have been mistaken?

Related to the infallibility problem is this difficulty: Cultural relativism implies that we cannot legitimately criticize other cultures. If a culture approves of its actions, then those actions are morally right—and it does not matter one bit whether another culture disapproves of them. Remember, there is no objective moral code to appeal to. Each society is its own maker of the moral law. It makes no sense for society X to accuse society Y of immorality, for what society Y approves of *is* moral. Some may be willing to accept this consequence of cultural relativism, but look at what it would mean. What if the people of Germany approved of the extermination of millions of Jews, Gypsies, and others during World War II? Then the extermination was morally right. Suppose the people of Libya approved of the terrorist bombing of Pan Am flight 103 over Lockerbie, Scotland, killing 270 people (a tragedy for which the Libyan government eventually took responsibility). Then the bombing was morally right, and those who placed the bomb on board did no wrong. But all this seems very much at odds with our moral experience. We

think it makes perfect sense sometimes to condemn other cultures for morally wrong actions.

Now consider the notion of moral progress. We sometimes compare what people did in the past with what they do now, noting that current practices are morally better than they used to be. We no longer countenance such horrors as massacres of native peoples, slavery, and lynchings, and we think that these changes are signs of moral progress. But cultural relativism implies that there cannot be any such thing as moral progress. To claim legitimately that there has been moral progress, there must be an objective, transcultural standard for comparing cultures of the past and present. But according to cultural relativism, there are no objective moral standards, just norms relative to each culture. On the other hand, if there is moral progress as we think there is, then there must be objective moral standards.

Cultural relativism also has a difficult time explaining the moral status of social reformers. We tend to believe they are at least sometimes right and society is wrong. When we contemplate social reform, we think of such moral exemplars as Martin Luther King, Jr., Mahatma Gandhi, and Susan B. Anthony, all of whom agitated for justice and moral progress. But one of the consequences of cultural relativism is that social reformers could *never* be morally right. By definition, what society judges to be morally right is morally right, and since social reformers disagree with society, they could not be right—ever. But surely on occasion it's the reformers who are right and society is wrong.

There is also the serious difficulty of using cultural relativism to make moral decisions. Cultural relativism says that moral rightness is whatever a culture or society approves of, but determining which culture or society one truly belongs to seems almost impossible. The problem is that we each belong to many social groups, and there is no fact of the matter regarding which one is our "true" society. Suppose you are an African-American Catholic Republican living in an artists colony in Alabama and enjoying the advantages of membership in an extremely large extended family. What is your true society? If you cannot identify your proper society, you cannot tell which cultural norms apply to you.

Some people may be willing to overlook these problems of cultural relativism because they believe it promotes cultural tolerance, an attitude that seems both morally praiseworthy and increasingly necessary in a pluralistic world. After all, human history has been darkened repeatedly by the intolerance of one society toward another, engendering vast measures of bloodshed, pain, oppression, injustice, and ignorance. The thought is that because all cultures are morally equal, there is no objective reason for criticizing any of them. Tolerance is then the best policy.

Cultural relativism, however, does not necessarily lead to tolerance and certainly does not logically entail it. In fact, cultural relativism can easily justify either tolerance or intolerance. It says that if a society sanctions tolerance, then tolerance is morally right for that society. But if a society approves of intolerance, then *intolerance* is morally right for that society—and the society cannot be legitimately criticized for endorsing such an attitude. According to cultural relativism, intolerance can be morally permissible just as tolerance can. In addition, though moral relativists may want to advocate universal tolerance, they cannot consistently do so. To say that all cultures should be tolerant is to endorse an objective moral norm, but cultural relativists insist that there are no objective moral norms. To endorse universal tolerance is to abandon cultural relativism.

ETHICS AND RELIGION

How is ethics related to religion? One obvious connection is that historically religion has always had moral content—mostly in the form of moral precepts, codes, or commandments to guide the conduct of adherents. In Western civilization, this content has been so influential in moral (and legal) matters that many now take for granted that religion is the fundamental basis of morality, that right and wrong, good and bad, are synonymous with the will of God. Secular or nontheistic systems of ethics (for example, the ethics of Stoicism, Confucianism, Buddhism, utilitarianism, and contractarianism) have also shaped how we think about morality. But for millions of people, religion is the fountainhead of the moral law.

An important query in ethics is whether this common view of morality is correct: whether morality depends fundamentally on religion, whether—to state the question in its traditional form—the moral law is constituted by the will of God. The view that morality does have this kind of dependence is known as the **divine command theory**. It says that right actions are those commanded by God, and wrong actions are those forbidden by God. God is the author of the moral law, making right and wrong by his will.

But many people—both religious and nonreligious—have found this doctrine troubling. Philosophers have generally rejected it, including some famous theistic thinkers such as Thomas Aquinas (1225–1274), Gottfried Leibniz (1646–1710), and Immanuel Kant (1724–1804).

The problem is that the theory presents us with a disconcerting dilemma first spelled out in Plato's *Euthyphro*. In this dialogue, Socrates asks a penetrating question that is often expressed like this: Are actions morally right because God commands them, or does God command them because they are morally right? In the first option, God creates the moral law (the divine command theory); in the second, the moral law is independent of God's will so that even God is subject to it. Critics of the divine command theory have argued that the first option implies the moral law is entirely arbitrary. The second option denies the theory.

The arbitrariness is thought to arise like this: If actions are morally right just because God commands them to be so, then it is possible that any actions whatsoever could be morally right. The murder and rape of innocents, the oppression of the weak, the abuse of the poor—these and many other awful deeds would be morally permissible if God so willed. There would be no independent standard to judge that these acts are wrong, no moral reasons apart from God's will to suggest that such deeds are evil. God would be free to establish arbitrarily any actions whatsoever as morally right.

Defenders of the divine command theory have replied to the arbitrariness charge by saying that God would never command something evil because God is all-good. But critics point out that if the theory is true, the assertion that God is all-good would be meaningless, and the traditional religious idea of the goodness of God would become an empty notion. If God makes the moral law, then the moral term *good* would mean "commanded by God." But then "God is good" would mean something like "God does what God commands" or even "God is what God is," which tells us nothing about the goodness of God. Likewise, "God's commands are good" would translate as "God's commands are God's commands." This attempt to escape the charge of arbitrariness seems to have intolerable implications.

Theists and nontheists alike find this horn of Socrates' dilemma—the idea of an arbitrary, divinely ordained morality—incredible. They therefore reject the divine command theory and embrace the other horn, the view that right and wrong are independent of God's will. Moral standards are external to God, binding on both God and mortals. If there are divine commands, they will conform to these independent moral norms. The religious may then claim that God is good—good because he abides perfectly by the moral law and guides the conduct of believers accordingly.

If moral standards are not grounded in the divine will, if they are logically independent of religion, then morality is a legitimate concern for the religious and nonreligious alike, and everyone has equal access to moral reflection and the moral life. The best evidence for the latter is ethics itself. The fact is that people *do ethics*. They use critical reasoning and experience to determine moral norms, explore ethical issues, test moral theories, and live a good life. The results of these explorations are moral outlooks and standards founded on good reasons and arguments and assented to by reflective people everywhere.

In bioethics, the informed opinions of religious people are as relevant as those of secularists. But all parties must be willing to submit their views to the tests and criteria of critical reasoning and evidence.

But even if ethics does not have this independent status, there are still good reasons for religious believers to know how to use the critical tools that ethics offers. First, like many secular moral rules, religious moral codes are often vague and difficult to apply to conflicts and issues, especially in complex fields such as bioethics. Getting around this problem requires interpreting the codes, and this task involves consideration of broader norms or theories, a typical job for ethics. Second, like everyone else, believers must deal with moral conflicts of all sorts—including clashes between the moral beliefs of religious adherents, religious leaders, and religious traditions. What is often needed is a neutral standard and critical analyses to arrive at a resolution—tools that ethics can easily provide. Third, public debate on ethical issues in a diverse society requires ground rules—chief among them being that positions must be explained and reasons must be given in their support. Unexplained assertions without supporting reasons or arguments are likely to be ignored. In this arena, ethics is essential.

MORAL ARGUMENTS

Critical reasoning is something we employ every time we carefully and systematically assess the truth of a statement or the merits of a logical argument. We ask: Are there good reasons for believing this statement? Is this a good argument—does it prove its case? These sorts of questions are asked in every academic field and in every serious human endeavor. Wherever there is a need to acquire knowledge, to separate truth from falsity, and to come to a reliable understanding of how the world works, these questions are asked and answers are sought. Ethics is no exception. Critical reasoning in ethics—called *moral reasoning*—employs the same general principles of logic and evidence that guide the search for truth in every other field. So we need not wonder whether we use critical reasoning in ethics but whether we use it well.

Argument Fundamentals

Most critical reasoning is concerned in one way or another with the construction or evaluation of arguments. As you may have guessed, here *argument* denotes not an altercation but a patterned set of assertions: at least one statement providing support for another statement. We have an argument when one or more statements give us reasons for believing another one. The supporting statements are *premises*, and the supported statement is the *conclusion*. In critical reasoning, the term *statement* also has a technical meaning. A statement (or claim) is an assertion that something is or is not the case and is therefore the kind of utterance that is either true or false.

You need to understand at the outset that *argument* in this sense is not synonymous with *persuasion*. An argument provides us with reasons for accepting a claim; it is an attempted "proof" for an assertion. But persuasion does not necessarily involve giving any reasons at all for accepting a claim. To persuade is to influence people's opinions, which can be accomplished by offering a good argument but also by misleading with logical fallacies, exploiting emotions and prejudices, dazzling with rhetorical gimmicks, hiding or distorting the facts, threatening or coercing people—the list is long. Good arguments prove something whether or not they persuade. Persuasive ploys can change minds but do not necessarily prove anything.

So we formulate an argument to try to show that a particular claim (the conclusion) should be believed, and we analyze an argument to see if it really does show what it purports to show. If the argument is good, we are entitled to believe its conclusion. If it is bad, we are not entitled to believe it.

Consider these two simple arguments:

ARGUMENT 1
Law enforcement in the city is a complete failure. Incidents of serious crime have doubled.

ARGUMENT 2
It's wrong to take the life of an innocent person. Abortion takes the life of an innocent person. So abortion is wrong.

In Argument 1, the conclusion is "Law enforcement in the city is a complete failure," which is supported by the premise "Incidents of serious crime have doubled." The conclusion of Argument 2 is "abortion is wrong," and it is backed by two premises: "It's wrong to take the life of an innocent person" and "Abortion takes the life of an innocent person." Despite the differences between these two passages (differences in content, the number of premises, and the order of their parts), they are both arguments because they exemplify basic argument structure: a conclusion supported by at least one premise.

Though the components of an argument seem clear enough, people often fail to distinguish between arguments and strong statements that contain no arguments at all. Suppose we change Argument 1 into this:

Law enforcement in the city is a complete failure. Nothing seems to work anymore. This situation is intolerable.

Now there is no argument, just an expression of annoyance or anger. There are no statements giving us reasons to believe a conclusion. What we have are some unsupported assertions that may merely *appear* to make a case. If we ignore the distinction between genuine arguments and nonargumentative material, critical reasoning is undone.

Assuming we can recognize an argument when we see it, how can we tell if it is a good one? Fortunately, the general criteria for judging the merits of an argument are simple and clear. A good argument—one that gives us good reasons for believing a claim—must have (1) solid logic and (2) true premises. Requirement (1) means that the conclusion should follow logically from the premises, that there must be a proper logical connection between supporting statements and the statement supported. Requirement (2) says that what the premises assert must in fact be the case. An argument that fails in either respect is a bad argument.

There are two basic kinds of arguments—deductive and inductive—and our two requirements hold for both of them, even though the logical connections in each type are distinct. **Deductive arguments** are intended to give *logically conclusive* support to their conclusions so that if the premises are true, the conclusion absolutely must be true. Argument 2 is a deductive argument and is therefore supposed to be constructed so that if the two premises are true, its conclusion cannot possibly be false. Here it is with its structure laid bare:

ARGUMENT 2
1. It's wrong to take the life of an innocent person.
2. Abortion takes the life of an innocent person.
3. Therefore, abortion is wrong.

Do you see that, given the form or structure of this argument, if the premises are true, then the conclusion *has to be true*? It would be very strange—illogical, in fact—to agree that the two premises are true but that the conclusion is false.

Now look at this one:

ARGUMENT 3
1. All dogs are mammals.
2. Rex is a dog.
3. Therefore, Rex is a mammal.

Again, there is no way for the premises to be true while the conclusion is false. The deductive form of the argument guarantees this.

So a deductive argument is intended to have this sort of airtight structure. If it actually does have this structure, it is said to be *valid*. Argu-

ment 2 is deductive because it is intended to provide logically conclusive support to its conclusion. It is valid because, as a matter of fact, it does offer this kind of support. A deductive argument that fails to provide conclusive support to its conclusion is said to be *invalid*. In such an argument, it is possible for the premises to be true and the conclusion false. Argument 3 is intended to have a deductive form, and because it actually does have this form, the argument is also valid.

An elementary fact about deductive arguments is that their validity (or lack thereof) is a separate issue from the truth of the premises. Validity is a structural matter, depending entirely on how an argument is put together. Truth concerns the nature of the claims made in the premises and conclusion. A deductive argument is supposed to be built so that *if* the premises are true, the conclusion must be true—but in a particular case, the premises might *not* be true. A valid argument can have true or false premises and a true or false conclusion. (By definition, of course, it cannot have true premises and a false conclusion.) In any case, being invalid or having false premises dooms a deductive argument.

Inductive arguments are supposed to give *probable* support to their conclusions. Unlike deductive arguments, they are not designed to support their conclusions decisively. They can establish only that, if their premises are true, their conclusions are probably true (more likely to be true than not). Argument 1 is an inductive argument meant to demonstrate the probable truth that "Law enforcement in the city is a complete failure." Like all inductive arguments (and unlike deductive ones), it can have true premises and a false conclusion. So the sole premise—"incidents of serious crime have doubled"—can be true while the conclusion is false.

If inductive arguments succeed in lending probable support to their conclusions, they are said to be *strong*. Strong arguments are such that if their premises are true, their conclusions are probably true. If they fail to provide this probable support, they are termed *weak*. Argument 1 is a weak argument because its premise, even if true, does not show that more likely than not law enforcement in the city is a complete failure. After all, even if incidents of serious crime have doubled, law enforcement may be successful in other ways, or incidents of serious crime may be up for reasons unrelated to the effectiveness of law enforcement.

But consider this inductive argument:

ARGUMENT 4
1. Eighty-five percent of the students at this university are Republicans.
2. Sonia is a student at this university.
3. Therefore, Sonia is probably a Republican.

This argument is strong. If its premises are true, its conclusion is likely to be true. If eighty-five percent of the university's students are Republicans, and Sonia is a university student, she is more likely than not to be a Republican, too.

When a valid (deductive) argument has true premises, it is a good argument. A good deductive argument is said to be *sound*. Argument 2 is valid, but we cannot say whether it is sound until we determine the truth of the premises. Argument 3 is valid, and if its premises are true, it is sound. When a strong (inductive) argument has true premises, it is also a good argument. A good inductive argument is said to be *cogent*. Argument 1 is weak, so there is no way it can be cogent. Argument 4 is strong, and if its premises are true, it is cogent.

Checking the validity or strength of an argument is often a plain, commonsense undertaking. Using our natural reasoning ability, we can examine how the premises are linked to the conclusion and can see quickly whether the conclusion follows from the premises. We are most likely to make an easy job of it when the arguments are simple. Many times, however, we need some help, and help is available in the form of methods and guidelines for evaluating arguments.

Having a familiarity with common argument patterns, or forms, is especially useful when assessing the validity of deductive arguments. We are likely to encounter these forms again and again in bioethics as well as in everyday life. Here is a prime example:

ARGUMENT 5
1. If the surgeon operates, then the patient will be cured.
2. The surgeon is operating.
3. Therefore, the patient will be cured.

This argument form contains a *conditional* premise—that is, a premise consisting of a conditional, or if-then, statement (actually a compound statement composed of two constituent statements). Premise 1 is a conditional statement. A conditional statement has two parts: the part beginning with *if* (called the *antecedent*) and the part beginning with *then* (known as the *consequent*). So the antecedent of premise 1 is "If the surgeon operates," and the consequent is "then the patient will be cured."

The best way to appreciate the structure of such an argument (or any deductive argument, for that matter) is to translate it into traditional argument symbols in which each statement is symbolized by a letter. Here is the symbolization for Argument 5:

1. If p, then q.
2. p.
3. Therefore, q.

We can see that p represents "the surgeon operates," and q represents "the patient will be cured." But notice that we can use this same symbolized argument form to represent countless other arguments—arguments with different statements but having the same basic structure.

It just so happens that the underlying argument form for Argument 5 is extremely common—common enough to have a name, *modus ponens* (or affirming the antecedent). The truly useful fact about *modus ponens* is that any argument having this form is valid. We can plug any statements we want into the formula and the result will be a valid argument, a circumstance in which if the premises are true, the conclusion must be true.

Another common argument form is *modus tollens* (or denying the consequent). For example:

ARGUMENT 6

1. If the dose is low, then the healing is slow.
2. The healing is not slow.
3. Therefore, the dose is not low.

1. If *p*, then *q*.
2. Not *q*.
3. Therefore, not *p*.

Modus tollens is also a valid form, and any argument using this form must also be valid.

There are also common argument forms that are *invalid*. Here are two of them:

AFFIRMING THE CONSEQUENT

ARGUMENT 7

1. If the patient is getting better, then drugs are unnecessary.
2. Drugs are unnecessary.
3. Therefore, the patient is getting better.

1. If *p*, then *q*.
2. *q*.
3. Therefore, *p*.

DENYING THE ANTECEDENT

ARGUMENT 8

1. If the rate of infection is increasing, then the patients will die.
2. The rate of infection is not increasing.
3. Therefore, the patients will not die.

1. If *p*, then *q*.
2. Not *p*.
3. Therefore, not *q*.

The advantage of being able to recognize these and other common argument forms is that you can use that skill to determine readily the validity of many deductive arguments. You know, for example, that any argument having the same form as *modus ponens* or *modus tollens* must be valid, and any argument in one of the common invalid forms must be invalid.

Patterns of Moral Arguments

All that you have learned about argument fundamentals thus far applies directly to that subspecies of argument we are most interested in: moral argument. A **moral argument** is an argument whose conclusion is a moral statement, an assertion that an action is right or wrong or that a person or motive is good or bad. We utter a moral statement when we say such things as "Physician-assisted suicide is wrong," or "Maria should not have had an abortion," or "Dr. Jones is a good person." We are constantly making moral statements and including them in our moral arguments, which we frequently devise and hold up for inspection and evaluation.

Recall Argument 2, a simple (and common) moral argument:

1. It's wrong to take the life of an innocent person.
2. Abortion takes the life of an innocent person.
3. Therefore, abortion is wrong.

Here we can see all the standard features of a typical moral argument: (1) At least one premise (premise 1) is a moral statement asserting a general moral norm such as a moral principle; (2) at least one premise (premise 2) is a nonmoral statement describing an action or circumstance; and (3) the conclusion is a moral statement expressing a moral judgment about a specific action or circumstance.

Notice how natural this pattern seems. If we want to argue that a particular action (or kind of action) is wrong, for example, we must provide a reason for this moral judgment. The natural (and logical) move is to reach for a general moral principle that supports the judgment. Why is performing surgery on Mrs. Johnson without her consent wrong? Because, we might say, treating people without their consent is a violation of their autonomy (a moral principle), and performing surgery on Mrs. Johnson without her consent would be an instance of such a violation (a nonmoral fact).

REVIEW **Valid and Invalid Argument Forms**

Valid Forms

Affirming the Antecedent (*Modus Ponens*)	Denying the Consequent (*Modus Tollens*)
If p, then q.	If p, then q.
p.	Not q.
Therefore, q.	Therefore, not p.

Example:	Example:
If Spot barks, a burglar is in the house.	If it's raining, the park is closed.
Spot is barking.	The park is not closed.
Therefore, a burglar is in the house.	Therefore, it's not raining.

Invalid Forms

Affirming the Consequent	Denying the Antecedent
If p, then q.	If p, then q.
q.	Not p.
Therefore, p.	Therefore, not q.

Example:	Example:
If the cat is on the mat, she is asleep.	If the cat is on the mat, she is asleep.
She is asleep.	She is not on the mat.
Therefore, she is on the mat.	Therefore, she is not asleep.

This natural way of proceeding reflects the logical realities of moral reasoning. In a moral argument, we *must* have at least one moral premise to draw a conclusion about the morality of a particular state of affairs. Without a moral premise, we cannot legitimately arrive at a moral conclusion. That is, from a nonmoral premise alone, a moral conclusion does not logically follow. For example, from the nonmoral fact that abortions are frequently performed, we cannot conclude that abortion is immoral. Nonmoral premises cannot support a conclusion expressing a moral judgment. Likewise, we cannot reason from a moral premise alone (one affirming a general moral principle) to a conclusion about the morality of a particular action. We need a nonmoral premise affirming that the particular action in question is an instance of the general class of actions referred to in the general moral premise. In Argument 2, the moral premise tells us it's wrong to take the life of an innocent person, but we need the nonmoral premise to assert that abortion is an instance of taking the life of an innocent person. After all, that a fetus is a person—the kind of entity that is deserving of full moral rights—is not obviously true and not assented to by everyone. We must spell out in a premise what we take to be the nonmoral fact of the matter.

This discussion underscores a previously mentioned fact about moral disagreements. When people disagree on a moral issue, they may or may not be disagreeing about moral principles. They may actually share the relevant moral principles but disagree about the nonmoral facts—or vice versa. So when people take contradictory stands on the conclusion of a moral argument,

IN DEPTH

FALLACIES IN MORAL REASONING

The world is full of bad arguments. Many of them occur again and again in different guises and contexts, being so common that they have been given names and are studied by those who wish to avoid such mistakes. These common, defective arguments are called *fallacies*. Here are a few that often crop up in moral reasoning:

STRAW MAN

The straw man fallacy is the misrepresentation of a person's views so they can be more easily attacked or dismissed. Suppose you argue that because an immunization program will save the lives of thousands of children and will likely cause the death of only 1 child out of every 500,000, we should fund the immunization program. But then your opponent replies that you think the life of a child isn't worth much. Thus your point has been distorted, made to look extreme or unsavory—and is now an easier target. The straw man fallacy, of course, proves nothing, though many people fall for it every day.

APPEAL TO THE PERSON

Closely related to the straw man fallacy is appeal to the person (also known as the *ad hominem* fallacy). Appeal to the person is the rejecting of a statement on the grounds that it comes from a particular person, not because the statement, or claim, itself is false or dubious. For example:

> *You can safely discard anything that Susan has to say about abortion. She's a Catholic.*

> *Johnson argues that our current health care system is defective. But don't listen to him—he's a liberal.*

These arguments are defective because they ask us to reject a claim because of a person's character, background, or circumstances—things that are generally irrelevant to the truth of claims. A statement must stand or fall on its own merits. The personal characteristics of the person espousing the view do not necessarily have a bearing on its truth. Only if we can show that someone's dubious traits somehow make the claim dubious are we justified in rejecting the claim because of a person's personal characteristics. Such a circumstance is rare.

APPEAL TO IGNORANCE

As its name implies, this fallacy tries to prove something by appealing to what we don't know. The appeal to ignorance is arguing either that (1) a claim is true because it has not been proven false or (2) a claim is false because it has not been proven true. For example:

> *No one has proven that a fetus is not a person, so it is in fact a person.*

> *It is obviously false that a fetus is a person because science has not proven that it is a person.*

The first argument tries to prove a claim by pointing out that it has not been proven false. The second argument tries to prove that a claim is false because it has not been proven true. Both kinds of arguments are bogus because they assume that a lack of evidence proves something. But a lack of evidence can prove nothing. Being ignorant of the facts does not enlighten us. Notice that if a lack of evidence could prove something, then you could prove just about anything you wanted. You could reason, for instance, that since no one can prove that horses cannot fly, horses must be able to fly.

BEGGING THE QUESTION

The fallacy of begging the question is trying to prove a conclusion by using that very same conclusion as support. It is arguing in a circle. This way of trying to prove something says, in effect, "X is true because X is true." Here is a classic example:

> *The Bible says that God exists.*

> *The Bible is true because God wrote it.*

> *Therefore, God exists.*

The conclusion here ("God exists") is supported by premises that assume that very conclusion.

Here's another one:

All citizens have the right to a fair trial because those whom the state is obliged to protect and give consideration are automatically due judicial criminal proceedings that are equitable by any reasonable standard.

This passage may at first seem like a good argument, but it isn't. It reduces to this unimpressive assertion: "All citizens have the right to a fair trial because all citizens have the right to a fair trial." The conclusion is "All citizens have the right to a fair trial," but that is more or less what the premise says. The premise—"those whom the state is obliged to protect and give consideration are automatically due judicial criminal proceedings that are equitable by any reasonable standard"—is equivalent to "All citizens have the right to a fair trial."

SLIPPERY SLOPE

The metaphor behind this fallacy suggests the danger of stepping on a dicey incline, losing your footing, and sliding to disaster. The fallacy of slippery slope, then, is arguing erroneously that a particular action should not be taken because it will lead inevitably to other actions resulting in some dire outcome. The key word here is *erroneously*. A slippery slope scenario becomes fallacious when there is no reason to believe that the chain of events predicted will ever happen. For example:

If dying patients are permitted to refuse treatment, then soon doctors will be refusing the treatment on their behalf. Then physician-assisted suicide will become rampant, and soon killing patients for almost any reason will become the norm.

This argument is fallacious because there are no reasons for believing that the first step will ultimately result in the chain of events described. If good reasons could be given, the argument might be salvaged.

---

the source of the conflict could lie with the moral premises or the nonmoral premises or both.

Unfortunately, in everyday life moral arguments do not come with their premises clearly labeled, so we need to be able to identify the premises ourselves. This job is made more difficult by a simple fact of the moral life: Often premises (moral and nonmoral) are left unsaid and are merely implied. Sometimes premises are unstated because they are obvious assumptions that need not be mentioned. But if we are to perform a thorough evaluation of an argument, we must drag the implicit premises into the open so they can be fully assessed. Such careful scrutiny is especially important in moral arguments because the implicit premises are often questionable assumptions—the secret, weak links in the chain of reasoning. For example:

ARGUMENT 9
1. In vitro fertilization is an entirely unnatural process, as far from natural reproduction as one could imagine.

2. Therefore, in vitro fertilization should not be used.

As it stands, this is a bad argument; the conclusion does not follow from the premise. But there is an implied (moral) premise lurking here, and if we make it explicit, the argument will be valid:

1. In vitro fertilization is an entirely unnatural process, as far from natural reproduction as one could imagine.
2. Any process that is unnatural should not be used.
3. Therefore, in vitro fertilization should not be used.

Now the argument is complete, and we can see both the nonmoral premise (premise 1) and the moral premise (premise 2), which is a moral principle. But now that we have brought the moral premise into the light of day, we can see that it is false or at least debatable. We use many processes and products that are unnatural (for example, modern pharmaceuticals, intravenous feeding, surgery, CAT scans, artificial limbs, and contact lenses), but we generally do not regard them as morally impermissible.

Very often we can tell that an argument has an unstated premise because there is a logical leap between the stated premises and the conclusion. The inference from stated premises to conclusion does not work unless the missing premise is supplied. A good candidate for the implicit premise will make the argument valid or strong and will be plausible in the context of the argument. The most straightforward approach, however, is to treat the argument as deductive and look for a premise that will make the argument valid, as we did in Argument 9.

Evaluating Premises

As we have seen, good arguments have true premises. But how do we know if the premises are true? Fortunately, there are ways to test, or evaluate, the truth of premises. The tests differ, however, depending on whether the premises are nonmoral or moral.

Checking the truth of nonmoral premises can involve the exploration of either empirical or conceptual matters. An empirical belief, or claim, is one that can be confirmed by sense experience—that is, by observation or scientific investigation. Most nonmoral premises are empirical claims that we can check by examining our own experience or that of others or by consulting the relevant scientific findings. By these methods we can test (and support) a wide variety of empirical assertions, such as many of the nonmoral premises examined earlier: "Incidents of serious crime have doubled"; "Eighty-five percent of the students at this university are Republicans"; "If the patient is getting better, then drugs are unnecessary."

In bioethics, among the most controversial nonmoral premises are those affirming that a medical treatment or program will or will not have a particular effect on people. The issue is whether it will help or harm and to what degree. Sometimes reliable data are available to resolve the issue. Sometimes no clear evidence exists, leaving people to make educated guesses that are often in dispute.

In any case, critical reasoning in bioethics demands that we always seek the most reliable evidence available and try to assess its worth objectively. It requires that our empirical claims be supported by good empirical evidence and that we expect the same from others who make empirical assertions.

A conceptual matter has to do with the meaning of terms, something we need to pay attention to because disputes in bioethics sometimes hinge on the meaning of a concept. For example, in disagreements about the moral permissibility of abortion, the crux of the matter is often how the disputants define *person* (as in Argument 2), or *human life*, or *human being*. Similarly, whether someone supports or opposes euthanasia often hangs on how it is defined. Some, for example, define it in the narrow sense of taking direct action to kill someone for his sake (mercy killing), while others insist on a wider sense that encompasses both mercifully killing and allowing to die. Whether we are devising our own arguments or evaluating those of others, being clear on the meaning of terms is essential, and any proposed definition must be backed by good reasons.

Moral premises are like nonmoral ones in that they too should be supported by good reasons and be subjected to serious scrutiny. But just how are moral premises supported and scrutinized?

Support for a moral premise (a moral principle or standard) can come from at least three sources: other moral principles, moral theories, or our most reliable moral judgments. Probably the most common way to support a moral principle is to appeal to a higher-level principle (which often turns out to be one of the four major moral principles discussed earlier). Suppose the moral premise in question is "The patient's wishes about whether surgery is performed on him should not be ignored." Some would argue that this principle is derived from, or is based on, the higher principle that autonomous persons should be allowed to exercise their capacity for self-determination.

Or let's say the premise is "Individuals in a persistent vegetative state should never have their feeding tubes removed so they can 'die with dignity.'" Many would base this assertion on the principle that human life is sacred and should be preserved at all costs. Frequently, the higher principle appealed to is plausible, seemingly universal, or accepted by all parties so that further support for the principle is not necessary. At other times, the higher principle itself may be controversial and in need of support.

Moral premises can also be supported by a moral theory, a general explanation of what makes an action right or a person or motive good. (In Chapter 2 we discuss moral theories in depth.) For example, traditional utilitarianism is a moral theory affirming that right actions are those that produce the greatest happiness for all concerned. Appealing to utilitarianism, then, someone might insist that a baby born with severe brain damage who will die within a few days should not be allowed to wither slowly away in pain but should be given a lethal injection. The justification for this policy is that it would produce the least amount of unhappiness (including pain and suffering) for all concerned, including baby, parents, and caregivers. Those who reject this policy would have to argue that there was something wrong with utilitarianism or that other considerations (including alternative theories) outweigh utilitarian concerns.

Another possible source of support for moral premises is what philosophers call our *considered moral judgments*. These are moral judgments we deem plausible or credible after careful reflection that is as unbiased as possible. They may apply to both particular cases and more general moral statements. For example, after deliberation we might conclude that "Inflicting undeserved and unnecessary pain on someone is wrong," or that "Emergency care for accident victims should be provided regardless of their race or religion," or that "Amputating a patient's leg for no good reason is never morally permissible." Like moral principles and theories, such judgments can vary in how much weight they carry in moral

arguments and can be given more or less credibility (or undermined completely) by relevant reasons. (We examine more closely the relationships among theories, principles, and considered judgments in Chapter 2.)

Moral premises can be called into question by showing that they somehow conflict with credible principles, theories, or judgments. One way to do this is to cite *counterexamples*, instances in which the moral principle in question seems not to hold. Recall that a counterexample helps us see that the moral premise in Argument 9 is dubious. The premise says "Any process that is unnatural should not be used," but we often use unnatural products or processes (CAT scans and contact lenses, for instance) and do not think these actions morally wrong. In the same way, we can use counterexamples to evaluate the moral premise in Argument 2:

1. It's wrong to take the life of an innocent person.
2. Abortion takes the life of an innocent person.
3. Therefore, abortion is wrong.

Are there no exceptions to premise 1? Is it always wrong to kill an innocent person? We can imagine cases in which this premise seems either doubtful or at least not obviously true. What about situations in which many lives can be saved by taking the life of one person? What if all 50 people in a lifeboat at sea will drown unless one of them is cast overboard? What if the one unlucky person *agrees* to be cast overboard to save all the others? Or suppose a person is dying of cancer and is suffering unspeakable pain that cannot be relieved by any medical means—and she begs for a lethal injection of morphine. Some would argue that these scenarios raise serious questions about premise 1, suggesting that at least in its current form, it may not be true. In response to these counterexamples, some who wish to defend the premise might modify it to take the scenarios into account or even try to show that despite its implications premise 1 is justified.

KEY TERMS

applied ethics
bioethics
cultural relativism
deductive argument
descriptive ethics
divine command theory
ethical relativism
ethics
inductive argument
metaethics
moral absolutism
moral argument
moral objectivism
morality
normative ethics
paternalism
subjective relativism

SUMMARY

Morality refers to beliefs about right and wrong actions and morally good and bad persons or character. Ethics is the study of morality using the tools and methods of philosophy. The study of morality using the methodology of science is known as descriptive ethics. Ethics has three main branches: (1) normative ethics, the search for, and justification of, moral standards, or norms; (2) metaethics, the study of the meaning and justification of basic moral beliefs; and (3) applied ethics, the use of moral norms and concepts to resolve practical moral issues. Bioethics is applied ethics focused on health care, medical science, and medical technology.

Moral norms differ from other kinds of norms because they are characterized by (1) normative dominance, (2) universality, (3) impartiality, and (4) reasonableness. We apply moral norms to two distinct spheres of our moral experience—obligations and values. Moral obligations concern our duty, what we are obligated to do or not do, and refer primarily to right and wrong actions. Moral values generally concern those things that we judge to be morally good, bad, praiseworthy, or blameworthy. A right action can be obligatory (one that would be wrong not to perform) or

permissible (one that is not wrong to perform). A prohibited action would be one that would be wrong to perform. A supererogatory action is one that is "above and beyond" our duty.

In bioethics, four moral principles have been extremely influential and particularly relevant: (1) autonomy (autonomous persons should be allowed to exercise their capacity for self-determination); (2) beneficence (we should do good to others and avoid doing them harm); (3) utility (we should produce the most favorable balance of good over bad for all concerned); and (4) justice (we should treat equals equally).

According to ethical relativism, moral standards are not objective but are relative to what individuals or cultures believe. A familiar argument for cultural relativism is that if people's moral judgments differ from culture to culture, then moral norms are relative to culture, and people's moral judgments obviously do differ from culture to culture. But the first premise in the argument is false. In addition, cultural relativism seems implausible because it implies moral infallibility, immunity of all cultures from moral criticism from the outside, the automatic wrongness of the moral stance of social reformers, and the incoherence of the idea of moral progress. Moreover, cultural relativism does not necessarily lead to tolerance and does not logically entail it.

The divine command theory says that right actions are those commanded by God, and wrong actions are those forbidden by God. But many religious and nonreligious people have rejected the theory because it seems to imply that God's commands are arbitrary.

Most critical reasoning is concerned in one way or another with the construction or evaluation of arguments. All the skills required in dealing with arguments generally can be applied directly to handling moral arguments in particular. A moral argument is one whose conclusion is a moral statement, an assertion that an action is right or wrong or that a person or motive is good or bad.

FURTHER READING

Anita L. Allen, *New Ethics: A Guided Tour of the Twenty-First Century Moral Landscape* (New York: Miramax, 2004).

Robert Audi, *Moral Knowledge and Ethical Character* (New York: Oxford University Press, 1997).

Tom L. Beauchamp and James F. Childress, *Principles of Biomedical Ethics*, 5th ed. (New York: Oxford University Press, 2001).

Richard B. Brandt, *Ethical Theory* (Englewood Cliffs, NJ: Prentice-Hall, 1959).

Steven M. Cahn and Joram G. Haber, *Twentieth Century Ethical Theory* (Upper Saddle River, NJ: Prentice-Hall, 1995).

Jean Bethke Elshtain, "Judge Not?," *First Things* 46 (October 1994): 36–41.

Fred Feldman, *Introductory Ethics* (Englewood Cliffs, NJ: Prentice-Hall, 1978).

Richard M. Fox and Joseph P. DeMarco, *Moral Reasoning*, 2nd ed. (New York: Harcourt, Inc., 2001).

William K. Frankena, *Ethics*, 2nd ed. (Englewood Cliffs, NJ: Prentice-Hall, 1973).

Bernard Gert, *Morality: Its Nature and Justification* (New York: Oxford, 1998).

Chris Gowans, "Moral Relativism," in *The Stanford Encyclopedia of Philosophy* (Spring 2004 ed.), ed. Edward N. Zalta, http://plato.stanford.edu/archives/spr2004/entries/moral-relativism/.

C. E. Harris, *Applying Moral Theories* (Belmont, CA: Wadsworth, 1997).

Melville Herskovits, *Cultural Relativism: Perspectives in Cultural Pluralism* (New York: Vintage, 1972).

Albert R. Jonsen, *The Birth of Bioethics* (New York: Oxford University Press, 1998).

Kai Nielsen, *Ethics Without God* (Buffalo, NY: Prometheus, 1973).

Louis P. Pojman, *Ethics: Discovering Right and Wrong*, 4th ed. (Belmont, CA: Wadsworth, 2002).

Louis P. Pojman and Lewis Vaughn, eds., *The Moral Life*, 3rd ed. (New York: Oxford University Press, 2007).

James Rachels, *The Elements of Moral Philosophy*, 4th ed. (New York: McGraw-Hill, 2003).

Theodore Schick, Jr., and Lewis Vaughn, *Doing Philosophy*, 2nd ed. (New York: McGraw-Hill, 2002), chap. 5.

Russ Shafer-Landau, *Whatever Happened to Good and Evil?* (New York: Oxford University Press, 2004).

Peter Singer, ed., *A Companion to Ethics* (Cambridge: Blackwell, 1993).

Walter T. Stace, "Ethical Relativism," in *The Concept of Morals* (New York: Macmillan, 1965), 8–58.

Bonnie Steinbock, ed., *The Oxford Handbook of Bioethics* (Oxford: Oxford University Press, 2007).

Paul Taylor, *Principles of Ethics* (Encino, CA: Dickenson, 1975).

Lewis Vaughn, *Doing Ethics: Moral Reasoning and Contemporary Issues* (New York: W.W. Norton, 2008).

Lewis Vaughn, *The Power of Critical Thinking*, 2nd ed. (New York: Oxford University Press, 2008).

Thomas F. Wall, *Thinking Critically About Moral Problems* (Belmont, CA: Wadsworth, 2003).

G. J. Warnock, *The Object of Morality* (London: Methuen & Co. Ltd., 1971).

NOTES

1. James Rachels, *The Elements of Moral Philosophy,* 4th ed. (New York: McGraw-Hill, 2003), 14.

2. This example is derived from James Rachels' unique description of the case in "Ethical Theory and Bioethics," from *A Companion to Bioethics,* ed. Helga Kuhse and Peter Singer (Oxford: Blackwell, 2001), 16–17.

3. W. D. Ross, *The Right and the Good* (Oxford: Clarendon Press, 1930).

4. In their classic text *Principles of Biomedical Ethics* (New York: Oxford University Press, 2001), Tom L. Beauchamp and James F. Childress work out a comprehensive approach to biomedical ethics using a framework of four moral principles like the ones discussed here. They choose to treat beneficence and nonmaleficence separately and regard utility as part of beneficence.

5. This is roughly William K. Frankena's analysis, offered in his *Ethics,* 2nd ed. (Englewood Cliffs, NJ: Prentice-Hall, 1973), 47.

6. Solomon Asch, *Social Psychology* (Englewood Cliffs, NJ: Prentice-Hall, 1952), 378–79.

CHAPTER 2

Bioethics and Moral Theories

As we have seen, the moral life is dynamic, complex, and inescapable. In it we wrestle with momentous questions of moral value and moral rightness. We assert, challenge, accept, and reject moral statements. We make moral judgments about the rightness of actions, the goodness of persons or their character, and the moral quality and worth of our lives. Through general moral norms or principles, we direct our actions and inform our choices. We formulate and critique moral arguments, thereby testing what we know or think we know about moral realities. We do all this and one thing more: We naturally and unavoidably venture into the realm of moral theory, trying to see the larger moral meaning behind particular situations and precepts. In this chapter, we explore this realm and try to discern how it fits into the moral life in general and into bioethics in particular.

THE NATURE OF MORAL THEORIES

In science, theories help us understand the empirical world by explaining the causes of events, why things are the way they are. The germ theory of disease explains how particular diseases arise and spread in a human population. The heliocentric (sun-centered) theory of planetary motion explains why the planets in our solar system behave the way they do. In ethics, moral theories have a similar explanatory role. A **moral theory** explains not why one event causes another but why an action is right or wrong or why a person or a person's character is good or bad. A moral theory tells us what it is about an action that *makes it right*, or what it is about a person that *makes him or her good*. The divine command

theory of morality, for example, says that right actions are those commanded or willed by God. Traditional utilitarianism says that right actions are those that produce the greatest happiness for all concerned. These and other moral theories are attempts to define rightness or goodness. In this way, they are both more general and more basic than moral principles or other general norms.

Moral theorizing—that is, making, using, or assessing moral theories or parts of theories—is normal and pervasive in the moral life, though it is often done without much recognition that theory is playing a part in the deliberations. Whenever we try to understand what a moral property such as rightness or goodness means, or justify a moral principle or other norm, or resolve a conflict between two credible principles, or explain why a particular action or practice is right or wrong, or evaluate the plausibility of specific moral intuitions or assumptions, we do moral theorizing. In fact, we *must* theorize if we are to make headway in such investigations. We must stand back from the situation at hand and try to grasp the larger pattern that only theory can reveal.

Moral theories that concentrate on right and wrong actions are known as theories of obligation (or duty) or simply as *theories of right action*. The divine command theory and utilitarianism are theories of right action. Philosophers often distinguish these from moral theories that focus on good and bad persons or character—so-called *virtue-based theories*. Virtue ethics (covered later in this chapter) is a prime example.

How do moral theories fit into our everyday moral reasoning? In answering that, let's focus on theories of right action, probably the most influential type in bioethics. First, moral theories can figure directly in our moral arguments. As we saw earlier, moral arguments contain both moral and nonmoral premises. A moral premise can consist of a moral principle, a moral rule (a less general norm derived from or based on a principle), or a claim expressing a central tenet of a moral theory. Using such a tenet, someone might argue, for example, that stem-cell research should be fully funded rather than halted altogether because such a step would eventually lead to a greater benefit for more people, and right actions (according to utilitarianism) are those that result in the greatest overall benefit for the greatest number. Thus the fundamental moral standard of utilitarianism becomes a premise in an argument for a specific action in a particular case.

Second, theories can have an indirect impact on moral arguments because principles appealed to are often supported in turn by a moral theory. The principles can be either derived from or supported by the theory's account of right and wrong action. Consider the prohibition against murder, the basic precept that it is wrong to take the life of an innocent person. This principle can be drawn from theories built around the fundamental notion of respect for persons. As one such theory would have it, murder is wrong because it treats people not as persons with inherent worth but as mere things to be used or dispensed with as one wishes.

Some people are tempted to deduce from all this that moral theories are the dominant force in moral reasoning as well as in the moral life. This view would be an oversimplification. By design, moral theories are certainly more general in scope than moral principles, rules, or judgments. But from this fact it does not follow that theories alone are the ultimate authority in moral deliberations. For one thing, to be truly useful, moral theories must be filled out with details about how to apply them in real life and the kinds of cases to which they are relevant. For another, there is more to morality than what can be captured in the general norms of a theory. There is also the testimony of the particular, the evidence of individual moral judgments.

Our moral deliberations, then, involve both the general and the particular. Suppose we embrace a moral theory that seems to offer us a plausible explanation of what makes an action right or wrong. When we must decide which action is morally right in a particular situation, we look to our theory for general guidance. From our theory we may glean a set of moral principles that seem to apply to the case at hand. If the principles lead us to conflicting choices, we look again to the theory for insight in resolving the conflict. But we also must take into account our considered judgments about the case. (We may also formulate considered judgments about the relevant principles or rules.) If our considered judgments and the deliverances of our theory are consistent with one another, we have additional assurance that our decision in the case is correct. If our judgments clash with our theory or principles, we must decide which to revise or discard—for critical reasoning demands that our beliefs be coherent, that they do not harbor contradictions. If we believe our judgments to be more credible than the implications of our theory (or principles), we may modify the theory accordingly (or, rarely, regard the theory as irreparable and give it up). But if the theory seems more credible in this case, we may conclude that our judgment is untrustworthy and set it aside.

So a moral theory can show us what is important and reasonable in morality, guiding our judgments through overarching insights that may help us with specific cases and issues, sometimes correcting erring judgments along the way. Our considered judgments are fallible indicators of moral common sense and are checks against wayward theory or flawed principle. In bioethics, both of these moral resources are highly respected and widely used.

INFLUENTIAL MORAL THEORIES

Several moral theories have played major roles in bioethics, and they continue to influence how people think about bioethical issues. Theories of right action (in contrast to virtue-based theories) have dominated the field, each usually based on one of two broad views about the essential character of right actions. **Consequentialist** moral theories insist that the rightness of actions depends solely on their consequences or results. The key question is what or how much good the actions produce, however *good* is defined. **Deontological** (or **nonconsequentialist**) theories say that the rightness of actions is determined not solely by their consequences but partly or entirely by their intrinsic nature. For some or all actions, rightness depends on the kind of actions they are, not on how much good they produce. A consequentialist theory, then, may say that stealing is wrong because it causes more harm than good. But a deontological theory may contend that stealing is inherently wrong regardless of its consequences, good or bad.

Utilitarianism

The leading consequentialist theory is **utilitarianism**, the view that right actions are those that result in the most beneficial balance of good over bad consequences for everyone involved. It says we should maximize the nonmoral good (the *utility*) of everyone affected, regardless of the contrary urgings of moral rules or unbending moral principles. Various forms of utilitarianism differ in how they define utility, with some equating it with happiness or pleasure (the hedonistic view), others with satisfaction of preferences or desires or some other intrinsically valuable things or states such as knowledge or perfection.

In applying the utilitarian moral standard (the greatest good, everyone considered), some moral philosophers concentrate on specific acts and some on rules covering kinds of acts. The former approach is called **act-utilitarianism**, the idea that the rightness of actions depends solely on the relative good produced by *individual actions*. An act is right if in a particular situation it produces a greater balance of good over bad than any alternative acts; determining rightness is a matter of weighing the effects of each possible act. The latter approach, known

as **rule-utilitarianism**, avoids judging rightness by specific acts and focuses instead on *rules governing categories of acts*. It says a right action is one that conforms to a rule that, if followed consistently, would create for everyone involved the most beneficial balance of good over bad. We are to adhere to the rules because they maximize the good for everyone considered—even though a given act may produce bad effects in a particular situation.

The classic version of utilitarianism was devised by English philosopher Jeremy Bentham (1748–1832) and given more detail and plausibility by another English philosopher, John Stuart Mill (1806–1873). Classic utilitarianism is hedonistic in that the utility to be maximized is pleasure, broadly termed happiness, the only intrinsic good. A right action produces more net happiness (amounts of happiness minus unhappiness) than any alternative action, everyone considered. As Mill put it,

> [Actions] are right in proportion as they tend to promote happiness, wrong as they tend to produce the reverse of happiness. By "happiness" is intended pleasure, and the absence of pain; by "unhappiness," pain and the privation of pleasure.[1]

Bentham and Mill, however, had different ideas about what happiness entailed, as do many philosophers today. Bentham thinks that happiness is one-dimensional: It is pleasure, pure and simple, something that varies only in the amount that an agent can experience. On this scheme, it seems that the moral ideal would be to experience maximum amounts of pleasure, as does the glutton or the debauchee. But Mill thinks that pleasures can vary in quality as well as quantity. For him, there are lower and higher pleasures— the lower and inferior ones indulged in by the glutton and his ilk and the higher and more satisfying ones found in such experiences as the search for knowledge and the appreciation of art and music. Mill famously sums up this contrast by saying, "It is better to be a human being dissatisfied than a pig satisfied; better to be Socrates dissatisfied than a fool satisfied."[2]

Like all forms of utilitarianism, the classic formulation demands a strong sense of impartiality. When promoting happiness, we must not only take into account the happiness of everyone affected but also give everyone's needs or interests equal weight. Mill explains:

[The] happiness which forms the utilitarian standard of what is right conduct, is not the agent's own happiness, but that of all concerned. As between his own happiness and that of others, utilitarianism requires him to be as strictly impartial as a disinterested and benevolent spectator.[3]

In classic utilitarianism, the emphasis is on maximizing the total quantity of net happiness, not insuring that it is rationed in any particular amounts among the people involved. This means that an action resulting in 1,000 units of happiness for 10 people is better than an action yielding only 900 units of happiness for those same 10 people—regardless of how the units of happiness are distributed among them. Classic utilitarians do want to allocate the total amount of happiness among as many people as possible (thus their motto, "the greatest happiness for the greatest number"). But maximizing total happiness is the fundamental concern whether everyone gets an equal portion or one person gets the lion's share.

How might utilitarianism apply to a bioethical issue? Consider this scenario: Johnny is a 10-year-old boy with cerebral palsy, emaciated and bed-ridden, hooked to feeding tubes and monitors, his body twisted in pain that is almost impossible to control, his days measured out by one agonizing surgical operation after another, locked in the mental life of an infant and acknowledged by all the experts to be without hope. His anguished parents, wanting desperately to end his suffering, beg the physician to give Johnny a lethal injection. What should the physician do?

Suppose in this case there are only two options: indefinitely maintaining Johnny in his present condition or carrying out the parents' wishes. An act-utilitarian might reason like this. Allowing the current situation to continue would cause enormous unhappiness—Johnny's own physical agony, the unimaginable misery of the distraught parents, the anxiety of other family members and friends, and the distress and frustration of the physician and nurses who can do little more than stand by as Johnny withers away. On the other hand, administering the lethal injection would immediately end Johnny's pain and prevent future suffering. The parents would grieve for Johnny but would at least find some relief—and perhaps peace—in knowing that his torture was over. The medical staff would probably also be relieved for the same reason. There would, of course, also be possible negative consequences to take into account. In administering the lethal injection, the physician would be risking both professional censure and criminal prosecution. If her actions were to become public, people might begin to mistrust physicians who treat severely impaired children, undermining the whole medical profession. Perhaps the physician's action would lead to a general devaluing of the lives of disabled or elderly people everywhere. These dire consequences, however, would probably not be very likely if the physician acted discreetly. On balance, the act-utilitarian might say, greater net happiness (the least unhappiness) would result from the mercy killing, which would therefore be the morally permissible course.

A rule-utilitarian might judge the situation differently. The key question would be which rule if consistently followed would produce the greatest net happiness. Let us say that there are only two rules to consider. One says "Do not kill seriously impaired children, regardless of their suffering or the wishes of their parents." The other one is "Killing seriously impaired children is permissible if they are suffering severely and improvement is hopeless." The rule-utilitarian might reason that consistently following the second rule would have terrible consequences. It would cause widespread suspicion about the actions and motives of physicians who treat seriously impaired and disabled children. People would come to distrust physicians, which in turn

IN DEPTH
UTILITARIANISM AND THE GOLDEN RULE

Probably much to the dismay of his religious critics, John Stuart Mill defended his radical doctrine of utilitarianism by arguing that it was entirely consistent with a fundamental Christian teaching:

> In the golden rule of Jesus of Nazareth, we read the complete spirit of the ethics of utility. To do as one would be done by, and to love one's neighbour as oneself, constitute the ideal perfection of utilitarian morality. As the means of making the nearest approach to this ideal, utility would enjoin, first, that laws and social arrangements should place the happiness, or (as speaking practically it may be called) the interest, of every individual, as nearly as possible in harmony with the interest of the whole; and secondly, that education and opinion, which have so vast a power over human character, should so use that power as to establish in the mind of every individual an indissoluble association between his own happiness and the good of the whole; especially between his own happiness and the practice of such modes of conduct, negative and positive, as regard for the universal happiness prescribes: so that not only he may be unable to conceive the possibility of happiness to himself, consistently with conduct opposed to the general good, but also that a direct impulse to promote the general good may be in every individual one of the habitual motives of action, and the sentiments connected therewith may fill a large and prominent place in every human being's sentient existence.[4]

would damage the entire health care system. Society might begin to devalue the lives of disabled people generally as well as the elderly and other vulnerable populations. The rule would also appear to entail a blatant violation of the cardinal principle of medical practice—do no harm. Adhering to it might therefore cause an erosion of all ethical codes and professional standards in medicine. But following the first rule would have no such consequences. It would permit the suffering of some impaired children, but this consequence seems not to be as catastrophic as those produced by consistently conforming to the second rule. For the rule-utilitarian, then, the morally right action would be *not* to administer the lethal injection, despite the parents' pleas.

Kantian Ethics

From the great German philosopher Immanuel Kant (1724–1804) comes what is widely regarded as probably the most sophisticated and influential deontological theory ever devised. It is the very antithesis of utilitarianism, holding that right actions do not depend in the least on consequences, the maximization of utility, the production of happiness, or the desires and needs of human beings. For Kant, the core of morality consists in following a rational and universally applicable moral rule and doing so solely out of a sense of duty. An action is right only if it conforms to such a rule, and we are morally praiseworthy only if we perform it for duty's sake alone.

In Kant's system, all our moral duties are expressed in the form of *categorical imperatives*. An imperative is a command to do something; it is categorical if it applies without exception and without regard for particular needs or purposes. A categorical imperative says, "Do this—regardless." In contrast, a *hypothetical imperative* is a command to do something if we want to achieve particular aims, as in "If you want good pay, work hard." The moral law, then, rests on absolute directives that do not depend on the contingencies of desire or utility.

Kant says that through reason and reflection we can derive our duties from a single moral principle, what he calls *the* categorical imperative. He formulates it in different ways, the first one being "Act only on that maxim through which you can at the same time will that it should become a universal law."[5] For Kant, our actions have logical implications—they imply general rules, or maxims, of conduct. If you tell a lie for financial gain, you are in effect acting according to a maxim like "It's okay to lie to someone when doing so benefits you financially." The question is whether the maxim corresponding to an action is a legitimate moral law. To find out, we must ask if we could consistently will that the maxim become a universal law applicable to everyone— that is, if everyone could consistently act on the maxim and we would be willing to have them do so. If we could do this, then the action described by the maxim is morally permissible; if not, it is prohibited. Thus moral laws embody two characteristics thought to be essential to morality itself: universality and impartiality.

To show us how to apply this formulation of the categorical imperative to a specific situation, Kant uses the example of a lying promise. Suppose you need to borrow money from a friend, but you know you could never pay her back. So to get the loan, you decide to lie, falsely promising to repay the money. To find out if such a lying promise is morally permissible, Kant would have you ask if you could consistently will the maxim of your action to become a universal law, to ask, in effect, "What would happen if everyone did this?" The maxim is "Whenever you need to borrow money you cannot pay back, make a lying promise to repay." So what *would* happen if everyone in need of a loan acted in accordance with this maxim? People would make lying promises to obtain loans, but everyone would also know that such promises were worthless, and the custom of loaning money on promises would disappear. So willing the maxim to be a universal law involves a contradiction: If everyone made lying promises, promise-making itself would be no more; you cannot consistently will the maxim to become a universal law. Therefore, your duty is clear: Making a lying promise to borrow money is morally wrong.

Kant's first formulation of the categorical imperative yields several other duties, some of which are particularly relevant to bioethics. Notably he argues that there is an absolute moral prohibition against killing the innocent, lying, committing suicide, and failing to help others when feasible.

Perhaps the most renowned formulation of the categorical imperative is the principle of respect for persons (a formulation distinct from the first one, though Kant thought them equivalent). As he puts it, "Act in such a way that you always treat humanity, whether in your own person or in the person of any other, never simply as a means, but always at the same time as an end."[6] People must never be treated as if they were mere instruments for achieving some further end, for people are ends in themselves, possessors of ultimate inherent worth. People have ultimate value because they are the ultimate source of value for other things. They bestow value; they do not have it bestowed upon them. So we should treat both ourselves and other persons with the respect that all inherently valuable beings deserve.

According to Kant, the inherent worth of persons derives from their nature as free, rational beings capable of directing their own lives, determining their own ends, and decreeing their own rules by which to live. Thus, the inherent value of persons does not depend in any way on their social status, wealth, talent, race, or culture. Moreover, inherent value is something that all persons possess equally. Each person deserves the same measure of respect as any other.

Kant explains that we treat people merely as a means instead of an end-in-themselves if we disregard these characteristics of personhood—if we thwart people's freely chosen actions by coercing them, undermine their rational decision-making by lying to them, or discount their equality by discriminating against them. In bioethics, clear-cut cases of not respecting persons in Kant's sense would normally include experimenting on people without their knowledge and consent, lying to them about their medical condition and prognosis, and forcing patients to receive treatment against their will.

Notice that this formulation of the categorical imperative does not actually prohibit treating a person as a means but forbids treating a person *simply*, or *merely*, as a means—as nothing but a means. Kant recognizes that in daily life we often must use people to achieve our various ends. To buy milk we use the cashier; to find books we use the librarian; to get well we use the doctor. But because their actions are freely chosen and we do not undermine their status as persons, we do not use them *solely* as instruments of our will. Medical researchers use their human subjects as a means to an end—but not merely as a means to an end if the subjects give their informed consent to participate in the research.

Natural Law Theory

From ancient times to the present day, many people have thought that the outlines of the moral law are plain to see because they are written large and true in nature itself. This basic notion has been developed over the centuries into what is known as **natural law theory**, the view that right actions are those that conform to moral standards discerned in nature through human reason. Undergirding this doctrine is the belief that all of nature (including humankind) is teleological, that it is somehow directed toward particular goals or ends, and that humans achieve their highest good when they follow their true, natural inclinations leading to these goals or ends. There is, in other words, a way things *are*—natural processes and functions that accord with the natural law—and how things are shows how things *should be*. The prime duty of humans, then, is to guide their lives toward these natural ends, acting in accordance with the requirements of natural law.

Implicit in all this is the element of rationality. According to natural law theory, humans are rational beings empowered by reason to perceive the workings of nature, determine the natural inclinations of humans, and recognize the implications therein for morally permissible actions. That is, reason enables human beings to ascertain the moral law implicit in nature and to apply that objective, universal standard to their lives.

Though natural law theory has both religious and nonreligious forms, the theistic formulation of theologian-philosopher Thomas Aquinas (1225–1274) has been the theory's dominant version. It is not only the official moral outlook of the Roman Catholic Church, but it has also been the intellectual starting point for many contemporary variations of the theory, secular and otherwise. For Aquinas, God is the author of the natural law who gave humans the gift of reason to discern the law for themselves and live accordingly. Aquinas argues that human beings naturally tend toward—and therefore have a duty of—preserving human life and health (and so must not kill the innocent), producing and raising children, seeking knowledge (including knowledge of God), and cultivating cooperative social relationships. In all this, Aquinas says, the overarching aim is to do and promote good and avoid evil.

Natural law theory does not provide a relevant moral rule covering every situation, but it does offer guidance through general moral principles, some of which are thought to apply universally and absolutely (admitting no exceptions). Among these principles are absolutist prohibitions against directly killing the innocent, lying, and using contraceptives. In his list of acts considered wrong no matter what, Aquinas includes adultery, blasphemy, and sodomy.

Of course, moral principles or rules often conflict, demanding that we fulfill two or more incompatible duties. We may be forced, for example, to either tell a lie and save people's lives or tell the truth and cause their death—but we cannot do both. Some moral theories address these problems by saying that all duties are prima facie: When duties conflict, we must decide which ones override the others. Theories that posit absolute duties—natural law theory being a prime example—often do not have this option. How does the natural law tradition resolve such dilemmas? Among other resources, it uses the **doctrine of double effect**.

This principle, a cornerstone of Roman Catholic ethics, affirms that performing a bad action to bring about a good effect is never morally acceptable but that performing a good action may sometimes be acceptable even if it produces a bad effect. More precisely, the principle says it is always wrong to intentionally perform a bad action to produce a good effect, but doing a good action that results in a bad effect may be permissible if the bad effect is not intended although foreseen. In the former case, a bad thing is said to be directly intended; in the latter, a bad thing is not directly intended.

These requirements have been detailed in four "tests" that an action must pass to be judged morally permissible. We can express a traditional version of these tests like this:

1. The action itself must be morally permissible.
2. Causing a bad effect must not be used to obtain a good effect (the end does not justify the means).
3. Whatever the outcome of an action, the intention must be to cause only a good effect (the bad effect can be foreseen but never intended).
4. The bad effect of an action must not be greater in importance than the good effect.

Consider the application of these tests to euthanasia. Suppose an 80-year-old hopelessly ill patient is in continuous, unbearable pain and begs to be put out of her misery. Is it morally permissible to grant her request (either by giving a lethal injection or ending all ordinary life-sustaining measures)? If we apply the doctrine of double effect as just outlined, we must conclude that the answer is *no*: Euthanasia—either active or passive—is not a morally permissible option here. (In the Roman Catholic view, all forms of euthanasia are wrong, although it is permissible not to treat a hopelessly ill person for whom ordinary life-sustaining treatments are useless.) Failing even one of the tests would render an action impermissible, but in this case let us run through all four as a natural law theorist might:

1. Taking steps to terminate someone's life is a clear violation of test 1. Whatever its effects, the action of taking a life is in itself immoral, a violation of the cardinal duty to preserve innocent life.
2. Ending the woman's life to save her from terrible suffering is an instance of causing a bad effect (the woman's death) as a means of achieving a good effect (cessation of pain)—a failure of test 2.
3. The death of the woman is intended; it is not merely a tragic side effect of the attempt solely to ease her pain. So the action fails test 3.
4. Causing the death of an innocent person is a great evil that cannot be counterbalanced by the good of pain relief. So the action does not pass test 4.

The verdict in such a case would be different, however, if the patient's death were not intentionally caused but unintentionally brought about. Suppose, for example, that the physician sees that the woman is in agony and so gives her a large injection of morphine to minimize her suffering—knowing full well that the dose will also probably speed her death. In this scenario, the act of easing the woman's pain is itself morally permissible (test 1). Her death is not a means to achieve some greater good; the goal is to ease her suffering (test 2). Her death is not intended; the intention is to alleviate her pain, though the unintended (but foreseen) side effect is her hastened death (test 3). Finally, the good effect of an easier death seems more or less equivalent in importance to the bad effect of a hastened death. Therefore, unintentionally but knowingly bringing about the woman's death in this way is morally permissible.

We get similar results if we apply the double-effect principle in the traditional way to abortion. We find that as the intentional destruction of an innocent human life, (so-called direct) abortion is always immoral (test 1). Moreover, it is wrong even (or especially) if it is performed to bring about some good result, such as saving the mother's life or preventing serious harm to her (tests 2 and 3). On the other hand, actions leading unintentionally to the death of a fetus (so-called indirect abortion) may be permissible in rare cases. Say a pregnant woman has an infectious disease that will kill her unless she gets injections of a powerful drug. But the drug will abort the fetus. According to the doctrine of double effect, receiving the injections may be morally permissible if the action itself is morally permissible, which it is (test 1); if the death of the fetus is not used to rescue the woman (test 2); if the injections are given with the intention of curing the woman's disease, not of inducing an abortion (test 3); and if the death of the fetus is balanced by the life of the woman (test 4).

Rawls' Contract Theory

In its broadest sense, **contractarianism** refers to moral theories based on the idea of a social contract, or agreement, among individuals for mutual advantage. The most influential contemporary form of contractarianism is that of philosopher John Rawls (1921–2002), who uses the notion of a social contract to generate and defend moral principles governing how members of a society should treat one another. He asks, in effect, by what principles should a just society structure itself to ensure a fair distribution of rights, duties, and advantages of social cooperation?

His answer is that the required principles—essentially principles of justice—are those that people would agree to under hypothetical conditions that ensure fair and unbiased choices. He believes that if the starting point for the social contract is fair—if the initial conditions and bargaining process for producing the principles are fair—then the principles themselves will be just and will define the essential makeup of a just society. As Rawls says,

> [The] guiding idea is that the principles of justice for the basic structure of society are the object of the original agreement. They are the principles that free and rational persons concerned to further their own interests would accept in an initial position of equality as defining the fundamental

terms of their association. These principles are to regulate all further agreements; they specify the kinds of social cooperation that can be entered into and the forms of government that can be established.[7]

At the hypothetical starting point—what Rawls calls the "original position"—a group of normal, self-interested, rational individuals come together to choose the principles that will determine their basic rights and duties and their share of society's benefits and burdens. But to ensure that their decisions are as fair and impartial as possible, they must meet behind a metaphorical "veil of ignorance." Behind the veil, no one knows his own social or economic status, class, race, sex, abilities, talents, level of intelligence, or psychological makeup. Since the participants are rational and self-interested but ignorant of their situation in society, they will not agree to principles that will put any particular group at a disadvantage because they might very well be members of that group. They will choose principles that are unbiased and nondiscriminatory. The assumption is that since the negotiating conditions in the original position are fair, the agreements reached will also be fair—the principles will be just.

Rawls contends that given the original position, the participants would agree to arrange their social relationships according to these fundamental principles:

1. Each person is to have an equal right to the most extensive total system of equal basic liberties compatible with a similar system of liberty for all.
2. Social and economic inequalities are to be arranged so that they are both:
    (a) to the greatest benefit of the least advantaged . . . and
    (b) attached to offices and positions open to all under conditions of fair equality of opportunity.[8]

The first principle—the equal liberty principle—says that everyone is entitled to the most freedom possible in exercising basic rights and duties (for example, the right to vote and hold office and freedom of speech, assembly, and thought). Each person should get a maximum degree of basic liberties but no more than anyone else. This principle takes precedence over all other considerations (including the second principle) so that basic liberties cannot be reduced or canceled just to improve economic well-being.

The second principle concerns social and economic goods such as income, wealth, opportunities, and positions of authority. Part (b) says that everyone is entitled to an equal chance to try to acquire these basic goods. No one is guaranteed an equal share of them, but opportunities to obtain these benefits must be open to all, regardless of social standing.

Rawls knows that social and economic inequalities will naturally arise in society. But as he asserts in part (a), they are not unjust if they work to everyone's benefit, especially to the benefit of the least well off in society. "[There] is no injustice," he says, "in the greater benefits earned by a few provided that the situation of persons not so fortunate is thereby improved."[9] For Rawls, such a policy is far more just than one in which some people are made to suffer for the greater good of others: "[I]t is not just that some should lave less in order that others may prosper."

In Rawls' scheme, the demands of the first principle must be satisfied before satisfying the second, and the requirements of part (b) must be met before those of part (a). In any just distribution of benefits and burdens, then, the first priority is to ensure equal basic liberties for all concerned, then equality of opportunity, then the arrangement of any inequalities to the benefit of the least advantaged.

As a theory of distributive justice, Rawls' contractarianism seems to have significant implications for the allocation of society's health care resources. For example, one prominent line of argument goes like this: As Rawls claims, everyone is entitled to fair equality of opportunity, and adequate (basic) health care enables fair equality of opportunity (by ensuring "normal species functioning"). Therefore, everyone is entitled to adequate health care, which includes all appropriate measures for eliminating or compensating for the disadvantages of disease and impairment.[10] In such a system, there would be universal access to a basic level of health care, while more elaborate or elective services would be available to anyone who could afford them.

Another implication: Suppose that to provide a basic level of health care to everyone (and meet the equality-of-opportunity requirement), society would have to spend 90 percent of its health care resources. But say that in the current system, 50 percent of the resources are being spent on acute care for the elderly—that is, expensive measures to extend the lives of people who have already lived a long time. According to Rawlsian principles, is the current system of health care unjust?

Virtue Ethics

Most moral theories—including all those just discussed—are theories of obligation. They emphasize the rightness of actions and the duties of moral agents. Their main concern is knowing and doing what's right, and their chief guide to these aims is moral principles or directives. **Virtue ethics**, however, is a radically different kind of moral theory: It focuses on the development of virtuous character. According to virtue ethics, character is the key to the moral life, for it is from a virtuous character that moral conduct and values naturally arise. Virtues are ingrained dispositions to act by standards of excellence, so having the proper virtues leads as a matter of course to right actions properly motivated. The central task in morality, then, is not knowing and applying principles but being and becoming a good person, someone possessing the virtues that define moral excellence. In virtue ethics, someone determines right action not by consulting rules but by asking what a truly virtuous person would do or whether an action would accord with the relevant virtues.

Aristotle (384–322 B.C.E.) is the primary inspiration for contemporary versions of virtue ethics. For him, as for many modern virtue ethicists, the highest goal of humanity is the good life, or "human flourishing" (what Aristotle calls *eudaimonia*, or happiness), and developing virtues is the way to achieve such a rich and satisfying life. Thus virtues are both the traits that make us good persons and the dispositions that enable us to live good lives. The good life is the virtuous life.

Unlike many theories of obligation, virtue ethics asks us to do more than just observe minimal moral rules—it insists that we *aspire to moral excellence*, that we cultivate the virtues that will make us better persons. In this sense, virtue ethics is goal-directed, not rule-guided. The moral virtues—benevolence, honesty, loyalty, compassion, fairness, and the like—are ideals that we must ever strive to attain. (There are also nonmoral virtues such as patience, prudence, and reasonableness, which need not concern us here.) By the lights of both Aristotle and modern virtue ethicists, character is not static. We can become more virtuous by reflecting on our lives and those of others, practicing virtuous behavior, or imitating moral exemplars such as Gandhi, Buddha, Jesus, Muhammad, and Socrates. We can—and should—be better than we are.

To the virtue ethicist, possessing the right virtues means having the proper motivations that naturally accompany those virtues. To act morally, we must act from virtue, and acting from virtue means acting with the appropriate motives. It is not enough to do right; we must do right for the right motivating reasons. If we save a drowning friend, we should do so out of genuine feelings of compassion, kindness, or loyalty—not because of the prodding of moral rules or social expectations. In contrast, some moral theories (notably Kant's) maintain that acting morally is solely a matter of acting for duty's sake—performing an action simply because duty requires it. Virtuous motives are irrelevant; we act morally if we do our duty regardless of our motivations. But this notion seems to many to offer a barren picture of the moral life. Surely, they say, motivations for acting are often relevant to our evaluations of people's character and actions. The friend we saved from drowning would probably be appalled if we declared that we saved her out of duty even though we did not really care whether she lived or died. Many moral philosophers agree that motivations are indeed important considerations in moral judgments, and they have incorporated virtues into their theories of obligation.

Virtue ethics fits well with the emphasis on virtues that has always been part of the healing arts. Physicians and nurses are expected to possess particular virtues, including compassion, trustworthiness, justice, and honesty. They are expected to be more than just technically skilled and knowledgeable and to do more than merely follow the rules of conduct or procedure. They are obliged to do right by their patients, and this obligation is most likely met through the cultivation and possession of virtues.

The virtue ethics approach to bioethical issues is distinctive. On abortion, for example, the virtue ethicist might argue that a woman's decision to have an abortion should be judged by the virtues (or lack thereof) that she draws on in deciding what to do. If she decides to have an abortion just because she is afraid of the responsibilities of parenthood, she shows cowardice. If she wants to go through with an abortion merely because pregnancy would disrupt her vacation plans, she shows self-centeredness and callousness. In neither case is the virtue ethicist likely to call the woman's decision virtuous.[11]

The Ethics of Care

The ethics of care is a distinctive moral perspective that arose out of feminist concerns and grew to challenge core elements of most other moral theories. Generally those theories emphasize abstract principles, general duties, individual rights, impartial judgments, and deliberative reasoning. But the ethics of care shifts the focus to the unique demands of specific situations and to the virtues and feelings that are central to close personal relationships—empathy, compassion, love, sympathy, and fidelity. The heart of

> ### IN DEPTH
> ### CAN VIRTUE BE TAUGHT?

Aristotle believes that moral virtues are not the sort of thing you can learn by merely studying them, as you would if you wanted to learn calculus. He insists that moral virtues can only be learned through practice, by *living* the virtues. As he says,

[M]oral virtue comes about as a result of habit.... From this it is also plain that none of the moral virtues arises in us by nature.... [B]ut the virtues we get by first exercising them, as also happens in the case of the arts as well. For the things we have to learn before we can do them, we learn by doing them, e.g., men become builders by building and lyreplayers by playing the lyre; so too we become just by doing just acts, temperate by doing temperate acts, brave by doing brave acts.[12]

---

the moral life is feeling for and caring for those with whom you have a special, intimate connection—an approach that especially resonates with physicians and nurses.

Early on, the ethics of care drew inspiration from the notion that men and women have dramatically different styles of moral decision-making, with men seizing on principles, duties, and rights, and women homing in on personal relationships, caring, and empathy. This difference was highlighted in research done by psychologist Carol Gilligan and published in her 1982 book *In a Different Voice*.[13] Typically men recognize an ethic of justice and rights, she says, and women are guided by an ethic of compassion and care. In her view the latter is as legitimate as the former, and both have their place in ethics.

Other research has suggested that the differences between men and women in styles of moral thinking may not be as great as Gilligan suggests. But the credibility of the empirical claim does not affect the larger insight that the research seemed to some writers to suggest: Caring is an essential part of morality, and the most influential theories have not fully taken it into account.

These points get support along several lines. First, virtue ethics reminds us that virtues are part of the moral life. If caring is viewed as a virtue—in the form of compassion, empathy, or kindness—then caring too must be an element of morality. A moral theory then would be deficient if it made no room for care.

Moreover many argue that unlike the ethics of care, most moral theories push the principle of impartiality too far. Recall that impartiality in morality requires us to consider everyone as equal, counting everyone's interests the same. The principle applies widely, especially in matters of public justice, but less so in personal relationships of love, family, friendship, and the like. We seem to have special obligations (partiality) to close friends, family members, and others we care for, duties that we do not have to strangers or to universal humanity. As some philosophers explain it,

> The care perspective is especially meaningful for roles such as parent, friend, physician, and nurse, in which contextual response, attentiveness to subtle clues, and deepening special relationships are likely to be more important morally than impartial treatment.[14]

> May I devote my time and resources to caring for my own friends and family, even if this means ignoring the needs of other people whom I could also help? From an impartial point of view, our duty is to promote the interests of everyone alike. But few of us accept that view. The ethics of care confirms the priority that we naturally give to our family and friends, and so it seems a more plausible moral conception.[15]

Most moral theories emphasize duties and downplay the role of emotions, attitudes, and motivations. Kant, for example, would have us do our duty for duty's sake, whatever our feelings. For him, to be a morally good parent, we need only act from duty. But taking care of our children as a matter of moral obligation alone seems an empty exercise. Surely being a morally good parent also involves having feelings of love and attitudes of caring. The ethics of care eagerly takes these emotional elements into account.

Many philosophers, including several writing from a feminist perspective, have lodged such criticisms against the most influential moral theories while suggesting that a mature morality should accommodate both an ethic of obligation and an ethic of care. Annette Baier, for example, has taken this approach:

> It is clear, I think, that the best moral theory has to be a cooperative product of women and men, has to harmonize justice and care. The morality it theorizes about is after all for all persons, for men and for women, and will need their combined insights. As Gilligan said, what we need now is a "marriage" of the old male and the newly articulated female insights.[16]

Feminist Ethics

Feminist ethics is an approach to morality aimed at advancing women's interests and correcting injustices inflicted on women through social oppression and inequality. It is defined by a distinctive focus on these issues, rather than by a set of doctrines or common ideology among feminists, many of whom may disagree on the nature of feminist ethics or on particular moral issues. A variety of divergent perspectives have been identified as examples of feminist ethics, including the ethics of care.

Feminist ethics generally downplays the role of moral principles and traditional ethical concepts, insisting instead that moral reflection must take into account the social realities—the relevant social practices, relationships, institutions, and power arrangements. Many feminists think that the familiar principles of Western ethics—autonomy, utility, freedom, equality, and so forth—are too broad and abstract to help us make moral judgments about specific persons who are enmeshed in concrete social situations. It is not enough, for example, to respect a woman's de-

cision to have an abortion if she is too poor to have one, or if her culture is so oppressive (or oppressed) as to make abortion impossible to obtain, or if social conditioning leads her to believe that she has no choice or that her views don't count. Theoretical autonomy does not mean much if it is so thoroughly undermined in reality.

Many theorists in feminist ethics also reject the traditional concept of the moral agent. Jan Crosthwaite says that the old notion is that of "abstract individuals as fundamentally autonomous agents, aware of their own preferences and values, and motivated by rational self-interest (though not necessarily selfish)."[17] But, she says, many feminists

> present a richer conception of persons as historically and culturally located, socially related and essentially embodied. Individuals are located in and formed by specific relationships (chosen and unchosen) and ties of affection and responsibility. . . . Such a conception of socially embedded selves refocuses thinking about autonomy, shifting the emphasis from independent self-determination towards ideals of integrity within relatedness. . . . Respecting autonomy becomes less a matter of protecting individuals from "coercive" influences than one of positive empowerment, recognizing people's interdependence and supporting individuals' development of their own understanding of their situation and options.[18]

Though all adherents of feminist ethics support liberation and equality for women, they disagree on how these values apply to specific moral issues. Most support unimpeded access to abortion, but some do not. As later chapters show, opinions among feminists also diverge on surrogacy and reproductive technologies such as in vitro fertilization.

CRITERIA FOR JUDGING MORAL THEORIES

As you can see, as explanations of what makes actions right or character good, moral theories can differ dramatically in both content and quality. In their own fashion, they try to identify the true determinants of rightness or goodness, and they vary in how close they seem to get to the mark. Most moral philosophers would readily agree: Some moral theories are better than others, and a vital task in ethics is to try to tell which is which. Moral theories can be useful and valuable to us only if there are criteria for judging their worth—and fortunately there are such standards.

In several ways, moral theories are analogous to scientific theories. Scientists devise theories to explain the causes of events. The germ theory is offered to explain the cause and spread of infectious diseases. The Big Bang theory is used to explain the structure and expansion of the universe. The "greenhouse effect" is put forth to explain climate change. For each phenomenon to be explained, scientists usually have several possible theories to consider, and the challenge is to determine which one is best (and is therefore most likely to be correct). The superior theory is the one that fares best when judged by generally accepted yardsticks known as the *scientific criteria of adequacy*. One criterion often invoked is *fruitfulness*—whether the theory makes successful predictions of previously unknown phenomena. All things being equal, a theory that makes successful predictions of novel phenomena is more likely to be true than one that does not. Another important criterion is *conservatism*—how well a theory fits with established facts, with what scientists already know. All things being equal, a theory that conflicts with what scientists already have good reasons to believe is less likely to be true than a theory that has no such conflicts. Of course, an unconservative theory can turn out to be correct, and a conservative theory wrong, but the odds are against this outcome. Analogously, moral theories are meant to explain what makes an action right or a person good, and to try to determine which moral theory is most likely correct we apply conceptual yardsticks—the *moral criteria of adequacy*. Any plausible moral theory must measure up to these critical standards.

An important criterion of adequacy for moral theories is *Criterion I: consistency with our considered moral judgments*. Any plausible scientific theory must be consistent with the data that the theory is supposed to explain; there should be no conflicts between the theory and the relevant facts. A theory put forth to explain planetary motion, for example, must account for the relevant data—scientific observations of the movements of the planets and related objects. Likewise, a moral theory must also be consistent with the data it is supposed to explain: our considered moral judgments, what some call our moral common sense. We arrive at these judgments after careful deliberation that is as free of bias, self-interest, and other distorting influences as possible. Moral philosophers grant these judgments considerable respect and try to take them into account in their moral theorizing. As we have seen, these judgments are fallible, and they are often revised under pressure from trustworthy principles or theories. But we are entitled to trust them unless we have good reason to doubt them. Therefore, any moral theory that is seriously inconsistent with our considered judgments must be regarded as badly flawed, perhaps fatally so, and in need of radical revision. Our considered judgments, for example, tell us that slavery, murder, rape, and genocide are wrong. A moral theory that implies otherwise fails this criterion and is a candidate for rejection.

In applying this standard, we must keep in mind that in both science and ethics, there is tension between theory and data. A good theory explains the data, which in turn influence the shape of the theory. Particularly strong data can compel scientists to alter a theory to account for the information, but a good theory can also give scientists reasons to question or reject particular data. In the same way, there is a kind of give and take between a moral theory and the relevant data. Our considered moral judgments may give us good reasons for altering or even rejecting our moral theory. But if our moral theory is coherent and well supported, it may oblige us to rethink or reject our considered judgments. In both science and ethics, the goal is to ensure that the fit between theory and data is as tight as possible. The

---

Review **Evaluating Moral Theories: Criteria of Adequacy**

Criterion I: consistency with our considered moral judgments
Criterion II: consistency with the facts of the moral life
Criterion III: resourcefulness in moral problem-solving

---

fit is acceptably close when no further changes in the theory or the data are necessary—when there is a kind of balance between the two that moral philosophers call "reflective equilibrium."

Another test of adequacy is *Criterion II: consistency with the facts of the moral life.* In science, good theories are consistent with scientific background knowledge, with what scientists already have good reasons to believe. They are, as mentioned earlier, conservative. This background knowledge includes other well-founded theories, highly reliable findings, and scientific (natural) laws. Moral theories should also be consistent with background knowledge—the *moral* background knowledge, the basic, inescapable experiences of the moral life. These experiences include making moral judgments, disagreeing with others on moral issues, being mistaken in our moral beliefs, and giving reasons for accepting moral beliefs. That we do in fact experience these things from time to time is a matter of moral common sense—seemingly obvious facts of the moral life. Thus, any moral theory that is inconsistent with these aspects of the moral life is deeply problematic. It is possible that we are deluded about the moral life—that we, for example, merely think we are disagreeing with others on moral issues but are actually just venting our feelings. But our experience gives us good grounds for taking the commonsense view until we are given good reasons to believe otherwise.

Finally, we have *Criterion III: resourcefulness in moral problem-solving.* If a scientific theory helps scientists answer questions, solve problems, and control facets of the natural world, it

demonstrates both its plausibility and usefulness. All things being equal, such a resourceful theory is better than one that has none of these advantages. Much the same is true for moral theories. A resourceful moral theory helps us solve moral problems. It can help us identify morally relevant aspects of conduct, judge the rightness of actions, resolve conflicts among moral principles and judgments, test and correct our moral intuitions, and understand the underlying point of morality itself. Any moral theory that lacks problem-solving resourcefulness is neither useful nor credible.

APPLYING THE CRITERIA

In this section, we apply the three moral criteria of adequacy to two theories we discussed earlier (one consequentialist, the other deontological). As we do, keep in mind that evaluating moral theories using these yardsticks is not a rote process. There is no standard procedure for applying the criteria to a theory and no set of instructions for assigning conceptual weight to each criterion as we judge a theory's worth. But the criteria do help us make broad judgments on rational grounds about a theory's strengths and weaknesses. We must use them as guides, relying on our best judgment in applying them, just as scientists must use their own educated judgment in wielding their kind of criteria of adequacy. In neither case is there a neat algorithm for theory assessment, but nonetheless in both arenas the process is objective, reasonable, and essential.

We should also remember that no moral theory is perfect, and none is likely to get the highest marks on every test. But there is much to learn even from flawed theories. If we look closely, we can see that each of the most influential theories of past centuries, even with its faults apparent, seems to have grasped at least a modest, gleaming piece of the truth about the moral life.

Utilitarianism

For simplicity's sake, let us try to apply the criteria to classic act-utilitarianism, the view that right actions are those that result in the greatest overall happiness for everyone involved. First, note that the theory seems to pass the test suggested by Criterion II (consistency with the facts of the moral life). Utilitarianism assumes that we can indeed make moral judgments, have moral disagreements, be mistaken in our moral beliefs, and provide supporting reasons for our moral judgments.

The theory, however, has been accused of a lack of usefulness—failing Criterion III (resourcefulness in moral problem-solving). The usual charge is that utilitarianism is a poor guide to the moral life because the theory demands too much of us and blurs the distinction between obligatory and supererogatory actions. Utilitarianism says that we should always try to maximize happiness for everyone considered, to do our utmost to increase overall utility. But some say this requirement would lead us to extreme beneficence—to, for example, give away most of our possessions, spend most of our time in charity work, and deem mandatory many acts that we would normally consider above and beyond the call of duty. Some defenders of the theory have suggested that it can be modified easily to ease the demands that it places on us. A few utilitarians have insisted that, contrary to the popular view, the commonsense distinction between obligatory and supererogatory acts is mistaken and that morality does demand the kind of sacrifice that utilitarianism implies.

The most serious accusation against classic utilitarianism is that it flies in the face of our considered moral judgments (Criterion I), especially concerning issues of justice and rights.

Consider the case of a medical researcher trying to develop a cure for Alzheimer's disease. To devise this cure that would save countless lives, she needs only to conduct a single, secret experiment in which she gives a lethal drug to 10 early-stage Alzheimer's patients (without their knowledge) and does a postmortem examination on their brains. By increasing the unhappiness of 10 people (and depriving them of all possible happiness in the future), she can maximize happiness for thousands. Should she conduct the experiment? According to classic utilitarianism, if her actions would go undetected and have no additional unhappy effects, the answer is yes. The experiment would be justified by the enormous amount of net happiness it would generate. But the utilitarian verdict seems to conflict strongly with our considered judgments about justice. Taking the lives of a few people to benefit many others appears unjust, regardless of the good consequences that would flow from the deed. Critics claim that cases like this show that utilitarianism is a seriously inadequate theory.

Now consider the case of a competent patient with a serious illness who refuses medical treatment on religious grounds. He knows that he would suffer much less pain and have a longer and happier life if he were treated, but he still objects. But his physician wants to maximize the happiness and well-being of all her patients, so she surreptitiously treats the patient anyway without his consent. (Let us assume that no additional legal, professional, or psychological consequences ensue.) Does the physician do right? The utilitarian seems obliged to say yes. But our commonsense judgment would likely be that the physician violated her patient's autonomy—specifically, his right of self-determination.

Some utilitarians have replied to such Criterion I criticisms by saying that scenarios like those just presented are unrealistic and misleading. In the real world, they say, actions that seem to conflict with our moral intuitions almost always produce such bad consequences that the actions cannot be justified even on utilitarian grounds. Once *all* the possible consequences are taken into account, it becomes clear that the proposed actions do not maximize happiness and that commonsense morality and utilitarianism coincide. In real life, for example, the deeds of the researcher and the physician would almost certainly be exposed, resulting in a great deal of unhappiness for all concerned. Critics respond to the utilitarian by admitting that many times the judgments of commonsense morality and utilitarianism do in fact coincide when all the facts are known—but not always. Even the utilitarian must admit that there could be cases in which actions that maximize utility do clash with our considered moral judgments, and this possibility raises doubts about the utilitarian standard.

Kant's Theory

Like utilitarianism, Kant's theory seems generally consistent with the basic facts of the moral life (Criterion II), but many philosophers argue that it is not consistent with moral common sense (Criterion I). A major cause of the problem, they say, is Kant's insistence that we have absolute (or "perfect") duties—obligations that must be honored without exception. Thus in Kantian ethics, we have an absolute duty not to lie or to break a promise or to kill the innocent, come what may. Imagine that a band of killers wants to murder an innocent man who has taken refuge in your house, and the killers come to your door and ask you point blank if he is in your house. To say no is to lie; to answer truthfully is to guarantee the man's death. What should you do? In a case like this, says Kant, you must *do your duty*—you must tell the truth though murder is the result and a lie would save a life. But in this case such devotion to moral absolutes seems completely askew, for saving an innocent life seems far more important morally than blindly obeying a rule. Our considered judgments suggest that sometimes the consequences of our actions do matter more than adherence to the letter of the law, even if the law is generally worthy of our respect and obedience.

Some have thought that Kant's theory can yield implausible results for another reason. Recall that the first formulation of the categorical imperative says that an action is permissible if persons could consistently act on the relevant maxim, and we would be willing to have them do so. This requirement seems to make sense if the maxim in question is something like "Do not kill the innocent" or "Treat equals equally." But what if the maxim is "Enslave all Christians" or "Kill all Ethiopians"? We could—without contradiction—will either one of these precepts to become a universal law. And if we were so inclined, we could be willing for everyone to act accordingly, even if we ourselves were Christians or Ethiopians. So by Kantian lights, these actions could very well be morally permissible, and their permissibility would depend on whether someone was willing to have them apply universally. Critics conclude that because the first formulation of the categorical imperative seems to sanction such obviously immoral acts, the theory is deeply flawed. Defenders of Kant's theory, on the other hand, view the problems as repairable and have proposed revisions.

This apparent arbitrariness in the first formulation can significantly lessen the theory's usefulness (Criterion III). The categorical imperative is supposed to help us discern moral directives that are rational, universal, and objective. But if it is subjective in the way just described, its helpfulness as a guide for living morally is dubious. There may be remedies for this difficulty, but Kant's theory in its original form seems problematic.

KEY TERMS

act-utilitarianism
consequentialist theory
contractarianism
deontological (or nonconsequentialist)
    theory
doctrine of double effect
moral theory
natural law theory
rule-utilitarianism
utilitarianism
virtue ethics

SUMMARY

A moral theory explains why an action is right or wrong or why a person or a person's character is good or bad. Making, using, or assessing moral theories is a normal, pervasive feature of the moral life.

Consequentialist moral theories assume that the rightness of actions depends on their consequences or results. Deontological theories say that the rightness of actions is determined partly or wholly by their intrinsic nature. The leading consequentialist theory is utilitarianism, the view that right actions are those that result in the most beneficial balance of good over bad consequences for everyone involved. The theory comes in two main types. Act-utilitarianism is the idea that the rightness of actions depends on the relative good produced by individual actions. Rule-utilitarianism says a right action is one that conforms to a rule that, if followed consistently, would create for everyone involved the most beneficial balance of good over bad. Kantian ethics is opposed to consequentialist theories, holding that morality consists in following a rational and universally applicable moral rule and doing so solely out of a sense of duty. An action is right only if it conforms to such a rule, and we are morally praiseworthy only if we perform it for duty's sake alone. Natural law theory is a centuries-old view of ethics that maintains that right actions are those conforming to moral standards discerned in nature through human reason. Rawls' theory is a form of contractarianism, which means it is based on the idea of a social contract, or agreement, among individuals for mutual advantage. He argues for a set of moral principles that he believes would be arrived at through a fair, but hypothetical, bargaining process. Virtue ethics focuses on the development of virtuous character. The central task in morality is not knowing and applying principles but being and becoming a good person, someone possessing the virtues that define moral excellence. The ethics of care emphasizes the virtues and feelings that are central to close personal relationships.

The worth of moral theories can be assessed through the application of the moral criteria of adequacy. Criterion I is consistency with our considered moral judgments; Criterion II, consistency with the facts of the moral life; and Criterion III, resourcefulness in moral problem-solving.

FURTHER READING

Thomas Aquinas, *Summa Theologica*, in *Basic Writings of St. Thomas Aquinas*, trans. A. C. Pegis (New York: Random House, 1945), volume II, 3–46.

Jeremy Bentham, "Of the Principle of Utility," in *An Introduction to the Principles of Morals and Legislation* (Oxford: Clarendon Press, 1879), 1–7.

Baruch A. Brody, *Moral Theory and Moral Judgments in Medical Ethics* (Dordrecht: Kluwer, 1988).

Stephen Buckle, "Natural Law," in *A Companion to Ethics*, ed. Peter Singer, (Cambridge: Blackwell, 1993), 161–74.

Steven M. Cahn and Joram G. Haber, *Twentieth Century Ethical Theory* (Upper Saddle River, NJ: Prentice-Hall, 1995).

Fred Feldman, "Act Utilitarianism: Pro and Con," in *Introductory Ethics* (Englewood Cliffs, NJ: Prentice-Hall, 1978), 30-60.

John Finnis, *Natural Law and Natural Rights* (New York: Oxford University Press, 1980).

William K. Frankena, *Ethics*, 2nd ed. (Englewood Cliffs, NJ: Prentice-Hall, 1973).

C. E. Harris, *Applying Moral Theories* (Belmont, CA: Wadsworth, 1997).

Dale Jamieson, "Method and Moral Theory," in *A Companion to Ethics*, ed. Peter Singer (Cambridge: Blackwell, 1993), 476–87.

Mark Murphy, "The Natural Law Tradition in Ethics," in *The Stanford Encyclopedia of Philosophy* (Winter 2002 ed.), ed. Edward N. Zalta, http://plato.stanford.edu/archives/win2002/entries/natural-law-ethics/.

Kai Nielsen, "A Defense of Utilitarianism," *Ethics* 82 (1972): 113–24.

Kai Nielsen, *Ethics Without God* (Buffalo, NY: Prometheus, 1973).

Robert Nozick, "The Experience Machine," in *Anarchy, State and Utopia* (New York: Basic Books, 1974).

Onora O'Neill, "Kantian Ethics," in *A Companion to Ethics*, ed. Peter Singer, (Cambridge: Blackwell, 1993), 175–85.

Louis P. Pojman and Lewis Vaughn, eds., *The Moral Life*, 3rd ed. (New York: Oxford University Press, 2007).

James Rachels, *The Elements of Moral Philosophy*, 4th ed. (New York: McGraw-Hill, 2003).

James Rachels, ed., *Ethical Theory 2: Theories About How We Should Live* (Oxford: Oxford University Press, 1998).

John Rawls, "Some Remarks About Moral Theory," in *A Theory of Justice* (Cambridge: Harvard University Press, 1999), 40–46.

J. J. C. Smart, "Extreme and Restricted Utilitarianism," in *Essays Metaphysical and Moral* (Oxford: Blackwell, 1987).

Bonnie Steinbock, ed., *The Oxford Handbook of Bioethics* (Oxford: Oxford University Press, 2007).

Paul Taylor, *Principles of Ethics* (Encino, CA: Dickenson, 1975).

Lewis Vaughn, *Doing Ethics: Moral Reasoning and Contemporary Issues* (New York: W.W. Norton, 2008).

Bernard Williams, "A Critique of Utilitarianism," in *Utilitarianism: For and Against*, ed. J. J. C. Smart and Bernard Williams (New York: Cambridge University Press, 1973), 82-117.

NOTES

1. John Stuart Mill, "What Utilitarianism Is," in *Utilitarianism*, 7th ed. (London: Longmans, Green, and Co., 1879), chap. 2.

2. *Ibid.*

3. *Ibid.*

4. Mill, *Utilitarianism,* chap. II.

5. Immanuel Kant, *Groundwork of the Metaphysics of Morals,* trans. H. J. Paton (New York: Harper & Row, 1964), 88.

6. *Ibid.,* 96.

7. John Rawls, *A Theory of Justice,* rev. ed. (Cambridge: Harvard University Press, 1999), 10.

8. *Ibid.,* 266.

9. *Ibid.,* 13.

10. Norman Daniels, *Just Health Care* (New York: Cambridge University Press, 1985), 34–58.

11. Examples from Rosalind Hursthouse, *Beginning Lives* (Oxford: Blackwell, 1987), cited in Justin Oakley, "A Virtue Ethics Approach," in *A Companion to Bioethics* (Oxford: Blackwell, 2001), 86–97.

12. Aristotle, *Nicomachean Ethics,* trans. W. D. Ross, revised by J. L. Ackrill and J. O. Urmson (Oxford: Oxford University Press, 1925, 1980), book II, chap. 1.

13. Carol Gilligan, *In a Different Voice: Psychological Theory and Women's Development* (Cambridge, MA: Harvard University Press, 1982).

14. Tom L. Beauchamp and James F. Childress, *Principles of Biomedical Ethics,* 5th ed. (New York: Oxford University Press, 2001), 372.

15. James Rachels, *The Elements of Moral Philosophy* (New York: McGraw-Hill, 2003), 168.

16. Annette C. Baier, "The Need for More Than Justice," *Canadian Journal of Philosophy,* suppl. vol. 13 (1988): 56.

17. Jan Crosthwaite, "Gender and Bioethics," in *A Companion to Bioethics,* ed. Helga Kuhse and Peter Singer (Malden, MA: Blackwell Publishing, 2001), 32–40.

18. *Ibid.,* 37.

2

Physician & Patient

CHAPTER 3

Paternalism and Patient Autonomy

On its face, the patient-physician relationship seems technically simple and morally clear. The physician has a duty of beneficence toward the patient, an obligation to use her medical expertise to do him good and to avoid doing him harm. The patient has a right to this skilled beneficence and to respect for his autonomous choices regarding what the physician does. But below the surface, complications simmer. The principles of beneficence and autonomy are frequently at odds. The values of physicians and patients can diverge. The cultures of patients and health care providers can clash. And often the stakes for everyone involved are extraordinarily high.

In this chapter we explore several moral issues arising from these conflicts, focusing on questions of medical paternalism, refusing treatment, and "futile" treatment. Chapter 4 delves into other aspects of patient-physician relationships, notably truth-telling, deception, and confidentiality. Chapter 5 examines the patient-physician relationship further by studying the many sides of informed consent and patient competence.

SHADES OF AUTONOMY AND PATERNALISM

Autonomy is a person's rational capacity for self-governance or self-determination. It is an individual's power to deliberate about available options, to choose freely among those possibilities, and to act accordingly. We fully exercise our autonomy when our choices and actions are truly our own, free from the overriding pressure of people and factors that rob us of control. The requirement to respect autonomy runs through all of bioethics, expressed in the *autonomy principle,* which we can state as *autonomous persons should be allowed to exercise their capacity for self-determination.* In bioethics it is considered a fundamental standard that can be violated only for good reasons and with explicit justification. In the name of the autonomy principle, medicine has developed the doctrine of informed consent and has devised countless procedures and guidelines to ensure that the principle is honored in the details.

Limitations on a person's autonomy can be physical or psychological, obvious or subtle, justified or unjustified, and generally accepted or widely controversial. Physically restraining a patient violates his autonomy, and so does misinforming him about the seriousness of his illness. Forcing a healthy woman to have a hysterectomy is obvious coercion. Using false information to persuade her to have the operation is a subtler kind of compulsion. We tend to think that physicians are sometimes justified in confining and treating a mentally ill man who is a danger to himself and others. We would not think so if the man were perfectly healthy. Giving a 12-year-old girl a blood transfusion to save her life seems like normal medical practice. Withholding the transfusion because her parents say it is an affront to their religious faith is controversial.

Conflicts between respect for patients' autonomy and physicians' duty of beneficence usually raise the issue of **paternalism**, which we can define as the overriding of a person's actions or decision-making for his own good. Early medical practice was strongly paternalistic, inspired by the Hippocratic tradition of devotion to the welfare of patients and fatherly insistence on deciding unilaterally what is best for them. The

Hippocratic Oath and many later professional codes of medical practice had much to say about obligations to help and not to harm patients but little or nothing to declare about patients' rights to decide about their own medical care. But over the last few decades, this kind of heavy-handed paternalism has abated as society has placed more value on the rights of patients to know important facts about their medical care, to make choices regarding their medical treatment, and even to refuse treatment that physicians recommend.

We can distinguish between two kinds of paternalism. **Weak paternalism** refers to paternalism directed at persons who cannot act autonomously or whose autonomy is greatly diminished—who may be, for example, dangerously psychotic, severely retarded, extremely depressed, or acutely addicted. Weak paternalism is not usually considered an objectionable violation of autonomy because patients are already substantially nonautonomous to some degree. Generally it is thought to be morally acceptable because its purpose is to protect people from harm while they are nonautonomous, to determine if they are in fact nonautonomous, or to restore them to full autonomy. **Strong paternalism** is the overriding of a person's actions or choices even though he is substantially autonomous. Cases involving strong paternalism often provoke debate and sometimes legal wrangling. A man who normally behaves autonomously and rationally is involuntarily committed to a mental institution because he occasionally becomes confused and disoriented and doctors fear that he might someday become a threat to himself or others. A physician discovers that his patient has a malignant breast tumor, but because he knows she is terrified of the disease, he tells her that the tumor is benign and should be surgically removed just in case. A woman who needs a life-saving blood transfusion refuses it on religious grounds, but when she lapses into a coma, surgeons operate and give her the transfusion anyway. These and other scenarios play out more

often than we might think and prompt not only ethical disagreement but also personal and professional anguish.

Many people are staunchly anti-paternalistic, condoning (as most do) acts of weak paternalism but rejecting all forms of strong paternalism. They argue that strong paternalism is wrong because it violates the rights of persons to determine for themselves what is good and what is right. Persons are sovereigns over their own lives, and overriding their sovereignty is impermissible regardless of the benefits gained by violating it. Others are more willing to countenance some acts of paternalism (including strong paternalism) on the grounds that the persons involved *would* consent to the acts if circumstances were ideal (if, say, the persons were thinking more rationally). These thinkers, for example, might be willing to commit a substantially autonomous person to a mental institution involuntarily if he would have trouble living independently and might be a danger to himself. Still others argue that the only satisfactory justification for paternalism is not consent but beneficence—intervening simply to promote someone's welfare. On this view, the benefits of paternalistic actions must be balanced against the importance of respecting autonomy. Actions that minimally restrict autonomy but benefit the person greatly would be justified; actions that seriously violate autonomy while offering only minor benefits would not be acceptable. Far less important would be concerns about what the individual would or would not consent to under different circumstances.[1]

REFUSING TREATMENT

Patients want physicians to treat them; physicians want to treat patients. But often when patients (or their surrogates) refuse treatment, patient autonomy and physician beneficence collide, sparking personal frustration and moral perplexity all around. In such cases the most vexing bioethical questions include: Is it ever morally permissible for a physician to treat a patient

IN DEPTH
THE HIPPOCRATIC OATH

For centuries the Hippocratic Oath has been one of the great inspirations for Western medical ethics. It is one of several writings attributed to an ancient Greek school of medicine whose head was Hippocrates, born about 460 B.C.

I swear by Apollo Physician and Asclepius and Hygieia and Panaceia and all the gods and goddesses, making them my witness, that I will fulfill according to my ability and judgment this oath and this covenant:

To hold him who has taught me this art as equal to my parents and to live my life in partnership with him, and if he is in need of money to give him a share of mine, and to regard his offspring as equal to my brothers in male lineage and to teach them this art—if they desire to learn it—without fee and covenant; to give a share of precepts and oral instruction and all the other learning to my sons and to the sons of him who has instructed me and to pupils who have signed the covenant and have taken an oath according to the medical law, but to no one else.

I will apply dietetic measures for the benefit of the sick according to my ability and judgment; I will keep them from harm and injustice.

I will neither give a deadly drug to anybody if asked for it, nor will I make a suggestion to this effect. Similarly I will not give to a woman an abortive remedy. In purity and holiness I will guard my life and my art.

I will not use the knife, not even on sufferers from stone, but will withdraw in favor of such men as are engaged in this work.

Whatever houses I may visit, I will come for the benefit of the sick, remaining free of all intentional injustice, of all mischief and in particular of sexual relations with both female and male persons, be they free or slaves.

What I may see or hear in the course of the treatment or even outside of the treatment in regard to the life of men, which on no account one must spread abroad, I will keep to myself holding such things shameful to be spoken about.

If I fulfill this oath and do not violate it, may it be granted to me to enjoy life and art, being honored with fame among all men for all time to come; if I transgress it and swear falsely, may the opposite of all this be my lot.

From Ludwig Edelstein, *Ancient Medicine: Selected Papers of Ludwig Edelstein,* ed. Owsei Temkin and C. Lillian Temkin (Baltimore: Johns Hopkins University Press, 1967), 3-65.

against her will? If so, what justifies the action, and under what conditions is it acceptable?

Until the late 1980s, the right of competent patients to turn down treatments ordered by physicians was unsettled. (Very roughly, competent patients are autonomous persons able to make decisions about treatment options.) In some situations, patients were thought to have no right to decline recommended treatments. Physicians sometimes forced pregnant patients to have cesarean deliveries if failure to do so put the fetuses at extreme risk. The courts frequently overruled the right to refuse treatment if the patient had

dependent children or if the patient was not terminally ill. But later court rulings reversed the trend and carved out the bedrock principle that a competent patient has a right to reject recommended treatments, even life-saving ones. The legal principle now parallels the prevailing view in bioethics, which shifts the weight to patient autonomy over physician beneficence.

The courts have also stretched this right of competent patients to situations in which they become incompetent, as when they lapse into coma. Through advance directives or other evidence of their preferences, they can refuse life-sustaining treatment. This expression of prior intentions is now widely recognized as a legitimate exercise of autonomous choice.

The right to refuse treatment seems a relatively straightforward issue when the patient is a competent adult, but what if the patient is a child whose parents reject the recommended medical treatment on religious grounds? Consider the case of 11-year-old Ian Lundman of Minneapolis, Minnesota, who died on May 9, 1989, after slipping into a diabetic coma. His diabetes had remained medically untreated, his mother and stepfather forgoing insulin in favor of prayers from Christian Science practitioners.[2] (Christian Scientists believe that disease is a spiritual disorder requiring spiritual healing, not medical treatment.) Or consider this scenario, typical of such cases: A 6-year-old girl is seriously injured in a traffic accident, and the only way to save her life is to give her a blood transfusion—which her Jehovah's Witness parents reject because the procedure is explicitly forbidden by their faith. The physicians proceed with the transfusion and save the girl's life, and the parents sue the physicians and the hospital.

Parents who for religious reasons reject medical treatment for their children insist on the right to decide what's best for them and sincerely believe what's best is avoiding medical interventions. They demand the freedom to practice their religion as they see fit. But others have argued (including the courts) that though parents may decide many matters on the well-being of their children, they do not have the right to bring serious harm to them, especially since children cannot decide such issues for themselves. This view was summed up in a famous 1944 Supreme Court decision: "Parents may be free to become martyrs themselves. But it does not follow they are free . . . to make martyrs of their children."[3]

The situation takes on a different hue when children are considered competent to decide for themselves. States differ on whether an adolescent can be a "mature minor" to make health decisions, and the courts have waffled on the issue. Judges have ruled, for example, that a 15-year-old Jehovah's Witness girl dying of leukemia could refuse a blood transfusion that would save her life—but that a 16-year-old boy injured in a train accident could not decline a transfusion needed during surgery to save his arm. Nevertheless, many argue that if adolescents are not competent to decide such things, competent adults (including physicians and nurses) should step in to protect their welfare, even if intervening means defying religious doctrine.

FUTILE TREATMENT

The classic pattern of paternalism involves a physician who wants to treat a patient who prefers not to be treated. But sometimes things happen the other way around—when the patient or the patient's family wants a treatment that the physician, typically from beneficent motives, does not want to provide. The main moral conflict is between patient autonomy and the physician's view of what constitutes morally acceptable care.

The most dramatic (and heart-rending) of such cases center on whether to supply life-sustaining treatment to the patient. Consider the much discussed story of 85-year-old Helga Wanglie, who in 1990 suddenly had to be placed on a respirator because of serious breathing problems. Over the following weeks, her condition worsened as she sank into unconsciousness and then into a persistent vegetative state (a deep coma that is usually irreversible). She received round-the-clock life-sustaining treatment consisting of respirator, antibiotics, tube feedings, and other measures. But physicians told Helga's husband and two children that the treatment was not helping her and should be stopped. Her family, however, demanded that the treatment continue. They hoped for a miracle and asserted that Helga was not better off dead and that physicians should not play God. Her husband claimed that Helga had never expressed an opinion about life-sustaining treatment for herself. Later a second team of physicians confirmed the views of the first, calling the respirator "nonbeneficial" because it could not ease Helga's suffering, repair her body, or help her experience life.

Refusing Treatment for Children on Religious Grounds

Since the 1970s, several children have died after their parents refused medical treatment because of religious beliefs. The deaths have sparked fierce debates and legal conflicts, with some jurisdictions offering religious parents exemptions from child abuse and neglect laws while medical organizations such as the American Academy of Pediatrics (AAP) and the American Medical Association (AMA) have opposed the laws. In its policy statement on the issue, the AAP declares, "Constitutional guarantees of freedom of religion do not permit children to be harmed through religious practices, nor do they allow religion to be a valid defense when an individual harms or neglects a child." According to a recent tally of the religious exemptions:

- Thirty-nine states and the District of Columbia have religious exemptions in their civil codes on child abuse or neglect, largely because of a federal government policy from 1974 to 1983 requiring states to pass such exemptions in order to get federal funding for child protection work. The states are Alabama, Alaska, Arizona, Arkansas, California, Colorado, Connecticut, Delaware, Florida, Georgia, Idaho, Illinois, Indiana, Iowa, Kansas, Kentucky, Louisiana, Maine, Michigan, Minnesota, Mississippi, Missouri, Montana, Nevada, New Hampshire, New Jersey, New Mexico, North Dakota, Oklahoma, Oregon, Pennsylvania, Rhode Island, South Carolina, Utah, Vermont, Virginia, Washington, Wisconsin, and Wyoming. Additionally, Tennessee exempts caretakers who withhold medical care from being adjudicated as negligent if they rely instead on nonmedical "remedial treatment" that is "legally recognized or legally permitted."
- Nineteen states have religious defenses to felony crimes against children: Arkansas, Delaware, Idaho, Indiana, Iowa, Kansas, Louisiana, Minnesota, New Jersey, Ohio, Oklahoma, Oregon, Rhode Island, Tennessee, Utah, Virginia, Washington, West Virginia, and Wisconsin.
- Eleven states have religious defenses to misdemeanors: Alabama, Alaska, California, Colorado, Georgia, Maine, Nevada, New Hampshire, New York, South Carolina, and South Dakota. Missouri exempts parents from the misdemeanor charges of endangerment and nonsupport if they provide "nonmedical remedial treatment recognized and permitted under the laws of this state" instead of medical care.
- Florida has a religious exemption only in the civil code, but the Florida Supreme Court nevertheless held that it caused confusion about criminal liability and required overturning a felony conviction of Christian Scientists for letting their daughter die of untreated diabetes.

States with a religious defense to the most serious crimes against children include:

- Iowa and Ohio, with religious defenses to manslaughter
- Delaware and West Virginia, with religious defenses to murder of a child
- Arkansas, with a religious defense to capital murder
- Oregon, with a religious defense to homicide by abuse[4]

The struggle over whether to discontinue Helga's treatment eventually moved into court, but its decision did little to resolve the stalemate. Three days after the court ruling, Helga died.[5]

Such physician-patient conflicts are commonly described as confrontations about **medical futility**, the alleged pointlessness or ineffectiveness of administering particular treatments.

IN DEPTH
CPR AND DNR

The medical procedure used to restart a person's heart and breathing is known as cardiopulmonary resuscitation, or *CPR*. It typically consists of mouth-to-mouth resuscitation and external chest compression but may involve more advanced procedures such as defibrillation (electric shock to restore normal heart rhythm). A do-not-resuscitate order, or *DNR*, is a directive telling the medical staff to forgo CPR on a patient if his heart or breathing stops. DNR orders are generally thought to be medically appropriate and morally permissible when the performing of CPR on seriously or terminally ill patients would be ineffective or futile and would only prolong dying or intensify the patient's pain and suffering. Patients can consent to DNR orders in person, in written instructions in an advance directive such as a living will, or through someone they designate as their representative, or proxy. The AMA declares, "The physician has an ethical obligation to honor the resuscitation preferences expressed by the patient. Physicians should not permit their personal value judgments about quality of life to obstruct the implementation of a patient's preferences regarding the use of CPR."

Physicians may claim that a treatment is futile and therefore should not be used or continued. Patients or their surrogates may reject the label of futility and insist that everything be done that can be done. But physicians and patients often have different ideas about what constitutes futility. The former may judge a treatment futile if it cannot achieve a specified physiological benefit (cannot, for example, repair tissue, restore functioning, or ease suffering); the latter may think a treatment futile only if it cannot keep the body alive. For both, the issue of futility is a question of values—of what should be done in the circumstances.

In tugs of war over the acceptability of treatment, physicians appeal to a widely recognized principle: Physicians are not obligated to provide treatments that are inconsistent with reasonable standards of medical practice. They are not morally bound to comply, for example, when a patient requests that his legs be amputated for no reason or demands injections of a worthless and dangerous cancer remedy. Not every patient request must be regarded as legitimate, and not every medical technology must be supplied.

Many times in futility cases, physicians and surrogates find resolution. They agree to an extension of the treatment for a specified period or to reasonable goals that the treatment can achieve, or the surrogates eventually view the treatment as useless, or the patient dies. But sometimes resolution eludes everyone. The sharpest clash of values is likely to occur between physicians and those who argue for the sanctity of human life. On this view, the moral imperative is to keep the body alive at all costs. For someone who accepts this principle, the physicians' claim that the treatment does not benefit the patient will carry little weight. A common argument against the position is that it makes no sense to treat a body when the person whose body it is no longer exists.

APPLYING MAJOR THEORIES

The major moral theories imply diverse stands on paternalism. As a theory driven by the principle of beneficence, utilitarianism demands that we maximize the good for everyone involved—a requirement that may justify paternalistic actions. To promote the greatest good for patients—to minimize suffering and maximize well-being—a physician or nurse may think it sometimes legitimate to breach confidentiality or mislead patients about their condition or proposed treatment. She may believe it morally permissible to override a patient's refusal of treatment or to reject the use of requested treatments thought to be futile.

Act- and rule-utilitarians can disagree dramatically on such matters. (They may also differ in their estimates of the probabilities involved and ideas about the nature of the good to be maximized.) In act-utilitarianism, the rightness of actions depends on the relative good produced by individual actions; in rule-utilitarianism, rightness depends on the good maximized by rules governing categories of actions. On act-utilitarian grounds, a physician may judge that it is morally permissible to lie to a patient about a beneficial treatment to overcome the patient's refusal to be treated. But based on rule-utilitarianism, a physician may believe that in the long run, lies do more harm than good because they erode public trust in the medical profession. Better to adhere to a rule barring deceit as a means of getting patients to accept a treatment.

Utilitarians who follow John Stuart Mill's lead, however, would reject such paternalism. Mill believes that the principle of utility implies a strong respect for individual self-determination and asserts that no one may interfere with a person's liberty except to prevent harm to others. As Mill says, "[A person] cannot rightfully be compelled to do or forbear because it will be better for him to do so, because it will make him happier, because, in the opinion of others, to do so would be wise, or even right."[6] On this view people should typically be permitted to decide what is to be done to their own bodies, to refuse treatments, and to give their informed consent.

Generally, Kantian ethics also rejects paternalism. The means-end form of the categorical imperative insists on respect for the rights and autonomy of persons—respect that must not be weakened by calculations of utility and paternalistic urges to act for the patient's own good. The principle would require physicians to honor a patient's decision to refuse treatment, even when they believe the treatment is life-saving. Informed consent of the patient for any treatment would be mandatory, and misleading the patient about treatment would be out of the question. To ignore any of these requirements would be to treat the patient merely as a means and not as an end.

In cases of medical futility, a Kantian could argue that if a physician believes a treatment is pointless and that giving it would be unethical or inappropriate, then the physician's withholding or withdrawing the treatment is morally permissible. Forcing the physician to do what she thinks is wrong would be a violation of her autonomy.

Natural law theory is more paternalistic than Kantian ethics, a characteristic we can see in cases involving euthanasia. A physician guided by the doctrine of double effect would deny a terminally ill patient's request to be given a lethal injection or to have ordinary life-sustaining measures stopped so she could die. The Roman Catholic corollary to this approach, however, is that a hopelessly ill patient has the right to refuse *extraordinary* life-sustaining treatments—measures that cause suffering or hardship but offer no medical benefit.

KEY TERMS

autonomy
medical futility
paternalism
strong paternalism
weak paternalism

SUMMARY

Autonomy is a person's rational capacity for self-governance or self-determination. The requirement to respect autonomy is expressed in the autonomy principle: Autonomous persons should be allowed to exercise their capacity for self-determination. In bioethics this principle is thought to be a fundamental standard that can be violated only for good reasons and with explicit justification.

Paternalism is the overriding of a person's actions or decision-making for his own good. Weak paternalism refers to paternalism directed at persons who cannot act autonomously or whose autonomy is greatly diminished. It is not usually considered an objectionable violation of autonomy because patients are already

Elizabeth Bouvia

The central issue in this famous case—both moral and legal—is whether a competent patient has the right to refuse life-sustaining medical treatment. In *Bouvia v. Superior Court*, the California Court of Appeal answered the question with an emphatic yes, and other courts soon followed with similar rulings.

In 1983 Elizabeth Bouvia was 25 years old, bright, articulate, and mentally competent. But she had cerebral palsy from birth and was quadriplegic, her whole body paralyzed except for her right hand and a few muscles allowing minor face and head movements. She also suffered from degenerative arthritis, which, despite her paralysis, caused constant pain that could not be relieved entirely even with doses of morphine. She needed continuous care, but her family would not oblige. She had no job, no income, no home, and no hope of getting help except through public assistance.

She finally got her father to drive her to a public hospital in Riverside County, California, where she asked to be given pain medicine and hygienic care while she slowly committed suicide by starving herself to death. The hospital admitted her but refused to be part of her plan for suicide. She then asked for legal help from the American Civil Liberties Union (ACLU), and her case went before a judge in Riverside County.

Her attending physician at the hospital declared at the first hearing that he would not allow her to die by starvation and that if necessary he would force-feed her. Bouvia asked the judge to disallow the force-feeding, but he ruled that it was permissible, saying that letting her starve to death would have a terrible effect on the hospital staff as well as on physically handicapped people generally. He asserted that she may have the right to commit suicide but not the right to compel others to help her do it. He said that society's interest in preserving life was more important than Elizabeth Bouvia's constitutional right to privacy, the right to be left alone.

So the force-feeding began. Liquid nourishment was pumped into her through a plastic tube snaked into her nose to her stomach, a procedure known as nasogastric feeding. Opinions among medical professionals about the practice were mixed, with some saying that it was necessary and others that it was horrible and coercive, amounting to battery.

Bouvia lost an appeal of the judge's decision, was later transferred to another hospital, and eventually ended up at High Desert Hospital, a public long-term care facility. At High Desert, her physicians ordered, against her will, that she be once again force-fed to head off possible starvation. They thought nasogastric feeding appropriate because her condition was life-threatening and because with adequate nutrition she could possibly live another 15 or 20 years.

She sued the hospital, asking the Superior Court of Los Angeles to order the force-feeding halted. But the court refused, saying that she clearly intended suicide and that the state could do whatever was necessary to preserve her life.

She appealed the decision to a higher court and, this time, won. In a 1986 ruling, the California Court of Appeal declared unequivocally that competent adults have a "constitutionally guaranteed right" to decide for themselves whether to submit to medical treatments:

> [S]uch a patient has the right to refuse *any* medical treatment, even that which may save or prolong her life. . . . The right to refuse medical treatment is basic and fundamental. It is recognized as a part of the right of privacy protected by both the state and federal constitutions. . . . Its exercise requires no one's approval. It is not merely one vote subject to being overridden by medical opinion. . . . A long line of cases, approved by the Supreme court in *Cobbs v. Grant* (1972) . . . have held that where a doctor performs treatment in the absence of informed consent, there is an actionable battery. The obvious corollary to this principle is that "*a competent patient has the legal right to refuse medical treatment.*"[7]

The court also held that the previous judge had put too much importance on the *length* of Elizabeth Bouvia's life if treated (15 to 20 years) without considering the *quality* of that extended life:

> We do not believe it is the policy of this State that all and every life must be preserved against the will of the sufferer. It is incongruous, if not monstrous, for medical practitioners to assert their right to preserve a life that someone else must live, or, more accurately, endure, for "15 to 20 years." We cannot conceive it to be the policy of this State to inflict such an ordeal upon anyone.... It is, therefore, immaterial that the removal of the nasogastric tube will hasten or cause Bouvia's eventual death.[8]

Throughout Bouvia's long ordeal, physicians had noted that her obvious intention was to commit suicide and that they did not want to be accomplices in such an act. But the court maintained that her intentions were irrelevant and that she had a right to refuse treatment regardless of her intentions. Moreover, caregivers who honored refusals of treatment in such cases would not be subject to legal penalty.

Thus *Bouvia v. Superior Court* tilted the moral and legal scales from physician beneficence to patient autonomy. No other judicial ruling had so strongly and unequivocally asserted that competent patients have a right to reject treatments needed to keep them alive—and that this right supersedes the interests of doctors, hospitals, and the state.

---

substantially nonautonomous and because the point is to protect people from harm while they are nonautonomous, to determine if they are in fact nonautonomous, or to restore them to full autonomy. Strong paternalism is the overriding of a person's actions or choices even though he or she is substantially autonomous.

Patient autonomy and physician beneficence often conflict when patients refuse treatment. The central question in such cases is whether it is ever permissible for a physician to treat a patient against her will. Both physicians and the courts now recognize the right of competent patients to refuse treatment. But controversy arises when the patient is a child whose parents refuse medical treatment on religious grounds.

Physician-patient conflicts also surface when patients demand treatments that the physician thinks is inappropriate. These clashes are about medical futility, the alleged pointless-

ness or ineffectiveness of administering particular treatments. Physicians often appeal to the principle that they are not obligated to provide treatments that are inconsistent with reasonable standards of medical practice. Patients may appeal to other principles such as the sanctity of life.

Utilitarianism demands that we maximize the good for everyone involved—a requirement that may justify paternalistic actions. But utilitarian opinions on paternalism can vary depending on whether they are based on act- or rule-utilitarian approaches. Kantian ethics generally rejects paternalism, insisting on the rights and autonomy of persons. Natural law theory is more paternalistic, denying through the doctrine of double effect a terminally ill patient's request to be given a lethal injection or to have ordinary life-sustaining measures stopped so she could die.

Cases for Evaluation

CASE 1

Prayer, Medicine, and a Child's Death

(*New York Times*, August 6, 1990)—David and Ginger Twitchell, a Christian Science couple from Massachusetts who relied on prayer rather than on doctors as their young son lay dying from an obstructed bowel, were convicted of involuntary manslaughter last month. It was a stunning verdict, coming as it did in the very shadow of the Mother Church in Boston.

But the death of 2-year-old Robyn Twitchell and the conviction that followed was only the latest of a number of successful prosecutions of Christian Scientists whose children died agonizing deaths after spiritual healing failed.

The prosecutions, like many historic constitutional cases, represent a clash of apparent absolutes: of religious liberty and parental autonomy on the one hand and the right of the states to protect children—and the rights of the children themselves—on the other.

While the tenets of the church, particularly its reliance on prayer in lieu of standard medical treatment, remain fundamentally unchanged since Mary Baker Eddy founded it in Boston in 1879, they have come under intense attack in courtrooms and state legislatures.

In the last 15 months Christian Scientist parents have been convicted of involuntary manslaughter, felony child abuse or child endangerment in two California cities, as well as in Arizona and Florida. Other prosecutions, in Santa Monica, Calif., and Minneapolis, have been dismissed, although prosecutors in Minnesota have appealed. . . .

Rita Swan of Sioux City, Iowa, a former Christian Scientist, has led the campaign for such prosecutions after being convinced that her reliance on spiritual healing was largely responsible for the death of her infant son. "I'm sure the church has never faced a challenge like this in its history," she said. "The church has been so sophisticated and so smooth that coroners and prosecutors and social workers have just assumed that Christian Scientists have the right to do this."

Christian Scientists counter that by seeking to smother a crucial tenet of their faith, law-enforcement officials are infringing on their religious liberties. Nathan Talbot, chairman of the church's committee on publications, said, "They are trying to prosecute out of existence this method of treatment."

———

(*New York Times*, August 12, 1993)—The Supreme Judicial Court of Massachusetts today reversed a manslaughter conviction against a Christian Scientist couple whose 2-year-old son died after they tried to heal him through prayer rather than medical treatment.

David and Ginger Twitchell called in spiritual healers instead of doctors when the boy, Robyn, came down with a fever on April 3, 1986. Robyn died of a bowel obstruction five days later.

After being convicted in 1990 of involuntary manslaughter, the Twitchells were sentenced to 10 years of probation and ordered to have their other three children checked regularly by doctors.

While the court ruled that the failure of parents to seek medical attention for their children can support a conviction of involuntary manslaughter if the parents' conduct is "wanton or reckless," it found that "there is a substantial risk of a miscarriage of justice in this case, and, therefore, the judgments must be reversed."

———

Do you agree with the court's decision to reverse the Twitchells' manslaughter conviction? Why or why not? Do you think that parents should have the right to reject medical treatment for their children on the basis of religious beliefs? What moral principle would support your judgment? Should religious liberty be construed to allow parents to do anything *with their children as long as the actions are based on religious considerations? If not, what sorts of actions should and should not be allowed?*

---

*David Margolick, "In Child Deaths, a Test for Christian Science," *New York Times*, 6 August 1990; "Christian Scientists Are Cleared of Manslaughter," *New York Times*, 12 August 1993.

CASE 2

State Paternalism and Pregnant Women

(AP)—Public hospitals cannot test pregnant women for drugs and turn the results over to police without consent, the Supreme Court said Wednesday in a ruling that buttressed the Constitution's protection against unreasonable searches [*Ferguson v. City of Charleston*].

Some women who tested positive for drugs at a South Carolina public hospital were arrested from their beds shortly after giving birth.

The justices ruled 6-3 that such testing without patients' consent violates the Constitution even though the goal was to prevent women from harming their fetuses by using crack cocaine.

"It's a very, very important decision in protecting the right to privacy of all Americans," said Priscilla Smith, lawyer for the Center for Reproductive Law and Policy, who represented the South Carolina women. "It reaffirms that pregnant women have that same right to a confidential relationship with their doctors."

Justice John Paul Stevens wrote for the court that while the ultimate goal of the hospital's testing program may have been to get women into drug treatment, "the immediate objective of the searches was to generate evidence for law enforcement purposes in order to reach that goal."

When hospitals gather evidence "for the specific purpose of incriminating those patients, they have a special obligation to make sure that the patients are fully informed about their constitutional rights," Stevens said.

South Carolina Attorney General Charles Condon, who as a local prosecutor in Charleston began the testing program, issued a statement saying the program can continue if police get a search warrant or the patient's consent. "There is no right of a mother to jeopardize the health and safety of an unborn child through her own drug abuse," Condon wrote.

Condon developed the policy along with officials at the Medical University of South Carolina, a Charleston hospital that treats indigent patients. The women were arrested under the state's child-endangerment law, but their lawyers contended the policy was counterproductive and would deter women from seeking prenatal care. . . .

The decision reversed a federal appeals court ruling that said the South Carolina hospital's drug-testing policy was a valid effort to reduce crack cocaine use by pregnant women.

The hospital began the drug testing in 1989 during the crack cocaine epidemic. If a woman's urine test indicated cocaine use, she was arrested for distributing the drug to a minor. In 1990 the hospital gave drug-using maternity patients a choice between arrest or enrolling for drug treatment.

Ten women sued the hospital in 1993, saying the policy violated the Constitution. The hospital dropped the policy the following year, but by then police had arrested 30 women.[*]

Do you agree with the Supreme Court's decision? Why or why not? Should the state force pregnant women to behave in certain ways while carrying a fetus? If pregnant women can be legally punished for "fetal abuse," how should it be defined? Is a pregnant woman guilty of fetal abuse if she refuses to eat properly? Drinks any amount of alcohol? Forgoes prenatal care? Whose interests should be given greater weight—the woman's or the fetus'?

---

[*]Associated Press, "Court: Consent Needed to Drug-Test Pregnant Women," CNN.com., 21 March 2001.

CASE 3

Medical Futility

(*Washington Post*)—A 17-month-old deaf, blind and terminally ill child on life support is the latest focus in an emotional fight against a Texas law that allows hospitals to withdraw care when a patient's ongoing treatment is declared "medically futile."

Since Dec. 28, baby Emilio Gonzales has spent his days in a pediatric intensive care unit, mostly asleep from the powerful drugs he is administered, and breathing with the help of a respirator. Children's

Hospital here declared his case hopeless last month and gave his mother 10 days, as legally required, to find another facility to take the baby. That deadline, extended once already, was due to expire Wednesday, at which time the hospital was to shut off Emilio's respirator. Without the machine, Emilio would die within minutes or hours, hospital officials have said.

But the child's mother, Catarina Gonzales, 23, and lawyers representing a coalition of state and national disability rights advocates and groups that favor prolonging life persuaded a Travis County judge Tuesday to force the hospital to maintain Emilio's care while the search for a facility to accept him continues. The group's attempt last week to persuade a federal judge to intervene in the case failed.

County Probate Judge Guy Herman appointed a guardian ad litem, or attorney, to represent Emilio's interests and issued a temporary restraining order prohibiting Children's Hospital from removing life-sustaining care from the child. He set an April 19 hearing on the mother's and lawyers' request for a temporary injunction against the hospital.

"I believe there is a hospital that is going to accept my son," said Gonzales following the brief hearing. "I just want to spend time with my son. . . . I want to let him die naturally without someone coming up and saying we're going to cut off on a certain day."

Michael Regier, senior vice president for legal affairs of the Seton Family of Hospitals, which includes Children's Hospital, said the child's condition continues to deteriorate although he has not met the criteria to be declared brain dead. He said the hospital has contacted 31 facilities "without any single indication of interest in taking the transfer."

Gonzales and her lawyers are seeking a transfer for the child, diagnosed with a terminal neurometabolic disorder called Leigh's disease, to a hospital that will perform a tracheotomy and insert a feeding tube so that he can live out his life in the facility or at home with his mother. But Children's Hospital doctors have declared that continuing treatment is potentially painful and is prolonging the child's suffering.

Emilio's case has drawn interest and support nationwide, including from the siblings of Terri Schiavo, the Florida woman who was in a persistent vegetative state and who died in 2005 after doctors, acting on a court order, removed her life-sustaining feeding tube.

Texas's six-year-old "futile-care" law is one of two in the country that allow a hospital's ethics committee to declare the care of a terminally ill patient to be of no benefit and to discontinue care within a certain time frame. The patient's family or guardian must be informed in advance of the ethics committee meeting and must be allowed to participate. The family must also be given 10 days to find a medical facility willing to accept their terminal relative. After that period, the hospital may withdraw life support. Virginia gives a family 14 days to transfer a patient once a futile-care decision is made.*

Do you agree with the hospital's reasons for wanting to withdraw care? Do you agree with the child's parents? Explain. Do you believe that life should be preserved at all costs (the sanctity of life view)? Why or why not? Do you believe that quality of life is more important than the preservation of life in cases like this? If so, how would you justify that view?

---

*Sylvia Moreno, "Case Puts Futile-Treatment Law Under a Microscope," *Washington Post*, 11 April 2007.

FURTHER READING

Tom L. Beauchamp and James F. Childress, *Principles of Biomedical Ethics*, 5th ed. (New York: Oxford University Press, 2001), 176–94, 283–336.

Dax Cowart and Robert Burt, "Confronting Death: Who Chooses, Who Controls? A Dialogue Between Dax Cowart and Robert Burt," *Hastings Center Report* 28.1 (1998): 14–17.

Helga Kuhse and Peter Singer, *A Companion to Bioethics* (Oxford: Blackwell, 2001).

Edmund D. Pellegrino, "The Virtuous Physician and the Ethics of Medicine," in *Virtue and Medicine: Explorations in the Character of Medicine*, ed. Earl E. Shelp (Dordrecht: D. Reidel Publishing, 1985), 248–53.

Gregory E. Pence, *The Elements of Bioethics* (New York: McGraw-Hill, 2007).

Robert M. Veatch, "The Dying Cancer Patient," in *Case Studies in Medical Ethics* (Cambridge: Harvard University Press, 1977), 141–47.

NOTES

1. This summary of positions takes its inspiration from Tom L. Beauchamp and James F. Childress, *Principles of Biomedical Ethics,* 5th ed. (New York: Oxford University Press, 2001), 182–87.
2. Linda Greenhouse, "Supreme Court Roundup: Christian Scientists Rebuffed in Ruling by Supreme Court," *New York Times,* 23 January 1996.
3. *Prince v. Commonwealth of Massachusetts,* 321 U.S. 1958 (1944).
4. CHILD, Inc., "Religious Exemptions from Health Care for Children," http://www.childrenshealthcare.org/ 11 November 2007.
5. Steven H. Miles, "Informed Consent for 'Non-Beneficial' Medical Treatment," *The New England Journal of Medicine* 325.7 (15 August 1991): 512–15; "Brain Damaged Woman at Center of Lawsuit over Life-Support Dies," *New York Times* (6 July 1991), 8.
6. John Stuart Mill, *On Liberty* (1859; rpt. Gateway ed., Chicago: Henry Regnery, 1955), 17–18.
7. *Bouvia v. Superior Court,* 179 Cal. 3d 1127, 1135–43, 225 Cal. Rptr. 297 (Ct. App. 1986).
8. *Ibid.*

READINGS

Paternalism

GERALD DWORKIN

Dworkin accepts the notion (famously articulated by John Stuart Mill) that society may sometimes justifiably restrict a person's liberty for purposes of self-protection or the prevention of harm to others. But he takes issue with Mill's related anti-paternalistic idea that a person "cannot rightfully be compelled to do or forbear because it will be better for him to do so." He argues that some limited forms of state paternalism can be justified, for "[u]nder certain conditions it is rational for an individual to agree that others should force him to act in ways which, at the time of action, the individual may not see as desirable." In a representative government, rational people could agree to restrict their liberty even when the interests of others are not affected. But in such cases the state bears a heavy burden of proof to show "the exact nature of the harmful effects (or beneficial consequences) to be avoided (or achieved) and the probability of their occurrence."

Neither one person, nor any number of persons, is warranted in saying to another human creature of ripe years, that he shall not do with his life for his own benefit what he chooses to do with it.

—MILL

I do not want to go along with a volunteer basis. I think a fellow should be compelled to become better and not let him use his discretion whether he wants to get smarter, more healthy or more honest.

—GENERAL HERSHEY

I take as my starting point the "one very simple principle" proclaimed by Mill in *On Liberty* . . . "That principle is, that the sole end for which mankind are warranted, individually or collectively, in interfering with the liberty of action of any of their number, is self-protection. That the only purpose for which power can be rightfully exercised over any member of a civilized community, against his will, is to prevent harm to others. He cannot rightfully be compelled to do or forbear because it will be better for him to do so, because it will make him happier, because, in the opinion of others, to do so would be wise, or even right."[1]

This principle is neither "one" nor "very simple." It is at least two principles; one asserting that self-protection or the prevention of harm to others is sometimes a sufficient warrant and the other claiming that the individual's own good is *never* a sufficient warrant for the exercise of compulsion either by the society as a whole or by its individual members. I assume that no one with the possible exception of extreme pacifists or anarchists questions the correctness of the first half of the principle. This essay is an examination of the negative claim embodied in Mill's principle—the objection to paternalistic interferences with a man's liberty.

I

By paternalism I shall understand roughly the interference with a person's liberty of action justified by reasons referring exclusively to the welfare, good, happiness, needs, interests or values of the person being coerced. One is always well-advised to illustrate one's definitions by examples but it is not easy to find "pure" examples of paternalistic interferences. For almost any piece of legislation is justified by several different kinds of reasons and even if historically a piece of legislation can be shown to have been introduced for purely paternalistic motives, it may be that advocates of the legislation with an anti-paternalistic outlook can find sufficient reasons justifying the legislation without appealing to the reasons which were originally adduced to support it. Thus, for example, it may be the original legislation requiring motorcyclists to wear safety helmets was introduced for purely paternalistic reasons. But the Rhode Island Supreme Court recently upheld such legislation on the grounds that it was "not persuaded that the legislature is powerless to prohibit individuals from pursuing a course of conduct which could conceivably result in their becoming public charges," thus clearly introducing reasons of a quite different kind. Now I regard this decision as being based on reasoning of a very dubious nature but it illustrates the kind of problem one has in finding examples. The following

is a list of the kinds of interferences I have in mind as being paternalistic.

II

1. Laws requiring motorcyclists to wear safety helmets when operating their machines.
2. Laws forbidding persons from swimming at a public beach when lifeguards are not on duty.
3. Laws making suicide a criminal offense.
4. Laws making it illegal for women and children to work at certain types of jobs.
5. Laws regulating certain kinds of sexual conduct, e.g. homosexuality among consenting adults in private.
6. Laws regulating the use of certain drugs which may have harmful consequences to the user but do not lead to anti-social conduct.
7. Laws requiring a license to engage in certain professions with those not receiving a license subject to fine or jail sentence if they do engage in the practice.
8. Laws compelling people to spend a specified fraction of their income on the purchase of retirement annuities. (Social Security)
9. Laws forbidding various forms of gambling (often justified on the grounds that the poor are more likely to throw away their money on such activities than the rich who can afford to).
10. Laws regulating the maximum rates of interest for loans.
11. Laws against duelling.

In addition to laws which attach criminal or civil penalties to certain kinds of action there are laws, rules, regulations, decrees, which make it either difficult or impossible for people to carry out their plans and which are also justified on paternalistic grounds. Examples of this are:

1. Laws regulating the types of contracts which will be upheld as valid by the courts, e.g. (an example of Mill's to which I shall return) no man may make a valid contract for perpetual involuntary servitude.
2. Not allowing as a defense to a charge of murder or assult the consent of the victim.

3. Requiring members of certain religious sects to have compulsory blood transfusions. This is made possible by not allowing the patient to have recourse to civil suits for assault and battery and by means of injunctions.

4. Civil commitment procedures when these are specifically justified on the basis of preventing the person being committed from harming himself. (The D. C. Hospitalization of the Mentally Ill Act provides for involuntary hospitalization of a person who "is mentally ill, and because of that illness, is likely to injure *himself* or others if allowed to remain at liberty." The term injure in this context applies to unintentional as well as intentional injuries.)

5. Putting fluorides in the community water supply.

All of my examples are of existing restrictions on the liberty of individuals. Obviously one can think of interferences which have not yet been imposed. Thus one might ban the sale of cigarettes, or require that people wear safety-belts in automobiles (as opposed to merely having them installed) enforcing this by not allowing motorists to sue for injuries even when caused by other drivers if the motorist was not wearing a seat-belt at the time of the accident. . . .

III

Bearing these examples in mind let me return to a characterization of paternalism. I said earlier that I meant by the term, roughly, interference with a person's liberty for his own good. But as some of the examples show the class of persons whose good is invoiced is not always identical with the class of persons whose freedom is restricted. Thus in the case of professional licensing it is the practitioner who is directly interfered with and it is the would-be patient whose interests are presumably being served. Not allowing the consent of the victim to be a defense to certain types of crime primarily affects the would-be aggressor but it is the interests of the willing victim that we are trying to protect. Sometimes a person may fall into both classes as would be the case if we banned the manufacture and sale of cigarettes and a given manufacturer happened to be a smoker as well.

Thus we may first divide paternalistic interferences into "pure" and "impure" cases. In "pure" paternalism the class of persons whose freedom is restricted is identical with the class of persons whose benefit is intended to be promoted by such restrictions. Examples: the making of suicide a crime, requiring passengers in automobiles to wear seat-belts, requiring a Christian Scientist to receive a blood transfusion. In the case of "impure" paternalism in trying to protect the welfare of a class of persons we find that the only way to do so will involve restricting the freedom of other persons besides those who are benefited. Now it might be thought that there are no cases of "impure" paternalism since any such case could always be justified on non-paternalistic grounds, i.e. in terms of preventing harm to others. Thus we might ban cigarette manufacturers from continuing to manufacture their product on the grounds that we are preventing them from causing illness to others in the same way that we prevent other manufacturers from releasing pollutants into the atmosphere, thereby causing danger to the members of the community. The difference is, however, that in the former but not the latter case the harm is of such a nature that it could be avoided by those individuals affected if they so chose. The incurring of the harm requires, so to speak, the active cooperation of the victim. It would be mistaken theoretically and hypocritical in practice to assert that our interference in such cases is just like our interference in standard cases of protecting others from harm. At the very least someone interfered with in this way can reply that no one is complaining about his activities. It may be that impure paternalism requires arguments or reasons of a stronger kind in order to be justified since there are persons who are losing a portion of their liberty and they do not even have the solace of having it be done "in their own interest." Of course in some sense, if paternalistic justifications are ever correct then we are protecting others, we are preventing some from injuring others, but it is important to see the differences between this and the standard case.

Paternalism then will always involve limitations on the liberty of some individuals in their own interest but it may also extend to interferences with the liberty of parties whose interests are not in question.

IV

Finally, by way of some more preliminary analysis, I want to distinguish paternalistic interferences with liberty from a related type with which it is often confused. Consider, for example, legislation which forbids employees to work more than, say, 40 hours per week. It is sometimes argued that such legislation is paternalistic for if employees desired such a restriction on their hours of work they could agree among themselves to impose it voluntarily. But because they do not the society imposes its own conception of their best interests upon them by the use of coercion. Hence this is paternalism.

Now it may be that some legislation of this nature is, in fact, paternalistically motivated. I am not denying that. All I want to point out is that there is another possible way of justifying such measures which is not paternalistic in nature. It is not paternalistic because as Mill puts it in a similar context such measures are "required not to overrule the judgment of individuals respecting their own interest, but to give effect to that judgment they being unable to give effect to it except by concert, which concert again cannot be effectual unless it receives validity and sanction from the law."[2]

The line of reasoning here is a familiar one first found in Hobbes and developed with great sophistication by contemporary economists in the last decade or so. There are restrictions which are in the interests of a class of persons taken collectively but are such that the immediate interest of each individual is furthered by his violating the rule when others adhere to it. In such cases the individuals involved may need the use of compulsion to give effect to their collective judgment of their own interest by guaranteeing each individual compliance by the others. In these cases compulsion is not used to achieve some benefit which is not recognized to be a benefit by those concerned, but rather because it is the only feasible means of achieving some benefit which *is* recognized as such by all concerned. This way of viewing matters provides us with another characterization of paternalism in general. Paternalism might be thought of as the use of coercion to achieve a good which is not recognized as such by those persons for whom the good is intended. Again while this formulation captures the heart of the matter—it is surely

what Mill is objecting to in *On Liberty*—the matter is not always quite like that. For example when we force motorcyclists to wear helmets we are trying to promote a good—the protection of the person from injury—which is surely recognized by most of the individuals concerned. It is not that a cyclist doesn't value his bodily integrity; rather, as a supporter of such legislation would put it, he either places, perhaps irrationally, another value or good (freedom from wearing a helmet) above that of physical well-being or, perhaps, while recognizing the danger in the abstract, he either does not fully appreciate it or he underestimates the likelihood of its occurring. But now we are approaching the question of possible justifications of paternalistic measures and the rest of this essay will be devoted to that question.

V

I shall begin for dialectical purposes by discussing Mill's objections to paternalism and then go on to discuss more positive proposals. . . . The stucture of Mill's argument is as follows:

1. Since restraint is an evil the burden of proof is on those who propose such restraint.
2. Since the conduct which is being considered is purely self-regarding, the normal appeal to the protection of the interests of others is not available.
3. Therefore we have to consider whether reasons involving reference to the individual's own good, happiness, welfare, or interests are sufficient to overcome the burden of justification.
4. We either cannot advance the interests of the individual by compulsion, or the attempt to do so involves evil which outweighs the good done.
5. Hence the promotion of the individual's own interests does not provide a sufficient warrant for the use of compulsion.

Clearly the operative premise here is 4 and it is bolstered by claims about the status of the individual as judge and appraiser of his welfare, interests, needs, etc.

With respect to his own feelings and circumstances, the most ordinary man or woman has means of knowledge immeasurably surpassing those that can be possessed by any one else.[3]

He is the man most interested in his own well-being: the interest which any other person, except in cases of strong personal attachment, can have in it, is trifling, compared to that which he himself has.[4]

These claims are used to support the following generalizations concerning the utility of compulsion for paternalistic purposes.

The interferences of society to overrule his judgment and purposes in what only regards himself must be grounded in general presumptions; which may be altogether wrong, and even if right, are as likely as not to be misapplied to individual cases.[5]

But the strongest of all the arguments against the interference of the public with purely personal conduct is that when it does interfere, the odds are that it interferes wrongly and in the wrong place.[6]

All errors which the individual is likely to commit against advice and warning are far outweighed by the evil of allowing others to constrain him to what they deem his good.[7]

Performing the utilitarian calculation by balancing the advantages and disadvantages we find that:

Mankind are greater gainers by suffering each other to live as seems good to themselves, than by compelling each other to live as seems good to the rest.[8]

From which follows the operative premise 4.

This classical case of a utilitarian argument with all the premises spelled out is not the only line of reasoning present in Mill's discussion. There are asides, and more than asides, which look quite different and I shall deal with them later. But this is clearly the main channel of Mill's thought and it is one which has been subjected to vigorous attack from the moment it appeared—most often by fellow Utilitarians. The link that they have usually seized on is, as Fitzjames Stephen put it, the absence of proof that the "mass of adults are so well acquainted with their own interests and so much disposed to pursue them that no compulsion or restraint put upon them by any others for the purpose of promoting their interest can really promote them."[9] . . .

Now it is interesting to note that Mill himself was aware of some of the limitations on the doctrine that the individual is the best judge of his own interests.

In his discussion of government intervention in general (even where the intervention does not interfere with liberty but provides alternative institutions to those of the market) after making claims which are parallel to those just discussed, e.g.

People understand their own business and their own interests better, and care for them more, than the government does, or can be expected to do.[10]

He goes on to an intelligent discussion of the "very large and conspicuous exceptions" to the maxim that:

Most persons take a juster and more intelligent view of their own interest, and of the means of promoting it than can either be prescribed to them by a general enactment of the legislature, or pointed out in the particular case by a public functionary.[11]

Thus there are things

of which the utility does not consist in ministering to inclinations, nor in serving the daily uses of life, and the want of which is least felt where the need is greatest. This is peculiarly true of those things which are chiefly useful as tending to raise the character of human beings. The uncultivated cannot be competent judges of cultivation. Those who most need to be made wiser and better, usually desire it least, and, if they desired it, would be incapable of finding the way to it by their own lights.

. . . A second exception to the doctrine that individuals are the best judges of their own interest, is when an individual attempts to decide irrevocably now what will be best for his interest at some future and distant time. The presumption in favor of individual judgment is only legitimate, where the judgment is grounded on actual, and especially on present, personal experience; not where it is formed antecedently to experience, and not suffered to be reversed even after experience has condemned it.[12]

The upshot of these exceptions is that Mill does not declare that there should never be government interference with the economy but rather that

. . . in every instance, the burden of making out a strong case should be thrown not on those who resist but on those who recommend government interference. Letting alone, in short, should be the general practice: every departure from it, unless required by some great good, is a certain evil.[13]

In short, we get a presumption not an absolute prohibition. The question is why doesn't the argument against paternalism go the same way?

A consistent Utilitarian can only argue against paternalism on the grounds that it (as a matter of fact) does not maximize the good. It is always a contingent question that may be refuted by the evidence. But there is also a non-contingent argument which runs through *On Liberty*. When Mill states that "there is a part of the life of every person who has come to years of discretion, within which the individuality of that person ought to rein uncontrolled either by any other person or by the public collectively" he is saying something about what it means to be a person, an autonomous agent. It is because coercing a person for his own good denies this status as an independent entity that Mill objects to it so strongly and in such absolute terms. To be able to choose is a good that is independent of the wisdom of what is chosen. A man's "mode" of laying out his existence is the best, not because it is the best in itself, but because it is his own mode.[14]

> It is the privilege and proper condition of a human being, arrived at the maturity of his faculties, to use and interpret experience in his own way.[15]

As further evidence of this line of reasoning in Mill consider the one exception to his prohibition against paternalism.

> In this and most civilised countries, for example, an engagement by which a person should sell himself, or allow himself to be sold, as a slave, would be null and void; neither enforced by law nor by opinion. The ground for thus limiting his power of voluntarily disposing of his own lot in life, is apparent, and is very clearly seen in this extreme case. The reason for not interfering, unless for the sake of others, with a person's voluntary acts, is consideration for his liberty. His voluntary choice is evidence that what he so chooses is desirable, or at least endurable, to him, and his good is on the whole best provided for by allowing him to take his own means of pursuing it. But by selling himself for a slave, he abdicates his liberty; he foregoes any further use of it beyond that single act.
>
> He therefore defeats, in his own case, the very purpose which is the justification of allowing him to dispose of himself. He is no longer free; but is thenceforth in a position which has no longer the presumption in its favour, that would be afforded by his voluntarily remaining in it. The principle of freedom cannot require that he should be free not to be free. It is not freedom to be allowed to alienate his freedom.[16]

Now leaving aside the fudging on the meaning of freedom in the last line it is clear that part of this argument is incorrect. While it is true that *future* choices of the slave are not reasons for thinking that what he chooses then is desirable for him, what is at issue is limiting his immediate choice; and since this choice is made freely, the individual may be correct in thinking that his interests are best provided for by entering such a contract. But the main consideration for not allowing such a contract is the need to preserve the liberty of the person to make future choices. This gives us a principle—a very narrow one, by which to justify some paternalistic interferences. Paternalism is justified only to preserve a wider range of freedom for the individual in question. How far this principle could be extended, whether it can justify all the cases in which we are inclined upon reflection to think paternalistic measures justified remains to be discussed. What I have tried to show so far is that there are two strains of argument in Mill—one a straightforward Utilitarian mode of reasoning and one which relies not on the goods which free choice leads to but on the absolute value of the choice itself. The first cannot establish any absolute prohibition but at most a presumption and indeed a fairly weak one given some fairly plausible assumptions about human psychology; the second while a stronger line of argument seems to me to allow on its own grounds a wider range of paternalism than might be suspected. I turn now to a consideration of these matters.

VI

We might begin looking for principles governing the acceptable use of paternalistic power in cases where it is generally agreed that it is legitimate. Even Mill intends his principles to be applicable only to mature individuals, not those in what he calls "non-age." What is it that justifies us in interfering with children? The fact that they lack some of the emotional and cognitive capacities required in order to make fully rational decisions. It is an empirical question to just what extent children have an adequate conception of their own present and future interests but there is not much doubt that there are many deficiencies. For example it is very difficult for a child to defer gratification for any considerable period of time. Given these deficiencies and given the very real and permanent dangers that may befall the child it becomes not only permissible but even a duty of the parent to restrict the child's freedom in various ways. There is however an important moral limitation on the exercise of such parental power which is provided by the notion of the child eventually coming to see the correctness of his parents interventions. Parental paternalism may be thought of as a wager by the parent on the child's subsequent recognition of the wisdom of the restrictions. There is an emphasis on what could be called future-oriented consent—on what the child will come to welcome, rather than on what he does welcome.

The essence of this idea has been incorporated by idealist philosophers into various types of "real-will" theory as applied to fully adult persons. Extensions of paternalism are argued for by claiming that in various respects, chronologically mature individuals share the same deficiencies in knowledge, capacity to think rationally, and the ability to carry out decisions that children possess. Hence in interfering with such people we are in effect doing what they would do if they were fully rational. Hence we are not really opposing their will, hence we are not really interfering with their freedom. The dangers of this move have been sufficiently exposed by Berlin in his "Two Concepts of Liberty." I see no gain in theoretical clarity nor in practical advantage in trying to pass over the real nature of the interferences with liberty that we impose on others. Still the basic notion of consent is important and seems to me the only acceptable way of trying to delimit an area of justified paternalism.

Let me start by considering a case where the consent is not hypothetical in nature. Under certain conditions it is rational for an individual to agree that others should force him to act in ways which, at the time of action, the individual may not see as desirable. If, for example, a man knows that he is subject to breaking his resolves when temptation is present, he may ask a friend to refuse to entertain his request at some later stage.

A classical example is given in the Odyssey when Odysseus commands his men to tie him to the mast and refuse all future orders to be set free because he knows the power of the Sirens to enchant men with their songs. Here we are on relatively sound ground in later refusing Odysseus' request to be set free. He may even claim to have changed his mind but since it is just such changes that he wishes to guard against we are entitled to ignore them.

A process analogous to this may take place on a social rather than individual basis. An electorate may mandate its representatives to pass legislation which when it comes time to "pay the price" may be unpalatable. I may believe that a tax increase is necessary to halt inflation though I may resent the lower pay check each month. However in both this case and that of Odysseus the measure to be enforced is specifically requested by the party involved and at some point in time there is genuine consent and agreement on the part of those persons whose liberty is infringed. Such is not the case for the paternalistic measures we have been speaking about. What must be involved here is not consent to specific measures but rather consent to a system of government, run by elected representatives, with an understanding that they may act to safeguard our interests in certain limited ways.

I suggest that since we are all aware of our irrational propensities, deficiencies in cognitive and emotional capacities and avoidable and unavoidable ignorance it is rational and prudent for us to in effect take out "social insurance policies." We may argue for and against proposed paternalistic measures in terms of what fully rational individuals would accept as forms of protection. Now, clearly since the initial agreement is not about specific measures we are dealing with a more-or-less blank check and therefore there have to be carefully defined limits. What I am looking for are certain kinds of conditions which make it plausible to suppose that rational men could reach agreement to limit their liberty even when other men's interests are not affected.

Of course as in any kind of agreement schema there are great difficulties in deciding what rational individuals would or would not accept. Particularly in sensitive areas of personal liberty, there is always a danger of the dispute over agreement and rationality being a disguised version of evaluative and normative disagreement.

Let me suggest types of situations in which it seems plausible to suppose that fully rational individuals would agree to having paternalistic restrictions imposed upon them. It is reasonable to suppose that there are "goods" such as health which any person would want to have in order to pursue his own good—no matter how that good is conceived. This is an argument that is used in connection with compulsory education for children but it seems to me that it can be extended to other goods which have this character. Then one could agree that the attainment of such goods should be promoted even when not recognized to be such, at the moment, by the individuals concerned.

An immediate difficulty that arises stems from the fact that men are always faced with competing goods and that there may be reasons why even a value such as health—or indeed life—may be overridden by competing values. Thus the problem with the Christian Scientist and blood transfusions. It may be more important for him to reject "impure substances" than to go on living. The difficult problem that must be faced is whether one can give sense to the notion of a person irrationally attaching weights to competing values.

Consider a person who knows the statistical data on the probability of being injured when not wearing seat-belts in an automobile and knows the types and gravity of the various injuries. He also insists that the inconvenience attached to fastening the belt every time he gets in and out of the car outweighs for him the possible risks to himself. I am inclined in this case to think that such a weighing is irrational. Given his life plans which we are assuming are those of the average person, his interests and commitments already undertaken, I think it is safe to predict that we can find inconsistencies in his calculations at some point. I am assuming that this is not a man who for some conscious or unconscious reasons is trying to injure himself nor is he a man who just likes to "live dangerously." I am assuming that he is like us in all the relevant respects but just puts an enormously high negative value on inconve-

nience—one which does not seem comprehensible or reasonable.

It is always possible, of course to assimilate this person to creatures like myself. I, also, neglect to fasten my seat-belt and I concede such behavior is not rational but not because I weigh the inconvenience differently from those who fasten the belts. It is just that having made (roughly) the same calculation as everybody else I ignore it in my actions. [Note: a much better case of weakness of the will than those usually given in ethics texts.] A plausible explanation for this deplorable habit is that athough I know in some intellectual sense what the probabilities and risks are I do not fully appreciate them in an emotionally genuine manner.

We have two distinct types of situation in which a man acts in a non-rational fashion. In one case he attaches incorrect weights to some of his values; in the other he neglects to act in accordance with his actual preferences and desires. Clearly there is a stronger and more persuasive argument for paternalism in the latter situation. Here we are really not—by assumption—imposing a good on another person. But why may we not extend our interference to what we might call evaluative delusions? After all in the case of cognitive delusions we are prepared, often, to act against the expressed will of the person involved. If a man believes that when he jumps out the window he will float upwards—Robert Nozick's example—would not we detain him, forcibly if necessary? The reply will be that this man doesn't wish to be injured and if we could convince him that he is mistaken as to the consequences of his actions he would not wish to perform the action. But part of what is involved in claiming that a man who doesn't fasten his seat-belts is attaching an irrational weight to the inconvenience of fastening them is that if he were to be involved in an accident and severely injured he would look back and admit that the inconvenience wasn't as bad as all that. So there is a sense in which if I could convince him of the consequences of his actions he also would not wish to continue his present course of action. Now the notion of consequences being used here is covering a lot of ground. In one case it's being used to indicate what will or can happen as a result of a course of action and in the other it's making a prediction about the future evaluation of the consequences—in the first sense—of a course of action. And whatever the difference between facts and values—whether it be hard and fast or soft and slow—we are genuinely more reluctant to consent to interferences where evaluative differences are the issue. Let me now consider another factor which comes into play in some of these situations which may make an important difference in our willingness to consent to paternalistic restrictions.

Some of the decisions we make are of such a character that they produce changes which are in one or another way irreversible. Situations are created in which it is difficult or impossible to return to anything like the initial stage at which the decision was made. In particular some of these changes will make it impossible to continue to make reasoned choices in the future. I am thinking specifically of decisions which involve taking drugs that are physically or psychologically addictive and those which are destructive of one's mental and physical capacities.

I suggest we think of the imposition of paternalistic interferences in situations of this kind as being a kind of insurance policy which we take out against making decisions which are far-reaching, potentially dangerous and irreversible. . . .

A second class of cases concerns decisions which are made under extreme psychological and sociological pressure. I am not thinking here of the making of the decision as being something one is pressured into—e.g. a good reason for making duelling illegal is that unless this is done many people might have to manifest their courage and integrity in ways in which they would rather not do so—but rather of decisions such as that to commit suicide which are usually made at a point where the individual is not thinking clearly and calmly about the nature of his decision. In addition, of course, this comes under the previous heading of all-too-irrevocable decision. Now there are practical steps which a society could take if it wanted to decrease the possibility of suicide—for example not paying social security benefits to the survivors or as religious institutions do, not allowing such persons to be buried with the same status as natural deaths. I think we may count these as interferences with the liberty of persons to attempt suicide and the question is whether they are justifiable.

Using my argument schema the question is whether rational individuals would consent to such limitations. I see no reason for them to consent to an absolute prohibition but I do think it is reasonable for them to agree to some kind of enforced waiting period. Since we are all aware of the possibility of temporary states, such as great fear or depression, that are inimical to the making of well-informed and rational decisions, it would be prudent for all of us if there were some kind of institutional arrangement whereby we were restrained from making a decision which is (all too) irreversible. What this would be like in practice is difficult to envisage and it may be that if no practical arrangements were feasible then we would have to conclude that there should be no restriction at all on this kind of action. But we might have a "cooling off" period, in much the same way that we now require couples who file for divorce to go through a waiting period. Or, more far-fetched, we might imagine a Suicide Board composed of a psychologist and another member picked by the applicant. The Board would be required to meet and talk with the person proposing to take his life, though its approval would not be required.

A third class of decisions—these classes are not supposed to be disjoint—involves dangers which are either not sufficiently understood or appreciated correctly by the persons involved. Let me illustrate, using the example of cigarette smoking, a number of possible cases.

1. A man may not know the facts—e.g. smoking between 1 and 2 packs a day shortens life expectancy 6.2 years, the cost and pain of the illness caused by smoking, etc.
2. A man may know the facts, wish to stop smoking, but not have the requisite willpower.
3. A man may know the facts but not have them play the correct role in his calculation because, say, he discounts the danger psychologically because it is remote in time and/or inflates the attractiveness of other consequences of his decision which he regards as beneficial.

In case 1 what is called for is education, the posting of warnings, etc. In case 2 there is no theoretical problem. We are not imposing a good on someone who rejects it. We are simply using coercion to enable people to carry out their own goals. (Note: There obviously is a difficulty in that only a subclass of the individuals affected wish to be prevented from doing what they are doing.) In case 3 there is a sense in which we are imposing a good on someone since given his current appraisal of the facts he doesn't wish to be restricted. But in another sense we are not imposing a good since what is being claimed—and what must be shown or at least argued for—is that an accurate accounting on his part would lead him to reject his current course of action. Now we all know that such cases exist, that we are prone to disregard dangers that are only possibilities, that immediate pleasures are often magnified and distorted.

If in addition the dangers are severe and far-reaching we could agree to allowing the state a certain degree of power to intervene in such situations. The difficulty is in specifying in advance, even vaguely, the class of cases in which intervention will be legitimate.

A related difficulty is that of drawing a line so that it is not the case that all ultra-hazardous activities are ruled out, e.g. mountain-climbing, bullfighting, sports-car racing, etc. There are some risks—even very great ones—which a person is entitled to take with his life.

A good deal depends on the nature of the deprivation—e.g. does it prevent the person from engaging in the activity completely or merely limit his participation—and how important to the nature of the activity is the absence of restriction when this is weighed against the role that the activity plays in the life of the person. In the case of automobile seatbelts, for example, the restriction is trivial in nature, interferes not at all with the use or enjoyment of the activity, and does, I am assuming, considerably reduce a high risk of serious injury. Whereas, for example, making mountain climbing illegal prevents completely a person engaging in an activity which may play an important role in his life and his conception of the person he is.

In general the easiest cases to handle are those which can be argued about in the terms which Mill thought to be so important—a concern not just for the happiness or welfare, in some broad sense, of the individual but rather a concern for the autonomy and freedom of the person. I suggest that we would be most likely to consent to paternalism in those instances in which it preserves and enhances for the individual his ability to rationally consider and carry out his own decisions.

I have suggested in this essay a number of types of situations in which it seems plausible that rational men would agree to granting the legislative powers of a society the right to impose restrictions on what Mill calls "self-regarding" conduct. However, rational men knowing something about the resources of ignorance, ill-will and stupidity available to the lawmakers of a society—a good case in point is the history of drug legislation in the United States—will be concerned to limit such intervention to minimum. I suggest in closing two principles designed to achieve this end.

In all cases of paternalistic legislation there must be a heavy and clear burden of proof placed on the authorities to demonstrate the exact nature of the harmful effects (or beneficial consequences) to be avoided (or achieved) and the probability of their occurrence. The burden of proof here is twofold—what lawyers distinguish as the burden of going forward and the burden of persuasion. That the authorities have the burden of going forward means that it is up to them to raise the question and bring forward evidence of the evils to be avoided. Unlike the case of new drugs where the manufacturer must produce some evidence that the drug has been tested and found not harmful, no citizen has to show with respect to self-regarding conduct that it is not harmful or promotes his best interests. In addition the nature and cogency of the evidence for the harmfulness of the course of action must be set at a high level. To paraphrase a formulation of the burden of proof for criminal proceedings—better 10 men ruin themselves than one man be unjustly deprived of liberty.

Finally I suggest a principle of the least restrictive alternative. If there is an alternative way of accomplishing the desired end without restricting liberty then although it may involve great expense, inconvenience, etc. the society must adopt it.

NOTES

1. J. S. Mill, *Utilitarianism* and *On Liberty* (Fontana Library Edition, ed. by Mary Warnock, London, 1962), p. 135. All further quotes from Mill are from this edition unless otherwise noted.

2. J. S. Mill, *Principles of Political Economy* (New York: P. F. Collier and Sons, 1900), p. 442.

3. Mill, *Utilitarianism* and *On Liberty*, p. 207.

4. *Ibid.*, p. 206.

5. *Ibid.*, p. 207.

6. *Ibid.*, p. 214.

7. *Ibid.*, p. 207.

8. *Ibid.*, p. 138.

9. J. F. Stephens, *Liberty, Equality, Fraternity* (New York: Henry Holt & Co., n.d.), p. 24.

10. *Ibid.*, p. 33.

11. Mill, *Principles*, II, 458.

12. *Ibid.*, II, 459.

13. *Ibid.*, II, 451.

14. Mill, *Utilitarianism* and *On Liberty*, p. 197.

15. *Ibid.*, p. 186.

16. *Ibid.*, pp. 235–236.

The Refutation of Medical Paternalism

ALAN GOLDMAN

Except in a few extraordinary cases, strong paternalism in medicine is unjustified, Goldman argues. Patients have a right of self-determination, a right of freedom to make their own choices. Decisions regarding their own futures should be left up to them because persons are the best judges of their own interests and because self-determination is valuable for its own sake regardless of its generally positive effects. This right implies "the right to be told the truth about one's condition, and the right to accept or refuse or withdraw from treatment on the basis of adequate information regarding alternatives, risks and uncertainties." The faulty premise in the argument for medical paternalism, says Goldman, is that health and prolonged life can be assumed to be the top priorities for patients (and so physicians may decide for patients accordingly). But very few people always prioritize these values in this way.

There are two ways to attack an argument in favor of paternalistic measures (while accepting our criteria for justified paternalism). One is to argue that honoring rather than overriding the right of the person will not in fact harm him. The other is to admit that the satisfaction of the person's right may harm in some way, but argue that the harm does not merit exception to the right, all things considered. The first is principally an empirical, the second a moral counterargument.

The latter is not a perfectly clear-cut distinction, either in general or in application to the question of paternalism. For one thing, the most inclusive notion of harm is relative to the values and preferences of the particular individual. (This point will be important in the argument to follow.) A person is

From *The Moral Foundations of Professional Ethics* by Alan Goldman, Rowman & Littlefield, 1980. Reprinted with permission of the publisher. Notes omitted.

harmed when a state of affairs below a certain level on his preference scale is realized rather than one higher up. Our notion of harm derives what objectivity it has from two sources, again one principally empirical and the other more purely moral. The first is the fact that certain states of affairs are such that the vast majority of us would wish to avoid them in almost all conceivable contexts: physical injury, hastened death, or depression itself for example. It is an empirical question whether these states of affairs result from certain courses of conduct, hence, when they are predicted results, principally an empirical question whether harm ensues. The second source of a concept of harm independent of individual differences in subjective preferences is ideal-regarding: when the development of an individual capable of freely and creatively formulating and acting to realize central life projects is blocked, that person is harmed, whether or not he realizes it, and whether or not any of his present desires are frustrated.

The first argument against paternalistic interference holds that allowing an individual free choice is not most likely to result in harm taken in its objective sense. The second argument is somewhat more complex. It admits likely harm in the objective sense—worsened health, depression, or even hastened death in the examples we are considering—but holds that even greater harm to the individual is likely to ensue from the interference, harm in the more inclusive sense that takes account of his whole range of value orderings and the independent value of his integrity as an individual. In this latter situation there is one sense in which the individual is likely to suffer harm no matter what others do, since a state of affairs will be realized that he would wish to avoid, other things being equal, a state of affairs well below the neutral level in his preference orderings. But from the point of view of others, they impose harm only by interfering, since only that action results in a state of affairs lower on his scale of preferences than would otherwise be realized. In this sense harm is a relative notion, first because it is relative to subjective value orderings, and second because it is imposed only when a situation *worse* that what would otherwise occur is caused. We appeal to this second more inclusive notion in the second type of argument against paternalism.

Empirical Arguments

Returning to the medical context, other philosophers have recently questioned the degree of truth in the empirical premise that patients are likely to be harmed when doctors fully inform them. Sissela Bok, for example, has noted that in general it appears to be false that patients do not really want bad news, cannot accept or understand it, or are harmed by it. Yet she does not deny that information can sometimes harm patients, can cause depression, prolong illness, or even hasten death; and she explicitly allows for concealment when this can be shown in terminal cases. Allen Buchanan questions the ability of the doctor to make a competent judgment on the probability of harm to the patient, a judgment that would require both psychiatric expertise and intimate knowledge of the patient himself. Doctors are not generally trained to judge long-term psychological reactions, and even if they were, they would

require detailed psychological histories of patients in order to apply this expertise in particular cases. As medical practices tend to become more impersonal, certainly a trend in recent years, such intimate knowledge of patients, even on a nontheoretical level, will normally be lacking. Physicians would then have to rely upon loose generalizations, based on prior impressions of other patients and folklore from colleagues, in order to predict the effect of information on particular patients.

Buchanan appears to consider this point sufficient to refute the argument for paternalism, eschewing appeal to patients' rights. But unless we begin with a strong presumption of a right of the patient to the truth, I do not see why the difficulties for the doctor in judging the effect of information on the patient recommends a practice of disclosure. If the decision is to be based upon risk-benefit calculation (as it would be without consideration of rights), then, just as in other decisions regarding treatment, no matter how difficult to make, it seems that the doctor should act on his best estimate. The decision on what to say must be made by him one way or the other; and without a right-based presumption in favor of revealing the truth, its difficulty is no argument for one outcome rather than the other. In fact, the difficulty might count against revelation, since telling the truth is generally more irreversible than concealment or delay.

One could, it is true, attempt to make out a case for full disclosure on strict risk-benefit grounds, without appeal to rights. As we have seen in earlier chapters, utilitarians can go to great lengths to show that their calculations accord with the intuitive recognition of particular rights. In the case of lying or deceiving, they standardly appeal to certain systematic disutilities that might be projected, e.g. effects upon the agent's trustworthiness and upon the trust that other people are willing to accord him if his lies are discovered. In the doctor's case, he might fear losing patients or losing the faith of patients who continue to consult him, if he is caught in lies or deceptions. A utilitarian could argue further that, even in situations in which these disutilities appear not to figure, this appearance tends to be misleading, and that potential liars should therefore resist the temptation on this ground. One problem with this argument, as pointed out in the chapter on political ethics, is that it is empirically falsified in many situations. It is not always so difficult to foretell the utilitarian effects of deception, at least no more difficult than is any other future-looking moral calculation. In the case of terminally ill patients, for example, by the time they realize that their doctors have been deceiving them, they will be in no condition to communicate this fact to other patients or potential patients, even if such communication were otherwise commonplace. Thus the doctor has little to fear in the way of losing patients or patients' faith from his policy of disclosure or concealment from the terminally ill. He can safely calculate risks and benefits with little regard for such systematic disutilities. Again we have little reason to prefer honoring a right, in this case a right to be told the truth, without appealing to the right itself. The only conclusion that I would draw from the empirical points taken in themselves is that doctors should perhaps be better trained in psychology in order to be better able to judge the effects of disclosure upon patients, not that they should make a practice of full disclosure and of allowing patients full control over decisions on treatment. These conclusions we must reach by a different rights-based route.

I shall then criticize the argument for paternalistic strong role differentiation on the more fundamental moral ground. To do so I shall restrict attention to cases in which there is a definite risk or probability of eventual harm (in the objective sense) to the patient's health from revealing the truth about his condition to him, or from informing him of all risks of alternative treatments and allowing him a fully informed decision. These cases are those in which the high probability of harm can be supported or demonstrated, but in which the patient asks to know the truth. Such cases are not decided by the points of Bok or Buchanan, and they are the crucial ones for the question of strong role differentiation. The issue is whether such projected harm is sufficient to justify concealment. If the patient's normal right to self-determination prevails, then the doctor, in having to honor this right, is acting within the same moral framework as the rest of us. If the doctor acquires the authority to decide for the patient, a normally competent adult, or to withhold the truth about his own condition from him, then he has special profes-

sional license to override otherwise obtaining rights, and his position is strongly differentiated.

Before presenting the case against strong role differentiation on this basis, I want to dispense quickly with a possible conceptual objection. One might claim that the justification of medical paternalism would not in itself satisfy the criteria for strong role differentiation as defined. Since paternalism is justified as well in other contexts, the exceptions to the rights in question need not be seen to derive from a special principle unique to medical ethics, but can be held simply to instantiate a generally recognized ground for restricting rights or freedoms. If serious harm to a person himself generally can be counted as overriding evidence that the projected action is contrary to his own true preferences or values, and if this generally justifies paternalistic interference or delegation of authority for decisions to others, if, for example, legislators assume authority to apply coercive sanctions to behavior on these grounds, then the authority to be paternalistic would not uniquely differentiate doctors.

The above may be true in so far as paternalism is sometimes justified in other than medical contexts, but that does not alter the import of the argument for medical paternalism to our perception of the doctor's role. If the argument were sound, the medical profession might still be the only one, or one of only a few, paternalistic in this way. This would differentiate medical ethics sufficiently. I argued earlier that legislators must in fact honor normal moral rights. While paternalistic legislation is sometimes justified, as in the requirement that motorcycle riders wear helmets, such legislation is so relatively small a part of the legislator's concerns, and the amount of coercion justified itself so relatively light, that this does not alter our perception of the legislator's general moral framework. If the paternalist argument were sound in relation to doctors, on the other hand, this would substantially alter the nature of their practice and our perception of their authority over certain areas of our lives. We can therefore view the paternalist argument as expressing the underlying moral purposes that elevate the Hippocratic principle and augment the doctor's authority to ignore systematically rights that would obtain against all but those in the medical profession. The values expressed and elevated are viewed by doctors themselves as central to their role, which again distinguishes this argument from claims of justified paternalism in other contexts. Furthermore, viewing the argument in this way brings out the interesting relations between positions of doctors and those in other professions and social roles. It brings out that doctors tend to assume broader moral responsibility for decisions than laymen, while those in certain other professions tend to assume less. In any case, while I shall not in the end view the doctor's role as strongly differentiated, I do not want to rely upon this terminological point, but rather to refute the argument for overriding patients' rights to further the medical goal of optimal treatment.

The Moral Argument

In order to refute an argument, we of course need to refute only one of its premises. The argument for medical paternalism, stripped to its barest outline, was:

1. Disclosure of information to the patient will sometimes increase the likelihood of depression and physical deterioration, or result in choice of medically inoptimal treatment.
2. Disclosure of information is therefore sometimes likely to be detrimental to the patient's health, perhaps even to hasten his death.
3. Health and prolonged life can be assumed to have priority among preferences for patients who place themselves under physicians' care.
4. Worsening health or hastening death can therefore be assumed to be contrary to patients' own true value orderings.
5. Paternalism is therefore justified: doctors may sometimes override patients' prima facie rights to information about risks and treatments or about their own conditions in order to prevent harm to their health.

The Relativity of Values: Health and Life

The fundamentally faulty premise in the argument for paternalistic role differentiation for doctors is that which assumes that health or prolonged life must take absolute priority in the patient's value orderings. In order for paternalistic interference to be justified, a person must be acting irrationally or inconsistently with his own long-range preferences. The value ordering violated by the action to be prevented must either be known to be that of the person himself, as in the train example, or else be uncontroversially that of any rational person, as in the motorcycle helmet case. But can we assume that health and prolonged life have top priority in any rational ordering? If these values could be safely assumed to be always overriding for those who seek medical assistance, then medical expertise would become paramount in decisions regarding treatment, and decisions on disclosure would become assimilated to those within the treatment context. But in fact very few of us act according to such an assumed value ordering. In designing social policy we do not devote all funds or efforts toward minimizing loss of life, on the highways or in hospitals for example.

If our primary goal were always to minimize risk to health and life, we should spend our entire federal budget in health-related areas. Certainly such a suggestion would be ludicrous. We do not in fact grant to individuals rights to minimal risk in their activities or to absolutely optimal health care. From another perspective, if life itself, rather than life of a certain quality with autonomy and dignity, were of ultimate value, then even defensive wars could never be justified. But when the quality of life and the autonomy of an entire nation is threatened from without, defensive war in which many lives are risked and lost is a rational posture. To paraphrase Camus, anything worth living for is worth dying for. To realize or preserve those values that give meaning to life is worth the risk of life itself. Such fundamental values (and autonomy for individuals is certainly among them), necessary within a framework in which life of a certain quality becomes possible, appear to take precedence over the value of mere biological existence.

In personal life too we often engage in risky activities for far less exalted reasons, in fact just for the pleasure or convenience. We work too hard, smoke, exercise too little or too much, eat what we know is bad for us, and continue to do all these things even when informed of their possibly fatal effects. To doctors in their roles as doctors all this may appear irrational, although they no more act always to preserve their own health than do the rest of us. If certain risks to life and health are irrational, others are not. Once more the quality and significance of one's life may take precedence over maximal longevity. Many people when they are sick think of nothing above getting better; but this is not true of all. A person with a heart condition may decide that important unfinished work or projects must take priority over increased risk to his health; and his priority is not uncontroversially irrational. Since people's lives derive meaning and fulfillment from their projects and accomplishments, a person's risking a shortened life for one more fulfilled might well justify actions detrimental to his health. . . .

To doctors in their roles as professionals whose ultimate concern is the health or continued lives of patients, it is natural to elevate these values to ultimate prominence. The death of a patient, inevitable as it is in many cases, may appear as an ultimate defeat to the medical art, as something to be fought by any means, even after life has lost all value and meaning for the patient himself. The argument in the previous section for assuming this value ordering was that health, and certainly life, seem to be necessary conditions for the realization of all other goods or values. But this point, even if true, leaves open the question of whether health and life are of ultimate, or indeed any, intrinsic value, or whether they are valuable *merely* as means. It is plausible to maintain that life itself is not of intrinsic value, since surviving in an irreversible coma seems no better than death. It therefore again appears that it is the quality of life that counts, not simply being alive. Although almost any quality might be preferable to none, it is not irrational to trade off quantity for quality, as in any other good.

Even life with physical health and consciousness may not be of intrinsic value. Consciousness and health may not be sufficient in themselves to make the life worth living, since some states of consciousness are intrinsically good and others bad. Furthermore, if a person has nothing before him but pain and depression, then the instrumental worth of being alive may be reversed. And if prolonging one's life can be accomplished only at the expense of incapacitation or ignorance, perhaps preventing lifelong projects from being completed, then the instrumental value of longer life again seems overbalanced. It

is certainly true that normally life itself is of utmost value as necessary for all else of value, and that living longer usually enables one to complete more projects and plans, to satisfy more desires and derive more enjoyments. But this cannot be assumed in the extreme circumstances of severe or terminal illness. Ignorance of how long one has left may block realization of such values, as may treatment with the best chance for cure, if it also risks incapacitation or immediate death.

Nor is avoidance of depression the most important consideration in such circumstances, as a shallow hedonism might assume. Hedonistic theories of value, which seek only to produce pleasure or avoid pain and depression, are easily disproven by our abhorrence at the prospect of a "brave new world," or our unwillingness, were it possible, to be plugged indefinitely into a "pleasure machine." The latter prospect is abhorrent not only from an ideal-regarding viewpoint, but, less obviously, for want-regarding reasons (for most persons) as well. Most people would in fact be unwilling to trade important freedoms and accomplishments for sensuous pleasures, or even for the illusion of greater freedoms and accomplishments. As many philosophers have pointed out, while satisfaction of wants may bring pleasurable sensations, wants are not primarily *for* pleasurable sensations, or even for happiness more broadly construed, per se. Conversely, the avoidance of negative feelings or depression is not uppermost among primary motives. Many people are willing to endure frustration, suffering, and even depression in pursuit of accomplishment, or in order to complete projects once begun. Thus information relevant to such matters, such as medical information about one's own condition or possible adverse effects of various treatments, may well be worth having at the cost of psychological pain or depression.

The Value of Self-Determination

We have so far focused on the inability of the doctor to assume a particular value ordering for his patient in which health, the prolonging of life, or the avoidance of depression is uppermost. The likelihood of error in this regard makes it probable that the doctor will not know the true interests of his patient as well as the patient himself. He is therefore less likely than the patient himself to make choices in accord with that overall interest, and paternalistic assumption of authority to do so is therefore unjustified. There is in addition another decisive consideration mentioned earlier, namely the independent value of self-determination or freedom of choice. Personal autonomy over important decisions in one's life, the ability to attempt to realize one's own value ordering, is indeed so important that normally no amount of other goods, pleasures or avoidance of personal evils can take precedence. This is why it is wrong to contract oneself into slavery, and another reason why pleasure machines do not seem attractive. Regarding the latter, even if people were willing to forego other goods for a life of constant pleasure, the loss in variety of other values, and in the creativity that can generate new sources of value, would be morally regrettable. The value of self-determination explains also why there is such a strong burden of proof upon those who advocate paternalistic measures, why they must show that the person would otherwise act in a way inconsistent with his own value ordering, that is irrationally. A person's desires are not simply evidence of what is in his interest—they have extra weight.

Especially when decisions are important to the course of our lives, we are unwilling to relinquish them to others, even in exchange for a higher probability of happiness or less risk of suffering. Even if it could be proven, for example, that some scientific method of matching spouses greatly increased chances of compatibility and happiness, we would insist upon retaining our rights over marriage decisions. Given the present rate of success in marriages, it is probable that we could in fact find some better method of matching partners in terms of increasing that success rate. Yet we are willing to forego increased chances of success in order to make our own choices, choices that tend to make us miserable in the long run. The same might be true of career choices, choices of schools, and others central to the course of our lives. Our unwillingness to delegate these crucial decisions to experts or computers, who might stand

a better chance of making them correctly (in terms of later satisfactions), is not to be explained simply in terms of our (sometimes mistaken) assumptions that we know best how to satisfy our own interests, or that we personally will choose correctly, even though most other people do not. If our retaining such authority for ourselves is not simply irrational, and I do not believe it is, this can only be because of the great independent value of self-determination. We value the exercise of free choice itself in personally important decisions, no matter what the effects of those decisions upon other satisfactions. The independent value of self-determination in decisions of great personal importance adds also to our reluctance to relinquish medical decisions with crucial effects on our lives to doctors, despite their medical expertise.

Autonomy or self-determination is independently valuable, as argued before, first of all because we value it in itself. But we may again add to this want-regarding or utilitarian reason a second ideal-regarding or perfectionist reason. What has value does so because it is valued by a rational and autonomous person. But autonomy itself is necessary to the development of such valuing individual persons or agents. It is therefore not to be sacrificed to other derivative values. To do so as a rule is to destroy the ground for the latter. Rights in general not only express and protect the central interests of individuals (the raison d'être usually emphasized in their exposition); they also express the dignity and inviolability of individuality itself. For this reason the most fundamental right is the right to control the course of one's life, to make decisions crucial to it, including decisions in life-or-death medical contexts. The other side of the independent value of self-determination from the point of view of the individual is the recognition of him by others, including doctors, as an individual with his own possibly unique set of values and priorities. His dignity demands a right to make personal decisions that express those values.

Why Doctors Should Intervene

TERRENCE F. ACKERMAN

Respect for patient autonomy is distorted when autonomy is understood as mere noninterference, says Ackerman. On this prevalent hands-off view, "[t]he doctor need be only an honest and good technician, providing relevant information and dispensing professionally competent care." But this approach fails to respect autonomy genuinely, he argues, for it does not recognize that many factors can compromise autonomy, including illness and a host of psychological, social, and cultural constraints. At times, true respect for autonomy may require the physician to intervene, to deviate from the patient's stated preferences. The goal of the physician-patient relationship should be "to resolve the underlying physical (or mental) defect, and to deal with cognitive, psychological, and social constraints in order to restore autonomous functioning."

Patient autonomy has become a watchword of the medical profession. According to the revised 1980 AMA Principles of Medical Ethics,[1] no longer is it permissible for a doctor to withhold information from a patient, even on grounds that it may be harmful. Instead the physician is expected to "deal honestly with patients" at all times. Physicians also have a duty to respect the confidentiality of the doctor-patient relationship. Even when disclosure to a third party may be in the patient's interests, the doctor is instructed to release information only when required by law. Respect for the autonomy of patients has given rise to many specific patient rights—among them the right to refuse treatment, the right to give informed consent, the right to privacy, and the right to competent medical care provided with "respect for human dignity."

While requirements of honesty, confidentiality, and patients' rights are all important, the underlying moral vision that places exclusive emphasis upon these factors is more troublesome. The profession's notion of respect for autonomy makes noninterference its essential feature. As the Belmont Report has described it, there is an obligation to "give weight to autonomous persons' considered opinions and choices while refraining from obstructing their actions unless

From *Hastings Center Report*, vol. 12, no. 4 (August 1982), pp. 14–17. Reprinted by permission of the author and the publisher.

they are clearly detrimental to others."[2] Or, as Tom Beauchamp and James Childress have suggested, "To respect autonomous agents is to recognize with due appreciation their own considered value judgments and outlooks even when it is believed that their judgments are mistaken." They argue that people "are entitled to autonomous determination without limitation on their liberty being imposed by others."[3]

When respect for personal autonomy is understood as noninterference, the physician's role is dramatically simplified. The doctor need be only an honest and good technician, providing relevant information and dispensing professionally competent care. Does noninterference really respect patient autonomy? I maintain that it does not, because it fails to take account of the transforming effects of illness.

"Autonomy," typically defined as self-governance, has two key features. First, autonomous behavior is governed by plans of action that have been formulated through deliberation or reflection. This deliberative activity involves processes of both information gathering and priority setting. Second, autonomous behavior issues, intentionally and voluntarily, from choices people make based upon their own life plans.

But various kinds of constraints can impede autonomous behavior. There are physical constraints—confinement in prison is an example—where internal or external circumstances bodily prevent a person from deliberating adequately or acting on life plans. Cognitive constraints derive from either a lack of information or an inability to understand that information. A consumer's ignorance regarding the merits or defects of a particular product fits the description. Psychological constraints, such as anxiety or depression, also inhibit adequate deliberation. Finally, there are social constraints—such as institutionalized roles and expectations ("a woman's place is in the home," "the doctor knows best") that block considered choices.

Edmund Pellegrino suggests several ways in which autonomy is specifically compromised by illness:

> In illness, the body is interposed between us and reality—it impedes our choices and actions and is no longer fully responsive. . . . Illness forces a reappraisal and that poses a threat to the old image; it opens up all the old anxieties and imposes new ones—often including the real threat of death or drastic alterations in life-style. This ontological assault is aggravated by the loss of . . . freedoms we identify as peculiarly human. The patient . . . lacks the knowledge and skills necessary to cure himself or gain relief of pain and suffering. . . . The state of being ill is therefore a state of "wounded humanity," of a person compromised in his fundamental capacity to deal with his vulnerability.[4]

The most obvious impediment is that illness "interposes" the body or mind between the patient and reality, obstructing attempts to act upon cherished plans. An illness may not only temporarily obstruct long-range goals; it may necessitate permanent and drastic revision in the patient's major activities, such as working habits. Patients may also need to set limited goals regarding control of pain, alteration in diet and physical activity, and rehabilitation of functional impairments. They may face considerable difficulties in identifying realistic and productive aims.

The crisis is aggravated by a cognitive constraint—the lack of "knowledge and skills" to overcome their physical or mental impediment. Without adequate medical understanding, the patient cannot assess his or her condition accurately. Thus the choice of goals is seriously hampered and subsequent decisions by the patient are not well founded.

Pellegrino mentions the anxieties created by illness, but psychological constraints may also include denial, depression, guilt, and fear. I recently visited an eighteen-year-old boy who was dying of a cancer that had metastasized extensively throughout his abdomen. The doctor wanted to administer further chemotherapy that might extend the patient's life a few months. But the patient's nutritional status was poor, and he would need intravenous feedings prior to chemotherapy. Since the nutritional therapy might also encourage tumor growth, leading to a blockage of the gastrointestinal tract, the physician carefully explained the options and the risks and benefits several times, each time at greater length. But after each explanation the young man would say only that he wished to do whatever was necessary to get better. Denial prevented him from exploring the alternatives.

Similarly, depression can lead patients to make choices that are not in harmony with their life plans. Recently, a middle-aged woman with a history of ovarian cancer in remission returned to the hospital for the biopsy of a possible pulmonary metastasis. Complications ensued and she required the use of an artificial respirator for several days. She became severely depressed and soon refused further treatment. The behavior was entirely out of character with her previous full commitment to treatment. Fully supporting her overt wishes might have robbed her of many months of relatively comfortable life in the midst of a very supportive family around which her activities centered. The medical staff stalled for time. Fortunately, her condition improved.

Fear may also cripple the ability of patients to choose. Another patient, diagnosed as having a cerebral tumor that was probably malignant, refused life-saving surgery because he feared the cosmetic effects of neurosurgery and the possibility of neurological damage. After he became comatose and new evidence suggested that the tumor might be benign, his family agreed to surgery and a benign tumor was removed. But he later died of complications related to the unfortunate delay in surgery. Although while competent he had agreed to chemotherapy, his fears (not uncommon among candidates for neurosurgery) prevented him from accepting the medical intervention that might have secured him the health he desired.

Social constraints may also prevent patients from acting upon their considered choices. A recent case involved a twelve-year-old boy whose rhabdomyosarcoma had metastasized extensively. Since all therapeutic interventions had failed, the only remaining option was to involve him in a phase 1 clinical trial. (A phase 1 clinical trial is the initial testing of a drug in human subjects. Its primary purpose is to identify toxicities rather than to evaluate therapeutic effectiveness.) The patient's course had been very stormy, and he privately expressed to the staff his desire to quit further therapy and return home. However, his parents denied the hopelessness of his condition, remaining steadfast in their belief that God would save their child. With deep regard for his parents' wishes, he refused to openly object to their desires and the therapy was administered. No antitumor effect occurred and the patient soon died.

Various social and cultural expectations also take their toll. According to Talcott Parsons, one feature of the sick role is that the ill person is obligated "... to seek *technically competent* help, namely, in the most usual case, that of a physician and to *cooperate* with him in the process of trying to get well."[5] Parsons does not describe in detail the elements of this cooperation. But clinical observation suggests that many patients relinquish their opportunity to deliberate and make choices regarding treatment in deference to the physician's superior educational achievement and social status ("Whatever you think, doctor!"). The physical and emotional demands of illness reinforce this behavior.

Moreover, this perception of the sick role has been socially taught from childhood—and it is not easily altered even by the physician who ardently tries to engage the patient in decision making. Indeed, when patients are initially asked to participate in the decision-making process, some exhibit considerable confusion and anxiety. Thus, for many persons, the institutional role of patient requires the physician to assume the responsibilities of making decisions.

Ethicists typically condemn paternalistic practices in the therapeutic relationship, but fail to investigate the features that incline physicians to be paternalistic. Such behavior may be one way to assist persons whose autonomous behavior has been impaired by illness. Of course, it is an open moral question whether the constraints imposed by illness ought to be addressed in such a way. But only by coming to grips with the psychological and social dimensions of illness can we discuss how physicians can best respect persons who are patients.

Returning Control to Patients

In the usual interpretation of respect for personal autonomy, noninterference is fundamental. In the medical setting, this means providing adequate information and competent care that accords with the patient's wishes. But if serious constraints upon autonomous behavior are intrinsic to the state of being ill, then noninterference is not the best course, since the patient's choices will be seriously limited. Under these conditions, real respect for autonomy entails a more inclusive understanding of the relationship between patients and physicians. Rather than restraining themselves so that patients can exercise whatever autonomy they retain in illness, physicians should actively seek to neutralize the impediments that interfere with patients' choices.

In *The Healer's Art*, Eric Cassell underscored the essential feature of illness that demands a revision in our understanding of respect for autonomy:

> If I had to pick the aspect of illness that is most destructive to the sick, I would choose the loss of control. Maintaining control over oneself is so vital to all of us that one might see all the other phenomena of illness as doing harm not only in their own right but doubly so as they reinforce the sick person's perception that he is no longer in control."[6]

Cassell maintains, "The doctor's job is to return control to his patient." But what is involved in "returning control" to patients? Pellegrino identifies two elements that are preeminent duties of the physician: to provide technically competent care and to fully inform the patient. The noninterference approach emphasizes these factors, and their importance is clear. Loss of control in illness is precipitated by a physical or mental defect. If technically competent therapy can fully restore previous health, then the patient will again be in control. Consider a patient who is treated with antibiotics for a routine throat infection of streptococcal origin. Similarly, loss of control is fueled by lack of knowledge—not knowing what is the matter, what it portends for life and limb, and how it might be dealt with. Providing information that will enable the patient to make decisions and adjust goals enhances personal control.

If physical and cognitive constraints were the only impediments to autonomous behavior, then Pellegrino's suggestions might be adequate. But providing information and technically competent care will not do much to alter psychological or social impediments. Pellegrino does not adequately portray the physician's role in ameliorating these.

How can the doctor offset the acute denial that prevented the adolescent patient from assessing the benefits and risk of intravenous feedings prior to his additional chemotherapy? How can he deal with the candidate for neurosurgery who clearly desired that attempts be made to restore his health, but feared cosmetic and functional impairments? Here strategies must go beyond the mere provision of information. Crucial information may have to be repeatedly shared with patients. Features of the situation that the patient has brushed over (as in denial) or falsely emphasized (as with acute anxiety) must be discussed in more detail or set in their proper perspective. And the physician may have to alter the tone of discussions with the patient, emphasizing a positive attitude with the overly depressed or anxious patient, or a more realistic, cautious attitude with the denying patient, in order to neutralize psychological constraints.

The physician may also need to influence the beliefs or attitudes of other people, such as family members, that limit their awareness of the patient's perspective. Such a strategy might have helped the parents of the dying child to conform with the patient's wishes. On the other hand, physicians may need to modify the patient's own understanding of the sick role. For example, they may need to convey that the choice of treatment depends not merely upon the physician's technical assessment, but on the quality of life and personal goals that the patient desires.

Once we admit that psychological and social constraints impair patient autonomy, it follows that physicians must carefully assess the psychological and social profiles and needs of patients. Thus, Pedro Lain-Entralgo insists that adequate therapeutic interaction consists in a combination of "objectivity" and "cooperation." Cooperation "is shown by psychologically reproducing in the mind of the doctor, insofar as that is possible, the meaning the patient's illness has for him."[7] Without such knowledge, the

physician cannot assist patients in restoring control over their lives. Ironically, some critics have insisted that physicians are not justified in acting for the well-being of patients because they possess no "expertise" in securing the requisite knowledge about the patient.[8] But knowledge of the patient's psychological and social situation is also necessary to help the patient to act as a fully autonomous person.

Beyond Legalism

Current notions of respect for autonomy are undergirded by a legal model of doctor-patient interaction. The relationship is viewed as a typical commodity exchange—the provision of technically competent medical care in return for financial compensation. Moreover, physicians and patients are presumed to have an equal ability to work out the details of therapy, *provided that* certain moral rights of patients are recognized. But the compromising effects of illness, the superior knowledge of physicians, and various institutional arrangements are also viewed as giving the physician an unfair power advantage. Since the values and interests of patients may conflict with those of the physician, the emphasis is placed upon noninterference.[9]

This legal framework is insufficient for medical ethics because it fails to recognize the impact of illness upon autonomous behavior. Even if the rights to receive adequate information and to provide consent are secured, affective and social constraints impair the ability of patients to engage in contractual therapeutic relationships. When people are sick, the focus upon equality is temporally misplaced. The goal of the therapeutic relationship is the "development" of the patient—helping to resolve the underlying physical (or mental) defect, and to deal with cognitive, psychological, and social constraints in order to restore autonomous functioning. In this sense, the doctor-patient interaction is not unlike the parent-child or teacher-student relationship.

The legal model also falls short because the therapeutic relationship is not a typical commodity exchange in which the parties use each other to accomplish mutually compatible goals, without taking a direct interest in each other. Rather, the status of patients as persons whose autonomy is compromised constitutes the very stuff of therapeutic art.

The physician is attempting to alter the fundamental ability of patients to carry through their life plans. To accomplish this delicate task requires a personal knowledge about and interest in the patient. If we accept these points, then we must reject the narrow focus of medical ethics upon noninterference and emphasize patterns of interaction that free patients from constraints upon autonomy.

I hasten to add that I am criticizing the legal model only as a *complete* moral framework for therapeutic interaction. As case studies in medical ethics suggest, physicians and patients *are* potential adversaries. Moreover, the disability of the patient and various institutional controls provide physicians with a distinct "power advantage" that can be abused. Thus, a legitimate function of medical ethics is to formulate conditions that assure noninterference in patient decision making. But various positive interventions must also be emphasized, since the central task in the therapeutic process is assisting patients to reestablish control over their own lives.

In the last analysis, the crucial matter is how we view the patient who enters into the therapeutic relationship. Cassell points out that in the typical view ". . . the sick person is seen simply as a well person with a disease, rather than as qualitatively different, not only physically but also socially, emotionally, and even cognitively." In this view, ". . . the physician's role in the care of the sick is primarily the application of technology . . . and health can be seen as a commodity."[10] But if, as I believe, illness renders sick persons "qualitatively different," then respect for personal autonomy requires a therapeutic interaction considerably more complex than the noninterference strategy.

Thus the current "Principles of Medical Ethics" simply exhort physicians to be honest. But the crucial requirement is that physicians tell the truth in a way, at a time, and in whatever increments are necessary to allow patients to effectively use the information in adjusting their life plans.[11] Similarly, respecting a patient's refusal of treatment maximizes autonomy only if a balanced and thorough deliberation precedes the decision. Again, the "Principles" suggest that physicians observe strict confidentiality. But the more complex moral challenge is to use confidential information in a way that will help to give the patient more freedom. Thus, the doctor can keep a patient's report on family dynamics private, and still use it to modify attitudes or actions of family members that inhibit the patient's control.

At its root, illness is an evil primarily because it compromises our efforts to control our lives. Thus, we must preserve an understanding of the physician's art that transcends noninterference and addresses this fundamental reality.

REFERENCES

1. American Medical Association, *Current Opinions of the Judicial Council of the American Medical Association* (Chicago, Illinois: American Medical Association, 1981). p. ix. Also see Robert Veatch, "Professional Ethics: New Principles for Physicians?," *Hastings Center Report* 10 (June 1980), 16–19.

2. The National Commission for the Protection of Human Subjects of Biomedical and Behavioral Research. *The Belmont Report: Ethical Principles and Guidelines for the Protection of Human Subjects of Research* (Washington, D.C.: U.S. Government Printing Office, 1978), p. 58.

3. Tom Beauchamp and James Childress, *Principles of Biomedical Ethics* (New York: Oxford University Press, 1980), p. 59.

4. Edmund Pellegrino, "Toward a Reconstruction of Medical Morality: The Primacy of the Act of Profession and the Fact of Illness," *The Journal of Medicine and Philosophy* 4 (1979), 44–45.

5. Talcott Parsons, *The Social System* (Glencoe, Illinois: The Free Press, 1951), p. 437.

6. Eric Cassell, *The Healer's Art* (New York: Lippincott. 1976), p. 44. Although Cassell aptly describes the goal of the healer's art, it is unclear whether he considers it to be based upon the obligation to respect the patient's autonomy or the duty to enhance the well-being of the patient. Some parts of his discussion clearly suggest the latter.

7. Pedro Lain-Entralgo, *Doctor and Patient* (New York: McGraw-Hill, 1969), p. 155.

8. See Allen Buchanan, "Medical Paternalism," *Philosophy and Public Affairs* 7 (1978), 370–90.

9. My formulation of the components of the legal model differs from, but is highly indebted to, John Ladd's stimulating analysis in "Legalism and Medical Ethics," in John Davis et al., editors, *Contemporary Issues in Biomedical Ethics* (Clifton, N.J.: The Humana Press, 1979), pp. 1–35. However, I would not endorse Ladd's position that the moral principles that define our duties in the therapeutic setting are of a different logical type from those that define our duties to strangers.

10. Eric Cassell, "Therapeutic Relationship: Contemporary Medical Perspective," in Warren Reich, editor, *Encyclopedia of Bioethics* (New York: Macmillan, 1978), p. 1675.

11. Cf. Norman Cousins, "A Layman Looks at Truth-telling," *Journal of the American Medical Association* 244 (1980), 1929–30. Also see Howard Brody, "Hope," *Journal of the American Medical Association* 246 (1981), pp. 1411–12.

Autonomy, Futility, and the Limits of Medicine

ROBERT L. SCHWARTZ

Does respecting the principle of autonomy require physicians to provide any treatment that an autonomous patient requests? Schwartz says that physicians are not obligated to give scientifically futile treatment (a worthless cancer therapy, for example). More importantly, neither are they morally required to provide treatment that is outside the scope of medical practice (such as surgical amputation of a limb for purely religious reasons). In many instances (including the famous Wanglie case), the central question was not whether the treatment requested by the patient was futile, but whether the treatment was beyond the proper limits of medicine. Schwartz contends that defining the scope of medicine should be left to physicians themselves.

SURGEON: I don't seem to understand; why, precisely, have you come to see me today?

PATIENT: I am here because I need to have my right arm amputated, and I have been told that you are one of the finest surgeons in town.

SURGEON: That is, of course, correct. Tell me, though—I do not see a referral here—what makes you think that you need your arm amputated?

PATIENT: It is the only way I can expiate my sins. I could describe those sins to you in detail, and I could tell you why this is the only way I can seek expiation, but that hardly seems appropriate or necessary. In any case, I am sure that the only way I can expiate them is by having my right arm amputated.

SURGEON: Do I understand this? You came to see me because you want a good surgeon to amputate your right arm so that you can expiate your sins.

PATIENT: Exactly; I knew you would understand. By the way, I am fully insured.

SURGEON: Are you crazy? You've come to a surgeon just because you want your arm lopped off?

PATIENT: I would be crazy if I went any place else. I mean, you wouldn't recommend a butcher or a chiropractor, would you?

SURGEON: I'm sorry; your request is simply unacceptable. My values do not permit me to provide the services you seek. I just don't think it would be right.

PATIENT: Wait just a minute. I am not hiring you for your ability to make moral judgments. I am hiring you because of your technical skill in removing limbs. We are talking about my arm, my life, and my values. I have decided I need the surgery and I ask you merely to respect my autonomy and to apply your medical skill so that my values can be served. If you want to expiate your sins in some other way, that's just fine with me. I don't want your religious and ethical peccadillos to interfere with a high-quality technical medical service that I am paying you to provide for me.

Most of us find the surgeon's surprise at this patient's request understandable, and it is hard to imagine any surgeon acceding to this patient's demand. On the other hand (the one left), the patient is right—the surgeon is denying his technical skill because his values are different from those of the patient, whose values the surgeon does not respect.[1] The autonomy of the patient is being limited by the values of the doctor whose own interests, other than his interest in practicing medicine according to his own ethical values, would remain unaffected by his decision to provide the service.

From *Cambridge Quarterly of Healthcare Ethics*, vol. 1, no. 2 (1992), pp. 159–64. Copyright © 1992. Reprinted with the permission of Cambridge University Press and the author.

Autonomy and Patient Control of Medical Decision Making

Autonomy is the authority to make decisions in accord with one's own values, unrestrained by the values of others who do not suffer the consequences of the decision. Ordinarily, the principle of autonomy authorizes patients to make healthcare decisions unrestrained by the values of their physicians, others in the healthcare industry, or the rest of society. Despite this, even the strongest supporters of the primacy of the principle of autonomy in healthcare decision making—even those who believe that autonomy virtually always trumps beneficence—would be likely to support (or even require) the surgeon's decision *not* to offer surgery in this case. But why?

The principle of autonomy has never been understood to authorize patients to choose from among an unrestricted range of alternatives, As Fenella Rouse points out in the next note on the *Wanglie* case, autonomy has often been misconstrued and improperly applied by courts in cases involving medical decision making. In any case, there are at least three kinds of limitations on the exercise of autonomy by those making healthcare choices. First, patients may not require that they be treated by nonmedical means. Second, patients may not require that they be given scientifically futile treatment. Finally, and most significantly, patients may not require that they be treated in ways that are inconsistent with the ends of medicine, that is, in ways that are outside of the scope of medicine.

First, for example, a tense and depressed streetcar operator is not denied autonomy by our healthcare system if he is not given the option of choosing three weeks on the beach in Tahiti as a cure for his condition, even though it may well be effective. Three weeks on the beach in Tahiti is simply not a medical means of treatment—it is not among the medical alternatives for the treatment of that (or any other) condition.

Second, where the issue is one of scientific futility, i.e., whether a medical procedure will have the scientific consequences that are expected, the issue is left entirely to the medical profession. Physicians are not required to prescribe pasque-flower tea for the treatment of cancer, for example, because, as a scientific matter, there is simply no efficacy in treatment

by pasque-flower tea. From a purely scientific perspective, the treatment of cancer by pasque-flower tea really is futile.

Unlike beach rest, amputation is within the therapeutic arsenal of the medical profession; it is a medical procedure. Unlike pasque-flower tea as a cure for cancer, surgical amputation is a proven effective way of removing a limb; thus, it is not futile in a scientific sense. Despite this, though, we would not allow the patient in the opening vignette to demand that his arm be amputated because patients are not permitted to demand surgery that is inconsistent with the definition of the scope of medical practice accepted by the surgeon.[2] In their exercise of autonomy, patients may choose only from among reasonable medical alternatives. The hard question is how doctors, patients, and others define which medically and scientifically proven procedures are among the reasonable medical alternatives.

The Wanglie Case

The limitations on a patient's autonomy to choose healthcare has come to the forefront of the bioethics debate over the past year. In December 1989, Helga Wanglie, an 87-year-old retired school teacher in Minneapolis, tripped on a rug in her home and fractured her hip.[3] One month later, after surgery in one hospital, she was transferred to Hennepin County Medical Center, where her doctors determined she needed assistance in breathing and placed her on a ventilator. Three months later, in May 1990, she was transferred to yet another hospital to see if she could be weaned from her ventilator. While there, she suffered cardiac arrest and was resuscitated, but only after she suffered severe and irreversible brain damage that put her in a persistent vegetative state. She was moved back to Hennepin County Medical Center, where she was maintained on a ventilator and fed through a gastrostomy tube. Mrs. Wanglie remained in a persistent vegetative state for several months before her physicians determined that the continuation of high-tech medical intervention was inappropriate. In essence, the doctors determined that the care Mrs. Wanglie was receiving was no longer among the reasonable medical alternatives for a person in her condition—it was, to her doctors, morally analogous to amputating a limb to expiate sins.

Mrs. Wanglie's husband and her two children disagreed. As Mrs. Wanglie's husband pointed out, "Only He who gave life has the right to take life." He also pointed out, "I am a pro-lifer. I take the position that human life is sacred."[4] He and the children agreed that Mrs. Wanglie would want treatment continued, even if the doctors believed that there were no chance of recovery. This was, as the family pointed out, a determination based on the patient's values, and there was no reason to defer to the doctors' collective ethical judgment.

The physicians and the hospital searched in vain for some healthcare facility in Minnesota that would be willing to take Mrs. Wanglie and continue to provide her care. None came forward. Frustrated by what they considered the continued inappropriate use of medicine, the hospital sought a court order appointing a conservator to replace Mr. Wanglie to make healthcare decisions for Mrs. Wanglie. On 1 July 1991, the trial court judge refused to issue an order and effectively confirmed Mr. Wanglie's right to continue to make healthcare decisions for his wife of 53 years.[5] Three days after the order was issued, Mrs. Wanglie died "of natural causes." Her hospitalization cost nearly 1 million dollars, which was paid by Medicare and her private medigap insurance carrier. Neither objected to the care for financial or cost-benefit reasons, and the cost properly did not enter into the judicial analysis of the case.

Asking the Wrong Question: Substitute Decision Makers and the Wanglie Court

Unfortunately, the litigation in this case obscured the real issue. The hospital's decision to seek a conservatorship did nothing more than raise the issue of whether Mr. Wanglie was the best decision maker for his wife. The lawsuit asked nothing more than whether Mr. Wanglie was the most able to apply his wife's values to the medical facts in this case.[6] Indeed, the hospital supplied no evidence that anyone else would be more likely to be able to determine and apply Mrs. Wanglie's values. To the extent that the litigation focused on how best to carry to fruition Mrs. Wanglie's autonomy, not on the limits of that autonomy, the hospital was left without a prayer of success.

The real question, however, should not have been what Mrs. Wanglie would have desired (or what was in her "best personal medical interest")—there was no reason to doubt her family on that point—but whether the continuation of ventilator support and gastrostomy feeding were among the reasonable medical alternatives that should have been available to Mrs. Wanglie or her surrogate decision maker, whoever that might be. The question, really, was whether the provision of this kind of treatment in this kind of case was outside the limits of medicine and, thus, beyond her power of choice.

Mrs. Wanglie's healthcare providers should have argued that medical practice simply did not include providing a ventilator and gastrostomy feeding under circumstances of this case, and that no surrogate decision maker—whether it be Mr. Wanglie or another substituted by the court—should be able to choose this option. If, for example, Mr. Wanglie requested that his wife be frozen and cryopreserved so that she could be brought back to life and "cured" when there were sufficient advances in the science of her underlying ailments, there is no doubt that this request would not have to be honored by Mrs. Wanglie's medical team. A request for cryopreservation, like a request for surgery that a patient believes will expiate his sins, may well reflect the true desires of the patient, but it is a request that asks something that is beyond the limits of medicine.[7] Why is the Wanglie family request in this case any different? The real question in the *Wanglie* case was whether the continuation of life-sustaining treatment for an 87-year-old woman in a persistent vegetative state with no hope of return to sentience constitutes treatment outside of the limits of medicine.

Although the question of the propriety of treatment for Mrs. Wanglie has been discussed as if it were a question of "futility," there is no doubt that the treatment was *not* futile in the purely scientific sense. The treatment was designed to keep Mrs. Wanglie alive, and it served this end effectively. Those who have viewed the *Wanglie* case as one dealing with futility in a scientific sense have brought the wrong perspective to the case. The question is not whether the treatment offered would successfully do what Mrs. Wanglie's family said she desired—keep her alive—but whether keeping her alive, under the circumstances, was beyond the proper scope of medicine. Like most questions in medicine, this is not purely a question of science or a question of values, but a hybrid question.

The Role of the Physician in Healthcare Decision Making

Even when the question is not a purely scientific one, even when it involves a determination of whether medical treatment justifies the quality of life that results, our society has generally left to physicians the determination of whether a particular treatment is among the reasonable medical alternatives. There are, of course, problems with this approach.[8] Why should physicians have the exclusive authority to define the extent of their own professional conduct? Does this lead to too much variation from doctor to doctor and from hospital to hospital? Could doctors decide that providing treatment to HIV-positive patients is beyond the limits of medicine? Leaving the question of what constitutes a reasonable medical alternative in the hands of Dr. Kevorkian yields a very different result than leaving that same question in the hands of the doctors who are associated with the right-to-life movement. As the national debate over euthanasia has demonstrated, doctors disagree over the appropriate scope of medicine with as much vigor, and probably with more concern, than the rest of us.

In the end, though, that is exactly why these decisions should be left to physicians. If a patient who desires a particular course of treatment can find a healthcare provider—*any* healthcare provider—who believes that the proposed course of treatment is within the realm of reasonable medical alternatives, that patient will have access to that course of treatment. It is only when a patient desires treatment that not a single healthcare provider believes to be within the limits of medicine that the patient will be denied that course of treatment. If a patient seeks amputation for the expiation of sins, for example, it is unlikely that the patient will find any surgeon willing to perform the task. When there is universal agreement among healthcare providers that the patient's request seeks something beyond the limits of medicine, that should constitute very strong evidence that the request is inappropriate.

The Wanglie family could not find any healthcare provider in Minnesota who would offer the medical services the family thought appropriate. Although the technical services that were sought (the ventilator, for example) were clearly within the scope of medical practice, there was no healthcare provider in Minnesota who believed that the provision of those services in Mrs. Wanglie's circumstance was within the range of reasonable medical alternatives—at least, no one who was capable of providing the services was willing to do so. In effect, the court required Hennepin County Medical Center to provide a service that was, in the universal conclusion of Minnesota healthcare providers, inappropriate.

Asking the Right Question: The Courts and Ethics Committees

Courts focus only on the best way to serve the autonomy of patients; after all, the courts are largely responsible for making the principle of autonomy the guiding principle for medical decision-making. The *Wanglie* court was simply unable to get beyond the question of who could best identify the values and interests of the patient and move on to the question of whether the proposed treatment was within the limits of medicine. The court did not decide that continued use of the ventilator and the continued gastrostomy feedings were reasonable medical alternatives for Mrs. Wanglie; it did not address these questions at all. Similarly, in October 1991, an Atlanta judge finessed the same issue in just the same way when she determined in the *Jane Doe* case that a 13-year-old with a degenerative neurologic condition must be continued on a treatment dictated by her father, who believed in miracles, despite the testimony of her pediatric neurologist that it was "ethically and morally unconscionable" to do so.[9]

If the courts continue to miss the real issue in these cases, as they will, that issue will have to be addressed in some other forum where there is both the moral and medical sophistication to understand the limits of medicine and the sensitivity to understand (and help define) society's reasonable expectations of medicine. Within their roles as educators, as mediators, and as sources for discussion of exactly these questions, broadly interdisciplinary ethics committees seem particularly well suited to the task. When a court is forced to face a determination by such a committee that a particular treatment, in a particular case, is beyond the limits of medicine—even though this treatment is exactly what the patient desires, even though the treatment employs a clearly medical procedure, and even though the treatment is not scientifically futile—that court may be forced to take the real question seriously.

NOTES

1. One might argue that the surgeon's only real concern is over the competency of the patient, but there is no reason outside of this medical request itself to question that competency. Indeed, we accept the fact that competent people can make unusual requests—requests that the vast majority of us find strange—and still be competent. We are even more likely to find unusual behavior (such as various kinds of abstinence and abnegation) consistent with competence when the behavior is religious, or quasi-religious, as it is here. In any case, there is very little left to any meaningful notion of competence if we determine a patient's competence to choose a particular form of treatment solely by reference to the treatment choice he makes.

2. Analogously, the American Medical Association has found it unacceptable to have physicians administer lethal doses of drugs to execute condemned prisoners, even if the condemned prisoners request the administration of the drugs because the alternative methods of execution are more painful or degrading. Although the administration of the relevant drugs is appropriately limited to physicians, their use *for this purpose* is simply outside of the scope of medicine, whatever the prisoner-patient may desire.

3. A great deal has been written about the *Wanglie* case. Several relevant articles are found in the July–August 1991 issue of the *Hastings Center Report*, which includes a summary of the facts prepared by Ronald Cranford of the Department of Neurology at the hospital in which Mrs. Wanglie remained a patient at her death. The facts are fleshed out in various newspaper articles: Colen. Fight over life. *Newsday* (1991 Jan. 29):

City p. 57; Belkin. As family protests, hospital seeks an end to woman's life support. *New York Times* (1991 Jan. 10): Sec A, p. 1; Steinbrook Hospital or family: who decides right to die? *Los Angeles Times* (1991 Feb. 17): Part A, p. 1.

4. See note 3. Colen (1991): 57.

5. *Conservatorship of Wanglie*, No. PX-91-283 (Minn., Hennepin Co. Dist. Ct., July 1, 1991).

6. The hospital argued that Mr. Wanglie should be disqualified from making the decision for his wife because his decision was not in the "patient's best *personal medical interest.*" Cranford. Helga Wanglie's ventilator. *Hastings Center Report* (1991; Jul.–Aug.): 23–4.

7. The courts have been unsympathetic to those who seek cryopreservation, as you might guess. For a description of the case of Thomas Donaldson, who did not convince a court to allow the removal and freezing of his head before his certain death from a brain tumor, see Corwin. Tumor victim loses bid to freeze head before death. *Los Angeles Times* (1990 Sept. 15): Sec. A, p. 28. As one might expect, the case was subsequently turned into an episode of *L. A. Law* (#7D08, copyright 1990).

8. To the extent these problems flow from the use of a "futility" exception to normal requirements of consent, they are cogently and thoughtfully expressed in Scofield. Is consent useful when resuscitation isn't. *Hastings Center Report* (1991; Nov.–Dec.): 28–6. As Scofield points out (in the context of CPR);

> In reality the futility exception is a dishonest solution to the tragic choice that decisions to limit treatment represent. It purports to represent, but in fact departs from the fundamental values consent is intended to serve. It will not generate the conversation we need if we are to attain consensus about limiting treatment; nor will it make physicians sensitive in their dealings with patients, especially dying patients. It promotes a model of consent that is antithetical to setting limits in a democratic, caring manner. (p. 30)

9. Colen. Judge bars letting girl in coma die. *Newsday* (1991 Oct. 18): News p. 4.1.

Whose Body Is It Anyway?

ATUL GAWANDE

Through a series of vignettes drawn from actual cases, surgeon and writer Atul Gawande offers a compelling meditation on the real-life conflicts between patient autonomy and physician duty. Autonomy is an important value, he says, "[b]ut there are times—and they are more frequent than we readily admit—when a doctor has to steer patients to do what's right for themselves." He believes that ethicists err when they promote patient autonomy as the ultimate value, when it is actually one moral consideration among many. Often patients want kindness, not autonomy, or they may want doctors to decide for them. Gawande maintains that sometimes the compassionate thing for a doctor to do is push a reluctant patient toward an option that she herself believes is in her own best interests.

The first time I saw the patient it was the day before his surgery, and I thought he might be dead. Joseph Lazaroff, as I'll call him, lay in bed, his eyes closed, a sheet pulled up over his thin, birdlike chest. When people are asleep—or even when they are anesthetized and not breathing by themselves—it does not occur to you to question whether they are alive. They exude life as if it were heat. It's visible in the tone of an arm muscle, the supple curve of their lips, the flush of their skin. But as I bent forward to tap Lazaroff on the shoulder I found myself stopping short with that instinctive apprehension of touching the dead. His color was all wrong—pallid, fading. His cheeks, eyes, and temples were sunken, and his skin was stretched over his face like a mask. Strangest of all, his head was suspended two inches above his pillow, as if rigor mortis had set in.

"Mr. Lazaroff?" I called out, and his eyes opened. He looked at me without interest, silent and motionless.

I was in my first year of surgical residency and was working on the neurosurgery team at the time. Lazaroff had a cancer that had spread throughout his body, and he had been scheduled for surgery to excise a tumor from his spine. The senior resident had sent me to "consent" him—that is, to get Lazaroff's signature giving final permission for the operation. No problem, I had said. But now, looking at this frail, withered man, I had to wonder if we were right to operate on him.

His patient chart told the story. Eight months earlier, he had seen his doctor about a backache. The doctor initially found nothing suspicious, but three months later the pain had worsened and he ordered a scan. It revealed extensive cancer—multiple tumors in Lazaroff's liver, bowel, and up and down his spine. A biopsy revealed it was an untreatable cancer.

Lazaroff was only in his early sixties, a longtime city administrator who had a touch of diabetes, the

occasional angina, and the hardened manner of a man who had lost his wife a few years earlier and learned to live alone. His condition deteriorated rapidly. In a matter of months, he lost more than fifty pounds. As the tumors in his abdomen grew, his belly, scrotum, and legs filled up with fluid. The pain and debility eventually made it impossible for him to keep working. His thirty-something son moved in to care for him. Lazaroff went on around-the-clock morphine to control his pain. His doctors told him that he might have only weeks to live. Lazaroff wasn't ready to hear it, though. He still talked about the day he'd go back to work.

Then he took several bad falls; his legs had become unaccountably weak. He also became incontinent. He went back to his oncologist. A scan showed that a metastasis was compressing his thoracic spinal cord. The oncologist admitted him to the hospital and tried a round of radiation, but it had no effect. Indeed, he became unable to move his right leg; his lower body was becoming paralyzed.

He had two options left. He could undergo spinal surgery. It wouldn't cure him—surgery or not, he had at the most a few months left—but it offered a last-ditch chance of halting the progression of spinal-cord damage and possibly restoring some strength to his legs and sphincters. The risks, however, were severe. We'd have to go in through his chest and collapse his lung just to get at his spine. He'd face a long, difficult, and painful recovery. And given his frail condition—not to mention the previous history of heart disease—his chances of surviving the procedure and getting back home were slim.

The alternative was to do nothing. He'd go home and continue with hospice care, which would keep him comfortable and help him maintain a measure of control over his life. The immobility and incontinence would certainly worsen. But it was his best chance of dying peacefully, in his own bed, and being able to say good-bye to his loved ones.

The decision was Lazaroff's.

From *Complications: A Surgeon's Notes on an Imperfect Science* by Atul Gawande, pp. 208–27, © 2002. Published by Picador.

———

That, in itself, is a remarkable fact. Little more than a decade ago, doctors made the decisions; patients did what they were told. Doctors did not consult patients about their desires and priorities, and routinely withheld information—sometimes crucial information, such as what drugs they were on, what treatments they were being given, and what their diagnosis was. Patients were even forbidden to look at their own medical records: it wasn't their property, doctors said. They were regarded as children: too fragile and simpleminded to handle the truth, let alone make decisions. And they suffered for it. People were put on machines, given drugs, and subjected to operations they would not have chosen. And they missed out on treatments that they might have preferred.

My father recounts that, through the 1970s and much of the 1980s, when men came to see him seeking vasectomies, it was accepted that he would judge whether the surgery was not only medically appropriate but also personally appropriate for them. He routinely refused to do the operation if the men were unmarried, married but without children, or "too young." In retrospect, he's not sure he did right by all these patients, and, he says, he'd never do things this way today. In fact, he can't even think of a patient in the last few years whom he has turned down for a vasectomy.

One of the reasons for this dramatic shift in how decisions are made in medicine was a 1984 book, *The Silent World of Doctor and Patient*, by a Yale doctor and ethicist named Jay Katz. It was a devastating critique of traditional medical decision making, and it had wide influence. In the book, Katz argued that medical decisions could and should be made by the patients involved. And he made his case using the stories of actual patients.

One was that of "Iphigenia Jones," a twenty-one-year-old woman who was found to have a malignancy in one of her breasts. Then, as now, she had two options: mastectomy (which would mean removing the breast and the lymph nodes of the nearby axilla) or radiation with minimal surgery (removing just the lump and the lymph nodes). Survival rates were equal, although in a spared breast the tumor can recur and ultimately make mastectomy necessary. This surgeon preferred doing mastectomies, and that's what he told her he'd do. In the days leading up to the operation, however, the surgeon developed misgivings about removing the breast of someone that young. So the night before the operation he did an unusual thing: he discussed the treatment options with her and let her choose. She chose the breast-preserving treatment.

Sometime later, both patient and surgeon appeared on a panel discussing treatment options for breast cancer. Their story drew a heated response. Surgeons almost uniformly attacked the idea that patients should be allowed to choose. As one surgeon asked, "If doctors have such trouble deciding which treatment is best, how can patients decide?" But, as Katz wrote, the decision involved not technical but personal issues: Which was more important to Iphigenia—the preservation of her breast or the security of living without a significant chance that the lump would grow back? No doctor was the authority on these matters. Only Iphigenia was. Yet in such situations doctors did step in, often not even asking about a patient's concerns, and made their own decisions—decisions perhaps influenced by money, professional bias (for example, surgeons tend to favor surgery), and personal idiosyncrasy.

Eventually, medical schools came around to Katz's position. By the time I attended, in the early 1990s, we were taught to see patients as autonomous decision makers. "You work for them," I was often reminded. There are still many old-school doctors who try to dictate from on high, but they are finding that patients won't put up with that anymore. Most doctors, taking seriously the idea that patients should control their own fates, lay out the options and the risks involved. A few even refuse to make recommendations, for fear of improperly influencing patients. Patients ask questions, look up information on the Internet, seek second opinions. And they decide.

In practice, however, matters aren't so straightforward. Patients, it turns out, make bad decisions, too. Sometimes, of course, the difference between one option and another isn't especially significant. But when you see your patient making a grave mistake, should you simply do what the patient wants? The current medical orthodoxy says yes. After all, whose body is it, anyway?

———

Lazaroff wanted surgery. The oncologist was dubious about the choice, but she called in a neurosurgeon. The neurosurgeon, a trim man in his forties with a stellar reputation and a fondness for bow ties, saw Lazaroff and his son that afternoon. He warned them at length about how terrible the risks were and how limited the potential benefit. Sometimes, he told me later, patients just don't seem to hear the dangers, and in those cases he tends to be especially explicit about them—getting stuck on a ventilator because of poor lung function, having a stroke, dying. But Lazaroff wasn't to be dissuaded. The surgeon put him on the schedule.

"Mr. Lazaroff, I'm a surgical resident, and I'm here to talk to you about your surgery tomorrow," I said. "You're going to be having a thoracic spine corpectomy and fusion," He looked at me blankly. "This means that we will be removing the tumor compressing your spine," I said. His expression did not change. "The hope is that it will keep your paralysis from worsening."

"I'm not paralyzed," he said at last. "The surgery is so I won't become paralyzed."

I quickly retreated. "I'm sorry—I meant, keep you from becoming paralyzed." Perhaps this was just semantics—he could still move his left leg some. "I just need you to sign a permission form so you can have the surgery tomorrow."

The "informed-consent form" is a relatively recent development. It lists as many complications as we doctors can think of—everything from a mild allergic reaction to death—and, in signing it, you indicate that you have accepted these risks. It has the mark of lawyerdom and bureaucracy, and I doubt that patients feel any better informed after reading it. It does, however, provide an occasion to review the risks involved.

The neurosurgeon had already gone over them in detail. So I hit the highlights. "We ask for your signature so we're sure you understand the risks," I said. "Although you're having this done to preserve your abilities, the operation could fail or leave you paralyzed." I tried to sound firm without being harsh. "You could have a stroke or a heart attack or could even die." I held the form and a pen out to him.

"No one said I could die from this," he said, tremulously. "It's my last hope. Are you saying I'm going to die?"

I froze, not knowing quite what to say. Just then, Lazaroff's son, whom I'll call David, arrived, with his wrinkled clothes, scraggly beard, and slight paunch. The father's mood changed abruptly, and I remembered from notes in the medical chart that David had recently raised the question with him of whether heroic measures were still appropriate. "Don't you give up on me," Lazaroff now rasped at his son. "'You give me every chance I've got." He snatched the form and the pen from my hand. We stood, chastised and silent, as Lazaroff made a slow, illegible scrawl near the line for his signature.

Outside the room, David told me that he wasn't sure this was the right move. His mother had spent a long time in intensive care on a ventilator before dying of emphysema, and since then his father had often said that he did not want anything like that to happen to him. But now he was adamant about doing "everything." David did not dare argue with him.

Lazaroff had his surgery the next day. Once under anesthesia, he was rolled onto his left side. A thoracic surgeon made a long incision, opening into the chest cavity from the front around to the back along the eighth rib, slipped in a rib spreader, cranked it open, and then fixed in place a retractor to hold the deflated lung out of the way. You could see right down into the back of the chest to the spinal column. A fleshy, tennis ball-size mass enveloped the tenth vertebra. The neurosurgeon took over and meticulously dissected around and under the tumor. It took a couple of hours, but eventually the tumor was attached only where it invaded the bony vertebral body. He then used a rongeur—a rigid, jawed instrument—to take small, painstaking bites in the vertebral body, like a beaver gnawing slowly through a tree trunk, ultimately removing the vertebra and, with it, the mass. To rebuild the spine, he filled the space left behind with a doughy plug of methacrylate, an acrylic cement, and let it slowly harden in place. He slipped a probe in behind the new artificial vertebra. There was plenty of space. It had taken more than four hours, but the pressure on the spinal cord was gone. The thoracic surgeon closed Lazaroff's chest, leaving a rubber chest tube jutting out to reinflate his lung, and he was wheeled into intensive care.

The operation was a technical success. Lazaroff's lungs wouldn't recover, however, and we struggled to get him off the ventilator. Over the next few days, they gradually became stiff and fibrotic, requiring higher ventilator pressures. We tried to keep him under sedation, but he frequently broke through and woke up wild-eyed and thrashing. David kept a despondent bedside vigil. Successive chest X rays showed worsening lung damage. Small blood clots lodged in Lazaroff's lungs, and we put him on a blood thinner to prevent more clots from forming. Then some slow bleeding started—we weren't sure from where—and we had to give him blood transfusions almost daily. After a week, he began spiking fevers, but we couldn't find where the infection was. On the ninth day after the operation, the high ventilator pressures blew small holes in his lungs. We had to cut into his chest and insert an extra tube to keep his lungs from collapsing. The effort and expense it took to keep him going were enormous, the results dispiriting. It became apparent that our efforts were futile. It was exactly the way Lazaroff hadn't wanted to die—strapped down and sedated, tubes in every natural orifice and in several new ones, and on a ventilator. On the fourteenth day, David told the neurosurgeon that we should stop.

The neurosurgeon came to me with the news. I went to Lazaroff's ICU room, one of eight bays arrayed in a semicircle around a nursing station, each with a tile floor, a window, and a sliding glass door that closed it off from the noise but not from the eyes of the nurses. A nurse and I slipped in. I checked to make sure that Lazaroff's morphine drip was turned up high. Taking my place at the bedside, I leaned close to him and, in case he could hear me, told him I was going to take the breathing tube out of his mouth. I snipped the ties securing the tube and deflated the balloon cuff holding it in his trachea. Then I pulled the tube out. He coughed a couple of times, opened his eyes briefly, and then closed them. The nurse suctioned out phlegm from his mouth. I turned the ventilator off, and suddenly the room was quiet except for the sound of his labored, gasping breaths. We watched as he tired out. His breathing slowed down until he took only occasional, agonal breaths, and then he stopped. I put my stethoscope on his chest and listened to his heart fade away. Thirteen minutes after I took him off the ventilator, I told the nurse to record that Joseph Lazaroff had died.

———

Lazaroff, I thought, chose badly. Not, however, because he died so violently and appallingly. Good decisions can have bad results (sometimes people must take terrible chances), and bad decisions can have good results ("Better lucky than good," surgeons like to say). I thought Lazaroff chose badly because his choice ran against his deepest interests—interests not as I or anyone else conceived them, but as he conceived them. Above all, it was clear that he wanted to live. He would take any risk—even death—to live. But, as we explained to him, life was not what we had to offer. We could offer only a chance of preserving minimal lower-body function for his brief remaining time—at a cost of severe violence to him and against extreme odds of a miserable death. But he did not hear us: in staving off paralysis, he seemed to believe that he might stave off death. There are people who will look clear-eyed at such odds and take their chances with surgery. But, knowing how much Lazaroff had dreaded dying the way his wife had, I do not believe he was one of them.

Could it have been a mistake, then, even to have told him about the surgical option? Our contemporary medical credo has made us exquisitely attuned to the requirements of patient autonomy. But there are still times—and they are more frequent than we readily admit—when a doctor has to steer patients to do what's right for themselves.

This is a controversial suggestion. People are rightly suspicious of those claiming to know better than they do what's best for them. But a good physician cannot simply stand aside when patients make bad or self-defeating decisions—decisions that go against their deepest goals.

I remember a case from my first weeks of internship. I was on the general surgical service, and among the patients I was responsible for was a woman in her fifties—I'll call her Mrs. McLaughlin—who had had a big abdominal operation just two days before. An incision ran the entire length of her belly. Fluids and pain medication dripped through an intravenous line into her arm. She was recovering according to schedule, but she wouldn't get out of bed. I explained why it was essential for her to get up and around: it cuts the risk of pneumonia, clot formation in leg veins, and other detrimental effects. She wasn't swayed. She was tired, she said, and didn't feel up to it. Did she understand that she was risking serious problems? Yes, she said. Just leave me be.

During rounds that afternoon, the chief resident asked me if the patient had gotten out of bed. Well, no, I said—she had refused. That's no excuse, the chief said, and she marched me back to Mrs. McLaughlin's room. The chief sat down on the edge of the bed and, as friendly as a country pastor, said, "Hi, how're you doing," made some small talk, took Mrs. McLaughlin by the hand, and then said, "It's time to get out of bed now." And I watched Mrs. McLaughlin get up without a moment's hesitation, shuffle over to a chair, plop herself down, and say. "You know, that wasn't so bad after all."

I had come into residency to learn how to be a surgeon. I had thought that meant simply learning the repertoire of moves and techniques involved in doing an operation or making a diagnosis. In fact, there was also the new and delicate matter of talking patients through their decisions—something that sometimes entailed its own repertoire of moves and techniques.

––––––

Suppose you're a doctor. You're in an examination room of your clinic—one of those cramped spaces with fluorescent lights, a Matisse poster on the wall, a box of latex gloves on the counter, and a cold, padded patient table as centerpiece—seeing a female patient in her forties. She's a mother of two and a partner in a downtown law firm. Despite the circumstances, and the flimsy paper gown she's in, she manages to maintain her composure. You feel no mass or abnormality in her breasts. She had a mammogram before seeing you, and now you review the radiologist's report, which reads, "There is a faint group of punctate, clustered calcifications in the upper outer quadrant of the left breast that were not clearly present on the prior examination. Biopsy must be considered to exclude the possibility of malignancy." Translation: worrisome features have appeared; they could mean breast cancer.

You tell her the news. Given the findings, you say, you think she ought to have a biopsy. She groans, and then stiffens. "Every time I see one of you people, you find something you want biopsied," she says. Three times in the past five years, her annual mammogram has revealed an area of "suspicious" calcifi-

cations. Three times a surgeon has taken her to the operating room and removed the tissue in question. And three times, under the pathologist's microscope, it has proved to be benign. "You just don't know when enough is enough," she says. "Whatever these specks are that keep turning up, they've proved to be normal." She pauses, and decides. "I'm not getting another goddam biopsy," she says, and she stands up to get dressed.

Do you let her go? It's not an unreasonable thing to do. She's an adult, after all. And a biopsy is not a small thing. Scattered across her left breast are the raised scars—one almost three inches long. Enough tissue has already been taken out that the left breast is distinctly smaller than the right one. And, yes, there are doctors who biopsy too much, who take out breast tissue on the most equivocal of findings. Patients are often right to push for explanations and second opinions.

Still, these calcifications are not equivocal findings. They commonly do indicate cancer—even if they don't always—and typically at an early and treatable stage. Now, if having control over one's life is to mean anything, people have to be permitted to make their own mistakes. But when the stakes are this high, and a bad choice may be irreversible, doctors are reluctant to sit back. This is when they tend to push.

So push. Your patient is getting ready to walk out the door. You could stop her in her tracks and tell her she's making a big mistake. Give her a heavy speech about cancer. Point out the fallacy in supposing that three negative biopsies proves that the fourth one will be negative as well. And in all likelihood you'll lose her. The aim isn't to show her how wrong she is. The aim is to give her the chance to change her own mind.

Here's what I've seen good doctors do. They don't jump right in. They step out for a minute and give the woman time to get dressed. They take her down to the office to sit and talk, where it's more congenial and less antiseptic—with comfortable chairs instead of a hard table, a throw rug instead of linoleum. And, often, they don't stand or assume the throne behind the big oak desk but pull up a chair and sit with her. As one surgical professor told me, when you sit close by, on the same level as your patients, you're no longer the rushed, bossy doctor with no time to talk;

patients feel less imposed upon and more inclined to consider that you may both be on the same side of the issue at hand.

Even at this point, many doctors won't fuss or debate. Instead, some have what can seem like strange, almost formulaic conversations with the patient, repeating, virtually word for word, what she tells them. "I see your point," they might say. "Every time you come in, we find something to biopsy. The specks keep coming up normal, but we never stop biopsying." Beyond this, many doctors say almost nothing until they're asked to. Whether one calls this a ruse or just being open to their patients, it works, oddly enough, nine times out of ten. People feel heard and like they have had an opportunity to express their beliefs and concerns. At that point, they may finally begin to ask questions, voice doubts, even work through the logic themselves. And once they do, they tend to come around.

A few still resist, though, and when doctors really think someone is endangering himself or herself, other tactics are not beyond the pale. They may enlist reinforcements. "Should we call the radiologist and see what he really thinks?" they might ask, or "Your family's out in the waiting room. Why don't we ask them to come in?" They might give the patient time "to think it over," knowing that people often waver and change their minds. Sometimes they resort to subtler dynamics. I once saw a doctor, faced with a heart disease patient who wouldn't consider quitting smoking, simply fall silent, letting the complete extent of his disappointment show. The seconds ticked by until a full minute had passed. Before a thoughtful, concerned, and, yes, sometimes crafty doctor, few patients will not eventually "choose" what the doctor recommends.

———

But it's misleading to view all this simply as the art of doctorly manipulation: when you see patients cede authority to the doctor, something else may be going on. The new orthodoxy about patient autonomy has a hard time acknowledging an awkward truth: patients frequently don't want the freedom that we've given them. That is, they're glad to have their autonomy respected, but the exercise of that autonomy means being able to relinquish it. Thus, it turns out that patients commonly prefer to have others make their medical decisions. One study found that although 64 percent of the general public thought they'd want to select their own treatment if they developed cancer, only 12 percent of newly diagnosed cancer patients actually did want to do so.

This dynamic is something I only came to understand recently. My youngest child, Hunter, was born five weeks early, weighing barely four pounds, and when she was eleven days old she stopped breathing. She had been home a week and doing well. That morning, however, she seemed irritable and fussy, and her nose ran. Thirty minutes after her feeding, her respiration became rapid, and she began making little grunting noises with each breath. Suddenly, Hunter stopped breathing. My wife, panicked, leaped up and shook Hunter awake, and the baby started breathing again. We rushed her to the hospital.

Fifteen minutes later, we were in a large, bright, emergency department examination room. With an oxygen mask on, Hunter didn't quite stabilize—she was still taking over sixty breaths a minute and expending all her energy to do it—but she regained normal oxygen levels in her blood and held her own. The doctors weren't sure what the cause of her trouble was. It could have been a heart defect, a bacterial infection, a virus. They took X rays, blood, and urine, did an electrocardiogram, and tapped her spinal fluid. They suspected—correctly, as it turned out—that the problem was an ordinary respiratory virus that her lungs were too little and immature to handle. But the results from the cultures wouldn't be back for a couple of days. They admitted her to the intensive care unit. That night, she began to tire out. She had several spells of apnea—periods of up to sixty seconds in which she stopped breathing, her heartbeat slowed, and she became pale and ominously still—but each time she came back, all by herself.

A decision needed to be made. Should she be intubated and put on a ventilator? Or should the doctors wait to see if she could recover without it? There were risks either way. If the team didn't intubate her now, under controlled circumstances, and she "crashed"—maybe the next time she would not wake up from an apneic spell—they would have to perform an emergency intubation, a tricky thing to do in a child so small. Delays could occur, the breathing tube could go down the wrong pipe, the doctors could inadvertently traumatize the airway and cause it to shut down, and then she might suffer brain damage or even die from lack of oxygen. The likelihood of such a disaster was slim but real. I myself had seen it happen. On the other hand, you don't want to put someone on a ventilator if you don't have to, least of all a small child. Serious and detrimental effects, such as pneumonia or the sort of lung blowout that Lazaroff experienced, happen frequently. And, as people who have been hooked up to one of these contraptions will tell you, the machine shoots air into and out of you with terrifying, uncomfortable force; your mouth becomes sore; your lips crack. Sedation is given, but the drugs bring complications, too.

So who should have made the choice? In many ways, I was the ideal candidate to decide what was best. I was the father, so I cared more than any hospital staffer ever could about which risks were taken. And I was a doctor, so I understood the issues involved. I also knew how often problems like miscommunication, overwork, and plain hubris could lead physicians to make bad choices.

And yet when the team of doctors came to talk to me about whether to intubate Hunter, I wanted them to decide—doctors I had never met before. The ethicist Jay Katz and others have disparaged this kind of desire as "childlike regression." But that judgment seems heartless to me. The uncertainties were savage, and I could not bear the possibility of making the wrong call. Even if I made what I was sure was the right choice for her, I could not live with the guilt if something went wrong. Some believe that patients should be pushed to take responsibility for decisions. But that would have seemed equally like a kind of harsh paternalism in itself. I needed Hunter's physicians to bear the responsibility: they could live with the consequences, good or bad.

I let the doctors make the call, and they did so on the spot. They would keep Hunter off the ventilator, they told me. And, with that, the bleary-eyed, stethoscope-collared pack shuffled onward to their next patient. Still, there was the nagging question: if I wanted the best decision for Hunter, was relinquishing my hard-won autonomy really the right thing to do? Carl Schneider, a professor of law and medicine

at the University of Michigan, recently published a book called *The Practice of Autonomy*, in which he sorted through a welter of studies and data on medical decision making, even undertaking a systematic analysis of patients' memoirs. He found that the ill were often in a poor position to make good choices: they were frequently exhausted, irritable, shattered, or despondent. Often, they were just trying to get through their immediate pain, nausea, and fatigue; they could hardly think about major decisions. This rang true to me. I wasn't even the patient, and all I could do was sit and watch Hunter, worry, or distract myself with busywork. I did not have the concentration or the energy to weigh the treatment options properly.

Schneider found that physicians, being less emotionally engaged, are able to reason through the uncertainties without the distortions of fear and attachment. They work in a scientific culture that disciplines the way they make decisions. They have the benefit of "group rationality"—norms based on scholarly literature and refined practice. And they have the key relevant experience. Even though I am a doctor, I did not have the experience that Hunter's doctors had with her specific condition.

In the end, Hunter managed to stay off the ventilator, although she had a slow and sometimes scary recovery. At one point, less than twenty-four hours after the doctors had transferred her to a regular floor, her condition deteriorated and they had to rush her back to the ICU. She spent ten days in intensive care and two weeks in the hospital. But she went home in fine shape.

———

Just as there is an art to being a doctor, there is an art to being a patient. You must choose wisely when to submit and when to assert yourself. Even when patients decide not to decide, they should still question their physicians and insist on explanations. I may have let Hunter's doctors take control, but I pressed them for a clear plan in the event that she should crash. Later, I worried that they were being too slow to feed her—she wasn't given anything to eat for more than a week, and I pestered them with questions as to why. When they took her off the oxygen monitor on her eleventh day in the hospital, I got nervous. What harm was there in keeping it on,

I asked. I'm sure I was obstinate, even wrongheaded, at times. You do the best you can, taking the measure of your doctors and nurses and your own situation, trying to be neither too passive nor too pushy for your own good.

But the conundrum remains: if both doctors and patients are fallible, who should decide? We want a rule. And so we've decided that patients should be the ultimate arbiter. But such a hard-and-fast rule seems ill-suited both to a caring relationship between doctor and patient and to the reality of medical care, where a hundred decisions have to be made quickly. A mother is in labor: should the doctor give hormones to stimulate stronger contractions? Should he or she break the bag of water? Should an epidural anesthetic be given? If so, at what point in labor? Are antibiotics needed? How often should the mother's blood pressure be checked? Should the doctor use forceps? Should the doctor perform an episiotomy? If things don't progress quickly, should the doctor perform a cesarean section? The doctor should not make all these decisions, and neither should the patient. Something must be worked out between them, one on one—a personal modus operandi.

Where many ethicists go wrong is in promoting patient autonomy as a kind of ultimate value in medicine rather than recognizing it as one value among others. Schneider found that what patients want most from doctors isn't autonomy per se; it's competence and kindness. Now, kindness will often involve respecting patients' autonomy, assuring that they have control over vital decisions. But it may also mean taking on burdensome decisions when patients don't want to make them, or guiding patients in the right direction when they do. Even when patients do want to make their own decisions, there are times when the compassionate thing to do is to press hard: to steer them to accept an operation or treatment that they fear, or forgo one that they'd pinned their hopes on. Many ethicists find this line of reasoning disturbing, and medicine will continue to struggle with how patients and doctors ought to make decisions. But, as the field grows ever more complex and technological, the real task isn't to banish paternalism; the real task is to preserve kindness.

———

One more case, again from my internship year. The patient—I'll call him Mr. Howe—was in his late thirties, stout, bald, and with a muted, awkward manner. I wanted to turn the sound up when he spoke, and pictured him as someone who worked alone, perhaps as an accountant or a computer programmer. He was in the hospital following an operation for a badly infected gallbladder. Whenever I saw him, he wore the sad look of someone caged, and he asked no questions. He could not wait to leave the hospital.

Late Saturday afternoon, maybe three days after his surgery, his nurse paged me. He had spiked a high fever and become short of breath. He didn't look well, she said.

I found him sweating profusely, his face flushed, eyes wide. He was sitting bent forward, propped up on his thick arms, panting. He had an oxygen mask on, and, even with the flow turned up to the maximum, the pulse-oximeter readings showed barely adequate oxygen levels in his blood. His heart was racing at well over a hundred beats a minute, and his blood pressure was much too low.

His wife, a small, thin, pale woman with lank black hair, stood to the side, rocking on her feet and hugging herself. I examined Mr. Howe, drew blood for tests and cultures, and asked the nurse to give him a bolus of intravenous fluid, trying to appear as confident as I could. Then I went out into the hall and paged K., one of the chief residents, for help.

When she called back, I filled her in on the details. I think he's septic, I said. Sometimes a bacterial infection gets into the bloodstream and triggers a massive, system-wide response: high fevers and dilation of the body's peripheral blood vessels, causing the skin to flush, the blood pressure to drop, and the heart to speed up. After abdominal surgery, a common cause of this is an infection of the surgical wound. But his incision was not red or hot or tender, and he had no pain in his belly. His lungs, however, had sounded like a washing machine when I listened with my stethoscope. Perhaps a pneumonia had started this disaster.

K. came right over. She was just past thirty, almost six feet tall, with short blond hair, athletic, exhaustingly energetic, and relentlessly can-do. She took one look at Howe and then murmured to the nurse to keep an intubation kit available at the bedside. I had started antibiotics, and the fluids had improved his blood pressure a bit, but he was still on maximal oxygen and working hard to maintain his breathing. She went over to him, put a hand on his shoulder, and asked how he was doing. It took a moment before he managed to reply. "Fine," he said—a silly answer to a silly question, but a conversation starter. She explained the situation: the sepsis, the likely pneumonia, and the probability that he would get worse before he got better. The antibiotics would fix the problem, but not instantly, she said, and he was tiring out quickly. To get him through it, she would need to put him to sleep, intubate him, and place him on a breathing machine.

"No," he gasped, and sat straight up. "Don't . . . put me . . . on a . . . machine."

It would not be for long, she said. Maybe a couple of days. We'd give him sedatives so he'd be as comfortable as possible the whole time. And—she wanted to be sure he understood—without the ventilator he would die.

He shook his head. "No . . . machine."

He was, we believed, making a bad decision—out of fear, maybe incomprehension. With antibiotics and some high-tech support, we had every reason to believe, he'd recover fully. Howe had a lot to live for—he was young and otherwise healthy, and he had a wife and a child. Apparently, he thought so, too, for he had cared enough about his well-being to accept the initial operation. If not for the terror of the moment, we thought, he would have accepted the treatment. Could we be certain we were right? No, but if we were right could we really just let him die?

K. looked over at Howe's wife, who was stricken with fear and, in an effort to enlist her in the cause, asked what she thought her husband should do. She burst into tears. "I don't know, I don't know," she

cried. "Can't you save him?" She couldn't take it anymore, and left the room. For the next few minutes, K. kept trying to persuade Howe. When it was clear that she was making no headway, she left to phone his attending surgeon at home, and then returned to the bedside. Soon Howe did tire out. He leaned back in his bed, pale, sweaty strands of hair sticking to his pate, oxygen levels dropping on the monitor. He closed his eyes, and he gradually fell into unconsciousness.

That was when K. went into action. She lowered the head of Howe's bed until he lay flat. She had a nurse draw up a tranquilizing agent and administer it in his IV. She pressed a bag mask to his face and squeezed breaths of oxygen down into his lungs. Then I handed her the intubation equipment, and she slipped a long, clear plastic breathing tube down into his trachea on the first try. We wheeled Howe in his bed to the elevator and took him down a few floors to the intensive care unit.

Later, I found his wife and explained that he was now on a ventilator in the ICU. She said nothing and went to see him.

Over the next twenty-four hours, his lungs improved markedly. We lightened up on the sedation and let him take over breathing from the machine. He woke up and opened his eyes, the breathing tube sticking out of his mouth. He did not struggle.

"I'm going to take this tube out of your mouth now, OK?" I said. He nodded. I cut the ties and deflated the balloon cuff holding the tube in place. Then I pulled it out, and he coughed violently a few times. "You had pneumonia," I told him, "but you're doing just fine now."

I stood there silent and anxious for a moment, waiting to see what he would say. He swallowed hard, wincing from the soreness. Then he looked at me, and, in a hoarse but steady voice, he said, "Thank you."

Bouvia v. Superior Court

CALIFORNIA COURT OF APPEAL

In this 1986 ruling, the court asserted that competent adults have a "constitutionally guaranteed right" to decide for themselves whether to submit to medical treatments, a right that outweighs the interests of physicians, hospitals, and the state. A competent patient may refuse treatments even if they are needed to keep her alive.

Petitioner. Elizabeth Bouvia, a patient in a public hospital, seeks the removal from her body of a nasogastric tube inserted and maintained against her will and without her consent by physicians who so placed it for the purpose of keeping her alive through involuntary forced feeding.

Petitioner has here filed a petition for writ of mandamus and other extraordinary relief after the trial court denied her a preliminary injunction requiring that the tube be removed and that the hospital and doctors be prohibited from using any other similar procedures. We issued an alternative writ. We have heard oral argument from the parties and now order issuance of a peremptory writ, granting petitioner, Elizabeth Bouvia, the relief for which she prayed. . . .

The trial court denied petitioner's request for the immediate relief she sought. It concluded that leaving the tube in place was necessary to prolong petitioner's life, and that it would, in fact, do so. With the tube in place petitioner probably will survive the time required to prepare for trial, a trial itself and an appeal, if one proved necessary. The real party-physicians also assert, and the trial court agreed, that physically petitioner tolerates the tube reasonably well and thus is not in great physical discomfort.

Real parties' counsel therefore argue that the normal course of trial and appeal provide a sufficient remedy. But petitioner's ability to tolerate physical discomfort does not diminish her right to immediate relief. Her mental and emotional feelings are equally entitled to respect. She has been subjected to the forced intrusion of an artificial mechanism into her body against her will. She has a right to refuse

From California Court of Appeal, *Bouvia v. Superior Court*, 225 Cal. Rptr. 297 (Ctr. App. 1986).

the increased dehumanizing aspects of her condition created by the insertion of a permanent tube through her nose and into her stomach.

To petitioner it is a dismal prospect to live with this hated and unwanted device attached to her, through perhaps years of the law's slow process. She has the right to have it removed immediately. This matter constitutes a perfect paradigm of the axiom: "Justice delayed is justice denied."

By refusing petitioner the relief which she sought, the trial court, with the most noble intentions, attempted to exercise its discretion by issuing a ruling which would uphold what it considered a lawful object, i.e., keeping Elizabeth Bouvia alive by a means which it considered ethical. Nonetheless, it erred for it had no discretion to exercise. Petitioner sought to enforce only a right which was exclusively hers and over which neither the medical profession nor the judiciary have any veto power. The trial court could but recognize and protect her exercise of that right.

In explanation of its ruling, the trial court stated that it considered petitioner's "motives" to be indicative of an attempt to commit suicide with the state's help rather than a bona fide exercise of her right to refuse medical treatment. No evidence supports this conclusion.

As previously noted, the legal remedies available to petitioner through the normal course of trial and appeal are wholly inadequate. Therefore, a prompt resolution, even though based upon a provisional ruling, is justified, particularly when it will probably completely resolve this tragic case.

Petitioner is a 28-year-old woman. Since birth she has been afflicted with and suffered from severe cerebral palsy. She is quadriplegic. She is now a patient at a public hospital maintained by one of the real parties in interest, the County of Los Angeles. Other parties are physicians, nurses and the medical and support staff employed by the County of Los Angeles. Petitioner's physical handicaps of palsy and quadriplegia have progressed to the point where she is completely bed-ridden. Except for a few fingers of one hand and some slight head and facial movements, she is immobile. She is physically helpless and wholly unable to care for herself. She is totally dependent upon others for all of her needs. These include feeding, washing, clean-ing, toileting, turning, and helping her with elimina-tion and other bodily functions. She cannot stand or sit upright in bed or in a wheelchair. She lies flat in bed and must do so the rest of her life. She suffers also from degenerative and severely crippling arthritis. She is in continual pain. Another tube permanently attached to her chest automatically injects her with periodic doses of morphine which relieves some, but not all of her physical pain and discomfort.

She is intelligent, very mentally competent. She earned a college degree. She was married but her husband has left her. She suffered a miscarriage. She lived with her parents until her father told her that they could no longer care for her. She has stayed in-termittently with friends and at public facilities. A search for a permanent place to live where she might receive the constant care which she needs has been unsuccessful. She is without financial means to sup-port herself and, therefore, must accept public assis-tance for medical and other care.

She has on several occasions expressed the desire to die. In 1983 she sought the right to be cared for in a pub-lic hospital in Riverside County while she intentionally "starved herself to death." A court in that county de-nied her judicial assistance to accomplish that goal. She later abandoned an appeal from that ruling. Thereafter, friends took her to several different facilities, both pub-lic and private, arriving finally at her present location. Efforts by the staff of real party in interest County of Los Angeles and its social workers to find her an apart-ment of her own with publicly paid live-in help or regu-lar visiting nurses to care for her, or some other suitable facility, have proved fruitless.

Petitioner must be spoon fed in order to eat. Her present medical and dietary staff have determined that she is not consuming a sufficient amount of nutri-ents. Petitioner stops eating when she feels she cannot orally swallow more, without nausea and vomiting. As she cannot now retain solids, she is fed soft liquid-like food. Because of her previously announced resolve to starve herself, the medical staff feared her weight loss might reach a life-threatening level. Her weight since admission to real parties' facility seems to hover be-tween 65 and 70 pounds. Accordingly, they inserted the subject tube against her will and contrary to her express written instructions.

Petitioner's counsel argue that her weight loss was not such as to be life threatening and therefore the tube is unnecessary. However, the trial court found to the contrary as a matter of fact, a finding which we must accept. Nonetheless, the point is immate-rial, for, as we will explain, a patient has the right to refuse any medical treatment or medical service, even when such treatment is labeled "furnishing nourishment and hydration." This right exists even if its exercise creates a "life threatening condition." . . .

The right to refuse medical treatment is basic and fundamental. It is recognized as a part of the right of privacy protected by both the state and federal con-stitutions. Its exercise requires no one's approval. It is not merely one vote subject to being overridden by medical opinion. . . .

[A]ddressing one part of the problem, California passed the "Natural Death Act," Health and Safety Code section 7185 et seq. Although addressed to ter-minally ill patients, the significance of this legislation is its expression as state policy "that adult persons have the fundamental right to control the deci-sions relating to the rendering of their own medical care. . . ." Section 7188 provides the method whereby an adult person may execute a directive for the with-holding or withdrawal of life-sustaining procedures. Recognition of the right of other persons who may not be terminally ill and may wish to give other forms of direction concerning their medical care is expressed in section 7193: "Nothing in this chapter shall impair or supersede any legal right or legal re-sponsibility which any person may have to effect the withholding or withdrawal of life-sustaining proce-dures in any lawful manner. In such respect the pro-visions of this chapter are cumulative."

Moreover, as the Bartling decision holds, there is no practical or logical reason to limit the exercise of this right to "terminal" patients. The right to refuse treatment does not need the sanction or approval by any legislative act, directing how and when it shall be exercised. . . .

A recent Presidential Commission for the Study of Ethical Problems in Medicine and Biomedical and Behavioral Research concluded in part: "The voluntary choice of a competent and informed patient should determine whether or not life-sustaining therapy will be undertaken, just as such choices provide the basis for other decisions about medical treatment. Health care institutions and professionals should try to enhance patients' abilities to make decisions on their own behalf and to promote understanding of the available treatment options. . . . Health care professionals serve patients best by maintaining a presumption in favor of sustaining life, while recognizing that competent patients are entitled to choose to forego any treatments, including those that sustain life."

On December 11, 1985, the Los Angeles County Bar Association, and on January 6, 1986, the Los Angeles County Medical Association recognized as general principles for decision making the conclusions as expressly stated in the cases of Barber and Bartling and endorsed the conclusion of the Presidential Commission cited above.

The American Hospital Association (AHA) Policy and Statement of Patients' Choices of Treatment Options, approved by the American Hospital Association in February of 1985 discusses the value of a collaborative relationship between the patient and the physician and states in pertinent part: "Whenever possible, however, the authority to determine the course of treatment, if any, should rest with the patient" and "the right to choose treatment includes the right to refuse a specific treatment or all treatment. . . ."

Again, this statement reflects the fact that the controlling decision belongs to a competent, informed patient. It also contains a discussion of how that consent should be documented, and the desirability of a cooperative effort. Of course, none of the problems of incapacity due to age, unconsciousness, mental disease or disability mentioned in the policy statement affect the case before us.

Significant also is the statement adopted on March 15, 1986, by the Council on Ethical and Judicial Affairs of the American Medical Association. It is entitled "Withholding or Withdrawing Life Prolonging Medical Treatment." In pertinent part, it declares: "The social commitment of the physician is to sustain life

and relieve suffering. Where the performance of one duty conflicts with the other, the choice of the patient, or his family or legal representative if the patient is incompetent to act in his own behalf, should prevail. Life prolonging medical treatment includes medication and artificially or technologically supplied respiration, nutrition or hydration. In treating a terminally ill or irreversibly comatose patient, the physician should determine whether the benefits of treatment outweigh its burdens. At all times, the dignity of the patient should be maintained."

We do not believe that all of the foregoing case law and statements of policy and statutory recognition are mere lip service to a fictitious right. As noted in Bartling "We do not doubt the sincerity of [the hospital and medical personnel's] moral and ethical beliefs, or their sincere belief in the position they have taken in this case. However, if the right of the patient to self-determination as to his own medical treatment is to have any meaning at all, it must be paramount to the interests of the patient's hospital and doctors. . . . The right of a competent adult patient to refuse medical treatment is a constitutionally guaranteed right which must not be abridged."

It is indisputable that petitioner is mentally competent. She is not comatose. She is quite intelligent, alert, and understands the risks involved. . . .

At bench the trial court concluded that with sufficient feeding petitioner could live an additional 15 to 20 years; therefore, the preservation of petitioner's life for that period outweighed her right to decide. In so holding the trial court mistakenly attached undue importance to the amount of time possibly available to petitioner, and failed to give equal weight and consideration for the quality of that life; an equal, if not more significant, consideration.

All decisions permitting cessation of medical treatment or life-support procedures to some degree hastened the arrival of death. In part, at least, this was permitted because the quality of life during the time remaining in those cases had been terribly diminished. In Elizabeth Bouvia's view, the quality of her life has been diminished to the point of hopelessness, uselessness, unenjoyability and frustration. She, as the patient, lying helplessly in bed, unable to care for herself, may consider her existence meaningless. She cannot be faulted for so concluding. If her right to choose may not be exercised because there remains to her, in the opinion of a court, a physician or some committee, a certain arbitrary number of years, months, or days, her right will have lost its value and meaning.

Who shall say what the minimum amount of available life must be? Does it matter if it be 15 to 20 years, 15 to 20 months, or 15 to 20 days, if such life has been physically destroyed and its quality, dignity and purpose gone? As in all matters lines must be drawn at some point, somewhere, but that decision must ultimately belong to the one whose life is in issue.

Here Elizabeth Bouvia's decision to forego medical treatment or life-support through a mechanical means belongs to her. It is not a medical decision for her physicians to make. Neither is it a legal question whose soundness is to be resolved by lawyers or judges. It is not a conditional right subject to approval by ethics committees or courts of law. It is a moral and philosophical decision that, being a competent adult, is hers alone.

Adapting the language of Satz v. Perlmutter, "It is all very convenient to insist on continuing [Elizabeth Bouvia's] life so that there can be no question of foul play, no resulting civil liability and no possible trespass on medical ethics. However, it is quite another matter to do so at the patient's sole expense and against [her] competent will, thus inflicting never ending physical torture on [her] body until the inevitable, but artificially suspended, moment of death. Such a course of conduct invades the patient's constitutional right of privacy, removes [her] freedom of choice and invades [her] right to self-determine."

Here, if force fed, petitioner faces 15 to 20 years of a painful existence, endurable only by the constant administration of morphine. Her condition is irreversible. There is no cure for her palsy or arthritis. Petitioner would have to be fed, cleaned, turned, bedded, toileted by others for 15 to 20 years. Although alert, bright, sensitive, perhaps even brave and feisty, she must lie immobile, unable to exist except through physical acts of others. Her mind and spirit may be free to take great flights but she herself is imprisoned and must lie physically helpless subject to the ignominy, embarrassment, humiliation and dehumanizing aspects created by her helplessness. We do not believe it is the policy of this state that all and every life must be preserved against the will of the sufferer. It is incongruous, if not monstrous, for medical practitioners to assert their right

to preserve a life that someone else must live, or, more accurately, endure, for "15 to 20 years." We cannot conceive it to be the policy of this state to inflict such an ordeal upon anyone.

It is, therefore, immaterial that the removal of the nasogastric tube will hasten or cause Bouvia's eventual death. Being competent she has the right to live out the remainder of her natural life in dignity and peace. It is precisely the aim and purpose of the many decisions upholding the withdrawal of life-support systems to accord and provide as large a measure of dignity, respect and comfort as possible to every patient for the remainder of his days, whatever be their number. This goal is not to hasten death, though its earlier arrival may be an expected and understood likelihood.

Real parties assert that what petitioner really wants is to "commit suicide" by starvation at their facility. The trial court in its statement of decision said: "It is fairly clear from the evidence and the court cannot close its eyes to the fact that [petitioner] during her stay in defendant hospital, and for some time prior thereto, has formed an intent to die. She has voiced this desire to a member of the staff of defendant hospital. She claims, however, she does not wish to commit suicide. On the evidence, this is but a semantic distinction. The reasonable inference to be drawn from the evidence is that [petitioner] in defendant facility has purposefully engaged in a selective rejection of medical treatment and nutritional intake to accomplish her objective and accept only treatment which gives her some degree of comfort pending her demise. Stated another way, [petitioner's] refusal of medical treatment and nutritional intake is motivated not by a bona fide exercise of her right of privacy but by a desire to terminate her life. . . . Here [petitioner] wishes to pursue her objective to die by the use of public facilities with staff standing by to furnish her medical treatment to which she consents and to refrain from that which she refuses."

Overlooking the fact that a desire to terminate one's life is probably the ultimate exercise of one's right to privacy, we find no substantial evidence to support the court's conclusion. Even if petitioner had the specific intent to commit suicide in 1983, while at Riverside, she did not carry out that plan. Then she apparently had the ability, without artificial aids, to consume sufficient nutrients to sustain herself; now she does not. That is to say, the trial court here made the following express finding, "Plaintiff, when she chooses, can orally ingest food by masticating 'finger food' though additional nutritional intake is required intravenously and by nasogastric tube. . . ." As a consequence of her changed condition, it is clear she has now merely resigned herself to accept an earlier death, if necessary, rather than live by feedings forced upon her by means of a nasogastric tube. Her decision to allow nature to take its course is not equivalent to an election to commit suicide with real parties aiding and abetting therein.

Moreover, the trial court seriously erred by basing its decision on the "motives" behind Elizabeth Bouvia's decision to exercise her rights. If a right exists, it matters not what "motivates" its exercise. We find nothing in the law to suggest the right to refuse medical treatment may be exercised only if the patient's motives meet someone else's approval. It certainly is not illegal or immoral to prefer a natural, albeit sooner, death than a drugged life attached to a mechanical device.

Fundamental Elements of the Patient-Physician Relationship

AMA COUNCIL ON ETHICAL AND JUDICIAL AFFAIRS

In this section of its medical code of ethics, the AMA declares that the patient-physician relationship is a collaborative alliance in which both parties have responsibilities. Physicians should serve as their patients' advocates and respect their rights, including the right to accept or refuse recommended treatment, to receive complete information about treatments and their alternatives, and to have their confidentiality protected.

From ancient times, physicians have recognized that the health and well-being of patients depends upon a collaborative effort between physician and patient. Patients share with physicians the responsibility for their own health care. The patient-physician relationship is of greatest benefit to patients when they bring medical problems to the attention of their physicians in a timely fashion, provide information about their medical condition to the best of their ability, and work with their physicians in a mutually respectful alliance. Physicians can best contribute to this alliance by serving as their patients' advocate and by fostering these rights:

1. The patient has the right to receive information from physicians and to discuss the benefits, risks, and costs of appropriate treatment alternatives. Patients should receive guidance from their physicians as to the optimal course of action. Patients are also entitled to obtain copies or summaries of their medical re-

cords, to have their questions answered, to be advised of potential conflicts of interest that their physicians might have, and to receive independent professional opinions.

2. The patient has the right to make decisions regarding the health care that is recommended by his or her physician. Accordingly, patients may accept or refuse any recommended medical treatment.

3. The patient has the right to courtesy, respect, dignity, responsiveness, and timely attention to his or her needs.

4. The patient has the right to confidentiality. The physician should not reveal confidential communications or information without the consent of the patient, unless provided for by law or by the need to protect the welfare of the individual or the public interest.

5. The patient has the right to continuity of health care. The physician has an obligation to cooperate in the coordination of medically indicated care with other health care providers treating the patient. The physician may not discontinue

treatment of a patient as long as further treatment is medically indicated, without giving the patient reasonable assistance and sufficient opportunity to make alternative arrangements for care.

6. The patient has a basic right to have available adequate health care. Physicians, along with the rest of society, should continue to work toward this goal. Fulfillment of this right is depen-dent on society providing resources so that no patient is deprived of necessary care because of an inability to pay for the care. Physicians should continue their traditional assumption of a part of the responsibility for the medical care of those who cannot afford essential health care. Physicians should advocate for patients in dealing with third parties when appropriate.

Code of Ethics for Nurses

AMERICAN NURSES ASSOCIATION

This statement of ethical principles details the moral responsibilities of nurses to patients, themselves, fellow health care professionals, and the larger community. It enjoins nurses to respect patients' dignity, values, beliefs, and rights of self-determination (autonomy), informed consent, and privacy. When conflicts arise between the patient's preferences and those of others, the nurse's primary duty is to the patient.

Preface

Ethics is an integral part of the foundation of nursing. Nursing has a distinguished history of concern for the welfare of the sick, injured, and vulnerable and for social justice. This concern is embodied in the provision of nursing care to individuals and the community. Nursing encompasses the prevention of illness, the alleviation of suffering, and the protection, promotion, and restoration of health in the care of individuals, families, groups, and communities. Nurses act to change those aspects of social structures that detract from health and well-being. Individuals who become nurses are expected not only to adhere to the ideals and moral norms of the profession but also to embrace them as a part of what it means to be a nurse. The ethical tradition of nursing is self-reflective, enduring, and distinctive. A code of ethics makes explicit the primary goals, values, and obligations of the profession. . . .

Provision 1.

The nurse, in all professional relationships, practices with compassion and respect for the inherent dignity, worth, and uniqueness of every individual, unrestricted by considerations of social or economic status, personal attributes, or the nature of health problems.

1.1. Respect for human dignity—A fundamental principle that underlies all nursing practice is respect for the inherent worth, dignity, and human rights of every individual. Nurses take into account the needs and values of all persons in all professional relationships.

1.2. Relationships to patients—The need for health care is universal, transcending all individual differences. The nurse establishes relationships and delivers nursing services with respect for human needs and values, and without prejudice. An individual's lifestyle, value system and religious beliefs should be considered in planning health care with and for each patient. Such consideration does not suggest that the nurse necessarily agrees with or condones certain individual choices, but that the nurse respects the patient as a person.

1.3. The nature of health problems—The nurse respects the worth, dignity and rights of all human beings irrespective of the nature of the health problem. The worth of the person is not affected by disease, disability, functional status, or proximity to death. This respect extends to all who require the services of the nurse for the promotion of health, the prevention of illness, the restoration of health, the alleviation of suffering, and the provision of supportive care to those who are dying. The measures nurses take to care for the patient enable the patient to live with as much physical, emotional, social, and spiritual well-being as possible. Nursing care aims to maximize the values that the patient has treasured in life and extends supportive care to the family and significant others. Nursing care is directed toward meeting the comprehensive needs of patients and their families across the continuum of care. This is particularly vital in the care of patients and their families at the end of life to prevent and relieve the cascade of symptoms and suffering that are commonly associated with dying. Nurses are leaders and vigilant advocates for the delivery of dignified and humane care. Nurses actively participate in assessing and assuring the responsible and appropriate use of interventions in order to minimize unwarranted or unwanted treatment and patient suffering. The acceptability and importance of carefully considered decisions regarding resuscitation status, withholding and withdrawing life-sustaining therapies, forgoing medically provided nutrition and hydration, aggressive pain and symptom management and advance directives are increasingly evident. The nurse should provide interventions to relieve pain and other symptoms in the dying patient even when those interventions entail risks of hastening death. However, nurses may not act with the sole intent of ending a patient's life even though such action may be motivated by compassion, respect for patient autonomy and quality of life considerations. Nurses have invaluable experience, knowledge, and insight into care at the end of life and should be actively involved in related research, education, practice, and policy development.

1.4. The right to self-determination—Respect for human dignity requires the recognition of specific patient rights, particularly, the right of self-determination. Self-determination, also known as autonomy, is the philosophical basis for informed consent in health care. Patients have the moral and legal right to determine what will be done with their own person; to be given accurate, complete, and understandable information in a manner that facilitates an informed judgment; to be assisted with weighing the benefits, burdens, and available options in their treatment, including the choice of no treatment; to accept, refuse, or terminate treatment without deceit, undue influence, duress, coercion, or penalty; and to be given necessary support throughout the decision-making and treatment process. Such support would include the opportunity to make decisions with family and significant others and the provision of advice and support from knowledgeable nurses and other health professionals. Patients should be involved in planning their own health care to the extent they are able and choose to participate.

Each nurse has an obligation to be knowledgeable about the moral and legal rights of all patients to self-determination. The nurse preserves, protects, and supports those interests by assessing the patient's comprehension of both the information presented and the implications of decisions. In situations in which the patient lacks the capacity to make a decision, a designated surrogate decision-maker should be consulted. The role of the surrogate is to make decisions as the patient would, based upon the patient's previously expressed wishes and known values. In the absence of a designated surrogate decision-maker, decisions should be made in the best interests of the patient, considering the patient's personal values to the extent that they are known. The nurse supports patient self-determination by participating in discussions with surrogates, providing guidance and referral to other resources as necessary, and identifying and addressing problems in the decision-making process. Support of autonomy in the broadest sense also includes recognition that people of some cultures place less weight on individualism and choose to defer to family or community values in decision-making. Respect not just for the specific decision but also for the patient's method of decision-making is consistent with the principle of autonomy.

Individuals are interdependent members of the community. The nurse recognizes that there are situations in which the right to individual self-determination may be outweighed or limited by the rights, health and welfare of others, particularly in relation to public health considerations. Nonetheless, limitation of individual rights must always be considered a serious deviation from the standard of care, justified only when there are no less restrictive means available to preserve the rights of others and the demands of justice.

Truth-Telling and Confidentiality

A major moral issue in patient-physician relationships is how to handle the truth—specifically, whether doctors should always tell the truth to patients and whether doctors should ever reveal the truth about their patients to others. The former question is about the presumed duty of physicians not to deceive patients or withhold relevant medical information from them. The latter is about confidentiality, a physician's obligation to protect a patient's privacy. In both, the issues raised are contentious and ongoing, reverberating among patients, families, and caregivers and often forcing shifts in the policies and culture of medical practice. Though the debates are complex, they usually come down to disagreements about the limits of paternalism and the proper balance between the principles of autonomy and beneficence.

PATERNALISM AND DECEPTION

From ancient times, the principle of nonmaleficence—the duty to do no harm—has been enshrined in codes of medical ethics. But not so with the duty of truthfulness. The Hippocratic Oath does not mention an obligation of truth-telling or disclosure, and until 1980 even the professional code of the American Medical Association did not say anything about dealing honestly with patients. Many physicians have viewed the truth as something to conceal or reveal for the therapeutic good of the patient. For them, the overriding principle was beneficence (or nonmaleficence), which was best honored by delicately managing what patients knew about their own cases. The truth could be harmful, unsettling, and depressing—so why inflict it on vulnerable patients? In a famously blunt formulation of this view, an early twentieth-century physician declared that to be compassionate and gracious, doctors "must frequently withhold the truth from their patients, which is tantamount to telling a lie. Moreover, the physician soon learns that the art of medicine consists largely in skillfully mixing falsehood and truth."[1]

Nowadays, in the age of patient autonomy and informed consent, such strong paternalistic sentiments are less common. Most physicians value truth-telling, and professional standards encourage it while counseling sensitivity in conveying vital information to patients. But the moral problem of truthfulness still presses both physicians and patients, prompting questions with which they still wrestle. Is it ever morally permissible for a physician to lie to a patient? Does a physician's duty of beneficence sometimes justify deception? Does respect for patient autonomy rule it out? If there are exceptions to a duty of truthfulness, what are they?

Consider how easily (and painfully) such questions can arise. Karen, a 30-year-old woman with two small children, is admitted to the hospital after experiencing headaches, vomiting, memory loss, and partial paralysis. Dr. Smith runs numerous tests and discovers that Karen has a malignant brain tumor. It is advanced and untreatable, leaving Karen with only weeks to live. Before the tests, she had told Dr. Smith that she was terrified of cancer because her husband died of lung cancer and her mother of breast cancer. And if she succumbed to cancer, what would happen to her children? Who would care for them?

Dr. Smith considers carefully whether to tell Karen of the dire prognosis. He thinks about

IN DEPTH
DO PATIENTS WANT THE TRUTH? DO PHYSICIANS TELL IT?

- In 1961, a survey of physicians found that 90 percent of them would avoid telling patients of a diagnosis of cancer. But in a similar 1979 survey, 97 percent of physicians said that they would disclose a diagnosis of cancer.

- More recent research suggests that most physicians in Western cultures inform their cancer patients of their diagnosis, but fewer of them tell cancer patients about their prognosis.
- Several studies indicate that most cancer patients want to know the details of their disease, whether the news is good or bad.
- Surveys suggest that patients differ in the kinds of medical information they would like to have and how it is communicated to them.

From L. J. Fallowfield, V. A. Jenkins, and H. A. Beveridge, "Truth May Hurt but Deceit Hurts More: Communication in Palliative Care," *Palliative Medicine* 16 (2002), 297–303.

---

the misery that full disclosure would cause her, the days spent in terror before the end, the dark depression that would likely spoil her remaining time with her children.

He decides to shield her from the terrible facts, shrouding them in vague statements and irrelevant details. He tells her that she has a brain disease requiring neither surgery nor radiation, and he assures her that he has many drugs at his disposal for treating her symptoms. Karen is relieved to hear the news and does not question Dr. Smith's explanation. Sensing that disturbing details might lie behind his murky pronouncements, she presses him no further and tries to rouse a sense of optimism. She is eager to go home so things can get back to normal.

The next day she does go home. But after two weeks of trying to resume her normal routine, after enduring more headaches and vomiting, she collapses and dies.[2]

Notice that in this scenario Dr. Smith does not actually lie to Karen (that is, intentionally give her false information), but he does deliberately mislead her by withholding crucial facts and avoiding definite statements. Either way, he handles her paternalistically. Notice also that this story is about protecting a patient from a dreadful prognosis, but such paternalism can also apply to the truth about diagnoses and treatments.

Some medical writers would agree with Dr. Smith's decision. They think there are good reasons for occasionally misleading or lying to patients. Their main argument is that truth-telling can be injurious, evoking in patients feelings of panic, hopelessness, fear, and depression—any of which can worsen the patient's condition, sap her will to live, or tempt her to suicide. Honest disclosure must be modulated to promote the patient's welfare. The physician's duty to do no harm must take precedence over the obligation of veracity.

Others reject this argument, contending that it exaggerates the harm done to patients by full disclosure (and underestimates the beneficial effects of truthfulness) and fails to recognize that misleading or lying to patients can also do damage. A common suggestion is that if patients knew the truth about their situation, they would likely live their lives very differently than if they remained ignorant. If so, not knowing the truth robs patients of informed life decisions. If they knew their prognosis was terminal, for example, they might try harder to make every remaining day meaningful, to put their financial and legal affairs in order, and to behave differently toward their family and friends.

Advocates of full disclosure (that is, honest communication of the essential facts) also insist that informed patients are better patients—that patients who know where they stand are more likely to comply with the requirements of their treatment.

Moreover, some argue that deception breeds distrust—and not just between patient and doctor:

> [T]he long-term effect of lies on the family and, perhaps most importantly, on society, is incalculable. If trust is gradually corroded, if the "wells are poisoned," progress is hard. Mistrust creates lack of communication and increased fear, and this generation has seen just such a fearful myth created around cancer.[3]

The impact of the truth on patients may also depend largely on how it's told. As one writer puts it, cases that seem to indicate that truth-telling is harmful to patients may instead

> argue, not for no telling, but for better telling, for sensitivity and care in determining how much the patient wants to know, explaining carefully in ways the patient can understand, and providing full support and "after-care" as in other treatments.[4]

Another argument against full disclosure is that patients do not want to know the truth, especially if the prognosis is grim. A common claim is that even when patients say they want all the facts, they actually do not. Many writers counter this view with data from surveys suggesting that most patients really do prefer to be told the truth about their diagnosis. In light of these findings, presuming that patients do not mean what they say seems questionable at best.

None of this implies that the truth should be forced upon patients who genuinely choose not to be informed about their medical condition. As one commentator notes, autonomy can be served by offering a patient "the opportunity to learn the truth, at whatever level of detail that patient desires."[5]

Many skeptics of full disclosure have argued that physicians have no duty to tell patients the truth because patients are incapable of understanding it anyway. The practice of medicine is technically complex—so complex that even when a physician tries to explain the relevant facts to patients, they cannot grasp them. Telling patients the whole truth, the skeptics say, is impossible.

Critics of this argument say that even if communicating the whole truth is impossible, physicians still have a duty of complete honesty—an obligation to try hard to convey to patients the essential and relevant information. What's more, some argue that conveying the "whole truth and nothing but the truth" is unnecessary:

> [T]he explanation of a complicated situation in ways a layperson can understand is not a challenge unique to physicians. The same problem is faced by lawyers, electricians, automobile mechanics, and computer help-line workers. In none of these fields, including medicine, is it necessary to provide the layperson with a complete explanation (the "complete truth") of a situation. All a patient requires is an understanding adequate to appreciate the nature and seriousness of his illness and the potential benefits and risks of the available therapies. A diabetic need not know the stages of oxidative phosphorylation to grasp the importance of insulin and the role of diet in maintaining her health.[6]

The main argument in favor of truth-telling rests on the principle of autonomy. The gist is that we must always respect people's autonomy—their rational capacity for self-determination. Autonomous persons must be allowed to freely exercise this capacity: to decide how to live their own lives and what can and cannot be done to their own bodies. To respect their autonomy is to respect their freedom to act by their own lights, as long as their actions accord with the freedom of others. When physicians deceive a patient, they fail to respect his autonomy by constraining his ability to make informed choices. They compel him to make important decisions in a fog of distorted or missing information.

Many who insist on truth-telling and respect for autonomy admit that deceiving a patient may sometimes be necessary, but they say that any deception requires strong justification and should be a last resort. Some contend that deceiving a patient is permissible only when the deception is small and the benefits to the patient are great (as when a minor lie will save the patient's life). Most who argue in this vein believe that cases of permissible deception are rare.

CONFIDENTIAL TRUTHS

Truth-telling, then, is about health professionals imparting relevant facts to patients. **Confidentiality** concerns patients imparting information to health professionals who promise, implicitly or explicitly, not to disclose that information to others. It is an obligation or pledge of physicians, nurses, and others to keep secret the personal health information of patients unless they consent to disclosure. Most people probably assume they have a right to confidentiality. Physicians also take seriously their duty to protect patient privacy, though they may differ on whether the duty is absolute or prima facie. Their respect for confidentiality goes back centuries, having been boldly expressed in a long line of medical codes from ancient Greece onward. The Hippocratic Oath has the physician swear that "Whatever I see or hear, professionally or privately, which ought not to be divulged, I will keep secret and tell no one."

Arguments for confidentiality can take both consequentialist and nonconsequentialist forms. The consequentialist can argue that unless patients are able to rely on a physician to keep their secrets, they would be reluctant to reveal truthful information about themselves—information needed if the physician is to correctly diagnose their illnesses, devise effective treatments, and provide informed prognoses. Without respect for confidentiality, physicians would have a difficult time fulfilling their duty of beneficence. Worse, trust between physician and patient would break down, and trust is what makes the practice of medicine possible. But beyond issues of trust, the consequentialist can offer other dire consequences to consider. Disclosure of confidential medical information could expose patients to discrimination from insurance companies and employers, disrupt their personal relationships, and subject them to shame or public ridicule.

The nonconsequentialist can argue from the principle of autonomy, the idea that people should be allowed to exercise their capacity for self-determination. Autonomous persons, the argument goes, have a right to determine what may or may not be done to them—not just to their bodies and to their property, but to their private lives. They therefore have a right to control access to information about themselves and to limit intrusion into their personal affairs. They have, in other words, a **right to privacy**, the authority of persons to control who may possess and use information about themselves.

A related argument is that the physician-patient relationship is based in part on the physician's implicit promise to patients to preserve confidentiality and to respect their privacy. Patients' confidentiality must therefore be protected because the physician has promised to do so. Confidentiality arises from the physician's obligation to keep promises, what some call a duty of fidelity. Others see this line as another argument from autonomy because, as Kant would have it, to break a promise is to violate autonomy.

As hinted earlier, an important issue is whether the obligation to respect confidentiality is absolute (applying in all cases) or prima facie (allowing exceptions when other duties obtain). Some argue for absolute confidentiality, insisting that *any* breech of it undermines trust between physicians and patients and amounts to impermissible deception. But many believe that exceptions are sometimes justified when confidentiality must be weighed against other duties, such as the duty to prevent serious harm to the patient and others. The law reflects this prima facie view of confidentiality. It recognizes that communication between physicians and patients is "privileged" and should generally be safeguarded from invasion—yet requires physicians to breech confidentiality in some cases. State law, for example, may oblige physicians to reveal information about a patient if she has a serious contagious disease, suffers

LEGAL BRIEF

Confidentiality and a Duty to Warn

In the landmark 1976 case *Tarasoff v. Regents of the University of California*, the court held that duties of patient-psychotherapist confidentiality can be overridden when "a patient poses a serious danger of violence to others." In related cases:

- In 1983 people who were shot by John Hinckley as he tried to assassinate Ronald Reagan sued the psychiatrist who had been treating Hinckley. In *Brady v. Hopper*, a federal district court ruled that unless a patient makes a specific threat to a readily identifiable person, the patient's therapist cannot be held responsible for injuries inflicted on third parties by the patient.
- In *Bradley Center Inc. v. Wessner* (1982) and *Hedlund v. Superior Court of Orange County* (1983), the courts found that therapists are obligated to take reasonable steps to determine the degree of danger posed by a patient.
- In *Ewing v. Goldstein* (2004) and *Ewing v. Northridge Hospital Medical Center* (2004), the California Court of Appeal held that a therapist has a duty to warn third parties of a possible danger posed by a patient even if the threat is communicated not by the patient but by the patient's family.

---

from gunshot wounds, or is the apparent victim of abuse or assault (whether she is a child or an adult). Thus physicians can find themselves pulled not only between clashing moral duties but also between moral duties and legal requirements.

These sorts of conflicts were drawn in high relief by the famous 1976 California Supreme Court case of *Tarasoff v. Regents of the University of California*. It concerned Prosenjit Poddar, a student at UC Berkeley who sought counseling from psychotherapists employed by the university hospital. He confided in them that he intended to kill another student, Tatiana Tarasoff, when she returned from a summer trip in Brazil. The psychotherapists told the police of Poddar's intentions but warned neither Tatiana nor her parents of the threat. Judging Poddar to be rational, the police soon released him. When Tatiana returned from Brazil, Poddar murdered her just as he said he would. Her parents sued the university for failing to warn them of the danger to Tatiana, and they won. The court recognized the importance of confidentiality but ruled that in this case the psychotherapists had a duty to breech it to warn a third party of a serious risk of harm. "We conclude," the majority opinion said,

"that the public policy favoring protection of the confidential character of patient-psychotherapist communications must yield to the extent to which disclosure is essential to avert danger to others. The protective privilege ends where the public peril begins."

High-stakes collisions between the duties of confidentiality and preventing harm are more common than *Tarasoff* may suggest. Prime examples are cases involving patients who are HIV positive. Let's say a physician tells her patient that he has tested positive for HIV infection, that his wife could also become infected through sexual intercourse, and that he should inform her of the risk. But he says he will not disclose his condition to anyone and demands full physician-patient confidentiality. Or suppose this patient has no sexual partner but will be cared for at home by people who are unaware of his HIV status (and may be exposed to his body fluids). He refuses to inform them and asks his physician to tell no one. In both cases, if the physician maintains confidentiality, there is a high risk of serious harm to people, but revealing the patient's diagnosis to others destroys confidentiality. What should the physician do?

Many physicians and ethicists say that violating confidentiality in such a case is morally permissible if there is no other way to avoid the harm to others. They assert that violations should be a last resort after exploring other alternatives, which include getting the patient to agree to notify those at risk or to cease behavior that produces the risk.

But even with such careful attention to protecting patient privacy, is complete confidentiality really feasible? According to some observers, despite the high value we put on confidentiality, it is not what it used to be. It has been eroded, they say—not by physicians and nurses, but by our computerized, bureaucratized health care systems. The number of people who need to know the intimate details of a patient's records—physicians, nurses, medical technicians, students, consultants, secretaries, financial officers, data managers, insurance auditors, administrators, and more—has grown beyond all expectation. And in a digitized, networked world, the opportunities for improper or unethical access to the records have multiplied at every step. Critics contend that the traditional ideal of complete confidentiality is no longer possible, if it ever was. So they suggest that we give up the traditional notion and try to salvage the features of confidentiality that matter to us most.

APPLYING MAJOR THEORIES

In Kantian ethics, the morality of truth-telling and confidentiality seems unambiguous. Physicians who adopt the means-end formulation of the categorical imperative, for example, seem committed to an absolute duty of preserving both. In the Kantian view, treating people merely as a means to an end is impermissible, a violation of the principle of autonomy. Lying to patients and breeching confidentiality (by breaking a promise to respect privacy) are clear instances of such violations. For a strict Kantian, these prohibitions would have no exceptions; there would be no allowances made for extraordinary circumstances. Arguments that truth-telling could be injurious to patients and must therefore be done with an

eye to medical consequences would carry no weight. Likewise, there would be no place for the notion that confidentiality may be set aside if there is a conflicting "duty to warn."

For an act-utilitarian, the morality of truth-telling and confidentiality must be judged case by case, the right action being the one that maximizes the good for all concerned. In each instance, physicians must decide carefully what to disclose to a patient, calculating the impact that any disclosure would have on the patient, her family, and everyone else involved. For each decision about confidentiality, physicians must weigh the effect of the choice on the patient, the physician-patient relationship, third parties who may be harmed by maintaining confidentiality, and themselves (who may have to contend with legal consequences).

Rule-utilitarianism tries to regulate actions by rules that, if generally followed, would result in the best consequences, everyone considered. A rule-utilitarian might argue that the greatest amount of good is produced by a rule stating that a physician should, with care and sensitivity, tell patients the truth about their condition. This rule would presumably not only be beneficial to patients, but also help foster trust in patients for their physicians and for medicine generally. A similar case could be made for a rule mandating strict adherence to the principle of confidentiality. But a rule-utilitarian could also reason that the best rules are those that require less than full disclosure to patients and less than absolute confidentiality—that is, rules with some exceptions built in. For example, the best confidentiality rule might demand full respect for a patient's privacy—except when maintaining confidentiality could put someone's life in danger.

Virtue ethics also has something to say about veracity and confidentiality. Many who favor this moral outlook might contend that if a physician cultivates the virtues of honesty and fidelity, he will be more likely to communicate truthfully with patients, to keep his promises to them, and to maintain their confidences. Moreover, if he possesses the virtue of compassion, he will be sensitive to the effect that blunt truthfulness

Carlos R.

For many who are HIV positive, their anguish only deepens if others know about their condition. They demand medical confidentiality, and physicians are obliged to comply—but the "duty to warn" others of the risk of infection haunts both physicians and patients. Typically those thought to need warning are sexual partners and spouses, but sometimes caregivers—whether professionals or family members—are the ones of concern. This case is of the latter kind. It recounts the events that lead up to the question at issue—whether the physician's weightier duty is confidentiality or warning—then provides the opposing views of two commentators.

Twenty-one-year-old Carlos R. entered the hospital for treatment of gunshot wounds received in gang violence. During his stay, he confided to the attending physician that he was HIV positive, and testing proved him correct. Eventually he recovered well enough to leave the hospital to have his wounds cared for at home. The attending physician advised Carlos to have daily visits from a nurse to tend to his wounds. But Carlos was uninsured, and Medicaid would not pay for the home nursing visits because his 22-year-old sister Consuela was willing and able to care for him. For 10 years since their mother died, Consuela had assumed the role of mother for both Carlos and their younger sister.

Carlos was willing to let Consuela be his nurse, but he was adamant that she not be told about his HIV status. She was unaware of his homosexual activity, and so too was his father. More than anything else he feared that his father would learn the truth. There was also the cultural factor. Among many Hispanics, homosexuality is a social stigma.

The choice for Carlos' physician, then, was between preserving confidentiality and breeching it to warn Consuela of the risks involved in caring for an HIV-positive patient.

One commentator on this case argues against violating confidentiality. He contends that for a physician to have a duty to warn, there must be (1) "an imminent threat of serious and irreversible harm," (2) no other way to avert that threat except by breeching confidentiality, and (3) a situation in which the harm done by the breech is on a par with the harm avoided by the breech. In his view, none of these conditions are fully met in this case. He does not believe that the risk of Consuela becoming infected with HIV is very great—and certainly not "imminent." He also thinks that there are alternatives to breeching confidentiality—the main one being instructing Consuela in safe wound care. Moreover, he insists that the risks to Consuela from not telling her about Carlos' HIV status are far outweighed by the awful disruption of family relations that breeching confidentiality would cause.

The second commentator argues for violating confidentiality to warn Consuela. She maintains that Consuela has a right to information whether or not there is an appreciable risk to her. One reason is that if Consuela is not being told the truth, she is being deceived. Most people in Consuela's situation would want to know the facts and would probably assume that Carlos was not HIV positive because no one said so. Furthermore, in getting Consuela to provide nursing care, "the health care system is using her to avoid providing a service it would otherwise be responsible for." If so, then the system has an obligation to give her the information she needs to decide whether to accept the responsibility.

In the end, the physician should require the patient to choose: "Carlos can decide to accept Consuela's generosity—in return for which he must tell her he is HIV-infected (or ask the doctor to tell her)—or he can decide not to tell her and do without her nursing care."[7]

could have on patients and will adapt his truth-telling accordingly. He will also be able to empathize with patients and understand why confidentiality matters so much to them.

KEY TERMS
confidentiality
right to privacy

SUMMARY
Some medical writers contend that there are good reasons for misleading or lying to patients, claiming that truth-telling can evoke in patients feelings of panic, hopelessness, and depression that can worsen the patient's condition or state of mind. Honest disclosure must be modulated to promote the patient's welfare. Others reject this argument, saying that it exaggerates the harm done to patients by full disclosure and does not recognize that misleading or lying to patients can also do damage. They maintain that informed patients are better patients and that deception breeds distrust. In these debates we often hear that patients do not want to know the truth, but scientific surveys suggest that most patients do want accurate information about their diagnosis. The main argument for truth-telling rests on the principle of autonomy, the idea that people should be allowed to exercise freely their rational capacity for self-determination.

Confidentiality concerns patients imparting information to health professionals who promise, implicitly or explicitly, not to disclose that information to others. Consequentialist arguments for confidentiality say that without it, physicians would be hard pressed to obtain information from patients that could help in treatment, and trust between physician and patient would break down. Moreover, disclosure of confidential medical information could expose patients to discrimination, disrupt their personal relationships, and subject them to shame or public ridicule. Nonconsequentialist arguments appeal to the principle of autonomy, contending that autonomous persons have a right to determine what may or may not be done to their bodies as well as to their private lives. They have a right to privacy, the authority of persons to control who may possess and use information about themselves.

A major issue is whether the obligation to respect confidentiality is absolute or prima facie. Some argue for absolute confidentiality, insisting that any breech of it undermines trust between physicians and patients and amounts to impermissible deception. But many believe that exceptions are sometimes justified when confidentiality must be weighed against other duties, such as the duty to prevent serious harm to the patient and others.

Cases for Evaluation

CASE 1

Cultural Differences in Truth-Telling

While reflecting on my responsibility to provide patients with information, which is an ethical duty of American physicians, I often thought of the different approaches used in my country of origin, Italy, where patients are not always informed of their diagnosis and prognosis. In medical school at the University of Turin in the late 1970s, I learned Italian Deontology Code, written by the Italian Medical Association, which included the following statement: "A serious or lethal prognosis can be hidden from the patient, but not from the family."

During my first year of oncology fellowship in Italy in 1983, a middle-aged businessman was told he had gastritis, when dying of cachexia from end-stage carcinoma; a young, divorced housewife was told she had arthritis while receiving palliative radiation therapy for chemotherapy-resistant metastatic breast cancer; and a college student was told he had drug-induced hepatitis, but he was indeed progressing toward liver failure from widespread hepatitic involvement with lymphoma. In each case the patient's family or only 1 family member was informed of the true diagnosis and prognosis. A ritual started, composed of sotto voce conversations between the physician and the family members outside the patient's room: "Doctor, don't speak too loud" or "Doctor, tell me how much time is left for my husband, because I have to prepare." In each case, the patients knew or at least strongly suspected the truth, but they were part of a generally accepted farce of deception that prevented open discussion about the truth and how to act on it. Consequences of such deception varied from the unresolved financial problems left at the businessman's death, to the stressful, secret, and unsuccessful attempt of the dying single mother to find a way to provide for the future of her 4 children.*

Do you believe that a policy of telling the truth to the patient's family but deceiving the patient is morally permissible? If so, why? If not, what policy should be adopted instead? Do you think that the possible "consequences of such deception" outweigh any possible benefit of deceiving the patient? Should the family's wishes always trump the patient's preferences? Why or why not? Is it legitimate to criticize the truth-telling practices of another culture? Explain.

---

*Antonella Surbone, "Truth Telling to the Patient," *Journal of the American Medical Association* 268 (7 October 1992), 1661–62.

CASE 2

HIV and a Researcher's Duty to Warn

John, a licensed psychologist, is Principal Investigator for the "Assist" Project. His project is designed to identify behavioral trends among HIV+ adults in the New York City area. Participants were recruited from HIV/AIDS support groups, HIV/AIDS advocacy and service organizations, and through publicity in local bars, clinics and media outlets. John uses several measures to identify patterns among these individuals. He looks at help-seeking behaviors, physical and emotional symptoms, nutrition and diet habits, sexual behavior and knowledge of HIV/AIDS.

John uses an individual interview format as the method for the study. Each participant is asked to sign an informed consent form, which guarantees that all information revealed during the interviews will be kept confidential. The consent form describes the study and informs participants of the risks in-

volved, which John identifies as minimal. Each participant is paid $50 for each interview. Participants in the study are also provided free psychological counseling and medical care. Participants are interviewed three times over a two-year period.

In accordance with the research protocol, John asks a participant during one of the initial interviews about her current sexual practices. The participant tells John that she is having unprotected sex with her boyfriend. She states that her boyfriend does not know about her HIV status and that she has no plans to reveal her condition. Later during the interview she mentions the name of her boyfriend. John notes the information and continues with the interview.

Upon going back to his office, John becomes anxious about what he was told by the participant. He ponders what he should do. John thinks about his moral responsibility from a relational perspective, assessing the ethical problem from the standpoint of his responsibility to preserve the scientific integrity of the project, the participants' confidentiality and the boyfriend's welfare.*

What moral principles seem to be in conflict in this scenario? How would you resolve the conflict? Suppose John's only options are either to maintain confidentiality or to violate it by revealing the subject's HIV status to her boyfriend (the subject refuses to notify him voluntarily). What should John do, and on what grounds could either action be justified? Suppose that state law prohibits researchers from revealing a subject's HIV status. Would this fact change your judgment? Should any such legal fact change your judgment?

---

*Brian Schrag, ed. (Association for Practical and Professional Ethics), "Graduate Research Ethics: Cases and Commentaries—Volume 3, 1999," Online Ethics Center for Engineering, 27 March 2006, www.onlineethics.org/CMS/research/rescases/gradres/gradresv3.aspx. (14 November 2007).

CASE 3

Emergency Department Dilemma

A 25-year-old young man is dropped off by a friend at the emergency department (ED) and states that he was in a motor vehicle accident 30 min before arriving. He says that his car was extensively damaged but that he was able to get out of the car and walk around at the scene. There was no loss of consciousness. He states that the police were at the scene investigating. He does not volunteer whether the police questioned him personally or why the police let him leave. Except for bumps and bruises, he is not significantly injured enough to justify a radiograph or computed tomography scan of his head. However, I detect the odor of ethanol on his breath, and so I order a blood ethanol to evaluate his capacity further. It is my opinion that if he is legally impaired, then he cannot leave the ED unless someone picks him up and assumes responsibility for him. He does not refuse the test and his blood ethanol level is 0.17 mg/dl, indicating that he is legally impaired.

Emergency physicians know that people who think they might be legally impaired have a strong incentive to leave the scene of accidents to avoid detection by investigating police. This patient's story about being involved in a multicar crash severe enough to cause significant property damage, and then the investigating police allowing him to leave the scene without checking him for potential ethanol intoxication does not ring true.*

Should the physician maintain doctor-patient confidentiality? Should he tell the police that his impaired patient probably broke the law and may have hurt others? What moral principles are relevant to deciding what to do? How much weight would you give to them? Should regard for public safety and the law ever outweigh doctor-patient confidentiality? Explain.

---

*"Ethics Roundtable Debate: Is a Physician-Patient Confidentiality Relationship Subservient to the Greater Good?" ccforum. com, 25 April 2005, http://ccforum.com/content/9/3/233 (15 November 2007).

FURTHER READING

Tom L. Beauchamp and James F. Childress, *Principles of Biomedical Ethics*, 6th ed. (New York: Oxford University Press, 2009), 288–98.

Benjamin Freedman, "Offering Truth: One Ethical Approach to the Uninformed Cancer Patient," *Archives of Internal Medicine* 153 (8 March 1993), 572–76.

Raanan Gillon, "Telling the Truth, Confidentiality, Consent, and Respect for Autonomy," in *Bioethics* (Oxford: Oxford University Press, 2001), 507–28.

Roger Higgs, "On Telling Patients the Truth," in *Moral Dilemmas in Modern Medicine,* ed. Michael Lockwood (New York: Oxford University Press, 1985), 187–91, 193–202.

Charles C. Lund, "The Doctor, the Patient, and the Truth," *Annals of Internal Medicine* 24 (1946), 955–59.

NOTES

1. Joseph Collins, "Should Doctors Tell the Truth?," *Harper's Monthly Magazine* 155 (1927), 320–26.

2. This scenario was inspired by one discussed in Susan Cullen and Margaret Klein, "Respect for Patients, Physicians, and the Truth," in Ronald Munson, *Intervention and Reflection* (Belmont, CA: Wadsworth/Thomson Learning, 2004), 157–58.

3. Roger Higgs, "On Telling Patients the Truth," in *Moral Dilemmas in Modern Medicine,* ed. Michael Lockwood (New York: Oxford University Press, 1985), 187–91, 193–202.

4. *Ibid.,* 201.

5. Benjamin Freedman, "Offering the Truth: One Ethical Approach to the Uninformed Cancer Patient," *Archives of Internal Medicine* 153 (8 March 1993), 572–76.

6. Cullen and Klein, "Respect for Patients," 161.

7. Leonard Fleck and Marcia Angell (commentators), "Please Don't Tell: A Case About HIV and Confidentiality," *Hastings Center Report* 21 (Nov.–Dec. 1991), 39–40.

READINGS

Telling the Truth to Patients:
A Clinical Ethics Exploration

DAVID C. THOMASMA

According to Thomasma, truth-telling is important because it is "a right, a utility, and a kindness," but it can be trumped by more important values. "[T]ruth is a secondary good," he says. "Although important, other primary values take precedence over the truth. The most important of these values is survival of the individual and the community. A close second would be preservation of the relationship itself."

In this essay I will examine why the truth is so important to human communication in general, the types of truth, and why truth is only a relative value. After those introductory points, I will sketch the ways in which the truth is overridden or trumped by other concerns in the clinical setting. I will then discuss cases that fall into five distinct categories. The conclusion emphasizes the importance of truth telling and its primacy among secondary goods in the healthcare professional-patient relationship.

Reasons for Telling the Truth

... In all human relationships, the truth is told for a myriad of reasons. A summary of the prominent reasons are that it is a right, a utility, and a kindness.

It is a right to be told the truth because respect for the person demands it. As Kant argued, human society would soon collapse without truth telling, because it is the basis of interpersonal trust, covenants, contracts, and promises.

The truth is a utility as well, because persons need to make informed judgments about their actions. It is a mark of maturity that individuals advance and grow morally by becoming more and more self-aware of their needs, their motives, and their limitations. All these steps toward maturity require honest and forthright communication, first from parents

From *Cambridge Quarterly of Healthcare Ethics*, vol. 3, no. 3 (1994), pp. 372–82. Copyright © 1994 Cambridge University Press. Reprinted with permission of Cambridge University Press.

and later also from siblings, friends, lovers, spouses, children, colleagues, co-workers, and caregivers.[1]

Finally, it is a kindness to be told the truth, a kindness rooted in virtue precisely because persons to whom lies are told will of necessity withdraw from important, sometimes life-sustaining and life-saving relationships. Similarly, those who tell lies poison not only their relationships but themselves, rendering themselves incapable of virtue and moral growth.[2] ... When we stop and think of it, there are times when, at least for the moment, protecting us from the truth can save our egos, our self-respect, and even our most cherished values. Not all of us act rationally and autonomously at all times. Sometimes we are under sufficient stress that others must act to protect us from harm. This is called necessary paternalism. Should we become seriously ill, others must step in and rescue us if we are incapable of doing it ourselves. ...

In General Relationships

In each of the three main reasons why the truth must be told, as a right, a utility, and a kindness, lurk values that may from time to time become more important than the truth. When this occurs, the rule of truth telling is trumped, that is, overridden by a temporarily more important principle. The ultimate value in all instances is the survival of the community and/or the well-being of the individual. Does this mean for paternalistic reasons, without the person's consent, the right to the truth, the utility, and the kindness, can be shunted aside? The answer is "yes." The truth in a relationship responds to a multivariate complexity of values, the context for which helps determine which values in that relationship should predominate.

Nothing I have said thus far suggests that the truth may be treated in a cavalier fashion or that it can be withheld from those who deserve it for frivolous reasons. The only values that can trump the truth are recipient survival, community survival, and the ability to absorb the full impact of the truth at a particular time. All these are only temporary trump cards in any event. They only can be played under certain limited conditions because respect for persons is a foundational value in all relationships.

In Healthcare Relationships

It is time to look more carefully at one particular form of human relationship, the relationship between the doctor and the patient or sometimes between other healthcare providers and the patient.

Early in the 1960s, studies were done that revealed the majority of physicians would not disclose a diagnosis of cancer to a patient. Reasons cited were mostly those that derived from nonmaleficence. Physicians were concerned that such a diagnosis might disturb the equanimity of a patient and might lead to desperate acts. Primarily physicians did not want to destroy their patients' hope. By the middle 1970s, however, repeat studies brought to light a radical shift in physician attitudes. Unlike earlier views, physicians now emphasized patient autonomy and informed consent over paternalism. In the doctor-patient relation, this meant the majority of physicians stressed the patient's right to full disclosure of diagnosis and prognosis.

One might be tempted to ascribe this shift of attitudes to the growing patients' rights and autonomy movements in the philosophy of medicine and in public affairs. No doubt some of the change can be attributed to this movement. But also treatment interventions for cancer led to greater optimism about modalities that could offer some hope to patients. Thus, to offer them full disclosure of their diagnosis no longer was equivalent to a death sentence. Former powerlessness of the healer was supplanted with technological and pharmaceutical potentialities.

A more philosophical analysis of the reasons for a shift comes from a consideration of the goal of medicine. The goal of all healthcare relations is to receive/provide help for an illness such that no further harm is done to the patient, especially in that patient's vulnerable state.[3] The vulnerability arises because of increased dependency. Presumably, the doctor will not take advantage of this vulnerable condition by adding to it through inappropriate use of power or the lack of compassion. Instead, the vulnerable person should be assisted back to a state of human equality, if possible, free from the prior dependency.[4]

First, the goal of the healthcare giver–patient relation is essentially to restore the patient's autonomy. Thus, respect for the right of the patient to the truth is measured against this goal. If nothing toward that goal can be gained by telling the truth at a particular time, still it must be told for other reasons. Yet, if the truth would impair the restoration of autonomy, then it may be withheld on grounds of potential harm. Thus the goal of the healing relationship enters into the calculus of values that are to be protected.

Second, most healthcare relationships of an interventionist character are temporary, whereas relationships involving primary care, prevention, and chronic or dying care are more permanent. These differences also have a bearing on truth telling. During a short encounter with healthcare strangers, patients and healthcare providers will of necessity require the truth more readily than during a long-term relation among near friends. In the short term, decisions, often dramatically important ones, need to be made in a compressed period. There is less opportunity to maneuver or delay for other reasons, even if there are concerns about the truth's impact on the person.

Over a longer period, the truth may be withheld for compassionate reasons more readily. Here, the patient and physician or nurse know one another. They are more likely to have shared some of their values. In this context, it is more justifiable to withhold the truth temporarily in favor of more important long-term values, which are known in the relationship.

Finally, the goal of healthcare relations is treatment of an illness. An illness is far broader than its subset, disease. Illness can be viewed as a disturbance in the life of an individual, perhaps due to many nonmedical factors. A disease, by contrast, is a medically caused event that may respond to more interventionist strategies.[5]

Helping one through an illness is a far greater personal task than doing so for a disease. A greater, more enduring bond is formed. The strength of this bond may justify withholding the truth as well, although in the end "the truth will always out."

Clinical Case Categories

The general principles about truth telling have been reviewed, as well as possible modifications formed from the particularities of the healthcare professional–patient relationship. Now I turn to some contemporary examples of how clinical ethics might analyze the hierarchy of values surrounding truth telling.

There are at least five clinical case categories in which truth telling becomes problematic: intervention cases, long-term care cases, cases of dying patients, prevention cases, and nonintervention cases.

Intervention Cases

Of all clinically difficult times to tell the truth, two typical cases stand out. The first usually involves a mother of advanced age with cancer. The family might beg the surgeon not to tell her what has been discovered for fear that "Mom might just go off the deep end." The movie *Dad*, starring Jack Lemmon, had as its centerpiece the notion that Dad could not tolerate the idea of cancer. Once told, he went into a psychotic shock that ruptured standard relationships with the doctors, the hospital, and the family. However, because this diagnosis requires patient participation for chemotherapeutic interventions and the time is short, the truth must be faced directly. Only if there is not to be intervention might one withhold the truth from the patient for a while, at the family's request, until the patient is able to cope with the reality. A contract about the time allowed before telling the truth might be a good idea.

The second case is that of ambiguous genitalia. A woman, 19 years old, comes for a checkup because she plans to get married and has not yet had a period. She is very mildly retarded. It turns out that she has no vagina, uterus, or ovaries but does have an undescended testicle in her abdomen. She is actu- ally a he. Should she be told this fundamental truth about herself? Those who argue for the truth do so on grounds that she will eventually find out, and more of her subsequent life will have been ruined by the lies and disingenuousness of others. Those who argue against the truth usually prevail. National standards exist in this regard. The young woman is told that she has something like a "gonadal mass" in her abdomen that might turn into cancer if not removed, and an operation is performed. She is assisted to remain a female.

More complicated still is a case of a young Hispanic woman, a trauma accident victim, who is gradually coming out of a coma. She responds only to commands such as "move your toes." Because she is now incompetent, her mother and father are making all care decisions in her case. Her boyfriend is a welcome addition to the large, extended family. However, the physicians discover that she is pregnant. The fetus is about 5 weeks old. Eventually, if she does not recover, her surrogate decision makers will have to be told about the pregnancy, because they will be involved in the terrible decisions about continuing the life of the fetus even if it is a risk to the mother's recovery from the coma. This revelation will almost certainly disrupt current family relationships and the role of the boyfriend. Further, if the mother is incompetent to decide, should not the boyfriend, as presumed father, have a say in the decision about his own child?

In this case, revelation of the truth must be carefully managed. The pregnancy should be revealed only on a "need to know" basis, that is, only when the survival of the young woman becomes critical. She is still progressing moderately towards a stable state.

Long-Term Cases

Rehabilitation medicine provides one problem of truth telling in this category. If a young man has been paralyzed by a football accident, his recovery to some level of function will depend upon holding out hope. As he struggles to strengthen himself, the motivation might be a hope that caregivers know to be false, that he may someday be able to walk again. Yet this falsehood is not corrected, lest he slip into despair. Hence, because this is a long-term relationship, the truth will be gradually discovered by the patient under the aegis of encouragement by his physical therapists, nurses, and physicians, who enter his life as near friends.

Cases of Dying Patients

Sometimes, during the dying process, the patient asks directly, "Doctor, am I dying?" Physicians are frequently reluctant to "play God" and tell the patient how many days or months or years they have left. This reluctance sometimes bleeds over into a less-than-forthright answer to the question just asked. A surgeon with whom I make rounds once answered this question posed by a terminally ill cancer patient by telling her that she did not have to worry about her insurance running out!

Yet in every case of dying patients, the truth can be gradually revealed such that the patient learns about dying even before the family or others who are resisting telling the truth. Sometimes, without directly saying "you are dying," we are able to use interpretative truth and comfort the patient. If a car driver who has been in an accident and is dying asks about other family members in the car who are already dead, there is no necessity to tell him the truth. Instead, he can be told that "they are being cared for" and that the important thing right now is that he be comfortable and not in pain. One avoids the awful truth because he may feel responsible and guilt ridden during his own dying hours if he knew that the rest of his family were already dead.

Prevention Cases

A good example of problems associated with truth telling in preventive medicine might come from screening. The high prevalence of prostate cancer among men over 50 years old may suggest the utility of cancer screening. An annual checkup for men over 40 years old is recommended. Latent and asymptomatic prostate cancer is often clinically unsuspected and is present in approximately 30% of men over 50 years of age. If screening were to take place, about 16.5 million men in the United States alone would be diagnosed with prostate cancer, or about 2.4 million men each year. As of now, only 120,000 cases are newly diagnosed each year. Thus, as Timothy Moon noted in a recent sketch of the disease, "a majority of patients with prostate cancer that

is not clinically diagnosed will experience a benign course throughout their lifetime."[6]

The high incidence of prostate cancer coupled with a very low malignant potential would entail a whole host of problems if subjected to screening. Detection would force patients and physicians to make very difficult and life-altering treatment decisions. Among them are removal of the gland (with impotence a possible outcome), radiation treatment, and most effective of all, surgical removal of the gonads (orchiectomy). But why consider these rather violent interventions if the probable outcome of neglect will overwhelmingly be benign? For this reason the U.S. Preventive Services Task Force does not recommend either for or against screening for prostate cancer. Quality-of-life issues would take precedence over the need to know.

Nonintervention Cases

This last example more closely approximates the kind of information one might receive as a result of gene mapping. This information could tell you of the likelihood or probability of encountering a number of diseases through genetic heritage, for example, adult onset or type II diabetes, but could not offer major interventions for most of them (unlike a probability for diabetes).

Some evidence exists from recent studies that the principle of truth telling now predominates in the doctor–patient relationship. Doctors were asked about revealing diagnosis for Huntington's disease and multiple sclerosis, neither of which is subject to a cure at present. An overwhelming majority would consider full disclosure. This means that, even in the face of diseases for which we have no cure, truth telling seems to take precedence over protecting the patient from imagined harms.

The question of full disclosure acquires greater poignancy in today's medicine, especially with respect to Alzheimer's disease and genetic disorders that may be diagnosed in utero. There are times when our own scientific endeavors lack a sufficient conceptual and cultural framework around which to assemble facts. The facts can overwhelm us without such conceptual frameworks. The future of genetics poses just such a problem. In consideration of the new genetics, this might be the time to stress values over the truth.

Conclusion

Truth in the clinical relationship is factored in with knowledge and values.

First, truth is contextual. Its revelation depends upon the nature of the relationship between the doctor and patient and the duration of that relationship.

Second, truth is a secondary good. Although important, other primary values take precedence over the truth. The most important of these values is survival of the individual and the community. A close second would be preservation of the relationship itself.

Third, truth is essential for healing an illness. It may not be as important for curing a disease. That is why, for example, we might withhold the truth from the woman with ambiguous genitalia, curing her disease (having a gonad) in favor of maintaining her health (being a woman).

Fourth, withholding the truth is only a temporary measure. *In vino, veritas* it is said. The truth will eventually come out, even if in a slip of the tongue. Its revelation, if it is to be controlled, must always aim at the good of the patient for the moment.

At all times, the default mode should be that the truth is told. If, for some important reason, it is not to be immediately revealed in a particular case, a truth-management protocol should be instituted so that all caregivers on the team understand how the truth will eventually be revealed.

NOTES

1. Bok S. *Lying: Moral Choice in Public and Personal Life.* New York: Vintage Books, 1989.
2. Pellegrino E. D., Thomasma D. C. *The Virtues in Medical Practice.* New York: Oxford University Press, 1993.
3. Cassell E. The nature of suffering and the goals of medicine. *New England Journal of Medicine* 1982; 306(11):639–45.
4. See Nordenfelt L., issue editor. Concepts of health and their consequences for health care. *Theoretical Medicine* 1993; 14(4).
5. Moon T. D. Prostate cancer. *Journal of the American Geriatrics Society* 1992; 40:622–7 (quote from 626).
6. See note 5. Moon. 1992; 40:622–7.

On Telling Patients the Truth

MACK LIPKIN

Lipkin urges a decidedly paternalistic attitude toward truth-telling. He argues that because the stress of being sick can distort patients' thinking and because they lack understanding of medical concepts, it is usually impossible to convey to patients the full medical truth. Many times, telling the whole truth can do more harm than good. Moreover, many patients prefer not to know the full details about their condition. "Often enough," Lipkin says, "the ethics of the situation, the true moral responsibility, may demand that the naked facts not be revealed." The critical question is not whether deception occurs, but whether the deception is meant to benefit the patient or the physician.

Should a doctor always tell his patients the truth? In recent years there has been an extraordinary increase in public discussion of the ethical problems involved in this question. But little has been heard from physicians themselves. I believe that gaps in understanding the complex interactions between doctors and patients have led many laymen astray in this debate.

From *Newsweek*, 4 June 1979, p. 13. Reprinted with permission.

It is easy to make an attractive case for always telling patients the truth. But as L. J. Henderson, the great Harvard physiologist-philosopher of decades ago, commented:

> To speak of telling the truth, the whole truth and nothing but the truth to a patient is absurd. Like absurdity in mathematics, it is absurd simply because it is impossible. . . . The notion that the truth, the whole truth, and nothing but the truth can be conveyed to the patient is a good specimen of that

class of fallacies called by Whitehead "the fallacy of misplaced concreteness." It results from neglecting factors that cannot be excluded from the concrete situation and that are of an order of magnitude and relevancy that make it imperative to consider them. Of course, another fallacy is also often involved, the belief that diagnosis and prognosis are more certain than they are. But that is another question.

Words, especially medical terms, inevitably carry different implications for different people. When these words are said in the presence of anxiety-laden illness, there is a strong tendency to hear selectively and with emphases not intended by the doctor. Thus, what the doctors means to convey is obscured.

Indeed, thoughtful physicians know that transmittal of accurate information to patients is often impossible. Patients rarely know how the body functions in health and disease, but instead have inaccurate ideas of what is going on; this hampers the attempts to "tell the truth."

Take cancer, for example. Patients seldom know that while some cancers are rapidly fatal, others never amount to much; some have a cure rate of 99 percent, others less than 1 percent; a cancer may grow rapidly for months and then stop growing for years; may remain localized for years or spread all over the body almost from the beginning; some can be arrested for long periods of time, others not. Thus, one patient thinks of cancer as curable, the next thinks it means certain death.

How many patients understand that "heart trouble" may refer to literally hundreds of different abnormalities ranging in severity from the trivial to the instantly fatal? How many know that the term "arthritis" may refer to dozens of different types of joint involvement? "Arthritis" may raise a vision of the appalling disease that made Aunt Eulalee a helpless invalid until her death years later; the next patient remembers Grandpa grumbling about the damned arthritis as he got up from his chair. Unfortunately but understandably, most people's ideas about the implications of medical terms are based on what they have heard about a few cases.

The news of serious illness drives some patients to irrational and destructive behavior; others handle it sensibly. A distinguished philosopher forestalled my telling him about his cancer by saying, "I want to know the truth. The only thing I couldn't take and wouldn't want to know about is cancer." For two years he had watched his mother die slowly of a painful form of cancer. Several of my physician patients have indicated they would not want to know if they had a fatal illness.

Most patients should be told "the truth" to the extent that they can comprehend it. Indeed, most doctors, like most other people, are uncomfortable with lies. Good physicians, aware that some may be badly damaged by being told more than they want or need to know, can usually ascertain the patient's preference and needs.

Discussions about lying often center about the use of placebos. In medical usage, a "placebo" is a treatment that has no specific physical or chemical action on the condition being treated, but is given to affect symptoms by a psychologic mechanism, rather than a purely physical one. Ethicists believe that placebos necessarily involve a partial or complete deception by the doctor, since the patient is allowed to believe that the treatment has a specific effect. They seem unaware that placebos, far from being inert (except in the rigid pharmacological sense), are among the most powerful agents known to medicine.

Placebos are a form of suggestion, which is a direct or indirect presentation of an idea, followed by an uncritical, i.e., not thought-out, acceptance. Those who have studied suggestion or looked at medical history know its almost unbelievable potency; it is involved to a greater or lesser extent in the treatment of every conscious patient. It can induce or remove almost any kind of feeling or thought. It can strengthen the weak or paralyze the strong; transform sleeping, feeding, or sexual patterns; remove or induce a vast array of symptoms; mimic or abolish the effect of very powerful drugs. It can alter the function of most organs. It can cause illness or a great sense of well-being. It can kill. In fact, doctors often add a measure of suggestion when they prescribe even potent medications for those who also need psychologic support. Like all potent agents, its proper use requires judgment based on experience and skill.

Communication between physician and the apprehensive and often confused patient is delicate and uncertain. Honesty should be evaluated not only in terms of a slavish devotion to language often misinterpreted by the patient, but also in terms of intent. *The crucial question is whether the deception was intended to benefit the patient or the doctor.*

Physicians, like most people, hope to see good results and are disappointed when patients do poorly. Their reputations and their livelihood depend on doing effective work; purely selfish reasons would dictate they do their best for their patients. Most important, all good physicians have a deep sense of responsibility toward those who have entrusted their welfare to them.

As I have explained, it is usually a practical impossibility to tell patients "the whole truth." Moreover, often enough, the ethics of the situation, the true moral responsibility, may demand that the naked facts not be revealed. The now popular complaint that doctors are too authoritarian is misguided more often than not. Some patients who insist on exercising their right to know may be doing themselves a disservice.

Judgment is often difficult and uncertain. Simplistic assertions about telling the truth may not be helpful to patients or physicians in times of trouble.

On a Supposed Right to Lie from Altruistic Motives

IMMANUEL KANT

Kant asks whether we could ever have a duty to lie if lying was the only way to prevent harm to ourselves or to others. His answer is an emphatic no. We must speak the truth no matter what injuries befall people. In fact, the act of lying itself causes injury: "For [a lie] always injures another; if not another individual, yet mankind generally, since it vitiates the source of justice." For Kant, to be truthful is an "unconditional command of reason."

In the work called *France*, for the year 1797, Part VI., No. 1, on Political Reactions, by *Benjamin Constant*, the following passage occurs, p. 123:—

"The moral principle that it is one's duty to speak the truth, if it were taken singly and unconditionally, would make all society impossible. We have the proof of this in the very direct consequences which have been drawn from this principle by a German philosopher, who goes so far as to affirm that to tell a falsehood to a murderer who asked us whether our friend, of whom he was in pursuit, had not taken refuge in our house, would be a crime."

The French philosopher opposes this principle in the following manner, p. 124:—"It is a duty to tell the truth. The notion of duty is inseparable from the notion of right. A duty is what in one being corresponds to the right of another. Where there are no rights there are no duties. To tell the truth then is

From Kant's *Critique of Practical Reason and Other Works on the Theory of Ethics*, translated by Thomas Kingsmill Abbot. 1909, Longmans, Green, and Co. publisher.

a duty, but only towards him who has a right to the truth. But no man has a right to a truth that injures others." The πρῶτον ψεῦδος here lies in the statement that "*To tell the truth is a duty, but only towards him who has a right to the truth.*"

It is to be remarked, first, that the expression "to have a right to the truth" is unmeaning. We should rather say, a man has a right to his own *truthfulness* (*veracitas*), that is, to subjective truth in his own person. For to have a right objectively to truth would mean that, as in *meum* and *tuum* generally, it depends on his *will* whether a given statement shall be true or false, which would produce a singular logic.

Now, the *first* question is whether a man—in cases where he cannot avoid answering Yes or No—has the *right* to be untruthful. The *second* question is whether, in order to prevent a misdeed that threatens him or some one else, he is not actually bound to be untruthful in a certain statement to which an unjust compulsion forces him.

Truth in utterances that cannot be avoided is the formal duty of a man to everyone, however great the disadvantage that may arise from it to him or any other; and although by making a false statement I do no wrong to him who unjustly compels me to speak, yet I do wrong to men in general in the most essential point of duty, so that it may be called a lie (though not in the jurist's sense), that is, so far as in me lies I cause that declarations in general find no credit, and hence that all rights founded on contract should lose their force; and this is a wrong which is done to mankind.

If, then, we define a lie merely as an intentionally false declaration towards another man, we need not add that it must injure another; as the jurists think proper to put in their definition (*mendacium est falsiloquium in praejudicium alterius*). For it always injures another; if not another individual, yet mankind generally, since it vitiates the source of justice. This benevolent lie *may*, however, by *accident (casus)* become punishable even by civil laws; and that which escapes liability to punishment only by accident may be condemned as a wrong even by external laws. For instance, if you have *by a lie* hindered a man who is even now planning a murder, you are legally responsible for all the consequences. But if you have strictly adhered to the truth, public justice can find no fault with you, be the unforeseen consequence what it may. It is possible that whilst you have honestly answered Yes to the murderer's question, whether his intended victim is in the house, the latter may have gone out unobserved, and so not have come in the way of the murderer, and the deed therefore have not been done; whereas, if you lied and said he was not in the house, and he had really gone out (though unknown to you), so that the murderer met him as he went, and executed his purpose on him, then you might with justice be accused as the cause of his death. For, if you had spoken the truth as well as you knew it, perhaps the murderer while seeking for his enemy in the house might have been caught by neighbours coming up and the deed been prevented. Whoever then *tells a lie*, however good his intentions may be, must answer for the consequences of it, even before the civil tribunal, and must pay the penalty for them, however unforeseen they may have been; because truthfulness is a duty that must be regarded as the basis of all duties founded on contract, the laws of which would be rendered uncertain and useless if even the least exception to them were admitted.

To be *truthful* (honest) in all declarations is therefore a sacred unconditional command of reason, and not to be limited by any expediency.

Respect for Patients, Physicians, and the Truth

SUSAN CULLEN AND MARGARET KLEIN

Cullen and Klein argue that deception to benefit patients is wrong because it disrespects them by restricting their freedom to make choices about their own lives. But if a patient explicitly states that she does not want to know the facts about her condition, generally physicians should respect her wishes. Those who claim that it's not possible to tell patients the truth are confusing the "whole truth" with the "wholly true." Patients cannot and need not understand the whole truth—that is, all the medical details of a disease process. But they can understand enough to appreciate the nature and seriousness of the disease and the benefits and risks of treatments. Cullen and Klein concede that in rare cases, it is permissible for doctors to deceive a patient— but only if the deception is for a short while and if the potential gain from the deception is probable and significant. By this criterion, a brief deception to save the patient's life may be justified.

A long tradition in medicine holds that because medicine aims to promote the health of patients, it is permissible for a physician to deceive a patient if the deception would contribute to that end. "The crucial question," as one writer observes, "is whether the deception is intended to benefit the patient."[1]

Thus, according to this view, if Dr. Allison tells Mr. Barton he is making a good recovery from a kidney transplant, when in fact the transplanted kidney is not functioning well and his recovery is slower than expected, Dr. Allison's action is justified on the grounds that she is trying to keep up her patient's spirits and encouraging him to fight to regain his health. A sick person isn't made better by gloomy assessments.

This deception-to-benefit-the-patient (DBP) view has a prima facie appeal. At the least it is motivated by the physician's effort to do something to help the patient. Were a physician to tell a healthy patient he had a vitamin deficiency so she could sell him vitamin supplements or recommend unneeded surgery so she could collect a fee for performing it, we would condemn such actions outright. The physician is practicing deception in such cases to benefit herself, not the patient.

We all realize that a physician wouldn't be justified in engaging in just any form of action to benefit her patients. We reject as morally grotesque, for example, the notion that a surgeon should remove the vital organs from a healthy person and use them to save the lives of four others. Having the aim of benefiting a patient does not license using any means whatsoever. Rather, the physician must use means that are morally acceptable. While deceiving a patient for his own good is very different from killing an innocent person to provide the patient a benefit, we will argue that such deception is nonetheless wrong. In all but the rarest cases, deceiving a patient "for his own good" is an unacceptable way for a physician to try to help her patient.

Respect for Persons

While the DBP view seems unobjectionable at first sight, it is wrong for the same reason it is wrong for a

physician to tell a healthy patient he needs vitamins so she can benefit from selling them to him. Such behavior is wrong (in both cases), because it doesn't treat a human being with respect.

Humans are, at the very least, rational beings. We have the capacity to guide our actions on the basis of deliberation, rather than being moved only by instinct or psychological conditioning. Our ability to reason makes all of us worth more than a tree, a dog, or maybe anything else in the natural world.[2]

If we are each special because of our ability to make choices, then others should not destroy this ability or interfere with our exercise of it. All of us have an equal right to choose how to lead our lives, and others have a responsibility to respect that right. (Working out arrangements allowing each person maximum freedom while also guaranteeing the freedom of others is a major task of social and political philosophy.) Treating humans with respect means recognizing their autonomy by allowing them the freedom to make choices about their lives. By contrast, to disrespect people means taking away their freedom to live as they choose.

Disrespect and the Physician's Good

If Dr. Mires, a gynecological surgeon, tells Ms. Sligh she needs a hysterectomy, when in fact the medical indications are insufficient to justify the surgery and he is recommending it only for the money he will receive for the operation, Dr. Mires is treating Ms. Sligh with disrespect. By lying to Ms. Sligh, Dr. Mires is damaging her autonomy. She is put in the position of having to make a decision on the basis of the false information Dr. Mires provides to her. Hence, the option of deciding to do what is most likely to contribute to protecting and promoting her health is closed off to her. She can only *believe* she is making that decision, for Dr. Mires has forced her to deliberate on the basis of a false assumption.

When knowledge is power, ignorance is slavery. When Dr. Mires deliberately misinforms Ms. Sligh, he cripples her ability to carry out any plans she might have. It doesn't matter if she decides she doesn't want to have a hysterectomy and so avoids the risks, pain, and expense of surgery. Not only has she been made to worry needlessly and perhaps agonize over her decision, Dr. Mires' deception has put her in a false

From Ronald Munson, *Intervention and Reflection: Basic Issues in Medical Ethics*, 8th edition. Wadsworth Publishing Company: Belmont, CA, 2008. Used with permission.

position with respect to making decisions about her life. Unknown to her, he has restricted her freedom to make meaningful choices. He has discounted her ability to reason and make decisions, and in this way, he has treated her with disrespect.

Disrespect and the Patient's Good

The most serious cases in which physicians have traditionally considered themselves justified (and perhaps even obligated) to deceive a patient are ones in which the patient is dying and the disease can no longer be treated effectively.[3] In the past, the question was most often one of whether to tell a patient he had cancer. Now that cancer treatments have become more effective, the question has usually become one of whether to tell a patient a treatment is not likely to be effective in extending his life. The central issue remains the same, because the physician must still decide whether to deceive the patient.

Consider the following case. Susan Cruz, a thirty-four-year-old single mother of a six-year-old boy, suffered for more than two months from excruciating headaches that were often accompanied by vomiting and dizziness. Yet it wasn't until after she lost control of the left side of her body and collapsed in the bathroom in what she thought of as a fit that she went to see her HMO doctor. He immediately referred her to Dr. Charles Lambert, a neurologist, who, after a detailed examination, ordered an MRI of her brain. Susan had two seizures in the hospital, right after the scan. She was admitted, and the MRI was followed by a brain biopsy performed by Dr. Clare Williams, a neurosurgeon.

The results of the tests showed Susan had an aggressive form of malignant brain cancer affecting the glial cells. The cancer was so extensive Dr. Williams advised Dr. Lambert that not only was a surgical cure out of the question, surgery to reduce the amount of cancerous tissue would not be worth the risk of additional brain damage. Radiation treatments might shrink some of the tumor, but Susan's disease was so far advanced they would have little effect on the outcome.

After reviewing all the information in Susan's case, Dr. Lambert concluded it was not likely that whatever was done would extend Susan's life to an appreciable extent. Most likely, she would be dead within a few weeks, a month or two at the most. But should he tell her this? Wouldn't it be better to allow her to spend her last days free of the dread and anxiety that knowledge of the imminence of her death was sure to cause her? She and her son, Bryan, could share sometime together free from the worst kind of worry. She could do nothing to prevent her death, so shouldn't he leave her feeling hopeful about the future? After all, he couldn't *know* she would die in a few weeks.

"You have a disease of the supporting cells in the brain," Dr. Lambert told Susan. "That's the reason for the headaches, dizziness, vomiting, muscular weakness, and seizures."

"Is there a treatment?" Susan asked. "Will I have to have brain surgery?"

"Not for your stage of the disease," Dr. Lambert said. To avoid explaining why, he quickly added, "Radiation therapy is the best treatment we can offer, because X-rays will help kill off the abnormal tissue putting pressure on your brain."

"Will that make the headaches and all the rest go away?"

"It will help," Dr. Lambert said. "But we have medications that will help also. I can give you steroids to reduce the brain swelling and an anticonvulsant to control your seizures. I can also treat the headaches with effective drugs."

"When do my treatments start?"

"I'll prescribe some drugs today and set you up with the therapeutic radiologists," Dr. Lambert said. "I imagine they can start your treatments in a day or so."

"Great," Susan said. "I've got to get well so I can take care of Bryan. He's staying with my mom, and she's got a heart problem. A six-year-old boy can be a real handful."

Susan followed the treatment plan outlined by Dr. Lambert. She took the drugs prescribed and, with the help of her friend Mandy, showed up at the hospital for her radiation treatments for four weeks. She missed the fifth treatment, because she began having uncontrollable seizures and was taken to the hospital. She died the day after her admission.

Dr. Lambert never told Susan she had brain cancer, nor that the reason surgery wasn't appropriate was that the disease was so far advanced it would be useless. He didn't tell her that, by his estimation, she had only a few weeks of life remaining. Dr. Lambert didn't lie to Susan, but he deceived her. What he told her about her medical condition was vague and limited. He didn't share with her information he possessed that was relevant to her condition. He chose his words so that she would believe she had a disease that might be either cured or controlled by the treatments he prescribed.

While Susan did not (we may suppose) press Dr. Lambert for more information than he provided or ask him questions about her illness, this does not mean Dr. Lambert was not engaged in deception.[4] Susan (like many people) may not have known enough about medicine or her own body to ask the right sort of questions, may have been so intimidated by doctors not to dare to ask questions, or may have been psychologically incapable of asking questions about her illness, preferring to leave everything in the hands of her physician. Dr. Lambert, at the least, should have found out from Susan how much she wanted to know. A willful ignorance is, after all, quite different from an enforced ignorance.

It was also disingenuous for Dr. Lambert to reason that because he cannot be *certain* Susan will die of her disease within a few weeks, he should withhold information from her. Uncertainty of that kind is an ineliminable part of medical practice, and Dr. Lambert has every reason to believe Susan has a relatively short time to live. Judges instructing juries in death penalty cases often distinguish between real doubt and philosophical doubt in explaining the meaning of "reasonable doubt." Dr. Lambert has no real doubt about Susan's fate, and she is entitled to his best medical judgment.

Dr. Lambert's deception of Susan Cruz, like Dr. Mires' deception of Ms. Sligh, is morally wrong. Dr. Lambert deceives Susan with the aim of doing something good for her, while Dr. Mires deceives Ms. Sligh with the aim of doing something good for himself. We might thus say that the deception practiced by Dr. Mires is morally worse than that practiced by Dr. Lambert. Even so, Dr. Lambert's deception of Susan Cruz is still wrong, because it treats her disrespectfully.

By failing to provide Susan with crucial information, Dr. Lambert violates Susan's right to shape what is left of her own life. He deceives her into believing that, with the treatments he prescribes, she can go back to living a normal life and might eventually become healthy again. Because this is not so, Susan is thus denied the opportunity to decide how to spend the final weeks of her life.

She is unable to do what she might prefer to do, if she knew she had a fatal disease and a relatively short time left to live. She might reestablish a connection with her ex-husband, complete the novel she was writing, or visit New York. Most important, she might arrange for someone to take care of her six-year-old son. Prevented by Dr. Lambert's deception from knowing she may soon die, Susan is barred from pursuing what she values most in the time she has remaining.

Respect for persons bars the deception of patients. When the deception is for the physician's benefit, the wrong is obvious. Yet even when the deception is intended to benefit the patient, the physician's good intention doesn't alter the fact that the deception violates the patient's autonomy.

Three Critical Questions

Three questions about physicians' telling the truth to their patients arise with sufficient frequency as to warrant their being addressed explicitly.

1. What if a Patient Doesn't Want to Know About His Disease or the State of His Health?

Some writers have argued that many patients don't want to know what's wrong with them.[5] Although they may say they do, some don't mean it. Part of the physician's job is to assess how much information and what sort a patient can handle, then provide him with an appropriate amount and kind. Thus, a physician may decide that a man in his mid-thirties doesn't want to know he is showing the first symptoms of (say) Huntington's disease. Although the disease is invariably fatal and essentially untreatable, it is slow acting, and the patient may have another ten or fifteen years of more-or-less normal life before the worst symptoms of the disease manifest themselves. The physician may decide to spare the patient the anguish of living with the knowledge that he is eventually going to develop a fatal and particularly nasty disease. The patient, she judges, really wants her to protect him from the years of agony and uncertainty.

But with no more than her own assessment to guide her, in making judgments about what a patient wants to know, the physician is taking too much on herself. Huntington's disease is a genetic disorder that occurs when a parent passes on the HD gene to a child. Someone with one parent who has HD may already know he has a fifty-fifty chance of developing the disorder. He may want to know whether the problems he is experiencing are symptoms of the disease. If they are, he may choose to live his life in a way very different than he might if the problems are not symptoms. He might decide, for example, not to have a child and to avoid the risk of passing on the gene for the disease. Or if he and his partner decide to have a child, they might opt for artificial insemination and embryo screening to eliminate embryos carrying the HD gene. The physician is generally in no position to decide what information needs to be withheld from a patient. Full disclosure should be the default position for physicians.

The Patient Is Explicit. If a patient clearly and explicitly expresses the wish not to know the truth about his medical condition physicians should generally respect this desire. No disrespect is involved in not telling the truth (not providing information) to someone who decides he does not want to know it. The ignorance he imposes on himself may be necessary for him to go on with his life in the way he wishes.

Thus, someone may know himself well enough to realize that if he were diagnosed with inoperable cancer, he wouldn't be able to think about anything else, and the remainder of his life would be a misery of anxiety and fear. His physician should respect such a wish to remain ignorant, for it is as much an expression of autonomy as is the wish to be informed.

When a patient expresses the desire not to be informed about his medical condition, this does not justify his physician's *deceiving* him about his condition. The physician is warranted in withholding the truth from a patient who has asked to be kept ignorant, but the physician is not warranted in telling the patient nothing is wrong with him when there is or falsely assuring him he doesn't have metastatic prostate cancer.

Overriding Considerations? Cases in which patients do not wish to know about their medical condition may not be as rare as they once were. Some patients don't want to know if they are infected with HIV, for example, and request that they not be informed of test results that might show they are HIV-positive.

Such cases raise the question of whether the respect for persons that grounds the physician's obligation to allow a patient to make his own decisions requires the physician always to be bound by a patient's explicit wish not to be informed about his medical condition. We think not.

Where HIV or some other contagious disease is involved, the patient has a need to know, not necessarily for his own sake, but for the sake of others. Those who do not want to know they are HIV-positive lack information crucial to decisions concerning their own behavior with respect to others. The physician has an obligation to a particular patient, but she also has an obligation to prevent harm to others who may come into contact with that patient. Failing to tell a patient he is HIV-positive, even if he has requested not to know, makes her complicitous in the spread of the disease. She is not responsible for her patient's actions, but she is responsible for making sure he has information relevant to decisions affecting others. Violating his autonomy to the extent needed to inform him is justified by the possibility that it may save the lives of others. (If she discovered an airline pilot suffered from a seizure disorder, it would be morally wrong for her not to make sure the airline was informed.)

A question similar to that about infectious diseases arises about the "vertical transmission" of genetic diseases. Suppose a thirty-four-year-old man whose mother died of Huntington's doesn't want to be tested to find out whether he is carrying the gene (and so will develop the disease). He is bothered by some movement problems and episodes of mental confusion. He wants his physician to treat him for these but not tell him whether they are symptoms of the onset of Huntington's. The man is about to be married, and he has told his physician he and his wife intend to have children.

After examination and testing, the physician believes the patient's problems are symptoms of HD and are likely to get progressively worse. Moreover, the physician knows that offspring of the man have a fifty percent chance of inheriting the gene that causes the disease. Should the physician go against the patient's explicit request and inform him it is likely he has HD?

Once again, violating a patient's autonomy to the extent of telling him something he does not want to hear seems warranted. If the patient knows he may have HD, he might decide either not to have children or to employ embryo screening to avoid having a child that inherits the HD gene. In the absence of this knowledge, he may be more likely to have a child who will inherit the gene and eventually develop a painful, lingering, and fatal disease. Decreasing the likelihood of bringing a child into the world who will eventually develop such a disease justifies the physician's going against her patient's wishes. (Before reaching this stage, the physician might talk to the patient and attempt to get him to change his mind by telling him what might be at stake and making sure he understands his reproductive options.)

In summary, we hold that while a physician has a prima facie obligation to withhold the truth about a patient's condition from the patient at the patient's request, in some circumstances the physician may have a duty to ignore the request and provide the patient with information he doesn't want to hear.

Patients Who Don't Say. What about patients like Susan Cruz who express neither a desire to be fully informed nor a wish to be kept ignorant? Physicians are justified in presuming that patients want to know about the state of their health, diseases they may have, and the appropriate treatments for them. This presumption is no less than the recognition that patients are persons, that they are rational agents who may be assumed to want to make informed decisions about matters affecting their lives. Setting aside this prior presumption requires that a patient explicitly inform a physician that he or she wishes to remain in ignorance. Informing patients about their medical condition is, again, the default position for physicians.

Further, if a physician has doubts about whether a patient wants to be informed about her medical condition (as we discussed earlier in connection with Susan Cruz), he should make an effort to de-termine at the beginning of the relationship whether the patient wants to know about the nature and seriousness of her disease. "Don't ask, don't tell" is by no means an appropriate model for physician-patient communication, and because the physician holds the stronger position in the relationship, it is up to him to find out about how much his patient wants to know.

Studies indicate that a significant majority of patients do want to know about the state of their health. In most studies, over eighty percent of patients surveyed reported that they would want to be informed if they were diagnosed with cancer or some other serious disease.[6] Thus, telling a patient the truth can be regarded as the default position for the physician on grounds that are empirical as well as moral.

2. What if a Physician Is Unable to Tell a Patient the Truth?

Physicians cannot tell patients what they don't know themselves. Nothing is wrong with a physician's admitting that little is known about the patient's disease or that the patient's symptoms don't point to a clear diagnosis. Patients are aware that physicians aren't omniscient, and a physician who confesses to ignorance or puzzlement may be showing respect for the patient. A physician must recognize his own limitations, as distinct from the limitations of the state of medicine, and be prepared to refer a patient to someone more able to address the patient's problem.

Actual ignorance and the consequent impossibility of telling a patient the truth is not the issue that physicians and patients typically focus on in the conflict over truth-telling. The issue is usually about whether physicians, when they know the truth, are able to tell it to their patients.

A complaint often expressed by physicians about the need to get a patient's informed consent before carrying out a surgical procedure is that patients are unable to understand their explanations. The notion underlying this complaint is that, even when physicians try, it is impossible to inform patients about their medical condition.

This notion lies at the base of the argument that physicians, even when they do their best, cannot tell their patients the truth. Patients (the argument goes) lack the technical background and experience of physicians, so even intelligent and educated patients are not able to understand the medical terms and concepts physicians must use to describe a patient's condition. Physicians, if they are to communicate at all with the patient, must then switch to using terms and concepts that neither adequately nor accurately convey to the patient what is wrong with him. Thus, it is impossible for physicians to tell patients the truth.

Critics have pointed out that this argument that physicians are not able even in principle to tell patients "the truth" rests on a confusion between "whole truth" and "wholly true." Physicians, we can agree, cannot tell patients the "whole truth," meaning that no patient is going to be able to understand all the known details of a disease process as it affects him. Medicine is an information-rich enterprise, and even physicians are quickly out of their depth in areas beyond their expertise. How many of us really understand the pancreas?

Even so, the explanation of a complicated situation in ways a layperson can understand is not a challenge unique to physicians. The same problem is faced by lawyers, electricians, automobile mechanics, and computer help-line workers. In none of these fields, including medicine, is it necessary to provide the layperson with a complete explanation (the "complete truth") of a situation. All a patient requires is an understanding adequate to appreciate the nature and seriousness of his illness and the potential benefits and risks of the available therapies. A diabetic need not know the stages of oxidative phosphorylation to grasp the importance of insulin and role of diet in maintaining her health.

The argument also does not support the claim endorsed by some writers that, because a physician cannot tell their patients "the truth" (the "whole truth"), it's all right to tell them what is not "wholly true"—that is, to deceive them. Such deception may involve using vague language to explain a patient's medical condition. Thus, Dr. Lambert tells Susan Cruz, "You have a disease of the supporting cells in the brain," when he should have explained to her that she had a particular kind of brain cancer, one that was aggressive and that had advanced to an inoperable stage. The view that the impossibility of telling a patient "the whole truth" makes it all right to tell

the patient something not wholly true is analogous to saying, "Because I can't pay you the money I owe you, it's okay for me to rob you." Not being able to tell "the truth" is not a license to deceive.

Respect for persons requires that physicians tell their patients the relevant facts about their medical condition in a comprehensible way. It doesn't require trying to tell patients all the facts. Telling the truth is no more an impossibility for physicians than it is for automobile mechanics.

3. Don't Physicians Sometimes Have a Duty to Lie to Their Patients?

Some writers have argued that respect for persons and their autonomy sometimes permits physicians to deliberately deceive their patients. Granting that a sick patient desires to regain his health, then if that desire can most likely be attained by his physician's deceiving him, the physician is justified in carrying out the deception.[7] Deceiving the patient in such a case assists him in securing his goal, so a respect for the patient's goal makes the deception permissible. The physician violates the patient's autonomy a little while the patient is sick so that he will regain his health.

This is not a view that can be dismissed as obviously flawed, but it is one we ought to be cautious about adopting without qualification.

First, it is easy to overestimate the extent to which lying to a patient will be useful in helping him regain his health. We certainly don't have any data that show the relative advantage of deceiving patients about their illnesses. The old notion that if a patient with a serious illness is protected from anxiety and worry about his condition, he will heal faster is no more than speculation. As such, it will not justify our infringing someone's autonomy for the sake of what is at best a hypothetical gain.

Second, it is easy to underestimate the benefits of informing patients about the character of disease and the aim of the treatment. Most treatments for serious diseases require the full cooperation of the patient. A woman diagnosed with metastatic breast cancer must go through a rigorous course of therapy, ranging from surgery through chemotherapy and radiation treatments. If she knows that her cancer has spread from the breast to other places in her body and knows her chances of survival, she is more likely to adhere to the treatment plan mapped out by her oncologist. Deceiving the patient about her medical problem is probably, in most cases, more likely to work against her goal of preserving her life and regaining her health. Thus, deception may not only violate her autonomy, it may contribute to the loss of her life.

Let us suppose, however, that in some cases we can know with reasonable certainty that if we deceive someone about her illness this will contribute to her recovery. Is it acceptable to use deception and violate autonomy in the short run, if the deception can be expected to promote autonomy in the longer run?

Recalling an example mentioned earlier should make us wary of answering this question in the affirmative. It would be wrong, we said, to kill one healthy person to obtain organs to save the lives of four people. Such examples suggest it is wrong to interfere with autonomy (that of the healthy person) for the sake of promoting autonomy (that of the four sick ones).

Yet we generally agree it is acceptable for the federal government to tax people with a certain income, then use part of the money to help feed starving foreigners. This suggests it is *not* wrong to interfere with autonomy (that of taxpayers) to promote autonomy (that of the starving). Are our responses in these two cases inconsistent, or is there a difference between the cases? We suggest there is a difference.

In both cases, the gain in autonomy is great (lives saved), but in the tax case, the infringement of autonomy needed to achieve a great gain is minor. Taxing us as citizens takes away some of our resources and thus counts as an infringement of our autonomy. Yet we still retain a substantial degree of control over the important parts of our lives.

The contrast between these two cases suggests the following principle: It does not show a disrespect for persons to violate their autonomy, if the violation is minor and the potential gain is both probable and significant. Thus, for example, if a physician is confident she can save a patient's life by deceiving him for a short while, it is not wrong for her to deceive him. Suppose Ms. Cohen has an irrational fear of taking antibiotics, yet if she is not treated for a bacte-

rial lung infection, she will, almost certainly die. Her physician, in such circumstances, would be justified in telling her something like, "The pills I'm giving you will help your body fight the infection."

Such cases are sure to be rare, however. In most cases, either the stakes will not be high enough (someone's life) to justify deception or deception will not be likely to help. Most often, the physician's only legitimate course is to respect her patient's status as an autonomous agent. This means not trying to deceive him and helping him make decisions by providing him with information relevant to his disease and the treatment options open to him.

Conclusion

We have argued that a principle of respect for persons requires that physicians not engage in deceiving patients. It is clearly wrong for physicians to tell patients they need surgery that they don't need. Such a lie is wrong, we have contended, because it prevents patients from making informed choices about their lives. This is also true of deception intended to benefit a patient. In all but the rarest cases, deceiving a patient "for his own good" is an unacceptable way for physicians to try to help their patients.

NOTES

1. Mark Lipkin, *Newsweek* (June 4, 1979), p. 13. See also Joseph Ellin, "Lying and Deception: The Solution to a Dilemma in Medical Ethics," *Westminster Institute Review* (May 1981), pp. 3–6, and Joseph Collins, "Should Doctors Tell the Truth?" in Samuel Gorovitz *et al.*, eds., *Moral Problems in Medicine*, 2nd ed (New York: Prentice-Hall, 1983), pp. 190–201.

2. Immanuel Kant was the first to articulate this idea. See his *Groundwork of the Metaphysic of Morals*, tr. H. Paton (New York: Harper Torchbooks, 1964), esp. p. 96.

3. Lipkin, *loc. cit.*

4. Sissela Bok, *Lying: Moral Choice in Public and Private Life* (New York: Pantheon Books, 1978), p. 229.

5. Lipkin, *loc. cit.* See also Lawrence Henderson, "Physician and Patient as a Social System," *New England Journal of Medicine* (1955), p. 212.

6. Bok, p. 227.

7. Jane Zembaty, "A Limited Defense of Paternalism in Medicine," *Proceedings of the 13th Conference on Value Inquiry: The Life Sciences and Human Values* (Geneseo, NY: State University of New York, 1979), pp. 145–158. See also Terence Ackerman, "Why Doctors Should Intervene," *Hastings Center Report* (August 1982), pp. 14–17.

Why Privacy Is Important

JAMES RACHELS

Why should we care so much about privacy? Rachels asks. He notes that we have a sense of privacy that cannot be explained fully by our fear of being embarrassed or our concerns about being disadvantaged in some material way. He argues that "privacy is necessary if we are to maintain the variety of social relationships with other people that we want to have, and that is why it is important to us." To manage the relationships that we have with people, we must have "control over who has access to us."

Privacy is one of those familiar values that seem unproblematic until we start thinking about them, and then puzzles appear at every turn. The first puzzle is why, exactly, privacy is important. According to Justice Brandeis, it is "the right most valued by civilized men."[1] But why should we care so much about it? At first it may appear that no unitary explanation is possible, because people have so many interests that may be harmed by invasions of their privacy:

1. Privacy is sometimes necessary to protect people's interests in competitive situations. For example, it obviously would be a disadvantage to Bobby Fischer if he could not analyze the adjourned position in a chess game in private, without his opponent learning his results.

2. In other cases someone may want to keep some aspect of his life or behavior private simply because it would be embarrassing for other people to know about it. There is a splendid example of this in John Barth's novel *End of the Road*. The narrator of the story, Jake Horner, is with Joe Morgan's wife, Rennie, and they are approaching the Morgan house where Joe is at home alone:

"Want to eavesdrop?" I whispered impulsively to Rennie. "Come on, it's great! See the animals in their natural habitat."

Rennie looked shocked. "What for?"

"You mean you never spy on people when they're alone? It's wonderful! Come on, be a sneak! It's the most unfair thing you can do to a person."

From *Philosophy & Public Affairs*, vol. 4, no. 4, 1975, pp. 323–33. Copyright © 1975. Reprinted with permission of Blackwell Publishing Ltd.

"You disgust me, Jake!" Rennie hissed. "He's just reading. You don't know Joe at all, do you?"

"What does that mean?"

"*Real* people aren't any different when they're alone. No masks. What you see of them is authentic."

. . . Quite reluctantly, she came over to the window and peeped in beside me.

It is indeed the grossest of injustices to observe a person who believes himself to be alone. Joe Morgan, back from his Boy Scout meeting, had evidently intended to do some reading, for there were books lying open on the writing table and on the floor beside the bookcase. But Joe wasn't reading. He was standing in the exact center of the bare room, fully dressed, smartly executing military commands. About *face!* Right *dress!* 'Tenshun! Parade *rest!* He saluted briskly, his cheeks blown out and his tongue extended, and then proceeded to cavort about the room—spinning, pirouetting, bowing, leaping, kicking. I watched entranced by his performance, for I cannot say that in my strangest moments (and a bachelor has strange ones) I have surpassed him. Rennie trembled from head to foot.[2]

The scene continues even more embarrassingly.

3. There are several reasons medical records should be kept private, having to do with the consequences to individuals of facts about them becoming public knowledge. The president of the American Medical Association warned, "The average patient doesn't realize the importance of the confidentiality of medical records. Passing out information on venereal disease can wreck a marriage. Revealing a pattern of alcoholism or drug abuse can result

in a man's losing his job or make it impossible for him to obtain insurance protection."[3]

4. When people apply for credit (or for large amounts of insurance or for jobs of certain types), they are often investigated, and the result is a fat file of information about them. There is something to be said in favor of such investigations, for business people surely do have the right to know whether credit applicants are financially reliable. The trouble is that all sorts of other information can find its way into such files—information about the applicant's sex life, his political views, and so on. Clearly, it is unfair for one's application for credit to be influenced by such irrelevant matters.

These examples illustrate the variety of interests that may be protected by guaranteeing people's privacy, and it would be easy to give further examples of the same general sort. However, I do not think that examining such cases will provide a complete understanding of the importance of privacy, for two reasons.

First, these cases all involve relatively unusual sorts of situations, in which someone has something to hide or in which information about a person might provide someone with a reason for mistreating him in some way. Thus, reflection on these cases gives us little help in understanding the value that privacy has in *normal* or *ordinary* situations. By this I mean situations in which there is nothing embarrassing or shameful or unpopular in what we are doing and nothing ominous or threatening connected with its possible disclosure. For example, even married couples whose sex lives are normal (whatever that is), and so who have nothing to be ashamed of, by even the most conventional standards, and certainly nothing to be blackmailed about, do not want their bedrooms bugged. We need an account of the value that privacy has for us not only in the few special cases but in the many common and remarkable cases as well.

Second, even those invasions of privacy that do result in embarrassment or in some specific harm are objectionable on other grounds. A woman may rightly be upset if her credit rating is adversely affected by a report about her sexual behavior, because the use of such information is unfair; however, she may also object to the report simply because she feels—as most of us would—that her sex life is *nobody else's business*. This is an extremely important point. We have a sense of privacy that is violated in such affairs, and this sense of privacy cannot adequately be explained merely in terms of our fear of being embarrassed or disadvantaged in one of the obvious ways. An adequate account of privacy should help us to understand what makes something "someone's business" and why intrusions into things that are "none of your business" are, as such, offensive.

These considerations suggest that there is something important about privacy that we will miss if we confine our attention to examples such as (1)–(4). In what follows I will try to bring out what this something is.

Social Relationships and Appropriate Behavior

I will give an account of the value of privacy based on the idea that there is a close connection between our ability to control who has access to us and to information about us and our ability to create and maintain different sorts of social relationships with different people. According to this account, privacy is necessary if we are to maintain the variety of social relationships with other people that we want to have, and that is why it is important to us. By a "social relationship" I do not mean anything unusual or technical; I mean the sort of thing that we usually have in mind when we say of two people that they are friends or that they are husband and wife or that one is the other's employer.

We may begin by noticing that there are fairly definite *patterns of behavior* associated with these relationships. Our relationships with other people determine, in large part, how we act toward them and how they behave toward us. Moreover, there are different patterns of behavior associated with different sorts of relationships. Thus a man may be playful and affectionate with his children (although sometimes firm), businesslike with his employees, and respectful and polite with his mother-in-law. And to his close friends he may show a side of his personality that others never see—perhaps he is secretly a poet, and rather shy about it, and shows his verse only to his closest friends.

It is sometimes suggested that there is something deceitful or hypocritical about such variations in behavior. It is suggested that underneath all the role-playing there is the "real" person and that the various "masks" that we wear are some sort of phony disguise that we use to conceal our "true" selves. I take it that this is what is behind Rennie's remark, in the passage from Barth: "*Real* people aren't any different when they're alone. No masks. What you see of them is authentic." According to this way of looking at things, the fact that we observe different standards of conduct with different people is merely a sign of dishonesty. Thus the coldhearted businessman who reads poetry to his friends is "really" a gentle, poetic soul whose businesslike demeanor in front of his employees is only a false front; and the man who curses and swears when talking to his friends, but who would never use such language around his mother-in-law, is just putting on an act for her.

This is wrong. Of course the man who does not swear in front of his mother-in-law may be just putting on an act so that, for example, she will not disinherit him, when otherwise he would curse freely in front of her without caring what she thinks. But it may be that his conception of how he ought to behave with his mother-in-law is simply different from his conception of how he may behave with his friends. (Or it may not be appropriate for him to swear around *her* because "she is not that sort of person.") Similarly, the businessman may be putting up a false front for his employees, perhaps because he dislikes his work and has to make a continual, disagreeable effort to maintain the role. But on the other hand he may be, quite comfortably and naturally, a businessman with a certain conception of how it is appropriate for a businessman to behave; and this conception is compatible with his also being a husband, a father, and a friend, with different conceptions of how it is appropriate to behave with his wife, his children, and his friends. There need be nothing dishonest or hypocritical in any of this, and neither side of his personality need be the "real" him, any more than any of the others.

It is not merely accidental that we vary our behavior with different people according to the different social relationships that we have with them. Rather, the different patterns of behavior are (partly) what define the different relationships; they are an important part of what makes the different relationships what they are. The relation of friendship, for example, involves bonds of affection and special obligations, such as the duty of loyalty, that friends owe to one another; but it is also an important part of what it means to have a friend that I welcome her company, confide in her, tell her things about myself, and show her sides of my personality that I would not tell or show to just anyone.[4] Suppose I believe someone is my close friend, and then I discover that she is worried about her job and is afraid of being fired. But while she has discussed this situation with several other people, she has not mentioned it at all to me. And then I learn that she writes poetry and that this is an important part of her life; but while she has shown her poems to other people, she has not shown them to me. Moreover, I learn that she behaves with her other friends in a much more informal way than she behaves with me, that she makes a point of seeing them socially much more than she sees me, and so on. In the absence of some special explanation of her behavior, I would have to conclude that we are not as close as I had thought.

The same general point can be made about other sorts of human relationships: employer to employee, minister to congregant, doctor to patient, husband to wife, parent to child, and so on. In each case, the sort of relationship that people have to one another involves a conception of how it is appropriate for them to behave with each other and, what is more, a conception of the kind and degree of knowledge concerning one another that it is appropriate for them to have. Of course such relationships are not structured in exactly the same way for everyone. Some parents are casual and easygoing with their children, while others are more formal and reserved. Some doctors want to be friends with at least some of their patients; others are businesslike with all. Moreover, the requirements of social roles may vary from community to community—the role of wife may not require exactly the same sort of behavior in rural Alabama that it does in New York or New Guinea. And the requirements of social roles may change; the women's movement, for example, has made a tremendous impact on our understanding of the husband-wife relationship. The examples that I have been giving are drawn, loosely speaking, from contemporary American society, but this is mainly a matter of convenience. The important point is that however one conceives one's relations with other people, there is inseparable from that conception an idea of how it is appropriate to behave with and around them and what information about oneself it is appropriate for them to have.

Privacy and Personal Relationships

All of this has to do with the way that a crucial part of our lives—our relations with other people—is organized, and as such, its importance to us can hardly be exaggerated. Therefore, we have good reason to object to anything that interferes with these relationships and makes it difficult or impossible for us to maintain them in the way that we want. That is why the loss of privacy is so disturbing. Our ability to control who has access to us and to information about us allows us to maintain the variety of relationships with other people that we want to have.

Consider what happens when close friends are joined by a casual acquaintance. The character of the group changes; one of the changes is that conversation about intimate matters is now out of order. Suppose these friends could never be alone; suppose there were always third parties (let us say casual acquaintances or strangers) intruding. Then they could do either of two things. They could carry on as close friends do, sharing confidences, freely expressing their feelings about things, and so on. But this would mean violating their sense of how it is appropriate to behave around casual acquaintances or strangers. Or they could avoid doing or saying anything that they think inappropriate to do or say around the third party. But this would mean that they could no longer behave with one another in the way that friends do and, further, that, eventually, they would no longer *be* close friends.

Again, consider the differences between the way that a husband and wife behave when they are alone and the way they behave in the company of third parties. Alone, they may be affectionate, sexually intimate, have their fights and quarrels, and so on; but with others, a more "public" face is in order. If they

could never be alone together, they would either have to abandon the relationship that they would otherwise have as husband and wife or else behave in front of others in ways they now deem inappropriate.[5]

These considerations suggest that we need to separate our associations, at least to some extent, if we are to maintain a system of different relationships with different people. Separation allows us to behave with certain people in the way that is appropriate to the sort of relationship we have with them, without at the same time violating our sense of how it is appropriate to behave with, and in the presence of, others with whom we have different kinds of relationships. Thus if we are to be able to control the relationships that we have with other people, we must have control over who has access to us.

We now have an explanation of the value of privacy in ordinary situations in which we have nothing to hide. The explanation is that even in the most common and unremarkable circumstances, we regulate our behavior according to the kinds of relationships we have with the people around us. If we cannot control who has access to us, sometimes including and sometimes excluding various people, then we cannot control the patterns of behavior we need to adopt (this is one reason that privacy is an aspect of liberty) or the kinds of relations with other people that we will have.

What about our feeling that certain facts about us are "nobody else's business"? Here, too, it is useful to consider the nature of our relationships. If someone is our doctor, then it literally is her business to keep track of our health; if someone is our employer, then it literally is his business to know what salary we are paid; our financial dealings literally are the business of the people who extend us credit; and so on. In general, a fact about ourselves is someone's business if there is a specific relationship between us that entitles him to know. We are often free to choose whether or not to enter into such relationships, and those who want to maintain as much privacy as possible will enter them only reluctantly. What we cannot do is accept such a social role with respect to another person and then expect to retain the same degree of privacy relative to him or her that we had before. Thus, if we are asked how much money we have in the bank, we cannot say "It's none of your business" to our banker, prospective creditors, or our spouses. But, at the risk of being boorish, we could say that to others with whom we have no such relationship.

Thomson's View

In an important essay,[6] Judith Jarvis Thomson suggests that the key to understanding the right to privacy is to realize that there is nothing special about it. She suggests, "as a simplifying hypothesis, that the right to privacy is itself a cluster of rights, and that it is not a distinct cluster of rights but itself intersects with the cluster of rights which the right over the person consists of, and also with the cluster of rights which owning property consists of." This is an appealing idea because these other rights seem less puzzling than the right to privacy. Therefore, if the simplifying hypothesis is correct, the right to privacy may be much easier to understand.

Thomson explains that "the right over the person" consists of such "un-grand" rights as the right not to have various parts of one's body looked at, the right not to have one's elbow painted green, and so on. She understands these rights as analogous to property rights. The idea is that our bodies are ours and so we have the same rights with respect to them that we have with respect to our other possessions.

Is this plausible? Is a woman's right to prevent a Peeping Tom from looking at her breasts no different from her right to control who drives her car or who uses her fountain pen? These seem importantly different because the kind of interest we have in controlling who looks at what parts of our bodies is different from the interest we have in our cars or pens. For most of us, physical intimacy is a part of special sorts of personal relationships. Exposing one's knee or one's face to someone does not count for us as physical intimacy, but exposing a breast, and allowing it to be seen and touched, does. Of course the details are to some extent a matter of social convention; it is easy to understand that for a Victorian woman an exposed knee could be a sign of intimacy. She would be right to be distressed at learning that she had left a knee uncovered and that someone was staring at it. By dissociating the body from ideas of physical intimacy and the complex of personal relationships of which such intimacies are a part, we

can make this "right over the body" seem to be an ungrand kind of property right; but that dissociation separates this right from the matters that make privacy important.

Thomson suggests the following case as a possible source of trouble for the simplifying hypothesis:

> Some acquaintances of yours indulge in some very personal gossip about you. Let us imagine that all of the information they share was arrived at without violation of any right of yours, and that none of the participants violates a confidence in telling what he tells. Do they violate a right of yours in sharing the information? If they do, there is trouble for the simplifying hypothesis, for it seems to me there is no right not identical with, or included in, the right to privacy cluster which they could be thought to violate.[7]

But, she adds, this case does not really cause trouble, because the gossips "don't violate any right of yours. It seems to me we simply do not have rights against others that they shall not gossip about us."

This is, as Thomson says, a debatable case, but if our account of why privacy is important is correct, we have at least some reason to think that your right to privacy can be violated in such a case. Let us fill in some details. Suppose you are recently divorced, and the reason your marriage failed is that you became impotent shortly after the wedding. You have shared your troubles with your closest friend, but this is not the sort of thing you want everyone to know. Not only would it be humiliating for everyone to know, it is none of their business. It is the sort of intimate fact about you that is not appropriate for strangers or casual acquaintances to know. But now the gossips have obtained the information. Perhaps one of them innocently overheard your conversation with a friend; it was not his fault, so he did not violate your privacy in the hearing, but then you did not know he was within earshot. And now the gossips are spreading it around to everyone who knows you and to some who do not. Are they violating your right to privacy? Surely they are. If so, it is not surprising, for the interest involved in this case is just the sort of interest that the right to privacy typically protects. Since the right that is violated in this case is not also a property right or a right over the person, the simplifying hypothesis fails. But this should not be surprising, either, for if the right to privacy has a different point than these other rights, we should not expect it always to overlap with them. And even if it did always overlap, we could still regard the right to privacy as a distinctive sort of right in virtue of the special kind of interest it protects.

NOTES

1. *Olmstead v United States*, 277 US 438,478 (1928).
2. John Barth, *End of the Road* (New York: Avon, 1960), 57–58.
3. Dr. Malcolm Todd, quoted in the *Miami Herald*, 26 October 1973, sec. A, p. 18.
4. This is similar to Charles Fried's view of the relation between friendship and privacy in his illuminating book *An Anatomy of Values* (Cambridge: Harvard University Press, 1970).
5. This is from a television program guide in the *Miami Herald*, 21 October 1973, p. 17:

"I think it was one of the most awkward scenes I've ever done," said actress Brenda Benet after doing a romantic scene with her husband, Bill Bixby, in his new NBC-TV series, "The Magician."

"It was even hard to kiss him," she continued. "It's the same old mouth, but it was terrible. I was so abnormally shy; I guess because I don't think it's anybody's business. The scene would have been easier had I done it with a total stranger because that would be real acting. With Bill, it was like being on exhibition."

On the view presented here, it is not "abnormal shyness" or shyness of any type that is behind such feelings. Rather, it is a sense of what is appropriate with and around people with whom one has various sorts of personal relationships. Kissing *another actor* in front of the camera crew, the director, and so on, is one thing; but kissing *one's husband* in front of all these people is quite another thing. What made Ms. Benet's position confusing was that her husband was another actor, and the behavior that was permitted by one relationship was discouraged by the other.

6. Judith Jarvis Thomson, "The Right to Privacy," *Philosophy and Public Affairs* 4 (1975): 295–314.
7. Thomson, "Right to Privacy," 311–12.

Confidentiality in Medicine—A Decrepit Concept

MARK SIEGLER

Siegler points out that in this age of high-technology health care, the traditional ideal of patient-physician confidentiality does not exist in practice. Modern health care involves teams of specialists—medical, financial, governmental, social, and more—and they all require access to, and dissemination of, a great deal of confidential information about patients. These developments seem to be in response to people's demand for better and more comprehensive care. But they also are changing our traditional concept of medical confidentiality. Confidentiality is important because it shows respect for the patient's individuality and privacy and nurtures the bond of trust between patient and doctor.

Medical confidentiality, as it has traditionally been understood by patients and doctors, no longer exists. This ancient medical principle, which has been included in every physician's oath and code of ethics since Hippocratic times, has become old, worn-out, and useless; it is a decrepit concept. Efforts to preserve it appear doomed to failure and often give rise

From *The New England Journal of Medicine*, vol. 307, no. 24, pp. 1518–1521. Copyright © 1982. Reprinted with permission of the Massachusetts Medical Society.

to more problems than solutions. Psychiatrists have tacitly acknowledged the impossibility of ensuring the confidentiality of medical records by choosing to establish a separate, more secret record. The following case illustrates how the confidentiality principle is compromised systematically in the course of routine medical care.

A patient of mine with mild chronic obstructive pulmonary disease was transferred from the surgical intensive-care unit to a surgical nursing floor two days after an elective cholecystectomy. On the day of transfer, the patient saw a respiratory therapist writing in his medical chart (the therapist was recording the results of an arterial blood gas analysis) and became concerned about the confidentiality of his hospital records. The patient threatened to leave the hospital prematurely unless I could guarantee that the confidentiality of his hospital record would be respected.

The patient's complaint prompted me to enumerate the number of persons who had both access to his hospital record and a reason to examine it. I was amazed to learn that at least 25 and possibly as many as 100 health professionals and administrative personnel at our university hospital had access to the patient's record and that all of them had a legitimate need, indeed a professional responsibility, to open and use that chart. These persons included 6 attending physicians (the primary physician, the surgeon, the pulmonary consultant, and others); 12 house officers (medical, surgical, intensive-care unit, and "covering" house staff); 20 nursing personnel (on three shifts); 6 respiratory therapists; 3 nutritionists; 2 clinical pharmacists; 15 students (from medicine, nursing, respiratory therapy, and clinical pharmacy); 4 unit secretaries; 4 hospital financial officers; and 4 chart reviewers (utilization review; quality assurance review, tissue review, and insurance auditor). It is of interest that this patient's problem was straightforward, and he therefore did not require many other technical and support services that the modern hospital provides. For example, he did not need multiple consultants and fellows, such specialized procedures as dialysis, or social workers, chaplains, physical therapists, occupational therapists, and the like.

Upon completing my survey I reported to the patient that I estimated that at least 75 health professionals and hospital personnel had access to his medical record. I suggested to the patient that these people were all involved in providing or supporting his health-care services. They were, I assured him, working for him. Despite my reassurances the patient was obviously distressed and retorted, "I always believed that medical confidentiality was part of a doctor's code of ethics. Perhaps you should tell me just what you people mean by 'confidentiality'!"

Two Aspects of Medical Confidentiality
Confidentiality and Third-Party Interests
Previous discussions of medical confidentiality usually have focused on the tension between a physician's responsibility to keep information divulged by patients secret and a physician's legal and moral duty, on occasion, to reveal such confidences to third parties, such as families, employers, public health authorities, or police authorities. In all these instances, the central question relates to the stringency of the physician's obligation to maintain patient confidentiality when the health, well-being, and safety of identifiable others or of society in general would be threatened by a failure to reveal information about the patient. The tension in such cases is between the good of the patient and the good of others.

Confidentiality and the Patient's Interest
As the example above illustrates, further challenges to confidentiality arise because the patient's personal interest in maintaining confidentiality comes into conflict with his personal interest in receiving the best possible health care. Modern high-technology health care is available principally in hospitals (often, teaching hospitals), requires many trained and specialized workers (a "health-care team"), and is very costly. The existence of such teams means that information that previously had been held in confidence by an individual physician will now necessarily be disseminated to many members of the team. Furthermore, since health-care teams are expensive and few patients can afford to pay such costs directly, it becomes essential to grant access to the patient's medical record to persons who are responsible for obtaining third-party payment. These persons include chart reviewers, financial officers, insurance auditors, and quality-of-care assessors. Finally, as medicine expands from a narrow, disease-based model to a model that encompasses psychological, social, and economic problems, not only will the size of the health-care team and medical costs increase, but more sensitive information (such as one's personal habits and financial condition) will now be included in the medical record and will no longer be confidential.

The point I wish to establish is that hospital medicine, the rise of health-care teams, the existence of third-party insurance programs, and the expanding limits of medicine all appear to be responses to the wishes of people for better and more comprehensive medical care. But each of these developments necessarily modifies our traditional understanding of medical confidentiality.

The Role of Confidentiality in Medicine

Confidentiality serves a dual purpose in medicine. In the first place, it acknowledges respect for the patient's sense of individuality and privacy. The patient's most personal physical and psychological secrets are kept confidential in order to decrease a sense of shame and vulnerability. Secondly, confidentiality is important in improving the patient's health care—a basic goal of medicine. The promise of confidentiality permits people to trust (i.e., have confidence) that information revealed to a physician in the course of a medical encounter will not be disseminated further. In this way patients are encouraged to communicate honestly and forthrightly with their doctors. This bond of trust between patient and doctor is vitally important both in the diagnostic process (which relies on an accurate history) and subsequently in the treatment phase, which often depends as much on the patient's trust in the physician as it does on medications and surgery. These two important functions of confidentiality are as important now as they were in the past. They will not be supplanted entirely either by improvements in medical technology or by recent changes in relations between some patients and doctors toward a rights-based, consumerist model.

Possible Solutions to the Confidentiality Problem

First of all, in all nonbureaucratic, noninstitutional medical encounters—that is, in the millions of doctor-patient encounters that take place in physicians' offices, where more privacy can be preserved—meticulous care should be taken to guarantee that patients' medical and personal information will be kept confidential.

Secondly, in such settings as hospitals or large-scale group practices, where many persons have opportunities to examine the medical record, we should aim to provide access only to those who have "a need to know." This could be accomplished through such administrative changes as dividing the entire record into several sections—for example, a medical and financial section—and permitting only health professionals access to the medical information.

The approach favored by many psychiatrists—that of keeping a psychiatric record separate from the general medical record—is an understandable strategy but one that is not entirely satisfactory and that should not be generalized. The keeping of separate psychiatric records implies that psychiatry and medicine are different undertakings and thus drives deeper the wedge between them and between physical and psychological illness. Furthermore, it is often vitally important for internists or surgeons to know that a patient is being seen by a psychiatrist or is taking a particular medication. When separate records are kept, this information may not be available. Finally, if generalized, the practice of keeping a separate psychiatric record could lead to the unacceptable consequence of having a separate record for each type of medical problem.

Patients should be informed about what is meant by "medical confidentiality." We should establish the distinction between information about the patient that generally will be kept confidential regardless of the interest of third parties and information that will be exchanged among members of the health-care team in order to provide care for the patient. Patients should be made aware of the large number of persons in the modern hospital who require access to the medical record in order to serve the patient's medical and financial interests.

Finally, at some point most patients should have an opportunity to review their medical record and to make informed choices about whether their entire record is to be available to everyone or whether certain portions of the record are privileged and should be accessible only to their principal physician or to others designated explicitly by the patient. This approach would rely on traditional informed-consent procedural standards and might permit the patient to balance the personal value of medical confidentiality against the personal value of high-technology, team health care. There is no reason that the same procedure should not be used with psychiatric records instead of the arbitrary system now employed, in which everything related to psychiatry is kept secret.

Afterthought: Confidentiality and Indiscretion

There is one additional aspect of confidentiality that is rarely included in discussions of the subject. I am referring here to the wanton, often inadvertent, but avoidable exchanges of confidential information that occur frequently in hospital rooms, elevators, cafeterias, doctors' offices, and at cocktail parties. Of course, as more people have access to medical information about the patient the potential for this irresponsible abuse of confidentiality increases geometrically.

Such mundane breaches of confidentiality are probably of greater concern to most patients than the broader issue of whether their medical records may be entered into a computerized data bank or whether a respiratory therapist is reviewing the results of an arterial blood gas determination. Somehow, privacy is violated and a sense of shame is heightened when intimate secrets are revealed to people one knows or is close to—friends, neighbors, acquaintances, or hospital roommates—rather than when they are disclosed to an anonymous bureaucrat sitting at a computer terminal in a distant city or to a health professional who is acting in an official capacity.

I suspect that the principles of medical confidentiality, particularly those reflected in most medical codes of ethics, were designed principally to prevent just this sort of embarrassing personal indiscretion rather than to maintain (for social, political, or economic reasons) the absolute secrecy of doctor-patient communications. In this regard, it is worth noting that Percival's Code of Medical Ethics (1803) includes the following admonition: "Patients should be interrogated concerning their complaint in a tone of voice which cannot be overheard" [Leake, C. D., ed., *Percival's Medical Ethics.* Baltimore: Williams and Wilkins, 1927]. We in the medical profession frequently neglect these simple courtesies.

Conclusion

The principle of medical confidentiality described in medical codes of ethics and still believed in by patients no longer exists. In this respect, it is a decrepit concept. Rather than perpetuate the myth of confidentiality and invest energy vainly to preserve it, the public and the profession would be better served if they devoted their attention to determining which aspects of the original principle of confidentiality are worth retaining. Efforts could then be directed to salvaging those.

Tarasoff v. Regents of the University of California

SUPREME COURT OF CALIFORNIA

In this 1976 case, the court held that the professional duties of confidentiality can be overridden when a patient poses a serious danger to others. It concluded that "the public policy favoring protection of the confidential character of patient-psychotherapist communications must yield to the extent to which disclosure is essential to avert danger to others. The protective privilege ends where the public peril begins."

On October 27, 1969, Prosenjit Poddar killed Tatiana Tarasoff. Plaintiffs, Tatiana's parents, allege that two months earlier Poddar confided his intention to kill Tatiana to Dr. Lawrence Moore, a psychologist employed by the Cowell Memorial Hospital at the University of California at Berkeley. They allege that

Supreme Court of California, 17 Cal.3d 423, July 1, 1976.

on Moore's request, the campus police briefly detained Poddar, but released him when he appeared rational. They further claim that Dr. Harvey Powelson, Moore's superior, then directed that no further action be taken to detain Poddar. No one warned plaintiffs of Tatiana's peril. . . .

Plaintiffs' complaints predicate liability on two grounds: defendants' failure to warn plaintiffs of the impending danger and their failure to bring about Poddar's confinement pursuant to the Lanterman-Petris-Short Act. Defendants, in turn, assert that they owed no duty of reasonable care to Tatiana and that they are immune from suit under the California Tort Claims Act of 1963.

We shall explain that defendant therapists cannot escape liability merely because Tatiana herself was not their patient. When a therapist determines, or pursuant to the standards of his profession should determine, that his patient presents a serious danger of violence to another, he incurs an obligation to use reasonable care to protect the intended victim against such danger. The discharge of this duty may require the therapist to take one or more of various steps, depending upon the nature of the case. Thus it may call for him to warn the intended victim or others likely to apprise the victim of the danger, to notify the police, or to take whatever other steps are reasonably necessary under the circumstances. . . .

Plaintiffs' Complaints

Plaintiffs, Tatiana's mother and father, filed separate but virtually identical second amended complaints. The issue before us on this appeal is whether those complaints now state, or can be amended to state, causes of action against defendants. We therefore begin by setting forth the pertinent allegations of the complaints.

. . . Plaintiffs' first cause of action, entitled "Failure to Detain a Dangerous Patient," alleges that on August 20, 1969, Poddar was a voluntary outpatient receiving therapy at Cowell Memorial Hospital. Poddar informed Moore, his therapist, that he was going to kill an unnamed girl, readily identifiable as Tatiana, when she returned home from spending the summer in Brazil. Moore, with the concurrence of Dr. Gold, who had initially examined Poddar, and Dr. Yandell, assistant to the director of the department of psychiatry, decided that Poddar should be committed for observation in a mental hospital. Moore orally notified Officers Atkinson and Teel of the campus police that he would request commitment. He then sent a letter to Police Chief William Beall requesting the assistance of the police department in securing Poddar's confinement.

Officers Atkinson, Brownrigg, and Halleran took Poddar into custody, but, satisfied that Poddar was rational, released him on his promise to stay away from Tatiana. Powelson, director of the department of psychiatry at Cowell Memorial Hospital, then asked the police to return Moore's letter, directed that all copies of the letter and notes that Moore had taken as therapist be destroyed, and "ordered no action to place Prosenjit Poddar in 72-hour treatment and evaluation facility."

Plaintiffs' second cause of action, entitled "Failure to Warn on a Dangerous Patient," incorporates the allegations of the first cause of action, but adds the assertion that defendants negligently permitted Poddar to be released from police custody without "notifying the parents of Tatiana Tarasoff that their daughter was in grave danger from Prosenjit Poddar." Poddar persuaded Tatiana's brother to share an apartment with him near Tatiana's residence; shortly after her return from Brazil, Poddar went to her residence and killed her.

Plaintiffs' third cause of action, entitled "Abandonment of a Dangerous Patient," seeks $10,000 punitive damages against defendant Powelson. Incorporating the crucial allegations of the first cause of action, plaintiffs charge that Powelson "did the things herein alleged with intent to abandon a dangerous patient, and said acts were done maliciously and oppressively."

Plaintiffs' fourth cause of action, for "Breach of Primary Duty to Patient and the Public," states essentially the same allegations as the first cause of action, but seeks to characterize defendants' conduct as a breach of duty to safeguard their patient and the public. Since such conclusory labels add nothing to the factual allegations of the complaint, the first and fourth causes of action are legally indistinguishable. . . .

. . . We direct our, attention . . . to the issue of whether Plaintiffs' second cause of action can be amended to state a basis for recovery.

Plaintiffs Can State a Cause of Action Against Defendant Therapists for Negligent Failure to Protect Tatiana

The second cause of action can be amended to allege that Tatiana's death proximately resulted from defendants' negligent failure to warn Tatiana or others likely to apprise her of her danger. Plaintiffs contend that as amended, such allegations of negligence and proximate causation, with resulting damages, establish a cause of action. Defendants, however, contend that in the circumstances of the present case they owed no duty of care to Tatiana or her parents and that, in the absence of such duty, they were free to act in careless disregard of Tatiana's life and safety.

In analyzing this issue, we bear in mind that legal duties are not discoverable facts of nature, but merely conclusory expressions that, in cases of a particular type, liability should be imposed for damage done. "The assertion that liability must . . . be denied because defendant bears no 'duty' to plaintiff 'begs the essential question—whether the plaintiff's interests are entitled to legal protection against the defendant's conduct. . . . [Duty] is not sacrosanct in itself, but only an expression of the sum total of those considerations of policy which lead the law to say that the particular plaintiff is entitled to protection.'"

In the landmark case of *Rowland v. Christian* (1968), Justice Peters recognized that liability should be imposed "for an injury occasioned to another by his want of ordinary care or skill" as expressed in section 1714 of the Civil Code. Thus, Justice Peters, quoting from *Heaven v. Pender* (1883) stated: "Whenever one person is by circumstances placed in such a position with regard to another . . . that if he did not use ordinary care and skill in his own conduct . . . he would cause danger of injury to the person or property of the other, a duty arises to use ordinary care and skill to avoid such danger."

We depart from "this fundamental principle" only upon the "balancing of a number of considerations"; major ones "are the foreseeability of harm to the plaintiff, the degree of certainty that the plaintiff suffered injury, the closeness of the connection between the defendant's conduct and the injury suffered, the moral blame attached to the defendant's conduct, the policy of preventing future harm, the extent of the burden to the defendant and consequences to the community of imposing a duty to exercise care with resulting liability for breach, and the availability, cost and prevalence of insurance for the risk involved."

The most important of these considerations in establishing duty is foreseeability. As a general prin-

ciple, a "defendant owes a duty of care to all persons who are foreseeably endangered by his conduct, with respect to all risks which make the conduct unreasonably dangerous." As we shall explain, however, when the avoidance of foreseeable harm requires a defendant to control the conduct of another person, or to warn of such conduct, the common law has traditionally imposed liability only if the defendant bears some special relationship to the dangerous person or to the potential victim. Since the relationship between a therapist and his patient satisfies this requirement, we need not here decide whether foreseeability alone is sufficient to create a duty to exercise reasonable care to protect a potential victim of another's conduct.

Although, as we have stated above, under the common law, as a general rule, one person owed no duty to control the conduct of another nor to warn those endangered by such conduct, the courts have carved out an exception to this rule in cases in which the defendant stands in some special relationship to either the person whose conduct needs to be controlled or in a relationship to the foreseeable victim of that conduct. Applying this exception to the present case, we note that a relationship of defendant therapists to either Tatiana or Poddar will suffice to establish a duty of care; as explained in section 315 of the Restatement Second of Torts, a duty of care may arise from either "(a) a special relation . . . between the actor and the third person which imposes a duty upon the actor to control the third person's conduct, or (b) a special relation . . . between the actor and the other which gives to the other a right of protection."

Although Plaintiffs' pleadings assert no special relation between Tatiana and defendant therapists, they establish as between Poddar and defendant therapists the special relation that arises between a patient and his doctor or psychotherapist. Such a relationship may support affirmative duties for the benefit of third persons. Thus, for example, a hospital must exercise reasonable care to control the behavior of a patient which may endanger other persons. A doctor must also warn a patient if the patient's condition or medication renders certain conduct, such as driving a car, dangerous to others.

Although the California decisions that recognize this duty have involved cases in which the defendant stood in a special relationship *both* to the victim and to the person whose conduct created the danger, we do not think that the duty should logically be constricted to such situations. Decisions of other jurisdictions hold that the single relationship of a doctor to his patient is sufficient to support the duty to exercise reasonable care to protect others against dangers emanating from the patient's illness. The courts hold that a doctor is liable to persons infected by his patient if he negligently fails to diagnose a contagious disease, or having diagnosed the illness, fails to warn members of the patient's family.

Since it involved a dangerous mental patient, the decision in *Merchants Nat. Bank & Trust Co. of Fargo v. United States* (1967) comes closer to the issue. The Veterans Administration arranged for the patient to work on a local farm, but did not inform the farmer of the man's background. The farmer consequently permitted the patient to come and go freely during non-working hours; the patient borrowed a car, drove to his wife's residence and killed her. Notwithstanding the lack of any "special relationship" between the Veterans Administration and the wife, the court found the Veterans Administration liable for the wrongful death of the wife.

In their summary of the relevant rulings Fleming and Maximov conclude that the "case law should dispel any notion that to impose on the therapists a duty to take precautions for the safety of persons threatened by a patient, where due care so requires, is in any way opposed to contemporary ground rules on the duty relationship. On the contrary, there now seems to be sufficient authority to support the conclusion that by entering into a doctor-patient relationship the therapist becomes sufficiently involved to assume some responsibility for the safety, not only of the patient himself, but also of any third person whom the doctor knows to be threatened by the patient." [Fleming & Maximov, *The Patient or His Victim: The Therapist's Dilemma* (1974) 62 Cal. L. Rev. 1025, 1030.]

Defendants contend, however, that imposition of a duty to exercise reasonable care to protect third persons is unworkable because therapists cannot accurately predict whether or not a patient will resort to violence. In support of this argument amicus representing the American Psychiatric Association and other professional societies cites numerous articles which indicate that therapists, in the present state of the art, are unable reliably to predict violent acts; their forecasts, amicus claims, tend consistently to overpredict violence, and indeed are more often wrong than right. Since predictions of violence are often erroneous, amicus concludes, the courts should not render rulings that predicate the liability of therapists upon the validity of such predictions.

The role of the psychiatrist, who is indeed a practitioner of medicine, and that of the psychologist who performs an allied function, are like that of the physician who must conform to the standards of the profession and who must often make diagnoses and predictions based upon such evaluations. Thus the judgment of the therapist in diagnosing emotional disorders and in predicting whether a patient presents a serious danger of violence is comparable to the judgment which doctors and professionals must regularly render under accepted rules of responsibility.

We recognize the difficulty that a therapist encounters in attempting to forecast whether a patient presents a serious danger of violence. Obviously we do not require that the therapist, in making the determination, render a perfect performance; the therapist need only exercise "that reasonable degree of skill, knowledge, and care ordinarily possessed and exercised by members of [that professional specialty] under similar circumstances." Within the broad range of reasonable practice and treatment in which professional opinion and judgment may differ, the therapist is free to exercise his or her own best judgment without liability; proof, aided by hindsight, that he or she judged wrongly is insufficient to establish negligence.

In the instant case, however, the pleadings do not raise any question as to failure of defendant therapists to predict that Poddar presented a serious danger of violence. On the contrary, the present complaints allege that defendant therapists did in fact predict that Poddar would kill, but were negligent in failing to warn.

Amicus contends, however, that even when a therapist does in fact predict that a patient poses a serious danger of violence to others, the therapist should be absolved of any responsibility for failing to act to protect the potential victim. In our view, however, once a therapist does in fact determine, or under applicable professional standards reasonably should have determined, that a patient poses a serious danger of violence to others, he bears a duty to exercise reasonable care to protect the foreseeable victim of that danger. While the discharge of this duty of due care will necessarily vary with the facts of each case, in each instance the adequacy of the therapist's conduct must be measured against the traditional negligence standard of the rendition of reasonable care under the circumstances. As explained in Fleming and Maximov, *The Patient or His Victim: The Therapist's Dilemma* (1974), ". . . the ultimate question of resolving the tension between the conflicting interests of patient and potential victim is one of social policy, not professional expertise. . . . In sum, the therapist owes a legal duty not only to his patient, but also to his patient's would-be victim and is subject in both respects to scrutiny by judge and jury. . . ."

The risk that unnecessary warnings may be given is a reasonable price to pay for the lives of possible victims that may be saved. We would hesitate to hold that the therapist who is aware that his patient expects to attempt to assassinate the President of the United States would not be obligated to warn the authorities because the therapist cannot predict with accuracy that his patient will commit the crime.

Defendants further argue that free and open communication is essential to psychotherapy; that "unless a patient . . . is assured that . . . information [revealed by him] can and will be held in utmost confidence, he will be reluctant to make the full disclosure upon which diagnosis and treatment . . . depends." The giving of a warning, defendants contend, constitutes a breach of trust which entails the revelation of confidential communications.

We recognize the public interest in supporting effective treatment of mental illness and in protecting the rights of patients to privacy and the consequent public importance of safeguarding the confidential character of psychotherapeutic communication. Against this interest, however, we must weigh the public interest in safety from violent assault. The Legislature has undertaken the difficult task of balancing the countervailing concerns. In Evidence Code section 1014, it established a broad rule of privilege

to protect confidential communications between patient and psychotherapist. In Evidence Code section 1024, the Legislature created a specific and limited exception to the psychotherapist-patient privilege: "There is no privilege . . . if the psychotherapist has reasonable cause to believe that the patient is in such mental or emotional condition as to be dangerous to himself or to the person or property of another and that disclosure of the communication is necessary to prevent the threatened danger."

We realize that the open and confidential character of psychotherapeutic dialogue encourages patients to express threats of violence, few of which are ever executed. Certainly a therapist should not be encouraged routinely to reveal such threats; such disclosures could seriously disrupt the patient's relationship with his therapist and with the persons threatened. To the contrary, the therapist's obligations to his patient require that he not disclose a confidence unless such disclosure is necessary to avert danger to others, and even then that he do so discreetly, and in a fashion that would preserve the privacy of his patient to the fullest extent compatible with the prevention of the threatened danger.

The revelation of a communication under the above circumstances is not a breach of trust or a violation of professional ethics; as stated in the Principles of Medical Ethics of the American Medical Association (1957), section 9: "A physician may not reveal the confidence entrusted to him in the course of medical attendance . . . *unless he is required to do so by law or unless it becomes necessary in order to protect the welfare of the individual or of the community.*" (Emphasis added.) We conclude that the public policy favoring protection of the confidential character of patient-psychotherapist communications must yield to the extent to which disclosure is essential to avert danger to others. The protective privilege ends where the public peril begins.

Our current crowded and computerized society compels the interdependence of its members. In this risk-infested society we can hardly tolerate the further exposure to danger that would result from a concealed knowledge of the therapist that his patient was lethal. If the exercise of reasonable care to protect the threatened victim requires the therapist to warn the endangered party or those who can reasonably be expected to notify him, we see no sufficient societal interest that would protect and justify concealment. The containment of such risks lies in the public interest. For the foregoing reasons, we find that Plaintiffs' complaints can be amended to state a cause of action against defendants Moore, Powelson, Gold, and Yandell and against the Regents as their employer, for breach of a duty to exercise reasonable care to protect Tatiana. . . .

CHAPTER 5

Informed Consent

Most who have thought carefully about the issue believe that there is more to the ethics of doctor-patient relationships than just a regard for truthfulness and confidentiality. A larger, more complex notion often guides such interactions: **informed consent**. At the simplest level, the term refers to the action of an autonomous, informed person agreeing to submit to medical treatment or experimentation. The idea arises from the intuition that patients, as autonomous persons, should have the ultimate say in what is done to their bodies, that they ought not to be treated without their voluntary, informed agreement. Informed consent, then, is thought to be an ethical ideal in which physicians are obligated to tell patients about possible medical interventions and to respect their choices regarding them. It is also a legal requirement, compelling health care providers to disclose information about interventions to patients and obtain their permission before proceeding. (Requirements of informed consent also apply to researchers and research subjects, as discussed in Chapter 6.) The ethical ideal has often proved difficult to define precisely, to apply in real-life cases, and to embody effectively in laws and policies. But among most health care professionals and many of the patients they serve, there is little doubt about its importance and influence.

AUTONOMY AND CONSENT

Philosophers and other thinkers have justified informed consent through appeals to the principles of autonomy and beneficence. The principle of autonomy tells us that we should respect people's capacity for self-determination. To ac-

cept this standard is to reject strong medical paternalism, in which physicians or nurses decide unilaterally what is best for patients. Honoring the principle means letting patients voluntarily choose—even when their choices conflict with medical advice. The principle of beneficence urges physicians and nurses to promote patient welfare, and this goal is thought to be consistent with respecting patient autonomy. Thus bioethicists argue that informed consent promotes the good for patients because knowledgeable, autonomous patients who choose for themselves will advance their own best interests as they themselves conceive them. They will likely avoid unacceptable risks, protect themselves from abuses, and comply with the demands of their chosen treatment.

The ethical underpinnings of informed consent may be old and revered, but the concept as we know it today is young. Throughout most of medical history, devoted physicians practiced the healing arts while paying little attention to notions of patient self-determination and full disclosure. Beginning in the early twentieth century, judicial rulings began to challenge that approach bit by bit. The 1914 case *Schloendorff v. Society of New York Hospital* made it clear that "Every human being of adult years and sound mind has a right to determine what shall be done with his own body," but there was no suggestion that any consent had to be informed.[1] Simple consent was sufficient. Not until 1957 in the California court case *Salgo v. Leland Stanford Junior University Board of Trustees* was the physician's disclosure of information firmly tied to the patient's consent. In a ruling that concocted the term "informed consent," the court held that "a physician violates his duty to his patient and subjects himself to liability if he withholds any facts which are necessary to form the basis of an intelligent consent by the patient to the proposed treatment."[2] In the 1960s other cases went further by identifying the basic features of informed consent: the patient's voluntary consent informed by physicians who have a duty to disclose information about the patient's illness, the proposed treatment, its risks and benefits, and treatment alternatives (including no treatment at all).

These rulings still left many unanswered questions about the legal doctrine, most conspicuous among them being how to judge the adequacy of the physician's disclosure. The prevailing view in the early rulings was that disclosure is adequate if it meets the customary standards of medical practice. Information given to patients is sufficient if the medical profession considers it sufficient. But in the 1970s, courts began to insist that the adequacy of disclosure should be judged by what patients themselves find relevant to their situation. The most influential ruling of this kind came in 1972 in the U.S. Court of Appeals case *Canterbury v. Spence.* "The scope of the physician's communication to the patient, then," says Judge Robinson, "must be measured by the patient's need, and that need is the information material to the decision."[3]

Despite such judicial clarifications (and the enactment of countless statutes and institutional policies), much about informed consent remains unsettled—and unsettling. For one thing, many critics see huge discrepancies between the ethical ideal of informed consent and the laws or rules meant to implement it. They know, for example, that too often a patient can sign a form disclosing treatment risks and thereby, according to local law and institutional policy, grant her informed consent. But she may be neither informed nor autonomous and may not intend to consent to anything. Laws and policies may require physicians merely to warn patients of the risks of treatment, a thin imitation of bone fide informed consent. Some observers also decry the gap between theory and everyday medical practice, contending that physicians view informed consent as a bureaucratic or legalistic burden instead of a way to promote patient self-determination and well-being. As one critic put it, "the idea of physicians making decisions *for*, rather than *with*, patients, is still deeply embedded in the ideology of medical professionalism."[4]

CONDITIONS OF INFORMED CONSENT

Theorists break down informed consent into components believed to be necessary to the concept. Typically, they maintain that an informed consent exists if and only if (1) the patient is *competent* to decide, (2) she gets an adequate *disclosure* of information, (3) she *understands* the information, (4) she decides about the treatment *voluntarily*, and (5) she *consents* to the treatment.[5] This analysis seems straightforward enough, but complications (and controversy) ensue when we try to specify precisely what these conditions entail and to apply them to real-life cases.

As it pertains to informed consent, **competence** is very roughly the ability to render decisions about medical interventions. Individuals who are incompetent in this sense cannot give their informed consent, in which case the burden of decision-making falls to a surrogate (often a court-appointed guardian or a proxy selected through the patient's advance directive). Most of the time, however, people are presumed to be competent unless there are good reasons to think otherwise. Patients are often judged incompetent in cases of mental retardation, dementia, psychosis, alcoholism, and minority (being underage). But they may also be thought incompetent in less clear-cut situations—when they are overwhelmed by fear or pain, for instance. In addition, they are sometimes considered incompetent because they lack only one or two particular mental capacities—for example, the ability to communicate a decision, to understand the implications of a choice, to provide reasons, to explain decision-making, or to understand disclosed information. Still, incompetence is not necessarily total, or global; it may be specific to particular aspects of life. A woman who has been legally declared incompetent to handle her personal finances may be fully competent to give her informed consent. A man who has been involuntarily institutionalized for mental illness may still be able to make decisions regarding his medical treatment.

Sometimes a court will formally determine someone to be incompetent. But in most cases, the judicial system never gets involved, and the task of making informal determinations of incompetence goes to physicians (often in consultation with the patient's family).

To give their informed consent, competent patients must receive an adequate disclosure of information from physicians—but what is an adequate disclosure? What kind and amount of information is sufficient? The ethical doctrine of informed consent says that disclosure is adequate if it allows patients to weigh intelligently the risks and benefits of available choices. But how to achieve this ideal in practice is not obvious. Early court decisions suggested that physicians should be the arbiters of adequate disclosure (the physician-based standard); later rulings insisted that adequate disclosure is whatever satisfies the information needs of a hypothetically reasonable person (the patient-based standard); and others called for a subjective standard in which disclosure is supposed to be based on the information needs of a particular patient. But a purely physician-based standard for disclosure would ignore the patient's needs for information relevant to her own personal decisions. The kind of disclosure suitable for a hypothetically reasonable person would probably be very difficult to determine—and might, like the physician-based standard, impose disclosure criteria that have little to do with the information requirements of a particular patient. And an entirely subjective standard naively assumes that patients can always decide for themselves what facts they do and do not need to evaluate treatment options. Some courts have combined these standards, but

no configuration of requirements has been entirely true to the spirit of informed consent.

Despite these difficulties, courts and legislatures have generally mandated the disclosure of several pieces of important information:

1. The nature of the procedure (for example, whether it is a test or treatment, whether it is invasive, and how long it will take to perform)
2. The risks of the procedure (what kind of risks are involved, their seriousness, their probability of occurring, and when they might happen)
3. The alternatives to the proposed procedure—including the option of no treatment (includes information on the options' nature, risks, and benefits)
4. The expected benefits of the proposed treatment—including their extent and their likelihood of being achieved

Physicians are not obligated to provide disclosure in all situations; the duty of physicians to obtain informed consent has exceptions. Disclosure is often dispensed with in emergencies when stopping to obtain consent could seriously harm the patient. As suggested earlier, informed consent is not required when a patient is incompetent. Neither is it obligatory in cases of **waiver**, the patient's voluntary and deliberate giving up of the right to informed consent. It is an exercise in autonomous choice—the choice not to choose or decide. Authority to decide medical issues is turned over to the physician or surrogates. A much more controversial exception is **therapeutic privilege**, the withholding of relevant information from a patient when the physician believes disclosure would likely do harm. The idea behind it is that some patients are so distraught, depressed, or weak that disclosure could make their condition worse. Laws regarding therapeutic privilege vary on when invoking it is justified, with some allowing it only when disclosure would be extremely dangerous for the patient or when it would seriously diminish the patient's

IN DEPTH
TWO VIEWS OF INFORMED CONSENT

While agreeing on the value of informed consent, theorists have differed on its core meaning. For example, some define informed consent as "autonomous authorization," and others seem to equate it with "shared decision-making." Consider these contrasting views:

> [The President's] Commission . . . believes that "shared decisionmaking" is the appropriate ideal for patient-professional relationships that a sound doctrine of informed consent should support. . . . [The doctor-patient interaction] should, at a minimum, provide the patient with a basis for effective participation in sound decision-making. . . . It will usually consist of discussions between professional and patient that bring the knowledge, concerns, and perspective of each to the process of seeking agreement on a course of treatment. Simply put, this means that the physician or other health professional invites the patient to participate in a dialogue in which the professional seeks to help the patient understand the medical situation and available courses of ac-

tion, and the patient conveys his or her concerns and wishes. This does not involve a mechanical recitation of abstruse medical information, but should include disclosures that give the patient an understanding of his or her condition and an appreciation of its consequences.[6]

> The idea of informed consent suggests that a patient or subject does more than express agreement with, acquiesce in, yield to, or comply with an arrangement or a proposal. He or she actively *authorizes* the proposal in the act of consent. John may *assent* to a treatment plan without authorizing it. The assent may be a mere submission to the doctor's authoritative order, in which case John does not call on his *own* authority in order to give permission, and thus does not authorize the plan. Instead, he acts like a child who submits, yields, or assents to the school principal's spanking and in no way gives permission for or authorizes the spanking. . . . There is of course an historical relationship in clinical medicine between medical decisionmaking and informed consent. The emergence of the legal doctrine of informed consent was instrumental in drawing attention to issues of decisionmaking as well as authority in the doctor-patient relationship. Nevertheless, it is a confusion to treat informed consent and shared decisionmaking as anything like *synonymous*.[7]

---

autonomy. Others permit physicians far more leeway in deciding when to claim the privilege.

Critics worry that too many physicians use therapeutic privilege when they should in fact tell patients the facts and that overuse of it can undo informed consent. In any case, informed consent seems to imply that physicians should not use therapeutic privilege merely to avoid giving patients unpleasant news or to prevent them from rejecting a treatment.

It seems obvious that there can be no informed consent unless patients understand the information disclosed to them (although the

law is equivocal on this point). But it is less clear what such understanding amounts to. At a minimum, informed consent seems to require that patients be able to take in the relevant information and assess it well enough to appreciate the consequences of their choices. They need not completely fathom all the information given, but they should comprehend what is most relevant to their decision. And their refusal to submit to a recommended treatment should not be taken as evidence of a lack of understanding.

Of course, impediments to sufficient understanding abound. It can be deficient if physicians

LEGAL BRIEF

Important Informed Consent Cases

- *Schloendorff v. Society of New York Hospital (1914)*—Justice Cardozo underscored the value of patient self-determination and voluntary consent, declaring that "every human being of adult years and sound mind has a right to determine what shall be done with his body."
- *Salgo v. Leland Stanford Jr. University Board of Trustees (1957)*—The California Supreme Court found that physicians "have the duty to disclose any facts which are necessary to form the basis of an intelligent consent by the patient to proposed treatment."

- *Natanson v. Kline* (1960) and *Mitchell v. Robinson* (1960)—These decisions further specified the information to be conveyed to patients, insisting that the risks involved in a medical procedure should be disclosed.
- *Cobb v. Grant* (1972)—The California Supreme Court held that disclosure must consist of "all information relevant to a meaningful decisional process."
- *Canterbury v. Spence* (1972)—The U.S. Court of Appeals ruled that the adequacy of disclosure by a physician should not be judged by what the medical profession thinks is appropriate but by what information the patient finds relevant to his or her decision.

overload the patient with information or frame it in misleading ways (by playing up minimal benefits while playing down significant risks, for instance). The patient's ability to process or appreciate information can be shattered by fear, denial, wishful thinking, magical thinking, and false beliefs. But these problems do not show that acquiring an understanding sufficient for informed consent is impossible—only that it can be difficult and that physicians cannot assume that mere disclosure is enough.

The consent of an informed, competent, understanding patient cannot be legitimate unless it is given voluntarily—that is, freely, without undue (autonomy-robbing) pressure from others. Coercion and manipulation are the most obvious examples of such pressure. Some philosophers have plausibly defined coercion as the intentional use of "a credible and severe threat of harm or force to control another."[8] We might therefore judge a patient to be coerced if her doctor threatens to abandon her unless she submits to treatment, or if he plays on her fear of disability to get her to be more cooperative. Manipulation refers to many noncoercive ways of controlling someone's actions—for example, giv-

ing false or misleading information or withholding relevant facts. The use of therapeutic privilege to control a patient's decisions is, of course, manipulative—and corrosive to informed consent. But note that these forms of undue pressure can come not just from health care providers, but also from the patient's family and friends.

Everyday life is filled with social influences on our actions, beliefs, and reasoning. But these pressures are typically not so powerful that they overwhelm our autonomy. Likewise, physicians can influence patients through reasoning, emotional appeals, and authority—yet these pressures are not necessarily undue. In any given case, the line may be difficult to draw between pressures that render consent involuntary and those that do not.

In the ethical ideal, consent is more than assent—more than the patient's giving into the physician's wishes or doing what is expected. As several theorists have insisted, it is a kind of authorization to proceed with a course of action. When a patient authorizes her physician to treat her, she does not merely say yes, but autonomously, knowledgeably decides and *assumes responsibility* for the decision.[9] Actual practice, however, usually falls far short of the ideal, with form-signing and acquiescence substituting for free, informed authorization.

APPLYING MAJOR THEORIES

In what light would the major moral theories have us view informed consent? To ask a more precise question, would they require physicians to obtain informed consent before treating patients? Utilitarianism wants us to judge actions involving informed consent by the overall good they would produce, everyone considered. For an act-utilitarian, this standard must be applied to each individual case, and whether a physician should try to obtain informed consent depends on the benefits generated for all concerned (patient, medical providers, family, and others). There is both good and bad to weigh. Providing relevant information to the patient and seeking her authorization for treatment might reduce her anxiety and depression, increase her compliance and cooperation, enhance her satisfaction with treatment, or encourage her to be actively involved in her own care. But the process might also frighten or confuse her, force her to make decisions that she would rather leave to the physician, prompt her to choose a treatment judged by her physician not to be in her best interests, or take up too much of the physician's time. Forgoing the process altogether might also exact a toll in patient confusion, anxiety, and depression, and there would be the possibility of an erosion of trust between doctor and patient and, in the worst scenarios of mistrust, lawsuits.

So by act-utilitarian lights, in some instances a physician may be obliged to obtain informed consent, but in others she may be justified in ignoring it, even invoking therapeutic privilege. On this view, though informed consent may be frequently used, it is not a moral requirement.

A rule-utilitarian might conclude that the best overall consequences would be achieved if physicians consistently followed a rule requiring informed consent (except in a few extraordinary circumstances). In some cases, adhering to the rule might have worse results than ignoring it, but overall it would produce the greatest good for patients, physicians, nurses, and the medical profession.

The requirement of informed consent can be derived directly from Kantian ethics. As autonomous beings, people are entitled to respect, to be treated as ends in themselves, never merely as a means to an end. They therefore cannot be subjected to medical treatment just because physicians believe it is in their best interests. They must voluntarily consent to be treated, and for the choice to be fully autonomous, they must be informed truthfully about what is involved. To lie to them, withhold relevant information from them, coerce them, or manipulate them is to treat them merely as a means.

From a strictly Kantian viewpoint, therapeutic privilege is never permissible, but waiver is allowed because it represents an autonomous choice not to choose. Some theorists make an exception to these restrictions if the therapeutic privilege or other manipulative tactic is used to help restore or enhance a person's autonomy.

Rawls' contract theory calls for equal liberties for all, a demand that seems to support the doctrine of informed consent. Treating people without their informed authorization would be a violation of such liberties, and manipulation and coercion to obtain consent would be impermissible. This would be the case even if treating a few patients without informed consent would somehow benefit all of society.

KEY TERMS
competence
informed consent
therapeutic privilege
waiver

SUMMARY
Informed consent refers to the action of an autonomous, informed person agreeing to submit to medical treatment or experimentation. It is a powerful notion that thinkers have justified by appealing to the principles of autonomy and

Jerry Canterbury

How much are physicians obligated to disclose to patients, and by what standard should the adequacy of the disclosure be judged? In 1972 some answers came in the turning-point case *Canterbury v. Spence*.

Nineteen-year-old Jerry Canterbury entered the hospital for tests to determine the cause of the excruciating pain he felt between his shoulder blades. He had been in pain for months, and the prescription medications he had been taking weren't helping. Dr. William Spence ordered a myelogram, an x-ray of the spinal column taken after the column is injected with a traceable dye. After seeing the test results, Dr. Spence told Canterbury that the problem was probably a ruptured disk, and he recommended surgery on the spinal column to correct the problem. Canterbury consented to the procedure.

After the operation, he seemed to be recovering normally, but then he fell in the hospital and became paralyzed from the waist down. He learned later that paralysis was a possible risk of the kind of surgery he had undergone, but Dr. Spence had not mentioned it. Eventually he regained some muscle control but, even years later, needed crutches to walk and suffered from paralysis of the bowels and urinary incontinence.

Canterbury sued Dr. Spence for failure to tell him before the surgery of the risk of paralysis, and the court found in his favor, marking out some tenets of informed consent along the way. The court strongly affirmed the doctrine and the rationale upon which it rests:

> True consent to what happens to one's self is the informed exercise of a choice, and that entails an opportunity to evaluate knowledgeably the options available and the risks attendant upon each. The average patient has little or no understanding of the medical arts, and ordinarily has only his physician to whom he can look for enlightenment with which to reach an intelligent decision. From these almost axiomatic considerations

springs the need, and in turn the requirement, of a reasonable divulgence by physician to patient to make such a decision possible.... And it is evident that it is normally impossible to obtain a consent worthy of the name unless the physician first elucidates the options and the perils for the patient's edification.[10]

In a departure from most other rulings on informed consent, the court declared that the standard for judging whether a physician's disclosure is acceptable should not be the customary practices of physicians but the patient's requirements for pertinent information. In many situations, the court said, no relevant customary practice may exist, and—more importantly—to let the professional customs of physicians decide is to undermine the patient's right of self-determination. The rights and needs of patients set the bar:

> In our view, the patient's right of self-decision shapes the boundaries of the duty to reveal. That right can be effectively exercised only if the patient possesses enough information to enable an intelligent choice. The scope of the physician's communications to the patient, then, must be measured by the patient's need, and that need is the information material to the decision. Thus the test for determining whether a particular peril must be divulged is its materiality to the patient's decision: all risks potentially affecting the decision must be unmasked.[11]

The court characterized the test as what a reasonable person would likely need to know to make an informed decision about a proposed treatment.

Nevertheless, the judges recognized that the physician's invoking of therapeutic privilege (withholding information) is sometimes reasonable and proper. But they rejected "the paternalistic notion that the physician may remain silent simply because divulgence might prompt the patient to forgo therapy the physician feels the patient really needs."[12] Dr. Spence had cited this very notion in his defense.

Some have accused the court of being unclear on the issues of therapeutic privilege and the customary-practice standard of disclosure. But whether or not that's true, *Canterbury v. Spence* helped delineate essential features of the doctrine of informed consent that are now widely accepted. After *Canterbury*, there seemed no going back to the old ideas about disclosure.

---

beneficence. Court decisions have helped to establish the doctrine in law and society, most notably the case of *Canterbury v. Spence*, which asserted that the adequacy of disclosure by physicians should be judged by what patients think is relevant to their situations.

Theorists maintain that an informed consent exists if and only if (1) the patient is competent to decide, (2) she gets an adequate disclosure of information, (3) she understands the information, (4) she decides about the treatment voluntarily, and (5) she consents to the treatment. Competence is the ability to render decisions about medical interventions. Incompetent patients cannot give their informed consent and must rely on surrogates. What constitutes an adequate disclosure of information to patients is controversial, but the courts have generally ruled that disclosure must include information about the nature of the procedure, its risks, its alternatives (including no treatment), and its expected benefits.

Informed consent is not obligatory in cases of waiver, the patient's voluntary and deliberate giving up of the right to informed consent. It is an exercise in autonomous choice; authority to decide medical issues is turned over to the physician or surrogates. A controversial exception to informed consent is therapeutic privilege, the withholding of relevant information from a patient when the physician believes disclosure would likely do harm. Laws regarding therapeutic privilege vary on when invoking it is justified, with some allowing it only when disclosure would be extremely dangerous for the patient or when it would seriously diminish the patient's autonomy. Others permit physicians far more leeway in deciding when to claim the privilege.

An act-utilitarian would judge whether a physician should try to obtain informed consent according to the benefits generated for all concerned. A rule-utilitarian might conclude that the best overall consequences would be achieved if physicians consistently followed a rule requiring informed consent. In Kantian ethics, informed consent is an absolute requirement, and therapeutic privilege is never permissible. Rawls' contract theory seems to support the doctrine of informed consent. Treating people without their informed authorization would be a violation of basic liberties.

Cases for Evaluation

CASE 1

Informed Consent or Not?

A 64-year-old woman with multiple sclerosis (MS) is hospitalized. The team feels she may need to be placed on a feeding tube soon to assure adequate nourishment. They ask the patient about this in the morning and she agrees. However, in the evening (before the tube has been placed), the patient becomes disoriented and seems confused about her decision to have the feeding tube placed. She tells the team she doesn't want it in. They revisit the question in the morning, when the patient is again lucid. Unable to recall her state of mind from the previous evening, the patient again agrees to the procedure.*

Explain your answers: Has the woman given her informed consent? Should she be judged competent? Should her final agreement to the procedure be sufficient to establish informed consent, or should her earlier waffling and confusion also be taken into account?

---

*"Informed Consent," *Ethics in Medicine* (University of Washington School of Medicine), http://depts.washington.edu/bioethx/topics/consent.html (17 November 2007).

CASE 2

Informed Consent and Organ Transplants

(AP)—A woman in her 30s who is one of the four organ transplant patients [who became] infected with HIV and hepatitis [because of the transplant] was not told that the infected donor was high risk, and had previously rejected another donor "because of his lifestyle," her attorney said.

Attorney Thomas Demetrio filed a petition Thursday in Cook County Circuit Court on behalf of the woman, asking officials to keep a hospital and an organ procurement center from destroying or altering any records involving the donation.

"She's really a mess right now," Demetrio said of the Chicago-area woman. "She's still in shock."

The patient, identified in court documents as Jane Doe, received a kidney transplant at the University of Chicago Medical Center on Jan. 9, Demetrio said.

Gift of Hope Organ & Tissue Donor Network in Elmhurst and the University of Chicago both knew the kidney donor was high-risk and did not inform the patient, Demetrio said.

University of Chicago spokesman John Easton responded in an e-mail: "We believe we follow

guidelines, and of course with the patient's consent we will provide necessary records and documents, as is consistent with our open process."

Gift of Hope did not immediately respond to requests for comment.

The woman had been told the donor was a healthy young man, her attorney said. But on Tuesday, hospital officials disclosed to the woman that he was actually high-risk, a 38-year-old gay man, Demetrio said. CDC guidelines say that gay men who are sexually active should not be used as organ donors unless the patient is in imminent danger of death.

The woman was told she had HIV and hepatitis on Nov. 1, he said.

"The (organ) procurement group knew, the hospital knew, but the most important person did not know," he said. "The people that dedicate their lives to these transplant surgeries, they're just great people, but they need to bring the patient into the mix and let them make an informed decision."

U.S. Centers for Disease Control and Prevention guidelines were violated twice, the attorney said. One violation was not informing the woman about the donor's status and then not testing her afterward for HIV until just recently, after HIV and hepatitis were found during tests on another patient who was being evaluated for a second transplant. . . .

She's been started on an HIV drug regimen "and unfortunately one of the side effects is it's not good for the kidneys," Demetrio said. She's not hospitalized.

Dr. Dan Berger, medical director of a large HIV-AIDS clinic in Chicago, said U.S. doctors have had several years of experience treating HIV-infected patients who went on to get transplant organs. Such patients need an HIV specialist and a transplant specialist to monitor their medications, which include anti-rejection drugs for the transplant and antiretrovirals for HIV, he said.

The four patients infected by the high-risk donor's organs have extra medical concerns, Berger said.

"When a patient first becomes infected with HIV there's a huge spike in viral load and (at the same time) severe immune compromise," he said. "The fact that they also are on immune-suppressive medications (after transplant) may put them at extreme risk for opportunistic infection."*

If Jane Doe had not become infected with HIV and hepatitis after her transplant, would the failure of the donor network and the university to fully inform her about the donor have been morally wrong? If so, why? Would her consenting to the transplant have been permissible if she had known that the donor was high risk? Should a patient have the right to consent to and undergo risky treatments? Explain.

---

*The Associated Press, "Atty: Woman Wasn't Told Donor Was a Risk," 16 November 2007.

CASE 3
Adolescent Informed Consent

In mid-summer, a 14-year-old youth was brought to the pediatric emergency department by his mother for evaluation for altered mental status. The mother returned from work to find her son acting strangely. She had last seen him the previous evening, and there were no problems or complaints at that time. Earlier in the week the child had sustained several mosquito bites. The child was now at times lethargic and at other times agitated. There were two episodes of vomiting. There was no history of fever trauma, medications, or known ingestions. The medical history was negative. The social history was significant for a high-achieving honor student who came from a very financially successful household. Physical examination revealed a drowsy and disoriented athletic male. The vital signs were temperature of 37.8° Celsius, heart rate of 107 beats per minute, respiratory rate of 20 per minute, and blood pressure of 123/87 mm Hg. The general physical examination was unremarkable. The neurologic examination revealed a disoriented teenager with ataxia, brisk reflexes throughout, reactive pupils, and intact cranial nerves II through XII. A bedside glucose test and pulse oximetry were both normal. Given the ongoing epidemic of West Nile virus at the time of presentation, the mother was convinced that the child

had contracted the insect-borne disease because of the combination of mosquito bites and altered mental status. The mother was absolutely insistent that a spinal tap (lumbar puncture) be performed immediately, to evaluate for the possibility of West Nile virus.

The patient's pediatrician was also concerned and requested a full and thorough evaluation. An intravenous line was started and routine blood evaluations were ordered. The patient seemed at times to be more lucid, but at other times was again disoriented. When interviewed alone, he denied having West Nile virus, but he agreed to tell the physician why he believed this to be the case, but only if his parents were not told. The physician explained that all information given by the patient would be kept in strict confidence. Because of the assurance of confidentiality, the patient disclosed that he had bought a large amount of dextromethorphan on the Internet and had taken it with his friends after school.

Dextromethorphan ingestion, even in large quantities, generally does not require anything but supportive care. The mother, not knowing about the ingestion of this drug, continued to be insistent that further tests be performed, including a spinal tap.*

Who, if anyone, in this scenario should be allowed to give informed consent to treatment (or no treatment)? Why? Should the physician regard the 14-year-old as a mature minor? What actions should the physician take if she regarded him as a mature minor? What actions would the physician likely take if she decided to set aside the issue of informed consent and act only in the patient's best interests?

---

*Reza Keshavarz, "Adolescents, Informed Consent and Confidentiality: A Case Study," *The Mount Sinai Journal of Medicine* 72.4 (4 July 2005), 232–35.

FURTHER READING

Jessica W. Berg et al., *Informed Consent: Legal Theory and Clinical Practice* (New York: Oxford University Press, 2001).

Tom L. Beauchamp and James F. Childress, "The Meaning and Justification of Informed Consent," in *Principles of*

Biomedical Ethics, 5th ed. (New York: Oxford University Press, 2001), 77–98.

President's Commission for the Study of Ethical Problems in Medicine and Biomedical and Behavioral Research, *Making Health Care Decisions,* vol. 1: *Report* (Washington, DC: Government Printing Office, 1982), 2–6, 41–46.

Robert Young, "Informed Consent and Patient Autonomy," in *A Companion to Bioethics,* ed. Helga Kuhse and Peter Singer (Oxford: Blackwell, 2001), 441–51.

NOTES

1. *Schloendorff v. Society of New York Hospitals,* 105 N.E. 92 (N.Y. 1914).

2. *Salgo v. Leland Stanford Jr. Univ. Bd. of Trustees,* 317 P.2d 170 (Cal. Ct. App. 1957).

3. *Canterbury v. Spence,* 464F.2d 772 (D.C. Cir. 1972).

4. Jay Katz, "Informed Consent to Medical Entrepreneurialism," in *Conflicts of Interest in Clinical Practice and Research,* ed. R. G. Speece et al. (New York: Oxford University Press, 1996).

5. Tom L. Beauchamp and James F. Childress, *Principles of Biomedical Ethics,* 5th ed. (New York: Oxford University Press, 2001), 79–80.

6. President's Commission for the Study of Ethical Problems in Medicine and Biomedical and Behavioral Research, *Making Health Care Decisions,* vol. 1: *Report* (Washington, DC: Government Printing Office, 1982), 38.

7. Ruth R. Faden and Tom L. Beauchamp, "The Concept of Informed Consent," in *A History and Theory of Informed Consent* (New York: Oxford University Press, 1986), 235–73.

8. Beauchamp and Childress, *Principles,* 94.

9. *Ibid.,* 77–79; Jessica W. Berg et al., *Informed Consent: Legal Theory and Clinical Practice* (New York: Oxford University Press, 2001), 15–17.

10. *Canterbury v. Spence.*

11. *Canterbury v. Spence.*

12. *Canterbury v. Spence.*

READINGS

The Concept of Informed Consent

RUTH R. FADEN AND TOM L. BEAUCHAMP

Faden and Beauchamp distinguish two common views of informed consent and argue that only one of them reflects the true meaning of the concept. Real informed consent involves more than a patient's merely agreeing to, or acquiescing in, some suggested course of action. An informed consent is a patient's autonomous action that *authorizes* a course of action. The other common meaning of the term is defined legally or institutionally and does not refer to autonomous authorization. Faden and Beauchamp also believe that the tendency to equate informed consent with shared decision-making is confused. Decision-making, which has been linked historically to informed consent, is not enough.

What is an informed consent? Answering this question is complicated because there are two common, entrenched, and starkly different meanings of "informed consent." That is, the term is analyzable in

From *A History and Theory of Informed Consent* by Ruth R. Faden and Tom L. Beauchamp, pp. 276–86. Copyright © 1986 Oxford University Press, reprinted with permission.

two profoundly different ways—not because of mere subtle differences of connotation that appear in different contexts, but because two different *conceptions* of informed consent have emerged from its history and are still at work, however unnoticed, in literature on the subject.

In one sense, which we label *sense₁,* "informed consent" is analyzable as a particular kind of action by individual patients and subjects: an autonomous authorization. In the second sense, *sense₂*, informed consent is analyzable in terms of the web of cultural and policy rules and requirements of consent that collectively form the social practice of informed consent in institutional contexts where *groups* of patients and subjects must be treated in accordance with rules, policies, and standard practices. Here, informed consents are not always *autonomous* acts, nor are they always in any meaningful respect *authorizations*.

Sense₁: Informed Consent as Autonomous Authorization

The idea of an informed consent suggests that a patient or subject does more than express agreement with, acquiesce in, yield to, or comply with an arrangement or a proposal. He or she actively *authorizes* the proposal in the act of consent. John may *assent* to a treatment plan without authorizing it. The assent may be a mere submission to the doctor's authoritative order, in which case John does not call on his own authority in order to give permission, and thus does not authorize the plan. Instead, he acts like a child who submits, yields, or assents to the school principal's spanking and in no way gives permission for or authorizes the spanking. Just as the child merely submits to an authority in a system where the lines of authority are quite clear, so often do patients.

Accordingly, an informed consent in sense₁ should be defined as follows: An informed consent is an autonomous action by a subject or a patient that authorizes a professional either to involve the subject in research or to initiate a medical plan for the patient (or both). We can whittle down this definition by saying that an informed consent in sense₁ is given if a patient or subject with (1) substantial understanding and (2) in substantial absence of control by others (3) intentionally (4) authorizes a professional (to do intervention I).

All substantially autonomous acts satisfy conditions 1–3; but it does not follow from that analysis alone that all such acts satisfy 4. The fourth condition is what distinguishes informed consent as one *kind* of autonomous action. (Note also that the definition restricts the kinds of authorization to medical and research contexts.) A person whose act satisfies conditions 1–3 but who refuses an intervention gives an *informed refusal*.

The Problem of Shared Decisionmaking

This analysis of informed consent in sense₁ is deliberately silent on the question of how the authorizer and agent(s) being authorized *arrive at an agreement* about the performance of "I." Recent commentators on informed consent in clinical medicine, notably Jay Katz and the President's Commission, have tended to equate the idea of informed consent with a model of "shared decisionmaking" between doctor and patient. The President's Commission titles the first chapter of its report on informed consent in the patient-practitioner relationship "Informed Consent as Active, Shared Decision Making," while in Katz's work "the idea of informed consent" and "mutual decisionmaking" are treated as virtually synonymous terms.[1]

There is of course an historical relationship in clinical medicine between medical decisionmaking and informed consent. The emergence of the legal doctrine of informed consent was instrumental in drawing attention to issues of decisionmaking as well as authority in the doctor-patient relationship. Nevertheless, it is a confusion to treat informed consent and shared decisionmaking as anything like *synonymous*. For one thing, informed consent is not restricted to clinical medicine. It is a term that applies equally to biomedical and behavioral research contexts where a model of shared decisionmaking is frequently inappropriate. Even in clinical contexts, the social and psychological dynamics involved in selecting medical interventions should be distinguished from the patient's *authorization*.

We endorse Katz's view that effective communication between professional and patient or subject is often instrumental in obtaining informed consents (sense₁), but we resist his conviction that the idea of informed consent entails that the patient and physician "share decisionmaking," or "reason together," or reach a consensus about what is in the patient's best interest. This is a manipulation of the concept from a too singular and defined moral perspective on the practice of medicine that is in effect a moral program for changing the practice. Although the patient and physician *may* reach a decision together, they need not. It is the essence of informed consent in sense, only that the patient or subject *authorizes autonomously*; it is a matter of indifference where or how the proposal being authorized originates.

For example, one might advocate a model of shared decisionmaking for the doctor-patient relationship without simultaneously advocating that every medical procedure requires the consent of patients. Even relationships characterized by an ample slice of shared decisionmaking, mutual trust, and respect would and should permit many decisions about routine and low-risk aspects of the patient's medical treatment to remain the exclusive province of the physician, and thus some decisions are likely always to remain subject exclusively to the physician's authorization. Moreover, in the uncommon situation, a patient could autonomously authorize the physician to make *all* decisions about medical treatment, thus giving his or her informed consent to an arrangement that scarcely resembles the sharing of decisionmaking between doctor and patient.

Authorization

In authorizing, one both assumes responsibility for what one has authorized and transfers to another one's authority to implement it. There is no informed consent unless one *understands* these features of the act and *intends* to perform that act. That is, one must understand that one is assuming responsibility and warranting another to proceed.

To say that one assumes responsibility does not quite locate the essence of the matter, however, because a *transfer* of responsibility as well as of authority also occurs. The crucial element in an authorization is that the person who authorizes uses whatever right, power, or control he or she possesses in the situation to endow another with the right to act. In so doing, the authorizer assumes some responsibility for the actions taken by the other person. Here one could either authorize *broadly* so that a person can act in accordance with general guidelines, or *narrowly* so as to authorize only a particular, carefully circumscribed procedure.

Sense$_2$: Informed-Consent as Effective Consent

By contrast to sense$_1$, sense$_2$, or *effective* consent, is a policy-oriented sense whose conditions are not derivable solely from analyses of autonomy and autho-

rization, or even from broad notions of respect for autonomy. "Informed consent" in this second sense does not refer to *autonomous* authorization, but to a legally or institutionally *effective* (sometimes misleadingly called *valid*) authorization from a patient or a subject. Such an authorization is "effective" because it has been obtained through procedures that satisfy the rules and requirements defining a specific institutional practice in health care or in research.

The social and legal practice of requiring professionals to obtain informed consent emerged in institutional contexts, where conformity to operative rules was and still is the sole necessary and sufficient condition of informed consent. Any consent is an informed consent in sense$_2$ if it satisfies whatever operative rules apply to the practice of informed consent. Sense$_2$ requirements for informed consent typically do not focus on the autonomy of the act of giving consent (as sense$_1$ does), but rather on regulating the behavior of the *consent-seeker* and on establishing *procedures and rules* for the context of consent. Such requirements of professional behavior and procedure are obviously more readily monitored and enforced by institutions.

However, because formal institutional rules such as federal regulations and hospital policies govern whether an act of authorizing is effective, a patient or subject can autonomously authorize an intervention, and so give an informed consent in sense$_1$, and yet *not effectively authorize* that intervention in sense$_2$.

Consider the following example. Carol and Martie are nineteen-year-old, identical twins attending the same university. Martie was born with multiple birth defects, and has only one kidney. When both sisters are involved in an automobile accident, Carol is not badly hurt, but her sister is seriously injured. It is quickly determined that Martie desperately needs a kidney transplant. After detailed discussions with the transplant team and with friends, Carol consents to be the donor. There is no question that Carol's authorization of the transplant surgery is substantially autonomous. She is well informed and has long anticipated being in just such a circumstance. She has had ample opportunity over the years to consider what she would do were she faced with such a decision. Unfortunately, Carol's parents, who were in Nepal at the time of the accident, do not approve of her decision. Furious that they were not consulted, they decide to sue the transplant team and the hospital for having performed an unauthorized surgery on their minor daughter. (In this state the legal age to consent to surgical procedures is twenty-one.)

According to our analysis, Carol gave her informed consent in sense$_1$ to the surgery, but she did not give her informed consent in sense$_2$. That is, she autonomously authorized the transplant and thereby gave an informed consent in sense$_1$ but did not give a consent that was effective under the operative legal and institutional policy, which in this case required that the person consenting be a legally authorized agent. Examples of other policies that can define sense$_2$ informed consent (but not sense$_1$) include rules that consent be witnessed by an auditor or that there be a one-day waiting period between solicitation of consent and implementation of the intervention in order for the person's authorization to be effective. Such rules can and do vary, both within the United States by jurisdiction and institution, and across the countries of the world.

Medical and research codes, as well as case law and federal regulations, have developed models of informed consent that are delineated entirely in a sense$_2$ format, although they have sometimes attempted to justify the rules by appeal to something like sense$_1$. For example, disclosure conditions for informed consent are central to the history of "informed consent" in sense$_2$, because disclosure has traditionally been a *necessary* condition of effective informed consent (and sometimes a *sufficient* condition!). The legal doctrine of informed consent is primarily a law of disclosure; satisfaction of disclosure rules virtually consumes "informed consent" in law. This should come as no surprise, because the legal system needs a generally applicable informed consent mechanism by which injury and responsibility can be readily and fairly assessed in court. These disclosure requirements in the legal and regulatory contexts are not conditions of "informed consent" in sense$_1$; indeed disclosure may be entirely irrelevant to giving an informed consent in sense$_1$. If a person has an adequate *understanding* of relevant information without benefit of a disclosure, then it makes no difference whether someone *discloses* that information.

Other sense$_2$ rules besides those of disclosure have been enforced. These include rules requiring evidence of adequate comprehension of information and the aforementioned rules requiring the presence of auditor witnesses and mandatory waiting periods. Sense$_2$ informed consent requirements generally take the form of rules focusing on disclosure, comprehension, the minimization of potentially controlling influences, and competence. These requirements express the present-day mainstream conception in the federal government of the United States. They are also typical of international documents and state regulations, which all reflect a sense$_2$ orientation.

The Relationship Between Sense$_1$ and Sense$_2$

A sense$_1$ "informed consent" can fail to be an informed consent in sense$_2$ by a lack of conformity to applicable rules and requirements. Similarly, an informed consent in sense$_2$ may not be an informed consent in sense$_1$. The rules and requirements that determine sense$_2$ consents need not result in autonomous authorizations at all in order to qualify as informed consents.

Such peculiarities in informed consent law have led Jay Katz to argue that the legal doctrine of "informed consent" bears a "name" that "promises much more than its construction in case law has delivered." He has argued insightfully that the courts have, in effect, imposed a mere duty to warn on physicians, an obligation confined to risk disclosures and statements of proposed interventions. He maintains that "This judicially imposed obligation must be distinguished from the *idea* of informed consent, namely, that patients have a decisive role to play in the medical decisionmaking process. The idea of informed consent, though alluded to also in case law, cannot be implemented, as courts have attempted, by only expanding the disclosure requirements." By their actions and declarations, Katz believes, the courts have made informed consent a "cruel hoax" and have allowed "the idea of informed consent . . . to wither on the vine."[2]

The most plausible interpretation of Katz's contentions is through the sense$_1$/sense$_2$ distinction. If a physician obtains a consent under the courts' criteria, then an informed consent (sense$_2$) has been obtained. But it does not follow that the courts are using the *right* standards, or *sufficiently rigorous* standards in light of a stricter autonomy-based model—or "idea" as Katz puts it—of informed consent (sense$_1$).[3] If Katz is correct that the courts have made a mockery of informed consent and of its moral justification in respect for autonomy, then of course his criticisms are thoroughly justified. At the same time, it should be recognized that people can proffer legally or institutionally effective authorizations under prevailing rules even if they fall far short of the standards implicit in sense$_1$.

Despite the differences between sense$_1$ and sense$_2$, a definition of informed consent need not fall into one or the other class of definitions. It may conform to both. Many definitions of informed consent in policy contexts reflect at least a strong and definite reliance on informed consent in sense$_1$. Although the conditions of sense$_1$ are not logically necessary conditions for sense$_2$, we take it as morally axiomatic that they *ought* to serve—and in fact have served—as the benchmark or model against which the moral adequacy of a definition framed for sense$_2$ purposes is to be evaluated. This position is, roughly speaking, Katz's position.

A defense of the moral viewpoint that policies governing informed consent in sense$_2$ *should* be formulated to conform to the standards of informed consent in sense$_1$ is not hard to express. The goal of informed consent in medical care and in research—that is, the purpose behind the obligation to obtain informed consent—is to enable potential subjects and patients to make autonomous decisions about whether to grant or refuse authorization for medical and research interventions. Accordingly, embedded in the reason for having the social institution of informed consent is the idea that institutional requirements for informed consent in sense$_2$ *should* be intended to maximize the likelihood that the conditions of informed consent in sense$_1$ will be satisfied.

A major problem at the policy level, where rules and requirements must be developed and applied in the aggregate, is the following: The obligations imposed to enable patients and subjects to make authorization decisions must be evaluated not only in terms of the demands of a set of abstract conditions of "true" or sense$_1$ informed consent, but also in terms of the impact of imposing such obligations or requirements on various institutions with their concrete concerns and priorities. One must take account of what is fair and reasonable to require of health care professionals and researchers, the effect of alternative consent requirements on efficiency and effectiveness in the delivery of health care and the advancement of science, and—particularly in medical care—the effect of requirements on the welfare of patients. Also relevant are considerations peculiar to the particular social context, such as proof, precedent, or liability theory in case law, or regulatory authority and due process in the development of federal regulations and IRB consent policies.

Moreover, at the sense$_2$ level, one must resolve not only which requirements will define effective consent; one must also settle on the rules stipulating the conditions under which effective consents must be obtained. In some cases, hard decisions must be made about whether requirements of informed consent (in sense$_2$) should be imposed at all, even though informed consent (in sense$_1$) *could* realistically and meaningfully be obtained in the circumstances and could serve as a model for institutional rules. For example, should there be any consent requirements in the cases of minimal risk medical procedures and research activities?

This need to balance is not a problem for informed consent in sense$_1$, which is not policy oriented. Thus, it is possible to have a *morally acceptable* set of requirements for informed consent in sense$_2$ that deviates considerably from the conditions of informed consent in sense$_1$. However, the burden of moral proof rests with those who defend such deviations since the primary moral justification of the obligation to obtain informed consent is respect for autonomous action.

NOTES

1. President's Commission, *Making Health Care Decisions*, Vol. 1, 15 and Jay Katz, *The Silent World of Doctor and Patient* (New York: The Free Press, 1984), 87 and "The Regulation of Human Research—Reflections and Proposals," *Clinical Research* 21 (1973): 758–91. Katz does not provide a sustained analysis of joint or shared decisionmaking, and it is unclear precisely how he would relate this notion to informed content.

2. Jay Katz, "Disclosure and Consent," in A. Milunsky and G. Annas, eds., *Genetics and the Law II* (New York: Plenum Press, 1980), 122, 128.

3. We have already noted that Katz's "idea" of informed consent—as the active involvement of patients in the medical decisionmaking process—is different from our sense.

Informed Consent—Must It Remain a Fairy Tale?

JAY KATZ

The ideal of informed consent with its presumptions of autonomy and joint decision-making is yet to be fully realized in practice, says Katz. The concept has been legally recognized, but genuine patient self-determination is still not the norm. Physicians acknowledge it but are likely to see it as a perfunctory fulfillment of legal requirements or as an enumeration of risks. The goal of joint decision-making between physicians and patients is still unfulfilled. Physicians must come to see that they have a "duty to respect patients as persons so that care will encompass allowing patients to live their lives in their own self-willed ways."

I. The Pre-History of Informed Consent in Medicine

The idea that, prior to any medical intervention, physicians must seek their patients' informed consent was introduced into American law in a brief paragraph in a 1957 state court decision,[1] and then elaborated on in a lengthier opinion in 1960.[2] The emerging legal idea that physicians were from now on obligated to share decisionmaking authority with their patients shocked the medical community, for it constituted a radical break with the silence that had been the hallmark of physician-patient interactions throughout the ages. Thirty-five years are perhaps not long enough for either law or medicine to resolve the tension between legal theory and medical practice, particularly since judges were reluctant to face up to implications of their novel doctrine, preferring instead to remain quite deferential to the practices of the medical profession.

Viewed from the perspective of medical history, the doctrine of informed consent, if taken seriously, constitutes a revolutionary break with customary practice. Thus, I must review, albeit all too briefly, the history of doctor-patient communication. Only then can one appreciate how unprepared the medical profession was to heed these new legal com-

Originally published in the *Journal of Contemporary Health Law and Policy*, vol. 10, Spring 1994. Used with permission.

mands. But there is more: Physicians could not easily reject what law had begun to impose on them, because they recognized intuitively that the radical transformation of medicine since the age of medical science made it possible, indeed imperative, for a doctrine of informed consent to emerge. Yet, bowing to the doctrine did not mean accepting it. Indeed, physicians could not accept it because, for reasons I shall soon explore, the nature of informed consent has remained in the words of Churchill, "an enigma wrapped in a mystery."

Throughout the ages physicians believed that they should make treatment decisions for their patients. This conviction inheres in the Hippocratic Oath: "I swear by Apollo and Aesculepius [that] I will follow that system of regimen which according to *my* ability and judgment *I* consider for the benefit of *my* patients . . . ."[3] The patient is not mentioned as a person whose ability and judgment deserve consideration. Indeed, in one of the few references to disclosure in the Hippocratic Corpus, physicians are admonished "to [conceal] most things from the patient while attending to him; [to] give necessary orders with cheerfulness and serenity, . . . revealing nothing of the patient's future or present condition."[4] When twenty-five centuries later, in 1847, the American Medical Association promulgated its first Code of Ethics, it equally admonished patients that their "obedience . . . to the prescriptions of [their] physician should be prompt and implicit. [They] should never permit [their] own crude opinions . . . to influence [their] attention to [their physicians]."[5]

The gulf separating doctors from patients seemed unbridgeable both medically and socially. Thus, whenever the Code did not refer to physicians and patients as such, the former were addressed as "gentlemen" and the latter as "fellow creatures." To be sure, caring for patients' medical needs and "abstain[ing] from whatever is deleterious and mischievous"[6] was deeply imbedded in the ethos of Hippocratic medicine. The idea that patients were also "autonomous" human beings, entitled to being partners in decisionmaking, was, until recently, rarely given recognition in the lexicon of medical ethics. The notion that human beings possess individual human rights, deserving of respect, of course, is of recent origin. Yet it antedates the twentieth century and therefore could have had an impact on the nature and quality of the physician-patient relationship.

It did not. Instead, the conviction that physicians should decide what is best for their patients, and, therefore, that the authority and power to do so should remain vested in them, continued to have a deep hold on the practices of the medical profession. For example, in the early 1950s the influential Harvard sociologist Talcott Parsons, who echoed physicians' views, stated that the physician is a technically competent person whose competence and specific judgments and measures cannot be competently judged by the layman and that the latter must take doctors' judgments and measures on 'authority.'[7] The necessity for such authority was supported by three claims:

First, *physicians' esoteric knowledge, acquired in the course of arduous training and practical experience, cannot be comprehended by patients.* While it is true that this knowledge, in its totality, is difficult to learn, understand and master, it does not necessarily follow that physicians cannot translate their esoteric knowledge into language that comports with patients' experiences and life goals (i.e., into language that speaks to quality of future life, expressed in words of risks, benefits, alternatives and uncertainties). Perhaps patients can understand this, but physicians have had too little training and experience with, or even more importantly, a commit-

ment to, communicating their "esoteric knowledge" to patients in plain language to permit a conclusive answer as to what patients may comprehend.

Second, *patients, because of their anxieties over being ill and consequent regression to childlike thinking, are incapable of making decisions on their own behalf.* We do not know whether the childlike behavior often displayed by patients is triggered by pain, fear, and illness, or by physicians' authoritarian insistence that good patients comply with doctors' orders, or by doctors' unwillingness to share information with patients. Without providing such information, patients are groping in the dark and their stumbling attempts to ask questions, if made at all, makes them appear more incapable of understanding than they truly are.

We know all too little about the relative contributions which being ill, being kept ignorant, or being considered incompetent make to these regressive manifestations. Thus, physicians' unexamined convictions easily become self-fulfilling prophesies. For example, Eric Cassell has consistently argued that illness robs patients of autonomy and that only subsequent to the act of healing is autonomy restored.[8] While there is some truth to these contentions, they overlook the extent to which doctors can restore autonomy prior to the act of healing by not treating patients as children but as adults whose capacity for remaining authors of their own fate can be sustained and nourished. Cassell's views are reminiscent of Dostoyevsky's Grand Inquisitor who proclaimed that "at the most fearful moments of life," mankind is in need of "miracle, mystery and authority."[9] While, in this modern age, a person's capacity and right to take responsibility for his or her conduct has been given greater recognition than the Grand Inquisitor was inclined to grant, it still does not extend to patients. In the context of illness, physicians are apt to join the Grand Inquisitor at least to the extent of asserting that, while patients, they can only be comforted through subjugation to miracle, mystery and authority.

Third, *physicians' commitment to altruism is a sufficient safeguard for preventing abuses of their professional authority.* While altruism, as a general professional commitment, has served patients well in their encounters with physicians, the kind of protection it does and does not provide has not been examined in any depth. I shall have more to say about this later on. For now, let me only mention one problem: Altruism can only promise that doctors will try to place their patients' medical needs over their own personal needs. Altruism cannot promise that physicians will know, without inquiry, patients' needs. Put another way, patients and doctors do not necessarily have an identity of interest about matters of health and illness. Of course, both seek restoration of health and cure, and whenever such ends are readily attainable by only one route, their interests indeed may coincide.

In many physician-patient encounters, however, cure has many faces and the means selected affect the nature of cure in decisive ways. Thus, since quality of life is shaped decisively by available treatment options (including no treatment), the objectives of health and cure can be pursued in a variety of ways. Consider, for example, differences in value preferences between doctors and patients about longevity versus quality of remaining life. Without inquiry, one cannot presume identity of interest. As the surgeon Nuland cogently observed: "A doctor's altruism notwithstanding, his agenda and value system are not the same as those of the patient. That is the fallacy in the concept of beneficence so cherished by many physicians."[10]

II. The Age of Medical Science and Informed Consent

During the millennia of medical history, and until the beginning of the twentieth century, physicians could not explain to their patients, or—from the perspective of hindsight—to themselves, which of their treatment recommendations were curative and which were not. To be sure, doctors, by careful bedside observation, tried their level best "to abstain from what is deleterious and mischievous," to help if they could, and to be available for comfort during the hours, days or months of suffering. Doing more curatively, however, only became possible with the advent of the age of medical science. The introduction of scientific reasoning into medicine, aided by the results of carefully conducted research, permitted doctors for the first time to discriminate more aptly between knowledge, ignorance and conjecture

in their recommendations for or against treatment. Moreover, the spectacular technological advances in the diagnosis and treatment of disease, spawned by medical science, provided patients and doctors with ever-increasing therapeutic options, each having its own particular benefits and risks.

Thus, for the first time in medical history it is possible, even medically and morally imperative, to give patients a voice in medical decisionmaking. It is possible because knowledge and ignorance can be better specified; it is medically imperative because a variety of treatments are available, each of which can bestow great benefits or inflict grievous harm; it is morally imperative because patients, depending on the lifestyle they wish to lead during and after treatment, must be given a choice.

All this seems self-evident. Yet, the physician-patient relationship—the conversations between the two parties—was not altered with the transformation of medical practice during the twentieth century. Indeed, the silence only deepened once laboratory data were inscribed in charts and not in patients' minds, once machines allowed physicians' eyes to gaze not at patients' faces but at the numbers they displayed, once x-rays and electrocardiograms began to speak for patients' suffering rather than their suffering voices.

What captured the medical imagination and found expression in the education of future physicians, was the promise that before too long the diagnosis of patients' diseases would yield objective, scientific data to the point of becoming algorithms. *Treatment*, however, required subjective data from patients and would be influenced by doctors' subjective judgments. This fact was overlooked in the quest for objectivity. Also overlooked was the possibility that greater scientific understanding of the nature of disease and its treatment facilitated better communication with patients. In that respect contemporary Hippocratic practices remained rooted in the past.

III. The Impact of Law

The impetus for change in traditional patterns of communication between doctors and patients came not from medicine but from law. In a 1957 California case,[11] and a 1960 Kansas case,[12] judges were astounded and troubled by these undisputed facts:

That without any disclosure of risks, new technologies had been employed which promised great benefits but also exposed patients to formidable and uncontrollable harm. In the California case, a patient suffered a permanent paralysis of his lower extremities subsequent to the injection of a dye, sodium urokan, to locate a block in the abdominal aorta. In the Kansas case, a patient suffered severe injuries from cobalt radiation, administered, instead of conventional x-ray treatment, subsequent to a mastectomy for breast cancer. In the latter case, Justice Schroeder attempted to give greater specifications to the informed consent doctrine, first promulgated in the California decision: "To disclose and explain to the patient, in language as simple as necessary, the nature of the ailment, the nature of the proposed treatment, the probability of success or of alternatives, and perhaps the risks of unfortunate results and unforeseen conditions within the body."[13]

From the perspective of improved doctor-patient communication, or better, shared decisionmaking, the fault lines inherent in this American legal doctrine are many:

One: The common law judges who promulgated the doctrine restricted their task to articulating new and more stringent standards of liability whenever physicians withheld material information that patients should know, particularly in light of the harm that the spectacular advances in medical technology could inflict. Thus, the doctrine was limited in scope, designed to specify those minimal disclosure obligations that physicians must fulfill to escape *legal* liability for alleged non-disclosures. Moreover, it was shaped and confined by legal assumptions about the objectives of the laws of evidence and negligence, and by economic philosophies as to who should assume the financial burdens for medical injuries sustained by patients.

Even though the judges based the doctrine on "Anglo-American law['s] . . . premise of thoroughgoing self-determination,"[14] the Kansas court put it, or on "the root premise . . . fundamental in American jurisprudence that 'every human being of adult years and sound mind has a right to determine what shall be done with his own body,'"[15] as the Circuit Court for the District of Columbia put it in a subsequent opinion, the doctrine was grounded not in battery

law (trespass); but in negligence law. The reasons are many. I shall only mention a compelling one: Battery law, based on unauthorized trespass, gives doctors only one defense—that they have made adequate disclosure. Negligence law, on the other hand, permits doctors to invoke many defenses, including "the therapeutic privilege" not to disclose when in their judgment, disclosure may prove harmful to patients' welfare.

Two recent opinions illustrate the problems identified here. First, in a rare opinion, the Supreme Court of Pennsylvania reconfirmed its adherence to the minority view among American jurisdictions that battery, not negligence, is the appropriate cause of action whenever lack of informed consent is alleged. The court held that whenever "the patient . . . demonstrated, and the jury found, that he was not advised of . . . material facts, risks, complications and alternatives to surgery which a reasonable man would have considered significant in deciding whether to have the operation . . . the causation inquiry ends. The sole issue remaining [is] a determination of damages."[16] Earlier in its opinion, the court quoted, with approval, a prior Pennsylvania decision:

> [W]here a patient is mentally and physically able to consult about his condition, in the absence of an emergency, the consent of the patient is "a prerequisite to a surgical operation by his physician, and an operation without the patient's consent is a *technical assault*."[17]

Second, the Court of Appeals of California, in a ground-breaking opinion, significantly reduced the scope of the therapeutic privilege by requiring that in instances of hopeless prognosis (the most common situation in which the privilege has generally been invoked) the patient be provided with such information by asking, "If not the physician's duty to disclose a terminal illness, then whose?"[18] The duty to disclose prognosis had never before been identified specifically as one of the disclosure obligations in an informed consent opinion.

Thus, the appellate court's ruling constituted an important advance. It established that patients have a right to make decisions not only about the fate of their bodies but about the fate of their lives as well. The California Supreme Court, however, reversed.

In doing so, the court made too much of an issue raised by the plaintiffs that led the appellate court to hold that doctors must disclose "statistical life expectancy information."[19] To be sure, disclosure of statistical information is a complex problem, but in focusing on that issue, the supreme court's attention was diverted from a more important new disclosure obligation promulgated by the appellate court: the duty to inform patients of their dire prognosis. The supreme court did not comment on that obligation. Indeed, it seemed to reverse the appellate court on this crucial issue by reinforcing the considerable leeway granted physicians to invoke the therapeutic privilege exception to full disclosure: "We decline to intrude further, either on the subtleties of the physician-patient relationship or in the resolution of claims that the physician's duty of disclosure was breached, by requiring the disclosure of information that may or may not be indicated in a given treatment context."[20]

Two: The doctrine of informed consent was not designed to serve as a *medical* blueprint for interactions between physicians and patients. The medical profession still faces the task of fashioning a "doctrine" that comports with its own vision of doctor-patient communication and that is responsive both to the realities of medical practices in an age of science and to the commands of law. As I said years ago,

> [T]ranslating the ingredients of [the informed consent] process into legal and useful medical prescriptions that respect patients' wishes to maintain and surrender autonomy, as well as physicians' unending struggles with omnipotence and impotence in the light of medical uncertainty, is a difficult task [which the medical profession] has not pursued . . . in any depth.[21]

Thus, disclosure practices only changed to the extent of physicians disclosing more about the risks of a proposed intervention in order to escape legal liability.

Three: Underlying the legal doctrine there lurks a broader assumption which has neither been given full recognition by judges nor embraced by physicians. The underlying idea is this: That from now on patients and physicians must make decisions jointly, with patients ultimately deciding whether to ac-

cede to doctors' recommendations. In *The Cancer Ward*, Solzhenitsyn captured, as only a novelist can, the fears that such an idea engenders. When doctor Ludmilla Afanasyevna was challenged by her patient, Oleg Kostoglotov, about physicians' rights to make unilateral decisions on behalf of patients, Afanasyevna gave a troubled, though unequivocal, answer: "But doctors *are* entitled to the right—doctors above all. Without that right, there'd be no such thing as medicine."[22]

If Afanasyevna is correct, then patients must continue to trust doctors silently. Conversation, to comport with the idea of informed consent, ultimately requires that both parties make decisions jointly and that their views and preferences be treated with respect. Trust, based on blind faith—on passive surrender to oneself or to another—must be distinguished from trust that is earned after having first acknowledged to oneself and then shared with the other what one knows and does not know about the decision to be made. If all of that had been considered by physicians, they would have appreciated that a new model of doctor-patient communication, that takes informed consent seriously required a radical break with current medical disclosure practice.

Four: The idea of joint decisionmaking is one thing, and its application in practice another. To translate theory into practice cannot be accomplished, as the Judicial Council of the American Medical Association attempted to do in one short paragraph. The Judicial Council stated that "[t]he patient should make his own determination on treatment. Informed consent is a basic *social* policy . . . ."[23] To translate social policy into *medical* policy is an inordinately difficult task. It requires a reassessment of the limits of medical knowledge in the light of medical uncertainty, a reassessment of professional authority to make decisions for patients in light of the consequences of such conduct for the well-being of patients, and a reassessment of the limits of patients' capacities to assume responsibility for choice in the light of their ignorance about medical matters and their anxieties when ill. Turning now to these problems, I wish to highlight that, in the absence of such reassessments, informed consent will remain a charade, and joint decisionmaking will elude us.

IV. Barriers to Joint Decisionmaking

A. Medical Uncertainty

The longer I reflect about doctor-patient decision-making, the more convinced I am that in this modern age of medical science, which for the first time permits sharing with patients the uncertainties of diagnosis, treatment, and prognosis, the problem of uncertainty poses the most formidable obstacle to disclosure and consent. By medical uncertainty I mean to convey what the physician Lewis Thomas observed so eloquently, albeit disturbingly:

> The only valid piece of scientific truth about which I feel totally confident is that we are profoundly ignorant about nature. . . . It is this sudden confrontation with the depth and scope of ignorance that represents the most significant contribution of twentieth-century science to the human intellect. *We are, at last facing up to it*. In earlier times, we either pretended to understand . . . or ignored the problem, or simply made up stories to fill the gap.[24]

Alvan Feinstein put this in more concrete language: "Clinicians are still uncertain about the best means of treatment for even such routine problems as . . . a fractured hip, a peptic ulcer, a stroke, a myocardial infarction. . . . At a time of potent drugs and formidable surgery, the exact effects of many therapeutic procedures are dubious or shrouded in dissension."[25]

Medical uncertainty constitutes a formidable obstacle to joint decisionmaking for a number of reasons: Sharing uncertainties requires physicians to be more aware of them than they commonly are. They must learn how to communicate them to patients and they must shed their embarrassment over acknowledging the true state of their own and of medicine's art and science. Thus, sharing uncertainties requires a willingness to admit ignorance about benefits and risks; to acknowledge the existence of alternatives, each with its own known and unknown consequences; to eschew one single authoritative recommendation; to consider carefully how to present uncertainty so that patients will not be overwhelmed by the information they will receive; and to explore the crucial question of how much uncertainty physicians themselves can tolerate without compromising their effectiveness as healers.

To so conduct oneself is most difficult. For, once doctors, on the basis of their clinical experience and knowledge, conclude which treatment is best, they tend to disregard, if not reject, the view of other colleagues who treat the same condition differently. Consider the current controversy over the management of localized prostate cancer: surgery, radiation or watchful waiting.[26] Some of the physicians involved in the debate are not even willing to accept that uncertainty exists, or at least they minimize its relevance to choice of treatment. Most who advocate treatment strongly prefer one type over another based on professional specialization (radiologists tend to recommend radiation; surgeons surgery).

Moreover, acknowledgement of uncertainty is undermined by the threat that it will undermine doctors' authority and sense of superiority. As Nuland put it, to feel superior to those dependent persons who are the sick, is after all a motivating factor that often influences their choice of medicine as a profession.[27] All of this suggests that implementation of the idea of informed consent is, to begin with, not a patient problem but a physician problem.

B. Patient Incompetence

Earlier, I touched on physicians' convictions that illness and medicine's esoteric knowledge rob patients of the capacity to participate in decisionmaking. Yet we do not know whether this is true. The evidence is compromised by the groping, half-hearted, and misleading attempts to inform patients about uncertainty and other matters which can make doctors' communications so confusing and incomprehensible. If patients then appear stupid and ignorant this should come as no surprise; nor should patients' resigned surrender to this dilemma: "You are the doctor, you decide."

It is equally debatable, as Thomas Duffy has contended, that "[p]aternalism exists in medicine . . . to fulfill a need created by illness."[28] It led him to argue, echoing Cassell, that "obviously autonomy cannot function as the cornerstone of the doctor-patient relationship [since] the impact of disease on personal integrity results in the patient's loss of autonomy. . . . In the doctor-patient relationship, the medical profession should always err on the side of beneficence."[29] If

Duffy is correct, however, then informed consent is *ab initio* fatally compromised.

C. Patient Autonomy

Duffy's invocation of beneficence as the guiding principle is deeply rooted in the history of Hippocratic medicine. It finds expression in the ancient maxim: *primum non nocere*, above all do no harm, with "harm" remaining undefined but in practice being defined only as physical harm. Before presenting my views on the controversy over the primacy of autonomy or beneficence, let me briefly define their meaning.

In their authoritative book *Principles of Biomedical Ethics*, Thomas Beauchamp and James Childress defined these principles:

> Autonomy is a form of personal liberty of action where the individual determines his or her own course of action in accordance with a plan chosen by himself or herself. [Respect for individuals as autonomous agents entitles them] to such autonomous determinations without limitation on their liberty being imposed by others.[30]

Beneficence, on the other hand,

> [r]equires not only that we treat persons autonomously and that we refrain from harming them, but also that we contribute to their welfare including their health. [Thus the principle asserts] the duty to help others further their important and legitimate interests . . . to *confer* benefits and actively to prevent and remove harms . . . [and] to *balance* possible goods against the possible harms of an action.[31]

Beauchamp and Childress' unequivocal and strong postulate on autonomy contrasts with the ambiguities contained in their postulate on beneficence. What do they mean by "benefits" and "harms" that allow invocation of beneficence? Do they mean only benefits and harms to patients' physical integrity, or to their dignitary integrity as choice-making individuals as well? Furthermore, what degree of discretion and license is permissible in the duty "to balance?" I have problems with balancing unless it is resorted to only as a *rare* exception to respect for autonomy. While human life is, and human interactions are, too complex to make any principle rule absolute, any exceptions must be rigorously justified.

I appreciate that mine is a radical proposal and constitutes a sharp break with Hippocratic practices. If informed consent, however, is ever to be based on the postulate of joint decisionmaking, the obligation "to respect the autonomous choices and actions of others,"[32] as Childress has put it, must be honored. Otherwise, informed consent is reduced to doctors providing more information but leaving decisionmaking itself to the authority of physicians.

As one physician once told me, echoing only an all too prevalent belief (and he was a physician allegedly deeply committed to informed consent), "I must first make the judgment which treatment alternative is best for patients, and only after I have exercised that professional judgment, will I discuss the risks and benefits of *the* recommended treatment." This story illustrates the emphasis doctors place on risk disclosures rather than alternatives. The latter, however, is more crucial to joint decisionmaking than the former. Such a view, however, again encounters the issue of disclosure of medical uncertainty inherent in any forthright discussion of treatment alternatives. Physicians remain most reluctant to acknowledge uncertainty to themselves, and even more to their patients.

V. Respect for Autonomy

It should be evident by now that physicians must embark on a prolonged period of self-examination about how to interact with patients in new ways in an age of medical science and informed consent. Physicians must cease to complain about lawyers forcing them "to do silly things." Whenever doctors do so, they often observe that they can easily present their disclosures in ways that lead patients to agree with what they had thought to be the best alternative in the first place. This contention is a correct assessment of what transpires in customary practices that continue to eschew joint decisionmaking. Therefore, as I have already suggested, informed consent in today's world, is largely a charade which misleads patients into thinking that they are making decisions when indeed they are not.

Any meaningful change in Hippocratic decisionmaking practices first requires a new and revolutionary commitment to one principle: that physicians must respect patients as autonomous persons. The most crucial reason for my placing such high value on autonomy and self-determination is because doing so safeguards, as nothing else can, the recognition by the other that the person before him or her is as much a person as he or she is. Beneficence can readily reduce persons to non-persons by "taking care of them" in all of the many not only caring, but also, non-caring meanings of this phrase.

VI. The Current State of Physician-Patient Decisionmaking

In his recent book, entitled *How We Die*, Sherwin Nuland, a distinguished surgeon, reflects with profundity and insight on his lifelong interactions with patients. In a chapter on cancer and its treatment he speaks movingly about "death belong[ing] to the dying and to those who love them."[33] Yet, that privilege is often wrested from them when,

> [d]ecisions about continuation of treatment are influenced by the enthusiasm of the doctors who propose them. Commonly, the most accomplished of the specialists are also the most convinced and unyielding believers in biomedicine's ability to overcome the challenge presented by a pathological process. . . . [W]hat is offered as objective clinical reality is often the subjectivity of a devout disciple of the philosophy that death is an implacable enemy. To such warriors, even a temporary victory justifies the laying waste of the fields in which a dying man has cultivated his life.[34]

Looking back at his work, he concludes that "more than a few of my victories have been Pyrrhic. The suffering was sometimes not worth the success. . . . [H]ad I been able to project myself into the place of the family and the patient, I would have been less often certain that the desperate struggle should be undertaken."[35]

In his view, a surgeon,

> [t]hough he be kind and considerate of the patient he treats . . . allows himself to push his kindness aside because the seduction of The Riddle [the quest for diagnosis and cure] is so strong and the failure to solve it renders him so weak. [Thus, at times he convinces] patients to undergo diagnostic or therapeutic measures at a point in illness so far beyond reason that The Riddle might better have remained unsolved.[36]

Speaking then about the kind of doctor he will seek out when afflicted with a major illness, Nuland does not expect him to "understand my values, my expectations for myself . . . my philosophy of life. *That is not what he is trained for and that is not what he will be good at.*[37] Doctors can impart information, but "[i]t behooves every patient to study his or her own disease and learn enough about it. [Patients] should no longer expect from so many of our doctors what they cannot give."[38]

Nuland's views, supported by a great many poignant clinical vignettes, sensitively and forthrightly describe the current state of physician-patient decisionmaking, so dominated by physicians' judgments as to what is best. He presents many reasons for this state of affairs. One is based on doctors' "fear of failure":

> A need to control that exceeds in magnitude what most people would find reasonable. When control is lost, he who requires it is also a bit lost and so deals badly with the consequences of his impotence. In an attempt to maintain control, a doctor, usually without being aware of it, convinces himself that he knows better than the patient what course is proper. He dispenses only as much information as he deems fit, thereby influencing a patient's decision-making in ways he does not recognize as self-serving.[39]

I have presented Nuland's observations at some length because they illustrate and support my contentions that joint decisionmaking between doctors and patients still eludes us. My critics had claimed earlier that work on informed consent was dated because informed consent had become an integral aspect of the practice of medicine. In the paperback edition of *The Silent World of Doctor and Patient*, I argued that they have dismissed too lightly my central arguments:

> [T]hat meaningful collaboration between physicians and patients cannot become a reality until physicians have learned (1) how to treat their patients not as children but as the adults they are; (2) how to distinguish between their ideas of the best treatment and their patients' ideas of what is best; (3) how to acknowledge to their patients (and often to themselves as well) their ignorance and uncertainties about diagnosis, treatment, and prognosis; [and to all this, I now want to add, (4) how to explain to patients

the uncertainties inherent in the state of the art and science of medicine which otherwise permits doctors on the basis of their clinical experience to leave unacknowledged that their colleagues on the basis of their clinical experience have different beliefs as to which treatment is best].[40]

Nuland pleads for the resurrection of the family doctor[41] because he believes that the specialist is inadequate to the task of shouldering the burdens of decision with his patients. About this I differ with him. I believe that physicians (and surgeons as well) *can*, and *must*, learn to converse with patients in the spirit of joint decisionmaking. Physicians can and must learn to appreciate better than they do now that the principle of respect for person speaks to the caring commitment of physicians in old and new ways: *Old* in that it highlights the ancient and venerable medical duty not to abandon patients, and *new* by requiring doctors to communicate with them and remain at their sides, not only while their bodies are racked with pain and suffering but also while their minds are beset by fear, confusion, doubt and suffering over decisions to be made; also *new* in that implementation of the principle of psychological autonomy imposes the obligations on physicians both to invite, and respond to, questions about the decisions to be made, and to do so by respecting patients' ultimate choices, a new aspect of the duty to care.

The moral authority of physicians will not be undermined by this caring view of interacting with patients. Doctors' authority resides in the medical knowledge they possess, in their capacity to diagnose and treat, in their ability to evaluate what can be diagnosed and what cannot, what is treatable and what is not, and what treatment alternatives to recommend, each with its own risks and benefits and each with its own prognostic implications as to cure, control, morbidity, exacerbation or even death.

The moral authority of physicians resides in knowing better than others the certainties and the uncertainties that accompany diagnosis, treatment, prognosis, health and disease, as well the extent and the limits of their *scientific* knowledge and *scientific* ignorance. Physicians must learn to face up to and acknowledge the tragic limitations of their own professional knowledge, their inability to impart all their insights to all patients, and their own personal

incapacities—at times more pronounced than others—to devote themselves fully to the needs of their patients. They must learn not to be unduly embarrassed by their personal and professional ignorance and to trust their patients to react appropriately to such acknowledgment. From all this it follows that ultimately the moral authority of physicians resides in their capacity to sort out *with* patients the choices to be made.

It is in this spirit that duty and caring become interwoven. Bringing these strands together imposes upon physicians the duty to respect patients as persons so that care will encompass allowing patients to live their lives in their own self-willed ways. To let patients follow their own lights is not an abandonment of them. It is a professional duty that, however painful, doctors must obey.

Without fidelity to these new professional duties, true caring will elude physicians. There is much new to be learned about caring that in decades to come will constitute the kind of caring that doctors in the past have wished for but have been unable to dispense, and that patients may have always yearned for.

I do not know whether my vision of a new physician-patient relationship defies medical reality. Thus, I may be wrong and I am willing to entertain this possibility as long as my critics are willing to admit that they too may be wrong. *As a profession we have never examined and tested in a committed manner what I have proposed.* It is this fact which, in conclusion, I want to highlight. For, I believe that in this age of medical science and informed consent the category of patient is in need of a radical reconceptualization. Throughout medical history, patients have been viewed as passive, ignorant persons whose welfare was best protected by their following doctors' orders, and physicians and patients were socialized to interact with one another on that basis. Throughout this essay, I have argued that such a view of the physician-patient relationship was dictated by doctors' inability to explain to themselves what was therapeutic and what was not in the practice of medicine. The advent of the age of medical science has changed all that and for the first time in medical history doctors now can distinguish better between knowledge, ignorance and conjecture. In turn, this permits physicians to take patients into their confidence.

Finally, my purpose in writing this essay is twofold: (1) To argue, notwithstanding any theories of tort law and cost containment to the contrary,[42] that patients must ultimately be given the deciding vote in matters that effect their lives; and (2) to suggest that informed consent will remain a fairy tale as long as the idea of joint decisionmaking, based on a commitment to patient autonomy and self-determination, does not become an integral aspect of the ethos of medicine and the law of informed consent. Until then, physicians, patients and judges can only deceive themselves or be deceived about patients having a vital voice in the medical decisionmaking process. Of course, there are alternatives to joint decisionmaking. One that I have briefly explored elsewhere suggested that we need a number of informed (and uninformed) consent doctrines depending on the nature of the decisions to be made, with the implication that only in certain medical contexts must informed consent rise to the rigor advanced in this essay.[43] Another alternative is to fashion an informed consent doctrine for law and medicine that is *not* based on "[t]he root premise . . . fundamental in American jurisprudence, that '[e]very human being of adult years and sound mind has a right to determine what shall be done with his own body.'"[44] It is not a road on which I would like to travel and thus, I leave that task to others. It is important that those who disagree with me set forth their premises about who decides what; otherwise physicians and patients are condemned to interact with one another, under the rubric of what is now called "informed consent," by deception of both self and the other.

NOTES

1. Salgo v. Leland Stanford Jr. Univ. Bd. of Trustees, 317 P.2d 170, 181 (Cal. Dist. Ct. App. 1957).

2. Natanson v. Kline, 350 P.2d 1093 (Kan. 1960).

3. Hippocrates, *Oath of Hippocrates, in* 1 Hippocrates 299–301 (W.H.S. Jones trans., 1962).

4. 2 Hippocrates 297 (W.H.S. Jones trans., 1962).

5. American Medical Association: Code of Ethics (1847), reprinted in Jay Katz, The Silent World of Doctor and Patient 2 (1984), at 232.

6. Hippocrates, *supra* note 3, at 301.

7. Talcott Parsons, The Social System 464–65 (1951).

8. Eric Cassell, *The Function of Medicine*, Hastings Center Rep., Dec. 1977, at 16, 18.

9. Fyodor Dostoyevsky, The Brothers Karamazov 307 (A.P. MacAndrew trans., 1970).

10. Interview with Sherwin Nuland (1993).

11. Salgo v. Leland Stanford Jr. Univ. Bd. of Trustees, 317 P.2d 170 (Cal. Dist. Ct. App. 1957).

12. Natanson v. Kline, 350 P.2d 1093 (Kan. 1960).

13. *Id.* at 1106.

14. *Id.* at 1104.

15. Canterbury v. Spence, 464 F.2d 772, 780 (D.C. Cir. 1972).

16. Gouse v. Cassel, 615 A.2d 331, 335 (Pa. 1992).

17. *Id.* at 333–34 (emphasis added) (quoting Moscicki v. Shor, 163 A. 341, 342 (Pa. Super. Ct. 1932)).

18. Arato v. Avedon, 11 Cal. Rptr. 2d 169, 181 n.19 (Cal. Ct. App. 1992), *vacated*, 858 P.2d 598 (Cal. 1993).

19. *Arato*, 11 Cal. Rptr. 2d at 177.

20. *Arato*, 858 P.2d at 607.

21. Katz, *supra* note 5, at 84.

22. Alexander Solzhenitsyn, The Cancer Ward 77 (N. Bethell & D. Burg trans., 1969).

23. Judicial Council of the Am. Medical Ass'n, Current Opinions of the Judicial Council of the American Medical Association 25 (1981) (*emphasis added*).

24. Lewis Thomas, The Medusa and the Snail 73–74 (1979).

25. Alvan R. Feinstein, Clinical Judgment 23–24 (1967). Even though written 27 years ago, he has not changed his views. Interview with Alvan R. Feinstein (1994).

26. Gerald W. Chodak et al., *Results of Conservative Management of Clinically Localized Prostate Cancer*, 330 New Eng. J. Med. 242 (1994).

27. Interview with Sherwin B. Nuland (1994).

28. Thomas P. Duffy, *Agamemnon's Fate and the Medical Profession*, 9 W. New Eng. L. Rev. 21, 27 (1987).

29. *Id.* at 30.

30. Thomas L. Beauchamp & James F. Childress, Principles of Biomedical Ethics 56, 58 (1st ed. 1979).

31. Thomas L. Beauchamp & James F. Childress, Principles of Biomedical Ethics 148–49 (2d ed. 1983).

32. James F. Childress, *The Place of Autonomy in Bioethics*, Hastings Center Rep., Jan.–Feb. 1990, at 12, 12–13.

33. Sherwin B. Nuland, How We Die 265 (1994).

34. *Id.*

35. *Id.* at 266.

36. *Id.* at 249.

37. *Id.* at 266 (emphasis added).

38. *Id.* at 260.

39. *Id.* at 258.

40. Jay Katz, The Silent World of Doctor and Patient xi (1986).

41. Nuland, *supra* note 33, at 266.

42. *See, e.g.*, Peter H. Schuck, *Rethinking Informed Consent*, 103 Yale L.J. 899 (1994).

43. Jay Katz, *Physician-Patient Encounters "On a Darkling Plain,"* 9 W. New Eng. L. Rev. 207, 221–22 (1987).

44. Canterbury v. Spence, 464 F.2d 772, 780 (D.C. Cir. 1972).

Transparency: Informed Consent in Primary Care

HOWARD BRODY

Brody observes that the theory and the practice of informed consent are far apart and that accepted legal standards send physicians the wrong message about what they are supposed to do. He thinks that a conversation standard of informed consent does send the right message but is probably legally unworkable. He proposes instead a "transparency standard," which says that "disclosure is adequate when the physician's basic thinking has been rendered transparent to the patient."

While the patient's right to give informed consent to medical treatment is now well-established both in U.S. law and in biomedical ethics, evidence continues to suggest that the concept has been poorly integrated into American medical practice, and that in many instances the needs and desires of patients are not being well met by current policies.[1] It appears that the theory and the practice of informed consent are out of joint in some crucial ways. This is particularly true for primary care settings, a context typically ignored by medical ethics literature, but where the majority of doctor-patient encounters occur. Indeed, some have suggested that the concept of informed consent is virtually foreign to primary care medicine where benign paternalism appropriately reigns and where respect for patient autonomy is almost completely absent.[2]

It is worth asking whether current legal standards for informed consent tend to resolve the problem or to exacerbate it. I will maintain that accepted legal standards, at least in the form commonly employed by courts, send physicians the wrong message about what is expected of them. An alternative standard that would send physicians the correct message, a conversation standard, is probably unworkable legally. As an alternative, I will propose a transparency standard as a compromise that gives physicians a doable task and allows courts to review appropriately. I must begin, however, by briefly identifying some assumptions crucial to the development of this position even though space precludes complete argumentation and documentation.

Crucial Assumptions

Informed consent is a meaningful ethical concept only to the extent that it can be realized and promoted within the ongoing practice of good medicine. This need not imply diminished respect for patient autonomy, for there are excellent reasons to regard respect for patient autonomy as a central feature of good medical care. Informed consent, properly understood, must be considered an essential ingredient of good patient care, and a physician who lacks the skills to inform patients appropriately and obtain proper consent should be viewed as lacking essential medical skills necessary for practice. It is not enough to see informed consent as a nonmedical, legalistic exercise designed to promote patient autonomy, one that interrupts the process of medical care.

However, available empirical evidence strongly suggests that this is precisely how physicians currently view informed consent practices. Informed consent is still seen as bureaucratic legalism rather than as part of patient care. Physicians often deny the existence of realistic treatment alternatives, thereby attenuating the perceived need to inform the patient of meaningful options. While patients may be informed, efforts are seldom made to assess accurately the patient's actual need or desire for information, or what the patient then proceeds to do with the information provided. Physicians typically underestimate patients' desire to be informed and overestimate their desire to be involved in decisionmaking. Physicians may also view informed consent as an empty charade, since they are confident in their abilities to manipulate consent by how they discuss or divulge information.[3]

A third assumption is that there are important differences between the practice of primary care medicine and the tertiary care settings that have been most frequently discussed in the literature on informed consent. The models of informed consent discussed below typically take as the paradigm case something like surgery for breast cancer or the performance of an invasive and risky radiologic procedure. It is assumed that the risks to the patient are significant, and the values placed on alternative forms of treatment are quite weighty. Moreover, it is assumed that the specialist physician performing the procedure probably does a fairly limited number of procedures and thus could be expected to know exhaustively the precise risks, benefits, and alternatives for each.

Primary care medicine, however, fails to fit this model. The primary care physician, instead of performing five or six complicated and risky procedures frequently, may engage in several hundred treatment modalities during an average week of practice. In many cases, risks to the patient are negligible and conflicts over patient values and the goals of treatment or non-treatment are of little consequence. Moreover, in contrast to the tertiary care patient, the typical ambulatory patient is much better able to exercise freedom of choice and somewhat less likely to be intimidated by either the severity of the disease or the expertise of the physician; the opportunities for changing one's mind once treatment has begun are also much greater. Indeed, in primary care, it is much more likely for the full process of informed consent to treatment (such as the beginning and the dose adjustment of an anti-hypertensive medication) to occur over several office visits rather than at one single point in time.

It might be argued that for all these reasons, the stakes are so low in primary care that it is fully appropriate for informed consent to be interpreted only with regard to the specialized or tertiary care setting. I believe that this is quite incorrect for three reasons. First, good primary care medicine ought to embrace respect for patient autonomy, and if patient autonomy is operationalized in informed consent, prop-

erly understood, then it ought to be part and parcel of good primary care. Second, the claim that the primary care physician cannot be expected to obtain the patient's informed consent seems to undermine the idea that informed consent could or ought to be part of the daily practice of medicine. Third, primary care encounters are statistically more common than the highly specialized encounters previously used as models for the concept of informed consent.[4]

Accepted Legal Standards

Most of the literature on legal approaches to informed consent addresses the tension between the community practice standard, and the reasonable patient standard, with the latter seen as the more satisfactory, emerging legal standard.[5] However, neither standard sends the proper message to the physician about what is expected of her to promote patient autonomy effectively and to serve the informational needs of patients in daily practice.

The community practice standard sends the wrong message because it leaves the door open too wide for physician paternalism. The physician is instructed to behave as other physicians in that specialty behave, regardless of how well or how poorly that behavior serves patients' needs. Certainly, behaving the way other physicians behave is a task we might expect physicians to readily accomplish; unfortunately, the standard fails to inform them of the end toward which the task is aimed.

The reasonable patient standard does a much better job of indicating the centrality of respect for patient autonomy and the desired outcome of the informed consent process, which is revealing the information that a reasonable person would need to make an informed and rational decision. This standard is particularly valuable when modified to include the specific informational and decisional needs of a particular patient.

If certain things were true about the relationship between medicine and law in today's society, the reasonable patient standard would provide acceptable guidance to physicians. One feature would be that physicians esteem the law as a positive force in guiding their practice, rather than as a threat to their well-being that must be handled defensively. Another element would be a prospective consideration by the law of what the physician could reasonably have been expected to do in practice, rather than a retrospective review armed with the foreknowledge that some significant patient harm has already occurred.

Unfortunately, given the present legal climate, the physician is much more likely to get a mixed or an undesirable message from the reasonable patient standard. The message the physician hears from the reasonable patient standard is that one must exhaustively lay out all possible risks as well as benefits and alternatives of the proposed procedure. If one remembers to discuss fifty possible risks, and the patient in a particular case suffers the fifty-first, the physician might subsequently be found liable for incomplete disclosure. Since lawsuits are triggered when patients suffer harm, disclosure of risk becomes relatively more important than disclosure of benefits. Moreover, disclosure of information becomes much more critical than effective patient participation in decisionmaking. Physicians consider it more important to document what they said to the patient than to document how the patient used or thought about that information subsequently.

In specialty practice, many of these concerns can be nicely met by detailed written or videotaped consent documents, which can provide the depth of information required while still putting the benefits and alternatives in proper context. This is workable when one engages in a limited number of procedures and can have a complete document or videotape for each.[6] However, this approach is not feasible for primary care, when the number of procedures may be much more numerous and the time available with each patient may be considerably less. Moreover, it is simply not realistic to expect even the best educated of primary care physicians to rattle off at a moment's notice a detailed list of significant risks attached to any of the many drugs and therapeutic modalities they recommend.

This sets informed consent apart from all other aspects of medical practice in a way that I believe is widely perceived by nonpaternalistic primary care physicians, but which is almost never commented upon in the medical ethics literature. To the physician obtaining informed consent, *you never know when you are finished.* When a primary care physi-cian is told to treat a patient for strep throat or to counsel a person suffering a normal grief reaction from the recent death of a relative, the physician has a good sense of what it means to complete the task at hand. When a physician is told to obtain the patient's informed consent for a medical intervention, the impression is quite different. A list of as many possible risks as can be thought of may still omit some significant ones. A list of all the risks that actually have occurred may still not have dealt with the patient's need to know risks in relation to benefits and alternatives. A description of all benefits, risks, and alternatives may not establish whether the patient has understood the information. If the patient says he understands, the physician has to wonder whether he really understands or whether he is simply saying this to be accommodating. As the law currently *appears* to operate (in the perception of the defensively minded physician), there never comes a point at which you can be certain that you have adequately completed your legal as well as your ethical task.

The point is not simply that physicians are paranoid about the law; more fundamentally, physicians are getting a message that informed consent is very different from any other task they are asked to perform in medicine. If physicians conclude that informed consent is therefore not properly part of medicine at all, but is rather a legalistic and bureaucratic hurdle they must overcome at their own peril, blame cannot be attributed to paternalistic attitudes or lack of respect for patient autonomy.

The Conversation Model

A metaphor employed by Jay Katz, informed consent as conversation, provides an approach to respect for patient autonomy that can be readily integrated within primary care practice.[7] Just as the specific needs of an individual patient for information, or the meaning that patient will attach to the information as it is presented, cannot be known in advance, one cannot always tell in advance how a conversation is going to turn out. One must follow the process along and take one's cues from the unfolding conversation itself. Despite the absence of any formal rules for carrying out or completing a conversation on a specific subject, most people have a good intuitive grasp of what it means for a conversation to be finished, what it means to change the subject in the middle of a conversation, and what it means to later reopen a conversation one had thought was completed when something new has just arisen. Thus, the metaphor suggests that informed consent consists not in a formal process carried out strictly by protocol but in a conversation designed to encourage patient participation in all medical decisions to the extent that the patient wishes to be included. The idea of informed consent as physician-patient conversation could, when properly developed, be a useful analytic tool for ethical issues in informed consent, and could also be a powerful educational tool for highlighting the skills and attitudes that a physician needs to successfully integrate this process within patient care.

If primary care physicians understand informed consent as this sort of conversation process, the idea that exact rules cannot be given for its successful management could cease to be a mystery. Physicians would instead be guided to rely on their own intuitions and communication skills, with careful attention to information received from the patient, to determine when an adequate job had been done in the informed consent process. Moreover, physicians would be encouraged to see informed consent as a genuinely mutual and participatory process, instead of being reduced to the one-way disclosure of information. In effect, informed consent could be demystified, and located within the context of the everyday relationships between physician and patient, albeit with a renewed emphasis on patient participation.[8]

Unfortunately, the conversation metaphor does not lend itself to ready translation into a legal standard for determining whether or not the physician has satisfied her basic responsibilities to the patient. There seems to be an inherently subjective element to conversation that makes it ill-suited as a legal standard for review of controversial cases. A conversation in which one participates is by its nature a very different thing from the same conversation described to an outsider. It is hard to imagine how a jury could be instructed to determine in retrospect whether or not a particular conversation was adequate for its purposes. However, without the possibility for legal review, the message that patient autonomy is an important value and that patients have important rights within primary care would seem

to be severely undermined. The question then is whether some of the important strengths of the conversation model can be retained in another model that does allow better guidance.

The Transparency Standard

I propose the transparency standard as a means to operationalize the best features of the conversation model in medical practice. According to this standard, adequate informed consent is obtained when a reasonably informed patient is allowed to participate in the medical decision to the extent that patient wishes. In turn, "reasonably informed" consists of two features: (1) the physician discloses the basis on which the proposed treatment, or alternative possible treatments, have been chosen; and (2) the patient is allowed to ask questions suggested by the disclosure of the physician's reasoning, and those questions are answered to the patient's satisfaction.

According to the transparency model, the key to reasonable disclosure is not adherence to existing standards of other practitioners, nor is it adherence to a list of risks that a hypothetical reasonable patient would want to know. Instead, disclosure is adequate when the physician's basic thinking has been rendered transparent to the patient. If the physician arrives at a recommended therapeutic or diagnostic intervention only after carefully examining a list of risks and benefits, then rendering the physician's thinking transparent requires that those risks and benefits be detailed for the patient. If the physician's thinking has not followed that route but has reached its conclusion by other considerations, then what needs to be disclosed to the patient is accordingly different. Essentially, the transparency standard requires the physician to engage in the typical patient-management thought process, only to *do it out loud in language understandable to the patient.*[9]

To see how this might work in practice, consider the following as possible general decision-making strategies that might be used by a primary physician:

1. The intervention, in addition to being presumably low-risk, is also routine and automatic. The physician, faced with a case like that presented by the patient, almost always chooses this treatment.

2. The decision is not routine but seems to offer clear benefit with minimal risk.

3. The proposed procedure offers substantial chances for benefit, but also very substantial risks.

4. The proposed intervention offers substantial risks and extremely questionable benefits. Unfortunately, possible alternative courses of action also have high risk and uncertain benefit.

The exact risks entailed by treatment loom much larger in the physician's own thinking in cases 3 and 4 than in cases 1 and 2. The transparency standard would require that physicians at least mention the various risks to patients in scenarios 3 and 4, but would not necessarily require physicians exhaustively to describe risks, unless the patient asked, in scenarios 1 and 2.

The transparency standard seems to offer some considerable advantages for informing physicians what can legitimately be expected of them in the promotion of patient autonomy while carrying out the activities of primary care medicine, We would hope that the well-trained primary care physician generally thinks before acting. On that assumption, the physician can be told exactly when she is finished obtaining informed consent—first, she has to share her thinking with the patient; secondly, she has to encourage and answer questions; and third, she has to discover how participatory he wishes to be and facilitate that level of participation. This seems a much more reasonable task within primary care than an exhaustive listing of often irrelevant risk factors.

There are also considerable advantages for the patient in this approach. The patient retains the right to ask for an exhaustive recital of risks and alternatives. However, the vast majority of patients, in a primary care setting particularly, would wish to supplement a standardized recital of risks and benefits of treatment with some questions like, "Yes, doctor, but what does this really mean for me? What meaning am I supposed to attach to the information that you've just given?" For example, in scenarios 1 and 2, the precise and specific risk probabilities and possibilities are very small considerations in the thinking of the physician, and reciting an exhaustive list of risks

would seriously misstate just what the physician was thinking. If the physician did detail a laundry list of risk factors, the patient might very well ask, "Well, doctor, just what should I think about what you have just told me?" and the thoughtful and concerned physician might well reply, "There's certainly a small possibility that one of these bad things will happen to you; but I think the chance is extremely remote and in my own practice I have never seen anything like that occur." The patient is very likely to give much more weight to that statement, putting the risks in perspective, than he is to the listing of risks. And that emphasis corresponds with an understanding of how the physician herself has reached the decision.

The transparency standard should further facilitate and encourage useful questions from patients. If a patient is given a routine list of risks and benefits and then is asked "Do you have any questions?" the response may well be perfunctory and automatic. If the patient is told precisely the grounds on which the physician has made her recommendation, and then asked the same question, the response is much more likely to be individualized and meaningful.

There certainly would be problems in applying the transparency standard in the courtroom, but these do not appear to be materially more difficult than those encountered in applying other standards; moreover, this standard could call attention to more important features in the ethical relationship between physician and patient. Consider the fairly typical case, in which a patient suffers harm from the occurrence of a rare but predictable complication of a procedure, and then claims that he would not have consented had he known about that risk. Under the present 'enlightened' court standards, the jury would examine whether a reasonable patient would have needed to know about that risk factor prior to making a decision on the proposed intervention. Under the transparency standard, the question would instead be whether the physician thought about that risk factor as a relevant consideration prior to recommending the course of action to the patient. If the physician did seriously consider that risk factor, but failed to reveal that to the patient, he was in effect making up the patient's mind in advance about what risks were worth accepting. In that situation, the physician could easily be held liable. If, on the other hand, that risk was considered too insignificant to play a role in determining which intervention ought to be performed, the physician may still have rendered his thinking completely transparent to the patient even though that specific risk factor was not mentioned. In this circumstance, the physician would be held to have done an adequate job of disclosing information.[10] A question would still exist as to whether a competent physician ought to have known about that risk factor and ought to have considered it more carefully prior to doing the procedure. But that question raises the issue of negligence, which is where such considerations properly belong, and removes the problem from the context of informed consent. Obviously, the standard of informed consent is misapplied if it is intended by itself to prevent the practice of negligent medicine.

Transparency in Medical Practice

Will adopting a legal standard like transparency change medical practice for the better? Ultimately only empirical research will answer this question. We know almost nothing about the sorts of conversations primary care physicians now have with their patients, or what would happen if these physicians routinely tried harder to share their basic thinking about therapeutic choices. In this setting it is possible to argue that the transparency standard will have deleterious effects. Perhaps the physician's basic thinking will fail to include risk issues that patients, from their perspective, would regard as substantial. Perhaps how physicians think about therapeutic choice will prove to be too idiosyncratic and variable to serve as any sort of standard. Perhaps disclosing basic thinking processes will impede rather than promote optimal patient participation in decisions.

But the transparency standard must be judged, not only against ideal medical practice, but also against the present-day standard and the message it sends to practitioners. I have argued that that message is, "You can protect yourself legally only by guessing all bad outcomes that might occur and warning each patient explicitly that he might suffer any of them." The transparency standard is an attempt to send the message, "You can protect yourself legally by conversing with your patients in a way that promotes their participation in medical decisions, and more

specifically by making sure that they see the basic reasoning you used to arrive at the recommended treatment." It seems at least plausible to me that the attempt is worth making.

The reasonable person standard may still be the best way to view informed consent in highly specialized settings where a relatively small number of discrete and potentially risky procedures are the daily order of business. In primary care settings, the best ethical advice we can give physicians is to view informed consent as an ongoing process of conversation designed to maximize patient participation after adequately revealing the key facts. Because the conversation metaphor does not by itself suggest measures for later judicial review, a transparency standard, or something like it, may be a reasonable way to operationalize that concept in primary care practice. Some positive side-effects of this might be more focus on good diagnostic and therapeutic decisionmaking on the physician's part, since it will be understood that the patient will be made aware of what the physician's reasoning process has been like, and better documentation of management decisions in the patient record. If these occur, then it will be clearer that the standard of informed consent has promoted rather than impeded high quality patient care.

REFERENCE

1. Charles W. Lidz *et al.*, "Barriers to Informed Consent," *Annals of Internal Medicine* 99:4 (1983), 539–43.

2. Tom L. Beauchamp and Laurence McCullough, *Medical Ethics: The Moral Responsibilities of Physicians* (Englewood Cliffs, NJ: Prentice-Hall, 1984).

3. For a concise overview of empirical data about contemporary informed consent practices see Ruth R. Faden and Tom L. Beauchamp, *A History and Theory of Informed Consent* (New York: Oxford University Press, 1986), 98–99 and associated footnotes.

4. For efforts to address ethical aspects of primary care practice, see Ronald J. Christie and Barry Hoffmaster, *Ethical Issues in Family Medicine* (New York: Oxford University Press, 1986); and Harmon L. Smith and Larry R. Churchill, *Professional Ethics and Primary Care Medicine* (Durham, NC: Duke University Press, 1986).

5. Faden and Beauchamp, *A History and Theory of Informed Consent*, 23–49 and 114–50. I have also greatly benefited from an unpublished paper by Margaret Wallace.

6. For a specialty opinion to the contrary, see W. H. Coles *et al.*, "Teaching Informed Consent," in *Further Developments in Assessing Clinical Competence*, Ian R. Hart and Ronald

M. Harden, eds. (Montreal: Can-Heal Publications, 1987), 241–70. This paper is interesting in applying to specialty care a model very much like the one I propose for primary care.

7. Jay Katz, *The Silent World of Doctor and Patient* (New York: Free Press, 1984).

8. Howard Brody, *Stories of Sickness* (New Haven: Yale University Press, 1987), 171–81.

9. For an interesting study of physicians' practices on this point, see William C. Wu and Robert A Pearlman,

"Consent in Medical Decisionmaking: The Role of Communication," *Journal of General Internal Medicine* 3:1 (1988), 9–14.

10. A court case that might point the way toward this line of reasoning is *Precourt v. Frederick*, 395 **Mass.** 689 (1985). See William J. Curran, "Informed Consent in Malpractice Cases: A Turn Toward Reality," *New England Journal of Medicine* 314:7 (1986), 429–31.

Should Informed Consent Be Based on Rational Beliefs?

JULIAN SAVULESCU AND RICHARD W. MOMEYER

Savulescu and Momeyer maintain that being autonomous requires that a person hold rational beliefs. In informed consent, what passes for respecting autonomy often consists of little more than giving the patient information. But "[b]eing fully autonomous requires not only that we are informed, but that we exercise our theoretical rationality." Thus to ensure true informed consent, physicians should not only provide relevant information but also "assist patients to think more clearly and rationally. [Physicians] should care more about the rationality of patients' beliefs."

I. Introduction

Medical ethics places great emphasis on physicians respecting patient autonomy. It encourages tolerance even towards harmful choices patients make on the basis of their own values. This ethic has been defended by consequentialists and deontologists.

Respect for autonomy finds expression in the doctrine of consent. According to that doctrine, no medical procedure may be performed upon a competent patient unless that patient has consented to have that procedure, after having been provided with the relevant facts.

We have no quarrel with these principles. We do, however, question their interpretation and application. Our contention is that being autonomous requires that a person hold rational beliefs. We distinguish between rational choice and rational belief. Being autonomous may not require that one's choices

From *Medical Ethics* by Michael Boylan, "Should Informed Consent Be Based on Rational Beliefs?" by Julian Savulescu and Richard W. Momeyer, pp. 128–40. Copyright © 2000. Reprinted by permission of Pearson Education, Inc., Upper Saddle River, NJ.

and actions are rational. But it does require that one's beliefs which ground those choices are rational. If this is right, what passes for respecting autonomy sometimes consists of little more than providing information, and stops short of assessing whether this information is rationally processed. Some of what purports to be medical deference to a patient's values is not this at all: rather, it is acquiescence to irrationality. Some of what passes for respecting patient autonomy may turn out to be less respect than abandonment. Abandonment of patients has never been regarded as a morally admirable practice.

We will outline three ways in which patients hold irrational beliefs: (1) ignorance, (2) not caring enough about rational deliberation, and (3) making mistakes in deliberation. We argue that it is the responsibility of physicians not only to provide relevant information (which addresses 1), but to improve the rationality of belief that grounds consent (2 and 3).

II. Rationality and Autonomy
II.I True Belief and Autonomy
The word, "autonomy," comes from the Greek: autos (self) and nomos (rule or law).[1] Autonomy

is self-government or self-determination. Being autonomous involves freely and actively making one's own evaluative choices about how one's life should go.

It is a familiar idea that it is necessary to hold true beliefs if we are to get what we want. For example, John loves Northern Indian dishes and loathes Southern Indian dishes. Yet he is very confused about which dishes belong to which area. He consistently orders Southern Indian dishes thinking he is ordering Northern Indian dishes. His false beliefs cause him to fail to get what he wants.

However, true beliefs are important for evaluative choice in a more fundamental way: we cannot form an idea of *what* we want without knowing what the options on offer are *like*. Consider a person with gangrene of the foot. She is offered an amputation. In evaluating "having an amputation" she is attempting to evaluate a complete state of affairs: how much pain she will experience, whether she will be able to live by herself, visit her grandchildren, and so on. (Importantly, knowing the name of one's disease and the nature of the operation are less important facts.)

II.II True Belief and Practical Rationality

Practical rationality is concerned with what we have reason to care about and do. Let's distinguish between what there is good reason to do and what it is rational to do. Paul sits down after work to have a relaxing evening with his wife. She gives him a glass of what he believes is wine, but is in fact poison. There is a good reason for Paul not to drink it, even if this is not known to Paul. However, if he believes that it is wine, it is rational for him to drink it.[2] Thus:

> It is rational for a person to perform some act if there would be a good reason to perform that act if the facts were as he/she believes them to be.

Thus holding true beliefs is important in two ways: (1) it promotes our autonomy and (2) allows us to see that there is good reason to do. This does not collapse autonomous choice with rational choice. Even holding all the relevant true beliefs, a person may autonomously choose some course which he or she has no good reason to choose. For example, assume that the harms of smoking outweigh the benefits. Jim has

good reason to give up smoking. However, he may choose to smoke knowing all the good and bad effects of smoking. His choice is then irrational but his beliefs may be rational and he may be autonomous. His choice is not an expression of his autonomy if he believes that smoking is not only pleasurable, but good for your health.

II.III Coming to Hold True Beliefs

One important way to hold true beliefs is via access to relevant information. For example, one way to get Paul to believe that the wine is poisoned is to provide him with evidence that it is poisoned.

We can never know for certain that our beliefs are true. We can only be confident of their truth. Confidence is the likelihood that a belief is true. Beliefs which are based on evidence (rational beliefs) are more likely to be true than unfounded (irrational) beliefs. The likelihood that our beliefs are true is a function both of how informed they are and of how we think about that information.

Theoretical rationality is concerned with what it is rational to believe.

> It is rational for a person to believe some proposition if he/she ought to believe that proposition if he/she were deliberating rationally about the evidence available and his/her present beliefs, and those beliefs are not themselves irrational.

Let's say that a person is "deliberating rationally" if:[3]

1. She holds a degree of belief in a proposition which is responsive to the evidence supporting that proposition. For example, the firmer the evidence, the greater the degree of belief ought to be.
2. She examines her beliefs for consistency. If she detects inconsistency, she ought appropriately to contract her set of beliefs or adjust her degree of belief in the relevantly inconsistent beliefs.
3. She exposes her reasoning to the norms of inductive and deductive logic. Valid logic is important because it helps us to have the broadest range of true beliefs.

Consider the following example. Peter is trying to decide whether to have an operation. Suppose that he is provided with certain information and reasons in the following way.

1. There is a risk of dying from anaesthesia. (true)
2. I will require an anaesthetic if I am to have this operation. (true)

Therefore, if I have this operation, I will probably die.

———

The conclusion does not follow from the premises. Peter comes to hold an irrational belief because he commits a logical error. Irrational beliefs are less likely to be true than rational beliefs. Since knowledge of truth is elusive for subjective beings like us, the best we can hope for is informed, rational belief.

If we are right that information is important to evaluative choice because of its contribution to a person holding the relevant true beliefs necessary for evaluation, then deliberating rationally is as important as being informed, since this also affects the likelihood that one's beliefs are true. Being fully autonomous requires not only that we are informed, but that we exercise our theoretical rationality.

III. An Example of Irrational Belief: Jehovah's Witnesses and Blood

Jehovah's Witnesses (JWs) who refuse life-saving blood transfusions for themselves are often taken to be paradigm cases of autonomous, informed choice based on different (non-medically shared) values that require respect and deference.

Jehovah's Witnesses refuse life-saving blood transfusions because they believe that if they die and have received blood, they will turn to dust. But if they refuse blood (and keep Jehovah's other laws) and die, they will enjoy eternal life in Paradise.[4]

Jehovah's Witnesses interpret The Bible as forbidding the sustaining of life with blood in any manner. They base this belief on passages such as:

> "Every creature that lives and moves shall be food for you . . . But you must not eat the flesh with the life, which is the blood, still in it."[5]

Anyone eating the blood of an animal would be "cutoff" or executed.[6] The only legitimate use of animal blood was as a sacrifice to God. Leviticus 17:11 states:

> "... the life of the creature is the blood, and I appoint it to make expiation on the altar for yourselves: it is the blood, that is the life, that makes expiation."[7]

Jehovah's Witnesses believe these views concerning blood were important to the early Christian Church. At a meeting of the apostles and older men of Jerusalem to determine which laws would continue to be upheld in the new Church, blood was again proscribed:

> "... you are to abstain from meat that has been offered to idols, from blood, from anything that has been strangled. and from fornication."[8]

Jehovah's Witnesses believe that these passages imply more than a dietary proscription. They attach great symbolic significance to blood: it represents the life or soul. Thus they claim that the exhortation "abstain from blood" applies to all forms of blood, at all times. They argue that there is no moral difference between sustaining life by taking blood by mouth ("eating blood") and taking blood directly into the veins.

Relative to their beliefs, JWs are practically rational. Any (practically) rational person would choose to forgo earthly life if this ensured that one would enjoy a blissful eternal existence in the presence of God. If JWs are irrational, it is because their beliefs are irrational. A failure of theoretical rationality causes them to do what there is good reason not to do and frustrates their autonomy.

We believe that the beliefs of JWs are irrational. One way to show this is to question the rationality of belief in the existence of God or in the truth of some religious version of morality. For argument's sake, we will accept theism. However, the vast majority of those in the Judaeo-Christian tradition have not interpreted these passages from The Bible as proscribing blood transfusion. The beliefs of JWs are irrational on at least two counts: their particular beliefs are not responsive to evidence nor are their interpretations of Biblical text consistent. These failures of rationality are shared with other forms of religious "fundamentalism" and so-called "literal" interpretations of religious texts. It is worth noting that many JWs are also Creationists, believing all of Genesis to be literally true. Ignorance of historical context, the diverse intentions and circumstances of

Biblical peoples and authors, oral and written traditions in the Middle East, other religious traditions and interpretations of Biblical texts, inconsistencies between different canonised works and the like all help ground an unduly simplistic interpretation of The Bible.

Mere ignorance, however, is not to be equated with irrationality. Wilful ignorance is. And wilful ignorance is what lies behind grounding understanding of The Bible on faith rather than the kinds of knowledge suggested above. This sort of wilful ignorance cuts across educational levels as it is rooted in dogmatism and closed-mindedness rather than degrees of education.

However, we believe that JWs' beliefs are irrational even in terms that should be acceptable to JWs.

Firstly, their interpretation is inconsistent with other passages of The Bible and Christian practices. It is inconsistent with the Christian practice of communion. Communion is the holy ceremony of the Last Supper. At the Last Supper

> "Jesus took bread, and having said the blessing he broke it . . . with these words: 'Take this and eat; this is my body.' Then he took a cup [of wine], and having offered thanks to God . . . [said]. . . 'Drink from it . . . For this is my blood, the blood of the covenant, shed for many, for the forgiveness of sins.'"[9]

Secondly, Paul warns against slavish obedience to law:

> ". . . those who rely on obedience to the law are under a curse. . . ."[10] Christ bought us freedom from the curse of the law by becoming . . . an accursed thing."[11]

The answer is not obedience to law but faith.

> ". . . the law was a kind of tutor in charge of us until Christ should come, when we should be justified through faith; and now that faith has come, the tutor's charge is at an end."[12]

Paul himself does not understand The Bible to be literally true, as evidenced when he speaks of the story of the origin of Abraham's sons being "an allegory."[13] He goes on to say:

> "Mark my words: I, Paul, say to you that if you receive circumcision Christ will do you no good at all . . . [E]very man who receives circumcision is under obligation to keep the entire law. When you seek to be justified by way of law, your relation with Christ is completely severed . . . [O]ur hope of attaining that righteousness . . . is the work of the Spirit through faith . . . the only thing that counts is faith active in love."[14]

If the beliefs of JWs are irrational, why are they irrational?

IV. Three Examples of Holding a False Belief

In all three of the following cases, the person lacks a true belief which is relevant to choice. We describe how to help a person come to hold true beliefs, drawing out the parallels with patients and JWs.

Case 1. Lack of Information

Arthur 1 is burning rubbish in the garden. The fire grows rapidly. It begins to threaten surrounding buildings. They are not in imminent danger but Arthur wants to douse the fire with water before it gets out of hand. He goes to the shed where he keeps a jerry can of water for just such a situation. He has a high degree of belief that this can contains water. Unbeknownst to him, someone has substituted petrol for water in the can. He throws the liquid on the fire and the petrol ignites causing an explosion. He is badly burnt. Was Arthur irrational?

We need a more complete description of the state of affairs.

Arthur always locks the shed. There had been no signs of forced entry. There was only one jerry can in the shed. It was in the position where Arthur always kept it, next to the shovel. He had only the previous weekend refilled it with water after using it to put out another garden fire. If Arthur simply had no reason to suspect that the can contained anything but water, it was rational to believe that it contained water. A person who unavoidably lacks relevant information is neither theoretically nor practically irrational.

What should we do if we see Arthur about to throw the liquid onto the fire?

Arthur is rational, but he lacks a relevant true belief that he could have. In this case, the solution is simple. Provide information. Tell him, "Stop. The can contains petrol." If there were no time to provide this information, we ought to grab the can from his hands.

Many patients who hold false beliefs are like Arthur 1: uninformed. What we ought to do is provide them with information. If this is not possible, we should do what is best for them.

Are there any JWs like Arthur 1? Jehovah's Witnesses are remarkably well informed about blood transfusion, the effects of refusing it, and the Biblical context of their belief. But some may be unaware of the conflicting Biblical passages. These ought to be treated like Arthur 1. However, many are not like him. The provision of information is not alone an adequate response. What is required is rational argument.

Case 2. Not Engaging in Rational Deliberation

Arthur 2 is the same as Arthur 1, but in this case Arthur goes to the shed and finds it unlocked. He is not sure whether he left it locked last weekend. He thinks he probably did. The jerry can is next to the lawn mower. Arthur thinks that he normally keeps it next to the shovel. But, again, he is not sure. Is he irrational if he believes the can contains water?

Arthur clearly ought to believe that the door is open and the can is next to the lawnmower. But for these propositions to constitute evidence for the conclusion that the contents of the can are not water, Arthur must believe that the position of the can and door have changed. Should Arthur believe that he left the jerry can next to the shovel? This depends on the degree of belief Arthur has in his recollection of how things were. If he is vague, then there is no evidence.

Arthur may not lack information as much as a context for that information because he fails to remember relevant facts. This may be beyond control. In this case, Arthur 2 is like Arthur 1. But in some cases, a person fails to remember because he fails to think about the issue. And he may fail to think about the issue because he fails to care enough about the truth of his beliefs or the consequences of his actions.

Arthur could be directed to think more carefully about what he sees and of the possible implications of his actions. There may be other evidence he would find, if he looked, for believing the propositions that the door was locked and the can was next to the shovel. He may notice other items in the shed have been moved.

It is often thought that consultation in medicine involves presenting information so that it is understood. But even understanding is not enough. Facts must be assembled to tell a story or to construct an argument which stands in the foreground of deliberation. The arrangement and form of the facts is as important as their content.

Are there any JWs who are like Arthur 2? There is, we are assuming, evidence that their beliefs are false. However, being informed of these facts is not sufficient to cause them to hold the relevant true beliefs. They also need to care about thinking about that information in a rational way. The hallmark of faith is a stubbornness to respond to the evidence for a proposition. While this may be necessary for belief in God, it cannot be the appropriate paradigm for interpretation of God's word. The Bible, as a guide to how to live, aims to sanction some ways of living and proscribe others. Faith *in any interpretation* of God's word cannot be acceptable.[15] When interpreting the Biblical text, the appropriate paradigm for theists is rationality and not faith. Indeed, the efforts of JWs to argue for their interpretation of The Bible indicates that they subscribe to this paradigm. What they are required to do by that paradigm is to care more about the proper exercise of rationality.

Intervention in this case would include trying to persuade JWs to care more about rationality by showing how they themselves appeal to rational argument and why The Bible must be interpreted rationally.

We are often like Arthur 2 and some JWs: we fail to care enough about what we believe and what we commit to memory. This failing is at the interface of practical and theoretical rationality: we fail to care enough (a practical failing) about the rationality of our beliefs (a theoretical failing).

Case 3. Theoretical Irrationality

Arthur 3 is the same as Arthur 2 but in this case, Arthur is sure he left the door to the shed locked and sure that the jerry can is in a different position from where he left it. On entering the shed, he smells petrol. He doesn't normally keep petrol in the shed. None the less, he throws the fluid on the fire.

As the evidence mounts up, Arthur becomes more theoretically irrational if he fails to consider the possibility that the can contains petrol. At the limit, if the evidence is overwhelming, he is like a person who believes that p, and that if p then q, but fails to believe that q.

Why might Arthur be theoretically irrational?

He may simply fail to believe that what he smells is petrol. This would be an error of perception.

He may fail to examine his beliefs for inconsistency. He may fail to compare what he believes to what the evidence suggests is the case.

Most importantly of all, Arthur may not be very talented at theoretical reasoning. He may not be good at assembling the evidence and drawing conclusions from it. It is not enough for a person to throw up *any* explanation for evidence presented to him. To move from "I saw a light on the water" to "I saw a ghost at Dead Man's Bluff" is to make an unjustified and irrational leap. Ideally, we should infer to the best explanation.[16]

Physicians, concerned to promote theoretical rationality, may assemble facts in a way which together suggest a conclusion. But patients may still fail to draw the right conclusion. Telling a patient that he has "advanced cancer" may imply that he will die. But the patient may not conclude this. Indeed, even telling a patient that he will die may not convey "the message" that the physician intends to give: perhaps that the patient ought to sort out his affairs, that he will not offer any more curative treatments, and so on.

How would a person who is in a similar epistemic position to Arthur, but who is more theoretically rational than Arthur 3, convince him that the can contains petrol? He would engage Arthur in argument. He would provide reasons. He might say something like, "The can seems to be in a different position from how you left it. That might suggest that someone has used it. I can smell petrol. Perhaps someone has used the can to carry petrol."

The reason why most JWs hold an irrational belief is because they make mistakes in their theoretical reasoning. What is the best way to correct these mistakes? For many, it is a matter of someone versed in the relevant texts taking them through the argument.

In other cases, the route may be more indirect. A JW may be presented with some information, call it, I, which should or would cause him to conclude

that C if he also held other beliefs, B. However, he may fail to believe B or utilise B. He may have forgotten B in the urgent search for salvation, or had it drummed out of his head, or failed to see any longer its relevance. Intervention requires that we tap into these other beliefs. For an argument to be convincing for him may require the construction of the appropriate context: to show him that his belief should be rejected in his own terms.

Our object is the beliefs of JWs, not necessarily their choices. In some circumstances, JWs might autonomously choose to reject blood. We can autonomously adopt a course of action with a low probability of success, provided that we hold the relevant rational beliefs. Neither risk-takers nor the exceedingly cautious are necessarily non-autonomous, nor are they necessarily doing what there is good reason not to do.[17]

If JWs were to hold the relevant informed, rational beliefs, they might then autonomously choose to reject blood. But from their revised epistemic position, many would no doubt accept blood.

V. Summary and Implications

Where most rational agents differ from JWs is that they do not hold all of the following beliefs:

1. There is a God.
2. Divinely conferred immortality is possible for human beings after death.
3. God forbids eating blood.
4. Accepting a blood transfusion is no different from eating blood.
5. If one eats blood when alive, one turns to dust upon death.
6. We know 3–5 to be true based on faith that a (selectively) literal interpretation of The Bible reveals God's will.
7. If one lives a faithful life in accord with Jehovah's laws, eternal life is assured.

Many health care workers no doubt believe 1 and 2 and some variation on 7; it is 3, 4, 5, or especially 6 that is rejected. But this is a difference not in moral beliefs or values but about the structure of reality. This is a difference of opinion about metaphysics.

Hence if we are to respect JWs' refusals of life-prolonging blood transfusions, it is not on the grounds that we are obliged to respect decision-making that is based on a different value system from ours. Their values are the same as many other theists and atheists. They value earthly life and immortality as much as others do.

We often hear that we should allow people to do what there is no good reason to do out of respect for their nature as autonomous beings, as ends in themselves. But many such instances are something else entirely. They are cases in which people hold irrational beliefs. They are cases of theoretical irrationality. We do not respect autonomy when we encourage people to act on irrational beliefs. Rather, such beliefs limit a person's autonomy.

Rational Deliberation

Our aim has been to expand the regulative ideal governing consent. We have argued that true beliefs are necessary for evaluation. Information is important to choice insofar as it helps a person to hold the relevant true beliefs. But in order to hold the relevant true beliefs, competent people must also think rationally. Insofar as information is important, rational deliberation is important. Just as physicians should aim to provide relevant information regarding the medical procedures prior to patients consenting to have those procedures they should also assist patients to think more clearly and rationally. They should care more about the rationality of patients' beliefs.

Since holding true beliefs is necessary to be autonomous, we do not respect autonomy when we allow patients to act on irrational beliefs. Should physicians override choices based on irrational beliefs? Should life-saving blood transfusions be given to JWs against their wishes?

When we look at how informed medical decisions must be, we see that a requirement of informedness functions as an ideal to be striven for, and not as a requirement to be enforced. Society generally accepts that patients should be informed of all the relevant facts, but not that they must be compelled to accept information which they do not want. To force information on a person would be coercive.

The requirements of theoretical rationality should be on a par with requirements of informedness. This raises the question whether we should override both choices made in ignorance of relevant information or on the basis of irrational beliefs. We believe that there are reasons against taking this radical departure from the notion of informed consent as a regulative ideal.

The first reason is consequentialist: if we allow doctors to override choices based on some species of irrationality, then other JWs will be distressed at the thought their decisions will be overridden. The general misery and distrust of medicine that would result would reduce the value of such a policy. In the vast majority of cases, JWs' refusal of blood does not compromise their care. In fact, many may receive better care. Given the small numbers of people who would be saved by such a policy, it is not clear that it would be for the best. As is usually the case, education is better than compulsion.

Secondly, though a practice of allowing people to act out of wilful ignorance or irrationality may not promote their autonomy in the short term, respect for autonomy is not the only ground for noninterference in another person's life. It is surely enough that it is his life, and that he ought to be allowed to do what there is no good reason to do, if he chooses. Respect for persons is not restricted to respect for wholly rational persons.

In some cases, irrationality is so gross that it calls into question a person's competence. In these cases, intervention may be justified. But at lesser degrees of irrationality, we encourage the development of autonomy for all people in the long term by adopting a policy of empowering people to make their own choices.

Thirdly, *requiring* that choice be grounded on rational beliefs before it is respected is fraught with dangers. Those who claim to know Truth with certainty are at least as dangerous as those who claim to know Right and Good with certainty. Dogmatic ideologues of either sort show a lamentable propensity to use their "knowledge" to oppress others, sometimes "benignly" as paternalists, more often tyrannically as authoritarians. Hence a measure of epistemic scepticism about our own rationality or the lack of rationality in others is highly desirable.

In the end, deferral to irrationality, to partial autonomy, to imperfect consent and to unexplored values and metaphysical beliefs in patients may be necessary, even morally required. But before reaching this point, a physician committed to the highest standard of care will exercise her talents as an educator to promote greater rationality in patients. Not to make the effort to promote rational, critical deliberation is to risk a very contemporary form of patient abandonment: abandonment to human irrationality.

Duties as Educators

In important ways physicians have always been expected to be educators: about how bodies work, do not work, and go awry; about how to care for our bodies in sickness and health; about, in the end, how to live a mortal embodied existence. Our discussion suggests, however, that physician duties as educators are more extensive. For in order genuinely to respect autonomy and patients' values, physicians must be prepared to do more than provide patients with information relevant to making evaluative choices. They must attend to how that information is received, understood and used. Good education is not restricted to providing information. It requires encouraging in others the requisite skills for dealing with information rationally.

If an ethic of respect for persons in contemporary medicine rules out—except in the most extreme cases—coercion as a response to patient irrationality, it also makes more imperative a "critical educator" response to patient irrationality. One caveat, however: effective educators know when to promote critical enquiry. Physicians, whose primary obligations are to the medical wellbeing of patients, will do well to resist the secondary obligation to promote rational criticism of deeply held beliefs at a time when their patients are impaired and suffering greatly. Thus the time to engage a hypothetically irrational JW in a critical enquiry about her convictions on "eating blood" is not the time at which she might benefit from an immediate blood transfusion because her life is in jeopardy.

It may be a very contemporary form of physician abandonment of patients in need to accept wilfulness as autonomy, the mere provision of information as adequate for informed consent, and acceptance of any morally or metaphysically bizarre view held by patients as grounds for not pursuing a medically beneficial course of treatment. But if physicians are to promote autonomy, if they are to respect patients as persons, if they are to help patients to choose and do what there is good reason to do, they should care more about the rationality of their patients' beliefs. Physicians must concern themselves with helping patients to deliberate more effectively and, ultimately, must themselves learn to care more about theoretical rationality. To do any less is to abandon patients to autonomy-destroying, theoretical irrationality.

Acknowledgment

Thanks to Derek Parfit, Michael Lockwood and David Malyon for many helpful comments.

REFERENCES AND NOTES

1. Dworkin G. *The theory and practice of autonomy.* Cambridge: Cambridge University Press, 1988:. 12.

2. Adapted from Parfit D. *Reasons and persons.* Oxford: Clarendon Press, 1984: 153.

3. Forrest P. *The dynamics of belief: a normative logic.* Oxford: Basil Blackwell, 1986.

4. Watch Tower Bible and Tract Society of Pennsylvania. *Family care and medical management for Jehovah's Witnesses.* New York: Watch Tower Bible and Tract Society of New York, 1995.

5. *The new English Bible*: Genesis 9:3–4.

6. *The new English Bible*: Leviticus 17: 10, 13, 14; 7: 26, 7; Numbers 15: 30, 31; Deuteronomy 12: 23–5.

7. *The new English Bible*: Leviticus 17: 11.

8. *The new English Bible*: Acts 15: 29.

9. *The new English Bible*: Matthew 26: 26–9.

10. *The new English Bible*: Galatians 3: 10.

11. *The new English Bible*: Galatians 3: 13.

12. *The new English Bible*: Galatians 3: 24–5.

13. *The new English Bible*: Galatians 4: 24.

14. *The new English Bible*: Galatians 5: 2–6.

15. Belief in God may be a basic belief: a belief which does not rest on other beliefs. (Swinburne R. *Faith and reason.* Oxford: Clarendon Press, 1981: 33.) A basic rational belief is a belief in a proposition that is (1) self-evident or fundamental, (2) evident to the senses or memory, or (3) defensible by argument, inquiry or performance (Kenny A. *Faith and reason.* New York: Columbia University Press, 1983: 27). Beliefs about eating blood are secondary beliefs. They must be justified in terms of other beliefs. It is precisely this that cannot be rationally done.

16. Armstrong DM. *What is a law of nature?* Cambridge: Cambridge University Press, 1983: 59.

17. Pascal gave a rationalist argument for belief in God: we have more to lose if we do not believe in God, and we are wrong (eternal torment), than we have to lose if we do believe in God, and we are wrong (living under an illusion). So we ought to believe that God exists (Pascal B. *Pensées*. Geneve: Pierre Cailler, 1947: fragment 223). Theoretically rational JWs could give a similar justification for refusing blood.

Informed Consent: Some Challenges to the Universal Validity of the Western Model

ROBERT J. LEVINE

Levine says that since different countries and cultures may have vastly different perspectives on the nature of persons, and since the point of informed consent is to show respect for persons, it is not possible to provide a definition of informed consent that is universally applicable. The rules of the Western model of informed consent are not appropriate for many cultures. The ethical principle of respect for persons is universally applicable, but applying it to specific cultures with varying notions of *person* can be problematic. Levine suggests that instead of insisting on sticking to the rules, we use practical procedures to deal with the cultural differences when they arise.

Informed Consent

Informed consent holds a central place in the ethical justification of research involving human subjects. This position is signaled by the fact that it is the first-stated and, by far, the longest principle of the Nuremberg Code.[1]

> I. The voluntary consent of the human subject is absolutely essential. This means that the person involved should have the legal capacity to give consent; should be so situated as to be able to exercise free power of choice, without the intervention of any element of force, fraud, deceit, duress, overreaching, or other ulterior form of constraint or coercion; and should have sufficient knowledge and comprehension of the elements of the subject matter involved as to enable him to make an understanding and enlightened decision. This latter element requires that before the acceptance of an affirmative decision by the experimental subject there should be made known to him the nature, duration, and purpose of the experiment; the method and means by which it is to be conducted; all inconveniences and hazards reasonably to be expected; and the effects upon his health or person which may possibly come from his participation in the experiment. . . .

The Nuremberg Code identifies four attributes of consent without which consent cannot be considered valid: consent must be "voluntary," "legally competent," "informed," and "comprehending." These four attributes stand essentially unchanged to this day. . . .

The National Commission grounded the requirement for informed consent in the ethical principle of respect for persons which it defined as follows:

> Respect for persons incorporates at least two basic ethical convictions: First, that individuals should be treated as autonomous agents, and second, that persons with diminished autonomy and thus in need of protection are entitled to such protections.

The National Commission defined an "autonomous person" as ". . . an individual capable of deliberation about personal goals and of acting under the direction of such deliberation." To show respect for autonomous persons requires that we leave them alone, even to the point of allowing them to choose activities that might be harmful, unless they agree or consent that we may do otherwise. We are not to touch them or to encroach upon their private spaces

From *Law, Medicine, and Health Care*, vol. 19, no. 3–4 (1991), pp. 207–13. Reprinted with permission of the American Society of Law, Medicine & Ethics.

unless such touching or encroachment is in accord with their wishes. Our actions should be designed to affirm their authority and enhance their capacity to be self-determining; we are not to obstruct their actions unless they are clearly detrimental to others. We show disrespect for autonomous persons when we either repudiate their considered judgments or deny them the freedom to act on those judgments in the absence of compelling reasons to do so.

The National Commission's discussion of an autonomous person is consistent with the prevailing perception of the nature of the "moral agent" in Western civilization. A moral agent is an individual who is capable of forming a rational plan of life, capable of rational deliberation about alternative plans of action with the aim of making choices that are compatible with his or her life plan and who assumes responsibility for the consequences of his or her choices.

Although the National Commission did not cite either of the following sources as authoritative in developing its definition of respect for persons, it is clear to this observer that they found them influential: The first is the statement of the principle of respect for persons as articulated by the German philosopher, Immanuel Kant: "So act as to treat humanity, whether in thine own person or in that of any other, in every case as an end withal, never as a means only." A second influential statement is that of the American judge, Benjamin Cardozo: "Every human being of adult years and sound mind has the right to determine what will be done with his own body . . ."

[S]ince the late 1950s the idea of "informed consent" has been used in place of the original idea of "voluntary consent" as presented in the Nuremberg Code. In the actual process of negotiating informed consent and in the reviews of plans for informed consent conducted by Institutional Review Boards (IRBs), there is a tendency to concentrate on the information to be presented to the prospective subject. Among the IRB's principal concerns are the following questions: Is there a full statement of each of the elements of informed consent? Is the information presented in a style of language that one could expect the prospective subject to understand? Implicit in this is a vision of informed consent as a two step

process. First, information is presented to the subject by the investigator. Secondly, the subject satisfies himself or herself that he or she understands, and based upon this understanding either agrees or refuses to participate in the research project. . . .

In the paper I presented at an earlier CIOMS conference[2] I concluded:

> This brief survey of descriptions of relationships between health professionals and patients in three disparate cultures leads me to conclude that the informed consent standards of the Declaration of Helsinki are not universally valid. Imposition of these standards as they are now written will not accomplish their purposes; i.e., they will not guide physicians in their efforts to show respect for persons because they do not reflect adequately the views held in these cultures of the nature of the person in his or her relationship to society.

This conclusion was based on a review of observations of the doctor–patient relationship, subject–investigator relationship and perspectives on the nature of disease in three cultures: Western Africa, China, and a Central American Mayan Indian culture.

The concept of personhood as it exists in various cultures has been addressed in an excellent paper by Willy De Craemer.[3] De Craemer is a cross-cultural sociologist with extensive experience in the field in, among other places, Central Africa and Japan.

In this paper he makes it clear that the Western vision of the person is a minority viewpoint in the world. The majority viewpoint manifest in most other societies, both technologically developing (e.g., Central Africa) and technologically developed (e.g., Japan), does not reflect the American perspective of radical individualism. . . .

> The special status that the Japanese accord to human relationships, with its emphasis on the empathic and solidary interdependence of many individuals, rather than on the autonomous independence of the individual person, includes within it several other core attributes. To begin with, the kind of reciprocity (*on*) that underlies human relationships means that both concretely and symbolically what anthropologist Marcel Mauss . . . termed "the theme of the gift" is one of its dominant motifs. A continuous, gift-exchange-structured flow of material and nonmate-

rial "goods" and "services" takes place between the members of the enclosed human nexus to which each individual belongs. Through a never-ending process of mutual giving, receiving, and repaying . . . a web of relations develops that binds donor and recipients together in diffuse, deeply personal, and overlapping creditor-debtor ways. Generalized benevolence is involved, but so is generalized obligation, both of which take into account another crucial parameter of Japanese culture: the importance attached to status, rank, and hierarchical order in interpersonal relationships, and to . . . "proper-place occupancy" within them. The triple obligation to give, receive, and repay are tightly regulated by this status-formalism and sense of propriety. . . .

It is not difficult to imagine how a research ethics committee in the Western world—particularly in the United States—would evaluate the custom of exchange of gifts—both material and immaterial—in a system that recognized the legitimacy of "status, rank, and hierarchical order." Attention would soon be focused on the problems of "conflicts of interest." Questions would be raised as to whether consent would be invalidated by "undue inducement," or what the Nuremberg Code calls "other ulterior form(s) of constraint or coercion." In my views, it is impossible to evaluate the meaning of cash payments, provision of free services, and other "inducements" without a full appreciation of the cultural significance of such matters.

It is against this backdrop that I have been asked by the CIOMS Conference Programme Committee to "provide a definition [of informed consent] which is widely applicable to different countries and cultures." Given that the purpose of informed consent is to show respect for persons, in recognition of the vastly different perspectives of the nature of "person," I cannot do this. Since I cannot provide a substantive definition of informed consent, I shall suggest a procedural approach to dealing with the problem.

As an American I am firmly committed to the Western vision of the person and deeply influenced by my experience with the American variant of this vision. . . .

Thus, it would not be prudent to trust an American to provide a universally applicable definition of informed consent. I suggest further, that it would not be prudent to rely on any person situated in any culture to provide a universally applicable definition of informed consent.

Before proceeding, I wish to comment on the continuing controversy on the topic of ethical justification of research that crosses national boundaries. There are those who contend that all research, wherever it is conducted, should be justified according to universally applicable standards; I refer to them as "universalists." Those opposed to the universalist position, whom I call "pluralists," accept some standards as universal, but argue that other standards must be adapted to accommodate the mores of particular cultures. Pluralists commonly refer to the universalist position as "ethical imperialism," while universalists often call that of their opponents, "ethical relativism."

Universalists correctly point out that most therapeutic innovations are developed in industrialized nations. Investigators from these countries may go to technologically developing countries to test their innovations for various reasons; some of these reasons are good and some of them are not (e.g., to save money and to take advantage of the less complex and sophisticated regulatory systems typical to technologically developing countries). Moreover, universalists observe that, once the innovations have been proved safe and effective, economic factors often limit their availability to citizens of the country in which they were tested. Requiring investigators to conform to the ethical standards of their own country when conducting research abroad is one way to restrain exploitation of this type. Universalists also point to the Declaration of Helsinki as a widely accepted universal standard for biomedical research that has been endorsed by most countries, including those labeled "technologically developing." This gives weight to their claim that research must be conducted according to universal principles. Furthermore, the complex regulations characteristic of technologically developed countries are, in general, patterned after the Declaration of Helsinki.

Marcia Angell, in a particularly incisive exposition of the universalists' position, suggests this analogy[4]

> Does apartheid offend universal standards of justice, or does it instead simply represent the South African custom that should be seen as morally neutral? If the latter view is accepted, then ethical principles are

not much more than a description of the mores of a society. I believe they must have more meaning than that. There must be a core of human rights that we would wish to see honored universally, despite local variations in their superficial aspects . . . The force of local custom or law cannot justify abuses of certain fundamental rights, and the right of self-determination, on which the doctrine of informed consent is based, is one of them.

Pluralists join with universalists in condemning economic exploitation of technologically developing countries and their citizens.[5] Unlike the universalists, however, they see the imposition of ethical standards for the conduct of research by a powerful country on a developing country as another form of exploitation. In their view, it is tantamount to saying, "No, you may not participate in this development of technology, no matter how much you desire it, unless you permit us to replace your ethical standards with our own." Pluralists call attention to the fact that the Declaration of Helsinki, although widely endorsed by the nations of the world, reflects a uniquely Western view of the nature of the person; as such it does not adequately guide investigators in ways to show respect for all persons in the world.

An example of pluralism may be found in the diversity of national policies regarding blind HIV-seroprevalence studies. The United States Centers for Disease Control are now conducting anonymous tests of leftover blood drawn for other purposes without notification in studies designed to "determine the level of HIV-seroprevalence in a nationwide sample of hospital patients and clients at family planning, sexually transmitted disease, tuberculosis, and drug treatment clinics. . . ." No personal identifiers are kept.[6] Although there seems to be widespread agreement among US commentators that such anonymous testing without notification is ethically justified, different judgments have been reached in other countries, most notably in the United Kingdom and in the Netherlands.[7] Who is to say which of these nations has the correct ethical perspective that should be made part of the "universal standard?"

The legitimacy of the pluralists' position is recognized implicitly in U.S. policy on whether research subjects are required to be informed of the results of HIV antibody testing.[8] In general, this policy re-

quires that all individuals "whose test results are associated with personal identifiers must be informed of their own test results . . . individuals may not be given the option 'not to know' the result. . . ." This policy permits several narrowly defined exceptions. One of these provides that research "conducted at foreign sites should be carefully evaluated to account for cultural norms, the health resource capability and official health policies of the host country." Then "the reviewing IRB must consider if any modification to the policy is significantly justified by the risk/benefit evaluation of the research."

WHO/CIOMS Proposed International Guidelines provide specific guidance for the conduct of research in which an investigator or an institution in a technologically developed country serves as the "external sponsor" of research conducted in a technologically developing "host country."[9] In my judgment these guidelines strike a sensitive balance between the universalist and pluralist perspectives. They require that "the research protocol should be submitted to ethical review by the initiating agency. The ethical standards applied should be no less exacting than they would be for research carried out within the initiating country" (Article 28). They also provide for accommodation to the mores of the culture within the "host country." For example:

> Where individual members of a community do not have the necessary awareness of the implications of participation in an experiment to give adequately informed consent directly to the investigators, it is desirable that the decision whether or not to participate should be elicited through the intermediary of a trusted community leader. (Article 15).

The conduct of research involving human subjects must not violate any universally applicable ethical standards. Although I endorse certain forms of cultural relativism, there are limits to how much cultural relativism ought to be tolerated. Certain behaviors ought to be condemned by the world community even though they are sponsored by a nation's leaders and seem to have wide support of its citizens. For example, the Nuremberg tribunal appealed to universally valid principles in order to determine the guilt of the physicians (war criminals) who had conducted research according to standards approved by their nation's leaders.

I suggest that the principle of respect for persons is one of the universally applicable ethical standards. It is universally applicable when stated at the level of formality employed by Immanuel Kant: "So act as to treat humanity, whether in thine own person or in that of any other, in every case as an end withal, never as a means only." The key concept is that persons are never to be treated only or merely as means to another's ends. When one goes beyond this level of formality or abstraction, the principle begins to lose its universality. When one restates the principle of respect for persons in a form that reflects a peculiarly Western view of the person, it begins to lose its relevance to some people in Central Africa, Japan, Central America, and so on.

The Conference Programme Committee asked me to address the problem "of obtaining consent in cultures where non-dominant persons traditionally do not give consent, such as a wife." Having subscribed to the Western vision of the meaning of person, I believe that all persons should be treated as autonomous agents, wives included. Thus, I believe that we should show respect for wives in the context of research by soliciting their informed consent. But, if this is not permitted within a particular culture, would I exclude wives from participation in research?

Not necessarily. If there is a strong possibility either that the wife could benefit from participation in the research or that the class of women of which she is a representative could benefit (and there is a reasonable balance of risks and potential benefits), I would offer her an opportunity to participate. To do otherwise would not accomplish anything of value (e.g., her entitlement to self-determination); it would merely deprive her of a chance to secure the benefits of participation in the research. I would, of course, offer her an opportunity to decline participation, understanding that in some cultures she would consider such refusal "unthinkable."

. . . Lack of education in and of itself presents no problems that are unfamiliar to those experienced with negotiating informed consent with prospective subjects. These are barriers to comprehension which are not generally insurmountable. Greater problems are presented by those who hold beliefs about health and illness that are inconsistent with the concepts of Western medicine. It may, for example, be difficult to explain the purpose of vaccination to a person who believes that disease is caused by forces that Western civilization dismisses as supernatural or magical.[10] The meaning of such familiar (in the Western world) procedures as blood-letting may be vastly different and very disturbing in some societies.[11] Problems with such explanations can, I believe, be dealt with best by local ethical review committees.

Illiteracy, in and of itself, presents no problems to the process of informed consent which, when conducted properly, entails talking rather than reading. Rather, it presents problems with the documentation of informed consent. The process of informed consent, designed to show respect for persons, fosters their interests by empowering them to pursue and protect their own interests. The consent form, by contrast, is an instrument designed to protect the interests of investigators and their institutions and to defend them against civil or criminal liability. If it is necessary to have such protection of investigators, subjects may be asked to make their mark on a consent document and a witness may be required to countersign and attest to the fact that the subject received the information.

A Procedural Resolution

In "Proposal Guidelines for International Testing of Vaccines and Drugs Against HIV Infection and AIDS" (hereafter referred to as "Proposed HIV Guidelines"), reference is made to an ethical review system.[12] This system is based on that set forth in the WHO/CIOMS Proposed International Guidelines for Biomedical Research Involving Human Subjects. In the Proposed HIV Guidelines, there are suggestions for divisions of responsibility for ethical review. Here I shall elaborate how responsibilities should be divided for determining the adequacy of informed consent procedures.

This proposal presupposes the existence of an international standard for informed consent. I suggest that the standards for informed consent as set forth in the WHO/CIOMS Proposed International Guidelines and as elaborated in the Proposed HIV Guidelines, be recognized as the international standard for informed consent.

1. All plans to conduct research involving human subjects should be reviewed and approved by a research ethics committee (REC). Ideally the REC should be based in the community in which the research is to be conducted. However, as noted in CIOMS/WHO Proposed International Guidelines, under some circumstances regional or national committees may be adequate for these purposes. In such cases it is essential that regional or national committees have as members or consultants individuals who are highly familiar with the customs of the community in which the research is to be done.

The authority of the REC to approve research should be limited to proposals in which the plans for informed consent conform either to the international standard or to a modification of the international standard that has been authorized by a national ethical review body.

2. Proposals to employ consent procedures that do not conform to the international standard should be justified by the researcher and submitted for review and approval by a national ethical review body. Earlier in this paper I identified some conditions or circumstances that could justify such omissions or modifications.

The role of the national ethical review body is to authorize consent procedures that deviate from the international standard. The responsibility for review and approval of the entire protocol (with the modified consent procedure) remains with the REC. Specific details of consent procedures that conform to the international standard or to a modified version of the international standard approved by the national ethical review body should be reviewed and approved by the local ethical review committee.

3. There should be established an international ethical review body to provide advice, consultation and guidance to national ethical review bodies when such is requested by the latter.

4. In the case of externally sponsored research: Ethical review should be conducted in the initiating country. Although it may and should provide advice to the host country, its approval should be based on its finding that plans for informed consent are consistent with the international standard. If there has been a modification of consent procedures approved by the national ethical review body in the host country, the initiating country may either endorse the modification or seek consultation with the international review body.

NOTES

1. Reprinted in R. J. Levine: *Ethics and Regulation of Clinical Research.* Urban & Schwarzenberg, Baltimore & Munich, Second Edition, 1986.

2. R. J. Levine, "Validity of Consent Procedures in Technologically Developing Countries." In: *Human Experimentation and Medical Ethics.* Ed. by Z. Bankowski and N. Howard-Jones, Council for International Organizations of Medical Sciences, Geneva, 1982, pp. 16–30.

3. W. De Craemer, "A Cross-Cultural Perspective on Personhood." *Milbank Memorial Fund Quarterly* 61:19–34, Winter 1983.

4. M. Angell, "Ethical Imperialism? Ethics in International Collaborative Clinical Research." *New England Journal of Medicine* 319:1081–1083, 1988.

5. M. Barry, "Ethical Considerations of Human Investigation in Developing Countries: The AIDS Dilemma." *New England Journal of Medicine* 319:1083–1086. 1988; N. A. Christakis, "Responding to a Pandemic: International Interests in AIDS Control." *Daedalus* 118 (No. 2):113–114, 1989; and N. A. Christakis, "Ethical Design of an AIDS Vaccine Trial in Africa." *Hastings Center Report* 18 (No. 3):31–37, June/July, 1988.

6. M. Pappaioanou et al., "The Family of HIV Seroprevalence Studies: Objectives, Methods and Uses of Sentinel Surveillance in the United States." *Public Health Reports* 105(2):113–119, 1990.

7. R. Bayer, L. H. Lumey, and L. Wan, "The American, British and Dutch Responses to Unlinked Anonymous HIV Seroprevalence Studies: An International Comparison." *AIDS* 4:283–290, 1990, reprinted in this issue of *Laws, Medicine and Health Care,* 19:3–4.

8. R. E. Windom, Assistant Secretary for Health, policy on informing those tested about HIV serostatus, letter to PHS agency heads, Washington, DC, May 9, 1988.

9. Proposed International Guidelines for Biomedical Research Involving Human Subjects, A Joint Project of the World Health Organization and the Council for International Organizations of Medical Sciences, CIOMS. Geneva, 1982.

10. See De Craemer, *supra* note 3 and Levine, *supra* note 2.

11. A. J. Hall, "Public Health Trials in West Africa: Logistics and Ethics." *IRB: A Review of Human Subjects Research* 11 (No. 5):8–10, Sept/Oct 1989. See also Christakis, *supra* note 5.

12. R. J. Levine, and W. K. Mariner, "Proposed Guidelines for International Testing of Vaccines and Drugs Against HIV Infection and AIDS," prepared at the request of WHO, Global Programme on AIDS and submitted January 5, 1990.

Canterbury v. Spence

UNITED STATES COURT OF APPEALS

This 1972 case helped settle the question of what standard should be used to judge the adequacy of disclosure by a physician. The court ruled that adequacy should not be judged by what the medical profession thinks is appropriate but by what information the patient finds relevant to his decision. The scope of the communication to the patient "must be measured by the patient's need, and that need is the information material to the decision."

Suits charging failure by a physician adequately to disclose the risks and alternatives of proposed treatment are not innovations in American law. They date back a good half-century, and in the last decade they have multiplied rapidly. There is, nonetheless, disagreement among the courts and the commentators on many major questions, and there is no precedent of our own directly in point. For the tools enabling resolution of the issues on this appeal, we are forced to begin at first principles.

The root premise is the concept, fundamental in American jurisprudence, that "[e]very human being of adult years and sound mind has a right to determine what shall be done with his own body. . . ." True consent to what happens to one's self is the informed exercise of a choice, and that entails an opportunity to evaluate knowledgeably the options available and the risks attendant upon each. The average patient has little or no understanding of the medical arts, and ordinarily has only his physician to whom he can look for enlightenment with which to reach an intelligent decision. From these almost axiomatic considerations springs the need, and in turn the requirement, of a reasonable divulgence by physician to patient to make such a decision possible.

A physician is under a duty to treat his patient skillfully, but proficiency in diagnosis and therapy is not the full measure of his responsibility. The cases demonstrate that the physician is under an obligation to communicate specific information to the

From U. S. Court of Appeals, District of Columbia Circuit, *Canterbury v. Spence*, 464 F.2d 772 (D.C. Cir. 1972).

patient when the exigencies of reasonable care call for it. Due care may require a physician perceiving symptoms of bodily abnormality to alert the patient to the condition. It may call upon the physician confronting an ailment which does not respond to his ministrations to inform the patient thereof. It may command the physician to instruct the patient as to any limitations to be presently observed for his own welfare, and as to any precautionary therapy he should seek in the future. It may oblige the physician to advise the patient of the need for or desirability of any alternative treatment promising greater benefit than that being pursued. Just as plainly, due care normally demands that the physician warn the patient of any risks to his well-being which contemplated therapy may involve.

The context in which the duty of risk-disclosure arises is invariably the occasion for a decision as to whether a particular treatment procedure is to be undertaken. To the physician. whose training enables a self-satisfying evaluation, the answer may seem clear, but it is the prerogative of the patient, not the physician, to determine for himself the direction in which his interests seem to lie. To enable the patient to chart his course understandably, some familiarity with the therapeutic alternatives and their hazards becomes essential.

A reasonable revelation in these respects is not only a necessity but, as we see it, is as much a matter of the physician's duty. It is a duty to warn of the dangers lurking in the proposed treatment, and that is surely a facet of due care. It is, too, a duty to impart information which the patient has every right to expect. The patient's reliance upon the physician is a trust of the kind which traditionally has exacted obligations beyond those associated with arms-length transactions. His dependence upon the physician for information affecting his well-being, in terms of contemplated treatment, is well-nigh abject. As earlier noted, long before the instant litigation arose, courts had recognized that the physician had the responsibility of satisfying the vital informational needs of the patient. More recently, we ourselves have found "in the fiducial qualities of [the physician-patient] relationship the physician's duty to reveal to the patient that which in his best interests it is important that he should know." We now find, as a part of the physician's overall obligation to the patient, a similar duty of reasonable disclosure of the choices with respect to proposed therapy and the dangers inherently and potentially involved. . . .

Once the circumstances give rise to a duty on the physician's part to inform his patient, the next inquiry is the scope of the disclosure the physician is legally obliged to make. The courts have frequently confronted this problem but no uniform standard defining the adequacy of the divulgence emerges from the decisions. Some have said "full" disclosure, a norm we are unwilling to adopt literally. It seems obviously prohibitive and unrealistic to except physicians to discuss with their patients every risk of proposed treatment—no matter how small or remote—and generally unnecessary from the patient's viewpoint as well. Indeed, the cases speaking in terms of "full" disclosure appear to envision something less than total disclosure, leaving unanswered the question of just how much.

The larger number of courts, as might be expected, have applied tests framed with reference to prevailing fashion within the medical profession. Some have measured the disclosure by "good medical practice," others by what a reasonable practitioner would have bared under the circumstances, and still others by what medical custom in the community would demand. We have explored this rather considerable body of law but are unprepared to follow it. The duty to disclose, we have reasoned, arises from phenomena apart from medical custom and practice. The latter, we think, should no more establish the scope of the duty than its existence. Any

definition of scope in terms purely of a professional standard is at odds with the patient's prerogative to decide on projected therapy himself. That prerogative, we have said, is at the very foundation of the duty to disclose, and both the patient's right to know and the physician's correlative obligation to tell him are diluted to the extent that its compass is dictated by the medical profession.

In our view, the patient's right of self-decision shapes the boundaries of the duty to reveal. That right can be effectively exercised only if the patient possesses enough information to enable an intelligent choice. The scope of the physician's communications to the patient, then, must be measured by the patient's need, and that need is the information material to the decision. Thus the test for determining whether a particular peril must be divulged is its materiality to the patient's decision: all risks potentially affecting the decision must be unmasked. And to safeguard the patient's interest in achieving his own determination on treatment, the law must itself set the standard for adequate disclosure.

Optimally for the patient, exposure of a risk would be mandatory whenever the patient would deem it significant to his decision, either singly or in combination with other risks. Such a requirement, however, would summon the physician to second-guess the patient, whose ideas on materiality could hardly be known to the physician. That would make an undue demand upon medical practitioners, whose conduct, like that of others, is to be measured in terms of reasonableness. Consonantly with orthodox negligence doctrine, the physician's liability for nondisclosure is to be determined on the basis of foresight, not hindsight; no less than any other aspect of negligence, the issue on nondisclosure must be approached from the viewpoint of the reasonableness of the physician's divulgence in terms of what he knows or should know to be the patient's informational needs. If, but only if, the fact-finder can say that the physician's communication was unreasonably inadequate is an imposition of liability legally or morally justified.

Of necessity, the content of the disclosure rests in the first instance with the physician. Ordinarily it is only he who is in position to identify particular dangers; always he must make a judgment, in terms of materiality, as to whether and to what extent revelation to the patient is called for. He cannot know with complete exactitude what the patient would consider important to his decision, but on the basis of his medical training and experience he can sense how the average, reasonable patient expectably would react. Indeed, with knowledge of, or ability to learn, his patient's background and current condition, he is in a position superior to that of most others—attorneys, for example—who are called upon to make judgments on pain of liability in damages for unreasonable miscalculation.

From these considerations we derive the breadth of the disclosure of risks legally to be required. The scope of the standard is not subjective as to either the physician or the patient; it remains objective with due regard for the patient's informational needs and with suitable leeway for the physician's situation. In broad outline, we agree that "[a] risk is thus material when a reasonable person, in what the physician knows or should know to be the patient's position, would be likely to attach significance to the risk or cluster of risks in deciding whether or not to forgo the proposed therapy."

The topics importantly demanding a communication of information are the inherent and potential hazards of the proposed treatment, the alternatives to that treatment, if any, and the results likely if the patient remains untreated. The factors contributing significance to the dangerousness of a medical technique are, of course, the incidence of injury and the degree of the harm threatened. A very small chance of death or serious disablement may well be significant; a potential disability which dramatically outweighs the potential benefit of the therapy or the detriments of the existing malady may summon discussion with the patient.

There is no bright line separating the significant from the insignificant; the answer in any case must abide a rule of reason. Some dangers—infection, for example—are inherent in any operation; there is no obligation to communicate those of which persons of average sophistication are aware. Even more clearly, the physician bears no responsibility for discussion of hazards the patient has already discovered, or those having no apparent materiality to patients' decision on therapy. The disclosure doctrine, like

others marking lines between permissible and impermissible behavior in medical practice, is in essence a requirement of conduct prudent under the circumstances. Whenever nondisclosure of particular risk information is open to debate by reasonable-minded men, the issue is for the finder of the facts.

Two exceptions to the general rule of disclosure have been noted by the courts. Each is in the nature of a physician's privilege not to disclose, and the reasoning underlying them is appealing. Each, indeed, is but a recognition that, as important as is the patient's right to know, it is greatly outweighed by the magnitudinous circumstances giving rise to the privilege. The first comes into play when the patient is unconscious or otherwise incapable of consenting, and harm from a failure to treat is imminent and outweighs any harm threatened by the proposed treatment. When a genuine emergency of that sort arises, it is settled that the impracticality of conferring with the patient dispenses with need for it. Even in situations of that character the physician should, as current law requires, attempt to secure a relative's consent if possible. But if time is too short to accommodate discussion, obviously the physician should proceed with the treatment.

The second exception obtains when risk-disclosure poses such a threat of detriment to the patient as to become unfeasible or contraindicated from a medical point of view. It is recognized that patients occasionally become so ill or emotionally distraught on disclosure as to foreclose a rational decision, or complicate or hinder the treatment, or perhaps even pose psychological damage to the patient. Where that is so, the cases have generally held that the physician is armed with a privilege to keep the information from the patient, and we think it clear that portents of that type may justify the physician in action he deems medically warranted. The critical inquiry is whether the physician responded to a sound medical judgment that communication of the risk information would present a threat to the patient's well-being.

The physician's privilege to withhold information for therapeutic reasons must be carefully circumscribed, however, for otherwise it might devour the disclosure rule itself. The privilege does not accept the paternalistic notion that the physician may remain silent simply because divulgence might prompt the patient to forgo therapy the physician feels the patient really needs. That attitude presumes instability or perversity for even the normal patient, and runs counter to the foundation principle that the patient should and ordinarily can make the choice for himself. Nor does the privilege contemplate operation save where the patient's reaction to risk information, as reasonably foreseen by the physician, is menacing. And even in a situation of that kind, disclosure to a close relative with a view to securing consent to the proposed treatment may be the only alternative open to the physician. . . .

No more than breach of any other legal duty does nonfulfillment of the physician's obligation to disclose alone establish liability to the patient. An unrevealed risk that should have been made known must materialize, for otherwise the omission however unpardonable, is legally without consequence. Occurrence of the risk must be harmful to the patient, for negligence unrelated to injury is nonactionable. And, as in malpractice actions generally, there must be a causal relationship between the physician's failure to adequately divulge and damage to the patient.

CHAPTER 6

Human Research

Two noble values help shape the vast, extraordinary enterprise known as medical science: knowledge and beneficence—the unceasing quest to know, to find out, and the aspiration to act for people's good. When humans are the subjects of the research, these values assume their greatest importance, the stakes are at their highest, and the resulting ethical problems take on their sharpest edge. The chief difficulty is that these dual purposes do not fit together easily. Consequently, in its short history (dating from the early 1700s), systematized human research has engendered both great good and disturbing instances of evil. It has transformed our understanding of health and disease, magnified our power to treat and cure, saved millions of lives—and brought forth some astonishing moral outrages.

To medical science we owe the development of vaccines against polio, smallpox, measles, rubella, yellow fever, and hepatitis; treatments for heart disease, diabetes, cancer, and AIDS; strategies to prevent heart attacks, deadly infections, and birth defects; and diagnostic technology ranging from stethoscopes to MRIs to genetic tests. But the search for knowledge through medical research has also led down some dark paths:

• During World War II, Nazi physicians performed horrifying experiments on prisoners of war and civilians, killing and maiming many. At their 1947 trial in Nuremberg, Germany, the doctors were convicted of "murders, tortures, and other atrocities committed in the name of medical science."[1] Their unwilling victims were infected with cholera, smallpox, typhus, malaria,

and other diseases; given poisons to evaluate the deadly results; shot to simulate battle wounds; frozen to death; starved to death; sterilized; and mutilated. The infamous Nazi doctor Josef Mengele liked to study twins:

> He had collected children from the camps, measured their physical features, performed cross-transfusions, transplanted genitals, and other organs, and even created artificial Siamese twins. He also used his twin collection for comparative studies, infecting one child and then killing both for autopsy.[2]

• In 1932 the U.S. Public Health Service began a 40-year experiment to study the damaging effects of untreated syphilis in human beings. The research, known as the Tuskegee Study, involved around 600 poor black men, about 400 of whom had syphilis when they entered the experiment. The men were deceived about the nature of the study, were never told they had syphilis, and were never treated for it even when an effective treatment (penicillin) became readily available to the researchers. Several of the men died because of their untreated disease.

• From 1944 to 1974, the U.S. government sponsored secret experiments to determine the effects of radiation on thousands of human subjects, including children. Some of the subjects were exposed to dangerously high doses of radiation, and many never consented to the research and were not told of the potential harm.

• In 1956 researchers began a study of the natural course of hepatitis in institutionalized children, hoping to understand the disease better and to test a vaccine. Their experimental subjects were several hundred children housed at Willowbrook State Hospital in New York, the state's largest facility for retarded persons. In those days, conditions were such that most children admitted to Willowbrook eventually got hepatitis, which provoked flulike symptoms and immunity to future infections. For purposes of the experiment, the researchers infected the children with hepatitis when first admitted and monitored their bodies' responses. They were later condemned for using children—especially retarded children—in their study and for the methods they used to obtain consent from the children's parents.

Such stories shocked both the public and the medical world and provoked a sustained wave of soul-searching among policymakers and scientists about the ethics of human research. Out of the trial of Nazi doctors came the Nuremberg Code (one of the readings in this chapter), a set of minimal ethical principles meant to govern all scientific experiments involving humans. Later came other professional codes and government guidelines that reiterated and added to the principles. These included the Declaration of Helsinki, embraced by the World Medical Association (WMA) in 1964 (also a chapter reading); the 1979 Belmont Report (another selection), formulated by the congressionally established National Commission for the Protection of Human Subjects of Biomedical and Behavioral Research; and the 1993 international guidelines for biomedical human research, created by the World Health Organization (WHO) and the Council for International Organizations of Medical Sciences (CIOMS).

Obviously the moral dilemmas inherent in human research can be intense and difficult. But in this age of ambitious scientific inquiry, they cannot be safely ignored .

THE SCIENCE OF CLINICAL TRIALS

A scientific study designed to test a medical intervention in humans is known as a **clinical trial**. Normally the intervention is a drug or surgical procedure, and the point of the study is to de-termine the treatment's effects in the human body—specifically, whether it is safe and effective. Properly conducted, clinical trials provide the strongest and most trustworthy evidence of a treatment's impact on human health. Neither animal studies nor a physician's informal observations are as reliable and convincing.

Clinical trials can derive reliable answers because they are carefully configured to maximize objectivity, minimize bias, and avoid errors—all the problems that plague unscientific inquiries. A typical clinical trial devised to test the effectiveness of a treatment will consist of two groups of subjects: (1) an experimental group that gets the treatment to be evaluated and (2) a control group that closely resembles the experimental group but does not get the treatment. To learn anything useful about the treatment, researchers must study the relevant differences that arise between the two groups. Simply giving the treatment to the experimental group and observing what happens will not provide any useful answers. Usually, without a control group, the researchers cannot tell whether the subjects would have gotten better (or worse) without treatment, or if a factor other than the treatment was what most affected the subjects' condition (such as changes in their diet or behavior), or if the subjects' condition improved because of the placebo effect. (The placebo effect is a common phenomenon in which patients sometimes feel better after receiving treatment even when the treatment is inactive or fake.) With a control group, researchers can be more confident that relevant effects in the experimental group were brought about by the treatment and not by some extraneous element.

The control groups in clinical trials that investigate efficacy are of two kinds. In a placebo control group, subjects receive a **placebo**, an inactive or sham treatment—a "sugar pill," for example, or an inert pill that looks and tastes like the real drug. By using a placebo control group, researchers can take the placebo effect into account in assessing the worth of a treatment. For a treatment to be judged genuinely effective, subjects in the

IN DEPTH
THE TUSKEGEE TRAGEDY

The shocking revelations about the Tuskegee Study came decades after the research had been conducted. When finally told, the story provoked outrage, moral debate, and an apology from President Bill Clinton. Here is one of many recent news accounts:

> July 25, 2002—Thirty years ago today, the *Washington Evening Star* newspaper ran this headline on its front page:"Syphilis Patients Died Untreated." With those words, one of America's most notorious medical studies, the Tuskegee Syphilis Study, became public.
>
> "For 40 years, the U.S. Public Health Service has conducted a study in which human guinea pigs, not given proper treatment, have died of syphilis and its side effects," Associated Press reporter Jean Heller wrote on July 25, 1972."The study was conducted to determine from autopsies what the disease does to the human body."
>
> The next morning, every major U.S. newspaper was running Heller's story. . . .
>
> The Public Health Service, working with the Tuskegee Institute, began the study in 1932. Nearly 400 poor black men with syphilis from Macon County, Ala., were enrolled in the study. They were never told they had syphilis, nor were they ever treated for it. According to the Centers for Disease Control, the men were told they were being treated for "bad blood," a local term used to describe several illnesses, including syphilis, anemia and fatigue.
>
> For participating in the study, the men were given free medical exams, free meals and free burial insurance.

> At the start of the study, there was no proven treatment for syphilis. But even after penicillin became a standard cure for the disease in 1947, the medicine was withheld from the men. The Tuskegee scientists wanted to continue to study how the disease spreads and kills. The experiment lasted four decades, until public health workers leaked the story to the media.
>
> By then, dozens of the men had died, and many wives and children had been infected. In 1973, the National Association for the Advancement of Colored People (NAACP) filed a class-action lawsuit. A $9 million settlement was divided among the study's participants. Free health care was given to the men who were still living, and to infected wives, widows and children.
>
> But it wasn't until 1997 that the government formally apologized for the unethical study. President Clinton delivered the apology, saying what the government had done was deeply, profoundly and morally wrong:
>
> "To the survivors, to the wives and family members, the children and the grandchildren, I say what you know: No power on Earth can give you back the lives lost, the pain suffered, the years of internal torment and anguish.
>
> "What was done cannot be undone. But we can end the silence. We can stop turning our heads away. We can look at you in the eye and finally say, on behalf of the American people: what the United States government did was shameful.
>
> "And I am sorry."

National Public Radio, "Remembering Tuskegee," *NPR*, 25 July 2002, http://www.npr.org/programs/morning/features/2002/jul/tuskegee/ (1 March 2008).

---

treatment group must show significantly greater improvement than those in the placebo group. Studies using placebos in this way are called placebo-controlled trials. In an active control group, subjects get the standard treatment, one already proven to work. The results in the treatment group can then be compared to those in the active control group to see if the new treatment outperforms the old. Studies that use this type of control group are known as active-controlled trials. In general, placebo-controlled trials are more trustworthy than other types of clinical trials, but sometimes active-controlled trials can also yield reliable results, especially when they are used to find out which treatment is superior (rather than merely equivalent).

Another indispensible feature of most clinical trials is **blinding**, a procedure for ensuring that subjects and researchers don't know which interventions the subjects receive (standard treatment, new treatment, or placebo). If subjects know they have received a placebo, their assessment of how they feel may be skewed or they may change their health habits, try to obtain an active treatment, or even drop out of the study. If they know they have received an active treatment, they may experience improvement regardless of whether the treatment works. Knowledge of who receives what intervention can also affect researchers, moving them to unconscious bias in evaluating study results. Thus good clinical trials testing for treatment efficacy are blinded—preferably *double-blinded* (when both subjects and researchers are unaware of what treatments the subjects get), or at least *single-blinded* (in which only the subjects are unaware).

If clinical trials are to generate reliable data about a treatment's value, they must be not only blinded but also randomized. **Randomization** is the assigning of subjects randomly to both experimental and control groups. To draw reliable conclusions about the effects of a treatment, the control and experimental groups have to be comparable in relevant characteristics—and assigning subjects randomly helps ensure this. Randomization also minimizes the bias that can creep into a study when researchers unconsciously assign preferred subjects to a particular group. A new treatment can appear to be highly effective if healthier subjects are assigned to the experimental group and less healthy subjects to the control group.

Rarely, if ever, can a single clinical trial establish the safety and effectiveness of a treatment. Usually many studies must be conducted before scientists can be confident of such a conclusion. This hard fact is illustrated most clearly in drug research. By law and professional assent, research to establish the safety and effectiveness of new drugs must involve several clinical trials conducted in three stages, known formally as Phases I, II, and III. Before a drug is recognized as a proven treatment, it must pass muster in each phase. Usually before the human studies can even begin, the treatment must be studied in animals.

A Phase I trial tests the drug in a few people for safety and adverse reactions and ascertains safe and unsafe doses. Researchers do not try to evaluate the drug's efficacy. This kind of trial is said to be *nontherapeutic* because it is not expected to provide a therapeutic benefit to the subjects. In Phase II trials, investigators give the drug to larger groups of subjects to get a preliminary indication of its effectiveness and to do more assessments of safety. In Phase III trials, researchers hope finally to establish whether the drug is effective, determine how it compares in efficacy with other proven treatments, and learn how to employ it in the safest way. These trials are larger still, frequently having thousands of subjects, and are capable of providing definitive answers about a treatment's worth. Unlike Phase I trials, they are generally considered *therapeutic* if they are expected to provide a therapeutic benefit to at least some of the subjects. If a drug does well in Phase III trials, it can be approved for widespread use by patients. Sometimes further studies—Phase IV trials—are done after the approved drug is marketed. Their purpose is to assess the effectiveness and side effects of taking it for a long time.

BENEFICENCE, SCIENCE, AND PLACEBOS

Many of the key features of clinical trials have provoked moral debate, yet among the host of official codes issued on human research is a solid consensus on such trials' ethical requirements.[3] For a clinical trial to be morally permissible:

- Subjects must give their informed voluntary consent to participate.

- The study must be designed to minimize risks to subjects and offer an acceptable balance of risks and benefits. (Even if subjects give their informed consent, risks to them should not be unnecessary or excessive, and the risks must be offset by potential benefits derived from the research.)
- Subjects must be selected fairly to avoid exploiting or unjustly excluding them.
- The subjects' privacy should be protected, and the confidentiality of research data must be preserved.
- Before the research is conducted, it must be reviewed and approved by an independent panel (often an institutional review board, or IRB).

There is also substantial agreement in bioethics on the general moral principles that should apply to human research, standards from which the more specific requirements are derived: (1) autonomy, or respect for persons as autonomous agents; (2) beneficence, doing good for and avoiding harm to persons; and (3) justice, treating equals equally. When disagreements occur, they usually turn on how best to interpret, employ, or extend the requirements in specific kinds of cases.

The principle of beneficence is at the heart of many of the disputes because, as we have seen, the obligation to help or not harm subjects often seems to conflict with the aim of doing science. Physicians (or physician-researchers) have a duty of beneficence toward patients (or patient-subjects), but it is not obvious that clinical trials are always consistent with this duty. As we have seen, a widely accepted answer to this dilemma has been supplied in the official codes: Risks to subjects should be kept as low as possible, and the potential benefits of the research should be greater than the risks. These tenets have been joined with the further stipulations that no subject should be exposed to extreme risks even if the expected benefits are substantial; a subject's informed consent cannot justify research that is too risky; and potential benefits to both the subjects and soci-

ety should be considered, although the subjects' welfare must predominate. From this perspective, therapeutic trials—assuming the subjects' informed consent and acceptable risks and benefits—can be justified by the potential good to the subjects and future patients, or society. Nontherapeutic trials—assuming informed consent and minimal risks to the subjects—can be justified by significant potential good to society.

The use of control groups touches on most of these issues of beneficence. A clinical trial is conducted to find out which of two treatments is better for patients or whether a particular treatment has any worth, but of course this process entails that patients in the control group will often get less than the best available treatment or no genuine treatment at all (a placebo). Some argue that the permissibility of enrolling patients in such a study is questionable since by doing so they are being treated merely as a means to the end of scientific knowledge. But many reject this worry. For example:

[I]f there is uncertainty about the efficacy of any given treatment, a randomized trial is the best way to yield objectively valid results. It will tell the doctor which treatment is better for the patient. So, recruiting a patient to be a subject in a randomized clinical trial does not by itself compromise the researcher's duty as a doctor to care for the patient. The better treatment will be determined by the results of the trial. In fact, patients can benefit more from a research setting than from standard clinical care because they receive more attention with the resources available to the research team. By entering a patient in a randomized controlled clinical trial, a doctor is treating the patient as a means for the sake of generating scientific knowledge. But the doctor is also treating the patient as an end by obtaining consent to participate in the trial and by ensuring that the potential risks are commensurate with the potential benefits. The physician is at once fulfilling the primary duty of a doctor to the patient and the secondary duty of a researcher to the research subject.[4]

Frequently the issue is framed around the doctor's duty given what she knows about the treatments to be tested. As a physician, she has an obligation to act in the best interests of her patients, which requires that she offer to them only those treatments she judges to be the best. But in clinical trials, patients are randomized into experimental and control groups where they may not receive the treatment that the physician believes is best. Some bioethicists have concluded from this that randomized clinical trials are morally problematic because they "ask physicians to sacrifice the interests of their particular patients for the sake of the study and that of the information that it will make available for the benefit of society."[5]

But defenders of randomized studies contend that doctors breach no duty to their patients if the efficacy of the treatments being tested is unknown—that is, if there is no good evidence for preferring that patients be assigned to one group rather than another (control or experimental). Being in doubt about the relative merits of the treatments, physicians are said to be in *equipoise*, rationally balanced between the alternatives. They therefore cannot be guilty of offering treatments known to be less than the best available.

Still, critics insist that a physician owes patients her best judgment about available treatments, and if she believes (even on the basis of a hunch or suspicion) that one treatment is better or worse than another, then letting a randomized clinical trial choose the patients' treatment is wrong—a violation of trust. A physician with a preference is not in a state of equipoise.

Others argue that this view misunderstands the notion of equipoise. They contend that true equipoise does not depend on uncertainty in the mind of a physician, but on genuine disagreement about treatment efficacy in the medical and scientific community. The disagreement arises because of a lack of the kind of evidence generated by randomized clinical trials. As long as this form of equipoise exists, including patients in randomized studies is permissible.

Those who take this view also point out that a clinical trial may show that the physician's educated guess about a treatment is incorrect, making better care of the patient possible. As one philosopher explains,

> Properly carried out, with informed consent, clinical equipoise, and a design adequate to answer the question posed, randomized clinical trials protect physicians and their patients from therapies that are ineffective or toxic. Physicians and their patients must be clear about the vast gulf separating promising and proved therapies. The only reliable way to make this distinction in the face of incomplete information about pathophysiology and treatment mechanism is to experiment, and this will increasingly involve randomized trials. The alternative—a retreat to older methods—is unacceptable.[6]

Whatever the value of the scientific approach, many see no conflict between (1) physicians revealing to patients their honest preferences regarding treatments and (2) giving those patients the chance to enter a clinical trial. The key element here is full disclosure and informed consent:

> The physician has a strict therapeutic obligation to offer his or her best professional judgment, but also to obtain the patient's informed consent prior to initiating treatment. The latter obligation entails explaining the risks and benefits of all reasonable alternatives, including enrollment in an appropriate [randomized controlled trial] to test one treatment against another.[7]

Moral concern about control groups takes on added seriousness when their "treatment" is a placebo. Again the moral friction occurs at the point where beneficence and science collide. Recall that placebo-controlled trials are often the most scientifically reliable way to determine the effectiveness of a treatment. But in such studies, the placebo group receives no genuine treatment, while the experimental group gets one that is at least possibly, and perhaps probably, effective.

Can this deliberate nontreatment of patients be justified?

For many bioethicists and policy-making bodies, the answer is yes—but only in a restricted range of circumstances. The most widely accepted proviso is that the use of placebos is unethical when effective treatments are already available. In its 2004 version of the Declaration of Helsinki, the WMA asserts that in general a placebo-controlled trial "should only be used in the absence of existing proven therapy."[8] Testing a new, unproven treatment against a placebo is permissible, but usually only if no treatment has already been shown to work. If there is an established therapy, the new treatment must be pitted against it in an active-controlled trial.

This general rule has its greatest force in cases where the risks to subjects are large—when going without effective treatment can cause serious harm and threaten life. Some have argued that when the disease in question is potentially fatal, using placebo controls may be wrong even if there is no established treatment, just an unproven but promising one. A classic case seems to suggest this view. This is how bioethicists Tom Beauchamp and James Childress describe it:

> Promising laboratory tests led to a trial (phase I) to determine the safety of AZT among patients with AIDS. Several patients showed clinical improvement during this trial. Because AIDS was considered invariably fatal, many people argued that compassion dictated making it immediately available to all patients with AIDS. . . . However . . . as required by federal regulations, [the company] used a placebo-controlled trial of AZT to determine its effectiveness for certain groups of patients with AIDS. A computer randomly assigned some patients to AZT and others to a placebo. For several months, no major differences emerged in effectiveness, but then patients receiving the placebo began to die at a significantly higher rate. Of the 137 patients on the placebo, 16 died. Of the 145 patients on AZT, only one died. In view of these results, a data and safety monitoring board

advised terminating the trial. Subjects who had received the placebo in the trial were, as promised, the first to receive the drug.[9]

Many authorities recognize that the "no existing proven therapy" rule for placebo studies cannot be absolute. The WMA is among them, declaring in the Helsinki code that placebo-controlled trials may be permissible even when proven treatments exist, provided that the medical condition involved is minor. The WMA also implicitly acknowledges (as most authorities do) that sometimes the only way to identify the best therapies (and thereby ease the suffering of countless future patients) is to conduct a placebo-controlled trial, which may be a scientific necessity whether proven therapies exist or not. Bioethicists who accept this fact also typically believe that this research must be subject to at least two ethical restraints: Patients should never be exposed to undue risks (regardless of the potential benefits to society), and no research should be done without the patients' informed consent (which in itself cannot justify unsafe research).

SCIENCE AND INFORMED CONSENT

As discussed in the previous chapter, informed consent is the action of an autonomous, informed person agreeing to submit to medical treatment or experimentation. It is universally considered a moral prerequisite for medical treatment, and equally so for medical research. The first article of the Nuremberg Code asserts, "The voluntary consent of the human subject is absolutely essential"—an ethical requirement blatantly violated by the Nazi doctors. The underlying notion is that autonomous agents have the right to decide for themselves whether to expose their persons to the rigors and risks of clinical investigations. For bona fide informed consent, the person's decision must be informed by accurate information about the research, based on an adequate understanding of it, made voluntarily, and generated without coercion.

IN DEPTH
WOMEN IN CLINICAL TRIALS

Medical science has been accused of being unjust to women by frequently excluding them as subjects from studies of treatments that could help them. Too often in the past only men were included in studies of diseases that affected both men and women, and the treatments found to be effective in males would not necessarily have the same impact on females. The Institute of Medicine published a collection of papers on the ethical and legal problems arising from such research practices, including a critique by Susan Sherwin. She asserts that

[W]e can identify several specific areas of feminist concern, including: (1) some or all women may be unjustly excluded from some studies and suffer as a result; (2) women may be unjustly enrolled in studies that expose them to risk without offering appropriate benefits; (3) the research agenda may be unresponsive to the interests of oppressed groups; and (4) most generally, the process by which research decisions are made and carried out may maintain and promote oppressive practices....

...The exclusion of women from important clinical studies is the best known of the problems of injustice identified as falling within the scope of the topic of women's role in clinical studies. Historically, many studies of diseases that are common to both sexes have systematically excluded women from participation, so the necessary data for guiding treatment decisions for women are unavailable. Women's health care must often be based on untested inferences from data collected about men, but because there are important physiological differences between women and men, such inferences cannot always be presumed to be reliable; and, even when some data are collected about women's responses to the treatment in question, we may lack information about how a proposed treatment will affect specific groups of women (e.g., those who are disabled, elderly, or poor). Even according to traditional distributive conceptions of justice, it is clear that this sort of discrimination is unjust and bound to result in less effective health care for (some) women than for comparable men because the knowledge base which guides health care practices is unfairly skewed; if we accept the view that well-designed clinical studies are beneficial for a population, then the systematic exclusion of women from such studies must be seen as disadvantaging them unfairly. A social justice approach that is sensitive to matters of oppression helps us to recognize that this disadvantage is not random or accidental, but is a result and further dimension of women's generally oppressed status in society. According to the distributive models of justice, women ought to be represented proportionately to their health risk in any clinical studies likely to be of benefit to subject populations.

Susan Sherwin, "Women in Clinical Studies: A Feminist View," in *Women and Health Research: Ethical and Legal Issues of Including Women in Clinical Studies* (Washington, DC: National Academy Press, 1999), 11–17, http://www.nap.edu (16 June 2008).

The checklist of relevant information that researchers are expected to give subjects has become fairly standard. According to one international panel, it includes:

- That each individual is invited to participate as a subject in research and the aims and methods of the research

- The expected duration of the subject's participation
- The benefits that might reasonably be expected to result to the subjects or to others as an outcome of the research
- Any foreseeable risks or discomfort to the subject associated with participation in the research

- Any alternative procedures or courses of treatment that might be as advantageous to the subject as the procedure or treatment being tested
- The extent to which confidentiality of records in which the subject is identified will be maintained
- The extent of the investigator's responsibility, if any, to provide medical services to the subject
- That therapy will be provided free of charge for specified types of research-related injury
- Whether the subject or the subject's family or dependents will be compensated for disability or death resulting from such injury
- That the individual is free to refuse to participate and will be free to withdraw from the research at any time without penalty or loss of benefits to which he would otherwise be entitled[10]

Few doubt the reasonableness of such a list, but many have wondered whether the information can be conveyed to potential subjects so their consent is truly informed and voluntary. Probably the least plausible concern is an old paternalistic claim. Just as some physicians believe that patients are incapable of grasping the complexities of medical information, some researchers have argued that research subjects cannot fathom the alien language and arcane methods of science—so informed consent in clinical trials is impossible. Many bioethicists think this worry exaggerated (not to mention contemptuous of patient autonomy). They point out that subjects need not understand everything about a clinical study to give their informed consent; they need only comprehend enough to appreciate the most important implications, risks, and benefits of the research. Achieving this much understanding is possible although admittedly, in many situations and for many patients, extremely difficult.

Other concerns about informed consent relate to the unique circumstances that confront research volunteers. If patients are seriously ill and no proven treatment is available or none has helped them, they may consent to the research out of desperation, fear, wishful thinking, or hope. Against their own best interests, they may pay little attention to the information provided, ignore all the possible risks, expect to be cured, believe that a benefit is highly probable when it is only possible, even come to believe that a nontherapeutic trial will likely help them despite written disclosures to the contrary. Their consent therefore may not be fully voluntary and informed.

Another issue concerns payments to research subjects. It is generally agreed that, in the words of one international body, "Subjects may be paid for inconvenience and time spent, and should be reimbursed for expenses incurred, in connection with their participation in research; they may also receive free medical services."[11] But additional payments (especially large ones) to entice patients into entering a trial might get them to consent though they ordinarily would refuse. Some think the payment could be so tempting as to be coercive (to constitute, in legal terms, "undue inducement") and thus may undermine informed consent. Several policies and regulations try to restrict the use of these inducements, but some think these edicts go too far. "All of these rules seem to be excessively paternalistic," says Baruch Brody,

> If the independent review panel has already concluded that the risk-benefit ratio of the research is acceptable (otherwise, the research could not be approved), how can the large payment harm the subject? And in what way are large payments for acceptable research coercive or exploitative?[12]

RESEARCH ON THE VULNERABLE

Many moral issues arise from clinical research on people thought to be easily exploited or mistreated—the most vulnerable in society. These subjects include children, the mentally disabled, prisoners, minorities, and people in developing countries. The essential moral conflict is between (1) the duty to shield the vulnerable from abuse and (2) the aspiration to benefit them or society

IN DEPTH
WHY ENTER A CLINICAL TRIAL?

The National Cancer Institute sponsors many clinical trials and maintains the most extensive database of cancer trials in the nation. It publicizes them for cancer patients, saying, "Whenever you need treatment for your cancer, clinical trials may be an option for you." It acknowledges that there are benefits and risks to taking part in such research and describes them like this:

POSSIBLE BENEFITS
- Clinical trials offer high-quality cancer care. If you are in a randomized study and do not receive the new treatment being tested, you will receive the best known standard treatment. This may be as good as, or better than, the new approach.
- If a new treatment is proven to work and you are taking it, you may be among the first to benefit.
- By looking at the pros and cons of clinical trials and your other treatment choices, you are taking an active role in a decision that affects your life.

- You have the chance to help others and improve cancer treatment.

POSSIBLE DRAWBACKS
- New treatments under study are not always better than, or even as good as, standard care.
- If you receive standard care instead of the new treatment being tested, it may not be as effective as the new approach.
- New treatments may have side effects that doctors do not expect or that are worse than those of standard treatment.
- Even if a new treatment has benefits, it may not work for you. Even standard treatments, proven effective for many people, do not help everyone.
- Health insurance and managed care providers do not always cover all patient care costs in a study. What they cover varies by plan and by study. To find out in advance what costs are likely to be paid in your case, check with your insurance company and talk to a doctor, nurse or social worker from the study.

National Cancer Institute, "Taking Part in Cancer Research Studies," *National Cancer Institute,* 17 July 2007, http://www .cancer.gov/clinicaltrials/Taking-Part-in-Cancer-Treatment-Research-Studies/page1 (29 February 2008).

---

through needed research. Serious study of this clash of values has been goaded by a sad, historical fact: Many notorious cases in the ethics of clinical science involved research using vulnerable populations—among them the poor black men of Tuskegee, the children of Willowbrook, and the prisoners of the Nazi doctors.

The question of research on children acquires its edge partly because often the only way to devise treatments for children's diseases is to conduct clinical trials on these subjects. The physiology and pathology of children are so different from those of adults that trying to draw useful conclusions about the former from studies of the latter is frequently difficult, impossible, or dangerous. Many effective therapies now used to treat children could only have been developed

through clinical trials using children. Given the scientific necessity of this kind of research, important ethical questions exert their pressure: Is research on children ever permissible? How is informed consent to be handled? Can children give consent? What balance of risks and benefits for child subjects can justify experimentation on them? Can nontherapeutic trials ever be morally permissible? Are there limits to the risks that children should be allowed to bear?

Most official policies assert or assume that properly designed research in children is morally acceptable if it is conducted for their sake, if it is done to generate the therapies they need. The policies also agree on the necessity for consent before any research is begun and on the importance of a proper balance of risks and benefits for the research subjects. Disagreement comes in specifying the details of these requirements.

It is generally understood that consent to do research on children must in most cases be given by parents or guardians, who are supposed to decide in the children's best interests. Sometimes children may be allowed to give consent for themselves, provided they have reached the age of consent or maturity, but authorities disagree over when this point is reached. Existing policies require that in some circumstances child subjects must give their assent to the research (they must at least agree to it), even when parents or guardians have provided proxy informed consent. A few even claim that in some cases children may veto their participation in a trial. As one code phrases it, "the child's refusal to participate in research must always be respected unless according to the research protocol the child would receive therapy for which there is no medically-acceptable alternative."[13]

The prevailing view is that properly consented-to research involving children is permissible if it offers them benefits equaling or outweighing the risks and if the risks are limited. That is, therapeutic research is generally acceptable. Nontherapeutic research is another matter. Some oppose all such research, whether or not parents consent to it, on the grounds that it puts children at risk without hope of benefits for them in return. This position would rule out a great deal of science that could yield effective treatments for childhood diseases. Most official guidelines are less strict, allowing nontherapeutic research when the risk to the child subjects is minimal or close to it. The U.S. Department of Health and Human Services, for example, permits research that involves:

- No more than minimal risk to children, provided adequate steps are taken to solicit assent from the children and consent of the parents or guardians
- More than minimal risk to children and the prospect of direct benefits for them, provided (a) the benefits justify the risks, (b) no better alternative approaches exist,

and (c) adequate steps are taken to solicit assent from the children and consent of the parents or guardians
- More than minimal risk to children and no prospect of direct benefits for them, provided (a) the risk is only slightly greater than minimal risk, (b) the intervention involves experiences that are comparable to those that the subjects normally experience, (c) the intervention is likely to yield knowledge that is vitally important for understanding or treating the subjects' condition, and (d) adequate steps are taken to solicit assent from the children and consent of the parents or guardians[14]

Most of the pressing questions about research on children also apply to studies on the mentally impaired, and many of the answers are the same. This class of potential subjects includes adults who are severely retarded or suffer from psychiatric illness, in either situation being incompetent (at least much of the time) to make autonomous choices. As in the case of children, clinical research is scientifically necessary to develop therapies that could help these patients. There is widespread agreement that the research is justified if it is judged to be in their best interests and that appropriate surrogates must usually be the ones to make this judgment.

As might be expected, nontherapeutic research involving the mentally impaired is more contentious. Only if it entails minimal risk to the subjects, some argue, is this research legitimate. Others prefer a more relaxed policy. The National Institutes of Health, for example, permits studies on mentally impaired subjects if an appropriate consent process is used and if the research involves either (1) minimal risk, (2) greater than minimal risk but with the prospect of direct benefit to subjects, or (3) greater than minimal risk with no prospect of direct benefit to subjects but with the likelihood of gaining important knowledge about the subjects' illness.

An added complication in research on these vulnerable subjects is that their being in an institution can undermine attempts to obtain their voluntary consent. (Consent remains an issue with some mentally impaired patients because they may be competent though impaired, competent to decide some aspects of their care, or intermittently competent.) Institutionalized patients are especially susceptible to many forms of coercion or undue influence that can undermine the voluntariness of their decisions. They may feel intense pressure to submit to research because they have been conditioned to defer to people in authority, because they fear punishment or less consideration from caretakers for refusing to participate, or because the slightest advantages of being in a clinical trial (special attention or a change in routine, for example) can carry tremendous weight.

Official responses to these worries have emphasized close scrutiny of the research by independent review committees (and possibly other oversight panels) to identify sources of undue pressure on the subjects. Many contend that the alternative to continued (but closely monitored) research on the mentally impaired is no research at all, which is unacceptable.

A different set of ethical questions confronts us in research on vulnerable subjects in Third World countries. As the scientific testing of therapies in developing nations has increased, ethical controversy surrounding the research has also intensified. The main points of moral conflict were dramatically illustrated a decade ago in clinical trials of HIV-infected pregnant women in several African countries and Thailand. Research had previously demonstrated that the drug AZT (zidovudine) could substantially reduce the transmission of HIV from pregnant women to their fetuses (known as vertical transmission). But the dose of AZT used in the research was expensive—too expensive for widespread use in poor countries with large numbers of people with HIV. So scientists were eager to find out if a lower, cheaper dose of AZT would work. They reasoned that the best way to discover which AZT regimens were most effective at halting vertical transmission was to test them

on women in the developing countries using placebo-controlled trials.

They ran the trials, and the results showed that a less expensive AZT treatment could indeed significantly reduce vertical transmission. Nevertheless, many observers charge on various grounds that the research was unethical. Probably the chief argument against the studies is that in using a placebo (no-treatment) group, some of the subjects were deprived of an effective treatment that could have prevented many babies from being infected with HIV. Thus the researchers violated the widely accepted moral tenet that the welfare of the human subjects should outweigh the concerns of science and society. Marcia Angell, the executive editor of the *New England Journal of Medicine*, compares the trials to the Tuskegee Study in which African-American men with syphilis were studied but never treated even after an effective treatment for syphilis was in wide use. "Only when there is no known effective treatment is it ethical to compare a potential new treatment with a placebo," she says. "When effective treatment exists, a placebo may not be used."[15] Yet before the AZT trials began, an effective treatment was already available. Thus the women in the studies were treated merely as a means to the end of scientific inquiry.

Other commentators defend the use of placebo control groups in the trials and reject the idea that it was morally problematic. They argue that those in the placebo groups were not deprived of treatment that they would have received under normal circumstances. Nothing was taken from them that they already had, and so no injustice was done. Baruch Brody takes this line and argues that an injustice is committed only if the study participants are "denied any treatment *that should otherwise be available to him or her in light of the practical realities of health care resources available in the country in question*."[16] Judged by this standard, he says, "the trials in question were probably not unjust." Some defenders of the trials add the further point that if the research had not been done, many women would never have received any AZT at all.

Some critics of such trials allege a pattern of exploitation of people in developing countries. They say that researchers use impoverished or desperate subjects to determine the best therapies, and then that information is used to help people in rich countries, not the developing ones. Reflecting this concern about exploitation, international policies insist that any therapies developed through research should be shared with the community or country where the research was done. Brody thinks that these policies miss the mark. To avoid exploitation, we need not ensure that the benefits of research go to the larger community, but only to the subjects themselves:

> [W]e need to ask who needs to be protected from being exploited by the trials in question. It would seem that it is the participants. Are they getting a fair share of the benefits from the trial if it proves successful? This is a particularly troubling question when we consider those in the control group, whose major benefit from participation may have been an unrealized possibility of getting treated. If we judge that the participants have not received enough, then it is they who must receive more.[17]

APPLYING MAJOR THEORIES

Utilitarianism says that right actions are those that result in the most beneficial balance of good over bad consequences, everyone considered (see Chapter 2). What are the implications of this stance for human research? First, utilitarianism can provide an unequivocal justification for it. Through medical research, the causes of disease are unmasked, disease preventives are devised, treatments are developed, and the true worth of common but untested therapies is determined. Thus human well-being is advanced, and an important moral principle—beneficence—is satisfied.

On the utilitarian view, the moral justification for conducting any particular clinical trial depends on its offering a net benefit to all concerned. The maximization of benefit, in turn,

hangs on the quality and aims of the research—on how well and why it is done. The utilitarian would agree then with the common ethical requirements that "The experiment should be such as to yield fruitful results for the good of society, unprocurable by other methods or means of study, and not random and unnecessary in nature. . . . The experiment should be so conducted as to avoid all unnecessary physical and mental suffering and injury."[18]

Ethical codes insist that people must not be included in clinical trials without their informed consent, but whether utilitarianism is consistent with this requirement is debatable. Some argue that there really is no inconsistency because informed consent is just another way to maximize utility. Others doubt that this tack is coherent.

In medical research, the utilitarian perspective often leads to the same conclusions about the permissibility of actions that other theories do. But frequently the judgments clash dramatically, as they did in disputes over the placebo-controlled AZT trials in developing countries. The utilitarians argued that the cheapest, fastest way to find out which treatment was best and to use it on the people who needed it most was to use a placebo group. But many rejected this view, arguing in Kantian fashion that subjects in the placebo (no-treatment) group were treated as a mere means to the end of scientific rigor, and many babies would become HIV-infected as a result.

The AZT episode was one of many in clinical research that illustrated the distinctive implications of a Kantian approach. Its means-ends requirement—the prohibition against using persons as if they were mere things—was implicit in the strong condemnations of the Nazi medical experiments, the Cold War radiation research, the Tuskegee Study, and many others. It proscribes the coercing of research subjects, deceiving them, deliberately harming them, and diminishing or destroying their autonomy. Kant's notion of the equal moral value of persons yields the imperative to treat equals equally, which seems to imply that even in research, some subjects should not be treated better (or worse) than others for no morally relevant reason. For some bioethicists, this means that research subjects in poor countries should receive the same treatments in clinical trials that they would get if they lived in rich countries.

Kant would insist that these limits on what can be done to subjects can never be weakened or ignored for the sake of utility. The categorical imperative must not be breached—even to find cures for humanity's ills.

The heart of the modern doctrine of informed consent is Kantian. Because persons are autonomous, rational agents, they must be allowed the freedom to make choices and to have them respected. They may give or withhold their consent to medical treatment or research, consent that is valid only if informed, competent, and voluntary. Within limits, informed consent can legitimize the indignities of clinical trials by ensuring that even though subjects are treated as a means to an end, they are not treated *solely* as a means to an end. But if a person refuses to give her informed consent, or if it is impeded by misinformation (or no information), coercion, or undue influence, using her in research would be wrong. Respect for persons also implies that obtaining their informed consent cannot justify subjecting them to substantial risk of reduced autonomy or death.

For Rawls, social and economic inequalities are not unjust if they work to everyone's benefit, especially to the benefit of the least well off in society. This implies that (1) research efforts should be aimed primarily at helping the neediest and (2) it is impermissible to conduct research on the neediest to provide therapeutic benefits only to those who are better off. Clinical trials, then, using poor, desperate, or mentally impaired subjects to develop treatments for the rest of society could not be condoned. Applied internationally, Rawls' principles would lead us to condemn research in developing countries to benefit only people in developed ones.

KEY TERMS
blinding
clinical trial
placebo
randomization

SUMMARY
Clinical trials are scientific studies designed to test medical interventions in humans. They can derive reliable answers because they maximize the objectivity of observations, minimize bias, and avoid errors. The main requirements for a scientifically adequate clinical trial are a control group (using either a placebo or an active treatment), blinding, and randomization.

Official ethical codes on human research agree that (1) subjects must give their informed voluntary consent to participate, (2) the study must be designed to minimize risks to subjects and offer an acceptable balance of risks and benefits, (3) subjects must be selected fairly to avoid exploiting or unjustly excluding them, (4) the subjects' privacy should be protected and the confidentiality of research data must be preserved, and (5) before the research is conducted, it must be reviewed and approved by an independent committee. There is also substantial agreement on the general moral principles that apply to human research—autonomy, beneficence, and justice.

The use of control groups has raised ethical concerns, with some critics arguing that controlled trials treat subjects merely as a means to the end of scientific knowledge. But many believe that physicians do no wrong to their patients who enter a clinical trial if the physicians are in equipoise, rationally balanced between the alternative treatments. Debate about using control groups intensifies in placebo-controlled trials. The most widely accepted view is that the use of placebos is unethical when effective treatments are already available.

Most agree that the informed consent of subjects is essential for morally acceptable research. But there is often concern about whether truly

The UCLA Schizophrenia Study

Studies in which researchers do not offer real treatment to subjects suffering from a serious illness or condition often raise troubling ethical questions. In 1994 one such study got the attention of the media, the federal government, Congress, the legal system, and clinical researchers.

In the early 1980s, scientists at the University of California at Los Angeles (UCLA) Medical School began a study to determine how well schizophrenic patients could function without their antipsychotic medication, prolyxin decanoate. This knowledge would have been very valuable in treating schizophrenic patients because the drug is both boon and bane. In most patients the medication can ease (but not entirely banish) psychotic symptoms, including acute psychotic episodes. But it can also cause awful side effects, most notably tardive dyskinesia, a condition of involuntary muscle movements varying from mild to disabling and possibly becoming permanent.

People with schizophrenia are afflicted with delusions, hallucinations, depression, bizarre behavior, hostility, and—in a few cases—suicide. For many patients, taking prolyxin decanoate and enduring the side effects is preferable to experiencing the symptoms of schizophrenia left untreated. But the UCLA researchers wanted to find a way around these problems. They knew that some patients who are taken off their medication can function adequately for a long time before full-blown symptoms return. Identifying these patients early would enable a physician to withdraw their medication so they could benefit from it while avoiding its drawbacks. So the ultimate aim of the study was to uncover these identifying characteristics, and that required discontinuing the medication of the schizophrenic subjects to observe the recurrence of symptoms (relapse).

In this double-blind study, subjects were randomly assigned to either a placebo control group or a group receiving doses of prolyxin decanoate. For 12 weeks the groups received their respective doses (placebo or active drug). Then the groups switched treatments and continued that way for another 12 weeks. At the end of the 24 weeks, subjects whose symptoms were still under control were taken off the drug (or allowed to continue untreated) and monitored for up to one year until they experienced full relapse or severe symptoms. Shortly after the no-drug phase began, one subject had an extreme psychotic breakdown, and after the phase ended, another subject committed suicide.

Complaints were lodged against the UCLA researchers, alleging, among other things, that the informed consent process was invalid and that the study design was too risky because it made relapses very likely. In 1994 an office in the National Institutes of Health released a report concerning the matter. It charged that the informed consent process failed to adequately explain to subjects the distinction between regular medical care and the treatment that might be provided in the study. Other observers faulted the consent process for obscuring some vital information—the probability and severity of relapse.

---

informed and voluntary consent can be obtained from certain kinds of patients, chief among them children, the very ill, the mentally disabled, prisoners, minorities, and people in developing countries.

Regarding all these groups there is often disagreement about the proper balance of risk and benefits in clinical trials. Research involving subjects in Third World countries raises issues of justice, especially whether these subjects are entitled to the same level of care that subjects in developed countries get.

Cases for Evaluation

CASE 1
Giving Placebos to Children

(*New York Times*)—Researchers give a 6-year-old girl who suffers from asthma attacks a promising new drug in addition to her old medicine, then withdraw it to see how she will do without it. A depressed teenager enrolls in a study for an antidepressant, but does not know if he will get a sugar pill or the real thing. The parents of an epileptic youngster enroll her in a test of a new drug that has worked well in adults. But no one knows whether she will get the new medication, or the one that has worked only moderately well for her in the past.

These quandaries, all based on actual experiences, are likely to be faced by an increasing number of parents, children, and medical researchers around the country as the federal government steps up its efforts to test drugs on children.

Over the last three years, largely because of financial incentives that Congress has given pharmaceutical companies, pediatric studies of new drugs have boomed. In December, the Food and Drug Administration will begin mandating that such tests be done on certain drugs, and the agency wants to make sure researchers protect child participants.

"What level of discomfort or risk should a child in a study be exposed to?" asked Dr. Steven Hirschfeld, a medical officer at the F.D.A.'s Center for Drug Research and Evaluation. "If a child gets an asthma attack and starts to wheeze, are people willing to tolerate that to get complete information about a potentially helpful drug for children?"

Today, an F.D.A. advisory panel met in Bethesda, Md., to begin discussions aimed at setting the first guidelines for researchers on the controversial use of placebos in drug trials for children. Placebos are sugar pills, injections, or other treatments that resemble the drug that is being tested without having any of the same effects.

Dr. Hirschfeld said that the particular vulnerability of children often makes placebo controls necessary. "Children are not only very susceptible to their own expectations," he said in an interview. "They are very susceptible to their parents' expectations."

But a panelist, Dr. Charles Weijer, a bioethicist and an assistant professor of medicine at Dalhousie University in Halifax, Nova Scotia, said it was wrong to submit children to risks while providing them no immediate benefit.

"An investigator's chief concern ought to be the health and well-being of her patients," Dr. Weijer said at the hearing. . . .

The panel of 27 researchers that met today included several researchers from Europe who are working on international standards for clinical trials in children.

"What you people decide will affect directly not only children in the U.S., but children in Europe and the world at large," said Francis Crawley, chairman of a group working to set standards in Europe.

Dianne Murphy, the associate director for pediatrics at the F.D.A.'s Center for Drug Evaluation and Research, said that use of placebos can reduce the number of children needed in a study and can ensure the most conclusive outcome. "If you need a placebo trial to get an answer, and you don't do it, then you've wasted that child's blood, time and possible chance, in a trial that won't give them an answer," she said. . . .

But experts disagree on the ethics of withholding effective treatment from children when studying nonfatal conditions such as allergies or skin rashes. And there is no consensus for how to treat children with other serious ailments, such as depression, where the best treatment is unknown.*

Is giving children placebos in clinical trials ever morally permissible? If so, under what conditions should placebos be used? What if in a clinical trial some children suffer asthma attacks because effective treatment is withheld from them—is that acceptable? What if no effective treatments for some childhood diseases could be developed without using children in placebo-controlled trials. Would that fact outweigh any objections to such trials? Give reasons for your answers.

---

*Alexis Jetter, "Efforts to Test Drugs on Children Hasten Drive for Research Guidelines," *New York Times,* 12 September 2000, http://www.nytimes.com/2000/09/12/science/12ETHI.html (6 March 2008).

CASE 2
Research and Medicine Collide in Haiti

(*New York Times*)—The impoverished patients who step from the dirt sidewalk into the modern AIDS research clinic run by Cornell Medical College in Port-au-Prince, Haiti, are offered a seemingly simple arrangement.

"We would like to test your blood because you live in an area where AIDS may be common," the English version of the clinic's consent form reads. "We will provide you with medicine if you fall sick and cannot afford such care."

But the transaction is not as straightforward as it sounds. Many Haitians who visit the clinic are at once patients and subjects of United States-financed medical research, and circumstances that are bad for their health are sometimes best for research results.

That conflict is especially true in Cornell's most tantalizing research in Haiti, a study of sex partners, only one of whom is infected with the AIDS virus. Researchers, seeking clues to developing a vaccine, study the blood of both partners, particularly the uninfected ones who continue to be exposed to the virus through unprotected sex. They are trying to find out whether some people have natural protections against infection with the AIDS virus that could be replicated in a vaccine.

The Haitians are ideal research subjects, largely because they are not receiving the kind of care now standard in the world's developed countries. Condom use is low in Haiti, for cultural and other reasons. Anti-retroviral drugs that are successful at suppressing the virus are unavailable except to the very wealthy, and are not included in Cornell's promise to provide medicine.

Nearly 20 years after Cornell opened the clinic, it provides some of the best AIDS treatment available in a country devastated by the epidemic, fighting the myriad illnesses that result from AIDS. But that is a lower standard of care than patients receive routinely at American institutions, including the hospital affiliated with Cornell in New York City.

If the research were done in the United States, experts agree, the physicians would be obligated to prescribe the anti-retrovirals and deliver the most effective possible counseling against unprotected sex.

The ethical questions posed by Cornell's work among Haiti's poor are at the heart of a global debate about AIDS research that is roiling international health organizations from Geneva to Thailand, challenging ethics formulations established decades ago.

"It's really like a Faustian bargain," said Marc Fleisher, a member of the committee at Cornell that reviews research on humans. "It's like, since we're making this a better place, we're going to exploit it in a way we could never get away with in the United States," said Mr. Fleisher, the outside member on a board made up mostly of university employees who are doctors.

Cornell doctors defended the couples study as vitally important and stressed that its subjects receive the same counseling about the dangers of AIDS and the same care as other patients at the Haitian clinic.

United States standards for research on humans were strongly influenced by outrage over the Tuskegee syphilis study earlier this century, which misled impoverished black subjects for years while tracking their disease, and withheld treatment even after penicillin was discovered.

Today's subjects are not to be pressured to participate in research, according to Federal regulations. They are to be fully informed about the research's purposes and risks. They must receive the best available therapy for their illnesses and be told about any findings relevant to their health.

In theory, the same rules apply to federally financed studies overseas. But an examination of 15 years of records related to the Haiti couples research shows that it has received scant scrutiny from Government officials in Washington.

And the Government's rules barely address the moral ambiguities of AIDS research in indigent countries. . . .

Dr. Warren D. Johnson, the chief of international medicine and infectious diseases at Cornell, called the couples study "a very high priority," though he said it had been temporarily suspended while the university concentrated on other research in Haiti. "This is the critical group in the world—couples—that's where the war is to be fought," he said.

At least 97 couples have been enrolled in the blood study since 1991, records show, but Dr. Johnson said only 30 couples are still being followed. The study will be expanded to new couples early next year, he said, and coordinated with AIDS vaccine trials, which are expected to start in Haiti this fall using similar couples as subjects.

Cornell's clinic in Haiti offers strong inducements to subjects. It is the only center in the country providing free screening and treatment for H.I.V., venereal disease, and tuberculosis, a common complication of AIDS. The thousands who flock to it are too poor to buy food, let alone the simple medicines and vitamins that serve as "a powerful incentive for study participation," in the words of one Cornell grant report.

The head of the clinic, Dr. Jean William Pape, is a Haiti native and Cornell professor who has studied AIDS in Haiti for two decades. Dr. Pape, who trained at Cornell, defended the treatment of research subjects in the couples study, saying they benefited from the same counseling and free condoms available to everyone who visits the clinic.

Dr. Pape said that offering the life-saving drugs to the handful of research subjects would be an unethical lure to participate. Treating all H.I.V.-infected citizens, he said, would cost 10 times Haiti's health budget.

If the research on couples succeeds, he said, it could help lead to a vaccine against AIDS. "You have to take into account people who mean well for their country and not impose on them things that you feel are good for Western ideas," he said. . . .

The Haitians were valuable for another reason. Unlike AIDS patients in the United States and Europe, they were not receiving the anti-retroviral drugs that proved effective in halting the disease's progress.

The lack of those drugs "may allow identification of novel findings not easily studied in the U.S.A.," Dr. John L. Ho, a Cornell immunologist, wrote in an application for Federal funds. In 1995, the Federal Government awarded Cornell an extra $60,000 to expand this part of the Haitian couples study. . . .

Ethical standards for Federally financed studies require that patients be told why researchers want to study them. But the written consent form approved at Cornell and read aloud in Creole to each potential subject does not mention that the study focuses on couples in which one sexual partner has tested positive for H.I.V.

The form tells subjects their blood is being tested because "you live in an area where AIDS may be common." It promises all patients that H.I.V. test results will be kept confidential. . . .

After reviewing clinic materials, Marie Saint Cyr, a native of Haiti who now directs an AIDS program for women in Harlem, said there was a "clear conflict of interest" between the desire to collect information from research subjects and the obligation to effectively warn patients at risk.

"If you know somebody is positive and is having sex with a partner who is negative, you have a life and death situation in front of you," she said. "You have to do individualized counseling to really tap into what those people value in life, to confront them with the reality of H.I.V. and AIDS. This in no way addresses those serious things."*

Is the Cornell research ethical? Should subjects in the study get the same AIDS treatment available to people in the United States? Should the researchers provide stronger warnings to subjects about the dangers of not using condoms? Is the informed consent process morally acceptable? Explain your answers.

---

*Nina Bernstein, "Strings Attached: For Subjects in Haiti Study, Free AIDS Care Has a Price," *New York Times*, 6 June 1999, http://www.nytimes.com/pages/health (6 March 2008).

CASE 3

To Stop or Not to Stop a Clinical Trial

(*New York Times*)—Recently, scientists made the startling decision to halt a large multinational clinical trial that was testing a new drug regimen for breast cancer. The five-year trial was stopped after just two and a half years when results showed that the study drug cut the yearly rate of breast cancer recurrence by nearly half.

The decision has already provoked controversy: breast cancer recurrence is not necessarily the same as death, the critics say, so it is not clear whether the new drug actually saves lives.

The National Breast Cancer Coalition, a patient advocacy group, argued that researchers should have continued the study to see if the new drug prolonged lives.

The issue gets to the core of biomedical research. What is ideal for researchers may not always be ideal for subjects or for the demands of public health.

In this study, the researchers were looking to see if letrozole, which blocks estrogen synthesis, was more effective than a placebo in preventing the recurrence of breast cancer in women who had already taken the estrogen-blocking drug tamoxifen.

Because the advantage of letrozole on disease-free survival was apparent early on, the researchers had to halt the study.

Dr. James N. Ingle of the Mayo Clinic and a principal investigator in the study said he was surprised by the criticism over ending the study. "Preventing disease recurrence is a valid endpoint," he said. "If you sit down with patients, they will tell you that they don't want their cancer to come back. That's their first concern.

"In fact, I can't think of a study of breast cancer where actual survival is the primary endpoint. Disease-free survival is a well-accepted outcome with strong precedence in cancer research."

But to some researchers, the study stopped short of answering important questions. Does letrozole promote actual survival? What are its long-term adverse effects? How long should women continue to take it?

The results, for example, suggest a slight increase in osteoporosis in women taking letrozole compared with a placebo. So, other side effects may emerge over time.

The pursuit of perfect data may be the researcher's dream, but the perspective of a woman with breast cancer is vastly different. If you were privy to the interim analysis, you would most likely choose the new drug over the placebo.

Imagine the outcry if investigators had withheld the early evidence of the drug's benefit and finished the study, hoping for better data. Millions of women with breast cancer could then have correctly claimed they were denied a new treatment.

"A woman with breast cancer who wakes up the next morning without a recurrence of her disease is a survivor," said Dr. Paul Goss of Princess Margaret Hospital and lead author of the study. "What most people and even doctors don't understand about the course of breast cancer is that it is a chronic relapsing disease over many years."

Proving that letrozole saves lives will require a study lasting many years, Dr. Goss said. "We've done the first step, which is to show that letrozole works in preventing breast cancer recurrence," he said. "The next step is to do an extended trial to find out the optimal duration of treatment and long-term side effects."

When people enroll in research studies they sign informed consent agreements explaining the potential risks and benefits. In this case, the form promised subjects that they would be told if new information about their disease was discovered in the study. This virtually mandated early disclosure.

And although subjects are explicitly told in a consent form that they themselves may receive no direct benefit, many continue to hope for it. At the very least, they reasonably expect to be kept from all foreseeable harm.

But avoiding harm is not the same thing as getting benefit. In fact, in many clinical trials subjects are randomly assigned to take the drug or a placebo.

This has prompted some researchers to question whether the use of placebos is even ethical because some very sick people will essentially get no active treatment and may get worse.

What about using placebos in studies of serious illnesses like depression? Treatments for it are known to be effective, though imperfect. There is little doubt that the most powerful way to show a drug's efficacy and safety is to assign patients at random to the drug or a placebo. But depressed patients who get a placebo may not improve; they may get worse and even become suicidal.

Sure, scientists could compare an experimental drug with a proven standard drug, but this would require a much larger sample and would expose more people to risks of the new drug. That's because research results differ more widely between the use of placebos and active drugs, than between two active treatments.*

Were the researchers right to halt the breast cancer study early? Suppose by extending the trial the scientists could gain valuable knowledge that would help save many women's lives in the future. Would halting the trial early then be wrong? Suppose extending the trial would save lives in the future but also result in the deaths of some women in the study. Would the extension then be permissible? Was the use of placebos ethical? Explain your answers.

---

*Richard Friedman, "Cases: Long-Term Questions Linger in Halted Breast Cancer Trial," *New York Times*, 21 October 2003, http://www.nytimes.com/pages/health (6 March 2008).

FURTHER READING

Jessica W. Berg, Paul S. Appelbaum, et al., *Informed Consent: Legal Theory and Clinical Practice*, 2nd ed. (New York: Oxford University Press, 2001).

Baruch A. Brody, *The Ethics of Biomedical Research: An International Perspective* (New York: Oxford University Press, 1998).

A. M. Capron, "Human Experimentation," in *Medical Ethics*, ed. Robert M. Veatch (Sudbury, MA: Jones and Bartlett, 1997), 135–84.

Steven S. Coughlin and Tom L. Beauchamp, eds., *Ethics and Epidemiology* (New York: Oxford University Press, 1996).

Council for International Organizations of Medical Sciences in Collaboration with the World Health Or-

ganization, *International Ethical Guidelines for Biomedical Research Involving Human Subjects* (Geneva: CIOMS, 1993), 1–45.

Leonardo D. DeCastro, "Ethical Issues in Human Experimentation," in *A Companion to Bioethics*, ed. Helga Kuhse and Peter Singer (Oxford: Blackwell, 2001), 379–96.

John H. Fennick, *Studies Show: A Popular Guide to Understanding Scientific Studies* (Amherst, NY: Prometheus Books, 1997).

Walter Glannon, *Biomedical Ethics* (New York: Oxford University Press, 2005), chap. 6, 47–70.

Jay Katz, ed., *Experimentation with Human Beings* (New York: Russell Sage Foundation, 1972).

Alex John London, "Clinical Equipoise: Foundational Requirement or Fundamental Error?" in *The Oxford Handbook of Bioethics*, ed. Bonnie Steinbock (Oxford: Oxford University Press, 2007), 572–96.

National Bioethics Advisory Commission, "Protecting Research Participants—A Time for Change," in *Ethical and Policy Issues in Research Involving Human Participants: Summary* (Bethesda, MD: NBAC, 2001), i–ix.

Paul Ramsey, *The Patient as Person* (New Haven, CT: Yale University Press, 1970).

Adil E. Shamoo and David B. Resnik, *Responsible Conduct of Research* (New York: Oxford University Press, 2003).

Lewis Vaughn, *The Power of Critical Thinking* (New York: Oxford University Press, 2008), chap. 10, 382–441.

NOTES

1. Quoted in Albert R. Jonson, *The Birth of Bioethics* (New York: Oxford University Press, 1998), 135.

2. *Ibid.*

3. Baruch A. Brody, *The Ethics of Biomedical Research: An International Perspective* (New York: Oxford University Press, 1998), 31–54.

4. Walter Glannon, *Biomedical Ethics* (New York: Oxford University Press, 2005), 52–53.

5. Samuel Hellman and Deborah S. Hellman, "Of Mice but Not Men: Problems of the Randomized Clinical Trial," *New England Journal of Medicine* 324.22 (1991), 1585–89.

6. Eugene Passamani, "Clinical Trials: Are They Ethical?," *New England Journal of Medicine* 324.22 (1991), 1589–91.

7. Tom L. Beauchamp and James F. Childress, *Principles of Biomedical Ethics,* 5th ed. (New York: Oxford University Press, 2001), 324.

8. World Medical Association, *Declaration of Helsinki*, (2004), http:www.wma.net/e/policy/b3.html (17 October 2008).

9. Beauchamp and Childress, *Principles,* 324.

10. The Council for International Organizations of Medical Sciences (CIOMS) in Collaboration with the World Health Organization (WHO), *International Ethical Guidelines for Biomedical Research Involving Human Subjects* (Geneva: CIOMS, 1993).

11. *Ibid.*

12. Brody, *Ethics of Biomedical Research*, 44.

13. CIOMS in Collaboration with the WHO, *International Ethical Guidelines,* guideline 5.

14. Department of Health and Human Services, *Regulations for the Protection of Human Subjects* (1991), 46.401–46.406.

15. Marcia Angell, "The Ethics of Clinical Research in the Third World," *New England Journal of Medicine* 337.12 (1997), 847–49.

16. Baruch Brody, "Ethical Issues in Clinical Trials in Developing Countries," *Statistics in Medicine* 21 (2002), 2853–58.

17. Brody, "Ethical Issues."

18. The Nuremberg Code.

READINGS

The Nuremberg Code

1. The voluntary consent of the human subject is absolutely essential.

This means that the person involved should have legal capacity to give consent; should be so situated as to be able to exercise free power of choice, without the intervention of any element of force, fraud, deceit, duress, overreaching, or other ulterior form of constraint or coercion; and should have sufficient knowledge and comprehension of the elements of the subject matter involved as to enable him to make an understanding and enlightened decision. This latter element requires that before the acceptance of an affirmative decision by the experimental subject there should be made known to him the nature, duration, and purpose of the experiment; the method and means by which it is to be conducted; all inconveniences and hazards reasonably to be expected; and the effects upon his health or person which may possibly come from his participation in the experiment.

The duty and responsibility for ascertaining the quality of the consent rests upon each individual who initiates, directs or engages in the experiment. It is a personal duty and responsibility which may not be delegated to another with impunity.

2. The experiment should be such as to yield fruitful results for the good of society, unprocurable by other methods or means of study, and not random and unnecessary in nature.

3. The experiment should be so designed and based on the results of animal experimentation and a knowledge of the natural history of the disease or other problem under study that the anticipated results will justify the performance of the experiment.

4. The experiment should be so conducted as to avoid all unnecessary physical and mental suffering and injury.

5. No experiment should be conducted where there is an *a priori* reason to believe that death or disabling injury will occur; except, perhaps, in those experiments where the experimental physicians also serve as subjects.

6. The degree of risk to be taken should never exceed that determined by the humanitarian importance of the problem to be solved by the experiment.

7. Proper preparations should be made and adequate facilities provided to protect the experimental

From *Trials of War Criminals Before the Nuremberg Military Tribunals under Control Council Law No. 10,* vol. 2 (Washington, D.C.: U.S. Government Printing Office, 1949), 181–182.

subject against even remote possibilities of injury, disability, or death.

8. The experiment should be conducted only by scientifically qualified persons. The highest degree of skill and care should be required through all stages of the experiment of those who conduct or engage in the experiment.

9. During the course of the experiment the human subject should be at liberty to bring the experiment to an end if he has reached the physical or mental state where continuation of the experiment seems to him to be impossible.

10. During the course of the experiment the scientist in charge must be prepared to terminate the experiment at any stage, if he has probable cause to believe, in the exercise of the good faith, superior skill and careful judgment required of him that a continuation of the experiment is likely to result in injury, disability, or death to the experimental subject.

Declaration of Helsinki: Ethical Principles for Medical Research Involving Human Subjects
WORLD MEDICAL ASSOCIATION

This international ethical code echoes principles in the Nuremberg Code and breaks some new ground as well. In addition to affirming the importance of informed consent, it provides guidelines for conducting research on subjects who cannot give their informed consent, insists on the review of research protocols by "independent committees," discusses the use of placebo controls, and declares that "considerations related to the well-being of the human subject should take precedence over the interests of science and society."

A. Introduction

1. The World Medical Association has developed the Declaration of Helsinki as a statement of ethical principles to provide guidance to physicians and other participants in medical research involving human subjects. Medical research involving human subjects includes research on identifiable human material or identifiable data.

2. It is the duty of the physician to promote and safeguard the health of the people. The physician's knowledge and conscience are dedicated to the fulfillment of this duty.

3. The Declaration of Geneva of the World Medical Association binds the physician with the words, "The health of my patient will be my first consideration," and the International Code of Medical Ethics declares that, "A physician shall act only in the patient's interest when providing medical care which might have the effect of weakening the physical and mental condition of the patient."

4. Medical progress is based on research which ultimately must rest in part on experimentation involving human subjects.

5. In medical research on human subjects, considerations related to the well-being of the human subject should take precedence over the interests of science and society.

6. The primary purpose of medical research involving human subjects is to improve prophylactic, diagnostic and therapeutic procedures and the understanding of the aetiology and pathogenesis of disease. Even the best proven prophylactic, diagnostic, and therapeutic methods must continuously be challenged through research for their effectiveness, efficiency, accessibility, and quality.

7. In current medical practice and in medical research, most prophylactic, diagnostic, and therapeutic procedures involve risks and burdens.

From *Declaration of Helsinki*, World Medical Association, http://www.net/e/policy/b3.html. Copyright and permission, World Medical Association. All rights reserved.

8. Medical research is subject to ethical standards that promote respect for all human beings and protect their health and rights. Some research populations are vulnerable and need special protection. The particular needs of the economically and medically disadvantaged must be recognized. Special attention is also required for those who cannot give or refuse consent for themselves, for those who may be subject to giving consent under duress, for those who will not benefit personally from the research and for those for whom the research is combined with care.

9. Research Investigators should be aware of the ethical, legal and regulatory requirements for research on human subjects in their own countries as well as applicable international requirements. No national ethical, legal or regulatory requirement should be allowed to reduce or eliminate any of the protections for human subjects set forth in this Declaration.

B. Basic Principles for All Medical Research

10. It is the duty of the physician in medical research to protect the life, health, privacy, and dignity of the human subject.

11. Medical research involving human subjects must conform to generally accepted scientific principles, be based on a thorough knowledge of the scientific literature, other relevant sources of information, and on adequate laboratory and, where appropriate, animal experimentation.

12. Appropriate caution must be exercised in the conduct of research which may affect the environment, and the welfare of animals used for research must be respected.

13. The design and performance of each experimental procedure involving human subjects should be clearly formulated in an experimental protocol. This protocol should be submitted for consideration, comment, guidance, and where appropriate, approval to a specially appointed ethical review committee, which must be independent of the investigator, the sponsor or any other kind of undue influence. This independent committee should be in conformity with the laws and regulations of the country in which the research experiment is performed. The committee has the right to monitor ongoing trials. The researcher has the obligation to provide monitoring information to the committee, especially any serious adverse events. The researcher should also submit to the committee, for review, information regarding funding, sponsors, institutional affiliations, other potential conflicts of interest and incentives for subjects.

14. The research protocol should always contain a statement of the ethical considerations involved and should indicate that there is compliance with the principles enunciated in this Declaration.

15. Medical research involving human subjects should be conducted only by scientifically qualified persons and under the supervision of a clinically competent medical person. The responsibility for the human subject must always rest with a medically qualified person and never rest on the subject of the research, even though the subject has given consent.

16. Every medical research project involving human subjects should be preceded by careful assessment of predictable risks and burdens in comparison with foreseeable benefits to the subject or to others. This does not preclude the participation of healthy volunteers in medical research. The design of all studies should be publicly available.

17. Physicians should abstain from engaging in research projects involving human subjects unless they are confident that the risks involved have been adequately assessed and can be satisfactorily managed. Physicians should cease any investigation if the risks are found to outweigh the potential benefits or if there is conclusive proof of positive and beneficial results.

18. Medical research involving human subjects should only be conducted if the importance of the objective outweighs the inherent risks and burdens to the subject. This is especially important when the human subjects are healthy volunteers.

19. Medical research is only justified if there is a reasonable likelihood that the populations in which the research is carried out stand to benefit from the results of the research.

20. The subjects must be volunteers and informed participants in the research project.

21. The right of research subjects to safeguard their integrity must always be respected. Every precaution should be taken to respect the privacy of the

subject, the confidentiality of the patient's information and to minimize the impact of the study on the subject's physical and mental integrity and on the personality of the subject.

22. In any research on human beings, each potential subject must be adequately informed of the aims, methods, sources of funding, any possible conflicts of interest, institutional affiliations of the researcher, the anticipated benefits and potential risks of the study, and the discomfort it may entail. The subject should be informed of the right to abstain from participation in the study or to withdraw consent to participate at any time without reprisal. After ensuring that the subject has understood the information, the physician should then obtain the subject's freely given informed consent, preferably in writing. If the consent cannot be obtained in writing, the non-written consent must be formally documented and witnessed.

23. When obtaining informed consent for the research project the physician should be particularly cautious if the subject is in a dependent relationship with the physician or may consent under duress. In that case the informed consent should be obtained by a well-informed physician who is not engaged in the investigation and who is completely independent of this relationship.

24. For a research subject who is legally incompetent, physically or mentally incapable of giving consent or is a legally incompetent minor, the investigator must obtain informed consent from the legally authorized representative in accordance with applicable law. These groups should not be included in research unless the research is necessary to promote the health of the population represented and this research cannot instead be performed on legally competent persons.

25. When a subject deemed legally incompetent, such as a minor child, is able to give assent to decisions about participation in research, the investigator must obtain that assent in addition to the consent of the legally authorized representative.

26. Research on individuals from whom it is not possible to obtain consent, including proxy or advance consent, should be done only if the physical/mental condition that prevents obtaining informed consent is a necessary characteristic of the research

population. The specific reasons for involving research subjects with a condition that renders them unable to give informed consent should be stated in the experimental protocol for consideration and approval of the review committee. The protocol should state that consent to remain in the research should be obtained as soon as possible from the individual or a legally authorized surrogate.

27. Both authors and publishers have ethical obligations. In publication of the results of research, the investigators are obliged to preserve the accuracy of the results. Negative as well as positive results should be published or otherwise publicly available. Sources of funding, institutional affiliations, and any possible conflicts of interest should be declared in the publication. Reports of experimentation not in accordance with the principles laid down in this Declaration should not be accepted for publication.

C. Additional Principles for Medical Research Combined with Medical Care

28. The physician may combine medical research with medical care, only to the extent that the research is justified by its potential prophylactic, diagnostic, or therapeutic value. When medical research is combined with medical care, additional standards apply to protect the patients who are research subjects.

29. The benefits, risks, burdens, and effectiveness of a new method should be tested against those of the best current prophylactic, diagnostic, and therapeutic methods. This does not exclude the use of placebo, or no treatment, in studies where no proven prophylactic, diagnostic, or therapeutic method exists.[1]

30. At the conclusion of the study, every patient entered into the study should be assured of access to the best proven prophylactic, diagnostic, and therapeutic methods identified by the study.[2]

31. The physician should fully inform the patient which aspects of the care are related to the research. The refusal of a patient to participate in a study must never interfere with the patient-physician relationship.

32. In the treatment of a patient, where proven prophylactic, diagnostic, and therapeutic methods do not exist or have been ineffective, the physician, with informed consent from the patient, must be free to use unproven or new prophylactic, diagnostic, and therapeutic measures, if in the physician's judgement

it offers hope of saving life, reestablishing health or alleviating suffering. Where possible, these measures should be made the object of research, designed to evaluate their safety and efficacy. In all cases, new information should be recorded and, where appropriate, published. The other relevant guidelines of this Declaration should be followed.

NOTES

1. Note of clarification on paragraph 29 of the WMA Declaration of Helsinki:

> The WMA hereby reaffirms its position that extreme care must be taken in making use of a placebo-controlled trial and that in general this methodology should only be used in the absence of existing proven therapy. However, a placebo-controlled trial may be ethically acceptable, even if proven therapy is available, under the following circumstances:
>
> • Where for compelling and scientifically sound methodological reasons its use is necessary to determine

the efficacy or safety of a prophylactic, diagnostic, or therapeutic method; or
• Where a prophylactic, diagnostic, or therapeutic method is being investigated for a minor condition and the patients who receive placebo will not be subject to any additional risk of serious or irreversible harm.

All other provisions of the Declaration of Helsinki must be adhered to, especially the need for appropriate ethical and scientific review.

2. Note of clarification on paragraph 30 of the WMA Declaration of Helsinki:

> The WMA hereby reaffirms its position that it is necessary during the study planning process to identify post-trial access by study participants to prophylactic, diagnostic, and therapeutic procedures identified as beneficial in the study or access to other appropriate care. Post-trial access arrangements or other care must be described in the study protocol so the ethical review committee may consider such arrangements during its review.

The Belmont Report

THE NATIONAL COMMISSION FOR THE PROTECTION OF HUMAN SUBJECTS OF BIOMEDICAL AND BEHAVIORAL RESEARCH

In 1974 Congress created the commission to provide guidance on the ethical issues that arise in research on human subjects. The result of the commission's work is this report, which lays out a general approach to thinking about research ethics and elucidates the three most relevant moral principles—respect for persons, beneficence, and justice.

Ethical Principles and Guidelines for Research Involving Human Subjects

A. Boundaries Between Practice and Research
It is important to distinguish between biomedical and behavioral research, on the one hand, and the practice of accepted therapy on the other, in order to know what activities ought to undergo review for the protection of human subjects of research. The

From *The Belmont Report: Ethical Principles and Guidelines for the Protection of Human Subjects of Research* (April 18, 1979), The National Commission for the Protection of Human Subjects of Biomedical and Behavioral Research, http://ohsr.od.nih.gov/guidelines/belmont.html.

distinction between research and practice is blurred partly because both often occur together (as in research designed to evaluate a therapy) and partly because notable departures from standard practice are often called "experimental" when the terms "experimental" and "research" are not carefully defined.

For the most part, the term "practice" refers to interventions that are designed solely to enhance the well-being of an individual patient or client and that have a reasonable expectation of success. The purpose of medical or behavioral practice is to provide diagnosis, preventive treatment or therapy to particular individuals. By contrast, the term "research" designates an activity designed to test an hypothesis, permit conclusions to be drawn, and thereby to develop or contribute to generalizable knowledge (expressed, for example, in theories, principles, and statements of relationships). Research is usually described in a formal protocol that sets forth an objective and a set of procedures designed to reach that objective.

When a clinician departs in a significant way from standard or accepted practice, the innovation does not, in and of itself, constitute research. The fact that a procedure is "experimental," in the sense of new, untested or different, does not automatically place it in the category of research. Radically new procedures of this description should, however, be made the object of formal research at an early stage in order to determine whether they are safe and effective. Thus, it is the responsibility of medical practice committees, for example, to insist that a major innovation be incorporated into a formal research project.

Research and practice may be carried on together when research is designed to evaluate the safety and efficacy of a therapy. This need not cause any confusion regarding whether or not the activity requires review; the general rule is that if there is any element of research in an activity, that activity should undergo review for the protection of human subjects.

B. Basic Ethical Principles

The expression "basic ethical principles" refers to those general judgments that serve as a basic justification for the many particular ethical prescriptions and evaluations of human actions. Three basic principles, among those generally accepted in our cultural tradition, are particularly relevant to the ethics of research involving human subjects: the principles of respect of persons, beneficence and justice.

1. Respect for Persons. Respect for persons incorporates at least two ethical convictions: first, that individuals should be treated as autonomous agents, and second, that persons with diminished autonomy are entitled to protection. The principle of respect for persons thus divides into two separate moral requirements: the requirement to acknowledge autonomy and the requirement to protect those with diminished autonomy.

An autonomous person is an individual capable of deliberation about personal goals and of acting under the direction of such deliberation. To respect autonomy is to give weight to autonomous persons' considered opinions and choices while refraining from obstructing their actions unless they are clearly detrimental to others. To show lack of respect for an autonomous agent is to repudiate that person's considered judgments, to deny an individual the freedom to act on those considered judgments, or to withhold information necessary to make a considered judgment, when there are no compelling reasons to do so.

However, not every human being is capable of self-determination. The capacity for self-determination matures during an individual's life, and some individuals lose this capacity wholly or in part because of illness, mental disability, or circumstances that severely restrict liberty. Respect for the immature and the incapacitated may require protecting them as they mature or while they are incapacitated.

Some persons are in need of extensive protection, even to the point of excluding them from activities which may harm them; other persons require little protection beyond making sure they undertake activities freely and with awareness of possible adverse consequence. The extent of protection afforded should depend upon the risk of harm and the likelihood of benefit. The judgment that any individual lacks autonomy should be periodically reevaluated and will vary in different situations.

In most cases of research involving human subjects, respect for persons demands that subjects enter into the research voluntarily and with adequate information. In some situations, however, application of the principle is not obvious. The involvement of prisoners as subjects of research provides an instructive example. On the one hand, it would seem that the principle of respect for persons requires that prisoners not be deprived of the opportunity to volunteer for research. On the other hand, under prison conditions they may be subtly coerced or unduly influenced to engage in research activities for which they would not otherwise volunteer. Respect for persons would then dictate that prisoners be protected. Whether to allow prisoners to "volunteer" or to "protect" them presents a dilemma. Respecting persons, in most hard cases, is often a matter of balancing competing claims urged by the principle of respect itself.

2. Beneficence. Persons are treated in an ethical manner not only by respecting their decisions and protecting them from harm, but also by making efforts to secure their well-being. Such treatment falls under the principle of beneficence. The term "beneficence" is often understood to cover acts of kindness or charity that go beyond strict obligation. In this document, beneficence is understood in a stronger sense, as an obligation. Two general rules have been formulated as complementary expressions of beneficent actions in this sense: (1) do not harm and (2) maximize possible benefits and minimize possible harms.

The Hippocratic maxim "do no harm" has long been a fundamental principle of medical ethics. Claude Bernard extended it to the realm of research, saying that one should not injure one person regardless of the benefits that might come to others. However, even avoiding harm requires learning what is harmful; and, in the process of obtaining this information, persons may be exposed to risk of harm. Further, the Hippocratic Oath requires physicians to benefit their patients "according to their best judgment." Learning what will in fact benefit may require exposing persons to risk. The problem posed by these imperatives is to decide when it is justifiable to seek certain benefits despite the risks involved, and when the benefits should be foregone because of the risks.

The obligations of beneficence affect both individual investigators and society at large, because they extend both to particular research projects and to the entire enterprise of research. In the case of particular projects, investigators and members of their institutions are obliged to give forethought to the maximization of benefits and the reduction of risk that might occur from the research investigation. In the case of scientific research in general, members of the larger society are obliged to recognize the longer term benefits and risks that may result from the improvement of knowledge and from the development of novel medical, psychotherapeutic, and social procedures.

The principle of beneficence often occupies a well-defined justifying role in many areas of research involving human subjects. An example is found in research involving children. Effective ways of treating childhood diseases and fostering healthy devel-opment are benefits that serve to justify research involving children—even when individual research subjects are not direct beneficiaries. Research also makes it possible to avoid the harm that may result from the application of previously accepted routine practices that on closer investigation turn out to be dangerous. But the role of the principle of beneficence is not always so unambiguous. A difficult ethical problem remains, for example, about research that presents more than minimal risk without immediate prospect of direct benefit to the children involved. Some have argued that such research is inadmissible, while others have pointed out that this limit would rule out much research promising great benefit to children in the future. Here again, as with all hard cases, the different claims covered by the principle of beneficence may come into conflict and force difficult choices.

3. Justice. Who ought to receive the benefits of research and bear its burdens? This is a question of justice, in the sense of "fairness in distribution" or "what is deserved." An injustice occurs when some benefit to which a person is entitled is denied without good reason or when some burden is imposed unduly. Another way of conceiving the principle of justice is that equals ought to be treated equally. However, this statement requires explication. Who is equal and who is unequal? What considerations justify departure from equal distribution? Almost all commentators allow that distinctions based on experience, age, deprivation, competence, merit and position do sometimes constitute criteria justifying differential treatment for certain purposes. It is necessary, then, to explain in what respects people should be treated equally There are several widely accepted formulations of just ways to distribute burdens and benefits. Each formulation mentions some relevant property on the basis of which burdens and benefits should be distributed. These formulations are (1) to each person an equal share, (2) to each person according to individual need, (3) to each person according to individual effort, (4) to each person according to societal contribution, and (5) to each person according to merit.

Questions of justice have long been associated with social practice such as punishment, taxation and political representation. Until recently these questions have not generally been associated with scientific research. However, they are foreshadowed even in the earliest reflections on the ethics of research involving human subjects. For example, during the 19th and early 20th centuries the burdens of serving as research subjects fell largely upon poor ward patients, while the benefits of improved medical care flowed primarily to private patients. Subsequently, the exploitation of unwilling prisoners as research subjects in Nazi concentration camps was condemned as a particularly flagrant injustice. In this country, in the 1940's, the Tuskegee syphilis study used disadvantaged, rural black men to study the untreated course of a disease that is by no means confined to that population. These subjects were deprived of demonstrably effective treatment in order not to interrupt the project, long after such treatment became generally available.

Against this historical background, it can be seen how conceptions of justice are relevant to research involving human subjects. For example, the selection of research subjects needs to be scrutinized in order to determine whether some classes (e.g., welfare patients, particular racial and ethnic minorities, or persons confined to institutions) are being systematically selected simply because of their easy availability, their compromised position, or their manipulability, rather than for reasons directly related to the problem being studied. Finally, whenever research supported by public funds leads to the development of therapeutic devices and procedures, justice demands both that these not provide advantages only to those who can afford them and that such research should not unduly involve persons from groups unlikely to be among the beneficiaries of subsequent applications of the research.

Final Report: Human Radiation Experiments

ADVISORY COMMITTEE ON HUMAN RADIATION EXPERIMENTS

This official report details the government-sponsored radiation experiments conducted on thousands of human subjects from 1944 to 1974. Subjects were exposed to harmful levels of radiation, often without their consent and without being told of the potential dangers. The report also reviews the safety of contemporary human research using radiation and recommends apologies and compensation to the victimized subjects or their next of kin.

The Creation of the Advisory Committee

On January 15, 1994, President Clinton appointed the Advisory Committee on Human Radiation Experiments. The President created the Committee to investigate reports of possibly unethical experiments funded by the government decades ago.

The members of the Advisory Committee were fourteen private citizens from around the country: a representative of the general public and thirteen experts in bioethics, radiation oncology and biology,

From Advisory Committee on Human Radiation Experiments, Department of Energy, *Final Report: Executive Summary,* 1995, http://www.hss.energy.gov/healthsafety/ohre/roadmap/achre/report.html.

nuclear medicine, epidemiology and biostatistics, public health, history of science and medicine, and law.

President Clinton asked us to deliver our recommendations to a Cabinet-level group, the Human Radiation Interagency Working Group, whose members are the Secretaries of Defense, Energy, Health and Human Services, and Veterans Affairs; the Attorney General; the Administrator of the National Aeronautics and Space Administration; the Director of Central Intelligence; and the Director of the Office of Management and Budget. Some of the experiments the Committee was asked to investigate, and particularly a series that included the injection of plutonium into unsuspecting hospital patients, were of special concern to Secretary of Energy Hazel O'Leary. Her department had its origins in the federal agencies that had sponsored the plutonium experiments. These agencies were responsible for the development of nuclear weapons and during the Cold War their activities had been shrouded in secrecy. But now the Cold War was over.

The controversy surrounding the plutonium experiments and others like them brought basic questions to the fore: How many experiments were conducted or sponsored by the government, and why? How many were secret? Was anyone harmed? What was disclosed to those subjected to risk, and what opportunity did they have for consent? By what rules should the past be judged? What remedies are due those who were wronged or harmed by the government in the past? How well do federal rules that today govern human experimentation work? What lessons can be learned for application to the future? Our Final Report provides the details of the Committee's answers to these questions. This Executive Summary presents an overview of the work done by the Committee, our findings and recommendations, and the contents of the Final Report.

The President's Charge

The President directed the Advisory Committee to uncover the history of human radiation experiments during the period 1944 through 1974. It was in 1944 that the first known human radiation experiment of interest was planned, and in 1974 that the Department of Health, Education and Welfare adopted regulations governing the conduct of human research, a watershed event in the history of federal protections for human subjects.

In addition to asking us to investigate human radiation experiments, the President directed us to examine cases in which the government had intentionally released radiation into the environment for research purposes. He further charged us with identifying the ethical and scientific standards for evaluating these events, and with making recommendations to ensure that whatever wrongdoing may have occurred in the past cannot be repeated.

We were asked to address human experiments and intentional releases that involved radiation. The ethical issues we addressed and the moral frame-

work we developed are, however, applicable to all research involving human subjects.

The breadth of the Committee's charge was remarkable. We were called on to review government programs that spanned administrations from Franklin Roosevelt to Gerald Ford. As an independent advisory committee, we were free to pursue our charge as we saw fit. The decisions we reached regarding the course of our inquiry and the nature of our findings and recommendations were entirely our own.

The Committee's Approach

At our first meeting, we immediately realized that we were embarking on an intense and challenging investigation of an important aspect of our nation's past and present, a task that required new insights and difficult judgments about ethical questions that persist even today.

Between April 1994 and July 1995, the Advisory Committee held sixteen public meetings, most in Washington, D.C. In addition, subsets of Committee members presided over public forums in cities throughout the country. The Committee heard from more than 200 witnesses and interviewed dozens of professionals who were familiar with experiments involving radiation. A special effort, called the Ethics Oral History Project, was under taken to learn from eminent physicians about how research with human subjects was conducted in the 1940s and 1950s.

We were granted unprecedented access to government documents. The President directed all the federal agencies involved to make available to the Committee any documents that might further our inquiry, wherever they might be located and whether or not they were still secret.

As we began our search into the past, we quickly discovered that it was going to be extremely difficult to piece together a coherent picture. Many critical documents had long since been forgotten and were stored in obscure locations throughout the country. Often they were buried in collections that bore no obvious connection to human radiation experiments. There was no easy way to identify how many experiments had been conducted, where they took place, and which government agencies had sponsored them. Nor was there a quick way to learn what rules applied to these experiments for the period prior to the mid-1960s. With the assistance of hundreds of federal officials and agency staff, the Committee retrieved and reviewed hundreds of thousands of government documents. Some of the most important documents were secret and were declassified at our request. Even after this extraordinary effort, the historical record remains incomplete. Some potentially important collections could not be located and were evidently lost or destroyed years ago.

Nevertheless, the documents that were recovered enabled us to identify nearly 4,000 human radiation experiments sponsored by the federal government between 1944 and 1974. In the great majority of cases, only fragmentary data was locatable; the identity of subjects and the specific radiation exposures involved were typically unavailable.

Given the constraints of information, even more so than time, it was impossible for the Committee to review all these experiments, nor could we evaluate the experiences of countless individual subjects. We thus decided to focus our investigation on representative case studies reflecting eight different categories of experiments that together addressed our charge and priorities. These case studies included:

- Experiments with plutonium and other atomic bomb materials
- The Atomic Energy Commission's program of radioisotope distribution
- Nontherapeutic research on children
- Total body irradiation
- Research on prisoners
- Human experimentation in connection with nuclear weapons testing
- Intentional environmental releases of radiation
- Observational research involving uranium miners and residents of the Marshall Islands

In addition to assessing the ethics of human radiation experiments conducted decades ago, it was also important to explore the current conduct of human radiation research. Insofar as wrongdoing may have occurred in the past, we needed to examine the likelihood that such things could happen today. We therefore undertook three projects:

- A review of how each agency of the federal government that currently conducts or funds

research involving human subjects regulates this activity and oversees it.
- An examination of the documents and consent forms of research projects that are today sponsored by the federal government in order to develop insight into the current status of protections for the rights and interests of human subjects.
- Interviews of nearly 1,900 patients receiving out-patient medical care in private hospitals and federal facilities throughout the country. We asked them whether they were currently, or had been, subjects of research, and why they had agreed to participate in research or had refused,

The Historical Context

Since its discovery 100 years ago, radioactivity has been a basic tool of medical research and diagnosis. In addition to the many uses of the x ray, it was soon discovered that radiation could be used to treat cancer and that the introduction of "tracer" amounts of radioisotopes into the human body could help to diagnose disease and understand bodily processes. At the same time, the perils of overexposure to radiation were becoming apparent.

During World War II the new field of radiation science was at the center of one of the most ambitious and secret research efforts the world has known—the Manhattan Project. Human radiation experiments were undertaken in secret to help understand radiation risks to workers engaged in the development of the atomic bomb.

Following the war, the new Atomic Energy Commission used facilities built to make the atomic bomb to produce radioisotopes for medical research and other peacetime uses. This highly publicized program provided the radioisotopes that were used in thousands of human experiments conducted in research facilities throughout the country and the world. This research, in turn, was part of a larger postwar transformation of biomedical research through the infusion of substantial government monies and technical support.

The intersection of government and biomedical research brought with it new roles and new ethical questions for medical researchers. Many of these researchers were also physicians who operated within a tradition of medical ethics that enjoined them to put the interests of their patients first. When the doctor also was a researcher, however, the potential for conflict emerged between the advancement of science and the advancement of the patient's wellbeing.

Other ethical issues were posed as medical researchers were called on by government officials to play new roles in the development and testing of nuclear weapons. For example, as advisers they were asked to provide human research data that could reassure officials about the effects of radiation, but as scientists they were not always convinced that human research could provide scientifically useful data. Similarly, as scientists, they came from a tradition in which research results were freely debated. In their capacity as advisers to and officials of the government, however, these researchers found that the openness of science now needed to be constrained.

None of these tensions were unique to radiation research. Radiation represents just one of several examples of the exploration of the weapons potential of new scientific discoveries during and after World War II. Similarly, the tensions between clinical research and the treatment of patients were emerging throughout medical science, and were not found only in research involving radiation. Not only were these issues not unique to radiation, but they were not unique to the 1940s and 1950s. Today society still struggles with conflicts between the openness of science and the preservation of national security, as well as with conflicts between the advancement of medical science and the rights and interests of patients.

Key Findings
Human Radiation Experiments

- Between 1944 and 1974 the federal government sponsored several thousand human radiation experiments. In the great majority of cases, the experiments were conducted to advance biomedical science; some experiments were conducted to advance national interests in defense or space exploration; and some experiments served both biomedical and defense or space exploration purposes. As noted, in the great majority of cases only fragmentary data are available.

- The majority of human radiation experiments identified by the Advisory Committee involved radioactive tracers administered in amounts that are likely to be similar to those used in research today. Most of these tracer studies involved adult subjects and are unlikely to have caused physical harm. However, in some nontherapeutic tracer studies involving children, radioisotope exposures were associated with increases in the potential lifetime risk for developing thyroid cancer that would be considered unacceptable today. The Advisory Committee also identified several studies in which patients died soon after receiving external radiation or radioisotope doses in the therapeutic range that were associated with acute radiation effects.

- Although the AEC, the Defense Department and the National Institutes of Health recognized at an early date that research should proceed only with the consent of the human subject, there is little evidence of rules or practices of consent except in research with healthy subjects. It was commonplace during the 1940s and 1950s for physicians to use patients as subjects of research without their awareness or consent. By contrast, the government and its researchers focused with substantial success on the minimization of risk in the conduct of experiments, particularly with respect to research involving radioisotopes. But little attention was paid during this period to issues of fairness in the selection of subjects.

- Government officials and investigators are blameworthy for not having had policies and practices in place to protect the rights and interests of human subjects who were used in research from which the subjects could not possibly derive direct medical benefit. To the extent that there was reason to believe that research might provide a direct medical benefit to subjects, government officials and biomedical professionals are less blameworthy for not having had such protections and practices in place.

Intentional Releases

- During the 1944–1974 period, the government conducted several hundred intentional releases of radiation into the environment for research purposes. Generally, these releases were not conducted for the purpose of studying the effects of radiation on humans. Instead they were usually conducted to test the operation of weapons, the safety of equipment, or the dispersal of radiation into the environment.

- For those intentional releases where dose reconstructions have been undertaken, it is unlikely that members of the public were directly harmed solely as a consequence of these tests. However, these releases were conducted in secret and despite continued requests from the public that stretch back well over a decade, some information about them was made public only during the life of the Advisory Committee.

Uranium Miners

- As a consequence of exposure to radon and its daughter products in underground uranium mines, at least several hundred miners died of lung cancer and surviving miners remain at elevated risk. These men, who were the subject of government study as they mined uranium for use in weapons manufacturing, were subject to radon exposures well in excess of levels known to be hazardous. The government failed to act to require the reduction of the hazard by ventilating the mines, and it failed to adequately warn the miners of the hazard to which they were being exposed.

Secrecy and the Public Trust

- The greatest harm from past experiments and intentional releases may be the legacy of distrust they created. Hundreds of intentional releases took place in secret, and remained secret for decades. Important discussion of the policies to govern human experimentation also took place in secret. Information about human experiments was kept secret out of concern for embarrassment to the government, potential legal liability, and worry that public misun-

derstanding would jeopardize government programs.

- In a few instances, people used as experimental subjects and their families were denied the opportunity to pursue redress for possible wrongdoing because of actions taken by the government to keep the truth from them. Where programs were legitimately kept secret for national security reasons, the government often did not create or maintain adequate records, thereby preventing the public, and those most at risk, from learning the facts in a timely and complete fashion.

Contemporary Human Subjects Research

- Human research involving radioisotopes is currently subjected to more safeguards and levels of review than most other areas of research involving human subjects. There are no apparent differences between the treatment of human subjects of radiation research and human subjects of other biomedical research.

- Based on the Advisory Committee's review, it appears that much of human subjects research poses only minimal risk of harm to subjects. In our review of research documents that bear on human subjects issues, we found no problems or only minor problems in most of the minimal-risk studies we examined.

- Our review of documents identified examples of complicated, higher-risk studies in which human subjects issues were carefully and adequately addressed and that included excellent consent forms. In our interview project, there was little evidence that patient-subjects felt coerced or pressured by investigators to participate in research. We interviewed patients who had declined offers to become research subjects, reinforcing the impression that there are often contexts in which potential research subjects have a genuine choice.

- At the same time, however, we also found evidence suggesting serious deficiencies in aspects of the current system for the protection of the rights and interests of human subjects. For example, consent forms do not always provide adequate information and may be misleading about the impact of research participation on people's lives. Some patients with serious illnesses appear to have unrealistic expectations about the benefits of being subjects in research.

Current Regulations on Secrecy in Human Research and Environmental Releases
- Human research can still be conducted in secret today, and under some conditions informed consent in secret research can be waived.
- Events that raise the same concerns as the intentional releases in the Committee's charter could take place in secret today under current environmental laws. . . .

Key Recommendations
Apologies and Compensation
The government should deliver a personal, individualized apology and provide financial compensation to those subjects of human radiation experiments, or their next of kin, in cases where:

- Efforts were made by the government to keep information secret from these individuals or their families, or the public, for the purpose of avoiding embarrassment or potential legal liability, and where this secrecy had the effect of denying individuals the opportunity to pursue potential grievances.
- There was no prospect of direct medical benefit to the subjects, or interventions considered controversial at the time were presented as standard practice, and physical injury attributable to the experiment resulted.

Uranium Miners
- The Interagency Working Group, together with Congress, should give serious consideration to amending the provisions of the Radiation Exposure Compensation Act of 1990 relating to uranium miners in order to provide compensation to *all* miners who develop lung cancer after some minimal duration of employment underground (such as one year), without requiring a specific level

of exposure. The act should also be reviewed to determine whether the documentation standards for compensation should be liberalized.

Improved Protection for Human Subjects
- The Committee found no differences between human radiation research and other areas of research with respect to human subjects issues, either in the past or the present. In comparison to the practices and policies of the 1940s and 1950s, there have been significant advances in the federal government's system for the protection of the rights and interests of human subjects. But deficiencies remain. Efforts should be under taken on a national scale to ensure the centrality of ethics in the conduct of scientists whose research involves human subjects.
- One problem in need of immediate attention by the government and the biomedical research community is unrealistic expectations among some patients with serious illnesses about the prospect of direct medical benefit from participating in research. Also, among the consent forms we reviewed, some appear to be overly optimistic in portraying the likely benefits of research, to inadequately explain the impact of research procedures on quality of life and personal finances, and to be incomprehensible to lay people.
- A mechanism should be established to provide for continuing interpretation and application in an open and public forum of ethics rules and principles for the conduct of human subjects research. Three examples of policy issues in need of public resolution that the Advisory Committee confronted in our work are: (1) Clarification of the meaning of minimal risk in research with healthy children; (2) regulations to cover the conduct of research with institutionalized children; and (3) guidelines for research with adults of questionable competence, particularly for research in which subjects are placed at more than minimal risk but are offered no prospect of direct medical benefit.

Secrecy: Balancing National Security and the Public Trust

Current policies do not adequately safeguard against the recurrence of the kinds of events we studied that fostered distrust. The Advisory Committee concludes that there may be special circumstances in which it may be necessary to conduct human research or intentional releases in secret. However, to the extent that the government conducts such activities with elements of secrecy, special protections of the rights and interests of individuals and the public are needed.

Research Involving Human Subjects. The Advisory Committee recommends the adoption of federal policies requiring:

- The informed consent of all human subjects of classified research. This requirement should not be subject to exemption or waiver.
- That classified research involving human subjects be permitted only after the review and approval of an independent panel of appro-

priate nongovernmental experts and citizen representatives, all with the necessary security clearances.

Environmental Releases. There must be independent review to assure that the action is needed, that risk is minimized, and that records will be kept to assure a proper accounting to the public at the earliest date consistent with legitimate national security concerns. Specifically, the Committee recommends that:

- Secret environmental releases of hazardous substances should be permitted only after the review and approval of an independent panel. This panel should consist of appropriate, nongovernmental experts and citizen representatives, all with the necessary security clearances.
- An appropriate government agency, such as the Environmental Protection Agency, should maintain a program directed at the oversight of classified programs, with suitably cleared personnel. . . .

Of Mice but Not Men: Problems of the Randomized Clinical Trial

SAMUEL HELLMAN AND DEBORAH S. HELLMAN

The Hellmans contend that randomized clinical trials place physician-scientists (physicians who simultaneously act as scientists) in a terrible ethical bind. As physicians, they have a duty to look out for the best interests of their patients; as scientists, they have an obligation to ensure the integrity of the research. But often they cannot do both, the Hellmans say. Before or during a trial, if a physician-scientist believes that a new treatment is better (or worse) than the alternative treatment, she has a physician's duty to communicate this judgment to her patient-subjects and ensure that they get the best treatment. But if she does so, the validity of the research will be compromised. Thus randomized trials often pit the good of patients against the good of society. The authors "urge that such situations be avoided and that other techniques of acquiring clinical information be adopted."

As medicine has become increasingly scientific and less accepting of unsupported opinion or proof by

From *The New England Journal of Medicine*, 324, no. 22, pp. 1585–1589. Copyright © 1991, Massachusetts Medical Society. All rights reserved. Reprinted with permission.

anecdote, the randomized controlled clinical trial has become the standard technique for changing diagnostic or therapeutic methods. The use of this technique creates an ethical dilemma.[1,2] Researchers participating in such studies are required to modify their ethical commitments to individual patients and do serious damage to the concept of the physician as a practicing, empathetic professional who is primarily concerned with each patient as an individual. Researchers using a randomized clinical trial can be described as physician-scientists, a term that expresses the tension between the two roles. The physician, by entering into a relationship with an individual patient, assumes certain obligations, including the commitment always to act in the patient's best interests. As Leon Kass has rightly maintained, "the physician must produce unswervingly the virtues of loyalty and fidelity to his patient."[3] Though the ethical requirements of this relationship have been modified by legal obligations to report wounds of a suspicious nature and certain infectious diseases, these obligations in no way conflict with the central ethical obligation to act in the best interests of the patient medically. Instead, certain nonmedical interests of the patient are preempted by other social concerns.

The role of the scientist is quite different. The clinical scientist is concerned with answering questions—i.e., determining the validity of formally constructed hypotheses. Such scientific information, it is presumed, will benefit humanity in general. The clinical scientist's role has been well described by Dr. Anthony Fauci, director of the National Institute of Allergy and Infectious Diseases, who states the goals of the randomized clinical trial in these words: "It's not to deliver therapy. It's to answer a scientific question so that the drug can be available for everybody once you've established safety and efficacy."[4] The demands of such a study can conflict in a number of ways with the physician's duty to minister to patients. The study may create a false dichotomy in the physician's opinions; according to the premise of the randomized clinical trial, the physician may only know or not know whether a proposed course of treatment represents an improvement; no middle position is permitted. What the physician thinks, suspects, believes, or has a hunch about is assigned to the "not knowing" category, because knowing is defined on the basis of an arbitrary but accepted statistical test performed in a randomized clinical trial. Thus, little credence is given to information gained beforehand in other ways or to information accrued during the trial but without the required statistical

degree of assurance that a difference is not due to chance. The randomized clinical trial also prevents the treatment technique from being modified on the basis of the growing knowledge of the physicians during their participation in the trial. Moreover, it limits access to the data as they are collected until specific milestones are achieved. This prevents physicians from profiting not only from their individual experience, but also from the collective experience of the other participants.

The randomized clinical trial requires doctors to act simultaneously as physicians and as scientists. This puts them in a difficult and sometimes untenable ethical position. The conflicting moral demands arising from the use of the randomized clinical trial reflect the classic conflict between rights-based moral theories and utilitarian ones. The first of these, which depend on the moral theory of Immanuel Kant (and seen more recently in neo-Kantian philosophers, such as John Rawls[5]), asserts that human beings, by virtue of their unique capacity for rational thought, are bearers of dignity. As such, they ought not to be treated merely as means to an end; rather, they must always be treated as ends in themselves. Utilitarianism, by contrast, defines what is right as the greatest good for the greatest number—that is, as social utility. This view, articulated by Jeremy Bentham and John Stuart Mill, requires that pleasures (understood broadly, to include such pleasures as health and well-being) and pains be added together. The morally correct act is the act that produces the most pleasure and the least pain overall.

A classic objection to the utilitarian position is that according to that theory, the distribution of pleasures and pains is of no moral consequence. This element of the theory severely restricts physicians from being utilitarians, or at least from following the theory's dictates. Physicians must care very deeply about the distribution of pain and pleasure, for they have entered into a relationship with one or a number of individual patients. They cannot be indifferent to whether it is these patients or others that suffer for the general benefit of society. Even though society might gain from the suffering of a few, and even though the doctor might believe that such a benefit is worth a given patient's suffering (i.e., that utilitarianism is right in the particular case), the ethical obligation created by the covenant between doctor and patient requires the doctor to see the interests of the individual patient as primary and compelling. In essence, the doctor-patient relationship requires doctors to see their patients as bearers of rights who cannot be merely used for the greater good of humanity.

As Fauci has suggested,[4] the randomized clinical trial routinely asks physicians to sacrifice the interests of their particular patients for the sake of the study and that of the information that it will make available for the benefit of society. This practice is ethically problematic. Consider first the initial formulation of a trial. In particular, consider the case of a disease for which there is no satisfactory therapy—for example, advanced cancer or the acquired immunodeficiency syndrome (AIDS). A new agent that promises more effectiveness is the subject of the study. The control group must be given either an unsatisfactory treatment or a placebo. Even though the therapeutic value of the new agent is unproved, if physicians think that it has promise, are they acting in the best interests of their patients in allowing them to be randomly assigned to the control group? Is persisting in such an assignment consistent with the specific commitments taken on in the doctor-patient relationship? As a result of interactions with patients with AIDS and their advocates, Merigan[6] recently suggested modifications in the design of clinical trials that attempt to deal with the unsatisfactory treatment given to the control group. The view of such activists has been expressed by Rebecca Pringle Smith of Community Research Initiative in New York: "Even if you have a supply of compliant martyrs, trials must have some ethical validity."[4]

If the physician has no opinion about whether the new treatment is acceptable, then random assignment is ethically acceptable, but such lack of enthusiasm for the new treatment does not augur well for either the patient or the study. Alternatively, the treatment may show promise of beneficial results but also present a risk of undesirable complications. When the physician believes that the severity and likelihood of harm and good are evenly balanced, randomization may be ethically acceptable. If the physician has no preference for either treatment (is in a state of equipoise[7,8]), then randomization is ac-

ceptable. If, however, he or she believes that the new treatment may be either more or less successful or more or less toxic, the use of randomization is not consistent with fidelity to the patient.

The argument usually used to justify randomization is that it provides, in essence, a critique of the usefulness of the physician's beliefs and opinions, those that have not yet been validated by a randomized clinical trial. As the argument goes, these not-yet-validated beliefs are as likely to be wrong as right. Although physicians are ethically required to provide their patients with the best available treatment, there simply is no best treatment yet known.

The reply to this argument takes two forms. First, and most important, even if this view of the reliability of a physician's opinions is accurate, the ethical constraints of an individual doctor's relationship with a particular patient require the doctor to provide individual care. Although physicians must take pains to make clear the speculative nature of their views, they cannot withhold these views from the patient. The patient asks from the doctor both knowledge and judgment. The relationship established between them rightfully allows patients to ask for the judgment of their particular physicians, not merely that of the medical profession in general. Second, it may not be true, in fact, that the not-yet-validated beliefs of physicians are as likely to be wrong as right. The greater certainty obtained with a randomized clinical trial is beneficial, but that does not mean that a lesser degree of certainty is without value. Physicians can acquire knowledge through methods other than the randomized clinical trial. Such knowledge, acquired over time and less formally than is required in a randomized clinical trial, may be of great value to a patient.

Even if it is ethically acceptable to begin a study, one often forms an opinion during its course—especially in studies that are impossible to conduct in a truly double-blinded fashion—that makes it ethically problematic to continue. The inability to remain blinded usually occurs in studies of cancer or AIDS, for example, because the therapy is associated by nature with serious side effects. Trials attempt to restrict the physician's access to the data in order to prevent such unblinding. Such restrictions should make physicians eschew the trial, since their ability to act in the patient's best interests will be limited. Even supporters of randomized clinical trials, such as Merigan, agree that interim findings should be presented to patients to ensure that no one receives what seems an inferior treatment.[6] Once physicians have formed a view about the new treatment, can they continue randomization? If random assignment is stopped, the study may be lost and the participation of the previous patients wasted. However, if physicians continue the randomization when they have a definite opinion about the efficacy of the experimental drug, they are not acting in accordance with the requirements of the doctor-patient relationship. Furthermore, as their opinion becomes more firm, stopping the randomization may not be enough. Physicians may be ethically required to treat the patients formerly placed in the control group with the therapy that now seems probably effective. To do so would be faithful to the obligations created by the doctor-patient relationship, but it would destroy the study.

To resolve this dilemma, one might suggest that the patient has abrogated the rights implicit in a doctor-patient relationship by signing an informed-consent form. We argue that such rights cannot be waived or abrogated. They are inalienable. The right to be treated as an individual deserving the physician's best judgment and care, rather than to be used as a means to determine the best treatment for others, is inherent in every person. This right, based on the concept of dignity, cannot be waived. What of altruism, then? Is it not the patient's right to make a sacrifice for the general good? This question must be considered from both positions—that of the patient and that of the physician. Although patients may decide to waive this right, it is not consistent with the role of a physician to ask that they do so. In asking, the doctor acts as a scientist instead. The physician's role here is to propose what he or she believes is best medically for the specific patient, not to suggest participation in a study from which the patient cannot gain. Because the opportunity to help future patients is of potential value to a patient, some would say physicians should not deny it. Although this point has merit, it offers so many opportunities for abuse that we are extremely uncomfortable about accepting it. The responsibilities of physicians are much clearer; they are to minister to the current patient.

Moreover, even if patients could waive this right, it is questionable whether those with terminal illness would be truly able to give voluntary informed consent. Such patients are extremely dependent on both their physicians and the health care system. Aware of this dependence, physicians must not ask for consent, for in such cases the very asking breaches the doctor-patient relationship. Anxious to please their physicians, patients may have difficulty refusing to participate in the trial the physicians describe. The patients may perceive their refusal as damaging to the relationship, whether or not it is so. Such perceptions of coercion affect the decision. Informed-consent forms are difficult to understand, especially for patients under the stress of serious illness for which there is no satisfactory treatment. The forms are usually lengthy, somewhat legalistic, complicated, and confusing, and they hardly bespeak the compassion expected of the medical profession. It is important to remember that those who have studied the doctor-patient relationship have emphasized its empathetic nature.

> [The] relationship between doctor and patient partakes of a peculiar intimacy. It presupposes on the part of the physician not only knowledge of his fellow men but sympathy. . . . This aspect of the practice of medicine has been designated as the art; yet I wonder whether it should not, most properly, be called the essence.[9]

How is such a view of the relationship consonant with random assignment and informed consent? The Physician's Oath of the World Medical Association affirms the primacy of the deontologic view of patients' rights: "Concern for the interests of the subject must always prevail over the interests of science and society."[10]

Furthermore, a single study is often not considered sufficient. Before a new form of therapy is generally accepted, confirmatory trials must be conducted. How can one conduct such trials ethically unless one is convinced that the first trial was in error? The ethical problems we have discussed are only exacerbated when a completed randomized clinical trial indicates that a given treatment is preferable. Even if the physician believes the initial trial was in error, the physician must indicate to the patient the full results of that trial.

The most common reply to the ethical arguments has been that the alternative is to return to the physician's intuition, to anecdotes, or to both as the basis of medical opinion. We all accept the dangers of such a practice. The argument states that we must therefore accept randomized, controlled clinical trials regardless of their ethical problems because of the great social benefit they make possible, and we salve our conscience with the knowledge that informed consent has been given. This returns us to the conflict between patients' rights and social utility. Some would argue that this tension can be resolved by placing a relative value on each. If the patient's right that is being compromised is not a fundamental right and the social gain is very great, then the study might be justified. When the right is fundamental, however, no amount of social gain, or almost none, will justify its sacrifice. Consider, for example, the experiments on humans done by physicians under the Nazi regime. All would agree that these are unacceptable regardless of the value of the scientific information gained. Some people go so far as to say that no use should be made of the results of those experiments because of the clearly unethical manner in which the data were collected. This extreme example may not seem relevant, but we believe that in its hyperbole it clarifies the fallacy of a utilitarian approach to the physician's relationship with the patient. To consider the utilitarian gain is consistent neither with the physician's role nor with the patient's rights.

It is fallacious to suggest that only the randomized clinical trial can provide valid information or that all information acquired by this technique is valid. Such experimental methods are intended to reduce error and bias and therefore reduce the uncertainty of the result. Uncertainty cannot be eliminated, however. The scientific method is based on increasing probabilities and increasingly refined approximations of truth.[11] Although the randomized clinical trial contributes to these ends, it is neither unique nor perfect. Other techniques may also be useful.[12]

Randomized trials often place physicians in the ethically intolerable position of choosing between the good of the patient and that of society. We urge that such situations be avoided and that other techniques of acquiring clinical information be adopted.

For example, concerning trials of treatments for AIDS, Byar et al.[13] have said that "some traditional approaches to the clinical-trials process may be unnecessarily rigid and unsuitable for this disease." In this case, AIDS is not what is so different; rather, the difference is in the presence of AIDS activists, articulate spokespersons for the ethical problems created by the application of the randomized clinical trial to terminal illnesses. Such arguments are equally applicable to advanced cancer and other serious illnesses. Byar et al. agree that there are even circumstances in which uncontrolled clinical trials may be justified: when there is no effective treatment to use as a control, when the prognosis is uniformly poor, and when there is a reasonable expectation of benefit without excessive toxicity These conditions are usually found in clinical trials of advanced cancer.

The purpose of the randomized clinical trial is to avoid the problems of observer bias and patient selection. It seems to us that techniques might be developed to deal with these issues in other ways. Randomized clinical trials deal with them in a cumbersome and heavy-handed manner, by requiring large numbers of patients in the hope that random assignment will balance the heterogeneous distribution of patients into the different groups. By observing known characteristics of patients, such as age and sex, and distributing them equally between groups, it is thought that unknown factors important in determining outcomes will also be distributed equally. Surely, other techniques can be developed to deal with both observer bias and patient selection. Prospective studies without randomization, but with the evaluation of patients by uninvolved third parties, should remove observer bias. Similar methods have been suggested by Royall.[12] Prospective matched-pair analysis, in which patients are treated in a manner consistent with their physicians' views, ought to help ensure equivalence between the groups and thus mitigate the effect of patient selection, at least with regard to known covariates. With regard to unknown covariates, the security would rest, as in randomized trials, in the enrollment of large numbers of patients and in confirmatory studies. This method would not pose ethical difficulties, since patients would receive the treatment recommended by their physician. They would be included in the study by independent observers matching patients with respect to known characteristics, a process that would not affect patient care and that could be performed independently any number of times.

This brief discussion of alternatives to randomized clinical trials is sketchy and incomplete. We wish only to point out that there may be satisfactory alternatives, not to describe and evaluate them completely. Even if randomized clinical trials were much better than any alternative, however, the ethical dilemmas they present may put their use at variance with the primary obligations of the physician. In this regard, Angell cautions, "If this commitment to the patient is attenuated, even for so good a cause as benefits to future patients, the, implicit assumptions of the doctor-patient relationship are violated."[14] The risk of such attenuation by the randomized trial is great. The AIDS activists have brought this dramatically to the attention of the academic medical community. Techniques appropriate to the laboratory may not be applicable to humans. We must develop and use alternative methods for acquiring clinical knowledge.

NOTES

1. Hellman S. Randomized clinical trials and the doctor-patient relationship: an ethical dilemma. *Cancer Clin Trials* 1979; 2:189–93.

2. *Idem.* A doctor's dilemma: the doctor-patient relationship in clinical investigation. In: Proceedings of the Fourth National Conference on Human Values and Cancer, New York, March 15–17, 1984. New York: American Cancer Society, 1984:144–6.

3. Kass LR. *Toward a more natural science: biology and human affairs.* New York: Free Press, 1985:196.

4. Palca J. AIDS drug trials enter new age. *Science* 1989; 246:19–21.

5. Rawls J. *A theory of justice.* Cambridge, Mass.: Belknap Press of Harvard University Press, 1971:183–92, 446–52.

6. Merigan TC. You *can* teach an old dog new tricks—how AIDS trials are pioneering new strategies. *N Engl J Med* 1990; 323:1341–3.

7. Freedman B. Equipoise and the ethics of clinical research *N Engl J Med* 1987; 317:141–5.

8. Singer PA, Lantos JD, Whitington PF, Broelsch CE, Siegler M. Equipoise and the ethics of segmental liver transplantation. *Chin Res* 1988; 36:539–45.

9. Longcope WT. Methods and medicine. *Bull Johns Hopkins Hosp* 1932; 50:4–20.

10. Report on medical ethics. *World Med Assoc Bull* 1949; 1:109, 111.

11. Popper K. The problem of induction. In: Miller D, ed., *Popper selections.* Princeton, N.J.: Princeton University Press, 1985:101–17.

12. Royall RM. Ethics and statistics in randomized clinical trials. *Stat Sci* 1991; 6(1):52–62.

13. Byar DP, Schoenfeld DA, Green SB, et al. Design considerations for AIDS trials. *N Engl J Med* 1990; 323:1343–8.

14. Angell M. Patients' preferences in randomized clinical trials *N Engl J Med* 1984; 310:1385–7.

A Response to a Purported Ethical Difficulty with Randomized Clinical Trials Involving Cancer Patients

BENJAMIN FREEDMAN

Defenders of randomized clinical trials claim that physician-scientists do not violate a duty of fidelity to patients if the effectiveness of the treatments being tested is unknown and if the physicians are therefore in doubt (in a state of equipoise) about the treatments' merits. But critics say that if a physician suspects even for flimsy reasons that one treatment is better or worse than another, he cannot be in equipoise. Freedman thinks this view of equipoise is mistaken. He argues that true equipoise does not depend on uncertainty in the physician but on genuine disagreement in the medical community about a treatment's value because of a lack of good evidence gleaned from randomized clinical trials. When this kind of doubt exists, randomized clinical studies are permissible.

In recent years, for a variety of reasons, the mainstay of clinical investigation—the randomized controlled clinical trial (RCT)—has increasingly come under attack. Since Charles Fried's influential monograph,[1] the opponents of controlled trials have claimed the moral high ground. They claim to perceive a conflict between the medical and scientific duties of the physician-investigator, and between the conduct of the trial and a patient's rights. Samuel and Deborah Hellman write, for example, that "the randomized clinical trial routinely asks physicians to sacrifice the interests of their particular patients for the sake of the study and that of the information that it will make available for the benefit of society."[2] Maurie Markman's attraction to this point of view is clear when he writes that "the individual physician's principal ethical responsibility is to the *individual patient* that he or she is treating, and *not* to future patients [emphases in original]." In the interests of returning Markman to the fold, I will concentrate on resolving this central challenge to the ethics of RCTs.

It is unfortunately true that the most common responses from pro-trialists, by revealing fundamental misunderstandings of basic ethical concepts, do not inspire confidence in the ethics of human research as it is currently conducted. Proponents of clinical trials will commonly begin their apologia by citing benefits derived from trials—by validating the safety and efficacy of new treatments, and, at least as important, by discrediting accepted forms of treatment. So far so good. But they often go on to argue that there is a need to balance the rights of subjects against the needs of society. By this tactic, the proponents of clinical trials have implicitly morally surrendered, for to admit that something is a right is to admit that it represents a domain of action protected from the claims or interests of other individuals or of society itself. A liberal society has rightly learned to look askance at claims that rights of individuals need to yield to the demands of the collective. Patients' claims, then, because of their nature as rights, supersede the requirements of the collectivity.

Sometimes, indeed, the surrender is explicit. At the conclusion of a symposium on the ethics of research on human subjects, Sir Colin Dollery, a major figure in clinical trials, complained to the speaker: "You assume a dominant role for ethics—I think to the point of arrogance. Ethical judgments will be of little value unless the scientific innovations about which they are made . . . are useful."[3] But it is the nature of ethical judgments that they are, indeed, "dominant" as normative or accepted guides to action. One may say, "I know that X is the ethical thing to do, but I won't X." That expresses no logical contradiction, but simply weakness of will. But it is, by contrast, plainly contradictory to admit that X is ethical, yet to deny or doubt that one ought to X.

Closer examination and finer distinctions reveal, however, that the conflict between patients' rights and social interests is not at all at issue in controlled clinical trials. There is no need for proponents of clinical trials to concede the moral high ground.

What is the patient right that is compromised by clinical trials? The fear most common to patients who are hesitant about enrolling is that they would not receive the best care, that their right to treatment would be sacrificed in the interests of science. This presumes, of course, that the patient has a right to treatment. Such a right must in reason be grounded in patient need (a patient who is not ill has no right to treatment) and in medical knowledge and capability (a patient with an incurable illness has rights to be cared for, but no right to be cured).

That granted, we need to specify the kind of treatment to which a patient might reasonably claim a right. It was in this connection that I introduced the concept of *clinical equipoise* as critical to understanding the ethics of clinical trials.[4] Clinical equipoise is a situation in which there exists (or is pending) an honest disagreement in the expert clinical community regarding the comparative merits of two or more forms of treatment for a given condition. To be ethical, a controlled clinical trial must begin and be conducted in a continuing state of clinical equipoise—as between the arms of the study—and must, moreover, offer some reasonable hope that the successful conclusion of the trial will disturb equipoise (that is, resolve the controversy in the expert clinical community).

This theory presumes that a right to a specific medical treatment must be grounded in a professional judgment, which is concretized in the term *clinical equipoise*. A patient who has rights to medical treatment has rights restricted to, though not necessarily exhaustive of, those treatments that are understood by the medical community to be appropriate for his condition. A patient may eccentrically claim some good from a physician that is not recognized by the medical community as appropriate treatment. A physician may even grant this claim; but in so doing, he must realize that he has not provided medical treatment itself. Contrariwise, by failing to fulfill this request, the physician has not failed to satisfy the patient's right to medical treatment.

Provided that a comparative trial is ethical, therefore, it begins in a state of clinical equipoise. For that reason, by definition, nobody enrolling in the trial is denied his or her right to medical treatment, for no medical consensus for or against the treatment assignment exists.

(The modern climate requires that I introduce two simple caveats. First, I am ignoring economic and political factors that go into the grounding of a right to treatment. This is easy enough for one in Canada to write, but may be difficult for someone in the United States to read. Second, when speaking of treatment that is recognized to be condition-appropriate by the medical community, I mean to include only those judgments grounded in medical knowledge rather than social judgments. I would hope to avoid the current bioethical muddle over "medical futility," but if my claims need to be translated into terms appropriate to that controversy, "physiological futility" is close but not identical to what I mean by "inappropriate." For simplicity's sake, the best model to have in mind is the common patient demand for antibiotic treatment of an illness diagnosed as viral.)

Two errors are commonly committed in connection with the concept of clinical equipoise. The first mistake is in thinking that clinical equipoise (or its disturbance) relates to a single endpoint of a trial—commonly, efficacy. As a function of expert clinical judgment, clinical equipoise must incorporate all of the many factors that go into favoring one regimen over its competitors. Treatment *A* may be favored over *B* because it is more effective; or, because it is

almost as effective but considerably less toxic; or, because it is easier to administer, allowing, for example, treatment on an outpatient basis; or, because patients are more compliant with it; and so forth.

Just as equipoise may be based upon any one or a combination of these or other factors, it may be disturbed in the same way. Markman's second example, which discusses the efficacy of a multidrug combination chemotherapy regimen, seems vulnerable to this objection. Even were the results of the Mayo trial convincing with regard to the efficacy of this approach, it has not disturbed clinical equipoise in its favor unless other issues, such as toxicity, have been resolved as well. It is well worth pointing out that the endpoints of trials, particularly in cancer treatment, are far too narrow to disturb clinical equipoise in and of themselves, but they are necessary steps along a seriatim path. For that matter, in ignoring the compendious judgment involved in ascertaining equipoise, some studies spuriously claim that all of their arms are in equipoise on the basis of one variable (such as five-year survival rates), when they are clearly out of equipoise because of other factors (such as differences in pain and disfigurement).

The second mistake occurs in identifying clinical equipoise with an individual physician's point of indifference between two treatments. Citing the article in which I developed the concept and another article applying it, for example, the Hellmans write, "If the physician has no preference for either treatment (is in a state of equipoise), then randomization is acceptable."[5] But an individual physician is not the arbiter of appropriate or acceptable medical practice.

There are numerous occasions outside of clinical trials where outsiders need to determine whether the treatment provided was appropriate to the patient's condition. Regulators, as well as third-party payers—private or governmental—need to answer the question, as do health planners and administrators of health-care facilities. Disciplinary bodies of professional associations, and, most tellingly, courts judging allegations of malpractice, have to ascertain this as well. It is never the case that the judgment of an individual physician concerning whether a treatment is condition-appropriate (that is, whether it belongs within the therapeutic armamentarium) is sufficient. In all of these instances, however varied might be their rules of investigation and procedure, the ultimate question is: Does the expert professional community accept this treatment as appropriate for this condition? Since clinical equipoise and its disturbance applies to putative medical treatments for given conditions, this is a matter that is determined legally, morally, and reasonably by that medical community with the recognized relevant expertise.

Markman may have fallen into this error, writing repeatedly of the judgment of the treating or enrolling physician (and, in the first page, of the responsibility of "the individual physician") with respect to the clinical trial. There is, however, another way of looking at this. Whereas the status of a putative treatment within the medical armamentarium must be settled by the medical *community*, the application of that judgment *vis-à-vis* a given patient is, of course, the judgment (and the responsibility) of the *individual physician*. This individual clinical judgment must be exercised when enrolling a subject, rather than subjugated to the judgment of those who constructed the trial. Indeed, many studies will list this as a criterion of exclusion: "Those subjects who, in the judgment of the accruing physician, would be put at undue risk by participating."

Another point: the Hellmans write of a physician's duty in treating a patient to employ what he "thinks, suspects, believes, or has a hunch about."[6] This is clearly overstated as a duty: why not add to the list the physician's hopes, fantasies, fond but dotty beliefs, and illusions? Yet patients do choose physicians, in part, because of trust in their tacit knowledge and inchoate judgment, and not merely their sapient grasp of the current medical consensus. It would be a disservice to patients for a physician to see his or her role simply as a vehicle for transmitting the wisdom received from the expert medical community in all cases (though when a departure is made, this is done at the legal peril of the doctor!).

But what follows from this inalienable duty of the treating physician? Not as much as the opponents of trials would have us believe. A physician certainly has the right to refuse to participate in a trial that he believes places some participants at a medical disadvantage. Moreover, if he or she is convinced of that, he or she has a *duty* to abstain from participating. But that only speaks to the physician, and does not necessarily affect the patient. What opponents of trials forget is that the patient—the subject—is the ultimate decision maker—in fact, in law, and in ethics. In at least some cases, the fact that there is an open trial for which a patient meets the eligibility criteria needs to be disclosed as one medical alternative, to satisfy ethical norms of informed consent. A physician with convictions that the trial will put subjects at undue risk should inform the prospective subject of that conviction and the reasons for it, and may well recommend to the subject to decline participation. It will then be up to the patient whether to seek enrollment via another physician.

Most commonly at issue, though, is a physician's preference rather than conviction. In such cases, it is perfectly ethical—and becomingly modest—for a physician to participate in a trial, setting aside private misgivings based upon anecdote as overbalanced by the medical literature.

Finally, something should be said about the underlying philosophical buttress on which anti-trialists rely. Following Kant, the Hellmans argue that the underlying issue is that persons "ought not to be treated merely as means to an end; rather, they must always be treated as ends in themselves."[7] Clinical trials, however, are designed to yield reliable data and to ground scientifically valid inferences. In that sense, the treatments and examinations that a subject of a clinical trial undergoes are means to a scientific end, rather than interventions done solely for the subject's own benefit.

But the Kantian formulation is notoriously rigoristic, and implausible in the form cited. We treat others as means all the time, in order to achieve ends the others do not share, and are so treated in return. When buying a carton of milk or leaving a message, I am treating the cashier or secretary as means to an end they do not share. Were this unvarnished principle to hold, all but purely altruistic transactions would be ethically deficient. Clinical trials would be in very good (and, indeed, very bad) company. Those who follow the Kantian view are not concerned about treating another as a means, but rather about treating someone in a way that contradicts the other's personhood itself—that is, in a way that denies the fact that the person is not simply a means but is also an end. A paradigm case is when I treat someone in a way that serves my ends but, at the same time, is contrary to the other's best interests. It is time that a subject's participation in a clinical trial serves scientific ends, but what has not been shown is that it is contrary to the best interests of the subject. In cases where the two equipoise conditions are satisfied, this cannot be shown.

However, in some cases we are uncertain about whether an intervention will serve the best interests of the other, and so we ask that person. That is one reason for requiring informed consent to studies. There is another. By obtaining the consent of the other party to treat him as an end to one's own means, in effect, an identity of ends between both parties has been created. Applying this amended Kantian dictum, then, we should ask: Is there anything about clinical trials that necessarily implies that subjects are treated contrary to their personhood? And the answer is, of course, no—provided a proper consent has been obtained.

There remain many hard questions to ask about the ethics of controlled clinical studies. Many talents will be needed to address those questions and to reform current practice. Since those questions will only be asked by those who understand that such studies rest upon a sound ethical foundation, I am hopeful that Markman and others will reconsider their misgivings.

NOTES

1. C. Fried, *Medical Experimentation: Personal Integrity and Social Policy* (New York: Elsevier, 1974).
2. S. Hellman and D.S. Hellman, "Of Mice but Not Men," *New England Journal of Medicine* 324 (1991):1585–89, at 1586.
3. Comment by Sir Colin Dollery in discussion following H.-M. Sass, "Ethics of Drug Research and Drug Development," *Arzneimittel Forschung/Drug Research* 39 (II), Number 8a (1989):1041–48, at 1048.
4. B. Freedman, "Equipoise and the Ethics of Clinical Research," *New England Journal of Medicine* 317 (1987):141–45.
5. Hellman and Hellman, "Of Mice," 1586.
6. *Ibid.*
7. *Ibid.*

How to Resolve an Ethical Dilemma Concerning Randomized Clinical Trials

DON MARQUIS

Marquis addresses the well-known ethical dilemma of randomized clinical trials: A physician has a duty to see that her patients get a treatment that she judges best, but if she enters them in a clinical trial, they may not receive the treatment she prefers. He argues that a solution to the problem lies in the use of informed consent. By taking informed consent seriously, "a physician can both recommend a treatment and ask whether the patient is willing to enroll in the randomized clinical trial."

An apparent ethical dilemma arises when physicians consider enrolling their patients in randomized clinical trials. Suppose that a randomized clinical trial comparing two treatments is in progress, and a physician has an opinion about which treatment is better. The physician has a duty to promote the patient's best medical interests and therefore seems to be obliged to advise the patient to receive the treatment that the physician prefers. This duty creates a barrier to the enrollment of patients in randomized clinical trials.[1–10] Two strategies are often used to resolve the dilemma in favor of enrolling patients in clinical trials.

The "Either You Know Which Is Better or You Don't" Strategy

According to one strategy, physicians should not recommend one treatment over another if they do not really know which one is better, and they do not really know which treatment is better in the absence

From *The New England Journal of Medicine*, vol. 341, no. 9, pp. 691–93. Copyright © 1999 Massachusetts Medical Society. Reprinted with permission of the publisher.

of data from randomized clinical trials.[11] Data from uncontrolled studies are often influenced by the desire on both the investigator's part and the patient's part to obtain positive results.[12] Journal editors are more likely to publish reports of studies with positive results than reports of studies with negative results.[13] A treatment recommendation based on weaker evidence than that obtained from a randomized clinical trial is like a recommendation based on a mere hunch or an idiosyncratic preference.[14] Thus, according to this argument, in the absence of data from a randomized clinical trial, evidence that provides an adequate basis for recommending a treatment rarely exists, and the enrollment dilemma is based on a mistake.

This strategy for resolving the dilemma is simplistic. It assumes that evidence available to physicians can be only one of two kinds: gold standard evidence or worthless prejudice. But clinical judgments may be based on evidence of intermediate quality, including physicians' experience with their own patients, their conversations with colleagues concerning their colleagues' experience, their evaluation of the results of nonrandomized studies reported in the literature, their judgment about the mechanism of action of one or both treatments, or their view of the natural history of a given disease. Evidence need not be conclusive to be valuable; it need not be definitive to be suggestive. Because all good physicians allow evidence of intermediate quality to influence their professional judgment when a relevant randomized clinical trial is not being conducted, it is unreasonable to claim that such evidence has no worth when a relevant randomized clinical trial is being conducted. Therefore, the "either you know which is better or you don't" strategy for dealing with the enrollment dilemma is not persuasive.

Adopting a Less Strict Therapeutic Obligation

The dilemma about enrolling patients in randomized clinical trials is generated by the claim that a physician has a strict therapeutic obligation to inform the patients of the physician's treatment preference, even when the preference is based on evidence that is not of the highest quality. The dilemma could be resolved if the physician's therapeutic

obligation were less strict. This strategy was developed by Freedman.[14,15] He argued that the standard for determining whether a physician has engaged in medical malpractice or committed some other violation punishable by a professional disciplinary body is the standard of good practice as determined by a consensus of the medical community. There is no consensus about which of two treatments being compared in a randomized clinical trial is superior. (Otherwise, why conduct the trial?) Therefore, enrolling a patient in the trial does not violate the physician's therapeutic obligation to the patient, regardless of the physician's treatment preference. In addition, a patient who consults a physician with a preference for treatment A could have consulted a physician who preferred treatment B. Therefore, enrolling a patient in a randomized clinical trial in order to be randomly assigned (perhaps) to treatment B does not make such a patient worse off than he or she would otherwise have been.

Despite these points, compelling arguments for the stricter interpretation of therapeutic obligation remain. In the first place, consider what physicians expect when they seek professional advice from their malpractice attorneys, their tax advisors, or for that matter, their own physicians. Surely they expect—and believe they have a right to expect—not merely minimally competent advice, but the best professional judgments of the professionals they have chosen to consult. In the second place, patients choose physicians in order to obtain medical advice that is, in the judgment of those physicians, the best available. If physicians do not provide such advice, then they tacitly deceive then patients, unless they disclose to their patients that they are not bound by this strict therapeutic obligation. Physicians should adopt the strict therapeutic obligation.

A Resolution

The clash between a strict therapeutic obligation and a less strict one is only apparent. On the one hand, the less strict therapeutic obligation is supported by the argument that it is morally permissible to offer to enroll a patient in a randomized clinical trial. On the other hand, the strict therapeutic obligation is supported by the arguments concerning treatment recommendations. Recommending is different from offering to enroll. A recognition of this difference provides the basis for a solution to the dilemma.

Suppose that a randomized clinical trial is being conducted to compare treatments A and B and that a physician prefers A and informs the patient of this preference. All physicians have an obligation to obtain their patients' informed consent to treatment. A physician has respected this right only if he or she explains to the patient the risks and benefits of reasonable alternatives to the recommended treatment and offers the patient an opportunity to choose an alternative, if that is feasible. Either treatment B or enrollment in the trial comparing A and B is a reasonable alternative to treatment A, because presumably, A is not known to be superior to B: Indeed, there is some evidence that enrollment in a randomized clinical trial is a superior therapeutic alternative when a trial is available.[16] Respect for a patient's values is a central purpose of informed consent. A particular patient may place a greater value on participation in a study that will contribute to medical progress and to the well-being of patients in the future than on the unproved advantages of following the physician's recommendation. Therefore, a physician can both recommend a treatment and ask whether the patient is willing to enroll in the randomized clinical trial.

This resolution is based on the recognition that there can be evidence of the superiority of a treatment that falls short of the gold standard for evidence but is better than worthless. It also takes into account the good arguments for the view that physicians have a strict obligation to recommend the best treatment on the basis of their professional judgment, even when the recommendation is based on evidence that falls short of the gold standard. Nevertheless, because all physicians have an obligation to take informed consent seriously, because respect for informed consent entails offering a patient the reasonable alternatives to the recommended treatment, and because enrollment in an appropriate randomized clinical trial is often a reasonable therapeutic option, one could argue that offering a patient the opportunity to be enrolled in a clinical trial is not only morally permissible but, in many cases, also morally obligatory, if a relevant trial is being conducted and if enrollment in it is feasible. Taking informed consent seriously resolves the dilemma about whether to enroll patients in randomized clinical trials.

Is this analysis clinically realistic? Some may argue that if clinicians inform their patients that they prefer treatment A, then few of their patients will consent to participate in a trial comparing A with B. Furthermore, many clinicians may be unwilling to invest the time necessary to explain the option of enrollment in a trial, particularly if it seems unlikely that a patient, knowing the physician's preference for one of the treatments, will choose to participate in the trial.

On the other hand, in recent years the public has been exposed to a barrage of medical information and misinformation. Explaining to patients the difference between solid scientific evidence of the merits of a treatment and weaker evidence of its merits is worthwhile, whether or not a relevant randomized clinical trial is being conducted. When a relevant trial is being conducted, offering the patient enrollment in the trial should not impose on the physician a large, additional burden of explanation. Physicians can promote enrollment by explaining that their preference is based only on limited evidence, which may or may not be reliable. They can also explain that data from randomized clinical trials have often shown that the initial studies of new treatments were overly optimistic.[17]

In addition, using this informed-consent strategy to resolve the enrollment dilemma may not be morally optional. My analysis is based on two important obligations of physicians. The first is the strict obligation to recommend the treatment that is, in the physician's professional judgment, the best choice for the patient. The second is the obligation to obtain the patient's informed consent to the recommended treatment. The duty of obtaining informed consent implies that the physician is obligated to offer the patient the opportunity to enroll in a clinical trial when one is available, even if the physician has a treatment preference. The physician owes this duty to the individual patient, not simply to future patients who may benefit from advances in medical knowledge. Thus, the informed-consent strategy for resolving the dilemma about enrolling patients in randomized clinical trials leads to the conclusion that physicians have a greater duty to offer their patients enrollment in trials than has previously been realized. A strict, thoroughly defensible, therapeutic obligation need not interfere with the conduct of randomized clinical trials.

REFERENCES

I am indebted to Erin Fitz-Gerald, Nina Ainslie, Stephen Williamson, Sarah Taylor, Jerry Menikoff, Don Hatton, and Ron Stephens for their criticisms.

1. Chalmers T. C. The ethics of randomization as a decision-making technique and the problem of informed consent. Report of the 14th conference of cardiovascular training grant program directors, June 3–4, 1967. Bethesda, Md.: National Heart Institute, 1967:87–93.

2. Shaw L. W., Chalmers T. C. Ethics in cooperative clinical trials. Ann NY Acad Sci 1970; 169:487–95.

3. Kolata G. B. Clinical trials: methods and ethics are debated. Science 1977; 198:1127–31.

4. Walker D. Ethical considerations in randomized clinical trials. Semin Oncol 1981; 8:437–41.

5. Schafer A. The ethics of the randomized clinical trial. N Engl J Med 1982; 307:719–24.

6. Marquis D. Leaving therapy to chance. Hastings Cent Rep 1983; 13: 40–7.

7. Gifford R. The conflict between randomized clinical trials and the therapeutic obligation. J Med Philos 1986; 11:347–66.

8. Hellman S., Hellman D. S. Of mice but not men: problems of the randomized clinical trial. N Engl J Med 1991; 324:1585–9.

9. Gifford R. Community equipoise and the ethics of randomized clinical trials. Bioethics 1995; 9:127–48.

10. Markman M. Ethical difficulties with randomized clinical trials involving cancer patients: examples from the field of gynecologic oncology. J Clin Ethics 1992; 3:193–5.

11. Spodick D. H. Ethics of the randomized clinical trial. N Engl J Med 1983; 308:343.

12. Passamani E. Clinical trials—are they ethical? N Engl J Med 1991; 324:1589–92.

13. Altman L. Negative results: a positive viewpoint. New York Times, April 29, 1986:B6.

14. Freedman B. Equipoise and the ethics of clinical research. N Engl J Med 1987; 317:141–5.

15. *Idem.* A response to a purported ethical difficulty with randomized clinical trials involving cancer patients. J Clin Ethics 1992; 3:231–4.

16. Davis S., Wright P. W., Schulman S. F., et al. Participants in prospective, randomized clinical trials for resected non-small cell lung cancer have improved survival compared with nonparticipants in such trials. Cancer 1985; 56:1710–8.

17. Sacks H., Chalmers T. C., Smith H. Jr. Randomized versus historical controls for clinical trials. Am J Med 1982; 72:233–40.

Clinical Trials: Are They Ethical?

EUGENE PASSAMANI

Passamani rejects the view that randomized clinical trials are unethical because they prevent individual physicians from playing their hunches about particular patients. Hunches are unreliable guides to treatment efficacy. Clinical trials are done because the competent medical community is unpersuaded by existing data that one treatment is better than another, and the trials are the only reliable way to make this distinction. The ethical uneasiness arising from these studies can be put to rest, Passamani says, when they are "properly carried out, with informed consent, clinical equipoise, and a design adequate to answer the question posed."

Biomedical research leads to better understanding of biology and ultimately to improved health. Physicians have for millenniums attempted to understand disease, to use this knowledge to cure or palliate, and to relieve attendant suffering. Improving strategies

for prevention and treatment remains an ethical imperative for medicine. Until very recently, progress depended largely on a process of carefully observing groups of patients given a new and promising therapy; outcome was then compared with that previously observed in groups undergoing a standard treatment. Outcome in a series of case patients as compared with that in nonrandomized controls can be used to assess the treatment of disorders in which

From *The New England Journal of Medicine*, vol. 324, no. 22, pp. 1589–92. Copyright © 1991 Massachusetts Medical Society. Reprinted with permission of the publisher.

therapeutic effects are dramatic and the pathophysiologic features are relatively uncomplicated, such as vitamin deficiency or some infectious diseases. Observational methods are not very useful, however, in the detection of small treatment effects in disorders in which there is substantial variability in expected outcome and imperfect knowledge of complicated pathophysiologic features (many vascular disorders and most cancers, for example). The effect of a treatment cannot easily be extracted from variations in disease severity and the effects of concomitant treatments. Clinical trials have thus become a preferred means of evaluating an ever increasing flow of innovative diagnostic and therapeutic maneuvers. The randomized, double-blind clinical trial is a powerful technique because of the efficiency and credibility associated with treatment comparisons involving randomized concurrent controls.

The modern era of randomized trials began in the early 1950s with the evaluation of streptomycin in patients with tuberculosis.[1] Since that time trial techniques and methods have continuously been refined.[2] In addition, the ethical aspects of these experiments in patients have been actively discussed.[3-7]

In what follows I argue that randomized trials are in fact the most scientifically sound and ethically correct means of evaluating new therapies. There is potential conflict between the roles of physician and physician-scientist, and for this reason society has created mechanisms to ensure that the interests of individual patients are served should they elect to participate in a clinical trial.[6]

Clinical Research

The history of medicine is richly endowed with therapies that were widely used and then shown to be ineffective or frankly toxic. Relatively recent examples of such therapeutic maneuvers include gastric freezing for peptic ulcer disease, radiation therapy for acne, MER-29 (triparanol) for cholesterol reduction, and thalidomide for sedation in pregnant women. The 19th century was even more gruesome, with purging and bloodletting. The reasons for this march of folly are many and include, perhaps most importantly, the lack of complete understanding of human biology and pathophysiology, the use of observational methods coupled with the failure to appreciate substantial variability between patients in their response to illness and to therapy, and the shared desire of physicians and their patients for cure or palliation.

Chance or bias can result in the selection of patients for innovative treatment who are either the least diseased or the most severely affected. Depending on the case mix, a treatment that has no effect can appear to be effective or toxic when historical controls are used. With the improvement in diagnostic accuracy and the understanding of disease that has occurred with the passage of time, today's patients are identified earlier in the natural history of their disease. Recently selected case series therefore often have patients who are less ill and an outcome that is considerably better than that of past case series, even without changes in treatment.

Randomization tends to produce treatment and control groups that are evenly balanced in both known and unrecognized prognostic factors, which permits a more accurate estimate of treatment effect in groups of patients assigned to experimental and standard therapies. A number of independent randomized trials with congruent results are powerful evidence indeed.

A physician's daily practice includes an array of preventive, diagnostic, and therapeutic maneuvers, some of which have been established by a plausible biologic mechanism and substantial evidence from randomized clinical trials (e.g., the use of beta-blockers, thrombolytic therapy, and aspirin in patients with myocardial infarction).[8] It is unlikely that our distant descendants in medicine will discover that we late-20th-century physicians were wrong in these matters. However, new therapeutic maneuvers that have not undergone rigorous assessment may well turn out to be ineffective or toxic. Every therapy adopted by common consent on the basis of observational studies and plausible mechanism, but without the benefit of randomized studies, may be categorized by future physicians as useless or worse. Physicians are aware of the fragility of the evidence supporting many common therapies, and this is why properly performed randomized clinical trials have profound effects on medical practice. The scientific importance of randomized, controlled trials is in safeguarding current and future patients from our therapeutic passions. Most physicians recognize this fact.

Like any human activity, experimentation involving patients can be performed in an unethical and even criminal fashion. Nazi war crimes led to substantial efforts to curb abuse, beginning with the Nuremberg Code and the Helsinki Declaration and culminating in the promulgation of clearly articulated regulations in the United States and elsewhere.[4–6] There are abuses more subtle than those of the Gestapo and the SS. Involving patients in experiments that are poorly conceived and poorly executed is unethical. Patients who participate in such research may incur risk without the hope of contributing to a body of knowledge that will benefit them or others in the future. The regulations governing human experimentation are very important, as is continuing discussion and debate to improve the scientific and ethical aspects of this effort.

Several general features must be part of properly designed trials. The first is informed consent, which involves explicitly informing a potential participant of the goals of the research, its potential benefits and risks, the alternatives to participating, and the right to withdraw from the trial at any time. Whether informed consent is required in all trials has been debated.[9] I believe that patients must always be aware that they are part of an experiment. Second, a state of clinical equipoise must exist. Clinical equipoise means that on the basis of the available data, a community of competent physicians would be content to have their patients pursue any of the treatment strategies being tested in a randomized trial, since none of them have been clearly established as preferable.[7] The chief purpose of a data-monitoring committee is to stop the trial if the accumulating data destroy the state of clinical equipoise—that is, indicate efficacy or suggest toxicity. Finally, the trial must be designed as a critical test of the therapeutic alternatives being assessed. The question must be clearly articulated, with carefully defined measures of outcome; with realistic estimates of sample size, including probable event rates in the control group and a postulated and plausible reduction in the event rates in the treatment group; with Type I and II errors specified; and with subgroup hypotheses clearly stated if appropriate. The trial must have a good chance of settling an open question.[2]

Ethical Dimensions of Properly Constituted Trials

Experimentation in the clinic by means of randomized, controlled clinical trials has been periodically attacked as violating the covenant between doctor and patient.[10–12] Critics have charged that physicians engaged in clinical trials sacrifice the interests of the patient they ask to participate to the good of all similarly affected patients in the future. The argument is that physicians have a personal obligation to use their best judgment and recommend the "best" therapy, no matter how tentative or inconclusive the data on which that judgment is based. Physicians must play their hunches. According to this argument, randomized clinical trials may be useful in seeking the truth, but carefully designed, legitimate trials are unethical and perhaps even criminal because they prevent individual physicians from playing their hunches about individual patients. Therefore, it is argued, physicians should not participate in such trials.

It is surely unethical for physicians to engage knowingly in an activity that will result in inferior therapy for their patients. It is also important that the community of physicians be clear in distinguishing between established therapies and those that are promising but unproved. It is this gulf between proved therapies and possibly effective therapies (all the rest) that defines the ethical and unethical uses of randomized clinical trials. Proved therapies involve a consensus of the competent medical community that the data in hand justify using a treatment in a given disorder. It is this consensus that defines an ethical boundary. The physician-investigator who asks a patient to participate in a randomized, controlled trial represents this competent medical community in asserting that the community is unpersuaded by existing data that an innovative treatment is superior to standard therapy. Arguments that a physician who believes that such a treatment *might be* useful commits an unethical act by randomizing patients are simply wrong. Given the history of promising but discarded therapies, hunches about potential effectiveness are not the ideal currency of the patient-doctor interchange.

Lest readers conclude that modern hunches are more accurate than older ones, I have selected an example from the current cardiovascular literature that reveals the problems inherent in relying on hunches to the exclusion of carefully done experiments.

The Cardiac Arrhythmia Suppression Trial

Sudden death occurs in approximately 300,000 persons in the United States each year and is thus a problem worthy of our best efforts. In the vast majority of cases the mechanism is ventricular fibrillation superimposed on a scarred or ischemic myocardium. It had been observed that the ventricular extrasystoles seen on the ambulatory electrocardiographic recordings of survivors of myocardial infarction were independently and reproducibly associated with an increased incidence of subsequent mortality.[13,14] It had been established that a variety of antiarrhythmic drugs can suppress ventricular extrasystoles. Accordingly, physicians had the hunch that suppressing ventricular extrasystoles in the survivors of myocardial infarction would reduce the incidence of ventricular fibrillation and sudden death.

The Cardiac Arrhythmia Suppression Trial (CAST) investigators decided to test this hypothesis in a randomized, controlled trial. They sought survivors of myocardial infarction who had frequent extrasystoles on electrocardiographic recordings. The trial design included a run-in period during which one of three active drugs was administered and its effect on extrasystoles noted. Those in whom arrhythmias were suppressed were randomly assigned to active drug or placebo. The trial had to be stopped prematurely because of an unacceptable incidence of sudden death in the treatment group.[15] During an average follow-up of 10 months, 56 of 730 patients (7.7 percent) assigned to active drug and 22 of 725 patient (3.0 percent) assigned to placebo died. Clinical equipoise was destroyed by this striking effect. It is quite unlikely that observational (nonrandomized) methods would have detected this presumably toxic effect.

The CAST trial was a major advance in the treatment of patients with coronary disease and ventricular arrhythmia. It clearly revealed that the hunches of many physicians were incorrect. The trial's results are applicable not only to future patients with coronary disease and ventricular arrhythmia but also to the patients who participated in the study. By ran-

domizing, investigators ensured that half the participants received the better therapy—in this case placebo—and, contrary to intuition, most of them ultimately received the better therapy after the trial ended prematurely and drugs were withdrawn.

To summarize, randomized clinical trials are an important element in the spectrum of biomedical research. Not all questions can or should be addressed by this technique; feasibility, cost, and the relative importance of the issues to be addressed are weighed by investigators before they elect to proceed. Properly carried out, with informed consent, clinical equipoise, and a design adequate to answer the question posed, randomized clinical trials protect physicians and their patients from therapies that are ineffective or toxic. Physicians and their patients must be clear about the vast gulf separating promising and proved therapies. The only reliable way to make this distinction in the face of incomplete information about pathophysiology and treatment mechanism is to experiment, and this will increasingly involve randomized trials. The alternative—a retreat to older methods—is unacceptable.

Physicians regularly apply therapies tested in groups of patients to an individual patient. The likelihood of success in an individual patient depends on the degree of certainty evident in the group and the scientific strength of the methods used. We owe patients involved in the assessment of new therapies the best that science and ethics can deliver. Today, for most unproved treatments, that is a properly performed randomized clinical trial.

NOTES

1. Streptomycin in Tuberculosis Trials Committee, Medical Research Council. Streptomycin treatment of pulmonary tuberculosis: a Medical Research Council investigation *BMJ* 1948: 2:769–82.

2. Friedman LM, Furberg CD, DeMets DL. *Fundamentals of clinical trials.* Boston: John Wright/PSG, 1981.

3. Beecher HK. Ethics and clinical research. *N Engl J Med* 1966: 274: 1354–60.

4. Appendix II (The Nuremberg Code). In: Beauchamp TL, Childress JF. *Principles of biomedical ethics.* New York: Oxford University Press, 1979: 287–9.

5. Appendix II (The World Medical Association Declaration of Helsinki). In: Beauchamp TL, Childress JF. *Principles of biomedical ethics.* New York: Oxford University Press, 1979: 289–93.

6. The National Commission for the Protection of Human Subjects of Biomedical and Behavioral Research. The Belmont report: ethical principles and guidelines for the protection of human subjects of research. Washington, D.C.: Government Printing Office, 1978. (DHEW publication no. (05) 78-0012.)

7. Freedman B. Equipoise and the ethics of clinical research. *N Engl J Med* 1987: 317:141–5.

8. Yusuf S, Wittes J, Friedman L. Overview of results of randomized clinical trials in heart disease. I. Treatments following myocardial infarction. *JAMA* 1988: 260:2088–93.

9. Brahams D. Randomized trials and informed consent. *Lancet* 1988: 1033–4.

10. Burkhardt R, Kienle G. Controlled clinical trials and medical ethics. *Lancet* 1978: 2:1356–9.

11. Marquis D. Leaving therapy to chance. *Hastings Cent Rep* 1983: 13(4):40–7.

12. Gifford F. The conflict between randomized clinical trials and the therapeutic obligation. *J Med Philos* 1986: 1:347–66.

13. Ruberman W, Weinblatt E, Goldberg JD, Frank CW, Shapiro S. Ventricular premature beats and mortality after myocardial infarction. *N Engl J Med* 1977: 297:750–7.

14. Lown B. Sudden cardiac death: the major challenge confronting contemporary cardiology. *Am J Cardiol* 1979: 43:313–28.

15. The Cardiac Arrhythmia Suppression Trial (CAST) investigators. Preliminary report: effect of encainide and flecainide on mortality in a randomized trial of arrhythmia suppression after myocardial infarction. *N Engl J Med* 1989: 321:406–12.

The Ethics of Clinical Research in the Third World

MARCIA ANGELL

Angell maintains that randomized clinical trials comparing two treatments are morally permissible only when investigators are in a state of equipoise—that is, when there is "no good reason for thinking one [treatment] is better than another." So studies comparing a potential new treatment with a placebo are unethical if an effective treatment exists. If there is an effective treatment, subjects in the control group must receive the best known treatment. By this standard, some ongoing trials in the Third World must be judged impermissible—namely, the trials testing regimens to prevent the mother-infant transmission of HIV infection. The studies use placebo control groups even though a proven preventive exists. Angell concludes that the research community needs to bolster its commitment to the highest ethical standards "no matter where the research is conducted."

An essential ethical condition for a randomized clinical trial comparing two treatments for a disease is that there be no good reason for thinking one is better than the other.[1, 2] Usually, investigators hope and even expect that the new treatment will be better, but there should not be solid evidence one way or the other. If there is, not only would the trial be scientifically redundant, but the investigators would be guilty of knowingly giving inferior treatment to some participants in the trial. The necessity for investigators to be in this state of equipoise,[2] applies to placebo-controlled trials, as well. Only when there is

no known effective treatment is it ethical to compare a potential new treatment with a placebo. When effective treatment exists, a placebo may not be used. Instead, subjects in the control group of the study must receive the best known treatment. Investigators are responsible for all subjects enrolled in a trial, not just some of them, and the goals of the research are always secondary to the well-being of the participants. Those requirements are made clear in the Declaration of Helsinki of the World Health Organization (WHO), which is widely regarded as providing the fundamental guiding principles of research involving human subjects.[3] It states, "In research on man [sic], the interest of science and society should never take precedence over considerations related to the well-being of the subject," and "In any medical

From *The New England Journal of Medicine*, vol. 337, no. 12, pp. 847–49. Copyright © 1997 Massachusetts Medical Society. Reprinted with permission of the publisher.

study, every patient—including those of a control group, if any—should be assured of the best proven diagnostic and therapeutic method."

One reason ethical codes are unequivocal about investigators' primary obligation to care for the human subjects of their research is the strong temptation to subordinate the subjects' welfare to the objectives of the study. That is particularly likely when the research question is extremely important and the answer would probably improve the care of future patients substantially. In those circumstances, it is sometimes argued explicitly that obtaining a rapid, unambiguous answer to the research question is the primary ethical obligation. With the most altruistic of motives, then, researchers may find themselves slipping across a line that prohibits treating human subjects as means to an end. When that line is crossed, there is very little left to protect patients from a callous disregard of their welfare for the sake of research goals. Even informed consent, important though it is, is not protection enough, because of the asymmetry in knowledge and authority between researchers and their subjects. And approval by an institutional review board, though also important, is highly variable in its responsiveness to patients' interests when they conflict with the interests of researchers.

A textbook example of unethical research is the Tuskegee Study of Untreated Syphilis.[4] In that study, which was sponsored by the U.S. Public Health Service and lasted from 1932 to 1972, 412 poor African-American men with untreated syphilis were followed and compared with 204 men free of the disease to determine the natural history of syphilis. Although there was no very good treatment available at the time the study began (heavy metals were the standard treatment), the research continued even after penicillin became widely available and was known to be highly effective against syphilis. The study was not terminated until it came to the attention of a reporter and the outrage provoked by front-page stories in the *Washington Star* and *New York Times* embarrassed the Nixon administration into calling a halt to it.[5] The ethical violations were multiple: Subjects did not provide informed consent (indeed, they were deliberately deceived); they were denied the best known treatment; and the study was con-

tinued even after highly effective treatment became available. And what were the arguments in favor of the Tuskegee study? That these poor African-American men probably would not have been treated anyway, so the investigators were merely observing what would have happened if there were no study; and that the study was important (a "never-to-be-repeated opportunity," said one physician after penicillin became available).[6] Ethical concern was even stood on its head when it was suggested that not only was the information valuable, but it was especially so for people like the subjects—an impoverished rural population with a very high rate of untreated syphilis. The only lament seemed to be that many of the subjects inadvertently received treatment by other doctors.

Some of these issues are raised by Lurie and Wolfe elsewhere. They discuss the ethics of ongoing trials in the Third World of regimens to prevent the vertical transmission of human immunodeficiency virus (HIV) infection.[7] All except one of the trials employ placebo-treated control groups, despite the fact that zidovudine has already been clearly shown to cut the rate of vertical transmission greatly and is now recommended in the United States for all HIV-infected pregnant women. The justifications are reminiscent of those for the Tuskegee study: Women in the Third World would not receive antiretroviral treatment anyway, so the investigators are simply observing what would happen to the subjects' infants if there were no study. And a placebo-controlled study is the fastest, most efficient way to obtain unambiguous information that will be of greatest value in the Third World. Thus, in response to protests from Wolfe and others to the secretary of Health and Human Services, the directors of the National Institutes of Health (NIH) and the Centers for Disease Control and Prevention (CDC)—the organizations sponsoring the studies—argued, "It is an unfortunate fact that the current standard of perinatal care for the HIV-infected pregnant women in the sites of the studies does not include any HIV prophylactic intervention at all," and the inclusion of placebo controls "will result in the most rapid, accurate, and reliable answer to the question of the value of the intervention being studied compared to the local standard of care."[8]

Whalen et al. report the results of a clinical trial in Uganda of various regimens of prophylaxis against tuberculosis in HIV-infected adults, most of whom had positive tuberculin skin tests.[9] This study, too, employed a placebo-treated control group, and in some ways it is analogous to the studies criticized by Lurie and Wolfe. In the United States it would probably be impossible to carry out such a study, because of long-standing official recommendations that HIV-infected persons with positive tuberculin skin tests receive prophylaxis against tuberculosis. The first was issued in 1990 by the CDC's Advisory Committee for Elimination of Tuberculosis.[10] It stated that tuberculin-test-positive persons with HIV infection "should be considered candidates for preventive therapy." Three years later, the recommendation was reiterated more strongly in a joint statement by the American Thoracic Society and the CDC, in collaboration with the Infectious Diseases Society of America and the American Academy of Pediatrics.[11] According to this statement, ". . . the identification of persons with dual infection and the administration of preventive therapy to these persons is of great importance." However, some believe that these recommendations were premature, since they were based largely on the success of prophylaxis in HIV-negative persons.[12]

Whether the study by Whalen et al. was ethical depends, in my view, entirely on the strength of the preexisting evidence. Only if there was genuine doubt about the benefits of prophylaxis would a placebo group be ethically justified. This is not the place to review the scientific evidence, some of which is discussed in the editorial of Msamanga and Fawzi.[13] Suffice it to say that the case is debatable. Msamanga and Fawzi conclude that "future studies should not include a placebo group, since preventive therapy should be considered the standard of care." I agree. The difficult question is whether there should have been a placebo group in the first place.

Although I believe an argument can be made that a placebo-controlled trial was ethically justifiable because it was still uncertain whether prophylaxis would work, it should not be argued that it was ethical because no prophylaxis is the "local standard of care" in sub-Saharan Africa. For reasons discussed by Lurie and Wolfe, that reasoning is badly flawed.[7]

As mentioned earlier, the Declaration of Helsinki requires control groups to receive the "best" current treatment, not the local one. The shift in wording between "best" and "local" may be slight, but the implications are profound. Acceptance of this ethical relativism could result in widespread exploitation of vulnerable Third World populations for research programs that could not be carried out in the sponsoring country.[14] Furthermore, it directly contradicts the Department of Health and Human Services' own regulations governing U.S.-sponsored research in foreign countries,[15] as well as joint guidelines for research in the Third World issued by WHO and the Council for International Organizations of Medical Sciences,[16] which require that human subjects receive protection at least equivalent to that in the sponsoring country. The fact that Whalen et al. offered isoniazid to the placebo group when it was found superior to placebo indicates that they were aware of their responsibility to all the subjects in the trial.

The *Journal* has taken the position that it will not publish reports of unethical research, regardless of their scientific merit.[14, 17] After deliberating at length about the study by Whalen at al., the editors concluded that publication was ethically justified, although there remain differences among us. The fact that the subjects gave informed consent and the study was approved by the institutional review board at the University Hospitals of Cleveland and Case Western Reserve University and by the Ugandan National AIDS Research Subcommittee certainly supported our decision but did not allay all our misgivings. It is still important to determine whether clinical studies are consistent with preexisting, widely accepted ethical guidelines, such as the Declaration of Helsinki, and with federal regulations, since they cannot be influenced by pressures specific to a particular study.

Quite apart from the merits of the study by Whalen et al., there is a larger issue. There appears to be a general retreat from the clear principles enunciated in the Nuremberg Code and the Declaration of Helsinki as applied to research in the Third World. Why is that? Is it because the "local standard of care" is different? I don't think so. In my view, that is merely a self-serving justification after the fact. Is it because diseases and their treatments are very different in the Third World, so that information gained in the industrialized world has no relevance and we have to start from scratch? That, too, seems an unlikely explanation, although here again it is often offered as a justification. Sometimes there may be relevant differences between populations, but that cannot be assumed. Unless there are specific indications to the contrary, the safest and most reasonable position is that people everywhere are likely to respond similarly to the same treatment.

I think we have to look elsewhere for the real reasons. One of them may be a slavish adherence to the tenets of clinical trials. According to these, all trials should be randomized, double-blind, and placebo-controlled, if at all possible. That rigidity may explain the NIH's pressure on Marc Lallemant to include a placebo group in his study, as described by Lurie and Wolfe.[7] Sometimes journals are blamed for the problem, because they are thought to demand strict conformity to the standard methods. That is not true, at least not at this journal. We do not want a scientifically neat study if it is ethically flawed, but like Lurie and Wolfe we believe that in many cases it is possible, with a little ingenuity, to have both scientific and ethical rigor.

The retreat from ethical principles may also be explained by some of the exigencies of doing clinical research in an increasingly regulated and competitive environment. Research in the Third World looks relatively attractive as it becomes better funded and regulations at home become more restrictive. Despite the existence of codes requiring that human subjects receive at least the same protection abroad as at home, they are still honored partly in the breach. The fact remains that many studies are done in the Third World that simply could not be done in the countries sponsoring the work. Clinical trials have become a big business, with many of the same imperatives. To survive, it is necessary to get the work done as quickly as possible, with a minimum of obstacles. When these considerations prevail, it seems as if we have not come very far from Tuskegee after all. Those of us in the research community need to redouble our commitment to the highest ethical standards, no matter where the research is conducted, and sponsoring agencies need to enforce those standards, not undercut them.

NOTES

1. Angell, M. "Patients' preferences in randomized clinical trials." *N Engl J Med* 1984; 310:1385–7.

2. Freedman, B. "Equipoise and the ethics of clinical research." *N Engl J Med* 1987;317:141–5.

3. Declaration of Helsinki IV, 41st World Medical Assembly, Hong Kong, September 1989. In: Annas GJ, Grodin MA, eds. The Nazi doctors and the Nuremberg Code: human rights in human experimentation. New York: Oxford University Press, 1992: 339–42.

4. "Twenty years after: the legacy of the Tuskegee syphilis study." *Hastings Cent Rep* 1992;22(6):29–40.

5. Caplan, A.L. "When evil intrudes." *Hastings Cent Rep* 1992; 22(6):29–32.

6. "The development of consent requirements in research ethics." In: Faden, R.R., Beauchamp, T.L. *A History and Theory of Informed Consent.* New York: Oxford University Press, 1986: 151–99.

7. Lurie, P., Wolfe, S.M. "Unethical trials of interventions to reduce perinatal transmission of the human immunodeficiency virus in developing countries." *N Engl J Med* 1997; 337:853–6.

8. The conduct of clinical trials of maternal-infant transmission of HIV supported by the United States Department of Health and Human Services in developing countries. Washington, D.C.: Department of Health and Human Services, July 1997.

9. Whalen, C.C., Johnson, J.L., Okwera, A., et al. "A trial of three regimens to prevent tuberculosis in Ugandan adults infected with the human immunodeficiency virus." *N Engl J Med* 1997; 337:801–8.

10. "The use of preventive therapy for tuberculosis infection in the United States: recommendations of the Advisory Committee for Elimination of Tuberculosis." *MMWR Morb Mortal Wkly Rep* 1990; 39(RR-8):9–12.

11. Bass, J.B. Jr, Farer, L.S., Hopewell, P.C., et al. "Treatment of tuberculosis and tuberculosis infection in adults and children." *Am J Respir Crit Care Med* 1994; 149:1359–74.

12. De Cock, K.M., Grant, A., Porter, J.D. "Preventive therapy for tuberculosis in HIV-infected persons: international recommendations, research, and practice." *Lancet* 1995; 345:833–6.

13. Msamanga, G.I., Fawzi, W.W., "The double burden of HIV infection and tuberculosis in sub-Saharan Africa." *N Engl J Med* 1997; 337:849–51.

14. Angell, M. "Ethical imperialism? Ethics in international collaborative clinical research." *N Engl J Med* 1988; 319:1081–3.

15. "Protection of human subjects," 45 CFR 46 (1996).

16. International ethical guidelines for biomedical research involving human subjects. Geneva: Council for International Organizations of Medical Sciences, 1993.

17. Angell, M. "The Nazi hypothermia experiments and unethical research today." *N Engl J Med* 1990; 322:1462–4.

Ethical Issues in Clinical Trials in Developing Countries

BARUCH BRODY

Brody responds to major doubts raised about the ethics of some Third World clinical trials conducted to evaluate a regimen to prevent mother-to-infant transmission of HIV. He argues that the use of placebo control groups was ethical because no subjects were denied "any treatment that should otherwise be available to him or her in light of the practical realities of health care resources available in the country in question." According to a reasonable understanding of coercion, he says, no subjects were coerced into participating in the trials. Finally, some have claimed that the trials exploit developing countries "because the interventions in question, even if proven successful, will not be available in these countries." But such trials will not be exploitative, Brody says, if after the studies the subjects themselves are given access to any treatment proven effective.

Since the publication of the results of AIDS Clinical Trials Group (ACTG) 076, it has been known that an extensive regimen of Zidovudine provided to the mother and to the newborn can drastically reduce (25.5 to 8.3%) the vertical transmission of HIV.[1] Unfortunately, the regimen in question is quite expensive and beyond the means of most developing countries, some of which are the countries most in need of effective techniques for reducing vertical transmission. This realization led to a series of important clinical trials designed to test the effectiveness of less extensive and less expensive regimens of antiretroviral drugs. These trials were conducted by researchers from developed countries in the developing countries which were in need of these less expensive regimens.

These new trials have been very successful. The Thai CDC trial showed a 50% reduction (18.9 to 9.4%) in transmission from a much shorter antepartum regimen of Zidovudine combined with a more modest intrapartum regmen.[2] The PETRA trial showed that Zidovudine and Lamivudine provided in modest intrapartum and postpartum regimens also significantly reduced transmission, whether or not they were provided antepartum.[3] There was a trend to more reduction of transmission if they

were provided in a short antepartum regimen (16.5 to 7.8%) than if they were not (16.5 to 10.8%). Most crucially, there was no reduction (16.5 to 15.7%) if they were not provided postpartum. Finally, a single dose of nevirapine provided intrapartum and postpartum was shown in HIVNET 012 to significantly reduce transmission (21.3 to 11.9%).[4] In all cases except HIVNET 012, the control group received only a placebo. In HIVNET 012, the control group received a modest regimen of intrapartum and postpartum Zidovudine.

As a result of these trials, developing countries with some financial capabilities have the opportunity to drastically reduce vertical transmission by proven less expensive regimens. This constitutes an important contribution of these trials. Unfortunately, the poorest developing countries (including some in which these trials have been run) may not be able to afford even these shorter regimens unless the drugs in question are priced far less expensively for those countries. Efforts have begun to make that possible.[5]

There have been many critics of these trials who have argued that they were unethical. Some have gone on to attempt to explain how the information might have been obtained in other more ethical trials while others have not. My focus in this paper is not on that question. Instead, *I want to focus on the arguments offered in support of the claim that these*

From *Statistics in Medicine*, vol. 21, no. 19 (2002), pp. 2853–58. Copyright © John Wiley & Sons Ltd.

trials were unethical. I see the critics as advancing three very different criticisms, although the critics often do not carefully distinguish them. We will do so to enable each criticism to be analyzed. The *first criticism* is that an *injustice was done to the control group* in each of these trials (with perhaps the exception of HIVNET 012) since they were denied proven effective therapy as they only received a placebo. The *second criticism* is that the *participants in the trial were coerced* into participating, and did not give voluntary consent, because they had no real choice about participating since antiretroviral therapy was otherwise unavailable to them. The *third criticism* is that the *countries in question were exploited* by the investigators from the developed countries since they were testing the effectiveness of regimens that would not be available after the trial to the citizens of the countries in which the trials were conducted.

The Justice of the Use of the Placebo Control Group

The scientific importance of the use of concurrent placebo control groups is well illustrated by the PETRA trial. If there had been no such control group, and the various regimens had been compared to the historical control group in ACTG 076, then the intrapartum only arm would have been judged a success, since its transmission rate was only 15.7% as compared to the 25.5% transmission rate in the control group in ACTG 076. But it actually was no better than the placebo control group in PETRA (16.5%). When the rate of transmission varies from one setting to another, you really cannot use historical control groups. Despite this scientific value, the critics have argued that it was wrong to use a placebo control arm because the patients in that arm were being denied a proven therapy (the 076 regimen) and were being offered nothing in its place.[6] The critics claim that this did not meet the standard found in *earlier versions* of the Declaration at Helsinki: "In any medical study, every patient, including those of a control group, if any, should be assured of the best proven diagnostic and therapeutic method."[7]

Defenders of these trials quite properly note that none of the participants in these trials would otherwise have received any antiretroviral therapy, so nothing was being denied to them that they would otherwise have received. How then, ask the defenders, can the members of the control group have been treated unjustly? This led to a proposed, very controversial and eventually rejected, revision of the Declaration of Helsinki which read: "In any biomedical research protocol every patient-subject, including those of a control group, if any, should be assured that he or she will not be denied access to the best proven diagnostic, prophylactic, or therapeutic method that would otherwise be available to him or her."[8] The point is then that the justice or injustice of what is done to the control group depends on what the members of that group *would* have received if the trial had not been conducted.

While the reality of what the members of the control group would have received is obviously relevant, I am not satisfied that this proposed revision would have properly taken that into account. Would it be just, for example, to use such a placebo control group in a trial in a developed country where the antiretroviral therapy is widely available except to members of some persecuted minority, from whom the control group is drawn? They *would* not have received the treatment if the trial had not been conducted, although they *should* have been given the resources available in the developed country. Their use in a placebo control group is not therefore justified. The proposed revision made too much reference to what would have occurred and not enough to what should have occurred.

A recent workshop proposed instead that "study participants should be assured the highest standard of care practically attainable in the country in which the trial is being carried out."[9] This seems better, although it may suggest too much. Suppose that the treatment is practically attainable but only by inappropriately cutting corners on other forms of health care which may have a higher priority. I would suggest therefore that the normative nature of the standard be made explicit. It would then read that all participants in the study, including those in the control group, should not be denied any treatment *that should otherwise be available to him or her in light of the practical realities of health care resources available in the country in question.* The question for IRBs reviewing proposals for such research is then precisely the question of justice.

On that standard, the trials in question were probably not unjust, although there is some debate about the Thai CDC trial in light of donated resources that became available in Thailand between its being planned and its being implemented.[10] Such trials will be harder to justify in the future given the current availability of proven much less expensive therapies which should be available even in some of the poorest countries. It is of interest to note that HIVNET 012 was not a placebo-controlled trial, but it was a superiority trial, and active controlled trials are less problematic scientifically when they are superiority trials. That may well be the way future transmission trials will be run.

Coercive Offers

It has been suggested by other critics that the participants in these trials were coerced into participating because of their desperation. "The very desperation of women with no alternatives to protect their children from HIV infection can be extremely coercive," argue one set of critics.[11] One of the requirements of an ethical trial is that the participants voluntarily agree to participate, and how can their agreement to participate be voluntary if it was coerced?

This line of thinking is analogous to the qualms that many have about paying research subjects substantial sums of money for their participation in research. Such inducements are often rejected on the grounds that they are coercive, because they are too good to refuse. The ICH [International Conference on Harmonization] Guidelines for Good Clinical Practice is one of many standards which incorporate this approach when it stipulates that the "IRB/IEC should review both the amount and method of payment to subjects to assure that neither present problems of coercion or undue influences on the research subject."[12]

Normally, coercion involves a threat to put someone below their baseline unless they cooperate with the demands of the person issuing the threat.[13] As the researchers were not going to do anything to those who chose not to participate, they were clearly not threatening them. Further evidence of this comes from the reflection that threats are unwelcome to the parties being threatened, and there is no reason to suppose that the potential subjects saw the request to participate as something unwelcome. Even the critics recognize this. The potential subjects were being offered an opportunity that might improve their situation. This was an offer "too good to refuse," not a threat.

Should we expand the concept of coercion to include these very favorable offers? There are several reasons for thinking that we should not. First, it is widely believed that offering people valuable new opportunities is desirable. Moreover, the individuals in question want to receive these offers, and denying them the opportunity to receive them seems paternalistic or moralistic.[14] It is important that participants understand that what they are being offered is a chance to receive a treatment that may reduce transmission (since this is a randomized placebo-controlled trial of a new regimen), and ensuring that is essential for the consent to be informed. As long as care is taken to ensure that this information is conveyed in a culturally sensitive fashion, and is understood, then there seems to be little reason to be concerned about coercion simply because a good opportunity is being offered to those with few opportunities.

A colleague and I are currently working on one residual concern in this area. It has to do with studies in which there is a potential for long-term harms to subjects which they inappropriately discount because the very substantial short-term benefits cloud their judgment. This may be a ground for concern in some cases, but it is difficult to see how it would apply to the vertical transmission trials. For those trials, it is appropriate to conclude that concerns about coercion were unfounded.

Exploitation of Subjects

The final criticism of the trials is that they are exploitative of developing countries and their citizens because the interventions in question, even if proven successful, will not be available in these countries. To quote one of the critics: "To use a population as research subjects because of its poverty and its inability to obtain care, and then to not use that knowledge for the direct benefit of that population, is the very definition of exploitation. This exploitation is made worse by the fact that richer nations will unquestionably benefit from this research . . . [they]

will begin to use these lower doses, thereby receiving economic benefit.[15]

There are really two claims being advanced in that quotation. The second, that the developed countries ran these trials to discover cheaper ways of treating their own citizens, is very implausible since pregnant women in developed countries are receiving even more expensive cocktails of drugs both to treat the woman and to reduce transmission. The crucial issue is whether the trials are exploitative of the developing countries.

There seems to be a growing consensus that they are exploitative unless certain conditions about future availability in the country in question are met. The Council for International Organizations of Medical Sciences (CIOMS) is the source of this movement, as it declared in its 1992 guidelines that "as a general rule, the initiating agency should insure that, at the completion of successful testing, any products developed will be made reasonably available to residents of the host community or country."[16] A slightly weaker version of this requirement was adopted by a recent workshop which concluded that "studies are only appropriate if there is a reasonable likelihood that the populations in which they are carried out stand to benefit from successful results."[17]

This growing consensus is part of what lies behind the effort to secure these benefits by negotiating more favorable prices for the use of the tested drugs in developing countries. It seems highly desirable that this goal be achieved. But I want to suggest that it should be viewed as an aspiration, rather than a requirement, and that a different, more modest requirement must be met to avoid charges of exploitation.

A good analysis of exploitation is that it is a wrong done to individuals who do not receive a fair share of the benefits produced by an activity in which they take part, even if they receive some benefit.[18] This is why a mutually beneficial activity, one from which both parties will be better off, can still be exploitative if one of the parties uses their greater bargaining power to harvest most of the benefits and the other party agrees because they need whatever modest benefit is being left for them.

As we apply this concept to the trials in question, we need to ask who needs to be protected from being exploited by the trials in question. It would seem that it is the participants. Are they getting a fair share of the benefits from the trial if it proves successful? This is a particularly troubling question when we consider those in the control group, whose major benefit from participation may have been an unrealized possibility of getting treated. If we judge that the participants have not received enough, then it is they who must receive more. An obvious suggestion is that they be guaranteed access to any regimen proved efficacious in any future pregnancies (or perhaps even that they be granted access to antiretroviral therapy for their own benefit). This would be analogous to familiar concepts of subjects receiving continued access to treatment after their participation in a trial is completed.

I certainly support every reasonable effort to increase access to treatments which will reduce vertical transmission. But imposing the types of community-wide requirements that have been suggested, but not necessarily justified if the above analysis is correct, may prevent important trials from being run because of the potential expense. Such proposals should be treated as moral aspirations, and exploitation should be avoided by focusing on what is owed to the subjects who have participated in the trials. It is they, after all, who are primarily at risk for being exploited.

These observations are about research in developing countries in general, and not just about research on vertical transmission. Three lessons have emerged. The standard for when a placebo control group is justified is a normative standard (what they should have received if they were not in the trial) rather than a descriptive standard (what they would have received it they were not in the trial). Coercion is not a serious concern in trials simply because attractive offers are made to the subjects. Legitimate concerns about exploiting subjects should be addressed by ensuring their future treatment, rather than by asking what will happen in their community at large.

NOTES

1. E. M. Connor, R. S. Sperling, R. Gelber, et al, "Reduction of Maternal-Infant Transmission of Human Immunodeficiency Virus Type I with Zidovudine Treatment," *New England Journal of Medicine,* 331 (1984):1173–80.

2. N. Shaffer, R. Chuachoowong, P. A. Mock, et al., "Short-Course Zidovudine for Perinatal HIV Transmission in Bangkok, Thailand: A Randomised Controlled Trial," *Lancet*, 353 (1999): 773–80.

3. Conference data cited in K. DeCock, M. Fowler, E. Mercier, et al., "Prevention of Mother-to-Child HIV Transmission in Resource Poor Countries," *JAMA* 283 (2000): 1175–82.

4. L. A. Guay, P. Musoke, T. Fleming, et al., "Intrapartum and Neonatal Single-Dose Nevirapine Compared with Zidovudine for Prevention of Mother-to-Child Transmission of HIV-1 in Kampala, Uganda," *Lancet*, 354 (2000): 795–802.

5. P. Brown, "Cheaper AIDS Drugs Due for Third World," *Nature*, 405 (2000): 263.

6. P. Lurie and S. M. Wolfe, "Unethical Trials of Interventions to Reduce Perinatal Transmission of the Human Immunodeficiency Virus in Developing Countries," *New England Journal of Medicine*, 337 (1997): 853–56.

7. World Medical Association, Declaration of Helsinki, Principle 11.3.

8. "Proposed Revision of the Declaration of Helsinki," *Bulletin of Medical Ethics*, 18–21 (1999).

9. Perinatal HIV Intervention Research in Developing Countries Workshop Participants, "Science Ethics and the Future of Research into Maternal Infant Transmission of HIV-1," *Lancet*, 353 (1999): 832–35.

10. P. Phanuphak, "Ethical Issues in Studies in Thailand of the Vertical Transmission of HIV," *New England Journal of Medicine*, 338 (1998): 834–35.

11. E. Tafesse and T. Murphy, Letter, *New England Journal of Medicine*, 338 (1998): 838.

12. ICH. *Guideline for Good Clinical Practice* (Geneva: IFPMA, 1996), guideline 3.1.8.

13. R. Nozick, "Coercion." In Morgenbesser S., ed. *Philosophy, Science, and Method* (New York: St Martin's, 1969).

14. M. Wilkinson and A. Moore, "Inducement in Research," *Bioethics*, 11 (1997): 373–89.

15. I. Glantz and M. Grodin, Letter, *New England Journal of Medicine*, 338 (1998): 839.

16. CIOMS, *International Ethical Guidelines for Biomedical Research Involving Subjects* (Geneva: CIOMS, 1992), 68.

17. Perinatal HIV Intervention Research in Developing Countries Workshop Participants, "Science Ethics and the Future of Research into Maternal Infant Transmission of HIV-1," *Lancet*, 353 (1999): 832–35.

18. A. Wertheimer, *Exploitation* (Princeton, N.J.: Princeton University Press, 1996).

3

LIFE & DEATH

CHAPTER 7

Abortion

Abortion is the most contentious and complex issue in bioethics. It has divided the public, exercised politicians, occupied the courts, busied the media, and engendered violence. Much of the public debate has been bitter and irrational, driven by partisans bent on racking up political points and by popular media obsessed with keeping score. But away from the scuffle and out of earshot of the quarrelers, a more useful debate has been going on—the philosophical give and take among thinkers who test claims about the morality of abortion through reasoned argument and careful reflection. They have achieved no grand consensus on the issue, but they have plumbed it, clarified it, and wrung from it some thoughtful answers worth considering. They have, in other words, done bioethics. Let us see, then, what this work can tell us.

STARTING POINT: THE BASICS

Views on abortion—whether held by church, state, or citizenry—have varied dramatically through time and across cultures. Abortions in the ancient world were common, and there was no shortage of methods for effecting them. Some writers of the time condemned the practice, and some recommended it. "Let there be a law that no deformed child shall live," says Aristotle, "and if couples have children in excess, let abortion be procured before life and sense have begun."[1] The Hippocratic Oath proscribed the use of abortifacients (substances or devices for inducing abortions), a prohibition respected by many physicians but ignored by others.

The Hebrew and Christian scriptures do not denounce abortion and do not suggest that the fetus is a person. A passage in Exodus Chapter 21 touches on the topic and implies that the unborn entity is not a full human being. The passage comes after the emphatic "You shall not murder" of the Ten Commandments and after a warning that the penalty for murder is death. But Exodus 21:22 says that if a man causes a woman to have a miscarriage "but [she] is not harmed in any other way," the penalty is just a fine. Causing the death of a fetus was not considered murder.

Christians have generally condemned abortion, though their ideas about the personhood of the fetus have changed through the centuries. Many contemporary Christians, especially Roman Catholics, assume that the unborn is a full human being from the moment of conception. But in the twelfth century, the church came to the view that an embryo cannot have a soul until several weeks after conception. The rationale, inspired by Aristotle, was that the unborn cannot have a soul until it is "formed"—that is, until it has a human shape, a stage that is reached long after conception. Thomas Aquinas accepted this view and maintained that male embryos are formed (and thus given a soul, or "ensouled") 40 days after conception; female embryos, 90 days. Thus, killing a fetus, though always sinful, is not murder until after it is formed. In 1312, this doctrine became the church's official position. Only in the late nineteenth century did the church decide that ensoulment happens at conception and that any abortion after that point is the killing of a human person.

In English common law, abortion was considered a crime only if performed after **quickening** (when the mother first detects fetal movement). From its beginnings through the nineteenth

Fact File **U.S. Abortions**

- Almost half of all pregnancies are unintended.
- 4 in 10 of unintended pregnancies end in abortions.
- In 2005, 1.21 million abortions were performed.
- Each year, approximately 2 percent of women aged 15–44 have an abortion.
- Most Western industrialized countries have lower abortion rates than the United States does.
- 43 percent of women having abortions say they are Protestant; 27 percent, Catholic.
- 54 percent of women who have abortions had used contraception during the month they became pregnant.
- The risk of death associated with abortion is one death per million abortions performed at eight weeks or earlier; one death in 29,000 abortions performed at 16-20 weeks; and one death per 11,000 performed at 21 weeks or later.
- Less than 0.3 percent of women having abortions suffer medical complications requiring hospitalization.
- 50 percent of women who have abortions are younger than 25; 17 percent are teenagers.

The Alan Guttmacher Institute, "Facts on Induced Abortion in the United States," January 2008, http://www.guttmacher. org/pubs/fb_induced_abortion.html#14 (30 March 2008); L. A. Bartlett et al., "Risk Factors for Legal Induced Abortion-Related Mortality in the United States," *Obstetrics & Gynecology* 103.4 (2004), 729–37; S. K. Henshaw, "Unintended Pregnancy and Abortion: A Public Health Perspective," in *A Clinician's Guide to Medical and Surgical Abortion*, ed. M. Paul et al. (New York: Churchill Livingstone, 1999), 11–22; American College of Obstetricians and Gynecologists, "Induced Abortion," June 2007.

century, American law mostly reflected this tradition. Accordingly, in the early 1800s, several states passed statutes outlawing abortion after quickening except to save the life of the mother. But in the next 100 years, abortion laws gradually became stricter, dropping the quickening cutoff point and banning all abortions but those thought to preserve the life (or, rarely, the health) of the mother. The medical profession generally supported the tougher laws, and the views of physicians on abortion carried great weight.

In the 1950s, a trend toward liberalized laws began, and by 1970 the American Medical Association (AMA) and the American College of Obstetricians and Gynecologists were officially advocating less severe abortion policies. The latter declared, "It is recognized that abortion may be performed at a patient's request, or upon a physician's recommendation."[2] By that time, 12 states had amended their abortion statutes to make them less restrictive, and the public had warmed considerably to the idea of legalized abortion. The culmination of all these changes was the 1973 Supreme Court case of *Roe v. Wade*, which made abortions before viability legal.

The abortion policies of previous eras were handicapped by poor understanding of human development. But in modern times the facts are clear: *Fertilization*, or conception, happens when a sperm cell penetrates an egg, or ovum, forming a single cell known as a *zygote*, or conceptus. This meeting of sperm and egg usually takes place in one of the two fallopian tubes, the narrow tunnels linking the egg-producing ovaries with the uterus. For three to five days, the zygote moves down the fallopian tube to the uterus, dividing continually and thus getting larger along the way. In the fluid-filled uterus, it divides further, becoming a hollow sphere of cells known as a *blastocyst*. Within about five days, the blastocyst lodges firmly in the lining of the uterus (a feat called implantation) and is then known as an *embryo*.

The embryonic stage lasts until eight weeks after fertilization. During this time most of the embryo's internal organs form, the brain and spinal cord start to generate, and external features such as limbs and ears begin to appear. At eight weeks, though it is only about the size of a raspberry, the embryo has a rudimentary human shape.

From the end of the eighth week until birth, the unborn is technically known as a *fetus*. (In this text, however, we use the term to refer to the unborn at any stage from conception to birth.) At about 14 weeks of pregnancy, doctors can determine the fetus' sex. Around 16 to 20 weeks, the mother can feel the fetus moving inside her. Quickening was once thought to be a threshold event in pregnancy, signaling ensoulment or the presence of a human being. But it is of doubtful importance (except to the mother) since the fetus moves undetected before quickening, and the mother's sensing fetal movement is not associated with any significant change in development. A more meaningful benchmark is **viability**, the development stage at approximately 23 to 24 weeks of pregnancy when the fetus may survive outside the uterus. Babies born at this point, however, are at high risk of severe disabilities (mental retardation and blindness, among others) and death.

Development from fertilization to birth (called gestation) is nine months long, or about 40 weeks. This span of pregnancy is calculated from the first day of the woman's last menstrual period and is traditionally divided into three 3-month intervals—first trimester (0–12 weeks), second trimester (13–24 weeks), and third trimester (25 weeks to delivery). Babies delivered in the third trimester but before 37 weeks are considered premature.

Abortion is the ending of a pregnancy. Abortion due to natural causes—birth defect or injury,

for example—is known as **spontaneous abortion** or **miscarriage**. The intentional termination of pregnancy through drugs or surgery is called **induced abortion** or, more commonly, simply abortion. Abortion in this sense is the issue over which most of the ideological and judicial struggles are waged. Such is generally not the case for **therapeutic abortion**—abortion performed to preserve the life or health of the mother. Most people believe therapeutic abortion to be morally permissible.

Several methods are used to perform abortions, some of them surgical and some pharmaceutical. The method used depends on, among other things, the woman's health and the length of her pregnancy. The most common technique is known as *suction curettage* (also, *vacuum aspiration*), which is used in the first 12 weeks of pregnancy (when nearly 90 percent of abortions are performed). A doctor inserts a thin, bendable tube through the opening of the cervix into the uterus and, using a vacuum syringe or a machine or hand pump, suctions the contents of the uterus out through the tube. The method used most often after the first 12 weeks is *dilation and evacuation*. It involves widening the cervix and employing both suction and forceps to extract the fetus and placenta.

Abortions can be induced with drugs (often referred to as "medical abortions") but only in the first seven to nine weeks of pregnancy. The most common regimen uses two medications: mifepristone (RU-486, the so-called abortion pill) and misoprostol, a prostaglandin (hormone-like substance). Mifepristone interferes with the hormone progesterone, thinning the lining of the uterus and preventing implantation of the embryo. Misoprostol prompts the uterus to contract, forcing the embryo out. A woman sees her physician to take mifepristone, then up to three days later takes misoprostol (either at home or in the physician's office). This two-step procedure causes abortion about 95 percent of the time.

The risk of complications (such as serious bleeding or internal injury) from abortion is low and varies directly with the length of pregnancy—the

IN DEPTH
ABORTION AND PUBLIC OPINION

Do you think abortions should be legal under any circumstances, legal only under certain circumstances, or illegal in all circumstances?

Always Legal	**Sometimes Legal**	**Always Illegal**
26%	55%	18%

With respect to the abortion issue, would you consider yourself to be pro-choice or pro-life?

Pro-Choice	**Pro-Life**	**Mixed/Neither**
49%	45%	3%

Would you like to see the Supreme Court overturn its 1973 *Roe v. Wade* decision concerning abortion, or not?

Yes, Overturn	**No, Not Overturn**	**Unsure**
35%	53%	12%

Gallup Poll, May 10–13, 2007. N = 1,007 adults nationwide. Margin of error = ±3.

earlier an abortion is performed, the lower the risk. Less than 1 percent of women having early abortions experience complications; less than 2 percent of those having later abortions do. Death is a risk in any surgical procedure; the risk of death for suction curettage is less than 1 in 100,000 women. The risk for medical abortion is virtually the same. The chances of a woman dying in childbirth are at least 10 times higher.[3]

Over half of women having abortions are under 25 years old, and almost one-fifth of these are teenagers. Fifty-seven percent of abortions are performed on women who have never married; 17 percent, on married women; and 16 percent, on women who are separated, divorced, or widowed.

Their reasons for terminating a pregnancy are varied. According to a recent survey of women who had abortions, the reasons include:

- Having a baby would change my life (interfere with education, employment, etc.).—74 percent

- I can't afford a baby now (I'm unmarried, unemployed, destitute, etc.).—73 percent
- I don't want to be a single mother, or I'm having relationship problems.—48 percent
- My relationship or marriage may break up soon.—11 percent
- I've already completed my childbearing.—38 percent
- My husband or partner wants me to have an abortion.—14 percent
- There are possible problems affecting the health of the fetus.—13 percent
- There are physical problems with my health.—12 percent
- I was a victim of rape.—1 percent
- I became pregnant as a result of incest.—less than 0.5 percent[4]

Polls gauging the attitudes of the American public toward abortion have revealed many divisions but also remarkable agreement on some points. Only a small minority of people (5–20 percent) think that abortion should be illegal or unavailable in all circumstances. Most reject a total ban but differ on the existence or extent of restrictions placed on abortion. Roughly half consider themselves to be "pro-life" and half "pro-choice." A sizeable majority would not like to see *Roe v. Wade* completely overturned.

THE LEGAL STRUGGLE

As we have seen, abortion is both a moral and legal issue, and these two lines of debate must not be confused. But we cannot ignore how the legal conflict has influenced the ethical arguments, and vice versa. The former seized the attention of the nation when *Roe v. Wade* was handed down. Roe was "Jane Roe," a.k.a. Norma McCorvey, who had sought a nontherapeutic abortion in Texas where she lived. But Texas law forbade all abortions except those necessary to save the mother's life. So Roe sued the state of Texas in federal court, which ruled that the law was unconstitutional. Texas appealed the decision to the U.S. Supreme Court, and the Court sided with the federal court, declaring in *Roe v. Wade* that no state can ban abortions performed before viability.

The Court saw in the Constitution (most notably the Fourteenth Amendment, which grants due process and equal protection under the law) a guaranteed right of personal privacy that limits interference by the state in people's private lives, and the majority believed that the right encompassed a woman's decision to terminate her pregnancy. But, the Court noted, "this right is not unqualified and must be considered against important state interests in regulation." So it balanced the woman's right and state interests according to trimester of pregnancy. In the first trimester, the woman's right to end her pregnancy cannot be curtailed by the state. Her decision must be respected, and "its effectuation must be left to the medical judgment of the pregnant woman's attending physician." In the second trimester, the state may limit—but not entirely prohibit—the woman's right by regulating abortion for the sake of her health. After viability, the state

may regulate and even ban abortion except when it is necessary to preserve her life or health. The Court affirmed that its ruling "leaves the State free to place increasing restrictions on abortion as the period of pregnancy lengthens, so long as those restrictions are tailored to the recognized state interests."

The Court noted that the Constitution does not define "person" and that "the word 'person,' as used in the Fourteenth Amendment, does not include the unborn." In fact, the law has never maintained that the unborn are persons "in the whole sense."

After this historic case, the Supreme Court handed down numerous other decisions that circumscribed, but did not invalidate, the right to abortion defined in *Roe*. In these rulings, the Court held that (1) a woman can be required to give her written informed consent to abortion, (2) the government is not obliged to use taxpayer money to fund abortion services, (3) parental consent or a judge's authorization can be demanded of minors under age 18 who seek abortions, (4) a state can forbid the use of public facilities to perform abortions (except to save the woman's life), (5) a woman who consents to an abortion can be required to wait 24 hours before the procedure is performed, and (6) a state can mandate that a woman be given abortion information. Eventually the court came to a key doctrine concerning such limitations: Before viability, abortion can be restricted in many ways as long as the constraints do not amount to an "undue burden" on a woman trying to get an abortion. A state regulation constitutes an undue burden if it "has the purpose or effect of placing a substantial obstacle in the path of a woman seeking an abortion of a nonviable fetus."

PERSONS AND RIGHTS

People generally take one of three positions on the moral permissibility of abortion. The conservative view is that abortion is never morally acceptable (except possibly to preserve the mother's life), for the unborn is a human being in the full

Abortions performed late in pregnancy using a controversial surgical procedure have been the flashpoint for intense debate, legislative action, and court rulings. The procedure is known technically as *intact dilation and extraction* (D&X) and disparagingly as *partial-birth abortion*. Physicians use the first term; abortion opponents tend to use the latter. Late-term abortions are performed after the twentieth week of gestation and are uncommon, comprising around 1 percent of all abortions. Some women have them to protect their life or health and some to avoid having a severely impaired infant. Others have late abortions because they would not or could not have them earlier (these include teenagers, the poor, drug addicts, and women who were unaware of their pregnancy).

In the principal form of D&X, the woman's cervix is dilated, the fetus' torso is drawn manually or with medical instruments through the birth canal, and the brain is suctioned out and the skull collapsed so the head can also be withdrawn. Depending on the length of gestation and many other variables, some of the fetuses aborted in this way may be viable, and many are not.

In 2003 President Bush signed the Partial-Birth Abortion Ban Act, which outlawed a type of late-term abortion. But several federal courts declared the law unconstitutional because it lacks a "health exception" for women whose health is threatened. In 2007 the U.S. Supreme Court upheld the law, effectively banning D&X abortions (and arguably some other late-term procedures).

sense. The liberal view is that abortion is acceptable whenever the woman wants it, for the unborn is not a human being in the full sense. The moderate stance falls between these two stands, rejecting both the conservative's zero-tolerance for abortion and the liberal's idea of abortion on request. For the moderate, some—but not all—abortions may be morally justified. (These labels are common but sometimes misleading; being a conservative or liberal on the abortion issue does not necessarily mean you are a conservative or liberal in the broader political sense.)

Despite appearances, between the conservatives and the liberals there is at least a patch of common ground. Both sides agree on some basic moral principles—for example, that murder is wrong, that persons have a right to life, and that personal freedom should not be curtailed except for very important reasons. Conflicts arise not over such fundamentals but over the nonmoral facts (such as the nature of the fetus) and over the meaning and application of moral standards.

The main conservative argument against abortion is straightforward and based on a widely shared intuition about the wrongness of killing innocents. One popular formulation says that (1) the killing of an innocent human being is wrong; (2) the unborn is an innocent human being; (3) therefore, it is wrong to kill the unborn (abortion is immoral). At first glance, this argument may seem sound, but critics point out that the term *human being* improperly switches meanings in mid-argument, invalidating the inference (and thus committing what is known as the fallacy of equivocation). The problem is that in premise 2, *human being* means an entity that is biologically human, a member of the genetically distinct human species. But in premise 1, *human being* refers to an entity having all the psychological attributes and capacities that we normally associate with the possession of full moral rights (including a right to life)—what philosophers call a *person*. If *human being* referred to the same thing throughout the argument, the argument would be valid. But the argument equivocates on the term and is therefore invalid.

The conservative, however, avoids these difficulties by offering an improved version of the argument: (1) The killing of an innocent person is wrong; (2) the unborn is an innocent person from the moment of conception; (3) therefore, it is wrong to kill the unborn (abortion is immoral). This argument is valid, and premise 1 is obviously true. The crux of the matter is premise 2, which the conservative asserts and the liberal denies. What arguments can the conservative offer to support it?

One option is to start with this observation: In the continuous process of development from zygote to adult human, there seems to be no precise point at which the entity becomes unmistakably a bone fide human being (with a right to life). No clear line between nonperson and person can be found. Any point we select to indicate the nonperson/person boundary would be arbitrary and unsupportable. The conservative argues that the most plausible view then would be that personhood (and the right to life) begins at conception. It is at conception that, for example, a full complement of genetic information is present to propel development of a completely formed, mature human. As one philosopher puts it,

> The positive argument for conception as the decision moment of humanization is that at conception the new being receives the genetic code. It is this genetic information which determines his characteristics, which is the biological carrier of the possibility of human wisdom, which makes him a self-evolving being. A being with a human genetic code is man.[5]

Critics respond in various ways to this view. They point out, for example, that just because no nonperson/person line can be drawn doesn't mean there is no difference to be observed between the two phenomena. We may not be able to specify the precise moment when a tadpole turns into a frog, but we know there is a real difference between the two states. The failure to pinpoint a distinct moment when the unborn becomes a person does not show that it must be a person from the moment of conception.

Some philosophers argue on empirical grounds that the zygote cannot be an individual human being:

> [T]he very early conceptus cannot be identified with the embryo that may develop from it. This is because, for about the first two weeks of existence, it consists of a set of undifferentiated cells, any one of which could give rise to an embryo under certain circumstances. This "pre-embryo" may spontaneously divide, resulting in twins or triplets; alternatively, it may combine with another pre-embryo, giving rise to a single fetus.[6]

Some conservatives avoid such complications by arguing not that the fetus is a person, but that it is a *potential* person and thus has the same right to life as any existing person. The unborn may not be a person now, but its status as a possible future person puts it in the same moral category as any normal adult human being. One ethicist expresses the point like this:

> What makes the difference between human beings and other life is the capacity human beings enjoy for a specially rich kind of life. The life already enjoyed by a human being cannot be taken away from him, only the prospect of such life in the future. But this prospect is possessed as much by an infant or fetus as by a full-grown adult.[7]

A common response to this potentiality argument is that there is a world of difference between (1) possessing a particular trait that gives you a right and (2) *having the potential* to develop a trait that gives you a right. "[T]he right to vote in political elections may be granted to citizens who have reached the age of 18," says Mary Anne Warren, "but not to pre-adolescents—even though most of them clearly have the potential to reach the age of 18." From the fact that someone has the potential to become a Supreme Court justice does not follow that we should treat her as if she were a justice now.

Michael Tooley provides a more striking example. Suppose there existed a special chemical that could be injected into a kitten's brain to cause the kitten to gradually become a cat with a mind that was indistinguishable from the kind possessed by adult humans. The cat could think, talk, and feel just as humans do, acquiring all the proper traits that give it a right to life. Now consider:

> [C]ompare a member of *Homo sapiens* that has not developed far enough to have those properties that in themselves give something a right to life, but which later will come to have them, with a kitten that has been injected with the special chemical but which has not yet had the chance to develop the relevant properties. It is clear that it cannot be any more seriously wrong to kill the human than to kill the kitten. The potentialities are the same in both cases.[8]

Some critics also think that the potentiality argument undermines itself because it seems to have bizarre implications. They argue, for example, that if a zygote is a potential person (and thus has the same right to life as an adult human), then other entities must also be potential persons with a right to life—human ovum and spermatozoa for starters but also countless other cells in the human body. There is no difference between a single-cell zygote and any other single diploid cell that, through cloning, could also become a human being.

The liberal says that the unborn is not a person, not a full human being, and therefore does not have a right to life. If the unborn is a person, then killing it would be murder, and its right to life would be at least as weighty as the mother's. How can the liberal show that fetuses are not persons?

To start, the liberal will insist that merely being a *Homo sapiens*—a creature with human DNA—is not sufficient for personhood. To think so is to be guilty of a kind of prejudice called *speciesism*. The liberal argues that since whatever properties make us persons (and thus grant us a right to life) could conceivably be manifested by a nonhuman species, merely being a member of the human species cannot be sufficient for personhood status. If we assume that an entity is a person just because it happens to belong to our favored biological classification, we stand convicted of speciesism, close cousin to racism. There are properties that do qualify an entity as

a person, but simply being human is not one of them.

The liberal tack is to identify these traits and point out that a fetus does not possess them. According to Louis Pojman,

> These properties are intrinsically valuable traits that allow us to view ourselves as selves with plans and projects over time, properties like self-consciousness and rationality. . . . Although it is difficult to specify exactly what are the necessary and sufficient conditions for personhood, and liberals have described these conditions differently—some emphasizing desires and interests, others emphasizing agency or the ability to project into the future, others emphasizing the capacity for a notion of the self—they all point to a cluster of characteristics which distinguish children and adults from fetuses, infants, and most animals.[9]

Mary Anne Warren famously identifies five traits that are "most central" to personhood: (1) consciousness and the capacity to feel pain, (2) reasoning, (3) self-motivated activity, (4) the capacity to communicate, and (5) "the presence of self-concepts, and self-awareness, either individual or racial or both." To be considered a person, she says, a being need not possess all these traits, but surely "any being which satisfies *none* of (1)–(5) is certainly not a person." A fetus in fact satisfies none and is therefore not yet a person and "cannot coherently be said to have full moral rights."[10]

The conservative will counter that the liberal's standards for personhood are set too high, for they imply that cognitively impaired individuals—victims of serious dementia, retardation, or schizophrenia, for instance—are not persons and therefore do not have a right to life. The liberal view seems to condone the killing of these unfortunates, a repugnant implication. The liberal response is that even if cognitively impaired individuals do not qualify as persons, we may still have good reasons for not killing them—for example, because people value them or because a policy allowing them to be killed would be harmful to society (perhaps encouraging unnecessary killings or causing a general devaluing of life). In addition, the liberal points out that the personhood status of many (or most) cognitively impaired individuals is unclear, so a policy of regarding them as less than persons would be risky.

The biggest challenge to the liberal notion of personhood is the charge that it sanctions infanticide. The argument is that if killing a fetus is morally permissible because it is not a person, then killing an infant must be acceptable as well, for it is not a person either. According to the liberal's personhood criteria mentioned earlier, neither a fetus nor an infant is a person. Moreover, there is a glaring problem with the common liberal assumption that birth is the point at which a fetus becomes a person: The fetus just before birth and the infant just after are biologically almost indistinguishable. Saying that the former has no right to life but the latter does seems hard to justify.

Liberals contend that even if infants are not persons, infanticide is rarely permissible (possible exceptions include cases of horrendous birth defects and terminal illness). Some (including Warren) say that this is so because infants, though not persons, do have some moral standing. For example:

> In this country, and in this period of history, the deliberate killing of viable newborns is virtually never justified. This is in part because neonates are so very *close* to being persons that to kill them requires a very strong moral justification—as does the killing of dolphins, whales, chimpanzees, and other highly personlike creatures. It is certainly wrong to kill such beings just for the sake of convenience, or financial profit, or "sport."[11]

Others say that infanticide is to be condemned for reasons of social utility. As Joel Feinberg explains,

> The moral rule that condemns these killings [infanticide] and the legal rule that renders them punishable are both supported by "utilitarian reasons," that is, considerations of what is called "social utility," "the common good," "the public interest," and the like. Nature has apparently implanted in us an instructive tenderness toward infants that has proven extremely useful to the species, not only because it leads us to protect our young from death, and thus keep our population up, but also because infants usually grow into adults, and in Benn's words, "if as infants *they* are not treated with some minimal degree of tenderness and consideration, they will suffer for it later, as persons." One might add that when they are adults, others will suffer for it, too, at their hands. Spontaneous warmth and sympathy toward babies then clearly has a great deal of social utility, and insofar as infanticide would tend to weaken that socially valuable response, it is, on utilitarian grounds, morally wrong.[12]

Moderate views on abortion can be sketched out in a variety of ways. Many moderates claim the middle ground by arguing that the fetus achieves personhood at a point somewhere *between* conception and birth—at viability, at the time when fetal brain waves occur, or at some other notable point. Other moderates reject the notion of a distinct developmental line separating persons from nonpersons. They argue instead that the moral standing or right to life of the fetus increases gradually as it develops (expanding from minimal rights to almost full rights, for example) or that there is an indistinct threshold stage (when sentience emerges, say) beyond which the fetus has significantly increased moral standing. Departing dramatically from these strategies, some moderates stake out their position without appealing to fetal personhood.

The most famous example of the latter comes from Judith Jarvis Thomson. She argues that even if the conservative view is correct that the unborn is a person from the moment of conception, abortion may still be morally justified. A fetus may have a right to life, but this right "does not guarantee having either a right to be given the use of or a right to be allowed continued use of another person's body—even if one needs it for life itself."[13] The unborn's right to life is not absolute. It implies not that killing a fetus is always wrong, but that killing it unjustly is always wrong. Thomson argues her point with this striking analogy:

> You wake up in the morning and find yourself back to back in bed with an unconscious violinist. A famous unconscious violinist. He has been found to have a fatal kidney ailment, and the Society of Music Lovers has canvassed all the available medical records and found that you alone have the right blood type to help. They have therefore kidnapped you, and last night the violinist's circulatory system was plugged into yours, so that your kidneys can be used to extract poisons from his blood as well as your own. The director of the hospital now tells you, "Look, we're sorry the Society of Music Lovers did this to you—we would never have permitted it if we had known. But still, they did it, and the violinist now is plugged into you. To unplug you would be to kill him. But never mind, it's only for nine months. By then he will have recovered from his ailment, and can safely be unplugged from you."[14]

Thomson believes that our intuitions would tell us that this arrangement is outrageous, that the violinist's right to life would not give him the right to exploit someone's body against her will. Analogously, a fetus' right to life would not guarantee it unauthorized use of the mother's body; the mother has a right of self-defense. Abortion, therefore, is justified when the fetus takes up residence without the woman's consent, as when pregnancy is due to rape or failed contraception.

Some reject Thomson's argument by contending that it holds only if the woman bears no responsibility for her predicament, if the attached violinist or fetus takes up residence through no fault of her own. She may not be responsible for the fetus if she becomes pregnant through rape; she does not, after all, consent to be raped. But she can be held responsible if she voluntarily engages in sexual intercourse; she therefore is obligated to carry the fetus to term. Others maintain that the woman is obliged to sustain the life of

the unborn because she has a filial obligation to it. The unborn has a natural claim to the woman's body.

APPLYING MAJOR THEORIES

A utilitarian can argue that abortion is morally permissible because without this option, women (and society) would suffer terrible consequences:

> Throughout history women have paid a terrible price for the absence of safe and legal contraception and abortion. Forced to bear many children, at excessively short intervals, they were often physically debilitated and died young—a common fate in most pre-twentieth-century societies and much of the Third World today. Involuntary childbearing aggravates poverty, increases infant and child death rates, and places severe strains upon the resources of families and states.[15]

To these calamities, a utilitarian might add the woman's physical and emotional distress caused by pregnancy; the risk of complications or death in childbirth; disruption of her employment, education, or other life plans; and unhappiness caused by a loss of personal control and freedom.

Utilitarian arguments for abortion can also appeal to the quality of life of the infant or child. By this reasoning, abortion may be acceptable if the fetus is likely to be born with severe defects—anencephalic (essentially without a brain), terminally ill, severely retarded, or seriously disabled. Abortion would be a way to avoid great suffering.

Utilitarians who take Mill's view of individual liberty might argue for abortion by claiming that a woman must be allowed the freedom to decide what happens to her own body, which includes the attached fetus. This position follows from Mill's liberty (or harm) principle: We may not interfere with a person's capacity for self-determination except to prevent harm to others.

Those opposed to abortion can appeal to consequences, too: Having an abortion can cause the woman tremendous emotional pain, and the child can bring much happiness to the family and to the world. Besides, as an alternative to abortion, there is always adoption.

A common response to utilitarian arguments for abortion is this: If the fetus is a person, the utilitarian considerations don't matter much, if at all. If fetuses have a right to life (the same as any normal adult human), then it does not matter that their presence will cause others grief or that their quality of life will be marginal. If it is not permissible to kill a normal adult human (a person) on such grounds, then it cannot be permissible to kill a fetus-person for the same reasons.

In Kantian ethics, much depends on whether the unborn is to be considered a person. If it is a person, it has inherent worth and therefore cannot be treated as merely a means to an end. It cannot be killed just for the convenience of the mother or of society. But if the unborn is not a person, then abortion would seem to be more easily justified. Since the woman is a person, she has a right to exercise her autonomy and sovereignty over her own body—which may include ending her pregnancy.

On Kantian grounds, some can claim justification for abortion even if the fetus is a person. According to Kant, persons have a right of self-defense, a right to preserve their own lives against those who would take them. This right includes killing another if necessary for self-protection. If so, perhaps a woman whose pregnancy threatens her life can kill the unborn person in self-defense—a therapeutic abortion. In addition, Kant's view can be plausibly construed as sanctioning abortion as a way of respecting a fetus' personhood. If the fetus is defective and faces a demeaning, miserable existence, we can show ultimate respect for its status by averting such indignities through abortion.

The natural law position on abortion as articulated in Roman Catholicism is clear and unequivocal. The fetus is an innocent person from conception (with a right to life equal to that of the mother), and directly killing any innocent person is wrong. Thus directly killing the unborn even for the purpose of saving the mother's life is impermissible, for "evil is never to be done that good may come of it." The doctrine of double effect, however, permits the *indirect* killing of the unborn—specifically, abortions done to save the mother's life while having the unintended yet foreseen effect of killing the fetus. Traditionally the only abortions thought to fit these requirements have involved ectopic pregnancies and uterine cancer.

KEY TERMS

abortion
induced abortion
quickening
spontaneous abortion (miscarriage)
therapeutic abortion
viability

SUMMARY

Abortion is the ending of a pregnancy. Abortion due to natural causes is known as spontaneous abortion, or miscarriage; intentional termination of pregnancy is called induced abortion; and abortion performed to preserve the life or health of the mother is referred to as therapeutic abortion. Over half of women having abortions are under 25 years old; one-fifth of these are teenagers. Women give varying reasons for having abortions, including that having a baby would interfere with their life, cause financial or social difficulties, or put their health or life at risk. They also cite possible problems affecting the health of the fetus.

Since 1973 the legal status of abortion in the United States has been dominated by the Supreme Court's ruling in *Roe v. Wade*. The justices held that in the first trimester, the woman's right to end her pregnancy cannot be curtailed by the state; in the second trimester, the state may limit—but not entirely prohibit—the woman's right by regulating abortion for the sake of her health; and after viability, the state may regulate and even ban abortion except when it's necessary to preserve her life or health. The Court affirmed that its ruling "leaves the State free to place increasing restrictions on abortion as the

Nancy Klein

The most contentious—and usually the most agonizing—abortion cases are those involving what people take to be clashes between fetal and maternal rights or interests. Such conflicts have played out in many closely watched stories, including this one that grabbed headlines in 1989 and outraged people on all sides of the issue.

On December 13, 1988, 32-year-old Nancy Klein, wife and mother of a young daughter, was in an auto accident that damaged her brain and put her in a coma. At the time, she was 10 weeks pregnant. After six weeks she was still in the coma and still pregnant, and her doctors doubted that she would ever recover. But they did believe that her chances of coming out of the coma might improve if she had an abortion and that she could then be treated with medications that could not be safely given in pregnancy. So her husband, Martin, asked a New York State court to designate him as her guardian empowered to grant permission for the abortion.

But abortion opponents went to court to try to block the abortion. One of them petitioned to be named Nancy Klein's guardian, while another asked to become guardian for the fetus. "These people are ruining our family," Martin Klein declared. But one of the anti-abortion petitioners said, "I don't see this as interfering in the family's business. What we're trying to do is protect and support Nancy Klein and her child."

For two weeks, the legal battles raged, but ultimately Martin Klein won, and the requests of the abortion opponents were turned down by three state courts as well as by U.S. Supreme Court justices Marshall and Scalia. Referring to the two anti-abortion petitioners, one court asserted, "The record confirms that these absolute strangers to the Klein family, whatever their motivation, have no place in the midst of this family tragedy."

Finally, at 18 weeks of pregnancy, the abortion was performed. Martin Klein and his wife's parents were relieved and said they expected that after the abortion Nancy would recover from her coma. Several weeks later, she did.

For the next two years, she struggled in rehabilitation hospitals to regain her memory and her ability to speak and walk. She eventually recovered much of what she had lost, though her speech and walking remained impaired. She condemned the actions of the abortion opponents: "I feel very strongly that it was my problem, not theirs, and that they had no right to interfere."

---

period of pregnancy lengthens, so long as those restrictions are tailored to the recognized state interests." In several cases after *Roe*, the Court circumscribed the right of abortion by, among other things, holding that a woman can be required to give her written informed consent to abortion, that the government is not obliged to use taxpayer money to fund abortion services, and that parental consent or a judge's authorization can be demanded of minors under age 18 who seek abortions. In 2007 the Court upheld the Partial-Birth Abortion Ban Act, which outlawed a type of late-term abortion (referred to rhetorically as "partial-birth abortion") even when a woman's health might be threatened.

There are three main positions on the moral permissibility of abortion. The conservative view is that abortion is never morally acceptable (except possibly to preserve the mother's life), for the unborn is a human being in the full sense. The liberal view is that abortion is acceptable whenever the woman wants it, for the unborn is not a human being in the full sense. The moderate stance falls between these two stands, rejecting both the conservative's zero-tolerance for abortion and the liberal's idea of abortion on request. All sides tend to accept that murder is wrong, that persons have a right to life, and that personal freedom should not be curtailed except for very important reasons. Conservatives try to establish that the unborn should be recognized as an innocent person from the moment of conception by appealing to the lack of a precise cutoff point between zygote and adult human and by arguing that the fetus is a potential person. Liberals contend that merely being biologically human is not sufficient to establish personhood and that a fetus does not possess the properties that qualify an entity as a person. Taking a moderate position, Judith Jarvis Thomson argues that even if the conservative view is correct that the unborn is a person from the moment of conception, abortion may still be morally justified in some cases. The unborn's right to life is not absolute; it implies not that killing a fetus is always wrong, but that killing it unjustly is always wrong.

A utilitarian position can be staked out either for abortion or against it, depending on how the overall consequences of abortion are calculated. Kantian ethics can also yield pro- or anti-abortion positions depending on whether the unborn is considered a person. The natural law position on abortion as articulated in Roman Catholicism is that the fetus is an innocent person from conception, and directly killing any innocent person is wrong. Thus directly killing the unborn even for the purpose of saving the mother's life is impermissible. The doctrine of double effect, however, permits the indirect killing of the unborn—specifically, abortions done to save the mother's life while having the unintended yet foreseen effect of killing the fetus.

Cases for Evaluation

CASE I

Abortions for Minor Disabilities

(*London Times*)—More than 50 babies with club feet were aborted in just one area of England in a three-year period, according to new statistics.

Thirty-seven babies with cleft lips or palates and 26 with extra or webbed fingers or toes were also aborted.

The data have raised concerns about abortions being carried out for minor disabilities that could be cured by surgery.

Abortions are allowed up to birth in Britain in cases of serious handicap, but the law does not define what conditions should be considered grave enough to allow a termination late in the pregnancy. That is left to the discretion of doctors.

The Commons science and technology committee is carrying out an inquiry into whether the law should be made more specific.

Some parents, doctors and campaign groups are worried by what they see as a tendency to stretch the definition of serious handicap.

In 2003 Joanna Jepson, a Church of England curate, instigated a legal challenge against West Mercia police for failing to prosecute doctors who carried out an abortion on a baby with a cleft palate at 28 weeks' gestation. The challenge failed but raised public concerns over terminations for minor disabilities.

However, the latest figures—released by the South West Congenital Register—show that dozens of abortions are still carried out after the condition is discovered.

Jepson, now vicar of St Peter's church in Fulham, west London, said: "These figures raise grave questions about how the law is being implemented for babies diagnosed with a disability. I have strong doubts that the law is being used to protect the unborn."

Julia Millington, political director of the ProLife Alliance, added: "It is incomprehensible that a baby would be rejected for what amounts to little more than a cosmetic imperfection. Equality for the disabled cannot be achieved until we remove this discriminatory provision in the law."*

Do you think it is ever morally permissible to perform an abortion on a defective fetus? What about a fetus that is so deformed that it will certainly die within a few days after birth? Or a fetus with deformities that will guarantee it a lifetime of pain and serious disability and years of emotional and financial trauma for its family? Can abortions performed on fetuses with minor disabilities such as a cleft lip ever be justified? Give reasons for your answers.

---

*Sarah-Kate Templeton, "Babies Aborted for Minor Disabilities," TimesOnline, 21 October 2007, http://www.timesonline.co.uk/tol/news/uk/health/article2689787.ece (24 November 2007).

CASE 2
Sex-Selection Abortions

(BBC)—More than 10 [million] female births in India may have been lost to abortion and sex selection in the past 20 years, according to medical research.

Researchers in India and Canada for the *Lancet* journal said prenatal selection and selective abortion was causing the loss of 500,000 girls a year.

Their research was based on a national survey of 1.1 [million] households in 1998.

The researchers said the "girl deficit" was more common among educated women but did not vary according to religion.

The unusual gender balance in India has been known about for some time.

In most countries, women slightly outnumber men, but separate research for the year 2001 showed that for every 1,000 male babies born in India, there were just 933 girls.

The latest research is by Prabhat Jha of St Michael's Hospital at the University of Toronto, Canada, and Rajesh Kumar of the Postgraduate Institute of Medical Research in Chandigarh, India.

They found that there was an increasing tendency to select boys when previous children had been girls.

In cases where the preceding child was a girl, the ratio of girls to boys in the next birth was 759 to 1,000.

This fell even further when the two preceding children were both girls. Then the ratio for the third child born was just 719 girls to 1,000 boys.

However, for a child following the birth of a male child, the gender ratio was roughly equal.

Prabhat Jha said conservative estimates in the research suggested half a million girls were being lost each year.

"If this practice has been common for most of the past two decades since access to ultrasound became widespread, then a figure of 10 [million] missing female births would not be unreasonable."

Sex selective abortions have been banned in India for more than a decade.

Experts in India say female foeticide is mostly linked to socio-economic factors.

It is an idea that many say carries over from the time India was a predominantly agrarian society where boys were considered an extra pair of hands on the farm.

The girl child has traditionally been considered inferior and a liability—a bride's dowry can cripple a poor family financially.

The BBC's Jill McGivering says the problem is complicated by advances in technology. Ultrasound machines must be officially registered but many are now so light and portable, they are hard to monitor.

Although doctors in India must not tell couples the sex of a foetus, in practice, some just use coded signals instead, our correspondent says.

Last year the well-known religious leader and social activist, Swami Agnivesh, began a campaign across five northern and western states against female foeticide.

"There's no other form of violence that's more painful, more abhorrent, more shameful," he said.*

Are sex-selection abortions ever justified? Is the practice of "female foeticide" a form of discrimination against females? If so, can it ever be morally permissible? Explain your answers.

---

*"India 'Loses 10m Female Births,'" BBC News, 9 January 2006, http://news.bbc.co.uk/2/hi/south_asia/4592890.stm (24 November 2007).

CASE 3
Abortions and Prenatal Testing

(New York Times) Sarah Itoh, a self-described "almost-eleven-and-a-half," betrayed no trace of nervousness as she told a roomful of genetic counselors and obstetricians about herself one recent afternoon.

She likes to read, she said. Math used to be hard, but it is getting easier. She plays clarinet in her school band. She is a junior girl scout and an aunt, and she likes to organize, so her room is very clean. Last year, she won three medals in the Special Olympics.

"I am so lucky I get to do so many things," she concluded. "I just want you to know, even though I have Down syndrome, it is O.K."

Sarah's appearance at Henry Ford Hospital here is part of an unusual campaign being undertaken by parents of children with Down syndrome who worry about their future in the face of broader pre-natal testing that could sharply reduce the number of those born with the genetic condition.

Until this year, only pregnant women 35 and older were routinely tested to see if their fetuses had the extra chromosome that causes Down syndrome. As a result many couples were given the diagnosis only at birth. But under a new recommendation from the American College of Obstetricians and Gynecolo-gists, doctors have begun to offer a new, safer screen-ing procedure to all pregnant women, regardless of age.

About 90 percent of pregnant women who are given a Down syndrome diagnosis have chosen to have an abortion.

Convinced that more couples would choose to continue their pregnancies if they better appreciated what it meant to raise a child with Down syndrome, a growing group of parents is seeking to insert their own positive perspectives into a decision often dom-inated by daunting medical statistics and doctors who feel obligated to describe the difficulties of life with a disabled child.

They are pressing obstetricians to send them couples who have been given a prenatal diagnosis and inviting prospective parents into their homes to meet their children. In Massachusetts, for ex-ample, volunteers in a "first call" network linking veteran parents to new ones are now offering sup-port to couples deciding whether to continue a pregnancy.

The parent evangelists are driven by a deep-seated fear for their children's well-being in a world where there are fewer people like them. But as prenatal tests become available for a range of other perceived genetic imperfections, they may also be heralding a broader cultural skirmish over where to draw the line between preventing disability and accepting hu-man diversity.

"We want people who make this decision to know our kids," said Lucy Talbot, the president of a sup-port group here who prevailed on the hospital to give Sarah and two teenage friends an audience. "We want them to talk to us."

The focus on the unborn is new for most parent advocates, who have traditionally directed their en-ergy toward support for the born. But after broader testing was recommended in January, the subject began to hijack agendas at local support group meetings.

A dwindling Down syndrome population, which now stands at about 350,000, could mean less insti-tutional support and reduced funds for medical re-search. It could also mean a lonelier world for those who remain.

"The impact of these changes on the Down syn-drome community is going to be huge," said Dani Archer, a mother in Omaha who has set aside other Down syndrome volunteer work to strategize about how to reach prospective parents.

The 5,500 children born with Down syndrome each year in the United States suffer from mild to moderate mental retardation, are at high risk for congenital heart defects and a variety of other medi-cal problems, and have an average life expectancy of 49. As adults, some hold jobs, but many have dif-ficulty living independently.

"There are many couples who do not want to have a baby with Down syndrome," said Deborah A. Driscoll, chief of the obstetrics department at the University of Pennsylvania and a lead author of the new recommendation from the obstetricians' group. "They don't have the resources, don't have the emo-tional stamina, don't have the family support. We are recommending this testing be offered so that parents have a choice."*

Is it right for parents to have abortions to avoid giv-ing birth to a Down syndrome baby? Should society encourage such abortions to prevent disabilities or discourage them to promote a respect for human di-versity? Should the quality of a Down syndrome baby's future life be a factor in deciding whether to have the abortion? Explain your answers.

---

*Amy Harmon, "Prenatal Test Puts Down Syndrome in Hard Focus," New York Times, 9 May 2007, http://www.nytimes.com/2007/05/09/us/09down.html (24 November 2007).

FURTHER READING

Sidney Callahan, "A Case for Pro-Life Feminism," *Commonweal* 25 (April 1986), 232–38.

Philip Devine, *The Ethics of Homicide* (Ithaca, NY: Cornell University Press, 1978).

Joel Feinberg, "Abortion," in *Matters of Life and Death*, 3rd ed., ed. Tom Regan (New York: McGraw-Hill, 1993), 183-217.

Jonathan Glover, "The Sanctity of Life," in *Bioethics: An Anthology*, ed. Helga Kuhse and Peter Singer (Oxford: Blackwell, 1999), 193–202.

John Harris and Søren Holm, "Abortion," in *The Oxford Handbook of Practical Ethics*, ed. Hugh LaFollette (Oxford: Oxford University Press, 2003), 112–35.

Don Marquis, "Abortion Revisited," in *The Oxford Handbook of Bioethics*, ed. Bonnie Steinbock (Oxford: Oxford University Press, 2007), 395–415.

Jeff McMahan, *The Ethics of Killing: Problems at the Margins of Life* (New York: Oxford University Press, 2002).

Mark Murphy, "The Natural Law Tradition in Ethics," *Stanford Encyclopedia of Philosophy*, 11 March 2008, http://plato.stanford.edu/entries/natural-law-ethics (9 June 2008).

Louis P. Pojman, *Life and Death: Grappling with the Moral Dilemmas of Our Time* (Boston: Jones and Bartlett, 1992).

Louis P. Pojman and Francis J. Beckwith, eds., *The Abortion Controversy: 25 Years After Roe v. Wade: A Reader*, 2nd ed. (Belmont, CA: Wadsworth, 1998).

James Rachels, "Killing, Letting Die, and the Value of Life," in *Can Ethics Provide Answers?* (Lanham, MD: Rowman & Littlefield, 1997), 69-79.

Stephen Schwarz, *The Moral Question of Abortion* (Chicago: Loyola University Press, 1990).

Susan Sherwin, *No Longer Patient: Feminist Ethics and Health Care* (Philadelphia: Temple University Press, 1992), 108–14.

L. W. Sumner, *Abortion and Moral Theory* (Princeton, NJ: Princeton University Press, 1981).

Michael Tooley, *Abortion and Infanticide* (New York: Oxford University Press, 1983).

NOTES

1. Aristotle, *Politics* VII, 16, 1335b.

2. American College of Obstetricians and Gynecologists, *Standards for Obstetric-Gynecological Hospital Services* (Washington, DC: ACOG, August 1970), 53; American College of Obstetrics and Gynecologists, *Statement of Policy: Abortion* (Washington, DC: ACOG, August 1970). Quoted in Albert R. Jonsen, *The Birth of Bioethics* (New York: Oxford University Press), 290.

3. Figures from the American College of Obstetricians and Gynecologists, *Induced Abortion,* June 2007, www.acog.org (20 June 2007).

4. Lawrence B. Finer et al., "Reasons U.S. Women Have Abortions: Quantitative and Qualitative Perspectives," *Perspectives on Sexual and Reproductive Health* 37.3 (2005), 110–18.

5. John T. Noonan, Jr., "An Almost Absolute Value in History," in *The Morality of Abortion: Legal and Historical Perspectives,* ed. John T. Noonan, Jr. (Cambridge: Harvard University Press, 1970), 51–59.

6. Mary Anne Warren, "Abortion," in *A Companion to Bioethics,* ed. Helga Kuhse and Peter Singer (Oxford: Blackwell, 2001), 130.

7. Philip Devine, "The Scope of the Prohibition Against Killing," in *The Ethics of Homicide* (Ithaca, NY: Cornell University Press, 1978), 57.

8. Michael Tooley, "In Defense of Abortion and Infanticide," in *The Abortion Controversy,* ed. Louis P. Pojman and Francis J. Beckwith (Belmont, CA: Wadsworth, 1998), 209–33.

9. Louis P. Pojman, "Abortion: A Defense of the Personhood Argument," in *The Abortion Controversy,* ed. Pojman and Beckwith, 281.

10. Mary Anne Warren, "On the Moral and Legal Status of Abortion," *The Monist* 57.1 (1973), 43–61.

11. Mary Anne Warren, "Postscript on Infanticide," in *The Problem of Abortion,* 2nd ed., ed. Joel Feinberg (Belmont, CA: Wadsworth, 1984), 71–74.

12. Joel Feinberg, "Abortion," in *Matters of Life and Death: New Introductory Essays in Moral Philosophy,* ed. Tom Regan (New York: Random House, 1980); quoted in *The Abortion Controversy,* ed. Pojman and Beckwith, 287.

13. Judith Jarvis Thomson, "A Defense of Abortion," *Philosophy and Public Affairs* 1.1 (1971), 47–50, 54–66.

14. *Ibid.*

15. Mary Anne Warren, "Abortion," in A *Companion to Ethics,* ed. Peter Singer (Oxford: Blackwell, 1993), 303.

A Defense of Abortion

JUDITH JARVIS THOMSON

In this classic essay, Thomson argues that even if a fetus is a person at conception, at least some abortions could still be morally permissible. A fetus may have a right to life, but this right "does not guarantee having either a right to be given the use of or a right to be allowed continued use of another person's body—even if one needs it for life itself." A woman has a right not to have her body used by someone else against her will, which is essentially the case when she is pregnant due to no fault of her own (as a result of rape, for instance). The correct lesson about the unborn's right to life is not that killing a fetus is always wrong, but that killing it unjustly is always wrong.

Most opposition to abortion relies on the premise that the fetus is a human being, a person, from the moment of conception. The premise is argued for, but, as I think, not well. Take, for example, the most common argument. We are asked to notice that the development of a human being from conception through birth into childhood is continuous; then it is said that to draw a line, to choose a point in this development and say "before this point the thing is not a person, after this point it is a person" is to make an arbitrary choice, a choice for which in the nature of things no good reason can be given. It is concluded that the fetus is, or anyway that we had better say it is, a person from the moment of conception. But this conclusion does not follow. Similar things might be said about the development of an acorn into an oak tree, and it does not follow that acorns are oak trees, or that we had better say they are. Arguments of this form are sometimes called "slippery slope arguments"—the phrase is perhaps self-explanatory— and it is dismaying that opponents of abortion rely on them so heavily and uncritically.

I am inclined to agree, however, that the prospects for "drawing a line" in the development of the fetus look dim. I am inclined to think also that we shall probably have to agree that the fetus has already be-

come a human person well before birth. Indeed, it comes as a surprise when one first learns how early in its life it begins to acquire human characteristics. By the tenth week, for example, it already has a face, arms and legs, fingers and toes; it has internal organs, and brain activity is detectable.[1] On the other hand, I think that the premise is false, that the fetus is not a person from the moment of conception. A newly fertilized ovum, a newly implanted clump of cells, is no more a person than an acorn is an oak tree. But I shall not discuss any of this. For it seems to me to be of great interest to ask what happens if, for the sake of argument, we allow the premise. How, precisely, are we supposed to get from there to the conclusion that abortion is morally impermissible? Opponents of abortion commonly spend most of their time establishing that the fetus is a person, and hardly any time explaining the step from there to the impermissibility of abortion. Perhaps they think the step too simple and obvious to require much comment. Or perhaps instead they are simply being economical in argument. Many of those who defend abortion rely on the premise that the fetus is not a person, but only a bit of tissue that will become a person at birth; and why pay out more arguments than you have to? Whatever the explanation, I suggest that the step they take is neither easy nor obvious, that it calls for closer examination than it is commonly given, and that when we do give it this closer examination we shall feel inclined to reject it.

From "A Defense of Abortion," *Philosophy & Public Affairs*, vol. 1, no. 1 (Fall 1971). Copyright © 1971. Reprinted with permission of Blackwell Publishing. (Notes edited.)

I propose, then, that we grant that the fetus is a person from the moment of conception. How does the argument go from here? Something like this, I take it. Every person has a right to life. So the fetus has a right to life. No doubt the mother has a right to decide what shall happen in and to her body; everyone would grant that. But surely a person's right to life is stronger and more stringent than the mother's right to decide what happens in and to her body, and so outweighs it. So the fetus may not be killed; an abortion may not be performed.

It sounds plausible. But now let me ask you to imagine this. You wake up in the morning and find yourself back to back in bed with an unconscious violinist. A famous unconscious violinist. He has been found to have a fatal kidney ailment, and the Society of Music Lovers has canvassed all the available medical records and found that you alone have the right blood type to help. They have therefore kidnapped you, and last night the violinist's circulatory system was plugged into yours, so that your kidneys can be used to extract poisons from his blood as well as your own. The director of the hospital now tells you, "Look, we're sorry the Society of Music Lovers did this to you—we would never have permitted it if we had known. But still, they did it, and the violinist now is plugged into you. To unplug you would be to kill him. But never mind, it's only for nine months. By then he will have recovered from his ailment, and can safely be unplugged from you." Is it morally incumbent on you to accede to this situation? No doubt it would be very nice of you if you did, a great kindness. But do you *have* to accede to it? What if it were not nine months, but nine years? Or longer still? What if the director of the hospital says, "Tough luck, I agree, but you've now got to stay in bed, with the violinist plugged into you, for the rest of your life. Because remember this. All persons have a right to life, and violinists are persons. Granted you have a right to decide what happens in and to your body, but a person's right to life outweighs your right to decide what happens in and to your body. So you cannot ever be unplugged from him." I imagine you would regard this as outrageous, which suggests that something really is wrong with that plausible-sounding argument I mentioned a moment ago.

In this case, of course, you were kidnapped; you didn't volunteer for the operation that plugged the violinist into your kidneys. Can those who oppose abortion on the ground I mentioned make an exception for a pregnancy due to rape? Certainly. They can say that persons have a right to life only if they didn't come into existence because of rape; or they can say that all persons have a right to life, but that some have less of a right to life than others, in particular, that those who came into existence because of rape have less. But these statements have a rather unpleasant sound. Surely the question of whether you have a right to life at all, or how much of it you have, shouldn't turn on the question of whether or not you are the product of a rape. And in fact the people who oppose abortion on the ground I mentioned do not make this distinction, and hence do not make an exception in case of rape.

Nor do they make an exception for a case in which the mother has to spend the nine months of her pregnancy in bed. They would agree that would be a great pity, and hard on the mother; but all the same, all persons have a right to life, the fetus is a person, and so on. I suspect, in fact, that they would not make an exception for a case in which, miraculously enough, the pregnancy went on for nine years, or even the rest of the mother's life.

Some won't even make an exception for a case in which continuation of the pregnancy is likely to shorten the mother's life; they regard abortion as impermissible even to save the mother's life. Such cases are nowadays very rare, and many opponents of abortion do not accept this extreme view. All the same, it is a good place to begin: a number of points of interest come out in respect to it.

1. Let us call the view that abortion is impermissible even to save the mother's life "the extreme view." I want to suggest first that it does not issue from the argument I mentioned earlier without the addition of some fairly powerful premises. Suppose a woman has *become pregnant,* and now learns that she has a cardiac condition such that she will die if she carries the baby to term. What may be done for her? The fetus, being a person, has a right to life, but as the mother is a person too, so has she a right to life. Presumably they have an equal right to life. How is it supposed to come out that an abortion may not be performed? If mother and child have an equal right

to life, shouldn't we perhaps flip a coin? Or should we add to the mother's right to life her right to decide what happens in and to her body, which everybody seems to be ready to grant—the sum of her rights now outweighing the fetus' right to life?

The most familiar argument here is the following. We are told that performing the abortion would be directly killing[2] the child, whereas doing nothing would not be killing the mother, but only letting her die. Moreover, in killing the child, one would be killing an innocent person, for the child has committed no crime, and is not aiming at his mother's death. And then there are a variety of ways in which this might be continued. (1) But as directly killing an innocent person is always and absolutely impermissible, an abortion may not be performed. Or, (2) as directly killing an innocent person is murder, and murder is always and absolutely impermissible, an abortion may not be performed.[3] Or, (3) as one's duty to refrain from directly killing an innocent person is more stringent than one's duty to keep a person from dying, an abortion may not be performed. Or, (4) if one's only options are directly killing an innocent person or letting a person die, one must prefer letting the person die, and thus an abortion may not be performed.[4]

Some people seem to have thought that these are not further premises which must be added if the conclusion is to be reached, but that they follow from the very fact that an innocent person has a right to life.[5] But this seems to me to be a mistake, and perhaps the simplest way to show this is to bring out that while we must certainly grant that innocent persons have a right to life, the theses in (1) through (4) are all false. Take (2), for example. If directly killing an innocent person is murder, and thus is impermissible, then the mother's directly killing the innocent person inside her is murder, and thus is impermissible. But it cannot seriously be thought to be murder if the mother performs an abortion on herself to save her life. It cannot seriously be said that she *must* refrain, that she *must* sit passively by and wait for her death. Let us look again at the case of you and the violinist. There you are, in bed with the violinist, and the director of the hospital says to you, "It's all most distressing, and I deeply sympathize, but you see this is putting an additional strain on your kidneys, and

you'll be dead within the month. But you *have* to stay where you are all the same. Because unplugging you would be directly killing an innocent violinist, and that's murder, and that's impermissible." If anything in the world is true, it is that you do not commit murder, you do not do what is impermissible, if you reach around to your back and unplug yourself from that violinist to save your life.

The main focus of attention in writings on abortion has been on what a third party may or may not do in answer to a request from a woman for an abortion. This is in a way understandable. Things being as they are, there isn't much a woman can safely do to abort herself. So the question asked is what a third party may do, and what the mother may do, if it is mentioned at all, is deduced, almost as an after-thought, from what it is concluded that third parties may do. But it seems to me that to treat the matter in this way is to refuse to grant to the mother that very status of person which is so firmly insisted on for the fetus. For we cannot simply read off what a person may do from what a third party may do. Suppose you find yourself trapped in a tiny house with a growing child. I mean a very tiny house, and a rapidly growing child—you are already up against the wall of the house and in a few minutes you'll be crushed to death. The child on the other hand won't be crushed to death; if nothing is done to stop him from growing he'll be hurt, but in the end he'll simply burst open the house and walk out a free man. Now I could well understand it if a bystander were to say, "There's nothing we can do for you. We cannot choose between your life and his, we cannot be the ones to decide who is to live, we cannot intervene." But it cannot be concluded that you too can do nothing, that you cannot attack it to save your life. However innocent the child may be, you do not have to wait passively while it crushes you to death. Perhaps a pregnant woman is vaguely felt to have the status of house, to which we don't allow the right of self-defense. But if the woman houses the child, it should be remembered that she is a person who houses it.

I should perhaps stop to say explicitly that I am not claiming that people have a right to do anything whatever to save their lives. I think, rather, that there are drastic limits to the right of self-defense.

If someone threatens you with death unless you torture someone else to death, I think you have not the right, even to save your life, to do so. But the case under consideration here is very different. In our case there are only two people involved, one whose life is threatened, and one who threatens it. Both are innocent: the one who is threatened is not threatened because of any fault, the one who threatens does not threaten because of any fault. For this reason we may feel that we bystanders cannot intervene. But the person threatened can.

In sum, a woman surely can defend her life against the threat to it posed by the unborn child, even if doing so involves its death. And this shows not merely that the theses in (1) through (4) are false; it shows also that the extreme view of abortion is false, and so we need not canvass any other possible ways of arriving at it from the argument I mentioned at the outset.

2. The extreme view could of course be weakened to say that while abortion is permissible to save the mother's life, it may not be performed by a third party, but only by the mother herself. But this cannot be right either. For what we have to keep in mind is that the mother and the unborn child are not like two tenants in a small house which has, by an unfortunate mistake, been rented to both: the mother *owns* the house. The fact that she does adds to the offensiveness of deducing that the mother can do nothing from the supposition that third parties can do nothing. But it does more than this: it casts a bright light on the supposition that third parties can do nothing. Certainly it lets us see that a third party who says "I cannot choose between you" is fooling himself if he thinks this is impartiality. If Jones has found and fastened on a certain coat, which he needs to keep him from freezing, but which Smith also needs to keep him from freezing, then it is not impartiality that says "I cannot choose between you" when Smith owns the coat. Women have said again and again "This body is *my* body!" and they have reason to feel angry, reason to feel that it has been like shouting into the wind. Smith, after all, is hardly likely to bless us if we say to him, "Of course it's your coat, anybody would grant that it is. But no one may choose between you and Jones who is to have it."

We should really ask what it is that says "no one may choose" in the face of the fact that the body that houses the child is the mother's body. It may be simply a failure to appreciate this fact. But it may be something more interesting, namely the sense that one has a right to refuse to lay hands on people, even where it would be just and fair to do so, even where justice seems to require that somebody do so. Thus justice might call for somebody to get Smith's coat back from Jones, and yet you have a right to refuse to be the one to lay hands on Jones, a right to refuse to do physical violence to him. This, I think, must be granted. But then what should be said is not "no one may choose," but only "*I* cannot choose," and indeed not even this, but "*I* will not *act*," leaving it open that somebody else can or should, and in particular that anyone in a position of authority, with the job of securing people's rights, both can and should. So this is no difficulty. I have not been arguing that any given third party must accede to the mother's request that he perform an abortion to save her life, but only that he may.

I suppose that in some views of human life the mother's body is only on loan to her, the loan not being one which gives her any prior claim to it. One who held this view might well think it impartiality to say "I cannot choose." But I shall simply ignore this possibility. My own view is that if a human being has any just, prior claim to anything at all, he has a just, prior claim to his own body. And perhaps this needn't be argued for here anyway, since, as I mentioned, the arguments against abortion we are looking at do grant that the woman has a right to decide what happens in and to her body.

But although they do grant it, I have tried to show that they do not take seriously what is done in granting it. I suggest the same thing will reappear even more clearly when we turn away from cases in which the mother's life is at stake, and attend, as I propose we now do, to the vastly more common cases in which a woman wants an abortion for some less weighty reason than preserving her own life.

3. Where the mother's life is not at stake, the argument I mentioned at the outset seems to have a much stronger pull. "Everyone has a right to life, so the unborn person has a right to life." And isn't the child's right to life weightier than anything other than the mother's own right to life, which she might put forward as ground for an abortion?

This argument treats the right to life as if it were unproblematic. It is not, and this seems to me to be precisely the source of the mistake.

For we should now, at long last, ask what it comes to, to have a right to life. In some views having a right to life includes having a right to be given at least the bare minimum one needs for continued life. But suppose that what in fact *is* the bare minimum a man needs for continued life is something he has no right at all to be given? If I am sick unto death, and the only thing that will save my life is the touch of Henry Fonda's cool hand on my fevered brow, then all the same, I have no right to be given the touch of Henry Fonda's cool hand on my fevered brow. It would be frightfully nice of him to fly in from the West Coast to provide it. It would be less nice, though no doubt well meant, if my friends flew out to the West Coast and carried Henry Fonda back with them. But I have no right at all against anybody that he should do this for me. Or again, to return to the story I told earlier, the fact that for continued life that violinist needs the continued use of your kidneys does not establish that he has a right to be given the continued use of your kidneys. He certainly has no right against you that *you* should give him continued use of your kidneys. For nobody has any right to use your kidneys unless you give him such a right; and nobody has the right against you that you shall give him this right—if you do allow him to go on using your kidneys, this is a kindness on your part, and not something he can claim from you as his due. Nor has he any right against anybody else that *they* should give him continued use of your kidneys. Certainly he had no right against the Society of Music Lovers that they should plug him into you in the first place. And if you now start to unplug yourself, having learned that you will otherwise have to spend nine years in bed with him, there is nobody in the world who must try to prevent you, in order to see to it that he is given something he has a right to be given.

Some people are rather stricter about the right to life. In their view, it does not include the right to be given anything, but amounts to, and only to, the right not to be killed by anybody. But here a related difficulty arises. If everybody is to refrain from killing that violinist, then everybody must refrain from doing a great many different sorts of things. Everybody must refrain from slitting his throat, everybody must refrain from shooting him—and everybody must refrain from unplugging you from him. But does he have a right against everybody that they shall refrain from unplugging you from him? To refrain from doing this is to allow him to continue to use your kidneys. It could be argued that he has a right against us that *we* should allow him to continue to use your kidneys. That is, while he had no right against us that we should give him the use of your kidneys, it might be argued that he anyway has a right against us that we shall not now intervene and deprive him of the use of your kidneys. I shall come back to third-party interventions later. But certainly the violinist has no right against you that *you* shall allow him to continue to use your kidneys. As I said, if you do allow him to use them, it is a kindness on your part, and not something you owe him.

The difficulty I point to here is not peculiar to the right to life. It reappears in connection with all the other natural rights; and it is something which an adequate account of rights must deal with. For present purposes it is enough just to draw attention to it. But I would stress that I am not arguing that people do not have a right to life—quite to the contrary, it seems to me that the primary control we must place on the acceptability of an account of rights is that it should turn out in that account to be a truth that all persons have a right to life. I am arguing only that having a right to life does not guarantee having either a right to be given the use of or a right to be allowed continued use of another person's body—even if one needs it for life itself. So the right to life will not serve the opponents of abortion in the very simple and clear way in which they seem to have thought it would.

4. There is another way to bring out the difficulty. In the most ordinary sort of case, to deprive someone of what he has a right to is to treat him unjustly. Suppose a boy and his small brother are jointly given a box of chocolates for Christmas. If the older boy takes the box and refuses to give his brother any of the chocolates, he is unjust to him, for the brother has been given a right to half of them. But suppose that, having learned that otherwise it means nine years in bed with that violinist, you unplug yourself from him. You surely are not being unjust to him, for

you gave him no right to use your kidneys, and no one else can have given him any such right. But we have to notice that in unplugging yourself, you are killing him; and violinists, like everybody else, have a right to life, and thus in the view we were considering just now, the right not to be killed. So here you do what he supposedly has a right you shall not do, but you do not act unjustly to him in doing it.

The emendation which may be made at this point is this: the right to life consists not in the right not to be killed, but rather in the right not to be killed unjustly. This runs a risk of circularity, but never mind: it would enable us to square the fact that the violinist has a right to life with the fact that you do not act unjustly toward him in unplugging yourself, thereby killing him. For if you do not kill him unjustly, you do not violate his right to life, and so it is no wonder you do him no injustice.

But if this emendation is accepted, the gap in the argument against abortion stares us plainly in the face: it is by no means enough to show that the fetus is a person, and to remind us that all persons have a right to life—we need to be shown also that killing the fetus violates its right to life, i.e., that abortion is unjust killing. And is it?

I suppose we may take it as a datum that in a case of pregnancy due to rape the mother has not given the unborn person a right to the use of her body for food and shelter. Indeed, in what pregnancy could it be supposed that the mother has given the unborn person such a right? It is not as if there were unborn persons drifting about the world, to whom a woman who wants a child says "I invite you in."

But it might be argued that there are other ways one can have acquired a right to the use of another person's body than by having been invited to use it by that person. Suppose a woman voluntarily indulges in intercourse, knowing of the chance it will issue in pregnancy, and then she does become pregnant; is she not in part responsible for the presence, in fact the very existence, of the unborn person inside her? No doubt she did not invite it in. But doesn't her partial responsibility for its being there itself give it a right to the use of her body?[6] If so, then her aborting it would be more like the boy's taking away the chocolates, and less like your unplugging yourself from the violinist—doing so would be depriving it

of what it does have a right to, and thus would be doing it an injustice.

And then, too, it might be asked whether or not she can kill it even to save her own life: If she voluntarily called it into existence, how can she now kill it, even in self-defense?

The first thing to be said about this is that it is something new. Opponents of abortion have been so concerned to make out the independence of the fetus, in order to establish that it has a right to life, just as its mother does, that they have tended to overlook the possible support they might gain from making out that the fetus is *dependent* on the mother, in order to establish that she has a special kind of responsibility for it, a responsibility that gives it rights against her which are not possessed by any independent person—such as an ailing violinist who is a stranger to her.

On the other hand, this argument would give the unborn person a right to its mother's body only if her pregnancy resulted from a voluntary act, undertaken in full knowledge of the chance a pregnancy might result from it. It would leave out entirely the unborn person whose existence is due to rape. Pending the availability of some further argument, then, we would be left with the conclusion that unborn persons whose existence is due to rape have no right to the use of their mothers' bodies, and thus that aborting them is not depriving them of anything they have a right to and hence is not unjust killing.

And we should also notice that it is not at all plain that this argument really does go even as far as it purports to. For there are cases and cases, and the details make a difference. If the room is stuffy, and I therefore open a window to air it, and a burglar climbs in, it would be absurd to say, "Ah, now he can stay, she's given him a right to the use of her house—for she is partially responsible for his presence there, having voluntarily done what enabled him to get in, in full knowledge that there are such things as burglars, and that burglars burgle." It would be still more absurd to say this if I had had bars installed outside my windows, precisely to prevent burglars from getting in, and a burglar got in only because of a defect in the bars. It remains equally absurd if we imagine it is not a burglar who climbs in, but an innocent person who blunders or falls in. Again, suppose it were like this: people-seeds drift about in the air like pollen, and if you open your windows, one may drift in and take root in your carpets or upholstery. You don't want children, so you fix up your windows with fine mesh screens, the very best you can buy. As can happen, however, and on very, very rare occasions does happen, one of the screens is defective; and a seed drifts in and takes root. Does the person-plant who now develops have a right to the use of your house? Surely not—despite the fact that you voluntarily opened your windows, you knowingly kept carpets and upholstered furniture, and you knew that screens were sometimes defective. Someone may argue that you are responsible for its rooting, that it does have a right to your house, because after all you *could* have lived out your life with bare floors and furniture, or with sealed windows and doors. But this won't do—for by the same token anyone can avoid a pregnancy due to rape by having a hysterectomy, or anyway by never leaving home without a (reliable!) army.

It seems to me that the argument we are looking at can establish at most that there are *some* cases in which the unborn person has a right to the use of its mother's body, and therefore *some* cases in which abortion is unjust killing. There is room for much discussion and argument as to precisely which, if any. But I think we should sidestep this issue and leave it open, for at any rate the argument certainly does not establish that all abortion is unjust killing.

5. There is room for yet another argument here, however. We surely must all grant that there may be cases in which it would be morally indecent to detach a person from your body at the cost of his life. Suppose you learn that what the violinist needs is not nine years of your life, but only one hour: all you need do to save his life is to spend one hour in that bed with him. Suppose also that letting him use your kidneys for that one hour would not affect your health in the slightest. Admittedly you were kidnapped. Admittedly you did not give anyone permission to plug him into you. Nevertheless it seems to me plain you *ought* to allow him to use your kidneys for that hour—it would be indecent to refuse.

Again, suppose pregnancy lasted only an hour, and constituted no threat to life or health. And suppose that a woman becomes pregnant as a result of rape. Admittedly she did not voluntarily do anything to bring about the existence of a child. Admittedly she did nothing at all which would give the unborn person a right to the use of her body. All the same it might well be said, as in the newly emended violinist story, that she *ought* to allow it to remain for that hour—that it would be indecent in her to refuse.

Now some people are inclined to use the term "right" in such a way that it follows from the fact that you ought to allow a person to use your body for the hour he needs, that he has a right to use your body for the hour he needs, even though he has not been given that right by any person or act. They may say that it follows also that if you refuse, you act unjustly toward him. This use of the term is perhaps so common that it cannot be called wrong; nevertheless it seems to me to be an unfortunate loosening of what we would do better to keep a tight rein on. Suppose that box of chocolates I mentioned earlier had not been given to both boys jointly, but was given only to the older boy. There he sits, stolidly eating his way through the box, his small brother watching enviously. Here we are likely to say "You ought not to be so mean. You ought to give your brother some of those chocolates." My own view is that it just does not follow from the truth of this that the brother has any right to any of the chocolates. If the boy refuses to give his brother any, he is greedy, stingy, callous—but not unjust. I suppose that the people I have in mind will say it does follow that the brother has a right to some of the chocolates, and thus that the boy does act unjustly if he refuses to give his brother any. But the effect of saying this is to obscure what we should keep distinct, namely the difference between the boy's refusal in this case and the boy's refusal in the earlier case, in which the box was given to both boys jointly, and in which the small brother thus had what was from any point of view clear title to half.

A further objection to so using the term "right" that from the fact that A ought to do a thing for B, it follows that B has a right against A that A do it for him, is that it is going to make the question of whether or not a man has a right to a thing turn on how easy it is to provide him with it; and this seems not merely unfortunate, but morally unacceptable. Take the case of Henry Fonda again. I said earlier that I had no right to the touch of his cool hand on my fevered brow, even though I needed it to save my life. I said it would be frightfully nice of him to fly in from the West Coast to provide me with it, but that I had no right against him that he should do so. But suppose he isn't on the West Coast. Suppose he has only to walk across the room, place a hand briefly on my brow—and lo, my life is saved. Then surely he ought to do it, it would be indecent to refuse. Is it to be said "Ah, well, it follows that in this case she has a right to the touch of his hand on her brow, and so it would be an injustice in him to refuse"? So that I have a right to it when it is easy for him to provide it, though no right when it's hard? It's rather a shocking idea that anyone's rights should fade away and disappear as it gets harder and harder to accord them to him.

So my own view is that even though you ought to let the violinist use your kidneys for the one hour he needs, we should not conclude that he has a right to do so—we should say that if you refuse, you are, like the boy who owns all the chocolates and will give none away, self-centered and callous, indecent in fact, but not unjust. And similarly, that even supposing a case in which a woman pregnant due to rape ought to allow the unborn person to use her body for the hour he needs, we should not conclude that he has a right to do so; we should conclude that she is self-centered, callous, indecent, but not unjust, if she refuses. The complaints are no less grave; they are just different. However, there is no need to insist on this point. If anyone does wish to deduce "he has a right" from "you ought," then all the same he must surely grant that there are cases in which it is not morally required of you that you allow that violinist to use your kidneys, and in which he does not have a right to use them, and in which you do not do him an injustice if you refuse. And so also for mother and unborn child. Except in such cases as the unborn person has a right to demand it—and we were leaving open the possibility that there may be such cases—nobody is morally *required* to make large sacrifices, of health, of all other interests and concerns, of all other duties and commitments, for nine years, or even for nine months, in order to keep another person alive.

6. We have in fact to distinguish between two kinds of Samaritan: the Good Samaritan and what we might call the Minimally Decent Samaritan. The

story of the Good Samaritan, you will remember, goes like this:

> A certain man went down from Jerusalem to Jericho, and fell among thieves, which stripped him of his raiment, and wounded him, and departed, leaving him half dead.
>
> And by chance there came down a certain priest that way; and when he saw him, he passed by on the other side.
>
> And likewise a Levite, when he was at the place, came and looked on him, and passed by on the other side.
>
> But a certain Samaritan, as he journeyed, came where he was; and when he saw him he had compassion on him.
>
> And went to him, and bound up his wounds, pouring in oil and wine, and set him on his own beast, and brought him to an inn, and took care of him.
>
> And on the morrow, when he departed, he took out two pence, and gave them to the host, and said unto him, "Take care of him; and whatsoever thou spendest more, when I come again, I will repay thee." (Luke 10:30–35)

The Good Samaritan went out of his way, at some cost to himself, to help one in need of it. We are not told what the options were, that is, whether or not the priest and the Levite could have helped by doing less than the Good Samaritan did, but assuming they could have, then the fact they did nothing at all shows they were not even Minimally Decent Samaritans, not because they were not Samaritans, but because they were not even minimally decent.

These things are a matter of degree, of course, but there is a difference, and it comes out perhaps most clearly in the story of Kitty Genovese, who, as you will remember, was murdered while thirty-eight people watched or listened, and did nothing at all to help her. A Good Samaritan would have rushed out to give direct assistance against the murderer. Or perhaps we had better allow that it would have been a Splendid Samaritan who did this, on the ground that it would have involved a risk of death for himself. But the thirty-eight not only did not do this, they did not even trouble to pick up a phone to call the police. Minimally Decent Samaritanism would call for doing at least that, and their not having done it was monstrous.

After telling the story of the Good Samaritan, Jesus said "Go, and do thou likewise." Perhaps he meant that we are morally required to act as the Good Samaritan did. Perhaps he was urging people to do more than is morally required of them. At all events it seems plain that it was not morally required of any of the thirty-eight that he rush out to give direct assistance at the risk of his own life, and that it is not morally required of anyone that he give long stretches of his life—nine years or nine months—to sustaining the life of a person who has no special right (we were leaving open the possibility of this) to demand it.

Indeed, with one rather striking class of exceptions, no one in any country in the world is *legally* required to do anywhere near as much as this for anyone else. The class of exceptions is obvious. My main concern here is not the state of the law in respect to abortion, but it is worth drawing attention to the fact that in no state in this country is any man compelled by law to be even a Minimally Decent Samaritan to any person; there is no law under which charges could be brought against the thirty-eight who stood by while Kitty Genovese died. By contrast, in most states in this country women are compelled by law to be not merely Minimally Decent Samaritans, but Good Samaritans to unborn persons inside them. This doesn't by itself settle anything one way or the other, because it may well be argued that there should be laws in this country—as there are in many European countries—compelling at least Minimally Decent Samaritanism.[7] But it does show that there is a gross injustice in the existing state of the law. And it shows also that the groups currently working against liberalization of abortion laws, in fact working toward having it declared unconstitutional for a state to permit abortion, had better start working for the adoption of Good Samaritan laws generally, or earn the charge that they are acting in bad faith.

I should think, myself, that Minimally Decent Samaritan laws would be one thing, Good Samaritan laws quite another, and in fact highly improper. But we are not here concerned with the law. What we should ask is not whether anybody should be compelled by law to be a Good Samaritan, but whether we must accede to a situation in which somebody is being compelled—by nature, perhaps—to be a Good

Samaritan. We have, in other words, to look now at third-party interventions. I have been arguing that no person is morally required to make large sacrifices to sustain the life of another who has no right to demand them, and this even where the sacrifices do not include life itself; we are not morally required to be Good Samaritans or anyway Very Good Samaritans to one another. But what if a man cannot extricate himself from such a situation? What if he appeals to us to extricate him? It seems to me plain that there are cases in which we can, cases in which a Good Samaritan would extricate him. There you are, you were kidnapped, and nine years in bed with that violinist lie ahead of you. You have your own life to lead. You are sorry, but you simply cannot see giving up so much of your life to the sustaining of his. You cannot extricate yourself, and ask us to do so. I should have thought that—in light of his having no right to the use of your body—it was obvious that we do not have to accede to your being forced to give up so much. We can do what you ask. There is no injustice to the violinist in our doing so.

7. Following the lead of the opponents of abortion, I have throughout been speaking of the fetus merely as a person, and what I have been asking is whether or not the argument we began with, which proceeds only from the fetus' being a person, really does establish its conclusion. I have argued that it does not.

But of course there are arguments and arguments, and it may be said that I have simply fastened on the wrong one. It may be said that what is important is not merely the fact that the fetus is a person, but that it is a person for whom the woman has a special kind of responsibility issuing from the fact that she is its mother. And it might be argued that all my analogies are therefore irrelevant—for you do not have that special kind of responsibility for that violinist, Henry Fonda does not have that special kind of responsibility for me. And our attention might be drawn to the fact that men and women both *are* compelled by law to provide support for their children.

I have in effect dealt (briefly) with this argument in section 4; but a (still briefer) recapitulation now may be in order. Surely we do not have any such "special responsibility" for a person unless we have assumed it, explicitly or implicitly. If a set of parents do not try to prevent pregnancy, do not obtain an abortion, and then at the time of birth of the child do not put it out for adoption, but rather take it home with them, then they have assumed responsibility for it, they have given it rights, and they cannot *now* withdraw support from it at the cost of its life because they now find it difficult to go on providing for it. But if they have taken all reasonable precautions against having a child, they do not simply by virtue of their biological relationship to the child who comes into existence have a special responsibility for it. They may wish to assume responsibility for it, or they may not wish to. And I am suggesting that if assuming responsibility for it would require large sacrifices, then they may refuse. A Good Samaritan would not refuse—or anyway, a Splendid Samaritan, if the sacrifices that had to be made were enormous. But then so would a Good Samaritan assume responsibility for that violinist; so would Henry Fonda, if he is a Good Samaritan, fly in from the West Coast and assume responsibility for me.

8. My argument will be found unsatisfactory on two counts by many of those who want to regard abortion as morally permissible. First, while I do argue that abortion is not impermissible, I do not argue that it is always permissible. There may well be cases in which carrying the child to term requires only Minimally Decent Samaritanism of the mother, and this is a standard we must not fall below. I am inclined to think it a merit of my account precisely that it does *not* give a general yes or a general no. It allows for and supports our sense that, for example, a sick and desperately frightened fourteen-year-old schoolgirl, pregnant due to rape, may *of course* choose abortion, and that any law which rules this out is an insane law. And it also allows for and supports our sense that in other cases resort to abortion is even positively indecent. It would be indecent in the woman to request an abortion, and indecent in a doctor to perform it, if she is in her seventh month, and wants the abortion just to avoid the nuisance of postponing a trip abroad. The very fact that the arguments I have been drawing attention to treat all cases of abortion, or even all cases of abortion in which the mother's life is not at stake, as morally on a par ought to have made them suspect at the outset.

Secondly, while I am arguing for the permissibility of abortion in some cases, I am not arguing for the right to secure the death of the unborn child. It is easy to confuse these two things in that up to a certain point in the life of the fetus it is not able to survive outside the mother's body; hence removing it from her body guarantees its death. But they are importantly different. I have argued that you are not morally required to spend nine months in bed, sustaining the life of that violinist; but to say this is by no means to say that if, when you unplug yourself, there is a miracle and he survives, you then have a right to turn round and slit his throat. You may detach yourself even if this costs him his life; you have no right to be guaranteed his death, by some other means, if unplugging yourself does not kill him. There are some people who will feel dissatisfied by this feature of my argument. A woman may be utterly devastated by the thought of a child, a bit of herself, put out for adoption and never seen or heard of again. She may therefore want not merely that the child be detached from her, but more, that it die. Some opponents of abortion are inclined to regard this as beneath contempt—thereby showing insensitivity to what is surely a powerful source of despair. All the same, I agree that the desire for the child's death is not one which anybody may gratify, should it turn out to be possible to detach the child alive.

At this place, however, it should be remembered that we have only been pretending throughout that the fetus is a human being from the moment of conception. A very early abortion is surely not the killing of a person, and so is not dealt with by anything I have said here.

NOTES
I am very much indebted to James Thomson for discussion, criticism, and many helpful suggestions.
1. Daniel Callahan, *Abortion: Law, Choice and Morality* (New York, 1970), p. 373. This book gives a fascinating survey of the available information on abortion. The Jewish tradition is surveyed in David M. Feldman, *Birth Control in Jewish Law* (New York, 1968), Part 5, the Catholic tradition in John T. Noonan, Jr., "An Almost Absolute Value in History," in *The Morality of Abortion*, ed. John T. Noonan, Jr. (Cambridge, Mass., 1970).
2. The term "direct" in the arguments I refer to is a technical one. Roughly, what is meant by "direct killing" is either kill-

ing as an end in itself, or killing as a means to some end, for example, the end of saving someone else's life. See note 5 for an example of its use.

3. Cf. *Encyclical Letter of Pope Pius XI on Christian Marriage*, St. Paul Editions (Boston, n.d.), p. 32: "however much we may pity the mother whose health and even life is gravely imperiled in the performance of the duty allotted to her by nature, nevertheless what could ever be a sufficient reason for excusing in any way the direct murder of the innocent? This is precisely what we are dealing with here." Noonan (*The Morality of Abortion*, p. 43) reads this as follows: "What cause can ever avail to excuse in any way the direct killing of the innocent? For it is a question of that."

4. The thesis in (4) is in an interesting way weaker than those in (1), (2), and (3): they rule out abortion even in cases in which both mother *and* child will die if the abortion is not performed. By contrast, one who held the view expressed in (4) could consistently say that one needn't prefer letting two persons die to killing one.

5. Cf. the following passage from Pius XII, *Address to the Italian Catholic Society of Midwives*: "The baby in the maternal breast has the right to life immediately from God.—Hence there is no man, no human authority, no science, no medical, eugenic, social, economic or moral 'indication' which can establish or grant a valid juridical ground for a direct deliberate position of an innocent human life, that is a disposition which looks to its destruction either as an end or as a means to another end perhaps in itself not illicit.—The baby, still not born, is a man in the same degree and for the same reason as the mother" (quoted in Noonan, *The Morality of Abortion*, p. 45).

6. The need for a discussion of this argument was brought home to me by members of the Society for Ethical and Legal Philosophy, to whom this paper was originally presented.

7. For a discussion of the difficulties involved, and a survey of the European experience with such laws, see *The Good Samaritan and the Law*, ed. James M. Ratcliffe (New York, 1966).

Why Abortion Is Immoral

DON MARQUIS

Marquis first identifies what it is that makes murder wrong, then applies this understanding to the case of abortion. He argues that murdering someone is wrong because it robs him or her of a future—a loss of all possible "experiences, activities, projects, and enjoyments." Likewise, abortion is almost always wrong because it deprives the fetus of all prospects of such future experiencing and being.

The view that abortion is, with rare exceptions, seriously immoral has received little support in the recent philosophical literature. No doubt most philosophers affiliated with secular institutions of higher education believe that the anti-abortion position is either a symptom of irrational religious dogma or a conclusion generated by seriously confused philosophical argument. The purpose of this essay is to undermine this general belief. This essay sets out an argument that purports to show, as well as any argument in ethics can show, that abortion is, except possibly in rare cases, seriously immoral, that it is in the same moral category as killing an innocent adult human being.

From *Journal of Philosophy*, LXXXVI, 4 (April 1989), pp. 183–202. Reprinted with permission of The Journal of Philosophy, Inc. and the author.

The argument is based on a major assumption. Many of the most insightful and careful writers on the ethics of abortion—such as Joel Feinberg, Michael Tooley, Mary Anne Warren, H. Tristram Engelhardt, Jr, L. W. Sumner, John T. Noonan, Jr, and Philip Devine[1]—believe that whether or not abortion is morally permissible stands or falls on whether or not a fetus is the sort of being whose life it is seriously wrong to end. The argument of this essay will assume, but not argue, that they are correct.

Also, this essay will neglect issues of great importance to a complete ethics of abortion. Some anti-abortionists will allow that certain abortions, such as abortion before implantation or abortion when the life of a woman is threatened by a pregnancy or abortion after rape, may be morally permissible. This essay will not explore the casuistry of these hard cases. The purpose of this essay is to develop a general argument for the claim that the overwhelming majority of deliberate abortions are seriously immoral.

I

A sketch of standard anti-abortion and pro-choice arguments exhibits how those arguments possess certain symmetries that explain why partisans of those positions are so convinced of the correctness of their own positions, why they are not successful in convincing their opponents, and why, to others, this issue seems to be unresolvable. An analysis of the nature of this standoff suggests a strategy for surmounting it.

Consider the way a typical anti-abortionist argues. She will argue or assert that life is present from the moment of conception or that fetuses look like babies or that fetuses possess a characteristic such as a genetic code that is both necessary and sufficient for being human. Anti-abortionists seem to believe that (1) the truth of all of these claims is quite obvious, and (2) establishing any of these claims is sufficient to show that abortion is morally akin to murder.

A standard pro-choice strategy exhibits similarities. The pro-choicer will argue or assert that fetuses are not persons or that fetuses are not rational agents or that fetuses are not social beings. Pro-choicers seem to believe that (1) the truth of any of these claims is quite obvious, and (2) establishing any of these claims is sufficient to show that an abortion is not a wrongful killing.

In fact, both the pro-choice and the anti-abortion claims do seem to be true, although the "it looks like a baby" claim is more difficult to establish the earlier the pregnancy. We seem to have a standoff. How can it be resolved?

As everyone who has taken a bit of logic knows, if any of these arguments concerning abortion is a good argument, it requires not only some claim characterizing fetuses, but also some general moral principle that ties a characteristic of fetuses to having or not having the right to life or to some other moral characteristic that will generate the obligation or the lack of obligation not to end the life of a fetus. Accordingly, the arguments of the anti-abortionist and the pro-choicer need a bit of filling in to be regarded as adequate.

Note what each partisan will say. The anti-abortionist will claim that her position is supported by such generally accepted moral principles as "It is always prima facie seriously wrong to take a human life" or "It is always prima facie seriously wrong to end the life of a baby." Since these are generally accepted moral principles, her position is certainly not obviously wrong. The pro-choicer will claim that her position is supported by such plausible moral principles as "Being a person is what gives an individual intrinsic moral worth" or "It is only seriously prima facie wrong to take the life of a member of the human community." Since these are generally accepted moral principles, the pro-choice position is certainly not obviously wrong. Unfortunately, we have again arrived at a standoff.

Now, how might one deal with this standoff? The standard approach is to try to show how the moral principles of one's opponent lose their plausibility under analysis. It is easy to see how this is possible. On the one hand, the anti-abortionist will defend a moral principle concerning the wrongness of killing which tends to be broad in scope in order that even fetuses at an early stage of pregnancy will fail under it. The problem with broad principles is that they often embrace too much. In this particular instance, the principle "It is always prima facie wrong to take a human life" seems to entail that it is wrong to end the existence of a living human cancer-cell culture, on the grounds that the culture is both living and human. Therefore, it seems that the anti-abortionist's favored principle is too broad.

On the other hand, the pro-choicer wants to find a moral principle concerning the wrongness of killing which tends to be narrow in scope in order that fetuses will *not* fall under it. The problem with narrow principles is that they often do not embrace enough. Hence, the needed principles such as "It is prima facie seriously wrong to kill only persons" or "It is prima facie wrong to kill only rational agents" do not explain why it is wrong to kill infants or young children or the severely retarded or even perhaps the severely mentally ill. Therefore, we seem again to have a standoff. The anti-abortionist charges, not unreasonably, that pro-choice principles concerning killing are too narrow to be acceptable; the pro-choicer charges, not unreasonably, that anti-abortionist principles concerning killing are too broad to be acceptable.

Attempts by both sides to patch up the difficulties in their positions run into further difficulties. The anti-abortionist will try to remove the problem in her position by reformulating her principle concerning killing in terms of human beings. Now we end up with: "It is always prima facie seriously wrong to end the life of a human being." This principle has the advantage of avoiding the problem of the human cancer-cell culture counterexample. But this advantage is purchased at a high price. For although it is clear that a fetus is both human and alive, it is not at all clear that a fetus is a human *being*. There is at least something to be said for the view that something becomes a human being only after a process of development, and that therefore first trimester fetuses and perhaps all fetuses are not yet human beings. Hence, the anti-abortionist, by this move, has merely exchanged one problem for another.[2]

The pro-choicer fares no better. She may attempt to find reasons why killing infants, young children, and the severely retarded is wrong which are independent of her major principle that is supposed to explain the wrongness of taking human life, but which will not also make abortion immoral. This is no easy task. Appeals to social utility will seem satisfactory only to those who resolve not to think of the enormous difficulties with a utilitarian account of the wrongness of killing and the significant social costs of preserving the lives of the unproductive.[3] A pro-choice strategy that extends the definition of "person" to infants or even to young children seems just as arbitrary as an anti-abortion strategy that extends the definition of "human being" to fetuses. Again, we find symmetries in the two positions and we arrive at a standoff.

There are even further problems that reflect symmetries in the two positions. In addition to counterexample problems, or the arbitrary application problems that can be exchanged for them, the standard anti-abortionist principle "It is prima facie seriously wrong to kill a human being," or one of its variants, can be objected to on the grounds of ambiguity. If "human being" is taken to be a *biological* category, then the anti-abortionist is left with the problem of explaining why a merely biological category should make a moral difference. Why, it is asked, is it any more reasonable to base a moral conclusion on the number of chromosomes in one's cells than on the color of one's skin?[4] If "human being," on the other hand, is taken to be a *moral* category, then the claim that a fetus is a human being cannot be taken to be a premise in the anti-abortion argument, for it is precisely what needs to be established. Hence, either the anti-abortionist's main category is a morally irrelevant, merely biological category, or it is of no use to the anti-abortionist in establishing (noncircularly, of course) that abortion is wrong.

Although this problem with the anti-abortionist position is often noticed, it is less often noticed that the pro-choice position suffers from an analogous problem. The principle "Only persons have the right to life" also suffers from an ambiguity. The term "person" is typically defined in terms of psychological characteristics, although there will certainly be disagreement concerning which characteristics are most important. Supposing that this matter can be settled, the pro-choicer is left with the problem of explaining why *psychological* characteristics should make a *moral* difference. If the pro-choicer should attempt to deal with this problem by claiming that an explanation is not necessary, that in fact we do treat such a cluster of psychological properties as having moral significance, the sharp-witted anti-abortionist should have a ready response. We do treat being both living and human as having moral significance. If it is legitimate for the pro-choicer to demand that the anti-abortionist provide an explanation of the connection between the biological character of being a human being and the wrongness of being killed (even though people accept this connection), then it is legitimate for the anti-abortionist to demand that the pro-choicer provide an explanation of the connection between psychological criteria for being a person and the wrongness of being killed (even though that connection is accepted).[5]

Feinberg has attempted to meet this objection (he calls psychological personhood "commonsense personhood"):

The characteristics that confer commonsense personhood are not arbitrary bases for rights and duties, such as race, sex or species membership; rather they are traits that make sense out of rights and duties and without which those moral attributes would have no point or function. It is because people are conscious; have a sense of their personal identities; have plans, goals, and projects; experience emotions; are liable to pains, anxieties, and frustrations; can reason and bargain, and so on—it is because of these attributes that people have values and interests, desires and expectations of their own, including a stake in their own futures, and a personal well-being of a sort we cannot ascribe to unconscious or nonrational beings. Because of their developed capacities they can assume duties and responsibilities and can have and make claims on one another. Only because of their sense of self, their life plans, their value hierarchies, and their stakes in their own futures can they be ascribed fundamental rights. There is nothing arbitrary about these linkages. ("Abortion," p. 270)

The plausible aspects of this attempt should not be taken to obscure its implausible features. There is a great deal to be said for the view that being a psychological person under some description is a necessary condition for having duties. One cannot have a duty unless one is capable of behaving morally, and a being's capability of behaving morally will require having a certain psychology. It is far from obvious, however, that having rights entails consciousness or rationality, as Feinberg suggests. We speak of the rights of the severely retarded or the severely mentally ill, yet some of these persons are not rational. We speak of the rights of the temporarily unconscious. The New Jersey Supreme Court based their decision in the Quinlan case on Karen Ann Quinlan's right to privacy, and she was known to be permanently unconscious at that time. Hence, Feinberg's claim that having rights entails being conscious is, on its face, obviously false.

Of course, it might not make sense to attribute rights to a being that would never in its natural history have certain psychological traits. This modest connection between psychological personhood and moral personhood will create a place for Karen Ann Quinlan and the temporarily unconscious. But then it makes a place for fetuses also. Hence, it does not serve Feinberg's pro-choice purposes. Accordingly, it seems that the pro-choicer will have as much difficulty bridging the gap between psychological personhood and personhood in the moral sense as the anti-abortionist has bridging the gap between being a biological human being and being a human being in the moral sense.

Furthermore, the pro-choicer cannot any more escape her problem by making person a purely moral category than the anti-abortionist could escape by the analogous move. For if person is a moral category, then the pro-choicer is left without the resources for establishing (noncircularly, of course) the claim that a fetus is not a person, which is an essential premise in her argument. Again, we have both a symmetry and a standoff between pro-choice and anti-abortion views.

Passions in the abortion debate run high. There are both plausibilities and difficulties with the standard positions. Accordingly, it is hardly surprising that partisans of either side embrace with fervor the moral generalizations that support the conclusions they preanalytically favor, and reject with disdain the moral generalizations of their opponents as being subject to inescapable difficulties. It is easy to believe that the counterexamples to one's own moral principles are merely temporary difficulties that will dissolve in the wake of further philosophical research, and that the counterexamples to the principles of one's opponents are as straightforward as the contradiction between *A* and *O* propositions in traditional logic. This might suggest to an impartial observer (if there are any) that the abortion issue is unresolvable.

There is a way out of this apparent dialectical quandary. The moral generalizations of both sides are not quite correct. The generalizations hold for the most part, for the usual cases. This suggests that they are all *accidental* generalizations, that the moral claims made by those on both sides of the dispute do not touch on the *essence* of the matter.

This use of the distinction between essence and accident is not meant to invoke obscure metaphysical categories. Rather, it is intended to reflect the rather atheoretical nature of the abortion discussion. If the generalization a partisan in the abortion dispute adopts were derived from the reason why ending the life of a human being is wrong, then there could not be exceptions to that generalization unless some special case obtains in which there are even more powerful countervailing reasons. Such generalizations would not be merely accidental generalizations; they would point to, or be based upon, the essence of the wrongness of killing, what it is that makes killing wrong. All this suggests that a necessary condition of resolving the abortion controversy is a more theoretical account of the wrongness of killing. After all, if we merely believe, but do not understand, why killing adult human beings such as ourselves is wrong, how could we conceivably show that abortion is either immoral or permissible?

II

In order to develop such an account, we can start from the following unproblematic assumption concerning our own case: it is wrong to kill *us*. Why is it wrong? Some answers can be easily eliminated. It might be said that what makes killing us wrong is that a killing brutalizes the one who kills. But the brutalization consists of being inured to the performance of an act that is hideously immoral; hence, the brutalization does not explain the immorality. It might be said that what makes killing us wrong is the great loss others would experience due to our absence. Although such hubris is understandable, such an explanation does not account for the wrongness of killing hermits, or those whose lives are relatively independent and whose friends find it easy to make new friends.

A more obvious answer is better. What primarily makes killing wrong is neither its effect on the murderer nor its effect on the victim's friends and relatives, but its effect on the victim. The loss of one's life is one of the greatest losses one can suffer. The loss of one's life deprives one of all the experiences, activities, projects, and enjoyments that would otherwise have constituted one's future. Therefore, killing someone is wrong, primarily because the killing inflicts (one of) the greatest possible losses on the victim. To describe this as the loss of life can be misleading, however. The change in my biological state does not by itself make killing me wrong. The effect of the loss of my biological life is the loss to me of all those activities, projects, experiences, and enjoyments which would otherwise have constituted my future personal life. These activities, projects, experiences, and enjoyments are either valuable for their own sakes or are means to something else that is valuable for its own sake. Some parts of my future

are not valued by me now, but will come to be valued by me as I grow older and as my values and capacities change. When I am killed, I am deprived both of what I now value which would have been part of my future personal life, but also what I would come to value. Therefore, when I die, I am deprived of all of the value of my future. Inflicting this loss on me is ultimately what makes killing me wrong. This being the case, it would seem that what makes killing *any* adult human being prima facie seriously wrong is the loss of his or her future.[6]

How should this rudimentary theory of the wrongness of killing be evaluated? It cannot be faulted for deriving an "ought" from an "is," for it does not. The analysis assumes that killing me (or you, reader) is prima facie seriously wrong. The point of the analysis is to establish which natural property ultimately explains the wrongness of the killing, given that it is wrong. A natural property will ultimately explain the wrongness of killing, only if (1) the explanation fits with our intuitions about the matter and (2) there is no other natural property that provides the basis for a better explanation of the wrongness of killing. This analysis rests on the intuition that what makes killing a particular human or animal wrong is what it does to that particular human or animal. What makes killing wrong is some natural effect or other of the killing. Some would deny this. For instance, a divine-command theorist in ethics would deny it. Surely this denial is, however, one of those features of divine-command theory which renders it so implausible.

The claim that what makes killing wrong is the loss of the victim's future is directly supported by two considerations. In the first place, this theory explains why we regard killing as one of the worst of crimes. Killing is especially wrong, because it deprives the victim of more than perhaps any other crime. In the second place, people with AIDS or cancer who know they are dying believe, of course, that dying is a very bad thing for them. They believe that the loss of a future to them that they would otherwise have experienced is what makes their premature death a very bad thing for them. A better theory of the wrongness of killing would require a different natural property associated with killing which better fits with the attitudes of the dying. What could it be?

The view that what makes killing wrong is the loss to the victim of the value of the victim's future gains additional support when some of its implications are examined. In the first place, it is incompatible with the view that it is wrong to kill only beings who are biologically human. It is possible that there exists a different species from another planet whose members have a future like ours. Since having a future like that is what makes killing someone wrong, this theory entails that it would be wrong to kill members of such a species. Hence, this theory is opposed to the claim that only life that is biologically human has great moral worth, a claim which many anti-abortionists have seemed to adopt. This opposition, which this theory has in common with personhood theories, seems to be a merit of the theory.

In the second place, the claim that the loss of one's future is the wrong-making feature of one's being killed entails the possibility that the futures of some actual nonhuman mammals on our own planet are sufficiently like ours that it is seriously wrong to kill them also. Whether some animals do have the same right to life as human beings depends on adding to the account of the wrongness of killing some additional account of just what it is about my future or the futures of other adult human beings which makes it wrong to kill us. No such additional account will be offered in this essay. Undoubtedly, the provision of such an account would be a very difficult matter. Undoubtedly, any such account would be quite controversial. Hence, it surely should not reflect badly on this sketch of an elementary theory of the wrongness of killing that it is indeterminate with respect to some very difficult issues regarding animal rights.

In the third place, the claim that the loss of one's future is the wrong-making feature of one's being killed does not entail, as sanctity of human life theories do, that active euthanasia is wrong. Persons who are severely and incurably ill, who face a future of pain and despair, and who wish to die will not have suffered a loss if they are killed. It is, strictly speaking, the value of a human's future which makes killing wrong in this theory. This being so, killing does not necessarily wrong some persons who are sick and dying. Of course, there may be other reasons for a prohibition of active euthanasia, but that is another

matter. Sanctity-of-human-life theories seem to hold that active euthanasia is seriously wrong even in an individual case where there seems to be good reason for it independently of public policy considerations. This consequence is most implausible, and it is a plus for the claim that the loss of a future of value is what makes killing wrong that it does not share this consequence.

In the fourth place, the account of the wrongness of killing defended in this essay does straightforwardly entail that it is prima facie seriously wrong to kill children and infants, for we do presume that they have futures of value. Since we do believe that it is wrong to kill defenseless little babies, it is important that a theory of the wrongness of killing easily account for this. Personhood theories of the wrongness of killing, on the other hand, cannot straightforwardly account for the wrongness of killing infants and young children.[7] Hence, such theories must add special ad hoc accounts of the wrongness of killing the young. The plausibility of such ad hoc theories seems to be a function of how desperately one wants such theories to work. The claim that the primary wrong-making feature of a killing is the loss to the victim of the value of its future accounts for the wrongness of killing young children and infants directly; it makes the wrongness of such acts as obvious as we actually think it is. This is a further merit of this theory. Accordingly, it seems that this value of a future-like-ours theory of the wrongness of killing shares strengths of both sanctity-of-life and personhood accounts while avoiding weaknesses of both. In addition, it meshes with a central intuition concerning what makes killing wrong.

The claim that the primary wrong-making feature of a killing is the loss to the victim of the value of its future has obvious consequences for the ethics of abortion. The future of a standard fetus includes a set of experiences, projects, activities, and such which are identical with the futures of adult human beings and are identical with the futures of young children. Since the reason that is sufficient to explain why it is wrong to kill human beings after the time of birth is a reason that also applies to fetuses, it follows that abortion is prima facie seriously morally wrong.

This argument does not rely on the invalid inference that, since it is wrong to kill persons, it is wrong to kill potential persons also. The category that is morally central to this analysis is the category of having a valuable future like ours; it is not the category of personhood. The argument to the conclusion that abortion is prima facie seriously morally wrong proceeded independently of the notion of person or potential person or any equivalent. Someone may wish to start with this analysis in terms of the value of a human future, conclude that abortion is, except perhaps in rare circumstances, seriously morally wrong, infer that fetuses have the right to life, and then call fetuses "persons" as a result of their having the right to life. Clearly, in this case, the category of person is being used to state the *conclusion* of the analysis rather than to generate the *argument* of the analysis.

The structure of this anti-abortion argument can be both illuminated and defended by comparing it to what appears to be the best argument for the wrongness of the wanton infliction of pain on animals. This latter argument is based on the assumption that it is prima facie wrong to inflict pain on me (or you, reader). What is the natural property associated with the infliction of pain which makes such infliction wrong? The obvious answer seems to be that the infliction of pain causes suffering and that suffering is a misfortune. The suffering caused by the infliction of pain is what makes the wanton infliction of pain on me wrong. The wanton infliction of pain on other adult humans causes suffering. The wanton infliction of pain on animals causes suffering. Since causing suffering is what makes the wanton infliction of pain wrong and since the wanton infliction of pain on animals causes suffering, it follows that the wanton infliction of pain on animals is wrong.

This argument for the wrongness of the wanton infliction of pain on animals shares a number of structural features with the argument for the serious prima facie wrongness of abortion. Both arguments start with an obvious assumption concerning what it is wrong to do to me (or you, reader). Both then look for the characteristic or the consequence of the wrong action which makes the action wrong. Both recognize that the wrong-making feature of these immoral actions is a property of actions sometimes directed at individuals other than postnatal human beings. If the structure of the argument for the wrongness of the wanton infliction of pain on animals is sound, then

the structure of the argument for the prima facie serious wrongness of abortion is also sound, for the structure of the two arguments is the same. The structure common to both is the key to the explanation of how the wrongness of abortion can be demonstrated without recourse to the category of person. In neither argument is that category crucial.

This defense of an argument for the wrongness of abortion in terms of a structurally similar argument for the wrongness of the wanton infliction of pain on animals succeeds only if the account regarding animals is the correct account. Is it? In the first place, it seems plausible. In the second place, its major competition is Kant's account. Kant believed that we do not have direct duties to animals at all, because they are not persons. Hence, Kant had to explain and justify the wrongness of inflicting pain on animals on the grounds that "he who is hard in his dealings with animals becomes hard also in his dealing with men."[8] The problem with Kant's account is that there seems to be no reason for accepting this latter claim unless Kant's account is rejected. If the alternative to Kant's account is accepted, then it is easy to understand why someone who is indifferent to inflicting pain on animals is also indifferent to inflicting pain on humans, for one is indifferent to what makes inflicting pain wrong in both cases. But, if Kant's account is accepted, there is no intelligible reason why one who is hard in his dealings with animals (or crabgrass or stones) should also be hard in his dealings with men. After all, men are persons: animals are no more persons than crabgrass or stones. Persons are Kant's crucial moral category. Why, in short, should a Kantian accept the basic claim in Kant's argument?

Hence, Kant's argument for the wrongness of inflicting pain on animals rests on a claim that, in a world of Kantian moral agents, is demonstrably false. Therefore, the alternative analysis, being more plausible anyway, should be accepted. Since this alternative analysis has the same structure as the anti-abortion argument being defended here, we have further support for the argument for the immorality of abortion being defended in this essay.

Of course, this value of a future-like-ours argument, if sound, shows only that abortion is prima facie wrong, not that it is wrong in any and all circumstances. Since the loss of the future to a standard fetus, if killed, is, however, at least as great a loss as the loss of the future to a standard adult human being who is killed, abortion, like ordinary killing, could be justified only by the most compelling reasons. The loss of one's life is almost the greatest misfortune that can happen to one. Presumably abortion could be justified in some circumstances, only if the loss consequent on failing to abort would be at least as great. Accordingly, morally permissible abortions will be rare indeed unless, perhaps, they occur so early in pregnancy that a fetus is not yet definitely an individual. Hence, this argument should be taken as showing that abortion is presumptively very seriously wrong, where the presumption is very strong—as strong as the presumption that killing another adult human being is wrong.

III

How complete an account of the wrongness of killing does the value of a future-like-ours account have to be in order that the wrongness of abortion is a consequence? This account does not have to be an account of the necessary conditions for the wrongness of killing. Some persons in nursing homes may lack valuable human futures, yet it may be wrong to kill them for other reasons. Furthermore, this account does not obviously have to be the sole reason killing is wrong where the victim did have a valuable future. This analysis claims only that, for any killing where the victim did have a valuable future like ours, having that future by itself is sufficient to create the strong presumption that the killing is seriously wrong.

One way to overturn the value of a future-like-ours argument would be to find some account of the wrongness of killing which is at least as intelligible and which has different implications for the ethics of abortion. Two rival accounts possess at least some degree of plausibility. One account is based on the obvious fact that people value the experience of living and wish for that valuable experience to continue. Therefore, it might be said, what makes killing wrong is the discontinuation of that experience for the victim. Let us call this the *discontinuation account*.[9] Another rival account is based upon the obvious fact that people strongly desire to continue to live. This suggests that what makes killing us so wrong is that it interferes with the fulfillment of a

strong and fundamental desire, the fulfillment of which is necessary for the fulfillment of any other desires we might have. Let us call this the *desire account*.[10]

Consider first the desire account as a rival account of the ethics of killing which would provide the basis for rejecting the anti-abortion position. Such an account will have to be stronger than the value of a future-like-ours account of the wrongness of abortion if it is to do the job expected of it. To entail the wrongness of abortion, the value of a future-like-ours account has only to provide a sufficient, but not a necessary, condition for the wrongness of killing. The desire account, on the other hand, must provide us also with a necessary condition for the wrongness of killing in order to generate a pro-choice conclusion on abortion. The reason for this is that presumably the argument from the desire account moves from the claim that what makes killing wrong is interference with a very strong desire to the claim that abortion is not wrong because the fetus lacks a strong desire to live. Obviously, this inference fails if someone's having the desire to live is not a necessary condition of its being wrong to kill that individual.

One problem with the desire account is that we do regard it as seriously wrong to kill persons who have little desire to live or who have no desire to live or, indeed, have a desire not to live. We believe it is seriously wrong to kill the unconscious, the sleeping, those who are tired of life, and those who are suicidal. The value-of-a-human-future account renders standard morality intelligible in these cases; these cases appear to be incompatible with the desire account.

The desire account is subject to a deeper difficulty. We desire life, because we value the goods of this life. The goodness of life is not secondary to our desire for it. If this were not so, the pain of one's own premature death could be done away with merely by an appropriate alteration in the configuration of one's desires. This is absurd. Hence, it would seem that it is the loss of the goods of one's future, not the interference with the fulfillment of a strong desire to live, which accounts ultimately for the wrongness of killing.

It is worth noting that, if the desire account is modified so that it does not provide a necessary, but only a sufficient, condition for the wrongness of killing, the desire account is compatible with the value of a future-like-ours account. The combined accounts will yield an anti-abortion ethic. This suggests that one can retain what is intuitively plausible about the desire account without a challenge to the basic argument of this paper.

It is also worth noting that, if future desires have moral force in a modified desire account of the wrongness of killing, one can find support for an anti-abortion ethic even in the absence of a value of a future-like-ours account. If one decides that a morally relevant property, the possession of which is sufficient to make it wrong to kill some individual, is the desire at some future time to live—one might decide to justify one's refusal to kill suicidal teenagers on these grounds, for example—then, since typical fetuses will have the desire in the future to live, it is wrong to kill typical fetuses. Accordingly, it does not seem that a desire account of the wrongness of killing can provide a justification of a pro-choice ethic of abortion which is nearly as adequate as the value of a human-future justification of an anti-abortion ethic.

The discontinuation account looks more promising as an account of the wrongness of killing. It seems just as intelligible as the value of a future-like-ours account, but it does not justify an anti-abortion position. Obviously, if it is the continuation of one's activities, experiences, and projects, the loss of which makes killing wrong, then it is not wrong to kill fetuses for that reason, for fetuses do not have experiences, activities, and projects to be continued or discontinued. Accordingly, the discontinuation account does not have the anti-abortion consequences that the value of a future-like-ours account has. Yet, it seems as intelligible as the value of a future-like-ours account, for when we think of what would be wrong with our being killed, it does seem as if it is the discontinuation of what makes our lives worthwhile which makes killing us wrong.

Is the discontinuation account just as good an account as the value of a future-like-ours account? The discontinuation account will not be adequate at all, if it does not refer to the *value* of the experience that may be discontinued. One does not want the discontinuation account to make it wrong to kill

a patient who begs for death and who is in severe pain that cannot be relieved short of killing. (I leave open the question of whether it is wrong for other reasons.) Accordingly, the discontinuation account must be more than a bare discontinuation account. It must make some reference to the positive value of the patient's experiences. But, by the same token, the value of a future-like-ours account cannot be a bare future account either. Just having a future surely does not itself rule out killing the above patient. This account must make some reference to the value of the patient's future experiences and projects also. Hence, both accounts involve the value of experiences, projects, and activities. So far we still have symmetry between the accounts.

The symmetry fades, however, when we focus on the time period of the value of the experiences, etc., which has moral consequences. Although both accounts leave open the possibility that the patient in our example may be killed, this possibility is left open only in virtue of the utterly bleak future for the patient. It makes no difference whether the patient's immediate past contains intolerable pain, or consists in being in a coma (which we can imagine is a situation of indifference), or consists in a life of value. If the patient's future is a future of value, we want our account to make it wrong to kill the patient. If the patient's future is intolerable, whatever his or her immediate past, we want our account to allow killing the patient. Obviously, then, it is the value of that patient's future which is doing the work in rendering the morality of killing the patient intelligible.

This being the case, it seems clear that whether one has immediate past experiences or not does no work in the explanation of what makes killing wrong. The addition the discontinuation account makes to the value of a human future account is otiose. Its addition to the value-of-a-future account plays no role at all in rendering intelligible the wrongness of killing. Therefore, it can be discarded with the discontinuation account of which it is a part.

IV

The analysis of the previous section suggests that alternative general accounts of the wrongness of killing are either inadequate or unsuccessful in getting around the anti-abortion consequences of the value of a future-like-ours argument. A different strategy for avoiding these anti-abortion consequences involves limiting the scope of the value of a future argument. More precisely, the strategy involves arguing that fetuses lack a property that is essential for the value-of-a-future argument (or for any anti-abortion argument) to apply to them.

One move of this sort is based upon the claim that a necessary condition of one's future being valuable is that one values it. Value implies a valuer. Given this one might argue that, since fetuses cannot value their futures, their futures are not valuable to them. Hence, it does not seriously wrong them deliberately to end their lives.

This move fails, however, because of some ambiguities. Let us assume that something cannot be of value unless it is valued by someone. This does not entail that my life is of no value unless it is valued by me. I may think, in a period of despair, that my future is of no worth whatsoever, but I may be wrong because others rightly see value—even great value—in it. Furthermore, my future can be valuable to me even if I do not value it. This is the case when a young person attempts suicide, but is rescued and goes on to significant human achievements. Such young people's futures are ultimately valuable to them, even though such futures do not seem to be valuable to them at the moment of attempted suicide. A fetus's future can be valuable to it in the same way. Accordingly, this attempt to limit the anti-abortion argument fails.

Another similar attempt to reject the anti-abortion position is based on Tooley's claim that an entity cannot possess the right to life unless it has the capacity to desire its continued existence. It follows that, since fetuses lack the conceptual capacity to desire to continue to live, they lack the right to life. Accordingly, Tooley concludes that abortion cannot be seriously prima facie wrong.

What could be the evidence for Tooley's basic claim? Tooley once argued that individuals have a prima facie right to what they desire and that the lack of the capacity to desire something undercuts the basis of one's right to it. This argument plainly will not succeed in the context of the analysis of this essay, however, since the point here is to establish the fetus's right to life on other grounds. Tooley's argument assumes that the right to life cannot be established in general on some basis other than the desire for life. This position was considered and rejected in the preceding section of this paper.

One might attempt to defend Tooley's basic claim on the grounds that, because a fetus cannot apprehend continued life as a benefit, its continued life cannot be a benefit or cannot be something it has a right to or cannot be something that is in its interest. This might be defended in terms of the general proposition that, if an individual is literally incapable of caring about or taking an interest in some X, then one does not have a right to X or X is not a benefit or X is not something that is in one's interest.[11]

Each member of this family of claims seems to be open to objections. As John C. Stevens[12] has pointed out, one may have a right to be treated with a certain medical procedure (because of a health insurance policy one has purchased), even though one cannot conceive of the nature of the procedure. And, as Tooley himself has pointed out, persons who have been indoctrinated, or drugged, or rendered temporarily unconscious may be literally incapable of caring about or taking an interest in something that is in their interest or is something to which they have a right, or is something that benefits them. Hence, the Tooley claim that would restrict the scope of the value of a future-like-ours argument is undermined by counterexamples.[13]

Finally, Paul Bassen[14] has argued that, even though the prospects of an embryo might seem to be a basis for the wrongness of abortion, an embryo cannot be a victim and therefore cannot be wronged. An embryo cannot be a victim, he says, because it lacks sentience. His central argument for this seems to be that, even though plants and the permanently unconscious are alive, they clearly cannot be victims. What is the explanation of this? Bassen claims that the explanation is that their lives consist of mere metabolism and mere metabolism is not enough to ground victimizability. Mentation is required.

The problem with this attempt to establish the absence of victimizability is that both plants and the permanently unconscious clearly lack what Bassen calls "prospects" or what I have called "a future life like ours." Hence, it is surely open to one to argue that the real reason we believe plants and the permanently unconscious cannot be victims is that killing them cannot deprive them of a future life like ours; the real reason is not their absence of present mentation.

Bassen recognizes that his view is subject to this difficulty, and he recognizes that the case of children seems to support this difficulty, for "much of what we do for children is based on prospects." He argues, however, that, in the case of children and in other such cases, "potentiality comes into play only where victimizability has been secured on other grounds" (p. 333).

Bassen's defense of his view is patently question-begging, since what is adequate to secure victimizability is exactly what is at issue. His examples do not support his own view against the thesis of this essay. Of course, embryos can be victims: when their lives are deliberately terminated, they are deprived of their futures of value, their prospects. This makes them victims, for it directly wrongs them.

The seeming plausibility of Bassen's view stems from the fact that paradigmatic cases of imagining someone as a victim involve empathy, and empathy requires mentation of the victim. The victims of flood, famine, rape, or child abuse are all persons with whom we can empathize. That empathy seems to be part of seeing them as victims.[15]

In spite of the strength of these examples, the attractive intuition that a situation in which there is victimization requires the possibility of empathy is subject to counterexamples. Consider a case that Bassen himself offers: "Posthumous obliteration of an author's work constitutes a misfortune for him only if he had wished his work to endure" (p. 318). The conditions Bassen wishes to impose upon the possibility of being victimized here seem far too strong. Perhaps this author, due to his unrealistic standards of excellence and his low self-esteem, regarded his work as unworthy of survival, even though it possessed genuine literary merit. Destruction of such work would surely victimize its author. In such a case, empathy with the victim concerning the loss is clearly impossible.

Of course, Bassen does not make the possibility of empathy a necessary condition of victimizability; he requires only mentation. Hence, on Bassen's actual view, this author, as I have described him, can

be a victim. The problem is that the basic intuition that renders Bassen's view plausible is missing in the author's case. In order to attempt to avoid counterexamples, Bassen has made his thesis too weak to be supported by the intuitions that suggested it.

Even so, the mentation requirement on victimizability is still subject to counterexamples. Suppose a severe accident renders me totally unconscious for a month, after which I recover. Surely killing me while I am unconscious victimizes me, even though I am incapable of mentation during that time. It follows that Bassen's thesis fails. Apparently, attempts to restrict the value of a future-like-ours argument so that fetuses do not fall within its scope do not succeed.

V

In this essay, it has been argued that the correct ethic of the wrongness of killing can be extended to fetal life and used to show that there is a strong presumption that any abortion is morally impermissible. If the ethic of killing adopted here entails, however, that contraception is also seriously immoral, then there would appear to be a difficulty with the analysis of this essay.

But this analysis does not entail that contraception is wrong. Of course, contraception prevents the actualization of a possible future of value. Hence, it follows from the claim that if futures of value should be maximized that contraception is prima facie immoral. This obligation to maximize does not exist, however; furthermore, nothing in the ethics of killing in this paper entails that it does. The ethics of killing in this essay would entail that contraception is wrong only if something were denied a human future of value by contraception. Nothing at all is denied such a future by contraception, however.

Candidates for a subject of harm by contraception fall into four categories: (1) some sperm or other, (2) some ovum or other, (3) a sperm and an ovum separately, and (4) a sperm and an ovum together. Assigning the harm to some sperm is utterly arbitrary, for no reason can be given for making a sperm the subject of harm rather than an ovum. Assigning the harm to some ovum is utterly arbitrary, for no reason can be given for making an ovum the subject of harm rather than a sperm. One might attempt to avoid these problems by insisting that contraception deprives both the sperm and the ovum separately of a valuable future like ours. On this alternative, too many futures are lost. Contraception was supposed to be wrong, because it deprived us of one future of value, not two. One might attempt to avoid this problem by holding that contraception deprives the combination of sperm and ovum of a valuable future like ours. But here the definite article misleads. At the time of contraception, there are hundreds of millions of sperm, one (released) ovum and millions of possible combinations of all of these. There is no actual combination at all. Is the subject of the loss to be a merely possible combination? Which one? This alternative does not yield an actual subject of harm either. Accordingly, the immorality of contraception is not entailed by the loss of a future-like-ours argument simply because there is no nonarbitrarily identifiable subject of the loss in the case of contraception.

VI

The purpose of this essay has been to set out an argument for the serious presumptive wrongness of abortion subject to the assumption that the moral permissibility of abortion stands or falls on the moral status of the fetus. Since a fetus possesses a property, the possession of which in adult human beings is sufficient to make killing an adult human being wrong, abortion is wrong. This way of dealing with the problem of abortion seems superior to other approaches to the ethics of abortion, because it rests on an ethics of killing which is close to self-evident, because the crucial morally relevant property clearly applies to fetuses, and because the argument avoids the usual equivocations on "human life," "human being," or "person." The argument rests neither on religious claims nor on Papal dogma. It is not subject to the objection of "speciesism." Its soundness is compatible with the moral permissibility of euthanasia and contraception. It deals with our intuitions concerning young children.

Finally, this analysis can be viewed as resolving a standard problem—indeed, *the* standard problem—concerning the ethics of abortion. Clearly, it is wrong to kill adult human beings. Clearly, it is not wrong to end the life of some arbitrarily chosen single human

cell. Fetuses seem to be like arbitrarily chosen human cells in some respects and like adult humans in other respects. The problem of the ethics of abortion is the problem of determining the fetal property that settles this moral controversy. The thesis of this essay is that the problem of the ethics of abortion, so understood, is solvable.

NOTES

1. Feinberg, "Abortion," in *Matters of Life and Death: New Introductory Essays in Moral Philosophy*, Tom Regan, ed. (New York: Random House, 1986), pp. 256–93; Tooley, "Abortion and Infanticide," *Philosophy and Public Affairs*, II, 1 (1972): 37–65, Tooley, *Abortion and Infanticide* (New York: Oxford, 1984); Warren, "On the Moral and Legal Status of Abortion," *The Monist*, 1. VII, 1 (1973): 43–61; Engelhardt, "The Ontology of Abortion," *Ethics*, I. XXXIV, 3 (1974): 217–34; Sumner, *Abortion and Moral Theory* (Princeton: University Press, 1981); Noonan, "An Almost Absolute Value in History," in *The Morality of Abortion: Legal and Historical Perspectives*, Noonan, ed. (Cambridge: Harvard, 1970); and Devine, *The Ethics of Homicide* (Ithaca: Cornell, 1978).

2. For interesting discussions of this issue, see Warren Quinn, "Abortion: Identity and Loss," *Philosophy and Public Affairs*, XIII, 1 (1984): 24–54; and Lawrence C. Becker, "Human Being: The Boundaries of the Concept," *Philosophy and Public Affairs*, IV, 4 (1975): 334–59.

3. For example, see my "Ethics and the Elderly: Some Problems," in Stuart Spicker, Kathleen Woodward, and David Van Tassel, eds., *Aging and the Elderly: Humanistic Perspectives in Gerontology* (Atlantic Highlands, NJ: Humanities, 1978), pp. 341–55.

4. See Warren, "On the Moral and Legal Status of Abortion," and Tooley, "Abortion and Infanticide."

5. This seems to be the fatal flaw in Warren's treatment of this issue.

6. I have been most influenced on this matter by Jonathan Glover, *Causing Death and Saving Lives* (New York: Penguin, 1977), ch. 3; and Robert Young, "What Is So Wrong with Killing People?" *Philosophy*, LIV, 210 (1979): 515–28.

7. Feinberg, Tooley, Warren, and Engelhardt have all dealt with this problem.

8. Kant "Duties to Animals and Spirits," in *Lectures on Ethics*, trans. Louis Infeld (New York: Harper, 1963), p. 239.

9. I am indebted to Jack Bricke for raising this objection.

10. Presumably a preference utilitarian would press such an objection. Tooley once suggested that his account has such a theoretical underpinning. See his "Abortion and Infanticide," pp. 44–5.

11. Donald VanDeVeer seems to think this is self-evident. See his "Whither Baby Doe?" in *Matters of Life and Death*, p. 233.

12. "Must the Bearer of a Right Have the Concept of That to Which He Has a Right?" *Ethics*, XCV, 1 (1984): 68–74.

13. See Tooley again in "Abortion and Infanticide," pp. 47–9.

14. "Present Sakes and Future Prospects: The Status of Early Abortion," *Philosophy and Public Affairs*, XI, 4 (1982): 322–6.

15. Note carefully the reasons he gives on the bottom of p. 316.

On the Moral and Legal Status of Abortion

MARY ANNE WARREN

In this famous essay, Warren defends the view that abortion is always morally permissible. It is permissible, she says, because the unborn is not a person. Merely being human—a creature with human DNA—is not sufficient for personhood. To qualify as a person, an entity must possess certain intrinsically valuable traits. She identifies several traits that seem "most central" to personhood: (1) consciousness and the capacity to feel pain, (2) reasoning, (3) self-motivated activity, (4) the capacity to communicate, and (5) "the presence of self-concepts, and self-awareness, either individual or racial or both." Warren argues that any being that has none of these traits is surely not a person; a fetus has none of them and is therefore not yet a person and "cannot coherently be said to have full moral rights."

We will be concerned with both the moral status of abortion, which for our purposes we may define as the act which a woman performs in voluntarily terminating, or allowing another person to terminate, her pregnancy, and the legal status which is appropriate for this act. I will argue that, while it is not possible to produce a satisfactory defense of a woman's right to obtain an abortion without showing that a fetus is not a human being, in the morally relevant sense of that term, we ought not to conclude that the difficulties involved in determining whether or not a fetus is human make it impossible to produce any satisfactory solution to the problem of the moral status of abortion. For it is possible to show that, on the basis of intuitions which we may expect even the opponents of abortion to share, a fetus is not a person, and hence not the sort of entity to which it is proper to ascribe full moral rights.

Of course, while some philosophers would deny the possibility of any such proof,[1] others will deny that there is any need for it, since the moral permissibility of abortion appears to them to be too obvious to require proof. But the inadequacy of this attitude should be evident from the fact that both the friends and the foes of abortion consider their position to be morally self-evident. Because proabortionists have never adequately come to grips with the conceptual issues surrounding abortion, most if not all, of the arguments which they advance in opposition to laws restricting access to abortion fail to refute or even weaken the traditional antiabortion argument, i.e., that a fetus is a human being, and therefore abortion is murder.

These arguments are typically of one of two sorts. Either they point to the terrible side effects of the restrictive laws, e.g., the deaths due to illegal abortions, and the fact that it is poor women who suffer the most as a result of these laws, or else they state that to deny a woman access to abortion is to deprive her of her right to control her own body. Unfortunately, however, the fact that restricting access to abortion has tragic side effects does not, in itself, show that the restrictions are unjustified, since murder is wrong regardless of the consequences of prohibiting it; and the appeal to the right to control one's body, which is generally construed as a property right, is at best a rather feeble argument for the permissibility of abortion. Mere ownership does not give me the right to kill innocent people whom I find on my property,

From *The Monist*, vol. 57, no. 1, 1973, 43–61. Copyright © 1973 *The Monist*, La Salle, IL 61301.

and indeed I am apt to be held responsible if such people injure themselves while on my property. It is equally unclear that I have any moral right to expel an innocent person from my property when I know that doing so will result in his or her death.

Furthermore, it is probably inappropriate to describe a woman's body as her property, since it seems natural to hold that a person is something distinct from her property, but not from her body. Even those who would object to the identification of a person with her body, or with the conjunction of her body and her mind, must admit that it would be very odd to describe, say, breaking a leg, as damaging one's property, and much more appropriate to describe it as injuring one*self*. Thus it is probably a mistake to argue that the right to obtain an abortion is in any way derived from the right to own and regulate property.

But however we wish to construe the right to abortion, we cannot hope to convince those who consider abortion a form of murder of the existence of any such right unless we are able to produce a clear and convincing refutation of the traditional antiabortion argument, and this has not, to my knowledge, been done. With respect to the two most vital issues which that argument involves, i.e., the humanity of the fetus and its implication for the moral status of abortion, confusion has prevailed on both sides of the dispute. Thus, both proabortionists and antiabortionists have tended to abstract the question of whether abortion is wrong to that of whether it is wrong to destroy a fetus, just as though the rights of another person were not necessarily involved. This mistaken abstraction has led to the almost universal assumption that if a fetus is a human being, with a right to life, then it follows immediately that abortion is wrong (except perhaps when necessary to save the woman's life), and that it ought to be prohibited. It has also been generally assumed that unless the question about the status of the fetus is answered, the moral status of abortion cannot possibly be determined.

Two recent papers, one by B. A. Brody,[2] and one by Judith Thomson,[3] have attempted to settle the question of whether abortion ought to be prohibited apart from the question of whether or not the fetus is human. Brody examines the possibility that the following two statements are compatible: (1) that abortion is the taking of innocent human life, and therefore wrong; and (2) that nevertheless it ought not to be prohibited by law, at least under the present circumstances.[4] Not surprisingly, Brody finds it impossible to reconcile these two statements, since, as he rightly argues, none of the unfortunate side effects of the prohibition of abortion is bad enough to justify legalizing the *wrongful* taking of human life. He is mistaken, however, in concluding that the incompatibility of (1) and (2), in itself, shows that "the legal problem about abortion cannot be resolved independently of the status of the fetus problem" (p. 369).

What Brody fails to realize is that (1) embodies the questionable assumption that if a fetus is a human being, then of course abortion is morally wrong, and that an attack on *this* assumption is more promising, as a way of reconciling the humanity of the fetus with the claim that laws prohibiting abortion are unjustified, than is an attack on the assumption that if abortion is the wrongful killing of innocent human beings then it ought to be prohibited. He thus overlooks the possibility that a fetus may have a right to life and abortion still be morally permissible, in that the right of a woman to terminate an unwanted pregnancy might override the right of the fetus to be kept alive. The immorality of abortion is no more demonstrated by the humanity of the fetus, in itself, than the immorality of killing in self-defense is demonstrated by the fact that the assailant is a human being. Neither is it demonstrated by the *innocence* of the fetus, since there may be situations in which the killing of innocent human beings is justified.

It is perhaps not surprising that Brody fails to spot this assumption, since it has been accepted with little or no argument by nearly everyone who has written on the morality of abortion. John Noonan is correct in saying that "the fundamental question in the long history of abortion is, How do you determine the humanity of a being?"[5] He summarizes his own antiabortion argument, which is a version of the official position of the Catholic Church, as follows:

> . . . it is wrong to kill humans, however poor, weak, defenseless, and lacking in opportunity to develop their potential they may be. It is therefore morally wrong to kill Biafrans. Similarly, it is morally wrong to kill embryos.[6]

Noonan bases his claim that fetuses are human upon what he calls the theologians' criterion of humanity: that whoever is conceived of human beings is human. But although he argues at length for the appropriateness of this criterion, he never questions the assumption that if a fetus is human then abortion is wrong for exactly the same reason that murder is wrong.

Judith Thomson is, in fact, the only writer I am aware of who has seriously questioned this assumption; she has argued that, even if we grant the anti-abortionist his claim that a fetus is a human being, with the same right to life as any other human being, we can still demonstrate that, in at least some and perhaps most cases, a woman is under no moral obligation to complete an unwanted pregnancy.[7] Her argument is worth examining, since if it holds up it may enable us to establish the moral permissibility of abortion without becoming involved in problems about what entitles an entity to be considered human, and accorded full moral rights. To be able to do this would be a great gain in the power and simplicity of the proabortion position, since, although I will argue that these problems can be solved at least as decisively as can any other moral problem, we should certainly be pleased to be able to avoid having to solve them as part of the justification of abortion.

On the other hand, even if Thomson's argument does not hold up, her insight, i.e., that it requires *argument* to show that if fetuses are human then abortion is properly classified as murder, is an extremely valuable one. The assumption she attacks is particularly invidious, for it amounts to the decision that it is appropriate, in deciding the moral status of abortion, to leave the rights of the pregnant woman out of consideration entirely, except possibly when her life is threatened. Obviously, this will not do; determining what moral rights, if any, a fetus possesses is only the first step in determining the moral status of abortion. Step two, which is at least equally essential, is finding a just solution to the conflict between whatever rights the fetus may have, and the rights of the woman who is unwillingly pregnant. While the historical error has been to pay far too little attention to the second step, Ms. Thomson's suggestion is that if we look at the second step first we may find that a woman has a right to obtain an abortion *regardless* of what rights the fetus has.

Our own inquiry will also have two stages. In Section I, we will consider whether or not it is possible to establish that abortion is morally permissible even on the assumption that a fetus is an entity with a full-fledged right to life. I will argue that in fact this cannot be established, at least not with the conclusiveness which is essential to our hopes of convincing those who are skeptical about the morality of abortion, and that we therefore cannot avoid dealing with the question of whether or not a fetus really does have the same right to life as a (more fully developed) human being.

In Section II, I will propose an answer to this question, namely, that a fetus cannot be considered a member of the moral community, the set of beings with full and equal moral rights, for the simple reason that it is not a person, and that it is personhood, and not genetic humanity, i.e., humanity as defined by Noonan, which is the basis for membership in this community. I will argue that a fetus, whatever its stage of development, satisfies none of the basic criteria of personhood, and is not even enough *like* a person to be accorded even some of the same rights on the basis of this resemblance. Nor, as we will see, is a fetus's *potential* personhood a threat to the morality of abortion, since, whatever the rights of potential people may be, they are invariably overridden in any conflict with the moral rights of actual people.

I

We turn now to Professor Thomson's case for the claim that even if a fetus has full moral rights, abortion is still morally permissible, at least sometimes, and for some reasons other than to save the woman's life. Her argument is based upon a clever, but I think faulty, analogy. She asks us to picture ourselves waking up one day, in bed with a famous violinist. Imagine that you have been kidnapped, and your bloodstream hooked up to that of the violinist, who happens to have an ailment which will certainly kill him unless he is permitted to share your kidneys for a period of nine months. No one else can save him, since you alone have the right type of blood. He will be unconscious all that time, and you will have to stay in bed with him, but after the nine months are over he may be unplugged, completely cured, that is provided that you have cooperated.

Now then, she continues, what are your obligations in this situation? The antiabortionist, if he is consistent, will have to say that you are obligated to stay in bed with the violinist: for all people have a right to life, and violinists are people, and therefore it would be murder for you to disconnect yourself from him and let him die. But this is outrageous, and so there must be something wrong with the same argument when it is applied to abortion. It would certainly be commendable of you to agree to save the violinist, but it is absurd to suggest that your refusal to do so would be murder. His right to life does not obligate you to do whatever is required to keep him alive; nor does it justify anyone else in forcing you to do so. A law which required you to stay in bed with the violinist would clearly be an unjust law, since it is no proper function of the law to force unwilling people to make huge sacrifices for the sake of other people toward whom they have no such prior obligation.

Thomson concludes that, if this analogy be an apt one, then we can grant the antiabortionist his claim that a fetus is a human being, and still hold that it is at least sometimes the case that a pregnant woman has the right to refuse to be a Good Samaritan towards the fetus, i.e., to obtain an abortion. For there is a great gap between the claim that x has a right to life, and the claim that y is obligated to do whatever is necessary to keep x alive, let alone that she ought to be forced to do so. It is y's duty to keep x alive only if she has somehow contracted a *special* obligation to do so; and a woman who is unwillingly pregnant, e.g., who was raped, has done nothing which obligates her to make the enormous sacrifice which is necessary to preserve the conceptus.

This argument is initially quite plausible, and in the extreme case of pregnancy due to rape it is probably conclusive. Difficulties arise, however, when we try to specify more exactly the range of cases in which abortion is clearly justifiable even on the assumption that the fetus is human. Professor Thomson considers it a virtue of her argument that it does not enable us to conclude that abortion is *always* permissible. It would, she says, be "indecent" for a woman in her seventh month to obtain an abortion just to avoid having to postpone a trip to Europe. On the other hand, her argument enables us to see that "a sick and desperately frightened schoolgirl pregnant due to rape may *of course* choose abortion, and that any law which rules this out is an insane law." So far, so good; but what are we to say about the woman who becomes pregnant not through rape but as a result of her own carelessness, or because of contraceptive failure, or who gets pregnant intentionally and then changes her mind about wanting a child? With respect to such cases, the violinist analogy is of much less use to the defender of the woman's right to obtain an abortion.

Indeed, the choice of a pregnancy due to rape, as an example of a case in which abortion is permissible even if a fetus is considered a human being, is extremely significant; for it is only in the case of pregnancy due to rape that the woman's situation is adequately analogous to the violinist case for our intuitions about the latter to transfer convincingly. The crucial difference between a pregnancy due to rape and the normal case of an unwanted pregnancy is that in the *normal* case we cannot claim that the woman is in no way responsible for her predicament; she could have remained chaste, or taken her pills more faithfully, or abstained on dangerous days, and so on. If, on the other hand, you are kidnapped by strangers, and hooked up to a strange violinist, then you are free of any shred of responsibility for the situation, on the basis of which it could be argued that you are obligated to keep the violinist alive. Only when her pregnancy is due to rape is a woman clearly just as nonresponsible.[8]

Consequently, there is room for the antiabortionist to argue that in the normal case of unwanted pregnancy a woman has, by her own actions, assumed responsibility for the fetus. For if x behaves in a way which she could have avoided, and which she knows involves, let us say, a 1 percent chance of bringing into existence a human being, with a right to life, and does so knowing that if this should happen then that human being will perish unless x does certain things to keep it alive, then it is by no means clear that when it does happen x is free of any obligation to what she knew in advance would be required to keep that human being alive.

The plausibility of such an argument is enough to show that the Thomson analogy can provide a clear and persuasive defense of a woman's right to obtain an abortion only with respect to those cases in which the woman is in no way responsible for her pregnancy, e.g., where it is due to rape. In all other cases, we would almost certainly conclude that it was necessary to look carefully at the particular circumstances in order to determine the extent of the woman's responsibility, and hence the extent of her obligation. This is an extremely unsatisfactory outcome, from the viewpoint of the opponents of restrictive abortion laws, most of whom are convinced that a woman has a right to obtain an abortion regardless of how and why she got pregnant.

Of course a supporter of the violinist analogy might point out that it is absurd to suggest that forgetting her pill one day might be sufficient to obligate a woman to complete an unwanted pregnancy. And indeed it *is* absurd to suggest this. As we will see, the moral right to obtain an abortion is not in the least dependent upon the extent to which the woman is responsible for her pregnancy. But unfortunately, once we allow the assumption that a fetus has full moral rights, we cannot avoid taking this absurd suggestion seriously. Perhaps we can make this point more clear by altering the violinist story just enough to make it more analogous to a normal unwanted pregnancy and less to a pregnancy due to rape, and then seeing whether it is still obvious that you are not obligated to stay in bed with the fellow.

Suppose, then, that violinists are peculiarly prone to the sort of illness the only cure for which is the use of someone else's bloodstream for nine months, and that because of this there has been formed a society of music lovers who agree that whenever a violinist is stricken they will draw lots and the loser will, by some means, be made the one and only person capable of saving him or her. Now then, would you be obligated to cooperate in curing the violinist if you had voluntarily joined this society, knowing the possible consequences, and then your name had been drawn and you had been kidnapped? Admittedly, you did not promise ahead of time that you would, but you did deliberately place yourself in a position in which it might happen that a human life would be lost if you did not. Surely this is at least a prima facie reason for supposing that you have an obligation to stay in bed with the violinist. Suppose that you had gotten your name drawn deliberately; surely that would be quite a strong reason for thinking that you have such an obligation.

It might be suggested that there is one important disanalogy between the modified violinist case and the case of an unwanted pregnancy, which makes the woman's responsibility significantly less, namely, the fact that the fetus *comes into existence* as the result of the woman's actions. This fact might give her a right to refuse to keep it alive, whereas she would not have had this right had it existed previously, independently, and then as a result of her actions become dependent upon her for its survival.

My own intuition, however, is that x has no more right to bring into existence, either deliberately or as a foreseeable result of actions she could have avoided, a being with full moral rights (y), and then refuse to do what she knew beforehand would be required to keep that being alive, than she has to enter into an agreement with an existing person, whereby she may be called upon to save that person's life, and then refuse to do so when so called upon. Thus, x's responsibility for y's existence does not seem to lessen her obligation to keep y alive, if she is also responsible for y's being in a situation in which only she can save him or her.

Whether or not this intuition is entirely correct, it brings us back once again to the conclusion that once we allow the assumption that a fetus has full moral rights it becomes an extremely complex and difficult question whether and when abortion is justifiable. Thus the Thomson analogy cannot help us produce a clear and persuasive proof of the moral permissibility of abortion. Nor will the opponents of the restrictive laws thank us for anything less; for their conviction (for the most part) is that abortion is obviously *not* a morally serious and extremely unfortunate, even though sometimes justified act, comparable to killing in self-defense or to letting the violinist die, but rather is closer to being a morally neutral act, like cutting one's hair.

The basis of this conviction, I believe, is the realization that a fetus is not a person, and thus does not have a full-fledged right to life. Perhaps the reason why this claim has been so inadequately defended is that it seems self-evident to those who accept it. And so it is, insofar as it follows from what I take to be perfectly obvious claims about the nature of personhood, and about the proper grounds for ascribing moral rights, claims which ought, indeed, to be obvious to both the friends and foes of abortion. Nevertheless, it is worth examining these claims, and showing how they demonstrate the moral innocuousness of abortion, since this apparently has not been adequately done before.

II

The question which we must answer in order to produce a satisfactory solution to the problem of the moral status of abortion is this: How are we to define the moral community, the set of beings with full and equal moral rights, such that we can decide whether a human fetus is a member of this community or not? What sort of entity, exactly, has the inalienable rights to life, liberty, and the pursuit of happiness? Jefferson attributed these rights to all *men*, and it may or may not be fair to suggest that he intended to attribute them *only* to men. Perhaps he ought to have attributed them to all human beings. If so, then we arrive, first, at Noonan's problem of defining what makes a being human, and, second, at the equally vital question which Noonan does not consider, namely, What reason is there for identifying the moral community with the set of all human beings, in whatever way we have chosen to define that term?

1. On the Definition of "Human"
One reason why this vital second question is so frequently overlooked in the debate over the moral status of abortion is that the term "human" has two distinct, but not often distinguished, senses. This fact results in a slide of meaning, which serves to conceal the fallaciousness of the traditional argument that since (1) it is wrong to kill innocent human beings, and (2) fetuses are innocent human beings, then (3) it is wrong to kill fetuses. For if "human" is used in the same sense in both (1) and (2) then, whichever of the two senses is meant, one of these premises is question-begging. And if it is used in two different senses then of course the conclusion doesn't follow.

Thus, (1) is a self-evident moral truth,[9] and avoids begging the question about abortion, only if "human

being" is used to mean something like "a full-fledged member of the moral community." (It may or may not also be meant to refer exclusively to members of the species *Homo sapiens*.) We may call this the *moral* sense of "human." It is not to be confused with what we will call the *genetic* sense, i.e., the sense in which *any* member of the species is a human being, and no member of any other species could be. If (1) is acceptable only if the moral sense is intended, (2) is non-question-begging only if what is intended is the genetic sense.

In "Deciding Who Is Human," Noonan argues for the classification of fetuses with human beings by pointing to the presence of the full genetic code, and the potential capacity for rational thought (p. 35). It is clear that what he needs to show, for his version of the traditional argument to be valid, is that fetuses are human in the moral sense, the sense in which it is analytically true that all human beings have full moral rights. But, in the absence of any argument showing that whatever is genetically human is also morally human, and he gives none, nothing more than genetic humanity can be demonstrated by the presence of the human genetic code. And, as we will see, the *potential* capacity for rational thought can at most show that an entity has the potential for *becoming* human in the moral sense.

2. Defining the Moral Community
Can it be established that genetic humanity is sufficient for moral humanity? I think that there are very good reasons for not defining the moral community in this way. I would like to suggest an alternative way of defining the moral community, which I will argue for only to the extent of explaining why it is, or should be, self-evident. The suggestion is simply that the moral community consists of all and only *people*, rather than all and only human beings;[10] and probably the best way of demonstrating its self-evidence is by considering the concept of personhood, to see what sorts of entities are and are not persons, and what the decision that a being is or is not a person implies about its moral rights.

What characteristics entitle an entity to be considered a person? This is obviously not the place to attempt a complete analysis of the concept of personhood, but we do not need such a fully adequate analysis just to determine whether and why a fetus is or isn't a person. All we need is a rough and approximate list of the most basic criteria of personhood, and some idea of which, or how many, of these an entity must satisfy in order to properly be considered a person.

In searching for such criteria, it is useful to look beyond the set of people with whom we are acquainted, and ask how we would decide whether a totally alien being was a person or not. (For we have no right to assume that genetic humanity is necessary for personhood.) Imagine a space traveler who lands on an unknown planet and encounters a race of beings utterly unlike any she has ever seen or heard of. If she wants to be sure of behaving morally toward these beings, she has to somehow decide whether they are people, and hence have full moral rights, or whether they are the sort of thing which she need not feel guilty about treating as, for example, a source of food.

How should she go about making this decision? If she has some anthropological background, she might look for such things as religion, art, and the manufacturing of tools, weapons, or shelters, since these factors have been used to distinguish our human from our prehuman ancestors, in what seems to be closer to the moral than the genetic sense of "human." And no doubt she would be right to consider the presence of such factors as good evidence that the alien beings were people, and morally human. It would, however, be overly anthropocentric of her to take the absence of these things as adequate evidence that they were not, since we can imagine people who have progressed beyond, or evolved without ever developing, these cultural characteristics.

I suggest that the traits which are most central to the concept of personhood, or humanity in the moral sense, are, very roughly, the following:

1. Consciousness (of objects and events external and/or internal to the being), and in particular the capacity to feel pain;
2. Reasoning (the *developed* capacity to solve new and relatively complex problems);
3. Self-motivated activity (activity which is relatively independent of either genetic or direct external control);

4. The capacity to communicate, by whatever means, messages of an indefinite variety of types, that is, not just with an indefinite number of possible contents, but on indefinitely many possible topics;
5. The presence of self-concepts, and self-awareness, either individual or racial, or both.

Admittedly, there are apt to be a great many problems involved in formulating precise definitions of these criteria, let alone in developing universally valid behavior criteria for deciding when they apply. But I will assume that both we and our explorer know approximately what (1)–(5) mean, and that she is also able to determine whether or not they apply. How, then, should she use her findings to decide whether or not the alien beings are people? We needn't suppose that an entity must have *all* of these attributes to be properly considered a person; (1) and (2) alone may well be sufficient for personhood, and quite probably (1)–(3) are sufficient. Neither do we need to insist that any one of these criteria is *necessary* for personhood, although once again (1) and (2) look like fairly good candidates for necessary conditions, as does (3), if "activity" is construed so as to include the activity of reasoning.

All we need to claim, to demonstrate that a fetus is not a person, is that any being which satisfies *none* of (1)–(5) is certainly not a person. I consider this claim to be so obvious that I think anyone who denied it, and claimed that a being which satisfied none of (1)–(5) was a person all the same, would thereby demonstrate that she had no notion at all of what a person is—perhaps because she had confused the concept of a person with that of genetic humanity. If the opponents of abortion were to deny the appropriateness of these five criteria, I do not know what further arguments would convince them. We would probably have to admit that our conceptual schemes were indeed irreconcilably different, and that our dispute could not be settled objectively.

I do not expect this to happen, however, since I think that the concept of a person is one which is very nearly universal (to people), and that it is common to both proabortionists and antiabortionists, even though neither group has fully realized the relevance of this concept to the resolution of their dispute. Furthermore, I think that on reflection even the antiabortionists ought to agree not only that (1)–(5) are central to the concept of personhood, but also that it is a part of this concept that all and only people have full moral rights. The concept of a person is in part a moral concept; once we have admitted that *x* is a person we have recognized, even if we have not agreed to respect, *x*'s right to be treated as a member of the moral community. It is true that the claim that *x* is a *human being* is more commonly voiced as part of an appeal to treat *x* decently than is the claim that *x* is a person, but this is either because "human being" is here used in the sense which implies personhood, or because the genetic and moral senses of "human" have been confused.

Now if (1)–(5) are indeed the primary criteria of personhood, then it is clear that genetic humanity is neither necessary nor sufficient for establishing that an entity is a person. Some human beings are not people, and there may well be people who are not human beings. A man or woman whose consciousness has been permanently obliterated but who remains alive is a human being which is no longer a person; defective human beings, with no appreciable mental capacity, are not and presumably never will be people; and a fetus is a human being which is not yet a person, and which therefore cannot coherently be said to have full moral rights. Citizens of the next century should be prepared to recognize highly advanced, self-aware robots or computers, should such be developed, and intelligent inhabitants of other worlds, should such be found, as people in the fullest sense, and to respect their moral rights. But to ascribe full moral rights to an entity which is not a person is as absurd as to ascribe moral obligations and responsibilities to such an entity.

3. Fetal Development and the Right to Life
Two problems arise in the application of these suggestions for the definition of the moral community to the determination of the precise moral status of a human fetus. Given that the paradigm example of a person is a normal adult human being, then (1) How like this paradigm, in particular how far advanced since conception, does a human being need to be before it begins to have a right to life by virtue, not of being fully a person as of yet, but of being *like* a

person? and (2) To what extent, if any, does the fact that a fetus has the *potential* for becoming a person endow it with some of the same rights? Each of these questions requires some comment.

In answering the first question, we need not attempt a detailed consideration of the moral rights of organisms which are not developed enough, aware enough, intelligent enough, etc., to be considered people, but which resemble people in some respects. It does seem reasonable to suggest that the more like a person, in the relevant respects, a being is, the stronger is the case for regarding it as having a right to life, and indeed the stronger its right to life is. Thus we ought to take seriously the suggestion that, insofar as "the human individual develops biologically in a continuous fashion . . . the rights of a human person might develop in the same way."[11] But we must keep in mind that the attributes which are relevant in determining whether or not an entity is enough like a person to be regarded as having some moral rights are no different from those which are relevant to determining whether or not it is fully a person—i.e., are no different from (1)–(5)—and that being genetically human, or having recognizably human facial and other physical features, or detectable brain activity, or the capacity to survive outside the uterus, are simply not among these relevant attributes.

Thus it is clear that even though a seven- or eight-month fetus has features which make it apt to arouse in us almost the same powerful protective instinct as is commonly aroused by a small infant, nevertheless it is not significantly more personlike than is a very small embryo. It is *somewhat* more personlike; it can apparently feel and respond to pain, and it may even have a rudimentary form of consciousness, insofar as its brain is quite active. Nevertheless, it seems safe to say that it is not fully conscious, in the way that an infant of a few months is, and that it cannot reason, or communicate messages of indefinitely many sorts, does not engage in self-motivated activity, and has no self-awareness. Thus, in the *relevant* respects, a fetus, even a fully developed one, is considerably less personlike than is the average mature mammal, indeed the average fish. And I think that a rational person must conclude that if the right to life of a fetus is to be based upon its resemblance to a person, then it cannot be said to have any more right to life than, let us say, a newborn guppy (which also seems to be capable of feeling pain), and that a right of that magnitude could never override a woman's right to obtain an abortion, at any stage of her pregnancy.

There may, of course, be other arguments in favor of placing legal limits upon the stage of pregnancy in which an abortion may be performed. Given the relative safety of the new techniques of artificially inducing labor during the third trimester, the danger to the woman's life or health is no longer such an argument. Neither is the fact that people tend to respond to the thought of abortion in the later stages of pregnancy with emotional repulsion, since mere emotional responses cannot take the place of moral reasoning in determining what ought to be permitted. Nor, finally, is the frequently heard argument that legalizing abortion, especially late in the pregnancy, may erode the level of respect for human life, leading, perhaps, to an increase in unjustified euthanasia and other crimes. For this threat, if it is a threat, can be better met by educating people to the kinds of moral distinctions which we are making here than by limiting access to abortion (which limitation may, in its disregard for the rights of women, be just as damaging to the level of respect for human rights).

Thus, since the fact that even a fully developed fetus is not personlike enough to have any significant right to life on the basis of its personlikeness shows that no legal restrictions upon the stage of pregnancy in which an abortion may be performed can be justified on the grounds that we should protect the rights of the older fetus; and since there is no other apparent justification for such restrictions, we may conclude that they are entirely unjustified. Whether or not it would be *indecent* (whatever that means) for a woman in her seventh month to obtain an abortion just to avoid having to postpone a trip to Europe, it would not, in itself, be *immoral*, and therefore it ought to be permitted.

4. Potential Personhood and the Right to Life

We have seen that a fetus does not resemble a person in any way which can support the claim that it has even some of the same rights. But what about its *potential*, the fact that if nurtured and allowed to develop naturally it will very probably become a person? Doesn't that alone give it at least some right to life? It is hard to deny that the fact that an entity is a potential person is a strong prima facie reason for not destroying it; but we need not conclude from this that a potential person has a right to life, by virtue of that potential. It may be that our feeling that it is better, other things being equal, not to destroy a potential person is better explained by the fact that potential people are still (felt to be) an invaluable resource, not to be lightly squandered. Surely, if every speck of dust were a potential person, we would be much less apt to conclude that every potential person has a right to become actual.

Still, we do not need to insist that a potential person has no right to life whatever. There may well be something immoral, and not just imprudent, about wantonly destroying potential people, when doing so isn't necessary to protect anyone's rights. But even if a potential person does have some prima facie right to life, such a right could not possibly outweigh the right of a woman to obtain an abortion, since the rights of any actual person invariably outweigh those of any potential person, whenever the two conflict. Since this may not be immediately obvious in the case of a human fetus, let us look at another case.

Suppose that our space explorer falls into the hands of an alien culture, whose scientists decide to create a few hundred thousand or more human beings, by breaking her body into its component cells, and using these to create fully developed human beings, with, of course, her genetic code. We may imagine that each of these newly created individuals will have all of the original individual's abilities, skills, knowledge, and so on, and also have an individual self-concept, in short that each of them will be a bona fide (though hardly unique) person. Imagine that the whole project will take only seconds, and that its chances of success are extremely high, and that our explorer knows all of this, and also knows that these people will be treated fairly. I maintain that in such a situation she would have every right to escape if she could, and thus to deprive all of these potential people of their potential lives; for her right to life outweighs all of theirs together, in spite of the fact that they are all genetically human, all innocent, and all have a very high probability of becoming people very soon, if only she refrains from acting.

Indeed, I think she would have a right to escape even if it were not her life which the alien scientists planned to take, but only a year of her freedom, or, indeed, only a day. Nor would she be obligated to stay if she had gotten captured (thus bringing all these people-potentials into existence) because of her own carelessness, or even if she had done so deliberately, knowing the consequences. Regardless of how she got captured, she is not morally obligated to remain in captivity for *any* period of time for the sake of permitting any number of potential people to come into actuality, so great is the margin by which one actual person's right to liberty outweighs whatever right to life even a hundred thousand potential people have. And it seems reasonable to conclude that the rights of a woman will outweigh by a similar margin whatever right to life a fetus may have by virtue of its potential personhood.

Thus, neither a fetus's resemblance to a person, nor its potential for becoming a person provides any basis whatever for the claim that it has any significant right to life. Consequently, a woman's right to protect her health, happiness, freedom, and even her life,[12] by terminating an unwanted pregnancy, will always override whatever right to life it may be appropriate to ascribe to a fetus, even a fully developed one. And thus, in the absence of any overwhelming social need for every possible child, the laws which restrict the right to obtain an abortion, or limit the period of pregnancy during which an abortion may be performed, are a wholly unjustified violation of a woman's most basic moral and constitutional rights.[13]

Postscript on Infanticide

Since the publication of this article, many people have written to point out that my argument appears to justify not only abortion, but infanticide as well. For a new-born infant is not significantly more person-like than an advanced fetus, and consequently it would seem that if the destruction of the latter is permissible so too must be that of the former. Inasmuch as most people, regardless of how they feel about the morality of abortion, consider infanticide a form of murder, this might appear to represent a serious flaw in my argument.

Now, if I am right in holding that it is only people who have a full-fledged right to life, and who can be murdered, and if the criteria of personhood are as I have described them, then it obviously follows that killing a new-born infant isn't murder. It does *not* follow, however, that infanticide is permissible, for two reasons. In the first place, it would be wrong, at least in this country and in this period of history, and other things being equal, to kill a new-born infant, because even if its parents do not want it and would not suffer from its destruction, there are other people who would like to have it, and would, in all probability, be deprived of a great deal of pleasure by its destruction. Thus, infanticide is wrong for reasons analogous to those which make it wrong to wantonly destroy natural resources, or great works of art.

Secondly, most people, at least in this country, value infants and would much prefer that they be preserved, even if foster parents are not immediately available. Most of us would rather be taxed to support orphanages than allow unwanted infants to be destroyed. So long as there are people who want an infant preserved, and who are willing and able to provide the means of caring for it, under reasonably humane conditions, it is, *ceteris paribus*, wrong to destroy it.

But, it might be replied, if this argument shows that infanticide is wrong, at least at this time and in this country, doesn't it also show that abortion is wrong? After all, many people value fetuses, and are disturbed by their destruction, and would much prefer that they be preserved, even at some cost to themselves. Furthermore, as a potential source of pleasure to some foster family, a fetus is just as valuable as an infant. There is, however, a crucial difference between the two cases: so long as the fetus is unborn, its preservation, contrary to the wishes of the pregnant woman, violates her rights to freedom, happiness, and self-determination. Her rights override the rights of those who would like the fetus preserved, just as if someone's life or limb is threatened by a wild animal, his right to protect himself by destroying the animal overrides the rights of those who would prefer that the animal not be harmed.

The minute the infant is born, however, its preservation no longer violates any of its mother's rights, even if she wants it destroyed, because she is free to put it up for adoption. Consequently, while the moment of birth does not mark any sharp discontinuity in the degree to which an infant possesses the right to life, it does mark the end of its mother's right to determine its fate. Indeed, if abortion could be performed without killing the fetus, she would never possess the right to have the fetus destroyed, for the same reasons that she has no right to have an infant destroyed.

On the other hand, it follows from my argument that when an unwanted or defective infant is born into a society which cannot afford and/or is not willing to care for it, then its destruction is permissible. This conclusion will, no doubt, strike many people as heartless and immoral; but remember that the very existence of people who feel this way, and who are willing and able to provide care for unwanted infants, is reason enough to conclude that they should be preserved.

NOTES

1. For example, Roger Wertheimer, who in "Understanding the Abortion Argument" (*Philosophy and Public Affairs*, 1, No. 1 [Fall, 1971], 67–95), argues that the problem of the moral status of abortion is insoluble, in that the dispute over the status of the fetus is not a question of fact at all, but only a question of how one responds to the facts.

2. B. A. Brody, "Abortion and the Law," *The Journal of Philosophy*, 68, No. 12 (June 17, 1971), 357–369.

3. Judith Thomson, "A Defense of Abortion," *Philosophy and Public Affairs*, 1, No. 1 (Fall, 1971), 47–66.

4. I have abbreviated these standards somewhat, but not in a way which affects the argument.

5. John Noonan, "Abortion and the Catholic Church: A Summary History," *Natural Law Forum*, 12 (1967), 125.

6. John Noonan, "Deciding Who Is Human," *Natural Law Forum*, 13 (1968), 134.

7. "A Defense of Abortion."

8. We may safely ignore the fact that she might have avoided getting raped, e.g., by carrying a gun, since by similar means you might likewise have avoided getting kidnapped, and in neither case does the victim's failure to take all possible precautions against a highly unlikely event (as opposed to reasonable precautions against a rather likely event) mean that she is morally responsible for what happens.

9. Of course, the principle that it is (always) wrong to kill innocent human beings is in need of many other modifications, e.g., that it may be permissible to do so to save a greater number of other innocent human beings, but we may safely ignore these complications here.

10. From here on, we will use "human" to mean genetically human, since the moral sense seems closely connected to, and perhaps derived from, the assumption that genetic humanity is sufficient for membership in the moral community.

11. Thomas L. Hayes, "A Biological View," *Commonwealth* 85 (March 17, 1967), 677–78; quoted by Daniel Callahan, in *Abortion, Law, Choice, and Morality* (London: Macmillan & Co., 1970).

12. That is, insofar as the death rate, for the woman, is higher for childbirth than for early abortion.

13. My thanks to the following people, who were kind enough to read and criticize an earlier version of this paper: Herbert Gold, Gene Glass, Anne Lauterbach, Judith Thomson, Mary Mothersill, and Timothy Binkley.

An Almost Absolute Value in History

JOHN T. NOONAN, JR.

Noonan asserts that a human entity becomes a person at fertilization. He points to problems with the notion that personhood arises at some other point in human development (at viability, the point of fetal experience, or social visibility). He argues that the most plausible view is that personhood (and the right to life) begins at conception, for it is at conception that the "new being receives the genetic code. It is this genetic information which determines his characteristics, which is the biological carrier of the possibility of human wisdom, which makes him a self-evolving being. A being with a human genetic code is man."

The most fundamental question involved in the long history of thought on abortion is: How do you determine the humanity of a being? To phrase the question that way is to put in comprehensive humanistic terms what the theologians either dealt with as an explicitly theological question under the heading of "ensoulment" or dealt with implicitly in their treatment of abortion. The Christian position as it originated did not depend on a narrow theological or philosophical concept. It had no relation to theories of infant baptism. It appealed to no special theory of instantaneous ensoulment. It took the world's view on ensoulment as that view changed from Aristotle to Zacchia. There was, indeed, theological influence affecting the theory of ensoulment finally adopted, and, of course, ensoulment itself was a theological concept, so that the position was always explained in theological terms. But the theological notion of ensoulment could easily be translated into humanistic language by substituting "human" for "rational soul"; the problem of knowing when a man is a man is common to theology and humanism.

If one steps outside the specific categories used by the theologians, the answer they gave can be analyzed as a refusal to discriminate among human beings on the basis of their varying potentialities. Once conceived, the being was recognized as man because he had man's potential. The criterion for humanity, thus, was simple and all-embracing: If you are conceived by human parents, you are human.

The strength of this position may be tested by a review of some of the other distinctions offered in the contemporary controversy over legalizing abortion. Perhaps the most popular distinction is in terms of viability. Before an age of so many months, the fetus is not viable, that is, it cannot be removed from the mother's womb and live apart from her. To that extent, the life of the fetus is absolutely dependent on the life of the mother. This dependence is made the basis of denying recognition to its humanity.

Reprinted by permission of the publisher from *The Morality of Abortion: Legal and Historical Perspectives*, by John T. Noonan, Jr., pp. 51–59, Cambridge, MA: Harvard University Press. Copyright © 1970 by the President and Fellows of Harvard College.

There are difficulties with this distinction. One is that the perfection of artificial incubation may make the fetus viable at any time: It may be removed and artificially sustained. Experiments with animals already show that such a procedure is possible. This hypothetical extreme case relates to an actual difficulty; there is considerable elasticity to the idea of viability. Mere length of life is not an exact measure. The viability of the fetus depends on the extent of its anatomical and functional development. The weight and length of the fetus are better guides to the state of its development than age, but weight and length vary. Moreover, different racial groups have different ages at which their fetuses are viable. Some evidence, for example, suggests that Negro fetuses mature more quickly than white fetuses. If viability is the norm, the standard would vary with race and with many individual circumstances.

The most important objection to this approach is that dependence is not ended by viability. The fetus is still absolutely dependent on someone's care in order to continue existence; indeed a child of one or three or even five years of age is absolutely dependent on another's care for existence; uncared for, the older fetus or the younger child will die as surely as the early fetus detached from the mother. The unsubstantial lessening in dependence at viability does not seem to signify any special acquisition of humanity.

A second distinction has been attempted in terms of experience. A being who has had experience, has lived and suffered, who possesses memories, is more human than one who has not. Humanity depends on formation by experience. The fetus is thus "unformed" in the most basic human sense.

This distinction is not serviceable for the embryo which is already experiencing and reacting. The embryo is responsive to touch after eight weeks and at least at that point is experiencing. At an earlier stage the zygote is certainly alive and responding to its environment. The distinction may also be challenged by the rare case where aphasia has erased adult memory: has it erased humanity? More fundamentally, this distinction leaves even the older fetus or the younger child to be treated as an unformed inhuman thing. Finally, it is not clear why experience as such confers humanity. It could be argued that certain central experiences such as loving or learning are necessary to make a man human. But then human beings who have failed to love or to learn might be excluded from the class called man.

A third distinction is made by appeal to the sentiments of adults. If a fetus dies, the grief of the parents is not the grief they would have for a living child. The fetus is an unnamed "it" till birth, and is not perceived as personality until at least the fourth month of existence when movements in the womb manifest a vigorous presence demanding joyful recognition by the parents.

Yet feeling is notoriously an unsure guide to the humanity of others. Many groups of humans have had difficulty in feeling that persons of another tongue, color, religion, sex are as human as they. Apart from reactions to alien groups, we mourn the loss of a ten-year-old boy more than the loss of his one-day-old brother or his 90-year-old grandfather. The difference felt and the grief expressed vary with the potentialities extinguished, or the experience wiped out; they do not seem to point to any substantial difference in the humanity of baby, boy, or grandfather.

Distinctions are also made in terms of sensation by the parents. The embryo is felt within the womb only after about the fourth month. The embryo is seen only at birth. What can be neither seen nor felt is different from what is tangible. If the fetus cannot be seen or touched at all, it cannot be perceived as man.

Yet experience shows that sight is even more untrustworthy than feeling in determining humanity. By sight, color became an appropriate index for saying who was a man, and the evil of racial discrimination was given foundation. Nor can touch provide the test; a being confined by sickness, "out of touch" with others, does not thereby seem to lose his humanity. To the extent that touch still has appeal as a criterion, it appears to be a survival of the old English idea of "quickening"—a possible mistranslation of the Latin *animatus* used in the canon law. To that extent touch as a criterion seems to be dependent on the Aristotelian notion of ensoulment, and to fall when this notion is discarded.

Finally, a distinction is sought in social visibility. The fetus is not socially perceived as human. It cannot communicate with others. Thus, both subjectively and objectively, it is not a member of society. As moral rules are rules for the behavior of members of society to each other, they cannot be made for be-

havior toward what is not yet a member. Excluded from the society of men, the fetus is excluded from the humanity of men.

By force of the argument from the consequences, this distinction is to be rejected. It is more subtle than that founded on an appeal to physical sensation, but it is equally dangerous in its implications. If humanity depends on social recognition, individuals or whole groups may be dehumanized by being denied any status in their society. Such a fate is fictionally portrayed in *1984* and has actually been the lot of many men in many societies. In the Roman empire, for example, condemnation to slavery meant the practical denial of most human rights; in the Chinese Communist world, landlords have been classified as enemies of the people and so treated as nonpersons by the state. Humanity does not depend on social recognition, though often the failure of society to recognize the prisoner, the alien, the heterodox as human has led to the destruction of human beings. Anyone conceived by a man and a woman is human. Recognition of this condition by society follows a real event in the objective order, however imperfect and halting the recognition. Any attempt to limit humanity to exclude some group runs the risk of furnishing authority and precedent for excluding other groups in the name of the consciousness or perception of the controlling group in society.

A philosopher may reject the appeal to the humanity of the fetus because he views "humanity" as a secular view of the soul and because he doubts the existence of anything real and objective which can be identified as humanity. One answer to such a philosopher is to ask how he reasons about moral questions without supposing that there is a sense in which he and the others of whom he speaks are human. Whatever group is taken as the society which determines who may be killed is thereby taken as human. A second answer is to ask if he does not believe that there is a right and wrong way of deciding moral questions. If there is such a difference, experience may be appealed to: to decide who is human on the basis of the sentiment of a given society has led to consequences which rational men would characterize as monstrous.

The rejection of the attempted distinctions based on viability and visibility, experience and feeling, may be buttressed by the following considerations: Moral judgments often rest on distinctions, but if the distinctions are not to appear arbitrary *fiat*, they should relate to some real difference in probabilities. There is a kind of continuity in all life, but the earlier stages of the elements of human life possess tiny probabilities of development. Consider for example, the spermatozoa in any normal ejaculate: There are about 200,000,000 in any single ejaculate, of which one has a chance of developing into a zygote. Consider the oocytes which may become ova: there are 100,000 to 1,000,00 oocytes in a female infant, of which a maximum of 390 are ovulated. But once spermatozoa and ovum meet and the conceptus is formed, such studies as have been made show that roughly in only 20 percent of the cases will spontaneous abortion occur. In other words, the chances are about 4 out of 5 that this new being will develop. At this stage in the life of the being there is a sharp shift in probabilities, an immense jump in potentialities. To make a distinction between the rights of spermatozoa and the rights of the fertilized ovum is to respond to an enormous shift in possibilities. For about twenty days after conception the egg may split to form twins or combine with another egg to form a chimera, but the probability of either event happening is very small.

It may be asked, What does a change in biological probabilities have to do with establishing humanity? The argument from probabilities is not aimed at establishing humanity but at establishing an objective discontinuity which may be taken into account in moral discourse. As life itself is a matter of probabilities, as most moral reasoning is an estimate of probabilities, so it seems in accord with the structure of reality and the nature of moral thought to found a moral judgment on the change in probabilities at conception. The appeal to probabilities is the most commonsensical of arguments, to a greater or smaller degree all of us based our actions on probabilities, and in morals, as in law, prudence and negligence are often measured by the account one has taken of the probabilities. If the chance is 200,000,000 to 1 that the movement in the bushes into which you shoot is a man's, I doubt if many persons would hold you careless in shooting; but if the chances are 4 out of 5 that the movement is a human being's, few would acquit you of blame. Would the argument be different if only one out of ten children conceived came to term? Of course this argument would be different. This argument is an appeal to probabilities that actually exist, not to any and all states of affairs which may be imagined.

The probabilities as they do exist do not show the humanity of the embryo in the sense of a demonstration in logic any more than the probabilities of the movement in the bush being a man demonstrate beyond all doubt that the being is a man. The appeal is a "buttressing" consideration, showing the plausibility of the standard adopted. The argument focuses on the decisional factor in any moral judgment and assumes that part of the business of a moralist is drawing lines. One evidence of the nonarbitrary character of the line drawn is the difference of probabilities on either side of it. If a spermatozoon is destroyed, one destroys a being which had a chance of far less than 1 in 200 million of developing into a reasoning being, possessed of the genetic code, a heart and other organs, and capable of pain. If a fetus is destroyed, one destroys a being already possessed of the genetic code, organs, and sensitivity to pain, and one which had an 80 percent chance of developing further into a baby outside the womb who, in time, would reason.

The positive argument for conception as the decisive moment of humanization is that at conception the new being receives the genetic code. It is this genetic information which determines his characteristics, which is the biological carrier of the possibility of human wisdom, which makes him a self-evolving being. A being with a human genetic code is man.

This review of current controversy over the humanity of the fetus emphasizes what a fundamental question the theologians resolved in asserting the inviolability of the fetus. To regard the fetus as possessed of equal rights with other humans was not, however, to decide every case where abortion might be employed. It did decide the case where the argument was that the fetus should be aborted for its own good. To say a being was human was to say it had a destiny to decide for itself which could not be taken from it by another man's decision. But human beings with equal rights often come in conflict with each other, and some decision must be made as to whose claims are to prevail. Cases of conflict involving the fetus are different only in two respects: the total inability of the fetus to speak for itself and the fact that the right of the fetus regularly at stake is the right to life itself.

The approach taken by the theologians to these conflicts was articulated in terms of "direct" and "indirect." Again, to look at what they were doing from outside their categories, they may be said to have been drawing lines or "balancing values." "Direct" and "indirect" are spatial metaphors; "line-drawing" is another. "To weigh" or "to balance" values is a metaphor of a more complicated mathematical sort hinting at the process which goes on in moral judgments. All the metaphors suggest that, in the moral judgments made, comparisons were necessary, that no value completely controlled. The principle of double effect was no doctrine fallen from heaven, but a method of analysis appropriate where two relative values were being compared. In Catholic moral theology, as it developed, life even of the innocent was not taken as an absolute. Judgments of acts affecting life issued from a process of weighing. In the weighing, the fetus was always given a value greater than zero, always a value separate and independent from its parents. This valuation was crucial and fundamental in all Christian thought on the subject and marked it off from any approach which considered that only the parents' interests needed to be considered.

Even with the fetus weighed as human, one interest could be weighed as equal or superior: that of the mother in her own life. The casuists between 1450 and 1895 were willing to weigh this interest as superior. Since 1895, that interest was given decisive weight only in the two special cases of the cancerous uterus and the ectopic pregnancy. In both of these cases the fetus itself had little chance of survival even if abortion were not performed. As the balance was once struck in favor of the mother whenever her life was endangered, it could be so struck again. The balance reached between 1895 and 1930 attempted prudentially and pastorally to forestall a multitude of exceptions for interests less than life.

The perception of the humanity of the fetus and the weighing of fetal rights against other human rights constituted the work of the moral analysts. But what spirit animated abstract judgments? For the Christian community it was the injunction of Scripture to love your neighbor as yourself. The fetus as human was a neighbor; his life had parity with one's own. The commandment gave life to what otherwise would have been only rational calculation.

The commandment could be put in humanistic as well as theological terms: do not injure your fellow man without reasons. In these terms, once the humanity of the fetus is perceived, abortion is never right except in self-defense. When life must be taken to save life, reason alone cannot say that a mother must prefer a child's life to her own. With this exception, now of great rarity, abortion violates the rational humanist tenet of the equality of human lives.

For Christians the commandment to love had received a special imprint in that the exemplar proposed of love was the love of the Lord for his disciples. In the light given by this example, self-sacrifice carried to the point of death seemed in the extreme situations not without meaning. In the less extreme cases, preference for one's own interests to the life of another seemed to express cruelty or selfishness irreconcilable with the demands of love.

Abortion Decisions: Personal Morality

DANIEL CALLAHAN

Arguing for a moderate position on abortion, Callahan finds good reasons to reject both the notion that the unborn has no more value than a piece of tissue as well as the view that abortion is the immoral destruction of a human person. The fetus has at least some moral value, "an important and valuable form of human life." The moral status of the fetus demands a bias "against a routine, unthinking employment of abortion." But a woman also has moral obligations to "herself, her family and her society," so in some cases an abortion may be justified.

To press the problem to a finer point, what ought [women] to think about as they try to work out their own views on abortion?

Only a few suggestions will be made here, taking the form of arguing for an ethic of personal responsibility which tries, in the process of decision-making, to make itself aware of a number of things. The biological evidence should be considered, just as the problem of methodology must be considered; the philosophical assumptions implicit in different uses of the word "human" need to be considered; a philosophical theory of biological analysis is required; the social consequences of different kinds of analyses and different meaning of the word "human" should be thought through; consistency of meaning and use should be sought to avoid ad hoc and arbitrary solutions.

It is my own conviction that the "developmental school" offers the most helpful and illuminating approach to the problem of the beginning of human life, avoiding, on the one hand, a too narrow genetic criterion of human life and, on the other, a too broad and socially dangerous social definition of the "human." Yet the kinds of problems which appear in any attempt to decide upon the beginning of life suggest that no one position can be either proved or disproved from biological evidence alone. It becomes a question of trying to do justice to the evidence while, at the same time, realizing that how the evidence is approached and used will be a function of one's way of looking at reality, one's moral policy, the values and rights one believes need balancing, and the type of questions one thinks need to be asked. At the very least, however, the genetic evidence for the uniqueness of zygotes and embryos (a uniqueness of a different kind than that of the uniqueness of sperm and ova), their potentiality for development into a human person, their early development of human characteristics, their genetic and organic distinctness from the organism of the mother, appear to rule out a treatment even of zygotes, much less the more developed stages of the conceptus, as mere pieces of

"tissue," of no human significance or value. The "tissue" theory of the significance of the conceptus can only be made plausible by a systematic disregard of the biological evidence. Moreover, though one may conclude that a conceptus is only potential human life, in the process of continually actualizing its potential through growth and development, a respect for the sanctity of life, with its bias in favor even of undeveloped life, is enough to make the taking of such life a moral problem. There is a choice to be made and it is a moral choice. In the near future, it is likely that some kind of simple, safe abortifacient drug will be developed, which either prevents implantation or destroys the conceptus before it can develop. It will be tempting then to think that the moral dilemma has vanished, but I do not believe it will have.

It is possible to imagine a huge number of situations where a woman could, in good and sensitive conscience, choose abortion as a moral solution to her personal or social difficulties. But, at the very least, the bounds of morality are overstepped when, either through a systematic intellectual negligence or a willful choosing of that moral solution most personally convenient, personal choice is deliberately made easy and problem-free. Yet it seems to me that a pressure in that direction is a growing part of the ethos of technological societies; it is easily possible to find people to reassure us that we need have no scruples about the way we act, whether the issue is war, the suppression of rebellion and revolution, discrimination against minorities or the use of technological advances. Pluralism makes possible the achieving of freer, more subtle moral thinking; but it is a possibility constantly endangered by cultural pressures which would simplify or dissolve moral doubts and anguish.

The question of abortion "indications" returns at the level of personal choice. I have contended that the advent of permissive laws should not mean a cessation of efforts to explore the problem of "indications." When a woman asks herself, as she ought, whether her reasons for wanting an abortion are sound reasons—which presumes abortion is a serious enough moral issue to warrant the need to provide oneself with good reasons for choosing it—she will be asking herself about justifiable indications.

Thus, transposed from the legal to the personal level, the kinds of concerns adumbrated in the earlier chapters on indications remain fully pertinent. It was argued in those chapters that, with the possible exception of exceedingly rare instances of a direct threat to the physical life of the mother, one cannot speak of general categories of abortion indications as *necessitating* an abortion. In a number of circumstances, abortion may be a wise and justifiable solution to a distressed pregnancy. But when the language of necessity is used, the implication is that no other conceivable alternative is available. It may be granted, willingly enough, that some set of practical circumstances in some (possibly very many) concrete cases may indicate that abortion is the only feasible option open. But these cases cannot readily be determined in advance, and, for that reason, it is necessary to say that no formal indication as such (e.g., a psychiatric indication) entails a necessary, predetermined choice in favor of abortion.

The word "indication" remains the best word, suggesting that a number of given circumstances will bring the possibility or desirability of abortion to the fore. But to escalate the concept of an indication into that of a required procedure is to go too far. Abortion is *one* way to solve the problem of an unwanted or hazardous pregnancy (physically, psychologically, economically or socially), but it is rarely the only way, at least in affluent societies (I would be considerably less certain about making the same statement about poor societies). Even in the most extreme cases—rape, incest, psychosis, for instance—alternatives will usually be available and different choices, open. It is not necessarily the end of every woman's chance for a happy, meaningful life to bear an illegitimate child. It is not necessarily the automatic destruction of a family to have a seriously defective child born into it. It is not necessarily the ruination of every family living in overcrowded housing to have still another child. It is not inevitable that every immature woman would become even more so if she bore a child or another child. It is not inevitable that a gravely handicapped child can hope for nothing from life. It is not inevitable that every unwanted child is doomed to misery. It is not written in the essence of things, as a fixed law of human nature, that a woman cannot come to accept, love and be a good mother to a child who was initially unwanted. Nor is it a fixed law that she could not come to cherish a grossly deformed child. Naturally, these are only generalizations. The point is only that human beings are as a rule flexible, capable of doing more than they sometimes think they can, able to surmount serious dangers and challenges, able to grow and mature, able to transform inauspicious beginnings into satisfactory conclusions. Everything in life, even in procreative and family life, is not fixed in advance; the future is never wholly unalterable.

Yet the problem of personal question-asking must be pushed a step farther. The way the questions are answered will be very much determined by a woman's way of looking at herself and at life. A woman who has decided, as a personal moral policy, that nothing should be allowed to stand in the way of her own happiness, goals and self-interest will have no trouble solving the moral problem. For her, an unwanted pregnancy will, by definition, be a pregnancy to be terminated. But only by a Pickwickian use of words could this form of reasoning be called moral. It would preclude any need to consult the opinion of others, any need to examine the validity of one's own viewpoint, any need to, for instance, ask when human life begins, any need to interrogate oneself in any way, intellectually or morally; will and desire would be king.

Assuming, however, that most women would seek a broader ethical horizon than that of their exclusively personal self-interest, what might they think about when faced with an abortion decision? A respect for the sanctity of human life should, I believe, incline them toward a general and strong bias against abortion. Abortion is an act of killing, the violent, direct destruction of potential human life, already in the process of development. That fact should not be disguised, or glossed over by euphemism and circumlocution. It is not the destruction of a human person—for at no stage of its development does the conceptus fulfill the definition of a person, which implies a developed capacity for reasoning, willing, desiring and relating to others—but it is the destruction of an important and valuable form of human life. Its value and its potentiality are not dependent upon the attitude of the woman toward it; it grows by its own biological dynamism and has a genetic and morphological potential distinct from that of the woman. It has its own distinctive and individual future. If contraception and abortion are both seen as forms of birth limitation, they are distinctly different acts; the former precludes the possibility of a conceptus being formed, while the latter stops a conceptus already in existence from developing. The bias implied by the principle of the sanctity of human life is toward the protection of all forms of human life, especially, in ordinary circumstances, the protection of the right to life. That right should be accorded even to doubtful life; its existence should not be wholly dependent upon the personal self-interest of the woman.

Yet she has her own rights as well, and her own set of responsibilities to those around her; that is why she may have to choose abortion. In extreme situations of overpopulation, she may also have a responsibility for the survival of the species or of a people. In many circumstances, then, a decision in favor of abortion—one which overrides the right to life of that potential human being she carries within—can be a responsible moral decision, worthy neither of the condemnation of others nor of self-condemnation. But the bias of the principle of the sanctity of life is against a routine, unthinking employment of abortion; it bends over backwards not to take life and gives the benefit of the doubt to life. It does not seek to diminish the range of responsibility toward life—potential or actual—but to extend it. It does not seek the narrowest definition of life, but the widest and the richest. It is mindful of individual possibility, on the one hand, and of a destructive human tendency, on the other, to exclude from the category of "the human" or deny rights to those beings whose existence is or could prove burdensome to others.

The language used to describe abortion will have an important bearing on the sensitivities and imagination of those women who must make abortion decisions. Abortion can be talked about in the language of medical technology and technique—as, say, "a therapeutic procedure involving the emptying of the uterine contents." That language is neutral, clinical, unemotional. Or abortion can be talked about in the emotive language of relieving woman from suffering, or meeting the need for freedom among

women, or saving a nation from a devastating overpopulation. Both kinds of language have their place, for abortion has more than one result and meaning and abortion can legitimately be talked about in more than one way. What is objectionable is a conscious manipulation of language to incite an irrational emotional response, to allay doubts or to mislead the imagination. Particularly misleading is one commonly employed mixture of rhetorical modes by advocates of abortion on request. That is the use of a detached, clinical language to describe the actual operation itself combined with an emotive rhetoric to evoke the personal and social goods which an abortion can bring about. Thus, when every effort is made to suggest that emotion and feeling are perfectly appropriate to describe the social and personal goals of abortion, but that a clinical language only is appropriate when the actual technique and medical objective of an abortion is described, then the moral imagination is being misled.

Any human act can be described in impersonal, technological language, just as any act can be described in emotive language. What is wanted is an equity in the language. It is fair enough and to the point to say that in many circumstances abortion will save a woman's health or her family. It only becomes misleading when the act itself, as distinguished from its therapeutic goal, is talked about in an entirely different way. For, abortion is not just an "emptying of the uterine contents." It is also an act of killing; there will be no abortion unless the conceptus is killed (or its further existence made impossible, which amounts to the same thing). If it is appropriate to evoke the imagination and elicit sympathy for those women in a distressed pregnancy who could be helped by abortion, it is no less appropriate to evoke the imagination about what actually occurs in an abortion "procedure."

Imagination should also come into play at another point. It is often argued by proponents of abortion that there is no need for a woman ever to take any chances in a distressed pregnancy, particularly in the instance of an otherwise healthy woman who, if she has an abortion on one occasion, could simply get pregnant again on another, more auspicious occasion. This might be termed the "replacement theory" of abortion indications: since fetus "x" can be replaced by fetus "y," then there is no reason why a woman should have any scruples about such a replacement. This way of conceiving the choices effectively dissolves them; it becomes important only to know whether a woman can get pregnant again when she wants to. But this strategy can be employed only at the price of convincing oneself that there is no difference whatever among embryos or fetuses, that they all have exactly the same potentiality. But even the sketchiest knowledge of the genetic uniqueness of each conceptus (save in the instance of monozygotic twins), and thus the different genetic potentialities of each, should raise doubts on that point. Yet, having said that, I would not want to deny that the possibility of a further pregnancy could have an important bearing on the moral reasoning of a woman whose present pregnancy was threatening. If, out of a sense of responsibility toward her present children or her present life situation, a woman decided that an abortion was the wisest, most moral course, then the possibility that she could become pregnant later, when these responsibilities would be less pressing, would be a pertinent consideration.

The goal of these remarks is to keep alive in the consciences of women who have an abortion choice a moral tension; and it is to hope that they will be willing to bear the pain and the uncertainty of having to make a moral choice. It is the automatic, unthinking and unimaginative personal solution of abortion questions which women themselves should be extremely wary of, either for or against an abortion. A woman can, with little trouble, find both people and books to reassure her that there is no problem about abortion at all; or people and books to convince her that she would be a moral monster if she chose abortion. A woman can choose in advance the views she will listen to and thus have her predispositions confirmed. Yet a willingness to keep alive a moral tension, and to be wary of precipitous solutions, presupposes two things. First, that the woman herself wants to do what is right, realizing that what is right may not always be that which is most convenient, most easy or most immediately apt to solve a pressing problem. It is simply not the case that what one wants to do, or would like to do, or is

predisposed to do is necessarily the right thing to do. A willingness seriously to entertain that moral perception—which, of course, does not in itself imply a decision for or against an abortion—is one sign of moral seriousness.

Second, moral seriousness presupposes one is concerned with the protection and furthering of life. This means that, out of respect for human life, one bends over backwards not to eliminate human life, not to desensitize oneself to the meaning and value of potential life, not to seek definitions of the "human" which serve one's self-interest only. A desire to respect human life in all of its forms means, therefore, that one voluntarily imposes upon oneself a pressure against the taking of life; that one demands of oneself serious reasons for doing so, even in the case of a very early embryo; that one uses not only the mind but also the imagination when a decision is being made; that one seeks not to evade the moral issues but to face them; that one searches out the alternatives and conscientiously entertains them before turning to abortion. A bias in favor of the sanctity of human life in all of its forms would include a bias against abortion on the part of women; it would be the last rather than the first choice when unwanted pregnancies occurred. It would be an act to be avoided if at all possible.

A bias of this kind, voluntarily imposed by a woman upon herself, would not trap her; for it is also part of a respect for the dignity of life to leave the way open for an abortion when other reasonable choices are not available. For she also has duties toward herself, her family and her society. There can be good reasons for taking the life even of a very late fetus; once that also is seen and seen as a counterpoise in particular cases to the general bias against the taking of potential life, the way is open to choose abortion. The bias of the moral policy implies the need for moral rules which seek to preserve life. But, as a policy which leaves room for choice—rather than entailing a fixed set of rules—it is open to flexible interpretation when the circumstances point to the wisdom of taking exception to the normal ordering of the rules in particular cases. Yet, in that case, one is not genuinely taking exception to the rules. More accurately, one would be deciding that, for the preservation or furtherance of other values or right—species-rights, person-rights—a choice in favor of abortion would be serving the sanctity of life. That there would be, in that case, conflict between

rights, with one set of rights set aside (reluctantly) to serve another set, goes without saying. A subversion of the principle occurs when it is made out that there is no conflict and thus nothing to decide.

Abortion and the Concept of a Person

JANE ENGLISH

English stakes out some middle ground in the abortion debate. Echoing points made by Judith Jarvis Thomson, she argues that whether or not a fetus is a person, a woman may be justified in some instances (most notably in early pregnancy) in having an abortion as a form of self-defense. But an abortion is not always permissible, for even if a fetus is not a person, it still has at least partial moral status—a status that increases the more the fetus resembles a person. So in the late months of pregnancy, abortion seems wrong except to spare a woman from great injury or death.

The abortion debate rages on. Yet the two most popular positions seem to be clearly mistaken. Conservatives maintain that a human life begins at conception and that therefore abortion must be wrong because it is murder. But not all killings of humans are murders. Most notably, self defense may justify even the killing of an innocent person.

Liberals, on the other hand, are just as mistaken in their argument that since a fetus does not become a person until birth, a woman may do whatever she pleases in and to her own body. First, you cannot do as you please with your own body if it affects other people adversely.[1] Second, if a fetus is not a person, that does not imply that you can do to it anything you wish. Animals, for example, are not persons, yet to kill or torture them for no reason at all is wrong.

At the center of the storm has been the issue of just when it is between ovulation and adulthood that a person appears on the scene. Conservatives draw the line at conception, liberals at birth. In this paper I first examine our concept of a person and conclude that no single criterion can capture the concept of a person and no sharp line can be drawn. Next I argue that if a fetus is a person, abortion is still justifiable in many cases; and if a fetus is not a person, kill-

ing it is still wrong in many cases. To a large extent, these two solutions are in agreement. I conclude that our concept of a person cannot and need not bear the weight that the abortion controversy has thrust upon it.

I

The several factions in the abortion argument have drawn battle lines around various proposed criteria for determining what is and what is not a person. For example, Mary Anne Warren[2] lists five features (capacities for reasoning, self-awareness, complex communication, etc.) as her criteria for personhood and argues for the permissibility of abortion because a fetus falls outside this concept. Baruch Brody[3] uses brain waves. Michael Tooley[4] picks having-a-concept-of-self as his criterion and concludes that infanticide and abortion are justifiable, while the killing of adult animals is not. On the other side, Paul Ramsey[5] claims a certain gene structure is the defining characteristic. John Noonan[6] prefers conceived-of-humans and presents counterexamples to various other candidate criteria. For instance, he argues against viability as the criterion because the newborn and infirm would then be non-persons, since they cannot live without the aid of others. He rejects any criterion that calls upon the sorts of sentiments a being can evoke in adults on the grounds that this would allow us to exclude other races as

From *Canadian Journal of Philosophy*, vol. 5, no. 2 (Oct. 1975), pp. 233–43. Copyright © 1975. Reprinted with permission of the University of Calgary Press.

non-persons if we could just view them sufficiently unsentimentally.

These approaches are typical: foes of abortion propose sufficient conditions for personhood which fetuses satisfy, while friends of abortion counter with necessary conditions for personhood which fetuses lack. But these both presuppose that the concept of a person can be captured in a strait jacket of necessary and/or sufficient conditions.[7] Rather, "person" is a cluster of features, of which rationality, having a self concept and being conceived of humans are only part.

What is typical of persons? Within our concept of a person we include, first, certain biological factors: descended from humans, having a certain genetic make-up, having a head, hands, arms, eyes, capable of locomotion, breathing, eating, sleeping. There are psychological factors: sentience, perception, having a concept of self and of one's own interests and desires, the ability to use tools, the ability to use language or symbol systems, the ability to joke, to be angry, to doubt. There are rationality factors: the ability to reason and draw conclusions, the ability to generalize and to learn from past experience, the ability to sacrifice present interests for greater gains in the future. There are social factors: the ability to work in groups and respond to peer pressures, the ability to recognize and consider as valuable the interests of others, seeing oneself as one among "other minds," the ability to sympathize, encourage, love, the ability to evoke from others the responses of sympathy, encouragement, love, the ability to work with others for mutual advantage. Then there are legal factors: being subject to the law and protected by it, having the ability to sue and enter contracts, being counted in the census, having a name and citizenship, the ability to own property, inherit, and so forth.

Now the point is not that this list is incomplete, or that you can find counterinstances to each of its points. People typically exhibit rationality, for instance, but someone who was irrational would not thereby fail to qualify as a person. On the other hand, something could exhibit the majority of these features and still fail to be a person, as an advanced robot might. There is no single core of necessary and sufficient features which we can draw upon with the assurance that they constitute what really makes a person; there are only features that are more or less typical.

This is not to say that no necessary or sufficient conditions can be given. Being alive is a necessary condition for being a person, and being a U.S. Senator is sufficient. But rather than falling inside a sufficient condition or outside a necessary one, a fetus lies in the penumbra region where our concept of a person is not so simple. For this reason I think a conclusive answer to the question whether a fetus is a person is unattainable.

Here we might note a family of simple fallacies that proceed by stating a necessary condition for personhood and showing that a fetus has that characteristic. This is a form of the fallacy of affirming the consequent. For example, some have mistakenly reasoned from the premise that a fetus is human (after all, it is a human fetus rather than, say, a canine fetus), to the conclusion that it is a human. Adding an equivocation on "being," we get the fallacious argument that since a fetus is something both living and human, it is a human being.

Nonetheless, it does seem clear that a fetus has very few of the above family of characteristics, whereas a newborn baby exhibits a much larger proportion of them—and a two-year-old has even more. Note that one traditional anti-abortion argument has centered on pointing out the many ways in which a fetus resembles a baby. They emphasize its development ("It already has ten fingers . . .") without mentioning its dissimilarities to adults (it still has gills and a tail). They also try to evoke the sort of sympathy on our part that we only feel toward other persons ("Never to laugh . . . or feel the sunshine?"). This all seems to be a relevant way to argue, since its purpose is to persuade us that a fetus satisfies so many of the important features on the list that it ought so be treated as a person. Also note that a fetus near the time of birth satisfies many more of these factors than a fetus in the early months of development. This could provide reason for making distinctions among the different stages of pregnancy, as the U.S. Supreme Court has done.[8]

Historically, the time at which a person has been said to come into existence has varied widely. Muslims date personhood from fourteen days after conception. Some medievals followed Aristotle in placing ensoulment at forty days after conception for a male fetus and eighty days for a female fetus.[9] In European common law since the Seventeenth Century, abortion was considered the killing of a person only after quickening, the time when a pregnant woman first feels the fetus move on its own. Nor is this variety of opinions surprising. Biologically, a human being develops gradually. We shouldn't expect there to be any specific time or sharp dividing point when a person appears on the scene.

For these reasons I believe our concept of a person is not sharp or decisive enough to bear the weight of a solution to the abortion controversy. To use it to solve that problem is to clarify *obscurum per obscurius.*

II

Next let us consider what follows if a fetus is a person after all. Judith Jarvis Thomson's landmark article, "A Defense of Abortion,[10] correctly points out that some additional argumentation is needed at this point in the conservative argument to bridge the gap between the premise that a fetus is an innocent person and the conclusion that killing it is always wrong. To arrive at this conclusion, we would need the additional premise that killing an innocent person is always wrong. But killing an innocent person is sometimes permissible, most notably in self defense. Some examples may help draw out our intuitions or ordinary judgments about self defense.

Suppose a mad scientist, for instance, hypnotized innocent people to jump out of the bushes and attack innocent passers-by with knives. If you are so attacked, we agree you have a right to kill the attacker in self defense, if killing him is the only way to protect your life or to save yourself from serious injury. It does not seem to matter here that the attacker is not malicious but himself an innocent pawn, for your killing of him is not done in a spirit of retribution but only in self defense.

How severe an injury may you inflict in self defense? In part this depends upon the severity of the injury to be avoided: you may not shoot someone merely to avoid having your clothes torn. This might lead one to the mistaken conclusion that the defense may only equal the threatened injury in severity; that to avoid death you may kill, but to avoid a black eye

you may only inflict a black eye or the equivalent. Rather, our laws and customs seem to say that you may create an injury somewhat, but not enormously, greater than the injury to be avoided. To fend off an attack whose outcome would be as serious as rape, a severe beating or the loss of a finger, you may shoot; to avoid having your clothes torn, you may blacken an eye.

Aside from this, the injury you may inflict should only be the minimum necessary to deter or incapacitate the attacker. Even if you know he intends to kill you, you are not justified in shooting him if you could equally well save yourself by the simple expedient of running away. Self defense is for the purpose of avoiding harms rather than equalizing harms.

Some cases of pregnancy present a parallel situation. Though the fetus is itself innocent, it may pose a threat to the pregnant woman's well-being, life prospects or health, mental or physical. If the pregnancy presents a slight threat to her interests, it seems self defense cannot justify abortion. But if the threat is on a par with a serious beating or the loss of a finger, she may kill the fetus that poses such a threat, even if it is an innocent person. If a lesser harm to the fetus could have the same defensive effect, killing it would not be justified. It is unfortunate that the only way to free the woman from the pregnancy entails the death of the fetus (except in very late stages of pregnancy). Thus a self defense model supports Thomson's point that the woman has a right only to be freed from the fetus, not a right to demand its death.[11]

The self defense model is most helpful when we take the pregnant woman's point of view. In the pre-Thomson literature, abortion is often framed as a question for a third party: do you, a doctor, have a right to choose between the life of the woman and that of the fetus? Some have claimed that if you were a passer-by who witnessed a struggle between the innocent hypnotized attacker and his equally innocent victim, you would have no reason to kill either in defense of the other. They have concluded that the self defense model implies that a woman may attempt to abort herself, but that a doctor should not assist her. I think the position of the third party is somewhat more complex. We do feel some inclination to intervene on behalf of the victim rather than the attacker, other things equal. But if both parties are innocent, other factors come into consideration. You would rush to the aid of your husband whether he was attacker or attackee. If a hypnotized famous violinist were attacking a skid row bum, we would try to save the individual who is of more value to society. These considerations would tend to support abortion in some cases.

But suppose you are a frail senior citizen who wishes to avoid being knifed by one of these innocent hypnotics, so you have hired a bodyguard to accompany you. If you are attacked, it is clear we believe that the bodyguard, acting as your agent, has a right to kill the attacker to save you from a serious beating. Your rights of self defense are transferred to your agent. I suggest that we should similarly view the doctor as the pregnant woman's agent in carrying out a defense she is physically incapable of accomplishing herself.

Thanks to modern technology, the cases are rare in which a pregnancy poses as clear a threat to a woman's bodily health as an attacker brandishing a switchblade. How does self defense fare when more subtle, complex and long-range harms are involved?

To consider a somewhat fanciful example, suppose you are a highly trained surgeon when you are kidnapped by the hypnotic attacker. He says he does not intend to harm you but to take you back to the mad scientist who, it turns out, plans to hypnotize you to have a permanent mental block against all your knowledge of medicine. This would automatically destroy your career which would in turn have a serious adverse impact on your family, your personal relationships and your happiness. It seems to me that if the only way you can avoid this outcome is to shoot the innocent attacker, you are justified in so doing. You are defending yourself from a drastic injury to your life prospects. I think it is no exaggeration to claim that unwanted pregnancies (most obviously among teenagers) often have such adverse lifelong consequences as the surgeon's loss of livelihood.

Several parallels arise between various views on abortion and the self defense model. Let's suppose further that these hypnotized attackers only operate at night, so that it is well known that they can be avoided completely by the considerable inconvenience of never leaving your house after dark.

One view is that since you could stay home at night, therefore if you go out and are selected by one of these hypnotized people, you have no right to defend yourself. This parallels the view that abstinence is the only acceptable way to avoid pregnancy. Others might hold that you ought to take along some defense such as Mace which will deter the hypnotized person without killing him, but that if this defense fails, you are obliged to submit to the resulting injury, no matter how severe it is. This parallels the view that contraception is all right but abortion is always wrong, even in cases of contraceptive failure.

A third view is that you may kill the hypnotized person only if he will actually kill you, but not if he will only injure you. This is like the position that abortion is permissible only if it is required to save a woman's life. Finally we have the view that it is all right to kill the attacker, even if only to avoid a very slight inconvenience to yourself and even if you knowingly walked down the very street where all these incidents have been taking place without taking along any Mace or protective escort. If we assume that a fetus is a person, this is the analogue of the view that abortion is always justifiable, "on demand."

The self defense model allows us to see an important difference that exists between abortion and infanticide, even if a fetus is a person from conception. Many have argued that the only way to justify abortion without justifying infanticide would be to find some characteristic of personhood that is acquired at birth. Michael Tooley, for one, claims infanticide is justifiable because the really significant characteristics of person are acquired some time after birth. But all such approaches look to characteristics of the developing human and ignore the relation between the fetus and the woman. What if, after birth, the presence of an infant or the need to support it posed a grave threat to the woman's sanity or life prospects? She could escape this threat by the simple expedient of running away. So a solution that does not entail the death of the infant is available. Before birth, such solutions are not available because of the biological dependence of the fetus on the woman. Birth is the crucial point not because of any characteristics the fetus gains, but because after birth the woman can defend herself by a means less drastic than killing the infant. Hence self defense can be used to justify abortion without necessarily thereby justifying infanticide.

III

On the other hand, supposing a fetus is not after all a person, would abortion always be morally permissible? Some opponents of abortion seem worried that if a fetus is not a full-fledged person, then we are justified in treating it in any way at all. However, this does not follow. Non-persons do get some consideration in our moral code, though of course they do not have the same rights as persons have (and in general they do not have moral responsibilities), and though their interests may be overridden by the interests of persons. Still, we cannot just treat them in any way at all.

Treatment of animals is a case in point. It is wrong to torture dogs for fun or to kill wild birds for no reason at all. It is wrong Period, even though dogs and birds do not have the same rights persons do. However, few people think it is wrong to use dogs as experimental animals, causing them considerable suffering in some cases, provided that the resulting research will probably bring discoveries of great benefit to people. And most of us think it all right to kill birds for food or to protect our crops. People's rights are different from the consideration we give to animals, then, for it is wrong to experiment on people, even if others might later benefit a great deal as a result of their suffering. You might volunteer to be a subject, but this would be supererogatory; you certainly have a right to refuse to be a medical guinea pig.

But how do we decide what you may or may not do to non-persons? This is a difficult problem, one for which I believe no adequate account exists. You do not want to say, for instance, that torturing dogs is all right whenever the sum of its effects on people is good—when it doesn't warp the sensibilities of the torturer so much that he mistreats people. If that were the case, it would be all right to torture dogs if you did it in private, or if the torturer lived on a desert island or died soon afterward, so that his actions had no effect on people. This is an inadequate account, because whatever moral consideration animals get, it has to be indefeasible, too. It will have

to be a general proscription of certain actions, not merely a weighing of the impact on people on a case-by-case basis.

Rather, we need to distinguish two levels on which consequences of actions can be taken into account in moral reasoning. The traditional objections to Utilitarianism focus on the fact that it operates solely on the first level, taking all the consequences into account in particular cases only. Thus Utilitarianism is open to "desert island" and "lifeboat" counterexamples because these cases are rigged to make the consequences of actions severely limited.

Rawls' theory could be described as a teleological sort of theory, but with teleology operating on a higher level.[12] In choosing the principles to regulate society from the original position, his hypothetical choosers make their decision on the basis of the total consequences of various systems. Furthermore, they are constrained to choose a general set of rules which people can readily learn and apply. An ethical theory must operate by generating a set of sympathies and attitudes toward others which reinforces the functioning of that set of moral principles. Our prohibition against killing people operates by means of certain moral sentiments including sympathy, compassion and guilt. But if these attitudes are to form a coherent set, they carry us further: we tend to perform supererogatory actions, and we tend to feel similar compassion toward person-like non-persons.

It is crucial that psychological facts play a role here. Our psychological constitution makes it the case that for our ethical theory to work, it must prohibit certain treatment of non-persons which are significantly person-like. If our moral rules allowed people to treat some person-like non-persons in ways we do not want people to be treated, this would undermine the system of sympathies and attitudes that makes the ethical system work. For this reason, we would choose in the original position to make mistreatment of some sorts of animals wrong in general (not just wrong in the cases with public impact), even though animals are not themselves parties in the original position. Thus it makes sense that it is those animals whose appearance and behavior are most like those of people that get the most consideration in our moral scheme.

It is because of "coherence of attitudes," I think, that the similarity of a fetus to a baby is very significant. A fetus one week before birth is so much like a newborn baby in our psychological space that we cannot allow any cavalier treatment of the former while expecting full sympathy and nurturative support for the latter. Thus, I think that anti-abortion forces are indeed giving their strongest arguments when they point to the similarities between a fetus and a baby, and when they try to evoke our emotional attachment to and sympathy for the fetus. An early horror story from New York about nurses who were expected to alternate between caring for six-week premature infants and disposing of viable 24-week aborted fetuses is just that—a horror story. These beings are so much alike that no one can be asked to draw a distinction and treat them so very differently.

Remember, however, that in the early weeks after conception, a fetus is not very much unlike a person. It is hard to develop these feelings for a set of genes which doesn't yet have a head, hands, beating heart, response to touch or the ability to move by itself. Thus it seems to me that the alleged "slippery slope" between conception and birth is not so very slippery. In the early stages of pregnancy, abortion can hardly be compared to murder for psychological reasons, but in the latest stages it is psychologically akin to murder.

Another source of similarity is the bodily continuity between fetus and adult. Bodies play a surprisingly central role in our attitudes toward persons. One has only to think of the philosophical literature on how far physical identity suffices for personal identity or Wittgenstein's remark that the best picture of the human soul is the human body. Even after death, when all agree the body is no longer a person, we still observe elaborate customs of respect for the human body; like people who torture dogs, necrophiliacs are not to be trusted with people.[13] So it is appropriate that we show respect to a fetus as the body continuous with the body of a person. This is a degree of resemblance to persons that animals cannot rival.

Michael Tooley also utilizes a parallel with animals. He claims that it is always permissible to drown newborn kittens and draws conclusions about infanticide.[14] But it is only permissible to drown kittens when their survival would cause some hardship. Per-haps it would be a burden to feed and house six more cats or to find other homes for them. The alternative of letting them starve produces even more suffering than the drowning. Since the kittens get their rights secondhand, so to speak, *via* the need for coherence in our attitudes, their interests are often overriden by the interests of full-fledged persons. But if their survival would be no inconvenience of people at all, then it is wrong to drown them, *contra* Tooley.

Tooley's conclusions about abortion are wrong for the same reason. Even if a fetus is not a person, abortion is not always permissible, because of the resemblance of a fetus to a person. I agree with Thomson that it would be wrong for a woman who is seven months pregnant to have an abortion just to avoid having to postpone a trip to Europe. In the early months of pregnancy when the fetus hardly resembles a baby at all, then, abortion is permissible whenever it is in the interests of the pregnant woman or her family. The reasons would only need to outweigh the pain and inconvenience of the abortion itself. In the middle months, when the fetus comes to resemble a person, abortion would be justifiable only when the continuation of the pregnancy or the birth of the child would cause harms—physical, psychological, economic or social—to the woman. In the late months of pregnancy, even on our current assumption that a fetus is not a person, abortion seems to be wrong except to save a woman from significant injury or death.

The Supreme Court has recognized similar gradations in the alleged slippery slope stretching between conception and birth. To this point, the present paper has been a discussion of the moral status of abortion only, not its legal status. In view of the great physical, financial and sometimes psychological costs of abortion, perhaps the legal arrangement most compatible with the proposed moral solution would be the absence of restrictions, that is, so-called abortion "on demand."

So I conclude, first, that application of our concept of a person will not suffice to settle the abortion issue. After all, the biological development of a human being is gradual. Second, whether a fetus is a person or not, abortion is justifiable early in pregnancy to avoid modest harms and seldom justifiable late in pregnancy except to avoid significant injury or death.[15]

NOTES

1. We also have paternalistic laws which keep us from harming our own bodies even when no one else is affected. Ironically, anti-abortion laws were originally designed to protect pregnant women from a dangerous but tempting procedure.

2. Mary Anne Warren, "On the Moral and Legal Status of Abortion," *Monist* 57 (1973), p. 55.

3. Baruch Brody, "Fetal Humanity and the Theory of Essentialism," in Robert Baker and Frederick Elliston (eds.), *Philosophy and Sex* (Buffalo, NY., 1975).

4. Michael Tooley, "Abortion and Infanticide," *Philosophy and Public Affairs* 2 (1971).

5. Paul Ramsey, "The Morality of Abortion," in James Rachels, ed., *Moral Problems* (New York, 1971).

6. John Noonan, "Abortion and the Catholic Church: A Summary History," *Natural Law Forum* 12 (1967), pp. 125–131.

7. Wittgenstein has argued against the possibility of fifty capturing the concept of a game, *Philosophical Investigations* (New York, 1958), §66–71.

8. Not because the fetus is partly a person and so has some of the rights of persons, but rather because of the rights of person-like non-persons.

9. Aristotle himself was concerned, however, with the different question of when the soul takes form. For historical data, see Jimmye Kimmey, "How the Abortion Laws Happened," *Ms.* 1 (April, 1973), pp. 48ff and John Noonan, *loc. cit.*

10. J. J. Thomson, "A Defense of Abortion," *Philosophy and Public Affairs* 1 (1971).

11. *Ibid.*, p. 52.

12. John Rawls, *A Theory of Justice* (Cambridge, Mass., 1971), §§ 3–4.

13. On the other hand, if they can be trusted with people, then our moral customs are mistaken. It all depends on the facts of psychology.

14. *Op. cit.*, pp. 40, 60–61.

15. I am deeply indebted to Larry Crocker and Arthur Kuflik for their constructive comments.

In Defense of Abortion and Infanticide

MICHAEL TOOLEY

Tooley argues that an individual cannot have a right to life unless it "possesses the concept of a continuing self or mental substance." It is unlikely that fetuses or unborn babies have any such concept, so they do not have a right to life. The fact that they will someday come to have the requisite concept does not in itself make it seriously wrong to destroy them. Thus abortion and even infanticide shortly after birth must be viewed as morally acceptable.

What reason is there for raising the question of the morality of infanticide? One reason is that it seems very difficult to formulate a completely satisfactory pro-abortion position without coming to grips with the infanticide issue. For the problem that the liberal on abortion encounters here is that of specifying a cutoff point that is not arbitrary: At what stage in the development of a human being does it cease to be morally permissible to destroy it, and why?

It is important to be clear about the difficulty here. The problem is not, as some have thought, that since there is a continuous line of development from

From *The Abortion Controversy: 25 Years After Roe v. Wade, a Reader*, 2nd ed. by Louis P. Pojman and Francis Beckwith. Copyright © 1998, pp. 209–233. Reprinted by permission of Michael Tooley.

a zygote to a newborn baby, one cannot hold that it is seriously wrong to destroy a newborn baby without also holding that it is seriously wrong to destroy a zygote, or any intermediate stage in the development of a human being. The problem is rather that if one says that it is wrong to destroy a newborn baby but not a zygote or some intermediate stage, one should be prepared to point to a *morally relevant* difference between a new-born baby and the earlier stage in the development of a human being.

Precisely the same difficulty can, of course, be raised for a person who holds that infanticide is morally permissible, since one can ask what morally relevant difference there is between an adult human being and a newborn baby. What makes it morally permissible to destroy a baby, but wrong to kill an adult? So the challenge remains. But I shall argue that in the latter case there is an extremely plausible answer.

Reflecting on the morality of infanticide forces one to face up to this challenge. In the case of abortion a number of events—quickening or viability, for instance—might be taken as cutoff points, and it is easy to overlook the fact that none of these events involves any morally significant change in the developing human. In contrast, if one is going to defend infanticide, one has to get very clear about what it is that gives something a right to life.

One of the interesting ways in which the abortion issue differs from most other moral issues is that the plausible positions on abortion appear to be extreme ones. For if a human fetus has a right to life, one is inclined to say that, in general, one would be justified in killing it only to save the life of the mother, and perhaps not even in that case.[1] Such is the extreme anti-abortion position. On the other hand, if the fetus does not have a right to life, why should it be seriously wrong to destroy it? Why would one need to point to special circumstance—such as the presence of genetic disease, or a threat to the woman's health—in order to justify such action? The upshot is that there does not appear to be any room for a moderate position on abortion as one finds, for example, in the Model Penal Code recommendations.[2]

Aside from the light it may shed on the abortion question, the issue of infanticide is both interesting and important in its own right. The theoretical interest has been mentioned earlier: It forces one to face up to the question of what it is that gives something a right to life. The practical importance need not be labored. Most people would prefer to raise children who do not suffer from gross deformities or from severe physical, emotional, or intellectual handicaps. If it could be shown that there is no moral objection to infanticide, the happiness of society could be significantly and justifiably increased.

The suggestion that infanticide may be morally permissible is not an idea that many people are able to consider dispassionately. Even philosophers tend to react in a way that seems primarily visceral—offering no arguments and dismissing infanticide out of hand.

Some philosophers have argued, however, that such a reaction is not inappropriate, on the ground that, first, moral principles must, in the final analysis, be justified by reference to our moral feelings, or intuitions, and secondly, infanticide is one practice that is judged wrong by virtually everyone's moral intuition. I believe, however, that this line of thought is unsound, and I have argued elsewhere that even if one grants, at least for the sake of argument, that moral intuitions are the final court of appeal regarding the acceptability of moral principles, the question of the morality of infanticide is not one that can be settled by an appeal to our intuitions concerning it.[3] If infanticide is to be rejected, an argument is needed, and I believe that the considerations advanced in this essay show that it is unlikely that such an argument is forthcoming.

What Sort of Being Can Possess a Right to Life?

The issues of the morality of abortion and of infanticide seem to turn primarily upon the answers to the following four questions:

1. What properties, other than potentialities, give something a right to life?
2. Do the corresponding potentialities also endow something with a right to life?
3. If not, do they at least make it seriously wrong to destroy it?
4. At what point in its development does a member of the biologically defined species *Homo sapiens* first possess those nonpotential properties that give something a right to life?

The argument to be developed in the present section bears upon the answers to the first two questions.

How can one determine what properties endow a being with a right to life? An approach that I believe is very promising starts from the observation that there appear to be two radically different sorts of reasons why an entity may lack a certain right. Compare, for example, the following two claims:

1. A child does not have a right to smoke.
2. A newspaper does not have a right not to be torn up.

The first claim raises a substantive moral issue. People might well disagree about it, and support their conflicting views by appealing to different moral theories. The second dispute, in contrast, seems an unlikely candidate for moral dispute. It is natural to say that newspapers just are not the sort of thing that can have any rights at all, including a right not to be torn up. So there is no need to appeal to a substantive moral theory to resolve the question whether a newspaper has a right not to be torn up.

One way of characterizing this difference, albeit one that will not especially commend itself to philosophers of a Quinean bent, is to say that the second claim, unlike the first, is true in virtue of a certain *conceptual* connection, and that is why no moral theory is needed in order to see that it is true. The explanation, then, of why it is that a newspaper does not have a right not to be torn up, is that there exists some property P such that, first, newspapers lack property P, and, second, it is a conceptual truth that only things with property P can be possessors of rights.

What might property P be? A plausible answer, I believe, is set out and defended by Joel Feinberg in his paper, "The Rights of Animals and Unborn Generations."[4] It takes the form of what Feinberg refers to as the *interest principle*: ". . . the sorts of beings who *can* have rights are precisely those who have (or can have) interests."[5] And then, since "interests must be compounded somehow out of conations,"[6] it follows that things devoid of desires, such as newspapers, can have neither interests nor rights. Here, then, is one account of the difference in status between judgments such as (1) and (2) above.

Let us now consider the right to life. The interest principle tells us that an entity cannot have any rights at all, and, *a fortiori*, cannot have a right to life, unless it is capable of having interests. This in itself may be a conclusion of considerable importance. Consider, for example, a fertilized human egg cell. Someday it will come to have desires and interests. As a zygote, however, it does not have desires, nor even the *capacity* for having desires. What about interests? This depends upon the account one offers of the relationship between desires and interests. It seems to me that a zygote cannot be properly spoken of as a subject of interests. My reason is roughly this. What is in a thing's interest is a function of its present and future desires, both those it will actually have and those it could have. In the case of an entity that is not presently capable of any desires, its interests must be based entirely upon the satisfaction of future desires. Then, since satisfaction of future desires presupposes the continued existence of the entity in question, anything which has an interest that is based upon the satisfaction of future desires must also have an interest in its own continued existence. Therefore, something that is not presently capable of having any desires at all—like a zygote—cannot have any interests at all unless it has interest in its own continued existence. I shall argue shortly, however, that a zygote cannot have such an interest. From this it will follow that it cannot have any interests at all, and this conclusion, together with the interest principle, entails that not all members of the species *Homo sapiens* have a right to life.

The interest principle involves, then, a thesis concerning a necessary condition that something must satisfy if it is to have a right to life, and it is a thesis that has important moral implications. It implies, for example, that abortions, if performed sufficiently early, do not involve any violation of a right to life. But on the other hand, the interest principle provides no help with the question of the moral status of human organisms once they have developed to the point where they do have desires, and thus are capable of having interests. The interest principle states that they *can* have rights. It does not state whether they *do* have rights—including, in particular, a right not to be destroyed.

It is possible, however, that the interest principle does not exhaust the connections between rights and interests. It formulates only a very general connection: A thing cannot have any rights at all unless it is capable of having at least some interest. May there not be more specific connections, between particular rights and particular sorts of interests? The following line of thought lends plausibility to this suggestion. Consider animals such as cats. Some philosophers are inclined to hold that animals such as cats do not have any rights at all. But let us assume, for the purpose of the present discussion, that cats do have some rights, such as a right not to be tortured, and consider the following claim:

3. A cat does not have a right to a university education.

How is this statement to be regarded? In particular, is it comparable in status to the claim that children do not have a right to smoke, or, instead, to the claim that newspapers do not have a right to be torn up? To the latter, surely. Just as a newspaper is not the sort of thing that can have any rights at all, including a right not to be destroyed, so one is inclined to say that a cat, though it may have some rights, such as a right not to be tortured, is not the sort of thing that can possibly have a right to a university education.

This intuitive judgment about the status of claims such as (3) is reinforced, moreover, if one turns to the question of the grounds of the interest principle. Consider, for example, the account offered by Feinberg, which he summarizes as follows:

> Now we can extract from our discussion of animal rights a crucial principle for tentative use in the resolution of the other riddles about the applicability of the concept of a right, namely, that the sorts of beings who *can* have rights are precisely those who have (or can have) interests. I have come to this tentative conclusion for two reasons: (1) because a right holder must be capable of being represented and it is impossible to represent a being that has no interests, and (2) because a right holder must be capable of being a beneficiary in his own person, and a being without interests is a being that is incapable of being harmed or benefited, having no good or "sake" of its own. Thus a being without interests has no "behalf" to act in, and no "sake" to act for.[7]

If this justification of the interest principle is sound, it can also be employed to support principles connecting particular rights with specific sorts of interests. Just as one cannot represent a being that has no interests at all, so one cannot, in demanding a university education for a cat, be representing the cat unless one is thereby representing some interest that the cat has, and that would be served by its receiving a university education. Similarly, one cannot be acting for the sake of a cat in arguing that it should receive a university education unless the cat has some interest that will thereby be furthered. The conclusion, therefore, is that if Feinberg's defense of the interest principle is sound, other, more specific principles must also be correct. These more specific principles can be summed up, albeit somewhat vaguely, by the following, *particular-interests principle.*

It is a conceptual truth that an entity cannot have a particular right, R, unless it is at least capable of having some interest, I, which is furthered by its having right R.

Given this particular-interests principle, certain familiar facts, whose importance has not often been appreciated, become comprehensible. Compare an act of killing a normal adult human being with an act of torturing one for five minutes. Though both acts are seriously wrong, they are not equally so. Here, as in most cases, to violate an individual's right to life is more seriously wrong than to violate his right not to have pain inflicted upon him. Consider, however, the corresponding actions in the case of a newborn kitten. Most people feel that it is seriously wrong to torture a kitten for five minutes, but not to kill it painlessly. How is this difference in the moral ordering of the two types of acts, between the human case and the kitten case, to be explained? One answer is that while normal adult human beings have both a right to life and a right not to be tortured, a kitten has only the latter. But why should this be so? The particular-interest principle, however, suggests a possible explanation. Though kittens have some interests, including, in particular, an interest in not being tortured, which derives from their capacity to feel pain, they do not have an interest in their own continued existence and, hence, do not have a right not to be destroyed. This answer contains, of course, a large promissory element. One needs a defense of the view that kittens have no interest in continued existence. But the point here is simply that there is an important question about the rationale underlying the moral ordering of certain sorts of acts, and that the particular-interests principle points to a possible answer.

This fact lends further plausibility, I believe, to the particular-interests principle. What one would ultimately like to do, of course, is to set out an analysis of the concept of a right, show that the analysis is indeed satisfactory, and then show that the particular-interests principle is entailed by the analysis. Unfortunately, it will not be possible to pursue such an approach here, since formulating an acceptable analysis of the concept of a right is a far from trivial matter. What I should like to do, however, is to touch briefly upon the problem of providing such an analysis, and then to indicate the account that seems to me most satisfactory—an account which does entail the particular-interests principle.

It would be widely agreed, I believe, both that rights impose obligations and that the obligations they impose upon others are *conditional* upon certain factors. The difficulty arises when one attempts to specify what the obligations are conditional upon. There seems to be two main views in this area. According to the one, rights impose obligations that are conditional upon the interests of the possessor of the right. To say that Sandra has a right to something is thus to say, roughly, that if it is in Sandra's interest to have that thing, then others are under an obligation not to deprive her of it. According to the second view, rights impose obligations that are conditional upon the right's not having been waived. To say that Sandra has a right to something is to say, roughly, that if Sandra has not given others permission to take the thing, then they are under an obligation not to deprive her of it.

Both views encounter serious difficulties. On the one hand, in the case of minors, and nonhuman animals, it would seem that the obligations that rights impose must be taken as conditional upon the interests of those individuals, rather than upon whether they have given one permission to do certain things. On the other, in the case of individuals who are capable of making informed and rational decisions, if that person has not given one permission to take something that belongs to him, it would seem that one is, in general, still under an obligation not to deprive him of it, even if having that thing is no longer in his interest.

As a result, it seems that a more complex account is needed of the factors upon which the obligations imposed by rights are conditional. The account which I now prefer, and which I have defended elsewhere,[8] is this: "A has a right to X" means the same as:

> A is such that it can be in A's interest to have X, and either (1) A is not capable of making an informed and rational choice whether to grant others permission to deprive him of X, in which case, if it is in A's interest not to be deprived of X, then, by this fact alone, others are under a prima facie obligation not to deprive A of X, *or* (2) A is capable of making an informed and rational choice whether to grant others permission to deprive him of X, in which case

the others are under a prima facie obligation not to deprive A of X if and only if A has not granted them permission to do so.

And if this account, or something rather similar is correct, then so is the particular-interests principle.

What I now want to do is simply apply the particular-interests principle to the case of the right to life. First, however, one needs to notice that the expression, "right to life," is not entirely happy, since it suggests that the right in question concerns the continued existence of a biological organism. That this is incorrect can be brought out by considering possible ways of violating an individual's right to life. Suppose, for example, that future technological developments make it possible to change completely the neural networks in a brain, and that the brain of some normal adult human being is thus completely reprogrammed so that the organism in question winds up with memories (or rather, apparent memories), beliefs, attitudes, and personality traits totally different from those associated with it before it was subjected to programming. (The Pope is reprogrammed, say, on the model of Bertrand Russell.) In such a case, however beneficial the change might be, one would surely want to say that *someone* had been destroyed, that an adult human being's right to life had been violated, even though no biological organism had been killed. This shows that the expression, "right to life," is misleading, since what one is concerned about is not just the continued existence of a biologicial organism.

How, then, might the right in question be more accurately described? A natural suggestion is that the expression, "right to life," refers to the right of a subject of experiences and other mental states to continue to exist. It might be contended, however, that this interpretation begs the question against certain possible views. For someone might hold—and surely some people in fact do—that while continuing subjects of experiences and other mental states certainly have a right to life, so do some other organisms that are only potentially such continuing subjects, such as human fetuses. A right to life, on this view, is *either* the right of a subject of experiences to continue to exist *or* the right of something that is only potentially a continuing subject of experiences to become such an entity.

This view is, I believe, to be rejected, for at least two reasons. First, this view appears to be clearly incompatible with the interest principle. Second, this position entails that the destruction of potential persons is, in general, prima facie seriously wrong, and I shall argue, in the next section, that the latter view is incorrect.

Let us consider, then, the right of a subject of experiences and other mental states to continue to exist. The particular-interests principle implies that something cannot possibly have such a right unless its continued existence can be in its interest. We need to ask, then, what must be the case if the continued existence of something is to be in its interest.

It will help to focus our thinking, I believe, if we consider a crucial case, stressed by Derek Parfit. Imagine a human baby that has developed to the point of being sentient, and of having simple desires, but that is not yet capable of having any desire for continued existence. Suppose, further, that the baby will enjoy a happy life and will be glad that it was not destroyed. Can we or can we not say that it is in the baby's interest not to be destroyed?

To approach this case, let us consider a closely related one, namely, that of a human embryo that has not developed sufficiently far to have any desires, or even any states of consciousness at all, but that will develop into an individual who will enjoy a happy life, and who will be glad that his mother did not have an abortion. Can we or can we not say that it is the embryo's interest not to be destroyed?

Why might someone be tempted to say that it is in the embryo's interest that it not be destroyed? One line of thought which, I believe, tempts some people, is this. Let Mary be an individual who enjoys a happy life. Then, though some philosophers have expressed serious doubts about this, it might very well be said that it was certainly in Mary's interest that a certain embryo was not destroyed several years earlier. And this claim, together with the tendency to use expressions such as "Mary before she was born" to refer to the embryo in question, may lead one to think that it was in the embryo's interest not to be destroyed. But this way of thinking involves conceptual confusion. A subject of interests, in the relevant sense of "interest," must necessarily be a subject of concious states, including experiences and desires. This means that

in identifying Mary with the embryo, and attributing to it her interest in its earlier nondestruction, one is treating the embryo as if it were itself a subject of consciousness. But by hypothesis, the embryo being considered has not developed to the point where there is any subject of consciousness associated with it. It cannot, therefore, have any interests at all, and *a fortiori*, it cannot have any interest in its own continued existence.

Let us now return to the first case—that of a human baby that is sentient, and that has simple desires, but which is not yet capable of having more complex desires, such as a desire for its own continued existence. Given that it will develop into an individual who will lead a happy life and who will be glad that the baby was not destroyed, does one want to say that the baby's not being destroyed is in the baby's own interest?

Again, the following line of thought may seem initially tempting. If Mary is the resulting individual, then it was in Mary's interest that the baby not have been destroyed. But the baby just *is* Mary when she was young. So it must have been in the baby's interest that it not have been destroyed.

Indeed, this argument is considerably more tempting in the present case than in the former, since here there is something that is a subject of consciousness, and which it is natural to identify with Mary. I suggest, however, that when one reflects upon the case, it becomes clear that such an identification is justified only if certain further things are the case. Thus, on the one hand, suppose that Mary is able to remember quite clearly some of the experiences that the baby enjoyed. Given that sort of causal and psychological connection, it would seem perfectly reasonable to hold that Mary and the baby are one and the same subject of consciousness, and thus, that if it is in Mary's interest that the baby not have been destroyed, then this must also have been in the baby's interest. On the other hand, suppose that not only does Mary, at a much later time, not remember any of the baby's experiences, but the experiences in question are not psychologically linked, either via memory or in any other way, to mental states enjoyed by the human organism in question at *any* later time. Here it seems to me clearly incorrect to say that Mary and the baby are one and the same subject of consciousness and therefore it cannot be correct to transfer, from Mary to the baby, Mary's interest in the baby's not having been destroyed.

Let us now return to the question of what must be the case if the continued existence of something is to be in its own interest. The picture that emerges from the two cases just discussed is this. In the first place, nothing at all can be in an entity's interest unless it has desires at some time or other. But more than this is required if the continued existence of the entity is to be in its own interest. One possibility, which will generally be sufficient, is that the individual have, at the time in question, a desire for its own continued existence. Yet it also seems clear that an individual's continued existence can be in its own interest even when such a desire is not present. What is needed, apparently, is that the continued existence of the individual will make possible the satisfaction of some desires existing at other times. But not just any desires existing at other times will do. Indeed, as is illustrated both by the case of the baby just discussed and by the deprogramming/reprogramming example, it is not even sufficient that they be desires associated with the same physical organism. It is crucial that they be desires that belong to one and the same subject of consciousness.

The critical question, then, concerns the conditions under which desires existing at different times can be correctly attributed to a single, continuing subject of consciousness. This question raises a number of difficult issues that cannot be considered here. Part of the rationale underlying the view I wish to advance will be clear, however, if one considers the role played by memory in the psychological unity of an individual over time. When I remember a past experience, what I know is not merely that there was a certain experience which someone or other had, but that there was an experience that belonged to the *same* individual as the present memory beliefs, and it seems clear that this feature of one's memories is, in general, a crucial part of what it is that makes one a continuing subject of experiences, rather than merely a series of psychologically isolated, momentary subjects of consciousness. This suggests something like the following principle:

Desires existing at different times can belong to a single, continuing subject of consciousness only if that subject of consciousness possesses, at some time, the concept of a continuing self or mental substance.[9]

Given this principle, together with the particular-rights principle, one can set out the following argument in support of a claim concerning a necessary condition that an entity must satisfy if it is to have a right to life:

1. The concept of a right is such that an individual cannot have a right at time *t* to continued existence unless the individual is such that it can be in its interest at time *t* that it continue to exist.

2. The continued existence of a given subject of consciousness cannot be in that individual's interest at time *t* unless *either* that individual has a desire, at time *t*, to continue as a subject of consciousness, *or* that individual can have desires at other times.

3. An individual cannot have a desire to continue to exist as a subject of consciousness unless it possesses the concept of continuing self or mental substance.

4. An individual existing at one time cannot have desires at other times unless there is at least one time at which it possesses the concept of a continuing self or mental substance.

Therefore,

5. An individual cannot have a right to continued existence unless there is at least one time at which it possesses the concept of a continuing self or mental substance.

This conclusion is obviously significant. But precisely what implications does it have with respect to the morality of abortion and infanticide? The answer will depend upon what relationship there is between, on the one hand, the behavioral and neurophysiological development of a human being, and, on the other, the development of that individual's mind. Some people believe that there is no relationship at all. They believe that a human mind, with all its mature capacities, is present in a human from conception onward, and so is there before the brain has even begun to develop, and before the individual has begun to exhibit behavior expressive of higher mental functioning. Most philosophers, however, reject this view. They believe, on the one hand, that there is, in general, a rather close relation between an individual's behavioral capacities and its mental functioning, and, on the other, that there is a very intimate relationship between the mind and the brain. As regards the latter, some philosophers hold that the mind is in fact identical with the brain. Others maintain that the mind is distinct from the brain, but causally dependent upon it. In either case, the result is a view according to which the development of the mind and the brain are necessarily closely tied to one another.

If one does adopt the view that there is a close relation between the behavioral and neurophysiological development of a human being, and the development of its mind, then the previous conclusion has a very important, and possibly decisive implication with respect to the morality of abortion and infanticide. For when human development, both behavioral and neurophysiological, is closely examined, it is seen to be most unlikely that human fetuses, or even newborn babies, possess any concept of a continuing self.[10] And in the light of the above conclusion, this means that such individuals do not possess a right to life.

But is it reasonable to hold that there is a close relation between human behavioral and neurophysiological development, and the development of the human mind? Approached from a scientific perspective, I believe that there is excellent reason for doing so. Consider, for example, what is known about how, at later stages, human mental capacities proceed in step with brain development, or what is known about how damage to different parts of the brain can affect, in different ways, an individual's intellectual capacities.

Why, then, do some people reject the view that there is a close relationship between the development of the human mind, and the behavioral and neurophysiological development of human beings? There are, I think, two main reasons. First, some philosophers believe that the scientific evidence is

irrelevant because they believe that it is possible to establish, by means of a purely metaphysical argument, that a human mind, with its mature capacities, is present in a human from conception onward. I have argued elsewhere that the argument in question is unsound.[11]

Second, and more commonly, some people appeal to the idea that it is a divinely revealed truth that human beings have minds from conception onward. There are a number of points to be made about such an appeal. First, the belief that a mind, or soul, is infused into a human body at conception by God is not an essential belief within many of the world's religions. Second, even with religious traditions, such as Roman Catholicism, where the belief is a very common one, it is by no means universally accepted. Thus, for example, the well-known Catholic philosopher, Joseph Donceel, has argued very strongly for the claim that the correct position on the question of ensoulment is that the soul enters the body only when the human brain has undergone a sufficient process of development.[12] Third, there is the question of whether it is reasonable to accept the religious outlook that is being appealed to in support of the contention that humans have minds that are capable of higher intellectual activities from conception onward. This question raises very large issues in philosophy of religion, which cannot be pursued here. But it should at least be said that most contemporary philosophers who have reflected upon religious beliefs have come to the view that there is not sufficient reason even for believing in the existence of God, let alone for accepting the much more detailed religious claims which are part of a religion such as Christianity. Finally, suppose that one nonetheless decides to accept the contention that it is a divinely revealed truth that humans have, from conception onward, minds that are capable of higher mental activities, and that one appeals to this purported revelation in order to support the claim that all humans have a right to life. One needs to notice that if one then goes on to argue, not merely that abortion is wrong, but that there should be a law against it, one will encounter a very serious objection. For it is surely true that it is inappropriate, at least in a pluralistic society, to appeal to specific religious beliefs of a nonmoral sort—such as the belief that God infuses souls into human bodies at conception—in support of legislation that will be binding upon everyone, including those who either accept different religious beliefs, or none at all.

Is It Morally Wrong to Destroy Potential Persons?

In this section I shall consider the question of whether it can be seriously wrong to destroy an entity, not because of the nonpotential properties it presently possesses, but because of the properties it will later come to have, if it is not interfered with. First, however, we need to be clear why this is such a crucial question. We can do this by considering a line of thought that has led some people to feel that the anti-abortionist position is more defensible than that of the pro-abortionist. The argument in question rests upon the gradual and continuous development of an organism as it changes from a zygote into an adult human being. The anti-abortionist can point to this development, and argue that it is morally arbitrary for a pro-abortionist to draw a line at some point in this continuous process—such as at birth, or viability—and to say that killing is permissible before, but not after, that particular point.

The pro-abortionist reply would be, I think, that the emphasis on the continuity of the process is misleading. What the anti-abortionist is really doing is simply challenging the pro-abortionist to specify what properties a thing must have in order to have a right to life, and to show that the developing organism does acquire those properties at the point in question. The pro-abortionist may then be tempted to argue that the difficulty in meeting this challenge should not be taken as grounds for rejecting his position. For the anti-abortionist cannot meet this challenge either; he is equally unable to say what properties something must have if it is to have a right to life.

Although this rejoinder does not dispose of the anti-abortionist argument, it is not without bite. For defenders of the view that abortion is almost always wrong have failed to face up to the question of the *basic* moral principles on which their position rests, where a basic moral principle is one whose acceptability does not rest upon the truth of any factual claim of a nonmoral sort.[13] They have been content to assert the wrongness of killing any organism, from a zygote on, if that organism is a member of the biologically defined species *Homo sapiens*. But they have overlooked the point that this cannot be an acceptable *basic* moral principle, since difference in species is not in itself a morally relevant difference.[14]

The anti-abortionist can reply that it is possible to defend his position, but not a pro-abortionist position, *without* getting clear about the properties a thing must possess if it is to have a right to life. For one can appeal to the following two claims: First, that there is a property, even if one is unable to specify what it is, that (1) is possessed by normal adult humans, and (2) endows any being possessing it with a right to life. Second, that there are properties that satisfy (1) and (2), at least one of those properties will be such that any organism potentially possessing that property has a right to life even now, simply in virtue of that potentiality—where an organism possesses a property potentially if it will come to have it in the normal course of its development.

The second claim—which I shall refer to as the potentiality principle—is crucial to the anti-abortionist's defense of his position. Given that principle, the anti-abortionist can defend his position without grappling with the very difficult question of what nonpotential properties an entity must possess in order to have a right to life. It is enough to know that adult members of *Homo sapiens* do have such a right. For then one can employ the potentiality principle to conclude that any organism that belongs to the species *Homo sapiens*, from a zygote on—with the possible exception of those that suffer from certain gross neurophysiological abnormalities—must also have a right to life.

The pro-abortionist, in contrast, cannot mount a comparable argument. He cannot defend his position without offering at least a partial answer to the question of what properties a thing must possess in order to have a right to life.

The importance of the potentiality principle, however, goes beyond the fact that it provides support for an anti-abortion position. For it seems that if the potentiality principle is unsound, then there is no acceptable defense of an extreme conservative view on abortion.

The reason is this: Suppose that the claim that an organism's having certain potentialities is sufficient grounds for its having a right to life cannot be sustained. The claim that a fetus that is a member of *Homo sapiens* has a right to life can then be attacked as follows. The reason an adult member of *Homo sapiens* has a right to life, but an infant ape, say, does not, is that there are certain physiological properties that the former possesses and the latter does not. Now even if one is unsure exactly what the relevant psychological characteristics are, it seems clear that an organism in the early stages of development from a zygote into an adult member of *Homo sapiens* does not possess those properties. One need merely compare a human fetus with an ape fetus. In early stages of development, neither will have any mental life at all. (Does a zygote have a mental life? Does it have experiences? Or beliefs? Or desires?) In later stages of fetal development some mental events presumably occur, but these will be of a very rudimentary sort. The crucial point, however, is that given what we know through comparative studies of, on the one hand, brain development, and, on the other behavior after birth, it is surely reasonable to hold that there are no significant differences in the respective mental lives of a human fetus and an ape fetus. There are, of course, physiological differences, but these are not in themselves morally significant. *If* one held that potentialities were relevant to the ascription of a right to life, one could argue that the physiological differences, though not morally relevant in themselves, are morally relevant in virtue of their causal consequences: They will lead to later psychological differences that are morally relevant, and for this reason the physiological differences are themselves morally significant. But if the potentiality principle is not available, this line of argument cannot be used, and there will then be no differences between a human and an ape fetus that the anti-abortionist can use as grounds for ascribing a right to life to the former but not to the latter.

This argument assumes, of course, that the anti-abortionist cannot successfully argue that there are religious reasons for holding that, even when potentialities are set aside, there is a morally relevant difference between human fetuses and ape fetuses. In the previous section I indicated, however, why it is

very unlikely that any religious line of argument can be satisfactory in the present context.

The conclusion seems to be then, that the anti-abortionist position is defensible only if the potentiality principle is sound. Let us now consider what can be said against that principle. One way of attacking it is by appealing to the conclusion advanced in the previous section, to the effect that an individual cannot have a right to continued existence unless there is at least one time at which it possesses the concept of continuing self or mental substance. This principle entails the denial of the potentiality principle. Or more precisely, it does so in conjunction with the presumably uncontroversial empirical claim that a fertilized human egg cell, which does possess the relevant potentialities, does not possess the concept of a continuing self or mental substance.

Alternatively, one could appeal to the more modest claim involved in the interest principle and use it to argue that since a fertilized human egg cell cannot have any interests at all, it cannot have any rights, and *a fortiori* cannot have a right to life. So potentialities alone cannot endow something with a right to life.

Given these lines of argument, is there any reason not to rest the case at this point? I want to suggest that there are at least two reasons why one needs to take a closer look at the potentiality principle. The first is that some people who are anti-abortionists may wish to reject not only the particular-interests principle, but also the more modest interest principle, and although I believe that this response to the above arguments is unsound, I think it is important to see whether there aren't other arguments that are untouched by this reply.

A second, and more important, reason why it is unwise to base one's case against the anti-abortionist entirely upon an appeal to principles such as the interest principle is this. The anti-abortionist can modify his position slightly and avoid the arguments in question. Specifically, he can abandon his claim that a human fetus has a right to life, but contend that it is nevertheless seriously wrong to kill it. Some philosophers would feel that such modification cannot possibly be acceptable, on the ground that no action can be seriously wrong unless it violates someone's right to something. It seems to me, however, that this latter view is in fact mistaken.[15] In any case, let us consider the position that results from this modification. An anti-abortionist who is willing to adopt this position can then appeal, not to the potentiality principle, but to the following, *modified potentiality principle:*

> If there are properties possessed by normal adult human beings that endow any organism possessing them with a right to life, then at least one of those properties is such that it is seriously wrong to kill any organism that potentially possesses that property, simply in virtue of that potentiality.

Since this modified potentiality principle is not concerned with the attribution of rights to organisms, it cannot be attacked by appealing to the interest principle, or to the particular-interests principle, or to some analysis of the concept of a right.

Let us now consider how the case against the anti-abortionist position can be strengthened. I shall advance three arguments that are objections to both the original and the modified potentiality principles. Since the original potentiality principle cannot be correct unless the modified one is, it will suffice to consider only the modified principle. The basic issue, then, is this: Is there any property J which satisfies the following three conditions:

1. There is a property, K, such that any individual possessing property K has a right to life, and there is a scientific law, L, to the effect that any organism possessing property J will, in the normal course of events, come to possess property K at some later time.
2. Given the relationship just described between property J and property K, it is seriously wrong to kill anything possessing property J.
3. If property J were not related to property K in the way indicated, the fact that an organism possessed property J would not make it seriously wrong to kill it.

In short, the question is whether there is a property, J, that makes it seriously wrong to kill something *only because* J stands in a certain causal relation to a second property, K, which is such that anything possessing that property *ipso facto* has a right to life.

My first objection turns upon the claim that if one accepts the modified potentiality principle, one ought also to accept the following, *generalized potentiality principle.*

> If there are any properties possessed by normal adult human beings that endow any organism possessing them with a right to life, then at least one of those properties is such that it is seriously wrong to perform any action that will prevent some system, which otherwise would have developed the property, from doing so.

This generalized potentiality principle differs from the original and the modified potentiality principles in two respects. First, it applies to systems of objects and not merely to organisms. I think that this first generalization is one that ought to be accepted by anyone who accepts either the original or the modified principle. For why should it make any difference whether the potentiality resides in a single organism, or in a system of organisms that are so interrelated that they will in the normal course of affairs, due to the operation of natural laws, causally give rise to something that possesses the property in question? Surely it is only the potentiality for a certain outcome that matters and not whether there are one or more objects interacting and developing in a predetermined way to produce that outcome.

In thinking about this issue, it is important not to confuse *potentialities* with mere *possibilities*. The generalized potentiality principle does not deal with a collection of objects that merely have the capacity to interact in certain ways. The objects must already be interrelated in such a way that in the absence of external interference, the laws governing their future interaction and development will bring it about that the system will develop the property in question.

The second difference is that the original and modified potentiality principles deal only with the *destruction* of organisms, while the generalized principle deals with any action that prevents an organism, or system, from developing the relevant property. I think that the anti-abortionist will certainly want to accept this generalization. For suppose that by exposing a human zygote to appropriate radiation one could transform it into a frog zygote. A woman could then undergo a two-step abortion: first the human zygote would be transformed into a frog zygote and then the frog zygote would be destroyed. Assuming that one doesn't view the destruction of a frog zygote as seriously wrong, one must either hold that it is seriously wrong to prevent a human zygote from developing its potentialities, or else conclude that the two-step abortion technique is morally permissible. The latter option would not appear to be viable, let alone a welcome one, for the anti-abortionist. For why should it be morally permissible to destroy a human organism in two steps, one of which limits its potentialities and the other of which destroys the resulting organism, but seriously wrong to collapse these two steps into one limiting its potentialities and destroying it by a single action? I think that the anti-abortionists would agree that there is no significant moral distinction here, and thus would accept the second generalization involved in the expanded potentiality principle.

Suppose, now, that artificial wombs have been perfected. A healthy, unfertilized human egg cell has been placed in one, along with a large number of spermatozoa. If the device is turned on, the spermatozoa will be carried, via a conveyor belt, to the unfertilized egg cell, where, we can assume, fertilization will take place. The device is such, moreover, that no outside assistance will be needed at any future stage, and nine months later a normal human baby will emerge from the artificial womb. Given these assumptions—all of which are certainly empirically possible—once such a device has been turned on, there will exist an active potentiality that will, if not interfered with, give rise to something that will become an adult human being, and so will have a right to life. But would it be seriously wrong to destroy that potentiality—as might be done, for example, by turning off the machine, or by cutting the conveyor belt, so that fertilization does not take place? Most people, I believe, would certainly not think that such actions were seriously wrong. If that view is correct, the generalized potentiality principle must be rejected as unsound.

In short, the first argument against the modified potentiality principle, and hence against the original potentiality principle, is as follows. It is reasonable to accept the modified principle only if it is also reasonable to accept the generalized potentiality principle because whether the potentialities reside in a single organism or in a system does not seem to be a morally significant difference. But to accept the generalized potentiality principle is to commit oneself to the view that interference with an artificial womb so as to prevent fertilization from taking place is just as seriously wrong as abortion, and for precisely the same reason. If, as seems plausible, this is not an acceptable view, then one cannot reasonably accept either the original or the modified potentiality principle.

Let us now turn to my second argument against the modified potentiality principle. This argument turns upon the following crucial claim:

> Let C be any type of causal process where there is some type of occurrence, E, such that processes of type C would possess no intrinsic moral significance were it not for the fact that they result in occurrences of type E.

Then,

> The characteristic of being an act of intervening in a process of type C that prevents the occurrence of an outcome of type E makes an action intrinsically wrong to precisely the same degree as does the characteristic of being an act of ensuring that a causal process of type C, which it was in one's power to initiate, does not get initiated.

This principle, which I shall refer to as the moral symmetry principle with respect to action, would be rejected by some philosophers. They would argue that there is an important distinction to be drawn between "what we owe people in the form of aid, and what we owe them in the way of noninterference,"[16] and that the latter, "negative duties," are duties that it is more serious to neglect than the former, "positive" ones. This view arises from an intuitive response to examples such as the following. Even if it is wrong not to send food to starving people in other parts of the world, it is more wrong still to kill someone. And isn't the conclusion, then, that one's obligation to refrain from killing someone is a more serious obligation than one's obligation to save lives?

I want to argue that this is not the correct conclusion. I think that it is tempting to draw this conclusion if one fails to consider the motivation likely to be associated with the respective actions. If someone performs an action he knows will kill someone else, this will usually be good reason for concluding that he wanted the death of the person in question. In contrast, failing to help someone may indicate only apathy, laziness, selfishness, or an amoral outlook: the fact that a person knowingly allows another to die is not normally grounds for concluding that he desired that person's death. Someone who knowingly kills another is thus more likely to be seriously defective from a moral point of view than someone who fails to save another's life.

If we are not to be led to false conclusions by our intuitions about certain cases, we must explicitly assume identical motivations in the two situations. Compare, for example, the following: (1) Jones sees that Smith will be killed by a bomb unless he warns him. Jones' reaction is, "How fortunate, this will save me the trouble of killing Smith myself." So Jones allows Smith to be killed by the bomb, even though he could have easily warned him. (2) Jones wants Smith dead, and therefore shoots him. Is one to say that there is a significant difference between the wrongness of Jones' behavior in these two cases? I suggest that is not plausible to hold that there is a significant difference here.

If this is right, then it would appear to be a mistake to draw a distinction between positive and negative duties and to hold the latter impose stricter obligations than the former. The differences in our intuitions about situations that involve giving aid to others, and corresponding situations that involve not interfering with others, is to be explained by reference to probable differences in the motivations that are likely to be present in the two sorts of situations, and not by reference to a distinction between positive and negative duties. For once it is specified that the motivation is the same in the two situations, it seems clear that inaction is as wrong in the one case as action is in the other.

There is another point that may be relevant. Action involves effort, whereas inaction usually does not. It does not usually require any effort to refrain from killing someone, but saving someone's life may require a considerable effort. One needs to ask, then, how large a sacrifice a person is morally required to make to save the life of another. If the sacrifice is a very significant one, it may be that one is not morally obliged to save the life of another in that situation. Superficial reflection upon such cases might easily lead one to introduce the distinction between positive and negative duties, but again it seems clear that this would be a mistake. The point is not that one has a greater duty to refrain from killing others than to perform actions that will save them. It is rather that positive actions require effort, and this means that in deciding what to do a person has to take into account his own right to do what he wants with his life, and not only the other person's right to life. In order to avoid this confusion, then, one needs to confine oneself to consideration of situations in which the positive action requires no greater sacrifice than is involved in the inaction.

What I have been arguing, in brief, is this. It is probably true, for example, that most cases of killing are morally worse than most cases of merely letting die. This, however, is not an objection to the moral symmetry principle, since that principle does not imply that, all things considered, acts of killing are, in general, morally on a par with cases of allowing someone to die. What the moral symmetry principle implies is rather that, *other things being equal*, it is just as wrong to fail to save someone as it is to kill someone. If one wants to test this principle against one's moral intuitions, one has to be careful to select pairs of situations in which all other morally relevant factors—such as motivation, and risk to the agent—are equivalent. And I have suggested that when this is done, the moral symmetry principle is by no means counterintuitive.[17]

My argument against the modified potentiality principle can now be stated. Suppose at some future time a chemical were to be discovered which, when injected into the brain of a kitten, would cause the kitten to develop into a cat possessing a brain of the sort possessed by humans, and consequently into a cat having all the psychological capabilities characteristic of normal adult humans. Such cats would be able to think, to use language, and so on. Now it would surely be morally indefensible in such a situation to hold that it is seriously wrong to kill an adult member of the species *Homo sapiens* without also holding that it is wrong to kill any cat that has undergone such a process of development: There would be no morally significant differences.

Second, imagine that one has two kittens, one of which has been injected with a special chemical, but which has not yet developed those properties that in themselves endow something with a right to life, and the other of which has not been injected with the special chemical. It follows from the moral symmetry principle that the action of injecting the former with a "neutralizing" chemical that will interfere with the transformation process and prevent the kitten from developing those properties that in themselves would give it a right to life is prima facie no more seriously wrong than the action of intentionally refraining from injecting the second kitten with the special chemical.

It perhaps needs to be emphasized here that the moral symmetry principle does not imply that neither action is morally wrong. Perhaps both actions are wrong, even seriously so. The moral symmetry principle implies only that if they are wrong, they are so to precisely the same degree.

Third, compare a kitten that has been injected with the special chemical and then had it neutralized, with a kitten that has never been injected with the chemical. It is clear that it is no more seriously wrong to kill the former than to kill the latter. For although their bodies have undergone different processes in the past, there is no reason why the kittens need differ in any way with respect to either their present properties or their potentialities.

Fourth, again consider two kittens, one of which has been injected with the special chemical, but which has not yet developed those properties that in themselves would give it a right to life, and the other of which has not been injected with the chemical. It follows from the previous two steps in the argument that the combined action of injecting the first kitten with a neutralizing chemical and then killing it is no more seriously wrong than the combined action of intentionally refraining from injecting the second kitten with the special chemical and then killing it.

Fifth, one way of neutralizing the action of the special chemical is simply to kill the kitten. And since there is surely no reason to hold that it is more seriously wrong to neutralize the chemical and to kill the kitten in a single step than in two successive steps, it must be the case that it is no more seriously wrong to kill a kitten that has been injected with the special chemical, but which has not developed those properties that in themselves would give it a right to life, than it is to inject such a kitten with a neutralizing chemical and then to kill it.

Next, compare a member of *Homo sapiens* that has not developed far enough to have those properties that in themselves give something a right to life, but which later will come to have them, with a kitten that has been injected with the special chemical but which has not yet had the chance to develop the relevant properties. It is clear that it cannot be any more seriously wrong to kill the human than to kill the kitten. The potentialities are the same in both cases. The only difference is that in the case of a human fetus the potentialities have been present from the beginning of the organism's development, while in the case of the kitten they have been present only from the time it was injected with the special chemical. This difference in the time at which the potentialities were acquired is not a morally relevant one.

It follows from the previous three steps in the argument that it is no more seriously wrong to kill a human being that lacks properties that in themselves, and irrespective of their causal consequences, endow something with a right to life, but which will naturally develop those properties, than it would be to intentionally refrain from injecting a kitten with the special chemical, and to kill it. But if it is the case that normal adult humans do possess properties that in themselves give them a right to life, it follows in virtue of the modified potentiality principle that it is seriously wrong to kill any human organism that will naturally develop the properties in question. Thus, if the modified potentiality principle is sound, we are forced by this argument to conclude that if there were a chemical that would transform kittens into animals having the psychological capabilities possessed by adult humans, it would be seriously wrong to intentionally refrain from injecting kittens with the chemical and to kill them instead.

But is it clear that this final conclusion is unacceptable? I believe that it is. It turns out, however, that this issue is *much* more complex than most people take it to be.[18] Here, however, it will have to suffice to note that the vast majority of people would certainly view this conclusion as unacceptable. For although there are at present no special chemicals that will transform kittens in the required way, there are other biological organisms, namely unfertilized human egg cells, and special chemicals, namely human spermatozoa, that will transform those organisms in the required way. So if one were to hold that it was seriously wrong to intentionally refrain from injecting kittens with the special chemical and instead to kill them, one would also have to maintain that it was prima facie seriously wrong to refrain from injecting human egg cells with spermatozoa, and instead to kill them. So unless the anti-abortionist is prepared to hold that any woman, married or unmarried, does something seriously wrong every month that she intentionally refrains from getting pregnant, he cannot maintain that it would be seriously wrong to refrain from injecting the kitten with the special chemical, and instead to kill it.

In short, the previous argument shows that anyone who wants to defend the original or the modified potentiality principle must either argue against the moral symmetry principle, or hold that in a world in which kittens could be transformed into "rational animals," it would be seriously wrong to kill newborn kittens. But we have just seen that if one accepts the latter claim, one must also hold that it is seriously wrong to intentionally refrain from fertilizing a human egg cell and to kill it instead. Consequently, it seems very likely that any anti-abortionist rejoinder to the present argument will be directed against the moral symmetry principle. In the present essay I have not attempted to offer a thorough defense of that principle, although I have tried to show that what is perhaps the most important objection to it—the one that appeals to a distinction between positive and negative duties—rests upon a superficial analysis of our moral intuitions. Elsewhere, however, I have argued that a thorough examination of the moral symmetry principle sustains the conclusion that that principle is in fact correct.

There is one final point that needs to be made about the present argument, and that is that there are variations of it which do not involve the moral symmetry principle, but which also tell against the anti-abortionist position. These variations are suggested by the reflection that someone not quite convinced, for example, that failing to save is, in itself,

just as seriously wrong as killing, may very well accept one of the following, more modest claims:

1. Failing to save someone is, in itself, almost as seriously wrong as killing.
2. Killing and failing to save are *comparable* in the technical sense of there being some number n such that failing to save n people is in itself, at least as seriously wrong as killing one person.

These claims can be generalized into principles similar to, but less controversial than, the moral symmetry principle. In the case of the second, we have the following, *moral comparability principle.*

> Let C be any type of causal process where there is some type of occurrence, E, such that processes of type C would possess no intrinsic moral significance were it not for the fact that they result in occurrences of type E.

Then,

> There is some number n such that the characteristic of being an act of ensuring that n causal processes of type C, which it was within one's power to initiate, do not get initiated, makes an action intrinsically wrong to at least the degree that the characteristic of being an act of intervening in a process of type C which prevents the occurrence of an event of type E does.

Given this moral comparability principle, one way of proceeding is simply to parallel the argument involving the moral symmetry principle. This will lead to the conclusion that there is some number n such that intentionally refraining from fertilizing n human egg cells is in itself at least as seriously wrong as destroying a human before it has acquired those nonpotential properties that would give it a right to life. Then, if it is granted that it is not seriously wrong to refrain from fertilizing n human egg cells, it follows that it is not in itself seriously wrong to destroy a human before it has acquired nonpotential properties that would give it a right to life.

Most people would readily grant the claim that it is not seriously wrong to intentionally refrain from fertilizing n human egg cells. It is worth noting, however, that there is a variant of the argument that avoids this assumption. Consider the moral status of destroying a human organism that has not yet acquired the nonpotential properties that would give it a right to life, and that, if allowed to survive, will lead an unhappy life. The moral comparability principle implies that there is some number *n* such that the destruction of such an entity is, in itself, no more seriously wrong than intentionally refraining from fertilizing *n* human egg cells that will result in *n* individuals who will lead unhappy lives. Since the latter is surely not even wrong, let alone seriously so, it follows that it is not seriously wrong to destroy a human organism that has not yet acquired those nonpotential properties that would give it a right to life, and that, if allowed to survive, will lead an unhappy life.

This variation of the comparability argument has led to a more modest conclusion. However, it is still a conclusion that tells against the view advanced by anti-abortionists, since they reject the claim that abortion is morally permissible in cases where the resulting individual will lead an unhappy life.

To sum up, what I have argued in the present section is this. The anti-abortionist position is defensible only if some version of the potentiality principle is sound. The original version of that principle is incompatible, however, both with the particular-interests principle and with the interest principle, and also with the account of the concept of a right offered above. The modified potentiality principle avoids these problems. There are, however, at least three other serious objections that tell against both the original potentiality principle and the modified one. It would seem, therefore, that there are excellent reasons for rejecting the potentiality principle, and with it, the anti-abortionist position.

Summary and Conclusions

In this paper I have advanced three main philosophical contentions:

1. An entity cannot have a right to life unless it is capable of having an interest in its own continued existence.
2. An entity is not capable of having an interest in its own continued existence unless it possesses, at some time, the concept of a continuing self, or subject of experiences and other mental states.
3. The fact that an entity will, if not destroyed, come to have properties that would give it a right to life does not in itself make it seriously wrong to destroy it.

If these philosophical contentions are correct, the crucial question is a factual one: At what point does a developing human being acquire the concept of a continuing self, and at what point is it capable of having an interest in its own continued existence? I have not examined this issue in detail here, but I have suggested that careful scientific studies of human development both behavioral and neurophysiological, strongly support the view that even newborn humans do not have the capacities in question. If this is right, then it would seem that infanticide during a time interval shortly after birth must be viewed as morally acceptable.

But where is the line to be drawn? And what is the precise cutoff point? If one maintained, as some philosophers do, that an individual can possess a concept only if it is capable of expressing that concept linguistically, then it would be a relatively simple matter to determine whether a given organism possessed the concept of a continuing subject of experiences and other mental states. It is far from clear, however, that this claim about the necessary connection between the possession of concepts and the having of linguistic capabilities is correct. I would argue, for example, that one wants to ascribe mental states of a conceptual sort—such as beliefs and desires—to animals that are incapable of learning a language, and that an individual cannot have beliefs and desires unless it possesses the concepts involved in those beliefs and desires. And if that view is right—if an organism can acquire concepts without thereby acquiring a way of expressing those concepts linguistically—then the question of whether an individual possesses the concept of a continuing self may be one that requires quite subtle experimental techniques to answer.

If this view of the matter is roughly correct, there are two worries that one is left with at the level of practical moral decisions, one of which may turn out to be deeply disturbing. The lesser worry is the question just raised: Where is the line to be drawn in the case of infanticide? This is not really a troubling question since there is no serious need to know the exact point at which a human infant acquires a right to life. For in the vast majority of cases in which infanticide is desirable due to serious defects from which the baby suffers, its desirability will be apparent at birth or within a very short time thereafter. Since it seems clear that an infant at this point in its development is not capable of possessing the concept of a continuing subject of experiences and other mental states, and so is incapable of having an interest in its own continued existence, infanticide will be morally permissible in the vast majority of cases in which it is, for one reason or another, desirable. The practical moral problem can thus be satisfactorily handled by choosing some short period of time, such as a week after birth, as the interval during which infanticide will be permitted.

The troubling issue that arises out of these reflections concerns whether adult animals belonging to species other than *Homo sapiens* may not also possess a right to life. For once one allows that an individual can possess concepts, and have beliefs and desires, without being able to express those concepts, or those beliefs and desires, linguistically, then it becomes very much an open question whether animals belonging to other species do not possess properties that give them a right to life. Indeed, I am strongly inclined to think that adult members of at least some nonhuman species do have a right to life. My reason is that, first, I believe that some nonhuman animals are capable of envisaging a future for themselves, and of having desires about future states of themselves. Second, that anything which exercises these capacities has an interest in its own continued existence. And third, that having an interest in one's own continued existence is not merely necessary, but also a sufficient condition, for having a right to life.

The suggestion that at least some nonhuman animals have a right to life is not unfamiliar, but is one that most of us are accustomed to dismissing very casually. The line of thought advanced here suggests that this attitude may very well turn out to be tragically mistaken. Once one reflects upon the question of the *basic* moral principles involved in the ascription of a right to life to organisms, one may find

oneself driven to the conclusion that our everyday treatment of members of other species is morally indefensible and that we are in fact murdering innocent persons.

NOTES

1. Judith Jarvis Thomson, in her article "A Defense of Abortion," *Philosophy & Public Affairs* 1, 1971, 47–66, argues very forcefully for the view that this conclusion is incorrect. For a critical discussion of her argument, see Chapter 3 of *Abortion and Infanticide*.

2. America Law Institute, *Model Penal Code* (Philadelphia, 1962), section 230.3.

3. *Abortion and Infanticide*, Chapter 10.

4. In *Philosophy and Environmental Crisis*, ed. William T. Blackstone, Athens, Ga., 1974, 43–68.

5. Ibid., 51.

6. Ibid., 49–50.

7. Ibid., 51.

8. *Abortion and Infanticide*, section 5.2.

9. For a fuller discussion, and defense of this principle, see ibid., section 5.3.

10. For a detailed survey of the scientific evidence concerning human development, see ibid., section 11.5.

11. Ibid., section 11.42.

12. For a brief discussion, see Joseph F. Donceel, "A Liberal Catholic's View," *Abortion in a Changing World*, 1, ed. R. E. Hal, New York, 1970. A more detailed philosophical discussion can be found in Donceel's "Immediate Animation and Delayed Hominization," *Theological Studies*, 31, 1970, 76–105.

13. Consider the belief that it is prima facie wrong to pull cats' tails. Here is a belief that is almost universally accepted, but very few people, if any, would regard it as a basic moral belief. For this belief rests upon a nonmoral belief, to the effect that pulling cats' tails causes them pain. If one came to believe that cats actually enjoy this, one would abandon the moral belief in question. So the belief, though widely and firmly accepted, is a derived moral belief, rather than a basic one.

14. For a much more extended discussion of this point, see, for example, Peter Singer's essay, "Animals and the Value of Life," *Matters of Life and Death*, ed. by Tom Regan (Philadelphia, 1980), or my own discussion in section 4.2 of *Abortion and Infanticide*.

15. *Abortion and Infanticide*, section 7.33.

16. Philippa Foot, "The Problem of Abortion and the Doctrine of the Double Effect," *The Oxford Review*, 5 (1967): 5–15. *See* the discussion of 11ff.

17. For a much more detailed defense of this view, see section 6.5 of *Abortion and Infanticide*.

18. A discussion of why this is so can be found in Chapter 7 of *Abortion and Infanticide*.

Abortion Through a Feminist Ethics Lens

SUSAN SHERWIN

Sherwin says that a central moral feature of pregnancy is that it takes place in women's bodies and has a tremendous impact on women's lives. Policies about abortion affect women uniquely. So we must evaluate how proposed abortion policies "fit into general patterns of oppression for women," and a decision to have or not to have an abortion must be left to the individual woman, the one who best understands the circumstances of the decision. A fetus has moral significance, but its moral standing depends on its relationship to the pregnant woman. Feminist views, says Sherwin, stress "the importance of protecting women's right to continue as well as to terminate pregnancies as each sees fit."

Abortion has long been a central issue in the arena of applied ethics, but, the distinctive analysis of feminist ethics is generally overlooked in most philosophic discussions. Authors and readers commonly presume a familiarity with the feminist position and equate it with liberal defences of women's right to choose abortion, but, in fact, feminist ethics yields a different analysis of the moral questions surrounding abortion than that usually offered by the more familiar liberal defenders of abortion rights. Most feminists can agree with some of the conclusions that arise from certain non-feminist arguments on abortion, but they often disagree about the way the issues are formulated and the sorts of reasons that are invoked in the mainstream literature.

Among the many differences found between feminist and non-feminist arguments about abortion, is the fact that most non-feminist discussions of abortion consider the questions of the moral or legal permissibility of abortion in isolation from other questions, ignoring (and thereby obscuring) relevant connections to other social practices that oppress women. They are generally grounded in masculinist conceptions of freedom (e.g., privacy, individual choice, individuals' property rights in their own bodies) that do not meet the needs, interests, and intuitions of many of the women concerned. In

From *Dialogue: Canadian Philosophical Review*, vol. XXX, no. 1–2 (1991), pp. 327–342. Copyright © the Canadian Philosophical Association.

contrast, feminists seek to couch their arguments in moral concepts that support their general campaign of overcoming injustice in all its dimensions, including those inherent in moral theory itself.[1] There is even disagreement about how best to understand the moral question at issue: non-feminist arguments focus exclusively on the morality and/or legality of performing abortions, whereas feminists insist that other questions, including ones about accessibility and delivery of abortion services must also be addressed.

Although feminists welcome the support of non-feminists in pursuing policies that will grant women control over abortion decisions, they generally envision very different sorts of policies for this purpose than those considered by non-feminist sympathizers. For example, Kathleen McDonnell (1984) urges feminists to develop an explicitly "'feminist morality' of abortion. . . . At its root it would be characterized by the deep appreciations of time complexities of life, the refusal to polarize and adopt simplistic formulas" (p. 52). Here, I propose one conception of the shape such an analysis should take.

Women and Abortion

The most obvious difference between feminist and non-feminist approaches to abortion can be seen in the relative attention each gives to the interests and experiences of women in its analysis. Feminists consider it self-evident that the pregnant woman is a subject of principal concern in abortion decisions.

In most non-feminist accounts, however, not only is she not perceived as central, she is rendered virtually invisible. Non-feminist theorists, whether they support or oppose women's right to choose abortion, focus almost all their attention on the moral status of the developing embryo or the fetus.

In pursuing a distinctively feminist ethics, it is appropriate to begin with a look at the role of abortion in women's lives. Clearly, the need for abortion can be very intense; women have pursued abortions under appalling and dangerous conditions, across widely diverse cultures and historical periods. No one denies that if abortion is not made legal, safe, and accessible, women will seek out illegal and life-threatening abortions to terminate pregnancies they cannot accept. Anti-abortion activists seem willing to accept this price, but feminists judge the inevitable loss of women's lives associated with restrictive abortion policies to be a matter of fundamental concern.

Although anti-abortion campaigners imagine that women often make frivolous and irresponsible decisions about abortion, feminists recognize that women have abortions for a wide variety of reasons. Some women, for instance, find themselves seriously ill and incapacitated throughout pregnancy; they cannot continue in their jobs and may face enormous difficulties in fulfilling their responsibilities at home. Many employers and schools will not tolerate pregnancy in their employees or students, and not every woman is able to put her job, career, or studies on hold. Women of limited means may be unable to take adequate care of children they have already borne and they may know that another mouth to feed will reduce their ability to provide for their existing children. Women who suffer from chronic disease, or who feel too young, or too old, or who are unable to maintain lasting relationships may recognize that they will not be able to care properly for a child at this time. Some who are homeless, or addicted to drugs, or who are diagnosed as carrying the AIDS virus may be unwilling to allow a child to enter the world under such circumstances. If the pregnancy is a result of rape or incest, the psychological pain of carrying it to term may be unbearable, and the woman may recognize that her attitude to the child after birth will always be tinged with bit-

terness. Some women have learned that the fetuses they carry have serious chromosomal anomalies and consider it best to prevent them from being born with a condition bound to cause suffering. Others, knowing the fathers to be brutal and violent, may be unwilling to subject a child to the beatings or incestuous attacks they anticipate; some may have no other realistic way to remove the child (or themselves) from the relationship.

Or a woman may simply believe that bearing a child is incompatible with her life plans at this time, since continuing a pregnancy is likely to have profound repercussions throughout a woman's entire life. If the woman is young, a pregnancy will very likely reduce her chances of education and hence limit her career and life opportunities: "The earlier a woman has a baby, it seems, the more likely she is to drop out of school; the less education she gets, the more likely she is to remain poorly paid, peripheral to the labour market, or unemployed, and the more children she will have—between one and three more than her working childless counterpart" (Petchesky 1984, p. 150). In many circumstances, having a child will exacerbate the social and economic forces already stacked against her by virtue of her sex (and her race, class, age, sexual orientation, or the effects of some disability, etc.). Access to abortion is a necessary option for many women if they are to escape the oppressive conditions of poverty.

Whatever the reason, most feminists believe that a pregnant woman is in the best position to judge whether abortion is the appropriate response to her circumstances. Since she is usually the only one able to weigh all the relevant factors, most feminists reject attempts to offer any general abstract rules for determining when abortion is morally justified. Women's personal deliberations about abortion include contextually defined considerations reflecting their commitment to the needs and interests of everyone concerned—including herself, the fetus she carries, other members of her household, etc. Because there is no single formula available for balancing these complex factors through all possible cases, it is vital that feminists insist on protecting each woman's right to come to her own conclusions. Abortion decisions are, by their very nature, dependent on specific features of each woman's experience; theoretically dispassionate philosophers and other moralists should not expect to set the agenda for these considerations in any universal way. Women must be acknowledged as full moral agents with the responsibility for making moral decisions about their own pregnancies.[2] Although I think that it is possible for a woman to make a mistake in her moral judgment on this matter (i.e., it is possible that a woman may come to believe that she was wrong about her decision to continue or terminate a pregnancy), the intimate nature of this sort of decision makes it unlikely that anyone else is in a position to arrive at a more reliable conclusion; it is, therefore, improper to grant others the authority to interfere in women's decisions to seek abortions.

Feminist analysis regards the effects of unwanted pregnancies on the lives of women individually and collectively as a central element in the moral evaluation of abortion. Even without patriarchy, bearing a child would be a very important event in a woman's life. It involves significant physical, emotional, social, and (usually) economic changes for her. The ability to exert control over the incidence, timing, and frequency of child-bearing is often tied to her ability to control most other things she values. Since we live in a patriarchal society, it is especially important to ensure that women have the authority to control their own reproduction.[3] Despite the diversity of opinion among feminists on most other matters, virtually all feminists seem to agree that women must gain full control over their own reproductive lives if they are to free themselves from male dominance.[4] Many perceive the commitment of the political right wing to opposing abortion as part of a general strategy to reassert patriarchal control over women in the face of significant feminist influence (Petchesky 1980, p. 112).

Women's freedom to choose abortion is also linked with their ability to control their own sexuality. Women's subordinate status often prevents them from refusing men sexual access to their bodies. If women cannot end the unwanted pregnancies that result from male sexual dominance, their sexual vulnerability to particular men can increase, because caring for an(other) infant involves greater financial needs and reduced economic opportunities for women.[5] As a result, pregnancy often forces women to become dependent on men. Since a woman's dependence on a man is assumed to entail that she will remain sexually loyal to him, restriction of abortion serves to channel women's sexuality and further perpetuates the cycle of oppression.

In contrast to most non-feminist accounts, feminist analyses of abortion direct attention to the question of how women get pregnant. Those who reject abortion seem to believe that women can avoid unwanted pregnancies by avoiding sexual intercourse. Such views show little appreciation for the power of sexual politics in a culture that oppresses women. Existing patterns of sexual dominance mean that women often have little control over their sexual lives. They may be subject to rape by strangers, or by their husbands, boyfriends, colleagues, employers, customers, fathers, brothers, uncles, and dates. Often, the sexual coercion is not even recognized as such by the participants, but is the price of continued "good will"—popularity, economic survival, peace, or simple acceptance. Few women have not found themselves in circumstances where they do not feel free to refuse a man's demands for intercourse, either because he is holding a gun to her head or because he threatens to be emotionally hurt if she refuses (or both). Women are socialized to be compliant and accommodating, sensitive to the feelings of others, and frightened of physical power; men are socialized to take advantage of every opportunity to engage in sexual intercourse and to use sex to express dominance and power. Under such circumstances, it is difficult to argue that women could simply "choose" to avoid heterosexual activity if they wish to avoid pregnancy. Catherine MacKinnon neatly sums it up: "the logic by which women are supposed to consent to sex [is]: preclude the alternatives, then call the remaining option 'her choice'" (MacKinnon 1989, p. 192).

Nor can women rely on birth control alone to avoid pregnancy. There simply is no form of reversible contraception available that is fully safe and reliable. The pill and the IUD are the most effective means offered, but both involve significant health hazards to women and are quite dangerous for some. No woman should spend the 30 to 40 years of her reproductive life on either form of birth control. Further, both have been associated with subsequent problems of involuntary infertility, so they are far from optimum for women who seek to control the timing of their pregnancies.

The safest form of birth control involves the use of barrier methods (condoms or diaphragms) in combination with spermicidal foams or jelly. But these methods also pose difficulties for women. They may be socially awkward to use: young women are discouraged from preparing for sexual activity that might never happen and are offered instead romantic models of spontaneous passion. (Few films or novels interrupt scenes of seduction for the fetching of contraceptives.) Many women find their male partners unwilling to use barrier methods of contraception and they do not have the power to insist. Further, cost is a limiting factor for many women. Condoms and spermicides are expensive and are not covered under most health care plans. There is only one contraceptive option which offers women safe and fully effective birth control: barrier methods with the back-up option of abortion.[6]

From a feminist perspective, a central moral feature of pregnancy is that it takes place in *women's bodies* and has profound effects on *women's* lives. Gender-neutral accounts of pregnancy are not available; pregnancy is explicitly a condition associated with the female body.[7] Because the need for abortion is experienced only by women, policies about abortion affect women uniquely. Thus, it is important to consider how proposed policies on abortion fit into general patterns of oppression for women. Unlike non-feminist accounts, feminist ethics demands that the effects on the oppression of women be a principal consideration when evaluating abortion policies.

The Fetus

In contrast, most non-feminist analysts believe that the moral acceptability of abortion turns on the question of the moral status of the fetus. Even those who support women's right to choose abortion tend to accept the central premise of the anti-abortion proponents that abortion can only be tolerated if it can be proved that the fetus is lacking some criterion of full personhood.[8] Opponents of abortion have structured the debate so that it is necessary to define the status of the fetus as either valued the same as other humans (and hence entitled not to be killed) or as lacking in all value. Rather than challenging the logic of this formulation, many defenders of abortion have concentrated on showing that the fetus is indeed without significant value (Tooley 1972, Warren 1973); others, such as Wayne Sumner (1981), offer a more subtle account that reflects the gradual development of fetuses whereby there is some specific criterion that determines the degree of protection to be afforded them which is lacking in the early stages of pregnancy but present in the later stages. Thus, the debate often rages between abortion opponents who describe the fetus as an "innocent," vulnerable, morally important, separate being whose life is threatened and who must be protected at all costs, and abortion supporters who try to establish some sort of deficiency inherent to fetuses which removes them from the scope of the moral community.

The woman on whom the fetus depends for survival is considered as secondary (if she is considered at all) in these debates. The actual experiences and responsibilities of real women are not perceived as morally relevant (unless they, too, can be proved innocent by establishing that their pregnancies are a result of rape or incest). It is a common assumption of both defenders and opponents of women's right to choose abortion that many women will be irresponsible in their choices. The important question, though, is whether fetuses have the sort of status that justifies interfering in women's choices at all. In some contexts, women's role in gestation is literally reduced to that of "fetal containers"; the individual women disappear or are perceived simply as mechanical life-support systems.[9]

The current rhetoric against abortion stresses the fact that the genetic make-up of the fetus is determined at conception and the genetic code is incontestably human. Lest there be any doubt about the humanity of the fetus, we are assailed with photographs of fetuses at various stages of development demonstrating the early appearance of recognizably human characteristics, e.g., eyes, fingers, and toes. The fact that the fetus in its early stages is microscopic, virtually indistinguishable from other primate fetuses to the untrained eye, and lacking in the capacities that make human life meaningful and valuable is not deemed relevant by the self-appointed defenders of fetuses. The anti-abortion campaign is directed at evoking sympathetic attitudes towards this tiny, helpless being whose life is threatened by its own mother; it urges us to see the fetus as entangled in an adversarial relationship with the (presumably irresponsible) woman who carries it. We are encouraged to identify with the "unborn child" and not with the (selfish) woman whose life is also at issue.

Within the non-feminist literature, both defenders and opponents of women's right to choose abortion agree that the difference between a late term fetus and a newborn infant is "merely geographical" and cannot be considered morally significant. But a fetus inhabits a woman's body and is wholly dependent on her unique contribution to its maintenance while a newborn is physically separate though still in need of a lot of care. One can only view the distinction between being in or out of a woman's womb as morally irrelevant if one discounts the perspective of the pregnant woman; feminists seem to be alone in recognizing her perspective as morally important.[10]

Within anti-abortion arguments, fetuses are identified as individuals; in our culture which views the (abstract) individual as sacred, fetuses *qua* individuals should be honoured and preserved. Extraordinary claims are made to try to establish the individuality and moral agency of fetuses. At the same time, the women who carry these fetal individuals are viewed as passive hosts whose only significant role is to refrain from aborting or harming their fetuses. Since it is widely believed that the woman does not actually have to *do* anything to protect the life of the fetus, pregnancy is often considered (abstractly) to be a tolerable burden to protect the life of an individual so like us.[11]

Medicine has played its part in supporting these sorts of attitudes. Fetal medicine is a rapidly expanding specialty, and it is commonplace in professional medical journals to find references to pregnant women as "fetal environments." Fetal surgeons now have at their disposal a repertory of sophisticated technology that can save the lives of dangerously ill fetuses; in light of such heroic successes, it is perhaps understandable that women have disappeared from their view. These specialists see fetuses as their patients, not the women who nurture them. Doctors perceive themselves as the *active* agents in saving fetal lives and, hence, believe that they are the ones in direct relationship with the fetuses they treat.

Perhaps even more distressing than the tendency to ignore the woman's agency altogether and view her as a purely passive participant in the medically controlled events of pregnancy and childbirth is the growing practice of viewing women as genuine threats to the well-being of the fetus. Increasingly, women are viewed as irresponsible or hostile towards their fetuses, and the relationship between them is characterized as adversarial (Overall 1987, p. 60). Concern for the well-being of the fetus is taken as licence for doctors to intervene to ensure that women comply with medical "advice." Courts are called upon to enforce the doctors' orders when moral pressure alone proves inadequate, and women are being coerced into undergoing unwanted Caesarean deliveries and technologically monitored hospital births. Some states have begun to imprison women for endangering their fetuses through drug abuse and other socially unacceptable behaviours. An Australian state recently introduced a bill that makes women liable to criminal prosecution "if they are found to have smoked during pregnancy, eaten unhealthful foods, or taken any other action which can be shown to have adversely affected the development of the fetus" (Warren 1989, p. 60).

In other words, physicians have joined with anti-abortionist activists in fostering a cultural acceptance of the view that fetuses are distinct individuals, who are physically, ontologically, and socially separate from the women whose bodies they inhabit, and who have their own distinct interests. In this picture, pregnant women are either ignored altogether or are viewed as deficient in some crucial respect and hence subject to coercion for the sake of their fetuses. In the former case, the interests of the women concerned are assumed to be identical with those of the fetus; in the latter, the women's interests are irrelevant because they are perceived as immoral, unimportant, or unnatural. Focus on the fetus as an independent entity has led to presumptions which deny pregnant women their roles as active, independent, moral agents with a primary interest in what becomes of the fetuses they carry. Emphasis on the fetus's status has led to an assumed licence to interfere with women's reproductive freedom.

A Feminist View of the Fetus

Because the public debate has been set up as a competition between the rights of women and those of fetuses, feminists have often felt pushed to reject claims of fetal value in order to protect women's claims. Yet, as Addelson (1987) has argued, viewing abortion in this way "tears [it] out of the context of women's lives" (p. 107). There are other accounts of fetal value that are more plausible and less oppressive to women.

On a feminist account, fetal development is examined in the context in which it occurs, within women's bodies rather than in the imagined isolation implicit in many theoretical accounts. Fetuses develop in specific pregnancies which occur in the lives of particular women. They are not individuals housed in generic female wombs, nor are they full persons at risk only because they are small and subject to the whims of women. Their very existence is relational, developing as they do within particular women's bodies, and their principal relationship is to the women who carry them.

On this view, fetuses are morally significant, but their status is relational rather than absolute. Unlike other human beings, fetuses do not have any independent existence; their existence is uniquely tied to the support of a specific other. Most non-feminist commentators have ignored the relational dimension of fetal development and have presumed that the moral status of fetuses could be resolved solely in terms of abstract metaphysical criteria of personhood. They imagine that there is some set of properties (such as genetic heritage, moral agency, self-consciousness, language use, or self-determination) which will entitle all who possess them to be granted the moral status of persons (Warren 1973, Tooley 1972). They seek some particular feature by which we can neatly divide the world into the dichotomy of moral persons (who are to be valued and protected) and others (who are not entitled to the same group privileges); it follows that it is a merely empirical question whether or not fetuses possess the relevant properties.

But this vision misinterprets what is involved in personhood and what it is that is especially valued about persons. Personhood is a social category, not an isolated state. Persons are members of a community; they develop as concrete, discrete, and specific individuals. To be a morally significant category, personhood must involve personality as well as biological integrity.[12] It is not sufficient to consider persons simply as Kantian atoms of rationality; persons are all embodied, conscious beings with particular social histories. Annette Baier (1985) has developed a concept of persons as "second persons" which helps explain the sort of social dimension that seems fundamental to any moral notion of personhood:

> A person, perhaps, is best seen as one who was long enough dependent upon other persons to acquire the essential arts of personhood. Persons essentially are *second* persons, who grow up with other persons. . . . The fact that a person has a life *history*, and that a people collectively have a history depends upon the humbler fact that each person has a childhood in which a cultural heritage is transmitted, ready for adolescent rejection and adult discriminating selection and contribution. Persons come after and before other persons. (P. 84–85; her emphasis.)

Persons, in other words, are members of a social community which shapes and values them, and personhood is a relational concept that must be defined in terms of interactions and relationships with others.

A fetus is a unique sort of being in that it cannot form relationships freely with others, nor can others readily form relationships with it. A fetus has a primary and particularly intimate relationship with the woman in whose womb it develops; any other relationship it may have is indirect, and must be mediated through the pregnant woman. The relationship that exists between a woman and her fetus is clearly asymmetrical, since she is the only party to the relationship who is capable of making a decision about whether the interaction should continue and since the fetus is wholly dependent on the woman who sustains it while she is quite capable of surviving without it.

However much some might prefer it to be otherwise, no one else can do anything to support or harm a fetus without doing something to the woman who nurtures it. Because of this inexorable biological reality, she bears a unique responsibility and privilege in determining her fetus's place in the social scheme of things. Clearly, many pregnancies occur to women who place very high value on the lives of the particular fetuses they carry, and choose to see their pregnancies through to term despite the possible risks and costs involved; hence, it would be wrong of anyone to force such a woman to terminate her pregnancy under these circumstances. Other women, or some of these same women at other times, value other things more highly (e.g., their freedom, their health, or previous responsibilities which conflict with those generated by the pregnancies), and choose not to continue their pregnancies. The value that women ascribe to individual fetuses varies dramatically from case to case, and may well change over the course of any particular pregnancy. There is no absolute value that attaches to fetuses apart from their relational status determined in the context of their particular development.

Since human beings are fundamentally relational beings, it is important to remember that fetuses are characteristically limited in the relationships in which they can participate; within those relationships, they can make only the most restricted "contributions."[13] After birth, human beings are capable of a much wider range of roles in relationships with an infinite variety of partners; it is that very diversity of possibility and experience that leads us to focus on the abstraction of the individual as a constant through all her/his relationships. But until birth, no such variety is possible, and the fetus is defined as an entity within a woman who will almost certainly be principally responsible for it for many years to come.

No human, and especially no fetus, can exist apart from relationships; feminist views of what is valuable about persons must reflect the social nature of their existence. Fetal lives can neither be sustained nor destroyed without affecting the women who support them. Because of a fetus's unique physical status— *within* and dependent on a particular woman—the responsibility and privilege of determining its specific social status and value must rest with the woman carrying it. Fetuses are not persons because they have not developed sufficiently in social relationships to be persons in any morally significant sense (i.e., they are not yet second persons). Newborns, although just beginning their development into persons, are immediately subject to social relationships, for they are capable of communication and response in interaction with a variety of other persons. Thus, feminist accounts of abortion stress the importance of protecting women's right to continue as well as to terminate pregnancies as each sees fit.

Feminist Politics and Abortion

. . . Feminists support abortion on demand because they know that women must have control over their reproduction. For the same reason, they actively oppose forced abortion and coerced sterilization, practices that are sometimes inflicted on the most powerless women, especially those in the Third World. Feminist ethics demands that access to voluntary, safe, effective birth control be part of any abortion discussion, so that women have access to other means of avoiding pregnancy.[14]

Feminist analysis addresses the context as well as the practice of abortion decisions. Thus, feminists also object to the conditions which lead women to abort wanted fetuses because there are not adequate financial and social supports available to care for a child. Because feminist accounts value fetuses that are wanted by the women who carry them, they oppose practices which force women to abort because of poverty or intimidation. Yet, the sorts of social changes necessary if we are to free women from having abortions out of economic necessity are vast; they include changes not only in legal and health-care policy, but also in housing, child care, employment, etc. (Petchesky 1980, p. 112). Nonetheless, feminist ethics defines reproductive freedom as the condition under which women are able to make truly voluntary choices about their reproductive lives, and these many dimensions are implicit in the ideal.

Clearly, feminists are not "pro-abortion," for they are concerned to ensure the safety of each pregnancy to the greatest degree possible; wanted fetuses should not be harmed or lost. Therefore, adequate pre- and post-natal care and nutrition are also important elements of any feminist position on reproductive freedom. Where anti-abortionists direct their energies to trying to prevent women from obtaining abortions, feminists seek to protect the health of wanted fetuses. They recognize that far more could be done to protect and care for fetuses if the state directed its resources at supporting women who continue their pregnancies, rather than draining away resources in order to police women who find that they must interrupt their pregnancies. Caring for the women who carry fetuses is not only a more legitimate policy than is regulating them; it is probably also more effective at ensuring the health and well-being of more fetuses.

Feminist ethics also explores how abortion policies fit within the politics of sexual domination. Most feminists are sensitive to the fact that many men support women's right to abortion out of the belief that women will be more willing sexual partners if they believe that they can readily terminate an unwanted pregnancy. Some men coerce their partners into obtaining abortions the women may not want.[15] Feminists understand that many women oppose abortion for this very reason, being unwilling to support a practice that increases women's sexual vulnerability (Luker 1984, pp. 209–15). Thus, it is important that feminists develop a coherent analysis of reproductive freedom that includes sexual freedom (as women choose to define it). That requires an analysis of sexual freedom that includes women's right to refuse sex; such a right can only be assured if women have equal power to men and are not subject to domination by virtue of their sex.[16]

In sum, then, feminist ethics demands that moral discussions of abortion be more broadly defined than they have been in most philosophic discussions. Only by reflecting on the meaning of ethical pronouncements on actual women's lives and the connections between judgments on abortion and the conditions of domination and subordination can we come to an adequate understanding of the moral status of abortion in our society. As Rosalind Petchesky (1980) argues, feminist discussion of abortion "must be moved beyond the framework of a 'woman's right to choose' and connected to a much broader revolutionary movement that addresses all of the conditions of women's liberation" (p. 113).

NOTES

Earlier versions of this paper were read to the Department of Philosophy, Dalhousie University and to the Canadian Society for Women in Philosophy in Kingston. I am very grateful for the comments received from colleagues in both forums: particular thanks go to Lorraine Code, David Bray-brooke, Richmond Campbell, Sandra Taylor, Terry Tomkow and Kadri Vihvelin for their patience and advice.

1. For some idea of the ways in which traditional moral theory oppresses women, see Morgan (1987) and Hoagland (1988).

2. Critics continue to want to structure the debate around the *possibility* of women making frivolous abortion decisions and hence want feminists to agree to setting boundaries on acceptable grounds for choosing abortion. Feminists ought to resist this injunction, though. There is no practical way of drawing a line fairly in the abstract; cases that may appear "frivolous" at a distance, often turn out to be substantive when the details are revealed, i.e., frivolity is in the eyes of the beholder. There is no evidence to suggest that women actually make the sorts of choices worried critics hypothesize about: e.g., a woman eight months pregnant who chooses to abort because she wants to take a trip or gets in "a tiff" with her partner. These sorts of fantasies, on which demands to distinguish between legitimate and illegitimate personal reasons for choosing abortion chiefly rest, reflect an offensive conception of women as irresponsible; they ought not to be perpetuated. Women, seeking moral guidance in their own deliberations about choosing abortion, do not find such hypothetical discussions of much use.

3. In her monumental historical analysis of the early roots of Western patriarchy, Gerda Lerner (1986) determined that patriarchy began in the period from 3100 to 600 B.C. when men appropriated women's sexual and reproductive capacity; the earliest states entrenched patriarchy by institutionalizing the sexual and procreative subordination of women to men.

4. There are some women who claim to be feminists against choice in abortion. See, for instance, Callahan (1987), though few spell out their full feminist program. For reasons I develop in this paper, I do not think this is a consistent position.

5. There is a lot the state could do to ameliorate this condition. If it provided women with adequate financial support, removed the inequities in the labour market, and provided affordable and reliable childcare, pregnancy need not so often lead to a woman's dependence on a particular man. The fact that it does not do so is evidence of the state's complicity in maintaining women's subordinate position with respect to men.

6. See Petchesky (1984), especially Chapter 5, "Considering the Alternatives: The Problems of Contraception," where she documents the risks and discomforts associated with pill use and IUD's and the increasing rate at which women are choosing the option of diaphragm or condom with the option of early legal abortions as backup.

7. See Zillah Eisenstein (1988) for a comprehensive theory of the role of the pregnant body as the central element in the cultural subordination of women.

8. Thomson (1971) is a notable exception to this trend.

9. This seems reminiscent of Aristotle's view of women as "flower pots" where men implant the seed with all the

important genetic information and the movement necessary for development and women's job is that of passive gestation, like the flower pot. For exploration of the flower pot picture of pregnancy, see Whitbeck (1973) and Lange (1983).

10. Contrast Warren (1989) with Tooley (1972).

11. The definition of pregnancy as a purely passive activity reaches its ghoulish conclusion in the increasing acceptability of sustaining brain-dead women on life support systems to continue their functions as incubators until the fetus can be safely delivered. For a discussion of this new trend, see Murphy (1989).

12. This apt phrasing is taken from Petchesky (1986), p. 342.

13. Fetuses are almost wholly individuated by the women who bear them. The fetal "contributions" to the relationship are defined by the projections and interpretations of the pregnant woman in the latter stages of pregnancy if she chooses to perceive fetal movements in purposeful ways (e.g., it likes classical music, wine, exercise").

14. Therefore, the Soviet model, where women have access to multiple abortions but where there is no other birth control available, must also be opposed.

15. See CARAL/Halifax (1990), p. 20–21, for examples of this sort of abuse.

16. It also requires that discussions of reproductive and sexual freedom not be confined to "the language of control and sexuality characteristic of a technology of sex" (Diamond and Quinby 1988, p. 197), for such language is alienating and constrains women's experiences of their own sexuality.

REFERENCES

Addelson, Kathryn Pyne, 1987. "Moral Passages." In *Women and Moral Theory*. Edited by Eva Feder Kittay and Diana T. Meyers. Totowa, NJ: Rowman & Littlefield.

Baier, Annette, 1985. *Postures of the Mind: Essays on Mind and Morals*. Minneapolis: University of Minnesota Press.

Callahan, Sidney, 1987. "A Pro-life Feminist Makes Her Case." *Utne Reader* (March/April): 104–14.

CARAL/Halifax, 1990. *Telling Our Stories: Abortion Stories from Nova Scotia*. Halifax: CARAL/Halifax (Canadian Abortion Rights Action League).

Daly, Mary, 1973. *Beyond God the Father: Toward a Philosophy of Women's Liberation*. Boston: Beacon Press.

Diamond, Irene, and Lee Quinby, 1988. "American Feminism and the Language of Control." In *Feminism and Foucault: Reflections on Resistance*. Edited by Irene Diamond and Lee Quinby. Boston: Northeastern University Press.

Eisenstein, Zillah R., 1988. *The Female Body and the Law*. Berkeley: University of California Press.

Hoagland, Sara Lucia, 1988. *Lesbian Ethics: Toward New Value*. Palo Alto, CA: Institute of Lesbian Studies.

Lange, Lynda, 1983. "Woman Is Not a Rational Animal: On Aristotle's Biology of Reproduction." In *Discovering Reality: Feminist Perspectives on Epistemology, Metaphysics, Methodology, and Philosophy of Science*. Edited by Sandra Harding and Merill B. Hintikka. Dordrecht, Holland: D. Reidel.

Lerner, Gerda, 1986. *The Creation of Patriarchy*. New York: Oxford.

Luker, Kristin, 1984. *Abortion and the Politics of Motherhood*. Berkeley: University of California Press.

MacKinnon, Catherine, 1989. *Toward a Feminist Theory of the State*. Cambridge, MA: Harvard University Press.

McDonnell, Kathleen, 1984. *Not an Easy Choice: A Feminist Re-examines Abortion*. Toronto: The Women's Press.

McLaren, Angus, and Arlene Tigar McLaren, 1986. *The Bedroom and the State: The Changing Practices and Politics of Contraception and Abortion in Canada, 1880–1980*. Toronto: McClelland and Stewart.

Morgan, Kathryn Pauly, 1987. "Women and Moral Madness." In *Science, Morality and Feminist Theory*. Edited by Marsha Hanen and Kai Nielsen. *Canadian Journal of Philosophy*, Supplementary Volume 13: 201–26.

Murphy, Julien S., 1989. "Should Pregnancies Be Sustained in Brain-dead Women?: A Philosophical Discussion of Postmortem Pregnancy." In *Healing Technology: Feminist Perspectives*. Edited by Kathryn Srother Ratcliff et al. Ann Arbor: The University of Michigan Press.

Overall, Christine, 1987. *Ethics and Human Reproduction: A Feminist Analysis*. Winchester, MA: Allen & Unwin.

Petchesky, Rosalind Pollack, 1980. "Reproductive Freedom: Beyond 'A Woman's Right to Choose.'" In *Women: Sex and Sexuality*. Edited by Catharine R. Stimpson and Ethel Spector Person. Chicago: University of Chicago Press.

———1984. *Abortion and Woman's Choice: The State, Sexuality, and Reproductive Freedom*. Boston: Northeastern University Press.

Sumner, L. W., 1981. *Abortion and Moral Theory*. Princeton: Princeton University Press.

Thomson, Judith Jarvis, 1971. "A Defense of Abortion." *Philosophy and Public Affairs*, 1: 47–66.

Tooley, Michael, 1972. "Abortion and Infanticide." *Philosophy and Public Affairs*, 2, 1 (Fall): 37–65.

Van Wagner, Vicki, and Bob Lee, 1989. "'Principles into Practice: An Activist Vision of Feminist Reproductive Health Care." In *The Future of Human Reproduction*. Edited by Christine Overall. Toronto: The Women's Press.

Warren, Mary Anne, 1973. "On the Moral and Legal Status of Abortion." *The Monist*, 57: 43–61.

——1989. "The Moral Significance of Birth." *Hypatia*, 4, 2 (Summer): 46–65.

Whitbeck. Carolyn, 1973. "Theories of Sex Difference." *The Philosophical Forum*, 5, 1–2 (Fall/Winter 1973–74): 54–80.

Roe v. Wade

UNITED STATES SUPREME COURT

In this decision, the Court ruled that no state can ban abortions performed before viability. The Court thought that the Constitution implied a guaranteed right of personal privacy that limits interference by the state in people's private lives and that the right encompassed a woman's decision to have an abortion. But the woman's right is not absolute and must be balanced against important state interests. Thus the Court held that in the first trimester, the woman's right to an abortion cannot be restrained by the state. In the second trimester, the state may limit—but not entirely prohibit—the woman's right by regulating abortion for the sake of her health. After viability, the state may regulate and even ban abortion except when necessary to preserve her life or health.

Majority Opinion (Delivered by Justice Blackmun)

Three reasons have been advanced to explain historically the enactment of criminal abortion laws in the 19th century and to justify their continued existence.

It has been argued occasionally that these laws were the product of a Victorian social concern to discourage illicit sexual conduct. Texas, however, does not advance this justification in the present case, and it appears that no court or commentator has taken the argument seriously. The appellants and *amici* contend, moreover, that this is not a proper state purpose at all and suggest that, if it were, the Texas statutes are overbroad in protecting it since the law fails to distinguish between married and unwed mothers.

A second reason is concerned with abortion as a medical procedure. When most criminal abortion laws were first enacted, the procedure was a hazardous one for the woman. This was particularly true prior to the development of antisepsis. Antiseptic techniques, of course, were based on discoveries by Lister, Pasteur, and others first announced in 1867,

but were not generally accepted and employed until about the turn of the century. Abortion mortality was high. Even after 1900, and perhaps until as late as the development of antibiotics in the 1940s, standard modern techniques such as dilation and curettage were not nearly so safe as they are today. Thus, it has been argued that a state's real concern in enacting a criminal abortion law was to protect the pregnant woman, that is, to restrain her from submitting to a procedure that placed her life in serious jeopardy.

Modern medical techniques have altered this situation. Appellants and various *amici* refer to medical data indicating that abortion in early pregnancy, that is, prior to the end of the first trimester, although not without its risk, is now relatively safe. Mortality rates for women undergoing early abortions, where the procedure is legal, appear to be as low as or lower than the rates for normal childbirth. Consequently, any interest of the state in protecting the woman from an inherently hazardous procedure except when it would be equally dangerous for her to forgo it, has largely disappeared. Of course, important state interests in the areas of health and medical standards do remain. The state has a legitimate interest in seeing to it that abortion, like any other medi-

United States Supreme Court, 410 U.S. 113, 93 S. Ct. 705. January 22, 1973.

cal procedure, is performed under circumstances that insure maximum safety for the patient. This interest obviously extends at least to the performing physician and his staff, to the facilities involved, to the availability of after-care, and to adequate provision for any complication or emergency that might arise. The prevalence of high mortality rates at illegal "abortion mills" strengthens, rather than weakens, the state's interest in regulating the conditions under which abortions are performed. Moreover, the risk to the woman increases as her pregnancy continues. Thus, the state retains a definite interest in protecting the woman's own health and safety when an abortion is proposed at a late stage of pregnancy.

The third reason is the state's interest—some phrase it in terms of duty—in protecting prenatal life. Some of the argument for this justification rests on the theory that a new human life is present from the moment of conception. The state's interest and general obligation to protect life then extends, it is argued, to prenatal life. Only when the life of the pregnant mother herself is at stake, balanced against the life she carries within her, should the interest of the embryo or fetus not prevail. Logically, of course, a legitimate state interest in this area need not stand or fall on acceptance of the belief that life begins at conception or at some other point prior to live birth. In assessing the state's interest, recognition may be given to the less rigid claim that as long as at least potential life is involved, the state may assert interests beyond the protection of the pregnant woman alone.

Parties challenging state abortion laws have sharply disputed in some courts the contention that a purpose of these laws, when enacted, was to protect prenatal life. Pointing to the absence of legislative history to support the contention, they claim that most state laws were designed solely to protect the woman. Because medical advances have lessened this concern, at least with respect to abortion in early pregnancy, they argue that with respect to such abortions the laws can no longer be justified by any state interest. There is some scholarly support for this view of original purpose. The few state courts called upon to interpret their laws in the late 19th and early 20th centuries did focus on the state's interest in protecting the woman's health rather than in preserving the embryo and fetus. Proponents of this view point out that in many states, including Texas, by statute or judicial interpretation, the pregnant woman herself could not be prosecuted for self-abortion or for cooperating in an abortion performed upon her by another. They claim that adoption of the "quickening" distinction through received common law and state statutes tacitly recognizes the greater health hazards inherent in late abortion and impliedly repudiates the theory that life begins at conception.

It is with these interests, and the weight to be attached to them, that this case is concerned.

The Constitution does not explicitly mention any right of privacy. In a line of decisions, however, going back perhaps as far as Union Pacific R. Co. v. Botsford, 141 U.S. 250, 251 (1891), the court has recognized that a right of personal privacy, or a guarantee of certain areas or zones of privacy, does exist under the Constitution. In varying contexts, the court or individual justices have, indeed, found at least the roots of that right in the first amendment, in the fourth and fifth amendments, in the penumbras of the Bill of Rights, in the ninth amendment, or in the concept of liberty guaranteed by the first section of the fourteenth amendment. These decisions make it clear that only personal rights that can be deemed "fundamental" or "implicit" in the concept of ordered liberty are included in this guarantee of personal privacy. They also make it clear that the right has some extension to activities relating to marriage, procreation, contraception, family relationships, and child rearing and education.

This right of privacy, whether it be founded in the fourteenth amendment's concept of personal liberty and restrictions upon state action, as we feel it is, or, as the district court determined, in the ninth amendment's reservation of rights to the people, is broad enough to encompass a woman's decision whether or not to terminate her pregnancy. The detriment that the state would impose upon the pregnant woman by denying this choice altogether is apparent. Specific and direct harm medically diagnosable even in early pregnancy may be involved. Maternity, or additional offspring, may force upon the woman a distressful life and future. Psychological harm may be imminent. Mental and physical health may be taxed by child care. There is also the distress, for all concerned, associated with the unwanted child, and there is the problem of bringing a child into a family already unable, psychologically and otherwise, to care for it. In other cases, as in this one, the additional difficulties and continuing stigma factors the woman and her responsible physician necessarily will consider in consultation.

On the basis of elements such as these, appellant and some *amici* argue that the woman's right is absolute and that she is entitled to terminate her pregnancy at whatever time, in whatever way, and for whatever reason she alone chooses. With this we do not agree. Appellant's arguments that Texas either has no valid interest strong enough to support any limitation upon the woman's sole determination are unpersuasive. The court's decisions recognizing a right of privacy also acknowledge that some state regulation in areas protected by that right is appropriate. As noted above, a state may properly assert important interests in safeguarding health, in maintaining medical standards, and in protecting potential life. At some point in pregnancy, to sustain regulation of the factors that govern the abortion decision. The privacy right involved, therefore, cannot be said to be absolute. In fact, it is not clear to us that the claim asserted by some *amici* that one has an unlimited right to do with one's body as one pleases bears a close relationship to the right of privacy previously articulated in the court's decisions. The court has refused to recognize an unlimited right of this kind in the past.

We, therefore, conclude that the right of personal privacy includes the abortion decision, but that this right is not unqualified and must be considered against important state interests in regulation.

We note that those federal and state courts that have recently considered abortion law challenges have reached the same conclusion. A majority, in addition to the district court in the present case, have held state laws unconstitutional, at least in part, because of vagueness or because of overbreadth and abridgment of rights.

Although the results are divided, most of these courts have agreed that the right of privacy, however based, is broad enough to cover the abortion decision; that the right, nonetheless, is not absolute and is subject to some limitations; and that at some point

the state interests as to protection of health, medical standards, and prenatal life, become dominant. We agree with this approach.

Where certain "fundamental rights" are involved, the court has held that regulation limiting these rights may be justified only by a "compelling state interest," and that legislative enactments must be narrowly drawn to express only the legitimate state interests at stake.

In the recent abortion cases, cited above, courts have recognized these principles. Those striking down state laws have generally scrutinized the state's interests in protecting health and potential life, and have concluded that neither interest justified broad limitations on the reasons for which a physician and his pregnant patient might decide that she should have an abortion in the early stages of pregnancy. Courts sustaining state laws have held that the state's determinations to protect health or prenatal life are dominant and constitutionally justifiable.

The district court held that the appellee failed to meet his burden of demonstrating that the Texas statute's infringement upon Roe's rights was necessary to support a compelling state interest, and that, although the appellee presented "several compelling justifications for state presence in the area of abortions," the statutes outstripped these justifications and swept "far beyond any areas of compelling state interest." Appellant and appellee both contest that holding. Appellant, as has been indicated, claims an absolute right that bars any state imposition of criminal penalties in the area. Appellee argues that the state's determination to recognize and protect prenatal life from and after conception constitutes a compelling state interest. As noted above, we do not agree fully with either formulation.

A. The appellee and certain *amici* argue that the fetus is a "person" within the language and meaning of the fourteenth amendment. In support of this, they outline at length and in detail the well-known facts of fetal development. If this suggestion of personhood is established, the appellant's case, of course, collapses, for the fetus' right to life would then be guaranteed specifically by the amendment. The appellant conceded as much on reargument. On the other hand, the appellee conceded on reargument that no case could be cited that holds that a fetus is a person within the meaning of the fourteenth amendment.

The Constitution does not define "person" in so many words. Section 1 of the fourteenth amendment contains three references to "person . . ." but in nearly all these instances, the use of the word is such that it has application only postnatally. None indicates, with any assurance, that it has any possible prenatal application.

All this, together with our observation, supra, that throughout the major portion of the 19th century prevailing legal abortion practices were far freer than they are today, persuades us that the word "person," as used in the fourteenth amendment, does not include the unborn. . . .

B. The pregnant woman cannot be isolated in her privacy. She carries an embryo and, later, a fetus, if one accepts the medical definitions of the developing young in the human uterus. See Dorland's Illustrated Medical Dictionary 478–479, 547 (7th ed. 1965). The situation therefore is inherently different from marital intimacy, or bedroom possession of obscene material, or marriage, or procreation, or education, with which *Eisenstadt, Griswold, Stanley, Loving, Skinner, Pierce*, and *Meyer* were respectively concerned. As we have intimated above, it is reasonable and appropriate for a state to decide that at some point in time another interest, that of health of the mother or that of potential human life, becomes significantly involved. The woman's privacy is no longer sole and any right of privacy she possesses must be measured accordingly.

Texas urges that, apart from the fourteenth amendment, life begins at conception and is present throughout pregnancy, and that, therefore, the state has a compelling interest in protecting that life from and after conception. We need not resolve the difficult question of when life begins. When those trained in the respective disciplines of medicine, philosophy, and theology are unable to arrive at any consensus, the judiciary, at this point in the development of man's knowledge, is not in a position to speculate as to the answer.

It should be sufficient to note briefly the wide divergence of thinking on this most sensitive and difficult question. There has always been strong support for the view that life does not begin until live birth.

This was the belief of the Stoics. It appears to be the predominant, though not the unanimous, attitude of the Jewish faith. It may be taken to represent also the position of a large segment of the Protestant community, insofar as that can be ascertained; organized groups that have taken a formal position on the abortion issue have generally regarded abortion as a matter for the conscience of the individual and her family. As we have noted, the common law found greater significance in quickening. Physicians and their scientific colleagues have regarded that event with less interest and have tended to focus either upon conception, upon live birth, or upon the interim point at which the fetus becomes "viable," that is, potentially able to live outside the mother's womb, albeit with artificial aid. Viability is usually placed at about seven months (28 weeks) but may occur earlier, even at 24 weeks. The Aristotelian theory of "mediate animation," that held sway throughout the Middle Ages and the Renaissance in Europe, continued to be official Roman Catholic dogma until the 19th century, despite opposition to this "ensoulment" theory from those in the church who would recognize the existence of life from the moment of conception. The latter is now, of course, the official belief of the Catholic church. As one brief *amicus* discloses, this is a view strongly held by many non-Catholics as well, and by many physicians. Substantial problems for precise definition of this view are posed, however, by new embryological data that purport to indicate that conception is a "process" over time, rather than an event, and by new medical techniques: implantation of embryos, artificial insemination, and even artificial wombs.

In areas other than criminal abortion, the law has been reluctant to endorse any theory that life, as we recognize it, begins before live birth or to accord legal rights to the unborn except in narrowly defined situations and except when the rights are contingent upon live birth. For example, the traditional rule of tort law denied recovery for prenatal injuries even though the child was born alive. That rule has been changed in almost every jurisdiction. In most states, recovery is said to be permitted only if the fetus was viable, or at least quick, when the injuries were sustained, though few courts have squarely so held. In a recent development, generally opposed by the commentators, some states permit the parents of a stillborn child to maintain an action for wrongful death because of prenatal injuries. Such an action, however, would appear to be one to vindicate the parents' interest and is thus consistent with the view that the fetus, at most, represents only the potentiality of life. Similarly, unborn children have been recognized as acquiring rights or interests by way of inheritance or other devolution of property, and have been represented by guardians ad litem. Perfection of the interests involved, again, has generally been contingent upon live birth. In short, the unborn have never been recognized in the law as persons in the whole sense.

In view of all this, we do not agree that, by adopting one theory of life, Texas may override the rights of the pregnant woman that are at stake. We repeat, however, that the state does have an important and legitimate interest in preserving and protecting the health of the pregnant woman, whether she be a resident of the state or a nonresident who seeks medical consultation and treatment there, and that it has still another important and legitimate interest in protecting the potentiality of human life. These interests are separate and distinct. Each grows in substantiality as the woman approaches term and, at a point during pregnancy, each becomes "compelling."

With respect to the state's important and legitimate interest in the health of the mother, the "compelling" point, in the light of present medical knowledge, is at approximately the end of the first trimester. This is so because of the now-established medical fact, referred to above at 149, that until the end of the first trimester mortality in abortion may be less than mortality in normal childbirth. It follows that, from and after this point, a state may regulate the abortion procedure to the extent that the regulation reasonably relates to the preservation and protection of maternal health. Examples of permissible state regulation in this area are requirements as to the qualifications of the person who is to perform the abortion; as to the licensure of that person; as to the facility in which the procedure is to be performed, that is, whether it must be a hospital or may be a clinic or some other place of less-than-hospital status; as to the licensing of the facility; and the like.

This means, on the other hand, that, for the period of pregnancy prior to this "compelling" point, the attending physician, in consultation with his patient, is free to determine, without regulation by the state, that, in his medical judgment, the patient's pregnancy should be terminated. If that decision is reached, the judgment may be effectuated by an abortion free of interference by the state.

With respect to the state's important and legitimate interest in potential life, the "compelling" point is at viability. This is so because the fetus then presumably has the capability of meaningful life outside the mother's womb. State regulation protective of fetal life after viability thus has both logical and biological justifications. If the state is interested in protecting fetal life after viability, it may go so far as to proscribe abortion during that period, except when it is necessary to preserve the life or health of the mother.

Measured against these standards, art. 1196 of the Texas penal code, in restricting legal abortions to those "procured or attempted by medical advice for the purpose of saving the life of the mother," sweeps too broadly. The statute makes no distinction between abortions performed early in pregnancy and those performed later, and it limits to a single reason, "saving" the mother's life, the legal justification for the procedure. The statute, therefore, cannot survive the constitutional attack made upon it here. . . .

To summarize and to repeat:

1. A state criminal abortion statute of the current Texas type, that excepts from criminality only a life-saving procedure on behalf of the mother, without regard to pregnancy stage and without recognition of the other interests involved, is violative of the due process clause of the fourteenth amendment.

a. For the stage prior to approximately the end of the first trimester, the abortion decision and its effectuation must be left to the medical judgment of the pregnant woman's attending physician.

b. For the stage subsequent to approximately the end of the first trimester, the state, in promoting its interest in the health of the mother, may, if it chooses, regulate the abortion procedure in ways that are reasonably related to maternal health.

c. For the stage subsequent to viability, the state in promoting its interest in the potentiality of human life may, if it chooses, regulate, and even proscribe, abortion except where it is necessary, in appropriate medical judgment, for the preservation of the life or health of the mother.

2. The state may define the term "physician," as it has been employed in the preceding paragraphs of this part XI of this opinion, to mean only a physician currently licensed by the state, and may proscribe any abortion by a person who is not a physician as so defined. . . .

This holding, we feel, is consistent with the relative weights of the respective interests involved, with the lessons and examples of medical and legal history, with the lenity of the common law, and with the demands of the profound problems of the present day. The decision leaves the state free to place increasing restrictions on abortion as the period of pregnancy lengthens, so long as those restrictions are tailored to the recognized state interests. The decision vindicates the right of the physician to administer medical treatment according to his professional judgment up to the points where important state interests provide compelling justifications for intervention. Up to those points, the abortion decision in all its aspects is inherently, and primarily, a medical decision, and basic responsibility for it must rest with the physician. If an individual practitioner abuses the privilege of exercising proper medical judgment, the usual remedies, judicial and intra-professional, are available. . . .

Planned Parenthood of Southeastern Pennsylvania v. Casey

UNITED STATES SUPREME COURT

In this 1992 ruling, the Court found that "The essential holding of Roe v. Wade should be retained and once again reaffirmed." But it rejected Roe's trimester framework and established an "undue burden" test for assessing the restrictions that states put on abortion. Before viability, abortion can be restricted in many ways as long as the constraints do not amount to an undue burden on a woman wishing to obtain an abortion. The Court held that several restrictions do not impose such burdens, including the requirement that a woman give her written informed consent to abortion and that minors under age 18 who seek abortions obtain parental consent or a judge's authorization. But a spousal notification provision does constitute an undue burden.

I

Liberty finds no refuge in a jurisprudence of doubt. Yet, 19 years after our holding that the Constitution protects a woman's right to terminate her pregnancy in its early stages, Roe v Wade (1973), that definition of liberty is still questioned. Joining the respondents as amicus curiae, the United States, as it has done in five other cases in the last decade, again asks us to overrule Roe.

At issue . . . are five provisions of the Pennsylvania Abortion Control Act of 1982, as amended in

United States Supreme Court, 505 U.S. 833, 112 S. Ct. 2791, June 29, 1992.

1988 and 1989. . . . The Act requires that a woman seeking an abortion give her informed consent prior to the abortion procedure, and specifies that she be provided with certain information at least 24 hours before the abortion is performed. Section 3205. For a minor to obtain an abortion, the Act requires the informed consent of one of her parents, but provides for a judicial bypass option if the minor does not wish to or cannot obtain a parent's consent. Section 3206. Another provision of the Act requires that, unless certain exceptions apply, a married woman seeking an abortion must sign a statement indicating that she has notified her husband of her intended abortion. Section 3209. The Act exempts compliance with these three requirements in the event of a "medical emergency," which is defined in Section 3 of the Act. See Section 3205(a), Section 3206(a), Section 3209(c). In addition to the above provisions regulating the performance of abortions, the Act imposes certain reporting requirements on facilities that provide abortion services.

Before any of these provisions took effect, the petitioners, who are five abortion clinics and one physician representing himself as well as a class of physicians who provide abortion services, brought this suit seeking declaratory and injunctive relief. Each provision was challenged as unconstitutional on its face. The District Court entered a preliminary injunction against the enforcement of the regulations, and, after a 3-day bench trial, held all the provisions at issue here unconstitutional, entering a permanent injunction against Pennsylvania's enforcement of them. The Court of Appeals for the Third Circuit affirmed in part and reversed in part, upholding all of the regulations except for the husband notification requirement. . . . [W]e find it imperative to review once more the principles that define the rights of the woman and the legitimate authority of the State respecting the termination of pregnancies by abortion procedures.

After considering the fundamental constitutional questions resolved by Roe, principles of institutional integrity, and the rule of stare decisis, we are led to conclude this: the essential holding of Roe v. Wade should be retained and once again reaffirmed.

It must be stated at the outset and with clarity that Roe's essential holding, the holding we reaffirm, has three parts. First is a recognition of the right of the woman to choose to have an abortion before viability and to obtain it without undue interference from the State. Before viability, the State's interests are not strong enough to support a prohibition of abortion or the imposition of a substantial obstacle to the woman's effective right to elect the procedure. Second is a confirmation of the State's power to restrict abortions after fetal viability if the law contains exceptions for pregnancies which endanger the woman's life or health. And third is the principle that the State has legitimate interests from the outset of the pregnancy in protecting the health of the woman and the life of the fetus that may become a child.

These principles do not contradict one another; and we adhere to each.

II

Constitutional protection of the woman's decision to terminate her pregnancy derives from the Due Process Clause of the Fourteenth Amendment. It declares that no State shall "deprive any person of life, liberty, or property, without due process of law." The controlling word in the cases before us is "liberty."

. . . It is a promise of the Constitution that there is a realm of personal liberty which the government may not enter. We have vindicated this principle before. Marriage is mentioned nowhere in the Bill of Rights, and interracial marriage was illegal in most States in the 19th century, but the Court was no doubt correct in finding it to be an aspect of liberty protected against state interference by the substantive component of the Due Process Clause. . . .

Neither the Bill of Rights nor the specific practices of States at the time of the adoption of the Fourteenth Amendment marks the outer limits of the substantive sphere of liberty which the Fourteenth Amendment protects. . . . It is settled now, as it was when the Court heard arguments in Roe v. Wade, that the Constitution places limits on a State's right to interfere with a person's most basic decisions about family and parenthood, as well as bodily integrity.

The inescapable fact is that adjudication of substantive due process claims may call upon the Court in interpreting the Constitution to exercise that same capacity which, by tradition, courts always have exercised: reasoned judgment. Its boundaries are not susceptible of expression as a simple rule. That does not mean we are free to invalidate state policy choices with which we disagree; yet neither does it permit us to shrink from the duties of our office. . . .

III

. . . No evolution of legal principle has left Roe's doctrinal footings weaker than they were in 1973. No development of constitutional law since the case was decided has implicitly or explicitly left Roe behind as a mere survivor of obsolete constitutional thinking. . . .

We have seen how time has overtaken some of Roe's factual assumptions: advances in maternal health care allow for abortions safe to the mother later in pregnancy than was true in 1973, and advances in neonatal care have advanced viability to a point somewhat earlier. But these facts go only to the scheme of time limits on the realization of competing interests, and the divergences from the factual premises of 1973 have no bearing on the validity of Roe's central holding, that viability marks the earliest point at which the State's interest in fetal life is constitutionally adequate to justify a legislative ban on nontherapeutic abortions. The soundness or unsoundness of that constitutional judgment in no sense turns on whether viability occurs at approximately 28 weeks, as was usual at the time of Roe, at 23 to 24 weeks, as it sometimes does today, or at some moment even slightly earlier in pregnancy, as it may if fetal respiratory capacity can somehow be enhanced in the future. Whenever it may occur, the attainment of viability may continue to serve as the critical fact, just as it has done since Roe was decided; which is to say that no change in Roe's factual underpinning has left its central holding obsolete, and none supports an argument for overruling it.

The sum of the precedential enquiry to this point shows Roe's underpinnings unweakened in any way affecting its central holding. While it has engendered disapproval, it has not been unworkable. . . .

The Court's duty in the present case is clear. In 1973, it confronted the already-divisive issue of governmental power to limit personal choice to undergo abortion, for which it provided a new resolution based on the due process guaranteed by the Fourteenth Amendment. Whether or not a new social consensus is developing on that issue, its divisiveness is no less today than in 1973, and pressure to overrule the decision, like pressure to retain it, has grown only more intense. A decision to overrule Roe's essential holding under the existing circumstances would address error, if error there was, at the cost of both profound and unnecessary damage to the Court's legitimacy, and to the Nation's commitment to the rule of law. It is therefore imperative to adhere to the essence of Roe's original decision, and we do so today.

IV

From what we have said so far, it follows that it is a constitutional liberty of the woman to have some freedom to terminate her pregnancy. We conclude that the basic decision in Roe was based on a constitutional analysis which we cannot now repudiate. The woman's liberty is not so unlimited, however, that from the outset the State cannot show its concern for the life of the unborn, and at a later point in fetal development the State's interest in life has sufficient force so that the right of the woman to terminate the pregnancy can be restricted. . . .

We conclude the line should be drawn at viability, so that, before that time, the woman has a right to choose to terminate her pregnancy. We adhere to this principle for two reasons. First, as we have said, is the doctrine of stare decisis. Any judicial act of line-drawing may seem somewhat arbitrary, but Roe was a reasoned statement, elaborated with great care. We have twice reaffirmed it in the face of great opposition. . . .

The second reason is that the concept of viability, as we noted in Roe, is the time at which there is a realistic possibility of maintaining and nourishing a life outside the womb, so that the independent existence of the second life can, in reason and all fairness, be the object of state protection that now overrides the rights of the woman. . . . We must justify the lines we draw. And there is no line other than viability which is more workable. To be sure, as we have said, there may be some medical developments that affect the precise point of viability, see supra, but this is an imprecision within tolerable limits, given that the medical community and all those who must apply its discoveries will continue to explore the matter. The viability line also has, as a practical matter, an element of fairness. In some broad sense, it might be said that a woman who fails to act before viability has consented to the State's intervention on behalf of the developing child.

The woman's right to terminate her pregnancy before viability is the most central principle of Roe v. Wade. It is a rule of law and a component of liberty we cannot renounce. . . .

Yet it must be remembered that Roe v. Wade speaks with clarity in establishing not only the woman's liberty but also the State's "important and legitimate interest in potential life." That portion of the decision in Roe has been given too little acknowledgment and implementation by the Court in its subsequent cases. . . .

Roe established a trimester framework to govern abortion regulations. Under this elaborate but rigid construct, almost no regulation at all is permitted during the first trimester of pregnancy; regulations designed to protect the woman's health, but not to further the State's interest in potential life, are permitted during the second trimester; and, during the third trimester, when the fetus is viable, prohibitions are permitted provided the life or health of the mother is not at stake. Most of our cases since Roe have involved the application of rules derived from the trimester framework.

The trimester framework no doubt was erected to ensure that the woman's right to choose not become so subordinate to the State's interest in promoting fetal life that her choice exists in theory, but not in fact. We do not agree, however, that the trimester approach is necessary to accomplish this objective. A framework of this rigidity was unnecessary, and, in its later interpretation, sometimes contradicted the State's permissible exercise of its powers.

Though the woman has a right to choose to terminate or continue her pregnancy before viability, it does not at all follow that the State is prohibited from taking steps to ensure that this choice is thoughtful and informed. Even in the earliest stages of pregnancy, the State may enact rules and regulations designed to encourage her to know that there are philosophic and social arguments of great weight that can be brought to bear in favor of continuing the pregnancy to full term, and that there are procedures and institutions to allow adoption of unwanted children as well as a certain degree of state assistance if the mother chooses to raise the child herself. . . . It follows that the States are free to enact laws to provide a reasonable framework for a woman to make a decision that has such profound and lasting meaning. This, too, we find consistent with Roe's central premises, and indeed the inevitable consequence of our holding that the State has an interest in protecting the life of the unborn. . . .

Numerous forms of state regulation might have the incidental effect of increasing the cost or decreasing the availability of medical care, whether for abortion or any other medical procedure. The fact that a law which serves a valid purpose, one not designed to strike at the right itself, has the incidental effect of making it more difficult or more expensive to procure an abortion cannot be enough to invalidate it. Only where state regulation imposes an undue burden on a woman's ability to make this decision does the power of the State reach into the heart of the liberty protected by the Due Process Clause. . . .

. . . Before viability, Roe and subsequent cases treat all governmental attempts to influence a woman's decision on behalf of the potential life within her as unwarranted. This treatment is, in our judgment, incompatible with the recognition that there is a substantial state interest in potential life throughout pregnancy.

The very notion that the State has a substantial interest in potential life leads to the conclusion that not all regulations must be deemed unwarranted. Not all burdens on the right to decide whether to terminate a pregnancy will be undue. In our view, the undue burden standard is the appropriate means of reconciling the State's interest with the woman's constitutionally protected liberty. . . .

. . . We give this summary:

a. To protect the central right recognized by Roe v. Wade while at the same time accommodating the State's profound interest in potential life, we will employ the undue burden analysis as explained in this opinion. An undue burden exists, and therefore a provision of law is invalid, if its purpose or effect is to place a substantial obstacle in the path of a woman seeking an abortion before the fetus attains viability.

b. We reject the rigid trimester framework of Roe v. Wade. To promote the State's profound interest in potential life, throughout pregnancy, the State may take measures to ensure that the woman's choice is informed, and measures designed to advance this interest will not be invalidated as long as their purpose is to persuade the woman to choose childbirth over abortion. These measures must not be an undue burden on the right.

c. As with any medical procedure, the State may enact regulations to further the health or safety of a woman seeking an abortion. Unnecessary health regulations that have the purpose or effect of presenting a substantial obstacle to a woman seeking an abortion impose an undue burden on the right.

d. Our adoption of the undue burden analysis does not disturb the central holding of Roe v. Wade, and we reaffirm that holding. Regardless of whether exceptions are made for particular circumstances, a State may not prohibit any woman from making the ultimate decision to terminate her pregnancy before viability.

e. We also reaffirm Roe's holding that, "subsequent to viability, the State, in promoting its interest in the potentiality of human life, may, if it chooses, regulate, and even proscribe, abortion except where it is necessary, in appropriate medical judgment, for the preservation of the life or health of the mother."

These principles control our assessment of the Pennsylvania statute, and we now turn to the issue of the validity of its challenged provisions.

V

The Court of Appeals applied what it believed to be the undue burden standard, and upheld each of the provisions except for the husband notification requirement. We agree generally with this conclusion, but refine the undue burden analysis in accordance with the principles articulated above. We now consider the separate statutory sections at issue.

(B)

We next consider the informed consent requirement. Section 3205. Except in a medical emergency, the statute requires that at least 24 hours before performing an abortion a physician inform the woman of the nature of the procedure, the health risks of the abortion and of childbirth, and the "probable gestational age of the unborn child." The physician or a qualified nonphysician must inform the woman of the availability of printed materials published by the State describing the fetus and providing information about medical assistance for childbirth, information about child support from the father, and a list of agencies which provide adoption and other services as alternatives to abortion. An abortion may not be performed unless the woman certifies in writing that she has been informed of the availability of these printed materials and has been provided them if she chooses to view them.

Our prior decisions establish that, as with any medical procedure, the State may require a woman to give her written informed consent to an abortion. . . .

In *Akron v. Akron Center for Reproductive Health, Inc.* (1983) (*Akron I.*) we invalidated an ordinance which required that a woman seeking an abortion be provided by her physician with specific information "designed to influence the woman's informed choice between abortion or childbirth." As we later described the *Akron I* holding in *Thornburgh* v. *American College of Obstetricians and Gynecologists*, there were two purported flaws in the Akron ordinance: the information was designed to dissuade the woman from having an abortion, and the ordinance imposed "a rigid requirement that a specific body of information be given in all cases, irrespective of the particular needs of the patient. . . .

. . . It cannot be questioned that psychological wellbeing is a facet of health. Nor can it be doubted that most women considering an abortion would deem the impact on the fetus relevant, if not dispositive, to the decision. In attempting to ensure that a woman apprehend the full consequences of her decision, the State furthers the legitimate purpose of reducing the risk that a woman may elect an abortion, only to discover later, with devastating psychological consequences, that her decision was not fully informed. If the information the State requires to be made available to the woman is truthful and not misleading, the requirement may be permissible.

We also see no reason why the State may not require doctors to inform a woman seeking an abortion of the availability of materials relating to the consequences to the fetus, even when those consequences have no direct relation to her health. An example illustrates the point. We would think it constitutional for the State to require that, in order for there to be informed consent to a kidney transplant operation, the recipient must be supplied with information about risks to the donor as well as risks to himself or herself. A requirement that the physician make available information similar to that mandated by the statute here was described in *Thornburgh* as an outright attempt to wedge the Commonwealth's message discouraging abortion into the privacy of the informed consent dialogue between the woman and her physician. We conclude, however, that informed choice need not be defined in such narrow terms that all considerations of the effect on the fetus are made irrelevant. As we have made clear, we depart from the holdings of *Akron I* and *Thornburgh* to the extent that we permit a State to further its legitimate goal of protecting the life of the unborn by enacting legislation aimed at ensuring a decision that is mature and informed, even when, in so doing, the State expresses a preference for childbirth over abortion. In short, requiring that the woman be informed of the availability of information relating to fetal development and the assistance available should she decide to carry the pregnancy to full term is a reasonable measure to ensure an informed choice, one which might cause the woman to choose childbirth over abortion. This requirement cannot be considered a substantial obstacle to obtaining an abortion, and, it follows, there is no undue burden. . . .

The Pennsylvania statute also requires us to reconsider the holding in *Akron I* that the State may not require that a physician, as opposed to a qualified assistant, provide information relevant to a woman's informed consent. Since there is no evidence on this record that requiring a doctor to give the information as provided by the statute would amount, in practical terms, to a substantial obstacle to a woman seeking an abortion, we conclude that it is not an undue burden. Our cases reflect the fact that the Constitution gives the States broad latitude to decide that particular functions may be performed only by licensed professionals, even if an objective assessment might suggest that those same tasks could be performed by others. Thus, we uphold the provision as a reasonable means to ensure that the woman's consent is informed.

Our analysis of Pennsylvania's 24-hour waiting period between the provision of the information deemed necessary to informed consent and the performance of an abortion under the undue burden standard requires us to reconsider the premise behind the decision in *Akron I* invalidating a parallel requirement. In *Akron I* we said: Nor are we convinced that the State's legitimate concern that the woman's decision be informed is reasonably served by requiring a 24-hour delay as a matter of course. We consider that conclusion to be wrong. The idea that important decisions will be more informed and deliberate if they follow some period of reflection does not strike us as unreasonable, particularly where the statute directs that important information become part of the background of the decision. The statute, as construed by the Court of Appeals, permits avoidance of the waiting period in the event of a medical emergency, and the record evidence shows that, in the vast majority of cases, a 24-hour delay does not create any appreciable health risk. In theory, at least, the waiting period is a reasonable measure to implement the State's interest in protecting the life of the unborn, a measure that does not amount to an undue burden.

Whether the mandatory 24-hour waiting period is nonetheless invalid because, in practice, it is a substantial obstacle to a woman's choice to terminate her pregnancy is a closer question. The findings of fact by the District Court indicate that, because of the distances many women must travel to reach an abortion provider, the practical effect will often be a delay of much more than a day because the waiting period requires that a woman seeking an abortion make at least two visits to the doctor. The District Court also found that, in many instances, this will increase the exposure of women seeking abortions to "the harassment and hostility of anti-abortion protestors demonstrating outside a clinic." As a result, the District Court found that, for those women who have the fewest financial resources, those who must travel long distances, and those who have difficulty explaining their whereabouts to husbands, employers, or others, the 24-hour waiting period will be "particularly burdensome."

These findings are troubling in some respects, but they do not demonstrate that the waiting period constitutes an undue burden. . . .

(C)

Section 3209 of Pennsylvania's abortion law provides, except in cases of medical emergency, that no physician shall perform an abortion on a married woman without receiving a signed statement from the woman that she has notified her spouse that she is about to undergo an abortion. The woman has the option of providing an alternative signed statement certifying that her husband is not the man who impregnated her; that her husband could not be located; that the pregnancy is the result of spousal sexual assault which she has reported; or that the woman believes that notifying her husband will cause him or someone else to inflict bodily injury upon her. A physician who performs an abortion on a married woman without receiving the appropriate signed statement will have his or her license revoked, and is liable to the husband for damages. . . .

. . . In well-functioning marriages, spouses discuss important intimate decisions such as whether to bear a child. But there are millions of women in this country who are the victims of regular physical and psychological abuse at the hands of their husbands. Should these women become pregnant, they may have very good reasons for not wishing to inform their husbands of their decision to obtain an abortion. Many may have justifiable fears of physical abuse, but may be no less fearful of the consequences of reporting prior abuse to the Commonwealth of Pennsylvania. Many may have a reasonable fear that notifying their husbands will provoke further instances of child abuse; these women are not exempt from Section 3209's notification requirement. Many may fear devastating forms of psychological abuse from their husbands, including verbal harassment, threats of future violence, the destruction of possessions, physical confinement to the home, the withdrawal of financial support, or the disclosure of the abortion to family and friends. These methods of psychological abuse may act as even more of a deterrent to notification than the possibility of physical violence, but women who are the victims of the abuse are not exempt from Section 3209's notification requirement. And many women who are pregnant as a result of sexual assaults by their husbands will be unable to avail themselves of the exception for spousal sexual assault, because the exception requires that the woman have notified law enforcement authorities within 90 days of the assault, and her husband

will be notified of her report once an investigation begins. If anything in this field is certain, it is that victims of spousal sexual assault are extremely reluctant to report the abuse to the government; hence, a great many spousal rape victims will not be exempt from the notification requirement imposed by Section 3209. . . .

(D)

We next consider the parental consent provision. Except in a medical emergency, an unemancipated young woman under 18 may not obtain an abortion unless she and one of her parents (or guardian) provides informed consent as defined above. If neither a parent nor a guardian provides consent, a court may authorize the performance of an abortion upon a determination that the young woman is mature and capable of giving informed consent and has, in fact, given her informed consent, or that an abortion would be in her best interests.

We have been over most of this ground before. Our cases establish, and we reaffirm today, that a State may require a minor seeking an abortion to obtain the consent of a parent or guardian, provided that there is an adequate judicial bypass procedure. Under these precedents, in our view, the one-parent consent requirement and judicial bypass procedure are constitutional.

The only argument made by petitioners respecting this provision and to which our prior decisions do not speak is the contention that the parental consent requirement is invalid because it requires informed parental consent. For the most part, petitioners' argument is a reprise of their argument with respect to the informed consent requirement in general, and we reject it for the reasons given above. Indeed, some of the provisions regarding informed consent have particular force with respect to minors: the waiting period, for example, may provide the parent or parents of a pregnant young woman the opportunity to consult with her in private, and to discuss the consequences of her decision in the context of the values and moral or religious principles of their family.

CHAPTER 8

Reproductive Technology

For most of human history, there was only one way to conceive a child (through sexual intercourse), one way to gestate it (in the womb of the woman who conceived it), and—according to common practice—one way to raise it (under the control of those contributing the egg and sperm).

Not anymore. The revered, time-tested order of procreation and parenthood has changed, thanks to an explosion of innovation in what is known as assisted reproductive technology (ART). Through ART procedures, doctors can fertilize a woman's egg in a laboratory dish to produce an embryo that can be implanted in any normal uterus; test ART embryos for genetic abnormalities before implantation (and cull defective ones); mechanically bring together selected sperm and eggs in fallopian tubes for fertilization; freeze embryos, eggs, and sperm for later use (and possible destruction); create embryos from donor eggs and sperm to offer up for adoption; and, in a sterile laboratory container, fertilize an egg by injecting into it a single sperm cell. The technology has also made possible the novel role of reproductive surrogate, a woman who contracts to gestate a baby for others who may or may not be genetically related to it. And behind these new realities lurks the theoretical possibility of what some believe will be the ultimate ART, both intriguing and disturbing: human reproductive cloning.

Assisted reproductive technologies are meant to address the agonizing problem of infertility and the powerful desire that many people have for children of their own, especially children with whom they have a biological link. The point of these advances is widely understood, but their uses are controversial. At every turn, they generate ethical questions and serious debate about the nature and meaning of the family, the welfare of children, the treatment of women, the moral status of embryos, the value of human life, the sanctity of natural procreation, and the legitimacy of reproductive rights.

But despite the complexity and seriousness of these issues, it's possible to make at least modest progress in sorting them out. Historically the field of bioethics cut its teeth on the moral problems arising from reproductive technology and has much to offer those who want to try to make sense of them.

IN VITRO FERTILIZATION

In normal (unassisted) reproduction, sperm inches through the woman's uterus and into one of the fallopian tubes, where a single sperm cell penetrates and thus fertilizes the egg released that month from an ovary. The resulting embryo (technically a zygote) backtracks through the fallopian tube, returning to the uterus where it implants itself in the uterine lining. At successful implantation, pregnancy begins. **Infertility** (usually defined as the inability to get pregnant after one year of unprotected sex) can befall a couple if there is a problem with any one of these processes. That is, a couple can become infertile if ovulation does not happen, either sperm or egg is of low quality, the fallopian tubes are blocked (often because of malformation or injury), the embryo is abnormal, or implantation is unsuccessful. In up to 90 percent of cases, physicians can treat such problems with conventional methods—drugs and surgery. But increasingly they turn to some form of ART, which usually means in vitro fertilization.

Fact File **Assisted Reproduction**

- In 2002, 10 percent of the 62 million women of reproductive age had sought fertility services in the past; 7 percent of married couples including reproductive-age women (2.1 million couples) had not achieved pregnancy even after forgoing contraception for 12 months.
- About half of infertility cases can be traced to problems in the woman, half to problems in the man.
- 85 to 90 percent of infertility cases are treated not with ART but with conventional medical approaches such as drugs and surgery.
- 99 percent of ART procedures performed are IVF (in vitro fertilization).
- Approximately 28 percent of IVF cycles using the woman's own eggs result in live births. In 1989, the rate was 14 percent.
- 33.5 percent of ART pregnancies are multiple-fetus (twins, triplets, or more).
- In the United States, by 2003 nearly 300,000 babies had been born through the use of ART methods.
- The average cost of a single IVF cycle is $12,400.

Data compiled from the Centers for Disease Control and Prevention (CDC) and the American Society of Reproductive Medicine.

In vitro fertilization (IVF) is the uniting of sperm and egg in a laboratory dish, instead of inside a woman's body. (*In vitro* means "in glass" and refers to such outside-the-body containers; the term contrasts with *in utero*, or "in the uterus.") The idea is to create embryos that can be transferred to the woman's uterus, where they can develop to term. (In the much older technique known as artificial insemination, sperm is mechanically inserted into the uterus without sexual intercourse in hopes of achieving fertilization in the woman's body.) The process of IVF and embryo transfer is technically complex, typically consisting of five main steps:

1. **Ovarian stimulation (superovulation).** The woman takes ovulation stimulants (fertility drugs) to prompt her ovaries to produce several eggs at once instead of the usual one per month. Standard IVF procedure calls for multiple eggs because often some of them will be defective, and not every embryo may implant or develop properly once transferred to the uterus.

2. **Egg retrieval.** When the eggs are ready, they are extracted from the egg sacs, or follicles, of the ovaries—usually a 30-minute outpatient surgery. In a typical egg retrieval, an ultrasound-guided needle is inserted into the vagina, through the vaginal wall, and into the ovaries to the egg-bearing follicles. One by one, the eggs are suctioned out through the needle.

3. **Insemination/fertilization.** The retrieved eggs are inspected, and the ones judged to be of highest quality are mixed with sperm (a step called insemination), which results within a few hours in sperm cells penetrating the eggs (fertilization). Typically some eggs will not fertilize, and occasionally none will. Sometimes the chances of fertilization are greatly increased by a technique known as intracytoplasmic sperm injection (ICSI),

in which an egg is pierced and a single sperm cell is injected into it.

4. **Embryo culture.** After fertilization, the embryos are left to grow in a culture medium. Within 48 hours each one consists of 2 to 4 cells; in three days, 6 to 10 cells. Around the third day, fertility experts can screen the embryos for genetic diseases using a technique known as pre-implantation genetic diagnosis (PGD). Only embryos found to be free of defective genes are selected to be transferred to the uterus.

5. **Embryo transfer.** Delivery of embryos to the uterus is generally painless and is performed in the doctor's office up to six days after egg retrieval. To increase the chances of pregnancy, two or more embryos are usually transferred at once. The embryos, along with the fluid surrounding them, are placed in a long, strawlike tube called a transfer catheter. Then the catheter is eased into the vagina and through the cervix, and the embryos are pushed from the tube into the uterus. If all goes well, an embryo implants in the uterine lining.

Fertility experts have developed numerous variations on these steps. One is gamete intrafallopian transfer (GIFT). In this process, ovarian stimulation and egg retrieval proceed as they do in IVF, but then the eggs and sperm (gametes) are transferred together to a fallopian tube to fertilize. GIFT is rarely used (less than 1 percent of ART procedures performed are GIFTs), but it is an option for some who prefer that fertilization take place inside the body. Another variant of IVF is zygote intrafallopian transfer (ZIFT). Like IVF, this procedure depends on fertilization occurring in vitro, but an embryo (zygote) is transferred not to the uterus but to a fallopian tube. Some people believe that ZIFT offers an increased chance of implantation, but it too constitutes less than 1 percent of attempts at assisted reproduction.

Couples are generally not limited to using their own sperm and eggs in IVF and its variations. They can also rely on donors, either anonymous or known, primarily to avoid the transmission of a genetic disorder or to substitute donor sperm or eggs for their own abnormal or absent gametes. Sperm donors are screened for sexually transmitted diseases and other health problems, and donor sperm is collected, frozen, analyzed, stored (in sperm banks), and used when needed. Egg donors are screened in the same way that sperm donors are, and donor eggs are acquired through standard ovarian stimulation and egg retrieval. The eggs are checked for maturity and, usually soon after retrieval, fertilized with donor sperm or sperm from the partner of the woman trying to become pregnant. (Increasingly eggs are also being frozen and stored for later use in achieving pregnancy.)

As with all forms of reproductive technology, in vitro fertilization (plus embryo transfer) brings with it a long list of risks and benefits—most of which have provoked or underscored a raft of thorny ethical questions. On the plus side is IVF's indisputable power to help many people overcome infertility, to enable desperate couples to do what they otherwise could not: have healthy, biologically related children. The need is great; at last count, in the United States there were over 2 million infertile couples. But since 1981, when the technology was introduced in America, the country has seen the birth of hundreds of thousands of IVF babies.

The other side of the ledger includes two disconcerting facts: IVF is expensive, and its success rates are much lower than most people think. The average cost of a single attempt to overcome infertility using IVF is $12,400. (An attempt, called a cycle, typically includes the steps from retrieval to transfer, a sequence lasting about two weeks.) Some couples end up paying tens of thousands of dollars. On average, a live birth is the outcome in only about 28 percent of IVF cycles in which the woman's own eggs are used. This rate varies with age: The older the woman, the lower the chances of a live birth. In most cases, then, more than one (expensive) cycle is required to achieve a live birth, and many health insurance plans will not cover the cost.

IVF cycles pose health risks for both woman and child. For the woman, the physical demands of the IVF process—the surgery, the monitoring, the waiting—can be uncomfortable, inconvenient, and stressful. The surgery itself comes with a risk, however low, of side effects such as bleeding, infection, and damaged tissue. There is also a chance of complications from taking the fertility drugs that instigate superovulation, including abdominal pain, memory loss, mood swings, and headaches. The most worrisome among these is a rare but potentially dangerous condition known as ovarian hyperstimulation syndrome, characterized by swollen and painful ovaries. Multiple pregnancies—caused mainly by transferring several embryos at once—increase the chances of high blood pressure, anemia, gestational diabetes, and uterine rupture. For the child, there are concerns that ART techniques may lead to birth defects, low birth weight, and diseases such as cancer. Some research has suggested a link between ART and a higher incidence of such problems than occurs in non-ART children, although the disorders are still rare. Researchers are generally not sure, however, if the link is causal, and they have been unable so far to rule out the possibility that these problems are related not to ART but to the infertility itself.

Multiple pregnancies—a common result of IVF cycles—dramatically raise the risks to children's life and health. The chances of prenatal and postnatal death are higher than for single pregnancies, and premature birth is much more likely. Prematurity increases the risk of cerebral palsy, blindness, heart defects, serious infection, respiratory distress syndrome, and other grave maladies. Even aside from prematurity, babies born after a multiple pregnancy have an elevated risk of birth defects and low birth weight, the latter being a separate risk factor for many diseases. One way that practitioners try to lower the risks of multiple pregnancy is to use fetal reduction

(also known as selective abortion) to eliminate some of the fetuses in utero. But the procedure itself carries with it a risk of miscarriage.

Several issues—technological and ethical—arise from the handling of the unused embryos that inevitably result from IVF. The common practice is to freeze, or cryopreserve, the extra embryos for possible transfer in the future. Fertility clinics freeze thousands of embryos every year, and hundreds of thousands of them are now in cryostorage. Freezing a woman's leftover embryos gives her the option of using them in future IVF cycles rather than going through another arduous (and expensive) round of ovarian stimulation and egg retrieval. By having her embryos frozen, she can also select the timing of embryo transfer to avoid causing or aggravating any health problems in pregnancy. A significant drawback to the process is that cryopreserved embryos are less likely to result in live births than unfrozen embryos are. Another is that many embryos do not live through freezing and thawing.

Frozen embryos can remain in cryostorage for years—because the couple divorces, because one or both of them die, because they disagree about what to do with the embryos (for example, if one wants to donate them but the other does not), or because they have changed their minds about getting pregnant. The moral and legal implications of these possibilities are being debated now. One alternative is to donate the unused embryos to an infertile couple, which means that the prospective parents will have no genetic connection to the child born to them. Such an arrangement seems unproblematic to some people but is morally or legally questionable to others. Without legal guidance and ethical consensus, fertility clinics must decide what to do with frozen embryos that are unused, unclaimed, or undonated. Often they either donate the embryos for research or destroy them. To those who believe that embryos have a right to life, both of these options are morally impermissible. But even people who don't believe that embryos are persons may think that embryonic life should not be treated as if it has no moral worth at all.

Many of the moral arguments about IVF have involved objections only to a particular step or outcome of the technology, but much of the debate has been about the moral acceptability of IVF itself—about whether it should be used at all. A host of arguments against IVF have been based on alleged harm to children, harm to families or the natural order of procreation, and harm to women. The strongest arguments for IVF have appealed to individual autonomy or reproductive rights.

Some have objected to IVF because of its potential for causing birth defects and disease in children. As we have seen, research supports this worry, though the exact degree of risk is unknown. One commentator argues that

> it would be wrong to use reproductive technologies to create children if this bore a significant chance of producing serious disease and impairments in these very children. Questions are being raised about whether in vitro fertilization (IVF) and other reproductive technologies do, in fact, create serious illness and deficits in a small but significant proportion of children who are born of them. If these technologies were found to do so, it would be wrong to forge ahead with their use.[1]

For many, much depends on the magnitude of the risk. A low level of risk may be acceptable since even normal methods of conception carry a small risk of birth defects and other problems. To insist that IVF and its variants be safer than the usual way of bringing children into the world (or even risk free) seems unreasonable.

Several writers argue that it would not be wrong to use reproductive technology to bring forth severely damaged children because if the technology had not been used, the children would not be alive—and being alive is better than not being alive. That is, compared to not existing at all, being brought into the world—even to suffer horribly—is a net gain. As one proponent of this view says,

> [A] higher incidence of birth defects in such offspring would not justify banning the [reproductive] technique in order to protect the offspring, because without these techniques these children would not have been born at all. Unless their lives are so full of suffering as to be worse than no life at all, a very unlikely supposition, the defective children of such a union have not been harmed if they would not have been born healthy.[2]

Others believe this view is confused. One critic says that it is based on the false assumption that nonexistence before birth is bad while existence is good and that the two can be meaningfully compared. The view assumes, she says,

> that children with an interest in existing are waiting in a spectral world of nonexistence where their situation is less desirable than it would be were they released into this world. . . . Their admission into this realm is thwarted by the failure to use available new reproductive technologies. This failure negates their interest in existing and thereby harms them.[3]

On the contrary, she says, nonexistence before birth is neither good nor bad. Moreover, the notion that children cannot really be harmed by ART "justifies allowing the new technologies to create almost any harm to children conceived as a result of their use—as long as this is not devastating harm in which death is preferable to life with it."[4]

Some people claim that the use of ART undermines the value we place on offspring. They argue that children are supposed to be regarded as inherently valuable but that reproductive technology tempts us to view them as manufactured products and as commodities acquired in the marketplace for a price. But others see no reason to assume that a couple who creates a child through ART would not love and care for it as they would a child produced through the usual means. They also maintain that the mere involvement of money does not necessarily entail the treatment of children as commodities—otherwise adoption, which involves prices and payments, would also have to be considered morally unacceptable.

IVF has been condemned by some religious groups because it breaks the natural connection between procreation and sexual intercourse in marriage. The only morally permissible way to conceive a child, they say, is through sexual union between husband and wife. According to the Vatican, IVF and other forms of assisted reproduction are "contrary to the unity of marriage, to the dignity of the spouses, to the vocation proper to parents, and to the child's right to be conceived and brought into the world in marriage and from marriage."[5] Some critics, however, think this view has little credibility outside the particular religious tradition espousing it. According to Peter Singer,

> Few infertile couples will take seriously the view that their marital relationship will be damaged if they use the technique [IVF] which offers them the best chance of having their own child. It is in any case extraordinarily paternalistic for anyone else to tell a couple that they should not use IVF because it will harm their marriage. That, surely, is for them to decide.[6]

Whether or not IVF harms marriages, it surely changes family relationships, and that is a pressing concern for many. Through ART, a child can have many parents—genetic (those who contribute egg or sperm), gestational (the woman who carries the baby to term), and social (the people who raise the child). With all these possibilities, the family can take forms that were unthinkable a few decades ago. These changes have prompted some to argue that by weakening the *biological* connections between parents and children, reproductive technology will also loosen the *social* bonds between them—the values, commitments, and feelings that have characterized families in the past. A common reply is that such a claim requires empirical support, for it is not at all obvious that new family structures will be bad for all concerned. Research is scarce on the harm and benefits of new parental arrangements, and to assume the worst is unreasonable.

Many people insist that IVF is a boon to women because it enhances their freedom by multiplying their reproductive choices. But some feminists have repudiated this view. They argue that the pressure from patriarchal society for women to establish their worth by becoming mothers is so powerful that their choices regarding reproduction are not truly free but coerced. If so, then the existence of IVF and other reproductive technologies does not bring more freedom—it just reinforces social stereotypes.

Mary Anne Warren disagrees. She acknowledges that IVF comes with substantial risks and burdens but denies that women are too constrained or coerced by society to decide about the technology for themselves:

> Neither the patriarchal power structure nor pronatalist [pro-childbearing] ideology makes women incapable of reasoned choice about childbearing. Rather, the social pressures upon some women to have children—and the pressures upon others not to have children—are circumstances which we must take into account in our deliberations. . . . In deliberating about either "natural" motherhood or the use of IVF, we may sometimes be wrong about what is in our own interests, and perhaps some of us are excessively influenced by pronatalist ideology. But it does not follow that we would benefit from additional paternalistic restraints. Autonomy necessarily implies the right to make our own mistakes.[7]

To defend the use of IVF, many commentators appeal to autonomy or individual rights. John Robertson, for example, argues for what he calls "procreative liberty"—the freedom to reproduce or not to reproduce. This amounts to a right to make a reproductive choice without interference from others, including a choice about use of reproductive technologies. He contends that only very weighty considerations can override a person's procreative liberty:

> If procreative liberty is taken seriously, a strong presumption in favor of using technologies that centrally implicate reproductive interests should be recognized. Although procreative rights are not absolute, those who would limit procreative

choice should have the burden of establishing substantial harm. . . . This will give persons directly involved the final say about use of a particular technology, unless tangible harm to the interests of others can be shown.[8]

As we have seen, many would argue that such substantial harms are inherent in reproductive technologies—most notably, harms to children, women, and families. Others would insist that at least some moral or religious rules (those concerning the treatment of embryos or the role of reproduction in marriage, for example) can always trump autonomy.

SURROGACY

A **surrogate** is a woman who gestates a fetus for others, usually for a couple or another woman. She contracts with them to carry the pregnancy to term, to relinquish the baby at birth, and to let them legally adopt it. The surrogacy can take two different forms. In what has been called *traditional surrogacy*, sperm from either the couple's male partner or a donor is used to artificially inseminate the surrogate (the "surrogate mother"). Since the egg fertilized is the surrogate's, the baby produced from this arrangement is genetically related only to the surrogate and to whoever supplies the sperm. In *gestational surrogacy*, the surrogate receives a transferred embryo created through IVF using the sperm and egg of others (the contracting couple or donors). Because the gestational surrogate (also called the gestational carrier) does not contribute her own egg, she has no genetic connection to the baby.

In surrogacy relationships, we can distinguish between genetic (or biological), gestational, and social (or rearing) parents. Thus we can say that a traditional surrogate is the genetic mother because she contributes her egg to conception. She is also the gestational mother because she carries the pregnancy. But she is not meant to be the social mother who raises the child; the contractual, or intended, parents plan to do that. The man who contributes the sperm (typically the intended father) is the genetic father. In

gestational surrogacy, the surrogate is the gestational mother while the prospective mother and father are usually the genetic parents, who are also likely to be the social parents. In moral and legal disputes over surrogacy arrangements, these distinctions come up again and again and are often used to parse questions about who the "real" parents are.

A woman may opt for gestational surrogacy because she has an abnormal uterus or no uterus (because of hysterectomy or congenital defect) or because she suffers from health problems that make pregnancy dangerous, such as cystic fibrosis and serious forms of diabetes and heart disease. A couple may turn to a traditional surrogate for many of the same reasons. In both kinds of surrogacy, the intended parents generally want more than just a child—they want a biologically related child. For them, then, adoption may be less attractive. (Couples may also decide against adoption for other reasons, including its expense and the scarcity of adoptable children.)

Surrogate arrangements are generally complex and legally unsettled. Surrogacy contracts may specify all of the surrogate's prenatal duties (including those regarding her alcohol consumption, smoking, prenatal testing, medical treatment, and sexual intercourse), the involvement of the intended parents in the pregnancy (for example, their presence or absence at the birth), the permissibility of abortion in case of fetal abnormalities, the arrangements for adoption of the child, and the money to be paid to the surrogate (including prorated compensation if there is a miscarriage). Whatever the financial arrangements, they cannot be construed as transactions involving the buying or selling of children, which is illegal. (Some states forbid surrogacy agreements allowing any kind of payment.) So money paid to surrogates—now probably in the range of $10,000 to $30,000—is supposed to be regarded as compensation for such things as her time and effort or her diminished job opportunities. (A few women agree to become surrogates for altruistic reasons and do not expect payment.) Complicating the picture fur-

IVF and the technology for freezing embryos have opened up an array of possibilities for treating infertility that until recently were unthinkable. Here is one example, one of many stunning reports from this new frontier:

(BBC News)—Israeli scientists say that they have extracted and matured eggs from girls as young as five to freeze for possible fertility treatment in the future.

The team said that the technique could give child cancer sufferers left infertile by chemotherapy treatment a shot at parenthood later in life.

The team took eggs from a group of girls between the ages of five and 10 who had cancer.

They artificially matured the eggs to make them viable and froze them.

Experts had previously thought the eggs of pre-pubescent girls could not be used in this way.

Dr. Ariel Revel, from Hadassah University Hospital in Jerusalem, is to present the team's findings at a fertility conference in Lyon, France, this week.

"No eggs have yet been thawed, so we do not know whether pregnancies will result," he said in a statement.

"But we are encouraged by our results so far, particularly the young ages of the patients from whom we have been able to collect eggs."

Childhood cancers have a good cure rate— between 70% and 90%—but often require aggressive chemotherapy which can mean the child will be sterile in later life.

Geoff Thaxter, of the children's cancer charity CLIC Sargent, said: "This report represents interesting initial research into potential fertility treatments for children being treated for cancer, and could help to make sure that childhood cancer does not have a lifelong impact."

But Josephine Quintavalle, of Comment on Reproductive Ethics, expressed concern that if the eggs were donated to a woman of childbearing age, a resulting child could have a biological mother who was only a few years older.[9]

---

ther is the hodgepodge of surrogacy laws from state to state and the absence of national laws. Some states have outlawed surrogacy, some allow it with varying restrictions, some allow it but declare that the contracts are unenforceable, and some have no relevant legislation.

The kinds of questions and conflicts that surrogacy can engender have been accentuated in numerous cases, the most famous one being that of "Baby M." Over 20 years ago Mary Beth Whitehead agreed to become a surrogate mother for William and Elizabeth Stern. For $10,000 she consented to be artificially inseminated with Mr. Stern's sperm, to carry the child to term, and to relinquish it to the Sterns after birth. The baby—named Melissa by the Sterns but known to the world as Baby M—was born on March 27, 1986. But then Whitehead had a change of heart.

After declaring that she could not give the infant up, she left the state with it. The case eventually ended up in a New Jersey court, where the judge ruled that the surrogate agreement was binding and that Whitehead had to turn over Baby M to the Sterns. Whitehead appealed the ruling to the New Jersey Supreme Court and won a reversal. The court ruled that the surrogacy contract was actually invalid and that Whitehead was the legal mother. Citing the best interests of the child, however, the court also held that Baby M should live with the Sterns and that Whitehead should have visitation rights.

Many of the arguments about surrogacy mirror those about IVF, clustering around reproductive autonomy and alleged harm to children, families, and women. But probably the most pervasive argument—and perhaps the strongest on the anti-surrogacy side—is that surrogacy arrangements amount to baby-selling, a blatant affront to human dignity. (The charge is usually made against commercial surrogacy, in which money changes hands, not against altruistic surrogacy, in which women volunteer their surrogate services.) As one surrogacy critic says,

> Commercial surrogacy substitutes market norms for some of the norms of parental love. Most importantly, it requires us to understand parental rights no longer as trusts but as things more like property rights—that is, rights of use and disposal over the things owned. For in this practice the natural mother deliberately conceives a child with the intention of giving it up for material advantage. . . . By engaging in the transfer of children by sale, all of the parties to the surrogate contract express a set of attitudes toward children which undermine the norms of parental love.[10]

Defenders of surrogacy deny that it constitutes baby-selling, claiming instead that a surrogate is simply relinquishing her right as a parent to have a relationship with the child. She is not selling an existing close relationship with someone; she is selling, or forfeiting, the right to enjoy a future parent-child relationship—and it is not obvious that doing so is wrong.

Moreover, says the surrogacy advocate, the practice is not that different from adoption, in which biological parents give away their children (as well as the hope of any relationship with them). On the contrary, says Elizabeth Anderson, adoption and surrogacy differ substantially:

> The purpose of adoption is to provide a means for placing children in families when their parents cannot or will not discharge their parental responsibilities. It is not a sphere for the existence of a supposed parental right to dispose of one's children for profit.[11]

Laura Purdy, however, reminds us that surrogacy provides a socially valuable service and asks,

> Why then must it be motivated by altruistic considerations? We do not frown upon those who provide other socially valuable services even when they do not have the "right" motives. Nor do we require them to be unpaid. For instance, no one expects physicians, no matter what their motivation, to work for beans. They provide an important service; their motivation is important only to the extent that it affects quality.[12]

Bonnie Steinbock thinks that surrogacy arrangements have sometimes involved baby-selling, and she points to the Baby M case as an example. But she argues that this unsavory element can be eliminated if we view surrogacy as prenatal adoption:

> The question, then, is whether we can reconcile paying the surrogate, beyond her medical expenses, with the idea of surrogacy as prenatal adoption. We can do this by separating the terms of the agreement, which include surrendering the infant at birth to the biological father, from the justification for payment. The payment should be seen as justification for the risks, sacrifice, and discomfort the surrogate undergoes during pregnancy. This means that if, through no fault on the part of the surrogate, the baby is stillborn, she should still be paid in full, since she has kept her part of the bargain. . . . If, on the other hand, the surrogate changes her mind and decides to keep the child, she would break the agreement, and would not be entitled to any fee, or compensation for expenses incurred during pregnancy.[13]

CLONING

Clones, in the sense used by biologists, are genetically identical entities, whether cells, DNA molecules, plants, animals, or humans. **Cloning** is the asexual production of a genetically identical entity from an existing one. In animals and humans, since the genetic blueprint for an individual is in each of its cells (mostly in the nucleus), all the cells of a clone contain the same blueprint as all the cells of the clone's progenitor. An animal or human clone is not a perfect copy of an individual—not like a photocopy of an original

LEGAL BRIEF
Surrogacy Contracts and the Law

- States permitting surrogacy agreements: Florida, Illinois, Massachusetts, New Mexico, Tennessee, Texas, Nevada, New Hampshire, New Jersey, Oregon, Virginia, Washington
- States forbidding surrogacy agreements: Indiana, Louisiana, Michigan, New York, North Dakota, Utah, Washington, DC
- States that have no laws on surrogacy: Alabama, Alaska, Arkansas, Colorado, Connecticut, Georgia, Idaho, Iowa, Kansas, Delaware, Kentucky, Maine, Montana, Minnesota, Mississippi, North Carolina, South Dakota, Rhode Island, Oklahoma, Vermont, West Virginia, Wyoming
- States whose laws are vague or unsettled on surrogacy agreements: Arizona, Maryland, Pennsylvania, South Carolina, Ohio, Missouri, Wisconsin

Source: Human Rights Campaign, http://www.hrc.org/index .htm (27 November 2007).

document—but a living thing that shares a set of genetic instructions with another.

In agriculture, cloning to propagate plant strains is commonplace, and for years scientists have been cloning human and animal cells for research purposes. Molecular biologists often clone fragments of DNA for study. Among animals and humans, clones appear naturally in the form of identical twins, individuals with identical sets of DNA. Scientists have managed to duplicate this process in a form of cloning known as *twinning*. Through in vitro fertilization they produce an embryo (zygote), and when it consists of two to four identical cells, they separate them and let them grow into discrete but genetically identical organisms.

The cloning that has provoked the most public consternation and media attention is the creation of a genetic duplicate of an adult animal or human, what has often been called **reproductive cloning**. The aim of this work is the live birth of an individual. (Cloning for other purposes is called **therapeutic**, or **research, cloning**, a topic we discuss further in Chapter 9.) This kind of cloning suddenly became front-page news in 1997 when scientists announced that they had managed to clone an adult sheep, resulting in the birth of an apparently healthy clone called Dolly. She was the genetic twin of her adult "parent" and the first mammal so cloned. After her, scientists cloned additional animals in similar fashion—cattle, goats, pigs, cats, rabbits, mice, and more—and are working on others.

The primary cloning method for producing live-birth mammals, and the one most likely to be considered for human cloning, is known as somatic cell nuclear transfer (SCNT). The usual steps are:

1. Extract the DNA-packed nucleus from an egg cell (creating an enucleated egg).
2. Replace the egg's nucleus with the donor nucleus of an ordinary body (somatic) cell from the adult individual to be cloned. (It's also possible to use cells from existing embryos.)
3. Stimulate the reconfigured cell with chemicals or electricity to start cell division and growth to the embryo stage.
4. Transfer the cloned embryo to a host uterus for development and birth.

The egg and somatic nucleus can come from two different individuals or the same individual. If from two different ones, the largest portion of the clone's DNA will be from the nucleus donor since almost all DNA resides in the nucleus, with only a tiny amount located outside the nucleus in the cell's mitochondria. If from the same individual, the clone will get its entire complement of DNA from the nucleus and mitochondria of the same individual.

To date, no human has been successfully cloned, and for technical and moral reasons none is likely to be cloned any time soon. At this stage of the technology, both scientists and policymakers have serious concerns about the safety and ethics of human reproductive cloning.

A typical response to the prospect of human cloning is moral outrage—which too often is based on misunderstandings. Chief among these is the notion that a human clone would be identical to an existing person, the clone's "parent." This idea has led to a host of silly fantasies played out in movies, literature, and the popular mind: an army of Hitler clones spawned from one of the führer's cells, a laboratory of Albert Einsteins discovering the secrets of the universe, the perfect team of Hank Aaron or Michael Jordan clones, a houseful of identical children who are exact copies of a rich, eccentric egotist. The underlying fallacy is that genes make the person, that genetics ordains all of an individual's characteristics. This view is known as genetic determinism, and it is a myth. The National Academy of Sciences makes the point this way:

> Even if clones are genetically identical with one another, they will not be identical in physical or behavioral characteristics, because DNA is not the only determinant of these characteristics. A pair of clones will experience different environments and nutritional inputs while in the uterus, and they would be expected to be subject to different inputs from their parents, society, and life experience as they grow up. If clones derived from identical nuclear donors and identical mitochondrial donors are born at different times, as is the case when an adult is the donor of the somatic cell nucleus, the environmental and nutritional differences would be expected to be more pronounced than for monozygotic (identical) twins. And even monozygotic twins are not fully identical genetically or epigenetically because mutations, stochastic [random] developmental variations, and varied imprinting effects (parent-specific

chemical marks on the DNA) make different contributions to each twin.[14]

Einstein's clone would have Einstein's genes but would not and could not be Einstein. The clone would be unique and probably not much like his famous progenitor at all.

At this stage of scientific knowledge, human cloning seems likely to result in high rates of serious birth defects.[15] Under these circumstances, most commentators agree that cloning should not be attempted. (A few question this conclusion, noting that even now parents who are certain to conceive and bear children with terrible genetic disorders are permitted to do so.) Nevertheless, since 1997 the dispute over the moral permissibility of cloning has raged on, fueled by the thought that, given the usual pace of scientific progress, the problem of congenital malformations will be solved and the efficient cloning of human beings will soon be technologically feasible.

As we would expect, many of those who favor the use of cloning rest their case on its likely benefits. For some people, their only hope of having a child with whom they are genetically related would be through cloning. Some men have no sperm; some women, no eggs; cloning could get around the problem. For couples who value this genetic connection and who also want to avoid passing on a genetic disease or health risk to their child, cloning would be an attractive option—perhaps the only option. Parents whose only child dies could have her cloned from a cell harvested from her body, ensuring that some part of her would live on. A boy who needs an organ transplant to live could be cloned so his clone could provide the needed organ, perfectly matched to avoid transplant rejection.

As in the case of IVF, many claim a moral right to use cloning, arguing that people have a basic right of reproductive liberty and that cloning is covered by that right. They deny that this right to cloning is absolute (overriding all other considerations) but believe that it carries great weight nonetheless. As one writer puts it:

IN DEPTH
CLONING TIME LINE

1970 British developmental biologist John Gurdon clones a frog.

1978 Louise Brown is born, the first baby conceived through IVF.

1980 The U.S. Supreme Court holds that a genetically engineered life form—a bacterium—can be patented.

1996 Through the work of Ian Wilmut and his colleagues, the first animal cloned from adult cells—a sheep named Dolly—is born.

1997 President Bill Clinton declares a five-year moratorium on federal funding for research into human cloning.

1997 Wilmut and his colleagues create Polly, a sheep with a human gene in each of its cells.

2001 Scientists in Massachusetts clone the first human embryo.

2002 The President's Council on Bioethics recommends a ban on reproductive cloning.

2003 In South Korea, human embryonic stems are cloned.

2003 Dolly, now 6 years old, is euthanized when she is found to have lung disease.

2004 A company called Genetics Savings and Clone says it will clone people's cats for them for $50,000 per cat.

2005 The creator of Dolly is licensed to clone human embryos for medical research.

[I]t is reasonable to hold that the freedom of infertile couples to use cloning is a form of procreative freedom. Procreative freedom is worthy of respect in part because freedom in general is worthy of respect. But more than this, procreative freedom is an especially important freedom because of the significance that procreative decisions can have for persons' lives. For these reasons, the freedom of infertile couples to use cloning is worthy of respect.[16]

Some critics of cloning have charged that it violates the rights of the resulting clone—specifically, the right to a unique identity. A clone by definition is not genetically unique; his genome is iterated in his "parent." Aside from doubts about whether such a right exists, the strongest reply to this worry is that genetic uniqueness is neither necessary nor sufficient for personal uniqueness:

What is the sense of identity that might plausibly be each person has a right to have uniquely, which constitutes the special uniqueness of each individual? Even with the same genes, two individuals,

for example homozygous twins, are numerically distinct and not identical, so what is intended must be the various properties and characteristics that make each individual qualitatively unique and different than others. Does having the same genome as another person undermine that unique qualitative identity? Only in the crudest genetic determinism. . . . But there is no reason whatever to believe in that kind of genetic determinism, and I do not think that anyone does.[17]

A similar rights argument says that cloning would be wrong because it violates what has been called a "right to ignorance" or a "right to an open future." Consider a situation in which a clone begins his life many years after his older twin does. The younger twin lives in the shadow of the older one, thinking—correctly or incorrectly—that his genetically identical sibling has already lived the life that he (the younger twin) has barely started. He believes that his future is already set. His sense of personal freedom and of a future of possibilities is diminished. In this way, the argument goes, his right to an open-ended life story has been flouted.

But some think this argument is built on flimsy assumptions:

> [A]ll of these concerns are not only quite speculative, but are directly related to certain specific cultural values. Someone created through the use of somatic cell nuclear transfer techniques may or may not believe that their future is relatively constrained. Indeed, they may believe the opposite. In addition, quite normal parenting usually involves many constraints on a child's behavior that children may resent.[18]

Would the younger twin's right to ignorance or to an open future be violated just because she *believes* her future is fated, although her belief is false? Dan W. Brock insists that the answer is no:

> I believe that if the twin's future in reality remains open and his to freely choose, then someone acting in a way that unintentionally leads him to believe that his future is closed and determined has not violated his right to ignorance or to an open future. . . . If we know that the twin will believe that his open future has been taken from him as a result of being cloned, even though in reality it has not, then we know that cloning will cause him psychological distress, but not that it will violate his right.[19]

Many oppose the use of cloning technology (and any other ART) because it is unnatural, a deviant way of bringing children into the world. But this view is criticized as narrowly dogmatic, for some natural processes are bad (such as bacterial infection), and some unnatural ones are good (such as medical treatment). A few believe that naturalness should be defined according to a thing's function. They reason that since each part of the human body has a natural function, we should not subvert that part by giving it an additional function. Cloning, then, would be unnatural and wrong. But this take on naturalness has many detractors. For example:

> Although there are certainly unhealthy or unwise uses of our body parts, there's no reason for us to always adhere to an organ's primary function.

> The bridge of a nose has the primary function of allowing us to exhale and inhale air, but do we sin if we use it to support our spectacles? . . . . By-pass surgery improves our cardiovascular systems. Kidney dialysis allows people with kidney failure to survive. Transplants replace increasing numbers of our organs. All of these are human artificial interventions in nature. They seem morally justified, if anything does. So why not extend this reasoning to genetic engineering? Why not use genetics to produce a healthy child rather than a sickly one?[20]

A kindred objection to cloning and other reproductive technologies holds that they replace natural procreation with the artificial *manufacture* of children as products—a demeaning process that erodes our respect for human beings. Cloning is thus profoundly dehumanizing. "Human nature," says Leon Kass, "becomes merely the last part of nature to succumb to the technological project, which turns all of nature into raw material at human disposal."[21]

But why assume cloning is dehumanizing? Dan Brock says that we should not:

> It would be a mistake, however, to conclude that a human being created by human cloning is of less value or is less worthy of respect than one created by sexual reproduction. It is the nature of a being, not how it is created, that is the source of its value and makes it worthy of respect.[22]

APPLYING MAJOR THEORIES

We have the power to control human reproduction as never before. The question is: Should we? In the name of reproductive freedom and control, is it morally permissible to employ ART, surrogacy, even cloning?

The utilitarian will answer yes if the benefits of the technology outweigh its harms, no if they do not. Based on current knowledge of the good and bad effects, most utilitarians would probably see a net gain in the use of IVF and surrogacy arrangements, and they would likely endorse cloning if its risks to children could be decreased to an acceptable level. They presumably would calculate that IVF's real but low risk of birth defects and maternal complications is outweighed by the happiness brought to infertile couples, and the loss of embryos in the process would not be a major factor. They would likely make a similar calculation regarding surrogacy, assuming that surrogacy arrangements are properly regulated.

On the other hand, if the widespread use of reproductive technologies would harm society—if, for example, surrogacy or cloning would result in a general disregard for human life and welfare, as some critics argue—a rule-utilitarian might oppose these innovations. She could, with logical consistency, acknowledge that the technologies often increase net happiness in particular cases but oppose a public policy that allowed their use.

From a Kantian perspective, it is possible to either oppose or defend reproductive technologies. Someone could argue, for example, that IVF, surrogacy, and cloning are impermissible because they treat children merely as a means, instead of an end in themselves. Children are "manufactured" and sold as commodities to serve the ends of others. But a Kantian could refuse to take this view, arguing instead that couples who create children do so precisely because they wish to respect and love their offspring as persons. What matters is not how children are brought into the world, but how they are treated after they arrive.

According to the Roman Catholic interpretation of natural law theory, reproductive technologies must be rejected across the board. IVF is wrong because it attempts reproduction outside the bonds of marriage and defies the natural link between procreation and sexual union. It also involves the destruction of human embryos, each of which has a right to life. Surrogacy is immoral because it too is procreation outside of marriage and an affront to the integrity of the family. Human cloning is to be repudiated because it unnaturally separates procreation from sex and is a violation of the rights of the child.

KEY TERMS

cloning
cloning, reproductive
cloning, therapeutic or research
cycle (in assisted reproductive technology)
infertility
in vitro fertilization
surrogate

SUMMARY

Assisted reproductive technology (ART) is designed to address the problem of infertility, which affects millions of couples in the United States and worldwide. In vitro fertilization (IVF) is one such technology, consisting of the uniting of sperm and egg in a laboratory dish, instead of inside a woman's body. There are numerous variations on basic IVF, including gamete intrafallopian transfer (GIFT) and zygote intrafallopian transfer (ZIFT). IVF can help many couples overcome infertility, but it is expensive, and IVF cycles pose health risks to both woman and child. Paramount among the risks are multiple pregnancies, a frequent result of IVF cycles. Problems also arise from the practice of cryopreserving extra embryos often left over after IVF, a key question being what ultimately should be done with them.

Critics contend that IVF should not be used because it leads to birth defects and disease in children, undermines the value we place on children, breaks the natural connection between procreation and sexual intercourse in marriage, and dramatically changes common family relationships. Others argue that IVF enhances women's freedom by multiplying their reproductive choices or that IVF should be allowed in the name of procreative liberty.

A surrogate is a woman who gestates a fetus for others, usually for a couple or another woman. She contracts with them to carry the pregnancy to term, to relinquish the baby at birth, and to let them legally adopt it. Thus, in surrogacy relationships, we can distinguish between genetic (or biological), gestational, and social (or rearing) parents. Probably the most pervasive argument

Baby M

In recent years, no issue in assisted reproduction has generated more controversy than surrogate pregnancy. The kinds of questions and conflicts that surrogacy can engender have been accentuated in numerous cases, the most famous one being that of "Baby M."

In 1985 Mary Beth Whitehead agreed to become a surrogate mother for William and Elizabeth Stern. For $10,000 she consented to be artificially inseminated with William Stern's sperm, to carry the child to term, to relinquish all rights to it, and to surrender it to the Sterns at birth. At the time, she was married and had two school-age children. She said that she had no desire for more children to raise and that her aim was to give a child to a couple who could not have any children of their own. The Sterns said that they decided on surrogacy because Mrs. Stern had a medical condition that made pregnancy risky for her.

The baby—named Melissa by the Sterns but known to the world as Baby M—was born on March 27, 1986. Whitehead turned over the baby to the Sterns as agreed, but then she had a change of heart. The next day she went to the Sterns and pleaded with them to allow her to take the baby home with her for a while. The Sterns quoted her as saying, "I just want her for a week and I'll be out of your lives forever." She was distraught and persistent, and the Sterns thought she was suicidal. "Something took over," Whitehead would say later. "I think it was just being a mother." Reluctantly the Sterns agreed to let Whitehead keep the baby for a few days.

Two weeks later Mary Beth Whitehead let the Sterns know that she was not going to give the baby back. With a court order granting them custody of the child and backed by several police officers, the Sterns went to Whitehead's home to take custody. But the Whiteheads took the baby and fled to Florida, where they eluded the authorities for weeks. On July 31, however, a private detective located the baby, and authorities turned her over to the Sterns.

Whitehead tried to regain legal custody, and the case eventually ended up in a New Jersey court, where the judge ruled that the surrogate agreement was binding and that Whitehead had to turn over Baby M to the Sterns. After the judge's ruling, he signed papers allowing Elizabeth Stern to adopt her.

Whitehead appealed the ruling to the New Jersey Supreme Court and, on February 3, 1988, won an almost total reversal of the earlier decision. The court held in a unanimous ruling that the surrogacy contract was actually invalid, that it violated the state's adoption laws against selling babies, and that Whitehead was to have parental rights. "We thus restore the surrogate as the mother of the child," declared the court. "She is not only the natural mother, but also the legal mother, and is not to be penalized one iota because of the surrogate contract." Citing the best interests of the child, however, the court also held that Baby M should live with the Sterns and that Whitehead should have visitation rights. The ruling made it clear that, in New Jersey at least, surrogacy was permitted as long as the surrogate was not paid and she had the right to change her mind about giving up the baby.

The decision made history as the first one from a state's top court on the rights of surrogate mothers.

---

against surrogacy is that surrogacy arrangements amount to baby-selling, a blatant affront to human dignity. Defenders of surrogacy deny that it constitutes baby-selling, claiming instead that a surrogate is simply relinquishing her right as a parent to have a relationship with the child. The surrogacy advocate says that the practice is not that different from adoption, in which biological parents give away their children (as well as the hope of any relationship with them).

Cloning is the asexual production of a genetically identical entity from an existing one. All the cells of a clone contain the same blueprint as all the cells of the clone's progenitor. The cloning that has provoked the most debate and media attention is human reproductive cloning, the creation of a genetic duplicate of an adult human. So far, no human has been successfully cloned and is not likely to be any time soon. Nevertheless, fear or outrage regarding human cloning is widespread, much of it based on incorrect information. A common myth is genetic determinism, the view that genes make the person, that genetics ordains all of an individual's characteristics.

Many in favor of human cloning appeal to reproductive liberty and to cloning's possible benefits, such as enabling infertile couples to have a child that is genetically related to them. Critics charge that cloning is unnatural, that it violates the right of the resulting clone to a unique identity or future, and that it will result in the demeaning artificial manufacture of children as products.

Cases for Evaluation

CASE 1

The Fate of Frozen Embryos

Abstract

BACKGROUND. The moral status of the human embryo is particularly controversial in the United States, where one debate has centered on embryos created in excess at in vitro fertilization (IVF) clinics. Little has been known about the disposal of these embryos.

METHODS. We mailed anonymous, self-administered questionnaires to directors of 341 American IVF clinics.

RESULTS. 217 of 341 clinics (64 percent) responded. Nearly all (97 percent) were willing to create and cryopreserve extra embryos. Fewer, but still a majority (59 percent), were explicitly willing to avoid creating extras. When embryos did remain in excess, clinics offered various options: continual cryopreservation for a charge (96 percent) or for no charge (4 percent), donation for reproductive use by other couples (76 percent), disposal prior to (60 percent) or following (54 percent) cryopreservation, and donation for research (60 percent) or embryologist training (19 percent). Qualifications varied widely among those personnel responsible for securing couples' consent for disposal and for conducting disposal itself. Some clinics performed a religious or quasi-religious disposal ceremony. Some clinics required a couple's participation in disposal; some allowed but did not require it; some others discouraged or disallowed it.

CONCLUSIONS. The disposal of human embryos created in excess at American IVF clinics varies in ways suggesting both moral sensitivity and ethical divergence.*

One study estimates that as many as 400,000 embryos remain frozen in fertility clinics in the United States; this survey tried to document what happens to them. If you were faced with trying to decide what to do with frozen embryos, which of the options described here would you choose? Why? Do you believe that parents should have a say in what happens to their embryos? Do you think embryos have a right to exist regardless of the parents' wishes? Explain. Given that a frozen embryo is minute (comprising only two to four cells), do you think it merits a disposal ceremony? Why or why not?

---

*Andrea D. Gurmankin, Dominic Sisti, and Arthur L. Caplan, "Embryo Disposal Practices in IVF Clinics in the United States," *Politics and Life Sciences* 22.2 (August 2004), 3–8.

CASE 2

Surrogate Versus Father

(MSNBC)—Despite a court ruling against them, a Florida couple vows to continue their legal battle to gain custody of a child born by the woman they hired as a surrogate, but who then decided to keep the baby.

The issue, Tom and Gwyn Lamitina say, is not about Florida surrogacy law, which clearly gives the woman the right to the child. They are fighting for Tom Lamitina's rights as the father of the child.

"We filed an appeal," Scott Alan Salomon, the attorney for the couple, told TODAY co-host Meredith Vieira when all three appeared on the program Tuesday. "The trial judge overstepped his bounds. He had no right whatsoever to terminate parental rights in a paternity action."

Gwyn Lamitina, 46, said the couple wants custody of the child they think is rightfully theirs.

"We would ultimately like to have primary custody," she said. "If the judge deems that [the surrogate] has visitation, we would be up for that."

The child, Emma Grace, was born five months ago to Stephanie Eckard, whom the Lamitinas had met through an online site on which women who want to be surrogates advertise their availability.

Eckard, 30, is a teacher and a single mother of two other children of her own. According to Salomon, she had delivered three surrogate children for other couples before meeting the Lamitinas. Eckard lives in Jacksonville, in the northeast corner of the state, while the Lamitinas live in the Central Florida town of Oviedo. Eckard has declined all requests to be interviewed.

But a month after Eckard became pregnant, she and the Lamitinas had a confrontation over Eckard's smoking. Eckard broke off contact and decided to keep the child as her own. The Lamitinas had paid her $1,500 to carry the child.

The Lamitinas have never seen the girl. "I haven't known anything about her," Gwyn Lamitina told Vieira. "I had to find out she was born through the press."

Because Emma Grace was conceived with Eckard's egg and not Gwyn Lamitina's, Florida law gives Eckard the absolute right to decide to keep the child up until 48 hours after the birth. The trial court upheld that law on Oct. 11.

For that reason, Florida surrogacy lawyer Charlotte Danciu told NBC News in a recorded interview, "Couples should never let a surrogate use her own egg." . . .

As Danciu said, the law in Florida is very clear: A surrogate pregnancy with the surrogate's own egg is treated as an adoption and the birth mother can decide to keep the child, even if there is a signed contract. Tom Lamitina is the father of the child, but

the law treats him as a sperm donor with no parental rights.

"That is absolutely incorrect," said Salomon. "A sperm donor is one that signs a contract that says 'I am waiving my parental rights.' Tom voluntarily paid money to give a woman his sperm. He is not a sperm donor. He was doing this with the sole intent to become a father. That's the biggest joke of this whole case."

He said the Lamitinas' case is rightly a paternity case in which Tom Lamitina is seeking custody of his own son.

"Half of this child's DNA is Tom's," Salomon said. "The judge unilaterally said, 'We don't care about that. You have no rights.'"

Vieira asked if there is a legal precedent for that claim, to which Salomon replied, "There will be one now."*

Should the father have any rights to the child in this case? Is Florida law correct in giving the surrogate the right to decide to keep the child up until 48 hours after the birth, even if she had signed a surrogacy contract? In determining the custody of a child, should who gestates it carry more weight than genetic links to it (that is, where the egg and sperm come from)? Should genetic or gestational links carry more weight than the ability to properly care for the child? Explain your answers.

---

*Mike Celizic, "Couple Vows to Fight Surrogate Who Kept Baby," *MSNBC.com*, 23 October 2007, http://www.msnbc.msn .com/id/21435600/ (29 November 2007).

CASE 3

Cloning to Bring Back a Child

(MSNBC)—Katherine Gordon of Great Falls, Mont., whose 17-year-old daughter, Emily, was killed by a drunk driver five years ago, says she became obsessed with bringing a part of her daughter back in some way. Spurred on by the news of [the birth of the cloned sheep Dolly], she had her daughter's cells frozen and stored for possible future cloning. "I started to spend all day researching on the Internet and contacting biologists," she recalls. "I really went off the deep end."

Now she's resigned herself to the fact that the technology probably won't be available in time to help her bear Emily's clone, as she's now 42. But she says that if it were possible in the next couple of years, she would do it.

"I know it wouldn't be Emily—it would be her twin sister," she says. "Emily was perfect—she was beautiful and smart, too, and most of that is genetic. Her predisposition was real kind. Even if the clone had some of her negative qualities that would be fine, too. I don't know what the new person would be like, but she would have a good start in life." . . .

Dr. William Hurlbut, a bioethicist at Stanford University and member of President Bush's Council on Bioethics, urges parents to look at cloning from the perspective of the child. "I don't think anyone should have to live their life in the footsteps of someone else," he says. "The baby may be held up in comparison with some idealized image of the lost child. It seems morbid and insensitive to the love of the child."

But Gregory Pence, a pro-cloning bioethicist at the University of Alabama, Birmingham, and author of "Who's Afraid of Human Cloning?" defends that choice. "People have replacement children all the time. It's as good a reason as any to have a child sexually. Why are people creating children anyway? To create a sense of family, someone to take care of them when they're older. There are many self-centered reasons people have kids, parents just normally don't have to [spell] out these reasons."*

If Katharine Gordon could give birth to a clone of her deceased daughter, should she? Is grief over the loss of a child a morally legitimate reason for wanting to clone him or her? Is there a morally relevant difference between sexually producing a child to replace a lost one and producing a child through cloning for the same reason? Explain your answers.

---

*Julia Sommerfeld, "Coveting a Clone," MSNBC.com, undated, 2006, http://www.msnbc.msn.com/id/3076918/ (29 November 2007).

FURTHER READING

Kenneth D. Alpern, ed., *The Ethics of Reproductive Technology* (New York: Oxford University Press, 1992).

American Society for Reproductive Medicine, "Assisted Reproductive Technologies: A Guide for Patients," undated, 2007, http://www.asrm.org/ (27 November 2007).

Elizabeth Anderson, "Is Women's Labor a Commodity?" *Philosophy and Public Affairs* 19 (Winter 1990), 71–92.

Dan W. Brock, "An Assessment of the Ethical Issues Pro and Con," in *Cloning Human Beings: Report and Recommendations of the National Bioethics Advisory Commission,* vol. II, sect. E (Rockville, MD: NBAC, June 1997), 1–23.

Justine Burley, ed., *The Genetic Revolution and Human Rights* (Oxford: Oxford University Press, 1999).

Walter Glannon, "Reproductive Rights and Technologies," in *Biomedical Ethics* (New York: Oxford University Press, 2005), 71–94.

Jonathan Glover, *Choosing Children: The Ethical Dilemmas of Genetic Intervention* (Oxford: Oxford University Press, 2006).

John Harris and Søren Holm, eds., *The Future of Human Reproduction: Ethics, Choice, and Regulation* (Oxford: Oxford University Press, 1998).

Mark Murphy, "The Natural Law Tradition in Ethics," in *Stanford Encyclopedia of Philosophy,* 11 March 2008, http://plato.stanford.edu/entries/natural-law-ethics (9 June 2008).

National Bioethics Advisory Commission, *Cloning Human Beings,* June 1997, http://bioethics.georgetown.edu (14 July 2007).

New York State Task Force on Life and the Law, *Assisted Reproductive Technologies: Analysis and Recommendations for Public Policy* (Albany: New York State Department of Health, April 1998).

President's Council on Bioethics, "Assisted Reproduction," in *Reproduction & Responsibility: The Regulation of New Biotechnologies* (Washington, DC: Government Printing Office, 2004).

President's Council on Bioethics, *Human Cloning and Human Dignity: An Ethical Inquiry,* undated, 2002, www.bioethics.gov (14 July 2007).

Laura Purdy, "Genetics and Reproductive Risk: Can Having Children Be Immoral?" in *Genetics Now,* ed. John L. Buckley (Washington, DC: University Press of America, 1978).

John Robertson, *Children of Choice: Freedom and the New Reproductive Technologies* (Princeton, NJ: Princeton University Press, 1994).

Susan Sherwin, "Feminist Ethics and In Vitro Fertilization," in *Science, Morality and Feminist Theory*, ed. Marsha Hanen and Kai Nielsen (Calgary, Alberta: University of Calgary Press, 1987), 265–84.

Bonnie Steinbock, "Surrogate Motherhood as Prenatal Adoption," *Law, Medicine, & Health Care* 16 (Spring/ Summer 1988), 4050.

Margaret Tighe, Nicholas Tonti-Filippini, Robyn Rowland, and Peter Singer, "IVF: A Debate," in *Bioethics: An Anthology*, ed., Helga Kuhse and Peter Singer (Oxford: Blackwell, 1999), 91–102.

Robert Wachbroit and David Wasserman, "Reproductive Technology," in *The Oxford Handbook of Practical Ethics*, ed. Hugh LaFollette (Oxford: Oxford University Press, 2003), 136–60.

NOTES

1. Cynthia B. Cohen, "'Give Me Children or I Shall Die!' New Reproductive Technologies and Harm to Children," *Hastings Center Report* 26.2 (1996), 19–27.

2. John A. Robertson, "Procreative Liberty and the Control of Conception, Pregnancy, and Childbirth," *University of Virginia Law Review* 69 (1983), 434.

3. Cohen, "'Give Me Children,'" 21.

4. *Ibid.*, 22.

5. Vatican Congregation for the Doctrine of the Faith, "Instruction on Respect for Human Life in Its Origin and on the Dignity of Procreation," *Origins* 16.40 (19 March 1987).

6. Peter Singer, "IVF: The Simple Case," in *Ethical Issues at the Outset of Life*, ed. William B. Weil, Jr., and Martin Benjamin (Boston: Blackwell Scientific Publications, 1989), 44–49.

7. Mary Anne Warren, "IVF and Women's Interests: An Analysis of Feminist Concerns," *Bioethics* 2.1 (1988), 37–57.

8. John Robertson, "The Presumptive Primacy of Procreative Liberty," in *Children of Choice: Freedom and the New Reproductive Technologies* (Princeton, NJ: Princeton University Press, 1994), 22–42.

9. Michelle Roberts, "IVF Hope for Child Cancer Cases," BBC News, 2 July 2007, http://news.bbc.co.uk/2/hi/health/6259864.stm (27 November 2007).

10. Elizabeth S. Anderson, "Is Women's Labor a Commodity?" *Philosophy and Public Affairs* 19 (Winter 1990), 71–92.

11. *Ibid.*

12. Laura M. Purdy, "Surrogate Mothering: Exploitation or Empowerment?" *Bioethics* 3 (January 1989), 18–34.

13. Bonnie Steinbock, "Surrogate Motherhood as Prenatal Adoption," *Law, Medicine & Health Care* 16 (Spring/ Summer 1988), 40–50.

14. National Academy of Sciences, Committee on Science, Engineering, and Public Policy, *Scientific and Medical Aspects of Human Reproductive Cloning* (Washington, DC: National Academy Press, 2002), 26.

15. Human Genome Project Information, "Cloning Fact Sheet," Genomics.Energy.Gov, 29 August 2006, www.ornl.gov/sci/techsources/Human_Genome/elsi/cloning.shtml (15 June 2008).

16. Carson Strong, "The Ethics of Human Reproductive Cloning," *Ethics, Law and Moral Philosophy of Reproductive Biomedicine* 1.1 (March 2005), 45–49.

17. Dan W. Brock, "Cloning Human Beings: An Assessment of the Ethical Issues Pro and Con," paper prepared for the National Bioethics Advisory Commission, 1997.

18. National Bioethics Advisory Commission, *Cloning Human Beings: Report and Recommendations* (Rockville, MD: NBAC, June 1997), 67.

19. Brock, "Cloning Human Beings."

20. Louis P. Pojman, "Cloning," in *Life and Death: Grappling with the Moral Dilemmas of Our Time* (Belmont, CA: Wadsworth, 2000), 124.

21. Leon R. Kass, "The Wisdom of Repugnance," *The New Republic*, 2 June 1997, 17–26.

22. Brock, "Cloning Human Beings."

IVF: The Simple Case

PETER SINGER

Singer addresses seven moral objections that have been lodged against in vitro fer-tilization (IVF), focusing on its use in the "simple case" ("a married, infertile couple use an egg taken from the wife and sperm taken from the husband, and all embryos created are inserted into the womb of the wife"). The objections include the charges that IVF is unnatural, that it is risky for the offspring, and that it separates the procre-ative and conjugal aspects of marriage and so damages the martial relationship. He concludes that all the objections are weak and that "[t]hey should not count against going ahead with IVF when it is the best way of overcoming infertility" and when the infertile couple decides against adoption.

The so-called simple case of IVF is that in which a married, infertile couple use an egg taken from the wife and sperm taken from the husband, and all embryos created are inserted into the womb of the wife. This case allows us to consider the eth-ics of IVF in itself, without the complications of the many other issues that can arise in different circumstances. Then we can go on to look at these complications separately.

The Technique

The technique itself is now well known and is fast becoming a routine part of infertility treatment in many countries. The infertile woman is given a hor-mone treatment to induce her ovaries to produce more than one egg in her next cycle. Her hormone levels are carefully monitored to detect the precise moment at which the eggs are ripening. At this time the eggs are removed. This is usually done by lapa-roscopy, a minor operation in which a fine tube is inserted into the woman's abdomen and the egg is sucked out up the tube. A laparoscope, a kind of

From *Ethical Issues at the Outset of Life* (1987), edited by William B. Weil, Jr., and Martin Benjamin, pp. 44–49. Based on work done with Deane Wells and previously published in *Making Babies* (revised edition, 1985). Published by Scribner, an imprint of Simon & Schuster Adult Publishing Group. Copyright © 1984, 1985 by Peter Singer and Deane Wells.

periscope illuminated by fiber optics, is also inserted into the abdomen so that the surgeon can locate the place where the ripe egg is to be found. Instead of laparoscopy, some IVF teams are now using ultra-sound techniques, which eliminate the need for a general anesthetic.

Once the eggs have been collected they are placed in culture in small glass dishes known as petri dishes, not in test tubes despite the popular label of "test-tube babies." Sperm is then obtained from the male partner by means of masturbation and placed with the egg. Fertilization follows, in at least 80 percent of the ripe eggs. The resulting embryos are allowed to cleave once or twice and are usually transferred to the woman some 48 to 72 hours after fertilization. The actual transfer is done via the vagina and is a simple procedure.

It is after the transfer, when the embryo is back in the uterus and beyond the scrutiny of medical sci-ence, that things are most likely to go wrong. Even with the most experienced IVF teams, the majority of embryos transferred fail to implant in the uterus. One pregnancy for every five transfers is currently considered to be a good working average for a com-petent IVF team. Many of the newer teams fail to achieve anything like this rate. Nevertheless, there are so many units around the world now practicing IVF that thousands of babies have been produced as a result of the technique. IVF has ceased to be experimental and is now a routine, if still "last re-sort" method of treating some forms of infertility.

Objections to the Simple Case

There is some opposition to IVF even in the simple case. The most frequently heard objections are as follows:

1. IVF is unnatural.
2. IVF is risky for the offspring.
3. IVF separates the procreative and the conjugal aspects of marriage and so damages the marital relationship.
4. IVF is illicit because it involves masturbation.
5. Adoption is a better solution to the problem of childlessness.
6. IVF is an expensive luxury and the resources would be better spent elsewhere.
7. IVF allows increased male control over reproduction and hence threatens the status of women in the community.

We can deal swiftly with the first four of these objections. If we were to reject medical advances on the grounds that they are "unnatural" we would be rejecting modern medicine as a whole, for the very purpose of the medical enterprise is to resist the ravages of nature which would otherwise shorten our lives and make them much less pleasant. If anything is in accordance with the nature of our species, it is the application of our intelligence to overcome adverse situations in which we find ourselves. The application of IVF to infertile couples is a classic example of this application of human intelligence.

The claim that IVF is risky for the offspring is one that was argued with great force before IVF became a widely used technique. It is sufficient to note that the results of IVF so far have happily refuted these fears. The most recent Australian figures, for example, based on 934 births, indicate that the rate of abnormality was 2.7%, which is very close to the national average of 1.5%. When we take into account the greater average age of women seeking IVF, as compared with the childbearing population as a whole, it does not seem that the *in vitro* technique itself adds to the risk of an abnormal offspring. This view is reinforced by the fact that the abnormalities

were all ones that arise with the ordinary method of reproduction; there have been no new "monsters" produced by IVF.[1] Perhaps we still cannot claim with statistical certainty that the risk of defect is no higher with IVF than with the more common method of conception; but if the risk is higher at all, it would appear to be only very slightly higher, and still within limits which may be considered acceptable.

The third and fourth objections have been urged by spokesmen for certain religious groups, but they are difficult to defend outside the confines of particular religions. Few infertile couples will take seriously the view that their marital relationship will be damaged if they use the technique which offers them the best chance of having their own child. It is in any case extraordinarily paternalistic for anyone else to tell a couple that they should not use IVF because it will harm their marriage. That, surely, is for them to decide.

The objection to masturbation comes from a similar source and can be even more swiftly dismissed. Religious prohibitions on masturbation are taboos from past times which even religious spokesmen are beginning to consider outdated. Moreover, even if one could defend a prohibition on masturbation for sexual pleasure—perhaps on the (very tenuous) ground that sexual activity is wrong unless it is directed either toward procreation or toward the strengthening of the bond between marriage partners—it would be absurd to extend a prohibition with that kind of rationale to a case in which masturbation is being used in the context of a marriage and precisely in order to make reproduction possible. (The fact that some religions do persist in regarding masturbation as wrong, even in these circumstances, is indicative of the folly of an ethical system based on absolute rules, irrespective of the circumstances in which those rules are being applied, or the consequences of their application.)

Overpopulation and the Allocation of Resources

The next two objections, however, deserve more careful consideration. In an overpopulated world in which there are so many children who cannot be properly fed and cared for, there is something incongruous about using all the ingenuity of modern medicine to create more children. And similarly, when there are so many deaths caused by preventable diseases, is there not something wrong with the priorities which lead us to develop expensive techniques for overcoming the relatively less serious problem of infertility?

These objections are sound to the following extent: in an ideal world we would find loving families for unwanted children before we created additional children; and in an ideal world we would clear up all the preventable ill-health and malnutrition-related diseases before we went on to tackle the problem of infertility. But is it appropriate to ask, of IVF alone, whether it can stand the test of measurement against what we would do in an ideal world? In an ideal world, none of us would consume more than our fair share of resources. We would not drive expensive cars while others die for the lack of drugs costing a few cents. We would not eat a diet rich in wastefully produced animal products while others cannot get enough to nourish their bodies. We cannot demand more of infertile couples than we are ready to demand of ourselves. If fertile couples are free to have large families of their own, rather than adopt destitute children from overseas, infertile couples must also be free to do what they can to have their own families. In both cases, overseas adoption, or perhaps the adoption of local children who are unwanted because of some impairment, should be considered; but if we are not going to make this compulsory in the former case, it should not be made compulsory in the latter.

There is a further question: to what extent do infertile couples have a right to assistance from community medical resources? Again, however, we must not single out IVF for harsher treatment than we give to other medical techniques. If tubal surgery is available and covered by one's health insurance, or is offered as part of a national health scheme, then why should IVF be treated any differently? And if infertile couples can get free or subsidized psychiatry to help them overcome the psychological problems of infertility, there is something absurd about denying them free or subsidized treatment which could overcome the root of the problem, rather than the symptoms. By today's standards, after all, IVF is not an inordinately expensive medical technique; and there is no country, as far as I know, which limits its provision of free or subsidized health care to those cases in which the patient's life is in danger. Once we extend medical care to cover cases of injury, incapacity, and psychological distress, IVF has a strong claim to be included among the range of free or subsidized treatments available.

The Effect on Women

The final objection is one that has come from some feminists. In a recently published collection of essays by women titled *Test-Tube Women: What Future for Motherhood?*, several contributors are suspicious of the new reproductive technology. None is more hostile than Robyn Rowland, an Australian sociologist, who writes:

> Ultimately the new technology will be used for the benefit of men and to the detriment of women. Although technology itself is not always a negative development, the real question has always been—who controls it? Biological technology is in the hands of men.[2]

And Rowland concludes with a warning as dire as any uttered by the most conservative opponents of IVF:

> What may be happening is the last battle in the long war of men against women. Women's position is most precarious . . . we may find ourselves without a product of any kind with which to bargain. For the history of "mankind" women have been seen in terms of their value as childbearers. We have to ask, if that last power is taken and controlled by men, what role is envisaged for women in the new world? Will women become obsolete? Will we be fighting to retain or reclaim the right to bear children—has patriarchy conned us once again? I urge you sisters to be vigilant.

I can see little basis for such claims. For a start, women have figured quite prominently in the leading IVF teams in Britain, Australia, and the United States: Jean Purdy was an early colleague of Edwards and Steptoe in the research that led to the birth of Louise Brown; Linda Mohr has directed the development of embryo freezing at the Queen Victoria

Medical Centre in Melbourne; and in the United States Georgeanna Jones and Joyce Vargyas have played leading roles in the groundbreaking clinics in Norfolk, Virginia, and at the University of Southern California, respectively. It seems odd for a feminist to neglect the contributions these women have made.

Even if one were to grant, however, that the technology remains predominantly in male hands, it has to be remembered that it was developed in response to the needs of infertile couples. From interviews I have conducted and meetings I have attended, my impression is that while both partners are often very concerned about their childlessness, in those cases in which one partner is more distressed than the other by this situation, that partner is usually the woman. Feminists usually accept that this is so, attributing it to the power or social conditioning in a patriarchal society; but the origin of the strong female desire for children is not really what is in question here. The question is: in what sense is the new technology an instrument of male domination over women? If it is true that the technology was developed at least as much in response to the needs of women as in response to the needs of men, then it is hard to see why a feminist should condemn it.

It might be objected that whatever the origins of IVF and no matter how benign it may be when used to help infertile couples, the further development of techniques such as ectogenesis—the growth of the embryo from conception totally outside the body, in an artificial womb—will reduce the status of women. Again, it is not easy to see why this should be so. Ectogenesis will, if it is ever successful, provide a choice for women. Shulamith Firestone argued several years ago in her influential feminist work *The Dialectic of Sex*[3] that this choice will remove the fundamental biological barrier to complete equality. Hence Firestone welcomed the prospect of ectogenesis and condemned the low priority given by our male-dominated society to research in this area.

Firestone's view is surely more in line with the drive to sexual equality than the position taken by Rowland. If we argue that to break the link between women and childbearing would be to undermine the status of women in our society, what are we saying about the ability of women to obtain true equality in other spheres of life? I am not so pessimistic about the abilities of women to achieve equality with men across the broad range of human endeavor. For that reason I think women will be helped, rather than harmed, by the development of a technology which makes it possible for them to have children without being pregnant. As Nancy Breeze, a very differently inclined contributor to the same collection of essays, puts it:

> Two thousand years of morning sickness and stretch marks have not resulted in liberation for women or children. If you should run into a Petri dish, it could turn out to be your best friend. So rock it; don't knock it![4]

So to sum up this discussion of the ethics of the simple case of IVF: the ethical objections urged against IVF under these conditions are not strong. They should not count against going ahead with IVF when it is the best way of overcoming infertility and when the infertile couple are not prepared to consider adoption as a means of overcoming their problems. There is, admittedly, a serious question about how much of the national health budget should be allocated to this area. But then, there are serious questions about the allocation of resources in other areas of medicine as well.

REFERENCES

1. Abstract. *Proceedings of the Fifth Scientific Meeting of the Fertility Society of Australia*, Adelaide, Dec 2–6, 1986.
2. Rowland R. Reproductive technologies: The final solution to the woman question? In: Arditti R., Klein R. D., Minden, S., eds., *Test-tube Women: What Future for Motherhood?* London: Pandora, 1984.
3. Firestone S. *The Dialectic of Sex*. New York: Bantam, 1971.
4. Breeze N. Who is going to rock the petri dish? In: Arditti R., Klein R. D., Minden S., eds, *Test-tube Women: What Future for Motherhood?* London: Pandora, 1984.

IVF and Women's Interests:
An Analysis of Feminist Concerns

MARY ANNE WARREN

In this essay, Warren examines some feminist objections to IVF and other new reproductive technologies. Because of the risks and costs to women from IVF, she says, it is not at all clear that it provides a net benefit to them. But if the disadvantages do not clearly outweigh the possible benefits, "then the matter is properly left to individual choice," and it would be wrong to conclude that women's interests demand an end to research in IVF and related technologies. She finds no merit in the argument by some feminists that because of the pressure from patriarchal society for women to have children (the "pronatalist" attitude), women cannot give genuine voluntary consent to IVF treatments even if well informed. On the contrary, "Neither the patriarchal power structure nor pronatalist ideology makes women incapable of reasoned choice about childrearing."

Thus far, little of the public and professional debate about the ethics of *in vitro* fertilization (IVF) and other new reproductive technologies (NRTs) has focused upon the possible negative effects of these technologies on women. There is endless discussion of the moral status of the fertilized ovum or pre-embryo, and its possible moral rights.[1] Theologians and nonreligious critics debate the propriety of conceiving human beings "artificially," that is, without heterosexual intercourse.[2] Concern is also voiced—and appropriately so—about the possible physical or mental effects of technologically assisted reproduction upon the resulting children. But with the exception of a small group of feminist critics, few have paid much attention to the dangers to the women who serve as experimental subjects in reproductive research and, indirectly, to all women.

In what follows, I will examine some of the feminist objections to IVF and other NRTs. I will argue that, although the NRTs pose some significant dangers for women, it would be wrong to conclude that women's interests demand an end to IVF and other reproductive research. But if we are to understand the ethics of IVF, we must ask not only whether it is in itself morally objectionable,

but also whether it is (part of) an adequate societal response to the problem of involuntary infertility among women. IVF is at best a small part of a solution to that problem; it can help only a small minority of infertile women, and does nothing to address the underlying social causes which contribute to the problem. Moreover, the publicity surrounding IVF and other NRTs may deflect attention and resources from the potentially more important tasks of understanding and counteracting the preventable causes of infertility.

1. Feminist Criticisms: The Microlevel

Feminist critiques of the NRTs operate in part on the microlevel, that is, the level of individual behavior, individual rights and wrongs; and in part on the macrolevel, the level of historical context and social implications. I will begin with the microlevel criticisms.

At the microlevel, the primary issue is whether IVF is sufficiently beneficial to IVF patients to justify the commercial marketing of the procedure, or even continued research and development. IVF is usually depicted as an astonishing success story: infertile women are enabled to have beautiful, healthy children. We hear far less about the associated dangers. We do not yet know the long-term side effects of the use of drugs and hormones to induce superovulation. The

From *Bioethics* 2, no. 1, 1988, 37–57. Reprinted by permission of Blackwell Publishing Ltd.

collection of ova through abdominal surgery, usually under general anaesthesia, carries a significant risk of mortality or morbidity.[3] The replacement of the fertilized ovum in the uterus may cause infection, physical damage, or ectopic pregnancy. An abnormally high percentage of IVF pregnancies end in spontaneous abortion or stillbirth. There are additional risks to mother and infant, associated not with the IVF procedure itself but with the ways in which IVF pregnancies are generally monitored (e.g., through ultrasound, amniocentesis, and endometrial biopsy), and with the exceptionally high rate of cesarean section which is typical of IVF births.[4]

In addition to these physical risks, women who undergo IVF bear personal and psychological burdens. These include the emotional ups and downs inherent in the cycle of hope and disappointment; the disruption of work and, often, personal relationships; and the humiliation and depersonalization that may result from the submission to painful and embarrassing invasions of their bodies. When these costs are considered in conjunction with the fact that only a small minority of women who undergo IVF treatments will give birth to a viable infant,[5] it is far from clear that IVF provides a net benefit to participating patients.

2. IVF and Informed Consent

Whether or not the benefits of IVF treatment will outweigh its costs and risks to female patients depends in part upon just how severe these costs and risks turn out to be, and in part upon whether success rates can be improved in existing programs and high standards maintained in new ones. It also depends upon just how great a boon motherhood is to those women for whom IVF leads to a successful pregnancy. Those who regard motherhood as the greatest pleasure or achievement of which (some) women are capable will be prepared to tolerate greater risks and uncertainties than those who see motherhood—or, rather, the way it is institutionalized—as a significant burden.

In spite of these uncertainties—indeed, precisely because of them—it may be argued that women have the right to undertake the risks associated with IVF if *they* judge those risks to be worth taking. If women's right to reproductive autonomy means anything, it must mean that we are entitled to take some risks with our physical and psychological health, in the attempt to either have or not have children. Neither abortion nor many forms of contraception are entirely safe, but women sometimes reasonably judge that the alternatives are even less desirable. Having a wanted child can be as important a goal as avoiding an unwanted birth. If the costs and dangers of IVF to individual women and children were so great that no informed and responsible person would attempt that route to parenthood, then perhaps the paternalistic protection of women through the prohibition of IVF would be appropriate. But if these costs and dangers are not, so far as we can now determine, so great as to *clearly* outweigh the possible benefits, then the matter is properly left to individual choice.

Of course, the right to the voluntary use of contraception, abortion, or the newer reproductive technologies is meaningless unless the requirements are met for informed and voluntary consent. Informed consent requires, among other things, an understanding of the medical and psychological risks, and the probability of success. There are troubling questions about whether all of the women who have been patients and experimental subjects in IVF programs have fully understood the risks to which they were being exposed and the often slight chances that they themselves would benefit from the research done.[6] Debate continues about the adequacy of the counselling and information received by women in current IVF programs.[7] However, many of these women are very well-informed, not only through counselling but through their own reading and investigation. For them, at least, participation in an IVF program would seem to be an exercise of the right to reproductive autonomy.

Some of the feminist critics of IVF accept this argument for reproductive autonomy, arguing only for the kinds of legal regulation and ethical supervision necessary to ensure that women's consent to IVF treatments is adequately informed and voluntary, and that necessary precautions are taken to make the procedure as safe as possible.[8] Others, however, reject this argument as superficial. In their view, women cannot give truly voluntary consent to IVF treatments, regardless of how well-informed they may be about the risks, costs, and odds of success. They argue that women's reproductive "choices" are conditioned by the patriarchal power structure and the pronatalist ideology with which it is associated. Having children is still commonly regarded as a duty or a prerequisite for adult status, especially for women. This pronatalist ideology makes it difficult for women to make genuinely free choices about reproduction in general, or IVF in particular. Gena Corea says,

> The propaganda . . . that women are nothing unless they bear children, that if they are infertile, they lose their most basic identity as women . . . has a coercive power. It conditions a woman's choices as well as her *motivations* to choose. Her most heartfelt desire, the pregnancy for which she so desperately yearns, has been—to varying degrees—conditioned.[9]

There is surely some truth in this response. The "desperation of women who cannot meet the cultural definition of womanhood by becoming mothers"[10] is, to some extent, a cultural artifact. We hear far less about the plight of infertile men. There are, in all probability, infertile men who are equally "desperate" to have children; some even undergo painful surgical procedures (e.g, vasectomy reversal) in the pursuit of that goal. But we do not often see photographs in the newspaper of smiling fathers, proudly displaying infants that they have conceived with the help of such surgery.

It is true that female infertility is, in some respects, a more severe problem for a heterosexual couple than male infertility. Male infertility, though no easier to cure, is more easily circumvented: it is much easier for the couple to use AID (artificial insemination with donated sperm) than to obtain a donor egg or to "rent" another woman's womb, if the infertility is on the female side—and much less legally and morally problematic. Nevertheless, the apparently greater desperation of many infertile women, and the attention paid to that supposed desperation,[11] probably also reflect the degree to which the perception of women's social worth is still tied to their function as childbearers.

The question is whether or not these points demonstrate that the opportunity to make their own choices about IVF and other NRTs is of no value to women. I think that they do not. Freedom is not an all-or-nothing affair. We can rarely be completely free of unjust or inappropriate social and economic pressures, but we can sometimes make sound and appropriate decisions, in the light of our own circumstances.

Neither the patriarchal power structure nor pronatalist ideology makes women incapable of reasoned choice about childbearing. Rather, the social pressures upon some women to have children—and the pressures upon others not to have children—are circumstances which we must take into account in our deliberations. Either having children or not having them can be socially (and financially) expensive. Motherhood is apt to interfere with other life goals to a degree that fatherhood usually does not. This is not so much because of female biology as because of the social expectation that mothers will also be the primary childrearers, and the shortage of adequate childcare facilities and flexible working arrangements which would enable women to combine parenting and paid working without heroic effort. Yet childlessness, especially when it is involuntary, can be a great and lasting grief. This is particularly true in a society like our own, in which most people who are not parents have little opportunity to have long-term nurturing relationships with children.

Women are not unaware of these social realities. In deliberating about either "natural" motherhood or the use of IVF, we may sometimes be wrong about what is in our own interests, and perhaps some of us are excessively influenced by pronatalist ideology. But it does not follow that we would benefit from additional paternalistic constraints. Autonomy necessarily implies the right to make our own mistakes.

Unfortunately, not all infertile women have the opportunity to make use of IVF. Some causes of infertility (e.g., some anatomical or hormonal abnormalities) cannot be circumvented by external fertilization. Worse, IVF—like AID—is often restricted, either by law or by medical practice, to married heterosexual women. It is often argued that this discrimination is pragmatically necessary, since making IVF available to all infertile women who can afford it might provoke so much conservative opposition that IVF programs would be eliminated altogether. It is nevertheless an injustice. Such discrimination could be justified only if there were some evidence that women who are single or lesbian are more likely to be inadequate parents than are married and heterosexual women; and there is no such evidence. It is also arguably unjust—and certainly unfortunate—that the high cost of IVF treatments effectively excludes many women. But denying IVF to all women, for paternalistic reasons, would also be an injustice. To be subject to inappropriate social pressures is not necessarily to be deprived of either judgment or will. We need to be suspicious of analyses which "deny our power and our ability to make choices, even within the constraints of patriarchy."[12]

Of course, the right of individuals to make their own choices must sometimes be constrained for the sake of the general welfare. If the advent of IVF and other NRTs can be proved detrimental to women or to society as a whole, then we shall have to regard women who serve as researchers or clinicians, patients or experimental subjects in IVF programs, as unwittingly working against women's larger interests. Their choices may be individually rational, but collectively harmful. Arguments to this effect are what I call macrolevel arguments.

3. The Macrolevel Critique

Some feminist critics have sought to place the NRTs in their social and historical context, by looking at the history of iatrogenic harms to women caused by male-dominated medicine, and at the possible future abuses of reproductive technologies. Mary O'Brien and others have argued that men suffer from an envy of the larger role that women play in human procreation, and from their own natural inability to know with certainty which children are genetically their own.[13] On this view, men have long sought to control women and women's reproductive processes, in order to assure themselves biological as well as social heirs. Patriarchal marriage, the sexual double standard, the confinement and legal disenfranchisement of women, the massacre of women healers and wise women during the witch-craze era, and the subsequent ascendancy of male-dominated obstetrics and gynecology, are all seen as part of this male project of control.[14]

It would be difficult to deny that women have suffered from the male domination of medicine, not only in the loss of control over their own reproductive processes, but in iatrogenic illness and death.

The entry of male physicians into obstetric practice in the seventeenth century led to a centuries-long plague of puerperal fever.[15] Male physicians in the nineteenth century campaigned successfully for the prohibition of abortion and contraception, and castrated thousands of women for supposed psychological problems. In this century, the DES, thalidomide, and Dalkon Shield disasters, the overuse of hysterectomy and other gynecological surgery,[16] and the over-technologization of birth,[17] all illustrate the same tendency to intervene in women's reproductive processes without good evidence of the safety and/or necessity of the intervention. Needless to say, modern obstetrics and gynecology have also produced some benefits for women. Many of the physical problems associated with pregnancy and birth can be more effectively treated than in the past. But we cannot know how much greater these benefits might have been had the medical profession not excluded women for many generations.

Given this history of iatrogenic harm to women, it is not surprising that many women regard the advent of IVF and other NRTs with suspicion. They fear that the new reproductive technologies will not only intensify male control of female reproductive processes, but may eventually remove women from the process of reproduction altogether. Irene Elia warns that,

> If men ever controlled parthenogenesis, using sperm nuclei placed in thawed or simulated egg cytoplasm and gestated in artificial or non-human wombs, they could enjoy total domination. With their gametes, they could produce either males or females—motherless all![18]

(There does, however, seem to be a biological problem here which Elia has overlooked: parthenogenesis using a sperm with a Y nucleus would produce a nonviable YY embryo; while the use of an X sperm would produce an XX—or female—offspring.)

Another cause for concern, not only among feminists, is that the NRTs are providing a means for the possible implementation of repressive eugenics programs. Many fear that the new methods for controlling the quality of our offspring, e.g., by embryo screening, prenatal diagnosis and selective abortion, or the use of donor gametes, will eventually become socially and/or legally mandatory. Corea asks, "Will those searching for perfect babies begin first by socially outlawing major . . . birth defects . . . and then . . . move on to ever lesser defects like asthma?"[19] Perhaps in the future women who try to reproduce without such eugenic interventions will be accused of child abuse, as are women today who give birth at home with the help of a midwife, rather than in a hospital setting.

4. The Shape of the Future

The dangers of male control of women's reproductive processes, and of the implementation of repressive eugenics programs, are real. There are, however, ways of resisting those dangers without calling for the termination of IVF and other reproductive research. None are simple, but all are morally essential for independent reasons.

Perhaps the most essential need is for more equal participation by women in all areas of medicine and biomedical research. It is difficult for any male-dominated profession either to understand women's needs or to serve them effectively. The new reproductive technologies should not be primarily in the hands of male physicians and researchers, but neither should any other form of medical treatment. It is equally essential that women (and men) from the various racial and ethnic groups and socioeconomic classes have a voice in determining the kinds of reproductive technologies that are developed and the ways in which they are used; for each of these groups may also be especially vulnerable to possible misuses of these technologies.

Many members of the medical professions would deny that the lesser participation of women in these fields is due to any remaining discrimination. The legal barriers to women's entry to medical studies and practice have been largely removed, and more or less nondiscriminatory criteria are increasingly used in the selection of medical students. But this is not enough. It would not even be enough if 50 percent of all medical *students* were women; for there are still powerful social and structural barriers to women's entry and success in such medical and scientific specialities as gynecology, obstetrics, embryology, neonatology, and endocrinology. These barriers include simple prejudice, as well as the excessively long hours required during the years of training and apprenticeship, and the difficulty of resuming that training after an extended break. All medical specializations need to be made more compatible with the needs of many women (and many men as well) for flexible working hours and interruptible career schedules. Otherwise, women in medicine will continue to be forced either to curtail their professional aspirations, or to forgo childbearing, or postpone it beyond the biologically optimal years.

Opening the medical and research professions to greater participation by women and other underrepresented groups is a long-term goal. In the meantime, it is essential that every government body with responsibility for the regulation of the NRTs, every ethical oversight committee, and every public agency which funds reproductive research be at least 50 percent composed of women. Among these, there should be some who have been on the receiving end of the new reproductive technologies—and some who have chosen not to be. An effort should also be made to include (proportionate numbers of) individuals from diverse racial, ethnic, and socioeconomic groups. This is probably the best immediate way of improving the likelihood that the interests of the consumers of reproductive technologies will be fairly represented in making of policy decisions.

But will this be enough to prevent the NRTs from being used coercively? Will women in the future be *required* to submit to IVF treatments, in order that their embryos may be screened for imperfections, genetically engineered, or replaced with embryos derived from "superior" individuals? This could happen only if our most basic civil liberties were lost. However, basic civil liberties, especially those affecting reproductive rights, are still far from adequate, and could easily be lost. In Australia, the legal status of abortion is still somewhat ambiguous.[20] And in the United States, the right to legal abortion may stand or fall upon the confirmation or rejection by the Senate of a single Supreme Court nominee.

This fact provides reason for continued feminist struggle; but it does not provide support for the suppression of all reproductive technologies that can be used coercively. Women's reproductive autonomy cannot be secured through such suppression. The history of coercive population control programs, e.g., in India and China, amply demonstrates that even the older—but still most important—reproductive technologies of contraception and abortion can be coercively used. Yet it is also clear that the *suppression* of contraception and abortion could virtually ensure the reproductive enslavement of women, as it has in the past. Nor do coercive eugenics programs require new reproductive technologies. The Nazi genocides of World War II, which are often cited as grounds for rejecting new technologies that could be used to implement immoral eugenics programs, clearly demonstrate that innovative biotechnology is not essential for the commission of atrocities in the name of eugenics. For these reasons, the defense of basic civil rights seems to be a more promising way of preventing the implementation of immoral eugenics programs than the suppression of reproductive technologies.

More to be feared, perhaps, is the covertly coercive force of social expectation. New technologies often have a momentum of their own; once they exist, they are likely to be seen as pragmatically and morally superior to any less highly technological option, even when the reverse may be the case. Some feminists argue that the very existence of IVF as a treatment for female infertility increases the pressures on infertile women to keep on trying until they have exhausted every possible treatment for their infertility.[21] The prevailing pronatalist ideology may thereby be strengthened, and the social stigma and suffering of all infertile women increased.

This is a realistic concern. The possibility of an IVF baby, however slight, may make it harder for infertile women to accept their condition and get on with their lives, or to defend the childlessness they may prefer. So too, the new methods for the prenatal diagnosis and selective abortion of defective fetuses may be eroding women's freedom *not* to try to control the quality of their children, but simply to accept them as they are.[22] But this subtle erosion of freedom is not inevitable. Women can learn to exercise the legal right to refuse medical interventions that they do not need or want. We shall also have to work to retain that legal right, and to extend it in some areas.[23] These are difficult tasks, but they are tasks that would be no less essential if there were no *new* reproductive technologies.

5. The Final Solution?

Perhaps the most alarming scenario suggested by some critics of the NRTs is that women may be altogether eliminated from the reproductive process.[24] Once ectogenesis is perfected, natural pregnancy may come to be seen as dangerous and irresponsible; it may even be outlawed. Some speculate further, that once men have ectogenesis they will see no reason for women to exist at all, and consequently will create an all-male world.

But neither of these scenarios is likely to come about. Even if there were a realistic prospect for the achievement of total (i.e., conception-to-birth) ectogenesis in the nonremote future—which there is not—there would be little danger that ectogenesis will replace uterine gestation as the usual way of making babies. It will almost certainly be economically impossible to replace natural wombs with artificial ones. Extrauterine gestation, should it become possible, could hardly be much less expensive than contemporary neonatal intensive care. Thus, it would be beyond the reach of all but the very wealthy. This is an excellent reason for not devoting massive public resources to the attempt to develop methods of total ectogenesis. But it also shows that even if ectogenesis were perfected tomorrow, the elimination of natural pregnancy would remain a remote possibility.

It is still less likely that artificial gestation would threaten women's continued existence. Robyn Rowland asks, as man gets closer to reproducing himself, what forces can possibly stop him? . . . Will this last act of power make women obsolete; permanently unemployed; disposable?[25] Ectogenesis would likely lead to women's perceived obsolescence only if women were valued exclusively or primarily for our reproductive function. But that is clearly false, even in the most highly patriarchal societies. There are, no doubt, many men who agree in principle with Thomas Aquinas's dictum that women were created to help men in the work of reproduction, and *only* in that work "since [a] man can be more efficiently helped by another man in other works."[26] There is, and perhaps has always been, a strong current of misogyny in much male culture. Yet most men still regard heterosexual practices as preferable to the alternatives—and not just because of the reproductive function of these practices. More importantly, perhaps, women's paid and unpaid labor is essential to the functioning of virtually every social and economic institution throughout the world. Few men are willing to undertake the tasks of homemaking and childrearing without female assistance. If there has been a central patriarchal project, it has been to control women and channel their energies into the service of male needs—not to eliminate women, which would be self-defeating.[27]

6. The Mystique of Motherhood

There is a deeper reason why some women are angered and alarmed by the NRTs. Some have argued the increased control of the female reproductive process which the NRTs give (certain) men will be detrimental to women's social status and sense of personal agency. These feminist critics maintain that women's procreativity has long been a source of social power, but that the NRTs are progressively robbing us of that power. Corea deplores the way that, "Woman, once deified as the life-creating Goddess, is now lying on a table with her mouth taped shut, having the eggs sucked out of her body."[28] Rowland says,

> How powerful we have always seemed; we who can bleed regularly and not die; we who can grow another human being inside our own bodies. Dubious though it has been in real terms, this has since "primitive" times been a source of mythical power for women when all else was kept from them. For many women it is the only experience of power they will ever have.[29]

Despite these eloquent pleas, I doubt that the NRTs are depriving women of any important source of social power which we now enjoy, or once enjoyed. The contrast between the hypothetical days when women were worshipped as the sole givers of life, and the new age in which some women need medical assistance in order to conceive, is probably less great than is sometimes supposed. Women may have sought supernatural or "professional" help in conceiving since prehistoric times. Neolithic images of fecund women predate the written word by tens of thousands of years. These images seem to express an awe of female procreativity; but they may have also had a practical use, e.g., as fertility charms. There is little reason to believe that early fertility magic was

entirely in the hands of women—though it may have been. In any case, the essential role of the male in conception has been known in most societies for at least several millennia. Thus, if the resort to male assistance inevitably undermines the awe of female fertility, then women in earlier times may have derived less social power from this source than is sometimes assumed.

There are other reasons for doubting the practical value of whatever mystical power may be ascribed to the female role in procreation. The power that supposedly flows from motherhood is often cited by apologists for patriarchy, as a reason why women have no need for other forms of power or even for personal autonomy. These apologists would have us believe that the hand that rocks the cradle rules the world—even if the hand's owner is deprived of the most basic civil liberties. But such "power" is a poor substitute for social, economic, and political equality. It may even make life worse for women. The suspicion of mystical or supernatural power, especially when associated with women, inspires not just respect, but fear and hostility. The women who were burned as witches at the dawn of the so-called age of reason had good reason to wish that they had not been credited with supernatural agency.

What feminists want, or should want, for women is not the largely symbolic power that comes from the awe of female procreativity, but respect for women as persons. Persons are due respect, not primarily because of the mystical powers that may act in or through them, but because of their capacity to think, feel, and act. The power to act effectively is achieved through the use of "our intellects, our imaginations, and our capacity for collective action."[30] The mystification of motherhood can do little to enhance that power. On the contrary, it would seem more apt to encourage the notion that women's "natural task . . . [is] accomplished by being rather than doing."[31] It may also reinforce the tendency to view women less as persons than as parts of "alien Nature," vessels of a force that is awesome but not entirely human.[32] If the new reproductive technologies, by subjecting some female reproductive processes to apparently greater control, serve to undermine that mystification, then the appropriate feminist reaction may be, "So much the better."

7. The Social Causes of Female Infertility

I have saved for last what may be the most important feminist objection to IVF. It is an objection not to the continuation of IVF programs at some level of funding, but rather to the relative neglect of potentially more effective ways of approaching the problem.

Involuntary infertility has always been a problem for some women, and (though this was less often recognized) some men. Whether it currently affects a larger proportion of women than in previous generations is unclear, though many believe that it does. The causes of human infertility are not well understood, but neither are they entirely mysterious. A study of 708 couples attending fertility clinics in one part of England found that in 28 percent of cases the cause of the failure to conceive could not be identified, while in 26 percent, the problem was on the male side.[33] The most common cause of female infertility was ovulatory failure, which apparently responded very well to treatment; the pregnancy rate after two years was approximately 96 percent. The next most common cause was infective damage to the fallopian tubes; here, the outlook was much poorer, with only about 19 percent conceiving after two years, despite surgery and other treatments. IVF was originally developed primarily for the treatment of this kind of female infertility, though it is now also used in some cases where the cause of the woman's infertility is unclear, or where the problem is due to some defect in the male's sperm.

For some infertile women or couples, for whom other treatments have failed, IVF probably offers the best remaining hope of biological parenthood—though it is often a rather slim hope. But it would obviously be better to prevent infertility in the first place, if this were possible. Much female infertility is socially caused, and probably could have been prevented. Prevention and cure are obviously not mutually exclusive approaches. But feminist critics have argued that the primary focus of the medical profession and the society as a whole has been too much on the treatment of infertility and too little on its prevention, and that the publicity given to IVF is symptomatic of this imbalance. In Heather Dietrich's words,

IVF is valenced towards a medical, high-tech solution rather than the prevention of infertility. . . . It will emphasize and extend the isolation and analysis of fertility, as a discrete process, rather than [contributing to] a holistic approach to fertility within a woman's body and life.[34]

A more holistic approach to the problem of infertility would include an investigation of the social, as well as the physiological, causes of involuntary infertility. One group of social causes comprises a large range of sexual and contraceptive practices. As noted above, much female infertility is caused by infective damage to the fallopian tubes. Such infections are, in the majority of cases, sexually transmitted; and sexual practices and modes of contraception can affect the likelihood of contracting such sexually transmitted diseases (STDs).

Other things being equal, the more sexual partners a woman has, and the more partners each of them has had, the greater her risk of contracting an infection which will eventually damage her fertility. Thus, some might be tempted simply to blame the apparent increase in this form of female infertility on the so-called sexual revolution, which has meant that more women have become sexually active earlier, and have had, on the average, more sexual partners. But this would be a mistake. The sexual revolution need not have led to an increase in the incidence of STDs, or in consequent infertility. If it has, this is due in part to the kinds of contraceptives and prophylactics that have—or have not—been used. Some contraceptives are known to increase the danger of pelvic inflammatory disease (PID). IUDs, for instance, can cause acute or chronic inflammation, and are associated with a 600 percent increase in PID.[35] Hormone-based contraceptives also appear, at least in some cases, to increase susceptibility to PID. In contrast, barrier methods, particularly condoms, and particularly when used in combination with spermicides, provide a fair degree of protection against most STDs—although they also tend to be somewhat less effective in preventing pregnancy. For maximum protection against both unwanted pregnancy and the transmission of infection, heterosexual couples who have not practiced long-term monogamy probably should use both condoms and some female contraceptive. But, for a variety of reasons, most do not.

The particular sexual activities in which people commonly engage may also increase the risk of infertility. Heterosexual intercourse, of the kind usually described as "normal" or "ordinary" is much more likely to transmit infection than either oral sex or masturbation (mutual or solitary). If the orientation of the majority of adults towards such "normal" sexual practice is an inalterable result of human biology, as most assume, then social mores can make little difference to this particular cause of infertility. But if, as some have argued, heterosexuality and the ways in which it is commonly expressed are social institutions rather than strictly natural phenomena,[36] then some of these institutions must be included among the social causes of infertility.

There are many other social causes of infertility. Exposure to toxic substances, in the workplace and the general environment, is certainly involved in some cases. Among the poor, inadequate nutrition, generally poor health, and limited access to health care are often contributing factors. Where abortion is illegal or beyond the reach of many women, improperly performed abortions are a common cause of infertility—and often death. Poor women are sometimes surgically sterilized against their will, or without an understanding of the permanence of the procedure. Because their other options are likely to be more limited, poor women are also more likely to choose surgical sterilization, and some of them may later regret that decision. Unnecessary hysterectomies and other surgical procedures are another cause of involuntary infertility. In parts of Africa and the Middle East, the complications of genital mutilation ("female circumcision") undoubtedly cause much infertility.[37]

While this is not a complete list of the social causes of female infertility, it is enough to show that they are many and varied. Some, such as involuntary sterilization and unnecessary surgery, are clear abuses. Few would dispute the need to prevent such abuses, though there is much debate about just how commonly they occur. Some, such as the lack of legal, safe, and affordable abortion in much of the world, could readily be remedied through changes in the law, but there is bitter controversy about the morality of such changes. And some, such as the relative frequency of "ordinary" heterosexual intercourse, would probably be extremely resistant to change, even if we could agree that such change would be desirable.

Thus, there can be no simple solution to the problem of socially caused involuntary infertility. Yet there is room for a wider societal response to that problem. That response should include a more concerted effort to develop safer new contraceptives and to improve the older barrier methods. Often, it will need to include a more equitable distribution of medical resources, and better access to contraception and abortion—and to some of the NRTs. But the first step should be the better dissemination of information about ways of protecting oneself and others from the more common and preventable causes of infertility.

The international AIDS epidemic has led to a widespread recognition of a distinction between "safe" and "unsafe" sex. Although AIDS can be transmitted in many ways besides sexual contact, that mode of transmission is common, and some sexual practices are evidently more dangerous than others in this regard. Thus, in many parts of the world, public information campaigns and school sex education programs are being created or supplemented to teach basic facts about AIDS, how it is transmitted, and how the danger of transmission can be minimized.

A skeptical feminist might wonder whether it is coincidental that this public concern with safer sexual practices has arisen only when—perhaps for the first time ever—more men than women are suffering some of the most lethal consequences of unsafe sexual practices.[38] On the other hand, gay rights advocates may be correct in their suspicion that more might have been done to help the victims of AIDS and to stop the spread of the illness, had not so many of these victims been homosexual males. Yet, however belated or inadequate, the new openness to the dissemination of information about relatively safe and unsafe sexual practices, prophylactics, and the like, is surely a positive development. This new openness may facilitate the prevention of other STDs as well, including those that—though not usually fatal—can lead to infertility.

But the idea that making sex safer is a legitimate public goal meets strong opposition from sexual and religious conservatives. Right-wing groups have long opposed attempts to ameliorate the harmful consequences of sexual activity, e.g., through the legalization of contraception and abortion, sex education in schools, or the public advertising of condoms and other contraceptives. They believe that women who do not want to have children should either avoid heterosexual intercourse altogether, or "accept the consequences," and that anyone who wants to avoid contracting a sexually transmitted disease should either remain celibate or practice lifelong monogamy with a partner who does likewise.

These attitudes have had a considerable influence, particularly in societies strongly influenced by Christianity. In effect, both "Pregnancy and disease have been pervasively and systematically used to inhibit sexual activity."[39] This punitive attitude is often based upon the distinctively—though not universally—Christian idea that all sexual activity is inherently sinful, except that which is apt for the production of children within a monogamous marriage. (This exception is only partial, since some Christian authorities have held that even procreative marital sexual intercourse can be sinful, if it is motivated by lust.) From this perspective, it can seem entirely appropriate, a kind of natural justice, that those who engage in nonmonogamous or nonprocreative sexual activities should be penalized by unwanted pregnancies, sexually transmitted diseases, and perhaps infertility. Attempts to prevent these harmful consequences of unsafe sex will therefore be seen as encouraging immoral sexual behavior.

Far from receding into the past, this punitive attitude towards much human sexual activity may currently be gaining strength, at least in some parts of the world. In this social context, it is doubly unrealistic to approach involuntary female infertility as though it were basically a medical problem. Improving IVF and other medical treatments for infertility would remain an important goal even if all of the social causes of infertility were eliminated, since not all infertility is socially caused. But there is some danger that the enormous publicity attendant upon the development of IVF and other NRTs will foster the illusion that the problem of involuntary infertility is being largely solved, when it is not.

8. Conclusion

Taken together, these objections are sufficient to cast some doubt upon the net value of IVF to women. They do not, however, support the conclusion that a just concern for women's interests demands the elimination of IVF and other NRTs. The costs and risks of IVF treatments to the female patient are substantial, but they are not known to be so great as to clearly outweigh the potential benefits in every case. Pronatalist ideology may put undue pressure upon infertile women to submit to IVF, but so long as potential IVF patients are adequately informed about the costs, risks, and odds of success, such covert social pressures need not make valid consent impossible.

Feminists are rightly concerned that if the NRTs continue to be developed and delivered by largely male teams, women's interests will not be as well served as they ought to be. The interests of women and men will be affected in different ways by the development of these technologies. Insofar as it is women who more often undergo invasive and/or potentially dangerous medical procedures associated with the NRTs, their interests are somewhat more centrally affected. Women should, therefore, be at least equally represented in the development of these technologies. Members of various racial, ethnic, or socioeconomic groups may also have special needs, or be especially vulnerable to harmful uses or abuses of the NRTs, and they too should be represented.

There is a need for more participation by women in all aspects of the practice, funding, and supervision of such biomedical research, as well as in the provision of medical care. Some of the ways in which the medical and research professions have been structured have served, perhaps inadvertently, as barriers to women, and other "minority" groups in these professions. The members of those professions have an obligation to remove those barriers—not by lowering standards, but by altering institutions and practices that discriminate needlessly against some competent individuals.

Even with greater participation by women in the development of the NRTs, there will remain some danger that the NRTs will contribute to the subtle erosion of women's reproductive autonomy. The use of new reproductive technologies might in time become legally or socially mandatory even for (some) fertile women, e.g., as a way of implementing eugenic goals. But this danger can better be counteracted by protecting individual civil rights than by seeking to eliminate the new reproductive technologies

If these conclusions are correct, then IVF is probably a justifiable means of attempting to overcome infertility. But IVF can help only a small proportion of infertile women and men, and it inflicts heavy costs and risks on all who undergo it. It can, therefore, be only a small part of an adequate societal response to the problem of involuntary infertility.

One major element of a more adequate societal response to that problem is the better dissemination of knowledge about the preventable causes of infertility, e.g., those associated with particular sexual practices and contraceptive methods. A more concerted effort should also be made to develop safer (and cheaper) contraceptives and prophylactics, especially of the kinds that protect against both pregnancy and the transmission of STDs. Contraceptives, safe abortion, and other kinds of medical care need to be available to all women, including those who are underage or unable to pay. These are practical goals, which need not be prohibitively expensive, and which have already been at least partially achieved in some places.

If more is done to counteract the social causes of infertility, there may eventually be less need for IVF. Yet IVF may remain the best (medical) approach to the treatment of some forms of infertility. Thus, it is too soon to conclude that this new reproductive technology will not serve women's interests. If women and other underrepresented groups can gain a larger presence in the medical and research professions, and if suitable modes of regulation can be implemented, then the NRTs may provide more benefits than dangers. If not, then feminists may be right to remain somewhat skeptical about the long-term value of these new technologies for women.

NOTES

1. See, for instance, G. R. Dunstan, 'The Ethical Debate,' in *In Vitro Fertilisation: Past, Present, Future*, edited by S. Fishel and E. M. Symonds (Oxford, Washington, D.C: IRL Press, 1986): and Brian Johnstone, Helga Kuhse and Peter Singer, 'The Moral Status of the Embryo: Two Viewpoints,' in *Test-Tube Babies: A Guide to the Moral Questions, Present Techniques, and Future Possibilities*, edited by William Walters and Peter Singer (Melbourne: Oxford University Press, 1982), pp. 49–64.

2. See Paul Ramsey, *Fabricated Man: The Ethics of Genetic Control* (New Haven and London, Yale University Press, 1974), and Leon Kass, 'New Beginnings in Life,' in *The New Genetics and the Future of Man* (Grand Rapids, Michigan: Eerdman's Publishing, 1972), pp. 53–54.

3. In some IVF programmes, e.g., that at the Monash Medical Centre in Victoria, the collection of ova through laparoscopy is being superceded by the use of ultrasound to guide the aspiration needle. This procedure can be performed without surgery, and usually with only local anaesthesia. However, laparoscopy remains the method in use in many other IVF programmes. (See H. Wickland, L. Hamberger and L. Enk, 'Ultrasound for Oocyte Recovery,' in *In Vitro Fertilisation*, edited by S. Fishel and E. M. Symonds (Oxford and Washington D.C: IRL Press, 1986), pp. 69–76.)

4. For a more extensive discussion of the medical risks of IVF treatment see Gena Corea, *The Mother Machine: Reproductive Technologies from Artificial Insemination to Artificial Wombs* (New York: Harper and Row, 1985), pp. 149–59.

5. Estimates of the success rate of IVF treatment range from 4% to 25%. Not surprisingly, the critics of IVF tend to favour the lower estimates, while the proponents favour the higher.

6. Corea, pp. 167–9.

7. See Janet Winfield, 'Reproduction, Technology and the Search for Reproduction Control and Freedom—A Question of Choice,' a paper presented at the National Conference on Reproductive Technologies, sponsored by the National Feminist Network on Reproductive Technology, Canberra, May 1986 (hereafter referred to as the "Canberra conference").

8. See Lori B. Andrews, 'Remaking Conception and Pregnancy: How the Laws Influence Reproductive Technology,' *Frontiers* 9:1 (1986), pp. 36–40, and Amadeo F. D'Adamo Jr. and Elaine Hoffman Baruch, 'Whither the Womb? Myths, Machines, and Mothers,' *op, cit,* pp. 72–79.

9. Corea, p. 170. See also Robyn Rowland, 'Choice or Control? Women and Our Relationship to the New Reproductive Technologies,' (Canberra conference, 1986).

10. Rebecca Albury, 'Who Owns the Embryo?' in *Test-Tube Women: What Future for Motherhood?*, edited by Rita Arditti, Renate Duelli Klein and Shelly Minden (London: Pandora Press, 1984), p. 57.

11. See, for instance, Lois Leiderman Davitz, *Baby Hunger: Every Woman's Longing for a Baby* (Minneapolis: Winston Press, 1984).

12. Lynne M. Foltrow, review of *Test-Tube Women, Women's Rights Law Reporter* 8:4 (1985), p. 307.

13. Mary O'Brien, *The Politics of Reproduction* (London and Boston: Routledge and Kegan Paul, 1981).

14. See Mary Daly, *Gynaecology: The Metaethics of Radical Feminism* (Boston: Beacon Press, 1978), p. 224. The history of the suppression of female healers and midwives is well documented in Barbara Ehrenreich and Deirdre English, *Witches, Midwives and Nurses: A History of Women Healers* (Old Westbury, New York: The Feminist Press, 1973).

15. The primary reason for the higher incidence of often-fatal puerperal fever among women attended by male physicians in the seventeenth through nineteenth centuries appears to be that male physicians, unlike traditional midwives, not only attended women in labour, but also treated persons with infectious diseases. Consequently, although they may not have washed their hands any less frequently than the midwives did, they spread far more infection. See Daly, pp. 236–7, and Adrienne Rich, *Of Woman Born: Motherhood as Experience and Institution* (London: Virago, 1977), p. 151.

16. See, for instance, Robert H. Keyser, *Women Under the Knife* (New York: Warner Books, Inc., 1984).

17. Obstetrics continues to impose upon birthing women a great many interventions, the therapeutic value of which has never satisfactorily been demonstrated. These include the routine induction and augmentation of labour; routine use of ultrasound; electronic fetal monitoring; artificial rupture of membranes; enemas and perineal shaves; routine episiotomy; the use of forceps and vacuum extraction; routine use of analgesic drugs and epidurals; and the current high rates of Caesarian section. (See Belinda Court and Carolyn Noble Spruel, 'Report on Discussion in Workshop on Politics of Homebirth,' (Canberra conference, 1986).

18. Irene Elia, *The Female Animal* (Oxford, New York, Tokyo: Oxford University Press, 1985), p. 280.

19. Corea, p. 93.

20. In all Australian states there are sections of various acts that make it a crime to *unlawfully* perform or procure an abortion. In most states, these statutes—which were once used to prohibit all or almost all abortions—remain in force, but case law has progressively expanded the class of abortions that are not considered unlawful. In South Australia, the statute dealing with abortion states specific exceptions to the general prohibition, e.g., abortions that are necessary to preserve the woman's life, or her physical or mental health, or when there is a substantial risk of fetal malformation. Such exceptions can be interpreted as including most actual abortions. However, because the exceptions cannot entirely negate the rule, there is necessarily in each state some class of abortions which remain illegal. The definition of that class is highly ambiguous, since each exception can be interpreted more or less liberally. Thus, although abortion is readily available in most of (the urban areas) of Australia, those who perform or procure abortions do so in the face of some uncertainty about the legality of their actions.

21. See, for example, Marion Brown, 'Female Infertility—Causes, Options, Priorites and IVF' (Canberra conference, 1986), p. 3.

22. Barbara Katz Rothman, *The Tentative Pregnancy: Prenatal Diagnosis and the Future of Motherhood* (New York: Viking Press, 1986), p. 11.

23. The legal right of competent adults to refuse medical treatment is not absolute. In the United States, a number of women have been forced by court order to undergo Caesarean sections against their will. A San Diego woman, whose son was born with brain damage and consequently died, was charged with negligent child abuse for not following physician's instructions during her pregnancy (she was, however, acquitted).

24. See Robyn Rowland, 'Reproductive Technologies: The Final Solution to the Woman Question?' in *Test-Tube Women*, pp. 356–369.

25. Rowland, 'Reproductive Technologies,' p. 365.

26. Thomas Aquinas, *Summa Theologica*, Vol. 1, Part 1, Question 92, Article I (New York: Benziger Brothers, 1947, p. 466).

27. This claim might appear to be contradicted by the widespread practice of female infanticide; generally speaking, the poorer a society, and the more severely patriarchal, the fewer female infants are likely to be raised. But female infanticide shows only that families are reluctant to raise female children, not that adult women are not in demand; where female infanticide creates a shortage of adult women, men often wage war to capture women from other groups.

28. Corea, p. 176.

29. Rowland, 'Reproductive Technologies,' p. 363.

30. Poltrow, p. 304.

31. John Stuart Mill, *Early Essays on Marriage and Divorce*, in *Essays on Sex Equality*, edited by Alice Rossi (Chicago and London: University of Chicago Press, 1979), p. 77.

32. See Simone de Beauvoir, *The Second Sex* (New York, London, Tornot: Bantam Books, 1961), p. 63.

33. M. G. R. Hill, 'Infertility: Nature and Extent of the Problem,' In *Human Embryo Research: Yes or No?* (London and New York: Tavistock Publications, 1986), pp. 25–34.

34. Heather Dietrich, 'IVF: What Can We Do?' (Canberra conference), p. 8.

35. Population Information Programme, Johns Hopkins University, 'Infertility and Sexually Transmitted Disease: A Public Health Challenge,' *Population Reports*, Series L(4), July 1983; cited by Adele Clark, 'Subtle Forms of Sterilisation Abuse: A Reproductive Rights Analysis', in *Test-Tube Women*, p. 199.

36. See for instance, Adrienne Rich, 'Compulsory Hetero-sexuality and Lesbian Existence,' *Signs: Journal of Women in Culture and Society* 5:4 (Summer 1980), pp. 631–60.

37. See Fran P. Hosken, *The Hosken Report: Genital and Sexual Mutilation of Females* (Lexington, Massachusetts: Women's International Network News, 1979), and Asma El Daree, *Woman Why Do You Weep? Circumcision and Its Consequences* (London: Zed Press, 1982).

38. While in much of the world, the great majority of AIDS victims are men, in some parts of Africa the disease seems to affect women and children just about as often.

39. Cindy Patton, *Sex and Germs: The Politics of AIDS* (Boston: South End Press, 1985), p. 10.

"Give Me Children or I Shall Die!" New Reproductive Technologies and Harm to Children

CYNTHIA B. COHEN

Cohen points out that some evidence indicates that reproductive technologies cause serious illness and defects in a small percentage of children. She argues that if these technologies do in fact cause such harm, it would be wrong to use them. Some who disagree put forth the "Interest in Existing Argument," which says that even if the new technologies caused children to be born with serious disorders, the harm done would be morally permissible (except in rare cases) because "it is better to be alive—even with serious disease and deficits—than not." Cohen sees several problems in this argument. For one thing, she says, it is based on the false assumption that "children with an interest in existing are waiting in a spectral world of nonexistence where their situation is less desirable than it would be were they released into this world."

"Be fruitful and multiply," God urged newly created humans. Those who take this command to heart cherish the opportunity to procreate and nurture children, to pass on their individual traits and family heritage to their offspring. Having children, for many, is a deeply significant experience that offers overall meaning for their lives. Not all who wish to do so, however, can fulfill the biblical injunction to multiply. Those who cannot often experience a terrible sense of loss. Rachel, in Genesis, felt such despair over her failure to conceive that she cried out to Jacob, "Give me children, or I shall die!" Some who echo her cry today turn to the new reproductive technologies.

There are ethical limits, however, to what may be done to obtain long-sought offspring. Having a deep desire and even a need for something does

not justify doing anything whatsoever to obtain it. If the means used to bring children into the world were to create substantial harm to others or to these very children, this would provide strong moral reason not to employ them. It would be wrong, for instance, for infertile couples to place women at risk of substantial harm by enticing those who are not in peak physical condition to "donate" eggs with handsome sums of money. By the same token, it would be wrong to use reproductive technologies to create children if this bore a significant chance of producing serious disease and impairments in these very children. Questions are being raised about whether in vitro fertilization (IVF) and other reproductive technologies do, in fact, create serious illness and deficits in a small but significant proportion of children who are born of them. If these technologies were found to do so, it would be wrong to forge ahead with their use.

Yet advocates of procreative liberty reject this seemingly inescapable conclusion. They contend that even if children were born with serious disorders traceable to their origin in the new reproductive technologies, this would not, except in rare cases, provide moral reason to refrain from using them. Those who conclude otherwise, they maintain, do not understand the peculiar sort of substantial harm to which children born of these novel reproductive means are susceptible. Surely, John Robertson and like-minded thinkers claim, it is better to be alive—even with serious disease and deficits—than not. And these children would not be alive, but for the use of the new reproductive techniques. Therefore, they argue, these children cannot be substantially harmed by the use of these means to bring them into the world. Only if they are caused by these technologies to suffer devastating illness that makes life worse than nonexistence can they be said to be substantially harmed by them.

This startling claim raises intriguing questions. What do we mean by substantial harm—particularly when children who might experience it have not yet been conceived? What degree of disease and suffering that a child would experience as a result of the application of these novel means of conception would make it wrong to use them? Would it be wrong if the child's life would be so terrible that nonexistence would be better? Few conditions would be excluded by this standard. Would it be wrong if the child's life would not be awful, but would include major physical impairments, severe mental disability and/or considerable pain and suffering?

In responding to such questions, we must consider the possibility that different standards of substantial harm may apply to children at the time when we consider conceiving them and after conception and birth. If so, we must develop a standard of substantial harm that applies to children who might be conceived that is distinct from one that applies to those already born—and must explain how children who are not born can be harmed. We must also address the concern that decisions not to conceive children because they would have serious deficits devalue the lives of those already living who were born with such deficits. Finally, we must grapple with the question of what parents and infertility specialists ought to do in the current state of inadequate knowledge about the effects of the new reproductive technologies on the children who result from their use.

The Harm to Children Argument

To ask what it means to attribute substantial harm to children who result from the new reproductive technologies is not just to pose an interesting abstract question. Studies indicate this may be a very practical, real question, as they raise the possibility that these technologies may create serious deficits in some proportion of the children born of them. To get a sense of the harms at issue, let us consider the claims of critics of the use of these technologies about their effect on the children born of them.

A primary harm that they attribute to the use of the new reproductive technologies is physical damage. Few long-term studies have been undertaken of the kinds and rates of physical diseases and abnormalities incurred by children born of the new reproductive technologies. Moreover, the evidence these investigations provide is conflicting. Australia is the only country that has kept statistics on the condition at birth *and* subsequent progress of children born of IVF since the inception of this technique in the late 1970s. Data from that country indicate that these children are two or three times more likely to suffer such serious diseases as spina bifida and transposition of the great vessels (a heart abnormality). Australian data also suggest that some drugs used to stimulate women's ovaries to produce multiple oocytes in preparation for IVF increase the risk of serious birth impairments in the resulting children. Other investigations and commentators support this finding.[1] Still other reports, however, suggest that there is no increase in disorders at birth among children resulting from the use of the new reproductive technologies.[2] One small American follow-up study of the health status of children born of IVF and gamete intrafallopian transfer (GIFT) could find no significant differences in the rate of physical or neurological abnormalities in children born of techniques of assisted conception.[3] No controlled study to date, however, has incorporated an adequate sample size or sufficiently long follow-up monitoring period to determine accurately the risk of physical disorders associated with children born of IVF.

And little is known about the physiological impact on children who result from such other procedures as embryo freezing, gamete donation, zona drilling, and intracytoplasmic sperm injection.

It is well known that the higher rate of multiple births in IVF due to the implantation of several embryos in the uterus at a time contributes to an increased rate of preterm and low birth-weight babies. This, in turn, is associated with a higher incidence of perinatal, neonatal, and infant mortality in children conceived by IVF than those conceived coitally.[4] In France, for instance, the rates of prematurity and intrauterine growth retardation among IVF births in a two-year period were 16 percent and 14 percent respectively, whereas the expected rates for the general population were 7 percent and 3 percent.[5] An analysis of IVF outcome data from France between 1986 and 1990 indicated that perinatal mortality among IVF births also was higher than that in the general population, even when data were stratified according to gestational number. French neonatologists who had worked to prevent low birth weight, congenital anomalies, and genetic disorders among newborns observed that "[n]ow, we suddenly find our NICU filled with high-risk newborns . . . [as a result of the expansion of IVF services]."

Critics also express concern that the new reproductive technologies may jeopardize the psychological and social welfare of the children who result from them, particularly when they involve third parties in donor or surrogacy arrangements and depend on secrecy.[6] These children, they hypothesize, will view themselves as manufactured products, rather than distinctive individuals born of love between a man and a woman.[7] They will be denied the stable sense of identity that comes from knowing their biological heritage and family lineage should their rearing parents differ from their genetic parents.[8] Moreover, the social stigma these children will experience when others learn that they were conceived by these novel means will increase their difficulties, opponents contend. Little research is available on the effect of the use of assisted reproduction on the psychosocial development of the resulting children. In the first controlled study of family relationships

and the psychological development of children created by the new reproductive technologies, no group differences in the emotions, behavior, or relationships with parents between children born of assisted reproduction and children conceived naturally or adopted could be found.[9]

One commentator summarizes the issues of harm raised by the use of the new reproductive technologies as follows:

> The technology for both IVF and GIFT as well as adjunct technologies such as zona drilling, embryo freezing, and gamete donation have not been accompanied by careful scrutiny and analysis of the risks involved. Indeed, even when risks are clearly established (as with multiple pregnancy), there has been no discernible attempt to reduce these risks by altering procedures and protocols. There also has been an appalling lack of follow-up studies to determine the long-term health, psychological, and social consequence of these procedures.[10]

In view of the current lack of systematic knowledge about difficulties these methods may create in children born of them, opponents of the new reproductive technologies maintain it is wrong to use them. Those who resort to these techniques, they claim, bear the burden of proof of their safety. They have an obligation to establish whether these ever-increasing methods of assisted reproduction do, in fact, harm a small but significant proportion of children before they are used. For ease of reference, we will call their claims the Harm to Children Argument against the use of the new reproductive technologies.

The Interest in Existing Argument

The basic response to the Harm to Children Argument by several proponents of the use of the new reproductive technologies,[11] of whom John Robertson is a respected spokesperson, is that even if children born of the new reproductive technologies were to suffer serious impairments as a result of their origin, this would not necessarily render it wrong to use these techniques. We might call this response the Interest in Existing Argument: since it is, in almost all cases, better to be alive than not, and these children would not be alive but for the employment of these techniques, using them to bring these children into the world is justified. Robertson writes:

> [A] higher incidence of birth defects in such off-spring would not justify banning the technique in order to protect the offspring, because without these techniques these children would not have been born at all. Unless their lives are so full of suffering as to be worse than no life at all, a very unlikely supposition, the defective children of such a union have not been harmed if they would not have been born healthy.[12]

Only where "from the perspective of the child, viewed solely in light of his interests as he is then situated, any life at all with the conditions of his birth would be so harmful to him that from his perspective he would prefer not to live,"[13] could it be said to be a substantial harm to have been brought into existence by means of the new reproductive technologies.

Robertson here implicitly distinguishes between *devastating harm*—harm that brings such suffering into a person's life that this life is worse than no life at all—[and] *serious harm*—harm that does not render life worse than death, but that includes such detriments as major physical impairments, severe mental disability, and/or considerable pain and suffering. He labels only the former *substantial harm*. Indeed, at certain points, Robertson maintains that children damaged by their origin in the new reproductive technologies cannot be said to suffer harm at all, since their birth is an overriding benefit.

The Harm to Children Argument is logically flawed, Robertson and like-minded thinkers maintain, because the benefit of life that children born of these techniques receive outweighs almost any detriment they might experience as a result of their origins. Robertson notes:

> Preventing harm would mean preventing the birth of the child whose interests one is trying to protect. Yet a child's interests are hardly protected by preventing the child's existence. If the child has no way to be born or raised free of that harm, a person is not injuring the child by enabling her to be born in the circumstances of concern.[14]

It is not open to children damaged by the use of the new reproductive technologies to live free of impairment, since they could not have existed without the use of these technologies. The alternative for them would have been not to live at all, a state which is not in their interests. Consequently, according to the Interest in Existing Argument, it is, in almost all instances, in the interests of children who might be born of the new reproductive technologies to be brought into the world by these means, even if this would risk serious harm to them.

This argument applies only to children who suffer harm that is a necessary result of the use of these techniques. Thus, if it were claimed that contract surrogacy creates psychological harm for a child because the biological mother and rearing parents would be in a constant state of conflict with each other, the Interest in Existing Argument could not be used in response. This is because the warring trio could behave in a different manner less likely to cause this sort of harm to the child. According to advocates of the Interest in Existing Argument it was not a necessary condition of the child's very existence that the conflict among these various parents occur.

The Harm of Not Existing

The Interest in Existing Argument assumes that children with an interest in existing are waiting in a spectral world of nonexistence where their situation is less desirable than it would be were they released into this world. This presupposition is revealed by such observations as "a child's interests are hardly protected by preventing the child's existence" and that it is a disadvantage to such children that they "have no way of being born." In the Interest in Existing Argument children who might be conceived are pictured as pale preexisting entities with an interest in moving into the more full-blooded reality of this world. Their admission into this realm is thwarted by the failure to use available new reproductive technologies. This failure negates their interest in existing and thereby harms them.

Before a person exists, however, he or she does not reside in some other domain. Prior to conception, there is *no one who waits to be brought into this world*. Joel Feinberg argues, "Since it is necessary to *be* if one is to *be better off*, it is a logical contradiction to say that someone could be better off though not in existence."[15] To say that it was good for someone already in existence to have been born does not imply that his existence in this world is better than his life in some other realm. Nor does it imply that if he had not been caused to exist, this would have been bad for him.[16] Although a wealth of possible children can be conceived, their interests cannot be diminished if they are not. Therefore, it cannot be coherently argued that it is "better" for children to be created by means of the new reproductive technologies, even when this would result in serious disorders to them, since there is no alternative state in which their lot could be worse.

Part of the confusion at the heart of the Interest in Existing Argument stems from an incoherence found in tort actions for "wrongful life," to which this argument has an acknowledged debt. In these suits, children born with impairments claim that their current condition is worse than the state of nonexistence they would have had were it not for negligence on the part of physicians, hospitals, or testing laboratories. The wrong done to them, they contend, is not that their impaired condition was negligently caused, but that their very existence was negligently caused. This, they maintain, is a serious injury, since they would have been better off not being born at all. They ask for compensation for the injury of being brought into this world.

In an early wrongful life case, *Gleitman v. Cosgrove*, a child born with impairments whose mother had been told erroneously that her exposure to German measles during pregnancy would not harm the fetus, brought suit for damages for the injury of being born.[17] The traditional method of measuring damages in tort is to compare the condition of the plaintiff before and after an injury and to compensate for the difference. When the putative wrong done to the plaintiff is to have been brought into existence in an impaired state, the court must measure the difference between nonexistence and existence with impairments. In *Gleitman*, the court found it "logically impossible" to "weigh the value of life with impairments against the nonexistence of life itself." We cannot, according to the court, conceptualize a world in which the plaintiff did not exist and ask what benefits and burdens he experienced in that world in order to compare it with his situation in this world.

Even so, the *Gleitman* court concluded that the value of life, no matter how burdened, outweighs the

disvalue of not existing, and that damages therefore could not be awarded to the child for "wrongful life." In drawing this conclusion, the court implicitly compared the world of existence with that of nonexistence and declared the former always preferable to the latter. Yet this is precisely the step the court had said it could not take. Similarly, in another leading case, *Berman v. Allan*, the court ruled against recognition of a "wrongful life" claim on grounds that "life—whether experienced with or without a major physical handicap—is more precious than non-life."[18] These courts were concerned that awarding damages for being alive would diminish the high value that the law places on human life. This public policy concern, however, caused them to lapse into incoherence. They claimed that the world of existence cannot be measured against that of nonexistence. However, if existence is better than nonexistence, as they also declared, nonexistence must be conceptually accessible in some sense so that an intelligible comparison can be made between it and existence.

Proponents of the Interest in Existing Argument adopt the two-world view underlying the logically impossible thesis of the early wrongful life cases when they claim that children are harmed if they are not brought out of the world of nonexistence into the world of existence. This leaves them with two problems: (1) explaining how to conceptualize and comprehend nonexistence and (2) justifying the claim that it is better to exist than not. Moreover, their dependence on the wrongful life decisions causes them to overlook an essential feature of their opponents' argument. The Harm to Children Argument is a *before-the-fact* one that applies to the time when a decision must be made about whether to employ the new reproductive technologies. *At this time, unlike the wrongful life cases, no child exists who could be harmed.* The Harm to Children Argument holds that at this preconception time, the morally right decision is not to use such technologies until further research establishes the degree of harm this might do to children who result. The Interest in Existing Argument, however, is an after-the-fact argument meant to apply at a time when children are already born. It must be used as a response to those who object to having already brought children into the world. Since the harm posited by the critics has not yet occurred when the decision is made whether to employ them, it is not an adequate response to say that without these technologies the resulting children would not have been born.[19] That is precisely what is at issue—*whether these children ought to have been conceived and born.*

A further difficulty is that the Interest in Existing Argument justifies allowing the new reproductive technologies to create almost any harm to children conceived as a result of their use—as long as this is not devastating harm in which death is preferable to life with it. As Bonnie Steinbock and Ron McClamrock observe, "Very few lives meet the stringent conditions imposed by the wrongful life analysis. . . . Even the most dismal sorts of circumstances of opportunity (including, for example . . . an extremely high chance of facing an agonizing death from starvation in the early years of life, severe retardation plus quadriplegia) fail to be covered"[20] by the standard of devastating harm. Yet it would strike many as ethically objectionable to proceed with reproductive techniques should such serious, but not devastating harms result from them in a significant proportion of cases.

The "Wrongful Life" Standard of Substantial Harm

Those who present the Interest in Existing Argument, adopting the standard applied in wrongful life cases, describe substantial harm as that which, in Robertson's words, puts one in a condition that renders life so "horrible"[21] and so "full of unavoidable suffering" (p. 169) that it is worse than "no life at all."[22] Robertson does not give a more precise definition of substantial harm, nor does he present specific examples of conditions which fall under that rubric in his discussion of harm to children and the new reproductive technologies. Feinberg expands on the "wrongful life" standard of substantial harm:

> Surely in most cases of suffering and impairment we think of death as even worse. This is shown by the widespread human tendency to "cling to life at all costs." And even for severe genetic handicaps and inherited maladies, most competent persons who suffer from them will not express regret that they were born in the first place. . . . In the most extreme cases, however, I think it is rational to prefer not to have

come into existence at all, and while I cannot prove this judgment, I am confident that most people will agree that it is at least plausible. I have in mind some of the more severely victimized sufferers from brain malformation, spina bifida, Tay-Sachs disease, polycystic kidney disease, Lesch-Nyhan syndrome, and those who, from whatever cause, are born blind and deaf, permanently incontinent, severely retarded, and in chronic pain or near-total paralysis, with life-expectancies of only a few years.[23]

To talk about death, both Feinberg and Robertson assume, is the same as to talk about "not coming into existence at all." They assimilate nonexistence before life and nonexistence after having lived. This is a mistake. *Nonexistence before coming into being* and *nonexistence after having lived* are two distinct concepts.

Lucretius observed that we do not express concern about nonexistence before creation, but we do fear our nonexistence after death. Why is this? The reason we perceive death as bad, Thomas Nagel proposes, is that it causes us to have fewer goods of this life than we would have had if we had continued to live.[24] Frances Kamm further observes that it is not only the absence of future goods in this life that leads us to fear death, but that death "takes away what already was and would have continued to be."[25] Preconception nonexistence, however, does not deprive us of what was ours already. In it there is no particular individual whose life ends and who thereby loses out on life's goods. Consequently, nonexistence before conception and birth does not seem as bad as death. We are indifferent to it.

Several other features of death that are also not characteristic of preconception nonexistence contribute to our assessment of it as bad. Death, for instance, happens to a person, whereas preconception nonexistence does not include an event in which nonexistence happens to a person. Death reveals our vulnerability in that through it a person is destroyed and deprived of life's goods. If a person does not exist, in contrast, this does not reflect negatively on "his" or "her" capacities.[26] Because of significant differences between them, preconception and posthumous nonexistence are qualitatively distinct concepts that are not interchangeable. Death has characteristics that lead us to evaluate it as bad, whereas preconception nonexistence strikes us as neither good nor bad.

Do we, too, fall into the trap of positing a shadowy world of nonexistence by distinguishing between preconception and posthumous nonexistence? We do not claim that either of these forms of nonexistence is a metaphysical locale. Instead, we view both as logical constructs built out of what we know about being alive. For both Nagel and Kamm, the meaning of death is derived from what we know about our existence in this world. The same is true of preconception nonexistence. Although the multitude of children whom it is possible for us to bring into the world do not exist, we can conceptualize certain things about them and what their lives would be like were we to conceive and bear them. We can also comprehend certain things about the negation of their existence were they to be born. That is, we can understand what they would lose if we decided not to conceive them and bring them into the world. Thus, we can meaningfully compare preconception nonexistence with life. We can consider children who might be brought into existence and ask whether we ought to conceive them without having to postulate a separate sphere of nonexistence in which they wait as we ponder the question.

While we can make sense of the notion of preconception nonexistence, can we also intelligibly claim that children who have not yet been conceived can have interests? It might be argued that those who do not exist cannot have interests and that therefore possible children can have no interest in not being conceived and brought into the world with serious disorders. Yet possible children can have interests, if these are taken in the sense of what contributes to their good, rather than as psychological states. We can conceive of what would promote their welfare were they to be brought into the world. To deny them such interests is mistakenly to reason by analogy with the dead. It has been supposed that the dead can have no interests because we cannot perform any actions that will affect the condition of their lives.[27] We cannot causally impinge on them for better or worse, it has been argued, for their lives have been completed. But this is not the case with possible children. We can affect them causally for better or worse by our present actions. Thus, we can ascribe to possible children certain interests that can be thwarted or fulfilled by actions that we take.

The interests of children who might be born of the new reproductive technologies are not adequately captured by the "wrongful life" standard. The comparison that parents and physicians must make when they assess whether use of these technologies would negatively affect the good of children who might result is not between *death* and the condition of these children were they to be born with certain deficits. The appropriate comparison is between *preconception nonexistence* and their condition were they to be born with certain deficits. If preconception nonexistence, unlike death, is neither good nor bad, then any life that will be worse than it *will not have to be as bad as the life of devastating deficits set out in the wrongful life standard.* A life with serious, but not devastating, deficits could be bad and therefore worse than preconception nonexistence, which is neither good nor bad. Therefore, we must modify the wrongful life standard of substantial harm to indicate that if new reproductive technologies were shown to cause a significant proportion of children born of them to suffer either devastating *or* serious deficits, they would cause substantial harm to these children and consequently ought not be used.

The Inadequate Opportunity for Health Standard of Substantial Harm

How are we to identify the serious deficits that—along with devastating deficits—would constitute substantial harm to these children? The boundary between moderate, serious, and devastating deficits is sufficiently blurred that reasonable people can disagree about where it lies in particular cases. Many would disagree with Feinberg that children knowingly conceived with such disorders as spina bifida, blindness, deafness, severe retardation, or permanent incontinence should be considered to be suffering from devastating deficits that make their lives worse than death. However, they might well view these disorders as amounting to serious deficits that make their lives worse than preconception nonexistence. What is needed is a conceptual framework that marks off those deficits that have such a negative impact on children that reasonable people would agree that knowingly to conceive children with these disorders would be to impose substantial harm on them in the vast majority of cases.

Laura Purdy suggests that we cause substantial harm to future children and therefore ought not knowingly conceive them "when there is a high risk of transmitting a serious disease or defect [of a sort that would deny them] a normal opportunity for health."[28] At points in Purdy's discussion, as when she states that "every parent should try to ensure normal health for his child," she can be taken to mean that having an abnormal state of health would constitute a disorder sufficiently serious to warrant not conceiving a child who would have it. On this approach, children with a particular biological, chemical, or mental state different from the norm would be said to lack "normal health" and therefore to suffer from a "serious disease or defect" that would justify not conceiving them. Yet it would not strike us as wrong knowingly to conceive children who are not "normal" because they have myopia or albinism. Normality does not appear to provide an adequate standard for deciding that a disorder is a serious deficit that substantially harms a child knowingly conceived with it.

At other points, however, Purdy seems to suggest that the focus for defining a serious deficit that falls under the substantial harm rubric should be on the failure to provide an adequate opportunity for a healthy life, as this is defined within a culture. Here she seems on the right track, for notions of health and disease—for better and for worse—are embedded within a society. What constitutes health and what represents a serious falling away from it varies from culture to culture and changes from time to time. As the notion of health and of an adequate opportunity for health vary according to the cultural context and conditions, so, too, does the meaning of a serious disease or deficit. Moreover, access to health services and the resulting opportunity for health—or lack of it—also affect what is meant by health, serious disorder, and substantial harm.

In our society, children who are color-blind are considered to have only a mild deficit and no diminution of their opportunity for health. However, in certain African cultures in which the capacity to distinguish a great variety of shades of green is needed to function at a minimal level for survival, color blindness is a serious deficit. Children born with this condition in such cultures do not have an adequate opportunity for health because their condition cannot be remedied. Thus, cultural values affect the meanings of health and of serious disorders. Stanley Hauerwas observes that "disease descriptions and remedies are relative to a society's values and needs. Thus 'retardation' might not 'exist' in a society which values cooperation more than competition and ambition."[29] Further, medical practices in different cultures reflect different views of what constitutes health and serious diseases. In Germany children with blood pressure that differs from the norm for their age on both the high and low end are suspected to be at risk of serious disease, whereas in America only high blood pressure is considered an indicator of serious disease.

What makes a disorder serious, however, is not only a matter of cultural needs, expectations, constructions, and practices. Some children are born with remediable conditions that are transformed into serious deficits when they are not ameliorated due to circumstances of injustice and neglect within a culture. The child born with spina bifida to poor parents in the hills of Appalachia has a minimal opportunity for health and a more serious disorder than the child born with this same condition to professional parents in Los Angeles. It might not be unfair to a child knowingly to conceive him or her with paralysis of the lower limbs if that child, once born, would have access to support structures giving him or her adequate mobility.[30] Nor would we have grounds for considering it wrong for parents knowingly to conceive a blind child if that child would receive compensatory education and ameliorative instruments enabling him or her to have an adequate opportunity for health within a society.

This relativity of the notion of health and of an adequate opportunity for health means that no definition of serious disease or disorder amounting to substantial harm that would apply across all cultures, times, and places can be given. Instead, the assessment of serious disease amounting to substantial harm must be made under specific circumstances within particular cultures. It must be defined not only in terms of a given physical or mental condition that damages a child's ability to function within a culture, but also in terms of the failure or inability of a culture to provide a child with access to ameliorative resources.

Sidney Callahan maintains that a principle of proportionality should be applied when making decisions concerning reproduction.[31] This would mean that the lower the risk and gravity of impairment to the child and the more would-be parents, family, and the institutional structures of a society are able and willing to ameliorate the impairment, the less the likelihood that a child would suffer a serious deficit and the more ethically justifiable it would be to conceive him or her. Should the probability and gravity of impairment be great, however, and the would-be parents, family, and social structure unwilling or unable to provide ameliorative measures for the child with such impairment, the higher the likelihood the child would suffer a serious deficit and the less ethically justifiable it would be to conceive that child. We do not end up with a black letter definition of a deficit serious enough to be termed substantial harm on this approach, but one that requires us to consider the nature of the disorder from which the child would suffer, the circumstances into which the child would be brought, and the ameliorative resources available for that child. Under current circumstances in our culture in which children born with disabling disorders have inadequate support, it would be morally questionable, at least, knowingly to conceive a child suffering from some of the deficits listed by Feinberg above.

Obligations to Actual and Possible Children

Although we consider it ethically necessary to provide treatment to keep children alive who have serious illnesses, we do not consider it ethically necessary knowingly to conceive children with those same disorders. Why is this? Why do we assume that our obligations to children who already exist differ from our obligations to children whom we might conceive?

The difference between an actual and possible child and between our evaluations of preconception nonexistence and death help to explain this distinction. Since we view death as an evil in relation to being alive, we tend to maintain that once children are born, only if they suffer devastating harms that make life worse than death would we be justified in not doing what we can to prevent their death. Being alive is better than being dead, except in rare circumstances. However, we do not believe that we have an obligation to do everything we can to conceive and bring into the world possible children who would suffer serious or devastating illness as a result. This is because no one exists who is wronged by not being conceived and also because preconception nonexistence does not strike us as being either bad or good. To fail to actualize a possible child, therefore, does not put that child in a worse situation or wrong that child.

Furthermore, we have no obligation to conceive children if this would detrimentally affect the good of the family or culture into which they would be born. We have no obligation, for instance, to conceive a sixth child if we believe our family can only function adequately with five. And we need not bring children into the world when this would contribute to a problem of overpopulation or of limited resources. It is morally acceptable, indeed, some would say, morally required, that *before* we bring children into the world, we consider not only their well-being were they to be born, but the good of those who would be affected by their birth. *After* birth, however, the interest in existing of the living child comes into play and morally outweighs remnants of a parental or societal interest in not having had that child.

These conclusions may appear to intimate that the lives of children born with serious or even devastating disorders are not valued or valuable. This conclusion does not follow from the preceding argument. Should parents, after receiving convincing evidence that use of the new reproductive technologies would harm the resulting children, decide against employing them, this could say one of two things to living children with serious or devastating disorders. It could suggest that it would have been better for their families if a different child had been born without these disorders and she was not. Or it could imply that it would have been better for this child to have been born without these disorders.[32] The first implication suggests that it would be better for others if children with these disorders were not born, whereas the second maintains that it would be better for the children themselves if they had not been born with them. The first implies that it is regrettable that these children are alive instead of "normal" children. The second implies that it is regrettable that these children have these disorders. The second implication is the one on which we tend to act. This is exhibited by efforts we make to avoid serious or devastating disorders in children during pregnancy and to treat and care for children with such disorders after they are born. All of this suggests that it is not the children we disvalue, but the disorders that they have sustained. Consequently, it is not necessarily a reproach to disabled children who are already born if decisions are made against knowingly conceiving children who would have the same disabilities.

It is, however, a reproach to us and to our social institutions that once children with serious and devastating disorders are born, we provide woefully insufficient services and resources to them and their families. Does this contradict the claim that we value living children with disabilities and have their interests at heart? Hauerwas provides one perceptive explanation of our ambivalent and complex attitude toward those who live with serious disabilities in the course of discussing those who are developmentally delayed. He observes:

> After all, what we finally seek is not simply to help the retarded better negotiate their disability but to be like us: not retarded. Our inability to accomplish that frustrates and angers us, and sometimes the retarded themselves become the object of our anger. We do not like to be reminded of the limits of our power, and we do not like those who remind us.[33]

We wish to remedy the disabilities with which children may be born, but find it difficult to cope with the recognition of our own vulnerability that they inadvertently call forth. Therefore, we relegate them to a separate domain within the world of existence where we believe unknown others will assist them to meet the special challenges they face. This is uncharitable and unjust. We have a responsibility to overcome our misplaced frustration about being unable to render those who have serious or devastating disorders more like those who do not. We have a responsibility to assist them to make their own way in the world unhampered by our irrational fears.

Taking Harms Seriously

The biblical injunction to multiply does not exhort us to do anything whatsoever to have children. It would be wrong to have children if it were known before conception that the means used to bring this about could inflict serious or devastating deficits on those very children. Yet the logic of the Interest in Existing Argument leads its proponents to brush aside the question whether these technologies might create such serious impairments. The thrust of this argument is that use of the new reproductive technologies provides its own justification—it produces children. This claim disregards the welfare of these children. Moreover, it creates a barrier to more extensive and detailed investigations of the effect of the new reproductive technologies on children born of them.

On the approach presented here, if it were known ahead of time that children conceived with the assistance of the new reproductive technologies would not have an adequate opportunity for health, it would be wrong to use them. Assessment of when and whether this could be the case would be carried out in light of the personal, familial, and social circumstances into which these children would be born. This means that would-be parents who consider resorting to the new reproductive technologies must be informed about the risks these techniques would present to the children born as a result of their use, the means available for ameliorating deficits these children might experience, and what social support would be available should they lack the resources to address such deficits on their own. Only then can they decide whether they ought to proceed with these techniques. To implement this recommendation, evidence for and against the contention that the new reproductive technologies cause serious or devastating physical, psychological, or social harm to the resulting children should be investigated more thoroughly than at present. Because of limited knowledge of the possible effects of these measures on their children, those who repeat Rachel's cry today face an agonizingly difficult decision when they consider whether to use the new reproductive technologies.

REFERENCES

1. National Perinatal Statistics Unit, Fertility Society of Australia, *In Vitro Fertilization Pregnancies. Australia and New Zealand* 1979–1985, Sydney, Australia, 1987; Paul L. Lancaster, "Congenital Malformations after In-Vitro Fertilisation,"

[letter] *Lancet* 2 (1987): 1392–93; see also AIHW National Perinatal Statistics Unit, Fertility Society of Australia, *Assisted Conception in Australia and New Zealand 1990* (Sydney: AIHW National Perinatal Statistics Unit, 1992); Gail Vines, "Shots in the Dark for Infertility," *New Scientist* 140 (1993): 13–15; Lene Koch, "Physiological and Psychosocial Risks of the New Reproductive Technologies," in *Tough Choices: In Vitro Fertilization and the Reproductive Technologies*, ed. Patricia Stephenson and Marsden G. Wagner (Philadelphia: Temple University Press, 1993), pp. 122–34.

2. U. B. Wennerholm et al., "Pregnancy Complications and Short-Term Follow-Up of Infants Born after In Vitro Fertilization and Embryo Transfer," *Acta Obstetrica et Gynecologicia Scandinavica* 70 (1991): 565–73; B. Rizk et al., "Perinatal Outcome and Congenital Malformations in In-Vitro Fertilization Babies from the Bourn-Hallam Group," *Human Reproduction* 6 (1991): 1259–64; S. Friedler, S. Mashiach, and N. Laufer, "Births in Israel Resulting from In-Vitro Fertilization/Embryo Transfer, 1982–1989: National Registry of the Israeli Association for Fertility Research," *Human Reproduction* 7 (1992): 1159–63; Society for Assisted Reproductive Technology, American Society for Reproductive Medicine, Assisted Reproductive Technology in the United States and Canada, "1993 Results Generated from the American Society for Reproductive Medicine/Society for Assisted Reproductive Technology Registry," *Fertility and Sterility* 64(1995): 13–21.

3. Norma C. Morin et al., "Congenital Malformations and Psychosocial Development in Children Conceived by In Vitro Fertilization," *Journal of Pediatrics* 115 (1989): 222–27.

4. V. Beral et al., "Outcome of Pregnancies Resulting from Assisted Conception," *British Medical Bulletin* 46, no. 3 (1990): 753–68; I. Craft and T. al-Shawaf, "Outcome and Complications of Assisted Reproduction," *Current Opinion in Obstetrics and Gynecology* 3 (1991): 668–73; Rizk et al., "Perinatal Outcome and Congenital Malformations in In-Vitro Fertilization Babies from the Bourn-Hallam Group"; P. Doyle, V. Beral, and N. Maconochie, "Preterm Delivery, Low Birthweight and Small-for-Gestational-Age in Liveborn Singleton Babies Resulting from In-Vitro Fertilization," *Human Reproduction* 7 (1992): 425–28; Friedler et al., "Births in Israel," pp. 1160–63.

5. Jean-Pierre Relier, Michele Couchard, and Catherine Huon, "The Neonatologist's Experience of In Vitro Fertilization Risks," *Tough Choices*, pp. 135–143; see also P. Rufat et al., "Task Force Report on the Outcome of Pregnancies and Children Conceived by In Vitro Fertilization (France: 1987 to 1989)," *Fertility and Sterility* 61 (1994): 324–30; FIVNAT (French In Vitro National), "Pregnancies and Births Resulting from In Vitro Fertilization: French National Registry, Analysis of Data 1986 to 1990," *Fertility and Sterility* 64 (1995): 746–56.

6. Cynthia B. Cohen, "Reproductive Technologies: Ethical Issues," in *Encyclopedia of Bioethics*, ed. Warren Thomas Reich (New York: Simon and Schuster Macmillan, 1995),

vol. 4, pp. 2233–41; A. Baran and R. Pannor, *Lethal Secrets: The Shocking Consequences and Unsolved Problems of Artificial Insemination* (New York: Warner Books, 1989); D. N. Mushin, J. Spensley, and M. Barreda-Hanson, "In Vitro Fertilization Children: Early Psychosocial Development," *Journal of In Vitro Fertilization and Embryo Transfer* 4 (1986): 247–52.

7. Margaret Radin, "Market-Inalienability," *Harvard Law Review* 100 (1987): 1921–36; Sidney Callahan, "The Ethical Challenges of the New Reproductive Technologies," in *Medical Ethics: A Guide for Health Professionals*, ed. J. Monagle and David Thomas (Rockville, Md.: Aspen, 1988), pp. 26–37.

8. Leon Kass, *Toward a More Natural Science: Biology and Human Affairs* (New York: Free Press, 1985), p. 113; Lisa Sowle Cahill, "The Ethics of Surrogate Motherhood: Biology, Freedom, and Moral Obligation," *Law, Medicine and Health Care* 16, nos. 1–2 (1988): 65–71, at 69; Cynthia B. Cohen, "Parents Anonymous," in *New Ways of Making Babies: The Case of Egg Donation*, ed. Cynthia B. Cohen (Bloomington: Indiana University Press, 1996).

9. Susan Golombok et al., "Parents and Their Children Happy with Assisted Conception," [letter] *British Medical Journal* 307 (1994): 1032.

10. Lene Koch, "Physiological and Psychosocial Risks of the New Reproductive Technologies," p. 128.

11. Ruth F Chadwick, "Cloning," *Philosophy* 57 (1982): 201–9; John A. Robertson, "Procreative Liberty and the Control of Conception, Pregnancy, and Childbirth," *University of Virginia Law Review* 69 (1983): 405–462, at 434; John A. Robertson, "Embryos, Families, and Procreative Liberty: The Legal Structure of the New Reproduction," *Southern California Law Review* 59 (1986): 942–1041, at 958, 988; John A. Robertson, "Procreative Liberty, Embryos, and Collaborative Reproduction: A Legal Perspective," in *Embryos, Ethics, and Women's Rights: Exploring the New Reproductive Technologies*, ed. E. F. Baruch, A. F. Adamo, Jr., and J. Seager (New York: Howarth Press, 1988), pp. 179–94; John A. Robertson, "The Question of Human Cloning," *Hastings Center Report* 24, no. 3 (1994): 6–14; John A. Robertson, *Children of Choice: Freedom and the New Reproductive Technologies* (Princeton, N.J.: Princeton University Press, 1994), pp. 75–76, 110–11, 122–23, 152, 169–70; Ruth Macklin, "Splitting Embryos on the Slippery Slope," *Kennedy Institute of Ethics Journal* 4 (1994): 209–25, at 219–20.

12. Robertson, "Procreative Liberty and the Control of Conception, Pregnancy, and Childbirth," p. 434.

13. Robertson, *Children of Choice*, pp. 75–76.

14. Robertson, *Children of Choice*, pp. 75–76.

15. Joel Feinberg, "Wrongful Life and the Counterfactual Element in Harming," *Social Philosophy and Policy* 4 (1988):145–78, at 158.

16. Derek Parfit, *Reasons and Persons* (Oxford: Oxford University Press, 1985), p. 487.

17. *Gleitman v. Cosgrove*, 49 N.J. 22, 227A. 2d 689 (1967).

18. *Berman v. Allan*, 80 N.J. 421, 404 A. 2d 8 (1979).

19. Robertson, *Children of Choice*, pp. 75, 117; "Embryos, Families, and Procreative Liberty," pp. 958, 988.

20. Bonnie Steinbock and Ron McClamrock, "When Is Birth Unfair to the Child?" *Hastings Center Report* 24, no. 6 (1994): 16–22, at 17.

21. Robertson, *Children of Choice*, pp. 82, 85.

22. Robertson, "Procreative Liberty and the Control of Conception, Pregnancy, and Childbirth," p. 434.

23. Feinberg, "Wrongful Life," p. 159.

24. Thomas Nagel, "Death," in *Mortal Questions* (Cambridge: Cambridge University Press: 1979), pp. 1–10.

25. Frances M. Kamm, *Morality, Mortality, Volume I. Death and Whom to Save from It* (New York: Oxford University Press, 1993), p. 40.

26. Kamm, *Morality, Mortality*, pp. 40–41.

27. Joan Callahan, "On Harming the Dead," *Ethics* 97 (1987): 341–52; Ernest Partridge, "Posthumous Interests and Posthumous Respect," *Ethics*, 91 (1981): 243–64.

28. Laura Purdy, "Genetic Diseases: Can Having Children Be Immoral?" in *Genetics Now: Ethical Issues in Genetic Research*, ed. John Buckly, Jr. (Washington, D.C.: University Press of America, 1978), pp. 25–39, at 25.

29. Stanley Hauerwas, "Suffering the Retarded: Should We Prevent Retardation?" in *Suffering Presence: Theological Reflections on Medicine, the Mentally Handicapped, and the Church*, ed. Stanley Hauerwas (Notre Dame: University of Notre Dame Press, 1986), pp. 159–81.

30. Steinbock and McClamrock, "When Is Birth Unfair to the Child?" and Sidney Callahan, "An Ethical Analysis of Responsible Parenthood," in *Genetic Counseling: Facts, Values, and Norms*, ed. Alexander M. Capron, Marc Lappé, and Robert F. Murray (New York: Alan R. Liss, 1979), pp. 217–38.

31. Callahan, "An Ethical Analysis of Responsible Parenthood."

32. Mary Warnock, "Ethical Challenges in Embryo Manipulation," *British Medical Journal* 304 (1992): 1045–49, at 1047.

33. Hauerwas, "Suffering the Retarded," p. 176.

Instruction on Respect for Human Life in Its Origin and on the Dignity of Procreation

CONGREGATION FOR THE DOCTRINE OF THE FAITH

This document articulates the official position of the Roman Catholic Church, declaring that many kinds of reproductive technology or practices are morally impermissible. Among other affirmations, it asserts that (1) nontherapeutic experimentation on embryos is illicit, (2) "it is immoral to produce embryos destined to be exploited as disposable 'biological material,'" (3) nontherapeutic genetic manipulations are contrary to human dignity, (4) artificial fertilization involving sperm and egg from unmarried individuals is illicit, and (5) in vitro fertilization is not morally legitimate.

Biomedical Research and the Teaching of the Church

The gift of life which God the Creator and Father has entrusted to man calls him to appreciate the inestimable value of what he has been given and to take responsibility for it: This fundamental principle must be placed at the center of one's reflection in order to clarify and solve the moral problems raised by artificial interventions on life as it originates and on the processes of procreation.

Thanks to the progress of the biological and medical sciences, man has at his disposal ever more ef-

From Congregation of the Doctrine of the Faith, *Instruction on Respect for Human Life in Its Origin and on the Dignity of Procreation*, February 22, 1987. © Libreria Editrice Vaticana.

fective therapeutic resources; but he can also acquire new powers, with unforeseeable consequences, over human life at its very beginning and in its first stages. Various procedures now make it possible to intervene not only in order to assist, but also to dominate the processes of procreation. These techniques can enable man to "take in hand his own destiny," but they also expose him "to the temptation to go beyond the limits of a reasonable dominion over nature." (1) They might constitute progress in the service of man, but they also involve serious risks. Many people are therefore expressing an urgent appeal that in interventions on procreation the values and rights of the human person be safeguarded. Requests for clarification and guidance are coming not only from the faithful, but also from those who recognize the church as "an expert in humanity" (2) with a mission to serve the "civilization of love" (3) and of life.

The church's magisterium does not intervene on the basis of a particular competence in the area of the experimental sciences; but having taken account of the data of research and technology, it intends to put forward, by virtue of its evangelical mission and apostolic duty, the moral teaching corresponding to the dignity of the person and to his or her integral vocation. It intends to do so by expounding the criteria of moral judgment as regards the applications of scientific research and technology, especially in relation to human life and its beginnings. These criteria are the respect, defence and promotion of man, his "primary and fundamental right" to life, (4) his dignity as a person who is endowed with a spiritual soul and with moral responsibility (5) and who is called to beatific communion with God. . . .

Anthropology and Procedures in the Biomedical Field

Which moral criteria must be applied in order to clarify the problems posed today in the field of biomedicine? The answer to this question presupposes a proper idea of the nature of the human person in his bodily dimension.

For it is only in keeping with his true nature that the human person can achieve self-realization as a "unified totality"; and this nature is at the same time corporal and spiritual. By virtue of its substantial union with a spiritual soul, the human body cannot be considered as a mere complex of tissues, organs and functions, nor can it be evaluated in the same way as the body of animals; rather, it is a constitutive part of the person who manifests and expresses himself through it.

The natural moral law expresses and lays down the purposes, rights and duties which are based upon the bodily and spiritual nature of the human person. Therefore this law cannot be thought of as simply a set of norms on the biological level; rather, it must be defined as the rational order whereby man is called by the Creator to direct and regulate his life and actions and in particular to make use of his own body.

A first consequence can be deduced from these principles: An intervention on the human body affects not only the tissues, the organs and their functions, but also involves the person himself on different levels. It involves, therefore, perhaps in an implicit but nonetheless real way, a moral significance and responsibility. . . .

Applied biology and medicine work together for the integral good of human life when they come to the aid of a person stricken by illness and infirmity and when they respect his or her dignity as a creature of God. No biologist or doctor can reasonably claim, by virtue of his scientific competence, to be able to decide on people's origin and destiny. This norm must be applied in a particular way in the field of sexuality and procreation, in which man and woman actualize the fundamental values of love and life.

God, who is love and life, has inscribed in man and woman the vocation to share in a special way in his mystery of personal communion and in his work as Creator and Father. For this reason marriage possesses specific goods and values in its union and in procreation which cannot be likened to those existing in lower forms of life. Such values and meanings are of the personal order and determine from the moral point of view the meaning and limits of artificial interventions on procreation and on the origin of human life. These interventions are not to be rejected on the grounds that they are artificial. As such, they bear witness to the possibilities of the art of medicine. But they must be given a moral evaluation in reference to the dignity of the human person, who is called to realize his vocation from God to the gift of love and the gift of life.

Fundamental Criteria for a Moral Judgment

The fundamental values connected with the techniques of artificial human procreation are two: the life of the human being called into existence and the special nature of the transmission of human life in marriage. The moral judgment on such methods of artificial procreation must therefore be formulated in reference to these values.

Physical life, with which the course of human life in the world begins, certainly does not itself contain the whole of a person's value, nor does it represent the supreme good of man, who is called to eternal life. However it does constitute in a certain way the "fundamental" value of life precisely because upon this physical life all the other values of the person are based and developed. The inviolability of the innocent human being's right to life "from the moment of conception until death" is a sign and requirement of the very inviolability of the person to whom the Creator has given the gift of life.

By comparison with the transmission of other forms of life in the universe, the transmission of human life has a special character of its own, which derives from the special nature of the human person. "The transmission of human life is entrusted by nature to a personal and conscious act and as such is subject to the all-holy laws of God: immutable and inviolable laws which must be recognized and observed. For this reason one cannot use means and follow methods which could be licit in the transmission of the life of plants and animals."

Advances in technology have now made it possible to procreate apart from sexual relations through the meeting *in vitro* of the germ cells previously taken from the man and the woman. But what is technically possible is not for that very reason morally admissible. Rational reflection on the fundamental values of life and of human procreation is therefore indispensable for formulating a moral evaluation of such technological interventions on a human being from the first stages of his development. . . .

I. Respect for Human Embryos

What respect is due to the human embryo, taking into account his nature and identity?
The human being must be respected—as a person—from the very first instant of his existence. . . .

This congregation is aware of the current debates concerning the beginning of human life, concerning the individuality of the human being and concerning the identity of the human person. The congregation recalls the teachings found in the Declaration on Procured Abortion:

"From the time that the ovum is fertilized, a new life is begun which is neither that of the father nor of the mother; it is rather the life of a new human being with his own growth. It would never be made human if it were not human already. To this perpetual evidence . . . modern genetic science brings valuable confirmation. It has demonstrated that, from the

first instant, the program is fixed as to what this living being will be: a man, this individual man with his characteristic aspects already well determined. Right from fertilization is begun the adventure of a human life, and each of its great capacities requires time . . . to find its place and to be in a position to act."

This teaching remains valid and is further confirmed, if confirmation were needed, by recent findings of human biological science which recognize that in the zygote (the cell produced when the nuclei of the two gametes have fused) resulting from fertilization the biological identity of a new human individual is already constituted.

Certainly no experimental datum can be in itself sufficient to bring us to the recognition of a spiritual soul; nevertheless, the conclusions of science regarding the human embryo provide a valuable indication for discerning by the use of reason a personal presence at the moment of this first appearance of a human life: How could a human individual not be a human person? The magisterium has not expressly committed itself to an affirmation of a philosophical nature, but it constantly reaffirms the moral condemnation of any kind of procured abortion. This teaching has not been changed and is unchangeable.

Thus the fruit of human generation from the first moment of its existence, that is to say, from the moment the zygote has formed, demands the unconditional respect that is morally due to the human being in his bodily and spiritual totality. The human being is to be respected and treated as a person from the moment of conception and therefore from that same moment his rights as a person must be recognized, among which in the first place is the inviolable right of every innocent human being to life. This doctrinal reminder provides the fundamental criterion for the solution of the various problems posed by the development of the biomedical sciences in this field: Since the embryo must be treated as a person, it must also be defended in its integrity, tended and cared for, to the extent possible, in the same way as any other human being as far as medical assistance is concerned. . . .

How is one to evaluate morally research and experimentation on human embryos and fetuses?
Medical research must refrain from operations on live embryos, unless there is a moral certainty or not caus-

ing harm to the life or integrity of the unborn child and the mother, and on condition that the parents have given their free and informed consent to the procedure. It follows that all research, even when limited to the simple observation of the embryo, would become illicit were it to involve risk to the embryo's physical integrity or life by reason of the methods used or the effects induced. As regards experimentation, and presupposing the general distinction between experimentation for purposes which are not directly therapeutic and experimentation which is clearly therapeutic for the subject himself, in the case in point one must also distinguish between experimentation carried out on embryos which are still alive and experimentation carried out on embryos which are dead. *If the embryos are living, whether viable or not, they must be respected just like any other human person; experimentations on embryos which is not directly therapeutic is illicit.* No objective, even though noble in itself such as a foreseeable advantage to science, to other human beings or to society, can in any way justify experimentation on living human embryos or fetuses, whether viable or not, either inside or outside the mother's womb. The informed consent ordinarily required for clinical experimentation on adults cannot be granted by the parents, who may not freely dispose of the physical integrity or life of the unborn child. Moreover, experimentation on embryos and fetuses always involves risk, and indeed in most cases it involves the certain expectation of harm to their physical integrity or even their death. To use human embryos or fetuses as the object or instrument of experimentation constitutes a crime against their dignity as human beings having a right to the same respect that is due to the child already born and to every human person. . . .

. . . The practice of keeping alive human embryos *in vivo* or *in vitro* for experimental or commercial purposes is totally opposed to human dignity. In the case of experimentation that is clearly therapeutic, namely, when it is a matter of experimental forms of therapy used for the benefit of the embryo itself in a final attempt to save its life and in the absence of other reliable forms of therapy, recourse to drugs or procedures not yet fully tested can be licit.

The corpses of human embryos and fetuses, whether they have been deliberately aborted or not, must be re- spected just as the remains of other human beings. In particular, they cannot be subjected to mutilation or to autopsies if their death has not yet been verified and without the consent of the parents or of the mother. Furthermore, the moral requirements must be safeguarded that there be no complicity in deliberate abortion and that the risk of scandal be avoided. Also, in the case of dead fetuses, as for the corpses of adult persons, all commercial trafficking must be considered illicit and should be prohibited. . . .

How is one to evaluate morally the use for research purposes of embryos obtained by fertilization "in vitro"? Human embryos obtained *in vitro* are human beings and subjects with rights: Their dignity and right to life must be respected from the first moment of their existence. *It is immoral to produce human embryos destined to be exploited as disposable "biological material."*

In the usual practice of *in vitro* fertilization, not all of the embryos are transferred to the woman's body; some are destroyed. Just as the church condemns induced abortion, so she also forbids acts against the life of these human beings. *It is a duty to condemn the particular gravity of the voluntary destruction of human embryos obtained "in vitro" for the sole purpose of research, either by means of artificial insemination or by means of "twin fission." By acting in this way the researcher usurps the place of God; and even though he may be unaware of this, he sets himself up as the master of the destiny of others inasmuch as he arbitrarily chooses whom he will allow to live and whom he will send to death and kills defenseless human beings.*

Methods of observation or experimentation which damage or impose grave and disproportionate risks upon embryos obtained *in vitro* are morally illicit for the same reasons. Every human being is to be respected for himself and cannot be reduced in worth to a pure and simple instrument for the advantage of others. *It is therefore not in conformity with the moral law deliberately to expose to death human embryos obtained "in vitro."* In consequence of the fact that they have been produced *in vitro*, those embryos which are not transferred into the body of the mother and are called "spare" are exposed to an absurd fate, with no possibility of their being offered safe means of survival which can be licitly pursued.

What judgment should be made on other procedures of manipulating embryos connected with the "techniques of human reproduction?"

Techniques of fertilization *in vitro* can open the way to other forms of biological and genetic manipulation of human embryos, such as attempts or plans for fertilization between human and animal gametes and the gestation of human embryos in the uterus of animals, or the hypothesis or project of constructing artificial uteruses for the human embryo. *These procedures are contrary to the human dignity proper to the embryo, and at the same time they are contrary to the right of every person to be conceived and to be born within marriage and from marriage. Also, attempts or hypotheses for obtaining a human being without any connection with sexuality through "twin fission," cloning or parthenogenesis are to be considered contrary to the moral law, since they are in opposition to the dignity both of human procreation and of the conjugal union.*

The freezing of embryos, even when carried out in order to preserve the life of an embryo—cryopreservation—*constitutes an offense against the respect due to human beings* by exposing them to grave risks of death or harm to their physical integrity and depriving them, at least temporarily, of maternal shelter and gestation, thus placing them in a situation in which further offenses and manipulation are possible.

Certain attempts to influence chromosomic or genetic inheritance are not therapeutic, but are aimed at producing human beings selected according to sex or other predetermined qualities. These manipulations are contrary to the personal dignity of the human being and his or her integrity and identity. . . .

II. Interventions upon Human Procreation

. . . A preliminary point for the moral evaluation of [*in vitro* fertilization and artificial insemination] is constituted by the consideration of the circumstances and consequences which those procedures involve in relation to the respect due the human embryo. Development of the practice of *in vitro* fertilization has required innumerable fertilizations and destructions of human embryos. Even today, the usual practice presupposes a hyperovulation on the part of the woman: A number of ova are withdrawn, fertilized and then cultivated *in vitro* for some days.

Usually not all are transferred into the genital tracts of the woman; some embryos, generally called "spare," are destroyed or frozen. On occasion, some of the implanted embryos are sacrificed for various eugenic, economic or psychological reasons. Such deliberate destruction of human beings or their utilization for different purposes to the detriment of their integrity and life is contrary to the doctrine on procured abortion already recalled. The connection between *in vitro* fertilization and the voluntary destruction of human embryos occurs too often. This is significant: Through these procedures, with apparently contrary purposes, life and death are subjected to the decision of man, who thus sets himself up as the giver of life and death by decree. This dynamic of violence and domination may remain unnoticed by those very individuals who, in wishing to utilize this procedure, become subject to it themselves. The facts recorded and the cold logic which links them must be taken into consideration for a moral judgment on *in vitro* fertilization and embryo transfer: The abortion mentality which has made this procedure possible thus leads, whether one wants it or not, to man's domination over the life and death of his fellow human beings and can lead to a system of radical eugenics. . . .

A. Heterologous* Artificial Fertilization

Why must human procreation take place in marriage? Every human being is always to be accepted as a gift and blessing of God. However, from the moral point of view a truly responsible procreation vis-à-vis the unborn child must be the fruit of marriage.

For human procreation has specific characteristics by virtue of the personal dignity of the parents and of the children: The procreation of a new person, whereby the man and the woman collaborate with the power of the Creator, must be the fruit and the sign of the mutual self-giving of the spouses, of their love and of their fidelity. *The fidelity of the spouses in the unity of marriage involves reciprocal respect of their right to become a father and a mother only through each other.* The child has the right to be conceived, carried in the womb, brought into the

---

*[Heterologous: using gametes coming from at least one donor other than the spouses who are married to each other.]

world and brought up within marriage: It is through the secure and recognized relationship to his own parents that the child can discover his own identity and achieve his own proper human development. The parents find in their child a confirmation and completion of their reciprocal self-giving: The child is the living image of their love, the permanent sign of their conjugal union, the living and indissoluble concrete expression of their paternity and maternity. By reason of the vocation and social responsibilities of the person, the good of the children and of the parents contributes to the good of civil society; the vitality and stability of society require that children come into the world within a family and that the family be firmly based on marriage. The tradition of the church and anthropological reflection recognize in marriage and in its indissoluble unity the only setting worthy of truly responsible procreation.

Does heterologous artificial fertilization conform to the dignity of the couple and to the truth of marriage?
Through *in vitro* fertilization and embryo transfer and heterologous artificial insemination, human conception is achieved through the fusion of gametes of at least one donor other than the spouses who are united in marriage. *Heterologous artificial fertilization is contrary to the unity of marriage, to the dignity of the spouses, to the vocation proper to parents, and to the child's right to be conceived and brought into the world in marriage and from marriage.* Respect for the unity of marriage and for conjugal fidelity demands that the child be conceived in marriage; the bond existing between husband and wife accords the spouses, in an objective and inalienable manner, the exclusive right to become father and mother solely through each other. Recourse to the gametes of a third person in order to have sperm or ovum available constitutes a violation of the reciprocal commitment of the spouses and a grave lack in regard to that essential property of marriage which is its unity. Heterologous artificial fertilization violates the rights of the child: it deprives him of his filial relationship with his parental origins and can hinder the maturing of his personal identity. Furthermore, it offends the common vocation of the spouses who are called to fatherhood and motherhood: It objectively deprives conjugal fruitfulness of its unity and integrity; it brings about and manifests

a rupture between genetic parenthood, gestational parenthood and responsibility for upbringing. Such damage to the personal relationships within the family has repercussions on civil society: What threatens the unity and stability of the family is a source of dissension, disorder and injustice in the whole of social life.

These reasons lead to a negative moral judgment concerning heterologous artificial fertilization: Consequently, fertilization of a married woman with the sperm of a donor different from her husband and fertilization with the husband's sperm of an ovum not coming from his wife are morally illicit. Furthermore, the artificial fertilization of a woman who is unmarried or a widow, whoever the donor may be, cannot be morally justified.

The desire to have a child and the love between spouses who long to obviate sterility which cannot be overcome in any other way constitute understandable motivations; but subjectively good intentions do not render heterologous artificial fertilization conformable to the objective and inalienable properties of marriage or respectful of the rights of the child and of the spouses.

Is "surrogate" motherhood morally licit?
No, for the same reasons which lead one to reject heterologous artificial fertilization: For it is contrary to the unity of marriage and to the dignity of the procreation of the human person. . . .

B. Homologous* Artificial Fertilization
Since heterologous artificial fertilization has been declared unacceptable, the question arises of how to evaluate morally the process of homologous artificial fertilization: *in vitro* fertilization and embryo transfer and artificial insemination between husband and wife. First a question of principle must be clarified.

What connection is required from the moral point of view between procreation and the conjugal act?

1. The church's teaching on marriage and human procreation affirms the "inseparable connection, willed by God and unable to be broken by man on

---

*[Homologous: using gametes of two spouses joined in marriage.]

his own initiative, between the two meanings of the conjugal act: the unitive meaning and the procreative meaning. Indeed, by its intimate structure the conjugal act, while most closely uniting husband and wife, capacitates them for the generation of new lives according to laws inscribed in the very being of man and of woman." . . . "By safeguarding both these essential aspects, the unitive and the procreative, the conjugal act preserves in its fullness the sense of true mutual love and its ordination toward man's exalted vocation to parenthood." The same doctrine concerning the link between the meanings of the conjugal act and between the goods of marriage throws light on the moral problem of homologous artificial fertilization, since "it is never permitted to separate these different aspects to such a degree as positively to exclude either the procreative intention or the conjugal relation." Contraception deliberately deprives the conjugal act of its openness to procreation and in this way brings about a voluntary dissociation of the ends of marriage. Homologous artificial fertilization, in seeking a procreation which is not the fruit of a specific act of conjugal union, objectively effects an analogous separation between the goods and the meanings of marriage. Thus, *fertilization is licitly sought when it is the result of a "conjugal act which is per se suitable for the generation of children to which marriage is ordered by its nature and by which the spouses become one flesh." But from the moral point of view procreation is deprived of its proper perfection when it is not desired as the fruit of the conjugal act, that is to say of the specific act of the spouses' union.*

2. The moral value of the intimate link between the goods of marriage and between the meanings of the conjugal act is based upon the unity of the human being, a unity involving body and spiritual soul. Spouses mutually express their personal love in the "language of the body," which clearly involves both "spousal meanings" and parental ones. The conjugal act by which the couple mutually express their self-gift at the same time expresses openness to the gift of life. It is an act that is inseparably corporal and spiritual. It is in their bodies and through their bodies that the spouses consummate their marriage and are able to become father and mother. In order to respect the language of their bodies and their natural generosity, the conjugal union must take place

with respect for its openness to procreation; and the procreation of a person must be the fruit and the result of married love. The origin of the human being thus follows from a procreation that is "linked to the union, not only biological but also spiritual, of the parents, made one by the bond of marriage." Fertilization achieved outside the bodies of the couple remains by this very fact deprived of the meanings and the values which are expressed in the language of the body and in the union of human persons.

3. Only respect for the link between the meanings of the conjugal act and respect for the unity of the human being make possible procreation in conformity with the dignity of the person. In his unique and irrepeatable origin, the child must be respected and recognized as equal in personal dignity to those who give him life. The human person must be accepted in his parents' act of union and love; the generation of a child must therefore be the fruit of that mutual giving which is realized in the conjugal act wherein the spouses cooperate as servants and not as masters in the work of the Creator, who is love.

In reality, the origin of a human person is the result of an act of giving. The one conceived must be the fruit of his parents' love. He cannot be desired or conceived as the product of an intervention of medical or biological techniques; that would be equivalent to reducing him to an object of scientific technology. No one may subject the coming of a child into the world to conditions of technical efficiency which are to be evaluated according to standards of control and dominion. *The moral relevance of the link between the meanings of the conjugal act and between the goods of marriage, as well as the unity of the human being and the dignity of his origin, demand that the procreation of a human person be brought about as the fruit of the conjugal act specific to the love between spouses.* . . .

Is homologous "in vitro" fertilization morally licit?
The answer to this question is strictly dependent on the principles just mentioned. Certainly one cannot ignore the legitimate aspirations of sterile couples. For some, recourse to homologous *in vitro* fertilization and embryo transfer appears to be the only way of fulfilling their sincere desire for a child. The question is asked whether the totality of conjugal life in

such situations is not sufficient to ensure the dignity proper to human procreation. It is acknowledged that *in vitro* fertilization and embryo transfer certainly cannot supply for the absence of sexual relations and cannot be preferred to the specific acts of conjugal union, given the risks involved for the child and the difficulties of the procedure. But it is asked whether, when there is no other way of overcoming the sterility which is a source of suffering, homologous *in vitro* fertilization may not constitute an aid, if not a form of therapy, whereby its moral licitness could be admitted. The desire for a child—or at least an openness to the transmission of life—is a necessary prerequisite from the moral point of view for responsible human procreation. But this good intention is not sufficient for making a positive moral evaluation of *in vitro* fertilization between spouses. The process of *in vitro* fertilization and embryo transfer must be judged in itself and cannot borrow its definitive moral quality from the totality of conjugal life of which it becomes part nor from the conjugal acts which may precede or follow it. . . .

It has already been recalled that, in the circumstances in which it is regularly practised, IVF and ET involves the destruction of human beings, which is something contrary to the doctrine on the illicitness of abortion previously mentioned. But even in a situation in which every precaution were taken to avoid the death of human embryos, homologous *in vitro* fertilization and embryo transfer dissociates from the conjugal act the actions which are directed to human fertilization. For this reason the very nature of homologous *in vitro* fertilization and embryo transfer also must be taken into account, even abstracting from the link with procured abortion. Homologous *in vitro* fertilization and embryo transfer is brought about outside the bodies of the couple through actions of third parties whose competence and technical activity determine the success of the procedure. Such fertilization entrusts the life and identity of the embryo into the power of doctors and biologists and establishes the domination of technology over the origin and destiny of the human person. Such a relationship of domination is in itself contrary to the dignity and equality that must be common to parents and children.

Conception *in vitro* is the result of the technical action which presides over fertilization. *Such fertil-* *ization is neither in fact achieved nor positively willed as the expression and fruit of a specific act of the conjugal union. In homologous "in vitro" fertilization and embryo transfer, therefore, even if it is considered in the context of de facto existing sexual relations, the generation of the human person is objectively deprived of its proper perfection: namely, that of being the result and fruit of a conjugal act* in which spouses can become "cooperators with God for giving life to a new person." . . . Although the manner in which human conception is achieved with *in vitro* fertilization and embryo transfer cannot be approved, every child which comes into the world must in any case be accepted as a living gift of the divine Goodness and must be brought up with love.

How is homologous artificial insemination to be evaluated from the moral point of view?
Homologous artificial insemination within marriage cannot be admitted except for those cases in which the technical means is not a substitute for the conjugal act but serves to facilitate and to help so that the act attains its natural purpose. . . .

"In its natural structure, the conjugal act is a personal action, a simultaneous and immediate cooperation on the part of the husband and wife, which by the very nature of the agents and the proper nature of the act is the expression of the mutual gift which, according to the words of Scripture, brings about union 'in one flesh.'" Thus moral conscience "does not necessarily proscribe the use of certain artificial means destined solely either to the facilitating of the natural act or to ensuring that the natural act normally performed achieves its proper end." If the technical means facilitates the conjugal act or helps it to reach its natural objectives, it can be morally acceptable. If, on the other hand, the procedure were to replace the conjugal act, it is morally illicit.

Artificial insemination as a substitute for the conjugal act is prohibited by reason of the voluntarily achieved dissociation of the two meanings of the conjugal act. Masturbation, through which the sperm is normally obtained, is another sign of this dissociation: Even when it is done for the purpose of procreation the act remains deprived of its unitive meaning: "It lacks the sexual relationship called for by the moral order, namely the relationship which realizes 'the full sense of mutual self-giving and human procreation in the context of true love.'" . . .

What moral criterion can be proposed with regard to medical intervention in human procreation?
The medical act must be evaluated not only with reference to its technical dimension, but also and above all in relation to its goal, which is the good of persons and their bodily and psychological health. The moral criteria for medical intervention in procreation are deduced from the dignity of human persons, of their sexuality and of their origin.

Medicine which seeks to be ordered to the integral good of the person must respect the specifically human values of sexuality. The doctor is at the service of persons and of human procreation. He does not have the authority to dispose of them or to decide their fate. A medical intervention respects the dignity of persons when it seeks to assist the conjugal act either in order to facilitate its performance or in order to enable it to achieve its objective once it has been normally performed.

On the other hand, it sometimes happens that a medical procedure technologically replaces the conjugal act in order to obtain a procreation which is neither its result nor its fruit. In this case the medical act is not, as it should be, at the service of conjugal union, but rather appropriates to itself the procreative function and thus contradicts the dignity and the inalienable rights of the spouses and of the child to be born.

The humanization of medicine, which is insisted upon today by everyone, requires respect for the integral dignity of the human person first of all in the act and at the moment in which the spouses transmit life to a new person. It is only logical therefore to address an urgent appeal to Catholic doctors and scientists that they bear exemplary witness to the respect due to the human embryo and to the dignity of procreation. The medical and nursing staff of Catholic hospitals and clinics are in a special way urged to do justice to the moral obligations which they have assumed, frequently also, as part of their contract. Those who are in charge of Catholic hospitals and clinics and who are often religious will take special care to safeguard and promote a diligent observance of the moral norms recalled in the present instruction.

The suffering caused by infertility in marriage.
The suffering of spouses who cannot have children or who are afraid of bringing a handicapped child into the world is a suffering that everyone must understand and properly evalutate.

On the part of the spouses, the desire for a child is natural: It expresses the vocation to fatherhood and motherhood inscribed in conjugal love. This desire can be even stronger if the couple is affected by sterility which appears incurable. Nevertheless, marriage does not confer upon the spouses the right to have a child, but only the right to perform those natural acts which are per se ordered to procreation.

A true and proper right to a child would be contrary to the child's dignity and nature. The child is not an object to which one has a right nor can he be considered as an object of ownership: Rather, a child is a gift, "the supreme gift" and the most gratuitous gift of marriage, and is a living testimony of the mutual giving of his parents. For this reason, the child has the right as already mentioned, to be the fruit of the specific act of the conjugal love of his parents; and he also has the right to be respected as a person from the moment of his conception.

Nevertheless, whatever its cause or prognosis, sterility is certainly a difficult trial. The community of believers is called to shed light upon and support the suffering of those who are unable to fulfill their legitimate aspiration to motherhood and fatherhood. Spouses who find themselves in this sad situation are called to find in it an opportunity for sharing in a particular way in the Lord's cross, the source of spiritual fruitfulness. Sterile couples must not forget that "even when procreation is not possible, conjugal life does not for this reason lose its value. Physical sterility in fact can be for spouses the occasion for other important services to the life of the human person, for example, adoption, various forms of educational work and assistance to other families and to poor or handicapped children." Many researchers are engaged in the fight against sterility. While fully safeguarding the dignity of human procreation, some have achieved results which previously seemed unattainable. Scientists therefore are to be encouraged to continue their research with the aim of preventing the causes of sterility and of being able to remedy them so that sterile couples will be able to procreate in full respect for their own personal dignity and that of the child to be born.

Surrogate Mothering: Exploitation or Empowerment?

LAURA M. PURDY

Taking a consequentialist approach, Purdy asserts that in some cases the benefits of surrogate mothering may outweigh its costs and thus be morally permissible. Some feminists argue that the practice is necessarily wrong because it transfers the burden and risks of pregnancy from one woman to another, because it separates sex from reproduction, or because it separates reproduction from child-rearing. But Purdy finds these arguments unconvincing. She examines the claim that surrogacy is baby-selling and concludes that "selling babies" is not an accurate description of what happens in surrogacy. A better characterization is that the birth mother is "giving up her parental right to have a relationship with the child." Certainly in some circumstances, surrogate mothering can be rendered immoral by coercion of the surrogate or by unjust surrogacy contracts. "Fair and reasonable regulations," she says, "are essential to prevent exploitation of women."

Introduction

"Pregnacy is barbaric"[1] proclaimed Shulamith Firestone in the first heady days of the new women's movement; she looked forward to the time when technology would free women from the oppression of biological reproduction. Yet as reproductive options multiply, some feminists are making common cause with conservatives for a ban on innovations. What is going on?

Firestone argued that nature oppresses women by leaving them holding the reproductive bag, while men are free of such burden; so long as this biological inequality holds, women will never be free (pp. 198–200). It is now commonplace to point out the naivety of her claim: it is not the biological difference per se that oppresses women, but its social significance. So we need not change biology, only attitudes and institutions.

This insight has helped us to see how to achieve a better life for women, but I wonder if it is the whole story. Has Firestone's brave claim no lesson at all for us?

Her point was that being with child is uncomfortable and dangerous, and it can limit women's lives. We have become more sensitive to the ways in which social arrangements can determine how much these difficulties affect us. However, even in feminist utopias, where sex or gender are considered morally irrelevant except where they may entail special needs, a few difficulties would remain. Infertility, for instance, would exist, as would the desire for a child in circumstances where pregnancy is impossible or undesirable.

At present, the problem of infertility is generating a whole series of responses and solutions. Among them are high-tech procedures like IVF, and social arrangements like surrogate motherhood. Both these techniques are also provoking a storm of concern and protest. As each raises a distinctive set of issues, they need to be dealt with separately, and I shall here consider only surrogate motherhood.

One might argue that no feminist paradise would need any practice such as this. As Susan Sherwin argues, it could not countenance "the capitalism, racism, sexism, and elitism of our culture [that] have combined to create a set of attitudes which views children as commodities whose value is derived from their possession of parental chromosomes."[2] Nor will society' define women's fulfilment as only in terms of their relationship to genetically-related children. No longer will children be needed as men's heirs or women's livelihood.

We will, on the contrary, desire relationships with children for the right reasons: the urge to nurture, teach and be close to them. No longer will we be

From *Bioethics*, vol. 3, no. 1 (1989), pp. 18–34. Copyright © Basil Blackwell Ltd. Reprinted with permission of Blackwell Publishing Ltd.

driven by narcissistic wishes for clones or immortality to seek genetic offspring no matter what the cost. Indeed, we will have recognized that children are the promise and responsibility of the whole human community. And child-rearing practices will reflect these facts, including at least a more diffuse family life that allows children to have significant relationships with others. Perhaps child-rearing will be communal.

This radically different world is hard to picture realistically, even by those like myself who—I think—most ardently wish for it. The doubts I feel are fanned by the visions of so-called cultural feminists who glorify traditionally feminine values. Family life can be suffocating, distorting, even deadly.[3] Yet there is a special closeness that arises from being a child's primary caretaker, just as there can be a special thrill in witnessing the unfolding of biologically-driven traits in that child. These pleasures justify risking neither the health of the child[4] nor that of the mother; nobody's general well-being should be sacrificed to them, nor do they warrant high social investment. However, they are things that, other things being equal, it would be desirable to preserve so long as people continue to have anything like their current values. If this is so, then evaluating the morality of practices that open up new ways of creating children is worthwhile.[5]

Moral or Immoral?

What is surrogate mothering exactly? Physically, its essential features are as follows: a woman is inseminated with the sperm of a man to whom she is not married. When the baby is born she relinquishes her claim to it in favour of another, usually the man from whom the sperm was obtained. As currently practiced, she provides the egg, so her biological input is at least equal to that of the man.[6] Surrogate mothering may not therefore be the best term for what she is doing.

By doing these things she also acts socially—to take on the burden and risk of pregnancy for another, and to separate sex and reproduction, reproduction and child-rearing, and reproduction and marriage. If she takes money for the transaction (apart from payment of medical bills), she may even be considered to be selling a baby.

The bare physical facts would not warrant the welter of accusation and counter-accusation that surrounds the practice.[7] It is the social aspects that have engendered the acrimony about exploitation, destruction of the family, and baby-selling. So far we have reached no consensus about the practice's effect on women or its overall morality.

I believe that the appropriate moral framework for addressing questions about the social aspects of contracted pregnancy is consequentialist.[8] This framework requires us to attempt to separate those consequences that invariably accompany a given act from those that accompany it only in particular circumstances. Doing this compels us to consider whether a practice's necessary features lead to unavoidable overridingly bad consequences. It also demands that we look at how different circumstances are likely to affect the outcome. Thus a practice which is moral in a feminist society may well be immoral in a sexist one. This distinction allows us to tailor morality to different conditions for optimum results without thereby incurring the charge of malignant relativism.

Before examining arguments against the practice of contracted pregnancy, let us take note of why people might favour it. First, as noted before, alleviating infertility can create much happiness. Secondly, there are often good reasons to consider transferring burden and risk from one individual to another. Pregnancy may be a serious burden or risk for one woman, whereas it is much less so for another. Some women love being pregnant, others hate it; pregnancy interferes with work for some, not for others; pregnancy also poses much higher levels of risk to health (or even life) for some than for others. Reducing burden and risk is a benefit not only for the woman involved, but also for the resulting child. High-risk pregnancies create, among other things, serious risk of prematurity, one of the major sources of handicap in babies. Furthermore, we could prevent serious genetic diseases by allowing carriers to avoid pregnancy. A third benefit of "surrogate mothering" is that it makes possible the creation of non-traditional families. This can be a significant source of happiness to single women and gay couples.

All of the above presuppose that there is some advantage in making possible at least partially genetically-based relationships between parents and offspring. Although, as I have argued above, we might be better off without this desire, I doubt that we will soon be free of it. Therefore, if we can satisfy it at little cost, we should try to do so.

Is Surrogate Mothering Always Wrong?

Despite the foregoing advantages, some feminists argue that the practice is *necessarily* wrong: it is wrong because it must betray women's and society's basic interests.[9]

What, if anything is wrong with the practice? Let us consider the first three acts I described earlier: transferring burden and risk, separating sex and reproduction, and separating reproduction and childrearing. Separation of reproduction and marriage will not be dealt with here.

Is it wrong to take on the burden of pregnancy for another? Doing this is certainly supererogatory, for pregnancy can threaten comfort, health, even life. One might argue that women should not be allowed to take these risks, but that would be paternalistic. We do not forbid mountain-climbing or riding a motorcycle on these grounds. How could we then forbid a woman to undertake this particular risk?

Perhaps the central issue is the transfer of burden from one woman to another. However, we frequently do just that—much more often than we recognize. Anyone who has her house cleaned, her hair done, or her clothes dry-cleaned is engaging in this procedure;[10] so is anyone who depends on agriculture or public works such as bridges.[11] To the objection that in this case the bargain includes the risk to life and limb, as well as use of time and skills, the answer is that the other activities just cited entail surprisingly elevated risk rates from exposure to toxic chemicals or dangerous machinery.[12]

Furthermore, it is not even true that contracted pregnancy merely shifts the health burden and risks associated with pregnancy from one woman to another. In some cases (infertility, for example) it makes the impossible possible; in others (for women with potentially high-risk pregnancies) the net risk is lowered.[13] As we saw, babies benefit, too, from better health and fewer handicaps. Better health and fewer handicaps in both babies and women also means that scarce resources can be made available for other needs, thus benefiting society in general.

I do think that there is, in addition, something suspect about all this new emphasis on risk. Awareness of risks inherent in even normal pregnancy constitutes progress: women have always been expected to forge ahead with child-bearing oblivious to risk. Furthermore, child-bearing has been thought to be something women owed to men or to society at large, regardless of their own feelings about a given—or any—pregnancy. When women had little say about these matters, we never heard about risk.[14] Why are we hearing about risk only now, now that women finally have some choices, some prospect of remuneration?[15] For that matter, why is our attention not drawn to the fact that surrogacy is one of the least risky approaches to non-traditional reproduction?[16]

Perhaps what is wrong about this kind of transfer is that it necessarily involves exploitation. Such exploitation may take the form of exploitation of women by men and exploitation of the rich by the poor. This possibility deserves serious consideration, and will be dealt with shortly.

Is there anything wrong with the proposed separation of sex and reproduction? Historically, this separation—in the form of contraception—has been beneficial to women and to society as a whole. Although there are those who judge the practice immoral, I do not think we need belabour the issue here.

It may be argued that not all types of separation are morally on a par. Contraception is permissible, because it spares women's health, promotes autonomy, strengthens family life, and helps make population growth manageable. But separation of sex and reproduction apart from contraception is quite another kettle of fish: it exploits women, weakens family life, and may increase population. Are these claims true and relevant?

Starting with the last first, if we face a population problem, it would make sense to rethink overall population policy, not exploit the problems of the infertile.[17] If family strengthing is a major justification for contraception, we might point out that contracted pregnancy will in some cases do the same. Whether or not having children can save a failing marriage, it will certainly prevent a man who wants children from leaving a woman incapable of providing them. We may bewail his priorities, but if his wife is sufficiently eager for the relationship to continue it would again be paternalistic for us to forbid "surrogacy" in such circumstances. That "surrogacy" reduces rather than promotes women's autonomy may be true under some circumstances, but there are good grounds for thinking that it can also enhance autonomy. It also remains to be shown that the practice systematically burdens women, or one class of women. In principle, the availability of new choices can be expected to nourish rather than stunt women's lives, so long as they retain control over their bodies and lives. The claim that contracted pregnancy destroys women's individuality and constitutes alienated labour, as Christine Overall argues, depends not only on a problematic Marxist analysis, but on the assumption that other jobs available to women are seriously less alienating.[18]

Perhaps what is wrong here is that contracted pregnancy seems to be the other side of the coin of prostitution. Prostitution is sex without reproduction; "surrogacy" is reproduction without sex. But it is difficult to form a persuasive argument that goes beyond mere guilt by association. Strictly speaking, contracted pregnancy is not prostitution; a broad-based Marxist definition would include it, but also traditional marriage. I think that in the absence of further argument, the force of this accusation is primarily emotional.

Perhaps the dread feature contracted pregnancy share with prostitution is that it is a lazy person's way of exploiting their own "natural resources." But I suspect that this idea reveals a touchingly naive view of what it takes to be a successful prostitute, not to mention the effort involved in running an optimum pregnancy. Overall takes up this point by asserting that it

> is not and cannot be merely one career choice among others. It is not a real alternative. It is implausible to suppose that fond parents would want it for their daughters. We are unlikely to set up training courses for surrogate mothers. Schools holding "career days" for their future graduates will surely not invite surrogate mothers to address the class on advantages of "vocation." And surrogate motherhood does not seem to be the kind of thing one would put on one's curriculum vitae. (p. 126)

But this seems to me to be a blatant *ad populum* argument.

Such an objection ought, in any case, to entail general condemnation of apparently effortless ways of life that involved any utilization of our distinctive characteristics.

We surely exploit our personal "natural resources" whenever we work. Ditchdiggers use their bodies, professors use their minds. Overall seems particularly to object to some types of "work": contracted pregnancy "is no more a real job option than selling one's blood or one's gametes or one's bodily organs can be real job options" (p. 126). But her discussion makes clear that her denial that such enterprises are "real" jobs is not based on any social arrangements that preclude earning a living wage doing these things, but rather on the moral judgement that they are wrong. They are wrong because they constitute serious "personal and bodily alienation." Yet her arguments for such alienation are weak. She contends that women who work as "surrogates" are deprived of any expression of individuality (p. 126), are interchangeable (p. 127), and that they have no choice about whose sperm to harbour (p. 128). It is true that, given a reasonable environment (partly provided by the woman herself), bodies create babies without conscious effort. This fact, it seems to me, has no particular moral significance: many tasks can be accomplished in similar ways yet are not thought valueless.[19]

It is also usually true that women involved in contracted pregnancy are, in some sense, interchangeable. But the same is true, quite possibly necessarily so, of most jobs. No one who has graded mounds of logic exams or introductory ethics essays could reasonably withhold their assent to this claim, even though college teaching is one of the most autonomous careers available. Even those of us lucky enough to teach upper-level courses that involve more expression of individual expertise and choice can be slotted into standardized job descriptions. Finally, it is just false that a woman can have no say about whose sperm she accepts: this could be guaranteed by proper regulation.

I wonder whether there is not some subtle devaluing of the physical by Overall. If so, then we are falling into the trap set by years of elitist equations of women, nature and inferiority.

What I think is really at issue here is the disposition of the fruit of contracted pregnancy: babies. However, it seems to be generally permissible to dispose of or barter what we produce with both our minds and our bodies—except for that which is created by our reproductive organs. So the position we are considering may just be a version of the claim that it is wrong to separate reproduction and child-rearing.

Why? It is true that women normally expect to become especially attached to the product of this particular kind of labour, and we generally regard such attachment as desirable. It seems to be essential for successfully rearing babies the usual way. But if they are to be reared by others who are able to form the appropriate attachment, then what is wrong if a surrogate mother fails to form it? It seems to me that the central question here is whether this "maternal instinct" really exists, and, if it does, whether suppressing it is always harmful.

Underlying these questions is the assumption that bonding with babies is "natural" and therefore "good." Perhaps so: the evolutionary advantage of such a tendency would be clear. It would be simpleminded, however, to assume that our habits are biologically determined: our culture is permeated with pronatalist bias.[20] "Natural" or not, whether a tendency to such attachment is desirable could reasonably be judged to depend on circumstance. When infant mortality is high[21] or responsibility for child-rearing is shared by the community, it could do more harm than good. Beware the naturalistic fallacy![22]

But surely there is something special about gestating a baby. That is, after all, the assumption behind the judgement that Mary Beth Whitehead, not William Stern, had a stronger claim to Baby M. The moral scoreboard seems clear: they both had the same genetic input, but she gestated the baby, and therefore has a better case for social parenthood.[23]

We need to be very careful here. Special rights have a way of being accompanied by special responsibilities: women's unique gestational relationship with babies may be taken as reason to confine them once more to the nursery. Furthermore, positing special rights entailed directly by biology flirts again with the naturalistic fallacy and undermines our capacity to adapt to changing situations and forge our destiny.[24]

Furthermore, we already except many varieties of such separation. We routinely engage in sending children to boarding school, foster parenting, daycare, and so forth; in the appropriate circumstances, these practices are clearly beneficial. Hence, any blanket condemnation of separating reproduction and child-rearing will not wash; additional argument is needed for particular classes of cases.

John Robertson points out that the arguments against separating reproduction and child-rearing used against contracted pregnancy are equally valid—but unused—with respect to adoption.[25] Others, such as Herbert Krimmel, reject this view by arguing that there is a big moral difference between giving away an already existing baby and deliberately creating one to give away. This remains to be shown, I think. It is also argued that as adoption outcomes are rather negative, we should be wary of extending any practice that shares its essential features. In fact, there seems to be amazingly little hard information about adoption outcomes. I wonder if the idea that they are bad results from media reports of offspring seeking their biological forebears. There is, in any case, reason to think that there are differences between the two practices such that the latter is likely to be more successful than the former.[26]

None of the social descriptions of surrogacy thus seem to clearly justify the outcry against the practice. I suspect that the remaining central issue is the crucial one: surrogacy is baby-selling and participating in this practice exploits and taints women.

Is Surrogacy Baby-Selling?

In the foregoing, I deliberately left vague the question of payment in contracted pregnancy. It is clear that there is a recognizable form of the practice that does not include payment; however, it also seems clear that controversy is focusing on the commercial form. The charge is that it is baby-selling and that this is wrong.

Is paid "surrogacy" baby-selling? Proponents deny that it is, arguing that women are merely making available their biological services. Opponents retort that as women are paid little or nothing if they fail to hand over a live, healthy child, they are indeed selling a baby. If they are merely selling their services they would get full pay, even if the child were born dead.

It is true women who agree to contracts relieving clients of responsibility in this case are being exploited. They, after all, have done their part, risked their risks, and should be paid—just like the physicians involved. Normal child-bearing provides no guarantee of a live, healthy child—why should contracted pregnancy?

There are further reasons for believing that women are selling their services, not babies. Firstly, we do not consider children property. Therefore, as we cannot sell what we do not own, we cannot be selling babies. What creates confusion here is that we do think we own sperm and ova. (Otherwise, how could men sell their sperm?) Yet we do not own what they become, persons. At what point, then, does the relationship cease to be describable as "ownership"?

Resolution of this question is not necessary to the current discussion. If we can own babies, there seems to be nothing problematic about selling them. If ownership ceases at some time before birth (and could thus be argued to be unconnected with personhood), then it is not selling of babies that is going on.

Although this response deals with the letter of the objection about baby-selling, it fails to heed its spirit, which is that we are trafficking in persons, and that such trafficking is wrong. Even if we are not "selling," something nasty is happening.

The most common analogy, with slavery, is weak. Slavery is wrong according to any decent moral theory: the institution allows people to be treated badly. Their desires and interests, whose satisfaction is held to be essential for a good life, are held in contempt. Particularly egregious is the callous disregard of emotional ties to family and self-determination generally. But the institution of surrogate mothering deprives babies of neither.[27] In short, as Robertson contends, "the purchasers do not buy the right to treat the child . . . as a commodity or property. Child abuse and neglect laws still apply" (p. 655).

If "selling babies" is not the right description of what is occurring, then how are we to explain what happens when the birth mother hands the child over to others? One plausible suggestion is that she is giving up her parental right to have a relationship with the child.[28] That it is wrong to do this for pay remains to be shown. Although it would be egoistic and immoral to "sell" an ongoing, friendly relationship (doing so would raise questions about whether it was friendship at all), the immorality of selling a relationship with an organism your body has created but with which you do not yet have a unique social bond, is a great deal less clear.[29]

People seem to feel much less strongly about the wrongness of such acts when motivated by altruism; refusing compensation is the only acceptable proof of such altruism. The act is, in any case, socially valuable. Why then must it be motivated by altruistic considerations? We do not frown upon those who provide other socially valuable services even when they do not have the "right" motive. Nor do we require them to be unpaid. For instance, no one expects physicians, no matter what their motivation, to work for beans. They provide an important service; their motivation is important only to the extent that it affects quality.

In general, workers are required to have appropriate skills, not particular motivations.[30] Once again, it seems that there is a different standard for women and for men.

One worry is that women cannot be involved in contracted pregnancy without harming themselves, as it is difficult to let go of a child without lingering concern. So far, despite the heavily-publicized Baby M case, this appears not to be necessarily true.[31]

Another worry is that the practice will harm children. Children's welfare is, of course, important. Children deserve the same consideration as other persons, and no society that fails to meet their basic needs is morally satisfactory. Yet I am suspicious of the objections raised on their behalf in these discussions: recourse to children's alleged well-being is once again being used as a trump card against women's autonomy.

First, we hear only about possible risks, never possible benefits, which, as I have been arguing, could be substantial.[32] Second, the main objection raised is the worry about how children will take the knowledge that their genetic mother conceived on behalf of another. We do not know how children will feel about having had such "surrogate" mothers. But as it is not a completely new phenomenon we might start our inquiry about this topic with historical evidence, not pessimistic speculation. In any case, if the practice is dealt with in an honest and common-sense way, particularly if it becomes quite common (and therefore "normal"), there is likely to be no problem. We are also hearing about the worries of existing children of women who are involved in the practice: there are reports that they fear their mother will give them away, too. But surely we can make clear to children the kinds of distinctions that distinguish the practice from slavery or baby-selling in the first place.

Although we must try to foresee what might harm children, I cannot help but wonder about the double standards implied by this speculation. The first double standard occurs when those who oppose surrogacy (and reproductive technologies generally) also oppose attempts to reduce the number of handicapped babies born.[33] In the latter context, it is argued that despite their problems handicapped persons are often glad to be alive. Hence it would be paternalistic to attempt to prevent their birth.

Why then do we not hear the same argument here? Instead, the possible disturbance of children born of surrogacy is taken as a reason to prevent their birth. Yet this potential problem is both more remote and most likely involves less suffering than such ailments as spina bifida, Huntington's Disease or cystic fibrosis, which some do not take to be reasons to refrain from child-bearing.[34]

Considering the sorts of reasons why parents have children, it is hard to see why the idea that one was conceived in order to provide a desperately-wanted child to another is thought to be problematic. One might well prefer that to the idea that one was an "accident," adopted, born because contraception or abortion were not available, conceived to cement a failing marriage, to continue a family line, to qualify for welfare aid, to sex-balance a family, or as an experiment in child-rearing. Surely what matters for a child's well-being in the end is whether it is being raised in a loving, intelligent environment.

The second double standard involves a disparity between the interests of women and children. Arguing that surrogacy is wrong because it may upset children suggests a disturbing conception of the moral order. Women should receive consideration at least equal to that accorded children. Conflicts of interest between the two should be resolved according to the same rules we use for any other moral subjects. Those rules should never prescribe sacrificing one individual's basic interest at the mere hint of harm to another.

In sum, there seems to be no reason to think that there is anything necessarily wrong with "surrogate mothering," even the paid variety. Furthermore, some objections to it depend on values and assumptions that have been the chief building blocks of women's inequality. Why are some feminists asserting them? Is it because "surrogacy" as currently practiced often exploits women?

Is "Surrogate Mothering" Wrong in Certain Situations?

Even if "surrogate mothering" is not necessarily immoral, circumstances can render it so. For instance, it is obviously wrong to coerce women to engage in the practice. Also, certain conditions are unacceptable. Among them are clauses in a contract that subordinate a woman's reasonable desires and judgements to the will of another contracting party,[35] clauses legitimating inadequate pay for the risks and discomforts involved, and clauses that penalize her for the birth of a handicapped or dead baby through no fault of her own. Such contracts are now common.[36]

One popular solution to the problem of such immoral contracts is a law forbidding all surrogacy agreements; their terms would then be unenforceable. But I believe that women will continue to engage in surrogate mothering, even if it is unregulated, and this approach leaves them vulnerable to those who change their mind, or will not pay. Fair and reasonable regulations are essential to prevent exploitation of women. Although surrogate mothering may seem risky and uncomfortable to middle-class persons safely ensconced in healthy, interesting, relatively well-paid jobs, with adequate regulation it becomes an attractive option for some women. That these women are more likely than not to be poor is no reason to prohibit the activity.

As I suggested earlier, poor women now face substantial risks in the workplace. Even a superficial survey of hazards in occupations available to poor women would give pause to those who would prohibit surrogacy on the grounds of risk.[37] Particularly shocking is the list of harmful substances and conditions to which working women are routinely exposed. For instance, cosmeticians and hairdressers, dry-cleaners and dental technicians are all exposed to carcinogens in their daily work (Stellman, Appendixes 1 and 2). Most low-level jobs also have high rates of exposure to toxic chemicals and dangerous machinery, and women take such jobs in disproportionate numbers. It is therefore unsurprising that poor women sicken and die more often than other members of society.[38]

This is not an argument in favour of adding yet another dangerous option to those already facing such women. Nor does it follow that the burdens they already bear justify the new ones. On the contrary, it is imperative to clean up dangerous workplaces. However, it would be utopian to think that this will occur in the near future. We must therefore attempt to improve women's lot under existing conditions. Under these circumstances it would be irrational to prohibit surrogacy on the grounds of risk when women would instead have to engage in still riskier pursuits.

Overall's emphatic assertion that contracted pregnancy is not a "real choice" for women is unconvincing. Her major argument, as I suggested earlier, is that it is an immoral, alienating option. But she also believes that such apparently expanded choices simply mask an underlying contraction of choice (p. 124). She also fears that by "endorsing an uncritical freedom of reproductive choice, we may also be implicitly endorsing all conceivable alternatives that an individual might adopt; we thereby abandon the responsibility for evaluating substantive actions in favour of advocating merely formal freedom of choice" (p. 125). Both worries are, as they stand, unpersuasive.

As I argued before, there is something troubling here about the new and one-sided emphasis on risk. If nothing else, we need to remember that contracted pregnancy constitutes a low-tech approach to a social problem, one which would slow the impetus toward expensive and dangerous high-tech solutions.[39]

A desire for children on the part of those who normally could not have them is not likely to disappear anytime soon. We could discount it, as many participants in debate about new reproductive technologies do. After all, nobody promised a rose garden to infertile couples, much less to homosexuals or to single women. Nor is it desirable to propagate the idea that having children is essential for human fulfilment.

But appealing to the sacrosanctity of traditional marriage or of blood ties to prohibit otherwise acceptable practices that would satisfy people's desires hardly makes sense, especially when those practices may provide other benefits. Not only might contracted pregnancy be less risky and more enjoyable than other jobs women are forced to take, but there are other advantages as well. Since being pregnant is not usually a full-time occupation, "surrogate mothering" could buy time for women to significantly improve their lot: students, aspiring writers, and social activists could make real progress toward their goals.

Women have until now done this reproductive labour for free.[40] Paying women to bear children should force us all to recognize this process as the socially useful enterprise that it is, and children as socially valuable creatures whose upbringing and welfare are critically important.

In short, "surrogate mothering" has the potential to empower women and increase their status in society. The darker side of the story is that it also has frightening potential for deepening their exploitation. The outcome of the current warfare over control of new reproductive possibilities will determine which of these alternatives comes to pass.

NOTES

1. Shulamith Firestone, *The Dialectic of Sex* (New York: Bantam Books, 1970), p. 198. A version of this paper was given at the Eastern SWIP meeting, 26 March 1988. I would like especially to thank Helen B. Holmes and Sara Ann Ketchum for their useful comments on this paper; they are, of course, in no way responsible for its perverse position! Thanks also to the editors and referees of *Bioethics* for their helpful criticisms.

2. Susan Sherwin, "Feminist Ethics and *In Vitro* Fertilization," *Science, Morality and Feminist Theory*, ed. Marsha Hanen and Kai Nielsen, *Canadian Journal of Philosophy*, supplementary volume 13 (1987), p. 277.

3. Consider the many accounts of the devastating things parents have done to children, in particular.

4. See L. M. Purdy. "Genetic Diseases: Can Having Children be Immoral?" *Moral Problems in Medicine*, ed. Samuel Gorovitz (Englewood Cliffs, NJ: Prentice-Hall, 1983), pp. 377–84.

5. Another critical issue is that no feminist utopia will have a supply of "problem" children whom no one wants. Thus the

proposal often heard nowadays that people should just adopt all those handicapped, non-white kids will not do. (Nor does it "do" now.)

6. I share with Sara Ann Ketchum the sense that this term is not adequate, although I am not altogether happy with her suggestion that we call it "contracted motherhood" ("New Reproductive Technologies and the Definition of Parenthood: A Feminist Perspective," paper given at the 1987 *Feminism and Legal Theory Conference*, at the University of Wisconsin at Madison, summer 1987, pp. 44ff.). It would be better, I think, to reserve terms like "mother" for the social act of nurturing. I shall therefore substitute the terms "contracted pregnancy" and "surrogacy" (in quotes).

7. This is not to say that no one would take the same view as I: the Catholic Church, for instance, objects to the masturbatory act required for surrogacy to proceed.

8. The difficulty in choosing the "right" moral theory to back up judgments in applied ethics, given that none are fully satisfactory, continues to be vexing. I would like to reassure those who lose interest at the mere sight of consequentialist—let alone utilitarian—judgement, that there are good reasons for considering justice an integral part of moral reasoning, as it quite obviously has utility.

A different issue is raised by the burgeoning literature on feminist ethics. I strongly suspect that utilitarianism could serve feminists well, if properly applied. (For a defence of this position, see my paper "Do Feminists Need a New Moral Theory," given at the University of Minnesota, Duluth, at the conference *Explorations in Feminist Ethics: Theory and Practice*, 8–9 October 1988.)

9. See for example Gena Corea, *The Mother Machine*, and Christine Overall, *Ethics and Human Reproduction* (Winchester, MA: Allen & Unwin, 1987).

10. These are just a couple of examples in the sort of risky service that we tend to take for granted.

11. Modern agricultural products are brought to us as some risk by farm workers. Any large construction project will also result in some morbidity and mortality.

12. Even something so mundane as postal service involves serious risk on the part of workers.

13. The benefit to both high-risk women, and to society is clear. Women need not risk serious deterioration of health or abnormally high death rates.

14. See Laura Purdy, "The Morality of New Reproductive Technologies," *Journal of Social Philosophy* (Winter 1987), 38–48.

15. For elaboration of this view, consider Jane Ollenburger and John Hamlin, "'All Birthing Should Be Paid Labor'"—a Marxist Analysis of the Commodification of Motherhood," in *On the Problem of Surrogate Parenthood: Analyzing the Baby M Case*, ed. Herbert Richardson, (Lewiston, NY: Edwin Mellen Press, 1987).

16. Compare the physical risk with that of certain contraceptive technologies, and high-tech fertility treatments like IVF.

17. Infertility is often a result of social arrangements. This process would therefore be especially unfair to those who have already been exposed to more than their share of toxic chemicals or other harmful conditions.

18. Christine Overall, *Ethics and Human Reproduction*, (Winchester, MA: Allen & Unwin, 1987), ch. 6. Particularly problematic are her comments about women's loss of individuality, as I will be arguing shortly.

19. Men have been getting handsome pay for sperm donation for years; by comparison with child-bearing, such donation is a lark. Yet there has been no outcry about its immorality. Another double standard?

20. See Ellen Peck and Judith Senderowitz, *Pronatalism: The Myth of Mom and Apple Pie* (New York: Thomas Y. Crowell, 1974).

20. As it has been at some periods in the past: see for example information about family relationships in Philippe Ariès, *Centuries of Childhood: A Social History of Family Life*, trans. Robert Baldick (New York, 1982), and Lloyd DeMause's work.

22. Consider the arguments in ch. 8 of *Women's Work*, by Ann Oakley (New York: Vintage Books, 1974).

23. One of the interesting things about the practice of contracted pregnancy is that it can be argued to both strengthen and weaken the social recognition of biological relationships. On the one hand, the pregnant woman's biological relationship is judged irrelevant beyond a certain point; on the other, the reason for not valuing it is to enhance that of the sperm donor. This might be interpreted as yet another case where men's interests are allowed to overrule women's. But it might also be interpreted as a salutary step toward awareness that biological ties can and sometimes should be subordinated to social ones. Deciding which interpretation is correct will depend on the facts of particular cases, and the arguments taken to justify the practice in the first place.

24. Science fiction, most notably John Wyndham's *The Midwich Cuckoos*, provides us with thought-provoking material.

25. John Robertson, "Surrogate Mothers: Not so Novel After All," *Hastings Center Report*, vol. 13, no. 5 (October 1983). This article is reprinted in *Bioethics*, ed. Rem B. Edwards and Glen C. Graber (San Diego, CA: Harcourt, Brace Jovanovich, 1988). Krimmel's article ("The Case Against Surrogate Parenting") was also originally published in the *Hastings Center Report* and is reprinted in *Bioethics*. References here are to the latter.

26. One major difference between adoption and contracted pregnancy is that the baby is handed over virtually at birth, thus ensuring that the trauma sometimes experienced by older adoptees is not experienced. Although children of contracted pregnancy might well be curious to know about their biological mother, I do not see this as a serious obstacle to the practice, since we could change our policy about this. There is also reason to believe that carefully-screened women undertaking a properly-regulated contracted pregnancy are less likely to experience lingering pain of separation. First, they have deliberately chosen to go through pregnancy, knowing

that they will give the baby up. The resulting sense of control is probably critical to their short- and long-term well-being. Second, their pregnancy is not the result of trauma. See also Monica B. Morris, "Reproductive Technology and Restraints," *Transaction/SOCIETY* (March/April 1988), 16–22, esp. p. 18.

27. There may be a problem for the woman who gives birth, as the Baby M case has demonstrated. There is probably a case for a waiting period after the birth during which the woman can change her mind.

28. Heidi Malm suggested this position in her comment on Sara Ann Ketchum's paper "Selling Babies and Selling Bodies: Surrogate Motherhood and the Problem of Commodificaton," at the Eastern Division *APA* meetings, 30 December 1987.

29. Mary Anne Warren suggests, alternately, that this objection could be obviated by women and children retaining some rights and responsibilities toward each other in contracted pregnancy. Maintaining a relationship of sorts might also, she suggests, help forestall and alleviate whatever negative feelings children might have about such transfers. I agree that such openness is probably a good idea in any case. (Referee's comment.)

31. Perhaps lurking behind the objections of surrogacy is some feeling that it is wrong to earn money by letting your body work, without active effort on your part. But this would rule out sperm selling, as well as using women's beauty to sell products and services.

31. See, for example, James Rachels, "A Report from America: The Baby M Case," *Bioethics*, vol. 1, n. 4 (October 1987), 365. He reports that there have been over 600 successful cases; see also the above note on adoption.

32. Among them the above-mentioned one of being born healthier.

33. To avoid the difficulties about abortion added by the assumption that we are talking about existing fetuses, let us consider here only the issue of whether certain couples should risk pregnancy.

34. There is an interesting link here between these two aspects of reproduction, as the promise of healthier children is, I think, one of the strongest arguments for contracted pregnancy.

35. What this may consist of naturally requires much additional elucidation.

36. See Susan Ince, "Inside the Surrogate Industry," *Test-Tube Women*, ed. Rita Arditti, Renate Duelli Klein, and Shelley Minden (London: Pandora Press, 1984).

37. See, for example, Jeanne Mager Stellman, *Women's Work, Women's Health* (New York: Pantheon, 1977).

38. See George L. Waldbott, *Health Effects of Environmental Pollutants* (St Louis: C. V. Mosby, 1973); Nicholas Ashford, *Crisis in the Workplace: Occupational Disease and Injury* (Cambridge: MIT Press, 1976); *Cancer and the Worker* (New York Academy of Science, 1977); *Environmental Problems in Medicine*, ed. William D. McKee (Springfield, IL: Charles C. Thomas, 1977).

39. These are the ones most likely to put women in the clutches of the paternalistic medical establishment. Exploitation by commercial operations such as that of Noel Keane could be avoided by tight regulation or prohibition altogether of for-profit enterprises.

40. The implications of this fact remain to be fully understood; I suspect that they are detrimental to women and children, but that this is a topic for another paper.

On "Surrogacy"[1]

BARBARA KATZ ROTHMAN

Rothman asserts that in the conflicts arising from surrogacy arrangements the central question is what makes a woman a mother. Her answer is that the gestational mother is the real mother: "Any pregnant woman is the mother of the child she bears. Her gestational relationship establishes her motherhood." Thus regardless of whose sperm or eggs are involved, paid surrogacy contracts amount to baby-selling and are illegitimate. "I cannot ever believe that a woman is pregnant with someone else's baby," Rothman says. "The idea is repugnant—it reduces the woman to a container."

A Question of Policy

The first thing to bear in mind is that surrogate motherhood is not a new procreative technology. The business of "surrogacy" has nothing to do with scientific progress, and everything to do with marketing. The procreative technology used is artificial insemination. Artificial insemination with donor sperm has been used in human beings for over a hundred years. The "technologies" involved are the technology of masturbation, and of the turkey baster or its equivalent.

It is important to remember that is the case, because we are sometimes overwhelmed with the developments of the new procreative technology, as with our other technologies. Sometimes we think—and sometimes we are encouraged to think—that there is nothing we can do to halt "progress." If science can produce "test-tube babies," how can we ever stop it? And if our new knowledge gives us these new powers, should we even want to stop it?

These are important questions. But they are not the questions of surrogate motherhood. Surrogate motherhood was not brought to us by the march of scientific progress. It was brought to us by brokers, by people who saw a new market and went after it. And the market is something we know we *can* control, and often *should* control.

When artificial insemination was introduced, it was used to support the traditional family structure, husbands and wives having and raising babies. In earlier times, when couples were unable to start a pregnancy, it was most often assumed to be the fault of the wife, and in some cultures husbands had the recourse of divorce. With expanding knowledge, infertility was shown to be sometimes a problem in the husband's body. Wives were not given the recourse of divorce under these circumstances, and artificial insemination became a way of maintaining the intact husband-wife unit. Wives were not encouraged to take a "surrogate," a substitute lover, but rather doctors used semen, given anonymously, to impregnate wives.

The process was undertaken with the greatest of secrecy. According to some accounts, the wife herself was not told what was done to her in the first American use of artificial insemination.[2] Certainly, no one outside of the couple and the doctor were told—artificial insemination was shrouded in silence. This enabled men to be the social fathers of the children their wives bore.

Social fatherhood is the key issue here. What makes a woman a mother has always been quite obvious. But what makes a man a father has been subject to some question. The formula our society (along with many others) has arrived at is that fatherhood is determined by the man's relationship to the child's mother. A man married to a woman is the recognized father of her children. This way of reckoning fatherhood builds on two things: the obvious and unquestioned nature of biological motherhood, and the traditional patriarchal relationship of men and their wives. This is a way of acknowledging parenthood that is based on relationships: the relationship of the woman to her baby as it grows within, and the relationship of the man to the woman.

And so it stood for over a hundred years: artificial insemination was a way of managing male infertility that kept the patriarchal family intact, that allowed children to be born to a couple, children who would be truly theirs, to bring into the world together, to raise and to cherish together.

So what changed? For one thing, infertility appears to be more of a social problem: the actual rates of infertility may or may not be rising, but societal concern certainly is. For another, the supply of babies available for adoption has dropped dramatically. Young women, faced with unwanted pregnancies, have been given choices: the choice of abortion and the choice of raising a child without a husband. Infertile couples can no longer benefit, no matter how innocently, from the tragedies of young mothers. Our attitude toward infertility has also changed—and this may indeed be an indirect result of scientific progress. Progress against infertility has become a newspaper and television staple. Remember the excitement that surrounded the first in vitro baby, the first American in vitro baby, the first in vitro twins, and so on. The first in vitro quints were the cover story of *People* magazine in 1988.[3] The idea began to be generated that infertility was curable, if only a couple tried hard enough, saw enough doctors, went through enough procedures. The reality is something quite different. Only 10 percent of those couples attempting in vitro fertilization will have a baby. There is a 90 percent failure rate with that technology.

What we have done is to create a population of desperate, heartbroken infertile people: people who cannot find babies to adopt, who have "tried everything" and cannot get pregnant, people who have devoted years of their lives to trying, one way or another, to get a baby.

The medical technology has enabled the couple to sort out "whose fault" the infertility is. When it is the husband who is infertile, the use of insemination with donor sperm remains a solution, enabling the couple to have a pregnancy and the much-wanted baby. When it is the wife who is infertile, the pressures mount on the woman to feel guilt at not being able to "give her husband" a child. A baby is what they want more than anything. And he could have one, if not for her.

It is in this context that the marketing of "surrogate" motherhood developed. Brokers entered the scene, telling the couple that they can indeed have a baby, and it will be "his" baby. "Surrogate motherhood" was sold as a solution to the tragedy of infertility and a way of resolving women's guilt at their own infertility. For couples who had spent untold thousands of dollars on medical treatments, the thousands more for surrogacy contracts may have seemed a bargain. For people living without these many thousands of dollars, infertility remains unsolved.

With this new use of artificial insemination, the relationships of the parties involved changed totally. The relationship of the mother to her baby within her no longer counts. The baby has become a commodity, something a woman can produce and sell. She is encouraged to think of the baby as no more hers than a factory worker thinks of the car he works on as his. The relationship of the father to the mother no longer counts: it will cease to exist as motherhood is made anonymous, handled by brokers and doctors. The relationships that will count are that of the father to his sperm donation and that of the market: the contracts and the fees. What makes a man a father is not his relationship to the mother, we are told, but that it is his sperm and his money.

The brokers tell us that this is not baby selling: how can a man buy his own baby? they ask. And true enough, how can someone buy something which is already his? But what makes the baby his? If the sperm donor in more traditional artificial insemination came up to the couple a year later, said he had had an accident and was now infertile, and would like to have their baby, he would have no right to it. If he offered them money, he would not be buying that which is his, but that which is theirs: producing a semen sample does not make a man a social father, does not make that his baby. Is it then his intention that makes the child his? The fathers in the surro-

gacy cases do not donate their sperm. They are not donating or giving or selling. They are buying. Then how is this different from any other example of baby buying and selling? The answer is it is not.

If we legalize surrogacy arrangements, then to buy a baby one will need sperm and money. Couples—or just men—who have both can buy babies. But what of lesbian couples? And what of men without adequate sperm? Many cases of infertility involve both partners. What of a couple desperate to have a baby in which the wife cannot carry a pregnancy and the husband has insufficient sperm, or carries a deadly disease? Sperm, too, is for sale: we literally have sperm banks. If we permit surrogate motherhood for the situation of men who produce their "own" sperm, then what of the men who must buy sperm? Broker Noel Keane says he is prepared to make such arrangements.[4] Once sperm is purchased, the owners of the sperm can use that sperm as their "own" to make their "own" baby with a surrogate. We are going to find ourselves selling babies in "kit" form, purchasing the pieces and services separately: sperm here, an egg there, a rented uterus somewhere else. This is of course a "slippery slope" kind of argument—once you permit some people to buy some babies under some conditions, it is very hard to justify any given person not being allowed to purchase a baby under other circumstances.

So surrogacy is baby selling. As Angela Holder has said, "If I order a widget from a widget maker, and I pay cash money for that widget, and a widget is delivered to me, I defy you to tell me I have not bought a widget."[5]

And what would be wrong with simply opening up a market economy in babies? Others have argued eloquently what the problems are with baby selling, and we have as a society accepted those arguments. Some things, we have felt, should simply not be sold—and certainly not people. One of the strongest arguments against baby selling is that we know that if we allowed babies to be sold, some people would be put under great pressure to sell their babies. This is the same reason that we do not allow organs to be sold from living people, even when we know that lives might actually be saved. If we allowed some people to sell, say, a kidney, we know that some might feel forced to do so. And so now and again someone with much money dies for lack of an organ that he or she was willing to buy and someone else was willing to sell because such a sale, such a contract, even if arguably in the best interests of the parties involved, would be against the best interests of the society as a whole. I believe that "surrogacy" presents a situation parallel to organ selling, and that the same arguments apply.

I began by saying that surrogacy is not a result of new procreative technology, but must be understood entirely as a marketing strategy Let me now amend that slightly. Most of the surrogate motherhood cases that reach the courts and the media are based on the old technology of artificial insemination. But some are using a newer technology. We must consider what these new developments in procreative technology will mean for the future of surrogacy contracts.

The new technologies are varied, but share in common the use of genetic material from one woman to create a pregnancy in the body of another woman. There are several ways this can be done. An egg from one woman can be removed, fertilized in vitro (in glass), and put into the body of another woman. Some in vitro fertilization clinics are doing this for women who want to become mothers but cannot produce eggs. Other women, who produce "extra" eggs, donate those eggs for the use of infertile women who cannot produce their own eggs. Sometimes the donors are other women in the program who are ovulating well, sometimes they are hired egg donors, and sometimes they are friends or relatives of the infertile woman. Whether donated or purchased, genetic material from outside of the couple is used to enable a woman and her husband to have a pregnancy and share in the birthing and rearing of a baby. The situation is most closely analogous to artificial insemination with donated or purchased sperm.

Another way that this same thing can be accomplished is by allowing fertilization to take place within the body of the woman who is donating the egg. A fertilized egg, what some call a pre-embryo or pre-implantation embryo, is moved from the donor and placed within the body of the woman who will be the mother. This, too, is much like artificial insemination. Some months later we look at a pregnant woman and her husband expecting their child. In these situations of embryo transfer or egg donation, like the situation of artificial insemination with donor sperm, genetic material from outside the couple is used to create the pregnancy, but social parenthood, from the point of early pregnancy on, is shared within the couple.

That then is the technology. And what of the marketing? Like the marketing of artificial insemination, egg donations can also be turned around and used to create a pregnancy not within the family, but in a hired woman, leading to the ultimate purchase of a baby.

With this technology, it is not necessary for the "surrogate" to be genetically related to the baby she bears. So one marketing strategy is to hire a woman to carry a pregnancy for a woman who can produce eggs but not carry a pregnancy for herself. Now something challenging happens to our thinking: we are forced to confront the question of what makes a woman a mother. Is it the egg, or is it the pregnancy? In the cases mentioned above, where a woman is unable to create an egg, the transfer of the egg or embryo left the pregnant woman the social mother: it was the pregnant woman who intended to be the mother, who not only intended to bear and birth the child, but to raise the child as well. But if we hire a woman to carry the pregnancy, who then is the mother? Is it the egg donor, or the pregnant woman?

In one court decision involving such a case, the egg donor was named as the mother, and the name of the pregnant woman—the gestational mother—was not put on the birth certificate. This is of course analogous to the marketing of surrogate motherhood with the old technology of artificial insemination. Relationships are discounted, and the genetic tie as well as the exchange of money are given primacy. We are asked to accept the idea that the mother is the person who owned the egg and paid for the service, just as we are asked to accept the man who owned the sperm and paid for the services as the father.

This opens up an enormous new profit potential for the brokers in the surrogacy market. The technologies of egg and embryo transfer, were surrogate motherhood contracts made enforceable, could be used to drive costs down and keep profits up for the baby brokers. As it stands now, the brokers are limited in their use of surrogate mothers. Because the women are genetically related to the babies they produce, the father-purchasers want only certain kinds of women: intelligent, attractive, and most assuredly of the same race as the couple. Since it is predominantly white couples who have the $25,000 and up that the brokers charge, and since it is particularly white babies that are in scarce supply for adoption, what brokers need are intelligent, attractive, healthy white women to act as surrogates. In our society, such women can command some money for their services, not enormous sums compared, say, to what corporate executives—or for that matter truck drivers—get, but at this moment the going rate is $10,000 to the mother.

But what will happen if the new technology allows brokers to hire women who are not related genetically to the babies that are to be sold? Like the poor and non-white women who are hired to do other kinds of nurturing and caretaking work, these mothers can be paid very little, with few benefits, and no long-term commitment. The same women who are pushing white babies in strollers, white old folks in wheelchairs, can be carrying white babies in their bellies. Poor, uneducated third-world women and women of color from the United States and elsewhere, with fewer economic alternatives, can be hired more cheaply. They can also be controlled more tightly. With a legally supported surrogate motherhood contract, and with the new technology, the marketing possibilities are enormous—and terrifying. Just as Perdue and Holly Farms advertise their chickens based on superior breeding and feeding, the baby brokers could begin to advertise their babies: brand name, state-of-the-art babies produced from the "finest" of genetic materials and an all-natural, vitamin-enriched diet.

I used to envision such "baby farms" located in third-world countries, supplying babies to American purchasers. But now I wonder: most European countries have outlawed surrogacy-for-hire. In the United States, as long as one state permits it, if we have no national legislation barring it, the business can be legally established. Remember, in the most famous surrogacy case to date, that of Baby M,

both the Sterns and the Whiteheads lived in New Jersey, the broker lived in Michigan, the clinic was located in New York, and the adoption was slated to go through Florida. If just one state exists for the legal paperwork, it may be the third-world women of America—the women of our inner-city ghettos—who grow babies for "export." It is in the United States that the rights of rich people to buy are most deeply held.

The time to stop such nightmare visions is now. We stop it by not acknowledging the underlying principle of surrogate contracts, by not accepting the very concept of "surrogacy" for motherhood. A surrogate is a substitute. In some human relations, we can accept no substitutes. Any pregnant woman is the mother of the child she bears. Her gestational relationship establishes her motherhood. We will not accept the idea that we can look at a woman, heavy with child, and say the child is not hers. The fetus is part of the woman's body, regardless of the source of the egg and sperm. Biological motherhood is not a service, not a commodity, but a relationship. Motherhood can remain obvious. If a woman is carrying a baby, then it is her baby and she is its mother. Of course it is true that a mother, any mother, can abdicate her motherhood, can give away a baby. But it is hers to give. And if we were to allow the selling of babies, then it is hers to sell, or refuse to sell.

And what can we do with fatherhood? How can we protect the relationship between a father and his child? What will make a man a father? One possibility is to stay with the model that we had: a father can continue to take his fatherhood from his relationship with the mother of the child. In a married couple, the father can continue to be, as hitherto, the husband of the mother.

That is not a perfect solution to the troubling question of fatherhood. It gives, in some ways, too much power to women over men's procreation. And it gives, in other ways, too much power to men over women's procreation. But this is not a new problem. We are not struggling here with questions of science and new technology. Here we are struggling with ago-old questions of relationships, of family, of how we are bound together. We have not found perfect ways of dealing with these issues in all of history. But we have, in this society, been clear in rejecting the use of money in these relationships. We have said that in our society husbands and wives, mothers and fathers, and babies are not for sale. Nothing in the new procreative technology need change that.

Those engaged in surrogacy brokering tell us that if we do not bring surrogacy into the open market, it, like adoption, will continue to exist in "gray-" or black-market forms. And they are probably right. Preventing the open sale of babies has not prevented couples from having to spend much money on getting babies, nor has it prevented brokers from making money out of matching babies to adopters.

I do not disagree with the brokers over acknowledging the problem, but over choosing the solution. There are grave costs to any form of open market in baby selling. If we wish to legalize baby selling, let us acknowledge what we are doing, and offer the appropriate protections to the parties involved. If we choose to allow a woman to sell her baby, so be it. But let us recognize that it is indeed her baby that she is selling. And if we do not wish to permit baby selling, then there is nothing in the new procreative technology that forces us to do so. We do not have to give the support of the state and of the courts to a view of babies as purchasable commodities or motherhood as a salable service.

In sum, the legislation I feel we need to develop as national policy in the United States would recognize that *the gestational mother is the mother.* Any pregnant woman is the mother of the child she bears, regardless of the source of the egg or the sperm. The rights and the responsibilities of motherhood are the same for all gestational mothers, regardless of the source of the egg and the sperm.

Therefore, *purchasing a baby from its mother, regardless of the source of the egg and the sperm, is purchasing a baby.* Until or unless we legalize baby selling, the law cannot acknowledge paid surrogacy contracts. Surrogacy is not to be used as a way around the laws against the sale of babies: it is itself a variation of baby selling.

Further, *accepting a baby as a gift from its mother, regardless of the source of the egg and the sperm, is a form of adoption.* The laws that govern the rights and responsibilities of all parties to an adoption must apply to so-called surrogate arrangements as well.

A Question of Values

People—friends, colleagues, maybe especially family—keep pointing out to me, with a bemused air, how strange it is to find me arguing on the same side as religious leaders in the debate on surrogacy arrangements. And I, too, occasionally find some amusement in the "strange bedfellows" phenomenon. Indeed, with carefully groomed "happy surrogates" and their equally well-groomed brokers placed on a TV or radio show by a professional public relations firm, I often find myself, side-by-side with some priest or rabbi, brought in by a producer to give a "balanced" view. And so we argue out the problems of surrogacy, sandwiched between car commercials, wine cooler ads, and other signs of the times.

The "tag" they use to identify me on television—the white line of print that shows up on the screen but which I never get to see in the studio—sometimes reads *author*, rarely reads *sociologist*, but most often they seem to use *feminist*. And so there we are, "feminist" and "priest" or "rabbi" arguing the same, antisurrogacy side.

But it is only on the very surface that I am on the same side as these religious leaders. We may have landed on the same side of this particular fence, but we've taken very different paths to get there, and we are headed in very different directions. The values that I use in my opposition to surrogacy are fundamentally different from those the religious leaders are using, and the goals I seek are just as different. And strangely enough, in many ways my values and goals are much the same as those used by those of my feminist colleagues who have come to an opposite conclusion.

The arguments against surrogacy that come out of traditional religious context most often rest on two basic principles: first that surrogacy is "unnatural," because it goes against the nature of women and especially of mothers; second, that it violates the sanctity of the family.

Feminists are a lot less sure about just what is "natural" for women, but on the whole we've concluded that the institution of motherhood as it exists in our society is pretty far from any natural state. Neither I nor my feminist colleagues are about to get caught up in any "maternal instincts" arguments. Women end pregnancies with abortions, or end their motherhood by giving a baby up for adoption, when that is what they feel they need to do. Being pregnant does not necessarily mean a woman is going to mother, to raise the child that might be born of that pregnancy. Nor are we going to claim that only a birth mother can mother, can nurture a baby. We know that loving people, men as well as women, can provide all the warm, caring, loving nurturance a baby needs.

Feminists are also not concerned with maintaining the "sanctity of the family," a pleasant enough phrase that has been used to cover an awful lot of damage. That was the argument used to stop funding day-care centers, the argument offered to allow men to beat their wives and children, the argument most generally used to stop women from controlling their own lives and their own bodies. The "family" whose "sanctity" is being maintained is the patriarchal, male-dominated family. Feminists have a different sense of family—we need to protect the single young mother and her child, the lesbian couple and their children, the gay man's family. As feminists, we are concerned not with the control and ownership and kinship issues of the traditional family, but with the *relationships* people establish with one another, with adults and with children.

So why then, as a feminist, do I oppose the surrogacy relationship? The "liberal" wing of feminism does not necessarily oppose those contracts. As long as the women entering them do so of their own volition, with fully informed consent, and as long as they maintain their control over their own bodies throughout the pregnancies, some feminists have said that surrogacy contracts should be supported by the state. Some even go as far as Lori Andrews, for instance, a noted feminist attorney, who says that these contracts should be binding with absolutely no opportunity for the mother to change her mind.

What then are the objections that I, out of my vision of feminism, raise to surrogacy? And more important, on what values am I basing my objections?

My values place relationships as central. Rather than the ownership or kinship ties that appear to epitomize the "traditional" or patriarchal family, I value the interpersonal relations people establish. A man does not own his wife, nor does he have ownership rights over the child she produces of her body. Men may own their sperm, but children are not sperm grown up. Children are not "owned," and they are not available for sale. On the other hand, children do not enter the world from Mars, or out of a black box. Children, as it says in the books for children, come from mothers. They enter the world in a relationship, a physical and social and emotional relationship with the woman in whose body they have been nurtured. The nurturance of pregnancy is a relationship, one that develops as a fetus becomes more and more a baby.

That does not mean that the maternal relationship cannot be ended. Nor does it mean that the relationship is the most overwhelming, all-powerful relationship on earth. In fact, we know it to be a fairly fragile relationship. The intimacy that a mother and her baby experience can be easily lost if they are separated. If a woman chooses to end this relationship, so be it. When a mother chooses to give a baby up to others who want to raise that baby as their own, she is doing what we have all done sometime in our lives—ending a relationship. Sometimes this is done with less and sometimes with more pain, but rarely is it an easy thing for a mother to do.

The relationship that a woman has established by the time she births her baby has more weight, in my value system, than claims of genetic ties, of contracts signed, or of down payments made.

When I make this argument with traditionally oriented people, I am often asked if this doesn't contradict my ideas about a woman's right to abort an unwanted pregnancy. Not at all, I think. When a woman chooses an abortion, she is choosing not to enter into a maternal relationship. Women want access to safe abortions as quickly as possible, before quickening, before a relationship can begin.

In sum, in my value system, I am placing the woman, her experiences and her relationships, at the very heart of my understanding of all pregnancies.

The second value I bring as a feminist to my understanding of surrogacy contracts is the value of women's bodily autonomy, our control over our own bodies. And I see the fetus as part of a woman's body. Traditional patriarchal values would see the fetus as part of its father's body, his "seed" planted in a woman's body. In a patriarchal system, the father—or the state or the church—is held to have special control over a woman's body and life because of that fetus she can bear. As a feminist, I reject that. The fetus is *hers*. Women never bear anybody else's baby: not their husband's, not the state's, and not the purchaser's in a surrogacy contract. Every woman bears her *own* baby. I believe that is true regardless of the source of the sperm, and regardless also of the source of the egg.

As I said earlier, most of the surrogacy arrangements we have seen so far, like the Stern-Whitehead case, were done not with elaborate new technology, but with the very old and very simple technology of artificial insemination. The "surrogate" has been in every possible way the mother to the baby she bore. But some newer technology will allow eggs to be transferred from woman to woman, allowing a woman to be pregnant with fetus grown of another woman's egg.

The Catholic Church and some other religious groups reject that technology. I do not. When that technology is used to enable a woman to enter motherhood with a pregnancy, in just the way that artificial insemination has been used to allow an infertile man to become a social father beginning with pregnancy, I have no problem with it. My concern is when that technology is used in a so-called surrogacy arrangement—when the birth mother, the pregnant woman, is declared to be only a "rented womb," a "surrogate," and the *real* mother is declared to be the woman who produced the egg.

The church and other conservative forces object to the technology because they value the fertilized egg itself as an object believed to be human. I object when women are "used," when parts of women are put up for sale or hire, when our relationships are discounted in favor of genetic and monetary ties.

Those feminists, like Lori Andrews, who would allow surrogacy contracts still demand rights of bodily autonomy for the pregnant woman. The compromise position they maintain is that it is indeed her body, and she must have all decision-making control over her pregnancy—but it is not her baby in her body, not if she has contracted it away. I feel that kind of "compromise" does a profound disservice to women. I cannot ever believe that a woman is pregnant with someone else's baby. The idea is repugnant—it reduces the woman to a container. Nor do I think that that kind of compromise, saying the pregnancy is indeed hers, but the fetus/baby theirs, the purchasers', can be workable. The "preciousness" of the very wanted, very expensive baby will far outweigh the value given to the "cheap labor" of the surrogate.

This is the inevitable result of thinking of pregnancy not as a relationship between a woman and her fetus but as a service she provides for others, and of thinking of the woman herself not as a person but as the container for another, often more valued, person. In that sense, surrogacy is the reductio ad absurdum of technological, patriarchal capitalism.

The values that I bring to motherhood, the values that I take from my feminism, all the values that I've tried to express in this book, all come together in my opposition to surrogacy. And this, to answer a question I began this book with, is what I think feminism has to offer the Mary Beth Whiteheads of the world.

NOTES

1. Portions of this chapter were presented as testimony to the Judiciary Committee of the New York State Senate hearings on "Surrogate Parenthood and New Reproductive Technology," October 16, 1986, and portions appeared in *Conscience*, May 1987, pp. 1–4.

2. Gena Corea, 1985, *The Mother Machine: Reproductive Technologies from Artificial Insemination to Artificial Wombs* (New York: Harper and Row).

3. *People*, February 15, 1988.

4. Noel Keane and I discussed this on the "MacNeil, Lehrer Newshour," March 31, 1987.

5. Angela Holder, 1984, presentation to the American Society of Law and Medicine conference, "What About the Children?" An International Conference on the Legal, Social, and Ethical Implications of New Reproductive and Prenatal Technologies," Boston, Massachusetts, October 29, 1984.

The Wisdom of Repugnance

LEON R. KASS

Kass contends that human cloning is both unethical and dangerous in its consequences. People are repelled by many aspects of human cloning, and although this revulsion is not an argument, it is "the emotional expression of deep wisdom, beyond reason's power fully to articulate it." Kass argues that human cloning should also be rejected because it is a major violation of our "given nature" and the social relations based in this nature, it creates serious issues of identity and individuality for the cloned person, it turns begetting into dehumanizing manufacture, and it is "inherently despotic" because it seeks to make children according to their parents' will and in their own image.

Our habit of delighting in news of scientific and technological breakthroughs has been sorely challenged by the birth announcement of a sheep named Dolly. Though Dolly shares with previous sheep the "softest clothing, woolly, bright," William Blake's question, "Little Lamb, who made thee?" has for her a radically different answer: Dolly was, quite literally, made. She is the work not of nature or nature's God but of man, an Englishman, Ian Wilmut, and his fellow scientists. What's more, Dolly came into being not only sexually—ironically, just like "He [who] calls Himself a Lamb"—but also as the genetically identical copy (and the perfect incarnation of the form or blueprint) of a mature ewe, of whom she is a clone. This long-awaited yet not quite expected success in cloning a mammal raised immediately the prospect—and the specter—of cloning human beings: "I a child and Thou a lamb," despite our differences, have always been equal candidates for creative making, only now, by means of cloning, we may both spring from the hand of man playing at being God.

After an initial flurry of expert comment and public consternation, with opinion polls showing overwhelming opposition to cloning human beings, President Clinton ordered a ban on all federal support for human cloning research (even though none was being supported) and charged the National Bioethics Advisory Commission to report in ninety days on the ethics of human cloning research. The com-

mission (an eighteen-member panel, evenly balanced between scientists and nonscientists, appointed by the president and reporting to the National Science and Technology Council) invited testimony from scientists, religious thinkers and bioethicists, as well as from the general public. It is now deliberating about what it should recommend, both as a matter of ethics and as a matter of public policy.

Congress is awaiting the commission's report, and is poised to act. Bills to prohibit the use of federal funds for human cloning research have been introduced in the House of Representatives and the Senate; and another bill, in the House, would make it illegal "for any person to use a human somatic cell for the process of producing a human clone." A fateful decision is at hand. To clone or not to clone a human being is no longer an academic question.

Taking Cloning Seriously, Then and Now

Cloning first came to public attention roughly thirty years ago, following the successful asexual production, in England, of a clutch of tadpole clones by the technique of nuclear transplantation. The individual largely responsible for bringing the prospect and promise of human cloning to public notice was Joshua Lederberg, a Nobel Laureate geneticist and a man of large vision. In 1966, Lederberg wrote a remarkable article in *The American Naturalist* detailing the eugenic advantages of human cloning and other forms of genetic engineering, and the following year he devoted a column in *The Washington Post*, where he wrote regularly on science and society, to the prospect of human cloning. He suggested that cloning could help us overcome the unpredictable variety that still rules human reproduction, and allow us to benefit from perpetuating superior genetic endowments. These writings sparked a small public debate in which I became a participant. At the time a young researcher in molecular biology at the National Institutes of Health (NIH), I wrote a reply to the *Post*, arguing against Lederberg's amoral treatment of this morally weighty subject and insisting on the urgency of confronting a series of questions and objections, culminating in the suggestion that "the programmed reproduction of man will, in fact, dehumanize him."

Much has happened in the intervening years. It has become harder, not easier, to discern the true meaning of human cloning. We have in some sense been softened up to the idea—through movies, cartoons, jokes and intermittent commentary in the mass media, some serious, most lighthearted. We have become accustomed to new practices in human reproduction: not just in vitro fertilization, but also embryo manipulation, embryo donation and surrogate pregnancy. Animal biotechnology has yielded transgenic animals and a burgeoning science of genetic engineering, easily and soon to be transferable to humans.

Even more important, changes in the broader culture make it now vastly more difficult to express a common and respectful understanding of sexuality, procreation, nascent life, family, and the meaning of motherhood, fatherhood and the links between the generations. Twenty-five years ago, abortion was still largely illegal and thought to be immoral, the sexual revolution (made possible by the extramarital use of the pill) was still in its infancy, and few had yet heard about the reproductive rights of single women, homosexual men and lesbians (Never mind shameless memoirs about one's own incest!) Then one could argue, without embarrassment, that the new technologies of human reproduction— babies without sex—and their confounding of normal kin relations—who's the mother: the egg donor, the surrogate who carries and delivers, or the one who rears?—would "undermine the justification and support that biological parenthood gives to the monogamous marriage." Today, defenders of stable,

monogamous marriage risk charges of giving offense to those adults who are living in "new family forms" or to those children who, even without the benefit of assisted reproduction, have acquired either three or four parents or one or none at all. Today, one must even apologize for voicing opinions that twenty-five years ago were nearly universally regarded as the core of our culture's wisdom on these matters. In a world whose once-given natural boundaries are blurred by technological change and whose moral boundaries are seemingly up for grabs, it is much more difficult to make persuasive the still compelling case against cloning human beings. As Raskolnikov put it, "man gets used to everything—the beast!"

———————

Indeed, perhaps the most depressing feature of the discussions that immediately followed the news about Dolly was their ironical tone, their genial cynicism, their moral fatigue: "AN UDDER WAY OF MAKING LAMBS" (*Nature*), "WHO WILL CASH IN ON BREAKTHROUGH IN CLONING?" (*The Wall Street Journal*), "IS CLONING BAAAAAAAAD?" (*The Chicago Tribune*). Gone from the scene are the wise and courageous voices of Theodosius Dobzhansky (genetics), Hans Jonas (philosophy) and Paul Ramsey (theology) who, only twenty-five years ago, all made powerful moral arguments against ever cloning a human being. We are now too sophisticated for such argumentation; we wouldn't be caught in public with a strong moral stance, never mind an absolutist one. We are all, or almost all, postmodernists now.

Cloning turns out to be the perfect embodiment of the ruling opinions of our new age. Thanks to the sexual revolution, we are able to deny in practice, and increasingly in thought, the inherent procreative teleology of sexuality itself. But, if sex has no intrinsic connection to generating babies, babies need have no necessary connection to sex. Thanks to feminism and the gay rights movement, we are increasingly encouraged to treat the natural heterosexual difference and its preeminence as a matter of "cultural construction." But if male and female are not normatively complementary and generatively significant, babies need not come from male and female complementarity. Thanks to the prominence and the acceptability of divorce and out-of-wedlock births, stable, monogamous marriage as the ideal home for procreation is no longer the agreed-upon cultural norm. For this new dispensation, the clone is the ideal emblem: the ultimate "single-parent child."

Thanks to our belief that all children should be *wanted* children (the more high-minded principle we use to justify contraception and abortion), sooner or later only those children who fulfill our wants will be fully acceptable. Through cloning, we can work our wants and wills on the very identity of our children, exercising control as never before. Thanks to modern notions of individualism and the rate of cultural change, we see ourselves not as linked to ancestors and defined by traditions, but as projects for our own self-creation, not only as self-made men but also man-made selves; and self-cloning is simply an extension of such rootless and narcissistic self-re-creation.

Unwilling to acknowledge our debt to the past and unwilling to embrace the uncertainties and the limitations of the future, we have a false relation to both: cloning personifies our desire fully to control the future, while being subject to no controls ourselves. Enchanted and enslaved by the glamour of technology, we have lost our awe and wonder before the deep mysteries of nature and of life. We cheerfully take our own beginnings in our hands and, like the last man, we blink.

————

Part of the blame for our complacency lies, sadly, with the field of bioethics itself, and its claim to expertise in these moral matters. Bioethics was founded by people who understood that the new biology touched and threatened the deepest matters of our humanity: bodily integrity, identity and individuality, lineage and kinship, freedom and self-command, eros and aspiration, and the relations and strivings of body and soul. With its capture by analytic philosophy, however, and its inevitable routinization and professionalization, the field has by and large come to content itself with analyzing moral arguments, reacting to new technological developments and taking on emerging issues of public policy, all performed with a naïve faith that the evils we fear can all be avoided by compassion, regulation and a respect for autonomy. Bioethics has made some major contributions in the protection of human subjects and in other areas where personal freedom is threatened; but its practitioners, with few exceptions, have turned the big human questions into pretty thin gruel.

One reason for this is that the piecemeal formation of public policy tends to grind down large questions of morals into small questions of procedure. Many of the country's leading bioethicists have served on national commissions or state task forces and advisory boards, where understandably, they have found utilitarianism to be the only ethical vocabulary acceptable to all participants in discussing issues of law, regulation and public policy. As many of these commissions have been either officially under the aegis of NIH or the Health and Human Services Department, or otherwise dominated by powerful voices for scientific progress, the ethicists have for the most part been content, after some "values clarification" and wringing of hands, to pronounce their blessings upon the inevitable. Indeed, it is the bioethicists, not the scientists, who are now the most articulate defenders of human cloning: the two witnesses testifying before the National Bioethics Advisory Commission in favor of cloning human beings were bioethicists, eager to rebut what they regard as the irrational concerns of those of us in opposition. One wonders whether this commission, constituted like the previous commissions, can tear itself sufficiently free from the accommodationist pattern of rubber-stamping all technical innovation, in the mistaken belief that all other goods must bow down before the gods of better health and scientific advance.

If it is to do so, the commission must first persuade itself, as we all should persuade ourselves, not to be complacent about what is at issue here. Human cloning, though it is in some respects continuous with previous reproductive technologies, also represents something radically new, in itself and in its easily foreseeable consequences. The stakes are very high indeed. I exaggerate, but in the direction of the truth, when I insist that we are faced with having to decide nothing less than whether human procreation is going to remain human, whether children are going to be made rather than begotten, whether it is a good thing, humanly speaking, to say yes in principle to the road which leads (at best) to the dehumanized rationality *of Brave New World*. This is not business as usual, to be fretted about for a while but finally to be given our seal of approval. We must rise to the occasion and make our judgments as if the future of our humanity hangs in the balance. For so it does.

The State of the Art

If we should not underestimate the significance of human cloning, neither should we exaggerate its imminence or misunderstand just what is involved. The procedure is conceptually simple. The nucleus of a mature but unfertilized egg is removed and replaced with a nucleus obtained from a specialized cell of an adult (or fetal) organism (in Dolly's case, the donor nucleus came from mammary gland epithelium). Since almost all the hereditary material of a cell is contained within its nucleus, the renucleated egg and the individual into which this egg develops are genetically identical to the organism that was the source of the transferred nucleus. An unlimited number of genetically identical individuals—clones—could be produced by nuclear transfer. In principle, any person, male or female, newborn or adult, could be cloned, and in any quantity. With laboratory cultivation and storage of tissues, cells outliving their sources make it possible even to clone the dead.

The technical stumbling block, overcome by Wilmut and his colleagues, was to find a means of reprogramming the state of the DNA in the donor cells, reversing its differentiated expression and restoring its full totipotency, so that it could again direct the entire process of producing a mature organism. Now that this problem has been solved, we should expect a rush to develop cloning for other animals, especially livestock, in order to propagate in perpetuity the champion meat or milk producers. Though exactly how soon someone will succeed in cloning a human being is anybody's guess. Wilmut's technique, almost certainly applicable to humans, makes *attempting* the feat an imminent possibility.

Yet some cautions are in order and some possible misconceptions need correcting. For a start, cloning is not Xeroxing. As has been reassuringly reiterated, the clone of Mel Gibson, though his genetic double, would enter the world hairless, toothless and peeing in his diapers, just like any other human infant. Moreover,

the success rate, at least at first, will probably not be very high: the British transferred 277 adult nuclei into enucleated sheep eggs, and implanted twenty-nine clonal embryos, but they achieved the birth of only one live lamb clone. For this reason, among others, it is unlikely that, at least for now, the practice would be very popular, and there is no immediate worry of mass-scale production of multicopies. The need of repeated surgery to obtain eggs and, more crucially, of numerous borrowed wombs for implantation will surely limit use, as will the expense; besides, almost everyone who is able will doubtless prefer nature's sexier way of conceiving.

Still, for the tens of thousands of people already sustaining over 200 assisted reproduction clinics in the United States and already availing themselves of in vitro fertilization, intracytoplasmic sperm injection and other techniques of assisted reproduction, cloning would be an option with virtually no added fuss (especially when the success rate improves). Should commercial interests develop in "nucleus-banking," as they have in sperm-banking; should famous athletes or other celebrities decide to market their DNA the way they now market their autographs and just about everything else; should techniques of embryo and germline genetic testing and manipulation arrive as anticipated, increasing the use of laboratory assistance in order to obtain "better" babies—should all this come to pass, then cloning, if it is permitted, could become more than a marginal practice simply on the basis of free reproductive choice, even without any social encouragement to upgrade the gene pool or to replicate superior types. Moreover, if laboratory research on human cloning proceeds, even without any intention to produce cloned humans, the existence of cloned human embryos in the laboratory, created to begin with only for research purposes, would surely pave the way for later baby-making implantations.

In anticipation of human cloning, apologists and proponents have already made clear possible uses of the perfected technology, ranging from the sentimental and compassionate to the grandiose. They include: providing a child for an infertile couple; "replacing" a beloved spouse or child who is dying or has died; avoiding the risk of genetic disease; permitting reproduction for homosexual men and lesbians who want nothing sexual to do with the opposite sex; securing a genetically identical source of organs or tissues perfectly suitable for transplantation; getting a child with a genotype of one's own choosing, not excluding oneself; replicating individuals of great genius, talent or beauty—having a child who really could "be like Mike"; and creating large sets of genetically identical humans suitable for research on, for instance, the question of nature versus nurture, or for special missions in peace and war (not excluding espionage), in which using identical humans would be an advantage. Most people who envision the cloning of human beings, of course, want none of these scenarios. That they cannot say why is not surprising. What is surprising, and welcome, is that, in our cynical age, they are saying anything at all.

The Wisdom of Repugnance

"Offensive." "Grotesque." "Revolting." "Repugnant." "Repulsive." These are the words most commonly heard regarding the prospect of human cloning. Such reactions come both from the man or woman in the street and from the intellectuals, from believers and atheists, from humanists and scientists. Even Dolly's creator has said he "would find it offensive" to clone a human being.

People are repelled by many aspects of human cloning. They recoil from the prospect of mass production of human beings, with large clones of look-alikes, compromised in their individuality; the idea of father-son or mother-daughter twins; the bizarre prospects of a woman giving birth to and rearing a genetic copy of herself, her spouse or even her deceased father or mother; the grotesqueness of conceiving a child as an exact replacement for another who has died; the utilitarian creation of embryonic genetic duplicates of oneself, to be frozen away or created when necessary, in case of need for homologous tissues or organs for transplantation; the narcissism of those who would clone themselves and the arrogance of others who think they know who deserves to be cloned or which genotype any child-to-be should be thrilled to receive; the Frankensteinian hubris to create human life and increasingly to control its destiny; man playing God. Almost no one finds any of the suggested reasons for human

cloning compelling; almost everyone anticipates its possible misuses and abuses. Moreover, many people feel oppressed by the sense that there is probably nothing we can do to prevent it from happening. This makes the prospect all the more revolting.

————

Revulsion is not an argument; and some of yesterday's repugnances are today calmly accepted—though, one must add, not always for the better. In crucial cases, however, repugnance is the emotional expression of deep wisdom, beyond reason's power fully to articulate it. Can anyone really give an argument fully adequate to the horror which is father-daughter incest (even with consent), or having sex with animals, or mutilating a corpse, or eating human flesh, or even just (just!) raping or murdering another human being? Would anybody's failure to give full rational justification for his or her revulsion at these practices make that revulsion ethically suspect? Not at all. On the contrary, we are suspicious of those who think that they can rationalize away our horror, say, by trying to explain the enormity of incest with arguments only about the genetic risks of inbreeding.

The repugnance at human cloning belongs in this category. We are repelled by the prospect of cloning human beings not because of the strangeness or novelty of the undertaking, but because we intuit and feel, immediately and without argument, the violation of things that we rightfully hold dear. Repugnance, here as elsewhere, revolts against the excesses of human willfulness, warning us not to transgress what is unspeakably profound. Indeed, in this age in which everything is held to be permissible so long as it is freely done, in which our given human nature no longer commands respect, in which our bodies are regarded as mere instruments of our autonomous rational wills, repugnance may be the only voice left that speaks up to defend the central core of our humanity. Shallow are the souls that have forgotten how to shudder.

The goods protected by repugnance are generally overlooked by our customary ways of approaching all new biomedical technologies. The way we evaluate cloning ethically will in fact be shaped by how we characterize it descriptively, by the context into which we place it, and by the perspective from which we view it. The first task for ethics is proper description. And here is where our failure begins.

———

Typically, cloning is discussed in one or more of three familiar contexts, which one might call the technological, the liberal and the meliorist. Under the first, cloning will be seen as an extension of existing techniques for assisting reproduction and determining the genetic makeup of children. Like them, cloning is to be regarded as a neutral technique, with no inherent meaning or goodness, but subject to multiple uses, some good, some bad. The morality of cloning thus depends absolutely on the goodness or badness of the motives and intentions of the cloners: as one bioethicist defender of cloning puts it, "the ethics must be judged [only] by the way the parents nurture and rear their resulting child and whether they bestow the same love and affection on a child brought into existence by a technique of assisted reproduction as they would on a child born in the usual way."

The liberal (or libertarian or liberationist) perspective sets cloning in the context of rights, freedoms and personal empowerment. Cloning is just a new option for exercising an individual's right to reproduce or to have the kind of child that he or she wants. Alternatively, cloning enhances our liberation (especially women's liberation) from the confines of nature, the vagaries of chance, or the necessity for sexual mating. Indeed, it liberates women from the need for men altogether, for the process requires only eggs, nuclei and (for the time being) uteri—plus, of course, a healthy dose of our (allegedly "masculine") manipulative science that likes to do all these things to mother nature and nature's mothers. For those who hold this outlook, the only moral restraints on cloning are adequately informed consent and the avoidance of bodily harm. If no one is cloned without her consent, and if the clonant is not physically damaged, then the liberal conditions for licit, hence moral, conduct are met. Worries that go beyond violating the will or maiming the body are dismissed as "symbolic"—which is to say, unreal.

The meliorist perspective embraces valetudinarians and also eugenicists. The latter were formerly more vocal in these discussions, but they are now generally happy to see their goals advanced under the less threatening banners of freedom and technological growth. These people see in cloning a new prospect for improving human beings—minimally, by ensuring the perpetuation of healthy individuals by avoiding the risks of genetic disease inherent in the lottery of sex, and maximally, by producing "optimum babies," preserving outstanding genetic material, and (with the help of soon-to-come techniques for precise genetic engineering) enhancing inborn human capacities on many fronts. Here the morality of cloning as a means is justified solely by the excellence of the end, that is, by the outstanding traits or individuals cloned—beauty, or brawn, or brains.

———

These three approaches, all quintessentially American and all perfectly fine in their places, are sorely wanting as approaches to human procreation. It is, to say the least, grossly distorting to view the wondrous mysteries of birth, renewal and individuality, and the deep meaning of parent-child relations, largely through the lens of our reductive science and its potent technologies. Similarly, considering reproduction (and the intimate relations of family life!) primarily under the political-legal, adversarial and individualistic notion of rights can only undermine the private yet fundamentally social, cooperative and duty-laden character of child-bearing, child-rearing and their bond to the covenant of marriage. Seeking to escape entirely from nature (in order to satisfy a natural desire or a natural right to reproduce!) is self-contradictory in theory and self-alienating in practice. For we are erotic beings only because we are embodied beings, and not merely intellects and wills unfortunately imprisoned in our bodies. And, though health and fitness are clearly great goods, there is something deeply disquieting in looking on our prospective children as artful products perfectible by genetic engineering, increasingly held to our willfully imposed designs, specifications and margins of tolerable error.

The technical, liberal and meliorist approaches all ignore the deeper anthropological, social and, indeed, ontological meanings of bringing forth new life. To this more fitting and profound point of view, cloning shows itself to be a major alteration, indeed, a major violation, of our given nature as embodied, gendered and engendering beings—and of the social relations built on this natural ground. Once this perspective is recognized, the ethical judgment on cloning can no longer be reduced to a matter of motives and intentions, rights and freedoms, benefits and harms, or even means and ends. It must be regarded primarily as a matter of meaning: Is cloning a fulfillment of human begetting and belonging? Or is cloning rather, as I contend, their pollution and perversion? To pollution and perversion, the fitting response can only be horror and revulsion; and conversely, generalized horror and revulsion are prima facie evidence of foulness and violation. The burden of moral argument must fall entirely on those who want to declare the widespread repugnances of humankind to be mere timidity or superstition.

Yet repugnance need not stand naked before the bar of reason. The wisdom of our horror at human cloning can be partially articulated, even if this is finally one of those instances about which the heart has its reasons that reason cannot entirely know.

The Profundity of Sex

To see cloning in its proper context, we must begin not, as I did before, with laboratory technique, but with the anthropology—natural and social—of sexual reproduction.

Sexual reproduction—by which I mean the generation of new life from (exactly) two complementary elements, one female, one male, (usually) through coitus—is established (if that is the right term) not by human decision, culture or tradition, but by nature; it is the natural way of all mammalian reproduction. By nature, each child has two complementary biological progenitors. Each child thus stems from and unites exactly two lineages. In natural generation, moreover, the precise genetic constitution of the resulting offspring is determined by a combination of nature and chance, not by human design: each human child shares the common natural human species genotype, each child is genetically (equally) kin to each (both) parent(s), yet each child is also genetically unique.

These biological truths about our origins foretell deep truths about our identity and about our hu-

man condition altogether. Every one of us is at once equally human, equally enmeshed in a particular familial nexus of origin, and equally individuated in our trajectory from birth to death—and, if all goes well, equally capable (despite our morality) of participating, with a complementary other, in the very same renewal of such human possibility through procreation. Though less momentous than our common humanity, our genetic individuality is not humanly trivial. It shows itself forth in our distinctive appearance through which we are everywhere recognized; it is revealed in our "signature" marks of fingerprints and our self-recognizing immune system; it symbolizes and foreshadows exactly the unique, never-to-be-repeated character of each human life.

Human societies virtually everywhere have structured child-rearing responsibilities and systems of identity and relationship on the bases of these deep natural facts of begetting. The mysterious yet ubiquitous "love of one's own" is everywhere culturally exploited, to make sure that children are not just produced but well cared for and to create for everyone clear ties of meaning, belonging and obligation. But it is wrong to treat such naturally rooted social practices as mere cultural constructs (like left- or right-driving, or like burying or cremating the dead) that we can alter with little human cost. What would kinship be without its clear natural grounding? And what would identity be without kinship? We must resist those who have begun to refer to sexual reproduction as the "traditional method of reproduction," who would have us regard as merely traditional, and by implication arbitrary, what is in truth not only natural but most certainly profound.

Asexual reproduction, which produces "single-parent" offspring, is a radical departure from the natural human way, confounding all normal understandings of father, mother, sibling, grandparent, etc., and all moral relations tied thereto. It becomes even more of a radical departure when the resulting offspring is a clone derived not from an embryo, but from a mature adult to whom the clone would be an identical twin; and when the process occurs not by natural accident (as in natural twinning), but by deliberate human design and manipulation; and when the child's (or children's) genetic constitution is preselected by the parent(s) (or scientists). Accordingly, as we will see, cloning is vulnerable to three kinds of concerns and objections, related to these three points: cloning threatens confusion of identity and individuality, even in small-scale cloning; cloning represents a giant step (though not the first one) toward transforming procreation into manufacture, that is, toward the increasing depersonalization of the process of generation and, increasingly, toward the "production" of human children as artifacts, products of human will and design (what others have called the problem of "commodification" of new life); and cloning—like other forms of eugenic engineering of the next generation—represents a form of despotism of the cloners over the cloned, and thus (even in benevolent cases) represents a blatant violation of the inner meaning of parent-child relations, of what it means to have a child, of what it means to say "yes" to our own demise and "replacement."

Before turning to these specific ethical objections, let me test my claim of the profundity of the natural way by taking up a challenge recently posed by a friend. What if the given natural human way of reproduction were asexual, and we now had to deal with a new technological innovation—artificially induced sexual dimorphism and the fusing of complementary gametes—whose inventors argued that sexual reproduction promised all sorts of advantages, including hybrid vigor and the creation of greatly increased individuality? Would one then be forced to defend natural asexuality because it was natural? Could one claim that it carried deep human meaning?

The response to this challenge broaches the ontological meaning of sexual reproduction. For it is impossible, I submit, for there to have been human life—or even higher forms of animal life—in the absence of sexuality and sexual reproduction. We find asexual reproduction only in the lowest forms of life: bacteria, algae, fungi, some lower invertebrates. Sexuality brings with it a new and enriched relationship to the world. Only sexual animals can seek and find complementary others with whom to pursue a goal that transcends their own existence. For a sexual being, the world is no longer an indifferent and largely homogeneous *otherness*, in part edible, in part dangerous. It also contains some very special and related and complementary beings, of the same kind but of opposite sex, toward whom one reaches out with special interest and intensity. In higher birds and mammals, the outward gaze keeps a lookout not only for food and predators, but also for prospective mates; the beholding of the many splendored world is suffused with desire for union, the animal antecedent of human eros and the germ of sociality. Not by accident is the human animal both the sexiest animal—whose females do not go into heat but are receptive throughout the estrous cycle and whose males must therefore have greater sexual appetite and energy in order to reproduce successfully—and also the most aspiring, the most social, the most open and the most intelligent animal.

———

The soul-elevating power of sexuality is, at bottom, rooted in its strange connection to mortality, which it simultaneously accepts and tries to overcome. Asexual reproduction may be seen as a continuation of the activity of self-preservation. When one organism buds or divides to become two, the original being is (doubly) preserved, and nothing dies. Sexuality, by contrast, means perishability and serves replacement; the two that come together to generate one soon will die. Sexual desire, in human beings as in animals, thus serves an end that is partly hidden from, and finally at odds with, the self-serving individual. Whether we know it or not, when we are sexually active we are voting with our genitalia for our own demise. The salmon swimming upstream to spawn and die tell the universal story: sex is bound up with death, to which it holds a partial answer in procreation.

The salmon and the other animals evince this truth blindly. Only the human being can understand what it means. As we learn so powerfully from the story of the Garden of Eden, our humanization is coincident with sexual self-consciousness, with the recognition of our sexual nakedness and all that it implies: shame at our needy incompleteness, unruly self-division and finitude; awe before the eternal; hope in the self-transcending possibilities of children and a relationship to the divine. In the sexually self-conscious animal, sexual desire can become eros, lust can become love. Sexual desire humanly regarded is thus sublimated into erotic longing for wholeness, completion and immortality which drives us knowingly into the embrace and its generative fruit—as well as into all the higher human possibilities of deed, speech and song.

Through children, a good common to both husband and wife, male and female achieve some genuine unification (beyond the mere sexual "union," which fails to do so). The two become one through sharing generous (not needy) love for this third being as good. Flesh of their flesh, the child is the parents' own commingled being externalized, and given a separate and persisting existence. Unification is enhanced also by their commingled work of rearing. Providing an opening to the future beyond the grave, carrying not only our seed but also our names, our ways and our hopes that they will surpass us in goodness and happiness, children are a testament to the possibility of transcendence. Gender duality and sexual desire, which first draws our love upward and outside of ourselves, finally provide for the partial overcoming of the confinement and limitation of perishable embodiment altogether.

Human procreation, in sum, is not simply an activity of our rational wills. It is a more complete activity precisely because it engages us bodily, erotically and spiritually, as well as rationally. There is wisdom in the mystery of nature that has joined the pleasure of sex, the inarticulate longing for union, the communication of the loving embrace and the deep-seated and only partly articulate desire for children in the very activity by which we continue the chain of human existence and participate in the renewal of human possibility. Whether or not we know it, the severing of procreation from sex, love and intimacy is inherently dehumanizing, no matter how good the product.

We are now ready for the more specific objections to cloning.

The Perversities of Cloning

First, an important if formal objection: any attempt to clone a human being would constitute an unethical experiment upon the resulting child-to-be. As the animal experiments (frog and sheep) indicate, there are grave risks of mishaps and deformities. Moreover, because of what cloning means, one cannot presume a future cloned child's consent to be a clone, even a healthy one. Thus, ethically speaking, we cannot even get to know whether or not human cloning is feasible.

I understand, of course, the philosophical difficulty of trying to compare a life with defects against nonexistence. Several bioethicists, proud of their philosophical cleverness, use this conundrum to embarrass claims that one can injure a child in its conception, precisely because it is only thanks to that complained-of conception that the child is alive to complain. But common sense tells us that we have no reason to fear such philosophisms. For we surely know that people can harm and even maim children in the very act of conceiving them, say, by paternal transmission of the AIDS virus, maternal transmission of heroin dependence or, arguably, even by bringing them into being as bastards or with no capacity or willingness to look after them properly. And we believe that to do this intentionally, or even negligently, is inexcusable and clearly unethical.

The objection about the impossibility of presuming consent may even go beyond the obvious and sufficient point that a clonant, were he subsequently to be asked, could rightly resent having been made a clone. At issue are not just benefits and harms, but doubts about the very independence needed to give proper (even retroactive) consent, that is, not just the capacity to choose but the disposition and ability to choose freely and well. It is not at all clear to what extent a clone will truly be a moral agent. For, as we shall see, in the very fact of cloning, and of rearing him as a clone, his makers subvert the cloned child's independence, beginning with that aspect that comes from knowing that one was an unbidden surprise, a gift, to the world, rather than the designed result of someone's artful project.

———

Cloning creates serious issues of identity and individuality. The cloned person may experience concerns about his distinctive identity not only because he will be in genotype and appearance identical to another human being, but, in this case, because he may also be twin to the person who is his "father" or "mother"—if one can still call them that. What would be the psychic burdens of being the "child" or "parent" of your twin? The cloned individual, moreover, will be saddled with a genotype that has already lived. He will not be fully a surprise to the world. People are likely always to compare his performances in life with that of his alter ego. True, his nurture and his circumstance in life will be different; genotype is not exactly destiny. Still, one must also expect parental and other efforts to shape this new life after the original—or at least to view the child with the original version always firmly in mind. Why else did they clone from the star basketball player, mathematician and beauty queen—or even dear old dad—in the first place?

Since the birth of Dolly, there has been a fair amount of doublespeak on this matter of genetic identity. Experts have rushed in to reassure the public that the clone would in no way be the same person, or have any confusions about his or her identity: as previously noted, they are pleased to point out that the clone of Mel Gibson would not be Mel Gibson. Fair enough. But one is shortchanging the truth by emphasizing the additional importance of the intrauterine environment, rearing and social setting: genotype obviously matters plenty. That, after all, is the only reason to clone, whether human beings or sheep. The odds that clones of Wilt Chamberlain will play in the NBA are, I submit, infinitely greater than they are for clones of Robert Reich.

Curiously, this conclusion is supported, inadvertently, by the one ethical sticking point insisted on by friends of cloning: no cloning without the donor's consent. Though an orthodox liberal objection, it is in fact quite puzzling when it comes from people (such as Ruth Macklin) who also insist that genotype is not identity or individuality, and who deny that a child could reasonably complain about being made a genetic copy. If the clone of Mel Gibson would not be Mel Gibson, why should Mel Gibson have grounds to object that someone had been made his clone? We already allow researchers to use blood and tissue samples for research purposes of no benefit to their sources: my falling hair, my expectorations, my urine and even my biopsied tissues are "not me" and not mine. Courts have held that the profit gained from uses to which scientists put my discarded tissues do not legally belong to me. Why, then, no cloning without consent—including, I assume, no cloning from the body of someone who just died? What harm is done the donor, if genotype is "not me"? Truth to tell, the only powerful justi-

fication for objecting is that genotype really does have something to do with identity, and everybody knows it. If not, on what basis could Michael Jordan object that someone cloned "him," say, from cells taken from a "lost" scraped-off piece of his skin? The insistence on donor consent unwittingly reveals the problem of identity in all cloning.

Genetic distinctiveness not only symbolizes the uniqueness of each human life and the independence of its parents that each human child rightfully attains. It can also be an important support for living a worthy and dignified life. Such arguments apply with great force to any large-scale replication of human individuals. But they are sufficient, in my view, to rebut even the first attempts to clone a human being. One must never forget that these are human beings upon whom our eugenic or merely playful fantasies are to be enacted.

Troubled psychic identity (distinctiveness), based on all-too-evident genetic identity (sameness), will be made much worse by the utter confusion of social identity and kinship ties. For, as already noted, cloning radically confounds lineage and social relations, for "offspring" as for "parents." As bioethicist James Nelson has pointed out, a female child cloned from her "mother" might develop a desire for a relationship to her "father," and might understandably seek out the father of her "mother," who is after all also her biological twin sister. Would "grandpa," who thought his paternal duties concluded, be pleased to discover that the clonant looked to him for paternal attention and support?

Social identity and social ties of relationship and responsibility are widely connected to, and supported by, biological kinship. Social taboos on incest (and adultery) everywhere serve to keep clear who is related to whom (and especially which child belongs to which parents), as well as to avoid confounding the social identity of parent-and-child or brother-and-sister) with the social identity of lovers, spouses and co-parents. True, social identity is altered by adoption (but as a matter of the best interest of already living children: we do not deliberately produce children for adoption). True, artificial insemination and in vitro fertilization with donor sperm, or whole embryo donation, are in some way forms of "prenatal adoption"—a not altogether unproblematic practice. Even here, though, there is in each case (as in all sexual reproduction) a known male source of sperm and a known single female source of egg—a genetic father and a genetic mother—should anyone care to know (as adopted children often do) who is genetically related to whom.

In the case of cloning, however, there is but one "parent." The usually sad situation of the "single-parent child" is here deliberately planned, and with a vengeance. In the case of self-cloning, the "offspring" is, in addition, one's twin; and so the dreaded result of incest—to be parent to one's sibling—is here brought about deliberately, albeit without any act of coitus. Moreover, all other relationships will be confounded. What will father, grandfather, aunt, cousin, sister mean? Who will bear what ties and what burdens? What sort of social identity will someone have with one whole side—"father's" or "mother's"—necessarily excluded? It is no answer to say that our society, with its high incidence of divorce, remarriage, adoption, extramarital childbearing and the rest, already confounds lineage and confuses kinship and responsibility for children (and everyone else), unless one also wants to argue that this is, for children, a preferable state of affairs.

————

Human cloning would also represent a giant step toward turning begetting into making, procreation into manufacture (literally, something "handmade"), a process already begun with in vitro fertilization and genetic testing of embryos. With cloning, not only is the process in hand, but the total genetic blueprint of the cloned individual is selected and determined by the human artisans. To be sure, subsequent development will take place according to natural processes; and the resulting children will still be recognizably human. But we here would be taking a major step into making man himself simply another one of the man-made things. Human nature becomes merely the last part of nature to succumb to the technological project, which turns all of nature into raw material at human disposal, to be homogenized by our rationalized technique according to the subjective prejudices of the day.

How does begetting differ from making? In natural procreation, human beings come together, complementarily male and female, to give existence to another being who is formed, exactly as we were, *by what we are*: living, hence perishable, hence aspiringly erotic, human beings. In clonal reproduction, by contrast, and in the more advanced forms of manufacture to which it leads, we give existence to a being not by what we are but by what we intend and design. As with any product of our making, no matter how excellent, the artificer stands above it, not as an equal but as a superior, transcending it by his will and creative prowess. Scientists who clone animals make it perfectly clear that they are engaged in instrumental making; the animals are, from the start, designed as means to serve rational human purposes. In human cloning, scientists and prospective "parents" would be adopting the same technocratic mentality to human children: human children would be their artifacts.

Such an arrangement is profoundly dehumanizing, no matter how good the product. Mass-scale cloning of the same individual makes the point vividly; but the violation of human equality, freedom and dignity are present even in a single planned clone. And procreation dehumanized into manufacture is further degraded by commodification, a virtually inescapable result of allowing baby-making to proceed under the banner of commerce. Genetic and reproductive biotechnology companies are already growth industries, but they will go into commercial orbit once the Human Genome Project nears completion. Supply will create enormous demand. Even before the capacity for human cloning arrives, established companies will have invested in the harvesting of eggs from ovaries obtained at autopsy or through ovarian surgery, practiced embryonic genetic alteration, and initiated the stockpiling of prospective donor tissues. Through the rental of surrogate-womb services, and through the buying and selling of tissues and embryos, priced according to the merit of the donor, the commodification of nascent human life will be unstoppable.

————

Finally, and perhaps most important, the practice of human cloning by nuclear transfer—like other anticipated forms of genetic engineering of the next generation—would enshrine and aggravate a profound and mischievous misunderstanding of the meaning of having children and of the parent-child relationship. When a couple now chooses to procreate, the partners are saying yes to the emergence of new life in its novelty, saying yes not only to having a child but also, tacitly, to having whatever child this child turns out to be. In accepting our finitude and opening ourselves to our replacement, we are tacitly confessing the limits of our control. In this ubiquitous way of nature, embracing the future by procreating means precisely that we are relinquishing our grip, in the very activity of taking up our own share in what we hope will be the immortality of human life and the human species. This means that our children are not *our* children: they are not our property, not our possessions. Neither are they supposed to live our lives for us, or anyone else's life but their own. To be sure, we seek to guide them on their way, imparting to them not just life but nurturing, love, and a way of life; to be sure, they bear our hopes that they will live fine and flourishing lives, enabling us in small measure to transcend our own limitations. Still, their genetic distinctiveness and independence are the natural foreshadowing of the deep truth that they have their own and never-before-enacted life to live. They are sprung from a past, but they take an uncharted course into the future.

Much harm is already done by parents who try to live vicariously through their children. Children are sometimes compelled to fulfill the broken dreams of unhappy parents; John Doe Jr. or the III is under the burden of having to live up to his forebear's name. Still, if most parents have hopes for their children, cloning parents will have expectations. In cloning, such overbearing parents take at the start a decisive step which contradicts the entire meaning of the open and forward-looking nature of parent-child relations. The child is given a genotype that has already lived, with full expectation that this blueprint of a past life ought to be controlling of the life that is to come. Cloning is inherently despotic, for it seeks to make one's children (or someone else's children) after one's own image (or an image of one's choosing) and their future according to one's will. In some cases, the despotism may be mild and benevolent. In other cases, it will be mischievous and downright tyrannical. But despotism—the control of another through one's will—it inevitably will be.

Meeting Some Objections

The defenders of cloning, of course, are not wittingly friends of despotism. Indeed, they regard themselves mainly as friends of freedom: the freedom of individuals to reproduce, the freedom of scientists and inventors to discover and devise and to foster "progress" in genetic knowledge and technique. They want large-scale cloning only for animals, but they wish to preserve cloning as a human option for exercising our "right to reproduce"—our right to have children, and children with "desirable genes." As law professor John Robertson points out, under our "right to reproduce" we already practice early forms of unnatural, artificial and extramarital reproduction, and we already practice early forms of eugenic choice. For this reason, he argues, cloning is no big deal.

We have here a perfect example of the logic of the slippery slope, and the slippery way in which it already works in this area. Only a few years ago, slippery slope arguments were used to oppose artificial insemination and in vitro fertilization using unrelated sperm donors. Principles used to justify these practices, it was said, will be used to justify more artificial and more eugenic practices, including cloning. Not so, the defender's retorted, since we can make the necessary distinctions. And now, without even a gesture at making the necessary distinctions, the continuity of practice is held by itself to be justificatory.

The principle of reproductive freedom as currently enunciated by the proponents of cloning logically embraces the ethical acceptability of sliding down the entire rest of the slope—to producing children ectogenetically from sperm to term (should it become feasible) and to producing children whose entire genetic makeup will be the product of parental eugenic planning and choice. If reproductive freedom means the right to have a child of one's own choosing, by whatever means, it knows and accepts no limits.

But, far from being legitimated by a "right to reproduce," the emergence of techniques of assisted reproduction and genetic engineering should compel us to reconsider the meaning and limits of such a putative right. In truth, a "right to reproduce" has always been a peculiar and problematic notion. Rights generally belong to individuals, but this is a right which (before cloning) no one can exercise alone. Does the right then inhere only in couples? Only in married couples? Is it a (woman's) right to carry or deliver or a right (of one or more parents) to nurture and rear? Is it a right to have your own biological child? Is it a right only to attempt reproduction, or a right also to succeed? Is it a right to acquire the baby of one's choice?

The assertion of a negative "right to reproduce" certainly makes sense when it claims protection against state interference with procreative liberty, say, through a program of compulsory sterilization. But surely it cannot be the basis of a tort claim against nature, to be made good by technology, should free efforts at natural procreation fail. Some insist that the right to reproduce embraces also the right against state interference with the free use of all technological means to obtain a child. Yet such a position cannot be sustained: for reasons having to do with the means employed, any community may rightfully prohibit surrogate pregnancy, or polygamy, or the sale of babies to infertile couples, without violating anyone's basic human "right to reproduce." When the exercise of a previously innocuous freedom now involves or impinges on troublesome practices that the original freedom never was intended to reach, the general presumption of liberty needs to be reconsidered.

———

We do indeed already practice negative eugenic selection, through genetic screening and prenatal diagnosis. Yet our practices are governed by a norm of health. We seek to prevent the birth of children who suffer from known (serious) genetic diseases. When and if gene therapy becomes possible, such diseases could then be treated, in utero or even before implantation—I have no ethical objection in principle to such a practice (though I have some practical worries), precisely because it serves the medical goal of healing existing individuals. But therapy, to be therapy, implies not only an existing "patient." It also implies a norm of health. In this respect, even germline gene "therapy," though practiced not on a human being but on egg and sperm, is less radical than cloning, which is in no way therapeutic. But once one blurs the distinction between health promotion and genetic enhancement, between so-called negative and positive eugenics, one opens the door to all future eugenic designs. "To make sure that a child will be healthy and have good chances in life": this is Robertson's principle, and owing to its latter clause it is an utterly elastic principle, with no boundaries. Being over eight feet tall will likely produce some very good chances in life, and so will having the looks of Marilyn Monroe, and so will a genius-level intelligence.

Proponents want us to believe that there are legitimate uses of cloning that can be distinguished from illegitimate uses, but by their own principles no such limits can be found. (Nor could any such limits be enforced in practice.) Reproductive freedom, as they understand it, is governed solely by the subjective wishes of the parents-to-be (plus the avoidance of bodily harm to the child). The sentimentally appealing case of the childless married couple is, on these grounds, indistinguishable from the case of an individual (married or not) who would like to clone someone famous or talented, living or dead. Further, the principle here endorsed justifies not only cloning but, indeed, all future artificial attempts to create (manufacture) "perfect" babies.

A concrete example will show how, in practice no less than in principle, the so-called innocent case will merge with, or even turn into, the more troubling ones. In practice, the eager parents-to-be will necessarily be subject to the tyranny of expertise. Consider an infertile married couple, she lacking eggs or he lacking sperm, that wants a child of their (genetic) own, and propose to clone either husband or wife. The scientist-physician (who is also co-owner of the cloning company) points out the likely difficulties—a cloned child is not really their (genetic) child, but the child of only *one* of them; this imbalance may produce strains on the marriage; the child might suffer identity confusion; there is a risk of perpetuating the cause of sterility; and so on—and he also points out the advantages of choosing a donor nucleus. Far better than a child of their own would be a child of their own choosing. Touting his own expertise in selecting healthy and talented donors, the doctor presents the couple with his latest catalog containing the pictures, the health records and the accomplishments of his stable of cloning donors, samples of whose tissues are in his deep freeze. Why not, dearly beloved, a more perfect baby?

The "perfect baby," of course, is the project not of the infertility doctors, but of the eugenic scientists and their supporters. For them, the paramount right is not the so-called right to reproduce but what biologist Bentley Glass called, a quarter of a century ago, "the right of every child to be born with a sound physical and mental constitution, based on a sound genotype . . . the inalienable right to a sound heritage." But to secure this right, and to achieve the requisite quality control over new human life, human conception and gestation will need to be brought fully into the bright light of the laboratory, beneath which it can be fertilized, nourished, pruned, weeded, watched, inspected, prodded, pinched, cajoled, injected, tested, rated, graded, approved, stamped, wrapped, sealed and delivered. There is no other way to produce the perfect baby.

Yet we are urged by proponents of cloning to forget about the science fiction scenarios of laboratory manufacture and multiple-copied clones, and to focus only on the homely cases of infertile couples exercising their reproductive rights. But why, if the single cases are so innocent, should multiplying their performance be so off-putting? (Similarly, why do others object to people making money off this practice, if the practice itself is perfectly acceptable?) When we follow the sound ethical principle of universalizing our choice—"would it be right if everyone cloned a Wilt Chamberlain (with his consent, of course)? Would it be right if everyone decided to practice asexual reproduction?"—we discover what is wrong with these seemingly innocent cases. The so-called science fiction cases make vivid the meaning of what looks to us, mistakenly, to be benign.

Though I recognize certain continuities between cloning and, say, in vitro fertilization, I believe that cloning differs in essential and important ways. Yet those who disagree should be reminded that the "continuity" argument cuts both ways. Sometimes we establish bad precedents, and discover that they were bad only when we follow their inexorable logic to places we never meant to go. Can the defenders of cloning show us today how, on their principles, we will be able to see producing babies ("perfect babies") entirely in the laboratory or exercising full control over their genotypes (including so-called enhancement) as ethically different, in any essential way, from present forms of assisted reproduction? Or are they willing to admit, despite their attachment to the principle of continuity, that the complete obliteration of "mother" or "father," the complete depersonalization of procreation, the complete manufacture of human beings and the complete genetic control of one generation over the next would be ethically problematic and essentially different from current forms of assisted reproduction? If so, where and how will they draw the line, and why? I draw it at cloning, for all the reasons given.

Ban the Cloning of Humans

What, then, should we do? We should declare that human cloning is unethical in itself and dangerous in its likely consequences. In so doing, we shall have the backing of the overwhelming majority of our fellow Americans, and of the human race, and (I believe) of most practicing scientists. Next, we should do all that we can to prevent the cloning of human beings. We should do this by means of an international legal ban if possible, and by a unilateral national ban, at a minimum. Scientists may secretly undertake to violate such a law, but they will be deterred by not being able to stand up proudly to claim the credit for their technological bravado and success. Such a ban on clonal baby-making, moreover, will not harm the progress of basic genetic science and technology. On the contrary, it will reassure the public that scientists are happy to proceed without violating the deep ethical norms and intuitions of the human community.

This still leaves the vexed question about laboratory research using early embryonic human clones, specially created only for such research purposes, with no intention to implant them into a uterus. There is no question that such research holds great promise for gaining fundamental knowledge about normal (and abnormal) differentiation, and for developing tissue lines for transplantation that might be used, say, in treating leukemia or in repairing brain or spinal cord injuries—to mention just a few of the conceivable benefits. Still, unrestricted clonal embryo research will surely make the production of living human clones much more likely. Once the genies put the cloned embryos into the bottles, who can strictly control where they go (especially in the absence of legal prohibitions against implanting them to produce a child)?

I appreciate the potentially great gains in scientific knowledge and medical treatment available from embryo research, especially with cloned embryos. At the same time, I have serious reservations about creating human embryos for the sole purpose of experimentation. There is something deeply repugnant and fundamentally transgressive about such a utilitarian treatment of prospective human life. This total, shameless exploitation is worse, in my opinion, than the "mere" destruction of nascent life. But I see no added objections, as a matter of principle, to creating and using *cloned* early embryos for research purposes, beyond the objections that I might raise to doing so with embryos produced sexually.

And yet, as a matter of policy and prudence, any opponent of the manufacture of cloned humans must, I think, in the end oppose also the creating of cloned human embryos. Frozen embryonic clones (belonging to whom?) can be shuttled around without detection. Commercial ventures in human cloning will be developed without adequate oversight. In order to build a fence around the law, prudence dictates that one oppose—for this reason alone—all production of cloned human embryos, even for research purposes. We should allow for all cloning research on animals to go forward, but the only safe trench that we can dig across the slippery slope, I suspect, is to insist on the inviolable distinction between animal and human cloning.

Some readers, and certainly most scientists, will not accept such prudent restraints, since they desire the benefits of research. They will prefer, even in fear and trembling, to allow human embryo cloning research to go forward.

Very well. Let us test them. If the scientists want to be taken seriously on ethical grounds, they must at the very least agree that embryonic research may proceed if and only if it is preceded by an absolute and effective ban on all attempts to implant into a uterus a cloned human embryo (cloned from an adult) to produce a living child. Absolutely no permission for the former without the latter.

The National Bioethics Advisory Commission's recommendations regarding this matter should be watched with the greatest care. Yielding to the wishes of the scientists, the commission will almost surely recommend that cloning human embryos for research be permitted. To allay public concern, it will likely also call for a temporary moratorium—not a legislative ban—on implanting cloned embryos to make a child, at least until such time as cloning techniques will have been perfected and rendered "safe" (precisely through the permitted research with cloned embryos). But the call for a moratorium rather than a legal ban would be a moral and a practical failure. Morally, this ethics commission would (at best) be waffling on the main ethical question, by refusing to declare the production of human clones unethical (or ethical). Practically, a moratorium on implantation cannot provide even the minimum protection needed to prevent the production of cloned humans.

Opponents of cloning need therefore to be vigilant. Indeed, no one should be willing even to consider a recommendation to allow the embryo research to proceed unless it is accompanied by a call for *prohibiting* implantation and until steps are taken to make such a prohibition effective.

———

Technically, the National Bioethics Advisory Commission can advise the president only on federal policy, especially federal funding policy. But given the seriousness of the matter at hand, and the grave public concern that goes beyond federal funding, the commission should take a broader view. (If it doesn't, Congress surely will.) Given that most assisted reproduction occurs in the private sector, it would be cowardly and insufficient for the commission to say, simply, "no federal funding" for such practices. It would be disingenuous to argue that we should allow federal funding so that we would then be able to regulate the practice; the private sector will not be bound by such regulations. Far better, for virtually everyone concerned, would be to distinguish between research on embryos and baby-making, and to call for a complete national and international ban (effected by legislation and treaty) of the latter, while allowing the former to proceed (at least in private laboratories).

The proposal for such a legislative ban is without American precedent, at least in technological matters, though the British and others have banned cloning of human beings, and we ourselves ban incest, polygamy and other forms of "reproductive freedom." Needless to say, working out the details of such a ban, especially a global one, would be tricky, what with the need to develop appropriate sanctions for violators. Perhaps such a ban will prove ineffective; perhaps it will eventually be shown to have been a mistake. But it would at least place the burden of practical proof where it belongs: on the proponents of this horror, requiring them to show very clearly what great social or medical good can be had only by the cloning of human beings.

We Americans have lived by, and prospered under, a rosy optimism about scientific and technological progress. The technological imperative—if it can be done, it must be done—has probably served us well, though we should admit that there is no accurate method for weighing benefits and harms. Even when, as in the cases of environmental pollution, urban decay or the lingering deaths that are the unintended by-products of medical success, we recognize the unwelcome outcomes of technological advance, we remain confident in our ability to fix all the "bad" consequences—usually by means of still newer and better technologies. How successful we can continue to be in such post hoc repairing is at least an open question. But there is very good reason for shifting the paradigm around, at least regarding those technological interventions into the human body and mind that will surely effect fundamental and likely irreversible) changes in human nature, basic human relationships, and what it means to be a human being. Here we surely should not be willing to risk everything in the naïve hope that, should things go wrong, we can later set them right.

The president's call for a moratorium on human cloning has given us an important opportunity. In a truly unprecedented way, we can strike a blow for the human control of the technological project, for wisdom, prudence and human dignity. The prospect of human cloning, so repulsive to contemplate, is the occasion for deciding whether we shall be slaves of unregulated progress, and ultimately its artifacts, or whether we shall remain free human beings who guide our technique toward the enhancement of human dignity. If we are to seize the occasion, we must, as the late Paul Ramsey wrote,

> raise the ethical questions with a serious and not a frivolous conscience. A man of frivolous conscience announces that there are ethical quandaries ahead that we must urgently consider before the future catches up with us. By this he often means that we need to devise a new ethics that will provide the rationalization for doing in the future what men are bound to do because of new actions and interventions science will have made possible. In contrast a man of serious conscience means to say in raising urgent ethical questions that there may be some things that men should never do. The good things that men do can be made complete only by the things they refuse to do.

Cloning Human Beings: An Assessment of the Ethical Issues Pro and Con

DAN W. BROCK

In this essay Brock reviews the arguments for and against human reproductive cloning. He maintains that there is probably a right to reproductive freedom that covers human cloning, but there could be other rights in conflict with this right, or serious enough harms involved to override it. The possible benefits of human cloning include the ability to relieve infertility, to avoid transmitting serious genetic disease to off-spring, and to clone someone (such as a child who died) who had special meaning to individuals. Arguments against the practice include that it violates a right to unique identity or to an open future, that it would cause psychological harm to the later twin, that it would carry unacceptable risks for the clone, and that it would lessen the worth of individuals and diminish respect for human life. Brock finds little merit in the identity and open-future arguments but thinks that human cloning does carry risk of significant harms, although most of the harms that people fear are based on common misconceptions.

The world of science and the public at large were both shocked and fascinated by the announcement in the journal *Nature* by Ian Wilmut and his colleagues that they had successfully cloned a sheep from a single cell of an adult sheep (Wilmut, 1997). But many were troubled or apparently even horrified at the prospect that cloning of adult humans by the same process might be possible as well. The response of most scientific and political leaders to the prospect of human cloning, indeed of Dr. Wilmut as well, was of immediate and strong condemnation.

A few more cautious voices were heard both suggesting some possible benefits from the use of human cloning in limited circumstances and questioning its too quick prohibition, but they were a clear minority. A striking feature of these early responses was that their strength and intensity seemed far to outrun the arguments and reasons offered in support of them—they seemed often to be "gut level" emotional reactions rather than considered reflections on the issues. Such reactions should not be simply dismissed, both because they may point us to important considerations otherwise missed and not easily articulated, and because they often have a major impact on public policy. But the formation of public policy should not ignore the moral reasons and arguments that bear on the practice of human cloning—these must be articulated in order to understand and inform people's more immediate emotional responses. This essay is an effort to articulate, and to evaluate critically, the main moral considerations and arguments for and against human cloning. Though many people's religious beliefs inform their views on human cloning, and it is often difficult to separate religious from secular positions, I shall

restrict myself to arguments and reasons that can be given a clear secular formulation.

On each side of the issue there are no distinct kinds of moral arguments brought forward. On the one hand, some opponents claim that human cloning would violate fundamental moral or human rights, while some proponents argue that its prohibition would violate such rights. While moral and even human rights need not be understood as absolute, they do place moral restrictions on permissible actions that an appeal to a mere balance of benefits over harms cannot justify overriding; for example, the rights of human subjects in research must be respected even if the result is that some potentially beneficial research is more difficult or cannot be done. On the other hand, both opponents and proponents also cite the likely harms and benefits, both to individuals and to society, of the practice. I shall begin with the arguments in support of permitting human cloning, although with no implication that it is the stronger or weaker position.

Moral Arguments in Support of Human Cloning

Is There a Moral Right to Use Human Cloning?

What moral right might protect at least some access to the use of human cloning? A commitment to individual liberty, such as defended by J. S. Mill, requires that individuals be left free to use human cloning if they so choose and if their doing so does not cause significant harms to others, but liberty is too broad in scope to be an uncontroversial moral right (Mill, 1859; Rhodes. 1995). Human cloning is a means of reproduction (in the most literal sense) and so the most plausible moral right at stake in its use is a right to reproductive freedom or procreative liberty (Robertson, 1994a; Brock, 1994), understood to include both the choice not to reproduce, for example, by means of contraception or abortion, and also the right to reproduce.

The right to reproductive freedom is properly understood to include the right to use various assisted reproductive technologies (ARTs), such as in vitro fertilization (IVF), oocyte donation, and so forth. The reproductive right relevant to human cloning is a negative right, that is, a right to use ARTs without interference by the government or others when made available by a willing provider. The choice of an assisted means of reproduction should be protected by reproductive freedom even when it is not the only means for individuals to reproduce, just as the choice among different means of preventing conception is protected by reproductive freedom. However, the case for permitting the use of a particular means of reproduction is strongest when it is necessary for particular individuals to be able to procreate at all, or to do so without great burdens or harms to themselves or others. In some cases human cloning could be the only means for individuals to procreate while retaining a biological tie to their child, but in other cases different means of procreating might also be possible.

It could be argued that human cloning is not covered by the right to reproductive freedom because whereas current ARTs and practices covered by that right are remedies for inabilities to reproduce sexually, human cloning is an entirely new means of reproduction; indeed, its critics see it as more a means of manufacturing humans than of reproduction. Human cloning is a different means of reproduction than sexual reproduction, but it is a means that can serve individuals' interest in reproducing. If it is not protected by the moral right to reproductive freedom, I believe that must be not because it is a new means of reproducing, but instead because it has other objectionable or harmful features; I shall evaluate these other ethical objections to it later.

When individuals have alternative means of procreating, human cloning typically would be chosen because it replicates a particular individual's genome. The reproductive interest in question then is not simply reproduction itself, but a more specific interest in choosing what kind of children to have. The right to reproductive freedom is usually understood to cover at least some choice about the kind of children one will have. Some individuals choose reproductive partners in the hope of producing offspring with desirable traits. Genetic testing of fetuses or preimplantation embryos for genetic disease or abnormality is done to avoid having a child with those diseases or abnormalities. Respect for individual self-determination, which is one of the grounds of a moral right to reproductive freedom, includes respecting individuals' choices about whether to have a child with a condition that will place severe burdens on them, and cause severe burdens to the child itself.

The less a reproductive choice is primarily the determination of one's own life, but primarily the determination of the nature of another, as in the case of human cloning, the more moral weight the interests of that other person, that is the cloned child, should have in decisions that determine its nature (Annas, 1994). But even then parents are typically accorded substantial, but not unlimited, discretion in shaping the persons their children will become, for example, through education and other childrearing decisions. Even if not part of reproductive freedom, the right to raise one's children as one sees fit, within limits mostly determined by the interests of the children, is also a right to determine within limits what kinds of persons one's children will become. This right includes not just preventing certain diseases or harms to children, but selecting and shaping desirable features and traits in one's children. The use of human cloning is one way to exercise that right.

Public policy and the law now permit prospective parents to conceive, or to carry a conception to term, when there is a significant risk or even certainty that the child will suffer from a serious genetic disease. Even when others think the risk or certainty of genetic disease makes it morally wrong to conceive, or to carry a fetus to term, the parents' right to reproductive freedom permits them to do so. Most possible harms to a cloned child are less serious than the genetic harms with which parents can now permit their offspring to be conceived or born.

I conclude that there is good reason to accept that a right to reproductive freedom presumptively includes both a right to select the means of reproduction, as well as a right to determine what kind of children to have, by use of human cloning. However, the specific reproductive interest of determining what kind of children to have is less weighty than are other reproductive interests and choices whose impact falls more directly and exclusively on the parents rather than the child. Even if a moral right to reproductive freedom protects the use of human cloning, that does not settle the moral issue about human cloning, since there may be other moral rights in conflict with this right, or serious enough harms from human cloning to override the right to use it; this right can be thought of as establishing a serious moral presumption supporting access to human cloning.

What Individual or Social Benefits Might Human Cloning Produce?

Largely Individual Benefits

The literature on human cloning by nuclear transfer or by embryo splitting contains a few examples of circumstances in which individuals might have good reasons to want to use human cloning. However, human cloning seems not to be the unique answer to any great or pressing human need and its benefits appear to be limited at most. What are the principal possible benefits of human cloning that might give individuals good reasons to want to use it?

1. *Human cloning would be a new means to relieve the infertility some persons now experience.* Human cloning would allow women who have no ova or men who have no sperm to produce an offspring that is biologically related to them (Eisenberg, 1976; Robertson, 1994b, 1997; LaBar, 1984). Embryos might also be cloned, by either nuclear transfer or embryo splitting, in order to increase the number of embryos for implantation and improve the chances of successful conception (NABER, 1994). The benefits from human cloning to relieve infertility are greater the more persons there are who cannot overcome their infertility by any other means acceptable to them. I do not know of data on this point, but the numbers who would use cloning for this reason are probably not large.

The large number of children throughout the world possibly available for adoption represents an alternative solution to infertility only if we are prepared to discount as illegitimate the strong desire of many persons, fertile and infertile, for the experience of pregnancy and for having and raising a child

biologically related to them. While not important to all infertile (or fertile) individuals, it is important to many and is respected and met through other forms of assisted reproduction that maintain a biological connection when that is possible; that desire does not become illegitimate simply because human cloning would be the best or only means of overcoming an individual's infertility.

2. *Human cloning would enable couples in which one party risks transmitting a serious hereditary disease to an offspring to reproduce without doing so* (Robertson, 1994b). By using donor sperm or egg donation, such hereditary risks can generally be avoided now without the use of human cloning. These procedures may be unacceptable to some couples, however, or at least considered less desirable than human cloning because they introduce a third party's genes into their reproduction instead of giving their offspring only the genes of one of them. Thus, in some cases human cloning could be a reasonable means of preventing genetically transmitted harms to offspring. Here too, we do not know how many persons would want to use human cloning instead of other means of avoiding the risk of genetic transmission of a disease or of accepting the risk of transmitting the disease, but the numbers again are probably not large.

3. *Human cloning to make a later twin would enable a person to obtain needed organs or tissues for transplantation* (Robertson, 1994b, 1997; Kahn, 1989; Harris, 1992). Human cloning would solve the problem of finding a transplant donor whose organ or tissue is an acceptable match and would eliminate, or drastically reduce, the risk of transplant rejection by the host. The availability of human cloning for this purpose would amount to a form of insurance to enable treatment of certain kinds of medical conditions. Of course, sometimes the medical need would be too urgent to permit waiting for the cloning, gestation, and development that is necessary before tissues or organs can be obtained for transplantation. In other cases, taking an organ also needed by the later twin, such as a heart or a liver, would be impermissible because it would violate the later twin's rights.

Such a practice can be criticized on the ground that it treats the later twin not as a person valued and loved for his or her own sake, as an end in itself in Kantian terms, but simply as a means for benefiting another. This criticism assumes, however, that only this one motive defines the reproduction and the relation of the person to his or her later twin. The well-known case some years ago in California of the Ayalas, who conceived in the hopes of obtaining a source for a bone marrow transplant for their teenage daughter suffering from leukemia, illustrates the mistake in this assumption. They argued that whether or not the child they conceived turned out to be a possible donor for their daughter, they would value and love the child for itself, and treat it as they would treat any other member of their family. That one reason they wanted it, as a possible means to saving their daughters life, did not preclude their also loving and valuing it for its own sake; in Kantian terms, it was treated as a possible means to saving their daughter, but not *solely as a means*, which is what the Kantian view proscribes.

Indeed, when people have children, whether by sexual means or with the aid of ARTs, their motives and reasons for doing so are typically many and complex, and include reasons less laudable than obtaining lifesaving medical treatment, such as having someone who needs them, enabling them to live on their own, qualifying for government benefit programs, and so forth. While these are not admirable motives for having children and may not bode well for the child's upbringing and future, public policy does not assess prospective parents' motives and reasons for procreating as a condition of their doing so.

4. *Human cloning would enable individuals to clone someone who had special meaning to them, such as a child who had died* (Robertson, 1994b). There is no denying that if human cloning were available, some individuals would want to use it for this purpose, but their desire usually would be based on a deep confusion. Cloning such a child would not replace the child the parents had loved and lost, but would only create a different child with the same genes. The child they loved and lost was a unique individual who had been shaped by his or her environment and choices, not just his or her genes, and more importantly who had experienced a particular relationship with them. Even if the later cloned child

could not only have the same genes but also be subjected to the same environment, which of course is impossible, it would remain a different child than the one they had loved and lost because it would share a different history with them (Thomas, 1974). Cloning the lost child might help the parents accept and move on from their loss, but another already existing sibling or a new child that was not a clone might do this equally well; indeed, it might do so better since the appearance of the cloned later twin would be a constant reminder of the child they had lost. Nevertheless, if human cloning enabled some individuals to clone a person who had special meaning to them and doing so gave them deep satisfaction, that would be a benefit to them even if their reasons for wanting to do so, and the satisfaction they in turn received, were based on a confusion.

Largely Social Benefits

5. *Human cloning would enable the duplication of individuals of great talent, genius, character, or other exemplary qualities.* Unlike the first four reasons for human cloning which appeal to benefits to specific individuals, this reason looks to benefits to the broader society from being able to replicate extraordinary individuals—a Mozart, Einstein, Gandhi, or Schweitzer (Lederberg, 1966; McKinnell, 1979). Much of the appeal of this reason, like much support and opposition to human cloning, rests largely on a confused and false assumption of genetic determinism, that is, that one's genes fully determine what one will become, do, and accomplish. What made Mozart, Einstein, Gandhi, and Schweitzer the extraordinary individuals they were was the confluence of their particular genetic endowments with the environments in which they were raised and lived and the particular historical moments they in different ways seized. Cloning them would produce individuals with the same genetic inheritances (nuclear transfer does not even produce 100 percent genetic identity, although for the sake of exploring the moral issues I have followed the common assumption that it does), but it is not possible to replicate their environments or the historical contexts in which they lived and their greatness flourished. We do not know the degree or specific respects in which any individual's greatness depended on "nature" or "nurture," but we

do know that it always depends on an interaction of them both. Cloning could not even replicate individuals' extraordinary capabilities, much less their accomplishments, because these too are the product of their inherited genes and their environments, not of their genes alone.

None of this is to deny that Mozart's and Einstein's extraordinary musical and intellectual capabilities, nor even Gandhi's and Schweitzer's extraordinary moral greatness, were produced in part by their unique genetic inheritances. Cloning them might well produce individuals with exceptional capacities, but we simply do not know how close their clones would be in capacities or accomplishments to the great individuals from whom they were cloned. Even so, the hope for exceptional, even if less and different, accomplishment from cloning such extraordinary individuals might be a reasonable ground for doing so.

Worries here about abuse, however, surface quickly. Whose standards of greatness would be used to select individuals to be cloned? Who would control use of human cloning technology for the benefit of society or mankind at large? Particular groups, segments of society, or governments might use the technology for their own benefit, under the cover of benefiting society or even mankind at large.

6. *Human cloning and research on human cloning might make possible important advances in scientific knowledge, for example, about human development* (Walters, 1982; Smith, 1983). While important potential advances in scientific or medical knowledge from human cloning or human cloning research have frequently been cited, there are at least three reasons for caution about such claims. First, there is always considerable uncertainty about the nature and importance of the new scientific or medical knowledge to which a dramatic new technology like human cloning will lead; the road to new knowledge is never mapped in advance and takes many unexpected turns. Second, we do not know what new knowledge from human cloning or human cloning research could also be gained by other means that do not have the problematic moral features to which its opponents object. Third, what human cloning research would be compatible with ethical and legal requirements for the use of human subjects in research

is complex, controversial, and largely unexplored. Creating human clones solely for the purpose of research would be to use them solely for the benefit of others without their consent, and so unethical. But if and when human cloning was established to be safe and effective, then new scientific knowledge might be obtained from its use for legitimate, nonresearch reasons.

Although there is considerable uncertainty concerning most of human cloning's possible individual and social benefits that I have discussed, and although no doubt it could have other benefits or uses that we cannot yet envisage, I believe it is reasonable to conclude at this time that human cloning does not seem to promise great benefits or uniquely to meet great human needs. Nevertheless, despite these limited benefits, a moral case can be made that freedom to use human cloning is protected by the important moral right to reproductive freedom. I shall turn now to what moral rights might be violated, or harms produced, by research on or use of human cloning.

Moral Arguments Against Human Cloning

Would the Use of Human Cloning Violate Important Moral Rights?

Many of the immediate condemnations of any possible human cloning following Wilmut's cloning of Dolly claimed that it would violate moral or human rights, but it was usually not specified precisely, or often even at all, what rights would be violated (WHO, 1997). I shall consider two possible candidates for such a right: a right to have a unique identity and a right to ignorance about one's future or to an open future. Claims that cloning denies individuals a unique identity are common, but I shall argue that even if there is a right to a unique identity, it could not be violated by human cloning. The right to ignorance or to an open future has only been explicitly defended, to my knowledge, by two commentators, and in the context of human cloning, only by Hans Jonas; it supports a more promising, but in my view ultimately unsuccessful, argument that human cloning would violate an important moral or human right.

Is there a moral or human right to a unique identity, and if so would it be violated by human cloning? For human cloning to violate a right to a unique identity, the relevant sense of identity would have to be genetic identity, that is, a right to a unique unrepeated genome. This would be violated by human cloning, but is there any such right? It might be thought that cases of identical twins show there is no such right because no one claims that the moral or human rights of the twins have been violated. However, this consideration is not conclusive (Kass, 1985; NABER, 1994). Only human actions can violate others' rights; outcomes that would constitute a rights violation if deliberately caused by human action are not a rights violation if a result of natural causes. If Arthur deliberately strikes Barry on the head so hard as to cause his death, he violates Barry's right not to be killed; if lightning strikes Cheryl, causing her death, her right not to be killed has not been violated. Thus, the case of twins does not show that there could not be a right to a unique genetic identity.

What is the sense of identity that might plausibly be what each person has a right to have uniquely, that constitutes the special uniqueness of each individual (Macklin 1994; Chadwick 1982)? Even with the same genes, homozygous twins are numerically distinct and not identical, so what is intended must be the various properties and characteristics that make each individual qualitatively unique and different from others. Does having the same genome as another person undermine that unique qualitative identity? Only on the crudest genetic determinism, according to which an individual's genes completely and decisively determine everything else about the individual, all his or her other nongenetic features and properties, together with the entire history or biography that constitutes his or her life. But there is no reason whatever to believe that kind of genetic determinism. Even with the same genes, differences in genetically identical twins' psychological and personal characteristics develop over time together with differences in their life histories, personal relationships, and life choices; sharing an identical genome does not prevent twins from developing distinct and unique personal identities of their own.

We need not pursue whether there is a moral or human right to a unique identity—no such right is found among typical accounts and enumerations of moral or human rights—because even if there is such a right, sharing a genome with another indi-

vidual as a result of human cloning would not violate it. The idea of the uniqueness, or unique identity, of each person historically predates the development of modern genetics. A unique genome thus could not be the ground of this long-standing belief in the unique human identity of each person.

I turn now to whether human cloning would violate what Hans Jonas called a right to ignorance, or what Joel Feinberg called a right to an open future (Jonas, 1974; Feinberg, 1980). Jonas argued that human cloning in which there is a substantial time gap between the beginning of the lives of the earlier and later twin is fundamentally different from the simultaneous beginning of the lives of homozygous twins that occur in nature. Although contemporaneous twins begin their lives with the same genetic inheritance, they do so at the same time, and so in ignorance of what the other who shares the same genome will by his or her choices make of his or her life.

A later twin created by human cloning, Jonas argues, knows, or at least believes she knows, too much about herself. For there is already in the world another person, her earlier twin, who from the same genetic starting point has made the life choices that are still in the later twin's future. It will seem that her life has already been lived and played out by another, that her fate is already determined; she will lose the sense of human possibility in freely and spontaneously creating her own future and authentic self. It is tyrannical, Jonas claims, for the earlier twin to try to determine another's fate in this way.

Jonas's objection can be interpreted so as not to assume either a false genetic determinism, or a belief in it. A later twin might grant that he is not determined to follow in his earlier twin's footsteps, but nevertheless the earlier twin's life might always haunt him, standing as an undue influence on his life, and shaping it in ways to which others' lives are not vulnerable. But the force of the objection still seems to rest on the false assumption that having the same genome as his earlier twin unduly restricts his freedom to create a different life and self than the earlier twin's. Moreover, a family environment also importantly shapes children's development, but there is no force to the claim of a younger sibling that the existence of an older sibling raised in that same family is an undue influence on the younger sibling's freedom to make his own life for himself in that environment. Indeed, the younger twin or sibling might gain the benefit of being able to learn from the older twin's or sibling's mistakes.

A closely related argument can be derived from what Joel Feinberg has called a child's right to an open future. This requires that others raising a child not so close off the future possibilities that the child would otherwise have as to eliminate a reasonable range of opportunities for the child autonomously to construct his or her own life. One way this right might be violated is to create a later twin who will believe her future has already been set for her by the choices made and the life lived by her earlier twin.

The central difficulty in these appeals to a right either to ignorance or to an open future is that the right is not violated merely because the later twin is likely to *believe* that his future is already determined, when that belief is clearly false and supported only by the crudest genetic determinism. If we know the later twin will falsely believe that his open future has been taken from him as a result of being cloned, even though in reality it has not, then we know that cloning will cause the twin psychological distress, but not that it will violate his right. Jonas's right to ignorance, and Feinberg's right of a child to an open future, are not violated by human cloning, though they do point to psychological harms that a later twin may be likely to experience and that I will take up later.

Neither a moral or human right to a unique identity, nor one to ignorance and an open future, would be violated by human cloning. There may be other moral or human rights that human cloning would violate, but I do not know what they might be. I turn now to consideration of the harms that human cloning might produce.

What Individual or Social Harms Might Human Cloning Produce?

There are many possible individual or social harms that have been posited by one or another commentator and I shall only try to cover the more plausible and significant of them.

Largely Individual Harms

1. *Human cloning would produce psychological distress and harm in the later twin.* No doubt knowing the path in life taken by one's earlier twin might often have several bad psychological effects (Callahan, 1993; LaBar, 1984; Macklin, 1994; McCormick, 1993; Studdard, 1978; Rainer, 1978; Verhey, 1994). The later twin might feel, even if mistakenly, that her fate has already been substantially laid out, and so have difficulty freely and spontaneously taking responsibility for and making her own fate and life. The later twin's experience or sense of autonomy and freedom might be substantially diminished, even if in actual fact they are diminished much less than it seems to her. She might have a diminished sense of her own uniqueness and individuality, even if once again these are in fact diminished little or not at all by having an earlier twin with the same genome. If the later twin is the clone of a particularly exemplary individual, perhaps with some special capabilities and accomplishments, she might experience excessive pressure to reach the very high standards of ability and accomplishment of the earlier twin (Rainer, 1978). These various psychological effects might take a heavy toll on the later twin and be serious burdens to her.

While psychological harms of these kinds from human cloning are certainly possible, and perhaps even likely in some cases, they remain at this point only speculative since we have no experience with human cloning and the creation of earlier and later twins. Nevertheless, if experience with human cloning confirmed that serious and unavoidable psychological harms typically occurred to the later twin, that would be a serious moral reason to avoid the practice. Intuitively at least, psychological burdens and harms seem more likely and more serious for a person who is only one of many identical later twins cloned from one original source, so that the clone might run into another identical twin around every street corner. This prospect could be a good reason to place sharp limits on the number of twins that could be cloned from any one source.

One argument has been used by several commentators to undermine the apparent significance of potential psychological harms to a later twin (Chadwick, 1982; Robertson, 1994b, 1997; Macklin, 1994). The point derives from a general problem, called the nonidentity problem, posed by the philosopher Derek Parfit, although not originally directed to human cloning (Parfit, 1984). Here is the argument. Even if all these psychological burdens from human cloning could not be avoided for any later twin, they are not harms to the twin, and so not reasons not to clone the twin. That is because the only way for the twin to avoid the harms is never to be cloned, and so never to exist at all. But these psychological burdens, hard though they might be, are not so bad as to make the twin's life, all things considered, not worth living. So the later twin is not harmed by being given a life even with these psychological burdens, since the alternative of never existing at all is arguably worse— he or she never has a worthwhile life—but certainly not better for the twin. And if the later twin is not harmed by having been created with these unavoidable burdens, then how could he or she be wronged by having been created with them? And if the later twin is not wronged, then why is any wrong being done by human cloning? This argument has considerable potential import, for if it is sound it will undermine the apparent moral importance of any bad consequence of human cloning to the later twin that is not so serious as to make the twin's life, all things considered, not worth living.

I defended elsewhere the position regarding the general case of genetically transmitted handicaps, that if one could have a *different* child without comparable burdens (for the case of cloning, by using a different method of reproduction which did not result in a later twin), there is as strong a moral reason to do so as there would be not to cause similar burdens to an already existing child (Brock, 1995). Choosing to create the later twin with serious psychological burdens instead of a different person who would be free of them, without weighty overriding reasons for choosing the former, would be morally irresponsible or wrong, even if doing so does not harm or wrong the later twin who could only exist with the burdens. These issues are too detailed and complex to pursue here and the nonidentity problem remains controversial and not fully resolved, but at the least, the argument for disregarding the psychological burdens to the later twin because he or she could not exist without them is controversial, and in my view mistaken. Such psychological harms, as I shall continue to call them, are speculative, but they should not be disregarded because of the nonidentity problem.

2. *Human cloning procedures would carry unacceptable risks to the clone.* There is no doubt that attempts to clone a human being at the present time would carry unacceptable risks to the clone. Further research on the procedure with animals, as well as research to establish its safety and effectiveness for humans, is clearly necessary before it would be ethical to use the procedure on humans. One risk to the clone is the failure to implant, grow, and develop successfully, but this would involve the embryo's death or destruction long before most people or the law consider it to be a person with moral or legal protections of its life.

Other risks to the clone are that the procedure in some way goes wrong, or unanticipated harms come to the clone; for example, Harold Varmus, director of the National Institutes of Health, raised the concern that a cell many years old from which a person is cloned could have accumulated genetic mutations during its years in another adult that could give the resulting clone a predisposition to cancer or other diseases of aging (Weiss, 1997). Risks to an ovum donor (if any), a nucleus donor, and a woman who receives the embryo for implantation would likely be ethically acceptable with the informed consent of the involved parties.

I believe it is too soon to say whether unavoidable risks to the clone would make human cloning forever unethical. At a minimum, further research is needed to better define the potential risks to humans. But we should not insist on a standard that requires risks to be lower than those we accept in sexual reproduction, or in other forms of ART.

Largely Social Harms

3. *Human cloning would lessen the worth of individuals and diminish respect for human life.* Unelaborated claims to this effect were common in the media after the announcement of the cloning of Dolly. Ruth Macklin explored and criticized the claim that human cloning would diminish the value we place on, and our respect for, human life because it would lead to persons being viewed as replaceable (Macklin, 1994). As I have argued concerning a right to a unique identity, only on a confused and indefensible notion of human identity is a person's identity determined solely by his or her genes, and so no

individual could be fully replaced by a later clone possessing the same genes. Ordinary people recognize this clearly. For example, parents of a child dying of a fatal disease would find it insensitive and ludicrous to be told they should not grieve for their coming loss because it is possible to replace him by cloning him; it is *their child who is dying* whom they love and value, and that child and his importance to them is not replaceable by a cloned later twin. Even if they would also come to love and value a later twin as much as they now love and value their child who is dying, that would be to love and value that *different child* for its own sake, not as a replacement for the child they lost. Our relations of love and friendship are with distinct, historically situated individuals with whom over time we have shared experience and our lives, and whose loss to us can never be replaced.

A different version of this worry is that human cloning would result in persons' worth or value seeming diminished because we would come to see persons as able to be manufactured or "handmade." This demystification of the creation of human life would reduce our appreciation and awe of human life and of its natural creation. It would be a mistake, however, to conclude that a person created by human cloning is of less value or is less worthy of respect than one created by sexual reproduction. At least outside of some religious contexts, it is the nature of a being, not how it is created, that is the source of its value and makes it worthy of respect. For many people, gaining a scientific understanding of the truly extraordinary complexity of human reproduction and development increases, instead of decreases, their awe of the process and its product.

A more subtle route by which the value we place on each individual human life might be diminished could come from the use of human cloning with the aim of creating a child with a particular genome, either the genome of another individual especially meaningful to those doing the cloning or an individual with exceptional talents, abilities, and accomplishments. The child then comes to be objectified, valued only as an object and for its genome, or at least for its genome's expected phenotypic expression, and no longer recognized

as having the intrinsic equal moral value of all persons, simply as persons. For the moral value and respect due all persons to come to be seen as resting only on the instrumental value of individuals and of their particular qualities to others would be to fundamentally change the moral status properly accorded to persons. Individuals would lose their moral standing as full and equal members of the moral community, replaced by the different instrumental value each has to others.

Such a change in the equal moral value and worth accorded to persons should be avoided at all costs, but it is far from clear that such a change would result from permitting human cloning. Parents, for example, are quite capable of distinguishing their children's intrinsic value, just as individual persons, from their instrumental value based on their particular qualities or properties. The equal moral value and respect due all persons simply as persons is not incompatible with the different instrumental value of different individuals; Einstein and an untalented physics graduate student have vastly different value as scientists, but share and are entitled to equal moral value and respect as persons. It is a confused mistake to conflate these two kinds of value and respect. If making a large number of clones from one original person would be more likely to foster it, that would be a further reason to limit the number of clones that could be made from one individual.

4. *Human cloning might be used by commercial interests for financial gain.* Both opponents and proponents of human cloning agree that cloned embryos should not be able to be bought and sold. In a science fiction frame of mind, one can imagine commercial interests offering genetically certified and guaranteed embryos for sale, perhaps offering a catalogue of different embryos cloned from individuals with a variety of talents, capacities, and other desirable properties. This would be a fundamental violation of the equal moral respect and dignity owed to all persons, treating them instead as objects to be differentially valued, bought, and sold in the marketplace. Even if embryos are not yet persons at the time they would be purchased or sold, they would be being valued, bought, and sold for the persons they will become. The moral consensus against any commer-

cial market in embryos, cloned or otherwise, should be enforced by law whatever the public policy ultimately is on human cloning.

5. *Human cloning might be used by governments or other groups for immoral and exploitative purposes.* In *Brave New World*, Aldous Huxley imagined cloning individuals who have been engineered with limited abilities and conditioned to do, and to be happy doing, the menial work that society needed done (Huxley, 1932). Selection and control in the creation of people was exercised not in the interests of the persons created, but in the interests of the society and at the expense of the persons created; nor did it serve individuals' interests in reproduction and parenting. Any use of human cloning for such purposes would exploit the clones solely as means for the benefit of others, and would violate the equal moral respect and dignity they are owed as full moral persons. If human cloning is permitted to go forward, it should be with regulations that would clearly prohibit such immoral exploitation.

Fiction contains even more disturbing or bizarre uses of human cloning, such as Mengele's creation of many clones of Hitler in Ira Levin's *The Boys from Brazil* (Levin, 1976), Woody Allen's science fiction cinematic spoof *Sleeper* in which a dictator's only remaining part, his nose, must be destroyed to keep it from being cloned, and the contemporary science fiction film *Blade Runner*. These nightmare scenarios may be quite improbable, but their impact should not be underestimated on public concern with technologies like human cloning. Regulation of human cloning must assure the public that even such far-fetched abuses will not take place.

Conclusion

Human cloning has until now received little serious and careful ethical attention because it was typically dismissed as science fiction, and it stirs deep, but difficult to articulate, uneasiness and even revulsion in many people. Any ethical assessment of human cloning at this point must be tentative and provisional. Fortunately, the science and technology of human cloning are not yet in hand, and so a public and professional debate is possible without the need for a hasty, precipitate policy response.

The ethical pros and cons of human cloning, as I see them at this time, are sufficiently balanced and uncertain that there is not an ethically decisive case either for or against permitting it or doing it. Access to human cloning can plausibly be brought within a moral right to reproductive freedom, but its potential legitimate uses appear few and do not promise substantial benefits. It is not a central component of the moral right to reproductive freedom and it does not uniquely serve any major or pressing individual or social needs. On the other hand, contrary to the pronouncements of many of its opponents, human cloning seems not to be a violation of moral or human rights. But it does risk some significant individual or social harms, although most are based on common public confusions about genetic determinism, human identity, and the effects of human cloning. Because most potential harms feared from human cloning remain speculative, they seem insufficient to warrant at this time a complete legal prohibition of either research on or later use of human cloning, if and when its safety and efficacy are established. Legitimate moral concerns about the use and effects of human cloning, however, underline the need for careful public oversight of research on its development, together with a wider public and professional debate and review before cloning is used on human beings.

REFERENCES

Annas, G. J. (1994). "Regulatory Models for Human Embryo Cloning: The Free Market, Professional Guidelines, and Government Restrictions." *Kennedy Institute of Ethics Journal* 4, 3:235–249.

Brock, D. W. (1994). "Reproductive Freedom: Its Nature, Bases and Limits," in *Health Care Ethics: Critical Issues for Health Professionals*, eds. D. Thomasma and J. Monagle. Gaithersburg, MD: Aspen Publishers.

Brock, D. W. (1995). "The Non-Identity Problem and Genetic Harm." *Bioethics* 9:269–275.

Callahan, D. (1993). "Perspective on Cloning: A Threat to Individual Uniqueness." *Los Angeles Times*, November 12, 1993:B7.

Chadwick, R. F. (1982). "Cloning." *Philosophy* 57:201–209.

Eisenberg. L. (1976). "The Outcome as Cause: Predestination and Human Cloning." *Journal of Medicine and Philosophy* 1:318–331.

Feinberg, J. (1980). "The Child's Right to an Open Future," in *Whose Child? Children's Rights, Patental Authority, and*

State Power, eds. W. Aiken and H. LaFollette. Totowa, NJ: Rowman and Littlefield.

Harris, J. (1992). *Wonderwoman and Superman: The Ethics of Biotechnology*. Oxford: Oxford University Press.

Huxley, A. (1932). *Brave New World*. London: Chalto and Winders.

Jonas, H. (1974). *Philosophical Essays: From Ancient Creed to Technological Man*. Englewood Cliffs, NJ: Prentice-Hall.

Kahn, C. (1989). "Can We Achieve Immortality?" *Free Inquiry* 9:14–18.

Kass, L. (1985). *Toward a More Natural Science*. New York: The Free Press.

LaBar, M. (1984). "The Pros and Cons of Human Cloning." *Thought* 57:318–333.

Lederberg, J. (1966). "Experimental Genetics and Human Evolution." *American Naturalist* 100:519–531.

Levin, I. (1976). *The Boys from Brazil*. New York: Random House.

Macklin, R. (1994). "Splitting Embryos on the Slippery Slope: Ethics and Public Policy." *Kennedy Institute of Ethics Journal* 4:209–226.

McCormick, R. (1993). "Should We Clone Humans?" *Christian Century* 110:1148–1149.

McKinnell, R. (1979). *Cloning: A Biologist Reports*. Minneapolis, MN: University of Minnesota Press.

Mill, J. S. (1859). *On Liberty*. Indianapolis, IN: Bobbs-Merrill Publishing.

NABER (National Advisory Board on Ethics in Reproduction) (1994). "Report on Human Cloning Through Embryo Splitting: An Amber Light." *Kennedy Institute of Ethics Journal* 4:251–282.

Parfit, D. (1984). *Reasons and Persons*. Oxford: Oxford University Press.

Rainer, J. D. (1978). "Commentary." *Man and Medicine: The Journal of Values and Ethics in Health Care* 3:115–117.

Rhodes, R. (1995). "Clones, Harms, and Rights." *Cambridge Quarterly of Healthcare Ethics* 4:285–290.

Robertson, J. A. (1994a). *Children of Choice: Freedom and the New Reproductive Technologies*. Princeton, NJ: Princeton University Press.

Robertson, J. A. (1994b). "The Question of Human Cloning." *Hastings Center Report* 24:6–14.

Robertson, J. A. (1997). "A Ban on Cloning and Cloning Research is Unjustified." Testimony Presented to the National Bioethics Advisory Commission, March 1997.

Smith, G. P. (1983). "Intimations of Immortality: Clones, Cyrons and the Law." *University of New South Wales Law Journal* 6:119–132.

Studdard, A. (1978). "The Lone Clone." *Man and Medicine: The Journal of Values and Ethics in Health Care* 3:109–114.

Thomas, L. (1974). "Notes of a Biology Watcher: On Cloning a Human Being." *New England Journal of Medicine* 291:1296–1297.

Verhey, A. D. (1994). "Cloning: Revisiting an Old Debate." *Kennedy Institute of Ethics Journal* 4:227–234.

Walters. W. A. W. (1982). "Cloning, Ectogenesis, and Hybrids: Things to Come?" in *Test-Tube Babies*, eds. W. A. W. Walters and P. Singer. Melbourne: Oxford University Press.

Weiss, R. (1997). "Cloning Suddenly Has Government's Attention." *International Herald Tribune*, March 7, 1997.

WHO (World Health Organization Press Office) (March 11, 1997). "WHO Director General Condemns Human Cloning." World Health Organization, Geneva, Switzerland.

Wilmut, I., et al. (1997). "Viable Offspring Derived from Fetal and Adult Mammalian Cells." *Nature* 385:810–813.

Opinion in the Matter of Baby M

NEW JERSEY SUPREME COURT

This case concerned the legal custody of "Baby M," an infant born to Mary Beth Whitehead in accordance with her agreement to become a surrogate mother for William and Elizabeth Stern. Whitehead consented to be artificially inseminated with Mr. Stern's sperm, to carry the child to term, and to hand it over to the Sterns after birth. But she refused to give up the baby and left the state with it. Eventually the dispute between Whitehead and the Sterns wound up in the New Jersey Supreme Court, which found that the surrogacy contract was invalid and that Whitehead was the legal mother. It also held that Baby M should live with the Sterns and that Whitehead should have visitation rights.

In this matter the Court is asked to determine the validity of a contract that purports to provide a new way of bringing children into a family. For a fee of $10,000, a woman agrees to be artificially inseminated with the semen of another woman's husband; she is to conceive a child, carry it to term, and after its birth surrender it to the natural father and his wife. The intent of the contract is that the child's natural mother will thereafter be forever separated from her child. The wife is to adopt the child, and she and the natural father are to be regarded as its parents for all purposes. The contract providing for this is called a "surrogacy contract," the natural mother inappropriately called the "surrogate mother."

We invalidate the surrogacy contract because it conflicts with the law and public policy of this State. While we recognize the depth of the yearning of infertile couples to have their own children, we find the payment of money to a "surrogate" mother illegal, perhaps criminal, and potentially degrading to women. Although in this case we grant custody to the natural father, the evidence having clearly proved such custody to be in the best interests of the infant, we void both the termination of the surrogate mother's parental rights and the adoption of the child by the wife/stepparent. We thus restore the "surrogate" as the mother of the child. We remand the issue of the natural mother's visitation rights to the trial court, since that issue was not reached below and the record before us is not sufficient to permit us to decide it *de novo*.

We find no offense to our present laws where a woman voluntarily and without payment agrees to act as a "surrogate" mother, provided that she is not subject to a binding agreement to surrender her child. Moreover, our holding today does not preclude the Legislature from altering the current statutory scheme, within constitutional limits, so as to permit surrogacy contracts. Under current law, however, the surrogacy agreement before us is illegal and invalid.

From New Jersey Supreme Court (1988) 109 N.J. 396, 537 A.2d 1227 (1988).

Facts

In February 1985, William Stern and Mary Beth Whitehead entered into a surrogacy contract. It recited that Stern's wife, Elizabeth, was infertile, that they wanted a child, and that Mrs. Whitehead was willing to provide that child as the mother with Mr. Stern as the father.

The contract provided that through artificial insemination using Mr. Stern's sperm, Mrs. Whitehead would become pregnant, carry the child to term, bear it, deliver it to the Sterns, and thereafter do whatever was necessary to terminate her maternal rights so that Mrs. Stern could thereafter adopt the child. Mrs. Whitehead's husband, Richard, was also a party to the contract; Mrs. Stern was not. Mr. Whitehead promised to do all acts necessary to rebut the presumption of paternity under the Parentage Act. Although Mrs. Stern was not a party to the surrogacy agreement, the contract gave her sole custody of the child in the event of Mr. Stern's death. Mrs. Stern's status as a nonparty to the surrogate parenting agreement presumably was to avoid the application of the baby-selling statute to this arrangement.

Mr. Stern, on his part, agreed to attempt the artificial insemination and to pay Mrs. Whitehead $10,000 after the child's birth, on its delivery to him. In a separate contract, Mr. Stern agreed to pay $7,500 to the Infertility Center of New York ("ICNY"). The Center's advertising campaigns solicit surrogate mothers and encourage infertile couples to consider surrogacy. ICNY arranged for the surrogacy contract by bringing the parties together, explaining the process to them, furnishing the contractual form, and providing legal counsel.

The history of the parties' involvement in this arrangement suggests their good faith. William and Elizabeth Stern were married in July 1974, having met at the University of Michigan, where both were Ph.D. candidates. Due to financial considerations and Mrs. Stern's pursuit of a medical degree and residency, they decided to defer starting a family until 1981. Before then, however, Mrs. Stern learned that she might have multiple sclerosis and that the disease in some cases renders pregnancy a serious health risk. Her anxiety appears to have exceeded the actual risk, which current medical authorities assess as minimal. Nonetheless that anxiety was evidently quite real, Mrs. Stern fearing that pregnancy might precipitate blindness, paraplegia, or other forms of debilitation. Based on the perceived risk, the Sterns decided to forgo having their own children. The decision had special significance for Mr. Stern. Most of his family had been destroyed in the Holocaust. As the family's only survivor, he very much wanted to continue his bloodline.

Initially the Sterns considered adoption, but were discouraged by the substantial delay apparently involved and by the potential problem they saw arising from their age and their differing religious backgrounds. They were most eager for some other means to start a family.

The paths of Mrs. Whitehead and the Sterns to surrogacy were similar. Both responded to advertising by ICNY. The Sterns' response, following their inquiries into adoption, was the result of their long-standing decision to have a child. Mrs. Whitehead's response apparently resulted from her sympathy with family members and others who could have no children (she stated that she wanted to give another couple the "gift of life"); she also wanted the $10,000 to help her family. . . .

. . . The two couples met to discuss the surrogacy arrangement and decided to go forward. On February 6, 1985, Mr. Stern and Mr. and Mrs. Whitehead executed the surrogate parenting agreement. After several artificial inseminations over a period of months, Mrs. Whitehead became pregnant. The pregnancy was uneventful and on March 27, 1986, Baby M was born.

Not wishing anyone at the hospital to be aware of the surrogacy arrangement, Mr. and Mrs. Whitehead appeared to all as the proud parents of a healthy female child. Her birth certificate indicated her name to be Sara Elizabeth Whitehead and her father to be Richard Whitehead. In accordance with Mrs. Whitehead's request, the Sterns visited the hospital unobtrusively to see the newborn child.

Mrs. Whitehead realized, almost from the moment of birth, that she could not part with this child. She had felt a bond with it even during pregnancy. Some indication of the attachment was conveyed to the Sterns at the hospital when they told Mrs. Whitehead what they were going to name the baby. She ap-

parently broke into tears and indicated that she did not know if she could give up the child. She talked about how the baby looked like her other daughter, and made it clear that she was experiencing great difficulty with the decision.

Nonetheless, Mrs. Whitehead was, for the moment, true to her word. Despite powerful inclinations to the contrary, she turned her child over to the Sterns on March 30 at the Whiteheads' home.

The Sterns were thrilled with their new child. They had planned extensively for its arrival, far beyond the practical furnishing of a room for her. It was a time of joyful celebration—not just for them but for their friends as well. The Sterns looked forward to raising their daughter, whom they named Melissa. While aware by then that Mrs. Whitehead was undergoing an emotional crisis, they were as yet not cognizant of the depth of that crisis and its implications for their newly enlarged family.

Later in the evening of March 30, Mrs. Whitehead became deeply disturbed, disconsolate, stricken with unbearable sadness. She had to have her child. She could not eat, sleep, or concentrate on anything other than her need for her baby. The next day she went to the Sterns' home and told them how much she was suffering.

The depth of Mrs. Whitehead's despair surprised and frightened the Sterns. She told them that she could not live without her baby, that she must have her, even if only for one week, that thereafter she would surrender her child. The Sterns, concerned that Mrs. Whitehead might indeed commit suicide, not wanting under any circumstances to risk that, and in any event believing that Mrs. Whitehead would keep her word, turned the child over to her. It was not until four months later, after a series of attempts to regain possession of the child, that Melissa was returned to the Sterns, having been forcibly removed from the home where she was then living with Mr. and Mrs. Whitehead, the home in Florida owned by Mary Beth Whitehead's parents.

The struggle over Baby M began when it became apparent that Mrs. Whitehead could not return the child to Mr. Stern. Due to Mrs. Whitehead's refusal to relinquish the baby, Mr. Stern filed a complaint seeking enforcement of the surrogacy contract. He alleged, accurately, that Mrs. Whitehead had not only refused to comply with the surrogacy contract but had threatened to flee from New Jersey with the child in order to avoid even the possibility of his obtaining custody. The court papers asserted that if Mrs. Whitehead were to be given notice of the application for an order requiring her to relinquish custody, she would, prior to the hearing, leave the state with the baby. And that is precisely what she did. After the order was entered, *ex parte*, the process server, aided by the police, in the presence of the Sterns, entered Mrs. Whitehead's home to execute the order. Mr. Whitehead fled with the child, who had been handed to him through a window while those who came to enforce the order were thrown off balance by a dispute over the child's current name.

The Whiteheads immediately fled to Florida with Baby M. They stayed initially with Mrs. Whitehead's parents, where one of Mrs. Whitehead's children had been living. For the next three months, the Whiteheads and Melissa lived at roughly twenty different hotels, motels, and homes in order to avoid apprehension. From time to time Mrs. Whitehead would call Mr. Stern to discuss the matter; the conversations, recorded by Mr. Stern on advice of counsel, show an escalating dispute about rights, morality, and power, accompanied by threats of Mrs. Whitehead to kill herself, to kill the child, and falsely to accuse Mr. Stern of sexually molesting Mrs. Whitehead's other daughter.

Eventually, the Sterns discovered where the Whiteheads were staying, commenced supplementary proceedings in Florida, and obtained an order requiring the Whiteheads to turn over the child. Police in Florida enforced the order, forcibly removing the child from her grandparents' home. She was soon thereafter brought to New Jersey and turned over to the Sterns. The prior order of the court, issued *ex parte*, awarding custody of the child to the Sterns *pendente lite*, was reaffirmed by the trial court after consideration of the certified representations of the parties (both represented by counsel) concerning the unusual sequence of events that had unfolded. Pending final judgment, Mrs. Whitehead was awarded limited visitation with Baby M.

The Sterns' complaint, in addition to seeking possession and ultimately custody of the child, sought enforcement of the surrogacy contract. Pursuant to the contract, it asked that the child be permanently placed in their custody, that Mrs. Whitehead's parental rights be terminated, and that Mrs. Stern be allowed to adopt the child, i.e., that, for all purposes, Melissa become the Sterns' child.

The trial took thirty-two days over a period of more than two months. . . . Soon after the conclusion of the trial, the trial court announced its opinion from the bench. It held that the surrogacy contract was valid; ordered that Mrs. Whitehead's parental rights be terminated and that sole custody of the child be granted to Mr. Stern; and, after hearing brief testimony from Mrs. Stern, immediately entered an order allowing the adoption of Melissa by Mrs. Stern, all in accordance with the surrogacy contract. Pending the outcome of the appeal, we granted a continuation of visitation to Mrs. Whitehead, although slightly more limited than the visitation allowed during the trial.

Although clearly expressing its view that the surrogacy contract was valid, the trial court devoted the major portion of its opinion to the question of the baby's best interests. . . .

On the question of best interests—and we agree, but for different reasons, that custody was the critical issue—the court's analysis of the testimony was perceptive, demonstrating both its understanding of the case and its considerable experience in these matters. We agree substantially with both its analysis and conclusions on the matter of custody. . . .

Invalidity and Unenforceability of Surrogacy Contract

We have concluded that this surrogacy contract is invalid. Our conclusion has two bases: direct conflict with existing statutes and conflict with the public policies of this State, as expressed in its statutory and decisional law.

One of the surrogacy contract's basic purposes, to achieve the adoption of a child through private placement, though permitted in New Jersey "is very much disfavored." Its use of money for this purpose—and we have no doubt whatsoever that the money is being paid to obtain an adoption and not, as the Sterns argue, for the personal services of Mary Beth Whitehead—is illegal and perhaps criminal. In addition to the inducement of money, there is the coercion of contract: the natural mother's irrevocable agreement, prior to birth, even prior to conception, to surrender the child to the adoptive couple. Such an agreement is totally unenforceable in private placement adoption. Even where the adoption is through an approved agency, the formal agreement to surrender occurs only after birth, and then, by regulation, only *after* the birth mother has been offered counseling. Integral to these invalid provisions of the surrogacy contract is the related agreement, equally invalid, on the part of the natural mother to cooperate with, and not to contest, proceedings to terminate her parental rights, as well as her contractual concession, in aid of the adoption, that the child's best interests would be served by awarding custody to the natural father and his wife—all of this before she has even conceived, and, in some cases, before she has the slightest idea of what the natural father and adoptive mother are like.

The foregoing provisions not only directly conflict with New Jersey statutes, but also offend long-established State policies. These critical terms, which are at the heart of the contract, are invalid and unenforceable, the conclusion therefore follows, without more, that the entire contract is unenforceable.

A. Conflict with Statutory Provisions

The surrogacy contract conflicts with: (1) laws prohibiting the use of money in connection with adoptions; (2) laws requiring proof of parental unfitness or abandonment before termination of parental rights is ordered or an adoption is granted; and (3) laws that make surrender of custody and consent to adoption revocable in private placement adoptions.

Our law prohibits paying or accepting money in connection with any placement of a child for adoption. Violation is a high misdemeanor. Excepted are fees of an approved agency (which must be a nonprofit entity) and certain expenses in connection with childbirth. . . .

B. Public Policy Considerations

The surrogacy contract's invalidity, resulting from its direct conflict with the above statutory provisions, is further underlined when its goals and means are measured against New Jersey's public policy. The contract's basic premise, that the natural parents can decide in advance of birth which one is to have custody of the child, bears no relationship to the settled law that the child's best interests shall determine custody. . . .

The surrogacy contract guarantees permanent separation of the child from one of its natural parents. Our policy, however, has long been that to the extent possible, children should remain with and be brought up by both of their natural parents. . . . This is not simply some theoretical ideal that in practice has no meaning. The impact of failure to follow that policy is nowhere better shown than in the results of this surrogacy contract. A child, instead of starting off its life with as much peace and security as possible, finds itself immediately in a tug-of-war between contending mother and father.

The surrogacy contract violates the policy of this State that the rights of natural parents are equal concerning their child, the father's right no greater than the mother's. . . . The whole purpose and effect of the surrogacy contract was to give the father the exclusive right to the child by destroying the rights of the mother.

The policies expressed in our comprehensive laws governing consent to the surrender of a child stand in stark contrast to the surrogacy contract and what it implies. Here there is no counseling, independent or otherwise, of the natural mother, no evaluation, no warning. . . .

Under the contract, the natural mother is irrevocably committed before she knows the strength of her bond with her child. She never makes a totally voluntary, informed decision, for quite clearly any decision prior to the baby's birth is, in the most important sense, uninformed, and any decision after that, compelled by a pre-existing contractual commitment, the threat of a lawsuit, and the inducement of a $10,000 payment, is less than totally voluntary. Her interests are of little concern to those who controlled this transaction. . . .

Worst of all, however, is the contract's total disregard of the best interests of the child. There is not the slightest suggestion that any inquiry will be made at any time to determine the fitness of the Sterns as custodial parents, of Mrs. Stern as an adoptive parent, their superiority to Mrs. Whitehead, or the effect on the child of not living with her natural mother.

This is the sale of a child, or, at the very least, the sale of a mother's right to her child, the only mitigating factor being that one of the purchasers is the father. Almost every evil that prompted the prohibition on the payment of money in connection with adoptions exists here. . . .

In the scheme contemplated by the surrogacy contract in this case, a middleman, propelled by profit, promotes the sale. Whatever idealism may have motivated any of the participants, the profit motive predominates, permeates, and ultimately governs the transaction. The demand for children is great and the supply small. The availability of contraception, abortion, and the greater willingness of single mothers to bring up their children has led to a shortage of babies offered for adoption. The situation is ripe for the entry of the middleman who will bring some equilibrium into the market by increasing the supply through the use of money.

Intimated, but disputed, is the assertion that surrogacy will be used for the benefit of the rich at the expense of the poor. In response it is noted that the Sterns are not rich and the Whiteheads not poor. Nevertheless, it is clear to us that it is unlikely that surrogate mothers will be as proportionately numerous among those women in the top twenty percent income bracket as among those in the bottom twenty percent. Put differently, we doubt that infertile couples in the low-income bracket will find upper income surrogates.

In any event, even in this case one should not pretend that disparate wealth does not play a part simply because the contrast is not the dramatic "rich versus poor." At the time of trial, the Whiteheads' net assets were probably negative—Mrs. Whitehead's own sister was foreclosing on a second mortgage. Their income derived from Mr. Whitehead's labors. Mrs. Whitehead is a homemaker, having previously held part-time jobs. The Sterns are both professionals, she a medical doctor, he a biochemist. Their combined income when both were working was about $89,500 a year and their assets sufficient to pay for the surrogacy contract arrangements.

The point is made that Mrs. Whitehead *agreed* to the surrogacy arrangement, supposedly fully understanding the consequences. Putting aside the issue of how compelling her need for money may have been, and how significant her understanding of the consequences, we suggest that her consent is irrelevant. There are, in a civilized society, some things that money cannot buy. In America, we decided long ago that merely because conduct purchased by money was "voluntary" did not mean that it was good or beyond regulation and prohibition. Employers can no longer buy labor at the lowest price they can bargain for, even though that labor is "voluntary," or buy women's labor for less money than paid to men for the same job, or purchase the agreement of children to perform oppressive labor, or purchase the agreement of workers to subject themselves to unsafe or unhealthful working conditions. There are, in short, values that society deems more important than granting to wealth whatever it can buy, be it labor, love, or life. Whether this principle recommends prohibition of surrogacy, which presumably sometimes results in great satisfaction to all of the parties, is not for us to say. We note here only that, under existing law, the fact that Mrs. Whitehead "agreed" to the arrangement is not dispositive.

The long-term effects of surrogacy contracts are not known, but feared—the impact on the child who learns her life was bought, that she is the offspring of someone who gave birth to her only to obtain money; the impact on the natural mother as the full weight of her isolation is felt along with the full reality of the sale of her body and her child; the impact on the natural father and adoptive mother once they realize the consequences of their conduct. Literature in related areas suggests these are substantial considerations, although, given the newness of surrogacy, there is little information.

The surrogacy contract is based on principles that are directly contrary to the objectives of our laws. It guarantees the separation of a child from its mother; it looks to adoption regardless of suitability; it totally ignores the child; it takes the child from the mother regardless of her wishes and her maternal fitness; and it does all of this, it accomplishes all of its goals, through the use of money.

Beyond that is the potential degradation of some women that may result from this arrangement. In many cases, of course, surrogacy may bring satisfaction, not only to the infertile couple, but to the surrogate mother herself. The fact, however, that many women may not perceive surrogacy negatively but rather see it as an opportunity does not diminish its potential for devastation to other women.

In sum, the harmful consequences of this surrogacy arrangement appear to us all too palpable. In New Jersey the surrogate mother's agreement to sell her child is void. Its irrevocability infects the entire contract, as does the money that purports to buy it.

Termination

We have already noted that under our laws termination of parental rights cannot be based on contract, but may be granted only on proof of the statutory requirements. That conclusion was one of the bases for invalidating the surrogacy contract. Although excluding the contract as a basis for parental termination, we did not explicitly deal with the question of whether the statutory bases for termination existed. We do so here.

As noted before, if termination of Mrs. Whitehead's parental rights is justified, Mrs. Whitehead will have no further claim either to custody or to visitation, and adoption by Mrs. Stern may proceed pursuant to the private placement adoption statute. If termination is not justified. Mrs. Whitehead remains the legal mother, and even if not entitled to custody, she would ordinarily be expected to have some rights of visitation. . . .

Nothing in this record justifies a finding that would allow a court to terminate Mary Beth Whitehead's parental rights under the statutory standard. It is not simply that obviously there was no "intentional abandonment or very substantial neglect of parental duties without a reasonable expectation of reversal of that conduct in the future," quite the contrary, but furthermore that the trial court never found Mrs. Whitehead an unfit mother and indeed affirmatively stated that Mary Beth Whitehead had been a good mother to her other children. . . .

Custody

. . . [T]he question of custody in this case, as in practically all cases, assumes the fitness of both parents, and no serious contention is made in this case that either is unfit. The issue here is which life would be *better* for Baby M, one with primary custody in the Whiteheads or one with primary custody in the Sterns.

The circumstances of this custody dispute are unusual and they have provoked some unusual contentions. The Whiteheads claim that even if the child's best interests would be served by our awarding custody to the Sterns, we should not do so, since that will encourage surrogacy contracts—contracts claimed by the Whiteheads, and we agree, to be violative of important legislatively stated public policies. Their position is that in order that surrogacy contracts be deterred, custody should remain in the surrogate mother unless she is unfit, regardless of the best interests of the child. We disagree. Our declaration that this surrogacy contract is unenforceable and illegal is sufficient to deter similar agreements. We need not sacrifice the child's interests in order to make that point sharper. . . .

Our custody conclusion is based on strongly persuasive testimony contrasting both the family life of the Whiteheads and the Sterns and the personalities and characters of the individuals. The stability of the Whitehead family life was doubtful at the time of trial. Their finances were in serious trouble (foreclosure by Mrs Whitehead's sister on a second mortagage was in process). Mr. Whitehead's employment, though relatively steady, was always at risk because of his alcoholism, a condition that he seems not to have been able to confront effectively. Mrs. Whitehead had not worked for quite some time, her last two employments having been part-time. One of the Whiteheads' positive attributes was their ability to bring up two children, and apparently well, even in so vulnerable a household. Yet substantial question was raised even about that aspect of their home life. The expert testimony contained criticism of Mrs. Whitehead's handling of her son's educational difficulties. Certain of the experts noted that Mrs. Whitehead perceived herself as omnipotent and omniscient concerning her children. She knew what they were thinking, what they wanted, and she spoke for them. As to Melissa, Mrs. Whitehead expressed the view that she alone knew what that child's cries and sounds meant. Her inconsistent stories about various things engendered grave doubts about her ability to explain honestly and sensitively to Baby M—and at the right time—the nature of her origin. Although faith in professional counseling is not a *sine qua non* of parenting, several experts believed that Mrs. Whitehead's contempt for professional help, especially professional psychological help, coincided with her feelings of omnipotence in a way that could be devastating to a child who most likely will need such help. In short, while love and affection there would be, Baby M's life with the Whiteheads promised to be too closely controlled by Mrs. Whitehead. The prospects for wholesome, independent psychological growth and development would be at serious risk.

The Sterns have no other children, but all indications are that their household and their personalities promise a much more likely foundation for Melissa to grow and thrive. There *is* a track record of sorts—during the one-and-a-half-years of custody Baby M has done very well, and the relationship between both Mr. and Mrs. Stern and the baby has become very strong. The household is stable, and likely to remain so. Their finances are more than adequate, their circle of friends supportive, and their marriage happy. Most important, they are loving, giving, nurturing, and open-minded people. They have demonstrated the wish and ability to nurture and protect Melissa, yet at the same time to encourage her independence. Their lack of experience is more than made up for by a willingness to learn and to listen, a willingness that is enhanced by their professional training, especially Mrs. Stern's experience as a pediatrician They are honest; they can recognize error, deal with it, and learn from it. They will try to determine rationally the best way to cope with problems in their relationship with Melissa. When the time comes to tell her about her origins, they will probably have found a means of doing so that accords with the best interests of Baby M. All in all, Melissa's future appear's solid, happy, and promising with them.

Based on all of this we have concluded, independent of the trial court's identical conclusion, that Melissa's best interests call for custody in the Sterns. Our above-mentioned disagreements with the trial court do not, as we have noted, in any way diminish our concurrence with its conclusions. . . .

Visitation

The trial court's decision to terminate Mrs. Whitehead's parental rights precluded it from making any determination on visitation. Our reversal of the trial court's order, however, requires delineation of Mrs. Whitehead's rights to visitation. It is apparent to us that this factually sensitive issue, which was never addressed below, should not be determined *de novo* by this Court. We therefore remand the visitation issue to the trial court for an abbreviated hearing and determination. . . .

The fact that the trial court did not address visitation is only one reason for remand. The ultimate question is whether, despite the absence of the trial court's guidance, the record before us is sufficient to allow an appellate court to make this essentially factual determination. We can think of no issue that is more dependent on a trial court's factual findings and evaluation than visitation.

We have decided that Mrs. Whitehead is entitled to visitation at some point, and that question is not open to the trial court on this remand. The trial court will determine what kind of visitation shall be granted to her, with or without conditions, and when and under what circumstances it should commence. . . .

Conclusion

This case affords some insight into a new reproductive arrangement: the artificial insemination of a surrogate mother. The unfortunate events that have unfolded illustrate that its unregulated use can bring suffering to all involved. Potential victims include the surrogate mother and her family, the natural father and his wife, and most importantly, the child. Although surrogacy has apparently provided positive results for some infertile couples, it can also, as this case demonstrates, cause suffering to participants, here essentially innocent and well-intended.

We have found that our present laws do not permit the surrogacy contract used in this case. Nowhere, however, do we find any legal prohibition against surrogacy when the surrogate mother volunteers, without any payment, to act as a surrogate and is given the right to change her mind and to assert her parental rights. Moreover, the Legislature remains free to deal with this most sensitive issue as it sees fit, subject only to constitutional constraints. . . .

CHAPTER 9

Genetic Choices

We are now in the Genetic Era, a time when the century-old trickle of scientific facts about our genetic selves has given way to a torrent. The rivulet widened suddenly in 1953 when Francis Crick and James Watson discovered that the double helix was the shape of DNA—the chemical compound that encodes the encyclopedic set of instructions for producing and maintaining all living things. It broadened into a flood in 2003 when scientists finally were able to chart the length and breadth of the human genome, determining the exact sequence of a human being's 3 billion letters of DNA code, all grouped into 20,000–25,000 genes. Now scientists are rapidly pinpointing genetic factors that cause or contribute to diseases, developing tests to identify and predict (even before conception) specific human conditions, researching ways to alter genes to effect cures or devise treatments, enabling parents to have control over the genetic makeup of their children, and peering into the future at the power to change profoundly the human genome itself.

At each step, moral questions press in, and they intersect with almost every major ethical concern in this text—paternalism, autonomy, beneficence, rights, confidentiality, abortion, killing, personhood, reproductive technology, justice in providing health care, research ethics, and more. Science has once again outpaced conventional moral understanding as genetics inserts a host of raw, hard questions into our lives: Should genetic testing be used to identify or predict diseases even when no treatment is available? Do carriers of a deadly genetic disease that is likely to be passed on to their children have a duty to warn those children of the risk?

Who should control genetic information about a person, and what is a physician's duty regarding truth-telling and confidentiality? Is it "playing God" to alter someone's genes to treat diseases or prevent them in future generations? Is it wrong for parents to use preconception genetic testing and embryo selection to avoid having a disabled baby? Do these practices discriminate against disabled people? Should genetic technology be used to select a child's gender or other attributes such as eye and hair color and musical or athletic ability? Should eugenics be employed? That is, should genetic knowledge be applied to whole populations in an attempt to improve the human genome?

Such questions could continue for several pages, but let us try to grapple with some of the main ones.

GENES AND GENOMES

Cells are the fundamental components of every living thing, and DNA (deoxyribonucleic acid) makes up the chemical coding that directs their construction, development, and operation. For nearly all organisms, DNA is the language of the genetic software that runs the cells and ensures the inheritance of traits from one generation to the next. Whether in ants, worms, gazelles, or humans, DNA consists of the same chemical ingredients and has the same molecular architecture: double, parallel strands linked together by chemical crossbars and twisted like a spiral staircase—the classic double helix. Each crossbar is formed by a matching pair of chemical bases, called a base pair. There are only four bases—

adenine (A), guanine (G), cytosine (C), and thymine (T)—yet they constitute the entire "alphabet" of the genetic code. Their order (the DNA sequence) along the strands (ATTCCGGA, for example) encodes all the instructions required for making and maintaining an organism. As it "reads" the code, a cell constructs, according to the precise specifications, various proteins, which carry out most biological processes and provide almost all of the material for building cells.

An organism's entire complement of DNA is known as its **genome**. The human genome consists of about 3 billion base pairs, and there is a complete genome in nearly every human cell. (A mouse genome has 2.6 billion base pairs; a fruit fly, 137 million; and an *E. coli* bacterium, 4.6 million.) In a typical human cell, the DNA strands total about six feet, coiled and crammed efficiently into an incredibly small space.

A cell does not "read" the 3 billion base pairs as one long stream of letters but as separate segments, or "words," of the stream, each segment providing instructions to the cell for manufacturing a customized protein or small group of proteins. These words of genetic code are **genes**, the fundamental units of biological inheritance. The human genome contains 20,000–25,000 genes, which vary in the length of their instructions from hundreds of DNA bases up to 2 million. Each gene has a duplicate, with one copy inherited from the male parent and one from the female parent.

In the cell's nucleus, the genes are neatly organized—bundled into 46 stringlike molecules known as **chromosomes**. These bundles are arranged into 23 pairs, with 22 of the pairs appearing the same for both males and females, and the twenty-third pair—the sex chromosomes—differing for males and females. Males have both an X and Y chromosome, while females have two X chromosomes.

Through the workings of all this genetic machinery, a human organism is produced and sustained, and a vast share of its characteristics is determined. (Genes have their say, but not nec-

essarily the final say, on how a person turns out, for he or she is also affected by the incredibly complex interactions between genetic systems and environmental factors.) When the machinery operates properly, the organism thrives. But flaws in the system—mistakes in the genes' coded instructions—can sometimes lead to devastating disease or disability. Mistakes (mutations or alterations) can arise when the order of bases in a DNA sequence is wrong or when bases have been added, deleted, or duplicated. Occasionally extra genes or chromosomes are added, or essential ones are left out.

Some genetic mutations are acquired—they happen in people randomly or because of exposure to noxious agents such as radiation, chemicals, or cigarette smoke. The exposure disorders can "run in families" not because they are hereditary but because family members are exposed to the same harmful environmental factors. But many mutations are indeed hereditary and are transmitted through families, triggering the same genetic disease in subsequent generations. The genetic errors are responsible for more than 4,000 hereditary diseases.

Unfortunately, the relation between genetic flaws and genetic disease is usually anything but simple. In most cases, genetic diseases arise not from a single gene defect but from many mutations in one or more genes, coupled with a person's lifestyle habits and environmental influences. Researchers believe that many common disorders such as heart disease, cancer, and diabetes are in this category.

GENETIC TESTING

Thanks to scientific advances in genetics (most notably the tracing of the human genome sequence by the Human Genome Project), it is now possible to check for genetic disorders by looking for changes in a person's DNA. This is the power of **genetic testing**, which is now available for over a thousand diseases, a number that is expected to increase by the hundreds in the next few years. With a small blood or tissue sample from a patient, clinicians can test for a host of genetic mutations that can unmask a variety of disorders. The testing is done for several reasons, including:

- *Newborn screening* to uncover genetic diseases for early treatment. Every state mandates some kind of genetic testing for newborns, with some states screening for as many as 30 disorders. The first mandatory genetic testing was for phenylketonuria (PKU), a disorder resulting in profound mental retardation when not treated early with a special diet.
- *Carrier testing* to determine whether someone is a carrier of a type of genetic disease known as an autosomal recessive disorder. A carrier possesses just one copy of a mutated gene and will not get the disease, but if two carriers together have a child, that child could inherit two copies of the mutated gene (one from each parent) and therefore greatly increase its chances of having the disease. PKU is such a disorder, and so is cystic fibrosis (a life-shortening illness affecting respiratory and gastrointestinal systems), sickle cell disease (a painful, debilitating blood cell disorder), and Tay-Sachs (a devastating metabolic disease usually causing death by age 5).
- *Predictive testing* to find out before any symptoms appear if someone is likely to develop a genetic disease later in life. This kind of testing is often recommended to people who have a family history of a genetic disorder. In a few cases, the testing can predict with high probability that a person will develop a disorder, but usually its implications are much more uncertain. For example, if testing shows that someone has the gene defect responsible for Huntington's disease (a life-shortening disorder causing dementia and physical deterioration), the chances that she will develop the disease are nearly 100 percent.

But someone found to have a single copy of the gene mutation linked to venous thrombosis (a blot-clotting disorder) has only a slightly higher risk of getting the disease than the general population.
- *Diagnostic testing* to confirm or rule out a genetic disorder in someone with symptoms.
- *Prenatal testing* to determine if a fetus has genetic abnormalities likely to cause physical or mental impairments. It is performed when there is reason to suspect genetic risk—for example, when the mother is age 35 or older (Down syndrome babies are more likely in this age group), when inherited disorders are evident in family history, or when ancestry or ethnicity suggests a greater chance of particular genetic disorders such as sickle cell and Tay-Sachs. Several prenatal genetic testing procedures are now used, the most common being amniocentesis, which analyzes a sample of amniotic fluid, and chorionic villus sampling (CVS), which tests a few cells from the placenta. Fetuses can now be tested for a long list of genetic disorders causing physical deformities, developmental defects, mental retardation, deafness, blindness, and death. Often if the news derived from prenatal testing is bad, parents must decide whether to terminate the pregnancy.
- *Preimplantation genetic diagnosis (PGD)* to test embryos produced through in vitro fertilization (IVF) for genetic abnormalities. Typically several embryos are produced in each cycle of IVF. Through PGD, those with genetic defects are screened out and only the mutation-free embryos are transferred to the woman's uterus for implantation. A typical procedure is to remove only one or two cells from a five- to eight-cell embryo for testing. PGD is costly and is usually reserved for cases in which there is a high probability of giving birth to a baby with serious disorders such as Down syndrome or Tay-Sachs disease.

Because genetics is bewilderingly complex, genetic testing itself is laden with complications that erode its usefulness and provoke medical and moral questions. For one thing, genetic tests almost never yield conclusive answers. In most cases, they can give only probabilities of developing a disease. Tests can identify a genetic mutation with certainty but usually can convey only in probabilities what ills that mutation might cause. For example, we can accurately determine that a woman has a mutation in the BRCA1 or BRCA2 gene, and this will tell us not that she will surely develop breast cancer but that she has a greater than 80 percent chance of doing so by age 70. So a positive test result (one identifying a mutation) does not guarantee the development of a genetic disorder. Moreover, though some disorders like Huntington's and Tay-Sachs are caused by mutations in a single gene (and thus are easier to predict), most genetic disorders result from abnormalities in several genes or in interactions between multiple genes and environmental factors. Scientists may not know about all the mutations responsible for a disorder, so available tests may identify only some of them. Or environmental influences later in life may cause mutations that earlier tests miss. So a negative test result (no mutation) does not guarantee a disease-free future.

Even when tests correctly predict a genetic disorder, they usually cannot foretell how severe its symptoms will be or when they will appear. Two people with mutations in the cystic fibrosis gene may differ dramatically in the severity of their respiratory and intestinal problems, and symptoms of Huntington's disease may arise in one person a decade before they appear in another.

Perhaps the most painful fact about genetic testing is that the power to identify and predict genetic disorders has outpaced our ability to do anything about them. We can now test for many diseases—and treat only some of them. We can ascertain that someone has a terrible disorder that has no treatment. Some argue that in such a situation, knowledge is not a blessing but a curse. A 2002 Harris poll found that 81 percent of adults would likely want a genetic test for a disease that was treatable or otherwise responsive to risk reduction. But only 49 percent would be likely to have the test if there was no known treatment or any other ways to cut risks.[1]

Genetic testing can also take an emotional toll. Though some people find it reassuring or empowering, others do not. After getting their test results, some feel depressed, angry, or frightened. If the testing shows they are at no or low risk of having a disorder, they may be tormented by survivor's guilt. If the news is bad, they may become fatalistic; if the news is good, they may develop a feeling of invulnerability. Either way, they may ignore opportunities to lower their risk (when that's possible), or they may make things worse by behaving recklessly. Though some people who test positive for being carriers take steps to avoid passing on the genetic defect, some also feel ashamed, guilty, or socially stigmatized for being carriers. Along with all these scenarios comes the possibility of family conflicts, for testing can divulge facts not just about the person tested but also about her relatives.

From all these complexities a multitude of ethical issues arise, including the following.

Personal Knowledge. Many moral quandaries begin when people suspect they might have a genetic disorder for which testing is available. Should a person choose to be tested when an incurable genetic disease is suspected (and no one else is affected)? This is a question about personal values and worldviews. If a young man suspects he might have a devastating disease like Huntington's (which has no cure and does not affect people until middle age), and he understands that testing could confirm or disconfirm his suspicions, he must decide whether to know or not know his status. In accordance with his values, he may choose to know because he wants to confront life's hazards with his eyes wide open and to exert as much control over his fortunes as he can. Or he may forgo the chance to learn his fate, seeking instead to live in hope as long

IN DEPTH
DIRECT-TO-CONSUMER
GENETIC TESTS

Many genetic tests are ordered for patients not by their physicians but by the patients themselves. The physician-ordered tests are widely used and trusted by medical professionals; the patient-ordered direct-to-the-consumer (DTC) tests often are not. DTC tests are typically sold on-line by numerous companies promising accurate, useful information about the presence of genetic mutations and the likelihood of developing particular diseases. But both scientists and government agencies have urged skepticism about such claims for several reasons:

- Claims made by DTC companies may be exaggerated or misleading. Contrary to advertising, the validity of many DTC tests is unproven. There may be no evidence establishing a link between specific genetic mutations and a risk of having a particular disorder.

- Clinical tests are heavily regulated by the federal government, but not DTC tests. No agency certifies the accuracy and validity of genetic tests sold directly to individuals.

- People who use DTC tests may get little or no help in properly interpreting test results. They therefore may not fully appreciate the uncertainty of the test results, or they may view the risks or disorders as more serious than they really are, or they may be left wondering what they should do about the information they get.

National Human Genome Research Institute, "Frequently Asked Questions About Genetic Testing," Genome.Gov, 1 October 2007, www.genome.gov/pfv.cfm?pageID=19516567 (14 December 2007); Genetics and Public Policy Center, "Direct-to-Consumer Genetic Testing: Empowering or Endangering the Public?" 25 July 2006, www.dnapolicy.org/policy.issue (22 December 2007).

---

as possible without the weight of a terrible diagnosis pressing down on him. This kind of choice is not merely hypothetical: Many symptomless people at risk for Huntington's disease decide not to be tested.

The moral equation changes when others are involved besides the one deciding whether to be tested. Imagine that a 45-year-old woman with grown children comes to believe that she probably has Huntington's disease because she has a family history and is beginning to experience some mild symptoms characteristic of the disease's early stages. If she has the gene mutation responsible for Huntington's, then each of her children has a 50 percent chance of inheriting it and thus having the disease. The average onset of the disorder is 35 to 44 years of age, with death usually occurring 13 to 15 years after that. Symptoms progress to extreme cognitive impairment and motor disability. The question is: Assuming she knows these facts, does she have a moral duty to be tested and, if the test is positive, to tell her children? Or, more generally, do we sometimes have a moral *obligation to know* and then a *duty to warn*?

Some might contend that she has no such obligation since the disease is untreatable. But others would disagree, arguing from the principle that we have a duty to prevent harm to others (especially those with whom we have a special relationship) if we are in a position to do so. Dutifully warned by their mother, the children could choose to be tested themselves and perhaps avoid transmitting the disorder to another generation by not having children or by using reproductive technology. In any case, the children could better arrange their lives to take the genetic facts into account, avoiding the harm of decisions made in ignorance.[2]

Often in genetic testing cases, people view the main ethical issue as a conflict between the duty to prevent harm to others and the principle of autonomy (typically construed as involving a right to privacy). Consider the case of three 20-something siblings, one of whom, Maria, has been diagnosed with Wilson's disease, an inherited metabolic disorder causing liver dysfunction and serious psychiatric problems. Wilson's is an autosomal recessive disorder, and since Maria definitely has it, her siblings each possess a one in four chance of also having it. Effective treatment is possible if it is started before symptoms appear. So far the siblings show no symptoms, and they are unaware that Wilson's has affected their family. Maria understands that her siblings could possibly be spared a dreadful disease if they are tested and treated early. But she is ashamed of her condition, especially the psychiatric symptoms, and insists that her privacy be respected and that her diagnosis not be disclosed to any of her relatives.

According to any plausible view of the principle of autonomy, Maria should be permitted to make choices affecting her own life, and her privacy should be respected. But many would assume that she also has an obligation to prevent harm—specifically, a duty to warn her siblings of the danger posed by Wilson's disease. Assuming this description of the ethical parameters is correct, which duty makes a stronger demand on Maria? Many would argue that the duty to prevent harm is stronger. Respect for autonomy is not absolute; we may—and often should—violate someone's autonomy to prevent harm to others. But some would say that autonomy is supreme or that we have no obligation at all to prevent harm, arguing that we do have a duty not to directly *harm* others but not a duty to *save* others.

Paternalism, Autonomy, and Confidentiality. Dilemmas of genetic knowledge also afflict clinicians—most sharply when the duty to maintain patient confidentiality clashes with a duty to warn family members of serious genetic peril. In Maria's case, a physician is caught in the middle, duty-bound to respect her privacy yet seeing clearly the harm that could befall her siblings if they are not told the very thing that Maria wants to keep secret. The law has been equivocal about disclosure of medical information against the patient's will, though some legal cases suggest that physicians may have a duty to warn people who are likely to be seriously harmed. A few physicians have been sued for their failure to inform relatives about genetic risks. Some physicians argue that breeching confidentiality may be morally permissible if the harm done by keeping silent outweighs the harm done by revealing private information about the patient. Others insist on strict adherence to a policy of nondisclosure. (Professional codes of ethics also differ on this issue.) But whatever view physicians take, they are likely to try to get around the dilemma by urging patients to warn their own family members.

In genetic testing, as in so many other areas of medicine, the principles of beneficence and autonomy collide, and the extent of physician paternalism is a live issue. For example, physicians have debated whether they should reveal to a patient the results of a genetic test showing that he or she is at high risk for an unpreventable, untreatable disease. They wonder if doing so is really in the patient's best interests. The question is especially keen when genetic testing targeted at one disorder incidentally uncovers a danger of falling prey to another—as when the APOE gene test for coronary heart disease shows a very high risk of eventually having Alzheimer's disease. The main argument against revealing this additional (and possibly unwanted) information is that it will not benefit the patient (because there is no way to prevent or treat Alzheimer's) and will cause the patient psychological harm. But many reject this view as strongly paternalistic and argue that the principle of autonomy gives patients the right to know their medical condition, including the results of genetic tests—even if the news is upsetting.

The same sorts of arguments are offered on the question of whether the public availability of genetic tests should be restricted. Most people can probably see the wisdom in restricting access to genetic tests that yield misleading, confusing, or otherwise unhelpful information. (Many genetic tests are like this and are useful only when combined with family history.) But some physicians favor restricting access to genetic tests for more paternalistic reasons, arguing that genetic self-knowledge causes psychological harms such as depression, anxiety, and panic or that patients cannot understand the complexities and implications of genetic information. Those who disagree with this view maintain that there is no reason to think that most patients will be psychologically wrecked by learning the truth about their genetic risks, that patient autonomy trumps any such concerns, and that the complexity of medical information is usually not considered an adequate justification for overriding patient autonomy.

Many people welcome the chance to discover the facts about their genetic predispositions, but others think they have good reasons to conceal such information or to decline testing altogether. Their wariness is prompted by the possibility of **genetic discrimination**, the use of genetic information by employers, insurance companies, and others to discriminate against or stigmatize people. Many fear that employers may use genetic information to decide whether to hire or fire them, weeding out those who may be healthy now but at risk for future diseases that could reduce productivity. They are also afraid that to cut costs, insurance companies will deny them health coverage or cancel it because genetic tests suggest a likelihood of eventual illness. These possibilities have left some people reluctant to undergo genetic testing because the results could be used as evidence against them, and this reluctance has been reinforced by some documented cases of genetic discrimination. Until recently, no comprehensive federal law addressed genetic discrimination, while state laws were inconsistent and limited in their approach to the issue. In 2008 the Genetic Information Nondiscrimination Act was signed into law, prohibiting genetic discrimination by either insurance companies or employers and barring them from requesting genetic tests.

The main ethical concern here is justice, whether people are being treated fairly. Employers and insurers have a plausible interest in con-trolling the costs of doing business, but can this interest legitimately include granting economic benefits to some people and not to others merely because of a difference in genes? Is it morally permissible to discriminate against people in this way because of factors over which they have no control? Can it be right to discriminate against people who are now healthy but may someday be unhealthy? If this type of discrimination is legitimate, for what genetic mutations and conditions would it be appropriate? In most cases, the chances that specific mutations will result in a particular disease are difficult or impossible to gauge. Is it acceptable to discriminate against people when the basis for that discrimination is so dubious?

Reproductive Decisions. The possibility of detecting genetic mutations in a fetus or in an embryo inspires both hope and anguish—the hope of avoiding birth impairments, the anguish of moral conflict. The moral issues arise primarily because prenatal testing is coupled with the option of abortion (called *selective* when done to avoid impairments), and PGD entails embryo selection. In nearly every case, selective abortion and embryo selection are the only options for avoiding the birth of a severely impaired baby. Once a genetic mutation is discovered, there is little or nothing that can be done to correct the mutation or the disorder. Those opposed to all abortions and the screening or destruction of embryos will judge these procedures morally impermissible, and they may see no wrong in permitting the birth of children with serious abnormalities. But many think that abortion and embryo selection may be justified when used to avoid having babies with such terrible defects.

A typical statement of the latter view is that it would be wrong not to prevent devastating diseases or disabilities in a child. Explaining exactly why a failure to prevent defects would be wrong, however, is not as easy as it might seem. We could say that failing to prevent an impairment is wrong because the child would be better off if the impairment were prevented, but philosophers have thought this notion incoherent. Bioethicist Dan W. Brock explains:

> The difficulty is that it would *not* be better for the person with the handicap to have had it prevented since that can only be done by preventing him from ever having existed at all; preventing the handicap would deny the individual a worthwhile, although handicapped, life. . . . But if [a mother's] failing to prevent the handicap has not made her child worse off, then failing to prevent the handicap does not harm her child. And if she does not harm her child by not preventing its handicap, then why does she wrong her child morally by failing to do so?[3]

Philosophers have responded to this incoherence problem by arguing that even if failing to prevent a serious disability does not wrong the child, the failure is still morally wrong for other reasons—for example, because it contributes to overall suffering in the world or because it treats children unfairly by disregarding their legitimate interests in having a decent chance at a good life.

A common charge against genetic testing to prevent birth impairments is that it amounts to disrespect or discrimination against people with disabilities. Some critics are adamantly opposed to testing, claiming that its purpose is to eliminate an entire class of people (the disabled), which puts genetic testing in the same moral category as heinous attempts to eradicate whole races of people. Even if not discriminatory, others say, genetic testing is meant to prevent the existence of the disabled and make possible the existence of the normal, and that fact sends a message of disrespect to people now living with disabilities. The message is that it would be better if disabled people did not exist.

Genetic testing is discriminatory if it involves violating people's rights, and it is disrespectful if it entails an attitude of contempt or condescension. But some bioethicists have insisted that discrimination or disrespect for persons is not entailed by genetic testing. For example:

> Much of what is involved in equality of respect is compatible with screening. Aiming for the con-

ception and birth of normal people, for instance, is perfectly compatible with insisting that the rights of disabled people are fully respected and with seeing them as equals. Medical treatment presupposes that health is better than sickness, but those who believe in it treat sick people as their equals.[4]

It has also been argued that anti-testing attitudes themselves have unsavory moral implications. Jeff McMahan points out that the critics of testing believe that "it is wrong for people to try to avoid having a disabled child and to have a non-disabled child instead." But this seems to imply that an action that most think is wrong must be permissible:

> [I]f it is morally *mandatory* to *allow* oneself to have a disabled child rather than to try, through screening, to have a child who would not be disabled, then it must be at least *permissible* to *cause* oneself to have a disabled rather than a non-disabled child.[5]

Yet most of us think it wrong deliberately to cause a disabled child to exist instead of a healthy child.

Even if we grant that embryo or prenatal testing is permissible, its use still raises a range of moral concerns. If a fetus has the gene for Huntington's disease, it is almost certain to suffer from the disease as an adult. The probability of being affected is extremely high, so we might conclude that testing (and possibly a selective abortion) is justified. But what if the chances of being affected are lower or uncertain (as is the case with the BRCA1 or BRCA2 gene)? Would abortion or embryo selection be justified? Would it be permissible if the odds of having the disease were low but the suffering it could cause was horrendous? Some diseases predicted by testing are late-onset (Huntington's and Alzheimer's, for instance); a person could live a satisfying life for decades before having symptoms. Is selective abortion permissible in such cases? Would it be permissible if the suffering at the end of life was likely to overshadow whatever happiness occurs earlier? Some predicted disorders are mild or treatable. Would parents have an obligation to screen out embryos with such disorders? Would it at least be permissible for parents to do so?

GENE THERAPY

After deciphering the vast codex of the human genome and peering into the rich patterning of genes, humans have taken the next, seemingly inevitable, step: to try to repair the genetic flaws they see. This incredible repair work is known as **gene therapy** (also referred to as genetic engineering), the manipulation of someone's genetic material to prevent or treat disease. It is an attempt to alter the workings of cells by, among other things, (1) replacing a missing or defective gene with a normal one, (2) repairing a faulty gene so it will function properly, or (3) activating or deactivating a gene (switching it on or off).

To date, most uses of gene therapy have been of the first kind, the insertion of a normal copy of a gene into cells to do the job that defective or absent genes should be doing. But delivering a gene to a cell is tricky and usually must be done with a carrier, or vector, such as a virus. Viruses can seek out particular cells and transfer pieces of DNA into them. Scientists put this natural talent of viruses to work by inactivating their harmful characteristics and modifying them to carry particular genes into designated cells. The genes can then induce the production of the proteins needed for normal functioning. A good example of this approach is the treatment of hemophilia (hemophilia A and B), a disorder that puts people at risk of bleeding to death because of impaired blood-clotting. The problem is caused by mutations in the genes that manufacture the proteins necessary for clotting (called blood-clotting factors), resulting in deficiencies of the proteins. In both animals and humans, scientists have used viruses to transfer normal copies of these genes into cells, enabling the genes to start producing the blood-clotting factors. The therapy has worked in animals and has shown promise in humans.

Gene therapy is of two types: somatic cell and germ-line cell. The former involves altering genes in a person's somatic (body) cells, such as liver or muscle cells, to treat an existing disorder. The alterations can help the person suffering from the disease but are not inheritable—they cannot be passed on to the person's offspring. They affect the person's genome but not the genomes of subsequent generations. The other type of gene therapy entails modifying genes in germ-line cells (egg and sperm cells) and zygotes—and these alterations are inheritable. Currently the scientific focus is on somatic-cell gene therapy, with most research evaluating treatments for cancer, heart disease, and infectious diseases. Gene therapy in germ-line cells is not yet feasible. But the ability to manipulate germ-line cells evokes both the dream of eradicating mutations from future generations (and thus permanently banishing particular disorders) and the nightmare of fabricating "designer" babies or introducing horrible errors into the human genome.

For scientists, physicians, and policymakers, the potential of gene therapy to effect cures is too great to ignore, so research will likely continue (and expand) indefinitely. But devising effective gene therapies is extremely difficult, and they can pose risks to patients. To develop any kind of effective gene therapy, scientists have to solve several technical problems. Chief among them are the difficulty of controlling viruses to accurately deliver genes to cells, the risk of virus carriers causing disease or provoking a harmful immune system response, and the complexity of treating disorders generated by multiple genes (such as diabetes, arthritis, heart diseases, and Alzheimer's). For these and other reasons, the field is still experimental, with hundreds of gene therapy studies in progress all over the world but few or no therapies approved for routine use. So far, scientific studies demonstrating success in using gene therapy have been intriguing and encouraging but preliminary. But there is little doubt among experts that safe and effective gene therapies (at least the somatic-cell kind) will be devised in the next few years.

Fact File **Genetic Tests**

Some available genetic tests (with their names and notes on the diseases or symptoms in parentheses):

- **Adult polycystic kidney disease** (APKD; kidney failure and liver disease)
- **Amyotrophic lateral sclerosis** (ALS; Lou Gehrig's disease; progressive motor function loss leading to paralysis and death)
- **Alzheimer's disease** (APOE; late-onset variety of senile dementia)
- **Gaucher disease** (GD; enlarged liver and spleen, bone degeneration)
- **Inherited breast and ovarian cancer** (BRCA1 and BRCA2; early-onset tumors of breasts and ovaries)
- **Hereditary nonpolyposis colon cancer** (CA; early-onset tumors of colon and sometimes other organs)
- **Central core disease** (CCD; mild to severe muscle weakness)
- **Cystic fibrosis** (CF; disease of lung and pancreas resulting in thick mucous accumulations and chronic infections)
- **Duchenne muscular dystrophy/Becker muscular dystrophy** (DMD; severe to mild muscle wasting, deterioration, weakness)
- **Dystonia** (DYT; muscle rigidity, repetitive twisting movements)
- **Emanuel syndrome** (severe mental retardation, abnormal development of the head, heart and kidney problems)
- **Factor V-Leiden** (FVL; blood-clotting disorder)
- **Fragile X syndrome** (FRAX; leading cause of inherited mental retardation)
- **Hemophilia A and B** (HEMA and HEMB; bleeding disorders)
- **Hereditary hemochromatosis** (HFE; excess iron storage disorder)
- **Huntington's disease** (HD; usually midlife onset; progressive, lethal, degenerative neurological disease)
- **Marfan syndrome** (FBN1; connective tissue disorder; tissues of ligaments, blood vessel walls, cartilage, heart valves, and other structures abnormally weak)
- **Myotonic dystrophy** (MD; progressive muscle weakness; most common form of adult muscular dystrophy)
- **Phenylketonuria** (PKU; progressive mental retardation due to missing enzyme; correctable by diet)
- **Prader Willi/Angelman syndromes** (PW/A; decreased motor skills, cognitive impairment, early death)
- **Sickle cell disease** (SS; blood cell disorder; chronic pain and infections)
- **Spinocerebellar ataxia, type 1** (SCA1; involuntary muscle movements, reflex disorders, explosive speech)
- **Spinal muscular atrophy** (SMA; severe, usually lethal progressive muscle-wasting disorder in children)
- **Tay-Sachs disease** (TS; fatal neurological disease of early childhood; seizures, paralysis)
- **Thalassemias** (THAL; anemias—reduced red blood cell levels)
- **Timothy syndrome** (CACNA1C; characterized by severe cardiac arrhythmia, webbing of the fingers and toes—called syndactyly, autism)

From Office of Science, U.S. Department of Energy, "Gene Testing," *Human Genome Product Information*, 24 July 2007, www.ornl.gov/sci/techresources/Human_Genome (18 December 2007).

In 1990 researchers conducted the first federally approved study of gene therapy, treating a 4-year-old girl suffering from adenosine deaminase (ADA) deficiency, a life-shortening disorder of severely weakened immunity. A normal gene generates ADA, an enzyme crucial to a healthy immune system, but in the girl the gene was missing, leaving her without any defense against life-threatening infections. Using a virus carrier, the researchers delivered the normal ADA gene to the girl's immune cells, hoping that it would produce the needed enzyme. The treatment worked. Her immune system soon began to function normally and did so for years.

Since that promising experiment, there have also been disappointments—and lessons to learn about the risks involved in gene therapy. In 1999 18-year-old Jesse Gelsinger experienced multiple organ failures and died during gene therapy to treat ornithine transcarboxylase deficiency (OTCD). The ultimate cause of death was traced back to his immune system's devastating reaction to the virus carrier. A few years later scientists used gene therapy to treat children with severe combined immunodeficiency (SCID), an intractable disorder that usually results in death by the age of 1. Amazingly, most of the children were cured. But two of these developed a condition like leukemia, so in 2003 the Food and Drug Administration (FDA) temporarily suspended clinical trials using these procedures. Later the trials resumed with closer FDA oversight and a greater appreciation among scientists generally of the inherent risks and the curative possibilities of gene therapy.

As you might suspect, many moral questions about gene therapy center on its potential for harm and help. In somatic-cell gene therapy, the risks and benefits of using the technology have become the primary moral concern, spurred on by much soul-searching after the early clinical mistakes. Regulatory agencies and review boards have sprung up to oversee clinical trials and to ensure an acceptable balance of risks and benefits for study subjects. The prevailing view is that if such steps are taken to minimize harm, and

if the potential benefits are substantial, somatic-cell therapy is morally permissible.

Germ-line therapy is a different matter. The safety concerns surrounding the technology are so worrisome that, at least in its current immature stage, it is generally thought to be morally unacceptable. The main problem is that scientists do not yet fully understand the likely ramifications of refashioning the genetic machinery of germ-line cells. The addition or modification of genes might make a condition worse or prevent one disease but cause others that are more severe. The result could be catastrophic or fatal to a child born of such engineering, and the calamities could happen at birth or years later. Worse, the resulting disorders could be passed on to future children. The nightmare scenario is that the genetic changes are inherited by many people, and the human genome itself is altered for the worse. These unknowns have compelled scientists not to renounce this research but to proceed with extreme caution and to forgo clinical trials until the genetics of germ-line cells is better understood.

Many moral arguments for and against gene therapy—perhaps the most controversial ones—do not appeal to the possibility of harm from the procedure itself, or they work from the assumption that the safety and effectiveness of gene therapy will eventually be established. Those arguments in favor of applying gene therapy (in either form) mirror many of those made for reproductive technology and genetic testing: If it is within our power to correct genetic flaws and thereby prevent or cure diseases, aren't we obligated to do so? If gene therapy offers us the chance to prevent harm to future people, don't we have a duty to try? If the principle of autonomy (or reproductive liberty) grants us the freedom to reproduce or not reproduce, doesn't it also give us the right to decide whether our offspring will have a disability or disease?

The responses to these views should also sound familiar: Reproductive freedom has limits, and germ-line therapy crosses the line; the manipulation or destruction of embryos that may occur in germ-line therapy shows disrespect for human life;

and gene therapy (especially germ-line) disrespects or discriminates against people with disabilities.

Some argue that gene therapy should not be permitted because it amounts to **eugenics**, the deliberate attempt to improve the genetic makeup of humans by manipulating reproduction. The word calls up images of the Nazi drive to racial purity through mandatory sterilization of undesirables as well as the early twentieth-century programs in the United States to forcibly sterilize criminals, "imbeciles," and other "defective persons." Such misdeeds are morally objectionable for several reasons, most notably because they violate people's autonomy, the central feature of state-sponsored coercion. But the term *eugenics* is broad, covering a range of practices that are not necessarily coercive and that have been called eugenics of either a *negative* or *positive* kind. Negative eugenics is thought to involve the prevention or treatment of diseases, typically through genetic testing, embryo selection, selective abortion, or germ-line therapy. By this definition, prenatal screening—which is a matter of public policy and generally considered morally permissible—is a type of negative eugenics. Positive eugenics is said to include attempts to improve on normal functions. It seeks not repair, but enhancement. Theoretically through germ-line therapy, parents could produce children who are smarter, taller, or more resistant to certain diseases than normal children are. Such enhancements are controversial, even though they may not be technically possible for many years.

The idea of a distinction between repair and enhancement is prominent in moral debates because some argue that the former is morally obligatory while the latter is not. That is, we may have a duty to use gene therapy to treat Tay-Sachs disease or cystic fibrosis, but not to give a child an abnormally long life or a super immune system. Several bioethicists reject this view. For example, John Harris:

> [S]uppose genes coding for repair enzymes which would not only repair radiation damage or damage by other environmental pollutants but would also prolong healthy life expectancy could be inserted into humans. Again, would it be permissible to let people continue suffering such damage when they could be protected against it? Would it in short be OK to let them suffer?
>
> It is not normal for the human organism to be self-repairing in this way; this must be eugenic if anything is. But if available, its use would surely, like penicillin before it, be more than merely [permissible].
>
> . . . There is in short no moral difference between attempts to cure dysfunction and attempts to enhance function where the enhancement protects life or health.[6]

Others insist that there is indeed a clear difference between the two, asserting that gene therapy is moral if it is intended to ensure or restore normal functions, but immoral if it is aimed at enhancing functions beyond normal. Their strongest objection to genetic enhancement is that it would lead to the most flagrant kind of social injustice. As Walter Glannon argues,

> The main moral concern about genetic enhancement of physical and mental traits is that it would give some people an unfair advantage over others with respect to competitive goods like beauty, sociability, and intelligence. . . . Enhancement would be unfair because only those who could afford the technology would have access to it, and many people are financially worse off than others through no fault of their own. Insofar as the possession of these goods gives some people an advantage over others in careers, income, and social status, the competitive nature of these goods suggests that there would be no limit to the benefits that improvements to physical and mental capacities would yield to those fortunate enough to avail themselves of the technology.[7]

STEM CELLS

There are over 200 different kinds of cells in the human body—muscle cells, blood cells, skin cells, nerve cells, and more. Yet all these cell types arise from just one sort of cell present in the

IN DEPTH
RECENT RESEARCH
IN GENE THERAPY

- **May 2007** A team of British doctors from Moorfields Eye Hospital and University College in London conduct first human gene therapy trials to treat Leber's congenital amaurosis, a type of inherited childhood blindness caused by a single abnormal gene. The procedure has already been successful at restoring vision for dogs. This is the first trial to use gene therapy in an operation to treat blindness in humans.
- **January 2007** A combination of two tumor-suppressing genes delivered in lipid-based nanoparticles drastically reduces the number and size of human lung cancer tumors in mice during trials conducted by researchers from The University of Texas M. D. Anderson Cancer Center and the University of Texas Southwestern Medical Center.
- **August 2006** Researchers at the National Cancer Institute (NCI), part of the National Institutes of Health, successfully reengineer immune cells, called lymphocytes, to target and attack cancer cells in patients with advanced metastatic melanoma. This is the first time that gene therapy is used successfully to treat cancer in humans.
- **March 2006** Gene therapy is used effectively to treat two adult patients for a disease affecting nonlymphocytic white blood cells called myeloid cells. Myeloid disorders are common and include a variety of bone marrow failure syndromes, such as acute myeloid leukemia. The study is the first to show that gene therapy can cure diseases of the myeloid system.
- **February 2005** Gene therapy cures deafness in guinea pigs. Each animal had been deafened by destruction of the hair cells in the cochlea that translate sound vibrations into nerve signals. A gene, called Atoh1, which stimulates the hair cells' growth, was delivered to the cochlea by an adenovirus. The genes triggered regrowth of the hair cells, and many of the animals regained up to 80 percent of their original hearing thresholds. This study, which many pave the way to human trials of the gene, is the first to show that gene therapy can repair deafness in animals..
- **March 2003** A University of California, Los Angeles, research team gets genes into the brain using liposomes coated in a polymer called polyethylene glycol (PEG). The transfer of genes into the brain is a significant achievement because viral vectors are too big to get across the "blood-brain barrier." This method has potential for treating Parkinson's disease.

From Office of Science, U.S. Department of Energy, "Gene Therapy," *Human Genome Project Information*, 6 August 2007, http://www.ornl.gov/sci/techresources/Human_Genome/medicine/genetherapy.shtml (31 December 2007).

early embryo, or blastocyst, five days after fertilization and before implantation in the uterus. These early cells are undifferentiated, having no specialized function as the other kinds of cells do; but they are also *pluripotent*, which means they are able to *become* differentiated, to turn into any of the body's specialty cells. They number only 30 or so inside the blastocyst, which is no larger than the dot on this letter *i*. Under normal conditions, they quickly differentiate into the various cell types. But when they are extracted from the blastocyst and nurtured in culture dishes, they can remain undifferentiated and retain their power to transform into any kind of cell, while replicating themselves continuously without limit. At this point they are *embryonic stem cells*. Because they can reproduce indefinitely, creating replicating cell lines, just a few of them are needed to generate a large supply.

Other stem cells in the developed human—*adult stem cells*—stand ever ready to differentiate themselves to replace worn out or damaged cells, constantly renewing and repairing the body's parts. Adult stem cells generate new bone, cartilage, skin, muscle, blood, and many other tissues. But their potential to produce diverse kinds of cells is constrained—unlike the nearly unbounded powers of differentiation found in embryonic stem cells.

It is this regenerative potential of stem cells (especially the embryonic kind) that has excited so much scientific and medical interest. Researchers have found that by getting stem cells to differentiate into particular kinds of cells, new cells and tissues can be generated to treat diseases and injuries characterized by a lack of functioning cell types. The therapeutic possibilities include Parkinson's disease, diabetes, heart disease, Alzheimer's, stroke, spinal cord injuries, burns, and arthritis. For example, type I diabetes occurs for lack of the cells that produce insulin, but scientists think it may be possible to prod embryonic stem cells into becoming insulin-producing cells and then to transplant those cells into patients with diabetes. On another front, researchers are now investigating the possibility of using stem cells to generate new heart muscle tissue to transplant to damaged hearts. These and many other stem-cell investigations are preliminary and may not yield effective treatments for years, and so far the established stem-cell therapies are few (only blood and skin cell transplants). But the amazing potential for treatments and cures of seemingly unstoppable diseases spurs on the research, raises the stakes, and makes debates about halting stem-cell research all the more volatile.

Most of the moral controversy over embryonic stem cells has focused on their source. The main source is, of course, embryos (blastocysts), which are inevitably destroyed in the process of retrieving the cells. The majority of the embryos are produced through IVF used in the treatment of infertility. IVF involves the production of multiple blastocysts, only some of which are eventually implanted in the uterus. The leftover blastocysts are frozen, and some that are neither implanted nor discarded may be used to extract stem cells. Another possibility is the use of IVF to create blastocysts specifically for stem-cell extraction in research—an option that is much more controversial than using the surplus blastocysts. Beyond the blastocyst stage there is one more stem-cell source: Researchers have been able to derive embryonic stem cells from fetuses obtained after elective abortions.

It is possible—but not yet technically feasible—to derive embryonic stem cells from blastocysts produced through what has been called *research* (or *therapeutic*) *cloning*. Many distinguish this kind of cloning-for-research-purposes from *reproductive cloning*, which aims at the live birth of a baby. In both forms, the underlying method is the same: Replace the nucleus of an egg cell with the nucleus of an ordinary somatic cell (a skin cell, for example) from an adult, then stimulate this reconstructed cell to start cell division and growth into a blastocyst. In research cloning, stem cells would be derived from the blastocyst; in reproductive cloning, the blastocyst would be implanted in the uterus to continue the reproductive process to birth. An advantage of research cloning is that body tissues derived from the stem cells would be genetically matched to the nucleus donor, so the new tissues could be used to treat the donor with less risk of tissue rejection by the donor's body. To date, no one has extracted human embryonic stem cells from cloned embryos successfully, but judging from research in animals, the feat eventually will be accomplished.

In the United States the availability of embryonic stem cells for research has been influenced heavily by existing laws and policies. A law enacted in 1995 bans the use of federal funds for any research involving the destruction of human embryos—a significant restriction since federal money drives an enormous portion of biomedical research. In 2001 President George W. Bush declared that no federal funding may support research that obtains stem cells by destroying embryos, although research may continue on the few existing stem-cell lines previously derived.

In 2007 a scientific breakthrough looked like it might solve the stem-cell source problem. Scientists announced that they were able to genetically reprogram ordinary human skin cells to take on the characteristics of embryonic stem cells. The findings seemed to promise an abundant future supply of embryonic stem cells for research without destroying embryos or using embryos already deceased. Many commentators immediately declared that science had finally ended the stem-cell debates that it began. Scientists everywhere welcomed the news of the breakthrough, but many also thought it premature to proclaim embryo research superfluous. They pointed out that it is not yet known whether the new engineered stem cells are as versatile, safe, or hearty as stem cells derived from embryos. They therefore favored pursuing, at least for now, both paths simultaneously.

Whether or not public disputes about embryonic stem cells subside, the underlying moral issues remain. The core question is this: Is it morally permissible to destroy human embryos in a search for cures? For those who believe that embryos have the moral status of persons, the answer must be no (just as it would be on the issue of abortion). The same goes for those who think using embryos as a source of stem cells shows disrespect for human life by reducing it to a mere commodity. In either case, people who grant embryos this special moral status are likely to argue that destroying them cannot be justified by any potential medical and scientific benefits. Some who take this view insist that just using or benefiting from stem cells previously derived from embryos or aborted fetuses is also impermissible. But to be involved in this way is to participate, however indirectly, in the immoral act of destroying innocent human life.

At the other end of the moral spectrum are those who maintain that blastocysts have no moral status at all and should be treated like any other human cell. They therefore contend that the use of embryos in stem-cell research is permissible, especially since it promises to help alleviate much human suffering. Their main concerns are the safety, integrity, and usefulness of the research and the resulting therapies.

For many who adopt intermediate positions, early embryos have less than full moral status but are still deserving of some respect. Stem-cell research using embryos is therefore morally acceptable—within limits. Bonnie Steinbock, for example, takes this view:

> Lacking the kinds of ends that persons have, embryos cannot be given the respect that is due to persons. Nevertheless, they have a significance and moral value that other bodily tissues do not have because they are "potent symbols of human life.". . . We show respect for human embryos by not using them in unimportant or frivolous ways, say, to teach high school biology or to make cosmetics or jewelry. However, respect for embryos does not require refraining from research likely to have significant benefits, such as treating disease and prolonging life.[8]

Some stake out some middle ground in the stem-cell debate in other ways. They may argue that mining stem cells from embryos is objectionable but that manipulating already available stem-cell lines is not. Or that taking stem cells from aborted fetuses or from embryos left over after reproductive IVF is permissible but that using embryos created for research through IVF or therapeutic cloning is wrong. Or that using IVF embryos, created originally for whatever reason, is moral but that generating embryos for stem-cell extraction through any kind of cloning is immoral.

APPLYING MAJOR THEORIES

The moral theories that have been applied to familiar ethical problems for generations also do work in the epoch of genetic testing and intervention. A utilitarian perspective is likely to favor genetic testing and gene therapy if they tend to promote the general welfare. A utilitarian might say that tests providing useful information about people's ge-

The Kingsburys

Increasing numbers of prospective parents are choosing to use PGD to screen their embryos for genetic diseases. In the past, many would-be parents who requested PGD knew this: They had a particular gene mutation, there was a good chance of passing it to their offspring, any child with the mutation is almost certain to develop the disease, and the disease is devastating and untreatable. The horrors in this category include cystic fibrosis, Huntington's disease, and Tay-Sachs. Now some couples in similar situations are taking PGD a step further: They are using it to screen for disorders that have much less than 100 percent probability of arising and that in many cases respond to treatment. The Kingsburys were among the first to face such a choice.

In their quest to have children, Chad and Colby Kingsbury were up against some dire genetic facts. Chad had inherited a genetic defect that causes a form of colon cancer—a disease that had already taken his mother and her two brothers, afflicted his cousin, and could very well soon affect him. For anyone with the mutation, the chances of having colon cancer are 20 times greater than normal. The disease generally appears in middle age, and most people can survive it if it's treated early. There is a 50 percent probability that any child of Chad's will inherit the mutation.

The Kingsburys understood these risks and knew that PGD could eliminate them. But there were other factors to weigh. PGD involves culling defective embryos (which are likely to be destroyed) and deliberating selecting those that are genetically acceptable. Is such a procedure morally permissible when the disorder to be avoided is not invariably lethal, not guaranteed to arise, and not likely to develop, if at all, until middle age?

As reported in the *New York Times*, to opt for PGD,

> [The Kingsburys] had to overcome their own misgivings about meddling with nature. They had to listen to the religious concerns of Mr. Kingsbury's family and to the insistence of Ms. Kingsbury's that the expense and physical demands of in vitro fertilization were not worth it, given that the couple could probably get pregnant without it. They had to stop asking themselves the unanswerable question of whether a cure would be found by the time their child grew up. . . . It took them two months to make the decision.[9]

In the end they chose PGD, and a healthy baby girl, Chloe, was the result. She will not get—and her children will not inherit from her—the kind of colon cancer that has ravaged Chad Kingsbury's family.

He says that he and his wife made the right decision: "I couldn't imagine them telling me my daughter has cancer when I could have stopped it."

Many people object to PGD and the embryo selection that it entails, arguing that it is morally equivalent to abortion, that it amounts to arrogant interference in natural processes, that it is eugenics run amok to create "designer babies," and that it demonstrates disrespect for people with disabilities. Nevertheless, the use of PGD is likely to increase—and to be applied to an ever widening range of diseases with varying degrees of severity.

netic risks are probably beneficial overall, though benefits must be weighed against the harm that can result from misleading test results, genetic discrimination, and breeches of doctor-patient confidentiality. She almost certainly would argue that prenatal testing and PGD (combined with selective abortion and embryo selection) are morally acceptable because they can prevent devastating diseases and disabilities in children as well as emotional or economic suffering in families. Gene therapy (both somatic and germ-line cell) is likely to be viewed in the same way—morally permissible if its benefits outweigh its risks. The utilitarian also would not hesitate to employ positive eugenics if altering the human genome would, on balance, increase human happiness and ease suffering. She would probably sanction the therapeutic use of embryonic stem cells (derived from any source) as long as there was a net benefit to society.

A natural law theorist might view some forms of genetic testing (newborn screening and predictive testing, for example) as morally acceptable ways to gain knowledge about health risks and to guide treatment. But a theorist in the Roman Catholic tradition would in most instances object to prenatal testing and PGD because they usually lead directly to selective abortion and embryo selection—clear violations of the unborn's right to life. Natural law theory would seem to countenance somatic-cell gene therapy because the aims are therapeutic, like conventional medical treatment. But germ-line gene therapy as a tool of positive eugenics would probably be condemned as contrary to nature. Research using stem cells derived from embryos would be considered immoral because it involves destroying innocent human life.

The Kantian notions of autonomy and of persons as ends-in-themselves support the right of patients to know (or not to know) the results of genetic tests, to have those results guarded according to rules of privacy and confidentiality, and to be treated fairly without fear of genetic discrimination. If by Kantian lights an embryo is a person, then destroying it after genetic testing may be impermissible—or permissible because preventing its future suffering could actually be an act of respect for its personhood. Likewise, positive eugenics could be seen through Kantian eyes as a way to improve human life while leaving personhood untouched.

KEY TERMS
chromosome
eugenics
genome
gene
gene therapy
genetic discrimination
genetic testing

SUMMARY
DNA makes up the chemical coding that directs the development and operation of cells, the fundamental components of every organism. Genes, the basic units of biological inheritance, are discrete segments of DNA strands. Genes in turn are organized into 46 chromosomes, arranged in 23 pairs. According to the instructions written in genes, a human organism is produced and sustained, and a large portion of its characteristics is determined. Mistakes, or mutations, in the DNA coding can lead to a variety of diseases and conditions, some of them grave.

Genetic testing involves procedures to check for genetic disorders by looking for changes in a person's DNA. Common forms of testing include newborn screening; carrier, predictive, diagnostic, and prenatal testing; and preimplantation genetic diagnosis (PGD). Genetic tests rarely yield certain predictions. For several reasons, a positive test result does not guarantee the presence of a disorder, and a negative test result does not ensure its absence. Unfortunately, our ability to detect diseases through genetic testing has outstripped our power to treat many of them. Many moral questions that arise from genetic testing are about duties to warn family members when an inherited disorder is discovered, the obligation of physicians regarding patient autonomy and confidentiality, the permissibility of genetic discrimination, and the morality of using testing to avoid causing seriously disabled persons to exist.

Gene therapy is the manipulation of someone's genetic material to prevent or treat disease. The somatic-cell type involves altering genes in a person's body cells; the germ-line type entails modifying genes in egg and sperms cells and zygotes. Ethical issues concern the medical risks and benefits of the therapy, duties to use the procedures to prevent suffering, reproductive freedom, and the morality of practicing positive genetics.

Embryonic stem cells can be derived from blastocysts, aborted fetuses, research cloning, and—apparently—genetically engineered somatic cells. The core issue regarding them is whether it is morally permissible to destroy them in a search for cures. Those who assign personhood status to embryos say no. Those who reject that view may grant embryos no special status at all, or they may say that embryos are not persons but are still worthy of some respect. In either case, embryonic stem-cell research is thought to be permissible.

Cases for Evaluation

CASE I

Designer Babies

(*TimesOnline*)—A British couple have won the right to test embryos for a gene that leads to high cholesterol levels and an increased risk of heart attacks, *The Times* has learnt.

The decision by the fertility watchdog will reopen controversy over the ethics of designer babies, as it allows doctors to screen embryos for a condition that is treatable with drugs and can be influenced by lifestyle as well as genes.

While the procedure is designed to detect a rare version of a disease called familial hypercholesterolaemia (FH), which often kills children before puberty, it will also identify a milder form that can be controlled by drugs and diet.

Critics argue that the test will allow couples to destroy embryos that would have had a good chance of becoming children with fulfilling and reasonably healthy lives.

The test will also create an unprecedented moral dilemma for some couples, as it could show that they have produced no embryos completely unaffected by the disease. This would force them to decide whether to implant embryos that they know have a genetic risk of premature heart disease and death, or to throw them away and deny them a chance of life.

Britain's first licence to test embryos for FH will be awarded next week to Paul Serhal, of University

College Hospital in London, by the Human Fertilisation and Embryology Authority (HFEA).

Its decision breaks new ground because it permits Mr. Serhal to screen out not only the severe form of the condition but also the milder type, which is usually treatable.

Embryo screening has previously been approved only for disorders in which a gene invariably causes a serious disease, or for conditions such as breast cancer in which mutations carry an 80 per cent lifetime risk.

FH occurs in two forms. The more common version, heterozygous FH, affects 1 in 500 people. It is caused by a single mutated gene, which raises cholesterol and thus the risk of hardened arteries, heart disease, and stroke. It can usually be managed with statin drugs and diet.

One in 250,000 people inherits two defective copies of the gene and develops homozygous FH, which is much more serious. Sufferers show severely elevated cholesterol from the age of 5, and can suffer angina by 6 or 7. Many die in childhood, and most have suffered at least one heart attack by the end of their twenties.

Mr. Serhal's patients, who are in their thirties, both have the milder heterozygous FH. They discovered their status only when they had a daughter, now 5, with the homozygous form, and they also have an unaffected son.

They said yesterday that they were delighted. "We had no idea that we both carried a gene for high cholesterol until the double gene was expressed in our first child. We are very lucky that our child has responded so well to the very high-dose drug regime. We have been led to understand that other children with the same double gene may not be so lucky." . . .

Mr. Serhal said: "This obnoxious disease can cause cardiovascular accidents at a very young age. Ideally, we will find embryos with no FH genes, but it is possible we will not and it will be up to the patients to choose. Some people would think twice about using embryos that they know have a risky gene, and others would say you shouldn't screen out a condition that can be managed so people can live with it. It will be an awkward choice."*

Is it wrong for parents to screen out embryos with disorders that are treatable? What about embryos that will probably—not certainly—develop a serious disease? Or those that will develop a fatal disease only in middle age? Is it morally permissible to cause to exist persons who are severely disabled and likely to suffer horribly throughout their lives? Give reasons for your answer.

*Mark Henderson, "Designer Baby Fear over Heart Gene Test," TimesOnline, 15 December 2007, http://www.timesonline.co.uk/tol/news/uk/science/article3054249.ece? (15 January 2008).

CASE 2

Causing Deaf Children

(*New Scientist*)—A few years ago, a lesbian couple in the U.S. sparked controversy when they chose a deaf sperm donor to ensure their children, like them, would be deaf. Now it appears that some would-be parents are resorting to pre-implantation genetic diagnosis (PGD) to achieve the same thing, by selecting and implanting embryos that will develop into deaf children.

This comes from a survey by the Genetics and Public Policy Center in Washington DC on how PGD is being used in the U.S.

Deep inside the report is this paragraph: "Some prospective parents have sought PGD to select an embryo for the presence of a particular disease or disability, such as deafness, in order that the child would share that characteristic with the parents. Three per cent of IVF-PGD clinics report having provided PGD to couples who seek to use PGD in this manner."

It is not clear how many, if any, children have been born after embryo selection for a disability, or which disabilities have been selected for. I asked Susannah Baruch, the lead author of the GPPC report, who told me that the team does not have any more details.

So let's do the sums: Since the survey included 137 IVF-PGD clinics, 3% means 4 couples at least, more if you assume some of the 200 clinics who did not respond to the survey have also provided this service. And since the success rate of IVF is roughly 30%, even if each couple made only one attempt at least

one child must have been born with a designer disability, most likely deafness, with the help of PGD.*

Is it right to deliberately cause a child to be deaf and thereby limit her opportunities in life? If so, why? If not, why not? Should medical authorities or the government restrict the use of IVF and PGD to selecting only healthy embryos? If both prospective parents have inherited deafness, there is a high probability that their child will be deaf. So their failing to use IVF/PGD to select healthy embryos would almost guarantee a deaf baby. Is such a failure morally wrong? If so, is deliberately selecting impaired embryos equally wrong? Explain.

*Michael Le Page, "Designer Deafness," *New Scientist*, 29 September 2006.

CASE 3

Cosmetic Embryo Selection

(*London Telegraph*)—Embryos are to be screened for a cosmetic defect for the first time in a British clinic.

Doctors have been given permission to create a baby free from a genetic disorder which would have caused the child to have a severe squint.

The Bridge Centre family clinic, in London, has been licensed to treat a businessman and his wife to create the baby. Both the businessman and his father suffer from the condition, which causes the eyes only to look downwards or sideways.

Critics have said that the permission is another step on the road to creating only perfect-looking babies in the laboratory.

The licence was granted by the Human Fertilisation and Embryology Authority (HFEA) to Prof. Gedis Grudzinskas, who believes the landmark ruling marks a shift away from granting licences only for life-threatening conditions.

He said: "We will increasingly see the use of embryo screening for severe cosmetic conditions."

He added that he would seek to screen for any genetic factor at all that would cause a family severe distress.

When asked if he would screen embryos for factors like hair colour, he said: "If there is a cosmetic aspect to an individual case I would assess it on its merits. [Hair colour] can be a cause of bullying which can lead to suicide. With the agreement of the HFEA, I would do it. "If a parent suffered from asthma, and it was possible to detect the genetic factor for this, I would do it. It all depends on the family's distress."

He argued that a baby born with the squint condition, congenital fibrosis of the extramacular muscles, would have to undergo several potentially dangerous operations from a young age. . . .

If successful, the screening could be the first case in the world where doctors have been able to select embryos without the condition. . . .

Until last year screening was restricted to life-threatening conditions such as cystic fibrosis or fatal blood disorders.*

Should prospective parents be permitted to screen their embryos for cosmetic reasons? Is there a moral difference between embryo selection against severe disabilities and embryo selection against cosmetic imperfections that cause the child to suffer psychological distress or social discrimination? Is embryo selection for cosmetic reasons a form of discrimination or disrespect for people with disabilities or imperfections? Explain your answers.

---

*Roland Hancock, "Clinic to Weed Out Embryos with a Squint," Telegraph.co.uk, 5 July 2007, http://www.telegraph .co.uk/news/main.jhtml?xml=/news/2007/05/07/nbaby07.xml (15 January 2008).

FURTHER READING

American Society for Reproductive Medicine, "Assisted Reproductive Technologies: A Guide for Patients," undated, 2007, http://www.asrm.org/ (27 November 2007).

Adrienne Asch, "Real Moral Dilemmas," *Christianity and Crisis* 46.10 (1986).

Dan W. Brock, "Genetic Engineering," in *A Companion to Applied Ethics*, ed. R. G. Frey and Christopher Heath Wellman (Oxford: Blackwell Publishing, 2003), 356–57, 361–67.

Ruth Chadwick, "Gene Therapy," in *A Companion to Bioethics*, ed. Helga Kuhse and Peter Singer (Oxford: Blackwell Publishing, 2001), 189–97.

Angus Clarke, "Genetic Screening and Counselling," in *A Companion to Bioethics,* ed. Helga Kuhse and Peter Singer (Oxford: Blackwell Publishing, 2001), 215-28.

Cold Spring Harbor Laboratory, "DNA from the Beginning: An Animated Primer on the Basics of DNA, Genes, and Heredity," undated, 2002, http://www .dnaftb.org/dnaftb/ (05 December 2007).

Department of Health and Human Services, *Regenerative Medicine*, August 2006, http://stemcells.nih.gov/ info/scireport/2006report.htm (1 January 2008).

Walter Glannon, *Genes and Future People: Philosophical Issues in Human Genetics* (Boulder, CO: Westview Press, 2001).

Jonathan Glover, "Future People, Disability, and Screening," in *Justice Between Age Groups and Generations*, ed. J. Fishkin and P. Laslett (New Haven, CT: Yale University Press, 1992).

Human Genome Program, U.S. Department of Energy, *Genomics and Its Impact on Science and Society: A 2003 Primer* (Washington, DC: U.S. Department of Energy, 2003).

National Academy of Sciences, *Understanding Stem Cells* (Washington, DC: National Academies Press, 2006).

National Bioethics Advisory Commission (NBAC), *Ethical Issues in Human Stem Cell Research: Executive Summary*, September 1999, http://bioethics.georgetown .edu/nbac (1 January 2008).

President's Council on Bioethics, *Human Cloning and Human Dignity: An Ethical Inquiry*, July 2002, http:// www.bioethics.gov/reports/cloningreport (9 January 2008).

John A. Robertson, "Extending Preimplantation Genetic Diagnosis: Medical and Non-Medical Uses," *Journal of Medical Ethics* 29 (August 2003), 213–16.

Bonnie Steinbock and Ron McClamrock, "When Is Birth Unfair to the Child?," *Hastings Center Report* 24.6 (November 1994), 15-21.

U.S. National Library of Medicine, *Handbook: Help Me Understand Genetics, Genetics Home Reference*, 26 November 2007, http:ghr.nlm.nih.gov (3 December 2007).

LeRoy Walters and Julie Gage Palmer, *The Ethics of Human Gene Therapy* (New York: Oxford University Press, 1997).

NOTES

1. The Harris Poll, Harris Interactive, 5 June 2002, www .harrisinteractive.com (18 December 2007).

2. This example and its analysis are inspired by Walter Glannon, in *Biomedical Ethics* (New York: Oxford University Press, 2005), 98–99.

3. Dan W. Brock, "The Non-Identity Problem and Genetic Harms—The Case of Wrongful Handicaps," *Bioethics* 9.3/4 (1995), 275–89.

4. Jonathan Glover, "Future People, Disability, and Screening," in *Justice Between Age Groups and Generations,* ed. J. Fishkin and P. Laslett (New Haven, CT: Yale University Press, 1992), 127–143.

5. Jeff McMahan, "The Morality of Screening for Disability," *Ethics, Law and Moral Philosophy of Reproductive Biomedicine* 1.1 (March 2005), 129–32.

6. John Harris, "Is Gene Therapy a Form of Eugenics?" in *Bioethics: An Anthology,* ed. Helga Kuhse and Peter Singer (Oxford: Blackwell Publishers, 1999), 165–70.

7. Walter Glannon, *Genes and Future People: Philosophical Issues in Human Genetics* (Boulder, CO: Westview Press, 2001), 94–101.

8. Bonnie Steinbock, "What Does 'Respect for Embryos' Mean in the Context of Stem Cell Research?" *Women's Health Issues* 10.3 (May/June 2000), 127–30.

9. Amy Harmon, "Couples Cull Embryos to Halt Heritage of Cancer," *New York Times,* 3 September 2006.

READINGS

Implications of Prenatal Diagnosis for the Human Right to Life

LEON R. KASS

In this article Kass explores the morality of aborting fetuses known through genetic testing to be defective. He condemns the practice, arguing that it could lead us to take a less sympathetic view toward people who are genetic "abnormals" and to embrace the insidious principle that "defectives should not be born." He concludes that "we should indeed be cautious and move slowly as we give serious consideration to the question 'What price the perfect baby?'"

It is especially fitting on this occasion to begin by acknowledging how privileged I feel and how pleased I am to be a participant in this symposium. I suspect that I am not alone among the assembled in considering myself fortunate to be here. For I was conceived after antibiotics yet before amniocentesis, late enough to have benefited from medicine's ability to prevent and control fatal infectious diseases, yet early enough to have escaped from medicine's ability to prevent me from living to suffer from my genetic diseases. To be sure, my genetic vices are, as far as I know them, rather modest, taken individually—myopia, asthma and other allergies, bilateral

forefoot adduction, bowleggedness, loquaciousness, and pessimism, plus some four to eight as yet undiagnosed recessive lethal genes in the heterozygous condition—but, taken together, and if diagnosable prenatally, I might never have made it.

Just as I am happy to be here, so am I unhappy with what I shall have to say. Little did I realize when I first conceived the topic, "Implications of Prenatal Diagnosis for the Human Right to Life," what a painful and difficult labor it would lead to. More than once while this paper was gestating, I considered obtaining permission to abort it, on the grounds that, by prenatal diagnosis, I knew it to be defective. My lawyer told me that I was legally in the clear, but my conscience reminded me that I had made a commitment to deliver myself of this paper, flawed or not. Next time, I shall practice better contraception.

From *Ethical Issues in Human Genetics*, edited by Bruce Hilton et al., 1973. Copyright © Plenum Publishing Corporation.

Any discussion of the ethical issues of genetic counseling and prenatal diagnosis is unavoidably haunted by a ghost called the morality of abortion. This ghost I shall not vex. More precisely, I shall not vex the reader by telling ghost stories. However, I would be neither surprised nor disappointed if my discussion of an admittedly related matter, the ethics of aborting the genetically defective, summons that hovering spirit to the reader's mind. For the morality of abortion is a matter not easily laid to rest, recent efforts to do so notwithstanding. A vote by the legislature of the State of New York can indeed legitimatize the disposal of fetuses, but not of the moral questions. But though the questions remain, there is likely to be little new that can be said about them, and certainly not by me.

Yet before leaving the general question of abortion, let me pause to drop some anchors for the discussion that follows. Despite great differences of opinion both as to what to think and how to reason about abortion, nearly everyone agrees that abortion is a moral issue.[1] What does this mean? Formally, it means that a woman seeking or refusing an abortion can expect to be asked to justify her action. And we can expect that she should be able to give reasons for her choice other than "I like it" or "I don't like it." Substantively, it means that, in the absence of good reasons for intervention, there is some presumption in favor of allowing the pregnancy to continue once it has begun. A common way of expressing this presumption is to say that "the fetus has a right to continued life."[2] In this context, disagreement concerning the moral permissibility of abortion concerns what rights (or interests or needs), and whose, override (take precedence over, or outweigh) this fetal "right." Even most of the "opponents" of abortion agree that the mother's right to live takes precedence, and that abortion to save her life is permissible, perhaps obligatory. Some believe that a woman's right to determine the number and spacing of her children takes precedence, while yet others argue that the need to curb population growth is, at least at this time, overriding.

Hopefully, this brief analysis of what it means to say that abortion is a moral issue is sufficient to establish two points. First, that the fetus is a living thing with some moral claim on us not to do it violence, and therefore, second, that justification must be given for destroying it.

Turning now from the general questions of the ethics of abortion, I wish to focus on the special ethical issues raised by the abortion of "defective" fetuses (so-called "abortion for fetal indications"). I shall consider only the cleanest cases, those cases where well-characterized genetic diseases are diagnosed with a high degree of certainty by means of amniocentesis, in order to side-step the added moral dilemmas posed when the diagnosis is suspected or possible, but unconfirmed. However, many of the questions I shall discuss could also be raised about cases where genetic analysis gives only a statistical prediction about the genotype of the fetus, and also about cases where the defect has an infectious or chemical rather than a genetic cause (e.g., rubella, thalidomide).

My first and possibly most difficult task is to show that there is anything left to discuss once we have agreed not to discuss the morality of abortion in general. There is a sense in which abortion for genetic defect is, after abortion to save the life of the mother, perhaps the most defensible kind of abortion. Certainly, it is a serious and not a frivolous reason for abortion, defended by its proponents in sober and rational speech—unlike justifications based upon the false notion that a fetus is a mere part of a woman's body, to be used and abused at her pleasure. Standing behind genetic abortion are serious and well-intentioned people, with reasonable ends in view: the prevention of genetic diseases, the elimination of suffering in families, the preservation of precious financial and medical resources, the protection of our genetic heritage. No profiteers, no sex-ploiters, no racists. No arguments about the connection of abortion with promiscuity and licentiousness, no perjured testimony about the mental health of the mother, no arguments about the seriousness of the population problem. In short, clear objective data, a worthy cause, decent men and women. If abortion, what better reason for it?

Yet if genetic abortion is but a happily wagging tail on the dog of abortion, it is simultaneously the nose of a camel protruding under a rather different tent. Precisely because the quality of the fetus is central to the decision to abort, the practice of genetic abortion has implications which go beyond those raised by abortion in general. What may be at stake here is the belief in the radical moral equality of all human beings, the belief that all human beings possess equally and independent of merit certain fundamental rights, one among which is, of course, the right to life.

To be sure, the belief that fundamental human rights belong equally to all human beings has been but an ideal, never realized, often ignored, sometimes shamelessly. Yet it has been perhaps the most powerful moral idea at work in the world for at least two centuries. It is this idea and ideal that animates most of the current political and social criticism around the globe. It is ironic that we should acquire the power to detect and eliminate the genetically unequal at a time when we have finally succeeded in removing much of the stigma and disgrace previously attached to victims of congenital illness, in providing them with improved care and support, and in preventing, by means of education, feelings of guilt on the part of their parents. One might even wonder whether the development of amniocentesis and prenatal diagnosis may represent a backlash against these same humanitarian and egalitarian tendencies in the practice of medicine, which, by helping to sustain to the age of reproduction persons with genetic disease has itself contributed to the increasing incidence of genetic disease, and with it, to increased pressures for genetic screening, genetic counseling, and genetic abortion. . . .

Genetic Abortion and the Living Defective

The practice of abortion of the genetically defective will no doubt affect our view of and our behavior toward those abnormals who escape the net of detection and abortion. A child with Down syndrome or with hemophilia or with muscular dystrophy born at a time when most of his (potential) fellow sufferers were destroyed prenatally is liable to be looked upon by the community as one unfit to be alive, as a second-class (or even lower) human type. He may be seen as a person who need not have been, and who would not have been, if only someone had gotten to him in time.

The parents of such children are also likely to treat them differently, especially if the mother would have wished but failed to get an amniocentesis because of ignorance, poverty, or distance from the testing station, or if the prenatal diagnosis was in error. In such cases, parents are especially likely to resent the child. They may be disinclined to give it the kind of care they might have before the advent of amniocentesis and genetic abortion, rationalizing that a second-class specimen is not entitled to first-class treatment. If pressed to do so, say by physicians, the parents might refuse, and the courts may become involved. This has already begun to happen.

In Maryland, parents of a child with Down syndrome refused permission to have the child operated on for an intestinal obstruction present at birth. The physicians and the hospital sought an injunction to require the parents to allow surgery. The judge ruled in favor of the parents, despite what I understand to be the weight of precedent to the contrary, on the grounds that the child was Mongoloid, that is, had the child been "normal," the decision would have gone the other way. Although the decision was not appealed to and hence not affirmed by a higher court, we can see through the prism of this case the possibility that the new powers of human genetics will strip the blindfold from the lady of justice and will make official the dangerous doctrine that some men are more equal than others.

The abnormal child may also feel resentful. A child with Down syndrome or Tay-Sachs disease will probably never know or care, but what about a child with hemophilia or with Turner's syndrome? In the past decade, with medical knowledge and power over the prenatal child increasing and with parental authority over the postnatal child decreasing, we have seen the appearance of a new type of legal action, suits for wrongful life. Children have brought suit against their parents (and others) seeking to recover damages for physical and social handicaps inextricably tied to their birth (e.g., congenital deformities, congenital syphilis, illegitimacy). In some of the American cases, the courts have recognized the justice of the child's claim (that he was injured due to parental negligence), although they have so far refused to award damages, due to policy considerations. In other countries, e.g., in Germany, judgments with compensation have gone for the plaintiffs. With the spread of amniocentesis and genetic abortion, we can only expect such cases to increase.

And here it will be the soft-hearted rather than the hard-hearted judges who will establish the doctrine of second-class human beings, out of compassion for the mutants who escaped the traps set out for them.

It may be argued that I am dealing with a problem which, even if it is real, will affect very few people. It may be suggested that very few will escape the traps once we have set them properly and widely, once people are informed about amniocentesis, once the power to detect prenatally grows to its full capacity, and once our "superstitious" opposition to abortion dies out or is extirpated. But in order even to come close to this vision of success, amniocentesis will have to become part of every pregnancy—either by making it mandatory, like the test for syphilis, or by making it "routine medical practice," like the Pap smear. Leaving aside the other problems with universal amniocentesis, we could expect that the problem for the few who escape is likely to be even worse precisely because they will be few.

The point, however, should be generalized. How will we come to view and act toward the many "abnormals" that will remain among us—the retarded, the crippled, the senile, the deformed, and the true mutants—once we embark on a program to root out genetic abnormality? For it must be remembered that we shall always have abnormls—some who escape detection or whose disease is undetectable *in utero*, others as a result of new mutations, birth injuries, accidents, maltreatment, or disease—who will require our care and protection. The existence of "defectives" cannot be fully prevented, not even by totalitarian breeding and weeding programs. Is it not likely that our principle with respect to these people will change from "We try harder" to "Why accept second best?" The idea of "the unwanted because abnormal child" may become a self-fulfilling prophecy, whose consequences may be worse than those of the abnormality itself.

Genetic and Other Defectives

The mention of other abnormals points to a second danger of the practice of genetic abortion. Genetic abortion may come to be seen not so much as the prevention of genetic disease, but as the prevention of birth of defective or abnormal children—and, in a way, understandably so. For in the case of what other diseases does preventive medicine consist in the elimination of the patient-at-risk? Moreover, the very language used to discuss genetic disease leads us to the easy but wrong conclusion that the afflicted fetus or person is rather than has a disease. True, one is partly defined by his genotype, but only partly. A person is more than his disease. And yet we slide easily from the language of possession to the language of identity, from "He has hemophilia" to "He is a hemophiliac," from "She has diabetes" through "She is diabetic" to "She is a diabetic," from "The fetus has Down syndrome" to "The fetus is a Down's." This way of speaking supports the belief that it is defective persons (or potential persons) that are being eliminated, rather than diseases.

If this is so, then it becomes simply accidental that the defect has a genetic cause. Surely, it is only because of the high regard for medicine and science, and for the accuracy of genetic diagnosis, that genotypic defectives are likely to be the first to go. But once the principle, "Defectives should not be born," is established, grounds other than cytological and biochemical may very well be sought. Even ignoring racialists and others equally misguided—of course, they cannot be ignored—we should know that there are social scientists, for example, who believe that one can predict with a high degree of accuracy how a child will turn out from a careful, systematic study of the socio-economic and psycho-dynamic environment into which he is born and in which he grows up. They might press for the prevention of sociopsychological disease, even of "criminality," by means of prenatal environmental diagnosis and abortion. I have heard rumor that a crude, unscientific form of eliminating potential "phenotypic defectives" is already being practiced in some cities, in that submission to abortion is allegedly being made a condition for the receipt of welfare payments. "Defectives should not be born" is a principle without limits. We can ill-afford to have it established.

Up to this point, I have been discussing the possible implications of the practice of genetic abortion for our belief in and adherence to the idea that, at least in fundamental human matters such as life and liberty, all men are to be considered as equals, that for these matters we should ignore as irrelevant the real qualitative differences amongst men, however important these differences may be for other purposes.

Those who are concerned about abortion fear that the permissible time of eliminating the unwanted will be moved forward along the time continuum, against newborns, infants, and children. Similarly, I suggest that we should be concerned lest the attack on gross genetic inequality in fetuses be advanced along the continuum of quality and into the later stages of life.

I am not engaged in predicting the future; I am not saying that amniocentesis and genetic abortion will lead down the road to Nazi Germany. Rather, I am suggesting that the principles underlying genetic abortion simultaneously justify many further steps down that road. The point was very well made by Abraham Lincoln:

> If A can prove, however conclusively, that he may, of right, enslave B—Why may not B snatch the same argument and prove equality, that he may enslave A?
>
> You say A is white, and B is black. It is color, then; the lighter having the right to enslave the darker? Take care. By this rule, you are to be slave to the first man you meet with a fairer skin than your own.
>
> You do not mean color exactly? You mean the whites are intellectually the superiors of the blacks, and, therefore have the right to enslave them? Take care again. By this rule, you are to be slave to the first man you meet with an intellect superior to your own.
>
> But, say you, it is a question of interest; and, if you can make it your interest, you have the right to enslave another. Very well. And if he can make it his interest, he has the right to enslave you.

Perhaps I have exaggerated the dangers; perhaps we will not abandon our inexplicable preference for generous humanitarianism over consistency. But we should indeed be cautious and move slowly as we give serious consideration to the question "What price the perfect baby?"[3]

NOTES

1. This strikes me as by far the most important inference to be drawn from the fact that men in different times and cultures have answered the abortion question differently. Seen in this light, the differing and changing answers themselves suggest that it is a question not easily put under, at least not for very long.

2. Other ways include: one should not do violence to living or growing things; life is sacred; respect nature; fetal life has value; refrain from taking innocent life; protect and preserve life. As some have pointed out, the terms chosen are of different weight, and would require reasons of different weight to tip the balance in favor of abortion. My choice of the "rights" terminology is not meant to beg the questions of whether such rights really exist, or of where they come from. However, the notion of a "fetal right to life" presents only a little more difficulty in this regard than does the notion of a "human right to life," since the former does not depend on a claim that the human fetus is already "human." In my sense of terms "right" and "life," we might even say that a dog or fetal dog has a "right to life," and that it would be cruel and immoral for a man to go around performing abortions even on dogs for no good reason.

3. For a discussion of the possible biological rather than moral price of attempts to prevent the birth of defective children see Motulsky, A. G., G. R. Fraser, and J. Felsenstein (1971).

Genetics and Reproductive Risk: Can Having Children Be Immoral?

LAURA M. PURDY

Purdy contends that it is morally wrong to "reproduce when we know there is a high risk of transmitting a serious disease or defect." This conclusion is based on the judgment that we have an obligation to provide each child with "something like a minimally satisfying life."

Is it morally permissible for me to have children?[1] A decision to procreate is surely one of the most significant decisions a person can make. So it would seem

Reprinted by permission of Laura M. Purdy.

that it ought not to be made without some moral soul-searching.

There are many reasons why one might hesitate to bring children into this world if one is concerned about their welfare. Some are rather general, like the deteriorating environment or the prospect of poverty. Others have a narrower focus, like continuing civil war in Ireland, or the lack of essential social support for child rearing persons in the United States. Still others may be relevant only to individuals at risk of passing harmful diseases to their offspring.

There are many causes of misery in this world, and most of them are unrelated to genetic disease. In the general scheme of things, human misery is most efficiently reduced by concentrating on noxious social and political arrangements. Nonetheless, we shouldn't ignore preventable harm just because it is confined to a relatively small corner of life. So the question arises: can it be wrong to have a child because of genetic risk factors?[2]

Unsurprisingly, most of the debate about this issue has focused on prenatal screening and abortion: much useful information about a given fetus can be made available by recourse to prenatal testing. This fact has meant that moral questions about reproduction have become entwined with abortion politics, to the detriment of both. The abortion connection has made it especially difficult to think about whether it is wrong to prevent a child from coming into being since doing so might involve what many people see as wrongful killing; yet there is no necessary link between the two. Clearly, the existence of genetically compromised children can be prevented not only by aborting already existing fetuses but also by preventing conception in the first place.

Worse yet, many discussions simply assume a particular view of abortion, without any recognition of other possible positions and the difference they make in how people understand the issues. For example, those who object to aborting fetuses with genetic problems often argue that doing so would undermine our conviction that all humans are in some important sense equal.[3] However, this position rests on the assumption that conception marks the point at which humans are endowed with a right to life. So aborting fetuses with genetic problems looks morally the same as killing "imperfect" people without their consent.

This position raises two separate issues. One pertains to the legitimacy of different views on abortion. Despite the conviction of many abortion activists to the contrary, I believe that ethically respectable views can be found on different sides of the debate, including one that sees fetuses as developing humans without any serious moral claim on continued life. There is no space here to address the details, and doing so would be once again to fall into the trap of letting the abortion question swallow up all others. Fortunately, this issue need not be resolved here. However, opponents of abortion need to face the fact that many thoughtful individuals do not *see* fetuses as moral persons. It follows that their reasoning process and hence the implications of their decisions are radically different from those envisioned by opponents of prenatal screening and abortion. So where the latter see genetic abortion as murdering people who just don't measure up, the former see it as a way to prevent the development of persons who are more likely to live miserable lives. This is consistent with a world view that values persons equally and holds that each deserves high quality life. Some of those who object to genetic abortion appear to be oblivious to these psychological and logical facts. It follows that the nightmare scenarios they paint for us are beside the point: many people simply do not share the assumptions that make them plausible.

How are these points relevant to my discussion? My primary concern here is to argue that conception can sometimes be morally wrong on grounds of genetic risk, although this judgment will not apply to those who accept the moral legitimacy of abortion and are willing to employ prenatal screening and selective abortion. If my case is solid, then those who oppose abortion must be especially careful not to conceive in certain cases, as they are, of course, free to follow their conscience about abortion. Those like myself who do not see abortion as murder have more ways to prevent birth.

Huntington's Disease

There is always some possibility that reproduction will result in a child with a serious disease or handicap. Genetic counselors can help individuals determine whether they are at unusual risk, and, as the Human Genome Project rolls on, their knowledge will increase by quantum leaps. As this knowledge becomes available, I believe we ought to use it to determine whether possible children are at risk *before* they are conceived.

I want in this paper to defend the thesis that it is morally wrong to reproduce when we know there is a high risk of transmitting a serious disease or defect. This thesis holds that some reproductive acts are wrong, and my argument puts the burden of proof on those who disagree with it to show why its conclusions can be overridden. Hence it denies that people should be free to reproduce mindless of the consequences.[4] However, as moral argument, it should be taken as a proposal for further debate and discussion. It is not, by itself, an argument in favor of legal prohibitions of reproduction.[5]

There is a huge range of genetic diseases. Some are quickly lethal; others kill more slowly, if at all. Some are mainly physical, some mainly mental; others impair both kinds of function. Some interfere tremendously with normal functioning, others less. Some are painful, some are not. There seems to be considerable agreement that rapidly lethal diseases, especially those, like Tay-Sachs, accompanied by painful deterioration, should be prevented even at the cost of abortion. Conversely, there seems to be substantial agreement that relatively trivial problems, especially cosmetic ones, would not be legitimate grounds for abortion.[6] In short, there are cases ranging from low risk of mild disease or disability to high risk of serious disease or disability. Although it is difficult to decide where the duty to refrain from procreation becomes compelling, I believe that there are some clear cases. I have chosen to focus on Huntington's Disease to illustrate the kinds of concrete issues such decisions entail. However, the arguments presented here are also relevant to many other genetic diseases.[7]

The symptoms of Huntington's Disease usually begin between the ages of thirty and fifty. It happens this way:

> Onset is insidious. Personality changes (obstinacy, moodiness, lack of initiative) frequently antedate or accompany the involuntary choreic movements. These usually appear first in the face, neck, and arms, and are jerky, irregular, and stretching in character. Contractions of the facial muscles result in grimaces; those of the respiratory muscles, lips, and tongue lead to hesitating, explosive speech. Irregular movements of the trunk are present; the gait is shuffling and dancing. Tendon reflexes are increased. . . .

> Some patients display a fatuous euphoria; others are spiteful, irascible, destructive, and violent. Paranoid reactions are common. Poverty of thought and impairment of attention, memory, and judgment occur. As the disease progresses, walking becomes impossible, swallowing difficult, and dementia profound. Suicide is not uncommon.[8]

The illness lasts about fifteen years, terminating in death.

Huntington's Disease is an autosomal dominant disease, meaning that it is caused by a single defective gene located on a non-sex chromosome. It is passed from one generation to the next via affected individuals. Each child of such an affected person has a fifty percent risk of inheriting the gene and thus of eventually developing the disease, even if he or she was born before the parent's disease was evident.[9]

Until recently, Huntington's Disease was especially problematic because most affected individuals did not know whether they had the gene for the disease until well into their childbearing years. So they had to decide about childbearing before knowing whether they could transmit the disease or not. If, in time, they did not develop symptoms of the disease, then their children could know they were not at risk for the disease. If unfortunately they did develop symptoms, then each of their children could know there was a fifty percent chance that they, too, had inherited the gene. In both cases, the children faced a period of prolonged anxiety as to whether they would develop the disease. Then, in the 1980s, thanks in part to an energetic campaign by Nancy Wexler, a genetic marker was found that, in certain circumstances, could tell people with a relatively high degree of probability whether or not they had the gene for the disease.[10] Finally, in March 1993, the defective gene itself was discovered.[11] Now individuals can find out whether they carry the gene for the disease, and prenatal screening can tell us whether a given fetus has inherited it. These technological developments change the moral scene substantially.

How serious are the risks involved in Huntington's Disease? Geneticists often think a ten percent risk is high.[12] But risk assessment also depends on what is at stake: the worse the possible outcome the more undesirable an otherwise small risk seems. In medicine, as elsewhere, people may regard the same result quite differently. But for devastating diseases like Huntington's this part of the judgment should be unproblematic: no one wants a loved one to suffer in this way.[13]

There may still be considerable disagreement about the acceptability of a given risk. So it would be difficult in many circumstances to say how we should respond to a particular risk. Nevertheless, there are good grounds for a conservative approach, for it is reasonable to take special precautions to avoid very bad consequences, even if the risk is small. But the possible consequences here *are* very bad: a child who may inherit Huntington's Disease has a much greater than average chance of being subjected to severe and prolonged suffering. And it is one thing to risk one's own welfare, but quite another to do so for others and without their consent.

Is this judgment about Huntington's Disease really defensible? People appear to have quite different opinions. Optimists argue that a child born into a family afflicted with Huntington's Disease has a reasonable chance of living a satisfactory life. After all, even children born of an afflicted parent still have a fifty percent chance of escaping the disease. And even if afflicted themselves, such people will probably enjoy some thirty years of healthy life before symptoms appear. It is also possible, although not at all likely, that some might not mind the symptoms caused by the disease. Optimists can point to diseased persons who have lived fruitful lives, as well as those who seem genuinely glad to be alive. One is Rick Donohue, a sufferer from the Joseph family disease: "You know, if my mom hadn't had me, I wouldn't be here for the life I have had. So there is a good possibility I will have children."[14] Optimists therefore conclude that it would be a shame if these persons had not lived.

Pessimists concede some of these facts, but take a less sanguine view of them. They think a fifty percent risk of serious disease like Huntington's appallingly high. They suspect that many children born into afflicted families are liable to spend their youth in dreadful anticipation and fear of the disease. They expect that the disease, if it appears, will be perceived as a tragic and painful end to a blighted life. They point out that Rick Donohue is still young, and has not experienced the full horror of his sickness. It is also well-known that some young persons have such a dilated sense of time that they can hardly envision themselves at thirty or forty, so the prospect of pain at that age is unreal to them.[15]

More empirical research on the psychology and life history of sufferers and potential sufferers is clearly needed to decide whether optimists or pessimists have a more accurate picture of the experiences of individuals at risk. But given that some will surely realize pessimists' worst fears, it seems unfair to conclude that the pleasures of these who deal best with the situation simply cancel out the suffering of those others when that suffering could be avoided altogether.

I think that these points indicate that the morality of procreation in situations like this demands further investigation. I propose to do this by looking first at the position of the possible child, then at that of the potential parent.

Possible Children and Potential Parents

The first task in treating the problem from the child's point of view is to find a way of referring to possible future offspring without seeming to confer some sort of morally significant existence upon them. I will follow the convention of calling children who might be born in the future but who are not now conceived "possible" children, offspring, individuals, or persons.

Now, what claims about children or possible children are relevant to the morality of childbearing in the circumstances being considered? Of primary importance is the judgment that we ought to try to provide every child with something like a minimally satisfying life. I am not altogether sure how best to formulate this standard but I want clearly to reject the view that it is morally permissible to conceive individuals so long as we do not expect them to be so miserable that they wish they were dead.[16] I believe that this kind of moral minimalism is thoroughly unsatisfactory and that not many people would really want to live in a world where it was the prevailing standard. Its lure is that it puts few demands on us, but its price is the scant attention it pays to human well-being.

How might the judgment that we have a duty to try to provide a minimally satisfying life for our children be justified? It could, I think, be derived fairly straightforwardly from either utilitarian or contractarian theories of justice, although there is no space here for discussion of the details. The net result of such analysis would be the conclusion that neglecting this duty would create unnecessary unhappiness or unfair disadvantage for some persons.

Of course, this line of reasoning confronts us with the need to spell out what is meant by "minimally satisfying" and what a standard based on this concept would require of us. Conceptions of a minimally satisfying life vary tremendously among societies and also within them. De rigueur in some circles are private music lessons and trips to Europe, while in others providing eight years of schooling is a major accomplishment. But there is no need to consider this complication at length here since we are concerned only with health as a prerequisite for a minimally satisfying life. Thus, as we draw out what such a standard might require of us, it seems reasonable to retreat to the more limited claim that parents should try to ensure something like normal health for their children. It might be thought that even this moderate claim is unsatisfactory since in some places debilitating conditions are the norm, but one could circumvent this objection by saying that parents ought to try to provide for their children health normal for that culture, even though it may be inadequate if measured by some outside standard.[17] This conservative position would still justify efforts to avoid the birth of children at risk for Huntington's Disease and other serious genetic diseases in virtually all societies.[18]

This view is reinforced by the following considerations. Given that possible children do not presently exist as actual individuals, they do not have a right to be brought into existence, and hence no one is maltreated by measures to avoid the conception of a possible person. Therefore, the conservative course that avoids the conception of those who would not be expected to enjoy a minimally satisfying life is at present the only fair course of action. The alternative is a laissez-faire approach which brings into existence the lucky, but only at the expense of the unlucky. Notice that attempting to avoid the creation of the unlucky does not necessarily lead to *fewer* people being brought into being; the question boils down to taking steps to bring those with better prospects into existence, instead of those with worse ones.

I have so far argued that if people with Huntington's Disease are unlikely to live minimally satisfying lives, then those who might pass it on should not have genetically related children. This is consonant with the principle that the greater the danger of serious problems, the stronger the duty to avoid them. But this principle is in conflict with what people think of as the right to reproduce. How might one decide which should take precedence?

Expecting people to forego having genetically related children might seem to demand too great a sacrifice of them. But before reaching that conclusion we need to ask what is really at stake. One reason for wanting children is to experience family life, including love, companionship, watching kids grow, sharing their pains and triumphs, and helping to form members of the next generation. Other reasons emphasize the validation of parents as individuals within a continuous family line, children as a source of immortality, or perhaps even the gratification of producing partial replicas of oneself. Children may also be desired in an effort to prove that one is an adult, to try to cement a marriage or to benefit parents economically.

Are there alternative ways of satisfying these desires? Adoption or new reproductive technologies can fulfil many of them without passing on known genetic defects. Replacements for sperm have been available for many years via artificial insemination by donor. More recently, egg donation, sometimes in combination with contract pregnancy,[19] has been used to provide eggs for women who prefer not to use their own. Eventually it may be possible to clone individual humans, although that now seems a long way off. All of these approaches to avoiding the use of particular genetic material are controversial and have generated much debate. I believe that tenable moral versions of each do exist.[20]

None of these methods permits people to extend both genetic lines, or realize the desire for immortality or for children who resemble both parents; nor is it clear that such alternatives will necessarily succeed in proving that one is an adult, cementing a marriage, or providing economic benefits. Yet, many people feel these desires strongly. Now, I am sympathetic to William James's dictum regarding desires: "Take any demand, however slight, which any creature, however weak, may make. Ought it not, for its own sole sake be satisfied? If not, prove why not."[21] Thus a world where more desires are satisfied is generally better than one where fewer are. However, not all desires can be legitimately satisfied since, as James suggests, there may be good reasons—such as the conflict of duty and desire—why some should be overruled.

Fortunately, further scrutiny of the situation reveals that there are good reasons why people should attempt—with appropriate social support—to talk themselves out of the desires in question or to consider novel ways of fulfilling them. Wanting to see the genetic line continued is not particularly rational when it brings a sinister legacy of illness and death. The desire for immortality cannot really be satisfied anyway, and people need to face the fact that what really matters is how they behave in their own lifetime. And finally, the desire for children who physically resemble one is understandable, but basically narcissistic, and its fulfillment cannot be guaranteed even by normal reproduction. There are other ways of proving one is an adult, and other ways of cementing marriages—and children don't necessarily do either. Children, especially prematurely ill children, may not provide the expected economic benefits anyway. Nongenetically related children may also provide benefits similar to those that would have been provided by genetically related ones, and expected economic benefit is, in many cases, a morally questionable reason for having children.

Before the advent of reliable genetic testing, the options of people in Huntington's families were cruelly limited. On the one hand, they could have children, but at the risk of eventual crippling illness and death for them. On the other, they could refrain from childbearing, sparing their possible children from significant risk of inheriting this disease, perhaps frustrating intense desires to procreate—only to discover, in some cases that their sacrifice was unnecessary because they did not develop the disease. Or they could attempt to adopt or try new reproductive approaches.

Reliable genetic testing has opened up new possibilities. Those at risk who wish to have children can get tested. If they test positive, they know their possible children are at risk. Those who are opposed to abortion must be especially careful to avoid conception if they are to behave responsibly. Those not opposed to abortion can responsibly conceive children, but only if they are willing to test each fetus and abort those who carry the gene. If individuals at risk test negative, they are home free.

What about those who cannot face the test for themselves? They can do prenatal testing and abort fetuses who carry the defective gene. A clearly positive test also implies that the parent is affected, although negative tests do not rule out that possibility. Prenatal testing can thus bring knowledge that enables one to avoid passing the disease to others, but only, in some cases, at the cost of coming to know with certainty that one will indeed develop the disease. This situation raises with peculiar force the question of whether parental responsibility requires people to get tested.

Some people think that we should recognize a right "not to know." It seems to me that such a right could be defended only where ignorance does not put others at serious risk. So if people are prepared to forego genetically related children, they need not get tested. But if they want genetically related children then they must do whatever is necessary to ensure that affected babies are not the result. There is, after all, something inconsistent about the claim that one has a right to be shielded from the truth, even if the price is to risk inflicting on one's children the same dread disease one cannot even face in oneself.

In sum, until we can be assured that Huntington's Disease does not prevent people from living a minimally satisfying life, individuals at risk for the disease have a moral duty to try not to bring affected babies into this world. There are now enough options available so that this duty needn't frustrate their reasonable desires. Society has a corresponding duty to facilitate moral behavior on the part of individuals. Such support ranges from the narrow and concrete (like making sure that medical testing and counseling is available to all) to the more general social environment that guarantees that all pregnancies are voluntary, that pronatalism is eradicated, and that women are treated with respect regardless of the reproductive options they choose.

NOTES

1. This paper is loosely based on "Genetic Diseases: Can Having Children Be Immoral?" originally published in *Genetics Now*, ed. John L. Buckley (Washington, DC: University

Press of America, 1978) and subsequently anthologized in a number of medical ethics texts. Thanks to Thomas Mappes and David DeGrazia for their helpful suggestions about updating the paper.

2. I focus on genetic considerations, although with the advent of AIDS the scope of the general question here could be expanded. There are two reasons for sticking to this relatively narrow formulation. One is that dealing with a smaller chunk of the problem may help us think more clearly, while realizing that some conclusions may nonetheless be relevant to the larger problem. The other is the peculiar capacity of some genetic problems to affect ever more individuals in the future.

3. For example, see Leon Kass, "Implications of Prenatal Diagnosis for the Human Right to Life," *Ethical Issues in Human Genetics*, eds. Bruce Hilton et al. (New York: Plenum Press, 1973).

4. This is, of course, a very broad thesis. I defend an even broader version in "Loving Future People," *Reproduction, Ethics and the Law*, ed. Joan Callahan (Bloomington: Indiana University Press, forthcoming).

5. Why would we want to resist legal enforcement of every moral conclusion? First, legal action has many costs, costs not necessarily worth paying in particular cases. Second, legal enforcement would tend to take the matter in question out of the realm of debate and treat it as settled. But in many cases, especially where mores or technology is rapidly evolving, we don't want that to happen. Third, legal enforcement would undermine individual freedom and decision-making capacity. In some cases, the ends envisioned are important enough to warrant putting up with these disadvantages, but that remains to be shown in each case.

6. Those who do not see fetuses as moral persons with a right to life may nonetheless hold that abortion is justifiable in these cases. I argue at some length elsewhere that lesser defects can cause great suffering. Once we are clear that there is nothing discriminatory about failing to conceive particular possible individuals, it makes sense, other things being equal, to avoid the prospect of such pain if we can. Naturally, other things rarely are equal. In the first place, many problems go undiscovered until a baby is born. Secondly, there are often substantial costs associated with screening programs. Thirdly, although women should be encouraged to consider the moral dimensions of routine pregnancy, we do not want it to be so fraught with tension that it becomes a miserable experience. (See "Loving Future People.")

7. It should be noted that failing to conceive a single individual can affect many lives: in 1916, nine hundred and sixty-two cases could be traced from six seventeenth-century arrivals in America. See Gordon Rattray Taylor, *The Biological Time Bomb* (New York, 1968), p. 176.

8. *The Merck Manual* (Rahway, NJ: Merck, 1972), pp. 1363, 1346. We now know that the age of onset and severity of the disease is related to the number of abnormal replications of the glutamine code on the abnormal gene. See Andrew

Revkin, "Hunting Down Huntington's," *Discover*, December 1993, p. 108.

9. Hymie Gordon, "Genetic Counseling," *JAMA*, Vol. 217, n. 9 (August 30, 1971), p. 1346.

10. See Revkin, "Hunting Down Huntington's," pp. 99–108.

11. "Gene for Huntington's Disease Discovered," *Human Genome News*, Vol. 5, n. 1 (May 1993), p. 5.

12. Charles Smith, Susan Holloway, and Alan E. H. Emery, "Individuals at Risk in Families—Genetic Disease," *Journal of Medical Genetics*, Vol. 8 (1971), p. 453.

13. To try to separate the issue of the gravity of the disease from the existence of a given individual, compare this situation with how we would assess a parent who neglected to vaccinate an existing child against a hypothetical viral version of Huntington's.

14. *The New York Times*, September 30, 1975, p. 1, col. 6. The Joseph family disease is similar to Huntington's Disease except that symptoms start appearing in the twenties. Rick Donohue was in his early twenties at the time he made this statement.

15. I have talked to college students who believe that they will have lived fully and be ready to die at those ages. It is astonishing how one's perspective changes over time, and how ages that one once associated with senility and physical collapse come to seem the prime of human life.

16. The view I am rejecting has been forcefully articulated by Derek Parfit, *Reasons and Persons* (Oxford: Oxford University Press, 1984). For more discussion, see "Loving Future People."

17. I have some qualms about this response since I fear that some human groups are so badly off that it might still be wrong for them to procreate, even if that would mean great changes in their cultures. But this is a complicated issue that needs its own investigation.

18. Again, a troubling exception might be the isolated Venezuelan group Nancy Wexler found where, because of in-breeding, a large proportion of the population is affected by Huntington's. See Revkin, "Hunting Down Huntington's."

19. Or surrogacy, as it has been popularly known. I think that "contract pregnancy" is more accurate and more respectful of women. Eggs can be provided either by a woman who also gestates the fetus or by a third party.

20. The most powerful objections to new reproductive technologies and arrangements concern possible bad consequences for women. However, I do not think that the arguments against them on these grounds have yet shown the dangers to be as great as some believe. So although it is perhaps true that new reproductive technologies and arrangements shouldn't be used lightly, avoiding the conceptions discussed here is well worth the risk. For a series of viewpoints on this issue, including my own "Another Look at Contract Pregnancy," see Helen B. Holmes, *Issues in Reproductive Technology I: An Anthology* (New York: Garland Press, 1992).

21. *Essays in Pragmatism*, ed. A. Castell (New York, 1948), p. 73.

The Morality of Screening for Disability

JEFF MCMAHAN

McMahan examines arguments against using screening technologies such as PGD to avoid giving birth to a disabled child. The most common objections are that screening and selection are discriminatory, diminish human diversity, cause disabled people social harms, and express a hurtful view toward them. McMahan says these objections imply that "it is wrong for people to try to avoid having a disabled child and to have a non-disabled child instead." This view in turn implies that it must be at least permissible to cause oneself to have a disabled rather than a non-disabled child. But, he argues, it is wrong to deliberately cause a disabled child to exist instead of a healthy child; therefore we must reject some or all of the objections against testing.

My topic is the morality of using screening technologies to enable potential parents to avoid having a disabled child. The relevant techniques include preconception genetic and non-genetic testing of potential parents, preimplantation genetic diagnosis (PGD), and prenatal screening with the option of abortion. Many people use these techniques and are grateful to have them. Others, however, object to their use, even when abortion is not an issue. The most common objections can be grouped into four basic types.

First, the opponents of screening and selection urge that these practices are perniciously discriminatory, in that their aim is to rid the world of people of a certain type, people who have increasingly come to share a sense of collective identity and solidarity. Some might even argue that for society to endorse and support screening for disability is analogous to promoting efforts to prevent the births of people of a particular racial group.

Second, the practices of screening and selection are not just detrimental to the disabled as a group but may also be harmful to individual disabled people in various ways. They may, for example, reinforce or seem to legitimize forms of discrimination against existing disabled people. And, if effective, they also reduce the *number* of disabled people, thereby making each disabled person a bit more unusual and a

bit more isolated. The reduction in numbers may, in addition, diminish the visibility and political power of disabled people generally.

Third, it is often held that a reduction in the number of disabled people would have an adverse effect on human diversity. To eliminate the disabled would be to eliminate a type of human being who makes a unique contribution to the world. For the disabled themselves, and indeed their mere presence among the rest of us, teach valuable lessons about respect for difference, about the nobility of achievement in the face of grave obstacles, and even about the value of life and what makes a life worth living.

Fourth, it is often held that practices of screening and selection express a view of disabled people that is hurtful to existing disabled people. Efforts to prevent disabled people from existing are said to express such views as that disabled people ought not to exist, that it is bad if disabled people exist, or at least worse than if normal people exist, that disabled people are not worth the burdens they impose on their parents and on the wider society, and so on. Screening and selection, in other words, seem to say to existing disabled people: The rest of us are trying to prevent the existence of other people like you.

One can respond to these objections to screening and selection, as some of the speakers at this conference have done, by appealing to rights of individual liberty. One could grant that the practices are objectionable for the reasons given but argue that those reasons are overridden by rights to reproductive freedom and by the benefits to those who are able to exercise

From *Ethics, Law and Moral Philosophy of Reproductive Biomedicine*, vol. 10, supp. 1, March 2005, pp. 129–32.

those rights. But I want to advance a reason for scepticism about the force of the objections themselves.

The objections do of course express serious and legitimate concerns, concerns that must be addressed in appropriate ways. But I will argue that they're insufficiently strong to show that screening and selection are wrong or should be prohibited. For if they were taken to show that, they would also have implications beyond the practices of screening and selection. They would also imply the permissibility of certain types of action that most people believe are impermissible.

Consider this hypothetical example: Suppose there is a drug that has a complex set of effects. It is an aphrodisiac that enhances a woman's pleasure during sexual intercourse. But it also increases fertility by inducing ovulation. If ovulation has recently occurred naturally, this drug causes destruction of the egg that is present in one of the fallopian tubes but also causes a new and different egg to be released from the ovaries. In addition, however, it has a very high probability of damaging the new egg in a way that will cause any child conceived through the fertilization of that egg to be disabled. The disability caused by the drug is, let us suppose, one that many potential parents seek to avoid through screening. But it is also, like virtually all disabilities, not so bad as to make life not worth living. Suppose that a woman takes this drug primarily to increase her pleasure but also with the thought that it may increase the probability of conception—for she wants to have a child. She is aware that the drug is likely to cause her to have a disabled child but she is eager for pleasure and reflects that it might be rather nice to have a child who might be more dependent than children usually are. Although she does not know it, she has in fact just ovulated naturally so the drug destroys and replaces the egg that was already present but also damages the new egg, thereby causing the child she conceives to be disabled.

Note that because the drug causes the woman's ovaries to release a new egg, the disabled child she conceives is a different individual from the child she would have had if she hadn't taken the drug.

Many people think that this woman's action is morally wrong. It is wrong to cause the existence of a disabled child rather than a child without a disability, just for the sake of one's own sexual pleasure. There are,

of course, some who think that rights to reproductive freedom make it permissible to choose to have a disabled child just as they also make it permissible to try to avoid having a disabled child. But most of us do not share that view. Most of us think that if it would be wrong to cause an already born child to become disabled, and if it would be wrong to cause a future child to be disabled through the infliction of prenatal injury, it should also be wrong to cause a disabled child to exist rather than a child without a disability.

There are of course differences. Whether they are morally significant and if so to what extent, are matters to which I will return shortly. For the moment, the important point to notice is that if the arguments I cited earlier show that screening and selection are wrong, they should also show that the action of the woman who takes the aphrodisiac is permissible. This is because if it is morally *mandatory* to *allow* oneself to have a disabled child rather than to try, through screening, to have a child who would not be disabled, than it must be at least *permissible* to *cause* oneself to have a disabled rather than a non-disabled child.

Let me try to explain this in greater detail. If it is wrong for the woman to take the aphrodisiac, that must be because there is a moral objection to voluntarily having a disabled child—an objection that's strong enough to make it wrong to cause oneself, by otherwise permissible means, to have a disabled rather than a non-disabled child. But if there is such an objection, it must surely be strong enough to make it at least permissible for people to try, by morally acceptable means, to avoid having a disabled child and to have a non-disabled child instead, and to make it impermissible for others to prevent them from making this attempt.

Yet the critics of screening believe not only that it is wrong for people to try to avoid having a disabled child and to have a non-disabled child instead, but even that it is permissible for others to prevent them from having a non-disabled rather than a disabled child. It would be inconsistent for these critics to condemn the woman in this example for causing herself to have a disabled rather than a non-disabled child and to condemn those who try to cause themselves *not* to have a disabled rather than a non-disabled child.

The crucial premise here is that if it would be morally objectionable to try to *prevent* a certain outcome, and permissible to deprive people of the means of preventing that outcome, then it ought to be permissible to *cause* that outcome, provided one does so by otherwise permissible means.

Note also that if we were to assert publicly that it would be wrong for this woman to do what would cause her to have a disabled child rather than a non-disabled child, or if we were to attempt to prevent her from taking the drug—for example, by making the drug illegal on the ground that it causes "birth defects"—our action would be vulnerable to the same objections that opponents of screening and selection urge against those practices.

If, for example, we were publicly to state the reasons why it would be objectionable for the woman to take the drug—that the disabled child's life might be likely to contain more hardship and less good than the life of a non-disabled child, that provision for the disabled child's special needs would involve greater social costs, and so on—the evaluations of disability and of disabled people that might be thought to be implicit in these claims could be deeply hurtful to existing disabled people, and if we were to prevent this woman and others from being able to take the drug, this would reduce the number of disabled people relative to the number there would otherwise have been, thereby threatening the collective identity and political power of existing disabled people.

In short, the arguments of the opponents of screening seem to imply not only that it would be permissible for the woman to take the aphrodisiac, thereby causing herself to have a disabled child, but also that it would be wrong even to voice objections to her action.

Some opponents of screening and selection may be willing to accept these implications. They might argue that there are relevant differences between causing oneself to have a disabled child rather than a different non-disabled child and causing an existing individual to be disabled. For example, in the latter case but not the former, there is a victim, someone for whom one's act is worse. So there are objections to causing an existing individual to be disabled that do not apply to merely causing a disabled person to exist, and to assert these objections merely expresses the view that it can be worse to be disabled than not to be, which seems unobjectionable, since it does not

imply any view of disabled people themselves. Screening and selection, by contrast, are held to express a pernicious and degrading view of disabled people.

Thus, opponents of screening and selection typically think that they can draw the line between action by a woman that may cause her to conceive a child who will be disabled and, for example, action taken by a pregnant woman that injures her fetus, causing it to be disabled when it otherwise would not have been. But in fact many people, especially among the disabled themselves, contend that it is no worse to be disabled than not to be. They claim that disabilities are "neutral" traits. So, for example, Harriet McBryde Johnson (2003), a disabled lawyer, emphatically repudiates the "unexamined assumption that disabled people are inherently 'worse off,' that we 'suffer,' that we have lesser 'prospects of a happy life.'"

The view that it is not bad to be disabled, apart from any ill effects caused by social discrimination, would be very difficult to sustain if it implied that to cause a person to become disabled would not harm that person, or that it is irrational to be averse to becoming disabled. But in fact those who claim that it is not bad in itself to *be* disabled can accept without inconsistency that it can be bad to *become* disabled. They can appeal to the *transition costs*. It is bad to become disabled because this can involve loss and discontinuity, requiring that one abandon certain goals and projects and adapt to the pursuit of different ones instead. It is these effects that make it rational to fear becoming disabled and they are a major part of the explanation of why it is wrong to cause someone to become disabled. The other major part is that the causation of disability involves a violation of the victim's autonomy.

But notice that these considerations do not count against causing disability through prenatal injury. For congenital disability does not have transition costs, and fetuses are not autonomous.

It seems, therefore, that opponents of screening and selection who also claim that it is not worse to be disabled have no basis for objecting to the infliction of prenatal injury that causes congenital disability. Moreover, to object to the infliction of disabling prenatal injury or to enact measures to prevent it would seem to express a negative view of disability and perhaps of the disabled themselves. At a minimum, it expresses the view that it is bad to be disabled, or at least worse than not to be disabled. And, if effective, efforts to prevent disabling prenatal injury would have other effects comparable to those of prohibiting or restricting screening for disability and selection, such as reducing the number of disabled people who would be born, thereby also threatening the sense of collective identity and solidarity among the disabled as well as diminishing their visibility and political power. Finally, prevention of prenatal injury would also threaten human diversity. It would deprive those who would have had contact with the person if he had been disabled of the unique benefits that disabled people offer to others.

So for those opponents of selection who also hold that it is not a harm or misfortune to be disabled, it seems that there are not only no reasons to object to the infliction of disabling prenatal injury but even positive reasons not to object to it and not to try to prevent it.

Suppose there were an aphrodisiac that would greatly enhance a woman's pleasure during sex but would, if taken during pregnancy, injure the fetus in a way that would cause it to be congenitally severely disabled. Those who oppose screening and selection for the reasons I cited earlier and who also hold that it is not bad in itself to be disabled are logically committed by their own arguments to accept that it would be permissible for a pregnant woman to take this aphrodisiac just to increase her own pleasure, and they are further committed to accept that it would be wrong to try to prevent the woman from taking the aphrodisiac or even to criticize her for doing so.

If we think that these conclusions are mistaken, which they surely are, we must reject some part of the case against screening and selection.

I will conclude by briefly suggesting a more positive way of addressing the concerns of those who oppose screening and selection. My sense is that the chief worry of those opposed to screening and selection has to do with the expressive effects of these practices. The worry is, as I noted earlier, that these practices give social expression to a negative view of disabled people, thereby reinforcing other forms of discrimination against them.

But notice that it is usually only people who have not had a disabled child who are averse to doing so.

Those people who actually have a disabled child tend overwhelmingly to be glad that they had the particular child they had. If any child they might have had would have been disabled, they tend to prefer having had their actual disabled child to having had no child at all. If they could have had a non-disabled child but it would have been a different child, they tend to prefer their actual disabled child. Of course, what they would usually most prefer is that their actual child had not been disabled. But it is almost invariably the case that any action that would have enabled them to avoid having a disabled child would have caused them to have a different child. When the parents appreciate this fact, they cease to wish that anything had been different in the past, and focus their hopes on the possibility of a cure.

In short, most people who currently have or have had a disabled child in the past do not regret having done so. They are, instead, glad to have had their actual child and frequently testify to the special joy and illumination afforded by being bound to a disabled child. This very different evaluation of having a disabled child by those who actually have experience of it is no less rational and no less authoritative than the evaluation that many people make prospectively that it would be bad or worse to have a disabled child.

We could therefore try to offset any negative expressive effects of screening and selection by giving public expression to these different and equally valid evaluations. I do not have any suggestions for how we might do this. That's a matter for specialists in public policy, not philosophers. But the crucial point is that it would be morally and strategically better for disabled people and their advocates to focus their efforts on positive proposals of this sort rather than to stigmatize and to seek to restrict or suppress practices such as screening and selection. By crusading against screening and selection, they risk making themselves appear to the wider public as fanatics bent on imposing harmful restrictions on others. That would certainly not serve the cause of obtaining justice for the disabled.

REFERENCE

Johnson HM. 2003. Unspeakable conversations. *New York Times Magazine* 16 February 2003, p. 79.

Disowning Knowledge: Issues in Genetic Testing

ROBERT WACHBROIT

Wachbroit considers whether physicians are justified in limiting patients' access to certain kinds of genetic tests or test results. He argues that sometimes such restrictions can be justified on scientific grounds, but too often they represent a "resurgent paternalism" in which physicians make nonmedical judgments out of concern that genetic information might cause social or psychological harm to patients. We should respect people's decisions to know—as well as their decisions not to know.

Last fall in Chicago, at a conference sponsored by the Alzheimer's Association and the National Institute on Aging, doctors and researchers met to discuss an ethical dilemma that has grown increasingly familiar as advances in diagnostic techniques outstrip the therapeutic abilities of the medical profession. The meeting focused on the use of a medical test for a particular heart condition—a test that can also, in some cases, predict with 90 percent accuracy whether someone will develop Alzheimer's disease by the age of 80. Should patients tested for the heart condition be told of their risk of contracting Alzheimer's disease, when there is little if anything medicine at present can do to prevent or ameliorate the condition?

Some people, including many of those attending the meeting, believe that the answer to this question is no: if the information is of little therapeutic value, it's of little value to the patient as well. It is wrong to burden the patient with troubling news when there is little or nothing that the physician can do about it.

At this stage in the history of medical practice, we may well be surprised to encounter such a response. Over the past few decades there has been an intense effort to articulate and defend a person's right to be informed of his or her medical condition. Not so long ago, this right was not widely acknowledged. Health professionals generally assumed that, in the case of certain diseases, patients didn't really want

to know. Moreover, even if they did want to, they wouldn't really understand the diagnosis; and even if they did want to know and could understand, they would be so psychologically harmed by the information that the result would likely be, if not suicide, then a clinical depression that would interfere with any sort of available care. Over the years the arguments attempting to defend this medical paternalism have been carefully examined and successfully undermined. The very idea of health professionals deciding whether a patient should know his or her medical condition is now routinely criticized in bioethics courses. Nonetheless, the advent of genetic testing appears to have provoked a resurgence of paternalistic thinking, especially in those cases where doctors can detect the genetic condition associated with a particular disease but are as yet unable to prevent or treat that disease.

The association between a genetic condition and a disease, and so the type of information a genetic test reveals, is subject to considerable variation. With results from the test for a specific mutation at the tip of chromosome 4, we can predict with near certainty whether an individual will suffer from Huntington's disease, a severe late-onset neurological disorder, but we can't yet tell when the disease will occur. With information from the test for mutations of the BRCA1 gene, we can, in particular situations, conclude that an individual has a susceptibility to a specific type of breast cancer, but we don't yet know what other conditions must be in place to trigger this susceptibility. With information from the test discussed in Chicago—a test that detects the presence of the apolipoprotein E genotype—we can, in particular

From "Disowning Knowledge: Issues in Genetic Testing," *Report from the Institute for Philosophy and Public Policy*, vol. 16, no. 3/4 (1996), pp. 14–18. Reprinted with permission.

situations, conclude that an individual is at an increased risk of contracting Alzheimer's disease, but there is still some controversy about the relative importance of this risk factor.

Recent concern has largely focused on these last two tests. At the Chicago meeting, the issue was the disclosure of certain additional information from a test already administered. In other cases, professional oganizations, as well as some advocacy groups, have proposed limits on the very availability of certain genetic tests. It is argued that tests for certain conditions should be restricted to research settings for the time being and not offered routinely or to all.

Are these proposals based on medical paternalism? Or can restrictions on genetic testing be defended on other grounds? I wish to examine possible justifications for limiting testing, distinguishing between those that are paternalistic and those that are not. I shall then consider the reasons and responsibilities that might influence patients in deciding whether to be tested or to receive genetic information.

Grounds for Restrictions
A discussion of reasons for restricting genetic testing should begin by acknowledging that there is no *right* to genetic testing. A right to be informed of test results (assuming that such a right exists) would not entail a right to *be* tested. And a "right to health care" (in the usual ways that phrase is understood) is not taken to include a right to have every diagnostic test, including genetic tests, performed. But though there is no right to genetic testing, a decision to withhold or restrict certain tests should be based on good public reasons (as opposed to private, economic reasons). This is especially true in the case of genetic tests, since in many cases genetic testing facilities, e.g., those connected with teaching hospitals, are supported, directly or indirectly, with public funds.

Reasons for restricting certain kinds of genetic tests can be divided into two broad categories. One set of reasons focuses on the *time and resources* that would be lost by the inappropriate use of genetic testing. Given the current state of knowledge, the results obtained from certain tests may include such a high number of false-positives or false-negatives, or be so difficult to interpret, that performing these tests would be a waste of the health professional's or laboratory's time, diverting resources from tests that are diagnostically more useful. For example, research has revealed a large number of possible mutations in BRCA1. Unless a woman's family history implicates a particular mutation in the occurrence of breast cancer, there is no point in testing her for that mutation; whatever the test result may be, it will not be interpretable. Thus, a decision not to offer BRCA1 testing to all women would be defensible on the grounds that widespread testing would needlessly draw upon society's limited resources of expertise and technology. Where the best available evidence shows that a given procedure would yield no meaningful information, it is entirely appropriate, so the argument goes, to restrict that procedure.

The second set of grounds for restricting the availability of genetic tests focuses on claims about the *social or psychological harms* that individuals might suffer from knowing their test results, where these harms are not offset by any corresponding medical benefit. Indeed, in many cases these harms are considered to be so palpable and the medical benefits so clearly nonexistent that it is assumed people would not want to know their genetic condition even if they had the opportunity.

One widely cited harm of knowing one's genetic condition arises from the prospect of discrimination in employment or insurance coverage. Someone with a known genetic condition indicating a susceptibility to breast cancer might be denied a job or a promotion, or denied health or life insurance, because she is regarded as a health risk and therefore as too great an economic risk. This concern about discrimination chiefly provides a reason why *third parties* should not be given access to an individual's genetic information. Yet an individual may well decide to forgo this information in order to maintain deniability. For example, suppose an insurance contract requires the individual to tell all she knows about her genetic condition, so that discovering that any information was withheld would constitute grounds for dismissing later claims. A person in this situation might well decide to remain ignorant, since she can't be penalized for withholding information she doesn't have.

However, a person can maintain ignorance of her genetic condition only up to a point, since genetic tests are not the only source of information about that condition. Standard family medical histories can sometimes tell a good deal, and claiming ignorance of this history may not be possible. If an individual suffers from Huntington's disease, then his or her children have a 50 percent probability of contracting it as well. If a woman's sister, mother, and aunt suffer from breast cancer, then it is likely that the woman is at greater risk than the general population of contracting breast cancer herself. Futhermore, genetic information is not always bad news. Someone who appears to be at risk for a certain disease because of her family history could discover, and so presumably assure an employer or insurer, that she is in fact not at risk because her test result was negative. Nevertheless, we should acknowledge that there can be perverse incentives to be ignorant, especially in the absence of appropriate laws regarding "genetic discrimination" or regulations regarding insurance and preexisting conditions.

A completely different harm that is associated with genetic information has to do with the psychological burden of knowing. Indeed, one writer refers to such infomation as "toxic knowledge." Unlike concerns about employment discrimination or insurance, fears about the burden of knowing speak directly to the question of the desirability of self-knowledge. For some people, the discovery that they have a genetic condition that places them at an especially high risk of suffering certain diseases could so depress them that the quality, joy, and purpose of their lives would evaporate. Moreover, even if the results of a genetic test were negative, some people might experience the reaction commonly known as "survivor's guilt," as they contemplate the prospects of their less fortunate siblings or other relatives.

The applicabilitiy of this reason will vary from person to person. Some people might be able to handle bad news calmly and move on, while others might become irrevocably incapacitated. We are individuals in how we each deal with the disappointments and tragedies in our lives. Genetic knowledge might be extremely toxic for one individual but less so for another. Presumably however, if a person does raise this issue in his own case, it probably applies.

Deciding for the Patient

It is this last set of reasons, when invoked to justify limits on the availability of genetic testing, that sug-

gests a resurgent paternalism with respect to medical information. They involve explicit judgments by medical professionals about what would be good for the patient, where the "good" (i.e., the avoidance of certain social and psychological harms) extends beyond matters of medical expertise. Whatever force they may have as reasons an *individual* might give for not wanting to know genetic information, their persuasiveness weakens considerably when they are offered by third parties as reasons for restrictions on genetic testing. While certain people might be psychologically devastated by their test results, there is no evidence to support the assumption that most people will be so devastated; indeed, such an assumption flies in the face of our commonsense knowledge of people's differences. Similarly, the likelihood that people will confront employment discrimination or insurance problems, and the seriousness with which they regard such a prospect, will vary with circumstances. It is therefore paternalistic to cite these concerns as grounds for restricting genetic testing.

The same can be said of arguments that the results of genetic tests are too complex or ambiguous for patients to understand. Test results may identify risk factors rather than yield predictions; the information may consist of probabilities rather than certainties. In other medical contexts, however, the complexity of information is not accepted as an excuse for taking decisions out of the patient's hands. For example, we require physicians to obtain informed consent before they engage in an intervention. However complex the relevant information might be, usefully communicating it to the patient is a challenge to which the professional must rise.

A rejection of the paternalistic arguments does not yield the conclusion that all genetic tests should be available to the public. As we have seen, restrictions on the availability of certain genetic tests, or of any medical procedure, need not be based on paternalism. For example, none of these comments affects the legitimacy or persuasiveness of the scientific reasons for restricting certain tests.

Unfortunately, some of the professional organizations and advocacy groups seeking to restrict genetic testing have allowed an admixture of paternalism to enter into what would otherwise be sound scientific arguments. Instead of simply pointing out that a test for BRCA1 mutations can yield no useful information about most women, they express worries about the "fear" and "panic" that widespread testing might provoke. The first objection to indiscriminate testing is valid; the second is not. By including arguments that would in other contexts be rejected as unwarranted medical paternalism, these organizations have inadvertently ceded the moral high ground to the for-profit laboratories that have rushed in to perform these tests. Whether the labs can provide testing with the appropriate care and counseling is an open question. But efforts to regulate or even comment upon their services are likely to be ineffectual so long as the laboratories can self-righteously affirm the patient's "right to know" against the paternalism of their critics.

Similarly, when the researchers in Chicago tried to formulate a policy regarding the disclosure of test results, paternalistic assumptions clouded the issue. It was agreed that a cardiac test yielding information about the risk of Alzheimer's disease poses an ethical problem for the physician, who must either inform patients of their condition or withhold that information. But there is another alternative: the physician can tell patients, before testing for one condition, that information about another condition will be available. Whether or not to be informed becomes the patient's decision. Indeed, this option is standard in communicating the results of various medical tests, including results where disease is not at issue. The obstetrician performing amniocentesis doesn't typically agonize over whether to inform the couple of the fetus's sex. The couple are simply asked whether they want to know. And in our society at this time, the patient's desire to know or not to know is taken to settle the matter.

A Responsibility to Know

It is mainly those who wish to know their genetic condition who are likely to object to paternalistic restrictions on genetic testing. We cannot assume, however, that most people would fall into this category. In one recent study, only 43 percent of research subjects who were offered the BRCA1 test agreed to have it performed. Many who refused the test cited the concerns about employment and insurance that I have already described, while others pointed to the psychological distress that knowledge might bring.

If the challenge to medical paternalism is based on the notion that people should be free to make their own choices with respect to information, then in general the decision not to know should be as fully respected as the decision *to* know. No one would be in favor of frog-marching people to a genetics lab, having them tested, and then compelling them to listen to the results. The widely acknowledged right people have to refuse treatment surely includes a right to refuse diagnostic tests. If some people simply don't want their decisions about how they live their lives to depend upon genetic information, it would seem that they have no reason, and certainly no obligation, to know.

Nevertheless, there are many circumstances in which people might have a moral responsibility to know—a responsibility that grows out of their professional or personal obligations. The case for professional obligations, though limited, is fairly clear. The same reasoning that supports drug testing of individuals in particular professions—air traffic controller, train conductor, airline pilot—also supports claiming that these individuals have an obligation to know their genetic information. If an individual might have a condition that, if manifested, would interfere with his job performance in such a way as to endanger other people, that person has an obligation to know and monitor that condition, whether he wants to or not.

Since most of us are not employed in such professions, however, this obligation attaches to relatively few people. Moreover, most genetic conditions are unlikely to have an impact on the safety of other people. It is difficult to argue that an airline pilot's refusal to know whether she is at special risk of contracting breast cancer would endanger the lives of the passengers.

The ways in which personal obligations may generate a responsibility to know one's genetic condition have not been given comparable attention, even though they are more widely applicable. Most of us are enmeshed in a network of personal obligations and commitments—to families, dependents, loved ones. In many cases, with information about our medical condition, we can more effectively discharge our obligations, or at least avoid measures that, under the circumstances, may be futile. Consider the case of a 50-year-old parent of minor children who refuses to know whether he is at high risk of contracting Alzheimer's disease within the next ten years. His refusal to know might be irresponsible; it might amount to a failure to engage fully in the (not just financial) planning that is part of a parent's commitment to his children. Whether one has a moral responsibility to know one's genetic condition, and the strength of that responsibility, will depend upon the particulars of the situation. In all likelihood, however, a person's *responsibility* to know will not depend upon the strength of his or her *desire* to know or not to know.

The idea of having a responsibility to know can seem jarring at first. We are drawn to a picture of an individual, faced with the prospect of knowing, weighing how that knowledge would affect her personally. The thought that someone ought to know seems to go against our cultural assumptions, as if such an obligation were an unwelcome interference in the private relationship a person has with her own life. The problem with this picture of solitary individuals contemplating whether to know about their future is that it fits so few of us.

How should the responsibility of knowing be balanced against the possible burden and cost of knowing? There is probably little of use that can be said at this level of generality, since much will depend on the circumstances. The 50-year-old who has minor children, by birth or adoption, is in a different situation from the footloose 20-year-old. In any event it should be clear that if we are to make responsible decisions about accepting or refusing medical information, we must begin by acknowledging that these decisions affect others as well as ourselves.

The Non-Identity Problem and Genetic Harms— The Case of Wrongful Handicaps

DAN W. BROCK

In this essay Brock scrutinizes the claim that it would be wrong not to prevent devastating genetic diseases or disabilities in a child. Some have held that failing to prevent an impairment is wrong because the child would be better off if the impairment were prevented. But Brock finds this view incoherent, arguing on logical grounds that a failure to prevent a serious disability cannot in fact *wrong the child.* He maintains instead that although failing to prevent a serious disability does not wrong the child, it is nevertheless wrong for "non-person-affecting" reasons.

The world-wide Human Genome Project (HGP) will produce information permitting genetic screening for an increasing number of genetic diseases and genetically based increased susceptibilities to diseases and other harmful conditions. In the foreseeable future, the capacities for preconception and prenatal screening for these diseases and conditions will almost certainly far outstrip our capacities for genetic therapy to correct for the harmful genes and their effects. The vast majority of decisions faced by prospective parents, consequently, will be whether to screen for par-

ticular genetic risks and/or conditions and when they are found to be present, whether to avoid conception or to terminate a pregnancy. Moreover, the vast majority of genetic risks that will be subject to screening will not be for diseases or conditions incompatible with life worth living—wrongful life cases—but rather for diseases and conditions sufficiently less severe or grave as to be compatible with having a life worth living. These genetic conditions and diseases will take different forms and many factors will affect the moral case for preventing them. But there is a systematic objection to all preconception wrongful handicap cases which must be resolved to clear the way for judgment about specific cases.

From *Bioethics*, vol. 9, no. 3, pp. 269–75, 1995. Reprinted with permission of Blackwell Publishing, Ltd. and the author.

To fix attention on the general sort of case and problem in question, which is not restricted to the context of genetic disease, let us alter slightly a case of Derek Parfit's, call it case P1, in which a woman is told by her physician that she should not attempt to become pregnant now because she has a condition that would be highly likely to result in mild retardation in her child.[1] Her condition is easily and fully treatable by taking a quite safe medication for one month. If she takes the medication and delays becoming pregnant for two months there is every reason to expect that she will have a normal child. Because she is impatient to begin a family she refuses to wait, gets pregnant now, and gives birth to a child who is mildly retarded. In common sense moral views, the woman in case P1 acts wrongly, and in particular wrongs her child, by not preventing its handicap for such a morally trivial reason. Most people would likely say that her action in P1 is no different morally than if she failed to take the medicine in a case, P2, identical to P1 except that the condition is discovered, and so the medicine must be taken, after conception and when she is already pregnant, or if, in a case, P3, she failed to provide a similar medication to her born child, in each case necessary to prevent a comparable degree of mental retardation to her child. On what Derek Parfit has called the "no difference" view, the view of common sense morality that he endorses, her failure to employ the medication to prevent her child's mental retardation would be equally and seriously wrong in each of the three cases. But her action in P1, which is analogous in relevant respects to genetic screening to prevent handicaps, has a special feature that makes it not so easily shown to be wrong as common sense morality might suppose.

In wrongful handicap cases such as this, the person's handicap leaves him with a worthwhile life, a life that is better than no life at all. The philosophical problem, as noted earlier, is how this judgment is compatible with the common view that it would be wrong not to prevent the handicap. The difficulty is that it would *not* be better for the person with the handicap to have had it prevented since that can only be done by preventing him from ever having existed at all; preventing the handicap would deny the individual a worthwhile, although handicapped,

life. The handicap could be prevented either by conceiving at a different time and/or under different circumstances, in which case a different child would be conceived, or by terminating the pregnancy, in which case this child never comes into existence and a different child may or may not be conceived instead. None of those possible means of preventing the handicap would be better for the child with the handicap—all would deny him or her a worthwhile life. But if the mother's failing to prevent the handicap has not made her child worse off, then failing to prevent the handicap does not harm her child. And if she does not harm her child by not preventing its handicap, then why does she wrong her child morally by failing to do so? How could making her child better off by giving it a life worth living, albeit a life with a significant handicap, wrong it? A wrong action must be bad for someone, but her choice to create her child with its handicap is bad for no one. So actions with effects for a child that would constitute seriously wrongful child abuse if done to an existing child are no harm, and so no wrong, if done to a child when they are inextricable from the choice to bring that child into existence with a worthwhile life. This argument threatens to undermine common and firmly held moral judgments, as well as public policy measures, concerning prevention of such handicaps to children.

Some philosophers accept the implications of this argument and hold that in choices of whether a particular individual will be brought into existence, only the interests of actual persons, not the interests of possible persons, which here means the individual whose existence is in question, are relevant to the choice.[2] So in case P1 above, the effects on the parents and the broader society, such as the greater childrearing costs and difficulties of having the mildly retarded child instead of taking the medication and having a normal child two months later are relevant to the decision; but the effects on and interests of the child itself who would be mildly retarded are not relevant. In P2 and P3, on the other hand, the fundamental reason the woman's action would be wrong is the easily preventable harm that she causes her child, or allows it to suffer.

I share with Parfit the no difference view that the woman's action would be equally wrong in P1,

P2, and P3. As Parfit notes, the difficulty is identifying and formulating the moral principle on the basis of which the woman's actions in all three cases are equally wrong, and which therefore remedies the limits of traditional ethical theories and their principles of beneficence—doing good—and non-maleficence—not causing or preventing harm. Perhaps the most natural way of trying to account for the moral wrong in wrongful handicap cases is to abandon the feature of the moral principles we appealed to above that generates the difficulty when we move from standard cases of prevention of harm to already existing persons, as in P3 above, to harm prevention in what David Heyd has called genesis cases like P1. That feature is what philosophers have called the person-affecting property of principles of beneficence and non-maleficence, such as principle M:

> M: Those individuals responsible for a child's, or other dependent person's, welfare are morally required not to let it suffer a serious harm or handicap that they could have prevented without imposing substantial burdens or costs on themselves or others.

Since harms to persons must always be harms to some person, it may seem that there is no alternative to principles that are person-affecting, but that is not so. The alternative is clearest if we follow Derek Parfit by distinguishing "same person" from "same number" choices. In same person choices, the same persons exist in each of the different alternative courses of action from which an agent chooses. Cases P2 and P3 above were same person choices; the harm of mild retardation prevented is to the woman's fetus or born child. In same number choices, the same number of persons exist in each of the alternative courses of action from which an agent chooses, but the identities of some of the persons who exist in those alternatives are affected by the choice. P1 is a same number, but not same person choice—the choice affects *who*, which child, will exist. If the woman does not take the medication nor wait to conceive, her child is born mildly retarded, whereas if she takes the medication and waits to conceive she gives birth to a different child who is not mildly retarded. Arguably, the concept of "harm" is necessarily comparative, and so the concept of "harm prevention" may seem neces-

sarily person-affecting, which is why harm prevention principles seem not to apply to different person choices like P1. But it is a mistake to believe that non person-affecting principles, even harm prevention principles, are not possible. Suppose for simplicity that the harm in question in P1 from the mild retardation is suffering and limited opportunity. Then there would be suffering and limited opportunity in P1 if the woman were to choose to have the mildly retarded child which will not exist and so would be prevented if she made the other choice and took the medication while waiting to conceive a different normal child. An example of a non person-affecting principle that applies to P1 is:

> N: Individuals are morally required not to let any possible child or other dependent person for whose welfare they are responsible experience serious suffering or limited opportunity if they can act so that, without imposing substantial burdens or costs on themselves or others, any alternative possible child or other dependent person for whose welfare they would be responsible will not experience serious suffering or limited opportunity.

Although, of course, suffering and limited opportunity must be experienced by some person—they cannot exist in disembodied form so in that sense N remains person-affecting, N does not require that the individuals who experience suffering and limited opportunity in one alternative exist without those effects in the other alternative; it is a same number, not same person principle. The non person-affecting nature of a moral principle concerning the evils of suffering and limited opportunity is clearer still in the following principle:

> N': It is morally good to act in a way that results in less suffering and less limited opportunity in the world.

On N', the woman in P1 acts in a morally good way by taking the medication and waiting to conceive a normal child. In the genetic screening analog, a couple acts in a morally good way by taking steps not to have a child whom they learn from genetic screening will experience suffering and limited opportunity that another child they could have instead would not experience. On N′, it is morally good to act in a way that makes the suffering and limited opportunity "avoidable by substitution," as Philip G. Peters, Jr. has put it.[3]

There is time to mention only one apparent difficulty with this way of avoiding the non-identity problem. It is that it does not account for the apparent aspect of the common sense moral judgment about P1 that the woman specifically wrongs her child by not preventing its handicap, that is, that her child is the victim of her wrong and so has a moral grievance against her. Her child is the person with the handicap which should have been prevented, but applying N or N′ the handicap should not have been prevented for the sake of that child since doing so would have made that child worse off (it would never have had its worthwhile life). Rather, applying N or N′, it should have been done only for the sake of less overall suffering and loss of opportunity.

This apparent difficulty with N and N′ is that they fail to identify a victim of the harm done who as victim has a special moral complaint against its mother. But when we appeal to non person-affecting principles to criticize the failure of the mother to prevent harm in P1, her child who suffers the harm is not a victim who is worse-off and so does not have a special moral complaint against her for her failure which must be accounted for. Unlike the typical cases of harm and rights violations, her child *cannot* claim that *he* has a special complaint against her because he is better, not worse, off as a result of her not meeting her obligation. It is therefore unclear that our moral principles must account for any special wrong done the woman's child, as opposed to a non person-affecting wrong done. This suggests that non person-affecting principles like N or N′ may not only be adequate for cases like P1, but that they are indeed preferable to person-affecting principles like M precisely because they do not direct us to the special standpoint and complaint of a victim who has been made worse-off; principles for P1 and other wrongful handicap cases should not direct us to a victim in that way because there is no victim who has been made worse-off and so has a special complaint.

Abandoning person-affecting principles of beneficence and non-maleficence to account for wrongful handicap cases may thus be a promising approach to those cases, especially if reflection on them leaves us confident of our judgment that the woman in P1 acts wrongly, but weakens our earlier confidence that she wrongs her child in letting it be born handicapped. The latter confidence that she wrongs her child may be further weakened by reflection on wrongful life, not wrongful handicap, cases. Wrongful life cases arise only when the child has a life that is overall not worth living, a life that is worse than no life at all. That is the correct threshold for the claim that the mother acted wrongly in conceiving and/or carrying the child to term knowing how bad its quality of life would be. But since her child's handicap in P1 could also be prevented only by not conceiving it, or by terminating her pregnancy after it had been conceived, she would not wrong it by allowing it to be born unless its life is not worth living, which by definition in wrongful handicap cases like P1 it is not. If she does act wrongly, then perhaps it is correct to insist that she nevertheless wrongs no one, as N and N′ imply, and that there is no wrong to her handicapped child for which our principles must account.

What principally explains resistance to this view, I believe, is the handicap that her child suffers, but if her child suffered a similar handicap as a result of an accident for which no one was at fault and which no one could have prevented, there would be no temptation to insist that it had been wronged. The difference, of course, is that she could, and I believe should, have prevented the handicap, but she could not have prevented this child from having the handicap except by never having conceived it, and so we should resist saying that she wrongs this child. In same number, but not same person, cases such as this, if anyone is wronged it is the class—her children—whom she permits without adequate reason or justification to be worse off than her children could have been.[4] But if this class—her children—has been wronged, it is in a sense from which it does not follow that any member of that class—that is, any one child—has been wronged. This is exactly the implication that N and N′ have. I conclude that the apparent difficulty with abandoning person-affecting principles—that they fail to identify a victim of the wrong who has a special moral complaint in favor of impersonal principles like N and N′ in wrongful handicap cases—is no difficulty after all.

It is worth pointing out one implication of my argument that any moral principle which best fits the features of wrongful handicap cases will be a non person-affecting principle. Others have attempted to solve Parfit's non-identity problem by seeking to show that person-affecting principles, such as appeal to moral rights, can be successfully applied to it.[5] But my argument has been that appeal to any person-affecting moral principles in cases of wrongful handicap like P1 will mischaracterize the wrong done. The very features of any appeal to person-affecting principles that are typically their advantage—that they make the wrong a wrong done *to the child* and the loss from the wrong a loss suffered *by the child*—mischaracterize wrongful handicap cases. Non person-affecting principles are correct for wrongful handicap cases because the non-identity problem at the heart of those cases makes the wrong that is done *not* done to the child and the handicap *not a loss* that is suffered by anyone. No person-affecting account of wrongful handicap cases will be correct. The general philosophical non-identity problem is not an obstacle to the position that a woman in cases like P1 is guilty of causing a wrongful handicap.

NOTES

1. Derek Parfit, *Reasons and Persons*, Oxford University Press, 1984, ch. 16.
2. David Heyd, *Genethics: Moral Issues in the Creation of People*, Berkeley, CA: University of California Press. 1992.
3. Philip G. Peters, "Protecting the Unconceived: Nonexistence, Avoidability, and Reproductive Technology," *Arizona Law Review* 31, 1989, 487–548.
4. Peters, *op cit.*; Michael D. Bayles, "Harm to the Unconceived." *Philosophy & Public Affairs* 5, 1976, 292–304.
5. James Woodward, "The Non-Identity Problem," *Ethics* 96, July 1986, 804–31; see also, Derek Parfit, "Comments," *Ethics* 96, July 1986, 854–62.

Is Gene Therapy a Form of Eugenics?

JOHN HARRIS

Harris addresses a common claim in debates about genetic therapy—that while we have a duty to cure disease (to restore normal functioning), we do not have a duty to enhance or improve upon a normal healthy life. He rejects this distinction, arguing that "[t]here is in short no moral difference between attempts to cure dysfunction and attempts to enhance function where the enhancement protects life or health."

Eugenic A. *adj.* Pertaining or adapted to the production of fine offspring. B. *sb.* in *pl.* The science which treats of this. (*The Shorter Oxford English Dictionary*, 3rd edn, 1965).

It has now become a serious necessity to better the breed of the human race. The average citizen is too base for the everyday work of modern civilization. Civilized man has become possessed of vaster powers than in old times for good or ill but has made no corresponding advance in wits and goodness to enable him to conduct his conduct rightly. (Sir Francis Galton)

From *Bioethics*, vol. 7, no. 2/3 (1993), pp. 178–187. Copyright © Basil Blackwell Ltd. 1993.

If, as I believe, gene therapy is in principle ethically sound except for its possible connection with eugenics, then there are two obvious ways of giving a simple and straightforward answer to a question such as this. The first is to say "yes it is, and so what?" The second is to say "no it isn't, so we shouldn't worry." If we accept the first of the above definitions we might well be inclined to give the first of our two answers. If, on the other hand, we accept the sort of gloss that Ruth Chadwick gives on Galton's account, "those who are genetically weak should simply be discouraged from reproducing," either by incentives or compulsory measures, we get a somewhat different flavour, and one which might incline a decent person who favours gene therapy towards the second answer.

The nub of the problem turns on how we are to understand the objective of producing "fine children." Does "fine" mean "as fine as children normally are," or does it mean "as fine as a child can be"? Sorting out the ethics of the connection between gene therapy and eugenics seems to involve the resolution of two morally significant issues. The first is whether or not there is a relevant moral distinction between attempts to remove or repair dysfunction on the one hand and measures designed to enhance function on the other, such that it would be coherent to be in favour of curing dysfunction but against enhancing function? The second involves the question of whether gene therapy as a technique involves something specially morally problematic.

The Moral Continuum

Is it morally wrong to wish and hope for a fine baby girl or boy? Is it wrong to wish and hope that one's child will not be born disabled? I assume that my feeling that such hopes and wishes are not wrong is shared by every sane decent person. Now consider whether it would be wrong to wish and hope for the reverse? What would we think of someone who hoped and wished that their child would be born with disability? Again I need not spell out the answer to these questions.

But now let's bridge the gap between thought and action, between hopes and wishes and their fulfilment. What would we think of someone who, hoping and wishing for a fine healthy child, declined to take the steps necessary to secure this outcome when such steps were open to them?

Again I assume that unless those steps could be shown to be morally unacceptable our conclusions would be the same.

Consider the normal practice at IVF clinics where a woman who has had say, five eggs fertilized *in vitro*, wishes to use some of these embryos to become pregnant. Normal practice would be to insert two embryos or at most three. If pre-implantation screening had revealed two of the embryos to possess disabilities of one sort or another, would it be right to implant the two embryos with disability rather than the others? Would it be right to choose the implantation embryos randomly? Could it be defensible for a doctor to override the wishes of the mother and implant the disabled embryos rather than the healthy ones—would we applaud her for so doing?[1]

The answer that I expect to all these rhetorical questions will be obvious. It depends, however, on accepting that disability is somehow disabling and therefore undesirable. If it were not, there would be no motive to try to cure or obviate disability in health care more generally. If we believe that medical science should try to cure disability where possible, and that parents would be wrong to withhold from their disabled children cures as they become available, then we will be likely to agree on our answers to the rhetorical questions posed.

What Is Disability?

It is notoriously hard to give a satisfactory definition of disability although I believe we all know pretty clearly what we mean by it. A disability is surely a physical or mental condition we have a strong rational preference not to be in; it is, more importantly, a condition which is in some sense a "harmed condition".[2] I have in mind the sort of condition in which if a patient presented with it unconscious in the casualty department of a hospital and the condition could be easily and immediately reversed, but not reversed unless the doctor acts without delay, a doctor would be negligent were she not to attempt reversal. Or, one which, if a pregnant mother knew that it affected her fetus and knew also she could remove the condition by simple dietary adjustment, then to fail to do so would be to knowingly harm her child.[3]

To make clearer what's at issue here let's imagine that as a result of industrial effluent someone had contracted a condition that she felt had disabled or harmed her in some sense. How might she convince a court say, that she had suffered disability or injury?

The answer is obvious but necessarily vague. Whatever it would be plausible to say in answer to such a question is what I mean (and what is clearly meant) by disability and injury. It is not possible to stipulate exhaustively what would strike us as plausible here, but we know what injury is and we know what disability or incapacity is. If the condition in question was one which set premature limits on their lifespan—made their life shorter than it would be with treatment—or was one which rendered her specially vulnerable to infection, more vulnerable than others, we would surely recognize that she had been harmed and perhaps to some extent disabled. At the very least such events would be plausible candidates for the description ''injuries'' or "disabilities."

Against a background in which many people are standardly protected from birth or before against pollution hazards and infections and have their healthy life expectancy extended, it would surely be plausible to claim that failure to protect in this way constituted an injury and left them disabled. Because of their vulnerability to infection and to environmental pollutants, there would be places it was unsafe for them to go and people with whom they could not freely consort. These restrictions on liberty are surely at least prima facie disabling as is the increased relative vulnerability.

These points are crucial because it is sometimes said that while we have an obligation to cure disease—to restore normal functioning—we do not have an obligation to enhance or improve upon a normal healthy life, that enhancing function is permissive but could not be regarded as obligatory. But, what constitutes a normal healthy life is determined in part by technological and medical and other advances (hygiene, sanitation, etc.). It is normal now, for example, to be protected against tetanus; the continued provision of such protection is not merely permissive. If the AIDS pandemic continues unabated and the only prospect, or the best prospect, for stemming its advance is the use of gene therapy to insert genes coding for antibodies to AIDS, I cannot think that it would be coherent to regard making available such therapy as permissive rather than mandatory.[4]

If this seems still too like normal therapy to be convincing, suppose genes coding for repair enzymes which would not only repair radiation damage or damage by other environmental pollutants but would also prolong healthy life expectancy could be inserted into humans. Again, would it be permissible to let people continue suffering such damage when they could be protected against it? Would it in short be OK to let them suffer?

It is not normal for the human organism to be self-repairing in this way, this must be eugenic if anything

is. But if available, its use would surely, like penicillin before it, be more than merely permissive.

Of course, there will be unclarity at the margins, but at least this conception of disability captures and emphasizes the central notion that a disability is disabling in some sense, that it is a harm to those who suffer it, and that to knowingly disable another individual or leave them disabled when we could remove the disability is to harm that individual.[5]

This is not an exhaustive definition of disability but it is a way of thinking about it which avoids certain obvious pitfalls. First it does not define disability in terms of any conception or normalcy. Secondly it does not depend on *post hoc* ratification by the subject of the condition—it is not a prediction about how the subject of the condition will feel. This is important because we need an account of disability we can use for the potentially self-conscious gametes, embryos, fetuses and neonates, and for the temporarily unconscious, which does not wait upon subsequent ratification by the person concerned.

With this account in mind we can extract the sting from at least one dimension of the charge that attempts to produce fine healthy children might be wrongful. Two related sorts of wrongfulness are often alleged here. One comes from some people and groups of people with disability or from their advocates. The second comes from those who are inclined to label such measures as attempts at eugenic control.

It is often said by those with disability or by their supporters[6] that abortion for disability, or failure to keep disabled infants alive as long as possible, or even positive infanticide for disabled neonates, constitutes discrimination against the disabled as a group, that it is tantamount to devaluing them as persons, to devaluing them in some existential sense. Alison Davis identifies this view with utilitarianism and comments further that "(i)t would also justify using me as a donor bank for someone more physically perfect (I am confined to a wheelchair due to spina bifida) and, depending on our view of relative worth, it would justify using any of us as a donor if someone of the status of Einstein or Beethoven, or even Bob Geldof, needed one of our organs to survive."[7] This is a possible version of utilitarianism, of course, but not I believe one espoused by anyone today. On the view assumed here and which I have defended in detail elsewhere,[8] all persons share the same moral status whether disabled or not. To decide not to keep a disabled neonate alive no more constitutes an attack on the disabled than does curing disability. To set the badly broken legs of an unconscious casualty who cannot consent does not constitute an attack on those confined to wheelchairs. To prefer to remove disability where we can is not to prefer non-disabled individuals as persons. To reiterate, if a pregnant mother can take steps to cure a disability affecting her fetus she should certainly do so, for to fail to do so is to deliberately handicap her child. She is not saying that she prefers those without disability as persons when she says she would prefer not to have a disabled child.

The same is analogously true of charges of eugenics in related circumstances. The wrong of practising eugenics is that it involves the assumption that "those who are genetically weak should be discouraged from reproducing" or are less morally important than other persons and that compulsory measures to prevent them reproducing might be defensible.

It is not that the genetically weak should be discouraged from reproducing but that everyone should be discouraged from reproducing children who will be significantly harmed by their genetic constitution.[9]

Indeed, gene therapy offers the prospect of enabling the genetically weak to reproduce and give birth to the genetically strong. It is to this prospect and to possible objections to it that we must now turn.

In so far as gene therapy might be used to delete specific genetic disorders in individuals or repair damage that had occurred genetically or in any other way, it seems straightforwardly analogous to any other sort of therapy and to fail to use it would be deliberately to harm those individuals whom its use would protect.

It might thus, as we have just noted, enable individuals with genetic defects to be sure of having healthy rather than harmed children and thus liberate them from the terrible dilemma of whether or not to risk having children with genetic defects.

Suppose now that it becomes possible to use gene therapy to introduce into the human genome genes coding for antibodies to major infections like AIDS,

hepatitis B, malaria and others, or coding for repair enzymes which could correct the most frequently occurring defects caused by radiation damage, or which could retard the ageing process and so lead to greater health longevity, or which might remove predispositions to heart disease, or which would destroy carcinogens or maybe permit human beings to tolerate other environmental pollutants?[10]

I have called individuals who might have these protections built into their germ line a "new breed."[11] It might be possible to use somatic cell therapy to make the same changes. I am not here interested in the alleged moral differences between germ line and somatic line therapy, though elsewhere I have argued strongly that there is no morally relevant difference.[12] The question we must address is whether it would be wrong to fail to protect individuals in ways like these which would effectively enhance their function rather than cure dysfunction, which would constitute improvements in human individuals or indeed to the human genome, rather than simple (though complex in another sense and sophisticated) repairs? I am assuming of course that the technique is tried, tested and safe.

To answer this question we need to know whether to fail to protect individuals whom we could protect in this way would constitute a harm to them.[13] The answer seems to be clearly that it would. If the gene therapy could enhance prospects for healthy longevity then just as today, someone who had a life expectancy of fifty years rather than one of seventy would be regarded as at a substantial disadvantage, so having one of only seventy when others were able to enjoy ninety or so would be analogously disadvantageous. However, even if we concentrate on increased resistance, or reduced susceptibility to disease, there would still be palpable harm involved. True, to be vulnerable is not necessaily to suffer the harm to which one is vulnerable, although even this may constitute some degree of psychological damage. However, the right analogy here seems to be drawn from aviation.

Suppose aircraft manufacturers could easily build in safety features which would render an aircraft immune to, or at least much less susceptible to, a wide range of aviation hazards. If they failed to do so we would regard them as culpable whether or not a particular aircraft did in fact succumb to any of these hazards in the course of its life. They would in short be like a parent who failed to protect her children from dangerous diseases via immunization or our imagined parent who fails to protect through gene therapy.

I hope enough has been said to make clear that where gene therapy will effect improvements to human beings or to human nature that provide protections from harm or the protection of life itself in the form of increases in life expectancy ("death postponing" is after all just "life saving" redescribed) then call it what you will, eugenics or not, we ought to be in favour of it. There is in short no moral difference between attempts to cure dysfunction and attempts to enhance function where the enhancement protects life or health.

What Sorts of Enhancement Protect Health?

I have drawn a distinction between attempts to protect life and health and other uses of gene therapy. I have done so mostly for the sake of brevity and to avoid the more contentious area of so-called cosmetic or frivolous uses of gene therapy. Equally and for analogous reasons I have here failed to distinguish between gene therapy on the germ line and gene therapy on the somatic line. I avoid contention here not out of distaste for combat but simply because to deploy the arguments necessary to defend cosmetic uses of gene therapy would take up more space than I have available now. Elsewhere I have deployed these arguments.[14] However, the distinction between preservation of life and health or normal medical uses and other uses of gene therapy is difficult to draw and it is worth here just illustrating this difficulty.

The British Government's "Committee on the Ethics of Gene Therapy" in its report to Parliament attempted to draw this distinction. The report, known by the surname of its chairman as *The Clothier Report*, suggested "in the current state of knowledge it would not be acceptable to attempt to change traits not associated with disease."[15] This was an attempt to rule out so called cosmetic uses of gene therapy which would include attempts to manipulate intelligence.[16]

Imagine two groups of mentally handicapped or educationally impaired children. In one the disability is traceable to a specific disease state or injury, in the other it has no obvious cause. Suppose now that gene therapy offered the chance of improving the intelligence of children generally and those in both these groups in particular. Those who think that using gene therapy to improve intelligence is wrong because it is not a dimension of health care would have to think that neither group of children should be helped, and those, like Clothier, who are marginally more enlightened would have to think that it might be ethical to help children in the first group but not those in the second.[17]

I must now turn to the question of whether or not gene therapy as a technique is specially morally problematic.

What's Wrong with Gene Therapy?

Gene therapy may of course be scientifically problematic in a number of ways and in so far as these might make the procedure unsafe we would have some reason to be suspicious of it. However, these problems are ethically uninteresting and I shall continue to assume that gene therapy is tried and tested from a scientific perspective. What else might be wrong with it?

One other ethical problem for gene therapy has been suggested and it deserves the small space left. Ruth Chadwick has given massive importance to the avoidance of doubt over one's genetic origins. Chadwick suggests that someone

> who discovers that her parents had an extra gene or genes added . . . may suffer from what today in the "problem pages" is called an "identity crisis" . . . Part of this may be an uncertainty about her genetic history. We have stressed the importance of this knowledge, and pointed out that when one does not know where 50 per cent of one's genes come from, it can cause unhappiness.[18]

Chadwick then asks whether this problem can be avoided if only a small amount of genetic makeup is involved. Her answer is equivocal but on balance she seems to feel that "we must be cautious about producing a situation where children feel they do not really belong anywhere, because their genetic history is confused."[19] This sounds mild enough until we examine the cash value of phrases like "can cause unhappiness" or "be cautious" as Chadwick uses them.

In discussing the alleged unhappiness caused by ignorance of 50 per cent of one's genetic origin, Chadwick argued strongly that such unhappiness was so serious that "it seems wise to restrict artificial reproduction to methods that do not involve donation of genetic material. This rules out AID, egg donation, embryo donation and partial surrogacy."[20]

In elevating doubt about one's genetic origin to a cause of unhappiness so poignant that it would be better that a child who might experience it had never been born, Chadwick ignores entirely the (in fact false) truism that, while motherhood is a fact, paternity is always merely a hypothesis. It is a wise child indeed that knows her father and since such doubt might reasonably cloud the lives of a high proportion of the population of the world, we have reason to be sceptical that its effects are so terrible that people should be prevented from reproducing except where such doubt can be ruled out.

The effect of Chadwick's conclusion is to deny gay couples and single people the possibility of reproducing. Chadwick denies this, suggesting "they are not being denied the opportunity to have children. If they are prepared to take the necessary steps ('the primitive sign of wanting is trying to get') their desire to beget can be satisfied." What are we to make of this? It seems almost self-consciously mischievous. In the first place, gay couples and single women resorting to what must, *ex hypothesi*, be distasteful sex with third parties merely for procreational purposes, are unlikely to preserve the identity of their sexual partners for the benefit of their offspring's alleged future peace of mind. If this is right then doubt over genetic origin will not be removed. Since Chadwick is explicitly addressing public policy issues she should in consistency advocate legislation against such a course of action rather than recommend it.

But surely, if we are to comtemplate legislating against practices which give rise to doubt about genetic origins we would need hard evidence not only that such practices harm the resulting children but that the harm is of such a high order that not only would it have been better that such children had never been born but also better that those who want

such children should suffer the unhappiness consequent on a denial of their chance to have children using donated genetic material?

Where such harm is not only unavoidable but is an inherent part of sexual reproduction and must affect to some degree or other a high percentage of all births, it is surely at best unkind to use the fear of it as an excuse for discriminating against already persecuted minorities in the provision of reproductive services.

Where, as in the case of gene therapy, such donated[21] material also protects life and health or improves the human condition, we have an added reason to welcome it.

NOTES

This paper was presented at the Inaugural Congress of the International Association of Bioethics, Amsterdam, The Netherlands, 5–7 October 1992. I am grateful to the audience at that meeting and particularly to Dan Brock, Norman Daniels, Raanan Gillon, Douglas Maclean and Maurice de Wachter for helpful comments.

1. The argument here follows that of my paper "Should We Attempt to Eradicate Disability," published in the Proceedings of the Fifteenth International Wittgenstein Symposium.

2. See my discussion of the difference between harming and wronging in my *Wonderwoman & Superman: The Ethics of Human Biotechnology* (Oxford, 1992), ch. 4.

3. This goes for relatively minor conditions like the loss of a finger or deafness and also for disfiguring conditions right through to major disability like paraplegia.

4. In this sense the definition of disability is like that of "poverty."

5. See my more detailed account of the relationship between harming and wronging in my *Wonderwoman & Superman* (Oxford: Oxford University Press, 1992), ch. 4.

6. Who should of course include us all.

7. Davis, "The Status of Anencephalic Babies: should their bodies be used as donor banks?" *Journal of Medical Ethics*, 14 (1988), p. 150.

8. See my *The Value of Life* (London: Routledge, 1985 and 1990), ch. 1 and my "Not all babies should be kept alive as long as possible" in Raanan Gillon and Anne Lloyd (eds), *Principles of Health Care Ethics* (Chichester: John Wiley, 1993).

9. I use the term "weak" here to echo Chadwick's use of the term. I take "genetically weak" to refer to those possessing a debilitating genetic condition or those who will inevitably pass on such a condition. All of us almost certainly carry some genetic abnormalities and are not thereby rendered "weak."

10. Here I borrow freely from my *Wonderwoman & Superman: The Ethics of Human Biotechnology* (Oxford University Press, 1992), ch. 9, where I discuss all these issues in greater depth than is possible here.

11. *Ibid.*

12. *Ibid.*, ch. 8.

13. For an elaboration on the importance of this distinction see my discussion of "the wrong of wrongful life" in *Wonderwoman & Superman*, ch. 4.

14. *Ibid.*, ch. 7.

15. *Report of the Committee on the Ethics of Gene Therapy*, presented to Parliament by Command of Her Majesty, January 1992. London HMSO para. 4. 22.

16. In fact intelligence is unlikely to prove responsive to such manipulation because of its multifactorial nature.

17. There would be analogous problems about attempts to block the use of gene therapy to change things like physical stature and height since it might be used in the treatment of achondroplasia or other forms of dwarfism.

18. Ruth Chadwick, *Ethics, Reproduction and Genetic Control* (London: Routledge, 1987), p. 126.

19 *Ibid.*, p. 127.

20. *Ibid.*, p. 39.

21. I use the term "donated" here, but I do not mean to rule out commerce in such genetic material. See my *Wonderwoman & Superman*, ch. 6.

Genetic Enhancement

WALTER GLANNON

On the question of genetic enhancement, Glannon argues that a line of demarcation can be drawn between treatment and enhancement. Gene therapy is permissible if it is intended to ensure or restore normal functions, but it is morally illegitimate if it is aimed at enhancing functions beyond normal. He thinks there are several moral problems with enhancement, but his main moral concern is "that it would give some people an unfair advantage over others with respect to competitive goods like beauty, sociability, and intelligence."

Gene therapy must be distinguished from genetic enhancement. The first is an intervention aimed at treating disease and restoring physical and mental functions and capacities to an adequate baseline. The second is an intervention aimed at improving functions and capacities that already are adequate. Genetic enhancement augments functions and capacities "that without intervention would be considered entirely normal."[1] Its goal is to "amplify 'normal' genes in order to make them better."[2] In chapter 1 [of *Genes and Future People*], I cited Norman Daniels's definitions of health and disease as well as what the notion of just health care entailed. This involved maintaining or restoring mental and physical functions at or to normal levels, which was necessary to ensure fair equality of opportunity for all citizens.

From *Genes and Future People: Philosophical Issues in Human Genetics* by Walter Glannon, pp. 94–101. Copyright © 2001. Reprinted by permission of Westview Press, a member of the Perseus Books Group.

Insofar as this aim defines the goal of medicine, genetic enhancement falls outside this goal. Furthermore, insofar as this type of intervention is not part of the goal of medicine and has no place in a just health care system, there are no medical or moral reasons for genetically enhancing normal human functions and capacities.

Some have argued that it is mistaken to think that a clear line of demarcation can be drawn between treatment and enhancement, since certain forms of enhancement are employed to prevent disease. LeRoy Walters and Julie Gage Palmer refer to the immune system as an example to make this point:

> In current medical practice, the best example of a widely accepted health-related physical enhancement is immunization against infectious disease.
>
> With immunization against diseases like polio and hepatitis B, what we are saying is in effect, "The immune system that we inherited from our parents may not be adequate to ward off certain viruses if we are exposed to them." Therefore, we will enhance the

capabilities of our immune system by priming it to fight against these viruses.

From the current practice of immunizations against particular diseases, it would seem to be only a small step to try to enhance the general function of the immune system by genetic means. . . . In our view, the genetic enhancement of the immune system would be morally justifiable if this kind of enhancement assisted in preventing disease and did not cause offsetting harms to the people treated by the technique.[3]

Nevertheless, because the goal of the technique would be to prevent disease, it would not, strictly speaking, be enhancement, at least not in terms of the definitions given at the outset of this section. Genetically intervening in the immune system as described by Walters and Palmer is a means of maintaining it in proper working order so that it will be better able to ward off pathogens posing a threat to the organism as a whole. Thus, it is misleading to call this intervention "enhancement." When we consider what is normal human functioning, we refer to the whole human organism consisting of immune, endocrine, nervous, cardiovascular, and other systems, not to these systems understood as isolated parts. The normal functioning in question here pertains to the ability of the immune system to protect the organism from infectious agents and thus ensure its survival. Any preventive genetic intervention in this system would be designed to maintain the normal functions of the organism, not to restore them or raise them above the norm. It would be neither therapy nor enhancement but instead a form of maintenance. Therefore, the alleged ambiguity surrounding what Walters and Palmer call "enhancing" the immune system does not impugn the distinction between treatment and enhancement.

If enhancement could make adequately functioning bodily systems function even better, then presumably there would be no limit to the extent to which bodily functions can be enhanced. Yet, beyond a certain point, heightened immune sensitivity to infectious agents can lead to an overly aggressive response, resulting in autoimmune disease that can damage healthy cells, tissues, and organs. In fact, there would be a limit to the beneficial effects of genetic intervention in the immune system, a limit be-

yond which the equilibrium between humoral and cellular response mechanisms would be disturbed.[4] If any intervention ensured that the equilibrium of the immune system was maintained in proper working order, then it would be inappropriate to consider it as a form of enhancement.

To further support the treatment-enhancement distinction, consider a nongenetic intervention, the use of a bisphosphonate such as alendronate sodium. Its purpose is to prevent postmenopausal women from developing osteoporosis, or to rebuild bone in women or men who already have osteoporosis. Some might claim that, because it can increase bone density, it is a form of enhancement. But its more general purpose is to prevent bone fractures and thus maintain proper bone function so that one can have normal mobility and avoid the morbidity resulting from fractures. In terms of the functioning of the entire organism, therefore, it would be more accurate to consider the use of bisphosphonates as prevention, treatment, or maintenance rather than enhancement.

Some might raise a different question. Suppose that the parents of a child much shorter than the norm for his age persuaded a physician to give him growth hormone injections in order to increase his height. Suppose further that the child's shortness was not due to an iatrogenic cause, such as radiation to treat a brain tumor. Would this be treatment or enhancement? The question that should be asked regarding this issue is not whether the child's height is normal for his age group. Rather, the question should be whether his condition implies something less than normal physical functioning, such that he would have fewer opportunities for achievement and a decent minimum level of well-being over his lifetime. Diminutive stature alone does not necessarily imply that one's functioning is or will be so limited as to restrict one's opportunities for achievement. Of course, being short might limit one's opportunities if one wanted to become a professional basketball player. But most of us are quite flexible when it comes to formulating and carrying out life plans. Robert Reich, the treasury secretary in President Clinton's first administration, is just one example of how one can achieve very much in life despite diminutive stature. If a child's stature significantly limited his functioning and opportunities, then growth-hormone injections should be considered therapeutic treatment. If his stature were not so limiting, then the injections should be considered enhancement.

Admittedly, there is gray area near the baseline of adequate functioning where it may be difficult to distinguish between treatment and enhancement. Accordingly, we should construe the baseline loosely or thickly enough to allow for some minor deviation above or below what would be considered normal functioning. An intervention for a condition near the baseline that would raise one's functioning clearly above the critical level should be considered an enhancement. An intervention for a condition making one's functioning fall clearly below the baseline, with the aim of raising one's functioning to the critical level, should be considered a treatment. For example, an athlete with a hemoglobin level slightly below the norm for people his age and mildly anemic may want to raise that level significantly in order to be more competitive in his sport. To the extent that his actual hemoglobin level does not interfere with his ordinary physical functioning, an intervention to significantly raise that level would be an instance of enhancement. In contrast, for a child who has severe thalassemia and severe anemia, with the risk of bone abnormalities and heart failure, an intervention to correct the disorder would be an instance of treatment.

The main moral concern about genetic enhancement of physical and mental traits is that it would give some people an unfair advantage over others with respect to competitive goods like beauty, sociability, and intelligence. . . . Enhancement would be unfair because only those who could afford the technology would have access to it, and many people are financially worse off than others through no fault of their own. Insofar as the possession of these goods gives some people an advantage over others in careers, income, and social status, the competitive nature of these goods suggests that there would be no limit to the benefits that improvements to physical and mental capacities would yield to those fortunate enough to avail themselves of the technology. This is altogether different from the example of immune-system enhancement. There would be no diminishing marginal value in the degree of competitive advantage that one could have over others for the social goods in question and presumably no limit to

the value of enhancing the physical and mental capacities that would give one this advantage. Not having access to the technology that could manipulate genetic traits in such a way as to enhance these capacities would put one at a competitive disadvantage relative to others who would have access to it.

Advancing an argument similar to the one used by those who reject the treatment-enhancement distinction, one might hold that competitive goods collapse the categorical distinction between correcting deficient capacities and improving normal ones. This is because competitive goods are continuous, coming in degrees, and therefore the capacities that enable one to achieve these goods cannot be thought of as either normal or deficient.[5] Nevertheless, to the extent that any form of genetic intervention is motivated by the medical and moral aim to enable people to have adequate mental and physical functioning and fair equality of opportunity for a decent minimum level of well-being, the goods in question are not *competitive* but *basic*. In other words, the aim of any medical intervention by genetic means is to make people better off than they were before by raising or restoring them to an absolute baseline of normal physical and mental functioning, not to make them comparatively better off than others. Competitive goods above the baseline may be continuous; but the basic goods that enable someone to reach or remain at the baseline are not. Given that these two types of goods are distinct, and that they result from the distinct aims and practices of enhancement and treatment, we can affirm that enhancement and treatment can and should be treated separately. We can uphold the claim that the purpose of any genetic intervention should be to treat people's abnormal functions and restore them to a normal level, not to enhance those functions that already are normal.

As I have mentioned, genetic enhancement that gave some people an advantage over others in possessing competitive goods would entail considerable unfairness. A likely scenario would be one in which parents paid to use expensive genetic technology to raise the cognitive ability or improve the physical beauty of their children. This would give them an advantage over other children with whom they would compete for education, careers, and income. Children of parents who could not afford to pay for the technology would be at a comparative disadvantage. Even if the goods in question fell above the normal functional baseline, one still could maintain that such an advantage would be unfair. It would depend on people's ability to pay, and inequalities in income are unfair to the extent that they result from some factors beyond people's control.

We could not appeal to the notion of a genetic lottery to resolve the problem of fairness regarding genetic enhancement. For, as I argued in the last section [of *Genes and Future People*], such a lottery is better suited to meeting people's needs than their preferences, and enhancements correspond to people's preferences. Moreover, a lottery might only exacerbate the problem by reinforcing the perception of unfairness, depending on how losers in the lottery interpreted the fact that others won merely as a result of a random selection. One suggestion for resolving the fairness problem (short of banning the use of the technology altogether) would be to make genetic enhancement available to all. Of course, how this system could be financed is a question that admits of no easy answer. But the more important substantive point is that universal access to genetic enhancement would not be a solution. Indeed, the upshot of such access would provide a reason for prohibiting it.

Universal availability of genetic enhancement would mean that many competitive goods some people had over others would be canceled out colletively. The idea of a competitive advantage gradually would erode, and there would be more equality among people in their possession of goods. There would not be complete equality, however. Differing parental attitudes toward such goods as education could mean differences in the extent to which cognitive enhancement was utilized. Some parents would be more selective than others in sending their children to better schools or arranging for private tutors. So, there still would be some inequality in the general outcome of the enhancement. But quite apart from this, the process of neutralizing competitive goods could end up being self-defeating on a collective level.[6] More specifically, one probable side-effect of boosting children's mental capacity on a broad scale would be some brain damage resulting in cognitive and affective impairment in some of the children who received the genetic enhancement. The net social cost of using the technology would outweigh any social advantage of everyone using it. If no one is made better off than others in their possession of social goods, but some people are made worse off than they were before in terms of their mental functioning, then the net social disadvantage would provide a reason for prohibiting collective genetic enhancement.

There is another moral aspect of enhancement that should be considered. I have maintained that inequalities above the baseline of normal physical and mental functioning are of no great moral importance and may be neutral on the question of fairness. Although equality and fairness are closely related, one does not necessarily imply the other. Again, fairness pertains to meeting people's needs. Once these needs have been met, inequalities in the possession of goods relating to preferences are not so morally significant. Thus, if the idea of an absolute baseline implies that people's basic physical and mental needs have been met, and if people who are comparatively better or worse off than others all have functioning at or above the baseline, then any inequalities in functioning above this level should not matter very much morally. If this is plausible, then it seems to follow that there would be nothing unfair and hence nothing morally objectionable about enhancements that made some people better off than others above the baseline. Nevertheless, this could undermine our belief in the importance of the fundamental equality of all people, regardless of how well off they are in absolute terms. Equality is one of the social bases of self-respect, which is essential for social harmony and stability.[7] Allowing inequalities in access to and possession of competitive goods at any level of functioning or welfare might erode this basis and the ideas of harmony and stability that rest on it. Although it would be difficult to measure, this type of social cost resulting from genetic enhancement could constitute another reason for prohibiting it.

Yet, suppose that we could manipulate certain genes to enhance our noncompetitive virtuous traits, such as altruism, generosity, and compassion.[8] Surely, these would contribute to a stable, well-ordered society and preserve the principle of fair equality of opportunity. Nothing in this program would be incompatible with the goal of medicine as the prevention and treatment of disease. But it would threaten the individual autonomy essential to us as moral agents who can be candidates for praise and blame, punishment and reward. What confers moral worth on our actions, and indeed on ourselves as agents, is our capacity to cultivate certain dispositions leading to actions. This cultivation involves the exercise of practical reason and a process of critical self-reflection, whereby we modify, eliminate, or reinforce dispositions and thereby come to identify with them as our own. Autonomy consists precisely in this process of reflection and identification. It is the capacity for reflective self-control that enables us to take responsibility for our mental states and the actions that issue from them. Given the importance of autonomy, it would be preferable to have fewer virtuous dispositions that we can identify with as our own than to have more virtuous dispositions implanted in us through genetic enhancement. These would threaten to undermine our moral agency because they would derive from an external source.[9] Even if our genes could be manipulated in such a way that our behavior always conformed to an algorithm for the morally correct course of action in every situation, it is unlikely that we would want it. Most of us would rather make autonomous choices that turned out not to lead to the best courses of action. This is because of the intrinsic importance of autonomy and the moral growth and maturity that come with making our own choices under uncertainty. The dispositions with which we come to identify, imperfect as they may be, are what make us autonomous and responsible moral agents. Enhancing these mental states through artificial means external to our own exercise of practical reason and our own process of identification would undermine our autonomy by making them alien to us.

In sum, there are four reasons why genetic enhancement would be morally objectionable. First, it would give an unfair advantage to some people over others because some would be able to pay for expensive enhancement procedures while others would not. Second, if we tried to remedy the first problem by making genetic enhancement universally accessible, then it would be collectively self-defeating. Although much competitive unfairness at the individual level would be canceled out at the collective level,

there would be the unacceptable social cost of some people suffering from adverse cognitive or emotional effects of the enhancement. Third, inequalities resulting from enhancements above the baseline of normal physical and mental functioning could threaten to undermine the conviction in the fundamental importance of equality as one of the bases of self-respect, and in turn social solidarity and stability. Fourth, enhancement of noncompetitive dispositions would threaten to undermine the autonomy and moral agency essential to us as persons.

NOTES

1. Jon Gordon, "Genetic Enhancement in Humans," *Science* 283 (March 26, 1999): 2023-2024.
2. Eric Juengst, "Can Enhancement Be Distinguished from Prevention in Genetic Medicine?" *Journal of Medicine and Philosophy* 22 (1997): 125-142, and "What Does Enhancement Mean?" in Erik Parens, ed., *Enhancing Human Traits: Ethical and Social Implications* (Washington, DC: Georgetown University Press, 1998): 27-47, at 27. Also, Dan Brock, "Enhancements of Human Function: Some Distinctions for Policymakers," *Ibid.*, 48-69.
3. *The Ethics of Human Gene Therapy* (New York: Oxford University Press, 1997), 110. Instead of distinguishing between treatments and enhancements, Walters and Palmer distinguish between health-related and non-health-related enhancements. But I do not find this distinction to be very helpful.
4. Brock points this out in "Enhancements of Human Function," 59. Marc Lappe makes a more compelling case for the same point in *The Tao of Immunology* (New York: Plenum Press, 1997).
5. Kavka develops and defends the idea that competitive goods are continuous in "Upside Risks: Social Consequences of Beneficial Biotechnology," in Carl Cranor, ed., *Are Genes Us? The Social Consequences of the New Genetics* (New Brunswick, NJ: Rutgers University Press, 1994): 155-179, at 164-165.
6. Kavka, "Upside Risks," 167. Also, Brock, "Enhancements of Human Function," 60; and Buchanan et al., *From Chance to Choice* (New York: Cambridge University Press, 2000), chap. 8.
7. Rawls makes this point in *A Theory of Justice* (Cambridge, MA: Harvard Belknap Press, 1971), 7-11, and in "Social Unity and Primary Goods," in A. Sen and B. Williams, eds., *Utilitarianism and Beyond* (Cambridge: Cambridge University Press, 1982), 162. See also Daniels, *Just Health Care* (New York: Cambridge University Press, 1985).
8. Walters and Palmer present this thought-experiment in *The Ethics of Human Gene Therapy*, 123-128. As they note, Jonathan Glover introduced this idea in *What Sort of People Should There Be?* (Harmondsworth: Penguin, 1984).

9. Drawing on the work of Lionel Trilling and Charles Taylor, Carl Elliott discusses cognitive and affective enhancements that undermine what he calls the "ethics of authenticity" in "The Tyranny of Happiness: Ethics and Cosmetic Psychophar-macology," in Parens, *Enhancing Human Traits*, 177–188. Also relevant to this issue is Harry Frankfurt, "Identification and Externality," in Frankfurt, *The Importance of What We Care About* (New York: Cambridge University Press, 1989): 58–68.

Germ-Line Gene Therapy

LEROY WALTERS AND JULIE GAGE PALMER

In this essay Walters and Palmer examine arguments for and against germ-line gene therapy. Major moral arguments in its favor include that it may be the only way to prevent damage to some people, that it may enable parents to avoid passing on a genetic disorder to children or grandchildren, and that this kind of therapy "best accords with the health professions' healing role and with the concern to protect rather than penalize individuals who have disabilities." Among the arguments against germ-line therapy are that any unanticipated negative effects will hurt not only the patient but also his descendants and that the intervention fails to show proper respect for preimplantation embryos and implanted fetuses. Walters and Palmer conclude that some of the pro arguments are strong and all of the con arguments are weak.

. . . Standard medical therapies, like somatic cell gene therapy, are somatic treatments and do not correct genetic defects in a patient's germ line. They may allow patients to live and to reproduce, passing on genetic mistakes which, without treatment, would not be perpetuated. Preimplantation and prenatal selection, like somatic medicine, may also result in a higher incidence of germ-line genetic defects because, unless they employ selective discard and selective abortion of unaffected carriers, both strategies increase the number of carriers of genetic defects that are born.

Successful germ-line gene replacement, on the other hand, will not perpetuate genetic mistakes. It will not only cure the patient at hand; it will also prevent the disease in question from arising in that patient's descendants. Applied to heterozygous carriers on a large scale, it could theoretically eliminate chosen disease-causing genes from the human gene pool.

As long as germ-line gene therapy must be performed on human zygotes or embryos one at a time

after in vitro fertilization, it is likely to remain an expensive technology with limited use. Only if a technique is developed for performing gene replacement or gene repair within the reproductive cells of human adults—perhaps through the injection of highly refined vectors that "home in" only on those cells (or their precursors in males)—are we likely to see the widespread diffusion of germ-line genetic intervention for disease prevention. . . .

For What Clinical Situations Will Germ-Line Gene Therapy Be Proposed?

It is difficult to predict the precise context in which germ-line gene therapy will first be considered. Tables 1 through 4 show four scenarios where the issue of germ-line intervention may at least be discussed at some point in the future.

TABLE I   MODE OF INHERITANCE I

Both the wife and the husband are afflicted with a recessive genetic disorder. That is, both have two copies of the same malfunctioning gene at a particular site in their chromosomes. Therefore, all of their offspring are likely to be affected with the same genetic disorder.

TABLE 2   MODE OF INHERITANCE 2

Both the wife and the husband are carriers of a recessive genetic disorder. That is, each has one copy of a properly functioning and one copy of a malfunctioning gene at a particular site in their chromosomes. Following Mendel's laws, 25% of the couple's offspring are likely to be "normal," 50% are likely to be carriers like their parents, and 25% are likely to be afflicted with the genetic disorder.

TABLE 3   DISEASE CONDITION 1

A diagnosable genetic disorder results in major irreversible damage to the brains of affected fetuses during the first trimester of pregnancy. There is no known method for making genetic repairs in the uterus during pregnancy. If any genetic repair is to be made, it must be completed before the embryo begins its intrauterine development.

TABLE 4   DISEASE CONDITION 2

A diagnosable genetic disorder affects many different cell types in many different parts of the bodies of patients affected by the disorder. Somatic cell gene therapy that targets a particular cell type is therefore unlikely to be successful in combating the disorder. Therefore, germ-line gene therapy delivered early enough to affect *all* cell types may be the only feasible way to prevent disease in a particular future person.

The kind of situation described in Table 1 is likely to arise as medical care succeeds in prolonging the lives of people with genetic disorders such as sickle cell disease or cystic fibrosis. If somatic cell gene therapy is employed in significant numbers of people afflicted with recessive genetic diseases, some of those people's somatic cells will be able to function normally, but their reproductive cells will remain unchanged, thus assuring that they will be carriers of genetic disease to the next generation. If two such phenotypically cured people marry and have children, all or almost all of their children will be afflicted with the disease which their parents had. Each succeeding generation of these children will

need somatic cell gene therapy for the treatment of their disease.

Table 2 sketches a scenario frequently encountered by genetic counselors. In this case, germ-line genetic intervention could be viewed as an alternative to prenatal diagnosis and selective abortion of affected fetuses or to preimplantation diagnosis and the selective discard of affected early embryos. A couple might also elect germ-line genetic intervention in order to avoid producing children who are *carriers* of genetic defects, even if the children are not themselves afflicted with genetic disease. The parents would know that children who are carriers may one day face precisely the kind of difficult reproductive decisions that they as parents are facing.

In the type of case outlined in Table 3, somatic cell gene therapy might be effective if one could deliver it to the developing embryo and fetus during the earliest stages of pregnancy, that is, shortly after the embryo has implanted in the uterus. However, there is no known method of administering intrauterine therapy to an early first-trimester embryo, and a deferral of treatment until the second or third trimester would probably allow irreversible damage to occur. Preimplantation treatment, which would almost certainly affect the future germ-line cells as well as the future somatic cells, could be the only feasible approach to producing children who are not brain damaged, especially for couples who reject the alternative of selectively discarding early embryos.[1]

The scenario presented in Table 4 may be especially relevant to the development of particular kinds of cancers as a result of inborn genetic factors and subsequent mutations. For example, about 40% of people with a cancer of the retina called *retinoblastoma* transmit a dominant gene for this disorder to their children. In patients with this germ-line type of retinoblastoma, somatic mutational events that occur after birth seem to activate the cancer-causing gene and can result in multiple types of cancer developing in different cell types within the patient's body. For example, a kind of cancer called *osteogenic sarcoma* frequently develops later in life in patients who have been successfully treated for retinoblastoma.[2] With germ-line retinoblastoma, the only effective antidote to the development of multiple types of cancers may be early germ-line gene therapy that effectively repairs *all* of the cells in a developing embryo.[3]

The Needed Technological Breakthough: Gene Replacement or Gene Repair

As we noted earlier in this chapter [of *The Ethics of Human Gene Therapy*], the current technique for somatic-cell gene therapy relies on rather imprecise methods of gene addition. For safe and effective germ-line gene therapy, it seems likely that a more precisely targeted method of gene replacement or gene repair will be necessary. The most obvious reason for preferring gene replacement is that gene addition in embryos would result in their (later-developing) sperm or egg cells containing *both* the malfunctioning and the properly functioning genes. Thus, one undesirable effect of researchers' treating present or future reproductive cells by gene addition is that the researchers would be directly contributing to an increase in the number of malfunctioning genes in future generations. In addition, if any of the germ-line disorders are dominant, as retinoblastoma seems to be, then only gene replacement is likely to eradicate the deleterious effects of the malfunctioning gene.

Major Ethical Arguments in Favor of Germ-Line Gene Therapy

In this and the following section we will analyze the major ethical arguments[4] for and against germ-line gene therapy.[5] For this analysis we will make the optimistic assumption that germ-line intervention methods will gradually be refined until they reach the point where gene replacement or gene repair is technically feasible and able to be accomplished in more than 95% of attempted gene transfer procedures. Thus, the following analysis presents the arguments for and against germ-line intervention under the most favorable conditions for such intervention.

A first argument in favor of germ-line intervention is that it may be the only way to prevent damage to particular biological individuals when that damage is caused by certain kinds of genetic defects. This argument is most closely related to the last two scenarios presented above. That is, only genetic modifications introduced into preimplantation embryos are likely to be early enough to affect all of the important cell types (as in retinoblastoma), or to reach

a large enough fraction of brain cells, or to be in time to prevent irreversible damage to the developing embryo. In these circumstances the primary intent of gene therapy would, or at least could, be to provide gene therapy for the early embryo. A side effect of the intervention would be that all of the embryonic cells, including the reproductive cells that would later develop, would be genetically modified.[6]

A second moral argument for germ-line genetic intervention might be advanced by parents. It is that they wish to spare their children and grandchildren from either (1) having to undergo somatic cell gene therapy if they are born affected with a genetic defect or (2) having to face difficult decisions regarding possibly transmitting a disease-related gene to their own children and grandchildren. In our first scenario, admittedly a rare case, two homozygous parents who have a genetic disease know in advance that all of their offspring are likely to be affected with the same genetic disease. In the second scenario, there is a certain probability that the parents' offspring will be affected or carriers. An assumption lying behind this second argument is that parents should enjoy a realm of moral and legal protection when they are making good-faith decisions about the health of their children. Only if their decisions are clearly adverse to the health interests of the children should moral criticism or legal intervention be considered.

A third moral argument for germ-line intervention is more likely to be made by health professionals, public-health officials, and legislators casting a wary eye toward the expenditures for health care. This argument is that, from a social and economic point of view, germ-line intervention is more efficient than repeating somatic cell gene therapy generation after generation. From a medical and public health point of view, germ-line intervention fits better with the increasingly preferred model of disease prevention and health promotion. In the very long run, germ-line intervention, if applied to both affected individuals and asymptomatic carriers of serious genetic defects, could have a beneficial effect on the human gene pool and the frequency of genetic disease.[7]

A fourth argument refers to the roles of researchers and health professionals. As a general rule, researchers deserve to have the freedom to explore new modes of treating and/or preventing human disease.[8] To be sure, moral rules set limits on how this research is conducted. For example, animals involved in the preclinical stages of the research should be treated humanely. In addition, the human subjects involved in the clinical trials should be treated with respect. When and if germ-line gene therapy is some day validated as a safe and effective intervention, health care providers should be free to, and may have a moral obligation to, offer it to their patients as a possible treatment. This freedom is based on the professional's general obligation to seek out and offer the best possible therapeutic alternatives to patients and society's recognition of a sphere in which health professionals are at liberty to exercise their best judgment on behalf of their patients.

A fifth and final argument in favor of germ-line gene therapy is that this kind of intervention best accords with the health professions' healing role and with the concern to protect rather than penalize individuals who have disabilities. This argument is not simply a plea for protecting all embryos and fetuses from the time of fertilization forward. Both authors of this book [*The Ethics of Human Gene Therapy*] think that abortion is morally justifiable in certain circumstances. However, prenatal diagnosis followed by selective abortion and preimplantation diagnosis followed by selective discard seem to us to be uncomfortable and probably discriminatory halfway technologies that should eventually be replaced by effective modes of treatment. The options of selective abortion and selective discard essentially say to prospective parents, "There is nothing effective that the health care system has to offer. You may want to give up on this fetus or embryo and try again." To people with disabilities that are diagnosable at the prenatal or preimplantation stages of development the message of selective abortion and selective discard may seem more threatening. That message may be read as, "If we health professionals and prospective parents had known you were coming, we would have terminated your development and attempted to find or create a nondisabled replacement."

This argument is not intended to limit the legal access of couples to selective abortion in the case of serious health problems for the fetus. We support such access. Rather, it is an argument about what the long-term goal of medicine and society should be. In our view, that long-term goal should be to prevent disability and disease wherever possible. Where prevention is not possible, the second-best alternative is a cure or other definitive remedy. In cases where neither prevention nor cure is possible, our goal should be to help people cope with disability and disease while simultaneously seeking to find a cure.

Major Arguments Against Germ-Line Gene Therapy

First, if the technique has unanticipated negative effects, those effects will be visited not only on the recipient of the intervention himself or herself but also on all of the descendants of that recipient. This argument seems to assume that a mistake, once made, could not be corrected, or at least that the mistake might not become apparent until the recipient became the biological parent of at least one child. For that first child, at least, the negative effects could be serious, as well as uncorrectable.

Second, some critics of germ-line genetic intervention argue that this technique will never be necessary because of available alternative strategies for preventing the transmission of diagnosable genetic diseases. Specifically, critics of germ-line gene therapy have sometimes suggested that preimplantation diagnosis and the selective discard of affected embryos might be a reasonable alternative to the high-technology, potentially risky attempt to repair genetic defects in early human embryos. Even without in vitro fertilization and preimplantation diagnosis, the option of prenatal diagnosis and selective abortion is available for many disorders. According to this view, these two types of selection, before embryos or fetuses have reached the stage of viability, are effective means for achieving the same goal.

The third argument is closely related to the second: this technique will always be an expensive option that cannot be made available to most couples, certainly not by any publicly funded health care system. Therefore, like in vitro fertilization for couples attempting to overcome the problem of infertility, germ-line gene therapy will be available only to wealthy people who can afford to pay its considerable expense on their own.

The fourth argument builds on the preceding two: precisely because germ-line intervention will be of such limited utility in preventing disease, there will be strong pressures to use this technique for genetic enhancement at the embryonic stage, when it could reasonably be expected to make a difference in the future life prospects of the embryo. Again in this case, only the affluent would be able to afford the intervention. However, if enhancement interventions were safe and efficacious, the long-term effect of such germ-line intervention would probably be to exacerbate existing differences between the most-well-off and the least-well-off segments of society.

Fifth, even though germ-line genetic intervention aims in the long run to treat rather than to abort or discard, the issue of appropriate respect for preimplantation embryos and implanted fetuses will nonetheless arise in several ways. After thoroughgoing studies of germ-line intervention have been conducted in nonhuman embryos, there will undoubtedly be a stage at which parallel studies in human embryos will be proposed. The question of human embryo research was recently studied by a committee appointed by the director of the National Institutes of Health.[9] Although the committee specifically avoided commenting on germ-line intervention, its recommendation that certain kinds of human embryo research should be continued and that such research should be funded by NIH provoked considerable controversy. Critics of the committee's position would presumably also oppose the embryo research that would be proposed to prepare the way for germ-line gene therapy in humans.[10] Their principal argument would be that the destruction or other harming of preimplantation embryos in research is incompatible with the kind of respect that should be shown to human embryos.

Even after the research phase of germ-line genetic intervention is concluded, difficult questions about the treatment of embryos will remain. For example, preimplantation diagnosis may continue to involve the removal of one or two totipotential cells from a four- to eight-cell embryo. While the moral status of totipotential human embryonic cells has received scant attention in bioethical debates, there is at least a plausible argument that a totipotential cell, once separated from the remainder of a preimplantation embryo, is virtually equivalent to a zygote; that is, under favorable conditions it could develop into an embryo, a fetus, a newborn, and an adult. This objection to the destruction of totipotential embryonic cells will only be overcome if a noninvasive genetic diagnostic test for early embryos (like an x-ray or a CT scan) can be developed. Further, even if a noninvasive diagnostic test is available, as we have noted above, a postintervention diagnostic test will probably be undertaken with each embryo to verify that the intervention has been successful. Health professionals and prospective parents will probably be at least open to the possibility of selective discard or selective abortion if something has gone radically wrong in the intervention procedure. Thus, germ-line genetic intervention may remain foreclosed as a moral option to those who are conscientiously opposed to any action that would directly terminate the life of a preimplantation embryo or a fetus.

The sixth argument points to potential perils of concentrating great power in the hands of human beings. According to this view, the technique of germ-line intervention would give human beings, or a small group of human beings, too much control over the future evolution of the human race. This argument does not necessarily attribute malevolent intentions to those who have the training that would allow them to employ the technique. It implies that there are built-in limits that humans ought not to exceed, perhaps for theological or metaphysical reasons, and at least hints that corruptibility is an ever-present possibility for the very powerful.

The seventh argument explicitly raises the issue of malevolent use. If one extrapolates from Nazi racial hygiene programs, this argument asserts, it is likely the germ-line intervention will be used by unscrupulous dictators to produce a class of superior human beings. The same techniques could be also used in precisely the opposite way, to produce humanlike creatures who would willingly perform the least-attractive and the most-dangerous work for a society. According to this view, Aldous Huxley's *Brave New World* should be updated, for modern molecular biology provides tyrants with tools for modifying human beings that Huxley could not have imagined in 1932.

The eighth and final argument against germ-line genetic intervention is raised chiefly by several European authors who place this argument in the context of human rights.[11] According to these commentators, human beings have a moral right to receive from their parents a genetic patrimony that has not been subjected to artificial tampering. Although the term "tampering" is not usually defined, it seems to mean any intentional effort to introduce genetic changes into the germ line, even if the goal is to reduce the likelihood that a genetic disease will be passed on to the children and grandchildren of a particular couple. The asserted right to be protected against such tampering may be a slightly different formulation of the sixth argument noted above—namely, that there are built-in limits, embedded in the nature of things, beyond which not even the most benevolent human beings should attempt to go.

A Brief Evaluation of the Arguments

In our view, the effort to cure and prevent serious disease and premature death is one of the noblest of all human undertakings. For this reason the first pro argument—that germ-line intervention may be the only way to treat or prevent certain diseases—seems to us to be of overriding importance. We also find the third pro argument to be quite strong, that a germ-line correction, if demonstrated to be safe and effective, would be more efficient than repeated applications of somatic cell gene therapy. In addition, the final pro argument about the overall mission of the health professions and about society's approach to disabilities seems to us to provide a convincing justification for the germ-line approach, when gene replacement is available.

Our replies to the objections raised by critics of germ-line intervention are as follows:

1. *Irreversible mistakes.* While we acknowledge that mistakes may be made in germ-line gene therapy, we think that the same sophisticated techniques that were employed to introduce the new genes will be able to be used to remove those genes or to compensate for their presence in some other way. Further, in any sphere of innovative therapy, a first step into human beings must be taken at some point.

2. *Alternative strategies.* Some couples, perhaps even most couples, will choose the alternative strategies of selective abortion or selective discard. In our view, a strategy of attempting to prevent or treat potential disease or disability in the particular biological individual accords more closely with the mission of the health sciences and shows greater respect for children and adults who are afflicted with disease or disability.

3. *High cost, limited availability.* It is too early to know what the relative cost of germ-line intervention will be when the technique is fully developed. In addition, the financial costs and other personal and social harms of preventable diseases will need to be compared with the financial costs of germ-line gene therapy. It is at least possible that this new technology could become widely diffused and available to many members of society.

4. *Use for enhancement.* Prudent social policy should be able to set limits on the use of germ-line genetic intervention. Further, some enhancements of human capabilities may be morally justifiable, especially when those enhancements are health related. We acknowledge that the distribution of genetic enhancement is an important question for policy makers.

5. *Human embryos.* In our view, research with early human embryos that is directed toward the development of germ-line gene therapy is morally justifiable in principle. Further, we acknowledge the potential of a totipotential cell but think that the value of a genetic diagnosis outweighs the value of such a cell. We also accept that, if a serious error is made in germ-line gene therapy, terminating the life of the resulting embryo or fetus may be morally justifiable. In short, there is a presumption in favor of fostering the continued development of human embryos and fetuses, but that presumption can in our view be overridden by other considerations like serious harm to the developing individual or others and the needs of preclinical research.

6. *Concentration of power.* We acknowledge that those who are able to use germ-line intervention will have unprecedented ability to introduce precise changes into the germ lines of particular individuals and families. However,

in our view, it is better for human beings to possess this ability and to use it for constructive purposes like preventing disease in families than not to possess the ability. The central ethical question is public accountability by the scientists, health providers, and companies that will be involved with germ-line intervention. Such accountability presupposes transparency about the use of the technology and an ongoing monitoring process aimed at preventing its misuse.

7. *Misuse by dictators.* This objection focuses too much attention on technology and too little on politics. There is no doubt that bona fide tyrants have existed in the 20th century and that they have made use of all manner of technologies—whether the low-tech methods of surgical sterilization or the annihilation of concentration camp inmates with poison gas or high-tech weapons like nuclear warheads and long-range missiles—to terrify and to dominate. However, the best approach to preventing the misuse of genetic technologies may not be to discourage the development of the technologies but rather to preserve and encourage democratic institutions that can serve as an antidote to tyranny. A second possible reply to the tyrannical misuse objection is that germ-line intervention requires a long lead time, in order to allow the offspring produced to grow to adulthood. Tyrants are often impatient people and are likely to prefer the more instantaneous methods of propaganda, intimidation, and annihilation of enemies to the relatively slow pace of germ-line modification.

8. *Human rights and tampering.* It is a daunting task to imagine what the unborn and as-yet-unconceived generations of people coming after us will want.[12] Even more difficult is the effort to ascribe rights to [future] human beings. Insofar as we can anticipate the needs and wants of future generations, we think that any reasonable future person would prefer health to serious disease and would therefore welcome a germ-line intervention in his or her family line that effectively prevented cystic fibrosis from being transmitted to him or her.

In our view, such a person would not regard this intervention as tampering and would regard as odd the claim that his or her genetic patrimony has been artificially tampered with. Cystic fibrosis was not a part of his or her family's heritage that the future person was eager to receive or to claim. . . .

NOTES

1. It is perhaps worth noting that researchers performing somatic-cell gene therapy have carefully avoided diseases and subtypes of diseases that affect mental functioning. One thinks, for example, of Lesch-Nyhan syndrome, of certain subtypes of Gaucher disease and Hunter syndrome, of Tay-Sachs disease, and of metachromatic leukodystrophy.

2. We owe the suggestion of retinoblastoma as a candidate disorder to Kevin FitzGerald, S. J. We are also indebted to Nelson A. Wivel for information on the genetics of retinoblastoma. See Nelson A. Wivel and LeRoy Walters, "Germ-Line Gene Modification and Disease Prevention: Some Medical and Ethical Perspectives," *Science* 262(5133): 533–538; 22 October 1993. See also Stephen H. Friend et al., "A Human DNA Segment with Properties of the Gene That Predisposes to Retinoblastoma and Osteosarcoma," *Nature* 323(6089): 643–646; 16 October 1986; and Ei Matsunaga, "Hereditary Retinoblastoma: Host Resistance and Second Primary Tumors," *Journal of the National Cancer Institute* 65(1): 47–51; July 1980.

3. Although the genetics of the germ-line p53 gene mutation are more complex than the genetics of the germ-line mutation that causes retinoblastoma, p53 may turn out to be another important tumor suppressor gene to which the same comments apply. On the germ-line p53 mutation, see Frederick P. Li et al., "Recommendations on Predictive Testing for Germ Line p53 Mutations Among Cancer-Prone Individuals," *Journal of the National Cancer Institute* 84(15): 1156–1160; 5 August 1992; and Curtis C. Harris and Monica Hollstein, "Clinical Implications of the *p53* Tumor-Suppressor Gene," *New England Journal of Medicine* 329(18): 1318–1327; 28 October 1993.

4. Eric T. Juengst, "Germ-Line Gene Therapy: Back to Basics," *Journal of Medicine and Philosophy* 16(6): 589–590; December 1991.

5. Burke K. Zimmerman, "Human Germ-Line Therapy: The Case for Its Development and Use," *Journal of Medicine and Philosophy* 16(6): 596–598; December 1991.

6. For a detailed discussion of and justification for germ-line intervention in this setting, see Marc Lappé, "Ethical Issues in Manipulating the Human Germ Line," *Journal of Medicine and Philosophy* 16(6): 621–639; December 1991.

7. As noted above, already in 1962 Joshua Lederberg was arguing against H. J. Muller's proposals for improving the human gene pool through programs of "voluntary germinal

choice" by appealing to the prospect of rapid, global genetic intervention by means of germ-line gene therapy. See Joshua Lederberg, "Biological Future of Man," in Gordon Wolstenholme, ed., *Man and His Future* (London: J. & A. Churchill, 1963), pp. 265 and 269.

8. On the general issue of the freedom of scientific inquiry, see Loren R. Graham, "Concerns About Science and Attempts to Regulate Inquiry," *Daedalus* 107(2): 1–21; Spring 1978.

9. National Institutes of Health, Human Embryo Research Panel, *Report* (Bethesda, MD: NIH, 27 September 1994).

10. See, for example, the following critiques of human embryo research: "The Inhuman Use of Human Beings," *First Things* 49: 17–21; January 1995; Dianne N. Irving, "Testimony Before the NIH Human Embryo Research Panel," *Linacre Quarterly* 61(4): 82–89; November 1994; and Kevin O'Rourke, "Embryo

Research: Ethical Issues," *Health Care Ethics USA* 2(4): 2–3; Fall 1994.

11. Alex Mauron and Jean-Marie Thévoz, "Germ-Line Engineering: A Few European Voices," *Journal of Medicine and Philosophy* 16(6): 654–655; December 1991.

12. There is a rather substantial literature on this topic. See, for example, Ruth Faden, Gail Geller, and Madison Powers, eds., *AIDS, Women and the Next Generation* (New York: Oxford University Press, 1991); LeRoy Walters, "Ethical Issues in Maternal Serum Alpha-Fetoprotein Testing and Screening: A Reappraisal," in Mark I. Evans et al., eds., *Fetal Diagnosis and Therapy: Science, Ethics and the Law* (Philadelphia: J.B. Lippincott, 1989), pp. 54–60; and Lori B. Andrews et al., eds., *Assessing Genetic Risks: Implications for Health and Social Policy: Report* (Washington, DC: National Academy Press, 1994).

What Does "Respect for Embryos" Mean in the Context of Stem Cell Research?

BONNIE STEINBOCK

Steinbock examines the question of whether embryonic stem-cell research is consistent with proper respect for embryos. She argues that early embryos have less than full moral status—they are not due the same respect that we give persons—but they still have a "significance and moral value that other bodily tissues do not have." We must not use embryos in frivolous ways, she says, but "respect for embryos does not require refraining from research likely to have significant benefits, such as treating disease and prolonging life."

Like abortion, embryo research polarizes those who believe that embryos have as much of a right to life as any born human being, and those who maintain that embryos are not the kinds of entities that can have rights, because rights are restricted either to persons or to sentient beings.[1] However, those who deny that embryos can be possessors of rights need not strip them of moral significance altogether. There is a "third alternative," which is that although human embryos do not have full moral status, or human moral status, they are a form of human life and, as such, deserving of respect. This is the view that virtually every commission considering the issue has taken, including the

From *Women's Health Issues*, vol. 10, no. 3 (May/June 2000), pp. 127–30. Copyright © 2000 The Jacobs Institute of Women's Health. Reprinted with permission from Elsevier.

Human Embryo Research Panel of the National Institutes of Health (NIH)[2] and the Warnock Committee[3] in Great Britain. But what does "respect for embryos" mean? Is this simply an empty phrase, solemnly invoked by national commissions to soften or conceal the fact that they are endorsing killing embryos?

This was charged by Daniel Callahan,[4] who took the NIH Human Embryo Research Panel to task for failing to demonstrate (as opposed to merely asserting) that progress in scientific research depends on using human embryos. Callahan's point is not that respect for embryos entails that they never be destroyed or used in research. Rather, it is that the interests or goals to be accomplished by using human embryos in research must be shown to be compelling, and unreachable by other means. If less than compelling purposes can justify the destruction of embryos, or if compelling goals could be reached without destroying embryos, the idea that embryos are due profound respect rings hollow.

A similar view regarding embryonic stem (ES) cell research was expressed by Richard M. Doerflinger.[5] He cited advances in isolating and culturing adult stem (AS) cells and suggested that AS cells might be more clinically useful than embryonic cells because treatments based on a patient's own cells would avoid problems of tissue rejection[5]:

> No one can say with certainty at this time whether embryonic stem cells will have any clinical use that cannot equally well be addressed by other means. . . . At a minimum, an ethic that demands serious respect for human embryonic life will also demand that other, morally accepted alternatives be explored first. (p. 144)

The suggestion that other alternatives should be explored first makes sense only if there is some reason to believe that these alternatives are likely to yield comparable results. As a nonscientist, I cannot evaluate the research cited by Doerflinger. A recent article in *Science*[6] says, "Scientists are now speeding ahead with work on adult stem cells, hoping to discover whether their promise will rival that of embryonic stem (ES) cells." If that is so, it is possible that it will not be necessary to use ES cells for therapeutic purposes. At the same time, no one can accuse the National Bioethics Advisory Commission of simply assuming that there will be scientific benefits from embryonic stem cell research, or ignoring the possibility that AS could be used instead of ES cells. Its report, *Ethical Issues in Human Stem Cell Research*,[7] examines at great length the scientific evidence, and the possibility that AS cells can replace embryonic cells. It concludes that this is unlikely because ES cells have a property that AS cells do not: the ability to differentiate into all cell types. The report states[7]:

> . . . although much promising research currently is being conducted with stem cells obtained from adult organisms, studies in animals suggest that this approach will be scientifically and technically limited. . . . Moreover, because important biological differences exist between embryonic and adult stem cells, this source of stem cells should not be considered an alternative to ES and EG [embryonic germ] cell research. (p. ii)

This raises the intriguing question of how promising evidence for the utility of AS cells must be to pursue that line of research while delaying research using ES cells, out of respect for embryos. Certainly, if current research indicated that significant medical benefit was just as likely from research using AS, as opposed to ES, cells, respect for embryos would require us to use AS cells. However, no one is making this claim. Although no one can say for sure, the likelihood is that stopping research using ES cells and exploring instead the therapeutic possibilities of AS cells will result in the loss of significant medical benefits for people. A better alternative would be to conduct both kinds of research simultaneously. In any event, Doerflinger's reference to doing research with AS cells appears to be a red herring because it is clear from what he says in his Abstract that he rejects absolutely stem cell research that involves the destruction of human embryos. If such research is never morally acceptable, why go on about doing other research "first"? Doerflinger's views about embryo research derive from the right-to-life position on the moral status of the human embryo. They are unrelated to the "third alternative" which accords respect, but not full moral status, to the human embryo.

What, then, does respect for embryos require? It is important, first, to differentiate respect for embryos from respect for persons. Respect for persons means, as Kant instructs us, never treating persons as mere means to our ends, but always treating them as ends in themselves. This obscure phrase means that we must take seriously the ends—the projects, the goals—that other people have (at least if they are morally permissible ends). We cannot do this with embryos as they do not have ends of their own. Lacking the kinds of ends that persons have, embryos cannot be given the respect that is due to persons. Nevertheless, they have a significance and moral value that other bodily tissues do not have because they are "potent symbols of human life."[8] In this respect, embryos are like dead bodies, which also do not have interests.[9] Unlike dead bodies, embryos are potential human beings in the sense that, under certain conditions, embryos can develop into human persons. This potential gives them a significance and importance that does not belong to other cells of the body, and imposes restrictions on what it is permissible to do to embryos. We show respect for human embryos by not using them in unimportant or frivolous ways, say, to teach high school biology or to make cosmetics or jewelry. However, respect for embryos does not require refraining from research likely to have significant benefits, such as treating disease and prolonging life.

Embryonic stem cells can be derived from embryos remaining after infertility treatment (sometimes called "spare" embryos), or they can be derived from embryos made solely for research purposes using in vitro fertilization (IVF). Both involve the destruction of embryos. However, the NBAC report distinguished morally between the two. It recommended that an exception should be made to the present ban on federal funding of embryo research to permit funding of research using spare embryos, but it recommended that federal agencies should not fund research involving the derivation of human ES cells from embryos made solely for research purposes[7]:

> The primary objection to creating embryos specifically for research is that there is a morally relevant difference between generating an embryo for the sole purpose of creating a child and producing an embryo with no such goal. Those who object to creating embryos for research often appeal to arguments about respecting human dignity by avoiding instrumental use of human embryos (i.e., using embryos merely as a means to some other goal does not treat them with appropriate respect or concern as a form of human life). (p. v)

Certainly, if one takes the right-to-life view of human embryos, it is morally wrong to create embryos and then destroy them, regardless of the purpose. However, according to the right-to-life view, it is also wrong to create more embryos than will be transferred for implantation; that is, it is wrong to create spare embryos and also wrong to use them in research. Because NBAC does not reject using spare embryos in research, but only creating embryos for the purpose of research, the question is, what justifies this distinction? Here is NBAC's argument[7]:

> Embryos that are discarded following the completion of IVF treatment were presumably created by individuals who had the primary intention of implanting them for reproductive purposes. . . . By contrast, research embryos are created for use in research and, in the case of stem cell research, their destruction in the process of research. Hence, one motivation that encourages serious consideration of the "discarded-created" distinction is a concern about instrumentalization—treating the embryo as a mere object—a practice that may increasingly lead us to think of embryos generally as means to our ends rather than as ends in themselves. (p. 56)

The first part of this paragraph simply reiterates the difference between spare and created embryos; it does not explain why there is a moral difference between the two. The last part attempts to provide a justification for a moral difference, but it relies on the view I have argued is conceptually confused: namely, that embryos should be treated as ends in themselves.

If we reject the view that embryos are ends in themselves, what follows? In my view, it makes no moral difference whether one creates an embryo for reproductive purposes but ends up using it in research, or whether one creates an embryo for the explicit purpose of research. Respect for embryos is demonstrated by restricting their use to important ends. Research that promises to cure disease and save lives clearly qualifies.

The acceptability of this view depends, of course, on one's view of the moral status of the embryo. If embryos are people, there is a moral difference between creating embryos for reproductive purposes and creating them for research purposes. Creating embryos for birth benefits the embryo, whereas creating them for research purposes harms (kills) the embryos to benefit others. But if you reject the idea that preimplantation embryos are the kinds of beings who can be benefited or harmed,[1] creating embryos for research purposes is just as acceptable as creating them for reproductive purposes. Both are valid; neither is frivolous. Therefore, neither contravenes the principle of respect for embryos as a form of human life.

REFERENCES

1. Steinbock B. Life before birth: The moral and legal status of embryos and fetuses. New York: Oxford University Press, 1992.
2. National Institutes of Health. Report of the human embryo research panel. Bethesda (MD): National Institutes of Health, 1994.

3. Warnock M. A question of life: The Warnock report on human fertilisation and embryology. New York: Basil Blackwell. 1985:63–4.

4. Callahan D. The puzzle of profound respect. Hastings Center Rep 1995;25:39–40.

5. Doerflinger R. The ethics of funding embryonic stem cell research: A Catholic viewpoint. Kennedy Inst Ethics J 1999; 9:137–50.

6. Vogel G. Capturing the promise of youth. Science 1999; 286:2238–9.

7. National Bioethics Advisory Commission. Ethical issues in human stem cell research, Vol 1. Rockville (MD), 1999.

8. Robertson J. A. Symbolic issues in embryo research. Hastings Center Rep 1995; 2 5:37–8.

9. Feinberg J. The mistreatment of dead bodies. Hastings Center Rep 1985; 15:31–7.

Declaration on the Production and the Scientific and Therapeutic Use of Human Embryonic Stem Cells

PONTIFICAL ACADEMY FOR LIFE

In this official position statement on embryonic stem cells, the Roman Catholic Church declares that it is morally impermissible to produce or use living human embryos to obtain embryonic stem (ES) cells, to produce and then destroy cloned human embryos to acquire ES cells, or to use ES cells that others have already derived.

Ethical Problems

. . . Given the nature of this article, the key ethical problems implied by these new technologies are presented briefly, with an indication of the responses which emerge from a careful consideration of the human subject from the moment of conception. It is this consideration which underlies the position affirmed and put forth by the Magisterium of the Church.

The *first ethical problem*, which is fundamental, can be formulated thus: *Is it morally licit to produce and/or use living human embryos for the preparation of ES cells?*

The answer is negative, for the following reasons:

1. On the basis of a complete biological analysis, the living human embryo is—from the moment of the union of the gametes—a *human subject* with a well defined identity, which from that point begins its own *coordinated, continuous and gradual development*, such that at no later stage can it be considered as a simple mass of cells.

2. From this it follows that as a "*human individual*" it has the *right* to its own life; and there-fore every intervention which is not in favour of the embryo is an act which violates that right. Moral theology has always taught that in the case of "*jus certum tertii*" the system of probabilism does not apply.

3. Therefore, the ablation of the inner cell mass (ICM) of the blastocyst, which critically and irremediably damages the human embryo, curtailing its development, is a *gravely immoral* act and consequently is *gravely illicit*.

4. *No end believed to be good*, such as the use of stem cells for the preparation of other differentiated cells to be used in what look to be promising therapeutic procedures, *can justify an intervention of this kind*. A good end does not make right an action which in itself is wrong.

5. For Catholics, this position is explicitly confirmed by the Magisterium of the Church which, in the Encyclical *Evangelium Vitae*, with reference to the Instruction *Donum Vitae* of the Congregation for the Doctrine of the Faith, affirms: "The Church has always taught and continues to teach that the result of human procreation, from the first moment of its existence, must be guaranteed that unconditional respect which is morally due

From Pontifical Academy for Life, Vatican City, August 25, 2000.

to the human being in his or her totality and unity in body and spirit: The human being is to be respected and treated as a person from the moment of conception; and therefore from that same moment his right as a person must be recognized, among which in the first place is the inviolable right of every innocent human being to life."

The **second ethical problem** can be formulated thus: *Is it morally licit to engage in so-called "therapeutic cloning"* by producing cloned human embryos and then destroying them in order to produce ES cells?

The answer is negative, for the following reason: Every type of therapeutic cloning, which implies producing human embryos and then destroying them in order to obtain stem cells, is illicit; for there is present the ethical problem examined above, which can only be answered in the negative.

The **third ethical problem** can be formulated thus: *Is it morally licit to use ES cells, and the differentiated cells obtained from them, which are supplied by other researchers or are commercially obtainable?*

The answer is negative, since: prescinding from the participation—formal or otherwise—in the morally illicit intention of the principal agent, the case in question entails a proximate material cooperation in the production and manipulation of human embryos on the part of those producing or supplying them.

In conclusion, it is not hard to see the seriousness and gravity of the ethical problem posed by the desire to extend to the field of human research the production and/or use of human embryos, even from an humanitarian perspective.

The possibility, now confirmed, of using **adult stem cells** to attain the same goals as would be sought with embryonic stem cells—even if many further steps in both areas are necessary before clear and conclusive results are obtained—indicates that adult stem cells represent a more reasonable and human method for making correct and sound progress in this new field of research and in the therapeutic applications which it promises. These applications are undoubtedly a source of great hope for a significant number of suffering people.

CHAPTER 10

Euthanasia and Physician-Assisted Suicide

No one escapes death—or the ethical issues that come with it. Advances in medicine now raise the old life-and-death questions anew, force new ones more unsettling, and provoke answers that are disturbing even when plausible. In euthanasia and physician-assisted suicide, the bioethical heart of the matter is the moral rightness of killing or letting die for the good of the patient. The countless disputes on this terrain are often fierce and elemental, for they are the visible signs of deep conflicts among fundamental moral principles and perspectives. Doctors and nurses have sworn to preserve life and relieve suffering—but how to do this when the only way to end suffering is to end life? They understand the need to respect patient autonomy, the right of self-determination—but what should they do when the patient freely chooses to forgo all their best efforts and to embrace extinction? Or if the terminal patient, inching in agony toward destruction, asks them to cut short her torment by killing her with a lethal injection? Or if she begs only for some help in dying by her own hand? Or if she has never expressed a choice about such matters and has slipped into permanent unconsciousness, withering in pain to the inevitable? In such cases, what does beneficence or mercy or respect for autonomy or regard for the sanctity of life demand?

More so than most other issues in bioethics, the morality of euthanasia and physician-assisted suicide is tangled with legal and policy debates. The ethical questions are, of course, logically distinct from these concerns. You are not necessarily guilty of inconsistency if you think some instances of physician-assisted suicide are morally permissible but believe the practice should never be legalized because legalization might lead to abuses. Or you may, without contradicting yourself, favor legalization to protect patient autonomy but argue that suicide in any form is almost never morally acceptable. In the heat of controversy, these distinctions often get blurred, and a major task of good moral reasoning is to keep the focus sharp.

Nowhere was moral reasoning and conceptual clarity needed more and used less than in the recent case of Terri Schiavo. In 1990, when she was 26, Schiavo's heart stopped suddenly for reasons that are still unclear; by the time she was resuscitated, she had suffered catastrophic and irreversible brain damage. She was left in what doctors call a persistent vegetative state—wakeful but without consciousness or intentional behavior and almost no chance of significant improvement. In this condition she was sustained for years by food and water injected into her body through tubes. The question arose: Would Terri have wanted to be kept alive like this? Would she have chosen death over this perpetual darkness? She could not answer and had left no written record of her preferences. Her husband, Michael Schiavo, became her legal guardian and claimed that Terri had once told him that she would rather die than be artificially sustained as she eventually was. He said he wanted to have Terri's feeding tube removed so she could die with dignity. Terri's parents would have none of this and insisted that efforts to keep her alive should continue because she could eventually regain consciousness. Across the country people debated the moral questions. Would removing Terri's feeding tube be murder? Would allowing her to die be a permissible act of mercy? All the while, the legal war between Michael Schiavo and Terri's parents dragged on, with the former seeking permission to disconnect the feeding tube and the latter trying to thwart him. The essential legal issue was who had the legal right to decide Terri Schiavo's fate. The list of people who weighed in on both the legal and moral questions is long and diverse—President George W. Bush, state legislators, members of the U.S. Congress, bioethicists, religious leaders, pro-life groups, the governor of Florida, disability rights organizations, and a vast assortment of media commentators. Time after time, state and federal courts sided with Michael Schiavo, and in the end a judge gave permission to remove Terri's feeding tube. Thirteen days after its removal, on March 31, 2005, Terri Schiavo was dead.

In some ways the Schiavo case is unique, but several of its more disturbing features are not. Many compelling end-of-life dramas are being played out right now behind closed hospital doors, away from news cameras, the posturing of politicians, and the gaze of unaffected people. The need for informed moral reasoning to come to terms with the heart-breaking realities is acute—and likely to grow.

DECIDING LIFE AND DEATH

Almost all of the terms used to discuss the morality of killing and letting die are controversial to some degree. Even the meaning of *death*—a seemingly straightforward concept to most people—has been a point of dispute. Nevertheless, some helpful distinctions are possible. For the sake of clarity (and neutrality), **euthanasia** can be characterized as directly or indirectly bringing about the death of another person for that person's sake.[1] The term derives from the Greek words meaning "good death" and evokes the idea that causing or contributing to someone's end may bestow on that person a good. Death is usually considered an evil, perhaps the greatest evil, but many think it can be a blessing if it spares someone from a slow, horrific dying or a hopeless, vegetative sleep.

Many philosophers maintain that there are two forms of euthanasia. **Active euthanasia** is said to involve performing an action that directly causes someone to die—what most people think of as "mercy killing." Giving a patient a lethal injection to end his suffering, then, is a case of active euthanasia. **Passive euthanasia** is allowing someone to die by *not* doing something that would prolong life. It includes removing a patient's feeding tube or respirator, failing to perform necessary surgery, and refraining from giving life-saving antibiotics. The distinction between the two is thought to be essentially this: Active euthanasia is *killing*, but passive euthanasia is *letting die*.

To some people, this conceptual border between active and passive euthanasia is crucial for assessing the morality of euthanasia. They point out that whereas letting a patient die is sometimes morally permissible, deliberately and directly killing a patient is always wrong. The former practice is legal and officially endorsed by the medical profession; the latter is illegal and officially condemned. The American Medical Association sanctioned this dichotomy in a 1973 policy statement:

> The intentional termination of the life of one human being by another—mercy killing—is contrary to that for which the medical profession stands and is contrary to the policy of the American Medical Association.
>
> . . . The cessation of the employment of extraordinary means to prolong the life of the body when there is irrefutable evidence that biological death is imminent is the decision of the patient and/or immediate family.[2]

For many (including most physicians), passive euthanasia may be moral, but active euthanasia is not.

But not everyone thinks this active-passive distinction makes sense. Some argue that there is no morally significant difference between mercifully killing a patient and mercifully letting the patient die. In both situations the doctor causes the patient's death—by either intentionally doing something in the one instance or intentionally refraining from doing something in the other. Thus an act of euthanasia may be morally right or wrong, but the rightness or wrongness does not depend purely on this active-passive divide. Moreover in practice, distinguishing examples of active and passive euthanasia may not be as easy as some think. The usual view is that passive euthanasia can sometimes be performed by disconnecting a dying patient's feeding tube and respirator. But this event can also be seen as an instance of performing an action that directly causes someone to die—that is, active euthanasia.

If euthanasia in some form is morally permissible, its permissibility must be linked to the patient's consent. Thus bioethicists talk about euthanasia that is voluntary, nonvoluntary, or involuntary. **Voluntary euthanasia** refers to situations in which competent patients voluntarily request or agree to euthanasia, communicating their wishes either while competent or through instructions to be followed if they become incompetent (if they fall into a persistent vegetative state, for example). Patients can indicate what is to be done in incompetence by formulating an advance directive—usually a living will or a document designating a surrogate, or proxy, to act on their behalf. **Nonvoluntary euthanasia** is performed when patients are not competent to chose death for themselves and have not previously disclosed their preferences. (Incompetent patients include not only incapacitated adults but infants and small children as well.) In these circumstances, the patient's family, physician, or other officially designated persons decide for the patient. **Involuntary euthanasia** is bringing about someone's death against her will or without asking for her consent while she is competent to decide. It is illegal and considered morally impermissible by both those who approve and disapprove of euthanasia. It is therefore generally left out of moral debates, except perhaps in slippery-slope arguments warning that voluntary or nonvoluntary euthanasia will inevitably become involuntary.

Combining the terms *active*, *passive*, *voluntary*, and *nonvoluntary*, we can identify four kinds of euthanasia that have been the main focus in bioethics:

1. **Active voluntary**—Directly causing death (mercy killing) with the consent of the patient
2. **Active nonvoluntary**—Directly causing death (mercy killing) without the consent of the patient
3. **Passive voluntary**—Withholding or withdrawing life-sustaining measures with the consent of the patient
4. **Passive nonvoluntary**—Withholding or withdrawing life-sustaining measures without the consent of the patient

Legally and ethically, the starkest contrast among these is between active and passive euthanasia. Active euthanasia (whether voluntary or nonvoluntary) is unlawful, while passive euthanasia (both voluntary and nonvoluntary) is legal provided certain conditions are met. Judicial rulings have firmly established a right of patients to refuse treatment—and thus to have life-sustaining treatment withheld or withdrawn—even though the patient dies as a result. Withdrawing or withholding treatment from an incompetent patient is generally legal if the patient has left instructions or if an appropriate person can be chosen to make the necessary decisions. Contemporary moral debate centers more on active than on passive euthanasia. There is considerable agreement about the moral rightness of allowing a patient to die but intense controversy about the permissibility of deliberately causing a patient's death (by administering a lethal injection, for example), whether the act is considered voluntary or nonvoluntary.

Recently, disputes over euthanasia have raged alongside arguments about **physician-assisted suicide**, in which a patient takes his own life with the aid of a physician. In a typical scenario, a patient asks the physician for help in committing suicide, the physician assists the patient by prescribing lethal doses of drugs or explaining a

LEGAL BRIEF

Euthanasia and Assisted Suicide: Major Developments

1990 In *Cruzan v. Director, Missouri Department of Health*, the U.S. Supreme Court recognizes the right of patients to refuse treatment (essentially a "right to die") and finds constitutional justification for living wills and surrogates who make medical decisions for incompetent patients.

1994 Oregon passes the Death With Dignity Act, legalizing the use of physician-assisted suicide under specific conditions. It permits doctors to prescribe drugs that terminally ill patients can use to commit suicide.

1997 In separate cases—*Washington v. Glucksberg* and *Vacco v. Quill*—the Supreme Court rules that there is no constitutional right to physician-assisted suicide but notes that each state may establish its own policy on the issue. It explicitly acknowledges a distinction between assisted suicide and the withdrawal of life-sustaining treatment.

2001 U.S. Attorney General John Ashcroft tries to thwart the Oregon right-to-die law by authorizing the Drug Enforcement Agency to act against physicians prescribing drugs for assisted suicide.

2006 The Supreme Court rules that the Justice Department (headed by Ashcroft and later Alberto Gonzales) had no authority to interfere with physicians acting under the Oregon law.

---

method of suicide, and the patient—not the physician—performs the final act that causes death. In contrast, in active euthanasia the physician performs the final act. Many argue that this difference in the ultimate cause of death implies a difference in moral responsibility. In physician-assisted suicide, the patient is thought to bear ultimate moral responsibility for the taking of life. Others doubt that any distinction in ultimate causes can amount to a moral difference. Thus they contend that physician-assisted suicide and active voluntary euthanasia are morally equivalent. What is the moral difference, they ask, between a physician helping a patient die by (1) administering a lethal injection upon request or (2) prescribing a lethal dose of medications upon request?

The American Medical Association has denounced physician-assisted suicide as unethical and inconsistent with physicians' duty to promote healing and preserve life. Surveys suggest, however, that many doctors support the use of physician-assisted suicide, and up to half of adults believe it should be legal in cases of terminal illness or incurable disease with severe pain. To date, it is legal only in Oregon, but the Supreme Court has ruled that states may legalize or prohibit it as they see fit.

Part of the difficulty of making everyday moral decisions about end-of-life situations is that death itself is not so easy to define. Traditionally death was understood to occur when breathing and heartbeat ceased. A person who wasn't breathing and had no heartbeat was dead. But thanks to modern medicine, machines can maintain someone's breathing and heartbeat indefinitely—even though there is permanent loss of all brain function. Heart and lungs keep going, but the individual is irreversibly brain-dead and can remain that way for decades. By the traditional standard, the individual is alive, but this seems counterintuitive.

We seem to need a new concept of death—an important consideration since any notion we adopt would dramatically influence our judgments about morally permissible behavior toward

IN DEPTH
EUTHANASIA AND ASSISTED SUICIDE: WHAT DOCTORS THINK AND DO

In 2000 a large survey of oncologists revealed that:

- **22.5%** supported the use of physician-assisted suicide for a terminally ill patient

with "unremitting pain"; **6.5%** favored active euthanasia in these circumstances.
- **56.2%** had received requests from patients for physician-assisted suicide; **38.2%**, for active euthanasia.
- **10.8%** had performed physician-assisted suicide; **3.7%**, active euthanasia.

Ezekiel J. Emanuel, Diane Fairclough, Brian Clarridge, et al., "Attitudes and Practices of U.S. Oncologists Regarding Euthanasia and Physician-Assisted Suicide," *Annals of Internal Medicine* 133.7 (3 October 2000), 527–32.

the living and the dead. If we judge an individual to be dead, then we would presumably think her no longer a person. If she is no longer a person, then it would seem to be permissible to disconnect all life support, harvest organs from the body for transplant, or prepare the body for burial. But if, despite appearances, she is still a person, wouldn't doing any of these things be murder? If so, those who perform these acts would be morally and legally culpable.

In 1968 a committee at Harvard Medical School formulated a new way of conceiving death, a perspective that has since become the standard in legal and medical matters. According to this *whole brain* view of death, an individual should be judged dead when all brain functions permanently cease. Brain death means genuine death. But several experts take issue with this view. They point out that some physiological processes such as respiration are partly independent of brain functions, and individuals that many would regard as dead (those in persistent vegetative states, for example) may have some residual brain activity. By the whole brain standard, Terri Schiavo, being wakeful but lacking consciousness, was alive until all brain activity stopped. To some, this consequence makes sense; to others, it seems odd. A better notion of death, some argue, is the *higher brain* view, which says that an individual should be considered dead when the higher brain operations responsible for consciousness permanently shut down. The thought

behind this standard is that individuals are dead when they are no longer persons, regardless of what physiological activity persists, and individuals are no longer persons when consciousness permanently terminates. By the higher brain criterion, Terri Schiavo died when her higher brain functions permanently stopped, even though other brain activity continued for years. Again, some would find this judgment plausible; others, bizarre.

AUTONOMY, MERCY, AND HARM

Let us examine the two main flashpoints in end-of-life bioethics: active voluntary euthanasia and physician-assisted suicide. We can focus mostly on the former since arguments for and against it are largely relevant to the latter.

What arguments might be offered to support active voluntary euthanasia? The strongest one derives from the principle of autonomy—a person's inherent right of self-determination. Proponents say that respecting autonomous persons means respecting their autonomous choices, including the choice to end their lives in their own way. Their right is preeminent, its only limit marking the point where their choices bring harm to others. As one philosopher explains it,

People have an interest in making important decisions about their lives in accordance with their own conception of how they want their lives to go. In exercising autonomy or self-determination, people take responsibility for their lives; since dying is a part of life, choices about the manner of their dying and the timing of their death are, for many people, part of what is involved in taking responsibility for their lives. Many people are concerned about what the last phase of their lives will be like, not merely because of fears that their dying might involve them in great suffering, but also because of the desire to retain dignity and as much control over their lives as possible during this phase. . . . There is no single, objectively correct answer as to when, if at all, life becomes a burden and unwanted. But that simply points up the importance of individuals being able to decide autonomously for themselves whether their own lives retain sufficient quality and dignity to make life worth living.[3]

Proponents believe that this right to die, though strong, does not necessarily compel others. Almost no one who seriously urges the autonomy argument thinks that having a right to die forces a duty on others (physicians, for example) to help in the dying.

Another major argument for active euthanasia appeals to the principle of beneficence, or mercy: If we are in a position to relieve the severe suffering of another without excessive cost to ourselves, we have a duty to do so. To refuse would be cruel, inhumane, and wrong. The argument would run something like this: If a competent, hopelessly ill patient in unrelieved agony requests help to be put out of his misery, we may have a duty to bring about his death. As bioethicist Dan W. Brock says,

> When there is a life-sustaining treatment that, if forgone, will lead relatively quickly to death [passive euthanasia], then doing so can bring an end to these patients' suffering without recourse to [active] euthanasia. For patients receiving no such treatment, however, [active] euthanasia may be the only release from their otherwise prolonged suffering and agony. This argument from mercy has always been the strongest argument for euthanasia in those cases to which it applies.[4]

By these lights, active euthanasia is sometimes better than passive, for withholding or withdrawing treatment from a dying patient in unspeakable pain may only draw out his agony.

The argument from beneficence taps into very deep intuitions about the point of mercy killing. Consider this variation of a twice-told tale in bioethics: A truck overturns on the highway, pinning the screaming driver under the cabin as the wreckage bursts into flames. He is burning alive, and there is no hope of pulling him out of the fire. To avoid slow incineration, he begs the lone onlooker to smash him in the head with a rock to kill him immediately. Should the onlooker oblige him?

A common response to such horrific suffering, at least in cases of medical euthanasia, is to insist that the torment can almost always be relieved without resort to lethal means. It is likely that most patients who request euthanasia because of unrelenting pain and deep depression can get relief through improved pain treatment and enlightened psychiatric care. Therefore euthanasia or physician-assisted suicide is unnecessary. But many bioethicists are not convinced. They argue that there will always be some patients whose pain cannot be eased by any means short of death, or who have no access to adequate palliative care, or whose suffering is neither physical nor psychiatric but social, philosophical, or spiritual. The main cause of the suffering may be loss of dignity or independence or concern for loved ones who will be left behind.

Those who oppose active voluntary euthanasia give moral weight to autonomy and beneficence but argue that other considerations undermine the pro-euthanasia arguments. One such matter is the supposed moral difference between killing and letting die, or between active and passive euthanasia. The thought is that killing a person is morally worse than letting that person die. Killing is wrong; letting die is permissible. Thus giving a patient a lethal injection is wrong, but unplugging his feeding tube or respirator may be morally acceptable. Some think that killing is morally worse because it involves a person causing the death of another person (murder), while letting die is a matter of allowing nature to do its work. In the first, a person kills; in the second, a disease kills.

But critics deny that there is a morally significant difference between killing and letting die. If there is no difference, they can argue that since passive euthanasia is permissible, and it is morally equivalent to active euthanasia, active euthanasia must be permissible as well. James Rachels tries to demonstrate this no-difference thesis in a famous thought experiment about parallel cases:

> In the first case, Smith stands to gain a large inheritance if anything should happen to his six-year-old cousin. One evening while the child is taking his bath, Smith sneaks into the bathroom, drowns the child, and arranges things so that it will look like an accident.
>
> In the second, Jones also stands to gain if anything should happen to his six-year-old cousin. Like Smith, Jones sneaks in, planning to drown the child in his bath. However, as he enters the bathroom Jones sees the child slip, hit his head and fall face down in the water. Jones is delighted; he stands by, ready to push the child's head back under if it is necessary, but it is not necessary. With only a little thrashing about, the child drowns all by himself, "accidentally," as Jones watches and does nothing.
>
> Now Smith killed the child, while Jones merely let the child die. That is the only difference between them. Did either man behave better, from a moral point of view?[5]

Rachels concludes that any dissimilarity between killing and letting die does not make a moral difference.

Winston Nesbitt rejects Rachels' no-difference view, arguing that the real reason Smith and Jones seem equally reprehensible is that they are both *prepared to kill*. If we assumed that Jones is ready to let his cousin die but is not prepared to kill him, we would judge Jones less harshly than Smith. If this is correct, Nesbitt says, then Rachels fails to make his case.[6]

Some argue against active voluntary euthanasia by advancing another kind of distinction—between *intending* someone's death and *not intending but foreseeing* it. This difference is emphasized in the doctrine of double effect, an essential feature of Roman Catholic ethics (see Chapter 2). Applying the distinction to euthanasia, we get this principle: It is wrong to intentionally harm someone (cause her death) to produce a good result (release from suffering, for example), but it is permissible to do something intended to produce a good result (release from suffering), even if the action leads to unintended but foreseen harm (her death). The difference is that in the former, a bad thing is directly intended; in the latter, a bad thing is not intended, only foreseen. By this formula, it would be wrong for a physician to try to relieve the chronic misery of a terminally ill patient by deliberately giving her high doses of morphine to hasten her death. But it would be morally acceptable for that physician to give the patient the same amount of morphine with the sole intention of easing her pain, even though the physician foresees that she will die as a result. (Giving a dying, suffering patient extremely high does of analgesics to the point of unconsciousness and accelerated death is known as terminal sedation; provided the patient consents, it is legal and generally considered morally permissible in medical practice.)

Many question whether in practice this intended/unintended distinction can always be drawn as clearly as proponents assume. For example:

> In the case of euthanasia, just as in pain and symptom control, critics maintain, the physician's end may be the good one of relieving the patient's suffering. In neither case would death be wanted by the patient or the physician if the suffering could be avoided without it, but both patient and physician may be prepared to accept the patient's earlier death in order to relieve his or her suffering. Although the patient's death in the case of euthanasia may be the necessary means taken in the causal path to relief of suffering, it is the unavoidable side-effect following upon the relief of the patient's suffering in the causal path taken to achieve pain and symptom control.[7]

IN DEPTH
OREGON'S DEATH WITH DIGNITY ACT

Under Oregon's Death With Dignity Act (DWDA), terminally ill adults may get prescriptions from their physicians for lethal drugs and self-administer them. In 2006, Oregon doctors wrote 65 such prescriptions, and 35 patients used the medications. From 1997 to 2006, 292 patients died under the law. The law specifies requirements for both doctor and patient.

To request a prescription for lethal medications, the DWDA requires that a patient must be:

- An adult (18 years of age or older)
- A resident of Oregon
- Capable (defined as able to make and communicate health care decisions)
- Diagnosed with a terminal illness that will lead to death within six months

Patients meeting these requirements are eligible to request a prescription for lethal medication from a licensed Oregon physician. To receive a prescrip-

tion for lethal medication, the following steps must be fulfilled:

- The patient must make two oral requests to his physician, separated by at least 15 days.
- The patient must provide a written request to his or her physician, signed in the presence of two witnesses.
- The prescribing physician and a consulting physician must confirm the diagnosis and prognosis.
- The prescribing physician and a consulting physician must determine whether the patient is capable.
- If either physician believes the patient's judgment is impaired by a psychiatric or psychological disorder, the patient must be referred for a psychological examination.
- The prescribing physician must inform the patient of feasible alternatives to DWDA, including comfort care, hospice care, and pain control.
- The prescribing physician must request, but may not require, the patient to notify his or her next-of-kin of the prescription request.

Oregon Department of Human Services, "Death With Dignity Act," Oregon.gov, March 2007, http://www.oregon.gov/DHS/ph/pas (2 February 2008).

Others are skeptical of the intended/unintended principle itself. Their view is that even if it is wrong to intentionally do harm to bring about good, directly intending a patient's death may still be permissible because to her, *death may not be a harm*. If her pain is unbearable and untreatable, and she makes an autonomous request to die, then active euthanasia may be a blessing—and therefore within ethical bounds.

Probably the most straightforward arguments against active euthanasia and physician-assisted suicide are appeals to bad consequences. They make their case at the policy level, asking us to consider the ramifications of legalizing or widely accepting these practices. Often their logical shape is the slippery slope: Allowing active euthanasia or physician-assisted suicide will inevitably lead to heinous extensions or perversions

of the original practices. The usual worries are that legalization will lead quickly from active voluntary euthanasia to active nonvoluntary euthanasia to outright involuntary forms of killing. Or that physicians or families will start pushing unwilling or unsure patients toward assisted suicide or voluntary euthanasia. Or that physicians and nurses will become increasingly willing to give lethal injections to people who are elderly, mentally ill, chronically ill, uninsured, and disabled. As one philosopher explains it,

> [E]uthanasia as a policy is a slippery slope. A person apparently hopelessly ill may be allowed to take his own life. Then he may be permitted to deputize others to do it for him should he no longer be able to act. The judgment of others then becomes the ruling factor. Already at this point

euthanasia is not personal and voluntary, for others are acting "on behalf of" the patient as they see fit. This may well incline them to act on behalf of other patients who have not authorized them to exercise their judgment. It is only a short step, then, from voluntary euthanasia (self-inflicted or authorized), to directed euthanasia administered to a patient who has given no authorization, to involuntary euthanasia conducted as part of a social policy.[8]

The key premise in most slippery-slope arguments, then, is an empirical claim that a policy permitting active voluntary euthanasia or assisted-suicide will lead to unjustified killing (involuntary euthanasia, for example). Much of the debate therefore has centered on whether any good empirical evidence supports such a premise. Unfortunately, scientific research on the issue has been scant, with most of it focused on the Netherlands, where physician-assisted suicide and active voluntary euthanasia have been legal since 2002. (There is even less data on Oregon, where a law permitting physician-assisted suicide was passed by Oregon voters in 1994 but not green-lighted until the Supreme Court decision of 2006.) Thus both those who favor and those who oppose euthanasia and assisted suicide try to make their case with data from the Dutch experience. One question they want the research to answer is whether legalization of voluntary euthanasia has expanded the use of nonvoluntary euthanasia, for a significant expansion would seem to support slippery-slope arguments. Opponents of legalization point to all the instances of Dutch physicians performing active euthanasia without the patient's consent (approximately 1000 per year, or about 0.8 percent of all deaths nationwide). Proponents reply that most of those patients were already near death or had become incompetent after initially asking for euthanasia or that the euthanasia was passive, consisting of withholding or withdrawing treatment. Most of all, they emphasize that the few studies done so far do not demonstrate that legalization has significantly multiplied the cases of nonvoluntary euthanasia.

The best minds on all sides of these debates recognize the need for better evidence to assess the slipperiness of the slippery slope. But they also know that the *mere possibility* of abuses arising from allowing euthanasia or assisted suicide is not in itself a good reason to ban the practices. If merely possible dangers or abuses justified prohibiting a practice, then we would have good reason to disallow advance directives, surrogate decision-making, and any kind of voluntary passive euthanasia. For a slippery-slope argument to work, there must be good evidence that the bad consequences of taking the first step are probable and serious.

APPLYING MAJOR THEORIES

Utilitarians can consistently adopt different views on active euthanasia and assisted suicide depending on how they define the good to be maximized, whether their moral focus is acts or rules, and how much importance they give to self-determination. Classic utilitarianism defines the good as happiness and would therefore judge the issues by how much happiness various actions might produce for everyone involved. From this perspective, euthanasia or assisted suicide for someone suffering horrible, inescapable pain might be permissible because ending life would bring about the most net happiness. Of course, the calculations would have to include other factors such as the psychological, social, and financial impact on the patient's family, friends, and caregivers. With everything factored in, the utilitarian answer could easily come out against euthanasia.

On the other hand, many utilitarians (following John Stuart Mill) think that there's more to consider in making moral judgments than just net happiness. As utilitarian philosopher Peter Singer says,

> Many people prefer to live a life with less happiness or pleasure in it, and perhaps even more pain and suffering, if they can thereby fulfill other important preferences. For example, they may choose to strive for excellence in art, or literature,

<table>
<tr><td colspan="4">

IN DEPTH
PHYSICIAN-ASSISTED SUICIDE AND PUBLIC OPINION

</td></tr>
</table>

Do you think it should be legal or illegal for doctors to help terminally ill patients end their own life by giving them a prescription for fatal drugs?

Legal	Illegal	Unsure
48%	44%	8%

If you were seriously ill with a terminal disease, would you consider ending your life, or not?

Yes	No	Probably	Maybe	Unsure
35%	55%	3%	2%	5%

Associated Press/Ipsos poll conducted by Ipsos-Public Affairs, May 22–24, 2007, 1000 adults nationwide; margin of error = ±3.

When a person has a disease that cannot be cured and is living in severe pain, do you think doctors should or should not be allowed by law to assist the patient to commit suicide if the patient requests it?

Should	Should Not	Unsure
56%	38%	6%

Regardless of whether or not you think it should be legal, please tell me whether you personally believe that in general doctor-assisted suicide is morally acceptable or morally wrong.

Morally Acceptable	Morally Wrong	Depends	Unsure
49%	44%	5%	2%

Gallup Poll, May 10–13, 2007, 1003 adults nationwide; margin of error = ±3.

Do you think a person has a moral right to end his or her own life under any of the following circumstances?

Yes	No	Unsure

When this person has a disease that is incurable?

| 53% | 39% | 8% |

When this person is suffering great pain and has no hope of improvement?

| 60% | 34% | 6% |

When this person is an extremely heavy burden on his or her family?

| 29% | 62% | 9% |

When this person is ready to die because living has become a burden?

| 33% | 58% | 9% |

Pew Research Center survey conducted by Princeton Survey Research Associates International, November 9–27, 2005, 1500 adults nationwide; margin of error = ±3.

or sport, even though they know that they are unlikely to achieve it, and may experience pain and suffering in the attempt.[9]

Those in utilitarianism's camp who take this view are known as *preference utilitarians*, holding that right actions are those that satisfy more of a person's preferences overall. To them, killing is bad when it prevents someone from satisfying his own preferences; it can be good (as in euthanasia) when more of the person's future preferences will be frustrated than satisfied. According to Singer,

[I]f the goods that life holds are, in general, reasons against killing, those reasons lose all their force when it is clear that those killed will not have such goods, or that the goods they have will be outweighed by bad things that will happen to them. When we apply this reasoning to the case of someone who is capable of judging the matter, and we add Mill's view that individuals are the best judges of their own interests, we can conclude that this reason against killing does not apply to a person who, with unimpaired capacities for judgment, comes to the conclusion that his or her future is so clouded that it would be better to die than to continue to live. Indeed, the reason against killing is turned into its opposite, a reason for acceding to that person's request.[10]

Rule-utilitarian approaches can lead to positions both favoring and opposing euthanasia and assisted suicide. Most slippery-slope arguments are essentially rule-utilitarian, asserting that a general policy of authorized killing will, step by step, take society down a path to awful consequences. The outcomes to be avoided are many, including increases in nonvoluntary or involuntary euthanasia, erosion of respect for the medical profession, and a weakening of society's abhorrence of homicide. Some also argue on rule-utilitarian grounds *for* a general policy, citing relief of suffering as the most obvious benefit.

The natural law view in Roman Catholicism condemns active and passive euthanasia, though the condemnation comes with qualifications. Directly intending to bring about a person's death to end suffering is prohibited, but the doctrine of double effect permits actions that have unintended but fatal results. As discussed earlier, the doctrine would not allow doctors to give high-dose analgesics to put patients out of their misery, but it would sanction their doing the same thing with the intention of easing pain though death is foreseen. In addition, under Catholic principles there is no obligation to use every means possible to prolong a person's life in every case. The Vatican declares:

> When inevitable death is imminent in spite of the means used, it is permitted in conscience to take the decision to refuse forms of treatment that would only secure a precarious and burdensome prolongation of life, so long as the normal care due to the sick person in similar cases is not interrupted.[11]

What is clear in Kant's theory is that suicide is prohibited because it treats persons as mere things and obliterates personhood. Kant asserts that "[T]he rule of morality does not admit of [suicide] under any condition because it degrades human nature below the level of animal nature and so destroys it." It is also apparent on Kant's view that competent persons must not be killed or permitted to die. But it is not obvious what Kant's opinion would be of individuals no longer regarded as persons because they have lapsed into a persistent vegetative state. Would respect for persons demand that they be kept alive at all costs—or that we perform nonvoluntary euthanasia to allow them to die with dignity?

KEY TERMS

active euthanasia
euthanasia
involuntary euthanasia
nonvoluntary euthanasia
passive euthanasia
physician-assisted suicide
voluntary euthanasia

SUMMARY

Euthanasia is directly or indirectly bringing about the death of another person for that person's sake. A common distinction is that active euthanasia involves performing an action that directly causes someone's death, while passive euthanasia is allowing someone to die by not doing something to prolong life. Voluntary euthanasia is performed when competent patients request or agree to it; nonvoluntary euthanasia, when patients are not competent to chose for themselves and have not previously disclosed their preferences. Involuntary euthanasia, both illegal and morally impermissible, is bringing about someone's death against her will or without asking for her consent. In physician-assisted suicide a patient takes his own life with the help of a physician.

Death traditionally has been understood as the cessation of breathing and heartbeat, but medical advances have rendered this notion problematic. The whole brain view is now the standard in legal and medical matters. It says that an individual should be judged dead when all brain functions permanently stop. Many experts object to this definition because some physiological processes such as respiration are partly independent of brain functions, a fact that would suggest on the whole brain view that individuals in persistent vegetative states with some brain activity must be considered alive. An alternative notion is the

Nancy Cruzan

In the 1990 case of *Cruzan v. Director, Missouri Depart-ment of Health*, the U.S. Supreme Court issued its first momentous ruling involving an individual's "right to die." The question was whether a feeding tube could be removed from a young woman named Nancy Cru-zan, who had been left in a persistent vegetative state after a terrible car crash.

On January 11, 1983, Nancy Cruzan's car over-turned on an icy road in Missouri, flinging her into a ditch and stopping her heart. By the time paramedics restarted it, her brain had been oxygen-deprived for at least 15 minutes. The resulting brain damage was profound and permanent. So at age 25 she fell into a persistent vegetative state, a benighted condition of minimal brain activity without consciousness or purposeful behavior. "The vegetative state," says an expert panel, "is a clinical condition of complete un-awareness of the self and the environment. . . . Recov-ery from a nontraumatic persistent vegetative state after three months is exceedingly rare."[12] Nancy lin-gered in that state for years, her body coiled into a rigid fetal position, nourished only by a surgically implanted feeding tube.

After three years of hoping that Nancy would somehow recover, her parents finally asked that the feeding tube be removed so she could die in peace. "You try your damnedest as long as there's hope," said Nancy's father, "and then when there is none anymore, you must let her go."

But authorities in the state of Missouri saw things differently. They sought to block the removal of Nancy's feeding tube. The Missouri Supreme Court said that the state has an extremely strong interest in preserv-ing life and that the Cruzans may not disconnect their daughter's feeding tube without "clear and convincing

evidence" of what Nancy would have wanted. At one time she had mentioned to a friend that she would not want to be kept alive like a "vegetable," but she had left no living will or other explicit instructions.

The Cruzans appealed to the U.S. Supreme Court, and in June 1990 it delivered its far-reaching decision in its first right-to-die case. The Court held that Mis-souri had a legitimate interest in demanding "clear and convincing evidence" of an incompetent individ-ual's preferences. By sanctioning this strict standard of evidence, the Court effectively ruled against the Cruzans. But in making its decision, it also laid out some weighty principles pertaining to a person's end-of-life choices.

The Court found that competent individuals have a constitutionally guaranteed "liberty interest" in re-fusing medical treatment, even when refusing could bring about their death. And for the first time, it ac-knowledged that if a person became incompetent, this right could be exercised through a living will or by a designated surrogate. States could still restrict this liberty interest, however, if a person's refusal of treatment was not stated clearly or strongly enough.

As part of its case, the state argued that there was a difference between withdrawing medical treatment and withdrawing food and fluids. But the Supreme Court recognized no such distinction.

A few months after the Court's ruling, Missouri said it would stop opposing the Cruzans' efforts, and a Missouri judge declared that the evidence of Nan-cy's intent was sufficiently convincing. In December 1990 he ordered her feeding tube removed.

On December 26, 1990, at the age of 33 and nearly eight years after her accident, Nancy Cruzan died peacefully.

---

higher brain standard, which asserts that indi-viduals are dead when the higher brain functions responsible for consciousness permanently close down. This view implies that those in persistent

vegetative states whose higher brain functions have irreversibly ceased are dead.

The main argument for the moral permissi-bility of active voluntary euthanasia is an appeal to autonomy. It contends that respecting people's inherent right of self-determination means respecting their autonomous choices about ending their lives. Another major argument appeals to the principle of beneficence, or mercy: If we are in a position to relieve the severe suffering of another without excessive cost to ourselves, we have an obligation to do so.

An important argument against active voluntary euthanasia appeals to the supposed moral difference between killing and letting die. Killing is thought to be worse than letting die, so giving a patient a lethal injection to effect an easy death is wrong, but disconnecting his feeding tube may be permissible. Critics argue that there is no morally significant difference between these two. Those opposed to voluntary euthanasia make a related distinction between intending someone's death and not intending but foreseeing it. The former is said to be wrong; the latter, permissible. Many are skeptical of this distinction as well.

Very often cases against active euthanasia and physician-assisted suicide are built on slippery-slope arguments, which contend that allowing these practices would inevitably lead to abuses, most notably unjustified killing. Typically, both those who make these arguments and those who criticize them appeal to empirical data on the legalized use of euthanasia or physician-assisted suicide in Oregon or the Netherlands. But the data are sparse and subject to much debate, leaving the key premise in most slippery-slope arguments weak.

Cases for Evaluation

CASE I

Doctor-Aided Suicide and "Vulnerable Groups"

(*ScienceDaily*)—Contrary to arguments by critics, a University of Utah–led study found that legalizing physician-assisted suicide in Oregon and the Netherlands did not result in a disproportionate number of deaths among the elderly, poor, women, minorities, uninsured, minors, chronically ill, less educated, or psychiatric patients.

Of 10 "vulnerable groups" examined in the study, only AIDS patients used doctor-assisted suicide at elevated rates.

"Fears about the impact on vulnerable people have dominated debate about physician-assisted suicide. We find no evidence to support those fears where this practice already is legal," says the study's lead author, bioethicist Margaret Battin, a University of Utah distinguished professor of philosophy and adjunct professor of internal medicine.

The study will be published in the October 2007 issue of the *Journal of Medical Ethics*. Battin conducted the research with public health physician Agnes van der Heide, of Erasmus Medical Center, Rotterdam; psychiatrist Linda Ganzini at Oregon Health & Science University, Portland; and physician Gerrit van der Wal and health scientist Bregje Onwuteaka-Philipsen, of the VU University Medical Center, Amsterdam. Van der Wal currently is inspector general of The Netherlands Health Care Inspectorate, which advises that nation's health minister.

The research deals with the so-called "slippery-slope" argument that has been made by critics of doctor-assisted suicide and has raised concern even among proponents. The argument is that by making it legal for medical doctors to help certain patients end their lives, vulnerable people will die in disproportionately large numbers.

"Would these patients be pressured, manipulated or forced to request or accept physician-assisted dying by overburdened family members, callous physicians, or institutions or insurers concerned about their own profits," the researchers asked.

The American College of Physicians said in 2005 that it was "concerned with the risks that legalization [of physician-assisted suicide] posed to vulnerable populations, including poor persons, patients with dementia, disabled persons, those from minority groups that have experienced discrimination, those confronting costly chronic illnesses, or very young children." . . .

Battin's team analyzed data on assisted suicide and voluntary active euthanasia in the Netherlands during 1985–2005—data taken from four government studies and several smaller ones. They analyzed Oregon Department of Human Services annual reports for 1998–2006, and surveys of physicians and hospice professionals.

The findings fell into three categories, based on the strength of the data. The researchers found:

- Direct evidence that elderly people, women, and uninsured people do not die in disproportionate numbers where physician-assisted death is legal, but AIDS patients do. (The insurance data is from Oregon only; everyone is insured in the Netherlands.)
- Evidence that is partly direct and partly inferred showing that physician-assisted death does not kill disproportionate numbers of people who are poor, uneducated, racial and ethnic minorities, minors, or people with chronic physical or mental disabilities or chronic but not terminal illnesses.
- Evidence that is based on inference or that is partly contested showing that people with psychiatric illness—including depression and Alzheimer's disease—are not likely to die in lopsided numbers.

"Those who received physician-assisted dying. . . appeared to enjoy comparative social, economic, educational, professional and other privileges," the researchers write.

The researchers noted that in both Oregon and the Netherlands, people who received a doctor's help in dying averaged 70 years old, and 80 percent were cancer patients.*

Suppose the data of this study are accurate. Would they show that all slippery-slope arguments against physician-assisted suicide are unsuccessful? Suppose the study proved that legalization did harm vulnerable populations. Would that finding support the conclusion that physician-assisted suicide should not be legalized under any circumstances? What might someone who is opposed to legalization say about this study? Or someone who favors legalization? How does the news of this study affect your own views on legalization? Give reasons for your answer.

*"Doctor-Aided Suicide: No Slippery Slope, Study Finds," *Science Daily*, 29 September 2007, http://www.sciencedaily .com/releases/2007/09/070926191348.htm (10 February 2008).

CASE 2

Suicide Pacts Among Friends

(*London Telegraph*)—Jenni Murray, the presenter of BBC Radio 4's *Woman's Hour*, has made plans to end her life if she becomes a burden to her family.

She said: "When my time comes I want to be able to decide about my destiny."

The last thing she wanted, she said, was for her children to suffer from her being desperately ill.

She is sealing a pact with two friends that they will assist each other to die if any of them is diagnosed with a debilitating and incurable illness. Methods they might use include injections or smothering with a pillow.

This is despite a law outlawing assisted suicide, which Murray says is sustained by a religious minority.

She speaks of the pact tomorrow night on a Channel 5 documentary, *Don't Get Me Started!*, that produces statistics to back the theory that many people in the country share her views on euthanasia.

Her appearance is part of a "personal rant" series in which noted people are given the chance to sound off about a subject they feel strongly about.

Publicity material for the show says that Murray "does not want to look after her sick and aging mother, and plans to end her own life when she becomes a burden to those around her."

The network said: "Jenni is angry that, having fought so hard to become liberated and independent, women are now being trapped into caring for dependent parents."

Murray, 56, from Barnsley, South Yorks, has been presenting *Woman's Hour* since 1987. In 1999 she was awarded an OBE for radio broadcasting.

Her pact is with Sally Feldman, a former editor of *Woman's Hour*, and Jane Wilton, another friend. They plan to sign a written agreement.

Murray is the vice-president of a society that concerns itself with Parkinson's disease, which her mother suffers from. Her father is a carer.

In the programme she emphasises that, while she supports her friends helping her to die, she would find it hard to do the same if her mother told her "Let me go."*

Do you agree with Murray's decision? Does she have a right to take her life for any reason? Is not wanting to be a burden to one's family a good reason? Should assisted-suicide pacts be legalized? Is it just as moral (or immoral) to assist in a friend's suicide as it is to directly kill her? Explain your answers.

---

*Hugh Davies, "Jenni Murray Makes a Suicide Pact," Telegraph.co.uk, 14 August 2006, http://www.telegraph.co.uk/news/main.jhtml?xml;eq/news/2006/08/14/nmurray14.xml (10 February 2008).

CASE 3

"Baby Euthanasia"

(*TimesOnline*)—When Frank and Anita's daughter Chanou was born with an extremely rare, incurable illness in August 2000, they knew that her life would be short and battled against the odds to make it happy.

They struggled around the clock against their baby's pain. "We tried all sorts of things," said Anita, a 37-year-old local government worker. "She cried all the time. Every time I touched her it hurt."

Chanou was suffering from a metabolic disorder that had resulted in abnormal bone development. Doctors gave her no more than 30 months to live. "We felt terrible watching her suffer," said Anita at their home near Amsterdam. "We felt we were letting her down."

Frank and Anita began to believe that their daughter would be better off dead. "She kept throwing up milk that was fed through a tube in her nose," said Anita. "She seemed to be saying, 'Mummy, I don't want to live any more. Let me go.'"

Eventually, doctors agreed to help the baby die at seven months. The feeding was stopped. Chanou was given morphine. "We were with her at that last moment," said Anita. "She was exhausted. She took a very deep last breath. It was so peaceful. It made me feel at peace inside to know that she wasn't suffering any more."

Even so, they felt that the suffering had gone on too long. Child euthanasia is illegal in Holland and doctors were afraid of being prosecuted. "It was a long road to find the humane solution that we reluctantly decided we wanted," said Frank, a bank worker.

Each year in Holland at least 15 seriously ill babies, most of them with severe spina bifida or chromosomal abnormalities, are helped to die by doctors acting with the parents' consent. But only a fraction of those cases are reported to the authorities because of the doctors' fears of being charged with murder.

Things are about to change, however, making it much easier for parents and doctors to end the suffering of an infant.

A committee set up to regulate the practice will begin operating in the next few weeks, effectively making Holland, where adult euthanasia is legal, the first country in the world to allow "baby euthanasia" as well.

The development has angered opponents of euthanasia who warn of a "slippery slope" leading to abuses by doctors and parents, who will be making decisions for individuals incapable of expressing a will.

Others welcome more openness about a practice that, according to doctors, goes on secretly anyway—even in Britain—regardless of the law. "It is a giant step forward and we are very happy about it," said Eduard Verhagen, clinical director of paediatrics at the University Medical Centre in Groningen, northern Holland.

Anti-euthanasia campaigners have been addressing hate mail to "Dr. Death," as they call him, ever since he admitted having personally overseen four "assisted neo-natal terminations." He then began drawing up guidelines for doctors carrying out euthanasia on babies.

It forced the government to confront the issue and Verhagen's so-called "Groningen protocol" has been adopted as the standard to be upheld by the regulatory committee.

It emphasises that life can be ended only in cases involving "unbearable suffering," with parental consent and after consultation with other physicians.

"If a child is untreatably ill," Verhagen explained, "there can be horrendous suffering that makes the last few days or weeks of this child's life unbearable. Now the question is: Are you going to leave the child like that or are you going to prevent that suffering?" He went on: "Does the child have to sit it out until the end? We think that the answer is no. There can be circumstances where, under very strict conditions, if all the requirements are fulfilled, active ending of life can be an option—but only in cases of untreatable disease and unbearable suffering."*

How would you respond to Verhagen's questions in the last paragraph? Do you believe that neonatal euthanasia performed under the strict conditions described by Verhagen is morally permissible? Why or why not? Should it be legalized?

---

*"Holland to Allow 'Baby Euthanasia,'" TimesOnline, 5 March 2006, http://www.timesonline.co.uk/article/0,,2089-2069963 ,00.html (10 February 2008).

FURTHER READING

Margaret Pabst Battin, *Ending Life: Ethics and the Way We Die* (New York: Oxford University Press, 2005).

Tom L. Beauchamp, ed., *Intending Death: The Ethics of Assisted Suicide and Euthanasia* (Upper Saddle River, NJ: Prentice-Hall, 1996).

R. B. Brandt, "The Morality and Rationality of Suicide," in *A Handbook for the Study of Suicide*, ed. Seymour Perlin (New York: Oxford University Press, 1975), 61–75.

Lonnie R. Bristow, President of the American Medical Association, "Statement on Physician-Assisted Suicide Before the United States House of Representatives Committee on the Judiciary, Subcommittee on the Constitution," *Congressional Record*, April 29, 1996.

Dan W. Brock, "Medical Decisions at the End of Life," in *A Companion to Bioethics*, ed. Helga Kuhse and Peter Singer (Malden, MA: Blackwell, 2001), 231–41.

Gerald Dworkin, "Physician-Assisted Death: The State of the Debate," in *The Oxford Handbook of Bioethics*, ed. Bonnie Steinbock (Oxford: Oxford University Press, 2007), 375–92.

Gerald Dworkin, R. Frey, and S. Bok, *Euthanasia and Physician-Assisted Suicide* (Cambridge: Cambridge University Press, 1998).

Philippa Foot, "Euthanasia," *Philosophy & Public Affairs* 6.2 (1977), 85–112.

Walter Glannon, "Medical Decisions at the End of Life," in *Biomedical Ethics* (New York: Oxford University Press, 2005), 119–42.

Jonathan Glover, "The Sanctity of Life," in *Bioethics: An Anthology*, ed. Helga Kuhse and Peter Singer (Oxford: Blackwell, 1999), 193–202.

Leon Kass, "Is There a Right to Die?" *Hastings Center Report* 23.1 (1993), 34–43.

Mark Murphy, "The Natural Law Tradition in Ethics," in *Stanford Encyclopedia of Philosophy*, 11 March 2008, http://plato.stanford.edu/entries/natural-law-ethics (9 June 2008).

New York State Task Force on Life and the Law, *When Death Is Sought: Assisted Suicide and Euthanasia in the Medical Context* (Albany: New York State Department of Health, April 1997).

Louis P. Pojman, "Euthanasia," in *Life and Death* (Belmont, CA: Wadsworth, 2000), 85–94.

The President's Commission for the Study of Ethical Problems in Medicine and Biomedical and Behavioral Research, *Defining Death* (Washington, DC: Government Printing Office, 1981).

Peter Singer, "Voluntary Euthanasia: A Utilitarian Perspective," *Bioethics* 17.5–6 (2003), 526–41.

Bonnie Steinbock and Alastair Norcross, ed., *Killing and Letting Die*, 2nd ed. (New York: Fordham University Press, 1994).

Robert Young, "Voluntary Euthanasia," in *The Stanford Encyclopedia of Philosophy* (Winter 2007 ed.), ed. Edward N. Zalta, http://plato.stanford.edu/archives/win2007/entries/euthanasia-voluntary/ (2008).

NOTES

1. A definition suggested by Philippa Foot (in "Euthanasia," *Philosophy & Public Affairs* 6.2 [1977], 85–112) and by Helga Kuhse (in "Euthanasia," in *A Companion to Ethics*, ed. Peter Singer [Oxford: Blackwell, 1933], 294–302.)

2. American Medical Association, *Opinions of the Judicial Council* (Chicago: American Medical Association, 1973).

3. Robert Young, "Voluntary Euthanasia," in *The Stanford Encyclopedia of Philosophy* (Winter 2007 ed.), ed. Edward N. Zalta, http://plato.stanford.edu/archives/win2007/entries/euthanasia-voluntary (28 January 2008).

4. Dan W. Brock, "Voluntary Active Euthanasia," *Hastings Center Report* 22.2 (March/April 1992), 11–12, 14–17, 19–21.

5. James Rachels, "Active and Passive Euthanasia," *New England Journal of Medicine* 292.2 (9 January 1975), 79.

6. Winston Nesbitt, "Is Killing No Worse Than Letting Die?" *Journal of Applied Philosophy* 12.1 (1995), 101–5.

7. Dan W. Brock, "Medical Decisions at the End of Life," in *A Companion to Bioethics,* ed. Helga Kuhse and Peter Singer (Malden, MA: Blackwell, 2001), 240.

8. J. Gay-Williams, "The Wrongfulness of Euthanasia," in *Intervention and Reflection: Basic Issues in Medical Ethics,* 7th ed., ed. Ronald Munson (Belmont, CA: Wadsworth, 2004), 710–11.

9. Peter Singer, "Voluntary Euthanasia: A Utilitarian Perspective," *Bioethics* 17.5–6 (2003), 526–41.

10. Sacred Congregation for the Doctrine of the Faith, *Declaration on Euthanasia* (Vatican City: The Vatican, 1980).

11. The Multi-Society Task Force on PVS, "Medical Aspects of the Persistent Vegetative State," *New England Journal of Medicine* 330.21 (26 May 1994), 1499–1508.

READINGS

The Wrongfulness of Euthanasia

J. GAY-WILLIAMS

Gay-Williams argues that deliberately killing a hopelessly ill person is morally wrong because such an act is inconsistent with natural law—it goes against the strong natural tendency of all humans to continue living. The practice is also in conflict with our own self-interest and is a treacherous slippery slope toward involuntary euthanasia.

My impression is that euthanasia—the idea, if not the practice—is slowly gaining acceptance within our society. Cynics might attribute this to an increasing tendency to devalue human life, but I do not believe this is the major factor. The acceptance is much more likely to be the result of unthinking sympathy and benevolence. Well-publicized, tragic stories like that of Karen Quinlan elicit from us deep feelings of compassion. We think to ourselves, "She and her family would be better off if she were dead." It is an easy step from the very human response to the view that if someone (and others) would be better off dead, then it might be all right to kill that person.[1] Although I respect the compassion that leads to this conclusion, I believe the conclusion is wrong. I want to show that euthanasia is wrong. It is inherently wrong, but it is also wrong judged from the standpoints of self-interest and of practical effects.

Before presenting my arguments to support this claim, it would be well to define "euthanasia." An essential aspect of euthanasia is that it involves taking a human life, either one's own or that of another. Also, the person whose life is taken must be someone who is believed to be suffering from some disease or injury from which recovery cannot reasonably be expected. Finally, the action must be deliberate and intentional. Thus, euthanasia is intentionally taking the life of a presumably hopeless person. Whether the life is one's own or that of another, the taking of it is still euthanasia.

It is important to be clear about the deliberate and intentional aspect of the killing. If a hopeless person is given an injection of the wrong drug by mistake and this causes his death, this is wrongful killing but not euthanasia. The killing cannot be the result of accident. Furthermore, if the person is given an injection of a drug that is believed to be necessary to treat his disease or better his condition and the person dies as a result, then this is neither wrongful killing nor euthanasia. The intention was to make the patient well, not kill him. Similarly, when a patient's condition is such that it is not reasonable to hope that any medical procedures or treatments will save his life, a failure to implement the procedures or treatments is not euthanasia. If the person dies, this will be as a result of his injuries or disease and not because of his failure to receive treatment.

The failure to continue treatment after it has been realized that the patient has little chance of benefiting from it has been characterized by some as "passive euthanasia." This phrase is misleading and mistaken.[2] In such cases, the person involved is not killed (the first essential aspect of euthanasia), nor is the death of the person intended by the withholding of additional treatment (the third essential aspect of euthanasia). The aim may be to spare the person additional and unjustifiable pain, to save him from the indignities of hopeless manipulations, and to avoid increasing the financial and emotional burden on his family. When I buy a pencil it is so that I can use it to write, not to contribute to an increase in the gross national product. This may be the unintended consequence of my action, but it is not the aim of my action. So it is with failing to continue the treatment of a dying person. I intend his death no more than I intend to reduce the GNP by not using medical supplies. His is an unintended dying, and so-called "passive euthanasia" is not euthanasia at all.

1. The Argument from Nature

Every human being has a natural inclination to continue living. Our reflexes and responses fit us to fight attackers, flee wild animals, and dodge out of the way of trucks. In our daily lives we exercise the caution and care necessary to protect ourselves. Our bodies are similarly structured for survival right down to the molecular level. When we are cut, our capillaries seal shut, our blood clots, and fibrogen is produced to start the process of healing the wound. When we are invaded by bacteria, antibodies are produced to fight against the alien organisms, and their remains are swept out of the body by special cells designed for clean-up work.

Euthanasia does violence to this natural goal of survival. It is literally acting against nature because all the processes of nature are bent towards the end of bodily survival. Euthanasia defeats these subtle mechanisms in a way that, in a particular case, disease and injury might not.

It is possible, but not necessary, to make an appeal to revealed religion in this connection.[3] Man as trustee of his body acts against God, its rightful possessor, when he takes his own life. He also violates the commandment to hold life sacred and never to take it without just and compelling cause. But since this appeal will persuade only those who are prepared to accept that religion has access to revealed truths, I shall not employ this line of argument.

It is enough, I believe, to recognize that the organization of the human body and our patterns of behavioral responses make the continuation of life a natural goal. By reason alone, then, we can recognize that euthanasia sets us against our own nature.[4] Furthermore, in doing so, euthanasia does violence to our dignity. Our dignity comes from seeking our ends. When one of our goals is survival, and actions are taken that eliminate that goal, then our natural dignity suffers. Unlike animals, we are conscious through reason of our nature and our ends. Euthanasia involves acting as if this dual nature—inclination towards survival and awareness of this as an end—did not exist. Thus, euthanasia denies our basic human character and requires that we regard ourselves or others as something less than fully human.

2. The Argument from Self-Interest

The above arguments are, I believe, sufficient to show that euthanasia is inherently wrong. But there are reasons for considering it wrong when judged by standards other than reason. Because death is final and irreversible, euthanasia maintains within it the possibility that we will work against our own interest if we practice it or allow it to be practiced on us.

Contemporary medicine has high standards of excellence and a proven record of accomplishment, but it does not possess perfect and complete knowledge. A mistaken diagnosis is possible, and so is a mistaken prognosis. Consequently, we may believe that we are dying of a disease when, as a matter of fact, we may not be. We may think that we have no hope of recovery when, as a matter of fact, our chances are quite good. In such circumstances, if euthanasia were permitted, we would die needlessly. Death is final and the chance of error too great to approve the practice of euthanasia.

Also, there is always the possibility that an experimental procedure or a hitherto untried technique will pull us through. We should at least keep this option open, but euthanasia closes it off. Furthermore, spontaneous remission does occur in many cases. For no apparent reason, a patient simply recovers when those all around him, including his physicians, expected him to die. Euthanasia would just guarantee their expectations and leave no room for the "miraculous" recoveries that frequently occur.

Finally, knowing that we can take our life at any time (or ask another to take it) might well incline us to give up too easily. The will to live is strong in all of us, but it can be weakened by pain and suffering and feelings of hopelessness. If during a bad time we allow ourselves to be killed, we never have a chance to reconsider. Recovery from a serious illness requires that we fight for it, and anything that weakens our determination by suggesting that there is an easy way out is ultimately against our own interest. Also, we may be inclined towards euthanasia because of our concern for others. If we see our sickness and suffering as an emotional and financial burden on our family, we may feel that to leave our life is to make their lives easier.[5] The very presence of the possibility of euthanasia may keep us from surviving when we might.

3. The Argument from Practical Effects

Doctors and nurses are, for the most part, totally committed to saving lives. A life lost is, for them, almost a personal failure, an insult to their skills and knowledge. Euthanasia as a practice might well alter this. It could have a corrupting influence so that in any case that is severe doctors and nurses might not try hard enough to save the patient. They might decide that the patient would simply be "better off dead" and take the steps necessary to make that come about. This attitude could then carry over to their dealings with patients less seriously ill. The result would be overall decline in the quality of medical care.

Finally, euthanasia as a policy is a slippery slope. A person apparently hopelessly ill may be allowed to take his own life. Then he may be permitted to deputize others to do it for him should he no longer be able to act. The judgment of others then becomes the ruling factor. Already at this point euthanasia is not personal and voluntary, for others are acting "on behalf of" the patient as they see fit. This may well incline them to act on behalf of other patients who have not authorized them to exercise their judgment. It is only a short step, then, from voluntary euthanasia (self-inflicted or authorized), to directed euthanasia administered to a patient who has given no authorization, to involuntary euthanasia conducted as part of a social policy.[6] Recently many psychiatrists and sociologists have argued that we define as "menial illness" those forms of behavior that we disapprove of.[7] This gives us license then to lock up those who display the behavior. The category "hopelessly ill" provides the possibility or even worse abuse. Embedded in a social policy, it would give society or its representatives the authority to eliminate all those who might be considered too "ill" to function normally any longer. The dangers of euthanasia are too great to all to run the risk of approving it in any form. The first slippery step may well lead to a serious and harmful fall.

I hope that I have succeeded in showing why the benevolence that inclines us to give approval of euthanasia is misplaced. Euthanasia is inherently wrong because it violates the nature and dignity of human beings. But even those who are not convinced by this must be persuaded that the potential personal and social dangers inherent in euthanasia are sufficient to forbid our approving it either as a personal practice or as a public policy.

Suffering is surely a terrible thing, and we have a clear duty to comfort those in need and to ease their suffering when we can. But suffering is also a natural part of life with values for the individual and for others that we should not overlook. We may legitimately seek for others and for ourselves an easeful death, as Arthur Dyck has pointed out.[8] Euthanasia, however, is not just an easeful death. It is a wrongful death. Euthanasia is not just dying. It is killing.

NOTES

1. For a sophisticated defense of this position see Philippa Foot, "Euthanasia," *Philosophy and Public Affairs*, vol. 6 (1977), pp. 85–112. Foot does not endorse the radical conclusion that euthanasia, voluntary and involuntary, is always right.
2. James Rachels rejects the distinction between active and passive euthanasia as morally irrelevant in his "Active and

Passive Euthanasia," *New England Journal of Medicine*, vol. 292, pp. 78–80. But see the criticism by Foot, pp. 100–103.

3. For a defense of this view see J. V. Sullivan, "The Immorality of Euthanasia," in *Beneficent Euthanasia*, ed. Marvin Kohl (Buffalo, N.Y.: Prometheus Books, 1975), pp. 34–44.

4. This point is made by Ray V. McIntyre in "Voluntary Euthanasia: The Ultimate Perversion," *Medical Counterpoint*, vol. 2, p. 26–29.

5. See McIntyre, p. 28.

6. See Sullivan, "Immorality of Euthanasia," pp. 34–44, for a fuller argument in support of this view.

7. See, for example, Thomas S. Szasz, *The Myth of Mental Illness*, rev. ed. (New York: Harper & Row, 1974).

8. Arthur Dyck, "Beneficent Euthanasia and Benemortasia," Kohl, op. cit., pp. 117–129.

Voluntary Active Euthanasia

DAN W. BROCK

Brock argues that the same two basic moral principles that support a patient's right to make choices about life-sustaining treatment also support the permissibility of voluntary active euthanasia. The first principle is individual self-determination; the second is individual well-being. Individual self-determination applies to the manner, circumstances, and timing of one's death and dying. A concern for individual well-being may justify euthanasia when a suffering patient determines that life is no longer a benefit.

. . . The central ethical argument for euthanasia is familiar. It is that the very same two fundamental ethical values supporting the consensus on patient's rights to decide about life-sustaining treatment also support the ethical permissibility of euthanasia. These values are individual self-determination or autonomy and individual well-being. By self-determination as it bears on euthanasia, I mean people's interest in making important decisions about their lives for themselves according to their own values or conceptions of a good life, and in being left free to act on those decisions. Self-determination is valuable because it permits people to form and live in accordance with their own conception of a good life, at least within the bounds of justice and consistent with others doing so as well. In exercising self-determination people take responsibility for their lives and for the kinds of persons they become. A central aspect of human dignity lies in people's capacity to direct their lives in this way. The value of exercising self-determination presupposes some minimum of decision making capacities or competence, which thus limits the scope of euthanasia sup-

© The Hastings Center. Reprinted by permission. This article originally appeared in the *Hastings Center Report*, vol. 22, no. 2 (1992).

ported by self-determination; it cannot justifiably be administered, for example, in cases of serious dementia or treatable clinical depression.

Does the value of individual self-determination extend to the time and manner of one's death? Most people are very concerned about the nature of the last stage of their lives. This reflects not just a fear of experiencing substantial suffering when dying, but also a desire to retain dignity and control during this last period of life. Death is today increasingly preceded by a long period of significant physical and mental decline, due in part to the technological interventions of modern medicine. Many people adjust to these disabilities and find meaning and value in new activities and ways. Others find the impairments and burdens in the last stage of their lives at some point sufficiently great to make life no longer worth living. For many patients near death, maintaining the quality of one's life, avoiding great suffering, maintaining one's dignity, and insuring that others remember us as we wish them to become of paramount importance and outweigh merely extending one's life. But there is no single, objectively correct answer for everyone as to when, if at all, one's life becomes all things considered a burden and unwanted. If self-determination is a fundamental value, then the great variability among people on this question makes it especially important that individuals control the manner, circumstances, and timing of their dying and death.

The other main value that supports euthanasia is individual well-being. It might seem that individual well-being conflicts with a person's self-determination when the person requests euthanasia. Life itself is commonly taken to be a central good for persons, often valued for its own sake, as well as necessary for pursuit of all other goods within a life. But when a competent patient decides to forgo all further life-sustaining treatment then the patient, either explicitly or implicitly, commonly decides that the best life possible for him or her with treatment is of sufficiently poor quality that it is worse than no further life at all. Life is no longer considered a benefit by the patient, but has now become a burden. The same judgment underlies a request for euthanasia: continued life is seen by the patient as no longer a benefit, but now a burden. Especially in the often severely compromised and debilitated states of many critically ill or dying patients, there is no objective standard, but only the competent patient's judgment of whether continued life is no longer a benefit.

Of course, sometimes there are conditions, such as clinical depression, that call into question whether the patient has made a competent choice, either to forgo life-sustaining treatment or to seek euthanasia, and then the patient's choice need not be evidence that continued life is no longer a benefit for him or her. Just as with decisions about treatment, a determination of incompetence can warrant not honoring the patient's choice; in the case of treatment, we then transfer decisional authority to a surrogate, though in the case of voluntary active euthanasia a determination that the patient is incompetent means that choice is not possible.

The value or right of self-determination does not entitle patients to compel physicians to act contrary to their own moral or professional values. Physicians are moral and professional agents whose own self-determination or integrity should be respected as well. If performing euthanasia became legally permissible, but conflicted with a particular physician's reasonable understanding of his or her moral or professional responsibilities, the care of a patient who requested euthanasia should be transferred to another.

Most opponents do not deny that there are some cases in which the values of patient self-determination and well-being support euthanasia. Instead, they commonly offer two kinds of arguments against it that on their view outweigh or override this support. The first kind of argument is that in any individual case where considerations of the patient's self-determination and well-being do support euthanasia, it is nevertheless always ethically wrong or impermissible. The second kind of argument grants that in some individual cases euthanasia may not be ethically wrong, but maintains nonetheless that public and legal policy should never permit it. The first kind of argument focuses on features of any individual case of euthanasia, while the second kind focuses on social or legal policy. In the next section I consider the first kind of argument.

Euthanasia Is the Deliberate Killing of an Innocent Person

The claim that any individual instance of euthanasia is a case of deliberate killing of an innocent person is, with only minor qualifications, correct. Unlike forgoing life-sustaining treatment, commonly understood as allowing to die, euthanasia is clearly killing, defined as depriving of life or causing the death of a living being. While providing morphine for pain relief at doses where the risk of respiratory depression and an earlier death may be a foreseen but unintended side effect of treating the patient's pain, in a case of euthanasia the patient's death is deliberate or intended even if in both the physician's ultimate end may be respecting the patient's wishes. If the deliberate killing of an innocent person is wrong, euthanasia would be nearly always impermissible.

In the context of medicine, the ethical prohibition against deliberately killing the innocent derives some of its plausibility from the belief that nothing in the currently accepted practice of medicine is deliberate killing. Thus, in commenting on the "It's Over, Debbie" case, four prominent physicians and bioethicists could entitle their paper "Doctors Must Not Kill."[1] The belief that doctors do not in fact kill requires the corollary belief that forgoing life-sustaining treatment, whether by not starting or by stopping treatment, is allowing to die, not killing. Common though this view is, I shall argue that it is confused and mistaken.

Why is the common view mistaken? Consider the case of a patient terminally ill with ALS disease. She is completely respirator dependent with no hope of ever being weaned. She is unquestionably competent but finds her condition intolerable and persistently requests to be removed from the respirator and allowed to die. Most people and physicians would agree that the patient's physician should respect the patient's wishes and remove her from the respirator, though this will certainly cause the patient's death. The common understanding is that the physician thereby allows the patient to die. But is that correct?

Suppose the patient has a greedy and hostile son who mistakenly believes that his mother will never decide to stop her life-sustaining treatment and that even if she did her physician would not remove her from the respirator. Afraid that his inheritance will be dissipated by a long and expensive hospitalization, he enters his mother's room while she is sedated, extubates her, and she dies. Shortly thereafter the medical staff discovers what he has done and confronts the son. He replies, "I didn't kill her, I merely allowed her to die. It was her ALS disease that caused her death." I think this would rightly be dismissed as transparent sophistry—the son went into his mother's room and deliberately killed her. But, of course, the son performed just the same physical actions, did just the same thing, that the physician would have done. If that is so, then doesn't the physician also kill the patient when he extubates her?

I underline immediately that there are important ethical differences between what the physician and the greedy son do. First, the physician acts with the patient's consent whereas the son does not. Second, the physician acts with a good motive—to respect the patient's wishes and self-determination—whereas the son acts with a bad motive—to protect his own inheritance. Third, the physician acts in a social role through which he is legally authorized to carry out the patient's wishes regarding treatment whereas the son has no such authorization. These and perhaps other ethically important differences show that what the physician did was morally justified whereas what the son did was morally wrong. What they do not show, however, is that the son killed while the physician allowed to die. One can either kill or allow to die with or without consent, with a good or bad motive, within or outside of a social role that authorizes one to do so.

The difference between killing and allowing to die that I have been implicitly appealing to here is roughly that between acts and omissions resulting in death.[2] Both the physician and the greedy son act in a manner intended to cause death, do cause death, and so both kill. One reason this conclusion is resisted is that on a different understanding of the distinction between killing and allowing to die, what the physician does is allow to die. In this account, the mother's ALS is a lethal disease whose normal progression is being held back or blocked by the life-sustaining respirator treatment. Removing this artificial intervention is then viewed as standing aside and allowing the patient to die of her underlying disease. I have argued elsewhere that this alternative account is deeply problematic, in part because it commits us to accepting that what the greedy son does is to allow to die, not kill.[3] Here, I want to note two other reasons why the conclusion that stopping life support is killing is resisted.

The first reason is that killing is often understood, especially within medicine, as unjustified causing of death; in medicine it is thought to be done only accidentally or negligently. It is also increasingly widely accepted that a physician is ethically justified in stopping life support in a case like that of the ALS patient. But if these two beliefs are correct, then what the physician does cannot be killing, and so must be allowing to die. Killing patients is not, to put it flippantly, understood to be part of physicians' job description. What is mistaken in this line of reasoning is the assumption that all killings are unjustified causings of death. Instead, some killings are ethically justified, including many instances of stopping life support.

Another reason for resisting the conclusion that stopping life support is often killing is that it is psychologically uncomfortable. Suppose the physician had stopped the ALS patient's respirator and had made the son's claim, "I didn't kill her, I merely allowed her to die. It was her ALS disease that caused her death." The clue to the psychological role here is how naturally the "merely" modifies "allowed her to die." The characterization as allowing to die is meant to shift felt responsibility away from the agent—the physician—and to the lethal disease process. Other language common in death and dying contexts plays a similar role; "letting nature take its course" or "stopping prolonging the dying process" both seem to shift responsibility from the physician who stops life support to the fatal disease process. However psychologically helpful these conceptualizations may be in making the difficult responsibility of a physician's role in the patient's death bearable, they nevertheless are confusions. Both physicians and family members can instead be helped to understand that it is the patient's decision and consent to stopping treatment that limits their responsibility for the patient's death and that shifts that responsibility to the patient.

Many who accept the difference between killing and allowing to die as the distinction between acts and omissions resulting in death have gone on to argue that killing is not in itself morally different from allowing to die.[4] In this account, very roughly, one kills when one performs an action that causes the death of a person (we are in a boat, you cannot swim, I push you overboard, and you drown), and one allows to die when one has the ability and opportunity to prevent the death of another, knows this, and omits doing so, with the result that the person dies (we are in a boat, you cannot swim, you fall overboard, I don't throw you an available life ring, and you drown). Those who see no moral difference between killing and allowing to die typically employ the strategy of comparing cases that differ in these and no other potentially morally important respects. This will allow people to consider whether the mere difference that one is a case of killing and the other of allowing to die matters morally, or whether instead it is other features that make most cases of killing worse than most instances of allowing to die. Here is such a pair of cases:

Case 1

A very gravely ill patient is brought to a hospital emergency room and sent up to the ICU. The patient begins to develop respiratory failure that is likely to require intubation very soon. At that point the patient's family members and long-standing physician arrive at the ICU and inform the ICU staff that there had been extensive discussion about future care with the patient when he was unquestionably competent. Given his grave and terminal illness, as well as his state of debilitation, the patient had firmly rejected being placed on a respirator under any circumstances, and the family and physician produce the patient's advance directive to that effect. The ICU staff do not intubate the patient, who dies of respiratory failure.

Case 2

The same as Case 1 except that the family and physician are slightly delayed in traffic and arrive shortly after the patient has been intubated and placed on the respirator. The ICU staff extubate the patient, who dies of respiratory failure.

In Case 1 the patient is allowed to die, in Case 2 he is killed, but it is hard to see why what is done in Case 2 is significantly different morally than what is done in Case 1. It must be other factors that make most killings worse than most allowings to die, and if so, euthanasia cannot be wrong simply because it is killing instead of allowing to die.

Suppose both my arguments are mistaken. Suppose that killing is worse than allowing to die and that withdrawing life support is not killing, although euthanasia is. Euthanasia still need not for that reason be morally wrong. To see this, we need to determine the basic principle for the moral evaluation of killing persons. What is it that makes paradigm cases of wrongful killing wrongful? One very plausible answer is that killing denies the victim something that he or she values greatly—continued life or a future. Moreover, since continued life is necessary for pursuing any of a person's plans and purposes, killing brings the frustration of all of these plans and desires as well. In a nutshell, wrongful killing deprives a person of a valued future, and of all the person wanted and planned to do in that future.

A natural expression of this account of the wrongness of killing is that people have a moral right not to be killed.[5] But in this account of the wrongness of killing, the right not to be killed, like other rights, should be waivable when the person makes a competent decision that continued life is no longer wanted or a good, but is instead worse than no further life at all. In this view, euthanasia is properly understood as a case of a person having waived his or her right not to be killed.

This rights view of the wrongness of killing is not, of course, universally shared. Many people's moral views about killing have their origins in religious views that human life comes from God and cannot be justifiably destroyed or taken away, either by the person whose life it is or by another. But in a pluralistic society like our own with a strong commitment to freedom of religion, public policy should not be grounded in religious beliefs which many in that society reject. I turn now to the general evaluation of public policy on euthanasia.

Would the Bad Consequences of Euthanasia Outweigh the Good?

The argument against euthanasia at the policy level is stronger than at the level of individual cases, though even here I believe the case is ultimately unpersuasive, or at best indecisive. The policy level is the place where the main issues lie, however, and where moral considerations that might override arguments in favor of euthanasia will be found, if they are found anywhere. It is important to note two kinds of disagreement about the consequences for public policy of permitting euthanasia. First, there is empirical or factual disagreement about what the consequences would be. This disagreement is greatly exacerbated by the lack of firm data on the issue. Second, since on any reasonable assessment there would be both good and bad consequences, there are moral disagreements about the relative importance of different effects. In addition to these two sources of disagreement, there is also no single, well-specified policy proposal for legalizing euthanasia on which policy assessments can focus. But without such specification, and especially without explicit procedures for protecting against well-intentioned misuse and ill-intentioned abuse, the consequences for policy are largely speculative. Despite these difficulties, a preliminary account of the main likely good and bad consequences is possible. This should help clarify where better data or more moral analysis and argument are needed, as well as where policy safeguards must be developed.

Potential Good Consequences of Permitting Euthanasia

What are the likely good consequences? First, if euthanasia were permitted it would be possible to respect the self-determination of competent patients who want it, but now cannot get it because of its illegality. We simply do not know how many such patients and people there are. In the Netherlands, with a population of about 14.5 million (in 1987), estimates in a recent study were that about 1,900 cases of voluntary active euthanasia or physician-assisted suicide occur annually. No straightforward extrapolation to the United States is possible for many reasons, among them, that we do not know how many people here who want euthanasia now get it, despite its illegality. Even with better data on the number of persons who want euthanasia but cannot get it, significant moral disagreement would remain about how much weight should be given to any instance of failure to respect a person's self-determination in this way.

One important factor substantially affecting the number of persons who would seek euthanasia is the extent to which an alternative is available. The widespread acceptance in the law, social policy, and medical practice of the right of a competent patient to forgo life-sustaining treatment suggests that the number of competent persons in the United States who would want euthanasia if it were permitted is probably relatively small.

A second good consequence of making euthanasia legally permissible benefits a much larger group. Polls have shown that a majority of the American public believes that people should have a right to obtain euthanasia if they want it.[6] No doubt the vast majority of those who support this right to euthanasia will never in fact come to want euthanasia for themselves. Nevertheless, making it legally permissible would reassure many people that if they ever do want euthanasia they would be able to obtain it. This reassurance would supplement the broader control over the process of dying given by the right to decide about life-sustaining treatment. Having fire insurance on one's house benefits all who have it, not just those whose houses actually burn down, by reassuring them that in the unlikely event of their house burning down, they will receive the money needed to rebuild it. Likewise, the legalization of euthanasia can be thought of as a kind of insurance policy against being forced to endure a protracted dying process that one has come to find burdensome and unwanted, especially when there is no life-sustaining treatment to forgo. The strong concern about losing control of their care expressed by many people who face serious illness likely to end in death suggests that they give substantial importance to the legalization of euthanasia as a means of maintaining this control.

A third good consequence of the legalization of euthanasia concerns patients whose dying is filled with severe and unrelievable pain or suffering. When there is a life-sustaining treatment that, if forgone, will lead relatively quickly to death, then doing so can bring an end to these patients' suffering without recourse to euthanasia. For patients receiving no such treatment, however, euthanasia may be the only release from their otherwise prolonged suffering and agony. This argument from mercy has always been the strongest argument for euthanasia in those cases to which it applies.[7]

The importance of relieving pain and suffering is less controversial than is the frequency with which patients are forced to undergo untreatable agony that only euthanasia could relieve. If we focus first on suffering caused by physical pain, it is crucial to distinguish pain that could be adequately relieved with modern methods of pain control, though it in fact is not, from pain that is relievable only by death.[8] For a variety of reasons, including some physicians' fear of hastening the patient's death, as well as the lack of a publicly accessible means for assessing the amount of the patient's pain, many patients suffer pain that could be, but is not, relieved.

Specialists in pain control, as for example the pain of terminally ill cancer patients, argue that there are very few patients whose pain could not be adequately controlled, though sometimes at the cost of so sedating them that they are effectively unable to interact with other people or their environment. Thus, the argument from mercy in cases of physical pain can probably be met in a large majority of cases by providing adequate measures of pain relief. This should be a high priority, whatever our legal policy on euthanasia—the relief of pain and suffering has long been, quite properly, one of the central goals of medicine. Those cases in which pain could be effectively relieved, but in fact is not, should only count significantly in favor of legalizing euthanasia if all reasonable efforts to change pain management techniques have been tried and have failed.

Dying patients often undergo substantial psychological suffering that is not fully or even principally the result of physical pain.[9] The knowledge about how to relieve this suffering is much more limited than in the case of relieving pain, and efforts to do so are probably more often unsuccessful. If the argument from mercy is extended to patients experiencing great and unrelievable psychological suffering, the numbers of patients to which it applies are much greater.

One last good consequence of legalizing euthanasia is that once death has been accepted, it is often more humane to end life quickly and peacefully, when that is what the patient wants. Such a death will often be seen as better than a more prolonged one. People who suffer a sudden and unexpected death, for example by dying quickly or in their sleep from a heart attack or stroke, are often considered lucky to have died in this way. We care about how we die in part because we care about how others remember us, and we hope they will remember us as we were in "good times" with them and not as we might be when disease has robbed us of our dignity as human beings. As with much in the treatment and care of the dying, people's concerns differ in this respect, but for at least some people, euthanasia will be a more humane death than what they have often experienced with other loved ones and might otherwise expect for themselves.

Some opponents of euthanasia challenge how much importance should be given to any of these good consequences of permitting it, or even whether some would be good consequences at all. But more frequently, opponents cite a number of bad consequences that permitting euthanasia would or could produce, and it is to their assessment that I now turn.

Potential Bad Consequences of Permitting Euthanasia

Some of the arguments against permitting euthanasia are aimed specifically against physicians, while others are aimed against anyone being permitted to perform it. I shall first consider one argument of the former sort. Permitting physicians to perform euthanasia, it is said, would be incompatible with their fundamental moral and professional commitment as healers to care for patients and to protect life. Moreover, if euthanasia by physicians became common, patients would come to fear that a medication was intended not to treat or care, but instead to kill, and would thus lose trust in their physicians. This position was forcefully stated in a paper by Willard Gaylin and his colleagues:

> The very soul of medicine is on trial. . . . This issue touches medicine at its moral center; if this moral center collapses, if physicians become killers or are even licensed to kill, the profession—and, therewith, each physician—will never again be worthy of trust and respect as healer and comforter and protector of life in all its frailty.

These authors go on to make clear that, while they oppose permitting anyone to perform euthanasia, their special concern is with physicians doing so:

> We call on fellow physicians to say that they will not deliberately kill. We must also say to each of our fellow physicians that we will not tolerate killing of patients and that we shall take disciplinary action against doctors who kill. And we must say to the broader community that if it insists on tolerating or legalizing active euthanasia, it will have to find non-physicians to do its killing.[10]

If permitting physicians to kill would undermine the very "moral center" of medicine, then almost certainly physicians should not be permitted to perform euthanasia. But how persuasive is this claim? Patients should not fear, as a consequence of permitting voluntary active euthanasia, that their physicians will substitute a lethal injection for what patients want and believe is part of their care. If active euthanasia is restricted to cases in which it is truly voluntary, then no patient should fear getting it unless she or he has voluntarily requested it. (The fear that we might in time also come to accept nonvoluntary, or even involuntary, active euthanasia is a slippery slope worry I address below.) Patients' trust of their physicians could be increased, not eroded, by knowledge that physicians will provide aid in dying when patients seek it.

Might Gaylin and his colleagues nevertheless be correct in their claim that the moral center of medi-

cine would collapse if physicians were to become killers? This question raises what at the deepest level should be the guiding aims of medicine, a question that obviously cannot be fully explored here. But I do want to say enough to indicate the direction that I believe an appropriate response to this challenge should take. In spelling out above what I called the positive argument for voluntary active euthanasia, I suggested that two principal values—respecting patients' self-determination and promoting their well-being—underlie the consensus that competent patients, or the surrogates of incompetent patients, are entitled to refuse any life-sustaining treatment and to choose from among available alternative treatments. It is the commitment to these two values in guiding physicians' actions as healers, comforters, and protectors of their patients' lives that should be at the "moral center" of medicine, and these two values support physicians' administering euthanasia when their patients make competent requests for it. . . .

A second bad consequence that some foresee is that permitting euthanasia would weaken society's commitment to provide optimal care for dying patients. We live at a time in which the control of health care costs has become, and is likely to continue to be, the dominant focus of health care policy. If euthanasia is seen as a cheaper alternative to adequate care and treatment, then we might become less scrupulous about providing sometimes costly support and other services to dying patients. Particularly if our society comes to embrace deeper and more explicit rationing of health care, frail, elderly, and dying patients will need to be strong and effective advocates for their own health care and other needs, although they are hardly in a position to do this. We should do nothing to weaken their ability to obtain adequate care and services.

This second worry is difficult to assess because there is little firm evidence about the likelihood of the feared erosion in the care of dying patients. There are at least two reasons, however, for skepticism about this argument. The first is that the same worry could have been directed at recognizing patients' or surrogates' rights to forgo life-sustaining treatment, yet there is no persuasive evidence that recognizing the right to refuse treatment has caused a serious erosion in the quality of care of dying patients. The second reason for skepticism about this worry is that only a very small proportion of deaths would occur from euthanasia if it were permitted. In the Netherlands, where euthanasia under specified circumstances is permitted by the courts, though not authorized by statute, the best estimate of the proportion of overall deaths that result from it is about 2 percent.[11] Thus, the vast majority of critically ill and dying patients will not request it, and so will still have to be cared for by physicians, families, and others. Permitting euthanasia should not diminish people's commitment and concern to maintain and improve the care of these patients.

A third possible bad consequence of permitting euthanasia (or even a public discourse in which strong support for euthanasia is evident) is to threaten the progress made in securing the rights of patients or their surrogates to decide about and to refuse life-sustaining treatment.[12] This progress has been made against the backdrop of a clear and firm legal prohibition of euthanasia, which has provided a relatively bright line limiting the dominion of others over patients' lives. It has therefore been an important reassurance to concerns about how the authority to take steps ending life might be misused, abused, or wrongly extended.

Many supporters of the right of patients or their surrogates to refuse treatment strongly oppose euthanasia, and if forced to choose might well withdraw their support of the right to refuse treatment rather than accept euthanasia. Public policy in the last fifteen years has generally let life-sustaining treatment decisions be made in health care settings between physicians and patients or their surrogates, and without the involvement of the courts. However, if euthanasia is made legally permissible greater involvement of the courts is likely, which could in turn extend to a greater court involvement in life-sustaining treatment decisions. Most agree, however, that increased involvement of the courts in these decisions would be undesirable, as it would make sound decisionmaking more cumbersome and difficult without sufficient compensating benefits.

As with the second potential bad consequence of permitting euthanasia, this third consideration too is speculative and difficult to assess. The feared erosion of patients' or surrogates' rights to decide about life-sustaining treatment, together with greater court involvement in those decisions, are both possible. However, I believe there is reason to discount this general worry. The legal rights of competent patients and, to a lesser degree, surrogates of incompetent patients to decide about treatment are very firmly embedded in a long line of informed consent and life-sustaining treatment cases, and are not likely to be eroded by a debate over, or even acceptance of, euthanasia. It will not be accepted without safeguards that reassure the public about abuse, and if that debate shows the need for similar safeguards for some life-sustaining treatment decisions they should be adopted there as well. In neither case are the only possible safeguards greater court involvement, as the recent growth of institutional ethics committees shows.

The fourth potential bad consequence of permitting euthanasia has been developed by David Velleman and turns on the subtle point that making a new option or choice available to people can sometimes make them worse off, even if once they have the choice they go on to choose what is best for them.[13] Ordinarily, people's continued existence is viewed by them as given, a fixed condition with which they must cope. Making euthanasia available to people as an option denies them the alternative of staying alive by default. If people are offered the option of euthanasia, their continued existence is now a choice for which they can be held responsible and which they can be asked by others to justify. We care, and are right to care, about being able to justify ourselves to others. To the extent that our society is unsympathetic to justifying a severely dependent or impaired existence, a heavy psychological burden of proof may be placed on patients who think their terminal illness or chronic infirmity is not a sufficient reason for dying. Even if they otherwise view their life as worth living, the opinion of others around them that it is not can threaten their reason for living and make euthanasia a rational choice. Thus the existence of the option becomes a subtle pressure to request it.

This argument correctly identifies the reason why offering some patients the option of euthanasia would not benefit them. Velleman takes it not as a reason for opposing all euthanasia, but for restricting it to circumstances where there are "unmistakable and overpowering reasons for persons to want the option of euthanasia," and for denying the option in all other cases. But there are at least three reasons why such restriction may not be warranted. First, polls and other evidence support that most Americans believe euthanasia should be permitted (though the recent defeat of the referendum to permit it in the state of Washington raises some doubt about this support). Thus, many more people seem to want the choice than would be made worse off by getting it. Second, if giving people the option of ending their life really makes them worse off, then we should not only prohibit euthanasia, but also take back from people the right they now have to decide about life-sustaining treatment. The feared harmful effect should already have occurred from securing people's right to refuse life-sustaining treatment, yet there is no evidence of any such widespread harm or any broad public desire to rescind that right. Third, since there is a wide range of conditions in which reasonable people can and do disagree about whether they would want continued life, it is not possible to restrict the permissibility of euthanasia as narrowly as Velleman suggests without thereby denying it to most persons who would want it; to permit it only in cases in which virtually everyone would want it would be to deny it to most who would want it.

A fifth potential bad consequence of making euthanasia legally permissible is that it might weaken the general legal prohibition of homicide. This prohibition is so fundamental to civilized society, it is argued, that we should do nothing that erodes it. If most cases of stopping life support are killing, as I have already argued, then the court cases permitting such killing have already in effect weakened this prohibition. However, neither the courts nor most people have seen these cases as killing and so as challenging the prohibition of homicide. The courts have usually grounded patients' or their surrogates' rights to refuse life-sustaining treatment in rights to privacy, liberty, self-determination, or bodily integrity, not in exceptions to homicide laws.

Legal permission for physicians or others to perform euthanasia could not be grounded in patients' rights to decide about medical treatment. Permitting euthanasia would require qualifying, at least in effect, the legal prohibition against homicide, a prohibition that in general does not allow the consent of the victim to justify or excuse the act. Nevertheless, the very same fundamental basis of the right to decide about life-sustaining treatment—respecting a person's self-determination—does support euthanasia as well. Individual self-determination has long been a well-entrenched and fundamental value in the law, and so extending it to euthanasia would not require appeal to novel legal values or principles. That suicide or attempted suicide is no longer a criminal offense in virtually all states indicates an acceptance of individual self-determination in the taking of one's own life analogous to that required for voluntary active euthanasia. The legal prohibition (in most states) of assisting in suicide and the refusal in the law to accept the consent of the victim as a possible justification of homicide are both arguably a result of difficulties in the legal process of establishing the consent of the victim after the fact. If procedures can be designed that clearly establish the voluntariness of the person's request for euthanasia it would under those procedures represent a carefully circumscribed qualification on the legal prohibition of homicide. Nevertheless, some remaining worries about this weakening can be captured in the final potential bad consequence, to which I will now turn.

This final potential bad consequence is the central concern of many opponents of euthanasia and, I believe, is the most serious objection to a legal policy permitting it. According to this "slippery slope" worry, although active euthanasia may be morally permissible in cases in which it is unequivocally voluntary and the patient finds his or her condition unbearable, a legal policy permitting euthanasia would inevitably lead to active euthanasia being performed in many other cases in which it would be morally wrong. To prevent those other wrongful cases of euthanasia we should not permit even morally justified performance of it.

Slippery slope arguments of this form are problematic and difficult to evaluate.[14] From one perspective, they are the last refuge of conservative defenders of the status quo. When all the opponent's objections to the wrongness of euthanasia itself have been met, the opponent then shifts ground and acknowledges both that it is not in itself wrong and that a legal policy which resulted only in its being performed would not be bad. Nevertheless, the opponent maintains, it should still not be permitted because doing so would result in its being performed in other cases in which it is not voluntary and would be wrong. In this argument's most extreme form, permitting euthanasia is the first and fateful step down the slippery slope to Nazism. Once on the slope we will be unable to get off.

Now it cannot be denied that it is possible that permitting euthanasia could have these fateful consequences, but that cannot be enough to warrant prohibiting it if it is otherwise justified. A similar possible slippery slope worry could have been raised to securing competent patients' rights to decide about life support, but recent history shows such a worry would have been unfounded. It must be relevant how likely it is that we will end with horrendous consequences and an unjustified practice of euthanasia. How likely and widespread would the abuses and unwarranted extensions of permitting it be? By abuses, I mean the performance of euthanasia that fails to satisfy the conditions required for voluntary active euthanasia, for example, if the patient has been subtly pressured to accept it. By unwarranted extensions of policy, I mean later changes in legal policy to permit not just voluntary euthanasia, but also euthanasia in cases in which, for example, it need not be fully voluntary. Opponents of voluntary euthanasia on slippery slope grounds have not provided the data or evidence necessary to turn their speculative concerns into well-grounded likelihoods.

It is at least clear, however, that both the character and likelihood of abuses of a legal policy permitting euthanasia depend in significant part on the procedures put in place to protect against them. I will not try to detail fully what such procedures might be, but will just give some examples of what they might include:

1. The patient should be provided with all relevant information about his or her medical condition, current prognosis, available alternative treatments, and the prognosis of each.
2. Procedures should ensure that the patient's request for euthanasia is stable or enduring (a brief waiting period could be required) and fully voluntary (an advocate for the patient might be appointed to ensure this).

3. All reasonable alternatives must have been explored for improving the patient's quality of life and relieving any pain or suffering.
4. A psychiatric evaluation should ensure that the patient's request is not the result of a treatable psychological impairment such as depression.[15]

These examples of procedural safeguards are all designed to ensure that the patient's choice is fully informed, voluntary, and competent, and so a true exercise of self-determination. Other proposals for euthanasia would restrict its permissibility further—for example, to the terminally ill—a restriction that cannot be supported by self-determination. Such additional restrictions might, however, be justified by concern for limiting potential harms from abuse. At the same time, it is important not to impose procedural or substantive safeguards so restrictive as to make euthanasia impermissible or practically infeasible in a wide range of justified cases.

These examples of procedural safeguards make clear that it is possible to substantially reduce, though not to eliminate, the potential for abuse of a policy permitting voluntary active euthanasia. Any legalization of the practice should be accompanied by a well-considered set of procedural safeguards together with an ongoing evaluation of its use. Introducing euthanasia into only a few states could be a form of carefully limited and controlled social experiment that would give us evidence about the benefits and harms of the practice. Even then firm and uncontroversial data may remain elusive, as the continuing controversy over what has taken place in the Netherlands in recent years indicates.[16]

The Slip into Nonvoluntary Active Euthanasia

While I believe slippery slope worries can largely be limited by making necessary distinctions both in principle and in practice, one slippery slope concern is legitimate. There is reason to expect that legalization of voluntary active euthanasia might soon be followed by strong pressure to legalize some nonvoluntary euthanasia of incompetent patients unable to express their own wishes. Respecting a person's self-determination and recognizing that continued life is not always of value to a person can support not only voluntary active euthanasia, but some nonvoluntary euthanasia as well. These are the same values that ground competent patients' right to refuse life-sustaining treatment. Recent history here is instructive. In the medical ethics literature, in the courts since Quinlan, and in norms of medical practice, that right has been extended to incompetent patients and exercised by a surrogate who is to decide as the patient would have decided in the circumstances if competent.[17] It has been held unreasonable to continue life-sustaining treatment that the patient would not have wanted just because the patient now lacks the capacity to tell us that. Life-sustaining treatment for incompetent patients is today frequently forgone on the basis of a surrogate's decision, or less frequently on the basis of an advance directive executed by the patient while still competent. The very same logic that has extended the right to refuse life-sustaining treatment from a competent patient to the surrogate of an incompetent patient (acting with or without a formal advance directive from the patient) may well extend the scope of active euthanasia. The argument will be, Why continue to force unwanted life on patients just because they have now lost the capacity to request euthanasia from us?

A related phenomenon may reinforce this slippery slope concern. In the Netherlands, what the courts have sanctioned has been clearly restricted to voluntary euthanasia. In itself, this serves as some evidence that permitting it need not lead to permitting the nonvoluntary variety. There is some indication, however, that for many Dutch physicians euthanasia is no longer viewed as a special action, set apart from their usual practice and restricted only to competent persons.[18] Instead, it is seen as one end of a spectrum of caring for dying patients. When viewed in this way it will be difficult to deny euthanasia to a patient for whom it is seen as the best or most appropriate form of care simply because that patient is now incompetent and cannot request it.

Even if voluntary active euthanasia should slip into nonvoluntary active euthanasia, with surrogates acting for incompetent patients, the ethical evaluation is more complex than many opponents of euthanasia allow. Just as in the case of surrogates' decisions to forgo life-sustaining treatment for incompetent patients, so also surrogates' decisions to request euthanasia for incompetent persons would often accurately reflect what the incompetent person would have wanted and would deny the person nothing that he or she would have considered worth having. Making nonvoluntary active euthanasia legally permissible, however, would greatly enlarge the number of patients on whom it might be performed and substantially enlarge the potential for misuse and abuse. As noted above, frail and debilitated elderly people, often demented or otherwise incompetent and thereby unable to defend and assert their own interests, may be especially vulnerable to unwanted euthanasia.

For some people, this risk is more than sufficient reason to oppose the legalization of voluntary euthanasia. But while we should in general be cautious about inferring much from the experience in the Netherlands to what our own experience in the United States might be, there may be one important lesson that we can learn from them. One commentator has noted that in the Netherlands families of incompetent patients have less authority than do families in the United States to act as surrogates for incompetent patients in making decisions to forgo life-sustaining treatment.[19] From the Dutch perspective, it may be we in the United States who are already on the slippery slope in having given surrogates broad authority to forgo life-sustaining treatment for incompetent persons. In this view, the more important moral divide, and the more important with regard to potential for abuse, is not between forgoing life-sustaining treatment and euthanasia, but instead between voluntary and nonvoluntary performance of either. If this is correct, then the more important issue is ensuring the appropriate principles and procedural safeguards for the exercise of decisionmaking authority by surrogates for incompetent persons in all decisions at the end of life. This may be the correct response to slippery slope worries about euthanasia.

I have cited both good and bad consequences that have been thought likely from a policy change permitting voluntary active euthanasia, and have tried to evaluate their likelihood and relative importance. Nevertheless, as I noted earlier, reasonable disagreement remains both about the consequences of permitting euthanasia and about which of these consequences are more important. The depth and strength of public and professional debate about whether, all things considered, permitting euthanasia would be desirable or undesirable reflects these disagreements. While my own view is that the balance of considerations supports permitting the practice, my principal purpose here has been to clarify the main issues.

NOTES

1. Willard Gaylin, Leon R. Kass, Edmund D. Pellegrino, and Mark Siegler, "Doctors Must Not Kill," *JAMA* 259 (1988): 2139–40.

2. Bonnie Steinbock, ed., *Killing and Allowing to Die* (Englewood Cliffs, N.J.: Prentice-Hall, 1980).

3. Dan W. Brock, "Forgoing Food and Water: Is It Killing?" in *By No Extraordinary Means: The Choice to Forgo Life-Sustaining Food and Water*, ed. Joanne Lynn (Bloomington: Indiana University Press, 1986), pp. 117–31.

4. James Rachels, "Active and Passive Euthanasia," *NEJM* 292 (1975): 78–80; Michael Tooley, *Abortion and Infanticide* (Oxford: Oxford University Press, 1983). In my paper, "Taking Human Life," *Ethics* 95 (1985): 851–65, I argue in more detail that killing in itself is not morally different from allowing to die and defend the strategy of argument employed in this and the succeeding two paragraphs in the text.

5. Dan W. Brock, "Moral Rights and Permissible Killing," in *Ethical Issues Relating to Life and Death*, ed. John Ladd (New York: Oxford University Press, 1979), pp. 94–117.

6. P. Painton and E. Taylor, "Love or Let Die," *Time*, 19 March 1990, pp. 62–71; *Boston Globe*/Harvard University Poll, *Boston Globe*, 3 November 1991.

7. James Rachels, *The End of Life* (Oxford: Oxford University Press, 1986).

8. Marcia Angell, "The Quality of Mercy," *NEJM* 306 (1982): 98–99; M. Donovan, P. Dillon, and L. Mcguire, Incidence and Characteristics of Pain in a Sample of Medical-Surgical Inpatients," *Pain* 30 (1987): 69–78.

9. Eric Cassell, *The Nature of Suffering and the Goals of Medicine* (New York: Oxford University Press, 1991).

10. Gaylin et al., "Doctors Must Not Kill."

11. Paul J. Van der Maas et al., "Euthanasia and Other Medical Decisions Concerning the End of Life," *Lancet* 338 (1991): 669–74.

12. Susan M. Wolf, "Holding the Line on Euthanasia," Special Supplement, *Hastings Center Report* 19, no. 1 (1989): 13–15.

13. My formulation of this argument derives from David Velleman's statement of it in his commentary on an earlier version of this paper delivered at the American Philosophical Association Central Division meetings; a similar point was made to me by Elisha Milgram in discussion on another occasion. For more general development of the point see Thomas Schelling, *The Strategy of Conflict* (Cambridge, Mass.: Harvard University Press, 1960); and Gerald Dworkin, "Is More Choice Better Than Less?" in *The Theory and Practice of Autonomy* (Cambridge: Cambridge University Press, 1988).

14. Frederick Schauer, "Slippery Slopes," *Harvard Law Review* 99 (1985): 361–83; Wibren van der Burg, "The Slippery Slope Argument," *Ethics* 102 (October 1991): 42–65.

15. There is evidence that physicians commonly fail to diagnose depression. See Robert I. Misbin, "Physicians Aid in Dying," *NEJM* 325 (1991): 1304–7.

16. Richard Fenigsen, "A Case against Dutch Euthanasia," Special Supplement, *Hastings Center Report* 19, no. 1 (1989): 22–30.

17. Allen E. Buchanan and Dan W. Brock, *Deciding for Others: The Ethics of Surrogate Decisionmaking* (Cambridge: Cambridge University Press, 1989).

18. Van der Maas et al., "Euthanasia and Other Medical Decisions."

19. Margaret P. Battin, "Seven Caveats Concerning the Discussion of Euthanasia in Holland," *American Philosophical Association Newsletter on Philosophy and Medicine* 89, no. 2 (1990).

When Self-Determination Runs Amok

DANIEL CALLAHAN

Callahan is opposed to the use of voluntary euthanasia and assisted suicide. He argues that a person's right of self-determination does not morally justify someone else killing that person, even for mercy's sake. He contends that, contrary to common opinion, there is indeed a moral difference between killing and letting die. A policy that lets physicians practice euthanasia will lead to dire consequences and pervert the profession of medicine.

The euthanasia debate is not just another moral debate, one in a long list of arguments in our pluralistic society. It is profoundly emblematic of three important turning points in Western thought. The first is that of the legitimate conditions under which one person can kill another. The acceptance of voluntary active euthanasia would morally sanction what can only be called "consenting adult killing." By the term I mean the killing of one person by another in the name of their mutual right to be killer and killed if they freely agree to play those roles. This turn flies in the face of a long-standing effort to limit the circumstances under which one person can take the life of another, from efforts to control the free flow of guns and arms, to abolish capital punishment, and to more tightly control warfare. Euthanasia would add a whole new category of killing to a society that already has too many excuses to indulge itself in that way.

The second turning point lies in the meaning and limits of self-determination. The acceptance of euthanasia would sanction a view of autonomy holding that individuals may, in the name of their own private, idiosyncratic view of the good life, call upon others, including such institutions as medicine, to help them pursue that life, even at the risk of harm to the common good. This works against the idea that the meaning and scope of our own right to lead our own lives must be conditioned by, and be compatible with, the good of the community, which is more than an aggregate of self-directing individuals.

The third turning point is to be found in the claim being made upon medicine: it should be prepared to make its skills available to individuals to help them achieve their private vision of the good life. This puts medicine in the business of promoting the individualistic pursuit of general human happiness and well-being. It would overturn the traditional belief that medicine should limit its domain to promoting and preserving human health, redirecting it instead to the relief of that suffering which stems from life itself, not merely from a sick body.

I believe that, at each of these three turning points, proponents of euthanasia push us in the wrong direction. Arguments in favor of euthanasia fall into four general categories, which I will take up in turn: (1) the moral claim of individual self-determination and well-being; (2) the moral irrelevance of the difference between killing and allowing to die; (3) the supposed paucity of evidence to show likely harmful consequences of legalized euthanasia; and (4) the compatibility of euthanasia and medical practice.

Self-Determination

Central to most arguments for euthanasia is the principle of self-determination. People are presumed to have an interest in deciding for themselves, according to their own beliefs about what makes life good, how they will conduct their lives. That is an important value, but the question in the euthanasia context is, What does it mean and how far should it extend? If it were a question of suicide, where a person takes their own life without assistance from another, that principle might be pertinent, at least for debate. But euthanasia is not that limited a matter. The self-determination in that case can only be effected by the moral and physical assistance of another. Euthanasia is thus no longer a matter only of self-determination, but of a mutual, social decision between two people, the one to be killed and the other to do the killing.

How are we to make the moral move from my right of self-determination to some doctor's right to kill me—from *my* right to *his* right? Where does the doctor's moral warrant to kill come from? Ought doctors to be able to kill anyone they want as long as permission is given by competent persons? Is our right to life just like a piece of property, to be given away or alienated if the price (happiness, relief of suffering) is right? And then to be destroyed with our permission once alienated?

In answer to all those questions, I will say this: I have yet to hear a plausible argument why it should be permissible for us to put this kind of power in the hands of another, whether a doctor or anyone else. The idea that we can waive our right to life, and then give to another the power to take that life, requires a justification yet to be provided by anyone.

Slavery was long ego outlawed on the ground that one person should not have the right to own another, even with the other's permission. Why? Because it is a fundamental moral wrong for one person to give over his life and fate to another, whatever the good consequences, and no less a wrong for another person to have that kind of total, final power. Like slavery, dueling was long ago banned on similar grounds: even free, competent individuals should not have the power to kill each other, whatever their motives, whatever the circumstances. Consenting adult killing, like consenting adult slavery or degradation, is a strange route to human dignity.

There is another problem as well. If doctors, once sanctioned to carry out euthanasia, are to be themselves responsible moral agents—not simply hired hands with lethal injections at the ready—then they must have their own *independent* moral grounds to kill those who request such services. What do I mean? As those who favor euthanasia are quick to point out, some people want it because their life has become so burdensome it no longer seems worth living.

The doctor will have a difficulty at this point. The degree and intensity to which people suffer from their diseases and their dying, and whether they find life more of a burden than a benefit, has very little directly to do with the nature or extent of their actual physical condition. Three people can have the same condition, but only one will find the suffering unbearable. People suffer, but suffering is as much a function of the values of individuals as it is of the physical causes of that suffering. Inevitably in that circumstance, the doctor will in effect be treating the patient's values. To be responsible, the doctor would have to share those values. The doctor would have to decide, on her own, whether the patient's life was "no longer worth living."

But how could a doctor possibly know that or make such a judgment? Just because the patient said so? I raise this question because, while in Holland at the euthanasia conference reported by Maurice de Wachter . . . , the doctors present agreed that there is no objective way of measuring or judging the claims of patients that their suffering is unbearable. And if it is difficult to measure suffering, how much more difficult to determine the value of a patient's statement that her life is not worth living?

However one might want to answer such questions, the very need to ask them, to inquire into the physician's responsibility and grounds for medical and moral judgment, points out the social nature of the decision. Euthanasia is not a private matter of self-determination. It is an act that requires two people to make it possible, and a complicit society to make it acceptable.

Killing and Allowing to Die

Against common opinion, the argument is sometimes made that there is no moral difference between stopping life-sustaining treatment and more active forms of killing, such as lethal injection. Instead I would contend that the notion that there is no morally significant difference between omission and commission is just wrong. Consider in its broad implications what the eradication of the distinction implies: that death from disease has been banished, leaving only the actions of physicians in terminating treatment as the cause of death. Biology, which used to bring about death, has apparently been displaced by human agency. Doctors have finally, I suppose, thus genuinely become gods, now doing what nature and the deities once did.

What is the mistake here? It lies in confusing causality and culpability, and in failing to note the way in which human societies have overlaid natural causes with moral rules and interpretations. Causality (by which I mean the direct physical causes of death) and culpability (by which I mean our attribution of moral responsibility to human actions) are confused under three circumstances.

They are confused, first, when the action of a physician in stopping treatment of a patient with an underlying lethal disease is construed as *causing* death. On the contrary, the physician's omission can only bring about death on the condition that the patient's disease will kill him in the absence of treatment. We may hold the physician morally responsible for the death, if we have morally judged such actions wrongful omissions. But it confuses reality and moral judgment to see an omitted action as having the same causal status as one that directly kills. A lethal injection will kill both a healthy person and a sick person. A physician's omitted treatment will have no effect on a healthy person. Turn off the machine on me, a healthy person, and nothing will happen. It will only, in contrast, bring the life of a sick person to an end because of an underlying fatal disease.

Causality and culpability are confused, second, when we fail to note that judgments of moral responsibility and culpability are human constructs. By that I mean that we human beings, after moral reflection, have decided to call some actions right or wrong, and to devise moral rules to deal with them. When physicians could do nothing to stop death, they were not held responsible for it. When, with medical progress, they began to have some power over death—but only its timing and circumstances, not its ultimate inevitability—moral rules were devised to set forth their obligations. Natural causes of death were not thereby banished. They were, instead, overlaid with a medical ethics designed to determine moral culpability in deploying medical power.

To confuse the judgments of this ethics with the physical causes of death—which is the connotation of the word *kill*—is to confuse nature and human action. People will, one way or another, die of some disease; death will have dominion over all of us. To say that a doctor "kills" a patient by allowing this to happen should only be understood as a moral judgment about the licitness of his omission, nothing more. We can, as a fashion of speech only, talk about a doctor *killing* a patient by omitting treatment he should have provided. It is a fashion of speech precisely because it is the underlying disease that brings death when treatment is omitted; that is its cause, not the physician's omission. It is a misuse of the word *killing* to use it when a doctor stops a treatment he believes will no longer benefit the patient—when, that is, he steps aside to allow an eventually inevitable death to occur now rather than later. The only deaths that human beings invented are those that come from direct killing—when, with a lethal injection, we both cause death and are morally responsible for it. In the case of omissions, we do not cause death even if we may be judged morally responsible for it.

This difference between causality and culpability also helps us see why a doctor who has omitted a treatment he should have provided has "killed" that patient while another doctor—performing precisely the same act of omission on another patient in different circumstances—does not kill her, but only allows her to die. The difference is that we have come, by moral convention and conviction, to classify unauthorized or illegitimate omissions as acts of "killing." We call them "killing" in the expanded sense of the term: a culpable action that permits the real cause of death, the underlying disease, to proceed to its lethal conclusion. By contrast, the doctor who, at the patient's request, omits or terminates unwanted treatment does not kill at all. Her underlying disease, not his action, is the physical cause of death; and we have agreed to consider actions of that kind to be morally licit. He thus can truly be said to have "allowed" her to die.

If we fail to maintain the distinction between killing and allowing to die, moreover, there are some disturbing possibilities. The first would be to confirm many physicians in their already too-powerful belief that, when patients die or when physicians stop treatment because of the futility of continuing it, they are somehow both morally and physically responsible for the deaths that follow. That notion needs to be abolished, not strengthened. It needlessly and wrongly burdens the physician, to whom should not be attributed the powers of the gods. The second possibility would be that, in every case where a doctor judges medical treatment no longer effective in prolonging life, a quick and direct killing of the patient would be seen as the next, most reasonable step, on grounds of both humaneness and economics. I do not see how that logic could easily be rejected.

Calculating the Consequences

When concerns about the adverse social consequences of permitting euthanasia are raised, its advocates tend to dismiss them as unfounded and overly speculative. On the contrary, recent data about the Dutch experience suggests that such concerns are right on target. From my own discussions in Holland, and from the articles on that subject in this issue and elsewhere, I believe we can now fully see most of the *likely* consequences of legal euthanasia.

Three consequences seem almost certain, in this or any other country: the inevitability of some abuse of the law; the difficulty of precisely writing, and then enforcing, the law; and the inherent slipperiness of the moral reasons for legalizing euthanasia in the first place.

Why is abuse inevitable? One reason is that almost all laws on delicate, controversial matters are to some extent abused. This happens because not everyone will agree with the law as written and will bend it, or ignore it, if they can get away with it. From explicit admissions to me by Dutch proponents of euthanasia, and from the corroborating information provided by the Remmelink Report and the outside studies of Carlos Gomez and John Keown, I am convinced that in the Netherlands there are a substantial number of cases of nonvoluntary euthanasia, that is, euthanasia undertaken without the explicit permission of the person being killed. The other reason abuse is inevitable is that the law is likely to have a low enforcement priority in the criminal justice system. Like other laws of similar status, unless there is an unrelenting and harsh willingness to pursue abuse, violations will ordinarily be tolerated. The worst thing to me about my experience in Holland was the casual, seemingly indifferent attitude toward abuse. I think that would happen everywhere.

Why would it be hard to precisely write, and then enforce, the law? The Dutch speak about the requirement of "unbearable" suffering, but admit that such a term is just about indefinable, a highly subjective matter admitting of no objective standards. A requirement for outside opinion is nice, but it is easy to find complaisant colleagues. A requirement that a medical condition be "terminal" will run aground on the notorious difficulties of knowing when an illness is actually terminal.

Apart from those technical problems there is a more profound worry. I see no way, even in principle, to write or enforce a meaningful law that can guarantee effective procedural safeguards. The reason is obvious yet almost always overlooked. The euthanasia transaction will ordinarily take place within the boundaries of the private and confidential doctor-patient relationship. No one can possibly know what takes place in that context unless the doctor chooses to reveal it. In Holland, less than 10 percent of the physicians report their acts of euthanasia and do so with almost complete legal impunity. There is no reason why the situation should be any better elsewhere. Doctors will have their own reasons for keeping euthanasia secret, and some patients will have no less a motive for wanting it concealed.

I would mention, finally, that the moral logic of the motives for euthanasia contain within them the ingredients of abuse. The two standard motives for euthanasia and assisted suicide are said to be our right of self-determination, and our claim upon the mercy of others, especially doctors, to relieve our suffering. These two motives are typically spliced together and presented as a single justification. Yet if they are considered independently—and there is no inherent reason why they must be linked—they reveal serious problems. It is said that a competent, adult person should have a right to euthanasia for the relief of suffering. But why must the person be suffering? Does not that stipulation already compromise the principle of self-determination? How can self-determination have any limits? Whatever the person's motives may be, why are they not sufficient?

Consider next the person who is suffering but not competent, who is perhaps demented or mentally retarded. The standard argument would deny euthanasia to that person. But why? If a person is suffering but not competent, then it would seem grossly unfair to deny relief solely on the grounds of incompetence. Are the incompetent less entitled to relief from suffering than the competent? Will it only be affluent, middle-class people, mentally fit and savvy about working the medical system, who can qualify? Do the incompetent suffer less because of their incompetence?

Considered from these angles, there are no good moral reasons to limit euthanasia once the principle of taking life for that purpose has been legitimated. If we really believe in self-determination, then any competent person should have a right to be killed by a doctor for any reason that suits him. If we believe in the relief of suffering, then it seems cruel and capricious to deny it to the incompetent. There is, in short, no reasonable or logical stopping point once the turn has been made down the road to euthanasia, which could soon turn into a convenient and commodious expressway.

Euthanasia and Medical Practice

A fourth kind of argument one often hears both in the Netherlands and in this country is that euthanasia and assisted suicide are perfectly compatible with the aims of medicine. I would note at the very outset that a physician who participates in another person's suicide already abuses medicine. Apart from depression (the main statistical cause of suicide), people commit suicide because they find life empty, oppressive, or meaningless. Their judgment is a judgment about the value of continued life, not only about health (even if they are sick). Are doctors now to be given the right to make judgments about the kinds of life worth living and to give their blessing to suicide for those they judge wanting? What conceivable competence, technical or moral, could doctors claim to play such a role? Are we to medicalize suicide, turning judgments about its worth and value into one more clinical issue? Yes, those are rhetorical questions.

Yet they bring us to the core of the problem of euthanasia and medicine. The great temptation of modern medicine, not always resisted, is to move beyond the promotion and preservation of health into the boundless realm of general human happiness and well-being. The root problem of illness and mortality is both medical and philosophical or religious. "Why must I die?" can be asked as a technical, biological question or as a question about the meaning of life. When medicine tries to respond to the latter, which it is always under pressure to do, it moves beyond its proper role.

It is not medicine's place to lift from us the burden of that suffering which turns on the meaning we assign to the decay of the body and its eventual death. It is not medicine's place to determine when lives are not worth living or when the burden of life is too great to be borne. Doctors have no conceivable way of evaluating such claims on the part of patients, and they should have no right to act in response to them. Medicine should try to relieve human suffering, but only that suffering which is brought on by illness and dying as biological phenomena, not that suffering which comes from anguish or despair at the human condition.

Doctors ought to relieve those forms of suffering that medically accompany serious illness and the threat of death. They should relieve pain, do what they can to allay anxiety and uncertainty, and be a comforting presence. As sensitive human beings, doctors should be prepared to respond to patients who ask why they must die, or die in pain. But here the doctor and the patient are at the same level. The doctor may have no better an answer to those old questions than anyone else; and certainly no special insight from his training as a physician. It would be terrible for physicians to forget this, and to think that in a swift, lethal injection, medicine has found its own answer to the riddle of life. It would be a false answer, given by the wrong people. It would be no less a false answer for patients. They should neither ask medicine to put its own vocation at risk to serve their private interests, nor think that the answer to suffering is to be killed by another. The problem is precisely that, too often in human history, killing has seemed the quick, efficient way to put aside that which burdens us. It rarely helps, and too often simply adds to one evil still another. That is what I believe euthanasia would accomplish. It is self-determination run amok.

When Abstract Moralizing Runs Amok

JOHN LACHS

In this response to Daniel Callahan's condemnation of voluntary euthanasia, Lachs argues that Callahan misunderstands the suffering and motivations of those who ask to die. Moreover, Lachs says, it is implausible to claim as Callahan does that a right to kill ourselves cannot be transferred to someone else. Callahan maintains that there are no good moral reasons to limit euthanasia once the practice has been legitimated, but Lachs contends that good moral reasons can come from our consideration of important distinctions and specific circumstances. Callahan suggests that self-determination will have us "run amok" in taking lives without restraint; Lachs declares, however, "No serious moralist has ever argued that self-determination must be absolute."

Moral reasoning is more objectionable when it is abstract than when it is merely wrong. For abstractness all but guarantees error by missing the human predicament that needs to be addressed, and worse, it is a sign that thought has failed to keep faith with its mission. The function of moral reflection is to shed light on the difficult problems we face; it cannot perform its job without a clear understanding of how and why certain of our practices come to seem no longer satisfactory.

It is just this grasp of the problem that is conspicuously lacking in Daniel Callahan's assault on euthanasia in "Self-Determination Run Amok."[1] The rhetoric Callahan unleashes gives not even a hint of the grave contemporary moral problems that euthanasia and assisted suicide, a growing number of people now think, promise to resolve.

Instead, we are offered a set of abstract principles, calculated to discredit euthanasia rather than to contribute to a sound assessment of it. Thus, Callahan informs us that suffering "brought on by illness and dying as biological phenomena"[2] is to be contrasted with suffering that comes from "anguish or despair at the human condition." The former constitutes the proper concern of medicine (so much for psychiatry!), the latter of religion and philosophy. Medication is the answer to physical pain; euthanasia can, therefore, be only a misconceived response to worries about the meaning of existence. Those who believe in it offer a "swift lethal injection" as "the answer to the riddle of life."

This way of putting the matter will come as a surprise to those who suffer from terrible diseases and who no longer find life worth living. It is grotesque to suppose that such individuals are looking for the meaning of existence and find it, absurdly, in a lethal injection. Their predicament is not intellectual but existential. They are not interested in the meaning of life but in acting on their belief that their own continued existence is, on balance, of no further benefit to them.

Those who advocate the legalization of euthanasia and the practice of assisted suicide propose them

as answers to a serious and growing social problem. We now have the power to sustain the biological existence of large numbers of very sick people, and we use this power freely. Accordingly, individuals suffering from painful terminal diseases, Alzheimer's patients, and those in a persistent vegetative state are routinely kept alive long past the point where they can function as human beings. They must bear the pain of existence without the ability to perform the activities that give life meaning. Some of these people feel intensely that they are a burden to others, as well as to themselves, and that their speedy and relatively dignified departure would be a relief to all concerned. Many observers of no more than average sensitivity agree that the plight of these patients is severe enough to justify such desires.

Some of these sufferers are physically not in a position to end their lives. Others could do so if they had the necessary instruments. In our culture, however, few have a taste for blowing out their brains or jumping from high places. That leaves drugs, which almost everyone is accustomed to taking, and which everyone knows can ease one peacefully to the other side.

The medical profession has, however, acquired monopoly power over drugs. And the danger of legal entanglement has made physicians wary of helping patients hasten their deaths in the discreet, humane way that has been customary for centuries. The result is that people who want to die and for whom death has long ceased to be an evil can find no way out of their misery. Current and growing pressures on the medical profession to help such sufferers are, therefore, due at least partly to medicine itself. People want physicians to aid in their suicides because, without such help, they cannot end their lives. This restriction of human autonomy is due to the social power of medicine; it is neither surprising nor morally wrong, therefore, to ask those responsible for this limitation to undo some of its most noxious effects. If the medical profession relinquished its hold on drugs, people could make effective choices about their future without the assistance of physicians. Even limited access to deadly drugs, restricted to single doses for those who desire them and who are certified to be of sound mind and near the end of life, would keep physicians away from dealing in death.

Unfortunately, however, there is little sensible public discussion of such policy alternatives. And these policy alternatives may, in any case, not satisfy Callahan, who appears to believe that there is something radically wrong with anyone terminating a human life. Because he plays coy, his actual beliefs are difficult to make out. He says the notion that self-determination extends to suicide "might be pertinent, at least for debate."[3] But his argument against euthanasia sidesteps this issue: he maintains that even if there is a right to kill oneself, it is not one that can be transferred. The reason for this is that doing so would lead to "a fundamental moral wrong"—that of one person giving over "his life and fate to another."

One might wonder how we know that transferring power over oneself is "a fundamental moral wrong." Callahan appears to entertain the idea with intuitive certainty, which gives him the moral and the logical high ground and entitles him to demand a justification from whoever disagrees. But such intuitions are problematic themselves: is fervent embrace of them enough to guarantee their truth? Morality would be very distant from the concerns of life if it depended on such guideposts placed here and there in the desert of facts, unrelated to each other or to anything else. Their message, moreover, makes the guideposts suspect: it comes closer to being an echo of tradition or an expression of current views than a revelation of eternal moral truths.

Most important, the very idea of a right that intrinsically *cannot* be handed on is difficult to grasp. Under normal circumstances, to have a right is to be free or to be entitled to have or to do something. I have a right, for example, to clean my teeth. No one else has the right to do that without my consent. But I can authorize another, say my sweetheart or my dental hygienist, to do it for me. Similarly, I can assign my right to my house, my left kidney, to raising my children, to deciding when I rise, when I go to sleep, and what I do in between (by joining the Army), and by a power of attorney even to pursuing my own interest.

To be sure, the transfer of rights is not without limits. My wife and I can, for example, give over our right to our children, though we cannot do so for money. I can contract to slave away for ten hours a day cooking hamburgers, but I cannot sell myself to be, once and for all, a slave. This does not mean, however, that some rights are intrinsically nontransferable. If my right to my left kidney were nontransferable, I could neither sell it nor give it away. But I can give it away, and the only reason I cannot sell it is because sales of this sort were declared, at some point, to be against public policy. We cannot sell ourselves into slavery for the same reason: human societies set limits to the transfer of rights on account of its unacceptable costs.

The case is no different with respect to authorizing another to end my life. If I have a right to one of my kidneys, I have a right to both. And if I can tell a needy person to take one of them, I can tell two needy people to take one each. There is nothing *intrinsically* immoral about this, even though when the second helps himself I die. Yet, by dying too soon, I may leave opportunities unexplored and obligations unmet. Unscrupulous operators may take advantage of my goodwill or naiveté. The very possibility of such acts invites abuse. For these and similar reasons, we may decide that giving the first kidney is morally acceptable, but giving the second is not. The difference between the two acts, however, is not that the first is generous while the second is "a fundamental moral wrong," but that the second occurs in a context and has consequences and costs that the first does not.

Only in terms of contest and cost, therefore, can we sensibly consider the issue of the morality of euthanasia. Moving on the level of abstract maxims, Callahan misses this point altogether. He declares: "There are no good moral reasons to limit euthanasia once the principle of taking life . . . has been legitimated."[4] Serious moral reflection, though it takes principles into account, is little interested in legitimating *them*. Its focus is on determining the moral acceptability of certain sorts of actions performed in complex contexts of life. Consideration of the circumstances is always essential: it is fatuous, therefore, to argue that if euthanasia is ever permissible, then "any competent person should have a right to be killed by a doctor for any reason that suits him."[5]

We can achieve little progress in moral philosophy without the ability and readiness to make relevant distinctions. Why, then, does Callahan refuse to acknowledge that there are important differences between the situation of a terminally ill patient in grave pain who wants to die and that of a young father in the dental chair who wishes, for a moment, that he were dead? Callahan's reason is that he thinks all judgments about the unbearability of suffering and the worthlessness of one's existence are subjective and, as such, parts of a "private, idiosyncratic view of the good life."[6] The amount of suffering "has very little directly to do" with our physical condition, and so the desire to end life is capricious and unreliable. If medicine honored such desires, it would "put its own vocation at risk" by serving "the private interests" of individuals.

I cannot imagine what the vocation of medicine might be if it is not to serve the private interests of individuals. It is, after all, my vision of the good life that accounts for my wish not to perish in a diabetic coma. And surgeons certainly pursue the private interests of their patients in removing cancerous growths and in providing face-lifts. Medicine does not surrender its vocation in serving the desires of individuals: since health and continued life are among our primary wishes, its career consists in just this service.

Nevertheless, Callahan is right that our judgments about the quality of our lives and about the level of our suffering have a subjective component. But so do the opinions of patients about their health and illness, yet physicians have little difficulty in placing these perceptions in a broader, objective context. Similarly, it is both possible and proper to take into account the objective circumstances that surround desires to terminate life. Physicians have developed considerable skill in relating subjective complaints to objective conditions; only by absurd exaggeration can we say that the doctor must accept either all or none of the patient's claims. The context of the young father in the dental chair makes it clear that only a madman would think of switching from novocaine to cyanide when he moans that he wants to be dead. Even people of ordinary sensitivity understand that the situation of an older person whose friends have all died and who now suffers the excruciating pain of terminal cancer is morally different.

The question of the justifiability of euthanasia, as all difficult moral questions, cannot be asked without specifying the details of context. Dire warnings of slippery slopes and of future large-scale, quietly conducted exterminations trade on overlooking differences of circumstance. They insult our sensitivity by the suggestion that a society of individuals of good will cannot recognize situations in which their fellows want and need help and cannot distinguish such situations from those in which the desire for death is rhetorical, misguided, temporary, or idiotic. It would indeed be tragic if medicine were to leap to the aid of lovelorn teenagers whenever they feel life is too much to bear. But it is just as lamentable to stand idly by and watch unwanted lives fill up with unproductive pain.

Callahan is correct in pointing out that, in euthanasia and in assisted suicide, the physician and the patient must have separate justifications for action. The patient's wish is defensible if it is the outcome of a sound reflective judgment. Such judgments take into account the current condition, pending projects, and long-term prospects of the individual and relate them to his or her permanent interests and established values. As all assessments, these can be in error. For this reason, persons soliciting help in dying must be ready to demonstrate that they are of sound mind and thus capable of making such choices, that their desire is enduring, and that both their subjective and their objective condition makes their wish sensible.

Physicians must first decide whether their personal values permit them to participate in such activities. If they do, they must diligently examine the justifiability of the patient's desire to die. Diagnosis and prognosis are often relatively easy to ascertain. But we are not without resources for a sound determination of the internal condition of individuals either: extensive questioning on multiple occasions, interviews with friends and loved ones, and exploration of life history and values of people contribute mightily to understanding their state of mind. Physicians who are prepared to aid individuals with this last need of their lives are not, therefore, in a position where they have to believe everything they hear and act on every request. They must make independent judgments instead of subordinating themselves as unthinking tools to the passing desires of those they wish to help. This does not attribute to doctors "the powers of the gods." It only requires that they be flexible in how they aid their patients and that they do so with due caution and on the basis of sound evaluation.

Callahan is once again right to be concerned that, if allowed, euthanasia will "take place within the boundaries of the private and confidential doctor–patient relationship."[7] This does, indeed, invite abuse and permit callous physicians to take a casual attitude to a momentous decision. Callahan is wrong, however, in supposing that this constitutes an argument against euthanasia. It is only a reason not to keep euthanasia secret, but to shed on it the wholesome light of publicity. Though the decision to terminate life is intensely private, no moral consideration demands that it be kept the confidential possession of two individuals. To the contrary, the only way we can minimize wrong decisions and abuse is to require scrutiny of the decision, prior to action on it, by a suitable social body. Such examination, including at least one personal interview with the patient, should go a long distance toward relieving Callahan's concern that any law governing euthanasia would have "a low enforcement priority in the criminal justice system."[8] With formal social controls in place, there should be very little need for the involvement of courts and prosecutors.

To suppose, as Callahan does, that the principle of autonomy calls for us to stand idly by, or even to assist, whenever and for whatever reason people want to end their lives is calculated to discredit both euthanasia and autonomy. No serious moralist has ever argued that self-determination must be absolute. It cannot hold unlimited sway, as Mill and other advocates of the principle readily admit, if humans are to live in a society. And morally, it would cut no ice if murderers and rapists argued for the legitimacy of their actions by claiming that they flow naturally and solely from who they are.

The function of the principle of autonomy is to affirm *a* value and to shift the burden of justifying infringements of individual liberty to established social and governmental powers. The value it affirms is that of individual agency expressed in the belief that, through action and suffering and death, the life of each person enjoys a sort of private integrity. This means that, in the end, our lives belong to no one but ourselves. The limits to such self-determination or self-possession are set by the demands of social life. They can be discovered or decided upon in the process of moral reflection. A sensible approach to euthanasia can disclose how much weight autonomy carries in that context and how it can be balanced against other, equally legitimate but competing values.

In the hands of its friends, the principle of self-determination does not run amok. What runs amok in Callahan's version of autonomy and euthanasia is the sort of abstract moralizing that forgets the problem it sets out to address and shuts its eye to need and suffering.

NOTES

1. D. Callahan, "Self-Determination Run Amok," *Hastings Center Report* 22 (March–April 1992): 52–55.
2. *Ibid.*, 55.
3. *Ibid.*, 52.
4. *Ibid.*, 54.
5. *Ibid.*
6. *Ibid.*, 52.
7. *Ibid.*, 54.
8. *Ibid.*

Physician-Assisted Suicide: A Tragic View

JOHN D. ARRAS

Arras is a firm believer in autonomy and finds himself "deeply sympathetic to the central values motivating the case for [physician-assisted suicide] and euthanasia." Nevertheless, he argues that legalizing the practices poses "too great a threat to the rights and welfare of too many people."

For many decades now, the calls for PAS and euthanasia have been perennial lost causes in American society. Each generation has thrown up an assortment of earnest reformers and cranks who, after attracting their fifteen minutes of fame, inevitably have been defeated by the combined weight of traditional law and morality. Incredibly, two recent federal appellate court decisions suddenly changed the legal landscape in this area, making the various states within their respective jurisdictions the first governments in world history, excepting perhaps the Nazi regime in Germany, to officially sanction PAS. Within the space of a month, both an eight-to-three majority of the United States Court of Appeals for the Ninth Circuit[1] on the West Coast, and a three-judge panel in the United States Court of Appeals for the Second Circuit,[2] in the Northeast, struck down long-standing state laws forbidding physicians to aid or abet their patients in acts of suicide. Within a virtual blink of an eye, the unthinkable had come to pass: PAS and euthanasia had emerged from their exile beyond the pale of law to occupy center stage in a dramatic public debate that eventually culminated in the United States Supreme Court's unanimous reversal of both lower court decisions in June 1997.[3]

Judge Reinhardt, writing for a majority of an *en banc* decision of the Ninth Circuit,[4] held that competent, terminally ill patients have a powerful "liberty interest," what used to be called a Constitutional right, to enlist the aid of their physicians in hastening death via prescriptions for lethal drugs.[5] He argued that, just as the right to privacy guarantees women the right to choose an abortion, this liberty interest protects a right to choose the time and manner of one's death.[6]

In response to warnings against the expansion of this right to broader categories of patients (e.g., to the mentally incapacitated) and against the great likelihood of mistake and abuse, Judge Reinhardt permitted the regulation of PAS in order to avoid such evils; however, he pointedly ruled out any and all blanket prohibitions.[7] In response to the traditional objections that allowing PAS would subvert the state's interests in preventing suicide and maintaining the integrity of the medical profession, Judge Reinhardt contended that our society already has effectively erased the distinction between merely allowing patients to die and killing them.[8] Reinhardt claimed that by allowing patients or their surrogates to forgo life-sustaining medical treatments, including artificially administered nutrition and hydration, and by sanctioning the administration of pain-killing drugs that might also hasten death, our society already permits a variety of "death inducing" practices. Thus, the social risks of allowing PAS are only different in degree, not in kind, from risks that we already countenance.

Writing for the Second Circuit in striking down a similar New York statute, Judge Miner explicitly rejected the claim of the Second Circuit majority that a "substantive due process" right of PAS exists in the Constitution. While presciently conceding that the Supreme Court was unlikely to extend the boundaries of the so-called right to privacy, Judge Miner found nevertheless that the statute violated the equal protection clause of the Constitution.[9] Echoing Judge Reinhardt's assertion that only a difference of degree separates PAS from the foregoing of life-sustaining treatments—claiming in effect that the administration of potentially death hastening analgesics constitutes a kind of suicide—Judge Miner observed that New York's law allowed some people relief from the ravages of terminal illness (i.e., those connected to some form of removable life-support) while denying relief to those not so connected, for whom PAS was the only remaining exit.[10] Concurring with Judge Reinhardt that the social risks of PAS are identical to those of our more socially approved "death inducing" practices, Judge Miner concluded that this kind of differential treatment serves no legitimate state purpose. Thus, he held that the law was unconstitutional even in the absence of a new fundamental right to PAS.[11]

What to think of these startling decisions? Were they harbingers of a new world brave enough to overcome centuries of religious censure and fear-mongering, a world that will no longer permit human beings to suffer unwillingly the torments of terminal illness? Or were they dangerous aberrations,

From *Physician Assisted Suicide: Expanding the Debate* by Margaret P. Battin, Rosamond Rhodes, and Anita Silvers. New York and London: Routledge 1998, pp. 279–300. Reprinted with permission.

decisions that simultaneously affirmed the autonomy of some, while endangering the lives of society's most vulnerable citizens?

The Supreme Court has finally left little doubt about where it stands on these questions. In a set of majority and concurring opinions remarkable for their ideological restraint, compassion, and thoughtfulness, the various Justices have concluded that extant state laws barring PAS and euthanasia violate neither the Fourteenth Amendment protection of liberty nor the Fifth Amendment's due process provision.[12] While thus issuing a painful rebuke to the partisans of liberalization, each of the Justices tempered his or her final judgment with the recognition that their collective decision would by no means end public debate, but would rather displace it onto the agendas of the fifty state legislatures.

As a firm believer in patient autonomy, I find myself to be deeply sympathetic to the central values motivating the case for PAS and euthanasia; I have concluded, however, that these practices pose too great a threat to the rights and welfare of too many people to be legalized in this country at the present time. Central to my argument in this essay will be the claim that the recently overturned decisions of the circuit courts employ a form of case-based reasoning that is ill-suited to the development of sound social policy in this area. I shall argue that in order to do justice to the very real threats posed by the widespread social practices of PAS and euthanasia, we need to adopt precisely the kind of policy perspective that the circuit courts rejected on principle. Thus, this essay presents the case for a forward-looking, legislative approach to PAS and euthanasia, as opposed to an essentially backward-looking, judicial or constitutional approach.[13] Although I suggest below that the soundest legislative policy at the present time would be to extend the legal prohibition of PAS into the near future, I remain open to the possibility that a given legislature, presented with sufficient evidence of the reliability of various safeguards, might come to a different conclusion.

Arguments and Motivations in Favor of PAS/Euthanasia

Let us begin, then, with the philosophical case for PAS and euthanasia, which consists of two distinct prongs, both of which speak simply, directly, and powerfully to our commonsensical intuitions. First, there is the claim of autonomy, that all of us possess a right to self-determination in matters profoundly touching on such religious themes as life, death, and the meaning of suffering. Just as we should each be free to make important choices bearing on how we shall live our own lives, so we should be equally free in choosing the time and manner of our deaths. For some, more life will always be welcome as a gift or perhaps even as a test of faith, but for others, continued life signifies only disfiguring suffering and the unrelenting loss of everything that invested their lives with meaning and dignity. As philosopher Ronald Dworkin has eloquently argued, it is a form of *tyranny* to force someone to endure terrible suffering at the end-of-life merely for the sake of someone else's values.[14] Each of us should be free to live or die as we see fit according to our own conceptions of the meaning of life and death.

Second, PAS and/or euthanasia are merciful acts that deliver terminally ill patients from a painful and protracted death. According to the utilitarian, acts are morally right insofar as they promote happiness and alleviate unhappiness, and wrong insofar as they cause or allow others to suffer needlessly. Even according to the traditional ethic of the medical profession, physicians have a solemn duty not merely to extend life whenever possible (and desirable), but also to alleviate pain and suffering whenever possible. For patients suffering from the final ravages of end-stage AIDS or cancer, a doctor's lethal prescription or injection can be, and often is, welcomed as a blessed relief. Accordingly, we should treat human beings at least as well as we treat grievously ill or injured animals by putting them, at their own request, out of their misery.

These philosophical reflections can be supplemented with a more clinical perspective addressed to the motivational factors lying behind many requests to die. Many people advocate legalization because they fear a loss of control at the end-of-life. They fear falling victim to the technological imperative; they fear dying in chronic and uncontrolled pain; they fear the psychological suffering attendant upon the relentless disintegration of the self; they fear, in short, a bad death. All of these fears, it so happens, are eminently justified. Physicians routinely ignore the documented wishes of patients and all too often allow patients to die with uncontrolled pain.[15] Studies of cancer patients have shown that over 50 percent suffer from unrelieved pain,[16] and many researchers have found that uncontrolled pain, particularly when accompanied by feelings of hopelessness and untreated depression, is a significant contributing factor for suicide and suicidal ideation.[17]

Clinical depression is another major factor influencing patients' choice of suicide.[18] Depression, accompanied by feelings of hopelessness, is the strongest predictor of suicide for both individuals who are terminally ill and those who are not.[19] Yet most doctors are not trained to notice depression, especially in complex cases such as the elderly suffering from terminal illnesses. Even when doctors succeed in diagnosing depression, they often do not successfully treat it with sufficient amounts of readily available medications.[20]

Significantly, the New York State Task Force on Life and Law found that the vast majority of patients who request PAS or euthanasia can be treated successfully both for their depression and their pain, and that when they receive adequate psychiatric and palliative care, their requests to die usually are withdrawn.[21] In other words, patients given the requisite control over their lives and relief from depression and pain usually lose interest in PAS and euthanasia.[22]

With all due respect for the power of modern methods of pain control, it must be acknowledged that a small percentage of patients suffer from conditions, both physical and psychological, that currently lie beyond the reach of the best medical and humane care. Some pain cannot be alleviated short of inducing a permanent state of unconsciousness in the patient, and some depression is unconquerable. For such unfortunate patients, the present law on PAS/euthanasia can represent an insuperable barrier to a dignified and decent death.[23]

Objections to PAS/Euthanasia

Opponents of PAS and euthanasia can be grouped into three main factions. One strongly condemns both practices as inherently immoral, as violations of the moral rule against killing the innocent. Most members of this group tend to harbor distinctly religious objections to suicide and euthanasia, viewing them as violations of God's dominion over human life.[24] They argue that killing is simply wrong in itself, whether or not it is done out of respect for the patient's autonomy or out of concern for her suffering. Whether or not this position ultimately is justifiable from a theological point of view, its imposition on believers and nonbelievers alike is incompatible with the basic premises of a secular, pluralistic political order.[25]

A second faction primarily objects to the fact that physicians are being called upon to do the killing. While conceding that killing the terminally ill or assisting in their suicides might not always be morally wrong for others to do, this group maintains that the participation of physicians in such practices undermines their role as healers and fatally compromises the physician-patient relationship.[26]

Finally, a third faction[27] readily grants that neither PAS nor active euthanasia, practiced by ordinary citizens or by physicians, are always morally wrong. On the contrary, this faction believes that in certain rare instances early release from a painful or intolerably degrading existence might constitute both a positive good and an important exercise of personal autonomy for the individual. Indeed, many members of this faction concede that should such a terrible fate befall them, they would hope to find a thoughtful, compassionate, and courageous physician to release them from their misery. But in spite of these important concessions, the members of this faction shrink from endorsing or regulating PAS and active euthanasia due to fears bearing on the social consequences of liberalization. This view is based on two distinct kinds of so-called "slippery slope" arguments. One bears on the inability to cabin PAS/euthanasia within the confines envisioned by its proponents; the other focuses on the likelihood of abuse, neglect, and mistake.

An Option Without Limits

The first version of the slippery slope argument contends that a socially sanctioned practice of PAS would in all likelihood prove difficult, if not impossible, to cabin within its originally anticipated boundaries. Proponents of legalization usually begin with a wholesomely modest policy agenda, limiting their suggested reforms to a narrow and highly specified range of potential candidates and practices.[28] "Give us PAS," they ask, "not the more controversial practice of active euthanasia, for presently competent patients who are terminally ill and suffering unbearable pain." But the logic of the case for PAS, based as it is upon the twin pillars of patient autonomy and mercy, makes it highly unlikely that society could stop with this modest proposal once it had ventured out on the slope. As numerous other critics have pointed out, if autonomy is the prime consideration, then additional constraints based upon terminal illness or unbearable pain, or both, would appear hard to justify.[29] Indeed, if autonomy is crucial, the requirement of unbearable suffering would appear to be entirely subjective. Who is to say, other than the patient herself, how much suffering is too much? Likewise, the requirement of terminal illness seems an arbitrary standard against which to judge patients' own subjective evaluation of their quality of life. If my life is no longer worth living, why should a terminally ill cancer patient be granted PAS but not me, merely because my suffering is due to my "nonterminal" arterio-lateral sclerosis ("ALS") or intractable psychiatric disorder?[30]

Alternatively, if pain and suffering are deemed crucial to the justification of legalization, it is hard to see how the proposed barrier of contemporaneous consent of competent patients could withstand serious erosion. If the logic of PAS is at all similar to that of forgoing life-sustaining treatments, and we have every reason to think it so, then it would seem almost inevitable that a case soon would be made to permit PAS for incompetent patients who had left advance directives. That would then be followed by a "substituted judgment" test for patients who "would have wanted" PAS, and finally an "objective" test would be developed for patients (including newborns) whose best interests would be served by PAS or active euthanasia even in the absence of any subjective intent.[31]

In the same way, the joint justifications of autonomy and mercy combine to undermine the plausibility of a line drawn between PAS and active euthanasia. As the authors of one highly publicized proposal have come to see, the logic of justification for active euthanasia is identical to that of PAS.[32]

Legalizing PAS, while continuing to ban active euthanasia, would serve only to discriminate unfairly against patients who are suffering and wish to end their lives, but cannot do so because of some physical impairment. Surely these patients, it will be said, are "the worst off group," and therefore they are the most in need of the assistance of others who will do for them what they can no longer accomplish on their own.

None of these initial slippery slope considerations amount to knock-down objections to further liberalization of our laws and practices. After all, it is not obvious that each of these highly predictable shifts (e.g., from terminal to "merely" incurable, from contemporaneous consent to best interests, and from PAS to active euthanasia), are patently immoral and unjustifiable. Still, in pointing out this likely slippage, the consequentialist opponents of PAS/euthanasia are calling on society to think about the likely consequences of taking the first tentative step onto the slope. If all of the extended practices predicted above pose substantially greater risks for vulnerable patients than the more highly circumscribed initial liberalization proposals, then we need to factor in these additional risks even as we ponder the more modest proposals.[33]

The Likelihood of Abuse

The second prong of the slippery slope argument argues that whatever criteria for justifiable PAS and active euthanasia ultimately are chosen, abuse of the system is highly likely to follow. In other words, patients who fall outside the ambit of our justifiable criteria will soon be candidates for death. This prong resembles what I have elsewhere called an "empirical slope" argument, as it is based not on the close logical resemblance of concepts or justifications, but rather on an empirical prediction of what is likely to happen when we insert a particular social practice into our existing social system.[34]

In order to reassure skeptics, the proponents of PAS/euthanasia concur that any potentially justifiable social policy in this area must meet at least the following three requirements.[35] The policy would have to insist: first, that all requests for death be truly voluntary; second, that all reasonable alternatives to PAS and active euthanasia must be explored before acceding to a patient's wishes; and, third, that a reliable system of reporting all cases must be established in order to effectively monitor these practices and respond to abuses. As a social pessimist on these matters, I believe, given social reality as we know it, that all three assumptions are problematic.

With regard to the voluntariness requirement, we pessimists contend that many requests would not be sufficiently voluntary. In addition to the subtly coercive influences of physicians and family members, perhaps the most slippery aspect of this slope is the highly predictable failure of most physicians to diagnose reliably and treat reversible clinical depression, particularly in the elderly population. As one geriatric psychiatrist testified before the New York Task Force, we now live in the "golden age" of treating depression, but the "lead age" of diagnosing it.[36] We have the tools, but physicians are not adequately trained and motivated to use them. Unless dramatic changes are effected in the practice of medicine, we can predict with confidence that many instances of PAS and active euthanasia will fail the test of voluntariness.

Second, there is the lingering fear that any legislative proposal or judicial mandate would have to be implemented within the present social system, one marked by deep and pervasive discrimination against the poor and members of minority groups.[37] We have every reason to expect that a policy that worked tolerably well in an affluent community like Scarsdale or Beverly Hills might not work so well in a community like Bedford-Stuyvesant or Watts, where your average citizen has little or no access to basic primary care, let alone sophisticated care for chronic pain at home or in the hospital. There is also reason to worry about any policy of PAS initiated within our growing system of managed care, capitation, and physician incentives for delivering less care.[38] Expert palliative care no doubt is an expensive and time-consuming proposition, requiring more, rather than less, time spent just talking with patients and providing them with humane comfort. It is highly doubtful that the context of physician-patient conversation within this new dispensation of "turnstile medicine" will be at all conducive to humane decisions untainted by subtle economic coercion.

In addition, given the abysmal and shameful track record of physicians in responding adequately to pain and suffering, we also can confidently predict that in many cases all reasonable alternatives will *not* have been exhausted.[39] Instead of vigorously addressing the pharmacological and psychosocial needs of such patients, physicians no doubt will continue to ignore, undertreat, or treat many of their patients in an impersonal manner. The result is likely to be more depression, desperation, and requests for physician-assisted death from patients who could have been successfully treated.[40] The root causes of this predictable failure are manifold, but high on the list is the inaccessibility of decent primary care to over thirty-seven million Americans. Other notable causes include an appalling lack of training in palliative care among primary care physicians and cancer specialists alike;[41] discrimination in the delivery of pain control and other medical treatments on the basis of race and economic status; various myths shared by both physicians and patients about the supposed ill effects of pain medications; and restrictive state laws on access to opioids.[42]

Finally, with regard to the third requirement, pessimists doubt that any reporting system would adequately monitor these practices. A great deal depends here on the extent to which patients and practitioners will regard these practices as essentially *private* matters to be discussed and acted upon within the privacy of the doctor-patient relationship. As the Dutch experience has conclusively demonstrated, physicians will be extremely loath to report instances of PAS and active euthanasia to public authorities, largely for fear of bringing the harsh glare of publicity upon the patients' families at a time when privacy is most needed.[43] The likely result of this predictable lack of oversight will be society's inability to respond appropriately to disturbing incidents and long-term trends. In other words, the practice most likely will not be as amenable to regulation as the proponents contend.

The moral of this story is that deeply seated inadequacies in physicians' training, combined with structural flaws in our healthcare system, can be reliably predicted to secure the premature deaths of many people who would in theory be excluded by the criteria of most leading proposals to legalize PAS. If this characterization of the status quo is at all accurate, then the problem will not be solved by well-meaning assurances that abuses will not be tolerated, or that patients will, of course, be offered the full range of palliative care options before any decision for PAS is ratified.[44] While such regulatory solutions are possible in theory, and may well justly prevail in the future, we should be wary of legally sanctioning any negative right to be let alone by the state when the just and humane exercise of that right will depend upon the provision of currently nonexistent services. The operative analogy here, I fear, is our failed and shameful policy of "deinstitutionalization," which left thousands of vulnerable and defenseless former residents of state psychiatric hospitals to fend for themselves on the streets, literally "rotting with their rights on."[45] It is now generally agreed that the crucial flaw in this well-intended but catastrophic policy was our society's willingness to honor such patients' negative right to be free of institutional fetters without having first made available reliable local alternatives to institutionalization. The operative lesson for us here is that judges and courts are much better at enunciating negative rights than they are at providing the services required for their successful implementation.

Two Approaches to Social Policy

We come now to the difficult task of assessing the capacity of various social policy approaches to address adequately all of the conflicting values implicated in this debate. This section shall contrast a forward-looking, policy-oriented legislative approach to the backward-looking, case-oriented judicial approach taken in the *Compassion in Dying* and *Vacco* cases. Before coming to that comparison, however, a crucial preliminary point must be noted. Central to any serious evaluation of competing policy approaches to PAS and euthanasia is the distinction between the morality of individual acts and the wisdom of social policy. Much of the debate in the popular media is driven by the depiction of especially dramatic and poignant instances of suffering humanity, desperate for release from the painful thrall of terminal illness.[46] Understandably, many of us are prompted to respond: "Should such a terrible fate ever befall me, I certainly would not want to suffer interminably; I would want the option of an early exit and the help of my trusted physician in securing it." The problem,

however, lies in getting from such compelling individual cases to social policy. The issue is not simply, "What would I want?" but rather, what is the best social policy, all things considered. Social pessimists warn that we cannot make this jump from individual case to policy without endangering the autonomy and the very lives of others, many of whom are numbered among our most vulnerable citizens.

A Judge-Made Policy Based on Constitutional Law

Appellate judges in the Ninth and Second Circuits authored powerful opinions giving constitutional protection to PAS for competent patients facing terminal illness. While these opinions fully vindicated patients' important stake in having a freely chosen and pain-free death, they seriously and fatally discounted the states' important interests in preventing the kinds of slippage and abuse catalogued above.

Dismissal of Social Consequences The opinion of the Ninth Circuit, *Compassion in Dying*, authored by Judge Reinhardt, is particularly troubling with regard to the dismissal of social consequences.[47] In response to the objection that legalizing PAS inevitably will prove "infinitely expansive," the court acknowledged the difficulty that it may be hard to distinguish the moral logic of PAS from that animating the call for direct physician-administered euthanasia. He further conceded that in some cases, patients will need the help of a physician in carrying out their choice of an autonomous and painless death.[48] Instead of carefully weighing this sobering possibility in the balance, or asking whether this likelihood of slippage should make us hesitate in taking the first step onto the slope, the court immediately dismissed it as a problem for future cases, not this one, noting that, "here we decide only the issue before us."[49] For those who worry that direct euthanasia carried out by physicians might impose too great a risk in the current social climate,[50] the dictum will prove less than comforting, especially in view of the judge's confession that "it [is] less important who administers the medication than who determines whether the terminally ill person's life shall end."[51]

Thus, although we have argued that this kind of forward-looking, policy-oriented perspective is crucial for adequately assessing the individual benefits and social risks involved in the proposal to legalize PAS, the judicial approach to the problem operates fully equipped with social blinders, and willfully dismisses the very real dangers lurking further down the slope, all in the name of individual rights. Indeed, at one point Judge Reinhardt implied that a refusal to contemplate such dangers is demanded by the judicial role itself.[52] To put it mildly and most charitably, this rights-orientated mind-set does not put us in a learning mode. When life and death are at stake, we need to base our social policy on a more comprehensive picture of the likely benefits and risks.

Judge Reinhardt's grasp of the clinical realities of depression and the ubiquitous absence of adequate pain control was no more impressive than the scope of his social vision. In response to the objection that the legalization of PAS eventually would lead physicians to treat requests to die in a routine and impersonal manner, Judge Reinhardt reassured us, in the face of massive evidence to the contrary, that "doctors would not assist a terminally ill patient to hasten his death as long as there were any reasonable chance of alleviating the patient's suffering or enabling him to live under tolerable conditions."[53] Judge Reinhardt's faith in professional and governmental regulations to ensure that all requests truly are voluntary (i.e., not due to depression), and free from the taint of untreated pain and suffering, is perhaps refreshing in the age of governmental regulation-bashing, but it is a naive and dangerous faith all the same.

Equal Protection and the Fate of Responsible Regulation
The ability of a constitutional right to assisted suicide to provide adequately for safeguards against abuse, neglect, and mistake is especially problematic within the context of the Second Circuit's equal protection analysis in *Vacco*. That court's assertion of the moral and legal equivalence of withholding life-sustaining treatments, the provision of potentially death-hastening analgesics, and assisted suicide raised extremely troubling questions about the constitutionality of a wide variety of possibly effective regulations.[54] The basic question is: If we have a constitutionally protected liberty interest in determining the time and manner of our deaths, then to

what extent will various regulatory schemes cut too deeply into our personal choices?

We actually have seen this script played out before in the context of abortion law. Prior to *Roe v. Wade*, many states already had begun liberalizing their statutes to allow women to opt for abortion under specified conditions.[55] One regulatory constraint that had been placed on women's choice in some jurisdictions was mandatory review by a hospital-based committee.[56] Now, whether or not we think that such committee review was a good idea in the context of abortion—I do not think it was—it is still interesting to note that this regulatory mechanism, along with a host of others, was discarded unceremoniously by the Supreme Court in *Doe v. Bolton*,[57] the companion case to *Roe v. Wade*.[58] In sum, the Court held that such mechanisms only serve to encumber the woman's choice, which really belongs to her (and perhaps also her doctor) alone.[59]

Now, if the Second Circuit's equal protection analysis had prevailed, and had the Supreme Court come to see no cognizable legal or moral differences between "allowing to die" and assisted suicide, then presumably the regulatory mechanisms surrounding the two sets of practices would have been subjected to identical standards of moral analysis and judicial review.[60] This kind of legally mandated parity would have had two likely consequences. First, all the paraphernalia of surrogate decision-making that currently surrounds decisions to forgo treatment would have been extended to PAS.[61] Just as most states presently allow family or close friends to make life-and-death decisions for loved ones on the basis of so-called "substituted judgment" ("What would the patient have wanted?") or best-interests or reasonable-person determinations, so we would have to allow family members the same role in those cases in which suicide "would have been chosen" by the patient or "would have been" in his best interest.[62] Obviously, this implication of the equal protection approach would have required proponents of PAS to bite a very large bullet indeed regarding the charge of indefinite expansion.

The second implication of the equal protection analysis is that a broad range of possibly helpful regulatory mechanisms, including waiting periods, committee review, second opinions, mandatory reporting, and perhaps even the requirement of terminal illness, might well have been swept aside in the name of individual liberty.[63] Currently, we do not require these kinds of substantive and procedural constraints for most decisions to forgo life-sustaining treatments by competent, terminally ill patients.[64] If, however, there is really no moral or legal difference between "allowing to die" and "assisting suicide"—if, as Judge Miner opines, adding PAS to our repertoire of choices would not add one iota of additional risk to individuals or society over and above those we already countenance—then encumbering the choice for PAS with all sorts of extra protective devices would seemingly lack constitutional validity.[65] In sum, then, the equal protection analysis championed in the Second Circuit threatened precisely those braking mechanisms that arguably might make the slippery slope a far safer place on which to practice physician-assisted death.

The Conflation of Killing and Allowing to Die Proceeding directly to the fulcrum of Judge Miner's analysis, we now consider the denial of a significant moral or legal difference between allowing a patient to die by means of forgoing life-sustaining treatments and assisting a patient in committing suicide. According to both circuit court opinions, there is no significant difference between withdrawing a ventilator, discontinuing a feeding tube, administering pain-killing but (potentially) life-shortening opioids, and prescribing a lethal dose of barbiturates.[66] In all these cases, the judges alleged, the intention is the same (i.e., to hasten death), the cause of death is the same (an *act* attributable to human agency), and the social risks of mistake and abuse are the same (e.g., misdiagnosis, undue pressure, etc.). Consequently, Judge Reinhardt concluded that PAS poses no greater threat to the state's interests in preventing suicide and in safeguarding the integrity of the medical profession than the already accepted practice of forgoing life-sustaining treatment.[67] For identical reasons Judge Miner saw no point in a more restrictive public policy towards PAS and based his entire Constitutional argument upon the purported identity of the intentions and effects of these two social practices.[68]

Along with a majority of the Supreme Court, I wish to uphold, for purposes of social policy analysis, the distinction between forgoing treatment and assisting suicide. Although the boundaries between these two practices at times are admittedly quite fuzzy, overlooking relevant differences between them leads proponents of legalization to ignore the very real social risks inherent in the judicial approach to policy.[69]

Whatever the outcome of our long-standing conceptual skirmishes bearing on the "intrinsic" distinctions between PAS, direct euthanasia, and forgoing life-sustaining treatments, the crucial question remains whether any of the purported distinctions between these activities constitute important differences for purposes of social policy.[70] As a slippery slope opponent of PAS and euthanasia, I have already conceded that individual acts involving either PAS or active euthanasia can be morally justified under certain circumstances. Having thus conceded that certain individual actions can be morally appropriate even when the intent is simply and unambiguously to end the patient's life, and even when "the cause" of death is simply and unambiguously attributable to the action of the physician, the crucial question is whether there are any remaining distinctions between allowing to die and actively killing (or assisting in a suicide) that might illuminate the negative policy implications of PAS and euthanasia.

Two points can be made in this connection. First, as the New York Task Force pointed out, the social consequences of not honoring requests to forgo treatment are very different from the consequences of failing to honor requests for PAS and euthanasia.[71] When society fails to honor requests to prescribe or deliver a lethal dose, the results can admittedly be very onerous for individual patients. The patient may face a prolonged period of deterioration before death, with increased pain and decreased dignity, contrary to what they otherwise would have wished. It is important to note, however, that in many such cases there are alternatives to prolonged and painful deaths. Under the present legal regime it is still permissible for a patient to seek out effective and compassionate hospice care, to refuse further administration of life-sustaining treatments, to request "terminal sedation" (inducing a loss of consciousness until death), and even to starve to death with the aid of a physician.[72] It is also legal for an individual truly to take matters into his own hands and to kill him-self, perhaps with the guidance of a popular "self-help" book.[73] Finally, it is possible for many patients with good and trusting relationships with compas-sionate physicians to achieve their objectives within the bounds of private and discreet relationships, but without the cover and consolations of law.[74]

By contrast, were society, systematically and as a matter of policy, to refuse to honor requests to forgo life-sustaining treatments in order to curb possible abuses, then everyone would have to submit to the imposition of unwanted and often invasive mea-sures. Whereas the refusal to honor a request for PAS or direct euthanasia amounts to a refusal of a posi-tive benefit or assistance, the imposition of medical treatment against one's will represents a violation of personal autonomy and physical integrity totally in-compatible with the deepest meaning of our tradi-tional respect for liberty. Such a refusal would entail the virtual imprisonment of the entire population of terminally ill and dying patients. While the failure to offer a deadly drug to a dying patient represents a failure of mercy requiring moral justification, the forced imposition of medical treatment against a patient's will arguably constitutes a trespass, or tech-nically a legal battery, so profound that it simply cannot be justified, especially at the level of broad gauged social policy.[75]

Without trying to sound especially hyperbolical, we can say that the practice of forgoing treatment is by now so deeply embedded in our social and medi-cal practices that a reversal of policy on this point would throw most of our major medical institutions into a state approaching chaos. The same cannot be said of a refusal to honor requests for PAS and eu-thanasia. Thus, while there may well be many over-lapping similarities between withholding treatment and participating in PAS or euthanasia, their respec-tive denial at the level of social policy would entail vastly different individual and social consequences. If our goal is to reduce the level of social risk sur-rounding all practices involving the treatment of in-curable and/or dying patients, a blanket prohibition of PAS can arguably advance this goal without totally unacceptable moral, legal, and social consequences. The same cannot be said of a blanket prohibition of forgoing life-sustaining treatments.

The second point in this connection is that the practice of PAS and/or active euthanasia would be bound to implicate many more persons than the practice of forgoing treatment.[76] While we should definitely worry about the possibility of error, ne-glect, and abuse in the context of allowing patients to die, it is at least somewhat comforting to realize that just about every patient in this category must be very badly off indeed. By the time that physicians discuss forgoing treatment with a patient or family, the patient is usually well into the process of dying.

With regard to PAS and euthanasia, however, we can expect that many candidates will be perfectly ambulatory and far from the dreaded scene of pain-ful terminal illness depicted by advocates. Depend-ing on how great the social slippage, this category may well come to encompass those with an incur-able condition but who are not presently "terminal," such as persons in the early stages of HIV infection or Alzheimer's disease.[77] It also may come to encom-pass patients suffering from prolonged and intrac-table depression who exhibit no other symptoms of physical illness. Although one important legislative proposal specifically excludes patients whose only symptoms are psychiatric in nature, this reluctance was likely motivated in no small measure by politi-cal considerations.[78] Once PAS or active euthana-sia, or both, are firmly in place, however, it will be extremely difficult to withhold them from persons whose suffering is every bit as real but whose source is entirely psychological rather than physical. That, Judge Miner and many others would surely object, would constitute an invidious distinction and thus a form of unconstitutional discrimination against the mentally ill.

If the States Are the Laboratory, What's the Experiment?

Although the Ninth Circuit was prepared to grant that states have a legitimate interest in avoiding the possibly adverse social consequences of PAS, the court insisted that regulation, rather than prohibi-tion, is the only constitutionally permissible means of so doing.[79] Toward that end, it would have as-signed the challenging task of crafting appropriate regulations to the "laboratory of the states." In view of the very real possibility that the social and individual harms attendant upon the legalization of PAS eventually would prove disproportionate to their benefits, this division of labor between the judiciary and the state legislatures is highly problematic. Had the Supreme Court affirmed the Ninth Circuit's reasoning in granting constitutional protection to the liberty interest in choosing death, states would have been deprived of their ability to put a stop to the widespread practice of PAS even if credible studies were to demonstrate that abuses were rampant and highly resistant to procedural safeguards. Short of a Constitutional amendment, there would have been no turning back had the right to PAS been guaranteed by either the due process or equal protection clauses.

Instead of putting ourselves into this precarious position, we should assign a different and more fundamental task to the laboratory of the states. Given the very real possibilities for extension and abuse of this liberty interest, state legislatures should be entrusted with the basic questions of whether, when, and under what circumstances such a risky social experiment should be attempted in the first place. State legislatures are in a better position than federal judges to study the social and clinical facts and come to a reasonable conclusion on the likely balance of individual benefit and social risks.[80] Given the social and medical realities of this country, I would hope that most states would follow the lead of the New York Task Force in refusing to countenance the legalization and routinization of PAS at this time. However, even if some states do decide to run these risks as a social experiment, i.e., to determine for themselves on the basis of empirical evidence and moral judgment whether more good than harm will come from legalizing PAS, they would have the flexibility, absent rigidly defined constitutional mandates, both to impose very strict regulations and, if necessary, to stop the experiment cold in the face of disconcerting evidence of serious moral slippage. Such an approach is, I believe, much better suited to asking the relevant policy questions and taking appropriate and prudent action.[81]

In addition to being safer, the legislative approach is also, at least potentially, much more democratic than the judicial, rights-based orientation. The legislature is the traditional site in this country for the resolution of most difficult and divisive questions of social policy, especially those marked by deep moral questions and highly troubling empirical uncertainties involving the lives and welfare of many citizens. A court-mandated solution to the question of PAS would, I believe, have secured a decisive and irrevocable victory for one side of this controversy before a thorough and robust public debate had taken place. One significant merit of a legislative approach is that, while it would not guarantee such a debate, it would at least be compatible with large-scale efforts at the state and local levels to foster a more democratically deliberative public dialogue on this matter. Such efforts could give citizens a chance to weigh the nature and value of the liberties at stake against the extent and probability of the social dangers posed by PAS. They could thus serve as a valuable *via media* between the judicial approach, which can often short circuit public debate, and decision-making by public referendum, which is more democratic in theory but often lacks an explicitly deliberative dimension that would allow citizens a deeper understanding of the issues involved before their legislatures took action.[82]

Toward a Policy of Prudent (Legal) Restraint and Aggressive (Medical) Intervention

In contrast to the judicial approach, which totally vindicates the value of patient autonomy at the expense of protecting the vulnerable, my own preferred approach to a social policy of PAS and euthanasia conceives of this debate as posing essentially a "tragic choice."[83] It frankly acknowledges that whatever choice we make, whether we opt for a reaffirmation of the current legal restraints or for a policy of legitimation and regulation, there are bound to be victims. The victims of the current policy are easy to identify: They are on the news, the talk shows, the documentaries, and often on Dr. Kevorkian's roster of so-called "patients." The victims of legalization, by contrast, will be largely hidden from view; they will include the clinically depressed eighty-year-old man who could have lived for another year of good quality if only he had been adequately treated, and the fifty-year-old woman who asks for death because doctors in her financially stretched HMO cannot, or will not, effectively treat her unrelenting, but mysterious, pelvic pain. Perhaps eventually, if we slide far enough down the slope, the uncommunicative stroke victim, whose distant children deem an earlier death to be a better death, will fall victim. There will be others besides these, many coming from the ranks of the uninsured and the poor. To the extent that minorities and the poor already suffer from the effects of discrimination in our healthcare system, it is reasonable to expect that any system of PAS and euthanasia will exhibit similar effects, such as failure to access adequate primary care, pain management, and psychiatric diagnosis and treatment. Unlike Dr. Kevorkian's "patients," these victims will not get their pictures in the papers, but they all will have faces and they will all be cheated of good months or perhaps even years.

This "tragic choice" approach to social policy on PAS/euthanasia takes the form of the following argument formulated at the legislative level. First, the number of "genuine cases" justifying PAS, active euthanasia, or both, will be relatively small. Patients who receive good personal care, good pain relief, treatment for depression, and adequate psychosocial supports tend not to persist in their desire to die.

Second, the social risks of legalization are serious and highly predictable. They include the expansion of these practices to nonvoluntary cases, the advent of active euthanasia, and the widespread failure to pursue readily available alternatives to suicide motivated by pain, depression, hopelessness, and lack of access to good primary medical care.

Third, rather than propose a momentous and dangerous policy shift for a relatively small number of "genuine cases"—a shift that would surely involve a great deal of persistent social division and strife analogous to that involved in the abortion controversy—we should instead attempt to redirect the public debate toward a goal on which we can and should all agree, namely the manifest and urgent need to reform the way we die in America. Instead of pursuing a highly divisive and dangerous campaign for PAS, we should attack the problem at its root with an ambitious program of reform in the areas of access to primary care and the education of physicians in palliative care. At least as far as the "slippery slope" opponents of PAS are concerned, we should thus first see to it that the vast majority of people in this country have access to adequate, affordable,

and nondiscriminatory primary and palliative care. At the end of this long and arduous process, when we finally have an equitable, effective, and compassionate healthcare system in place, one that might be compared favorably with that in the Netherlands, then we might well want to reopen the discussion of PAS and active euthanasia.

Finally, there are those few unfortunate patients who truly are beyond the pale of good palliative, hospice, and psychiatric care. The opponents of legalization must face up to this suffering remnant and attempt to offer creative and humane solutions. One possibility is for such patients to be rendered permanently unconscious by drugs until such time, presumably not a long time, as death finally claims them. Although some will find such an option to be aesthetically unappealing, many would find it a welcome relief.[84] Other patients beyond the reach of the best palliative and hospice care could take their own lives, either by well-known traditional means, or with the help of a physician who could sedate them while they refused further food and (life-extending) fluids. Those who find the latter option to be unacceptable might still be able to find a compassionate physician who, like Dr. Timothy Quill, will ultimately be willing, albeit in fear and trembling, to "take small risks for people [they] really know and care about."[85] Such actions will continue to take place within the privacy of the patient-physician relationship, however, and thus will not threaten vulnerable patients and the social fabric to the same extent as would result from full legalization and regulation.[86] As the partisans of legalized PAS correctly point out, the covert practice of PAS will not be subject to regulatory oversight, and is thus capable of generating its own abuses and slippery slope. Still, I believe that the ever-present threat of possible criminal sanctions and revocation of licensure will continue to serve, for the vast majority of physicians, as powerful disincentives to abuse the system. Moreover, as suggested earlier, it is highly unlikely that the proposals for legalization would result in truly effective oversight.

Conclusion

Instead of conceiving this momentous debate as a choice between, on the one hand, legalization and regulation with all of their attendant risks, and on the other hand, the callous abandonment of patients to their pain and suffering,[87] enlightened opponents must recommend a positive program of clinical and social reforms. On the clinical level, physicians must learn how to really listen to their patients, to unflinchingly engage them in sensitive discussions of their needs and the meaning of their requests for assisted death, to deliver appropriate palliative care, to distinguish fact from fiction in the ethics and law of pain relief, to diagnose and treat clinical depression, and finally, to ascertain and respect their patients' wishes for control regarding the forgoing of life-sustaining treatments. On the social level, opponents of PAS must aggressively promote major initiatives in medical and public education regarding pain control, in the sensitization of insurance companies and licensing agencies to issues of the quality of dying, and in the reform of state laws that currently hinder access to pain relieving medications.[88]

In the absence of an ambitious effort in the direction of aggressive medical and social reform, I fear that the medical and nursing professions will have lost whatever moral warrant and credibility they might still have in continuing to oppose physician-assisted suicide and active euthanasia. As soon as these reforms are in place, however, we might then wish to proceed slowly and cautiously with experiments in various states to test the overall benefits of a policy of legalization. Until that time, however, we are not well served as a society by court decisions allowing for legalization of PAS. The Supreme Court has thus reached a sound decision in ruling out a constitutional right to PAS. As the justices acknowledged, however, this momentous decision will not end the moral debate over PAS and euthanasia. Indeed, it should and hopefully will intensify it.

NOTES

The author would like to thank Carl Coleman, David DeGrazia, Yale Kamisar, Tom Murray, David Orentlicher, and Bonnie Steinbock for helpful discussions and exchanges on the issues dealt with in this paper. Longer versions of this article, published before the Supreme Court's decisions, appeared in *Biolaw* (July/August 1996), Special Section: 171–88 and *The Journal of Contemporary Health Law and Policy* 13 (1997): 361–89.

1. *Compassion in Dying* v. *Washington*, 79 F. 3d 790, 838 (9th Cir. 1996).

2. *Quill* v. *Vacco*, 80 F. 3d 716, 731 (2nd Cir. 1996).

3. *Vacco, Attorney General of New York, et al.* v. *Quill et al.*, certiorari to the United States Court of Appeals for the second circuit, No. 95–1858. Argued January 8, 1997—Decided June 26, 1997. *Washington et al.* v. *Glucksberg et al.*, certiorari to the United States Court of Appeals for the ninth circuit, No. 96–110. Argued January 8, 1997—Decided June 26, 1997.

4. See *Compassion in Dying*, 79 F. 3d at 790.

5. Ibid., 816.

6. Ibid., 813–14.

7. Ibid., 816–32, 836–37 (reviewing state interests and illustrating the application of the balancing test and holding).

8. Ibid., 822–23.

9. *Vacco* v. *Quill*, 80 F. 3d 716, 724–25 (2nd Cir. 1996).

10. Ibid., 727–29.

11. Ibid., 727.

12. *Washington* v. *Glucksberg*, 117 Sup. Ct. 2258 (1997). *Vacco* v. *Quill*, 117 Sup. Ct. 2293 (1997).

13. My stance on these issues has been profoundly influenced by my recent work with the New York State Task Force on Life and the Law (hereinafter "the Task Force") to come to grips with this issue. Following a thorough review of the moral, legal, and social arguments, this highly pluralistic advisory committee unanimously concluded against the legalization of either PAS or direct killing by physicians. A reading of the Supreme Court opinions in these cases suggests that the Task Force's analysis of the social policy of PAS was accepted by most, if not all, of the Justices. See Task Force, *When Death Is Sought: Assisted Suicide and Euthanasia in the Medical Context* (May 1994).

14. Ronald Dworkin, *Life's Dominion: An Argument About Abortion, Euthanasia, and Individual Freedom* (New York: Knopf, 1993), 217. While I agree with Professor Dworkin on the inadmissibility of religious rationales for the legal prohibition of PAS, we disagree on the availability of convincing secular justifications.

15. "A Controlled Trial to Improve Care for Seriously Ill Hospitalized Patients; The Study to Understand Prognoses and Preferences for Outcomes and Risks of Treatments (SUPPORT)," *Journal of the American Medical Association* 274 (Nov. 22, 1995): 1591–92.

16. Task Force, *When Death Is Sought*, x–xi.

17. Ibid., xiv.

18. Ezekiel J. Emanuel et al., "Euthanasia and Physician-Assisted Suicide: Attitudes and Experiences of Oncology Patients, Oncologists, and the Public," *Lancet* 347 (1996): 1805. See also D. Saltzburg et al., "The Relationship of Pain and Depression to Suicidal Ideation in Cancer Patients," *Proc. ASCO* 8 (1989): 312 (abstract).

19. W. Breitbart, "Cancer Pain and Suicide," in K. M. Foley, ed., *Advances in Pain Research and Therapy* 16 (1990): 399–412 (showing that studies indicate that depression "is present in 50 percent of all suicides, and those suffering from depression

are at 25 times greater risk for suicide than the general population").

20. New York State Task Force, *When Death Is Sought*, 127–28 (documenting the claim that doctors fail to diagnose and treat depression). See also Y. Conwell and E. D. Caine, "Rational Suicide and the Right to Die," *New England Journal of Medicine* 325 (1991): 1101.

21. New York State Task Force, *When Death Is Sought*, xiv.

22. As we shall see later, this fact is of enormous importance for our evaluation of PAS and euthanasia as social policies, for if the root causes or motivations for assisted death can be addressed successfully for most patients through the delivery of technically competent and compassionate medicine, the case for changing the law loses much of its urgency.

23. The above section thus signals two important points of agreement with the so-called Philosophers' Brief submitted to the Supreme Court in *Compassion in Dying* and *Vacco* by Ronald Dworkin, Thomas Nagel, Robert Nozick, John Rawls, Thomas Scanlon, and Judith Jarvis Thomson. I agree that individuals in the throes of a painful or degrading terminal illness may well have a very strong moral and even legal interest in securing PAS. I also agree that the pain and suffering of a small percentage of dying patients cannot be adequately controlled by currently available medical interventions. (*New York Review of Books* 44 (5) [March 27, 1997]: 41–47. See also appendix B of this volume.) As we shall see, however, I disagree with the philosophers' conclusion that this interest is sufficiently strong in the face of current medical and social inadequacies as to justify a legal right that would void the reasonably cautious prohibitions of PAS and euthanasia in effect in every State.

24. For religious objections to suicide and euthanasia, see St. Thomas Aquinas, "Whether It Is Lawful to Kill Oneself," in Tom L. Beauchamp and Robert Veatch, eds., *Ethical Issues in Death and Dying*, 2nd. ed. (1996), pp. 119–21. See also Dworkin, *Life's Dominion*, 193. See also Richard John Neuhaus, "The Return of Eugenics," *Commentary* 22 (1988) (arguing that life is a good of the person, not simply for the person).

25. Here too I agree with the Philosophers' Brief.

26. Willard Gaylin et al., "Doctors Must Not Kill," *Journal of the American Medical Association* 259 (1988): 2139–40. See also David Orentlicher, "Physician Participation in Assisted Suicide," *Journal of the American Medical Association* 262 (1989): 1844–45.

27. The author was a part of this faction during his tenure with the New York State Task Force.

28. See Christine Cassel et al., "Care of the Hopelessly Ill: Proposed Clinical Criteria for Physician-Assisted Suicide," *New England Journal of Medicine* 327 (1992): 1380–84 (approving of PAS but not of active euthanasia because it poses excessive social risks).

29. See Daniel Callahan, *The Troubled Dream of Life: Living With Mortality* (New York: Simon and Schuster, 1993). See also Yale Kamisar, "Against Assisted Suicide—Even a Very

Limited Form," *University of Detroit-Mercy Law Review* 72 (1995): 735.

30. ALS also is known as Lou Gehrig's disease.

31. *In re Conroy*, 486 A. 2d 1209 (1985) (summarizing the logic of foregoing life-sustaining treatments).

32. Cassel et al., "Care of the Hopelessly Ill," 1380–84. See also Franklin G. Miller et al., "Regulating Physician-Assisted Death," *New England Journal of Medicine* 331 (1994): 199–23 (conceding the untenability of the previous distinction).

33. Professors Dworkin, et al. consistently fail to mention the possibility, let alone the high likelihood, of this first sort of slippage; I take this to be a serious omission both in their joint brief and in Professor Dworkin's individually authored articles on this subject. These authors simply assume (with the plaintiffs and circuit court majority opinions) that this right will be restricted by means of procedural safeguards to presently competent, incurably ill individuals manifesting great pain and suffering due to physical illness. (For evidence of Professor Dworkin's continuing failure to acknowledge this problem, see his assessment of the Supreme Court opinions in "Assisted Suicide: What the Court Really Said," *New York Review of Books* 44 (14) (Sept. 25, 1997): 40–44.) Failure to notice this sort of dynamic might be due either to the philosophers' lack of familiarity with the recent history of bioethics or to their belief that the social risks of PAS are equivalent to the risks inherent in the widely accepted practice of foregoing life-sustaining treatments, and thus that such slippage would not present any additional risk. The latter assumption is, of course, vigorously contested by the opponents of PAS and euthanasia.

34. John Arras, "The Right to Die on the Slippery Slope," *Social Theory and Practice* 8 (1982): 285 (describing the "slippery slope" argument in favor of PAS).

35. See, e.g., Cassel et al., "Care of the Hopelessly Ill"; Miller et al., "Regulating Physician-Assisted Death"; Charles H. Baron et al., "Statute: A Model State Act to Authorize and Regulate Physician-Assisted Suicide," *Harvard Journal of Legislation* 33 (1996): 1.

36. Dr. Gary Kennedy, Division of Geriatrics, Montefiore Medical Center, Albert Einstein College of Medicine, Testimony before the New York Task Force on Life and the Law.

37. Task Force, *When Death Is Sought*, 143 (illustrating discrimination against minority groups). See also C. S. Cleeland et al., "Pain and Its Treatment in Outpatients with Metastic Cancer," *New England Journal of Medicine* 320 (1994): 592–96 (illustrating a study that found that patients treated for cancer at centers that care predominantly for minority individuals were three times more likely to receive inadequate therapy to relieve pain).

38. Susan M. Wolf, "Physician-Assisted Suicide in the Context of Managed Care," *Duquesne Law Review* 35 (1996): 455.

39. Task Force, *When Death Is Sought*, 43–47. "Despite dramatic advances in pain management, the delivery of pain relief is grossly inadequate in clinical practice. . . . Studies

have shown that only 2 to 60 percent of cancer pain, is treated adequately." Ibid., 43.

40. Wolf, "Physician-Assisted Suicide in the Context of Managed Care."

41. Task Force, *When Death Is Sought*, 44: "In general, researchers report that many doctors and nurses are poorly informed about, and have limited experience with, pain and symptom management. Health care professionals appear to have a limited understanding of the physiology of pain and the pharmacology of narcotic analgesics. Accordingly, many lack the understanding, skills, and confidence necessary for effective pain and symptom management." See also K. M. Foley, "The Relationship of Pain and Symptom Management to Patient Requests for Physician-Assisted Suicide," *Journal of Pain and Symptom Management* 6 (1991): 290.

42. Task Force, *When Death Is Sought*, 17.

43. One source estimates that in the early 1990s, no more than 30 percent of cases of PAS were reported. During 1994, the rate of reporting increased to roughly 50 percent of cases. See John Keown, "Further Reflections on Euthanasia in the Netherlands in the Light of the Remmelink Report and the Van Der Maas Survey," in Luke Gormally, ed., *Euthanasia: Clinical Practice and the Law* (1994) 219. See also Daniel Callahan and Margot White, "The Legalization of Physician-Assisted Suicide: Creating a Regulatory Potemkin Village," *University of Richmond Law Review* 30 (1996): 17.

44. See, e.g., Ronald Dworkin, "Introduction to the Philosophers' Brief," *New York Review of Books*, 41–42; and Dworkin, "Assisted Suicide: What the Court Really Said," 44.

45. Nancy Rhoden, "The Limits of Liberty: Deinstitutionalization, Homelessness, and Libertarian Theory," *Emory Law Journal* 32 (2) (Spring 1982): 375–440.

46. Tom Kuntz, "Helping a Man Kill Himself, As Shown on Dutch TV," *New York Times* (Nov. 13, 1994), at E–7 (describing the first national broadcast of an actual mercy killing in the Netherlands).

47. *Compassion in Dying* v. *Washington*, 79 F. 3d 790, 830–32 (9th Cir. 1996).

48. Ibid., 831.

49. Ibid., 832.

50. This group once included such distinguished physicians and advocates of PAS as Dr. Timothy Quill, Christine Cassel, and Diane Meier. See Cassel et al., "Care of the Hopelessly Ill."

51. *Compassion in Dying*, 79 F. 3d at 832.

52. Ibid., 831 ("In fact, the Court has never refused to recognize a substantive due process liberty right or interest merely because there were difficulties in determining when and how to limit its exercise or because others might someday attempt to use it improperly.").

53. Ibid., 827. Judge Reinhardt's optimism is contradicted by evidence amassed in the SUPPORT study. See note 15 above.

54. *Quill* v. *Vacco*, 80 F. 3d 716, 729 (2nd Cir. 1996).

55. 410 U.S. 113 (1973).

56. *Doe* v. *Bolton*, 410 U.S. 179, 184 (1973).

57. 410 U.S. 179 (1973).

58. Ibid., 198.

59. Ibid.

60. See Frank G. Miller, "Legalizing Physician-Assisted Suicide by Judicial Decision: A Critical Appraisal," *Biolaw* (Jul.–Aug. 1996).

61. Ibid., S–143.

62. For a comprehensive account of practices and laws governing the forgoing of life-sustaining treatment and surrogate decision making, see Alan Meisel, *The Right to Die*, 2d ed. (New York: Wiley Law Publications, 1995).

63. Miller, "Legalizing Physician-Assisted Suicide by Judicial Decision."

64. Meisel, *The Right to Die*.

65. Miller, "Legalizing Physician-Assisted Suicide by Judicial Decision."

66. *Quill* v. *Vacco*, 80 F. 3d 716, 729 (2nd Cir. 1996); see also *Compassion in Dying* v. *Washington*, 79 F. 3d 790, 822–24 (9th Cir. 1996).

67. Miller, "Legalizing Physician-Assisted Suicide by Judicial Decision," S-139.

68. *Quill* v. *Vacco*, 80 F. 3d 716, 729 (2nd Cir. 1996).

69. Dan Brock, "Voluntary Active Euthanasia," *Hastings Center Report* 22 (1992): 10. See also Brock, "Borderline Cases of Morally Justified Taking Life in Medicine," in Tom Beauchamp, ed., *Intending Death: The Ethics of Assisted Suicide and Euthanasia* (Upper Saddle River, NJ: Prentice Hall, 1996): 131–49.

70. For a helpful review of the arguments surrounding the distinction between "letting die" and PAS/euthanasia, see Kamisar, "Against Assisted Suicide—Even a Very Limited Form," 753–60. For those wishing to go deeper into these troubled waters, see B. Steinbock & Alastair Norcross, eds., *Killing and Letting Die* (New York: Fordham University Press, 1995). See also Beauchamp, ed., *Intending Death: The Ethics of Assisted Suicide and Euthanasia*.

71. Task Force, *When Death Is Sought*, 146–47.

72. David M. Eddy, "A Conversation with My Mother," *Journal of the American Medical Association* 272 (1994): 179 (illustrating the possibility of death by starvation).

73. Derek Humphrey, *Final Exit: The Practicalities of Self-deliverance and Assisted Suicide for the Dying*, 2nd ed., (New York: Bantam Doubleday, 1997).

74. Dick Lehr, "Death and the Doctor's Hand: Increasingly, Secretly, Doctors Are Helping the Incurably Ill to Die," *Boston Globe* (Apr. 25, 1993), p. 1 (featuring the experience of physicians who have helped patients to commit suicide).

75. *Restatement (second) of Torts*, sec. 13 (1965) (defining battery).

76. See also Seth Kreimer, "Does Pro-Choice Mean Pro-Kevorkian?: An Essay on Roe, Casey, and the Right to Die," *American University Law Review* 44 (1995): 803, 841.

77. The prospects for slippage here are excellent. The step from a requirement of terminal illness, viewed by these

courts as canonical, to one of merely "untreatable" or "incurable" illness, already has been recommended by a panel of distinguished proponents of PAS. See Miller et al., "Regulating Physician-Assisted Death." It is interesting to note in this connection that one of Jack Kevorkian's earliest "patients," Janet Atkins, reportedly was playing tennis a week or two before her assisted suicide.

78. Baron et al., "A Model State Act to Authorize and Regulate Physician-Assisted Suicide," 11. At an American Philosophical Association symposium on PAS in December, 1995, Professor Brock conceded that political-strategic considerations played a significant role in his group's decision not to sanction PAS for the chronically mentally ill.

79. *Compassion in Dying* v. *Washington*, 79 F. 3d 790, 832–33, 836–37 (9th Cir. 1996).

80. Carl E. Schneider, "Making Sausage: The Ninth Circuit's Opinion," *Hastings Center Report* 27 (1997): 27–28 (reviewing the shortcomings of judges in coming to terms with the complexities of highly contextualized social problems such as PAS).

81. For similar reasons, I am highly skeptical of state ballot initiatives, such as the 1994 initiative in Oregon, which do not make use of the legislatures' superior fact-finding capabilities or, for that matter, of the citizens' capacity for more deliberative approaches to democratic problem solving.

82. It does not speak well for the level of public understanding of this issue, as gauged by polls and referenda, that I, a middling public speaker at best, am unfailingly able to convert (or at least shake the confidence of) largely pro-PAS audiences by the end of a half-hour exploration of the social risks and available alternatives. For an excellent discussion of the promise of a more deliberative mode of democracy, see Amy Gutmann and Dennis Thompson, *Democracy and Disagreement* (Cambridge: Harvard University Press, 1996).

83. For an explication of the notion of a "tragic choice" in the sense that I employ here, see Guido Calabresi & Philip Bobbit, *Tragic Choices* (New York: W.W. Norton, 1978).

84. For a good example of how such "terminal sedation" can fit into an overall plan of palliative care, bringing relief to patients and families alike, see Ira Byock's compassionate and instructive account in *Dying Well: The Prospect for Growth at the End of Life* (New York: Riverhead Books, 1997), ch. 10.

85. Timothy Quill, "Death and Dignity: A Case of Individualized Decision Making," *New England Journal of Medicine* 324 (1991): 694.

86. Allowing for the occasional covert practice of PAS would, it is true, favor well-educated, middle-class individuals with access to willing physicians and would thus perpetuate an undesirable double standard that excludes the poor and unconnected from the benefit of a better death. (For a powerful formulation of this criticism, see Dworkin, "Introduction: The Philosophers' Brief," 41.) I take this double standard to be a definite liability of my approach, but one required by the moral necessity of avoiding other harms to other people. Describing my approach as informed by a "tragic" vision acknowledges the unhappy fact that no solution to the problem of dying in our society will be acceptable, fair, or humane to all. The most we can hope for here is "the least worst" policy.

87. In framing the question in just this way, Ronald Dworkin is guilty of posing a false dilemma in his otherwise admirable book. See Dworkin, *Life's Dominion*, p. 198.

88. This brief sketch of suggested reforms merely summarizes the careful work of the New York State Task Force. See *When Death Is Sought*, pp. 153–184.

Active and Passive Euthanasia

JAMES RACHELS

In this famous essay, Rachels argues that the traditional distinction between killing and letting die is untenable, that "killing is not in itself any worse than letting die." If so, then active euthanasia is no worse than passive euthanasia. Thus doctors may have to distinguish between active and passive euthanasia for legal reasons, but "they should not give the distinction any added authority and weight by writing it into official statements of medical ethics."

The distinction between active and passive euthanasia is thought to be crucial for medical ethics. The idea is that it is permissible, at least in some cases, to withhold treatment and allow a patient to die, but it is never permissible to take any direct action designed to kill the patient. This doctrine seems to be accepted by most doctors, and it is endorsed in a statement adopted by the House of Delegates of

From *The New England Journal of Medicine*, vol. 292, no. 2.

the American Medical Association on December 4, 1973:

> The intentional termination of the life of one human being by another—mercy killing—is contrary to that for which the medical profession stands and is contrary to the policy of the American Medical Association.
>
> The cessation of the employment of extraordinary means to prolong the life of the body when there is irrefutable evidence that biological death is imminent is the decision of the patient and/or his immediate family. The advice and judgment of the physician should be freely available to the patient and/or his immediate family.

However, a strong case can be made against this doctrine. In what follows I will set out some of the relevant arguments, and urge doctors to reconsider their views on this matter.

To begin with a familiar type of situation, a patient who is dying of incurable cancer of the throat is in terrible pain, which can no longer be satisfactorily alleviated. He is certain to die within a few days, even if present treatment is continued, but he does not want to go on living for those days since the pain is unbearable. So he asks the doctor for an end to it, and his family joins in the request.

Suppose the doctor agrees to withhold treatment, as the conventional doctrine says he may. The justification for his doing so is that the patient is in terrible agony, and since he is going to die anyway, it would be wrong to prolong his suffering needlessly. But now notice this. If one simply withholds treatment, it may take the patient longer to die, and so he may suffer more than he would if more direct action were taken and a lethal injection given. This fact provides strong reason for thinking that, once the initial decision not to prolong his agony has been made, active euthanasia is actually preferable to passive euthanasia, rather than the reverse. To say otherwise is to endorse the option that leads to more suffering rather than less, and is contrary to the humanitarian impulse that prompts the decision not to prolong his life in the first place.

Part of my point is that the process of being "allowed to die" can be relatively slow and painful, whereas being given a lethal injection is relatively quick and painless. Let me give a different sort of

example. In the United States about one in 600 babies is born with Down's syndrome. Most of these babies are otherwise healthy—that is, with only the usual pediatric care, they will proceed to an otherwise normal infancy. Some, however, are born with congenital defects such as intestinal obstructions that require operations if they are to live. Sometimes, the parents and the doctor will decide not to operate, and let the infant die. Anthony Shaw describes what happens then:

> . . . When surgery is denied [the doctor] must try to keep the infant from suffering while natural forces sap the baby's life away. As a surgeon whose natural inclination is to use the scalpel to fight off death, standing by and watching a salvageable baby die is the most emotionally exhausting experience I know. It is easy at a conference, in a theoretical discussion, to decide that such infants should be allowed to die. It is altogether different to stand by in the nursery and watch as dehydration and infection wither a tiny being over hours and days. This is a terrible ordeal for me and the hospital staff—much more so than for the parents who never set foot in the nursery.[*]

I can understand why some people are opposed to all euthanasia, and insist that such infants must be allowed to live. I think I can also understand why other people favor destroying these babies quickly and painlessly. But why should anyone favor letting "dehydration and infection wither a tiny being over hours and days"? The doctrine that says that a baby may be allowed to dehydrate and wither, but may not be given an injection that would end its life without suffering, seems so patently cruel as to require no further refutation. The strong language is not intended to offend, but only to put the point in the clearest possible way.

My second argument is that the conventional doctrine leads to decisions concerning life and death made on irrelevant grounds.

Consider again the case of the infants with Down's syndrome who need operations for congenital defects unrelated to the syndrome to live. Sometimes, there is no operation, and the baby dies, but when there is no such defect, the baby lives on. Now, an operation

---

[*]Shaw A: 'Doctor, Do We Have a Choice?' *The New York Times Magazine*, January 30, 1972. p. 54.

such as that to remove an intestinal obstruction is not prohibitively difficult. The reason why such operations are not performed in these cases is, clearly, that the child has Down's syndrome and the parents and doctor judge that because of that fact it is better for the child to die.

But notice that this situation is absurd, no matter what view one takes of the lives and potentials of such babies. If the life of such an infant is worth preserving, what does it matter if it needs a simple operation? Or, if one thinks it better that such a baby should not live on, what difference does it make that it happens to have an unobstructed intestinal tract? In either case, the matter of life and death is being decided on irrelevant grounds. It is the Down's syndrome, and not the intestines, that is the issue. The matter should be decided, if at all, on that basis, and not be allowed to depend on the essentially irrelevant question of whether the intestinal tract is blocked.

What makes this situation possible, of course, is the idea that when there is an intestinal blockage, one can "let the baby die," but when there is no such defect there is nothing that can be done, for one must not "kill" it. The fact that this idea leads to such results as deciding life or death on irrelevant grounds is another good reason why the doctrine should be rejected.

One reason why so many people think that there is an important moral difference between active and passive euthanasia is that they think killing someone is morally worse than letting someone die. But is it? Is killing, in itself, worse than letting die? To investigate this issue, two cases may be considered that are exactly alike except that one involves killing whereas the other involves letting someone die. Then, it can be asked whether this difference makes any difference to the moral assessments. It is important that the cases be exactly alike, except for this one difference, since otherwise one cannot be confident that it is this difference and not some other that accounts for any variation in the assessments of the two cases. So, let us consider this pair of cases:

In the first, Smith stands to gain a large inheritance if anything should happen to his six-year-old cousin. One evening while the child is taking his bath. Smith sneaks into the bathroom and drowns the child, and then arranges things so that it will look like an accident.

In the second, Jones also stands to gain if anything should happen to his six-year-old cousin. Like Smith, Jones sneaks in planning to drown the child in his bath. However, just as he enters the bathroom Jones sees the child slip and hit his head, and fall face down in the water. Jones is delighted; he stands by, ready to push the child's head back under if it is necessary, but it is not necessary. With only a little thrashing about, the child drowns all by himself, "accidentally," as Jones watches and does nothing.

Now Smith killed the child, whereas Jones "merely" let the child die. That is the only difference between them. Did either man behave better, from a moral point of view? If the difference between killing and letting die were in itself a morally important matter, one should say that Jones's behavior was less reprehensible than Smith's. But does one really want to say that? I think not. In the first place, both men acted from the same motive, personal gain, and both had exactly the same end in view when they acted. It may be inferred from Smith's conduct that he is a bad man, although that judgment may be withdrawn or modified if certain further facts are learned about him—for example, that he is mentally deranged. But would not the very same thing be inferred about Jones from his conduct? And would not the same further considerations also be relevant to any modification of this judgment? Moreover, suppose Jones pleaded, in his own defense, After all, I didn't do anything except just stand there and watch the child drown. I didn't kill him; I only let him die." Again, if letting die were in itself less bad than killing, this defense should have at least some weight. But it does not. Such a "defense" can only be regarded as a grotesque perversion of moral reasoning. Morally speaking, it is no defense at all.

Now, it may be pointed out, quite properly, that the cases of euthanasia with which doctors are concerned are not like this at all. They do not involve personal gain or the destruction of normal healthy children. Doctors are concerned only with cases in which the patient's life is of no further use to him, or in which the patient's life has become or will soon become a terrible burden. However, the point is the same in these cases: the bare difference between killing and letting die does not, in itself, make a moral difference. If a doctor lets a patient die, for humane reasons, he is in the same moral position as if he had given the patient a lethal injection for humane reasons. If his decision was wrong—if, for example, the patient's illness was in fact curable—the decision would be equally regrettable no matter which method was used to carry it out. And if the doctor's decision was the right one, the method used is not in itself important.

The AMA policy statement isolates the crucial issue very well; the crucial issue is "the intentional termination of the life of one human being by another." But after identifying this issue, and forbidding "mercy killing," the statement goes on to deny that the cessation of treatment is the intentional termination of a life. This is where the mistake comes in, for what is the cessation of treatment, in these circumstances, if it is not "the intentional termination of the life of one human being by another"? Of course it is exactly that, and if it were not, there would be no point to it.

Many people will find this judgment hard to accept. One reason, I think, is that it is very easy to conflate the question of whether killing is, in itself, worse than letting die, with the very different question of whether most actual cases of killing are more reprehensible than most actual cases of letting die. Most actual cases of killing are clearly terrible (think, for example, of all the murders reported in the newspapers), and one hears of such cases every day. On the other hand, one hardly ever hears of a case of letting die, except for the actions of doctors who are motivated by humanitarian reasons. So one learns to think of killing in a much worse light than of letting die. But this does not mean that there is something about killing that makes it in itself worse than letting die, for it is not the bare difference between killing and letting die that makes the difference in these cases. Rather, the other factors—the murderer's motive of personal gain, for example, contrasted with the doctor's humanitarian motivation—account for different reactions to the different cases.

I have argued that killing is not in itself any worse than letting die: if my contention is right, it follows that active euthanasia is not any worse than passive euthanasia. What arguments can be given on the other side? The most common, I believe, is the following:

"The important difference between active and passive euthanasia is that, in passive euthanasia, the doctor does not do anything to bring about the patient's death. The doctor does nothing, and the patient dies of whatever ills already afflict him. In active euthanasia, however, the doctor does something to bring about the patient's death: he kills him. The doctor who gives the patient with cancer a lethal injection has himself caused his patient's death: whereas if he merely ceases treatment, the cancer is the cause of the death."

A number of points need to be made here. The first is that it is not exactly correct to say that in passive euthanasia the doctor does nothing, for he does do one thing that is very important: he lets the patient die. "Letting someone die" is certainly different, in some respects, from other types of action—mainly in that it is a kind of action that one may perform by way of not performing certain other actions. For example, one may let a patient die by way of not giving medication, just as one may insult someone by way of not shaking his hand. But for any purpose of moral assessment, it is a type of action nonetheless. The decision to let a patient die is subject to moral appraisal in the same way that a decision to kill him would be subject to moral appraisal: it may be assessed as wise or unwise, compassionate or sadistic, right or wrong. If a doctor deliberately let a patient die who was suffering from a routinely curable illness, the doctor would certainly be to blame for what he had done, just as he would be to blame if he had needlessly killed the patient. Charges against him would then be appropriate. If so, it would be no defense at all for him to insist that he didn't "do anything." He would have done something very serious indeed, for he let his patient die.

Fixing the cause of death may be very important from a legal point of view, for it may determine whether criminal charges are brought against the doctor. But I do not think that this notion can be used to show a moral difference between active and passive euthanasia. The reason why it is considered bad to be the cause of someone's death is that death is regarded as a great evil—and so it is. However, if it has been decided that euthanasia—even passive euthanasia—is desirable in a given case, it has also been decided that in this instance death is no greater an evil than the patient's continued existence. And if this is true, the usual reason for not wanting to be the cause of someone's death simply does not apply.

Finally, doctors may think that all of this is only of academic interest—the sort of thing that philosophers may worry about but that has no practical bearing on their own work. After all, doctors must be concerned about the legal consequences of what they do, and active euthanasia is clearly forbidden by the law. But even so, doctors should also be concerned with the fact that the law is forcing upon them a moral doctrine that may well be indefensible, and has a considerable effect on their practices. Of course, most doctors are not now in the position of being coerced in this matter, for they do not regard themselves as merely going along with what the law requires. Rather, in statements such as the AMA policy statement that I have quoted, they are endorsing this doctrine as a central point of medical ethics. In that statement, active euthanasia condemned not merely as illegal but as "contrary to that for which the medical profession stands," whereas passive euthanasia is approved. However, the preceding considerations suggest that there is really no moral difference between the two, considered in themselves (there may be important moral differences in some cases in their *consequences*, but, as I pointed out, these differences may make active euthanasia, and not passive euthanasia, the morally preferable option). So, whereas doctors may have to discriminate between active and passive euthanasia to satisfy the law, they should not do any more than that. In particular, they should not give the distinction any added authority and weight by writing it into official statements of medical ethics.

The Distinction Between Refusing Medical Treatment and Suicide

NEW YORK STATE TASK FORCE ON LIFE AND THE LAW

In this report, the Task Force rejects the view that there is no significant difference between forgoing medical treatment and assisted suicide or euthanasia. It argues that equating the two would undermine patient autonomy and "make it impossible to limit physician-assisted suicide to competent, terminally ill patients, or to legalize physician-assisted suicide without also legalizing euthanasia."

The distinction between the refusal of life-sustaining medical treatment and suicide has been a critical component of all of our recommendations on end-of-life care. In our report on do-not-resuscitate orders, we grounded our legal analysis on the premise that suicide relates only to self-inflicted deaths and "not to a decision to refuse life-sustaining treatment." We reaffirmed this position in our report on the health care proxy, which found that "as a mat-

ter of public policy the taking of human life must not be granted legal sanction." Based on that conclusion, the health care proxy law, as enacted by the New York State Legislature, provides that "[t]his article is not intended to permit or promote suicide, assisted suicide, or euthanasia." Our proposed legislation on surrogate decision-making for incapacitated patients without advance directives contains a similar statement; the report accompanying the proposed legislation expressly states that surrogate decision-making is "not intended either as a step on the road to assisted suicide or as a vehicle to extend the authority of family members beyond the tradi-

From The New York State Task Force on Life and the Law, *When Death Is Sought: Assisted Suicide and Euthanasia in the Medical Context*, Supplement to Report, April 1997.

tional boundaries established by consent to provide treatment or not to treat." Most recently, our report on assisted suicide and euthanasia proposed "a clear line for public policies and medical practice between forgoing medical interventions and assistance to commit suicide or euthanasia," and outlined the legal, ethical, and policy considerations distinguishing the two practices.

We recognize that "the moral distinction between assisting to die and withdrawing treatment is hard to discern in certain cases." The alleged distinction between "acts" and "omissions," for example, is "particularly nebulous," given that physicians who comply with requests to refuse treatment are often required to undertake affirmative acts, such as disconnecting respirators or feeding tubes. Resting the distinction on a difference in intent is also not always persuasive, because "[i]n the act of disconnecting a life-sustaining ventilator . . . some physicians actually intend, not just to rid the patient of unwelcome technology, but to help the patient end her suffering by dying sooner.[1] Finally, as an empirical matter, it is undeniable that withdrawing or withholding life-sustaining treatment, at least in some cases, can play a causal role in any death that ensues. "When a doctor detaches a feeding tube from a patient who could have lived for an additional decade, albeit in a profoundly diminished state, she is certainly 'the cause' of death insofar as she determines when and how the patient dies.[2]

Nonetheless, the fact that the refusal of life-sustaining treatment and assisted suicide are similar in certain aspects does not mean that the practices implicate identical legal, clinical, ethical, and public policy concerns. The following factors, taken together, present compelling reasons to distinguish between the refusal of life-sustaining treatment and assisted suicide for law and public policy, despite the similarities that might exist in individual cases. Although these distinctions may not, in themselves, compel the conclusion that assisted suicide should remain illegal, they undermine the claim that the legal recognition of a broad right to refuse treatment requires recognition of a right to assisted suicide as a matter of constitutional law.

The Right to Refuse Medical Treatment Is Based on the Long-Standing Right to Resist Unwanted Physical Invasions, Not on a Right to "Hasten" Death.

Critics of the distinction between the refusal of life-sustaining treatment and assisted suicide contend that both practices are based on the position that dying patients have a right to "hasten death." For example, in Glucksberg, Judge Reinhardt characterized the judicial recognition of the right to refuse life-sustaining treatment as a "drastic change regarding acceptable medical practices," reflecting the courts' belief "that terminally ill persons are entitled . . . to hasten their deaths, and that . . . physicians may assist in the process.[3] This description of the development of the right to refuse treatment simply cannot be reconciled with the cases originally recognizing that right.

Courts that affirmed the right to refuse treatment, including life-sustaining measures, consistently grounded that right in the long-standing doctrine of informed consent, which forbids physicians from performing invasive medical procedures without the patient's knowing and voluntary agreement. That doctrine is based on the common-law concept of battery, under which any nonconsensual "touching" is a "tort"—a legal wrong—providing grounds for the victim to sue. While patients who refuse treatment may become sicker, and sometimes will die, that result has always been regarded as an unavoidable consequence of applying the doctrine of informed consent consistently and without exception, not as a reason to recognize individuals' right to refuse treatment capable of prolonging life. Contrary to Judge Reinhardt's assertion, the fact that courts did not explicitly recognize the right to refuse life-sustaining treatment until relatively recently does not mean that the right represented a "drastic change." Rather, the courts' recognition of the right to refuse life-sustaining treatment was simply an application of the long-standing prohibition of battery to "the advance of medical technology capable of sustaining life well past the point where natural forces would have brought certain death in earlier times." Until the widespread use of devices such as respirators, dialysis machines, and feeding tubes, there was simply no occasion for courts to consider the right to refuse life-sustaining treatment, outside the narrow context of "patients who refused medical treatment forbidden by their religious beliefs."

The fact that courts grounded the right to refuse treatment in the long-standing right to resist unwanted physical invasions, rather than in a broader "right" to "hasten death," strongly undermines the claim that the refusal of treatment and assisted suicide are legally and ethically the same. Prohibiting individuals from refusing medical treatment would represent "a violation of personal autonomy and physical integrity totally incompatible with the deepest meaning of our traditional respect for liberty. In some cases, such prohibitions would violate sincerely-held religious beliefs opposing certain medical interventions, such as the belief among Jehovah's Witnesses against receiving transfusions of blood. Decisions about assisted suicide do not implicate these interests. For this reason alone, assisted suicide is fundamentally different from the right to refuse treatment; moreover, the difference is not simply in degree but in kind.

Characterizing the Refusal of Medical Treatment as "The Cause" of Any Deaths That Result Would Undermine Society's Commitment to Respecting Patients' Decisions About Medical Care.

In case after case, courts have concluded that deaths following the refusal of treatment are caused primarily by the patient's underlying disease, not the patient's decision or act. As the New Jersey Supreme Court has held, "a patient does not die because of the withdrawal of a kidney dialysis machine, but because his underlying disease has destroyed the proper functioning of his kidney." Likewise, a patient does not die "from the withdrawal of a nasogastric tube, but because of her underlying medical problem, i.e., an inability to swallow."[4] If these statements were meant to suggest that the refusal of treatment plays absolutely no causal role in the patient's death, they would obviously be untrue. For example, when a physician withdraws a respirator or disconnects a feeding tube from a seriously ill patient, it is undeniable that these actions causally contribute to the patient's death: but for the withdrawal of treat-

ment, the patient would probably have continued to live. This empirical question of "but-for" causation, however, is clearly not what the courts had in mind. Instead, the law's traditional analysis of the cause of deaths following the refusal of life-sustaining treatment reflects important judgments about the nature and goals of medicine, which society should be extremely hesitant to revise, particularly in the guise of constitutional interpretation.

The law has long distinguished between the determination of causation as a factual matter and the determination of causation for the purpose of assessing legal and ethical accountability. When a variety of factual causes are necessary, but not individually sufficient, to bring about a particular result, the determination of which among them are properly cited as causative for legal purposes becomes a policy judgment, reflecting underlying assumptions about rights, duties, and moral blame. This is precisely the case when patients die following the refusal of life-sustaining treatment. In contrast to patients who take lethal drugs, patients who refuse life-sustaining treatment will not die unless they are suffering from a condition that makes it impossible to live without invasive medical support (such as an inability to breath, or an inability to swallow or assimilate food taken orally). As Daniel Callahan has put it, "there must he an underlying fatal pathology if allowing to die is even possible."[5] In light of the multiple causes of death following the refusal of life-sustaining treatment, the determination of legal causation cannot be based on simple empirical observation, but requires a deliberate judgment about legal and ethical accountability. The traditional view that the disease, not the refusal of treatment, is the primary cause of death affirms widely-shared beliefs about the nature of medical care—in particular, that consent to medical treatment is not obligatory, but a matter of individual choice. Because the technology is optional, patients who refuse it are not considered to be accountable for causing their own deaths.

By claiming that patients who refuse life-sustaining treatment are the primary cause of any deaths that result, the Second and Ninth Circuits unfairly stigmatize patients who choose not to submit to every available technology capable of prolonging life. The implication of assigning causal accountability to the patient, rather than the underlying injury or disease, is that consent to life-sustaining treatment is expected, and that those who refuse treatment are therefore responsible for bringing about their own deaths. In *Quill*, Judge Miner actually states that deaths following the refusal of life-sustaining treatment are unnatural: "[b]y ordering the discontinuance of . . . artificial life-sustaining processes or refusing to accept them in the first place, a patient hastens his death by means that are not natural in any sense."[6] This statement reflects a curious—and, we believe, dangerous—view of the relationship between nature and technology. Until the development of respirators and feeding tubes, patients who lost the ability to breathe or swallow would inevitably die, and no one would think to argue that such deaths were self-inflicted or anything but natural consequences of injury or disease. If, as Judge Miner claims, it is now "unnatural" to die from an inability to breathe or swallow, it is only because technologies have been developed that can forestall many of these deaths. The invention of new technology, however, does not make the choice to allow events to proceed without the technology "unnatural." To claim otherwise is to establish a "technological imperative," in which the very existence of technology becomes a mandate for its use. Such reasoning is actually more consistent with the claim that the use of life-sustaining treatment should be obligatory, and should be disturbing to those who support patients' right to control their own medical care.

Indeed, if patients who refuse life-sustaining treatment are responsible for "causing" the deaths that result, few deaths could be attributed to natural causes. Death often follows a decision to forgo an available medical treatment that could potentially prolong the patient's life. For example, death is typically preceded by the cessation of breathing and heartbeat, and only sometimes are efforts made to resuscitate dying patients by performing CPR. If deaths resulting from the failure to provide medical treatment are "nothing more nor less than assisted suicide," the consensual failure to perform CPR is a form of assisted suicide, and the doctor who does nothing when a patient's heart has stopped has

"caused" the patient's death.[7] Likewise, patients who refuse chemotherapy because they are unwilling to endure the painful and debilitating side effects, would no longer be victims of cancer, but of their own "unnatural" acts. While some might distinguish these examples of withholding life-sustaining treatment from more active instances of turning off respirators or disconnecting feeding tubes, it is widely accepted that "withdrawing" and "withholding" medical treatment implicate identical legal and ethical concerns. Thus, if turning off a respirator is suicide, so too is refusing to be connected to the respirator in the first place. And if refusing a respirator is suicide, the same must be true for refusing an organ transplant, or refusing any other grueling procedure with an uncertain outcome. Such characterizations defy common sense. There is an obvious difference between refusing invasive technologies that have the potential to prolong life long after the body is able to survive on its own, and deciding to commit suicide by causing the body to stop functioning before death would otherwise occur.

Finally, as a practical matter, telling physicians that they are the primary cause of death when patients refuse medical treatment is likely to backfire, by leading physicians, especially those opposed to assisted suicide, to question their participation in the withdrawal and withholding of medical care. Despite patients' clear legal right to refuse life-sustaining treatment, many doctors—particularly those who are opposed to any participation in efforts to "hasten death"—must still be persuaded to comply with patients' requests to forgo aggressive measures. By assuring doctors that they are not the legal cause of death when patients refuse treatment—in other words, by affirming that withholding and withdrawing treatment are not assisted suicide—existing legal and ethical standards allow physicians to honor patients' wishes about treatment without having to feel responsible for causing the patient's death. If physicians are told that deaths following the refusal of treatment are "unnatural," and that the refusal of treatment is the primary legal and ethical "cause of death," many physicians are likely to rethink their participation in the withholding and withdrawal of treatment. The result would be a disastrous setback for patient autonomy.

Equating the Refusal of Treatment with Suicide Would Make It Impossible to Limit Physician-Assisted Suicide to Competent, Terminally Ill Patients, or to Legalize Physician-Assisted Suicide Without Also Legalizing Euthanasia.

Equating the refusal of treatment with assisted suicide is also inconsistent with the claim that assisted suicide could be limited to competent, terminally ill patients, or that assisted suicide could be legalized while physician-administered lethal injections remain illegal. These practical consequences of abandoning the distinction between the refusal of treatment and suicide should not be ignored. In contrast to the broad right to refuse medical treatment, few proponents of legalizing assisted suicide argue that the practice should be available to anyone on demand. Instead, advocates of legalization have argued that assisted suicide should be treated as a "nonstandard medical practice reserved for extraordinary circumstances,"[8] or as a "response to medical failure," for those "few patients" who "will face a bad death despite all medical efforts.[9] In fact, most advocates of legalization acknowledge that laws prohibiting assisted suicide serve valuable societal interests, especially when applied to healthy individuals suffering from reversible physical or psychological problems. As Judge Reinhardt observed in *Glucksberg,* "the state has a clear interest in preventing anyone, no matter what age, from taking his own life in a fit of desperation, depression, or loneliness or as a result of any other problem, physical or psychological, which can be significantly ameliorated." In such cases, he wrote, "the heartache of suicide is the senseless loss of a life ended prematurely," and the state can legitimately take steps to prevent these suicides from taking place.[10]

Recognizing the need for limits, the plaintiffs in *Glucksberg* and *Quill* propose a right to physician-assisted suicide only for competent patients who are terminally ill. In addition, they argue that recognizing a right to a prescription for lethal drugs does not mean that patients should be permitted to direct their physicians to administer a lethal injection, even if they are unable to commit suicide by any other means. Legislative proposals to legalize assisted suicide now pending in many states contain similar limitations. In fact, these distinctions were critical to the success of the referendum to legalize physician-assisted suicide in Oregon.

Characterizing the refusal of life-sustaining treatment as a form of assisted suicide, however, would make it impossible (and probably unconstitutional) to limit assisted suicide to these narrow categories of cases, First, the claim that assisted suicide could be limited to terminally ill patients ignores the fact that the right to refuse treatment has not been limited to patients who are terminally ill. For example, in *Bouvia* v. *Superior Court,*[11] the California Court of Appeals authorized the removal of a feeding tube from a young woman afflicted with severe cerebral palsy, who had years of life ahead of her, rejecting efforts to limit the right to refuse treatment to patients who are terminally ill, As the *Bouvia* court observed, "if [the] right to choose may not be exercised because there remains to [the patient], in the opinion of a court, a physician or some committee, a certain arbitrary number of years, months, or days, [the] right will have lost its value and meaning." Other state courts have also rejected terminal illness as a constitutional benchmark, and the opinions of the Supreme Court justices in *Cruzan*—a case involving a patient who was not terminally ill—suggest that the United States Supreme Court would do the same thing if it were directly confronted with the question. If terminal illness is not an appropriate prerequisite for the refusal of life-sustaining treatment, and the refusal of treatment "is nothing more nor less than assisted suicide,"[12] how can other forms of assisted suicide be limited to patients who are terminally ill?

The same is true for the claim that assisted suicide could be limited to competent patients who make a contemporaneous request for physician-assisted death. As the New Jersey Supreme Court observed in the case of Karen Ann Quinlan, if a patient's decision to forgo life-sustaining treatment is deserving of legal recognition, "it should not be discarded solely on the basis that her condition prevents her conscious exercise of the choice."[13] To protect individuals' right to refuse unwanted life-sustaining treatment after a loss of capacity, the law has created mechanisms like living wills, health care proxies, and surrogate decision-making, all of which rely on a good-faith assessment of the incapacitated patient's wishes and/

or best interests by health care professionals, family members, and close friends. If the refusal of treatment is a form of suicide, and it is permitted for patients without decision-making capacity, other forms of suicide would have to be permitted for incapacitated patients as well. At a minimum, it would be impossible to deny the right to incapacitated patients who have specifically requested assisted suicide as part of an advance directive, or who have given a relative or friend explicit decision-making authority over treatment decisions by signing a health care proxy. In fact, a footnote in Judge Reinhardt's opinion in *Glucksberg* directly opens the door to such practices, by stating that "a decision of a duly appointed surrogate decision maker is for all legal purposes the decision of the patient himself."[14] What this means is that, even if the law is never changed to legalize euthanasia for the incapacitated, surrogate decision-makers could authorize the provision of lethal drugs to incapacitated patients by consenting to assisted suicide on the patient's behalf.

Moreover, characterizing the refusal of life-sustaining treatment as a form of suicide is inconsistent with the claim that physicians could be allowed to help patients commit suicide by prescribing lethal drugs, but not by providing lethal injections at a patient's request. If it is unfair to distinguish between "hastening death" by refusing life-sustaining treatment and "hastening death" by self-administering lethal drugs, how can it be acceptable to distinguish between self-administering lethal drugs and instructing a physician to administer those same drugs directly? Allowing physicians to prescribe lethal drugs but not to provide lethal injections would discriminate against patients who want to commit suicide but are physically unable to pick up or swallow a pill. These patients may in fact be suffering more than their able-bodied counterparts, and their claims for assistance may therefore appear more deserving of societal respect.

Finally, even what are characterized as "procedural" limitations on the right to physician-assisted suicide approved by the Second and Ninth Circuits and endorsed by virtually all supporters of legalization, would be difficult to defend if the refusal of life-sustaining treatment is seen as a form of assisted suicide as a matter of law. If, as Judge Miner claims,

any distinctions between the refusal of treatment and other forms of "hastening death" are arbitrary and unconstitutional, there would be no basis for requiring candidates for assisted suicide to submit to waiting periods, second opinions, and committee review. Such requirements are not imposed on individuals who seek to refuse life-sustaining treatment, and any effort to introduce them would undoubtedly be seen as burdensome and intrusive. "[I]f there is really no moral or legal difference between 'allowing to die' and 'assisting suicide'—if, as Judge Miner opines, adding [physician-assisted suicide] to our repertoire of choices would not add one iota of additional risk to individuals or society over and above those we already countenance—then it would seem that encumbering the choice for [physician-assisted suicide] with all sorts of extra protective devices would lack constitutional validity."[15]

The Balance Between the Benefits and Risks Likely to Result from the Legalization of Physician-Assisted Suicide Is Extremely Different from a Similar Balancing in the Context of Decisions to Refuse Medical Treatment.

In *When Death is Sought*, we concluded that the legalization of assisted suicide would create insurmountable risks of mistake and abuse. To the extent the Second and Ninth Circuit recognized these risks, they dismissed them as irrelevant, on the theory that similar risks apply when patients refuse life-sustaining medical treatment. The fact that similar risks exist in both situations, however, does not mean that the risks have the same implications for law and clinical practice. The critical question is whether the risks can be mitigated through careful regulation, and, if not, whether they outweigh the reasons advanced for changing the law. On both of these grounds, the risks associated with legalizing assisted suicide are fundamentally different from those involved in respecting patients' refusals of life-sustaining medical treatment.

First, the risks associated with legalizing assisted suicide would be far more difficult to regulate than the risks involved in refusing life-sustaining treatment. Many decisions to refuse life-sustaining treatment—particularly decisions to withdraw respirators and feeding tubes—take place in hospitals and nursing homes. By contrast, decisions about assisted suicide are likely to take place at home or in a physician's office. It is comparatively easy to require second opinions, committee oversights, and retrospective monitoring in institutional settings. Outside of hospitals and nursing homes, "effective oversight to minimize error or abuse would be more difficult, if not unrealizable."[16]

Second, with the refusal of treatment, the balance between the risks and the underlying individual right at stake yields different results from a similar balancing in the context of assisted suicide. On the risk side of the ledger, any harms that might result from the inappropriate refusal of treatment extend only to individuals who are suffering from an underlying condition that makes it impossible to live without invasive medical support. The size of this group, although not negligible, is inherently limited, and just about everyone in this category must be very bad off indeed. With assisted suicide, by contrast, the risk of mistake and abuse is considerably larger because anyone who takes lethal drugs will die, regardless of any underlying pathology. As Seth Kreimer has argued, "[t]he quantitative distinction between some and all can be a legitimate predicate for the qualitative distinction between permission and prohibition."[17]

At the same time, the individual and societal need for a broad right to refuse treatment is far greater than the need for changing the law to allow physicians to help patients commit suicide with lethal drugs. If the law did not permit patients to refuse life-sustaining treatment, dying patients would be forced to submit to any procedure that might potentially extend their lives, no matter how burdensome. The result—strapping patients down, pumping them with drugs, sticking tubes into them, and cutting them open to perform surgery—would be a brutal assault on individual rights and, in many cases, sincerely-held religious beliefs. By contrast, the legal prohibition of assisted suicide prevents patients from obtaining a physician's assistance in escaping a situation imposed by nature, but does not impose any additional harm not caused by the patient's own injury or disease. Moreover, "to the extent that laws prohibiting assisted suicide and euthanasia impose a burden, they do so only for individuals who make

an informed, competent choice to have their lives artificially shortened, and who cannot do so without another person's aid. As studies have confirmed, very few individuals fall into this group, particularly if appropriate pain relief and supportive care are provided." The refusal of treatment, by contrast, is an integral part of everyday medical practice. Prohibiting such decisions would therefore constitute a burden to individual autonomy in a significantly larger number of cases.

The Distinction Between Administering High Doses of Opioids to Relieve Pain and "Physician-Assisted Death."

Some proponents of legalizing assisted suicide argue that the practice is indistinguishable from another widely-accepted, aspect of medical care: the use of morphine and other opioids to relieve pain. In a 1994 article in *The New York Times,* Thomas Preston, a cardiologist, stated that the use of morphine drips "is undeniably euthanasia, hidden by the cosmetics of professional tradition and language." According to Dr. Preston, the continuous injection of morphine into a patient's vein will inevitably lead to the patient's death by "curtailing her breathing." Acceptance of the practice, he wrote, is "society's wink to euthanasia," and demonstrates that, despite existing legal prohibitions, "euthanasia is widespread now."[18]

Judge Reinhardt relied heavily on this argument in his opinion in *Glucksberg.* "As part of the tradition of administering comfort care," he wrote, "doctors have been supplying the causal agent of patients' deaths for decades." When physicians administer morphine drips for the relief of pain, "the actual cause of the patient's death is the drug administered by the physician or by a person acting under his supervision or direction. Because physicians are already causing patients' deaths by administering morphine drips, Judge Reinhardt concluded, the State cannot assert an interest in preventing physicians from causing death by prescribing lethal drugs for patients to self-administer.[19] The court dismissed the State's reliance on differences in intention, because "one of the known effects in each case is to hasten the end of the patient's life."[20]

The effort to characterize morphine drips as a form of covert euthanasia is extremely misguided.

First, as a factual matter, the causal relationship between morphine drips and patients' deaths is far less clear than Dr. Preston or Judge Reinhardt contend. While high doses of morphine can depress respiration when administered to patients who have not developed tolerance to the drug, physicians who treat patients with morphine for the relief of pain increase the doses gradually, so that tolerance can develop. Dr. Kathleen Foley, chief of the pain service at Memorial Sloan-Kettering Cancer Center, has concluded that "[t]he rapid development of tolerance to the respiratory depressant effects allows for escalation of the opioid dose in sonic patients to very high doses," and that "[t]here appears to be no limit to tolerance" when the drug is administered properly.[21] The claim that the use of morphine at properly titrated levels "hastens" patients' deaths, based on the effects of high doses of morphine on patients who have not developed tolerance, is entirely unfounded. It represents one of many myths about the consequences of using narcotics in the clinical setting, which have themselves contributed to the undermedication of patients experiencing treatable pain.

Second, and more importantly, the fact that morphine drips may accelerate patients' deaths in some cases does not make their use equivalent to assisted suicide or euthanasia. "Just as a surgeon might undertake risky heart surgery knowing that the patient may die on the table, so the conscientious physician can risk suppressing the patient's respiratory drive and thus hastening death so long as she is pursuing a valid medical objective and there are no better (less risky) options at hand."[22] As the President's Commission observed, "the moral issue is whether or not the decisionmakers have considered the full range of foreseeable effects, have knowingly accepted whatever risk of death is entailed, and have found the risk to be justified in light of the paucity and undesirability of other options."[23] These observations are consistent with the legal concept of recklessness, which is defined as the conscious disregard of a substantial and "unjustifiable" risk. "This definition necessarily excludes situations where the benefit of taking action outweighs the likelihood that the action cause harm." Thus, physicians are not permitted to prescribe morphine for minor headaches, when ordinary aspirin would work as well, but they can

(and. indeed, should) for the pain associated with terminal illness, assuming that no other less risky options exist. This does not mean that the physician can administer opioids indiscriminately: the doctrine of recklessness requires the physician to undertake a good-faith balancing of the benefits and risks. Instead, it recognizes that medical treatment sometimes requires significant trade-offs, and that acceptance of negative consequences for legitimate medical purposes is not equivalent to causing those consequences for their own sake.

Just as conflating the refusal of treatment with assisted suicide is likely to undermine patients' ability to control their medical treatment, telling physicians that an unintended death resulting from the provision of necessary palliative treatment is a form of covert euthanasia is likely to result in many more patients experiencing unrelieved pain. As John Arras has pointed out, "many physicians would sooner give up their allegiance to adequate pain control than their opposition to assisted suicide and euthanasia."[24] Characterizing the provision of pain relief as a form of euthanasia may well lead to an increase in needless suffering at the end of life. Advocates of legalizing assisted suicide should think carefully about the consequences of this argument for compassionate end-of-life care.

NOTES

1. J. Arras, "Physician-Assisted Suicide: A Tragic View," *J. Contemp. Health Law & Pol.* 13:361–389 (1997). In this volume, pp. 274–280.

2. Id.

3. 79 F.3d at 821–22.

4. *In re Peter*, 108 N.J. 365–529 A.2d 419 (1987).

5. D. Callahan, *The Troubled Dream of Life: In Search of a Peaceful Death* (New York. Simon & Schuster. 1993): 77.

6. 80 F.3d at 729.

7. G. J. Annas, "The Promised End—Constitutional Aspects of Physician-Assisted Suicide," *N. Eng. J. Med.* 335 (1996): 683–87 ("Since the failure to perform cardiopulmonary resuscitation always 'hastens death, . . . patients who refuse cardiopulmonary resuscitation would always be committing suicide (and doctors who write do-not-resuscitate orders would always be assisting suicide).").

8. F. G. Miller, T. E. Quill, H. Brody, J. C. Fletcher, L. O. Gostin, and D. E. Meier, "Regulating Physician-Assisted Death," *N. Eng. J. Med.* 331(1994): 119–23, at 119.

9. H. Brody, "Assisted Death—A Compassionate Response to a Medical Failure," *N. Eng. J. Med.* 327 (1992): 1384–88, at 1385.

10. 79 F.3d at 820.

11. 225 Cal. Rptr. 297 (Cal, Ct. App. 1986).

12. *Quill*, 80 F.3d at 729.

13. 70 N.J. at 41, 335 A.2d at 664.

14. 79 F.3d at 832, n.120.

15. Arras. "Physician-Assisted Suicide: A Tragic View."

16. C. H. Coleman & T. E. Miller. "Stemming the Tide: Assisted Suicide and the Constitution." *J. Law, Med. & Ethics* 23 (1995): 389–97, at 394.

17. S. Kreimer, "Does Pro-Choice Mean Pro Kevorkian? An Essay on *Roe, Casey*, and the Right to Die," *Am. U. L. Rev.* 44 (1995): 803, 841.

18. T. A. Preston. "Killing Pain. Ending Life," *The New York Times*, Nov. 1, 1994, at A27.

19. 79 F.3d at 823.

20. *Id.* at 824 (emphasis added).

21. K. M. Foley, "Controversies in Cancer Pain: Medical Perspectives," *Cancer* 63 (1989): 2257–65, at 2261–62; see also W. C. Wilson, N. G. Smedira, & C. Fink, "Ordering and Administering of Sedatives and Analgesics During the Withholding and Withdrawal of Life Support From Critically Ill Patients," *JAMA* 267 (1992) 949 53 (finding "no evidence that death actually was hastened by the administration of drugs," and that "if anything," the data "suggests that death occurred earlier in the patients who did not receive drugs").

22. Arras, "Physician-Assisted Suicide: A Tragic View."

23. President's Commission for the Study of Ethical Problems in Medicine and Biomedical and Behavioral Research. *Deciding to Forgo Life-Sustaining Treatment* (Washington: U.S. Government Printing Office. 1983) 82.

24. Arras, "Physician-Assisted Suicide: A Tragic View."

The Philosophers' Brief

RONALD DWORKIN, THOMAS NAGEL, ROBERT NOZICK, JOHN RAWLS,

THOMAS SCANLON, AND JUDITH JARVIS THOMSON

In the 1997 Supreme Court cases *Vacco v. Quill* and *Washington v. Glucksberg*, six prominent philosophers presented this amicus brief, urging that states should recognize a right to assisted suicide. They argued that "individuals have a constitutionally protected interest in making those grave decisions [about their own deaths] for themselves, free from the imposition of any religious or philosophical orthodoxy by court or legislature." They conceded that states have a legitimate interest in protecting people from irrational or unstable decisions about their dying but asserted that states cannot deny people wishing to die a chance to demonstrate that their decisions are informed, stable, and free. They maintained that there is no morally significant difference between a physician deliberately withdrawing medical treatment to let a patient die from a natural process and a physician hastening the patient's death by more active means.

Amici are six moral and political philosophers who differ on many issues of public morality and policy. They are united, however, in their conviction that respect for fundamental principles of liberty and justice, as well as for the American constitutional tradition, requires that the decisions of the Courts of Appeals be affirmed.

Brief for Ronald Dworkin, Thomas Nagel, Robert Nozick, John Rawls, Thomas Scanlon, and Judith Jarvis Thomson as *Amici Curiae* in Support of Respondents at 2, *Washington v. Glucksberg*, 117 S. Ct. 2258 (1997) (No. 96–110) and *Vacco v. Quill*, 117 S. Ct. 2293 (1997) (No. 95–1858).

Introduction and Summary of Argument

These cases do not invite or require the Court to make moral, ethical, or religious judgments about how people should approach or confront their death or about when it is ethically appropriate to hasten one's own death or to ask others for help in doing so. On the contrary, they ask the Court to recognize that individuals have a constitutionally protected interest in making those grave judgments for themselves, free from the imposition of any religious or philosophical orthodoxy by court or legislature. States have a constitutionally legitimate interest in protecting individuals from irrational, ill-informed, pressured, or unstable decisions to hasten their own death. To that end, states may regulate and limit the assistance that doctors may give individuals who express a wish to die. But states may not deny people in the position of the patient-plaintiffs in these cases the opportunity to demonstrate, through whatever reasonable procedures the state might institute—even procedures that err on the side of caution—that their decision to die is indeed informed, stable, and fully free. Denying that opportunity to terminally ill patients who are in agonizing pain or otherwise doomed to an existence they regard as intolerable could only be justified on the basis of a religious or ethical conviction about the value or meaning of life itself. Our Constitution forbids government to impose such convictions on its citizens.

Petitioners [i. e., the state authorities of Washington and New York] and the amici who support them offer two contradictory arguments. Some deny that the patient-plaintiffs have any constitutionally protected liberty interest in hastening their own deaths. But that liberty interest flows directly from this Court's previous decisions. It flows from the right of people to make their own decisions about matters "involving the most intimate and personal choices a person may make in a lifetime, choices central to personal dignity and autonomy," *Planned Parenthood* v. *Casey*, 505 U.S. 833, 851(1992).

The Solicitor General, urging reversal in support of Petitioners, recognizes that the patient-plaintiffs do have a constitutional liberty interest at stake in these cases. *See* Brief for the United States as Amicus Curiae Supporting Petitioners at 12, *Washington* v. *Vacco* (hereinafter Brief for the United States) ("The term 'liberty' in the Due Process Clause . . . is broad enough to encompass an interest on the part of terminally ill, mentally competent adults in obtaining relief from the kind of suffering experienced by the plaintiffs in this case, which includes not only severe physical pain, but also the despair and distress that comes from physical deterioration and the inability to control basic bodily functions."); *see also id.* at 13 ("*Cruzan* . . . supports the conclusion that a liberty interest is at stake in this case.")

The Solicitor General nevertheless argues that Washington and New York properly ignored this profound interest when they required the patient-plaintiffs to live on in circumstances they found in-

tolerable. He argues that a state may simply declare that it is unable to devise a regulatory scheme that would adequately protect patients whose desire to die might be ill informed or unstable or foolish or not fully free, and that a state may therefore fall back on a blanket prohibition. This Court has never accepted that patently dangerous rationale for denying protection altogether to a conceded fundamental constitutional interest. It would be a serious mistake to do so now. If that rationale were accepted, an interest acknowledged to be constitutionally protected would be rendered empty.

Argument
I. The Liberty Interest Asserted Here Is Protected by the Due Process Clause

The Due Process Clause of the Fourteenth Amendment protects the liberty interest asserted by the patient-plaintifis here.

Certain decisions are momentous in their impact on the character of a person's life decisions about religious faith, political and moral allegiance, marriage, procreation, and death, for example. Such deeply personal decisions pose controversial questions about how and why human life has value. In a free society, individuals must be allowed to make those decisions for themselves, out of their own faith, conscience, and convictions. This Court has insisted, in a variety of contexts and circumstances, that this great freedom is among those protected by the Due Process Clause as essential to a community of "ordered liberty." *Palko* v. *Connecticut*, 302 U.S. 319, 325 (1937). In its recent decision in *Planned Parenthood* v. *Casey*, 505 U.S. 833, 851(1992), the Court offered a paradigmatic statement of that principle:

> matters [] involving the most intimate and personal choices a person may make in a lifetime, choices central to a person's dignity and autonomy, are central to the liberty protected by the Fourteenth Amendment.

That declaration reflects an idea underlying many of our basic constitutional protections. As the Court explained in *West Virginia State Board of Education* v. *Barnette,* 319 U.S. 624, 642 (1943):

> If there is any fixed star in our constitutional constellation, it is that no official . . . can prescribe what

shall be orthodox in politics, nationalism, religion, or other matters of opinion or force citizens to confess by word or act their faith therein.

A person's interest in following his own convictions at the end of life is so central a part of the more general right to make "intimate and personal choices" for himself that a failure to protect that particular interest would undermine the general right altogether. Death is, for each of us, among the most significant events of life. As the Chief Justice said in *Cruzan v. Missouri*, 497 U.S. 261, 281(1990), "[t]he choice between life and death is a deeply personal decision of obvious and overwhelming finality." Most of us see death—whatever we think will follow it—as the final act of life's drama, and we want that last act to reflect our own convictions, those we have tried to live by, not the convictions of others forced on us in our most vulnerable moment.

Different people, of different religious and ethical beliefs, embrace very, different convictions about which way of dying confirms and which contradicts the value of their lives. Some fight against death with every weapon their doctors can devise. Others will do nothing to hasten death even if they pray it will come soon. Still others, including the patient-plaintiffs in these cases, want to end their lives when they think that living on, in the only way they can, would disfigure rather than enhance the lives they had created. Some people make the latter choice not just to escape pain. Even if it were possible to eliminate all pain for a dying patient—and frequently that is not possible—that would not end or even much alleviate the anguish some would feel at remaining alive, but intubated, helpless, and often sedated near oblivion.

None of these dramatically different attitudes about the meaning of death can be dismissed as irrational. None should be imposed, either by the pressure of doctors or relatives or by the fiat of government, on people who reject it. Just as it would be intolerable for government to dictate that doctors never be permitted to try to keep someone alive as long as possible, when that is what the patient wishes, so it is intolerable for government to dictate that doctors may never, under any circumstances, help someone to die who believes that further life means only degradation. The Constitution insists that people must be free to make these deeply personal decisions for themselves and must not be forced to end their lives in a way that appalls them, just because that is what some majority thinks proper.

II. This Court's Decisions in *Casey* and *Cruzan* Compel Recognition of a Liberty Interest Here

A. *Casey* Supports the Liberty Interest Asserted Here

In *Casey*, this Court, in holding that a state cannot constitutionally proscribe abortion in all cases, reiterated that the Constitution protects a sphere of autonomy in which individuals must be permitted to make certain decisions for themselves. The Court began its analysis by pointing out that "[a]t the heart of liberty is the right to define one's own concept of existence, of meaning, of the universe, and of the mystery of human life." 505 U.S. at 851. Choices flowing out of these conceptions, on matters "involving the must intimate and personal choices a person may make in a lifetime, choices central to personal dignity and autonomy, are central to the liberty protected by the Fourteenth Amendment." Id. "Beliefs about these matters," the Court continued, "could not define the attributes of personhood were they formed under compulsion of the State." Id.

In language pertinent to the liberty interest asserted here, the Court explained why decisions about abortion fall within this category of "personal and intimate" decisions. A decision whether or not to have an abortion, "originat[ing] within the zone of conscience and belief," involves conduct in which "the liberty of the woman is at stake in a sense unique to the human condition and so unique to the law." Id. at 852. As such, the decision necessarily involves the very "destiny of the woman" and is inevitably "shaped to a large extent on her own conception of her spiritual imperatives and her place in society." Id. Precisely because of these characteristics of the decision, "the State is [not] entitled to proscribe [abortion] in all instances." Id. Rather, to allow a total prohibition on abortion would be to permit a state to impose one conception of the meaning and value of human existence on all individuals. This the Constitution forbids.

The Solicitor General nevertheless argues that the right to abortion could be supported on grounds other than this autonomy principle, grounds that would not apply here. He argues, for example, that the abortion right might flow from the great burden an unwanted child imposes on its mother's life. Brief for the United States at 14-15. But whether or not abortion rights could be defended on such grounds, they were not the grounds on which this Court in fact relied. To the contrary, the Court explained at length that the right flows from the constitutional protection accorded all individuals to "define one's own concept of existence, of meaning, of the universe, and of the mystery of human life." *Casey*, 505 U.S. at 851.

The analysis in *Casey* compels the conclusion that the patient-plaintiffs have a liberty interest in this case that a state cannot burden with a blanket prohibition. Like a woman's decision whether to have an abortion, a decision to die involves one's very "destiny" and inevitably will be "shaped to a large extent on (one's) own conception of [one's] spiritual imperatives and [one's] place in society" *Id.* at 852. Just as a blanket prohibition on abortion would involve the improper imposition of one conception of the meaning and value of human existence on all individuals, so too would a blanket prohibition on assisted suicide. The liberty interest asserted here cannot be rejected without undermining the rationale of *Casey*. Indeed, the lower court opinions in the Washington case expressly recognized the parallel between the liberty interest in *Casey* and the interest asserted here. *See Compassion in Dying* v. *Washington*, 79 F.3d 790, 801(9th Cir. 1996) (en banc) ("In deciding right-to-die cases, we are guided by the Court's approach to the abortion cases. *Casey* in particular provides a powerful precedent, for in that case the Court had the opportunity to evaluate its past decisions and to determine whether to adhere to its original judgment."), *aff'g.* 850 F. Supp. 1454,1459 (W. D. Wash. 1994) ("[T]he reasoning in *Casey* [is] highly instructive and almost prescriptive . . ."). This Court should do the same.

B. Cruzan *Supports the Liberty Interest Asserted Here*

We agree with the Solicitor General that this Court's decision in "*Cruzan* . . . supports the conclusion that a liberty interest is at stake in this case." Brief for the United States at 8. Petitioners, however, insist that the present cases can be distinguished because the right at issue in Cruzan was limited to a right to reject an unwanted invasion of one's body.[1] But this Court repeatedly has held that in appropriate circumstances a state may require individuals to accept unwanted invasions of the body. See, e.g., Schmerber v. California, 384 U.S. 757 (1966) (extraction of blood sample from individual suspected of driving while intoxicated, notwithstanding defendant's objection, does not violate privilege against self-incrimination or other constitutional rights); Jacobson v. Massachusetts, 197 U.S. 11(1905) (upholding compulsory vaccination for smallpox as reasonable regulation for protection of public health).

The liberty interest at stake in *Cruzan* was a more profound one. If a competent patient has a constitutional right to refuse life-sustaining treatment, then, the Court implied, the state could not override that right. The regulations upheld in *Cruzan* were designed only to ensure that the individual's wishes were ascertained correctly. Thus, if *Cruzan* implies a right of competent patients to refuse life-sustaining treatment, that implication must be understood as resting not simply on a right to refuse bodily invasions but on the more profound right to refuse medical intervention when what is at stake is a momentous personal decision, such as the timing and manner of one's death. In her concurrence, Justice O'Connor expressly recognized that the right at issue involved a "deeply personal decision" that is "inextricably intertwined" with our notion of "self-determination." 497 U.S. at 287–89.

Cruzan also supports the proposition that a state may not burden a terminally ill patient's liberty interest in determining the time and manner of his death by prohibiting doctors from terminating life support. Seeking to distinguish *Cruzan*, Petitioners insist that a state may nevertheless burden that right in a different way by forbidding doctors to assist in the suicide of patients who are not on life-support machinery. They argue that doctors who remove life support are only allowing a natural process to end in death whereas doctors who prescribe lethal drugs are intervening to cause death. So, according to this argument, a state has an independent justification for forbidding doctors to assist in suicide that it does not have for forbidding them to remove life support.

In the former case though not the latter, it is said, the state forbids an act of killing that is morally much more problematic than merely letting a patient die.

This argument is based on a misunderstanding of the pertinent moral principles. It is certainly true that when a patient does not wish to die, different acts, each of which foreseeably results in his death, nevertheless have very different moral status. When several patients need organ transplants and organs are scarce, for example, it is morally permissible for a doctor to deny an organ to one patient, even though he will die without it, in order to give it to another. But it is certainly not permissible for a doctor to kill one patient in order to use his organs to save another. The morally significant difference between those two acts is not, however, that killing is a positive act and not providing an organ is a mere omission, or that killing someone is worse than merely allowing a "natural" process to result in death. It would be equally impermissible for a doctor to let an injured patient bleed to death, or to refuse antibiotics to a patient with pneumonia—in each case the doctor would have allowed death to result from a "natural" process—in order to make his organs available for transplant to others. A doctor violates his patient's rights whether the doctor acts or refrains from acting, against the patient's wishes, in a way that is designed to cause death.

When a competent patient does want to die, the moral situation is obviously different, because then it makes no sense to appeal to the patient's right not to be killed as a reason why an act designed to cause his death is impermissible. From the patient's point of view, there is no morally pertinent difference between a doctor's terminating treatment that keeps him alive, if that is what he wishes, and a doctor's helping him to end his own life by providing lethal pills he may take himself, when ready, if that is what he wishes—except that the latter may be quicker and more humane. Nor is that a pertinent difference from the doctor's point of view. If and when it is permissible for him to act with death in view, it does not matter which of those two means he and his patient choose. If it is permissible for a doctor deliberately to withdraw medical treatment in order to allow death to result from a natural process, then it is equally permissible for him to help his patient

hasten his own death more actively, if that is the patient's express wish.

It is true that some doctors asked to terminate life support are reluctant and do so only in deference to a patient's right to compel them to remove unwanted invasions of his body. But other doctors, who believe that their most fundamental professional duty is to act in the patient's interests and that, in certain circumstances, it is in their patient's best interests to die, participate willingly in such decisions: they terminate life support to cause death because they know that is what their patient wants. *Cruzan* implied that a state may not absolutely prohibit a doctor from deliberately causing death, at the patient's request, in that way and for that reason. If so, then a state may not prohibit doctors from deliberately using more direct and often more humane means to the same end when that is what a patient prefers. The fact that failing to provide life-sustaining treatment may be regarded as "only letting nature take its course" is no more morally significant in this context, when the patient wishes to die, than in the other, when he wishes to live. Whether a doctor turns off a respirator in accordance with the patient's request or prescribes pills that a patient may take when he is ready to kill himself, the doctor acts with the same intention: to help the patient die.

The two situations do differ in one important respect. Since patients have a right not to have life-support machinery attached to their bodies, they have, in principle, a right to compel its removal. But that is not true in the case of assisted suicide: patients in certain circumstances have a right that the state not forbid doctors to assist in their deaths, but they have no right to compel a doctor to assist them. The right in question, that is, is only a right to the help of a willing doctor.

III. State Interests Do Not Justify a Categorical Prohibition on All Assisted Suicide

The Solicitor General concedes that "a competent, terminally ill adult has a constitutionally cognizable liberty interest in avoiding the kind of suffering experienced by the plaintiffs in this case." Brief for the United States at 8. He agrees that this interest extends not only to avoiding pain, but to avoiding an existence the patient believes to be one of intolerable indignity or incapacity as well. *Id.* at 12. The Solicitor General argues, however, that states nevertheless have the right to "override" this liberty interest altogether, because a state could reasonably conclude that allowing doctors to assist in suicide, even under the most stringent regulations and procedures that could be devised, would unreasonably endanger the lives of a number of patients who might ask for death in circumstances when it is plainly not in their interests to die or when their consent has been improperly obtained.

This argument is unpersuasive, however, for at least three reasons. *First*, in *Cruzan*, this Court noted that its various decisions supported the recognition of a general liberty interest in refusing medical treatment, even when such refusal could result in death. 497 U.S. at 278–79. The various risks described by the Solicitor General apply equally to those situations. For instance, a patient kept alive only by an elaborate and disabling life-support system might well become depressed, and doctors might be equally uncertain whether the depression is curable: such a patient might decide for death only because he has been advised that he will die soon anyway or that he will never live free of the burdensome apparatus, and either diagnosis might conceivably be mistaken. Relatives or doctors might subtly or crudely influence that decision, and state provision for the decision may (to the same degree in this case as if it allowed assisted suicide) be thought to encourage it.

Yet there has been no suggestion that states are incapable of addressing such dangers through regulation. In fact, quite the opposite is true. In *McKay v. Bergstedt*, 106 Nev. 808, 801 P.2d 617 (1990), for example, the Nevada Supreme Court held that "competent adult patients desiring to refuse or discontinue medical treatment" must be examined by two nonattending physicians to determine whether the patient is mentally competent, understands his prognosis and treatment options, and appears free of coercion or pressure in making his decision. *Id.* at 827–28, 801 P.2d at 630. See also: *id.* (in the case of terminally ill patients with natural life expectancy of less than six months, [a] patient's right of self-determination shall be deemed to prevail over state interests, whereas [a] non-terminal patient's

decision to terminate life-support systems must first be weighed against relevant state interests by trial judge); [and] *In re Farrell*, 108 N.J. 335, 354, 529 A.2d 404, 413 (1987) ([which held that a] terminally-ill patient requesting termination of life-support must be determined to be competent and properly informed about [his] prognosis, available treatment options and risks, and to have made decision voluntarily and without coercion). Those protocols served to guard against precisely the dangers that the Solicitor General raises. The case law contains no suggestion that such protocols are inevitably insufficient to prevent deaths that should have been prevented.

Indeed, the risks of mistake are overall greater in the case of terminating life support. *Cruzan* implied that a state must allow individuals to make such decisions through an advance directive stipulating either that life support be terminated (or not initiated) in described circumstances when the individual was no longer competent to make such a decision himself, or that a designated proxy be allowed to make that decision. All the risks just described are present when the decision is made through or pursuant to such an advance directive, and a grave further risk is added: that the directive, though still in force, no longer represents the wishes of the patient. The patient might have changed his mind before he became incompetent, though he did not change the directive, or his proxy may make a decision that the patient would not have made himself if still competent. In *Cruzan*, this Court held that a state may limit these risks through reasonable regulation. It did not hold—or even suggest—that a state may avoid them through a blanket prohibition that, in effect, denies the liberty interest altogether.

Second, nothing in the record supports the [Solicitor General's] conclusion that no system of rules and regulations could adequately reduce the risk of mistake. As discussed above, the experience of states in adjudicating requests to have life-sustaining treatment removed indicates the opposite. The Solicitor General has provided no persuasive reason why the same sort of procedures could not be applied effectively in the case of a competent individual's request for physician-assisted suicide.

Indeed, several very detailed schemes for regulating physician-assisted suicide have been submitted to the voters of some states and one has been enacted. In addition, concerned groups, including a group of distinguished professors of law and other professionals, have drafted and defended such schemes. *See, e.g.*, Charles H. Baron, *et. al, A Model State Act to Authorize and Regulate Physician-Assisted Suicide*, 33 Harv. J. Legis. 1 (1996). Such draft statutes propose a variety of protections and review procedures designed to insure against mistakes, and neither Washington nor New York attempted to show that such schemes would be porous or ineffective. Nor does the Solicitor General's brief: it relies instead mainly on flat and conclusory statements. It cites a New York Task Force report, written before the proposals just described were drafted, whose findings have been widely disputed and were implicitly rejected in the opinion of the Second Circuit below. *See generally Quill* v. *Vacco*, 80 F.3d 716 (2d Cir. 1996). The weakness of the Solicitor General's argument is signaled by his strong reliance on the experience in the Netherlands which, in effect, allows assisted suicide pursuant to published guidelines. Brief for the United States at 23–24. The Dutch guidelines are more permissive than the proposed and model American statutes, however. The Solicitor General deems the Dutch practice of ending the lives of people like neonates who cannot consent particularly noteworthy, for example, but that practice could easily and effectively be made illegal by any state regulatory scheme without violating the Constitution.

The Solicitor General's argument would perhaps have more force if the question before the Court were simply whether a state has any rational basis for an absolute prohibition; if that were the question, then it might be enough to call attention to risks a state might well deem not worth running. But as the Solicitor General concedes, the question here is a very different one: whether a state has interests sufficiently compelling to allow it to take the extraordinary step of altogether refusing the exercise of a liberty interest of constitutional dimension. In those circumstances, the burden is plainly on the state to demonstrate that the risk of mistakes is very high, and that no alternative to complete prohibition would adequately and effectively reduce those risks. Neither of the Petitioners has made such a showing.

Nor could they. The burden of proof on any state attempting to show this would be very high. Consider, for example, the burden a state would have to meet to show that it was entitled altogether to ban public speeches in favor of unpopular causes because it could not guarantee, either by regulations short of an outright ban or by increased police protection, that such speeches would not provoke a riot that would result in serious injury or death to an innocent party. Or that it was entitled to deny those accused of crime the procedural rights that the Constitution guarantees, such as the right to a jury trial, because the security risk those rights would impose on the community would be too great. One can posit extreme circumstances in which some such argument would succeed. *See, e.g., Korematsu* v. *United States*, 323 U.S., 214 (1944) (permitting United States to detain individuals of Japanese ancestry during wartime). But these circumstances would be extreme indeed, and the *Korematsu* ruling has been widely and severely criticized.

Third, it is doubtful whether the risks the Solicitor General cites are even of the right character to serve as justification for an absolute prohibition on the exercise of an important liberty interest. The risks fall into two groups. The first is the risk of medical mistake, including a misdiagnosis of competence or terminal illness. To be sure, no scheme of regulation, no matter how rigorous, can altogether guarantee that medical mistakes will not be made. But the Constitution does not allow a state to deny patients a great variety of important choices, for which informed consent is properly deemed necessary, just because the information on which the consent is given may, in spite of the most strenuous efforts to avoid mistake, be wrong. Again, these identical risks are present in decisions to terminate life support, yet they do not justify an absolute prohibition on the exercise of the right.

The second group consists of risks that a patient will be unduly influenced by considerations that the state might deem it not in his best interests to be swayed by, for example, the feelings and views of close family members. Brief for the United States at

20. But what a patient regards as proper grounds for such a decision normally reflects exactly the judgments of personal ethics—of why his life is important and what affects its value—that patients have a crucial liberty interest in deciding for themselves. Even people who are dying have a right to hear and, if they wish, act on what others might wish to tell or suggest or even hint to them, and it would be dangerous to suppose that a state may prevent this on the ground that it knows better than its citizens when they should be moved by or yield to particular advice or suggestion in the exercise of their right to make fateful personal decisions for themselves. It is not a good reply that some people may not decide as they really wish—as they would decide, for example, if free from the "pressure" of others. That possibility could hardly justify the most serious pressure of all—the criminal law which tells them that they may not decide for death if they need the help of a doctor in dying, no matter how firmly they wish it.

There is a fundamental infirmity in the Solicitor General's argument. He asserts that a state may reasonably judge that the risk of "mistake" to some persons justifies a prohibition that not only risks but insures and even aims at what would undoubtedly be a vastly greater number of "mistakes" of the opposite kind—preventing many thousands of competent people who think that it disfigures their lives to continue living, in the only way left to them, from escaping that—to them—terrible injury. A state grievously and irreversibly harms such people when it prohibits that escape. The Solicitor General's argument may seem plausible to those who do not agree that individuals are harmed by being forced to live on in pain and what they regard as indignity. But many other people plainly do think that such individuals are harmed, and a state may not take one side in that essentially ethical or religious controversy as its justification for denying a crucial liberty.

Of course, a state has important interests that justify regulating physician-assisted suicide. It may be legitimate for a state to deny an opportunity for assisted suicide when it acts in what it reasonably judges to be the best interests of the potential suicide, and when its judgment on that issue does not rest on contested judgments about "matters involv-

ing the most intimate and personal choices a person may make in a lifetime, choices central to personal dignity and autonomy." *Casey*, 505 U.S. at 851. A state might assert, for example, that people who are not terminally ill, but who have formed a desire to die, are, as a group, very likely later to be grateful if they are prevented from taking their own lives. It might then claim that it is legitimate, out of concern for such people, to deny any of them a doctor's assistance [in taking their own lives].

This Court need not decide now the extent to which such paternalistic interests might override an individual's liberty interest. No one can plausibly claim, however—and it is noteworthy that neither Petitioners nor the Solicitor General does claim— that any such prohibition could serve the interests of any significant number of terminally ill patients. On the contrary, any paternalistic justification for an absolute prohibition of assistance to such patients would of necessity appeal to a widely contested religious or ethical conviction many of them, including the patient-plaintiffs, reject. Allowing *that* justification to prevail would vitiate the liberty interest.

Even in the case of terminally ill patients, a state has a right to take all reasonable measures to insure that a patient requesting such assistance has made an informed, competent, stable and uncoerced decision. It is plainly legitimate for a state to establish procedures through which professional and administrative judgments can be made about these matters, and to forbid doctors to assist in suicide when its reasonable procedures have not been satisfied. States may be permitted considerable leeway in designing such procedures. They may be permitted, within reason, to err on what they take to be the side of caution. But they may not use the bare possibility of error as justification for refusing to establish any procedures at all and relying instead on a flat prohibition.

Conclusion

Each individual has a right to make the "most intimate and personal choices central to personal dignity and autonomy." That right encompasses the right to exercise some control over the time and manner of one's death.

The patient-plaintiffs in these cases were all mentally competent individuals in the final phase of terminal illness and died within months of filing their claims.

Jane Doe described how her advanced cancer made even the most basic bodily functions such as swallowing, coughing, and yawning extremely painful and that it was "not possible for [her] to reduce [her] pain to an acceptable level of comfort and to retain an alert state." Faced with such circumstances, she sought to be able to "discuss freely with [her] treating physician [her] intention of hastening [her] death through the consumption of drugs prescribed for that purpose." *Quill* v. *Vacco*, 80 F.2d 716, 720 (2d Cir. 1996) (quoting declaration of Jane Doe).

George A. Kingsley, in advanced stages of AIDS which included, among other hardships, the attachment of a tube to an artery in his chest which made even routine functions burdensome and the development of lesions on his brain, sought advice from his doctors regarding prescriptions which could hasten his impending death. *Id.*

Jane Roe, suffering from cancer since 1988, had been almost completely bedridden since 1993 and experienced constant pain which could not be alleviated by medication. After undergoing counseling for herself and her family, she desired to hasten her death by taking prescription drugs. *Compassion in Dying* v. *Washington*, 850 F. Supp. 1454, 1456 (1994).

John Doe, who had experienced numerous AIDS-related ailments since 1991, was "especially cognizant of the suffering imposed by a lingering terminal illness because he was the primary caregiver for his long-term companion who died of AIDS" and sought prescription drugs from his physician to hasten his own death after entering the terminal phase of AIDS. *Id.* at 1456–57.

James Poe suffered from emphysema which caused him "a constant sensation of suffocating" as well as a cardiac condition which caused severe leg pain. Connected to an oxygen tank at all times but unable to calm the panic reaction associated with his feeling of suffocation even with regular doses of morphine, Mr. Poe sought physician-assisted suicide. *Id.* at 1457.

A state may not deny the liberty claimed by the patient-plaintiffs in these cases without providing them an opportunity to demonstrate, in whatever way the state might reasonably think wise and necessary, that the conviction they expressed for an early death is competent, rational, informed, stable, and uncoerced.

Affirming the decisions by the Courts of Appeals would establish nothing more than that there is such a constitutionally protected right in principle. It would establish only that some individuals, whose decisions for suicide plainly cannot be dismissed as irrational or foolish or premature, must be accorded a reasonable opportunity to show that their decision for death is informed and free. It is not necessary to decide precisely which patients are entitled to that opportunity. If, on the other hand, this Court reverses the decisions below, its decision could only be justified by the momentous proposition—a proposition flatly in conflict with the spirit and letter of the Court's past decisions—that an American citizen does not, after all, have the right, even in principle, to live and die in the light of his own religious and ethical beliefs, his own convictions about why his life is valuable and where its value lies.

NOTE

1. In that case, the parents of Nancy Cruzan, a woman who was in a persistent vegetative state following an automobile accident, asked the Missouri courts to authorize doctors to end life support and therefore her life. The Supreme Court held that Missouri was entitled to demand explicit evidence that Ms. Cruzan had made a decision that she would not wish to be kept alive in those circumstances, and to reject the evidence the family had offered as inadequate. But a majority of justices assumed, for the sake of the argument, that a competent patient has a right to reject life-preserving treatment, and it is now widely assumed that the Court would so rule in an appropriate case.

Vacco v. Quill

UNITED STATES SUPREME COURT

At issue in this case is whether a ban on assisted suicide enacted in New York state is constitutional—specifically whether the prohibition violates the Equal Protection Clause of the Fourteenth Amendment. The Court finds that it does not, that in fact there is no constitutional right to a physician's help in dying. But each state may establish its own policy on the issue.

In New York, as in most States, it is a crime to aid another to commit or attempt suicide, but patients may refuse even lifesaving medical treatment. The question presented by this case is whether New York's prohibition on assisting suicide therefore violates the Equal Protection Clause of the Fourteenth Amendment. We hold that it does not.

Petitioners are various New Yolk public officials. Respondents Timothy E. Quill, Samuel C. Klagsbrun, and Howard A. Grossman are physicians who practice in New York. They assert that although it would be "consistent with the standards of [their] medical practice[s]" to prescribe lethal medication for "mentally competent, terminally ill patients" who are suffering great pain and desire a doctor's help in taking their own lives, they are deterred from doing so by New York's ban on assisting suicide. Respondents, and three gravely ill patients who have since died, sued the State's Attorney General in the United States District Court. They urged that because New York permits a competent person to refuse life-sustaining medical treatment, and because the refusal of such treatment is "essentially the same thing" as physician-assisted suicide, New York's assisted-suicide ban violates the Equal Protection Clause.

The District Court disagreed: "[I]t is hardly unreasonable or irrational for the State to recognize a difference between allowing nature to take it course, even in the most severe situations, and intentionally using an artificial death-producing device." The court noted New York's "obvious legitimate interests in preserving life, and in protecting vulnerable persons," and concluded that "[u]nder the United States Constitution and the federal system it establishes,

the resolution of this issue is left to the normal democratic processes within the State."

The Court of Appeals for the Second Circuit reversed. The court determined that, despite the assisted-suicide ban's apparent general applicability, "New York law does not treat equally all competent persons who are in the final stages of fatal illness and wish to hasten their deaths," because "those in the final stages of terminal illness who are on life-support systems are allowed to hasten their deaths by directing the removal of such systems; but those similarly situated except for the previous attachment of life-sustaining equipment, are not allowed to hasten death by self-administering prescribed drugs." In the court's view, "[t]he ending of life by [the withdrawal of life-support systems] is *nothing more nor less than assisted suicide*" (emphasis added). The Court of Appeals then examined whether this supposed unequal treatment was rationally related to any legitimate state interest, and concluded that "to the extent that [New York's statutes] prohibit a physician from prescribing medications to be self-administered by a mentally competent, terminally-ill person in the final stages of his terminal illness, they are not rationally related to any legitimate state interest." We granted certiorari and now reverse.

The Equal Protection Clause commands that no State shall "deny to any person within its jurisdiction the equal protection of the laws." This provision creates no substantive rights. Instead, it embodies a general rule that States must treat like cases alike but may treat unlike cases accordingly. If a legislative classification or distinction "neither burdens a fundamental right nor targets a suspect class, we will uphold [it] so long as it bears a rational relation to some legitimate end."

United States Supreme Court. 521 U.S. 793 (1997).

New York's statutes outlawing assisting suicide affect and address matters of profound significance to all New Yorkers alike. They neither infringe fundmental rights nor involve suspect classifications. These laws are therefore entitled to a "strong presumption of validity."

On their faces, neither New York's ban on assisting suicide nor its statutes permitting patients to refuse medical treatment treat anyone differently than anyone else or draw any distinctions between persons. *Everyone*, regardless of physical condition, is entitled, if competent, to refuse unwanted lifesaving medical treatment; *no one* is permitted to assist a suicide. Generally speaking, laws that apply evenhandedly to all "unquestionably comply" with the Equal Protection Clause.

The Court of Appeals, however, concluded that some terminally ill people—those who are on life-support systems—are treated differently than those who are not, in that the former may "hasten death" by ending treatment, but the latter may not "hasten death" through physician-assisted suicide. This conclusion depends on the submission that ending or refusing lifesaving medical treatment "is nothing more nor less than assisted suicide." Unlike the Court of Appeals, we think the distinction between assisting suicide and withdrawing life-sustaining treatment, a distinction widely recognized and endorsed in the medical profession and in our legal traditions, is both important and logical: it is certainly rational. ("When the basic classification is rationally based, uneven effects upon particular groups within a class are ordinarily of no constitutional concern.")

The distinction comports with fundamental legal principles of causation and intent. First, when a patient refuses life-sustaining medical treatment, he dies from an underlying fatal disease or pathology, but if a patient ingests lethal medication prescribed by a physician, he is killed by that medication.

Furthermore, a physician who withdraws, or honors a patient's refusal to begin, life-sustaining medical treatment purposefully intends, or may so intend, only to respect his patient's wishes and "to cease doing useless and futile or degrading things to the patient when [the patient] no longer stands to benefit from them." Assisted Suicide in the United States, Hearing before the Subcommittee on the Constitution of the House Committee on the Judiciary, 104th Cong., 2d Sess., 368 (1996) (testimony of Dr. Leon R. Kass). The same is true when a doctor provides aggressive palliative care; in some cases, painkilling drugs may hasten a patient's death, but the physician's purpose and intent is, or may be, only to ease his patient's pain. A doctor who assists a suicide, however, "must, necessarily and indubitably, intend primarily that the patient be made dead." *Id.*, at 367. Similarly, a patient who commits suicide with a doctor's aid necessarily has the specific intent to end his or her own life, while a patient who refuses or discontinues treatment might not.

The law has long used actors' intent or purpose to distinguish between two acts that may have the same result. Put differently, the law distinguishes actions taken "because of" a given end from actions taken "in spite of" their unintended but foreseen consequences. ("When General Eisenhower ordered American soldiers onto the beaches of Normandy, he knew that he was sending many American soldiers to certain death. . . . His purpose, though, was to . . . liberate Europe from the Nazis.")

Given these general principles, it is not surprising that many courts, including New York courts, have carefully distinguished refusing life-sustaining treatment from suicide. In fact, the first state court decision explicitly to authorize withdrawing lifesaving treatment noted the "real distinction between the self-infliction of deadly harm and a self-determination against artificial life support." . . .

Similarly, the overwhelming majority of state legislatures have drawn a clear line between assisting suicide and withdrawing or permitting the refusal of unwanted lifesaving medical treatment by prohibiting the former and permitting the latter. And "nearly all states expressly disapprove of suicide and assisted suicide either in statutes dealing with durable powers of attorney in health-care situations, or in 'living will' statutes." Thus, even as the States move to protect and promote patients' dignity at the end of life, they remain opposed to physician-assisted suicide.

New York is a case in point. The State enacted its current assisted-suicide statutes in 1965.[1] Since then, New York has acted several times to protect patients common-law right to refuse treatment. In so doing, however, the State has neither endorsed a general right to "hasten death" not approved physician-assisted suicide. Quite the opposite: The State has reaffirmed the line between "killing" and "letting die." More recently the New York State Task Force on Life and the Law studied assisted suicide and euthanasia and, in 1994, unanimously recommended against legalization. When Death is Sought: Assisted Suicide and Euthanasia in the Medical Context vii (1994). In the Task Force's view. "allowing decisions to forego life-sustaining treatment and allowing assisted suicide or euthanasia have radically different consequences and meanings for public policy." *Id.*, at 146.

This Court has also recognized, at least implicitly, the distinction between letting a patient die and making that patient die. In *Cruzan v. Director, Mo. Dept. of Health* (1990), we concluded that "[t]he principle that a competent person has a constitutionally protected liberty interest in refusing unwanted medical treatment may be inferred from our prior decisions," and we assumed the existence of such a right for purposes of that case. But our assumption of a right to refuse treatment was grounded not, as the Court of Appeals supposed, on the proposition that patients have a general and abstract "right to hasten death," but on well established, traditional rights to bodily integrity and freedom from unwanted touching. In fact, we observed that "the majority of States in this country have laws imposing criminal penalties on one who assists another to commit suicide." *Cruzan* therefore provides no support for the notion that refusing life-sustaining medical treatment is "nothing more nor less than suicide."

For all these reasons we disagree with respondents' claim that the distinction between refusing lifesaving medical treatment and assisted suicide is "arbitrary" and "irrational."[2] Granted, in some cases, the line between the two may not be clear, but certainty is not required, even were it possible. Logic and contemporary practice support New York's judgment that the two acts are different, and New York may therefore, consistent with the Constitution, treat them differently. By permitting everyone to refuse unwanted medical treatment while prohibiting anyone from assisting a suicide, New York law follows a longstanding and rational distinction.

New York's reasons for recognizing and acting on this distinction—including prohibiting intentional killing and preserving life; preventing suicide; maintaining physicians' role as their patients' healers; protecting vulnerable people from indifference, prejudice, and psychological and financial pressure to end their lives; and avoiding a possible slide towards euthanasia—are discussed in greater detail in our opinion in *Glucksberg, ante.* These valid and important public interests easily satisfy the constitutional requirement that a legislative classification bear a rational relation to some legitimate end.

The judgment of the Court of Appeals is reversed.

NOTES

1. It has always been a crime, either by statute or under the common law, to assist a suicide in New York.

2. Respondents also argue that the State irrationally distinguishes between physician-assisted suicide and "terminal sedation," a process respondents characterize as "induc[ing] barbiturate coma and then starv[ing] the person to death." Petitioners insist, however, that "'[a]lthough proponents of physician-assisted suicide and euthanasia contend that terminal sedation is covert physician-assisted suicide or euthanasia, the concept of sedating pharmacotherapy is based on informed consent and the principle of double effect.'" Reply Brief for Petitioners 12 (quoting P. Rousseau, Terminal Sedation in the Care of Dying Patients, 156 Archives Internal Med. 1785, 1785–1786 ([1996]). Just as a State may prohibit assisting suicide while permitting patients to refuse unwanted lifesaving treatment, it may permit palliative care related to that refusal, which may have the foreseen but unintended "double effect" of hastening the patient's death. See New York Task Force, "When Death is Sought," at 163 ("It is widely recognized that the provision of pain medication is ethically and professionally acceptable even when the treatment may hasten the patient's death, if the medication is intended to alleviate pain and severe discomfort, not to cause death").

Washington v. Glucksberg

UNITED STATES SUPREME COURT

In this companion case to *Vacco v. Quill*, the question is whether Washington state's prohibition against causing or aiding a suicide offends the Due Process Clause of the Fourteenth Amendment. The Court determines that it does not and upholds Washington's law forbidding assisted suicide.

The question presented in this case is whether Washington's prohibition against "caus[ing]" or "aid[ing]" a suicide offends the Fourteenth Amendment to the United States Constitution. We hold that it does not.

It has always been a crime to assist a suicide in the State of Washington. In 1854, Washington's first Territorial Legislature outlawed "assisting another in the commission of self-murder." Today, Washington law provides: "A person is guilty of promoting a suicide attempt when he knowingly causes or aids another person to attempt suicide." Wash. Rev. Code 9A.36.060(l) (1994). "Promoting a suicide attempt" is a felony, punishable by up to five years' imprisonment and up to a $10,000 fine. At the same time, Washington's Natural Death Act, enacted in 1979, states that the "withholding or withdrawal of life-sustaining treatment" at a patient's direction "shall not, for any purpose, constitute a suicide."

Petitioners in this case are the State of Washington and its Attorney General. Respondents Harold Glucksberg, M.D., Abigail Halperin, M.D., Thomas A. Preston, M.D., and Peter Shalit, M.D., are physicians who practice in Washington. These doctors occasionally treat terminally ill, suffering patients, and declare that they would assist these patients in ending their lives if not for Washington's assisted-suicide ban. In January 1994, respondents, along with three gravely ill, pseudonymous plaintiffs who have since died and Compassion in Dying, a non-profit organization that counsels people considering physician-assisted suicide, sued in the United States District Court, seeking a declaration that Wash Rev. Code 9A.36.060(1) (1994) is, on its face, unconstitutional. *Compassion in Dying v. Washington* (WD Wash. 1994).

United States Supreme Court. 521 U.S. 702 (1997).

The plaintiffs asserted "the existence of a liberty interest protected by the Fourteenth Amendment which extends to a personal choice by a mentally competent, terminally ill adult to commit physician-assisted suicide." Relying primarily on *Planned Parenthood v. Casey* (1992) and *Cruzan v. Director, Missouri Dept. of Health* (1990), the District Court agreed and concluded that Washington's assisted-suicide ban is unconstitutional because it "places an undue burden on the exercise of [that] constitutionally protected liberty interest." The District Court also decided that the Washington statute violated the Equal Protection Clause's requirement that "'all persons similarly situated . . . be treated alike.'"

A panel of the Court of Appeals for the Ninth Circuit reversed, emphasizing that "[i]n the two hundred and five years of our existence no constitutional right to aid in killing oneself has ever been asserted and upheld by a court of final jurisdiction." *Compassion in Dying v. Washington* (1995). The Ninth Circuit reheard the case en banc, reversed the panel's decision, and affirmed the District Court. *Compassion in Dying v. Washington* (1996). Like the District Court, the en banc Court of Appeals emphasized our *Casey* and *Cruzan* decisions. The court also discussed what is described as "historical" and "current societal attitudes" toward suicide and assisted suicide, and concluded that "the Constitution encompasses a due process liberty interest in controlling the time and manner of one's death—that there is, in short, a constitutionally-recognized 'right to die.'" After "[w]eighing and then balancing" this interest against Washington's various interests, the court held that the State's assisted-suicide ban was unconstitutional "as applied to terminally ill competent adults who wish to hasten their deaths with medication prescribed by their physicians." The court did not reach the District Court's equal-protection holding. We granted certiorari and now reverse.

I

We begin, as we do in all due-process cases, by examining our Nation's history, legal traditions, and practices. In almost every State—indeed, in almost every western democracy—it is a crime to assist a suicide. The States' assisted-suicide bans are not innovations. Rather, they are longstanding expressions of the States' commitment to the protection and preservation of all human life. Indeed, opposition to and condemnation of suicide—and, therefore, of assisting suicide—are consistent and enduring themes of our philosophical, legal, and cultural heritages.

More specifically, for over 700 years, the Anglo-American common-law tradition has punished or otherwise disapproved of both suicide and assisting suicide. . . .

Over time, however, the American colonies abolished these harsh common-law penalties. . . . [But] the movement away from the common law's harsh sanctions did not represent an acceptance of suicide; rather, as Chief Justice Swift observed this change reflected the growing consensus that it was unfair to punish the suicide's family for his wrongdoing. . . .

That suicide remained a grievous, though nonfelonious, wrong is confirmed by the fact that colonial and early state legislatures and courts did not retreat from prohibiting assisting suicide. . . . And the prohibitions against assisting suicide never contained exceptions for those who were near death. . . .

The earliest American statute explicitly to outlaw assisting suicide was enacted in New York in 1828, and many of the new States and Territories followed New York's example. Between 1857 and 1865, a New York commission led by Dudley Field drafted a criminal code that prohibited "aiding" a suicide and, specifically, "furnish[ing] another person with any deadly weapon or poisonous drug, knowing that such person intends to use such weapon or drug in taking his own life." By the time the Fourteenth Amendment was ratified, it was a crime in most States to assist a suicide. . . .

Though deeply rooted, the States' assisted-suicide bans have in recent years been reexamined and, generally, reaffirmed. Because of advances in medicine and technology, Americans today are increasingly likely to die in institutions, from chronic illnesses. Public concern and democratic action are therefore sharply focused on how best to protect dignity and independence at the end of life, with the result that there have been many significant changes in state laws and in the attitudes these laws reflect. Many States, for example, now permit "living wills," surrogate health-care decisionmaking, and the withdrawal or refusal of life-sustaining medical treatment. At the same time, however, voters and legislators continue for the most part to reaffirm their States' prohibitions on assisting suicide. . . .

Attitudes toward suicide itself have changed since Bracton, but our laws have consistently condemned, and continue to prohibit, assisting suicide. Despite changes in medical technology and notwithstanding an increased emphasis on the importance of end-of-life decisionmaking, we have not retreated from this prohibition. Against this backdrop of history, tradition, and practice, we now turn to respondents' constitutional claim.

II

The Due Process Clause guarantees more than fair process, and the "liberty" it protects includes more than the absence of physical restraint. The Clause also provides heightened protection against government interference with certain fundamental rights and liberty interests. In a long line of cases, we have held that, in addition to the specific freedoms protected by the Bill of Rights, the "liberty" specially protected by the Due Process Clause includes the rights to marry, to have children, to direct the education and upbringing of one's children, to marital privacy, to use contraception, to bodily integrity, and to abortion. We have also assumed, and strongly suggested, that the Due Process Clause protects the traditional right to refuse unwanted lifesaving medical treatment.

But we "ha[ve] always been reluctant to expand the concept of substantive due process because guideposts for responsible decisionmaking in this unchartered area are scarce and open-ended." By extending constitutional protection to an asserted right or liberty interest, we, to a great extent, place the matter outside the arena of public debate and legislative action. We must therefore "exercise the utmost care whenever we are asked to break new ground in this field," lest the liberty protected by the Due Process Clause be subtly transformed into the policy preferences of the members of this Court.

Our established method of substantive-due-process analysis has two primary features: First, we have regularly observed that the Due Process Clause specially protects those fundamental rights and liberties which are, objectively, "deeply rooted in this Nation's history and tradition" and "implicit in the concept of ordered liberty," such that "neither liberty nor justice would exist if they were sacrificed." Second, we have required in substantive-due-process cases a "careful description" of the asserted fundamental liberty interest. Our Nation's history, legal traditions, and practices thus provide the crucial "guideposts for responsible decision-making" that direct and restrain our exposition of the Due Process Clause. As we stated recently . . . the Fourteenth Amendment "forbids the government to infringe . . . 'fundamental' liberty interests *at all*, no matter what process is provided, unless the infringement is narrowly tailored to serve a compelling state interest." . . .

Turning to the claim at issue here, the Court of Appeals stated that "[p]roperly analyzed, the first issue to be resolved is whether there is a liberty interest in determining the time and manner of one's death," or, in other words, "[i]s there a right to die?" Similarly, respondents assert a "liberty to choose how to die" and a right to "control of one's final days," and describe the asserted liberty as "the right to choose a humane, dignified death" and "the liberty to shape death." As noted above, we have a tradition of carefully formulating the interest at stake in substantive-due-process cases. For example, although *Cruzan* is often described as a "right to die" case, we were, in fact, more precise: we assumed that the Constitution granted competent persons a "constitutionally protected right to refuse lifesaving hydration and nutrition." The Washington statute at issue in this case prohibits "aid[ing] another person to attempt suicide," Wash. Rev. Code §9A.36.060(1) (1994), and, thus, the question before us is whether the "liberty" specially protected by the Due Process Clause includes a right to commit suicide which itself includes a right to assistance in doing so.

We now inquire whether this asserted right has any place in our Nation's traditions. Here, as discussed above, we are confronted with a consistent and almost universal tradition that has long rejected the asserted right, and continues explicitly to reject it today, even for terminally ill, mentally competent adults. To hold for respondents, we would have to reverse centuries of legal doctrine and practice, and strike down the considered policy choice of almost every State.

Respondents contend, however, that the liberty interest they assert is consistent with this Court's substantive-due-process line of cases, if not with this Nation's history and practice. Pointing to *Casey* and *Cruzan*, respondents read our jurisprudence in this area as reflecting a general tradition of "self-sovereignty" and as teaching that the "liberty" protected by the Due Process Clause includes "basic and intimate exercises of personal autonomy." According to respondents, our liberty jurisprudence, and the broad, individualistic principles it reflects, protects the "liberty of competent, terminally ill adults to make end-of-life decisions free of undue government interference." The question presented in this case, however, is whether the protections of the Due Process Clause include a right to commit suicide with another's assistance. With this "careful description" of respondents' claim in mind, we turn to *Casey* and *Cruzan*.

In *Cruzan*, we considered whether Nancy Beth Cruzan, who had been severely injured in an automobile accident and was in a persistive vegetative state, "ha[d] a right under the United States Constitution which would require the hospital to withdraw life-sustaining treatment" at her parents' request. We began with the observation that "[a]t common law, even the touching of one person by another without consent and without legal justification was a battery." We then discussed the related rule that "informed consent is generally required for medical treatment." After reviewing a long line of relevant state cases, we concluded that "the common-law doctrine of informed consent is viewed as generally encompassing the right of a competent individual to refuse medical treatment." Next, we reviewed our own cases on the subject, and stated that "[t]he principle that a competent person base constitutionally protected liberty interest in refusing unwanted medical treatment may be inferred from our prior decisions." Therefore, "for purposes, of [that] case, we assume[d] that the United States Constitution would grant a competent person a constitutionally protected right to refuse lifesaving hydration and nutrition." We concluded that, notwithstanding this right, the Constitution permitted Missouri to require clear and convincing evidence of an incompetent patient's wishes concerning the withdrawal of life-sustaining treatment.

Respondents contend that in *Cruzan* we "acknowledged that competent, dying persons have the right to direct the removal of life-sustaining medical treatment and thus hasten death," and that "the constitutional principle behind recognizing the patient's liberty to direct the withdrawal of artificial life support applies at least as strongly to the choice to hasten impending death by consuming lethal medication." Similarly, the Court of Appeals concluded that "*Cruzan*, by recognizing a liberty interest that includes the refusal of artificial provision of life-sustaining food and water, necessarily recognize[d] a liberty interest in hastening one's own death."

The right assumed in *Cruzan*, however, was not simply deduced from abstract concepts of personal autonomy. Given the common-law rule that forced medication was a battery, and the long legal tradition protecting the decision to refuse unwanted medical treatment, our assumption was entirely consistent with this Nation's history and constitutional traditions. The decision to commit suicide with the assistance of another may be just as personal and profound as the decision to refuse unwanted medical treatment, but it has never enjoyed similar legal protection. Indeed, the two acts are widely and reasonably regarded as quite distinct. See *Quill v. Vacco* (1997). In *Cruzan* itself, we recognized that most States outlawed assisted suicide—and even more do today—and we certainly gave no intimation that the right to refuse unwanted medical treatment could be somehow transmuted into a right to assistance in committing suicide.

Respondents also rely on *Casey*. There, the Court's opinion concluded that "the essential holding of *Roe v. Wade* should be retained and once again reaffirmed." We held, first, that a woman has a right, before her fetus is viable, to an abortion

"without undue interference from the State"; second, that States may restrict post-viability abortions, so long as exceptions are made to protect a woman's life and health; and third, that the State has legitimate interests throughout a pregnancy in protecting the health of the woman and the life of the unborn child. In reaching this conclusion, the opinion discussed in some detail this Court's substantive-due-process tradition of interpreting the Due Process Clause to protect certain fundamental rights and "personal decisions relating to marriage, procreation, contraception, family relationships, child rearing, and education," and noted that many of those rights and liberties "involv[e] the most intimate and personal choices a person may make in a lifetime."

The Court of Appeals, like the District Court, found *Casey* "'highly instructive'" and "'almost prescriptive'" for determining "'what liberty interest may inhere in a terminally ill person's choice to commit suicide'":

> Like the decision of whether or not to have an abortion, the decision how and when to die is one of "the most intimate and personal choices a person may make in a lifetime," a choice "central to personal dignity and autonomy."

. . . That many of the rights and liberties protected by the Due Process Clause sound in personal autonomy does not warrant the sweeping conclusion that any and all important, intimate, and personal decisions are so protected, and *Casey* did not suggest otherwise.

The history of the law's treatment of assisted suicide in this country has been and continues to be one of the rejection of nearly all efforts to permit it. That being the case, our decisions lead us to conclude that the asserted "right" to assistance in committing suicide is not a fundamental liberty interest protected by the Due Process Clause. The Constitution also requires, however, that Washington's assisted-suicide ban be rationally related to legitimate government interests. This requirement is unquestionably met here. As the court below recognized, Washington's assisted-suicide ban implicates a number of state interests.

First, Washington has an "unqualified interest in the preservation of human life." The State's prohibition on assisted suicide, like all homicide laws, both reflects and advances its commitment to this interest. This interest is symbolic and aspirational as well as practical:

> While suicide is no longer prohibited or penalized, the ban against assisted suicide and euthanasia shores up the notion of limits in human relationships. It reflects the gravity with which we view the decision to take one's own life or the life of another, and our reluctance to encourage or promote these decisions. New York State Task Force on Life and the Law, When Death is Sought: Assisted Suicide and Euthanasia in the Medical Context 131–132 (May 1994) (hereinafter New York Task Force).

Respondents admit that "[t]he State has a real interest in preserving the lives of those who can still contribute to society and enjoy life." The Court of Appeals also recognized Washington's interest in protecting life, but held that the "weight" of this interest depends on the "medical condition and the wishes of the person whose life is at stake." Washington, however, has rejected this sliding-scale approach and, through its assisted-suicide ban, insists that all persons' lives, from beginning to end, regardless of physical or mental condition, are under the full protection of the law. As we have previously affirmed, the States "may properly decline to make judgments about the 'quality' of life that a particular individual may enjoy." This remains true, as *Cruzan* makes clear, even for those who are near death.

Relatedly, all admit that suicide is a serious public-health problem, especially among persons in otherwise vulnerable groups. The State has an interest in preventing suicide, and in studying, identifying, and treating its causes.

Those who attempt suicide—terminally ill or not—often suffer from depression or other mental disorders. See New York Task Force 13–22, 126–128 (more than 95% of those who commit suicide had a major psychiatric illness at the time of death; among the terminally ill, uncontrolled pain is a "risk factor" because it contributes to depression). Research indicates . . . that many people who request physician-assisted suicide withdraw that request if their depression and pain are treated. The New York Task Force, however, expressed its concern that, because depression is difficult to diagnose, physicians and medical professionals often fail to respond adequately to seriously ill patients' needs. Thus, legal physician-assisted suicide could make it more difficult for the State to protect depressed or mentally ill persons, or those who are suffering from untreated pain, from suicidal impulses.

The State also has an interest in protecting the integrity and ethics of the medical profession. In contrast to the Court of Appeals' conclusion that "the integrity of the medical profession would [not] be threatened in any way by [physician-assisted suicide]," the American Medical Association, like many other medical and physicians' groups, has concluded that "[p]hysician-assisted suicide is fundamentally incompatible with the physician's role as healer." American Medical Association, Code of Ethics §2.211(1994). And physician-assisted suicide could, it is argued, undermine the trust that is essential to the doctor-patient relationship by blurring the time-honored line between healing and harming.

Next, the State has an interest in protecting vulnerable groups—including the poor, the elderly, and disabled persons—from abuse, neglect, and mistakes. The Court of Appeals dismissed the State's concern that disadvantaged persons might be pressured into physician-assisted suicide as "ludicrous on its face." We have recognized, however, the real risk of subtle coercion and undue influence in end-of-life situations. Similarly, the New York Task Force warned that "[l]egalizing physician-assisted suicide would pose profound risks to many individuals who are ill and vulnerable. . . . The risk of harm is greatest for the many individuals in our society whose autonomy and well-being are already compromised by poverty, lack of access to good medical care, advanced age, or membership in a stigmatized social group." New York Task Force 120. If physician-assisted suicide were permitted, many might resort to it to spare their families the substantial financial burden of end-of-life health-care costs.

The State's interest here goes beyond protecting the vulnerable from coercion; it extends to protecting disabled and terminally ill people from prejudice, negative and inaccurate stereotypes, and "societal indifference." The State's assisted-suicide ban reflects and reinforces its policy that the lives of terminally ill, disabled, and elderly people must be no less valued than the lives of the young and healthy, and that a seriously disabled person's suicidal impulses should be interpreted and treated the same way as anyone else's.

Finally, the State may fear that permitting assisted suicide will start it down the path to voluntary and perhaps even involuntary euthanasia. The Court of Appeals struck down Washington's assisted-suicide ban only "as applied to competent, terminally ill adults who wish to hasten their deaths by obtaining medication prescribed by their doctors." Washington insists, however, that the impact of the court's decision will not and cannot be so limited. If suicide is protected as a matter of constitutional right, it is argued, "every man and woman in the United States must enjoy it." The Court of Appeals' decision, and its expansive reasoning, provide ample support for the State's concerns. The court noted, for example, that the "decision of a duly appointed surrogate decision maker is for all legal purposes the decision of the patient himself," that "in some instances, the patient may be unable to self-administer the drugs and . . . administration by the physician . . . may be the only way the patient may be able to receive them," and that not only physicians, but also family members and loved ones, will inevitably partici-pate in assisting suicide. Thus, it turns out that what is couched as a limited right to "physician-assisted suicide" is likely, in effect, a much broader license, which could prove extremely difficult to police and contain. Washington's ban on assisting suicide prevents such erosion. . . .

We need not weigh exactly the relative strengths of these various interests. They are unquestionably important and legitimate, and Washington's ban on assisted suicide is at least reasonably related to their promotion and protection. We therefore hold that Wash. Rev. Code §9A.36.060(1) (1994) does not violate the Fourteenth Amendment, either on its face or "as applied to competent, terminally ill adults who wish to hasten their deaths by obtaining medication prescribed by their doctors."

Throughout the Nation, Americans are engaged in an earnest and profound debate about the morality, legality, and practicality of physician-assisted suicide. Our holding permits this debate to continue, as it should in a democratic society. The decision of the en banc Court of Appeals is reversed, and the case is remanded for further proceedings consistent with this opinion.

4

JUSTICE & HEALTH CARE

CHAPTER II

Dividing Up Health Care Resources

In this land of plenty, many are rich; many are poor. Many are healthy; many are not. Many who are afflicted by disease, disability, or injury can get the health care they need; many cannot—and they suffer and die for its lack. For any sensitive observer (and any decent society), these cold inequalities are surely cause for concern, dismay, even alarm. They also raise ethical questions of the most basic kind. To what are the less fortunate entitled, and what is society obligated to give? Are the needy due only the health care they can afford to buy for themselves, even if they can afford nothing? Or is society obligated to provide more? Is society obliged to provide everyone with access to health care regardless of ability to pay? Or is the claim on society's resources even stronger: Do people have a *right* to health care? If so, to what exactly are they entitled? To a guarantee of a state of well-being equal to that of everyone else? To an equal share of health care resources? To the best health care available? Or to something more modest—a decent minimum amount of health care? And what, exactly, is a decent minimum?

These are moral concerns on a larger scale than most of those we have grappled with in previous chapters. Here we ask not what is right or good in the person-to-person dramas of moral conflict; rather, we ask what is good or right in the policies and actions of society or government. The central issue is: Who should get health care, who should provide it, and who should pay for it? In other words, *what is just*? In the painful, complicated task of dividing up society's health care resources (including medical treatment, disease prevention, emergency care, and public health measures), what does justice demand?

Whatever answer is devised, it must take into account some hard realities. No system can provide maximum health care for everyone; there are limits—sometimes severe—to what any system can provide. Costs restrict how much health care can be delivered and how much can be obtained, and they can rise rapidly enough to destroy the best laid plans for fair access. Moreover, a society's finite resources must be allocated to satisfy many needs besides health care—education, defense, transportation, law enforcement, and others. Some kinds of health care can increase the well-being of more people to a greater degree than others, so considerations of efficiency will have to shape the allocation of resources. And somehow these quantitative factors must be reconciled with freedom of choice. In a free society, this value is paramount and cannot be entirely discarded for the sake of a more rational distribution of health care.

Most careful thinkers on the subject believe that a just apportioning of health care is possible. But how?

HEALTH CARE IN TROUBLE

The question is both grave and urgent because the current system for allocating health care is widely believed to be not only unjust but also ineffective and unsustainable. Many claim that, by several measures, it has failed or is failing.

Regardless of their political views, most tend to think that in this free and prosperous nation, all citizens should somehow have access to health care. But many people go without. Health care is so expensive that few can afford it unless they have some type of health insurance, which is itself expensive—so expensive in fact that the high cost is the main reason for lack of coverage. In 2006, almost 47 million people under the age of 65 were uninsured, and almost 9 million of those were children. Nearly a third of the under-65 population—almost 90 million people—had no health insurance for at least part of 2006 or 2007. The number of people without health insurance has been growing for years, rising by almost 9 million from 2000 to 2006.[1]

The consequences of going without health coverage are just what you might expect. The uninsured are less likely than the insured to get needed medical treatment, prescription drugs, preventive tests (pap smears and prostate exams, for example), and follow-up care when they do manage to see a doctor. Not surprisingly, researchers have estimated that the risk of death is 25 percent higher for the uninsured than the insured, resulting in about 18,000 more deaths in 2000 among those aged 25 to 64.[2]

Traditionally most people under age 65 got health coverage as a benefit of employment, but a smaller percentage of them are now obtaining insurance this way—69 percent in 2000 down to 60 percent in 2007. Fewer employers are offering this benefit (one-third of companies do not), and even when they do, many employees are either not eligible for it or cannot afford to pay their portion of the insurance premium. Over 70 percent of the uninsured are members of families with full-time workers.[3]

People who are age 65 and older and some adults under 65 with permanent disabilities are covered by the public health insurance program known as Medicare. It collects payroll taxes from workers during their employment years and provides coverage when they turn 65, paying many health care expenses including physician and hospital services and prescription drugs. Medicaid, another publicly supported program, covers some under-65 low-income people including children and the disabled. But coverage varies from state to state and, because of eligibility rules, does not extend to 37 percent of people below the federal poverty level. Together, all public health insurance programs—including Medicare, Medicaid, and other kinds of state insurance—cover 16 percent of people under age 65. The 47 million uninsured constitute 18 percent.[4]

Critics of the U.S. health care system point to discrepancies between the huge expenditures for health care and surprisingly low grades on standard measures of national health. According to the most recent data, the country's per capita spending on health care was $6,102—more than twice as much as the average amount spent by the richest nations in the world. (The list of the richest comprises 30 democracies in the Organization for Economic Cooperation and Development [OECD], including France, Germany, Switzerland, Denmark, Canada, the United Kingdom, Norway, and Japan.) The country coming closest to that level of spending was Luxembourg at $5,352; Canada spent $3,326; the United Kingdom, $2,724; and Japan, $2,358. Yet in the United States, life expectancy at birth (77.8 years) was lower than the average for the OECD countries (78.6 years) and lower than that of other economically advanced nations such as Canada, France, Japan, the United Kingdom, Switzerland, Iceland, Australia, and Spain. The infant mortality rate in the United States was also higher than the OECD average—6.8 deaths per 1000 live births compared to 5.4. In fact, it was higher than the rate of any of the other developed countries.[5]

Though the United States spends more on health care than any other country, the quality of the care is not obviously better overall than that of other countries. The U.S. system outshines them in some ways, but lags behind in others. For example, it excels in the development and use of medical technologies and has lower wait times for non-emergency surgeries. But it also has higher death rates from medical errors and fewer physicians per capita, and Americans have more trouble getting treated on nights and weekends and obtaining same-day appointments with doctors.[6] Research shows that for almost half of people who do receive care, that care is inadequate—that is, it does not meet established standards of recommended care.[7]

IN DEPTH
UNEQUAL HEALTH CARE FOR MINORITIES

Research has established that many minorities have much poorer health and higher mortality than the rest of the population. At the same time, they are also likely to receive lower quality health care. According to the Institute of Medicine, "Racial and ethnic minorities tend to receive lower-quality health care than whites do, even when insurance status, income, age, and severity of conditions are comparable." The CDC's Office of Minority Health and Health Disparities has detailed many of the differences between the health of minorities and that of others:

Current information about the biologic and genetic characteristics of minority populations does not explain the health disparities experienced by these groups compared with the white, non-Hispanic population in the United States....

- Even though the nation's infant mortality rate is down, the infant death rate among African Americans is still more than double that of whites. Heart disease death rates are more than 40 percent higher for African Americans than for whites. The death rate for all cancers is 30 percent higher for African Americans than for whites; for prostate cancer, it is more than double that for whites. African-American women have a higher death rate from breast cancer despite having a mammography screening rate that is nearly the same as the rate for white women. The death rate from HIV/AIDS for African Americans is more than seven times that for whites; the rate of homicide is six times that for whites.
- Hispanics living in the United States are almost twice as likely to die from diabetes as are non-Hispanic whites. Although constituting only 11 percent of the total population in 1996, Hispanics accounted for 20 percent of the new cases of tuberculosis. Hispanics also have higher rates of high blood pressure and obesity than non-Hispanic whites. There are differences among Hispanic populations as well. For example, whereas the rate of low birth weight infants is lower for the total Hispanic population compared with that of whites, Puerto Ricans have a low birth weight rate that is 50 percent higher than the rate for whites.
- American Indians and Alaska Natives have an infant death rate almost double that for whites. The rate of diabetes for this population group is more than twice that for whites. The Pima of Arizona have one of the highest rates of diabetes in the world. American Indians and Alaska Natives also have disproportionately high death rates from unintentional injuries and suicide.
- Asians and Pacific Islanders, on average, have indicators of being one of the healthiest population groups in the United States. However, there is great diversity within this population group, and health disparities for some specific segments are quite marked. Women of Vietnamese origin, for example, suffer from cervical cancer at nearly five times the rate for white women. New cases of hepatitis and tuberculosis also are higher in Asians and Pacific Islanders living in the United States than in whites.

The National Academies, "Minorities More Likely to Receive Lower-Quality Health Care, Regardless of Income and Insurance Coverage," 20 March 2002, http://www8.nationalacademies.org/onpinews/newsitem .aspx?RecordID=10260 (14 June 2008); CDC, Office of Minority Health & Health Disparities, "About Minority Health," 6 June 2007, http://www.cdc.gov/omhd/amh/amh.htm (14 June 2008).

Fact File U.S. Health Care

- In 2006, 46.5 million Americans had no health insurance—18 percent of people under age 65.
- Nearly 90 million were without health coverage for part of 2006 or 2007.
- Over 80 percent of the uninsured are members of working families.
- In 2006 one-third of companies did not offer health coverage.
- In 2006, there were 8.7 million uninsured children—nearly 12 percent of all children.
- According to data published in 2007, per capita spending on health care in the United States was $6,102; in Canada, $3,326; and in the United Kingdom, $2,724.
- Infant mortality in the United States was 6.8 deaths per 1000 live births, higher than that of all other developed countries.
- Almost half of the health care that people receive in the United States does not meet established standards of recommended care.

The Kaiser Commission on Medicaid and the Uninsured, "The Uninsured: A Primer," The Kaiser Family Foundation, October 2007, http://www.kff.org/uninsured/7451.cfm (21 March 2008); The National Coalition on Health Care, "Health Insurance Coverage," The National Coalition on Health Care, undated, 2008, http://www.nchc.org/facts/coverage.shtml (21 March 2008); Organization for Economic Cooperation and Development, OECD Health Data 2007, July 2007, http://www.oecd.org (27 March 2008); E. A. McGlynn et al., "The Quality of Health Care Delivered in the United States," *New England Journal of Medicine* 348.26 (2003), 2635–45; S. Asch et al., "Who Is at Greatest Risk for Receiving Poor-Quality Health Care?" *New England Journal of Medicine* 354.11 (2006), 1147–56.

In the United States most health care is allocated through **managed care**, a system for providing care to a particular group of patients (members of the system) using regulatory restraints to control costs and increase efficiency. People who enroll in a managed care plan—such as a health maintenance organization (HMO) or a preferred provider organization (PPO)—get health care at discounted prices from the plan's network of providers (physicians, hospitals, etc.). Managed care plans try to control costs by influencing the kind and amount of care that providers offer and by restricting the choices that members have. Though cost control and efficiency are laudable goals, many critics worry that they are at odds with patient welfare. The concern is that for the sake of economical medicine, providers may cut corners, decide not to order necessary tests, pay less attention to patients' needs, or refuse to treat certain serious health problems. Some charge that managed care as it is currently practiced forces physicians to try to serve both the patient and organizational efficiency, an impossible task that weakens the patient's trust in the physician.

THEORIES OF JUSTICE

All these difficulties bring us around again to the question of what is just. Justice in the most general sense refers to people getting what is fair or what is their due (see Chapter 1). At the heart of every plausible notion of justice is the principle that equals should be treated equally—that people should be treated the same unless there is a morally relevant reason for treating them differently. When we ask what justice demands in society's allocation of health care, we are dealing with matters of **distributive justice**—justice regarding the fair distribution of society's advantages and disadvantages, or benefits and burdens, including income, property, employment, rights, taxes, and public service.

Debates about ethical allocations of health care resources rely heavily on general theories of justice. To justify a particular scheme of allocation, philosophers, politicians, and others may appeal to a theory of justice, and those who criticize the scheme may do so by arguing against that underlying theory of justice or by offering an alternative theory they believe to be superior. Three types of theories have had—and continue to have—an enormous impact on the discussions: libertarian, utilitarian, and egalitarian.

According to **libertarian theories of justice**, the benefits and burdens of society should be distributed through the fair workings of a free market and the exercise of liberty rights of non-interference. The role of government is to protect the rights of individuals to freely pursue their own interests in the economic marketplace without violations of their liberty through coercion, manipulation, or fraud. Government may use coercion, but only to preserve liberty. Beyond these protections, the government has no obligation to adjust the distribution of benefits and burdens among people; the distribution is the responsibility of free and autonomous individuals. People may have equal rights or equal worth, but that does not entitle them to an equal distribution of society's benefits. The government acts unjustly if it coercively redistributes those benefits.

On this view, no one has a right to health care, and a government program using tax dollars to provide universal health care or even health care only for low-income families would be unjust. Such a program would be a coercive violation of people's right to use their resources as they see fit. The libertarian would accept a system of health care only if it is freely endorsed and financed by those who participate in it. So health insurance acquired through free choice by a group of private citizens to meet their own health care needs is acceptable. State-supported health insurance financed by taxes is not. But none of this would rule out voluntary charity by well-off citizens to provide health care for the poor.

In **utilitarian theories of justice**, a just distribution of benefits and burdens is one that maximizes the net good (utility) for society. Some al-locations (or principles of allocation) of society's resources are more beneficial overall than others, and these are what utilitarian justice demands. A utilitarian may grant some principles of allocation the status of rights—rules that can be enforced by society and that can override considerations of utility in specific situations. But the ultimate justification of the rules is utilitarian (actually, rule-utilitarian): Consistently following the rules may maximize utility generally, although rule adherence in some instances may not produce a net good.

On a utilitarian view, a just allocation of health care can take several forms depending on the facts about society's resources and needs and the likely effects of various allocation policies and programs. Thus, depending on calculations of net benefits, a utilitarian might endorse a system of universal health care insurance, or a qualified right to health care, or a two-tiered plan (like the U.S. arrangement) in which government-supported health insurance is combined with the option of privately purchased health coverage for those who can afford it.

Egalitarian theories of justice affirm that important benefits and burdens of society should be distributed equally. To achieve greater equality, the egalitarian (unlike the libertarian) would not be averse to mandating changes to the distribution of society's goods or to interfering in the workings of a free market. And the egalitarian (unlike the utilitarian) would not allow utility to be the ultimate overriding consideration in a system of distribution. From egalitarian premises, theorists have derived several schemes for allocating health care, including systems that give equal access to all legitimate forms of health care, that offer a guaranteed minimal level of health care for everyone, or that provide care only to those most in need.

A RIGHT TO HEALTH CARE

No matter what theory of justice people accept, they are likely to agree that it would be good for everyone to have adequate health care, or

An issue that has received attention in the news lately is the number of Americans who do not have health insurance. How serious do you think this problem is: very serious, somewhat serious, not too serious or not at all serious?

Very Serious	Somewhat Serious	Not Too Serious	Not at All Serious	Unsure
74%	19%	4%	2%	1%

NPR/Kaiser Foundation/Harvard School of Public Health survey, February 14–24, 2008, 1704 adults nationwide; margin of error = ±3.

Thinking again about health care in the country as a whole: Are you generally satisfied or dissatisfied with the total cost of health care in this country?

Satisfied	Dissatisfied	Unsure
17%	81%	2%

Which of these statements do you think best describes the U.S. health care system today? It is in a state of crisis, It has major problems, It has minor problems, or It does not have any problems.

State of Crisis	Major Problems	Minor Problems	No Problems	Unsure
17%	56%	24%	2%	1%

Do you think it is the responsibility of the federal government to make sure all Americans have health coverage, or is that not the responsibility of the federal government?

Is	Is Not	Unsure
64%	33%	3%

Gallup Poll, November 11–14, 2007, 1014 adults nationwide; margin of error = ±3.

Do you think the government should provide a national health insurance program for all Americans, even if this would require higher taxes?

Yes	No	Unsure
64%	35%	2%

CNN/Opinion Research Corporation Poll, May 4–6, 2007, 1028 adults nationwide; margin of error = ±3.

---

that beneficence may justify society's providing health care to the neediest, or that making particular kinds of health care available to certain groups may produce a net benefit for society. But some assert a much stronger claim: People have a moral *right* to health care. A right is an entitlement, a bona fide claim, to something. A person's rights impose duties on others—either (1) duties not to interfere with that person's obtaining something or (2) duties to help that person in her efforts to get something. Rights entailing the former obligations are called *negative rights*; those entailing the latter are called *positive rights*. Those who insist that an individual has a right to health care are referring to a positive right and are claiming that society has an obligation to provide that benefit in some way.

Libertarians are likely to deny that there is a right to health care, for generally they accept negative rights and disallow positive rights. Utilitarians can admit a right to health care, though it would be what some have called a *derivative right,* a rule ultimately justified by assessments of utility. Others, including egalitarians, can accommodate a right to health care and interpret it in the strong sense of being an entitlement that ultimately outweighs calculations of maximized utility.

But what reasons are there for believing that there is such a strong right to health care? Norman Daniels believes that such a right can be derived from one of the principles of justice articulated by John Rawls, specifically the right to "fair equality of opportunity."[8] Rawls maintains that everyone is entitled to an equal chance to obtain the basic goods of society, though there is no guarantee of an equal share of them (see the discussion of Rawls' theory in Chapter 2). A just society would ensure equal opportunities to its citizens. Daniels argues that disease and disability diminish people's "normal species functioning" and thus restrict the range of opportunities open to them. But "health care in all its forms, whether public health or medical, preventive or acute or chronic, aims to keep people functioning as close to normally as possible. . . . Health care thus preserves for us the range of opportunities we would have, were we not ill or disabled, given our talents and skills."[9] Since people are entitled to fair equality of opportunity, and adequate health care can protect or restore their normal range of opportunities, they have a positive right to adequate health care.

A pivotal question that confronts every serious advocate of a moral right to health care is what health care resources it includes. Some have thought the right encompasses universal equal access to all available health care resources. But this arrangement is not technically or economically feasible; a right to health care, it seems, must have limits. Recognizing this, many have argued for a weaker right to a "decent minimum" level of health care. On this view, everyone would have access to a minimal, basic array of health care resources. This tier of care would be universally available, publicly supported, and guaranteed for all in need. A second tier of additional health care services (elective or nonessential therapies, for example) would be available in the free marketplace for those who can afford them.

Allen Buchanan rejects the idea of a right to a decent minimum of care, but he understands its attractions:

> First, the notion that people have a right to a decent minimum or adequate level, rather than to *all* health care that produces any net benefit, clearly acknowledges that, because not all health care is of equal importance, allocational priorities must be set within health care and that resources

must also be allocated to goods other than health care. Second, this [decent minimum] position is also consonant with the intuitively plausible conviction that our obligations to the less fortunate, although fundamental enough to be expressed in the language of rights, are nonetheless *not unlimited*. Third, the decent minimum is a floor beneath which no one should be allowed to fall, not a ceiling above which the better-off are prohibited from purchasing services if they wish.[10]

But the implications of the decent-minimum standard have been extremely difficult to specify in a plausible way. What is, after all, a *decent minimum* of health care? We may assume it includes such things as immunizations, annual physical exams, and "routine" medical care. Should it also include heart transplants, treatments for rare or orphan diseases, cosmetic surgery, expensive but marginally effective care for very elderly or dying patients, and costly lifelong therapies for mentally impaired persons who will never reach "normal" functioning?

Buchanan believes that although there is no right to a decent minimum of health care, there are good reasons for supposing that society should nevertheless provide the kind and amount of health care that a decent-minimum right would demand. That is, there is no individual right, but there may be a societal duty. Among these reasons are arguments that people have special rights (as opposed to universal rights) to health care—rights of restitution to certain groups for past wrongs, rights of compensation for "those who have suffered unjust harm or who have been unjustly exposed to health risks by the assignable actions of private individuals or corporations," and rights to health care for honorable service to society (for wounded soldiers, for instance). There are also prudential arguments, Buchanan says, such as that "the availability of certain basic forms of health care make for a more productive labor force or improve the fitness of the citizenry for national defense." Arguments for what he calls "enforced beneficence" can also be made out.

To maximize the practical effect of our moral obligations of charity or beneficence regarding health care for those in need, "an enforced decent minimum principle is needed to achieve coordinated joint effort."[11] Thus, for example, the government could levy taxes to provide health care to the poor—not in the name of egalitarian justice, but for the sake of beneficence.

THE ETHICS OF RATIONING

Rationing has been a dirty word in debates about health care, laden as it is with images of extreme measures of last resort for managing a dearth of resources. But in health care, rationing—in the broad sense of parceling out important limited goods—has always been with us and probably always will be. People's health care needs are virtually boundless, yet the supply of health care resources is ever limited. So we ration: Medicare and Medicaid allot health care to the elderly and the poor; HMOs limit medical procedures, tests, and access to doctors to control costs; hospitals restrict the use of intensive care units (ICUs), cardiac surgical teams, emergency departments, hospital beds, and expensive drugs; organ transplants are doled out to the few because of shortages of usable organs; and the health care system as a whole rations a great deal of care by people's ability to pay for it.

Thus the tough choices of rationing fall hard upon us, and we are forced to ask: Who should get what share of limited health care goods and services? In countless troubling instances, the question reduces to this: Who should live and who must die? In nearly the same breath we have to ask: On what ethical grounds do we make these choices? The fundamental issue of the proper allocation of insufficient resources troubles on several levels at once. It arises both on the scale of the total health care system (concerning what portion of society's resources should go to health care and how this allotment should be used—so-called *macroallocation*) and on the scale of individual patients and providers (regarding who should receive specific resources—known as *microallocation*).

Let's consider just a few of the smaller scale (microallocation) questions raised by one of our scarcest life-saving resources—organ transplants. Transplant operations are incredibly expensive, organs are in very short supply, and transplants are desperately needed by far more people than can be accommodated. The waiting list for transplants is long, and thousands die every year for their lack. Screening committees at transplant centers decide whether someone should be placed on the waiting list and what ranking they should receive. They use various criteria to make these decisions, some explicit, some informal or unspoken, some plausible (such as the patient's need and likelihood of benefit), and some controversial (such as ability to pay, social worthiness, and health habits).

But what criteria *should* be used? What rationing policy for transplants is morally justified? Many proposed criteria are utilitarian, concerned with maximizing benefits to the patient and society. Many are egalitarian, focusing on justice and the moral equality of persons. Some philosophers propose rationing policies that emphasize one or the other, while some try systematically to accommodate both.[12] No policy is completely satisfactory, but some seem to capture our moral intuitions better than others.

One utilitarian approach to rationing care to patients is to measure objectively the benefits that a treatment is likely to give each patient, then selectively treat particular patients or conditions to maximize total benefits. The objective measure of benefits that has often been used in such calculations is known as QALY, or quality-adjusted life year. One QALY is equivalent to one year of life in good health, and a year of life in poor health is equal to less than 1 QALY. The lower the quality of life for a person in poor health, the lower the QALY value. A transplant operation that allows a patient to live seven years without disability or suffering is worth 7 QALYs; if it results in the patient's living seven years burdened by severe pain, it is worth less than 7 QALYs. Thus QALYs gauge a treatment's impact by, plausibly, trying to take into account both the length of life and its quality.

Intuitively this seems right because both quality of life and length of life matter to people. Most would probably rather enjoy a few years of good health than suffer through many years of terrible illness or disability. Suppose, then, that three people are awaiting heart transplants, without which they will die within six months, and only two transplants are possible. Two of the potential recipients are young, so a transplant for either one of them would yield 10 QALYs. The third person is much older; a transplant for her would yield only 5 QALYs. So a transplant selection committee using the QALY standard alone would likely allocate the available transplants to the two younger patients, maximizing total benefits.

The utilitarian purpose behind using QALYs is to do the most good with the resources available. But critics have charged that relying on QALYs to allocate or ration health care can lead to morally unacceptable decisions. John Harris argues, for example, that QALYs discriminate against older people:

> Maximizing QALYs involves an implicit and comprehensive ageist bias. For saving the lives of younger people is, other things being equal, always likely to be productive of more QALYs than saving older people. Thus on the QALY arithmetic we always have a reason to prefer, for example, neonatal or paediatric care to all "later" branches of medicine. This is because any calculation of the life-years generated for a particular patient by a particular therapy, must be based on the life expectancy of that patient. The older a patient is when treated, the fewer the life-years that can be achieved by the therapy.[13]

QALYs, he says, are also unfair to the disabled:

> Suppose for example that if an accident victim were treated, he would survive, but with paraplegia. This might always cash out at fewer QALYs than a condition which with treatment would give a patient perfect remission for about five years after which the patient would die. Suppose that both candidates wanted to go on living as long as they could and so both wanted, equally

fervently, to be given the treatment that would save their lives. Is it clear that the candidate with most QALYs on offer should always and inevitably be the one to have priority? To judge so would be to count the paraplegic's desire to live the life that was available to him as of less value than his rival's.[14]

Harris and others contend that a crucial failing of QALYs is that these objective measurements cannot accommodate the subjective nature of people's assessments of the value of their own lives. A paraplegic may value his life and think its quality extremely high despite his disability. A perfectly healthy person may think her life miserable despite a lack of physical ailments. The subjective valuation seems to be the important one; the objective measurement seems to be beside the point.

Policies for rationing transplants to a particular group of patients generally try to take into account the probability of transplant success or the urgency of the patients' needs. Both factors can be morally relevant. Regarding the former, because transplants are a scarce resource, fairness seems to demand that they be given to those who are likely to benefit from them—otherwise the resource will be wasted, and people will be deprived of a treatment that could have saved them. Regarding the latter, giving transplants to those who cannot survive for much longer without them fulfills a duty to preserve lives.

Nevertheless, some maintain that allocating resources in light of one of these considerations while disregarding the other is a mistake:

> For example, although heart-transplant surgeons sometimes list their patients as urgent priority candidates for an available heart because the patients will soon die if they do not receive a transplant, some of these patients are virtually certain to die even if they do receive the heart. High quality candidates are passed over in the process. A classification and queuing system that permits urgent need to determine priority exclusively is as unjust as it is inefficient.[15]

Neither probability of success nor urgent need seems to be as controversial as another kind of criterion: the *social value* of people's lives. Here the question is which potential recipients—if given the chance to live—are expected to contribute most to the good of society. To state the issue concretely: All things being equal, should the medical student get the transplant instead of the poet or prostitute? Nicholas Rescher thinks this question of social utility important and morally relevant:

> In "choosing to save" one life rather than another, "the society," through the mediation of the particular medical institution in question—which should certainly look upon itself as a trustee for the social interest—is clearly warranted in considering the likely pattern of future *services to be rendered* by the patient (adequate recovery assumed), considering his age, talent, training, and past record of performance. In its allocations of [exotic life-saving therapy], society "invests" a scarce resource in one person as against another and is thus entitled to look to the probable prospective "return" on its investment.[16]

Others reject this line altogether, arguing from an egalitarian or Kantian perspective that all persons have equal worth. Morally, the medical student is not worth more than the poet or prostitute, and vice versa. Education, achievement, occupation, and the like are not morally relevant.

Nevertheless, while generally taking this view, some philosophers maintain that in very rare cases, social worth can outweigh egalitarian concerns. It seems reasonable that in a natural disaster involving mass casualties, injured physicians or nurses should be treated first if they can aid the other survivors. We can imagine analogous situations involving organ transplants, says Walter Glannon:

> Suppose that Nelson Mandela needed a liver transplant in 1992. This was the time when he was leading the transition from apartheid to democracy in South Africa. The transition turned out to be peaceful; but the political situation was poten-

tially volatile. Mandela was essential to maintaining social stability. Suppose further that a younger individual also needed a liver and would have at least as good an outcome with a transplant. In the light of the political and social circumstances, Mandela should have been given priority over the younger patient in receiving a liver. His survival would have ensured the social stability of the country. It would have ensured that many people would not suffer a loss of welfare or life from the social instability that might have resulted otherwise. Mandela's social worth was a function of the dependence of many people's welfare and lives on his survival. That worth would have been a decisive factor in giving the organ to him rather than to another person with the same need.[17]

KEY TERMS
distributive justice
egalitarian theories of justice
libertarian theories of justice
managed care
utilitarian theories of justice

SUMMARY
The U.S. system of health care has been ailing—or failing, as some would say—for years. Its most obvious symptoms are 47 million uninsured people under age 65, soaring costs, and low grades on some measures of national health, such as infant mortality rates.

Debates about ethical allocations of health care resources often reduce to clashes between theories of distributive justice—that is, theories regarding the fair distribution of society's benefits and burdens. Libertarian theories of justice say that the benefits and burdens of society should be distributed through the fair workings of a free market and the exercise of liberty rights of noninterference. The role of government is to protect the rights of individuals to freely pursue their own interests in the economic marketplace without violations of their liberty through coercion, manipulation, or fraud. On this view, no one has a right to health care. In utilitarian theories of justice, a just distribution of benefits

Christine deMeurers

The era of managed care has changed health care in the United States radically—for the worse, many say. Whatever the case, it has surely set off a host of conflicts that were previously unimagined: clashes between patients and their insurance companies, between physicians and their cost-conscious managed care employers, and between the physicians' duty to put the patient's welfare first and the economic incentives to put it last. Out of this maelstrom many unsettling stories have come, including this one.

In 1992 Christine deMeurers—a 32-year-old wife, mother of two, and schoolteacher—found out that she had breast cancer. She fought back promptly and aggressively, enduring a radical mastectomy, radiation therapy, and chemotherapy. But in May 1993, a bone scan revealed that the cancer had spread and now rated the ominous label of Stage IV metastatic breast cancer. Every standard therapy available had been used against her disease with no apparent effect. She was running out of time.

Christine and her husband, Alan, were subscribers in an HMO, Health Net of Woodland Hills, California. They got the insurance through their employer (they both were teachers at the same school) and had opted for the least expensive coverage.

After the standard treatments failed, the deMeurers thought they had no options left, but Christine's oncologist, Dr. Mahesh Gupta, was hopeful. He held out the possibility that she could benefit from a promising new treatment, a bone marrow transplant. Its effectiveness against Christine's type of cancer was unproven, but it had been used successfully on other kinds of malignancies. In violation of Health Net rules on referrals, Dr. Gupta referred Christine directly to an expert he knew, an oncologist at the Scripps Clinic in La Jolla.

According to the deMeurers, the Scripps doctor was reluctant to help them or even to provide them with information about the bone marrow transplant. So they flew to Denver, where Christine was examined by Dr. Roy B. Jones at the University of Colorado. He told them that the bone marrow procedure might be beneficial to Christine. But about the time

that the deMeurers consulted with Dr. Jones, Health Net resolved that the company would not pay for the transplant because it was disallowed under the investigational clause in Christine's contract.

Increasingly desperate, the deMeurers started trying to raise the thousands of dollars needed to pay for the procedure, and they hired a lawyer to appeal Health Net's ruling. They also got permission to see another oncologist. He too encouraged Christine to consider the bone marrow transplant and referred her to the UCLA Medical Center, where Dr. John Glaspy presented the operation as an option and agreed to perform it.

This encounter between the deMeurers and Dr. Glaspy was strained by mutual ignorance of some significant facts. Wary of possible interference from Health Net, they did not tell Dr. Glaspy that they were Health Net subscribers and told him instead that they would pay for the transplant out of pocket. At the same time the deMeurers did not know that Dr. Glaspy was on the Health Net committee that had voted recently not to cover bone marrow transplants for Stage IV breast cancer patients.

Later, news came that Health Net had rejected the appeal filed by the deMeurers' lawyer.

Dr. Glaspy found himself caught between conflicting loyalties. As the deMeurers' physician, he felt a responsibility to help Christine get the transplant. But as a Health Net physician, he was required to uphold the regulations of the HMO, some of which he had helped make. Discussions ensued between Health Net administrators and UCLA physicians and officials. Finally, a way out of the conflict appeared when UCLA agreed that it would pay for Christine's operation.

Christine began the treatment on September 22, 1993, at UCLA Medical Center. She died March 10, 1995. Health Net officials expressed doubt that the treatment helped much. Alan deMeurers said that it gave Christine four disease-free months.

Eventually an arbitration panel ruled that Health Net should have paid for Christine's transplant and that the company had improperly interfered in the doctor-patient relationship.

and burdens is one that maximizes the net utility for society. Depending on calculations of net benefits, a utilitarian might endorse a system of universal health care insurance, or a qualified right to health care, or a two-tiered plan. Egalitarian theories of justice say that important benefits and burdens of society should be distributed equally. To achieve greater equality, the egalitarian would not be averse to mandating changes to the distribution of society's goods or to interfering in the workings of a free market. Egalitarian theorists could consistently endorse several schemes for allocating health care, including systems that give equal access to all legitimate forms of health care, that offer a guaranteed minimal level of health care for everyone, or that provide care only to those most in need.

Some theorists assert the strong claim that people have a positive moral right to health care. Libertarians would reject this view, utilitarians could endorse a derivative right to health care, and egalitarians could favor a bona fide entitlement to a share of society's health care resources. Some of the latter argue for a right to a decent minimum of health care.

Because people's health care needs are virtually limitless and the supply of resources is always bounded, rationing of health care in some form is ever with us. The dilemmas of rationing arise most visibly and acutely on the level of individual patients and providers who must contend with scarce life-saving resources such as organ transplants. The central moral issue in these cases is what criteria should be used to decide which patients get transplants and who should make the decisions.

Cases for Evaluation

CASE 1
Black Market in Organ Transplants

(*San Francisco Chronicle*)—Tears well up in P. Guna's eyes as he stares at a long scar running down his side. A year ago, he attempted to stave off mounting debt by swapping one of his healthy kidneys for quick cash.

"Humans don't need two kidneys, I was made to believe," he said. "I can sell my extra kidney and become rich, I thought."

At the time, an organ trader promised Guna, 38, a motorized-rickshaw driver with a fourth-grade education, $2,500 for the kidney, of which he eventually received only half. Since then, he has experienced excruciating pain in his hip that has kept him from working full time and pushed him deeper in debt.

In recent years, many Indian cities—like Chennai in southern India—have become hubs of a murky business in kidney transplants, despite a 1994 nationwide ban on human organ sales (the Transplant of Human Organ Act states only relatives of patients can donate kidneys).

An influx of patients, mainly foreigners, seeking the transplants has made the illicit market a lucrative business. Some analysts say the business thrives for the same reasons that have made India a top destination for medical tourism: low cost and qualified doctors. In fact, medical tourism is expected to reach $2.2 billion by 2012, according to government estimates.

Not surprisingly, an organized group of organ traders in cahoots with unscrupulous doctors is constantly on the prowl for donors like Guna.

In Gurgaon, a posh New Delhi suburb, police last month busted an illegal organ racket, which included doctors, nurses, pathology clinics, and hospitals. In the past 14 years, the participants allegedly removed kidneys from about 500 day laborers, the majority of them abducted or conned, before selling the organs to wealthy clients.

Police say the doctor believed to be the mastermind behind the operation, Amit Kumar, searched for donors by cruising in luxury cars outfitted with medical testing machines, and kept sophisticated surgical equipment in a residential apartment. In his office, police found letters and e-mail messages from 48 people from nine countries inquiring about transplants.

On Thursday, police arrested Kumar in Chitwan, a Nepalese jungle resort. Local news reports said he was identified by a hotel employee who recognized him from Indian television broadcasts seen in

Nepal. "I have not duped anybody," Kumar later told reporters in Kathmandu, according to the Associated Press.

Nepalese authorities say they won't extradite Kumar until they finish an investigation on whether he violated currency laws by not declaring $230,000 in cash and a check for $24,000 that he was carrying when arrested. He is scheduled to appear in a Nepalese court Sunday.

In another high-profile arrest, a renowned Chennai surgeon, Palani Ravichandran, was arrested in October in Mumbai for involvement in a kidney racket. He admitted to arranging organ transplants for wealthy foreigners—mainly from Persian Gulf states and Malaysia, whom he charged up to $25,000. Mumbai police say Ravichandran had performed between 40 and 100 illegal transplants since 2002.

Police say kidney donors can earn between $1,250 and $2,500, while recipients pay as much as $25,000, according to ActionAid India, an anti-poverty organization that has worked with kidney trade victims in the southern state of Tamil Nadu.

The same procedure can cost as much as $70,000 in China and $85,000 in the United States.

"These middlemen act more like cut-and-grab men whose only interest is to hack out the organ," said Annie Thomas, a field co-coordinator for ActionAid in Chennai, formerly known as Madras. "This is a reprehensible abuse of the poor, and this practice needs to be curbed."

Thomas says many middlemen typically masquerade the donors as relatives to circumvent the law while many foreigners in need of a kidney arrive on tourist visas rather than the required medical visas; some resort to false documents.*

Is it morally permissible to sell your own organs? Is it morally permissible to buy organs from consenting adult donors? Should organ selling be illegal in all cases? Are the Indian organ donors described in this article being exploited? How? Give reasons for your answers.

---

*Anuj Chopra, "Organ-Transplant Black Market Thrives in India," *SFGate*, 9 February 2008, http://www.sfgate.com (11 April 2008).

CASE 2

Expensive Health Care for a Killer

(*Statesman Journal*)—Oregon taxpayers are shelling out more than $120,000 a year to provide life-saving dialysis for a condemned killer.

Horacio Alberto Reyes-Camarena was sent to death row six years ago for stabbing to death an 18-year-old girl and dumping her body near the Oregon Coast.

At the Two Rivers Correctional Institution in Eastern Oregon, Reyes-Camarena, 47, gets hooked up to a dialysis machine for four hours three times a week to remove toxins from his blood.

Without dialysis, he would die because his kidneys are failing.

Each dialysis session costs $775.80 for treatment and medication, according to Corrections Department figures. At that rate, his dialysis costs $121,025 a year.

As the state keeps Reyes-Camarena alive, thousands of older, poor, sick and disabled Oregonians are trying to survive without medications and care that vanished amid state budget cuts.

Some Oregon hospitals are considering closing dialysis units because of Medicaid-related reductions.

Reyes-Camarena said he wants to sever his ties to the dialysis machine. The convicted killer wants to be the first Oregon inmate to receive a taxpayer-financed organ transplant.

"It's much better for me, and them, too," Reyes-Camarena said, referring to his desire for a kidney transplant, a procedure sought by nearly 57,000 Americans.

The prisoner cited medical reports indicating that transplant costs prove to be cheaper than dialysis in the long run.

Even so, transplant surgery is costly: $80,000 to $120,000. It also requires $500 to $1,200 a month in lifelong drugs to keep the recipient from rejecting the new organ.

Studies have found that the death rate for dialysis patients is about 23 percent a year. A successful transplant reduces that risk to about 3 percent a year.

But the number of transplants is severely limited by a national scarcity of available organs. As of this month, 56,895 Americans, including 192 Oregonians, were waiting for kidney transplants, according to the Virginia-based United Network for Organ Sharing, which maintains the nation's waiting list for organs.

Because the waiting list is long and there aren't enough organs to go around, some people die before a transplant becomes available.

Overall, 86,157 Americans are waiting for organ transplants—mostly kidneys, livers, pancreases and lungs. Officials estimate that about 700 will die this year while waiting.

Lifesaving care for Reyes-Camarena raises questions about the bounds of medical treatment for prisoners.*

Is society obligated to prolong the life of felons like Reyes-Camarena? As thousands of dollars are spent each year by the state to provide him with health care, many lawful citizens cannot afford critical care and die as a result. Is this arrangement just? Do prisoners have a right to health care? Does anyone have a right to health care? Explain your answers.

---

*Alan Gustafson, "Death Row Inmate Seeks Organ Transplant," *Statesman Journal*, 28 April 2003, http://news.statesmanjournal .com/article.cfm?i=59756 (11 April 2008).

CASE 3

Life, Death, and Money

(*Reader's Digest*)—Heart surgeon Mehmet Oz was set to go. On the operating table lay a 50-year-old man, dying from heart failure. He was anesthetized, out cold, and his chest was painted with sterile Betadine. In minutes, Dr. Oz and his team would implant a mechanical pump to keep him alive until a donor heart could be found.

All that remained was for Dr. Oz to scrub his hands. As he soaped up just outside the OR, he thought about the brief chat he'd had with the patient earlier that morning. The man, a mid-level executive with an agricultural company, was clearly terrified, knowing that he could die.

Just then someone called out. There was an urgent phone call for the surgeon. With suds dripping from his hands, Dr. Oz walked back into the OR and a nurse held the phone to his ear.

It was someone from the patient's health insurance company. His policy covered heart transplants, but not the cost of the mechanical pump. At the end of the operation, someone was going to owe a small fortune—and the insurers were insisting that it would not be them.

Dr. Oz's mind raced. What was he supposed to do, sacrifice this man's life because no one knew who'd pay for the surgery? A quick follow-up call to his department chairman confirmed his own instinct: Ethical decisions trump financial ones. He would proceed with the operation. They'd figure out who'd pay later.

In the end, the surgery was a success, but the hospital got stuck with most of the costs, which ultimately ran into the hundreds of thousands. If it hadn't picked up the tab, the patient would be drowning in debt.*

Did the surgeon make the right decision? Is it ever morally permissible to withhold critical care from someone for lack of payment? If the surgeon had stopped the surgery because the insurance company would not pay for it and the man died as a result, would anyone be morally culpable? If so, who? Explain your answers.

---

*Kerry Howley, "I Can't Afford to Get Sick," *Reader's Digest*, April 2006, http://www.rd.com/health/prevention/your-medical-care/the-cost-of-health-care-in-america/article26204 (11 April 2008).

FURTHER READING

Michael Boylan, "The Universal Right to Health Care," in *Medical Ethics*, ed. Michael Boylan (Upper Saddle River, NJ: Prentice-Hall, 2000), 391–402.

Tom L. Beauchamp and James F. Childress, "Justice," in *Principles of Biomedical Ethics*, 5th ed. (New York: Oxford University Press, 2001), 225–82.

Allen Buchanan, "Justice: A Philosophical Review," in *Justice and Health Care*, ed. Earl Shelp (Dordrecht: D. Reidel Publishing, 1981), 3–21.

Allen Buchanan, "Health-Care Delivery and Resource Allocation," in *Medical Ethics*, ed. Robert M. Veatch (Sudbury, MA: Jones and Bartlett, 1997), 321–61.

Norman Daniels, "Health-Care Needs and Distributive Justice," in *Justice and Justification* (Cambridge: Cambridge University Press, 1996), 179–207.

Norman Daniels, *Just Health Care* (Cambridge: Cambridge University Press, 1985).

Walter Glannon, "Allotting Scarce Medical Resources," in *Biomedical Ethics* (Oxford: Oxford University Press, 2005), 143–66.

The Kaiser Commission on Medicaid and the Uninsured, "The Uninsured: A Primer," October 2007, http://www.kff.org/uninsured/7451.cfm (21 March 2008).

Rosamond Rhodes, Margaret P. Battin, and Anita Silvers, eds., *Medicine and Social Justice* (New York: Oxford University Press, 2002).

NOTES

1. The Kaiser Commission on Medicaid and the Uninsured, "The Uninsured: A Primer," October 2007, http://www.kff.org/uninsured/7451.cfm (21 March 2008); The National Coalition on Health Care, "Health Insurance Coverage," undated, 2008, http://www.nchc.org/facts/coverage.shtml (21 March 2008).

2. Institute of Medicine, "Insuring America's Health: Principles and Recommendations," The National Academy Press, undated, 2004, http://www.nap.edu/catalog.php?record_id=10874#toc (21 March 2008).

3. The Kaiser Commission, "The Uninsured."

4. *Ibid.*

5. Organization for Economic Cooperation and Development, *OECD Health Data 2007,* July 2007, http://www.oecd.org (27 March 2008).

6. Congressional Research Service, *CRS Report for Congress: U.S. Health Care Spending: Comparison with Other OECD Countries* (Washington, DC: Congressional Research Service, 17 September 2007).

7. E. A. McGlynn et al., "The Quality of Health Care Delivered in the United States," *New England Journal of Medicine* 348.26 (2003), 2635–45; S. Asch et al., "Who Is at Greatest Risk for Receiving Poor-Quality Health Care?" *New England Journal of Medicine* 354.11 (2006), 1147–56.

8. John Rawls, *A Theory of Justice,* rev. ed. (Cambridge, MA: Harvard University Press, 1999).

9. Norman Daniels, "Is There a Right to Health Care and, if So, What Does It Encompass?" in *A Companion to Bioethics,* ed. Helga Kuhse and Peter Singer (Oxford: Blackwell Publishing, 1998), 316–25.

10. Allen Buchanan, "Health-Care Delivery and Resource Allocation," in *Medical Ethics,* ed. Robert M. Veatch (Boston: Jones and Bartlett Publishers, 1997), 351.

11. *Ibid.*

12. I owe this distinction to Tom L. Beauchamp and James F. Childress, *Principles of Biomedical Ethics,* 5th ed. (New York: Oxford University Press, 2001), 264–65.

13. John Harris, "QALYfying the Value of Life," *Journal of Medical Ethics* 13 (1987), 117–22.

14. *Ibid.*

15. *Ibid.* Beauchamp and Childress, *Principles of Biomedical Ethics,* 266.

16. Nicholas Rescher, "The Allocation of Exotic Medical Lifesaving Therapy," *Ethics* 79 (April 1969), 173–86.

17. Walter Glannon, *Biomedical Ethics* (New York: Oxford University Press, 2005), 158–59.

READINGS

Is There a Right to Health Care and, if So, What Does It Encompass?

NORMAN DANIELS

Daniels argues for a strong right to health care, deriving it from John Rawls' justice principle of "fair equality of opportunity." He reasons that disease and disability diminish people's "normal species functioning" and thus restrict the range of opportunities open to them. Since people are entitled to fair equality of opportunity, and adequate health care can protect or restore their normal range of opportunities, they have a positive right to adequate health care.

Is There a Right to Health Care?

Legal Versus Moral Rights to Health Care

One way to answer this question is to adopt the stance of legal positivists, who claim that there are no rights except those that are embodied in actual institutions through law. We would then be able to reply that in nearly every advanced industrial democracy in the world, there is a right to health care, since institutions exist in them that assure everyone access to needed services regardless of ability to pay. The notable exception is the United States, where many poor and near poor people have no insurance coverage for, and thus no assured access to, medically necessary services, although by law they cannot be denied emergency services.

The legal right to health care is embodied in a wide variety of types of health-care systems. These range from national health services, where the government is the provider of services, as in Great Britain, to public insurance schemes, where the government finances services, as in Canada, to mixed public and private insurance schemes, as in Germany and the Netherlands. Despite these differences in the design of systems, there is a broad overlap in the scope or content of the legal right to health care in these countries. Most cover "medically necessary" services, including a broad range of preventive, curative, rehabilitative and long-term care for physical and mental diseases, disorders and disabilities. Most exclude uses of medical technologies that enhance otherwise normal functioning or appearance, such as purely cosmetic surgery. The legal rights vary in significant ways, however, for example, in the degree to which they cover new reproductive technologies, or in the types of mental health and long-term care services that are offered.

In the context of rising costs and the rapid dissemination of new technologies there is growing debate in many countries about how to set limits on the scope of a right to health care. This debate about the scope of rights to health care pushes moral deliberation about such a right into the forefront, even where a legal right is recognized. Legal entitlements, most people believe, should reflect what society is morally obliged to provide by way of medical services. What, then, is the basis and scope of a moral right to health care?

Positive Versus Negative Rights

A right to health care is a *positive* as opposed to a *negative* right. Put quite simply, a positive right requires others to do something beneficial or enabling for right-bearers, whereas a negative right requires others to refrain from doing something, usually harmful or restrictive, to right-bearers. To say that others are required to do something or to refrain from doing something is to say they must so act or refrain even if they could produce more good or improve the world by not doing so (Thomson, 1990). For example, a negative right to free expression requires others to refrain from censuring the expression of the right-bearer even if censuring this speech would make a better world. Some public-health measures that protect people against interference with their health, such as environmental protections that protect people against polluters of air, water and food sources, might be construed as requirements of a negative right. More generally, however, a right to health care imposes an obligation on others to assist the right-bearers in obtaining needed and appropriate services. Specifically, claiming a right to health care includes these other claims; society has the duty to its members to allocate an adequate share of its total resources to health-related needs; society has the duty to provide a just allocation of different types of health care services, taking into account the competing claims of different types of health-care needs; each person is entitled to a fair share of such services, where a "fair share" includes an answer to the question, who should pay for the services? (Daniels, 1985). Health-care rights thus form a part of a broader family of positive "welfare" rights that includes rights to education and to income support. Because positive rights require other people to contribute their resources or skills to benefit right-bearers, rather than merely refraining from interfering with them, they have often been thought more difficult to justify than negative rights, and their scope and limits have been harder to characterize.

Theories of Justice and Rights to Health Care

If we are to think of a right to health care as a requirement of justice, then we should look to more general theories of justice as a way to specify the scope and limits of that right. On some theories of justice, however, there is little basis for requiring people to assist others by meeting their health care or other needs. Libertarians, for example, believe that fundamental rights to property, including rights to personal assets, such as talents and skills, are violated if society coerces individuals into providing "needed" resources or skills (Nozick, 1974). Libertarians generally recognize an "imperfect" duty to act beneficently or charitably, but this duty involves discretion. It can be discharged in different ways that are matters of choice. People denied charity have no right to it and have no complaint against people who act charitably in other ways. Though some have argued that the difficulty of coordinating the delivery of charitable assistance might justify coercive measures (Buchanan, 1984), and others have tried to show that even libertarians must recognize some forms of welfare rights (Sterba, 1985), most libertarians resist any weakening of the property rights at the core of their view (Brennan and Friedman, 1981).

A spectre sometimes raised by libertarians against the idea of a right to health care is that such a right is a "bottomless pit." Since new technologies continuously expand the scope of "medical needs," a right to health care would give rise to unlimited claims on the resources of others (Fried, 1969; Engelhardt, 1986). Protecting such an expansive right to health care would thus not be compatible with the function of a libertarian "minimal state" to assure the nonviolation of rights to liberty and property.

Though there remains controversy about whether utilitarians can provide a basis for recognizing true moral rights, there are strong utilitarian arguments in favour of governments assuring access to at least some broad range of effective medical services. Preventing or curing disease or disability reduces suffering and enables people to function in ways that contribute to aggregate welfare. In addition, knowing that health-care services are available increases personal security and strengthens the ties of community. Utilitarians can also justify redistributing the burden of delivering these benefits to society as a whole, citing the decreasing marginal utility of money to support progressive financing of health-care services (Brandt, 1979).

Beneath these quite general arguments, however, there lies a more specific controversy about the scope of utilitarian entitlements to health care. There seems to be little utilitarian justification for investing resources in health care if those resources would produce more net welfare when invested in other things, yet many people believe they have moral obligations to assist others with their health-care needs even at a net cost in utility. For example, some highly expensive and effective medical treatments that most people believe should be offered to people might not be "cost beneficial" and thus not defensible on utilitarian grounds. Similarly, many forms of long-term care, especially for those who cannot be restored to productive social activity, are also difficult to defend on utilitarian grounds, yet we insist our health-care systems are obliged to provide such services.

Lack of moral acceptance of the distributive implications of utilitarianism makes many uncomfortable with the use of methods, such as cost-effectiveness analysis, that are intended to guide decisions about resource allocation in health care. For example, an assumption of cost-effectiveness analysis is that a unit of health benefit, such as a quality-adjusted life year (QALY), is of equal value or importance regardless of where it is distributed. But this assumption does not capture the concerns many people have about how much priority to give to the sickest patients, or when aggregating modest benefits to large numbers of people it outweighs the moral importance of delivering more significant benefits to fewer people (Nord, 1993; Daniels, 1993).

Two points about a utilitarian framework for a right to health care are worth noting. Recognizing a right to health care is compatible with recognizing limits on entitlements that result from resource scarcity and the fact that there are competing uses of those resources. Consequently, recognizing a right to health care need not open a bottomless pit. Second, just what entitlements to services follow from a right to health care cannot be specified outside the context of a *system* properly designed to deliver health care in a way that promotes aggregate utility. For the utilitarian, entitlements are *system-relative*.

The same two points apply to other accounts of the foundations and limits of a right to health care.

Because many people reject the utilitarian rationales for health care (and other welfare) rights, theorists have explored other ways to ground such rights. Some claim that these rights are presupposed as enabling conditions for the exercise of other rights or liberties, or as practical presuppositions of all views of justice (Braybrooke, 1987) or as a way of avoiding vulnerability and exploitation (Goodin, 1988). One approach that has been developed in some detail views a right to health care as a special case of a right to equality of opportunity (Daniels, 1985). This approach shows how the most important contractarian theory of justice, Rawls' (1971) account of justice as fairness, can be extended to the problem of health care, since that theory gives prominence to a principle protecting equality of opportunity (Rawls, 1993). Without endorsing that account here, we shall use it to illustrate further the complexity surrounding the concept of a right to health care.

Equal Opportunity and a Right to Health Care

The central observation underlying this account of a right to health care is that disease and disability restrict the range of opportunities that would otherwise be open to individuals. This is true whether they shorten our lives or impair our ability to function, including through pain and suffering. Health care in all its forms, whether public health or medical, preventive or acute or chronic, aims to keep people functioning as close to normally as possible. Since we are complex social creatures, our normal functional capabilities include our capabilities for emotional and cognitive functioning and not just physical capabilities. Health care thus preserves for us the range of opportunities we would have, were we not ill or disabled, given our talents and skills.

The significant contribution health care makes to protecting the range of opportunities open to individuals is nevertheless *limited* in two important ways. It is limited because other things, such as the distribution of wealth and income and education, also profoundly affect equality of opportunity. It is also limited because health care, by restricting its aim to protecting normal functioning, leaves the normal distribution of talents and skills unmodified. It aims to help us function as "normal" competitors, not strictly equal ones.

Some argue that an equal opportunity account of health care should abandon the limit set by a focus on normal functioning (see Arneson, 1988; G. A. Cohen, 1989; Sen, 1992). They claim our concerns about equality, including equality of opportunity, require us to use health-care technologies whenever doing so would equalize opportunity for welfare or equalizes capabilities. For example, if through medical intervention we can "enhance" the otherwise normal capabilities of those who are at a competitive disadvantage, then our commitment to equality of opportunity requires us to do so. Obviously, this version of an equal opportunity account would vastly expand the moral requirements on medicine, yielding a right to health care much more expansive than any now embodied in actual systems and, arguably, one that would make administration of a health-care system unwieldy (Sabin and Daniels, 1994).

This expansive version of the appeal to equal opportunity ignores an important fact about justice: our concern for equality must be reconciled with considerations of liberty and efficiency in arriving at the overall requirements of justice (see Sen, 1992; Cohen, 1995; Daniels, 1996). Such a reconciliation seems to underlie the limits we commonly accept when we appeal to equality of opportunity. We generally believe that rights to equal opportunity are violated only if unfair social practices or preventable or curable diseases or disabilities interfere with the pursuit of reasonable plans of life within our society by making us lose competitive advantage. We accept, however, the fact that the natural distribution of talents and skills, working in an efficient market for them, will both enhance the social product and lead to inequalities in social outcomes. A just society will try to mitigate the effects of these inequalities in competitive advantage in other ways than by eliminating all eliminable differences in capabilities. For example, on Rawls' account, transfers that make the worst off as well off as they can be mitigate the effects on equality of allowing the natural distribution of talents and skills to enhance productivity. In what follows, the account of a right to health care rests on a more limited appeal to equal opportunity, one that takes the maintenance of normal functioning as a reasonable limit.

What Does a Right to Health Care Include?
System-Relative Entitlements
By making the right to health care a special case of rights to equality of opportunity, we arrive at a reasonable, albeit incomplete and imperfect, way of restricting its scope while still recognizing its importance. The account does not give individuals a basic right to have all of their health-care needs met. At the same time, there are social obligations to design a health-care system that protects opportunity through an appropriate set of health-care services. If social obligations to provide appropriate health care are not met, then individuals are definitely wronged. For example, if people are denied access—because of discrimination or inability to pay—to a basic tier of services adequate to protect normal functioning, injustice is done to them. If the basic tier available to people omits important categories of services without consideration of their effects on normal functioning, for example, whole categories of mental health or long-term care or preventive services, their rights are violated.

Still, not every medical need gives rise to an entitlement to services. The scope and limits of rights to health care, that is, the entitlements they actually carry with them, will be relative to certain facts about a given system. For example, a health-care system can protect opportunity only within the limits imposed by resource scarcity and technological development within a society. We cannot make a direct inference from the fact that an individual has a right to health care to the conclusion that this person is entitled to some specific health-care service, even if the service would meet a health-care need. Rather the individual is entitled to a specific service only if, in the light of facts about a society's technological capabilities and resource limitations, it should be a part of a system that appropriately protects fair equality of opportunity. The equal opportunity account of a right to health care, like the utilitarian account, makes entitlements to health care system-relative.

Effective Treatment of Disease and Disability
The health care we have strongest claim to is care that effectively promotes normal functioning by reducing the impact of disease and disability, thus protecting the range of opportunities that would otherwise be open to us. Just what counts as "effective," however? And what should we do about hard cases on the boundary between treatment of disease or disability and enhancement of capabilities?

It is a common feature of public and private insurance systems to limit care to treatments that are not "experimental" and have some "proven effectiveness." Unfortunately, many services that count as standard treatment have little direct evidence about outcomes to support their use (Hadorn, 1992). They are often just customary treatment. Furthermore, it is often controversial just when new treatments or technologies should count as "safe and efficacious." What counts as "reasonably effective" is then a matter of judgement and depends on the kind of condition and the consequences of not correcting it. We might, for example, want to lower our standards for effectiveness when we face a treatment of last resort, or raise them if resource scarcity is very great. On the other hand, we do not owe people a chance to obtain miracles through whatever unproven procedures they prefer to try.

By focusing a right to health care on the maintenance of normal functioning, a line is drawn between uses of medical technologies that count as legitimate "treatments" and those that we may want but which do not meet our "health-care needs." Although we may want medical services that can enhance our appearance, like cosmetic (as opposed to reconstructive) plastic surgery, or that can optimize our otherwise normal functioning, like some forms of counselling or some uses of Prozac, we do not truly need these services to maintain normal functioning. We are obliged to help others achieve normal functioning, but we do not "owe" each other whatever it takes to make us more beautiful or strong or completely happy (Daniels, 1985).

Though this line is widely used in both public and private insurance practices, it leaves us with hard cases. Some of the hardest issues involve reproductive technologies. Abortion, where there is no preventive or therapeutic need, does not count as "treatment" because an unwanted pregnancy is not a disease or disability. Some nevertheless insist that requirements of justice, including a right to control one's body, means that non-therapeutic abortion should be included as an entitlement in a health-care system. Some national health-insurance schemes do not cover infertility services. Yet infertility is a departure from normal functioning, even if some people never want to bear children. Controversy may remain about how much social obligation we have to correct this form of impaired opportunity, especially where the costs of some interventions, such as in vitro fertilization, are high and their effectiveness is modest. Different societies will judge this question differently, in part because they may place different values on the rearing of biologically related children or on the experience of child-bearing.

Hard cases involve non-reproductive technologies as well. In the United States, for example, many insurers will cover growth hormone treatment only for children deficient in growth hormone, not for those who are equally short but without any pathology. Yet the children denied therapy will suffer just as much as those who are eligible. Similar difficulties are involved in drawing a line between covered and non-covered uses of mental health services (Sabin and Daniels, 1994). As in the cases of reproductive technologies, there is room for different societies to "construct" the concept of mental disorder somewhat differently, with resulting variation in decisions about insurance coverage.

Rights and Limits on Effective Treatments

Even when some health-care service is reasonably effective at meeting a medical need, not all such needs are equally important. When a disease or disability has little impact on the range of opportunities open to someone, it is not as morally important to treat as other conditions that more seriously impair opportunity. The effect on opportunity thus gives us some guidance in thinking about resource allocation priorities.

Unfortunately, the impact on our range of opportunities gives only a crude and incomplete measure of the importance or priority we should give to a need or service. In making decisions about priorities

for purposes of resource allocation in health care, we face difficult questions about distributive fairness that are not answered by this measure of importance. For example, we must sometimes make a choice between investing in a technology that delivers a significant benefit to few people or one that delivers a more modest benefit to a larger number of people. Sometimes we must make a choice between investing in a service that helps the sickest, most impaired patients or one that helps those whose functioning is less impaired. Sometimes we must decide between the fairness of giving a scarce resource to those who derive the largest benefit or giving a broader range of people some chance at getting a benefit. In all of these cases, we lack clear principles for deciding how to make our choices, and the account of a right to health care we are discussing does not provide those principles either (Daniels, 1993). Some methodologies, like cost-effectiveness analysis, are intended to help us make appropriate resource allocation decisions in these kinds of cases. But these methodologies may themselves embody controversial moral assumptions about distributive fairness. This means they cannot serve as decision procedures for making these choices and can at best serve as aids to decision-makers who must be explicit about the moral reasoning that determines the distributive choices they make (Gold et al., 1996).

In any health-care system, then, some choices will have to be made by a fair, publicly accountable, decision-making process. Just what constitutes a fair decision-making procedure for resolving moral disputes about health care entitlements is itself a matter of controversy. It is a problem that has been addressed little in the literature. Our rights are not violated, however, if the choices that are made through fair decision-making procedures turn out to be ones that do not happen to meet our personal needs, but instead meet needs of others that are judged more important (Daniels and Sabin, 1997).

How Equal Must Our Rights to Health Care Be?

How equal must our rights to health care be? Specifically, must everyone receive exactly the same kinds of health-care services and coverage, or is fairness in health care compatible with a "tiered" system?

Around the world, even countries that offer universal health insurance differ in their answers to this question. In Canada and Norway, for example, no supplementary insurance is permitted. Everyone is served solely by the national health-insurance schemes, though people who seek additional services or more rapid service may go elsewhere, as some Canadians do by crossing the border. In Britain, supplementary private insurance allows about 10 per cent of the population to gain quicker access to services for which there is extensive queuing in the public system. Basing a right to health care on an obligation to protect equality of opportunity is compatible with the sort of tiering the British have, but it does not require it, and it imposes some constraints on the kind of tiering allowed.

The primary social obligation is to assure everyone access to a tier of services that effectively promotes normal functioning and thus protects equality of opportunity. Since health care is not the only important good, resources to be invested in the basic tier are appropriately and reasonably limited, for example, by democratic decisions about how much to invest in education or job training as opposed to health care. Because of their very high "opportunity costs," there will be some beneficial medical services that it will be reasonable not to provide in the basic tier, or to provide only on a limited basis, for example, with queuing. To say that these services have "high opportunity costs" means that providing them consumes resources that would produce greater health benefits and protect opportunity more if used in other ways.

In a society that permits significant income and wealth inequalities, some people will want to buy coverage for these additional services. Why not let them? After all, we allow people to use their after-tax income and wealth as they see fit to pursue the "quality of life" and opportunities they prefer. The rich can buy special security systems for their homes. They can buy safer cars. They can buy private schooling for their children. Why not allow them to buy supplementary health care for their families?

One objection to allowing a supplementary tier is that its existence might undermine the basic tier either economically or politically. It might attract better-quality providers away from the basic tier, or raise costs in the basic tier, reducing the ability of society to meet its social obligations. The supplementary tier might undermine political support for the basic tier, for example, by undercutting the social solidarity needed if people are to remain committed to protecting opportunity for all. These objections are serious, and where a supplementary tier undermines the basic tier in either way, economically or politically, priority must be given to protecting the basic tier. In principle, however, it seems possible to design a system in which the supplementary tier does not undermine the basic one. If that can be done, then a system that permits tiering avoids restricting liberty in ways that some find seriously objectionable.

A second objection is not to tiering itself but to the structure of inequality that results. Compare two scenarios. In one, most people are adequately served by the basic tier and only the best-off groups in society have the means and see the need to purchase supplementary insurance. That is the case in Great Britain. In the other, the basic tier serves only the poorest groups in society and most other people buy supplementary insurance. The Oregon plan to expand Medicaid eligibility partly through rationing the services it covers has aspects of this structure of inequality, since most people are covered by plans that avoid these restrictions (Daniels, 1991). The first scenario seems preferable to the second on grounds of fairness. In the second, the poorest groups can complain that they are left behind by others in society even in the protection of their health. In the first, the majority has less grounds for reasonable resentment or regret.

If the basic tier is not undermined by higher tiers, and if the structure of the inequality that results is not objectionable, then it is difficult to see why some tiering should not be allowed. There is a basic conflict here between concerns about equality and concerns about liberty, between wanting to make sure everyone is treated properly with regard to health care and wanting to give people the liberty to use their resources (after tax) to improve their lives as they see fit. In practice, the crucial constraint on the liberty we allow people seems to depend on the magnitude of the benefit available in the supplementary tier and unavailable in the basic tier. Highly visible forms of saving lives and improving function would be difficult to exclude from the basic tier while we make them available in a supplementary tier. In principle, however, some forms of tiering will not be unfair even when they involve medical benefits not available to everyone.

REFERENCES

Arneson, Richard (1988). Equality and equal opportunity for welfare. *Philosophical Studies*, 54, 79–95.

Brandt, Richard (1979). *A Theory of the Good and the Right*, Oxford: Oxford University Press.

Braybrooke, David (1987). *Meeting Needs*. Princeton, NJ: Princeton University Press.

Brennan, Geoffrey and Friedman, David (1981). A libertarian perspective on welfare. In Peter G. Brown, Conrad Johnson and Paul Vernier (eds), *Income Support: Conceptual and policy issues*. Totowa, NJ: Rowman and Littlefield.

Buchanan, Allen (1984). The right to a decent minimum of health care. *Philosophy and Public Affairs*, 13, 55–78.

Cohen, G. A. (1989). On the currency of egalitarian justice. *Ethics*, 99, 906–44.

Cohen, Joshua (1995). Amartya Sen: *Inequality Reexamined*. *Journal of Philosophy*, 92/5, 275–88.

Daniel, N. (1985). *Just Health Care*. Cambridge: Cambridge University Press.

——(1991). Is the Oregon rationing plan fair? *Journal of the American Medical Association*, 265, 2232–5.

——(1993). Rationing fairly: programmatic considerations. *Bioethics*, 7, 224–33.

——(1996). *Justice and Justification: reflective equilibrium in theory and practice*. Cambridge: Cambridge University Press.

Daniels, N. and Sabin, J. (1997). Limits to health care: fair procedures, democratic deliberation, and the legitimacy problem for insurers. *Philosophy and Public Affairs*. 26/4, 303–50.

Engelhardt, H. Tristram (1986). *The Foundations of Bioethics*. Oxford: Oxford University Press.

Fried, Charles (1969). *An Anatomy of Value*. Cambridge, MA: Harvard University Press.

Gold, Marthe, Siegel, Joanna. Russell, Louise and Weinstein, Milton (eds) (1996). *Cost-Effectiveness in Health and Medicine: recommendations of the Panel on Cost-Effectiveness in Health and Medicine*. New York: Oxford University Press.

Goodin, Robert (1988). *Reasons for Welfare*. Princeton, NJ: Princeton University Press.

Hadorn, David (ed.) (1992). *Basic Benefits and Clinical Guidelines*. Boulder, CO: Westview Press.

Nord, Eric (1993). The relevance of health state after treatment in prioritizing between different patients. *Journal of Medical Ethics*, 19, 37–42.

Nozick, R. (1974). *Anarchy, State, and Utopia*. New York: Basic Books.

Rawls, J. (1971). *A Theory of Justice*. Cambridge, MA: Harvard University Press.

——(1993). *Political Liberalism*. New York: Columbia University Press.

Sabin, James and Daniels, Norman (1994). Determining "medical necessity" in mental health practice. *Hastings Center Report*, 24/6, 5–13.

Sen. Amartya (1992). *Inequality Reexamined*. Cambridge, MA: Harvard University Press.

Sterba, James (1985). From liberty to welfare, *Social Theory and Practice*, 11, 285–305.

Thomson, Judith (1990). *The Realm of Rights*. Cambridge, MA: Harvard University Press.

The Right to a Decent Minimum of Health Care

ALLEN E. BUCHANAN

In this article Buchanan argues that the notion of a universal right to a decent minimum of health care cannot justify a mandatory decent minimum policy. But the combined weight of other arguments, he says, can establish that the state should provide certain individuals or groups with a decent minimum. The necessary arguments are from special rights, from the prevention of harm, from prudential considerations, and from enforced beneficence.

The Assumption That There Is a Right to a Decent Minimum

A consensus that there is (at least) a right to a decent minimum of health care pervades recent policy debates and much of the philosophical literature on health care. Disagreement centers on two issues. Is there a more extensive right than the right to a decent minimum of health care? What is included in the decent minimum to which there is a right?

Preliminary Clarification of the Concept

Different theories of distributive justice may yield different answers both to the question "Is there a right to a decent minimum?" and to the question "What comprises the decent minimum?" The justification a particular theory provides for the claim that there is a right to a decent minimum must at least cohere with the justifications it provides for other right-claims. Moreover, the character of this justification will determine, at least in part, the way in which the decent minimum is specified, since it will include an account of the nature and significance of health-care needs. To the extent that the concept of a decent minimum is theory-dependent, then, it would be naive to assume that a mere analysis of the concept of a decent minimum would tell us whether there is such a right and what its content is. Nonetheless, before we proceed to an examination of various theoretical attempts to ground and specify a right to a decent minimum, a preliminary analysis will be helpful.

Sometimes the notion of a decent minimum is applied not to health care but to health itself, the claim being that everyone is entitled to some minimal level, or welfare floor, of health. I shall not explore this variant of the decent minimum idea because I think its implausibility is obvious. The main difficulty is that assuring any significant level of health for all is simply not within the domain of social control. If the alleged right is understood instead as the right to everything which can be done to achieve some significant level of health for all, then the claim

From the President's Commission, *Securing Access to Health Care*, Vol. II. Washington, D.C. U.S. Government Printing Office, 1983.

that there is such a right becomes implausible simply because it ignores the fact that in circumstances of scarcity the total social expenditure on health must be constrained by the need to allocate resources for other goods.

Though the concept of a right is complex and controversial, for our purposes a partial sketch will do. To say that person A has a right to something, X, is first of all to say that A is entitled to X, that X is due to him or her. This is not equivalent to saying that if A were granted X it would be a good thing, even a morally good thing, or that X is desired by or desirable for A. Second, it is usually held that valid right-claims, at least in the case of basic rights, may be backed by sanctions, including coercion if necessary (unless doing so would produce extremely great disutility or grave moral evil), and that (except in such highly exceptional circumstances) failure of an appropriate authority to apply the needed sanctions is itself an injustice. Recent right-theorists have also emphasized a third feature of rights, or at least of basic rights or rights in the strict sense: valid right-claims "trump" appeals to what would maximize utility, whether it be the utility of the right-holder, or social utility. In other words, if A has a right to X, then the mere fact that infringing A's right would maximize overall utility or even A's utility is not itself a sufficient reason for infringing it.[1] Finally, a universal (or general) right is one which applies to all persons, not just to certain individuals or classes because of their involvement in special actions, relationships, or agreements.

The second feature—enforceability—is of crucial importance for those who assume or argue that there is a universal right to a decent minimum of health care. For, once it is granted that there is such a right and that such a right may be enforced (absent any extremely weighty reason against enforcement), the claim that there is a universal right provides the moral basis for using the coercive power of the state to assure a decent minimum for all. Indeed, the surprising absence of attempts to justify a coercively backed decent minimum policy by arguments that do *not* aim at establishing a universal right suggests the following hypothesis: advocates of a coercively based decent minimum have operated on the assumption that such a policy must be based on a universal right to a decent minimum. The chief aim of this article is to show that this assumption is false.

I think it is fair to say that many who confidently assume there is a (universal) right to a decent minimum of health care have failed to appreciate the significance of the first feature of our sketch of the concept of a right. It is crucial to observe that the claim that there is a right to a decent minimum is much stronger than the claim that everyone *ought* to have access to such a minimum, or that if they did it would be a good thing, or that any society which is capable, without great sacrifice, of providing a decent minimum but fails to do so is deeply morally defective. None of the latter assertions implies the existence of a right, if this is understood as a moral entitlement which ought to be established by the coercive power of the state if necessary. . . .

The Attractions of the Idea of a Decent Minimum

There are at least three features widely associated with the idea of a right to a decent minimum which, together with the facile consensus that vagueness promotes, help explain its popularity over competing conceptions of the right to health care. First, it is usually, and quite reasonably, assumed that the idea of a decent minimum is to be understood in a society-relative sense. Surely it is plausible to assume that, as with other rights to goods or services, the content of the right must depend upon the resources available in a given society and perhaps also upon a certain consensus of expectations among its members. So the first advantage of the idea of a decent minimum, as it is usually understood, is that it allows us to adjust the level of services to be provided as a matter of right to relevant social conditions and also allows for the possibility that as a society becomes more affluent the floor provided by the decent minimum should be raised.

Second, the idea of a decent minimum avoids the excesses of what has been called the strong equal access principle, while still acknowledging a substantive universal right. According to the strong equal access principle, everyone has an equal right to the best health-care services available. Aside from the weakness of the justifications offered in support of

it, the most implausible feature of the strong equal access principle is that it forces us to choose between two unpalatable alternatives. We can either set the publicly guaranteed level of health care lower than the level that is technically possible or we can set it as high as is technically possible. In the former case, we shall be committed to the uncomfortable conclusion that no matter how many resources have been expended to guarantee equal access to that level, individuals are forbidden to spend any of their resources for services not available to all. Granted that individuals are allowed to spend their after-tax incomes on more frivolous items, why shouldn't they be allowed to spend it on health? If the answer is that they should be so allowed, as long as this does not interfere with the provision of an adequate package of health-care services for everyone, then we have retreated from the strong equal access principle to something very like the principle of a decent minimum. If, on the other hand, we set the level of services guaranteed for all so high as to eliminate the problem of persons seeking extra care beyond this level, this would produce a huge drain on total resources, foreclosing opportunities for producing important goods other than health care.

So both the recognition that health care must compete with other goods and the conviction that beyond some less than maximal level of publicly guaranteed services individuals should be free to purchase additional services point toward a more limited right than the strong access principle asserts. Thus, the endorsement of a right to a decent minimum may be more of a recognition of the implausibility of the stronger right to equal access than a sign of any definite position on the content of the right to health care.

A third attraction of the idea of a decent minimum is that since the right to health care must be limited in scope (to avoid the consequences of a strong equal access right), it should be limited to the "most basic" services, those normally "adequate" for health, or for a "decent" or "tolerable" life. However, although this aspect of the idea of a decent minimum is useful because it calls attention to the fact that health-care needs are heterogeneous and must be assigned some order of priority, it does not itself provide any basis for determining which are most important.

The Need for a Supporting Theory

In spite of these attractions, the concept of a right to a decent minimum of health care is inadequate as a moral basis for a coercively backed decent minimum policy in the absence of a coherent and defensible theory of justice. Indeed, when taken together they do not even imply that there is a right to a decent minimum. Rather, they only support the weaker conditional claim that if there is a right to health care, then it is one that is more limited than a right of strong equal access, and is one whose content depends upon available resources and some scheme of priorities which shows certain health services to be more basic than others. . . .

My suggestion is that the combined weight of arguments from special (as opposed to universal) rights to health care, harm-prevention, prudential arguments of the sort used to justify public health measures, and two arguments that show that effective charity shares features of public goods (in the technical sense) is sufficient to do the work of an alleged universal right to a decent minimum of health care.

Arguments from Special Rights

The right-claim we have been examining (and find unsupported) has been a *universal* right-claim: one that attributes the same right to all persons. *Special* right-claims, in contrast, restrict the right in question to certain individuals or groups.

There are at least three types of arguments that can be given for special rights to health care. First, there are arguments from the requirements of rectifying past or present institutional injustices. It can be argued, for example, that American blacks and native Americans are entitled to a certain core set of health-care services owing to their history of unjust treatment by government or other social institutions, on the grounds that these injustices have directly or indirectly had detrimental effects on the health of the groups in question. Second, there are arguments from the requirements of compensation to those who have suffered unjust harm or who have been unjustly exposed to health risks by the assignable actions of private individuals or corporations— for instance, those who have suffered neurological damage from the effects of chemical pollutants.

Third, a strong moral case can be made for special rights to health care for those who have undergone exceptional sacrifices for the good of society as a whole—in particular those whose health has been adversely affected through military service. The most obvious candidates for such compensatory special rights are soldiers wounded in combat.

Arguments from the Prevention of Harm

The content of the right to a decent minimum is typically understood as being more extensive than those traditional public health services that are usually justified on the grounds that they are required to protect the citizenry from certain harms arising from the interactions of persons living together in large numbers. Yet such services have been a major factor—if not *the* major factor—in reducing morbidity and mortality rates. Examples include sanitation and immunization. The moral justification of such measures, which constitute an important element in a decent minimum of health care, rests upon the widely accepted Harm (Prevention) Principle, not upon a right to health care.

The Harm Prevention argument for traditional public health services, however, may be elaborated in a way that brings them closer to arguments for a universal right to health care. With some plausibility one might contend that once the case has been made for expending public resources on public health measures, there is a moral (and perhaps Constitutional) obligation to achieve some standard of *equal protection* from the harms these measures are designed to prevent. Such an argument, if it could be made out, would imply that the availability of basic public health services should not vary greatly across different racial, ethnic, or geographic groups within the country.

Prudential Arguments

Prudent arguments for health-care services typically emphasize benefits rather than the prevention of harm. It has often been argued, in particular, that the availability of certain basic forms of health care make for a more productive labor force or improve the fitness of the citizenry for national defense. This type of argument, too, does not assume that individuals have moral rights (whether special or universal) to the services in question.

It seems very likely that the combined scope of the various special health-care rights discussed above, when taken together with harm prevention and prudential arguments for basic health services and an argument from equal protection through public health measures, would do a great deal toward satisfying the health-care needs which those who advocate a universal right to a decent minimum are most concerned about. In other words, once the strength of a more pluralistic approach is appreciated, we may come to question the popular dogma that policy initiatives designed to achieve a decent minimum of health care for all must be grounded in a universal moral right to a decent minimum. This suggestion is worth considering because it again brings home the importance of the methodological difficulty encountered earlier. Even if, for instance, there is wide consensus on the considered judgment that the lower health prospects of inner city blacks are not only morally unacceptable but an injustice, it does not follow that this injustice consists of the infringement of a universal right to a decent minimum of health care. Instead, the injustice might lie in the failure to rectify past injustices or in the failure to achieve public health arrangements that meet a reasonable standard of equal protection for all.

Two Arguments for Enforced Beneficence

The pluralistic moral case for a legal entitlement to a decent minimum of health care (in the absence of a universal moral right) may be strengthened further by non-rights-based arguments from the principle of beneficence.[2] The possibility of making out such arguments depends upon the assumption that some principles may be justifiably enforced even if they are not principles specifying valid right-claims. There is at least one widely recognized class of such principles requiring contribution to the production of "public goods" in the technical sense (for example, tax laws requiring contribution to national defense). It is characteristic of public goods that each individual has an incentive to withhold his contribution to the collective goal even though the net result is that the goal will not be achieved. Enforcement of a principle requiring all individuals to contribute to the goal is necessary to overcome the individual's incentive to withhold contribu-

tion by imposing penalties for his own failure to contribute and by assuring him that others will contribute. There is a special subclass of principles whose enforcement is justified not only by the need to overcome the individual's incentive to withhold compliance with the principle but also to ensure that individuals' efforts are appropriately *coordinated*. For example, enforcing the rule of the road to drive only on the right not only ensures a joint effort toward the goal of safe driving but also coordinates individuals' efforts so as to make the attainment of that goal possible. Indeed, in the case of the "rule of the road" a certain kind of coordinated joint effort is the public good whose attainment justifies enforcement. But regardless of whether the production of a public good requires the solution of a coordination problem or not, there may be no *right* that is the correlative of the coercively backed obligation specified by the principle. There are two arguments for enforced beneficence, and they each depend upon both the idea of coordination and on certain aspects of the concept of a public good.

Both arguments begin with an assumption reasonable libertarians accept: there is a basic moral obligation of charity or beneficence to those in need. In a society that has the resources and technical knowledge to improve health or at least to ameliorate important health defects, the application of this requirement of beneficence includes the provision of resources for at least certain forms of health care. If we are sincere, we will be concerned with the efficacy of our charitable or beneficent impulses. It is all well and good for the libertarian to say that voluntary giving *can* replace the existing array of government entitlement programs, but this *possibility* will be cold comfort to the needy if, for any of several reasons, voluntary giving falters.

Social critics on the left often argue that in a highly competitive acquisitive society such as ours it is naive to think that the sense of beneficence will win out over the urgent promptings of self-interest. One need not argue, however, that voluntary giving fails from weakness of the will. Instead one can argue that even if each individual recognizes a moral duty to contribute to the aid of others and is motivationally capable of acting on that duty, some important forms of beneficence will not be forthcoming because each individual will rationally conclude that he should not contribute.

Many important forms of health care, especially those involving large-scale capital investment for technology, cannot be provided except through the contibutions of large numbers of persons. This is also true of the most important forms of medical research. But if so, then the beneficent individual will not be able to act effectively, in isolation. What is needed is a coordinated joint effort.

First argument. There are many ways in which I might help others in need. Granted the importance of health, providing a decent minimum of health care for all, through large-scale collective efforts, will be a more important form of beneficence than the various charitable acts A, B, and C, which I might perform *independently*, that is, whose success does not depend upon the contributions of others. Nonetheless, if I am rationally beneficent I will reason as follows: either enough others will contribute to the decent minimum project to achieve this goal, even if I do not contribute to it; or not enough others will contribute to achieve a decent minimum, even if I do contribute. In either case, my contribution will be wasted. In other words, granted the scale of the investment required and the virtually negligible size of my own contribution, I can disregard the minute possibility that my contribution might make the difference between success and failure. But if so, then the rationally beneficent thing for me to do is not to waste my contribution on the project of ensuring a decent minimum but instead to undertake an independent act of beneficence; A, B, or C—where I know my efforts will be needed and efficacious. But if everyone, or even many people, reason in this way, then what we each recognize as the most effective form of beneficence will not come about. Enforcement of a principle requiring contributions to ensuring a decent minimum is needed

The first argument is of the same form as standard public goods arguments for enforced contributions to national defense, energy conservation, and many other goods, with this exception. In standard public goods arguments, it is usually assumed that the individual's incentive for not contributing is self-interest and that it is in his interest not to contribute

because he will be able to partake of the good, if it is produced, even if he does not contribute. In the case at hand, however, the individual's incentive for not contributing to the joint effort is not self-interest, but rather his desire to maximize the good he can do for others with a given amount of his resources. Thus if he contributes but the goal of achieving a decent minimum for all would have been achieved without his contribution, then he has still failed to use his resources in a maximally beneficent way relative to the options of either contributing or not to the joint project, even though the goal of achieving a decent minimum is attained. The rationally beneficent thing to do, then, is not to contribute, even though the result of everyone's acting in a rationally beneficent way will be a relatively ineffective patchwork of small-scale individual acts of beneficence rather than a large-scale, coordinated effort.

Second argument. I believe that ensuring a decent minimum of health care for all is more important than projects A, B, or C, and I am willing to contribute to the decent minimum project, but only if I have assurance that enough others will contribute to achieve the threshold of investment necessary for success. Unless I have this assurance, I will conclude that it is less than rational—and perhaps even morally irresponsible—to contribute my resources to the decent minimum project. For my contribution will be wasted if not enough others contribute. If I lack assurance of sufficient contributions by others, the rationally beneficent thing for me to do is to expend my "beneficence budget" on some less-than-optimal project A, B, or C, whose success does not depend on the contribution of others. But without enforcement, I cannot be assured that enough others will contribute, and if others reason as I do, then what we all believe to be the most effective form of beneficence will not be forthcoming. Others may fail to contribute either because the promptings of self-interest overpower their sense of beneficence, or because they reason as I did in the First Argument, or for some other reason.

Both arguments conclude that an enforced decent minimum principle is needed to achieve coordinated joint effort. However, there is this difference. The Second Argument focuses on the *assurance problem*, while the first does not. In the Second Argument all that is needed is the assumption that rational beneficence requires assurance that enough others will contribute. In the First Argument the individual's reason for not contributing is not that he lacks assurance that enough others will contribute, but rather that it is better for him not to contribute regardless of whether others do or not.

Neither argument depends on an assumption of conflict between the individual's moral motivation of beneficence and his inclination of self-interest. Instead the difficulty is that in the absence of enforcement, individuals who strive to make their beneficence most effective will thereby fail to benefit the needy as much as they might.

A standard response to those paradoxes of rationality known as public goods problems is to introduce a coercive mechanism which attaches penalties to non-contribution and thereby provides each individual with the assurance that enough others will reciprocate so that his contribution will not be wasted and an effective incentive for him to contribute even if he has reason to believe that enough others will contribute to achieve the goal without his contribu-

tion. My suggestion is that the same type of argument that is widely accepted as a justification for enforced principles requiring contributions toward familiar public goods provides support for a coercively backed principle specifying a certain list of health programs for the needy and requiring those who possess the needed resources to contribute to the establishment of such programs, even if the needy have no *right* to the services those programs provide. Such an arrangement would serve a dual function: it would coordinate charitable efforts by focusing them on one set of services among the indefinitely large constellation of possible expressions of beneficence, and it would ensure that the decision to allocate resources to these services will become effective.

NOTES

1. Ronald Dworkin, *Taking Rights Seriously* (Cambridge, MA: Harvard University Press, 1977), pp. 184–205.
2. For an exploration of various arguments for a duty of beneficence and an examination of the relationship between justice and beneficence, in general and in health care, see Allen E. Buchanan, "Philosophical Foundations of Beneficence," *Beneficence and Health Care*, ed. Earl E. Shelp (Dordrecht, Holland: Reidel Publishing Co., 1982).

Multiculturalism and Just Health Care: Taking Pluralism Seriously

JEFFREY BLUSTEIN

Blustein examines the question of what justice requires regarding health care policies in pluralistic, democratic societies. He explores the implications of the influential theories of Engelhardt, Emanuel, Daniels, and Rawls and indicates the main issues that any adequate pluralistic theory must take into account.

Ours is a culturally diverse society. A major source of this diversity is the influx of foreign-born populations fleeing economic hardship and social deprivation and hoping for a better life and greater opportunities in the United States. Immigration to the United States is not a recent phenomenon, of course. The arrival of ethnic and minority populations from

From *Medicine and Social Justice: Essays on the Distribution of Health Care*, edited by Rosamond Rhodes, Margaret P. Battin, and Anita Silvers, pp. 38–52. Copyright © 2002 by Oxford University Press, Inc. Reprinted with permission.

various Asian and Hispanic countries is only the latest in a long history of immigration to America. In past years mainstream American society expected the new arrivals to quickly discard their distinctive beliefs, customs, and traditions and join the great "melting pot"; today this assimilationist expectation is increasingly being branded as "culturally insensitive." Not only do we now understand that, as a matter of sociological fact, ethnic and minority groups retain parts of their cultural belief systems while incorporating elements of the broader society, but there is also a growing appreciation of the *moral* claims of cultural pluralism. The call for assimilation has been replaced or supplemented by a new emphasis on respect for cultural diversity,[1] grounded in the recognition that it is insulting to the members of these cultural groups to neglect or belittle the importance of their cultural identities.

Multiculturalism, Pluralism, and Justice

Multiculturalism, as I understand it, is an amalgam of descriptive, pragmatic, and ethical claims.[2] The descriptive claim is that there are diverse culturally based and conditioned belief systems that help to shape the ways in which individuals view themselves, their relations with others, and their world. Pragmatically, multiculturalism advises us that efforts to communicate, to establish trust, and possibly to bring about change in the behavior of members of cultural groups are unlikely to be successful if those who interact with them are unfamiliar with the ways in which language is used in different cultures, with their particular cultural belief systems, and with the cultural context of their practices. The ethical claims are of two sorts. First, multiculturalism admonishes us to be humble. It is presumptuous of us to suppose that our moral values, rules, and practices are the best ones for human beings and that we have nothing to gain in terms of moral wisdom from communication with so-called inferior cultures. Our moral understanding of complex issues is furthered by respectful discussion with people with whom we disagree, especially when these people have cultural identities different from our own.[3] Second, multiculturalism espouses an egalitarian ethos. As Charles Taylor puts it, "Just as all must have equal civil rights, and equal voting rights, regardless of race and culture, so all should enjoy the presumption that their traditional culture has value" (Taylor, 1993, p. 68). The political implication of this presumption is that a state's institutions and policies should create a political framework that does not discriminate against individuals with different cultural belief systems merely because their conceptions of the good life are not shared by the majority culture.

As we shall see, a central question in debates about the proper scope of government action in general, and the role of government in the provision of health care in particular, is whether it is legitimate for the state to promote a particular conception of the good life. Because the term "conception of the good or the good life" has various meanings in these debates and is often not very clearly defined, it is necessary to indicate how I use the term in this chapter. Roughly, I understand it to refer to a way of life—that is, to a person's pattern of living—which embodies a particular ranking of goods or values that constitute or contribute to the good life for a person and a particular way of realizing them.[4] Multiculturalism is or should be a concern of theories of legitimate state action because a person's conception of the good, understood in this way, is partly constituted and shaped by aspects of his or her culture.

Cultural diversity is part of the explanation of the diverse conceptions of the good life among members of a pluralistic society such as ours, but not all the members of a particular cultural group necessarily share the same conception of the good life and not all differences in conceptions of the good life can be traced to distinctive cultural traditions and values. Indeed, as John Rawls and others have pointed out, modern constitutional democracies are characterized by an irreversible pluralism, that is, by often conflicting and incommensurable fundamental value systems, and this pluralism is only partly explained by culture and cultural diversity. Even in democratic societies that are much more culturally homogeneous than ours—certain European democracies, for example—pluralism "is the normal result of the exercise of human reason within the framework of the free institutions of a constitutional democratic regime" (Rawls, 1996, p. xviii).

The very pluralism that democratic regimes foster, however, creates the following serious problem for these societies: When people disagree so fundamentally about the good life, where are the grounds of social unity to be found? This is a quite general problem for liberal political theory, but in this chapter I want to focus on a related but narrower set of issues having to do with what justice requires with respect to the provision of health care in modern democratic societies. Rawls himself has not taken up this question, but a number of other philosophers, including Tristram Engelhardt (Engelhardt, 1991, 1999), Ezekiel Emanuel (Emanuel, 1991), and Norman Daniels in recent work (Daniels, 1990, 1996, 2000) have written on pluralism and its implications for a theory of just health care.

What these authors say about health-care justice, and their sensitivity to the problem of irresolvable pluralism, permit us to understand their proposals as varying responses to the problem posed by John Rawls in his later writing on political liberalism. Briefly put, the Rawlsian question is this: When full agreement on fundamental value conceptions cannot be reached among the members of society, conceived as free and equal persons who are concerned to live with one another on fair terms, can there be a societal consensus—what Rawls calls an "overlapping consensus"[5]—on the basic political arrangements for their society? The object of this consensus is, in Rawls's terminology, a *political conception* of justice. In the case of health care, the question is whether there can be general agreement among such persons on what they owe each other by way of medical assistance or health-care protection, that is, on a political conception of health-care justice. The oppressive use of state power to overcome pluralism might be able to impose uniformity, but, as in Rawls, this is ruled out by a normative commitment to noncoercion and to the achievement of free and willing agreement among citizens. Again as in Rawls, it is not sufficient that the consensus be a mere "modus vivendi," that is, the result of a political accommodation that is advantageous for parties with conflicting individual and group interests.

In contrast to an overlapping consensus, a modus vivendi is inherently unstable, for it is contingent on the balance of power remaining favorable to a political compromise, and it is affirmed on prudential, not principled, grounds. A theory of just health care of the right sort is a political conception of justice that can secure the voluntary and principled allegiance of persons who are divided by diverse conceptions of the good life, including, among other things, diverse understandings of disease and disability and the contributions different medical and health-related services make to the good life.

Pluralism is a general fact of political sociology that any political conception of justice in health care must accept and, in liberal societies with relatively permissive immigration policies, multiculturalism contributes significantly to that pluralism. But both the possibility of an overlapping consensus on a political conception and the content of that conception depend on how deep and extensive the plural-

ism is. Or rather, because not every conception of the good is compatible with basic tenets of a society of free institutions, the context within which these questions about an overlapping consensus are to be asked is a pluralism of what Rawls calls "reasonable" conceptions.[6] Engelhardt, for example, believes the pluralism of reasonable doctrines is so thoroughgoing that public agreement on a "content-full" or fully substantive political conception of justice for health care cannot be achieved except through state coercive measures.

Daniels, in contrast, is much more sanguine about the possibility, within a democratic society, of an overlapping consensus on a substantive criterion by which to determine the just distribution of health care resources. Emanuel, in contrast to Daniels, argues from the fact of pluralism against a substantive principle that determines an overarching set of medical services that citizens should be guaranteed by the polity as a matter of social justice. In contrast to Engelhardt, he argues for a conception of liberalism according to which society is entitled to differentially support and encourage those conceptions of the good life that embody certain substantive ideals, including political autonomy and individual self-development.[7]

The citizens of a democratic regime, in the free exercise of their reason, may come to espouse diverse theories of just health care that reflect their particular moral or religious or philosophical beliefs. But the justification of a theory of just health care for a democratic society of free institutions cannot rest on such doctrines as they are bound to be highly controversial. It must be independent of them, yet at the same time the theory must be one that citizens who affirm reasonable though opposing conceptions of the good have reason to endorse. Hence, it must not conflict too sharply with such reasonable conceptions. The three authors whose arguments I examine in this chapter have different views of the content of a theory of just health care that accommodates reasonable pluralism and multiculturalism insofar as cultural diversity contributes to reasonable pluralism. But they pose a similar question for themselves—namely, is there a theory of just health care for a democratic society that can win widespread support, where the basic fact of political life that constitutes the context of inquiry is a reasonable pluralism of conceptions of the human good, and if so, what does this theory require?

The two sections that follow deal with Engelhardt and Emanuel. Though as we shall see, there are some commonalities between them, their views on health care justice can be thought of as falling to the political right and the political left of liberalism, respectively. In expounding on their views, I have not dwelt at length on the conception of liberalism they reject, but have chosen instead to let the conception they are attacking emerge from their criticisms of it. In a later section, I turn to liberalism. After discussing recent developments in Rawlsian liberalism and fleshing out the Rawlsian problematic, I consider arguments for a liberal conception of just health care as the proper response to the political challenge Rawls poses.

A Libertarian Response to Pluralism

Great diversity in beliefs about philosophical, religious, and moral matters is especially likely in a liberal democratic society characterized by freedom of thought and expression, but the conditions that Tristram Engelhardt emphasizes as giving rise to value pluralism are quite general features of what he calls our "postmodern age." The contemporary world, he claims, is marked by two contrasting forces. There is a loss of faith in the power of human reason "to provide for morality and political theory what we long took for granted: a rationally justified content-full moral vision" (Engelhardt, 1991, p. xi). At the same time, "there remains a plurality of faith and moral commitments" that give rise to passionate conflicts among proponents of "irreconcilable competing moral visions" (1991, p. 9). Not only are there disagreements about such controversial matters as "contraception, abortion, third-party-assisted reproduction, and physician-assisted suicide," but in addition, "there are as many secular accounts of equality, justice, and fairness as there are religious groups, sects, and cults" (Engelhardt, 1999, p. 642). But if there are such deep disagreements about the requirements of justice itself, we have to wonder whether it is possible for diverse moral and religious communities to converge on a common conception of justice and just health care that can span differences among them, and whether such a conception can be justified to them, given

fundamental disagreements among them. Engelhardt believes that convergence on a common moral framework for deliberating about health care can be secured, despite the moral fragmentation characteristic of the postmodern age, and it is important to understand how he arrives at this conclusion.

As I interpret Engelhardt's argument, it draws a boundary between two domains with very different justificatory practices, the private and the public. Diverse conceptions of equality, justice, and fairness exist in the individual normative outlooks of members of a pluralistic society, conceptions that are grounded in and justified by (or taken to be justified by) particular religious, philosophical, and moral beliefs. Because these conceptions are justified by irreconcilable conceptions of the good, no theory of justice can possibly fit with all the particular beliefs that support these diverse conceptions. If the goal is convergence on a conception of justice that is *fully* justified to all reasonable members of a pluralistic society, plainly the goal can never be achieved. However, some kind of justification may still be possible, but this depends on putting aside particular moral, religious, and philosophical beliefs, as matters of *private* or group conviction, and recasting the problem of justifying a theory of justice as a problem of political justification in the *public* domain. Perhaps there is a basis for common agreement that forms a bridge across diverse communities with differing normative commitments, a conception of justice to regulate public life in a pluralistic society on which there can be an overlapping consensus. These are not exactly the terms in which Engelhardt articulates and defends his view, but I believe he could accept them as a faithful reconstruction.

Given the fact of pluralism, the only conception of justice that Engelhardt believes will be generally acceptable to reasonable people—that is, to people who are concerned to live with others on fair terms of association and who respect one another as free and equal persons—is a libertarian one:

> The necessary condition for participating in that world [i.e., a common moral world with moral strangers] is mutual respect, the non-use of others without their consent. This side-constraint is not grounded in a value given to autonomy, liberty, or to persons. . . . Mutual respect is accepted because it is

the one way to ground a common moral world for strangers without arbitrarily endorsing a particular ranking of values. (Engelhardt, 1991, p. 119)

There can be an overlapping consensus on a political conception of justice in a pluralistic society, but the conception is a limited and negative one. Coercion and deception are prohibited, but any more robust notion of what we owe to others as a matter of justice is ruled out as involving substantive moral intuitions about which individuals are deeply divided.

Engelhardt bases his libertarian response to pluralism on the claim that our postmodern age is defined in part by widespread rejection of the assumption that serious moral disagreements are in principle amenable to rational resolution. This skeptical thesis about the resolution of moral disagreements is controversial and libertarians are not committed to it. In any case, we might ask whether Engelhardt's political solution is sustainable if, as he claims, we live in a world characterized by a loss of faith in the power of reason to establish a common moral framework.[8] Perhaps such a loss of faith undercuts Engelhardt's own solution and dashes hopes for uncoerced general agreement on a content-less, as well as a content-full, political conception. But I will set aside questions about the foundation and coherence of Engelhardt's account and focus instead on the implications of his libertarianism for the delivery and conduct of health care.

The mechanism for the distribution of health care that, in Engelhardt's view, best exemplifies the only defensible political conception for a pluralistic society is the free market. He explains the connection between the conception and the free market this way:

> By requiring only peaceable, non-coerced, non-fraudulent exchanges, the market can allow strangers to transfer goods for services without endorsement of a particular morality. . . . Because a free market in health care requires. . . . only the consent of the participants, the market will always have an intellectual advantage over egalitarian health care systems that depend on a particular content-full vision of proper health care distributions. (1991, pp. 134–35)

In a just society, individuals would be able to join with like-minded others to form health-care systems or health-care delivery networks that are congenial to their normative outlooks. Their members would collectively decide how they will use common funds to insure themselves against various eventualities—in other words, what their health care entitlements will be—and because different systems would presumably reach different conclusions based on their particular vision of health care, there would be no universally mandated set of entitlements to health care. In addition, if some people wished to use their private resources to purchase more health care than that provided by common funds, they would be able to do so.

One question this proposal raises has to do with how the common funds are to be collected. If common funds are to be pooled from the private resources of the participants in each health-care delivery network, and if incomes are not fair, affluent networks would have an unfair advantage over poor ones in their ability to provide coverage for a more comprehensive set of benefits. In later writing, perhaps partly in recognition of this problem, Engelhardt added new details to his proposal by advocating the establishment of a system of vouchers or health-care purchase accounts. Two interrelated features of this proposal are worth underscoring. First, Engelhardt's voucher system is intended to attach to a free market system. Vouchers are introduced into this system for use by the pool to purchase health care from the delivery network of their choice. The vouchers function as specially dedicated money to be used by individuals to buy protection against health-care needs as defined by them. Second, the government's role with respect to the distribution of health care is confined to protecting the operation of the free market, and "a limited welfare right to health care"—involving government provision of vouchers—is defended on this basis. Under Engelhardt's proposal, there are no positive rights to health care that government should guarantee to all citizens as a matter of justice, for this "would involve the secular equivalent of establishing a particular religious morality" (1999, p. 650).

A further question about Engelhardt's libertarian solution to the lack of common agreement on a set of basic health-care entitlements concerns the extent to which reasonable people with diverse conceptions of the good life actually disagree about what is and is not a disease. If for the most part there is little controversy among reasonable people about this, then we might be able to mount an argument, at least with respect to the more important diseases, that society is obligated to provide people with medical services to treat them, resources permitting. At least Engelhardt could not object that recognition of a positive right to be given treatments for these conditions would involve the illicit imposition of a single "content-full" morality on a morally diverse society, *if* the way in which reasonable people draw the line between disease and its absence is largely independent of the fact of pluralism.

Engelhardt, however, believes that pluralism plays an important role here, and he takes this to provide further support for a libertarian solution: "The identification of a state of disease or health involves appeal to . . . particular rankings of human goals," and understandings of disease will therefore necessarily be "culture-influenced and relative" (1991, p. 113). It is relevant here to consider what the large body of cross-cultural and multicultural research on the interplay between culture and disease has shown us about the cultural relativity of disease.[9] We know from this literature that cultures vary in their understandings of how the human body works and how to fix it when it stops working properly. We also know that different cultures will use different terms to describe the diseases their members suffer from and that significant variations exist in how people from different cultures explain the causes of disease. None of this shows that there are significant differences across cultures with respect to what members count as a disease state. Indeed, Engelhardt himself is willing to concede that many diseases "(e.g., cancer of the lung or coronary artery disease) are identified as such because they tend to impede whatever goals humans might have" and that they will appear as diseases across cultures (1991, p. 113). Apparently more telling are those historical examples in which certain behaviors or conditions were once classified as diseases (e.g., masturbation and the running-away disease of slaves) (Engelhardt, 1974). But merely mentioning these cases does not establish that they were properly so classified or that no reasonable consensus on particular substantive health-care issues can

be achieved. Reasonable people recognize that the classification was erroneous and in doing so implicitly reject the view that, as Engelhardt puts its, disease categories are just "human cultural constructs" or "human social fabrications" (1991, p. 114).[10]

A Liberal Communitarian Response to Pluralism

A central tenet of many contemporary liberalisms—collectively referred to as "neutralist liberalism"—is that government may legitimately exercise a range of coercive powers, including the power of taxation, only if it uses these powers neutrally. Exactly what this *neutrality constraint* on government action involves has been a matter of considerable debate among liberals, but I shall understand the claim to be that government actions and policies should not intend to favor some conceptions of the good and some particular ways of life over others. State neutrality is appealing on two counts. The first is that neutrality is a moderately uncoercive means of securing the consent of persons who are concerned with living in a pluralistic society of free and equal citizens. Persons so conceived recognize that the government may not act on their behalf to coercively impose their particular way of life on others, but at the same time they reasonably want assurance that their own way of life will not be seriously threatened, and they are more likely to be confident of this when state coercive power is used on them neutrally than when it is used non-neutrally. The second source of the appeal is the requirement to treat people with equal respect and to protect their autonomy. When government uses coercive power on some citizens for reasons they morally reject, it is argued, they may reasonably feel that the government is failing to respect them as persons.[11]

Despite what many liberals regard as the powerful moral appeal of the notion of neutrality, Ezekiel Emanuel argues that it blocks solutions to crucial ethical questions about termination of medical care for incompetent individuals and rationing of scarce medical resources. We cannot solve these problems without appealing to some robust conception of the good, and liberalism, with its commitment to neutrality about what counts as the good life, cannot allow this. Only communities of individuals organized around shared visions of the good have the moral resources to make progress on these problems without violating the terms of their cooperative arrangement. But we live in a pluralistic society and so we must tolerate—indeed, as Emanuel sees it, more than just tolerate—a plurality of incompatible solutions, each driven by commitment to a particular conception of the good life. There are some similarities here with Engelhardt, but one significant difference between them is that Emanuel argues for a pluralistic system of health care on the ground that a commitment to neutrality precludes the solution of pressing questions in medical ethics, whereas Engelhardt bases it on the implausibility of supposing that serious moral disagreements, in medicine and elsewhere, can in principle be rationally resolved. In one case, neutrality is the problem, in the other, rationality.

"Liberalism accepts pluralism as a fact and permits individual diversity," Emanuel admits. But the neutrality condition, while it may yield a principle of toleration of diversity, provides no basis for positive encouragement of it. Emanuel's political vision, embracing elements of both liberalism and communitarianism, goes further in giving a more prominent place to pluralism: It "affirms pluralism as a positive value enhancing the realization of human potentialities and seeks not only to permit it but to foster it through political diversity" (Emanuel, 1991, p. 175).

Emanuel's conception of pluralism is communal and dynamic. From his perspective, conceptions of the good provide the framework for communal processes of deliberation among individuals who share the same basic normative commitments. They are not just held as matters of private conviction by those who may or may not participate with like-minded others in deliberations about their meaning and implications. Pluralism, for Emanuel, is decidedly not just a pluralism of conceptions of the good that guide people in the conduct of their private lives. It is also, and chiefly, a pluralism of *communities* with shared traditions, ideals, and practices, and liberalism, in his view, is ill-equipped to give the latter any special status. What is called for instead, he argues, is a political philosophy that, although liberal insofar as it recognizes the claim of pluralism and protects individual rights, is also communitarian in that it espouses a "pluralism of affirmation" whose realiza-

tion "requires recognizing a plurality of communities of deliberation" (1991, p. 161).

Liberal communitarianism also has important implications for how we are to understand the liberal commitment to respect cultural diversity, because respect for cultural diversity occupies an important place in liberal political thought as a way of acknowledging the claim of pluralism. On the liberal communitarian view, it is not enough to tolerate reasonable cultural diversity. Respect requires more—namely, conditions that support and promote ongoing collective deliberations within diverse cultural groups about fundamental elements of their communal life.

As with Engelhardt, we can think of Emanuel as engaged in the task of articulating a political conception of justice for a democratic pluralistic society (and perhaps a multicultural society as well). More specifically, both authors offer a political conception of justice in health care that is suitable for a society characterized by a reasonable pluralism of conceptions of the good. Further, both hold that, because there are deep disagreements regarding appropriate moral understandings of health care, there will be no general agreement on how to rank the value of different medical services, no consensus on which basic medical services society should guarantee to citizens as a matter of justice. A just society is not one that establishes some uniform set of equal basic health-care entitlements for all citizens. Rather, it is a society in which individuals are free to join and receive benefits from the health-care network of their choice (Engelhardt) or, with an important qualification to be mentioned below, a community health program of like-minded individuals, each group espousing and pursuing its own particular conception of the good insofar as it bears on health care (Emanuel).[12] Both writers therefore embrace a political conception of just health care that includes a universal right of citizens to participate in health care organizations they find congenial to their moral, religious, and cultural outlooks, and a corresponding obligation on the part of government to protect this right.

Unlike Engelhardt, however, Emanuel's political conception incorporates a substantive conception of the good, a communitarian conception. Communitarianism, as Emanuel conceives of it, makes a number of claims about the good of persons and how this is achieved:

> Informing this ideal [of liberal communitarianism] is a vision of a person who is (1) autonomous, (2) with fully developed capacities, including those capacities that can only be fully developed through participation in democratic deliberations, and (3) who has transcended his contingent existence through participation in the shaping and sustaining of his community. (Emanuel, 1991, p. 157)

Emanuel presumably believes that there can be a consensus among reasonable people on a political conception of justice that includes these liberal communitarian beliefs, and as his political conception includes them, he argues that government, acting on behalf of its citizens, may give extra support and encouragement to those community health programs with a philosophy and mode of operation that are congenial to the liberal communitarian vision. In doing so, of course, the neutrality constraint on government action is violated; but it is the commitment to neutrality, after all, that Emanuel regards as the principal problem with liberalism.

Emanuel is at pains to show that his vision of a health-care system organized along liberal communitarian lines is not just an exercise in utopian thinking, and he provides numerous details to flesh out his proposal. In his plan, several thousand individuals would devise their own community health program, possibly organized around preexisting neighborhood health centers, unions, community hospitals, or health maintenance organizations (HMOs), and based on a shared notion of the good. The programs would be funded by federal vouchers that are given to each person or family in the program and pooled in some sort of health-care trust fund supervised by a federal oversight board. What some may find particularly troubling are the significant exclusionary powers that community health programs have. In Emanuels (1991) scheme, the right of individuals to participate in this pluralistic health-care system does not entail that a particular community health program is obligated to accept them, even if they agree to live by its policies. A program may exclude them if this is "necessary to sustain a community's commitment to a particular conception of the good life" (p. 239).

Libertarians reject the liberal commitment to welfare rights in health care on the ground that, in a pluralistic and multicultural society, there can be no overlapping consensus on a substantive notion of equality or fairness. Liberal communitarians also believe that we cannot justify a criterion that specifies basic medical services that society should guarantee as a matter of justice, but rather than opt for a minimalist political conception they argue for a richer political conception that incorporates certain substantive ideals of the person and of democratic deliberation. Libertarians believe the liberal account goes too far; liberal communitarians believe that, in some respects, it does not go far enough. What might a liberal political conception look like and can it be the object of an overlapping consensus in a pluralistic, multicultural society?

Pluralism and Rawlsian Political Liberalism

Perhaps the most well-known and sophisticated liberal theory of just health-care is the one by Norman Daniels that builds on the early work of John Rawls. Though Rawls offers no theory of just health-care himself, Daniels believes that Rawls's principle of equal opportunity can be extended to provide a moral foundation for a right to health care. This might at first seem problematic, for as it is usually understood, Rawls' principle has to do with the impact of *social* structures, whether just or unjust, on opportunity, and much disease is the result of a natural lottery rather than social structure.[13] But diseases, no less than social structures, can preclude an individual from being able to compete with others for desirable social positions under conditions of fairness, Daniels argues, so we should think of equal opportunity as being concerned to counteract the opportunity-limiting effects of both sorts of impediments.

In the original formulation of his theory, Daniels pays little attention to the great diversity in beliefs about philosophical, religious, and moral matters characterizing democratic societies and to the implications of such diversity for a theory of just health care. Rawls himself recognizes the failure to take pluralism seriously as a shortcoming of his book *A Theory of Justice*: "Justice as fairness is presented there as a comprehensive liberal doctrine . . . in which all the members of its well-ordered society affirm that same doctrine. This kind of well-ordered society contradicts the fact of reasonable pluralism" (Rawls, 1999, p. 614). Rawls rectifies this shortcoming in his later work where he considers the justification of a conception of justice as a political enterprise whose aim is to show that it can be freely endorsed by citizens with different reasonable conceptions of the good from their particular perspectives.

According to Rawls, a liberal political conception of justice is characterized by three main features: (1) It consists of principles for evaluating the basic structure of social institutions; (2) the reasoning about matters of justice that it licenses does not rely on, but is independent of, comprehensive moral or religious views; and (3) it can be constructed out of certain key ideas that are already accepted by most people who share a democratic culture, such as the idea that society is a fair system of cooperation and that the terms of cooperation must be ones that free and equal persons can accept.[14] Justice as fairness—according to which the basic structure of society must maximize the long-term expectations of the least advantaged members of society, given background institutions that guarantee equal basic liberties and fair equality of opportunity—expresses and elaborates these key democratic ideas. In Rawls's view, this is a political conception of justice that can be justified to reasonable individuals with different systems of moral and other beliefs. But justice as fairness, Rawls now emphasizes, is not the only admissible liberal political conception:

> The content of public reason is given by a family of political conceptions of justice, and not by a single one. There are many liberalisms and related views, and therefore many forms of public reason specified by a family of reasonable political conceptions. Of these, justice as fairness, whatever its merits, is but one. (Rawls, 1999, p. 581)

The principles of every liberal political conception must specify and give priority to certain basic rights, liberties, and opportunities, and must assure "to all citizens adequate all-purpose means to make effective use of their liberties and opportunities" (1996, p. 6). But justice as fairness is only one way of understanding these requirements. Other reasonable liberal political conceptions include "Habermas's discourse conception of legitimacy . . . as well as

Catholic views of the common good and solidarity when they are expressed in terms of political values" (Rawls, 1999, pp. 582–83).

An important question for Daniels' view, if he accepts the recasting of the problem of just health care in the terms of Rawls's later work, is whether there are reasonable political conceptions that are significantly different from justice as fairness with respect to the principle of fair equality of opportunity. Justice as fairness may have, as Rawls claims in *Political Liberalism*, a special place among the family of reasonable political conceptions in that it is the *most* reasonable political conception that can be developed from certain key ideas implicit in the public culture of a democratic society. But Rawls acknowledges that it is not the only reasonable political conception that meets this condition and that justice as fairness, with its principle of fair equality of opportunity, expresses only a particular, "egalitarian form" or variant of political liberalism (Rawls, 1996, p. 6).

If we take this to suggest that there are reasonable liberal conceptions that do not contain the principle of fair equality of opportunity or do not give it the same weight that it has in justice as fairness, then it cannot be claimed that reasonable people (in Rawls's sense) will necessarily converge on a Daniels-type theory of just health care. In fact, reasonable people might converge on some other theory that contains a different conception of equal opportunity than the one Rawls advances in *Theory of Justice*, so that Daniels's equal opportunity account is only one of a number of competing accounts, each of which can lay claim to being a liberal theory of just health care. The question then arises whether there is a liberal argument for a right to health care that does not rely on the principle of fair equality of opportunity and that reasonable people cannot reasonably reject. Putting the question another way, are there any elements of liberal political conceptions *generally* upon which we can draw to ground such a right? A possible alternative to Daniels' approach is to argue for such a right from the general requirement that a liberal political conception of justice include measures to ensure for all citizens "adequate all-purpose means to make effective use" of their freedoms. On this view, health is conceived as a material precondition of the effective use of a wide range of freedoms, and health *care* is a right because it maintains or restores health, or where this is not possible, helps to ameliorate the effects of disease. It might also be argued that this generic liberal argument for a right to health care better accommodates the fact of reasonable pluralism than does Daniels's fair equality of opportunity argument.

Whatever the merits of this proposal might be, Daniels remains committed to his equal opportunity account, even though, like Rawls, he now takes the fact of pluralism more seriously than he did in the early formulation of his theory in *Just Health Care* (1985). The fair equality of opportunity view, earlier argued for on philosophical grounds, is now defended as the appropriate political conception for a democratic society characterized by a diversity of religious, philosophical, and moral doctrines.

This task is undertaken in chapter 4 of *From Chance to Choice: Genetics and Justice*, written by Daniels, Allen Buchanan, Dan Brock, and Daniel Wikler (2000; see also Daniels, 1990). Though a right to health care can be defended in various ways, it is the impact of disease and impairment on equal opportunity that for them has the greatest appeal as the foundation of such a right. But the authors also acknowledge that in a pluralistic society there may be various conceptions of equal opportunity, some more expansive than fair equality of opportunity. Two views of this sort are discussed at some length: In one, the target of egalitarian concerns is *welfare*, in the other, "positive freedom or *capability* of people to do or be what they choose" (Daniels, 1990, p. 273). The problem with these more demanding views, they claim, is that they derive from comprehensive moral or philosophical doctrines that not all reasonable people can accept.

A less demanding principle than fair equality of opportunity is the nondiscrimination view, which requires only the elimination of legal and informal barriers to access to desirable social positions. However, this weaker principle, they argue, does not adequately express a feature of the conception of equal opportunity that has considerable appeal in our public culture, namely, that competition for jobs or offices should not be unfairly distorted by one's initial social starting place, by one's family of origin, one's social class, and so forth. Working with this set of conceptions of equal opportunity, Daniels and colleagues attempt to show that there can be an overlapping consensus among reasonable people on a political conception of just health care that bases a right to health care on the principle of fair equality of opportunity, interpreted in terms of a notion of normal species functioning.[15] Proponents of the more expansive conceptions of equal opportunity can *at least* accept this, and proponents of the weaker conception can be shown to be unreasonable in so restricting the scope of the demands of equal opportunity.

Of course, an overlapping consensus on a political conception of just health care, or justice more generally, might not include everyone in the society, but universal inclusion is not a requirement of the Rawlsian project and it does not necessarily count against it or against a political theory of just health care defended along these lines, that some members of society are left out. For example, individuals who have immigrated to liberal democratic societies from authoritarian or tribal societies might not accept key elements of a public, democratic culture, at least for a time. (Arguably this is true of certain cultural groups in which women are socialized to be self-effacing and unconditionally obedient to their husbands or other male relatives.) They may retain conceptions of justice and equality that are the product of their native cultures, conceptions rooted in particular moral, religious, and philosophical belief systems. To the extent that they do not accept certain fundamental intuitive ideas present in the democratic political culture, they will have no reason to support a political conception of justice constructed out of these ideas. Or rather, they will have no reason of the *right type*, for it may be in their self-interest to comply with the norms of the democratic society if the state uses its coercive power to enforce obedience.

To the question, Why should we comply with democratic principles when our own conceptions of justice and equality do not recognize their validity? all that can be said is, this is how we do things here, and as long as you live here, you have to play by the rules. One would like to be able to show such individuals that they have reasons of a different sort for compliance, that it is not just because the superior power of the state leaves them no choice, but in Rawls's account this is not possible until they have assimilated fundamental normative ideas of the political culture.

Let us then confine the discussion to a pluralistic society of a certain sort, a society in which convergence on a liberal political conception of justice for the right reasons is possible among different cultural groups and adherents of different comprehensive doctrines. And let us suppose further that there will be a consensus in this society that health care is a requirement of justice because it is necessary to ensure fair equality of opportunity. It is still possible, indeed likely, that people's diverse cultural backgrounds and particular normative commitments will lead them to disagree about which scheme of medical and health services promotes fair equality of opportunity. Though Emanuel presents this as a serious problem for the liberal account,[16] it is not clear why a proponent of the fair equality of opportunity view cannot accept disagreement on this level, indeed why he cannot welcome this sort of disagreement, as long as it is constrained by basic agreement on the principle itself.[17] It need be no embarrassment to the liberal account that, given a reasonable pluralism, there will be a number of *sufficiently just* schemes of medical and health services, each of which can plausibly be regarded as living up to the principle of fair equality of opportunity. Different just health and medical schemes might assess differently the impact of particular medical services and technologies on the range of opportunities we enjoy. They might also assign different relative weights to categories of care: mental versus physical, preventive versus acute, and acute versus long-term care.

Of course, this does not show that Daniels' view is correct or that the reasoning by which he defends it, in both his early and more recent work, is sound. Engelhardt, for example, believes that in a pluralistic society there can only be consensus on a process of peaceable negotiation for resolving disputes, not on a substantive criterion. The point is a more modest one, namely the liberal account can allow a range of views about the importance of different medical and health services, and hence about what justice specifically requires in the realm of health care. The range is narrower than on some other accounts—for example, Engelhardt's and Emanuel's—but some measure of local variation can be accommodated.[18]

Conclusion

My main intention in canvassing the libertarian, liberal communitarian, and liberal responses to the fact of pluralism, and multiculturalism as an aspect of pluralism, has not been to advocate for one of them in particular. Too many important issues have been left unsettled to reach a conclusion about which is the better theory. Rather, I hope to have indicated the main issues that must be addressed by a theory of just health care for a pluralistic, multicultural society. I have assumed throughout that a theory of just health care must meet certain requirements, that the goal is not to provide the most philosophically compelling account of justice, but rather a conception of justice that reasonable people with diverse moral, philosophical, and religious belief systems can freely endorse despite their disagreements about other matters. In this sense, a theory of just health care that takes pluralism seriously must be political.

If we understand the task of constructing a political theory of justice the way John Rawls does, then an objection to Engelhardt might be that the fundamental intuitive ideas embedded in the public, democratic culture furnish us with sufficient materials for working up a more robust theory of just health care than the procedural one that Engelhardt defends. But we might not understand the task this way, and even if we do, these ideas may be too thin to support anything more than a libertarian solution. These are complex issues that I have not tried to resolve. Emanuel believes that, because of pluralism, any principle for determining what society should guarantee to citizens as a matter of justice, even if generally agreed upon, will be so abstract as to be of little practical use. The questions that pluralism and, secondarily, multiculturalism pose for a theory of just health care might therefore be formulated in the following ways: (1) What political conception (or conceptions) of just health care can secure the uncoerced allegiance of reasonable people—people who are committed to their own conceptions of the good but who recognize that they live in a pluralistic society and are concerned to live with one another on fair terms? And (2) Will this conception include a substantive and practically useful principle of health care entitlement?

NOTES

I want to thank Arthur Kuflik for spending many hours with me discussing the issues in this chapter and for helping me clarify and organize my thoughts on different approaches to a theory of justice for health care.

1. The notion of respect for cultural diversity is continuous with a familiar feature of liberal political thought, namely religious toleration.

2. See Ronald Bayer's helpful discussion of multiculturalism in "AIDS Prevention and Cultural Sensitivity: Are They Compatible?" *American Journal of Public Health* 84, no. 6, June 1994: 895–98.

3. This point is made by Amy Gutmann, "The Challenge of Multiculturalism in Political Ethics." *Philosophy and Public Affairs* 22, no. 3, summer 1993: 171–206.

4. Here I follow Joseph Chan, "Legitimacy, Unanimity, and Perfectionism." *Philosophy and Public Affairs* 29, no. 1, winter 2000: 3–42.

5. Rawls (1996) introduces the idea of an overlapping consensus on pp. 38–40 of *Political Liberalism*.

6. *Reasonable pluralism* is to be distinguished from *pluralism as such* and refers only to a pluralism of reasonable conceptions. Rawls discusses the latter notion in *Political Liberalism*, pp. 58–66.

7. The distinction between a substantive *principle* that determines an overarching set of medical services and substantive *ideals* incorporated into the political conception is discussed more fully in the section titled "a Liberal Communitarian Response to Pluralism."

8. What would Engelhardt say to a person who would rather force his views on others and who answers his critics this way: "To be sure, I cannot rationally convince you that I am right, but then you can't rationally convince me that you are right either"? The notion of rational justification that Engelhardt employs here seems to be something like rational *proof*, and it is questionable whether this is an appropriate way to understand how rational justification works in ethics.

9. The literature is vast. See, for example, Malcolm MacLachlan, *Culture and Health Care* (New York: John Wiley, 1997).

10. Whether diseases are social constructions determined by our positive or negative evaluations or whether they have some more "objective" basis is a long-standing controversy in the philosophy of medicine. For two opposing views, see Christopher Boorse, "On the Distinction between Disease and Illness," *Philosophy and Public Affairs* 5, no. 1, 1975: 49–68, and Peter Sedgwick, "Illness-Mental & Otherwise," *Hastings Center Studies*, 1, no. 3, 1973.

11. The discussion in this paragraph closely follows Harry Brighouse, "Neutrality, Publicity, and State Funding of the Arts." *Philosophy and Public Affairs* 24, no. 1, winter 1995: 35–63. I should note that I merely mention these as grounds of the appeal and do not take a position on the merits of the argument for neutrality.

12. Emanuel (1991) distinguishes among four conceptions of the good, each of which endorses a different scheme of health-care services. The *physical* conception justifies giving priority to the use of aggressive life-saving treatments for all patients; the *relational* conception favors an age-based scheme in which elderly patients receive palliative rather than life-saving care; the *autonomous* conception supports a system that focuses on providing medical care that has a reasonable prospect of enabling patients to live independent lives; and the *utilitarian* conception endorses the use of cost-effectiveness as the criterion for determining which services to provide and to whom (Emanuel, 1991, *The Ends of Human Life*, pp. 126–144).

13. Both the incidence and the distribution of disease are heavily influenced by socioeconomic factors that shape a person's relative social advantage. Recently, a number of bioethicists have called for greater attention to the social determinants of health, which, research has shown, do more to explain health differences between advantaged and disadvantaged members of society than do disparities in access to medical care. See, for example, James Hurowitz, "Toward a Social Policy for Health," *New England Journal of Medicine* 329, no. 2, July 8, 1993: 130–33.

14. See Rawls, (1999), "The Idea of Public Reason Revisited."

15. The normal species functioning interpretation of the principle of fair equality of opportunity is presented in chapter 4 of Daniels et al., *From Chance to Choice*, as well as in Daniels' (1981), "Health-Care Needs and Distributive Justice," and Daniels (1985) *Just Health Care*.

16. See chapter 4 of Emanuel (1991), *The Ends of Human Life*.

17. Here is where democratic political processes play an important role. Democratic deliberation is arguably the most appropriate way for citizens collectively to reach agreement on the specific requirements of the principle. Amy Gutmann and Dennis Thompson, in *Democracy and Disagreement* (1996), put democratic deliberation at the center of their attempt to solve the problem of reasonable pluralism.

18. See Daniels (1992), in which he offers this reply to Emanuel in his review of Emanuel's *The Ends of Human Life*.

REFERENCES

Bayer, R. (1994). AIDS prevention and cultural sensitivity: Are they compatible? *American Journal of Public Health* 84 (6), 895–98.

Boorse, C. (1975). On the distinction between disease and illness. *Philosophy and Public Affairs* 5 (1), 49–68.

Brighouse, H. (1995). Neutrality, publicity, and state funding of the arts. *Philosophy and Public Affairs* 24 (1), 35–63.

Chan, J. (2000). Legitimacy, unanimity, and perfectionism. *Philosophy and Public Affairs* 29 (1), 3–42.

Daniels, N. (1981). Health-care needs and distributive justice. *Philosophy and Public Affairs* 10 (2), 146–79.

Daniels, N. (1985). *Just Health Care*. Cambridge: Cambridge University Press.

Daniels, N. (1990). Equality of what: Welfare, resources, or capabilities? *Philosophy and Phenomenological Research*. 50 (Suppl), 273–96.

Daniels, N. (1992). Review of *The Ends of Human Life*. *Hastings Center Report* 22 (6), 41–42.

Daniels, N. (1996). Reflective equilibrium and justice as political. In Daniels, *Justice and Justification*. Cambridge: Cambridge University Press, pp. 144–75.

Daniels, N. (2000). With Allen Buchanan, Dan W. Brock, and Daniel Wikler. *From Chance to Choice: Genetics and Justice*. Cambridge: Cambridge University Press.

Emanuel, E. (1991). *The Ends of Human Life: Medical Ethics in a Liberal Polity*. Cambridge, MA: Harvard University Press.

Engelhardt, Jr., H.T. (1974). Disease of masturbation: Values and the concept of disease. *Bulletin of the History of Medicine* 48 (2), 234–48.

Engelhardt, Jr., H.T. (1991). *Bioethics and Secular Humanism: The Search for a Common Morality*. London: SCM Press.

Engelhardt, Jr., H.T. (1999). Freedom and moral diversity: the moral failures of health care in the welfare state. In J. Arras and B. Steinbock (eds.), *Ethical Issues in Modern Medicine*, 5th ed. Mountain View, CA: Mayfield, pp. 642–51. Reprinted from (1997). *Social Philosophy and Policy* 14 (2), 180–96.

Gutmann, A. (1993). The challenge of multiculturalism in political ethics. *Philosophy and Public Affairs* 22 (3), 171–206.

Gutmann, A. and Thompson, D. (1996). *Democracy and Disagreement*. Cambridge, MA: Harvard University Press.

Hurowitz, J. (1993). Toward a social policy for health. *New England Journal of Medicine* 329 (2), 130–33.

MacLachlan, M. (1997). *Culture and Health Care*. New York: John Wiley.

Rawls J. (1971). *A Theory of Justice*. Cambridge, MA: Harvard University Press.

Rawls, J. (1996). *Political Liberalism*. New York: Columbia University Press.

Rawls, J. (1999). The idea of public reason revisited. In *John Rawls: Collected Papers*. Cambridge, MA: Harvard University Press, pp. 573–615,

Sedgwick, P. (1973). "Illness-Mental and Otherwise," *Hastings Center Studies* 3 (1), 19–40.

Taylor, C. (1993). The Politics of Recognition. In A Gutmann (ed.), *Multiculturalism and the Politics of Recognition*. Princeton, NJ: Princeton University Press.

Rights to Health Care, Social Justice, and Fairness in Health Care Allocations: Frustrations in the Face of Finitude

H. TRISTRAM ENGELHARDT, JR.

Engelhardt asserts that "A basic human secular moral right to health care does not exist—not even to a 'decent minimum of health care.'" He distinguishes between losses that people suffer because of bad fortune and those due to unfairness. The former do not establish a duty of aid to the unfortunate (there is no moral right to such aid), but the latter may constitute claims on others. Out of compassion or benevolence, society may freely consent to help those in need, but there is no forced obligation to do so.

The imposition of a single-tier, all-encompassing health care system is morally unjustifiable. It is a coercive act of totalitarian ideological zeal, which fails to recognize the diversity of moral visions that frame interests in health care, the secular moral limits of state authority, and the authority of individuals over themselves and their own property. It is an act of secular immorality.

A basic human secular moral right to health care does not exist—not even to a "decent minimum of health care." Such rights must be created.

The difficulty with supposed right to health care, as well as with many claims regarding justice or fairness in access to health care, should be apparent. Since the secular moral authority for common action is derived from permission or consent, it is difficult (indeed, for a large-scale society, materially impossible) to gain moral legitimacy for the thoroughgoing imposition on health care of one among the many views of beneficence and justice. There are, after all, as many accounts of beneficence, justice, and fairness as there are major religions.

Most significantly, there is a tension between the foundations of general secular morality and the various particular positive claims founded in particular visions of beneficence and justice. It is materially impossible both to respect the freedom of all and to achieve their long-range best interests. Loose talk about justice and fairness in health care is therefore morally misleading, because it suggests that there is a particular canonical vision of justice or fairness that all have grounds to endorse. . . .

Rights to health care constitute claims on services and goods. Unlike rights to forbearance, which require others to refrain from interfering, which show the unity of the authority to use others, rights to beneficence are rights grounded in particular theories or accounts of the good. For general authority, they require others to participate actively in a particular understanding of the good life or justice. Without an appeal to the principle of permission, to advance such rights is to claim that one may press others into labor or confiscate their property. Rights to health care, unless they are derived from special contractual agreements, depend on particular understandings of beneficence rather than on authorizing permission. They may therefore conflict with the decisions of individuals who may not wish to participate in, and may indeed be morally opposed to, realizing a particular system of health care. Individuals always have the secular moral authority to use their own resources in ways that collide with fashionable understandings of justice or the prevailing consensus regarding fairness.

Health Care Policy: The Ideology of Equal, Optimal Care

It is fashionable to affirm an impossible commitment in health care delivery, as, for example, in the following four widely embraced health care policy goals, which are at loggerheads:

1. The best possible care is to be provided for all.
2. Equal care should be guaranteed.
3. Freedom of choice on the part of health care provider and consumer should be maintained.
4. Health care costs are to be contained.

From *Foundations of Bioethics*, 2d ed., by H. Tristram Engelhardt, Jr., (1996). Reprinted by permission of Oxford University Press.

One cannot provide the best possible health care for all and contain health care costs. One cannot provide equal health care for all and respect the freedom of individuals peaceably to pursue with others their own visions of health care or to use their own resources and energies as they decide. For that matter, one cannot maintain freedom in the choice of health care services while containing the costs of health care. One may also not be able to provide all with equal health care that is at the same time the very best care because of limits on the resources themselves. That few openly address these foundational moral tensions at the roots of contemporary health care policy suggests that the problems are shrouded in a collective illusion, a false consciousness, an established ideology within which certain facts are politically unacceptable.

These difficulties spring not only from a conflict between freedom and beneficence, but from a tension among competing views of what it means to pursue and achieve the good in health care (e.g., is it more important to provide equal care to all or the best possible health care to the least-well-off class?). The pursuit of incompatible or incoherent health care is rooted in the failure to face the finitude of secular moral authority, the finitude of secular moral vision, the finitude of human powers in the face of death and suffering, the finitude of human life, and the finitude of human financial resources. A health care system that acknowledges the moral and financial limitations on the provision of health care would need to

1. endorse inequality in access to health care as morally unavoidable because of private resources and human freedom;
2. endorse setting a price on saving human life as a part of establishing a cost-effective health care system established through communal resources.

Even though all health care systems de facto enjoy inequalities and must to some extent ration the health care they provide through communal resources, this is not usually forthrightly acknowledged. There is an ideological bar to recognizing and coming to terms with the obvious.

Only a prevailing collective illusion can account for the assumption in U.S. policy that health care may be provided (1) while containing costs (2) without setting a price on saving lives and preventing suffering when using communal funds and at the same time (3) ignoring the morally unavoidable inequalities due to private resources and human freedom. This false consciousness shaped the deceptions central to the Clinton health care proposal, as it was introduced in 1994. It was advanced to support a health care system purportedly able to provide all with (1) the best of care and (2) equal care, while achieving (3) cost containment, and still (4) allowing those who wish the liberty to purchase fee-for-service health care.[1] While not acknowledging the presence of rationing, the proposal required silent rationing in order to contain costs by limiting access to high-cost, low-yield treatments that a National Health Board would exclude from the "guaranteed benefit package."[2] In addition, it advanced mechanisms to slow technological innovation so as further to reduce the visibility of rationing choices.[3] One does not have to ration that which is not available. There has been a failure to acknowledge the moral inevitability of inequalities in health care due to the limits of secular governmental authority, human freedom, and the existence of private property, however little that may be. There was also the failure to acknowledge the need to ration health care within communal programs if costs are to be contained. It has been ideologically unacceptable to recognize these circumstances. . . .

Justice, Freedom, and Inequality

Interests in justice as beneficence are motivated in part by inequalities and in part by needs. That some have so little while others have so much properly evokes moral concerns of beneficence. Still, . . . the moral authority to use force to set such inequalities aside is limited. These limitations are in part due to the circumstance that the resources one could use to aid those in need are already owned by other people. One must establish whether and when inequalities and needs generate rights or claims against others.

The Natural and Social Lotteries

"Natural lottery" is used to identify changes in fortune that result from natural forces, not directly from the actions of persons. The natural lottery shapes the distribution of both naturally and socially conditioned assets. The natural lottery contrasts with the social lottery, which is used to identify changes in fortune that are not the result of natural forces but the actions of persons. The social lottery shapes the distribution of social and natural assets. The natural and social lotteries, along with one's own free decisions, determine the distribution of natural and social assets. The social lottery is termed a lottery, though it is the outcome of personal actions, because of the complex and unpredictable interplay of personal choices and because of the unpredictable character of the outcomes, which do not conform to an ideal pattern and because the outcomes are the results of social forces, not the immediate choices of those subject to them.

All individuals are exposed to the vicissitudes of nature. Some are born healthy and by luck remain so for a long life, free of disease and major suffering. Others are born with serious congenital or genetic diseases, others contract serious crippling fatal illnesses early in life, and yet others are injured and maimed. Those who win the natural lottery will for most of their lives not be in need of medical care. They will live full lives and die painless and peaceful deaths. Those who lost the natural lottery will be in need of health care to blunt their sufferings and, where possible, to cure their diseases and to restore function. There will be a spectrum of losses, ranging from minor problems such as having teeth with cavities to major tragedies such as developing childhood leukemia, inheriting Huntington's chorea, or developing amyelotrophic lateral sclerosis.

These tragic outcomes are the deliverances of nature, for which no one, without some special view of accountability or responsibility, is responsible (unless, that is, one recognizes them as the results of the Fall or as divine chastisements). The circumstance that individuals are injured by hurricanes, storms, and earthquakes is often simply no one's fault. When no one is to blame, no one may be charged with the responsibility of making whole those who lose the natural lottery on the ground of accountability for the harm. One will need an argument dependent on a particular sense of fairness to show that the readers of this volume should submit to the forcible redistribution of their resources to provide health care for

:hose injured by nature. It may very well be unfeel-
ng, unsympathetic, or uncharitable not to provide
such help. One may face eternal hellfires for failing to
provide aid.[4] But it is another thing to show in general secular moral terms that individuals owe others
such help in a way that would morally authorize state
force to redistribute their private resources and energies or to constrain their free choices with others.
To be in dire need does not by itself create a secular
moral right to be rescued from that need. The natural lottery creates inequalities and places individuals
at disadvantage without creating a straightforward
secular moral obligation on the part of others to aid
those in need.

Individuals differ in their resources not simply because of outcomes of the natural lottery, but
also due to the actions of others. Some deny themselves immediate pleasures in order to accumulate
wealth or to leave inheritances; through a complex
web of love, affection, and mutual interest, individuals convey resources, one to another, so that those
who are favored prosper and those who are ignored
languish. Some as a consequence grow wealthy and
others grow poor, not through anyone's malevolent
actions or omissions, but simply because they were
not favored by the love, friendship, collegiality, and
associations through which fortunes develop and individuals prosper. In such cases there will be neither
fairness nor unfairness, but simply good and bad
fortune.

In addition, some will be advantaged or disadvantaged, made rich, poor, ill, diseased, deformed,
or disabled because of the malevolent and blameworthy actions and omissions of others. Such will
be unfair circumstances, which just and beneficent
states should try to prevent and to rectify through
legitimate police protection, forced restitution, and
charitable programs. Insofar as an injured party has
a claim against an injurer to be made whole, not
against society, the outcome is unfortunate from the
perspective of society's obligations and obligations
of innocent citizens to make restitution. Restitution
is owed by the injurer, not society or others. There
will be outcomes of the social lottery that are on the
one hand blameworthy in the sense of resulting from
the culpable actions of others, though on the other
hand a society has no obligation to rectify them. The

social lottery includes the exposure to the immoral
and unjust actions of others. Again, one will need an
argument dependent on a particular sense of fairness
to show that the readers of this volume should submit to the forcible redistribution of their resources
to provide health care to those injured by others.

When individuals come to purchase health care,
some who lose the natural lottery will be able at least
in part to compensate for those losses through their
winnings at the social lottery. They will be able to
afford expensive health care needed to restore health
and to regain function. On the other hand, those
who lose in both the natural and the social lottery
will be in need of health care, but without the resources to acquire it.

The Rich and the Poor: Differences in Entitlements

If one owns property by virtue of just acquisition or
just transfer, then one's title to that property will not
be undercut by the tragedies and needs of others.
One will simply own one's property. On the other
hand, if one owns property because such ownership
is justified within a system that ensures a beneficent
distribution of goods (e.g., the achievement of the
greatest balance of benefits over harms for the greatest number or the greatest advantage for the least-
well-off class), one's ownership will be affected by
the needs of others. . . . Property is in part privately
owned in a strong sense that cannot be undercut by
the needs of others. In addition, all have a general
right to the fruits of the earth, which constitutes the
basis for a form of taxation as rent to provide fun-
gible payments to individuals, whether or not they
are in need. Finally, there are likely to be resources
held in common by groups that may establish bases
for their distribution to meet health care concerns.
The first two forms of entitlement or ownership exist
unconstrained by medical or other needs. The last
form of entitlement or ownership, through the decision of a community, may be conditioned by need.

The existence of any amount of private resources
can be the basis for inequalities that secular moral
authority may not set aside. Insofar as people own
things, they will have a right to them, even if others
need them. Because the presence of permission is
cardinal, the test of whether one must transfer one's

goods to others will not be whether such a redistribution will not prove onerous or excessive for the person subjected to the distribution, but whether the resources belong to that individual. Consider that you may be reading this book next to a person in great need. The test of whether a third person may take resources from you to help that individual in need will not be whether you will suffer from the transfer, but rather whether you have consented—at least this is the case if the principle of permission functions in general secular morality. . . . The principle of permission is the source of authority when moral strangers collaborate, because they do not share a common understanding of fairness or of the good. As a consequence, goal-oriented approaches to the just distribution of resources must be restricted to commonly owned goods, where there is authority to create programs for their use.

Therefore, one must qualify the conclusions of the 1983 American President's Commission for the Study of Ethical Problems that suggest that excessive burdens should determine the amount of tax persons should pay to sustain an adequate level of health care for those in need.[5] Further, one will have strong grounds for morally condemning systems that attempt to impose an all-encompassing health care plan that would require "equality of care [in the sense of avoiding] the creation of a tiered system [by] providing care based only on differences of need, not individual or group characteristics."[6] Those who are rich are always at secular moral liberty to purchase more and better health care.

Drawing the Line Between the Unfortunate and the Unfair

How one regards the moral significance of the natural and social lotteries and the moral force of private ownership will determine how one draws the line between circumstances that are simply unfortunate and those that are unfortunate and in addition unfair in the sense of constituting a claim on the resources of others.

Life in general, and health care in particular, reveal circumstances of enormous tragedy, suffering, and deprivation. The pains and sufferings of illness, disability, and disease, as well as the limitations of deformity, call on the sympathy of all to provide aid and give comfort. Injuries, disabilities, and diseases due to the forces of nature are unfortunate. Injuries, disabilities, and diseases due to the unconsented-to actions of others are unfair. Still, outcomes of the unfair actions of others are not necessarily society's fault and are in this sense unfortunate. The horrible injuries that come every night to the emergency rooms of major hospitals may be someone's fault, even if they are not the fault of society, much less that of uninvolved citizens. Such outcomes, though unfair with regard to the relationship of the injured with the injurer, may be simply unfortunate with respect to society and other citizens (and may licitly be financially exploited). One is thus faced with distinguishing the difficult line between acts of God, as well as immoral acts of individuals that do not constitute a basis for societal retribution on the one hand, and injuries that provide such a basis on the other.

A line must be created between those losses that will be made whole through public funds and those that will not. Such a line was drawn in 1980 by Patricia Harris, the then secretary of the Department of Health, Education, and Welfare, when she ruled that heart transplantations should be considered experimental and therefore not reimbursable through Medicare.[7] To be in need of a heart transplant and not have the funds available would be an unfortunate circumstance but not unfair. One was not eligible for a heart transplant even if another person had intentionally damaged one's heart. From a moral point of view, things would have been different if the federal government had in some culpable fashion injured one's heart. So, too, if promises of treatment had been made. For example, to suffer from appendicitis or pneumonia and not as a qualifying patient receive treatment guaranteed through a particular governmental or private insurance system would be unfair, not simply unfortunate.

Drawing the line between the unfair and the unfortunate is unavoidable because it is impossible in general secular moral terms to translate all needs into rights, into claims against the resources of others. One must with care decide where the line is to be drawn. To distinguish needs from mere desires, one must endorse one among the many competing visions of morality and human flourishing. One is forced to draw a line between those needs (or desires) that constitute claims on the aid of others and those that do not. The line distinguishing unfortunate from unfair circumstances justifies by default certain social and economic inequalities in the sense of determining who, if any one, is obliged in general secular immorality to remedy such circumstances or achieve equality. Is the request of an individual to have life extended through a heart transplant at great cost, and perhaps only for a few years, a desire for an inordinate extension of life? Or is it a need to be secure against a premature death? . . . Outside a particular view of the good life, needs do not create rights to the services or goods of others.[8] Indeed, outside of a particular moral vision there is no canonical means for distinguishing desires from needs.

There is a practical difficulty in regarding major losses at the natural and social lotteries as generating claims to health care: attempts to restore health indefinitely can deplete societal resources in the pursuit of ever-more incremental extensions of life of marginal quality. A relatively limited amount of food and shelter is required to preserve the lives of individuals. But an indefinite amount of resources can in medicine be committed to the further preservation of human life, the marginal postponement of death, and the marginal alleviation of human suffering and disability. Losses at the natural lottery with regard to health can consume major resources with little return. Often one can only purchase a little relief, and that only at great costs. Still, more decisive than the problem of avoiding the possibly overwhelming costs involved in satisfying certain health care desires (e.g., postponing death for a while through the use of critical care) is the problem of selecting the correct content-full account of justice in order canonically to distinguish between needs and desires and to translate needs into rights.

Beyond Equality: An Egalitarianism of Altruism Versus an Egalitarianism of Envy

The equal distribution of health care is itself problematic, a circumstance recognized in *Securing Access to Health Care*, the 1983 report of the President's Commission.[9] The difficulties are multiple:

1. Although in theory, at least, one can envisage providing all with equal levels of decent shelter, one cannot restore all to or preserve all in an equal state of health. Many health needs cannot be satisfied in the same way one can address most needs for food and shelter.

2. If one provided all with the same amount of funds to purchase health care or the same amount of services, the amount provided would be far too much for some and much too little for others who could have benefited from more investment in treatment and research.

3. If one attempts to provide equal health care in the sense of allowing individuals to select health care only from a predetermined list of available therapies, or through some managed health care plan such as accountable (to the government) health care plans or regional health alliances, which would be provided to all so as to prevent the rich from having access to better health care than the poor, one would have immorally confiscated private property and have restricted the freedom of individuals to join in voluntary relationships and associations.

That some are fortunate in having more resources is neither more nor less arbitrary or unfair than some having better health, better looks, or more talents. In any event, the translation of unfortunate circumstances into unfair circumstances, other than with regard to violations of the principle of permission, requires the imposition of a particular vision of beneficence or justice. . . .

Conflicting Models of Justice: From Content to Procedure

John Rawls's *A Theory of Justice* and Robert Nozick's *Anarchy, State, and Utopia* offer contrasting understandings of what should count as justice or fairness. They sustain differing suggestions regarding the nature of justice in health care. They provide a contrast between justice as primarily structural, a pattern of distributions that is amenable to rational disclosure, versus justice as primarily procedural, a matter of fair negotiation.[10] In *A Theory of Justice* Rawls forwards an expository device of an ahistorical perspective from which to discover the proper pattern for the distribution of resources, and therefore presumably for the distribution of health care resources. In this understanding, it is assumed that societally based entitlements have moral priority. Nozick, in contrast, advances a historical account of just distributions within which justice depends on what individuals have agreed to do with and for each other. Nozick holds that individually based entitlements are morally prior to societally based entitlements. In contrast with Rawls, who argues that one can discover a proper pattern for the allocation of resources, Nozick argues that such a pattern cannot be discovered and that instead one can only identify the characteristics of a just process for fashioning rights to health care. . . .

The differences between Nozick of *Anarchy, State, and Utopia* and Rawls of *A Theory of Justice* express themselves in different accounts of entitlements and ownership, and in different understandings of non-principled fortune and misfortune. For Rawls, one has justifiable title to goods if such a title is part of a system that ensures the greatest benefit to the least advantaged, consistent with a just-savings principle, and with offices and positions open to all under conditions of fair equality and opportunity, and where each person has an equal right to the most extensive total system of equal basic liberties compatible with a similar system of liberty for all. In contrast, for Nozick, one simply owns things: "Things come into the world already attached to people having entitlements over them."[11] If one really owns things, there will be freedom-based limitations on principles of distributive justice. One may not use people or their property without their permission or authorization. The needs of others will not erase one's property rights. The readers of this book should consider that they may be wearing wedding rings or other jewelry not essential to their lives, which could be sold to buy antibiotics to save identifiable lives in the third world. Those who keep such baubles may in part be acting in agreement with Nozick's account and claiming that "it is my right to keep my wedding ring for myself, even though the proceeds from its sale could save the lives of individuals in dire need."

Nozick's account requires a distinction between someone's secular moral rights and what is right, good, or proper to do. At times, selling some (perhaps all) of one's property to support the health care of those in need will be the right thing to do, even though one has a secular moral right to refuse to sell. This contrast derives from the distinction Nozick makes between *freedom as a side constraint*, as the very condition for the possibility of a secular moral community, and *freedom as one value among others*. This contrast can be understood as a distinction between those claims of justice based on the very possibility of a moral community, versus those claims of justice that turn on interests in particular goods and values, albeit interests recognized in the original position. For Nozick, one may not use innocent free persons without their consent, even if that use will save lives by providing needed health care or securing equality of opportunity. Even if such would be a good thing to do (e.g., in this sense of saving lives), no one has a right to do it. Because for Nozick one needs the *actual* consent of *actual* persons in order to respect them as free persons, their rights can morally foreclose the pursuit of many morally worthy goals. In contrast, Rawls treats freedom or liberty as a value. As a consequence, in developing just institutions, Rawls does not require actual consent of those involved. As a result, Rawls would allow rights to self-determination to be limited in order to achieve important social goals. . . .

This contrast between Rawls and Nozick can be appreciated more generally as a contrast between two quite different principles of justice, each of which has strikingly different implications for the allocation of health care resources.

1. Freedom- or permission-based justice is concerned with distributions of goods made in accord with the notion of the secular moral community as a peaceable social structure binding moral strangers, members of diverse concrete moral communities. Such justice will therefore require the consent of the individuals involved in a historical nexus of justice-regarding institutions understood in conformity with the principle of permission. The principle of beneficence may be pursued only within constraints set by the principle of permission.
2. Goals-based justice is concerned with the achievement of the good of individuals in society, where the pursuit of beneficence is not constrained by a strong principle of permis-

sion, but driven by some particular under-standing of morality, justice, or fairness. Such justice will vary in substance as one attempts, for example, to (a) give each person an equal share; (b) give each person what that person needs; (c) give each person a distribution as a part of a system designed to achieve the greatest balance of benefits over harms for the greatest number of persons; (d) give each person a distribution as a part of a system designed to maximize the advantage of the least-well-off class with conditions of equal liberty for all and of fair opportunity.

Allocations of health care in accord with freedom- or permission-based justice must occur within the constraint to respect the free choices of persons, in-cluding their exercise of their property rights. Allo-cations of health care in accord with goals-based jus-tice will need to establish what it means to provide a just pattern of health care, and what constitutes true needs, not mere desires, and how to rank the various health goals among themselves and in comparison with nonhealth goals. Such approaches to justice in health care will require a way of ahistorically dis-covering the proper pattern for the distribution of resources.

Permission-based and goals-based approaches to justice in health care contrast because they offer competing interpretations of the maxim, "Justitia est constans et perpetua voluntas jus suum cuique tribuens" (Justice is the constant and perpetual will to render everyone his due).[12] A permission-based approach holds that justice is first and foremost giv-ing to each the right to be respected as a free indi-vidual as the source of secular moral authority, in the disposition of personal services and private goods: that which is due (*ius*) to individuals is respect of their authority over themselves and their posses-sions. In contrast, a goals-based approach holds that justice is receiving a share of the goods, which is fair by an appeal to a set of ahistorical criteria specifying what a fair share should be, that is, what share is due to each individual. Since there are various senses of a fair share (e g., an equal share, a share in accordance with the system that maximizes the balance of ben-efits over harms, etc.), there will be various compet-

ing senses of justice in health care under the rubric of goals-based justice. . . .

The Moral Inevitability of a Multitier Health Care System

. . . In the face of unavoidable tragedies and contrary moral intuitions, a multitiered system of health care is in many respects a compromise. On the one hand, it provides some amount of health care for all, while on the other hand allowing those with resources to purchase additional or better services. It can endorse the use of communal resources for the provision of a decent minimal or basic amount of health care for all, while acknowledging the existence of private re-sources at the disposal of some individuals to pur-chase better basic as well as luxury care. While the propensity to seek more than equal treatment for oneself or loved ones is made into a vicious dispo-sition in an egalitarian system, a multitier system allows for the expression of individual love and the pursuit of private advantage, though still supporting a general social sympathy for those in need. Whereas an egalitarian system must suppress the widespread human inclination to devote private resources to the purchase of the best care for those whom one loves, a multitier system can recognize a legitimate place for the expression of such inclinations. A multitier system (1) should support individual providers and consumers against attempts to interfere in their free association and their use of their own resources, though (2) it may allow positive rights to health care to be created for individuals who have not been ad-vantaged by the social lottery.

The serious task is to decide how to define and provide a decent minimum or basic level of care as a floor of support for all members of so-ciety, while allowing money and free choice to fashion special tiers of services for the affluent. In addressing this general issue of defining what is to be meant by a decent minimum basic level or a minimum adequate amount of health care, the American President's Commission in 1983 suggested that in great measure content is to be created rather than discovered by democratic pro-cesses, as well as by the forces of the market. "In a democracy, the appropriate values to be assigned to the consequences of policies must ultimately be determined by people expressing their values through social and political processes as well as in the marketplace."[13] The Commission, however, also suggested that the concept of adequacy could in part be discovered by an appeal to that amount of care that would meet the standards of sound medical practice. "Adequacy does require that everyone receive care that meets standards of sound medical practice."[14] But what one means by "sound medical practice" is itself dependent on particular understandings within particular cultures. Criteria for sound medical practice are as much created as discovered. The moral inevitability of multiple tiers of care brings with it multiple standards of proper or sound medical practice and undermines the moral plausibility of various obiter dicta concerning the centralized allocation of medical resources. . . .

NOTES

1. The White House Domestic Policy Council, *The President's Health Security Plan* (New York: Times Books, 1993).

2. The White House Domestic Policy Council, *The President's Health Security Plan*, p. 43.

3. Innovation would be discouraged as drug prices are subject to review as reasonable. The White House Domestic Policy Council, *The President's Health Security Plan*, p. 45.

4. In considering how to respond to the plight of the impecunious, one might consider the story Jesus tells of the rich man who fails to give alms to "a certain beggar named Lazarus, full of sores, who was laid at his gate, desiring to be fed with the crumbs which fell from the rich man's table" (Luke 16:20–21). The rich man, who was not forthcoming with alms was condemned to a hell of excruciating torment.

5. President's Commission for the Study of Ethical Problems in Medicine and Biomedical and Behavioral Research, *Securing Access to Health Care* (Washington, DC.: U.S. Government Printing Office, 1983), vol. 1, pp. 43–46.

6. The White House Domestic Policy Council. "Ethical Foundations of Health Reform," in *The President's Health Security Plan*, p. 11.

7. H. Newman, "Exclusion of Heart Transplantation Procedures from Medicare Coverage," *Federal Register* 45 (Aug. 6, 1980): 52296. See also H. Newman, "Medicare Program: Solicitation of Hospitals and Medical Centers to Participate in a Study of Heart Transplants," *Federal Register* 46 (Jan. 22. 1981): 7072–75.

8. The reader should understand that the author holds that almsgiving is one of the proper responses to human suffering (in addition to being an appropriate expression of repentance, an act of repentance to which surely the author is obligated). It is just that the author acknowledges the limited secular moral authority of the state to compel charity coercively.

9. President's Commission, *Securing Access to Health Care*, vol. 1, pp. 18–19.

10. John Rawls, *A Theory of Justice* (Cambridge, Mass.: Harvard University Press, 1971), and Robert Nozick, *Anarchy, State, and Utopia* (New York: Basic Books, 1974).

11. Nozick, *Anarchy, State, and Utopia*, p. 160.

12. Flavius Petrus Sabbatius Justinianus, *The Institutes of Justinian*, trans. Thomas C. Sandars (1922; repr. Westport, Conn,: Greenwood Press, 1970), 1.1 p. 5.

13. President's Commission, *Securing Access to Health Care*, vol. 1, p. 37.

14. Ibid.

Rationing Fairly: Programmatic Considerations

NORMAN DANIELS

Daniels explores four problems of justice that arise in health care rationing—problems that afflict the Oregon rationing plan and that bioethics is still unsure how to solve. These are the problems of (1) fair chances/best outcomes, (2) priorities, (3) aggregation, and (4) democracy. He concludes with a plea against provincialism: "Being provincial about health care rationing will prevent us from seeing relationships among these rationing problems."

Despite its necessity, rationing raises troublesome questions about fairness. We ration in situations in which losers, as well as winners, have plausible claims to have their needs met. When we knowingly and deliberately refrain from meeting some legitimate needs, we had better have justification for the distributive choices we make. Not surprisingly, health planners and legislators appeal to bioethicists for help, asking what justice requires here. Can we help them? I think we are not ready to yet, and I will support this claim by noting four general rationing problems that we remain unsure how to solve, illustrating how they plague Oregon's rationing plan.

Before turning to the four problems, I want to make several preliminary remarks. First, philosophers (including me) have traditionally underestimated the importance of rationing, thinking of it as a peripheral, not central problem. Since we simply cannot afford, for example, to educate, treat medically, or protect legally people in all the ways their needs for these goods require or the accepted distributive principles seem to demand, rationing is clearly pervasive, not peripheral.

Rationing decisions share three key features. First, the goods we often must provide—legal services, health care, educational benefits—are not divisible without loss of benefit, unlike money. We thus cannot avoid unequal or "lumpy" distributions. Meeting the educational, health care or legal needs of some people, for example, will mean that the requirements of others will go unsatisfied. Second, when we ration, we deny benefits to some individuals who can plausibly claim they are owed them in principle. They can cite an accepted principle of distributive justice that governs their situation and should protect them. Third, the general distributive principles appealed to by claimants as well as by rationers do not by themselves provide adequate reasons for choosing among claimants: they are too schematic. This point was driven home to me by the way in which my "fair equality of opportunity" account of just health care (Daniels 1985, 1988) fails to yield specific solutions to the rationing problems I shall survey. Finally, even

the best work in the general theory of justice has not squarely faced the problems raised by the indeterminacy of distributive principles. Rawls (1971), for example, suggests that the problem of fleshing out the content of principles of distributive justice is ultimately procedural, falling to the legislature. Perhaps, but the claim that we must in general turn to a fair democratic procedure should not be an assumption, but the conclusion, either of a general argument or of a failed search for appropriate moral constraints on rationing. If however, there are substantive principles governing rationing, then the theory of justice is incomplete in a way we have not noticed. This point cuts across the debates between proponents of "local justice" (Walzer 1983; Elster 1992) and "global justice" (Rawls 1971; Gauthier 1986), and between liberalism and communitarianism (cf. Emanuel 1991; Daniels 1992).

Four Unsolved Rationing Problems: Illustrations from Oregon

The Fair Chances/Best Outcomes Problem

Before seeing how the fair chances/best outcomes problem arises in Oregon's macrorationing plan, consider its more familiar microrationing form: Which of several equally needy individuals should get a scarce resource, such as a heart transplant? Suppose, for example, that Alice and Betty are the same age, have waited on queue the same time, and that each will live only one week without a transplant. With the transplant, however, Alice is expected to live two years and Betty twenty. Who should get the transplant (cf. Kamm 1989)? Giving priority to producing best outcomes, a priority built into some point systems for awarding organs, would mean that Betty gets the organ and Alice dies (assuming persistent scarcity of organs, as Brock (1988) notes). But Alice might complain, "Why should I give up my only chance at survival—and two years of survival is not insignificant—just because Betty has a chance to longer? It is not fair that I give up everything that is valuable to me just so Betty can have more of what is valuable to her." Alice demands a lottery that gives her an equal chance with Betty.

Some people agree with Alice's complaint and agree with her demand for a lottery. Few would agree with her, however, if she had very little chance at survival; more would agree if her outcomes were only somewhat worse than Betty's. Still, at the level of intuitions, there is much disagreement about when and how much to favor best outcomes. Brock (1988), like Broome (1987) proposes breaking this deadlock by giving Alice and Betty chances proportional to the benefits they can get (e.g., by assigning Alice one side of a ten sided die). Kamm (1989, 1993) notes that Brock's proposal must be amended once we allow differences in urgency or need among patients. She favors assigning multiplicative weights to the degree of need or urgency. Then, the neediest might end up with no chance to receive a transplant if their outcomes were very poor, but, compared to Brock's "proportional chances" proposal, they have greater opportunity to get an organ if their outcomes were reasonably high. Both Brock's and Kamm's suggestions seem ad hoc. That there is some force to each of Alice's and Betty's demands does not, as Brock would have it, mean the force is clearly equal; similarly, assigning weights to more factors, as Kamm does, seems to add an element of prevision lacking in our intuitions about these cases. Our intuitions may fall short of giving us clear, orderly principles here.

We might try to break the deadlock at the level of intuitions by appealing to more theoretical considerations. For example, we might respond to Alice that she already has lost a "natural" lottery; she might have been the one with twenty years expected survival, but it turned out to be Betty instead. After the fact, however, Alice is unlikely to agree that there were no prior differences in access to care and so on. To undercut Alice's demand for a new lottery, we would have to persuade her that the proper perspective for everyone to adopt is *ex ante* not *ex post* information about her condition (cf Menzel 1989). But what should Alice know about herself *ex ante*? If Alice knows about her family history of heart disease, she might well not favor giving complete priority to best outcomes. Perhaps Alice should agree it is reasonable to adopt more radical *ex ante* position, one that denies her all information about herself, a thick "veil of ignorance." Controversy persists. Behind such a veil, some would argue that it would be irrational to forego the greater expected payoff that would result from giving priority to best out-comes. Citing Rawls's adoption of a maximin strategy, Kamm (1993) argues against such "gambling" behind the veil. Alternatively, she appeals to Scanlon (1982): if Alice would "reasonably regret" losing to Betty, then she should not be held to a scheme that favors best outcomes. Unclear about our intuitions, we are also stymied by a controversy at the deepest theoretical levels.

The best outcomes problem arises in macrorationing as well. Consider HSS Secretary Louis Sullivan's (1992) recent refusal to grant a Medicaid waiver to Oregon's rationing plan. Sullivan's main criticism of the Oregon plan is that in preferring treatments that provide greater net benefits the plan discriminates against the disabled. The clearest example of such discrimination would be this: Two groups of patients, both in need of a treatment that can give them a net benefit of a given magnitude; because one group has a disability, e.g., difficulty walking, that would not be affected by the treatment, we deny them the treatment. Neither Sullivan nor the NLC give an example, even hypothetical, of how this situation could arise in the Oregon scheme. The denial of coverage for aggressive treatment of very low birthweight ($<$500 gr) neonates, which they do cite as an example of discrimination, is not an appropriate example, because the denial is premised on the lack of benefit produced by aggressive treatment of such neonates.

Consider an example suggestive of the Oregon scheme. Suppose two treatments, T1 and T2, can benefit different groups of patients, G1 and G2 as follows. T1 preserves life for G1's (or provides some other major benefit), but it does not restore a particular function, such as walking, to G1s. T2 not only preserves life for G2s (or provides some other major benefit), but it also enables them to walk again. The Oregon Health Service Commission ranks T2 as a more important service than T1 because it produces a greater net benefit (I ignore the OTA (1991) argument that net benefit is not a major contributor to rank). Sullivan says that it is discriminatory to deny G1s T1, even though a single person would clearly consider relative benefit in deciding between T1 and T2.

The Sullivan/NLCMDD objection can, with charity, be interpreted as a version of Alice's complaint that favoring best outcomes denies her a fair chance t a benefit. Interpreted this way, the Sullivan/NLCMDD objection is that we cannot rule out giving G_1s any chance at the benefit treatment would bring them simply because G_2s would benefit more from the use of our limited resources. In effect, they seem to be saying we should give no weight to best outcomes. As I noted earlier, this extreme position does not seem to match our intuitions in the microrationing case. But neither does the alternative extreme position, that we must always give priority to better outcomes. The point is that a rationing approach that ranks services by net benefit, whether it turns out to be Oregon's scheme or simply Hadorn's (1991) alternative proposal, thus carries with it unsolved moral issues. To justify ranking by net benefit we must be prepared to address those underlying issues.

The Priorities Problem

Oregon's (intended) methodology of ranking by net benefit also ignores the moral issues I group here as the priorities problem. Suppose that two treatment condition pairs give equal net benefits. (Remember, this [does] not generally mean they produce the same health outcomes, only the same net benefits). Then the OHSC should rank them equal in importance. But now suppose that people with C_1 are more seriously impaired by their disease or disability than people with C_2. Though T_1 and T_2 produce equivalent net gains in benefit, people with C_2 will end up better off than people with C_1, since they started out better off. Nothing in the method of ranking treatment/condition pairs by net benefit responds to this difference between C_1s and C_2s. Nevertheless, most of us would judge it more important to give services to C_1s than it is to give them to C_2s under these conditions. We feel at least some inclination to help those worse off than those better off. For example, if C_1s after treatment were no better off than C_2s before treatment, we are more strongly inclined to give priority to the worse off. Our concern to respect that priority might decline if the effect of treating C_1s but not C_2s is that C_1s end up better off than C_2s. How troubled we would be by this outcome might depend on how great the new equality turned out to be, or on how significant the residual impairment of C_2s was.

Suppose now that there is greater net benefit from giving T_2 to C_2s than there is from giving T_1 to C_1s. If C_1s are sufficiently worse off to start with than T_2s, and if C_1s end up worse off or not significantly better off than C_2s, then our concern about priorities may compel us to forego the greater net benefit that results from giving T_2 to C_2s. But how much priority we give to the worst off still remains unclear. If we can only give a very modest improvement to the worst off, but we must forego a very significant improvement to those initially better off, then we may overrule our concern for the worst off. Our intuitions do not pull us toward a strict priority for the worst off.

Just what the structure of our concern about priority is, however, remains unclear. The unsolved priorities problem not only affects a methodology that ranks by net benefit or by net QLY's. It affects cost/benefit and cost/effectiveness rankings, including Eddy's (1991a) "willingness to pay" methodology. So too does the aggregation problem, to which I now briefly turn.

The Aggregation Problem

In June of 1990, the Oregon Health Services Commission released a list of treatment/condition pairs ranked by a cost/benefit calculation. Critics were quick to seize on rankings that seemed completely counter-intuitive. For example, as Hadorn noted (1991), toothcapping was ranked higher than appendectomy. The reason was simple: an appendectomy cost about $4,000, many times the cost of capping a tooth. Simply aggregating the net medical benefit of many capped teeth yielded a net benefit greater than that produced by one appendectomy.

Eddy (1991b) points out that our intuitions in these cases are largely based on comparing treatment/condition pairs for their importance on a one:one basis. One appendectomy is more important than one toothcapping because it saves a life rather than merely reduces pain and preserves dental function. But our intuitions are much less developed when it comes to making one:many comparisons (though we can establish indifference curves that capture trades we are willing to make; cf. Nord 1992). When does saving more lives through one technology mean we should forego saving fewer through another? The complex debate about whether "numbers count" has a bearing on rationing problems. How many legs should we be willing to forego saving in order to save one life? How many eyes? How many teeth? Can we aggregate *any* small benefits, or only those that are in some clear way significant, when we want to weigh these benefits against clearly significant benefits (e.g. saving a life) to a few? Kamm (1987, 1993) argues persuasively that we should not favor saving one life and curing a sore throat over saving a different life, because curing a sore throat is not a "competitor" with saving a life. She also argues that benefits that someone is morally not required to sacrifice in order to save another's life also have significant standing and can be aggregated. If we are not required to sacrifice an arm in order to save someone's life, then we can aggregate arms saved and weigh them against lives saved. She suggests that our judgments about aggregation differ if we are in contexts where saving lives rather than inducing harms (positive vs. negative duties) are at issue.

Kamm shows that we are not straightforward aggregators of all benefits and that our moral views are both complex and difficult to explicate in terms of well-ordered principles. These views are not compatible with the straightforward aggregation (sum ranking) that is presupposed by the dominant methodologies derived from welfare economies. Yet we do permit, indeed require, some forms of aggregation. Our philosophical task is to specify which principles governing aggregation have the strongest justification. If it appears there is no plausible, principled account of aggregation, then we have strong reason to rely instead on fair procedures and an obligation to give any of them.

The Democracy Problem

When Sullivan rejected Oregon's application for a Medicaid waiver, he complained that the methodology for assessing net medical benefit drew on biased or discriminatory public attitudes toward disabilities. Adapting Kaplan's (Kaplan and Anderson 1990) "quality of wellbeing" scale for use in measuring the benefit of medical treatments. Oregon surveyed residents, asking them to judge on a scale of 0 (death) to 100 (perfect health) what the impact would be of having to live the rest of one's life with some physical or mental impairment or symptom; for example, wearing eyeglasses was rated 95 out of 100, for a weighting of −0.05. Many of these judgments seem

downright bizarre, whether or not they reflect bias. For example, having to wear eyeglasses was rated slightly worse than the −0.046 weighting assigned to not being able to drive a car or use public transportation or the −0.049 assigned to having to stay at a hospital or nursing home. Other weightings clearly reflected cultural attitudes and possibly bias: having trouble with drugs or alcohol was given the second most negative weighting (−0.455) of all conditions, much worse than, for example, having a bad burn over large areas of your body (−0.372) or being so impaired that one needs help to eat or go to the bathroom (−0.106). Having to use a walker or wheelchair under your own control was weighted as much worse (−0.373) than having losses of consciousness from seizures, blackouts or coma (−0.114).

Claiming that people who experience a disabling condition, like being unable to walk, tend to give less negative ratings to them than people who have not experienced them, Sullivan argued Oregon was likely to underestimate the benefit of a treatment that left people with such disabilities. Excluding such treatments would thus be the result of public bias.[1] His complaint carries over to other methodologies, e.g., Eddy's (1991) willingness-to-pay approach and the use of QLY's in cost-effectiveness or cost-benefit analyses.

Sullivan's complaint raises an interesting question. Whose judgments about the effects of a condition should be used? Those who do not have a disabling condition may suffer from cultural biases, overestimating the impact of disability. But those who have the condition may rate it as less serious because they have modified their preferences, goals, and values in order to make a "healthy adjustment" to their condition. Their overall dissatisfaction—tapped by these methodologies—may not reflect the impact that would be captured by a measure more directly attuned to the range of capabilities they retain. Still, insisting on the more objective measure has a high political cost and may even seem paternalistic.

Sullivan simply assumes that we must give priority to the judgments made by those experiencing the condition, but that is not so obvious. Clearly, there is something attractive about the idea, embedded in all these methodologies, of assessing the relative impact of conditions on people by asking them what they think about that impact (cf. Menzel 1992). Should we give people what they actually want? Or should we give them what they should want, correcting for various defects in their judgment? What corrections to expressed preferences are plausible?

The democracy problem arises at another level in procedures that purport to be directly democratic. The Oregon plan called for the OHSC to respect "community values" in its ranking of services. Because prevention and family planning services were frequently discussed in community meetings, the OHSC assigned the categories including those services very high ranking. Consequently, in Oregon, vasectomies are ranked more important than hip replacements. Remember the priority and aggregation problems: it would seem more important to restore mobility to someone who cannot walk than to improve the convenience of birth control through vasectomy in several people. But, assuming that the Commissioners properly interpreted the wishes of Oregonians, that is not what Oregonians wanted the rankings to be. Should we treat this as error? Or must we abide by whatever the democratic process yields?

Thus far I have characterized the problem of democracy as a problem of error: a fair democratic process, or a methodology that rests in part on expressions of preferences, leads to judgments that deviate from either intuitive or theoretically based judgments about the relative importance of certain health outcomes or services. The problem is how much weight to give the intuitive or theoretically based judgments as opposed to the expressed preferences. The point should be put in another way as well. Should we in the end think of the democratic process as a matter of pure procedural justice? If so, then we have no way to correct the judgment made through the process, for what it determines to be fair is what counts as fair. Or should we really consider the democratic process as an impure and imperfect form of procedural justice? Then it is one that can be corrected by appeal to some prior notion of what constitutes a fair outcome of rationing. I suggest that we do not yet know the answer to this question, and we will not be able to answer it until we work harder at providing a theory of rationing.

Conclusion

I conclude with a plea against provincialism. The four problems I illustrated have their analogues in the rationing of goods other than health care. To flesh out a principle that says "people are equal before the law" will involve decisions about how to allocate legal services among all people who can make plausible claims to need them by citing that principle. Similarly, to give content to a principle that assumes equal educational opportunity will involve decisions about resource allocation very much like those involved in rationing health care. Being provincial about health care rationing will prevent us from seeing the relationships among these rationing problems. Conversely, a rationing theory will have greater force if it derives from consideration of common types of problems that are independent of the kinds of goods whose distribution is in question. I am suggesting that exploring a theory of rationing in this way is a prolegomenon to serious work in "applied ethics."

REFERENCES

Brock, Dan. 1988. "Ethical Issues in Recipient Selection for Organ Transplantation." In D. Mathieu (ed.) *Organ Substitution Technology: Ethical, Legal, and Public Policy Issues*. Boulder: Westview, pp. 86–99.

Broome, John. 1987. "Fairness and the Random Distribution of Goods." (unpublished manuscript).

Capron, Alexander. 1992. "Oregon's Disability: Principles or Politics?" *Hastings Center Report* 22: 6 November–December): 18–20.

Daniels, Norman. 1985. *Just Health Care*. Cambridge: Cambridge University Press.

Daniels, Norman. 1988. *Am I My Parents' Keeper? An Essay on Justice Between the Young and the Old*. New York: Oxford University Press.

Daniels, Norman. 1992. "Liberalism and Medical Ethics," *Hastings Center Report*. 22: 6 (November–December): 41–3.

Eddy, D. 1991a. "Rationing by Patient Choice," *JAMA* 265: 1 (January 2): 105–08.

Eddy, D. 1991b. "Oregon's Methods: Did Cost-Effectiveness Analysis Fail?" *JAMA* 266: 15 (October 16): 2135–41.

Elster, John. 1992. *Local Justice: How Institutions Allocate Scarce Goods and Necessary Burdens*. New York: Russel Sage.

Emanuel, Ezekiel. 1991. *The Ends of Human Life: Medical Ethics in a Liberal Polity*, Cambridge. MA: Harvard University Press.

Gauthier, D. 1986. *Morals By Agreement*, Oxford: Oxford University Press.

Hadorn, David. 1992. "The Problem of Discrimination in Health Care Priority Setting," *JAMA* 268: 11 (16 September): 1454–59.

Kamm, Frances. 1987. "Choosing Between People: Commonsense Morality and Doctors' Choices," *Bioethics* 1: 255–71.

Kamm, Frances. 1989. "The Report of the US Task Force on Organ Transplantation: Criticisms and Alternatives," *Mount Sinai Journal of Medicine* 56: 207–20.

Kamm, Frances. 1993. *Morality and Mortality, Vol. 1.* Oxford: Oxford University Press.

Kaplan, R. M. Anderson, J. P. 1990. "The General Health Policy Model: An Integrated Approach." In B. Spilker (ed.) *Quality of Life Assessments in Clinical Trials.* New York: Raven Press.

Menzel, Paul. 1989. *Strong Medicine.* New York: Oxford University Press.

Menzel, Paul. 1992. "Oregon's Denial: Disabilities and Quality of Life," *Hastings Center Report* 22: 6 (November–December): 21–25.

National Legal Center for the Medically Dependent and Disabled. 1991. Letter to Representative Christopher H. Smith.

Nord, Eric. 1992. "The Relevance of Health State After Treatment in Prioritising Between Different Patients," *Journal of Medical Ethics*, (forthcoming).

Office of Technology Assessment. 1991. *Evaluation of the Oregon Medicaid Proposal.* U.S. Congress (final draft in press).

Oregon Health Services Commission. 1991. *Prioritization of Health Services: A Report to the Governor and Legislature.*

Rawls, John. 1971. *A Theory of Justice.* Cambridge, MA: Harvard University Press.

Scanlon, Thomas. 1982. "Contractualism and Utilitarianism." In Amartya Sen and Bernard Williams, eds. *Utilitarianism and Beyond*, pp. 103–28. Cambridge: Cambridge University Press.

Sullivan, Louis. 1992. Press Release (August 3. 1992). Health and Human Services Press Office.

Walzer, Michael. 1983. *Spheres of Justice.* New York: Basic.

NOTE

1. The OTA (1991) notes that men gave dismenorhea a greater negative weight than women. The effect of this weighting is that greater net benefit, and thus higher rank accrues to treating dismenorhea if we include the judgments of men than if we counted only the judgments of women.

The Allocation of Exotic Medical Lifesaving Therapy

NICHOLAS RESCHER

Rescher addresses the problem of fairly allocating scarce medical resources when the critical question is: Whose life should be saved? He distinguishes between (1) criteria for selecting candidates to be seriously considered for a therapy and (2) criteria for choosing final recipients from the list of candidates. He maintains that five plausible criteria should be used to select the final recipients: (1) the relative likelihood of success of the therapy, (2) the life expectancy of the patient, (3) the nature of the patient's relationships with his immediate family, (4) the patient's likely pattern of future services to be rendered to society, and (5) the patient's past services and contributions.

I. The Problem

Technological progress has in recent years transformed the limits of the possible in medical therapy. However, the elevated state of sophistication of modern medical technology has brought the economists' classic problem of scarcity in its wake as an unfortunate side product. The enormously so-

phisticated and complex equipment and the highly trained teams of experts requisite for its utilization are scarce resources in relation to potential demand. The administrators of the great medical institutions that preside over these scarce resources thus come to be faced increasingly with the awesome choice: *Whose life to save?*

A (somewhat hypothetical) paradigm example of this problem may be sketched within the following set of definitive assumptions: We suppose that persons in some particular medically morbid condition re "mortally afflicted": It is virtually certain that they will die within a short time period (say ninety days). We assume that some very complex course of treatment (e.g., a heart transplant) represents a substantial probability of life prolongation for persons in this mortally afflicted condition. We assume that the facilities available in terms of human resources, mechanical instrumentalities, and requisite materials (e.g., hearts in the case of heart transplant) make it possible to give a certain treatment—this "exotic (medical) lifesaving therapy," or ELT for short—to a certain, relatively small number of people. And finally we assume that a substantially greater pool of people in the mortally afflicted condition is at hand. The problem then may be formulated as follows: How is one to select within the pool of afflicted patients the ones to be given the ELT treatment in question; how to select those "whose lives are to be saved"? Faced with many candidates for an ELT process that can be made available to only a few, doctors and medical administrators confront the decision of who is to be given a chance at survival and who is, in effect, to be condemned to die.

As has already been implied, the "heroic" variety of spare-part surgery can pretty well be assimilated to this paradigm. One can foresee the time when heart transplantation, for example, will have become pretty much a routine medical procedure, albeit on a very limited basis, since a cardiac surgeon with the technical competence to transplant hearts can operate at best a rather small number of times each week and the elaborate facilities for such operations will most probably exist on a modest scale. Moreover, in "sparepart" surgery there is always the problem of availability of the "spare parts" themselves. A report in one British newspaper gives the following picture: "Of the 150,000 who die of heart disease each year [in the U.K.], Mr. Donald Longmore, research surgeon at the National Heart Hospital [in London] estimated that 22,000 might be eligible for heart surgery. Another 30,000 would need heart and lung transplants. But there are probably only between 7,000 and 14,000 potential donors a year." Envisaging this situation in which at the very most something like one in four heart-malfunction victims can be saved, we clearly confront a problem in ELT allocation.

A perhaps even more drastic case in point is afforded by long-term haemodialysis, an ongoing process by which a complex device—an "artificial kidney machine"—is used periodically in cases of chronic renal failure to substitute for a nonfunctional kidney in "cleaning" potential poisons from the blood. Only a few major institutions have chronic haemodialysis units, whose complex operation is an extremely expensive proposition. For the present and foreseeable future the situation is that "the number of places available for chronic haemodialysis is hopelessly inadequate."

The traditional medical ethos has insulated the physician against facing the very existence of this problem. When swearing the Hippocratic Oath, he commits himself to work for the benefit of the sick in "whatsoever house I enter." In taking this stance, the physician substantially renounces the explicit choice of saving certain lives rather than others. Of course, doctors have always in fact had to face such choices on the battlefield or in times of disaster, but there the issue had to be resolved hurriedly, under pressure and in circumstances in which the very nature of the case effectively precluded calm deliberation by the decision maker as well as criticism by others. In sharp contrast, however, cases of the type we have postulated in the present discussion arise predictably, and represent choices to be made deliberately and "in cold blood."

It is, to begin with, appropriate to remark that this problem is not fundamentally a medical problem. For when there are sufficiently many afflicted candidates for ELT then—so we may assume—there will also be more than enough for whom the purely medical grounds for ELT allocation are decisively strong in any individual case, and just about equally strong throughout the group. But in this circumstance a selection of some afflicted patients over and against others cannot *ex hypothesi* be made on the basis of purely medical considerations.

The selection problem, as we have said, is in substantial measure not a medical one. It is a problem *for* medical men, which must somehow be solved by them, but that does not make it a medical issue—any more than the problem of hospital building is a medical issue. As a problem it belongs to the category of philosophical problems—specifically a problem of moral philosophy or ethics. Structurally, it bear's a substantial kinship with those issues in this field that revolve about the notorious whom-to-save-on-the-lifeboat and whom-to-throw-to the wolves-pursuing-the-sled questions. But whereas questions of this just-indicated sort are artificial, hypothetical, and farfetched, the ELT issue poses a genuine policy question for the responsible administrators in medical institutions, indeed a question that threatens to become commonplace in the foreseeable future.

Now what the medical administrator needs to have, and what the philosopher is presumably *ex officio* in a position to help in providing, is a body of *rational guidelines* for making choices in these literally life-or-death situations. This is an issue in which many interested parties have a substantial stake, including the responsible decision maker who wants to satisfy his conscience that he is acting in a reasonable way. Moreover; the family and associates of the man who is turned away—to say nothing of the man himself—have the right to an acceptable explanation. And indeed even the general public wants to know that what is being done is fitting and proper. All of these interested parties are entitled to insist that a reasonable code of operating principles provides a defensible rationale for making the life-and-death choices involved in ELT.

II. The Two Types of Criteria

Two distinguishable types of criteria are bound up in the issue of making ELT choices. We shall call these *Criteria of Inclusion* and *Crieria* of *Comparison*, respectively. The distinction at issue here requires some explanation. We can think of the selection as being made by a two-stage process: (1) the selection from among all possible candidates (by a suitable screening process) of a group to be taken under serious consideration as candidates for therapy, and then (2) the actual singling out, within this group, of the particular individuals to whom therapy is to be given. Thus the first process narrows down the range of comparative choices by eliminating en bloc whole categories of potential candidates. The second process calls for a more refined case-by-case comparison of those candidates that remain. By means of the first set of criteria one forms a selection group; by means of the second set, an actual selection is made within this group.

Thus what we shall call a "selection system" fo the choice of patients to receive therapy of the ELT type will consist of criteria of these two kinds. Such system will be acceptable only when the reasonable ness of its component criteria can be established.

III. Essential Features of an Acceptable ELT Selection System

To qualify as reasonable, an ELT selection must mee two important "regulative" requirements: it must be simple enough to be readily intelligible, and it mus be *plausible*, that is, patently reasonable in a way tha can be apprehended easily and without involving ramified subtleties. Those medical administrators responsible for ELT choices must follow a modus operandi that virtually all the people involved can readily understand to be acceptable (at a reasonable level of generality, at any rate). Appearances are critically important here. It is not enough that the choice he made in a *justifiable* way; it must be possible for people—plain people to "see" (i.e., understand without elaborate teaching or indoctrination) that *it is justified*, insofar as any mode of procedure can be justified in cases of this sort.

One "constitutive" requirement is obviously an essential feature of a reasonable selection system: all of its component criteria—those of inclusion and those of comparison alike—must be reasonable: in the sense of being *rationally defensible*. The ramifications of this requirement call for detailed consideration. But one of its aspects should be noted without further ado: it must be *fair*—it must treat relevantly like cases alike, leaving no room for "influence" or favoritism, etc.

IV. The Basic Screening Stage: Criteria of Inclusion (and Exclusion)

Three sorts of considerations are prominent among the plausible criteria of inclusion/exclusion at the basic screening stage: the constituency factor; the progress-of-science factor, and the prospect-of-success factor.

A. The Constituency Factor

It is a "fact of life" that ELT, can be available only in the institutional setting of a hospital or medical institute or the like. Such institutions generally have normal clientele boundaries. A veterans' hospital will not concern itself primarily with treating non-veterans, a children's hospital cannot be expected to accommodate the "senior citizen," an army hospital can regard college professors as outside its sphere. Sometimes the boundaries are geographic—a state hospital may admit only residents of a certain state. There are, of course, indefensible constituency principles—say race or religion, party membership, or ability to pay; and there are cases of borderline legitimacy e.g., sex. A medical institution is justified in considering for ELT only persons within its own constituency, provided this constituency is constituted upon a defensible basis. Thus the haemodialysis selection committee in Seattle "agreed to consider only those applications who were residents of the state of Washington. . . . They justified this stand on the grounds that since the basic: research . . . had been done at . . . a state-supported institution—the people whose taxes had paid for the research should be its first beneficiaries." While thus insisting that constituency considerations represent a valid and legitimate factor in ELT selection, I do feel there is much to be said for minimizing their role in life-or-death cases. Indeed a refusal to recognize them at all is a significant part of medical tradition, going back to the very oath of Hippocrates. They represent a departure from the ideal arising with the institutionalization of medicine, moving it away from its original status as an art practiced by an individual practitioner.

B. The Progress-of-Science Factor

The needs of medical research can provide a second valid principle of inclusion. The research interests of the medical staff in relation to the specific nature of the cases at issue is a significant consideration. It may be important for the progress of medical science—and thus of potential benefit to many persons in the future—to determine how effective the ELT at issue is with diabetics or persons over sixty or with a negative Rh factor. Considerations of this sort represent another type of legitimate factor in ELT selection.

A very definitely *borderline* case under this head would revolve around the question of a patient's willingness to pay, not in monetary terms, but in offering himself as an experimental subject, say by contracting to return at designated times for a series of tests substantially unrelated to his own health, but yielding data of importance to medical knowledge in general.

C. The Prospect-of-Success Factor

It may be that while the ELT at issue is not without *some* effectiveness in general, it has been established to be highly effective only with patients in certain specific categories (e.g., females under forty of a specific blood type). This difference in effectiveness—in the absolute or in the probability of success—is (we assume) so marked as to constitute virtually a difference in kind rather than in degree. In this case, it would be perfectly legitimate to adopt the general rule of making the ELT at issue available only or primarily to persons in this substantial-promise-of-success category. (It is on grounds of this sort that young children and persons over fifty are generally ruled out as candidates for haemodialysis.)

We have maintained that the three factors of constituency, progress of science, and prospect of success represent legitimate criteria of inclusion for ELT selection. But it remains to examine the considerations which legitimate them. The legitimating factors are in the final analysis practical or pragmatic in nature. From the practical angle it is advantageous—indeed to some extent necessary—that the arrangements governing medical institutions should embody certain constituency principles. It makes good pragmatic and utilitarian sense that progress-of-science considerations should be operative here. And, finally, the practical aspect is reinforced by a whole host of other considerations—including moral ones—in supporting the prospect-of-success criterion. The workings of each of these factors are of course conditioned by the ever-present element of limited availability. They are operative only in this context, that is, prospect of success is a legitimate consideration at all only because we are dealing with a situation of scarcity.

V. The Final Selection Stage: Criteria of Selection

Five sorts of elements must, as we see it, figure primarily among the plausible criteria of selection that are to be brought to bear in further screening the group constituted after application of the criteria of inclusion: the relative-likelihood-of-success factor, the life, expectancy factor, the family role factor, the potential contributions factor, and the services-rendered factor. The first two represent the *biomedical* aspect, the second three the *social* aspect.

A. The Relative-Likelihood-of-Success Factor

It is clear that the relative likelihood of success is a legitimate and appropriate factor in making a selection within the group of qualified patients that are to receive ELT. This is obviously one of the considerations that must count very significantly in a reasonable selection procedure.

The present criterion is of course closely related to item C of the preceding section. There we were concerned with prospect-of-success considerations categorically and en bloc. Here at present they come into play in a particularized case-by-case comparison among individuals. If the therapy at issue is not a once-and-for-all proposition and requires ongoing treatment, cognate considerations must be brought in. Thus, for example, in the case of a chronic ELT procedure such as haemodialysis it would clearly make sense to give priority, to patients with a potentially reversible condition (who would thus need treatment for only a fraction of their remaining lives).

B. The Life-Expectancy Factor

Even if the ELT is "successful" in the patient's case he may, considering his age and/or other aspects of his general medical condition, look forward to only a very short probable future life. This is obviously, another factor that must be taken into account.

C. The Family Role Factor

A person's life is a thing of importance not only to himself but to others—friends, associates, neighbors, colleagues, etc. But his (or her) relationship to his immediate family is a thing of unique intimacy and significance. The nature of his relationship to his wife, children, and parents, and the issue of their financial and psychological dependence upon him, are obviously matters that deserve to be given weight in the ELT selection. Other things being anything like equal, the mother of minor children must take priority over the middle-aged bachelor.

D. The Potential-Future-Contributions Factor (Prospective Service)

In "choosing to save" one life rather than another, "the society," through the mediation of the particular medical institution in question—which should certainly look upon itself as a trustee for the social interest—is clearly warranted in considering the likely pattern of future *services to be rendered* by the patient (adequate recovery assumed), considering his age, talent, training, and past record of performance. In its allocations of ELT, society "invests" a scarce resource in one person as against another and is thus entitled to look to the probable prospective "return" on its investment.

It may well be that a thoroughly egalitarian society is reluctant to put someone's social contribution into the scale in situations of the sort at issue. One popular article states that "the most difficult standard would be the candidate's value to society," and goes on to quote someone who said: "You can't just pick a brilliant painter over a laborer. The average citizen would be quickly eliminated." But what if it were not a brilliant painter but a brilliant surgeon or medical researcher that was at issue? One wonders if the author of the *obiter dictum* that one "can't just pick" would still feel equally sure of his ground. In any case, the fact that the standard is difficult to apply is certainly no reason for not attempting to apply it. The problem of ELT selection is inevitably burdened with difficult standards.

Some might feel that in assessing a patient's value to society one should ask not only who if permitted to continue living can make the greatest contribution to society in some creative or constructive way, but also who by dying would leave behind the greatest burden on society in assuming the discharge of their residual responsibilities. Certainly the philosophical utilitarian would give equal weight to both these considerations. Just here is where I would part ways with orthodox utilitarianism. For—though this is not the place to do so—I should be prepared to argue that a civilized society has an obligation to promote the furtherance of positive achievements in cultural and related areas even if this means the assumption of certain added burdens.

.The Past-Services-Rendered Factor (Retrospective Service)

A person's services to another person or group have always been taken to constitute a valid basis for a claim upon this person or group—of course a moral and not necessarily a legal claim. Society's obligation for the recognition and reward of services rendered—an obligation whose discharge is also very possibly conducive to self-interest in the long run—is thus another factor to be taken into account. This should be viewed as a morally necessary correlative of the previously considered factor of *prospective* service. It would be morally indefensible of society in effect to say: "Never mind about services you rendered yesterday—it is only the services to be rendered tomorrow that will count with us today." We live in very future-oriented times, constantly preoccupied in a distinctly utilitarian way with future satisfactions. And this disinclines us to give much recognition to past services. But parity considerations of the sort just adduced indicate that such recognition should be given *on grounds of equity*. No doubt a justification for giving weight to services rendered can also be attempted along utilitarian lines. ("The reward of past services rendered spurs people on to greater future efforts and is thus socially advantageous in the long-run future.") In saying that past services should be counted "on grounds of equity"—rather than "on grounds of utility"—I take the view that even if this utilitarian defense could somehow be shown to be fallacious, I should still be prepared to maintain the propriety of taking services rendered into account. The position does not rest on a utilitarian basis and so would not collapse with the removal of such a basis.

As we have said, these five factors fall into three groups: the biomedical factors *A* and *B*, the familial factor *C*, and the social factors *D* and *E*. With items *A* and *B* the need for a detailed analysis of the medical considerations comes to the fore. The age of the patient, his medical history, his physical and psychological condition, his specific disease, etc., will all need to be taken into exact account. These biomedical factors represent technical issues: they call for the physicians' expert judgment and the medical statisticians' hard data. And they are ethically uncontrover-

sial factors—their legitimacy and appropriateness are evident from the very nature of the case.

Greater problems arise with the familial and social factors. They involve intangibles that are difficult to judge. How is one to develop subcriteria for weighing the relative social contributions of (say) an architect or a librarian or a mother of young children? And they involve highly problematic issues. (For example, should good moral character be rated a plus and bad a minus in judging services rendered?) And there is something strikingly unpleasant in grappling with issues of this sort for people brought up in times greatly inclined towards maxims of the type "Judge not!" and "Live and let live!" All the same, in the situation that concerns us here such distasteful problems must be faced, since a failure to choose to save some is tantamount to sentencing all. Unpleasant choices are intrinsic to the problem of ELT selection; they are of the very essence of the matter.

But is reference to all these factors indeed inevitable? The justification for taking account of the medical factors is pretty obvious. But why should the social aspect of services rendered and to be rendered be taken into account at all? The answer is that they must be taken into account not from the *medical* but from the *ethical* point of view. Despite disagreement on many fundamental issues, moral philosophers of the present day are pretty well in consensus that the justification of human actions is to be sought largely and primarily—if not exclusively—in the principles of utility and of justice. But utility requires reference of services to be rendered and justice calls for a recognition of services that have been rendered. Moral considerations would thus demand recognition of these two factors. (This, of course, still leaves open the question of whether the point of view provides a valid basis of action: Why base one's actions upon moral principles—or, to put it bluntly—Why be moral? The present paper is, however, hardly the place to grapple with so fundamental an issue, which has been canvassed in the literature of philosophical ethics since Plato.)

VI. More Than Medical Issues Are Involved

An active controversy has of late sprung up in medical circles over the question of whether non-physician laymen should be given a role in ELT selection (in the specific context of chronic haemo-dialysis). One physician writes: "I think that the assessment of the candidates should be made by a senior doctor on the [dialysis] unit but I am sure that it would be helpful to him—both in sharing responsibility and in avoiding personal pressure—if a small unnamed group of people [presumably including laymen] officially made the final decision. I visualize the doctor bringing the data to the group, explaining the points in relation to each case, and obtaining their approval of his order of priority."

Essentially this procedure of a selection committee of laymen has for some years been in use in one of the most publicized chronic dialysis units, that of the Swedish Hospital of Seattle, Washington. Many physicians are apparently reluctant to see the choice of allocation of medical therapy pass out of strictly medical hands. Thus in a recent symposium on the "Selection of Patients for Haemodialysis," Dr. Ralph Shakman writes: "Who is to implement the selection? In my opinion it must ultimately be the responsibility of the consultants in charge of the renal units . . . I can see no reason for delegating this responsibility to lay persons. Surely the latter would be better employed if they could be persuaded to devote their time and energy to raise more and more money for us to spend on our patients." Other contributors to this symposium strike much the same note. Dr F. M. Parsons writes: In an attempt to overcome . . . difficulties in selection some have advocated introducing certain specified lay people into the discussions. Is it wise? I doubt whether a committee of this type can adjudicate as satisfactorily as two medical colleagues, particularly as successful therapy involves close cooperation between doctor and patient." And Dr. M. A. Wilson writes in the same symposium. "The suggestion has been made that lay panels should select individuals for dialysis from among a group who are medically suitable. Though this would relieve the doctor-in-charge of a heavy load of responsibility, it would place the burden on those who have no personal knowledge and have to base their judgments on medical or social reports. I do not believe this would result in better decisions for the group or improve the doctor–patient relationship in individual cases."

But no amount of flag waving about the doctor's facing up to his responsibility—or prostrations before the idol of the doctor-patient relationship and reluc-tance to admit laymen into the sacred precincts of the conference chambers of medical consultations—can obscure the essential fact that ELT selection is not wholly medical problem. When there are more tha[n] enough places in an ELT program to accommodate a[ll] who need it, then it will clearly be a medical questio[n] to decide who does have the need and which amon[g] these would successfully respond. But when an ad-mitted gross insufficiency of places exists, when ther[e] are ten or fifty or one hundred highly eligible candi-dates for each place in the program, then it is unreal-istic to take the view that purely medical criteria ca[n] furnish a sufficient basis for selection. The questio[n] of ELT selection becomes serious as a phenomeno[n] of scale—because, as more candidates present them-selves, strictly medical factors are increasingly les[s] adequate as a selection criterion precisely because b[y] numerical category-crowding there will be more an[d] more cases whose "status is much the same" so far a[s] purely medical considerations go.

The ELT selection problem clearly poses issues that transcend the medical sphere because—in the nature of the case—many residual issues remain to be dealt with once *all* of the medical questions have been faced. Because of this there is good reason why laymen as well as physicians should be involved in the selection process. Once the medical considerations have been brought to bear, fundamental social issues remain to be resolved. The instrumentalities of ELT have been created through the social investment of scarce resources, and the interests of the society deserve to play a role in their utilization. As representatives of their social interests, lay opinions should function to complement and supplement medical views once the proper arena of medical considerations is left behind. Those physicians who have urged the presence of lay members on selection panels can, from this point of view, be recognized as having seen the issue in proper perspective.

One physician has argued against lay representation on selection panels for haemodialysis as follows:

"If the doctor advises dialysis and the lay panel refuses, the patient will regard this as a death sentence passed by an anonymous court from which he has no right of appeal." But this drawback is not specific to the use of a lay panel. Rather, it is a feature inherent in every *selection* procedure, regardless of whether the selection is done by the head doctor of the unit, by a panel of physicians, etc. No matter who does the selecting among patients recommended for dialysis, the feelings of the patient who has been rejected and knows it) can be expected to be much the same, provided that he recognizes the actual nature of the choice (and is not deceived by the possibly convenient but ultimately poisonous fiction that because the selection was made by physicians it was made entirely on medical grounds).

In summary, then, the question of ELT selection would appear to be one that is in its very nature heavily laden with issues of medical research, practice, and administration. But it will not be a question that can be resolved on solely medical grounds. Strictly social issues of justice and utility will invariably arise in this area—questions going outside the medical area in whose resolution medical laymen can and should play a substantial role.

VII. The Inherent Imperfection (Non-Optimality) of Any Selection System

Our discussion to this point of the design of a selection system for ELT has left a gap that is a very fundamental and serious omission. We have argued that five factors must be taken into substantial and explicit account:

A. *Relative likelihood of success*. Is the chance of the treatment's being "successful" to be rated as high, good, average, etc.?

B. *Expectancy of future life*. Assuming the "success" of the treatment, how much longer does the patient stand a good chance (75 per cent or better) of living—considering his age and general condition?

C. *Family role*. To what extent does the patient have responsibilities to others in his immediate family?

D. *Social contributions rendered*. Are the patient's past services to his society outstanding, substantial, average, etc.?

E. *Social contributions to be rendered*. Considering his age, talents, training, and past record of performance, is there a substantial probability that the patient will—*adequate recovery being assured*—render in the future services to his society that can be characterized as outstanding, substantial, average, etc.?

This list is clearly insufficient for the construction of a reasonable selection system, since that would require not only *that these factors be taken into account* (somehow or other), but—going beyond this—would *specify a specific set of procedures for taking account of them*. The specific procedures that would constitute such a system would have to take account of the interrelationship of these factors (e.g., B and E), and to set out exact guidelines as to the relevant weight that is to be given to each of them. This is something our discussion has not as yet considered.

In fact, I should want to maintain that there is no such thing here as a single rationally superior selection system. The position of affairs seems to me to be something like this: (1) It is necessary (for reasons already canvassed) to have a system, and to have a system that is rationally defensible, and (2) to be rationally defensible, this system must take the factors *A–E* into substantial and explicit account. But (3) the exact manner in which a rationally defensible system takes account of these factors cannot be fixed in any one specific way on the basis of general considerations. Any of the variety of ways that give *A–E* "their due" will be acceptable and viable. One cannot hope to find within this range of workable systems some one that is optimal in relation to the alternatives. There is no one system that does "the (uniquely) best"—only a variety of systems that do "as well as one can expect to do" in cases of this sort.

The situation is structurally very much akin to that of rules of partition of an estate among the relations of a decedent. It is important that there be such rules. And it is reasonable that spouse, children, parents, siblings, etc., be taken account of in these rules. But the question of the exact method of division—say that when the decedent has neither living spouse nor living children then his estate is to be divided, dividing 60 per cent between parents, 40 per cent between siblings versus dividing 90 per cent between parents, 10 per cent between siblings—cannot be settled on the basis of any general abstract considerations of reasonableness. Within broad limits, a variety of resolutions are all perfectly acceptable—so that no one procedure can justifiably be regarded as "the (uniquely) best" because it is superior to all others.

VIII. A Possible Basis for a Reasonable Selection System

Having said that there is no such thing as *the optimal* selection system for ELT, I want now to sketch out the broad features of what I would regard as *one acceptable* system.

The basis for the system would be a point rating. The scoring here at issue would give roughly equal weight to the medical considerations A and B) in comparison with the extramedical considerations (C = family role, D = services rendered, and E = services to be rendered), also giving roughly equal weight to the three items involved here (C, D, and E).The result of such a scoring procedure would provide the essential starting point of our ELT selection mechanism. I deliberately say "starting point" because it seems to me that one should not follow the results of this scoring in an *automatic* way. I would propose that the actual selection should only be guided but not actually be dictated by this scoring procedure, along lines now to be explained.

IX. The Desirability of Introducing an Element of Chance

The detailed procedure I would propose—not of course as optimal (for reasons we have seen), but as eminently acceptable—would combine the scoring procedure just discussed with an element of chance. The resulting selection system would function as follows:

1. First the criteria of inclusion of Section IV above would be applied to constitute a *first phase selection group*—which (we shall suppose) is substantially larger than the number n of persons who can actually be accommodated with ELT.

2. Next the criteria of selection of Section V are brought to bear via a scoring procedure of the type described in Section VIII. On this basis a *second phase selection group* is constituted which is only *somewhat* larger—say by a third or a half—than the critical number n at issue.

3. If this second phase selection group is relatively homogeneous as regards rating by the scoring procedure—that is, if there are no really major disparities within this group (as would be likely if the initial group was significantly larger than n)—then the final selection

is made by *random* selection of n persons from within this group.

This introduction of the element of chance—in what could be dramatized as a "lottery of life and death"—must be justified. The fact is that such a procedure would bring with it three substantial advantages.

First, as we have argued above (in Section VII), any acceptable selection system is inherently nonoptimal. The introduction of the element of chance prevents the results that life-and-death choices are made by the automatic allocation of an admittedly imperfect selection method.

Second, a recourse to chance would doubtless make matters easier for the rejected patient and those who have a specific interest in him. It would surely be quite hard for them to accept his exclusion by relatively mechanical application of objective criteria in whose implementation subjective judgment is involved. But the circumstances of life have conditioned us to accept the workings of chance and to tolerate the element of luck (good or bad): human life is an inherently contingent process. Nobody, after all, has an absolute right to ELT—but most of us would feel that we have "every bit as much right" to it as anyone else in significantly similar circumstances. The introduction of the element of chance assures a like handling of like cases over the widest possible area that seems reasonable in the circumstances.

Third (and perhaps least), such a recourse to random selection does much to relieve the administrators of the selection system of the awesome burden of ultimate and absolute responsibility.

These three considerations would seem to build up a substantial case for introducing the element of chance into the mechanism of the system for ELT selection in a way limited and circumscribed by other weightier considerations, along some such lines as those set forth above.

It should be recognized that this injection of *man-made* chance supplements the element of *natural* chance that is present inevitably and in any case (apart from the role of chance in singling out certain persons as victims for the affliction at issue). As F. M. Parsons has observed: "any vacancies [in an ELT program—specifically haemodialysis] will be filled immediately by the first suitable patients, even though their claims r therapy may subsequently prove less than those of ther patients refused later." Life is a chancy business

and even the most rational of human arrangements can cover this over to a very limited extent at best.

QALYfying the Value of Life

JOHN HARRIS

One utilitarian approach to rationing is to measure objectively the benefits that a treatment is likely to give each patient, then selectively treat particular patients or conditions to maximize total benefits. An often-used objective measure of benefits is known as QALY, or quality-adjusted life year. Harris argues that QALYs discriminate against older people because "saving the lives of younger people is, other things being equal, always likely to be productive of more QALYs than saving older people." QALYs, he says, are also unfair to the disabled for similar reasons. Harris maintains that a crucial failing of QALYs is that these objective measurements cannot accommodate the subjective nature of people's assessments of the value of their own lives.

Against a background of permanently scarce resources it is clearly crucial that such health care resources as are available be not used wastefully. This point is often made in terms of "efficiency" and it is argued, not implausibly, that to talk of efficiency implies that we are able to distinguish between efficient and inefficient use of health care resources, and hence that we are in some sense able to measure the results of treatment. To do so of course we need a standard of measurement. Traditionally, in life-endangering conditions, that standard has been easy to find. Successful treatment removes the danger to life, or at least postpones it, and so the survival rates of treatment have been regarded as a good indicator of success.[1] However, equally clearly, it is also of crucial importance to those treated that the help offered them not only removes the threat to life, but leaves them able to enjoy the remission granted. In short, gives them reasonable quality, as well as extended quantity of life.

A new measure of quality of life which combines length of survival with an attempt to measure the quality of that survival has recently[2] been suggested and is becoming influential. The need for such a measure has been thus described by one of its chief architects: We need a simple, versatile, measure of success which incorporates both life expectancy and quality of life, and which reflects the values and ethics of the community

served. The 'Quality Adjusted Life Year' (QALY) measure fulfills such a role.[3] This is a large claim and an important one; if it can be sustained its consequences for health care will be profound indeed.

There are, however, substantial theoretical problems in the development of such a measure, and more important by far, grave dangers of its misuse. I shall argue that the dangers of misuse, which partly derive from inadequacies in the theory which generates them, make this measure itself a life-threatening device. In showing why this is so I shall attempt to say something positive about just what is involved in making scrupulous choices between people in situations of scarce resources, and I will end by saying something about the entitlement to claim in particular circumstances, that resources are indeed scarce.

We must first turn to the task of examining the QALY and the possible consequences of its use in resource allocation. A task incidentally which, because it aims at the identification and eradication of a life-threatening condition, itself (surprisingly perhaps for a philosophical paper) counts also as a piece of medical research,[4] which if successful will prove genuinely therapeutic.

The QALY
I. What Are QALYs?

It is important to be as clear as possible as to just what a QALY is and what it might be used for. I

From *Journal of Medical Ethics*, vol. 13, no. 3 (September 1987), pp. 117–23. Reprinted with permission from the BMJ Publishing Group.

cannot do better than let Alan Williams, the architect of QALYs referred to above, tell you in his own words:

> The essence of a QALY is that it takes a year of healthy life expectancy to be worth one, but regards a year of unhealthy life expectancy as worth less than 1. Its precise value is lower the worse the quality of life of the unhealthy person (which is what the "quality adjusted" bit is all about). If being dead is worth zero, it is, in principle, possible for a QALY to be negative, ie for the quality of someone's life to be judged worse than being dead.
>
> The general idea is that a beneficial health care activity is one that generates a positive amount of QALYs, and that an efficient health care activity is one where the cost-per-QALY is as low as it can be. A high priority health care activity is one where the cost-per-QALY is low, and a low priority activity is one where cost-per-QALY is high.[5]

The plausibility of the QALY derives from the idea that "given the choice, a person would prefer a shorter healthier life to a longer period of survival in a state of severe discomfort and disability."[6] The idea that any rational person would endorse this preference provides the moral and political force behind the QALY. Its acceptability as a measurement of health then depends upon its doing all the theoretical tasks assigned to it, and on its being what people want, or would want, for themselves.

II. How Will QALY Be Used?

There are two ways in which QALYs might be used. One is unexceptionable and useful, and fully in line with the assumptions which give QALYs their plausibility. The other is none of these.

QALYS might be used to determine which of rival therapies to give to a particular patient or which procedure to use to treat a particular condition. Clearly the one generating the most QALYs will be the better bet, both for the patient and for a society with scarce resources. However, QALYs might also be used to determine not what treatment to give *these* patients, but which group of patients to treat, or which conditions to give priority in the allocation of health care resources. It is clear that it is this latter use which Williams has in mind, for he specifically cites as one of the rewards of the development of QALYs, their use in "priority setting in the health care system in general."[7] It is this use which is likely to be of greatest interest to all those concerned with efficiency in the health service. And it is for this reason that it is likely to be both the most influential and to have the most far-reaching effects. It is this use which is I believe positively dangerous and morally indefensible. Why?

III. What's Wrong with QALYs?

It is crucial to realize that the whole plausibility of QALYS depends upon our accepting that they simply involve the generalization of the "truth"[8] that "given the choice a person would prefer a shorter healthier life to a longer period of survival in a state of severe discomfort." On this view giving priority to treatments which produce more QALYs or for which the cost-per-QALY is low, is both efficient and is also what the community as a whole, and those at risk in particular, actually want. But whereas it follows from the fact that given the choice a person would prefer a shorter healthier life to a longer one of severe discomfort, that the best treatment *for that person is* the one yielding the most QALYs, it does not follow that treatments yielding more QALYs are preferable to treatments yielding fewer where *different people* are to receive the treatments. That is to say, while it follows from the fact (if it is a fact) that I and everyone else would prefer to have, say one year of healthy life rather than three years of severe discomfort, that we value healthy existence more than uncomfortable existence for ourselves, it does not follow that where the choice is between three years of discomfort for *me* or immediate death on the one hand, and one year of health for you, or immediate death on the other, that I am somehow committed to the judgement that you ought to be saved rather than me.

Suppose that Andrew, Brian, Charles, Dorothy, Elizabeth, Fiona and George all have zero life-expectancy without treatment, but with medical care, all but George will get one year's complete remission and George will get seven years' remission. The costs of treating each of the six are equal but George's operation costs five times as much as the cost of the other operations. It does not follow that even if each person, if asked, would prefer seven years' remission to one for themselves, that they are all committed to the view that George should be treated rather than that they should. Nor does it follow that this is a preference that society should endorse. But it is the preference that QALYs dictate.

Such a policy does not value life or lives at all, for it is individuals who are alive, and individuals who lose their lives. And when they do the loss is principally their loss. The value of someone's life is, primarily and overwhelmingly, its value to him or her; the wrong done when an individual's life is cut short is a wrong to that individual. The victim of a murder or a fatal accident is the person who loses his life. A disaster is the greater the more victims there are, the more lives that are lost. A society which values the lives of its citizens is one which tries to ensure that as few of them die prematurely (that is when their lives could continue) as possible. Giving value to life-years or QALYs, has the effect in this case of sacrificing six lives for one. If each of the seven *wants* to go on living for as long as he or she can, if each values the prospective term of remission available, then to choose between them on the basis of life-years (quality adjusted or not), is in this case to give no value to the lives of six people.

IV. The Ethics of QALYs
Although we might be right to claim that people are not committed to QALYs as a measurement of health simply in virtue of their acceptance of the idea that each would prefer to have more QALYs rather than fewer for themselves, are there good moral reasons why QALYs should none the less be accepted?

The idea, which is at the root of both democratic theory and of most conceptions of justice, that each person is as morally important as any other and hence, that the life and interests of each is to be given equal weight, while apparently referred to and employed by Williams plays no part at all in the theory of QALYs. That which is to be given equal weight is not persons and their interests and preferences, but quality-adjusted life-years. And giving priority to the manufacture of QALYs can mean them all going to a few at the expense of the interests and wishes of the many. It will also mean that all available resources will tend to be deployed to assist those who will thereby gain the maximum QALYs—the young.

V. The Fallacy of Valuing Time
There is a general problem for any position which holds that time-spans are of equal value no matter who gets them, and it stems from the practice of valuing life-units (life-years) rather than people's lives.

If what matters most is the number of life-years the world contains, then the best thing we can do is devote our resources to increasing the population. Birth control, abortion and sex education come out very badly on the QALY scale of priorities.

In the face of a problem like this, the QALY advocate must insist that what he wants is to select the therapy that generates the most QALYs for those people who already exist, and not simply to create the maximum number of QALYs. But if it is people and not units of life-span that matter, if the QALY is advocated because it is seen as a moral and efficient way to fulfill our obligation to provide care for our fellows, then it does matter who gets the QALYs—because it matters how people are treated. And this is where the ageism of QALYs and their other discriminatory features become important.

VI. QALYs Are Ageist
Maximizing QALYs involves an implicit and comprehensive ageist bias. For saving the lives of younger people is, other things being equal, always likely to be productive of more QALYs than saving older people. Thus on the QALY arithmetic we always have a reason to prefer, for example, neonatal or pediatric care to all "later" branches of medicine. This is because any calculation of the life-years generated for a particular patient by a particular therapy, must be based on the life expectancy of that patient. The older a patient is when treated, the fewer the life-years that can be achieved by the therapy.

It is true that QALYs dictate that we prefer people, not simply who have *more life expectancy*, but rather people who have *more life expectancy to be gained from treatment*. But wherever treatment saves a life, and this will be frequently, for quite simple treatments, like a timely antibiotic, can be life-saving, it will, other things being equal, be the case that younger people have more life expectancy to gain from the treatment than do older people.

VII. Ageism and Aid
Another problem with such a view is that it seems to imply, for example, that when looking at societies from the outside, those with a lower average age have somehow a greater claim on our aid. This might have important consequences in looking at questions concerning aid policy on a global scale. Of course it is

true that a society's having a low average age might be a good indicator of its need for help, in that it would imply that people were dying prematurely. However, we can imagine a society suffering a disaster which killed off many of its young people (war perhaps) and which was consequently left with a high average age but was equally deserving of aid despite the fact that such aid would inevitably benefit the old. If QALYs were applied to the decision as to whether to provide aid to this society or another much less populous and perhaps with less pressing problems, but with a more normal age distribution, the "older" society might well be judged "not worth" helping.

VIII. QALYs Can Be Racist and Sexist

If a "high priority health care activity is one where the cost-per-QALY is low, and a low priority activity is one where cost-per-QALY is high" then people who just happen to have conditions which are relatively cheap to treat are always going to be given priority over those who happen to have conditions which are relatively expensive to treat. This will inevitably involve not only a systematic pattern of disadvantage to particular groups of patients, or to people afflicted with particular diseases or conditions, but perhaps also a systematic preference for the survival of some kinds of patients at the expense of others. We usually think that justice requires that we do not allow certain sections of the community or certain types of individual to become the victims of systematic disadvantage and that there are good moral reasons for doing justice, not just when it costs us nothing or when it is convenient or efficient, but also and particularly, when there is a price to be paid. We'll return shortly to this crucial issue of justice, but it is important to be clear about the possible social consequences of adopting QALYs.

Adoption of QALYs as the rationale for the distribution of health care resources may, for the above reasons, involve the creation of a systematic pattern of preference for certain racial groups or for a particular gender or, what is the same thing, a certain pattern of discrimination against such groups. Suppose that medical statistics reveal that say women, or Asian males, do better than others after a particular operation or course of treatment, or, that a particular condition that has a very poor prognosis in terms of QALYs afflicts only Jews, or gay men. Such statistics abound and the adoption of QALYs may well dictate very severe and systematic discrimination against groups identified primarily by race, gender or colour, in the allocation of health resources, where it turns out that such groups are vulnerable to conditions that are not QALY-efficient.[9]

Of course it is just a fact of life and far from sinister that different races and genders are subject to different conditions, but the problem is that QALYs may tend to reinforce and perpetuate these "structural" disadvantages.

IX. Double Jeopardy

Relatedly, suppose a particular terminal condition was treatable, and would, with treatment, give indefinite remission but with a very poor quality of life. Suppose for example that if an accident victim were treated, he would survive, but with paraplegia. This might always cash out at fewer QALYs than a condition which with treatment would give a patient perfect remission for about five years after which the patient would die. Suppose that both candidates wanted to go on living as long as they could and so both wanted, equally fervently, to be given the treatment that would save their lives. Is it clear that the candidate with most QALYs on offer should always and inevitably be the one to have priority? To judge so would be to count the paraplegic's desire to live the life that was available to him as of less value than his rival's—what price equal weight to the preferences of each individual?

This feature of QALYs involves a sort of double jeopardy. QALYs dictate that because an individual is unfortunate, because she has once become a victim of disaster, we are required to visit upon her a second and perhaps graver misfortune. The first disaster leaves her with a poor quality of life, and QALYs then require that in virtue of this she be ruled out as a candidate for life-saving treatment, or at best, that she be given little or no chance of benefiting from what little amelioration her condition admits of. Her first disaster leaves her with a poor quality of life and when she presents herself for help, along come QALYs and finish her off!

X. Life-Saving and Life-Enhancing

A distinction, consideration of which is long overdue, is that between treatments which are life-saving (or death-postponing) and those which e simply life-enhancing, in the sense that they improve the quality of life without improving life-expectancy. Most people think, and for good as well as for prudential reasons, that life-saving has priority over life-enhancement and that we should first allocate resources to those areas where they are immediately needed to save life and only when this has been done should the remainder be allocated to alleviating non-fatal conditions. Of course there are exceptions even here and some conditions, while not life-threatening, are so painful that to leave someone in a state of suffering while we attend even to the saving of life, would constitute unjustifiable cruelty. But these situations are rare and for the vast majority of cases we judge that life-saving should have priority.

It is important to notice that QALYs make no such distinction between types of treatment. Defenders of QALYs often cite with pride the example of hip-replacement operations which are more QALY-efficient than say kidney dialysis.[10] While the difficulty of choosing between treating very different groups of patients, some of whom need treatment simply to stay alive, while others need it to relieve pain and distress, is clearly very acute, and while it may be that life-saving should not *always* have priority over life-enhancement, the dangers of adopting QALYs which regard only one dimension of the rival claims, and a dubious one at that, as morally relevant, should be clear enough.

There is surely something fishy about QALYs. They can hardly form "an appropriate basis for health service policy." Can we give an account of just where they are deficient from the point of view of morality? We can, and indeed we have already started to do so. In addition to their other problems, QALYs and their use for priority setting in health care or for choosing not which treatment to give these patients, but for selecting which patients or conditions to treat, involve profound injustice, and if implemented would constitute a denial of the most basic civil rights. Why is this?

Moral Constraints

One general constraint that is widely accepted and that I think most people would judge should govern life and death decisions, is the idea that many people believe expresses the values animating the health service as a whole. These are the belief that the life and health of each person matters, and matters as much as that of any other and that each person is entitled to be treated with equal concern and respect both in the way health resources are distributed and in the way they are treated generally by health care professionals, however much their personal circumstances may differ from that of others.

This popular belief about the values which animate the health service depends on a more abstract view about the source and structure of such values and it is worth saying just a bit about this now.

I. The Value of Life

One such value is the value of life itself. Our own continued existence as individuals is the *sine qua non* of almost everything. So long as we want to go on living, practically everything we value or want depends upon our continued existence. This is one reason why we generally give priority to life-saving over life-enhancing.

To think that *life is valuable*, that in most circumstances, the worst thing that can happen to an individual is that she lose her life when this need not happen, and that the worst thing we can do is make decisions, a consequence of which, is that others die prematurely, we must think that *each life is valuable*. Each life counts for one and that is why more count for more. For this reason we should give priority to saving as many lives as we can, not as many life-years.[11]

One important point must be emphasized at this stage. We talk of "life-saving" but of course this must always be understood as "death-postponing." Normally we want to have our death postponed for as long as possible but where what's possible is the gaining of only very short periods of remission, hours or days, these may not be worth having. Even those who are moribund in this sense can usually recognize this fact, particularly if they are aware that the cost at postponing their death for a few hours or days at the most will mean suffering or death for others. However, even brief remission can be valuable in enabling the individual to put her affairs in order, make farewells and so on, and this can be important. It is for the individual to decide whether the remission that she can be granted is worth having. This is a delicate point that needs more discussion than I can give it here. However, inasmuch as QALYs do not help us to understand the features of a short and painful remission that might none the less make that period of vital importance to the individual, perhaps in terms of making something worthwhile out of her life as a whole, the difficulties of these sorts of circumstances, while real enough, do not undermine the case against QALYs.[12]

II. Treating People as Equals

If each life counts for one, then the life of each has the same value as that of any. This is why accepting the value of life generates a principle of equality. This principle does not of course entail that we treat each person equally in the sense of treating each person *the same*. This would be absurd and self-defeating. What it does involve is the idea that we treat each person with the same concern and respect. An illustration provided by Ronald Dworkin, whose work on equality informs this entire discussion, best illustrates this point: "If I have two children, and one is dying from a disease that is making the other uncomfortable, I do not show equal concern if I flip a coin to decide which should have the remaining dose of a drug."[13]

It is not surprising then that the pattern of protections for individuals that we think of in terms of civil rights[14] centres on the physical protection of the individual and of her most fundamental interests. One of the prime functions of the State is to protect the lives and fundamental interests of its citizens and to treat each citizen as the equal of any other. This is why the State has a basic obligation, *inter alia*, to treat all citizens as equals in the distribution of benefits and opportunities which affect their civil rights. The State must, in short, treat each citizen with equal concern and respect. The civil rights generated by this principle will of course include rights to the allocation of such things as legal protections and educational and health care resources. And this requirement that the State uphold the civil rights of citizens and deal justly between them, means that it must not choose between individuals, or permit choices to be made between individuals, that abridge their civil rights or in ways that attack their right to treatment as equals.

Whatever else this means, it certainly means that a society, through its public institutions, is not entitled to discriminate between individuals in ways that mean life or death for them on grounds which count the lives or fundamental interests of some as worth less than those of others. If for example some people were given life-saving treatment in preference others because they had a better quality of life tha those others, or more dependents and friends, or b cause they were considered more useful, this wou amount to regarding such people as more valuab than others on that account. Indeed it would be ta tamount, literally, to sacrificing the lives of others that they might continue to live.[15]

Because my own life would be better and eve of more value to me if I were healthier, fitter, ha more money, more friends, more lovers, more chil dren, more life expectancy, more everything I wan it does not follow that others are entitled to decid that because I lack some or all of these things I an less entitled to health care resources, or less worth to receive those resources, than are others, or tha those resources would somehow be wasted on me.

III. Civil Rights

I have spoken in terms of civil rights advisedly. If we think of the parallel with our attitude to the system of criminal justice the reasons will be obvious. We think that the liberty of the subject is of fundamental importance and that no one should be wrongfully detained. This is why there are no financial constraints on society's obligation to attempt to ensure equality before the law. An individual is entitled to a fair trial no matter what the financial costs to society (and the can be substantial). We don't adopt rubrics for the allocation of justice which dictate that only those for whom justice can be cheaply provided will receive it. And the reason is that something of fundamental importance is at stake—the liberty of the individual.

In health care something of arguably greater importance is often at stake—the very life of the individual. Indeed, since the abolition of capital punishment [in the United Kingdom], the importance of seeing that individuals' civil rights are respected in health care is pre-eminent.

IV. Discrimination

The only way to deal between individuals in a way which treats them as equals when resources are scarce, is to allocate those resources in a way which exhibits no preference. To discriminate between people on the grounds of quality of life, or QALY, or life-expectancy, is as unwarranted as it would be to discriminate on grounds of race or gender.

So, the problem of choosing how to allocate scarce resources is simple. And by that of course I mean "theoretically simple," not that the decisions will be easy to make or that it will be anything but agonisingly difficult actually to determine, however justly, who should live and who should die. Life-saving resources should simply be allocated in ways which do not violate the individual's entitlement to be treated as the equal of any other individual in the society: and that means the individual's entitlement to have his interests and desires weighed at the same value as those of anyone else. The QALY and the other bases of preference we have considered are irrelevant.

If health professionals are forced by the scarcity of resources, to choose, they should avoid unjust discrimination. But how are they to do this?

Just Distribution

If there were a satisfactory principle or theory of just distribution now would be the time to recommend its use.[14] Unfortunately there is not a satisfactory principle available. The task is to allocate resources between competing claimants in a way that does not violate the individual's entitlement to be treated as the equal of any other individual—and that means her entitlement to have her fundamental interests and desires weighed at the same value as those of anyone else. The QALY and other quality-of-life criteria are, as I we have seen, both dangerous and irrelevant as are considerations based on life-expectancy or on "life-years" generated by the proposed treatment. If health professionals are forced by the scarcity of resources to choose, not *whether* to treat but *who* to treat, they must avoid any method that amounts to unjust discrimination.

I do not pretend that the task of achieving this will be an easy one, nor that I have any satisfactory solution. I do have views on how to approach a solution, but the development of those ideas is a task for another occasion.[15] I will be content for the moment if I have shown that QALYs are not the answer and that efforts to find one will have to take a different direction.

I. Defensive Medicine

While it is true that resources will always be limited it is far from clear that resources for health care are justifiably as limited as they are sometimes made to appear. People within health care are too often forced to consider simply the question of the best way of allocating the *health care budget,** and consequently are forced to compete with each other for resources. Where lives are at stake however, the issue is a moral issue which faces the whole community, and in such circumstances, is one which calls for a fundamental reappraisal of priorities. The question should therefore be posed in terms, not of the health care budget alone, but of the *national budget.*[16] If this is done it will be clearer that it is simply not true that the resources necessary to save the lives of citizens are not available. Since the citizens in question are in real and present danger of death, the issue of the allocation of resources to life-saving is naturally one of, among other things, national defense. Clearly then health professionals who require additional resources simply to save the lives of citizens, have a prior and priority claim on the defense budget.

QALYs encourage the idea that the task for health economics is to find more efficient ways of doing the wrong thing—in this case sacrificing the lives of patients who could be saved. All people concerned with health care should have as their priority defensive medicine: defending their patients against unjust and lethal policies, and guarding themselves against devices that tend to disguise the immorality of what they are asked to do.

II. Priority in Life-Saving

It is implausible to suppose that we cannot deploy vastly greater resources than we do at present to save the lives of all those in immediate mortal danger. It should be only in exceptional circumstances—unforeseen and massive disasters for example—that we cannot achieve this. However, in such circumstances our first duty is to try to save the maximum number of lives possible. This is because, since each person's life is valuable, and since we are committed to treating each person with the same concern and respect that we show to any, we must preserve the lives of as many individuals as we can. To fail to do so would be to value at zero the lives and fundamental interests of those extra people we could, but do not, save. Where we cannot save all, we should select those who are not to be saved in a way that shows no unjust preference.

---

*NOTE: In the United Kingdom, most people receive health care through the publicly financed National Health Service.

We should be very clear that the obligation to save as many lives as possible is *not the obligation to save as many lives as we can cheaply or economically save*. Among the sorts of disasters that force us to choose between lives, is not the disaster of overspending a limited health care budget!

There are multifarious examples of what I have in mind here and just a couple must suffice to illustrate the point. Suppose, as is often the case, providing health care in one region of a country[17] is more expensive than doing so in another, or where saving the lives of people with particular conditions, is radically more expensive than other life-saving procedures, and a given health care budget won't run to the saving of all. Then any formula employed to choose priorities should do just that. Instead of attempting to measure the value of people's lives and select which are worth saving, any rubric for resource allocation should *examine the national budget afresh* to see whether there are any headings of expenditure that are more important to the community than rescuing citizens in mortal danger. For only if all other claims on funding are plausibly more important than that, is it true that resources for life-saving are limited.

III. Conclusion

The principle of equal access to health core is sustained by the very, same reasons that sustain both the principle of equality before the law and the civil rights required to defend the freedom of the individual. These are rightly considered so important that no limit is set on the cost of sustaining them. Equal access to health care is of equal importance and should be accorded the same priority for analogous reasons. Indeed, since the abolition of capital punishment, due process of law is arguably of less vital importance than is access to health care. We have seen that QALYs involve denying that the life and health of each citizen is as important as that of any. If, for example, we applied the QALY principle to the administration of criminal justice we might find that those with little life expectancy would have less to gain from securing their freedom and therefore should not be defended at all, or perhaps given a jury trial only if not in competition for such things with younger or fitter fellow citizens.

A recent BBC television programme calculated[18] that if a health authority had £200,000 to spend it would get 10 QALYs from dialysis of kidney patients, 266 QALYs from hip-replacement operations or 1197 QALYs from anti-smoking propaganda. While this information is undoubtedly useful and while advice to stop smoking is an important part of health care, we should be wary of a formula which seems to dictate that such a health authority would use its resources most efficiently if it abandoned hip replacements and dialysis in favor of advice to stop smoking.

NOTES

1. See the excellent discussion of the recent history of this line of thought in the Office of Health Economics publication *The measurement of health* London, 1985.

2. Williams A. Economics of coronary artery bypass grafting. *British medical journal* 1985; 291; and his contribution to the article, Centre eight—in search of efficiency. *Health and social service journal* 1985. These are by no means the first such attempts. See reference (1).

3. Williams A. The value of QALYs. *Health and social services journal* 1985.

4. I mention this in case anyone should think that it is only medical scientists who do medical research.

5. See reference (3): 3.

6. See reference (l): 16.

7. See reference (3): 5, and reference (3).

8. I'll assume this can be described as "true" for the sake of argument.

9. I am indebted to Dr S G Potts for pointing out to me some of these statistics and for other helpful comments.

10. For examples see reference (1) and reference (2).

11. See Parfit D. Innumerate ethics. *Philosophy and public affairs* 1978; 7, 4 Parfit's arguments provide a detailed defense of the principle that each is to count for one.

12. I consider these problems in more detail in my: eQALYty. In: Byrne P, ed. *King's College studies*. London: King's Fund Press, 1987/8. Forthcoming.

13. Dworkin R. *Taking rights seriously*. London: Duckworth, 1977: 227.

14. I do not of course mean to imply that there are such things as rights, merely that our use of the language of rights captures the special importance we attach to certain freedoms and protections. The term "civil rights" is used here as a "term of art" referring to those freedoms and protections that are customarily classed as "civil rights."

15. For an interesting attempt to fill this gap see Dworkin R. What is equality? *Philosophy and public affairs* 1981; 4 and 5.

16. And of course the international budget; see my *The value of life*. London: Routledge & Kegan Paul 1985: chapter 3.

17. See Townsend P, Davidson N, eds. *Inequalities in health: the Black Report*. Harmondsworth, Penguin: 1982.

18. BBC 1. *The heart of the matter* 1986, Oct.

abortion The ending of a pregnancy.

act-utilitarianism The view that the rightness of actions depends solely on the relative good produced by individual actions.

active euthanasia Performing an action that directly causes someone to die; "mercy killing."

applied ethics The use of moral norms and concepts to resolve practical moral issues.

autonomy A person's rational capacity for self-governance or self-determination.

bioethics Applied ethics focused on health care, medical science, and medical technology.

blinding A procedure for ensuring that subjects and researchers do not know which interventions the subjects receive (standard treatment, new treatment, or placebo).

chromosome A stringlike, gene-containing molecule in the nucleus of a cell.

clinical trial A scientific study designed to test systematically a medical intervention in humans.

cloning The asexual production of a genetically identical entity from an existing one.

cloning, reproductive Cloning aimed at the live birth of an individual.

cloning, therapeutic or research Cloning done for purposes other than producing a live individual.

competence The ability to render decisions about medical interventions.

confidentiality An obligation or pledge of physicians, nurses, and others to keep secret the personal health information of patients unless they consent to disclosure.

consequentialist theory A moral theory asserting that the rightness of actions depends solely on their consequences or results.

contractarianism Moral or political theories based on the idea of a social contract or agreement among individuals for mutual advantage.

cultural relativism The view that right actions are those sanctioned by one's culture.

cycle (in assisted reproductive technology) A sequence of steps involved in trying to achieve pregnancy through ART (assisted reproductive technology), typically extending from egg retrieval to embryo transfer.

deductive argument An argument intended to give logically conclusive support to its conclusion.

deontological (or nonconsequentialist) theory A moral theory asserting that the rightness of actions is determined partly or entirely by their intrinsic nature.

descriptive ethics The study of morality using the methodology of science.

distributive justice Justice regarding the fair distribution of society's advantages and disadvantages.

divine command theory The view that right actions are those commanded by God and wrong actions are those forbidden by God.

doctrine of double effect The principle that performing a bad action to bring about a good effect is never morally acceptable, but performing a good action may sometimes be acceptable even if it produces a bad effect.

egalitarian theories of justice Doctrines affirming that important benefits and burdens of society should be distributed equally.

ethical relativism The view that moral standards are not objective but are relative to what individuals or cultures believe.

ethics The study of morality using the tools and methods of philosophy.

eugenics The deliberate attempt to improve the genetic makeup of humans by manipulating reproduction.

euthanasia Directly or indirectly bringing about the death of another person for that person's sake.

gene The fundamental unit of biological inheritance.

gene therapy The manipulation of someone's genetic material to prevent or treat disease.

genetic discrimination The use of genetic information by employers, insurance companies, and others to discriminate against or stigmatize people.

genetic testing Procedures used to check for genetic disorders by looking for changes in a person's DNA.

genome An organism's entire complement of DNA.

in vitro fertilization The uniting of sperm and egg in a laboratory dish.

induced abortion The intentional termination of a pregnancy through drugs or surgery.

inductive argument An argument intended to give probable support to its conclusion.

infertility The inability to get pregnant after one year of unprotected sex.

informed consent The action of an autonomous, informed person agreeing to submit to medical treatment or experimentation.

in vitro fertilization The uniting of sperm and egg in a laboratory dish.

involuntary euthanasia Bringing about someone's death against her will or without asking for her consent while she is competent to decide.

libertarian theories of justice Doctrines holding that the benefits and burdens of society should be distributed through the fair workings of a free market and the exercise of liberty rights of noninterference.

managed care A system for providing health care to a particular group of patients (members of the system) using restraints to control costs and increase efficiency.

medical futility The alleged pointlessness or ineffectiveness of administering particular treatments.

metaethics The study of the meaning and justification of basic moral beliefs.

moral absolutism The belief that objective moral principles allow no exceptions or must be applied the same way in all cases and cultures.

moral argument An argument whose conclusion is a moral statement.

moral objectivism The view that there are moral norms or principles that are valid or true for everyone.

moral theory An explanation of why an action is right or wrong or why a person or a person's character is good or bad.

morality Beliefs regarding morally right and wrong actions and morally good and bad persons or character.

natural law theory The view that right actions are those that conform to moral standards discerned in nature through human reason.

nonvoluntary euthanasia Euthanasia performed when patients are not competent to choose it for themselves and have not previously disclosed their preferences.

normative ethics The search for, and justification of, moral standards, or norms.

passive euthanasia Allowing someone to die by not doing something that would prolong life.

paternalism The overriding of a person's actions or decision-making for his own good.

physician-assisted suicide A patient's taking her own life with the of aid of a physician.

placebo An inactive or sham treatment.

quickening At about 16 to 20 weeks of pregnancy, a pregnant woman's experience of fetal movement inside her.

randomization The assigning of subjects randomly to both experimental and control groups.

right to privacy The authority of persons to control who may possess and use information about themselves.

rule-utilitarianism The view that a right action is one that conforms to a rule that, if followed consistently, would create for everyone involved the most beneficial balance of good over bad.

spontaneous abortion (miscarriage) An abortion due to natural causes such as a birth defect or maternal injury.

strong paternalism The overriding of a person's actions or choices even though he is substantially autonomous.

subjective relativism The view that right actions are those sanctioned by a person.

surrogate A woman who gestates a fetus for others, usually for a couple or another woman.

therapeutic abortion Abortion performed to preserve the life or health of the mother.

therapeutic privilege The withholding of relevant information from a patient when the physician believes disclosure would likely do harm.

utilitarian theories of justice Doctrines asserting that a just distribution of benefits and burdens is one that maximizes the net good (utility) for society.

utilitarianism The view that right actions are those that result in the most beneficial balance of good over bad consequences for everyone involved.

viability The development stage when the fetus can survive outside the uterus.

virtue ethics A moral theory that focuses on the development of virtuous character.

waiver The patient's voluntary and deliberate giving up of the right to informed consent.

weak paternalism Paternalism directed at persons who cannot act autonomously or whose autonomy is greatly diminished.

voluntary euthanasia Euthanasia performed when competent patients voluntarily request or agree to it.

INDEX

Abortion, 253–68
  arguments for and against, 258–62
  definition, 255
  and infanticide, 261
  late-term, 258
  medical, 255
  and moral theories, 262–63
  and persons, 258–61
  and *Planned Parenthood v. Casey*, 347–53
  and potential persons, 259–60
  and religious belief, 253
  and *Roe v. Wade*, 254, 257
  selective, 466–68
  spontaneous, 255
  therapeutic, 255
Absolutism, moral, 13
  and Kant's theory, 46
Ackerman, Terrence F., 79–83
Angell, Marcia, 242–45
Aquinas, Thomas, 17, 36
Arguments, 19–26
  and counterexamples, 27
  deductive, 20
  and evaluating premises, 26–28
  inductive, 20–21
  modus ponens, 21–23
  modus tollens, 22–23
  moral, 18–28
Aristotle, 39–41
Assisted reproductive technology (ART), 354–66
Autonomy, 9–10, 51–57
  and confidentiality, 108–11
  and euthanasia, 539–31
  and futile treatment, 54–56
  and genetic testing, 465–66
  and informed consent, 144–48
  and paternalism, 51–57
  principle, 51
  and refusing treatment, 52–54
  and reproductive freedom, 358–60, 470
  and research, 196–99
  and truth-telling, 105–14

Baby M, 361, 368
Beauchamp, Tom L., 154–59, 199
Belmont Report, 217–20
Beneficence, 10–11
  and euthanasia, 530–31
  and research, 196–99
Bentham, Jeremy, 32–33
Bioethics, 3–13
  definition, 4
  and moral principles, 8–13
  and moral theories, 30–44
Blinding in clinical trials, 196
Bouvia v. Superior Court, 58–59, 98–102
Brock, Dan W., 366, 467, 531
Brody, Baruch, 246–50
Brody, Howard, 169–75
Buchanan, Allen, 619–20

Callahan, Daniel, 305–10
Canterbury v. Spence, 145, 150–51, 189–92

Categorical imperative, 34–35
Children and refusing medical treatment, 54–56
Children, research in, 203–04
Christian science, 54
Clinical trials, 194–96, 202
  nontherapeutic, 196
  placebo-controlled, 196–99
  women in, 200
Cloning, 362–66
  arguments for and against, 364–66
  and moral theories, 366–67
  myths about, 364
  reproductive, 362–66
  therapeutic, 473–74
Competence, 145
Confidentiality, 108–11
  and duty to warn, 108–10, 138–43
  and genetic testing, 465–66
  and HIV, 109, 111
  and moral theories, 110–12
  and *Tarasoff v. Regents*, 109–10, 138–43
Consequentialist theories, 32
Considered moral judgments, 27, 43
  and utilitarianism, 45–46
Criteria of adequacy, 42–43
  applying, 44–46
  moral, 43–46
  scientific, 43
Cruzan, Nancy, 537
Cruzan v. Director, Missouri Department of Health, 537
Cullen, Susan, 122–29
Cultural relativism, 13, 15–17
  argument for, 15
  arguments against, 16–17
  and tolerance, 17

Death, definition of, 529–30
deMeurers, Christine, 623
Deontological theories, 32
Divine command theory, 17–18
DNA, 460–71
DNR, 56
Doctrine of double effect, 36–38, 263
  and euthanasia, 532–33
Duty to warn, 108–10
Dworkin, Gerald, 63–73

Egalitarianism, 12–13
Embryonic stem cells, 471–74
English, Jane, 310–16
Equipoise, 198–99
Ethics, 3–18
  applied, 4
  of care, 40–42
  definition, 3–4
  descriptive, 4
  and divine command theory, 17–18
  and feelings, 6
  feminist, 42
  and God, 17–18
  and metaethics, 4
  and the moral life, 5–8

normative, 4
  and religion, 17–18
  virtue, 39–40
Eugenics, 471
Euthanasia, 526–36
  active, 527–28
  arguments for and against, 530–34
  definition, 527
  and doctrine of double effect, 532–33
  and moral theories, 534–36
  Oregon's Death with Dignity Act, 533–34
  passive, 527–28
  voluntary, 528

Faden, Ruth R., 154–59
Fallacies, 24–25
Feinberg, Joel, 261
Feminist ethics, 42
Freedman, Benjamin, 231–35
Futile treatment, 54–56

Gawande, Atul, 88–97
Gene therapy, 468–72
  arguments for and against, 470–71
  and eugenics, 471
Genetic discrimination, 466
Genetic testing, 461–68
  arguments over, 464–68
  and autonomy, 465–66
  and confidentiality, 465–66
  and discrimination, 466–67
  and duty to warn, 463–65
  limitations of, 463
  types of, 462–63, 469
Genetics, 460–76
  and moral theories, 474–76
Genomes, 460–461
Glannon, Walter, 471, 622
Goldman, Alan, 73–78
Good and bad, 7–8

Harris, John, 471, 621
Health care, 613–22
  and minorities, 615
  problems with, 613–16
  rationing, 620–22
  and Rawls, 618–19
  right to, 617–20
  and theories of justice, 616–17
Hellman, Samuel, 226–31
Helsinki, Declaration of, 199, 214–17
Hippocratic oath, 51–53, 253
HIV and confidentiality, 109, 111

Impartiality, 5–6
Infertility, 354–62
Informed consent, 105, 144–54
  and autonomy, 144–45
  and *Canterbury v. Spence*, 145, 150–51, 189–92
  conditions of, 145–48
  definition, 144
  and moral theories, 149
  and research, 199–201, 207
  and therapeutic privilege, 146–47

In vitro fertilization, 354–60
  arguments for and against, 358–60
  and moral theories, 366–67

Jehovah's Witness, 54
Justice, 12–13
  distributive, 12, 616–17
  egalitarian, 617
  and health care, 616–20
  libertarian, 617
  and Rawls' theory, 38–39
  and research, 196–99
  retributive, 12
  utilitarian, 617

Kant, Immanuel, 17, 34–35, 121–22
Kantian ethics, 34–36
  and abortion, 263
  applying, 57, 110, 149, 205–06, 263
  and ART, 366–67
  and euthanasia, 536
  evaluating, 46
  and genetics, 476
  and informed consent, 149
  and personhood, 35–36
  and research, 205–06
  and truth-telling, 110, 121–22
Katz, Jay, 159–68
Kingsbury, Chad and Colby, 475

Late-term abortion, 258
Levine, Robert J., 183–88
Libertarianism, 12–13
  and health care, 616–17
Lipkin, Mack, 119–21

Marquis, Don, 235–38, 279–90
McMahan, Jeff, 467
Medical futility, 55–56
Metaethics, 4
Mill, John Stuart, 32–33, 57
Morality, 3–13
  definition, 3
  and the law, 7
  and religion, 17–18
Moral life, 5–8
  elements of, 5–8
Moral arguments, 18–28. *See also* Arguments
Moral judgments, 27. *See also* Considered
    moral judgments
Moral principles, 8–13
  absolute, 8
  and evaluating premises, 26–27
  and genetic testing, 465–66
  and health care, 616–20
  and informed consent, 144–48
  prima facie, 8–9
  in research, 196–99
Moral theories, 30–46
  and considered moral judgments, 43
  definition, 30
  divine command theory, 17–18
  ethics of care, 40–42
  evaluating, 43–46
  and evaluating premises, 27
  feminist ethics, 42
  Kantian ethics, 34–36, 57, 110, 149, 205–06, 263
  natural law theory, 36–38, 57, 263
  Rawls' contract theory, 38–39, 149, 206
  utilitarianism, 32–34, 56–57, 110, 149, 205, 262–63
  virtue ethics, 39–40, 110–11

Natural law theory, 36–38
  and abortion, 263
  applying, 57, 263
  and ART, 366–67
  and the doctrine of double effect, 36–38, 263
  and euthanasia, 536
  and genetics, 476
  and IVF, 367
  and surrogacy, 367
Nesbitt, Winston, 532
Nonmaleficence, 10
Nonmoral, 7–8
Noonan, John T., 301–05
Normative dominance, 5
Norms, 5
Nuremberg Code, 193–94, 199–201, 213–14

Objectivism, 13
Oregon's Death with Dignity Act, 533–34

Passamani, Eugene, 238–42
Paternalism, 51–57
  arguments for and against, 106–08
  and autonomy, 51–56
  and confidentiality, 108–11
  definition, 10, 51
  and futile treatment, 54–56
  and moral theories, 56–57
  and refusing treatment, 52–54
  strong, 52
  and truth-telling, 105–14
  weak, 52
Personhood, 257
  and abortion, 257–62
  potential, 259–60
Physician-assisted suicide, 526–34
Placebos, 194–96
Planned Parenthood v. Casey, 347–53
Plato, 17
Preimplantation genetic diagnosis (PGD), 356, 462, 466, 475
Prima facie, 8–9
Principles. *See* Moral principles
Privacy, 108, 130–35

Quickening, 253–54

Rachels, James, 6, 130–35, 532
Radiation experiments, 220–26
Randomization, 196
Rationing, health care, 620–22
Rawls' contract theory, 38–39
  applying, 149, 206
  and health care resources, 39
  and informed consent, 149
  and the original position, 38
  and research, 206
Rawls, John, 38–39
  and health care, 618–19
Reasonableness, 6–8
Refusing treatment, 52–54, 58–59
  and deaths of children, 55
  and Elizabeth Bouvia, 58–59
Relativism, ethical, 13–17
  arguments for and against, 13–17
  cultural, 13, 15–17
  and moral diversity, 14
  subjective, 13–14
  and tolerance, 17
Religion and ethics, 17–18
Rescher, Nicholas, 622

Research, human, 193–206
  and children, 201–03
  and clinical trials, 194–99
  equipoise in, 198–99
  and informed consent, 199–201
  and moral principles, 197–99
  and moral theories, 205–06
  and placebos, 194, 196–99, 204–05
  in Third World countries, 204–05
  on the vulnerable, 201–05
Respect for persons, 35–36, 122–29
Right and wrong, 7–8
Robertson, John, 359–60
Roe v. Wade, 257, 342–47

Savulescu, Julian, 175–83
Schiavo, Terri, 526–27
Sherwin, Susan, 200, 333–42
Siegler, Mark, 135–38
Singer, Peter, 359, 535–36
Slippery slope arguments, 25. *See also* Fallacies
  and euthanasia, 533–34
Schwartz, Robert L., 84–88
Steinbock, Bonnie, 362, 474
Stem cells, 471–74
Surrogacy, 360–62
  arguments for and against, 361–62
  contracts, 360–61, 363
  and moral theories, 366–67

Tarasoff v. Regents, 109–10, 138–43
Theory. *See* Moral theory
Therapeutic privilege, 146–47
Thomasma, David C., 115–19
Thomson, Judith Jarvis, 261–62, 269–79
Tooley, Michael, 316–32
Truth-telling and paternalism, 105–14
  and moral theories, 110–12
Tuskegee Study, 193, 195
Twinning, 363

Universality, 5–6
Utilitarianism, 32–34
  and abortion, 262–63
  act, 32
  applying, 56–57, 110, 149, 205, 262–63
  and ART, 366–67
  classic, 32–34
  and confidentiality, 110
  and considered moral judgments, 45–46
  and euthanasia, 534–36
  evaluating, 45–46
  and health care, 617
  and genetics, 474–76
  and informed consent, 149
  and research, 205
  rule, 32
  and surrogacy, 366–67
  and truth-telling 110
Utility, 11–12, 32

Viability, fetal, 255
Virtue ethics, 39–40
  applying, 110–11
  and confidentiality, 110–12
  teaching, 41
  and truth-telling, 110–12
Virtues, 39–42

Warren, Mary Anne, 260–61, 291–301, 359
Willowbrook, 193–94

CPSIA information can be obtained at www.ICGtesting.com
Printed in the USA
BVOW030836310712

296633BV00004BA/5/P